The Oxford Annotated Mishnah

A New Translation of the Mishnah
With Introductions and Notes

Volume II

EDITED BY
Shaye J. D. Cohen
Robert Goldenberg
Hayim Lapin

UNIVERSITY PRESS

Great Clarendon Street, Oxford, OX2 6DP,
United Kingdom

Oxford University Press is a department of the University of Oxford.
It furthers the University's objective of excellence in research, scholarship,
and education by publishing worldwide. Oxford is a registered trade mark of
Oxford University Press in the UK and in certain other countries

© Oxford University Press 2022

The moral rights of the authors have been asserted

First Edition published in 2022

All rights reserved. No part of this publication may be reproduced, stored in
a retrieval system, or transmitted, in any form or by any means, without the
prior permission in writing of Oxford University Press, or as expressly permitted
by law, by licence or under terms agreed with the appropriate reprographics
rights organization. Enquiries concerning reproduction outside the scope of the
above should be sent to the Rights Department, Oxford University Press, at the
address above

You must not circulate this work in any other form
and you must impose this same condition on any acquirer

Published in the United States of America by Oxford University Press
198 Madison Avenue, New York, NY 10016, United States of America

British Library Cataloguing in Publication Data

Data available

Library of Congress Control Number: 2020946217

ISBN 978–0–19–284614–3 (Pack)
ISBN 978–0–19–923970–2 (Vol I)
ISBN 978–0–19–284612–9 (Vol II)
ISBN 978–0–19–284613–6 (Vol III)

Printed and bound by
CPI Group (UK) Ltd, Croydon, CR0 4YY

Links to third party websites are provided by Oxford in good faith and
for information only. Oxford disclaims any responsibility for the materials
contained in any third party website referenced in this work.

Contents

List of Figures   v

ORDER OF NASHIM   3

Tractate Yevamot   *Tal Ilan*   5

Tractate Ketubbot   *Robert Brody*   81

Tractate Nedarim   *Robert Goldenberg*   128

Tractate Nazir   *Robert Goldenberg*   181

Tractate Sotah   *Ishay Rosen-Zvi and Orr Scharf*   222

Tractate Gittin   *David Brodsky*   259

Tractate Qiddushin   *Gail Labovitz*   304

ORDER OF NEZIQIN   333

Tractate Bava Qamma   *Hayim Lapin*   335

Tractate Bava Metsi'a   *Hayim Lapin*   382

Tractate Bava Batra   *Hayim Lapin*   439

Tractate Sanhedrin   *Beth Berkowitz*   490

Tractate Makkot   *David C. Flatto*   557

Tractate Shevu'ot   *Elizabeth Shanks Alexander*   584

Tractate Eduyot   *Shaye J. D. Cohen*   628

Tractate Avodah Zarah   *Christine Hayes*   678

Tractate Avot   *Martin S. Jaffee*   710

Tractate Horayot   *Alyssa Gray*   759

List of Figures

1A   Women in *Yevamot* 1:1   8
1B   Women in *Yevamot* 1:3   8

THE MISHNAH

ORDER OF NASHIM
and
ORDER OF NEZIQIN

ORDER OF NASHIM

Tractate Yevamot   5
Tal Ilan

Tractate Ketubbot   81
Robert Brody

Tractate Nedarim   128
Robert Goldenberg

Tractate Nazir   181
Robert Goldenberg

Tractate Sotah   222
Ishay Rosen-Zvi and Orr Scharf

Tractate Gittin   259
David Brodsky

Tractate Qiddushin   304
Gail Labovitz

Tractate Yevamot

Tal Ilan

Introduction

Overview

Yevamot (singular *yevamah*), in this translation "levirate widows," refers to the case of a man who has died childless leaving both a wife and a surviving paternal brother (Latin, *levir*, "husband's brother, brother-in-law"). In keeping with Deuteronomy 25:5–10, the surviving brother is to marry the widow (*yibbum*, or "levirate marriage") or, if he refuses, to perform *halitsah*, literally, "the removal of the shoe," a formal and somewhat humiliating act of separation from the woman.

Structure and Organization of the Tractate

There is no single principle that defines the tractate's structure. Some large blocks of material are as follows. The Mishnah opens with a discussion of close kinship relationships that exempt a woman or her co-wives from levirate marriage (1:1–2.4). A series of complex hypothetical cases in chapter 3 refer back to the opening discussion. *Yevamot* 5:1 opens with a debate about the consequences of a second act of divorce, or betrothal, or performance of *halitsah*, with a co-wife. The rest of chapter 5 addresses this topic. *Yevamot* 6:2–7:6 deals with the consequences of levirate marriage and other forms of sexual union involving priests for making the woman eligible or ineligible to eat *terumah*. Chapter 8, which deals with men who cannot make legally valid sexual unions, in part continues this discussion. The consequences of priests' sexual unions, including the eating of priestly food by their spouses, is extended in chapter 9. Chapter 10:1–5, and again chapter 16, address testimony that a husband has died abroad. Chapter 10:6–9 considers the legal consequences of a sex act by a minor above the age of nine years and one day. Chapter 12 describes the rite of *halitsah* as the Mishnah recasts it. Cases involving diminished legal competence (minors, and especially deaf women) are the subject of much of the material in chapters 13 and 14, while chapters 15 and 16 involve circumstances in which the death of a husband (and the status of children if any) is uncertain due to travel abroad or imprisonment.

Main Ideas

The two key legal terms in the tractate are, levirate marriage (*yibbum*) and *halitsah*. The hypothetical cases of marriage rely heavily on the competing claims of co-wives (*tsarot*).

In addition, the Mishnah defines the finalization of levirate marriage through sexual intercourse, and introduces the concept of *ma'amar* ("statement") to refer to a verbal betrothal that does not have the full legal consequences of levirate marriage.

One notable feature throughout the tractate is the use of hypothetical situations involving, for instance, multiple sisters marrying multiple brothers creating overlapping or conflicting levirate obligations. Patterns that appear in the text include: (1) the statement of a law and its exposition over succeeding passages (e.g. "his brother who was never alive with him" listed in 1:1, is only explained and described in 2:2); (2) the use of the refrain "woe unto him on account of his wife and woe unto him on account of his brother's wife" (3:5, 13:7); (3) the use of narratives as precedents. Finally, (4) the tractate includes seven disputes between the House of Hillel and the House of Shammai that underscore the difference between these two views. While the Shammaite preference for levirate marriage may reflect an older law and practice, the Mishnah adopts the view of the Hillelites, who prefer *halitsah* even when it causes hardship for the levir.

Levirate marriage easily verges on incest, because a man is absolutely prohibited to have intercourse with his brother's wife or widow, if the brother had sired children (Leviticus 18:16). If not, he is commanded to marry the widow. More broadly, *Yevamot* is the locus for the discussion of all forms of permitted and forbidden marriages, such as incest, marriage into the priesthood (especially chapters 6 and 7) or in to the caste of the *netinim* (first in 2:4 but also in 6:2, 8:3, and 9:3), and the offspring of forbidden marriages such as *mamzerim* (4:12–13 and elsewhere) or *halalim* (9:1–2).

Because it is mostly interested in who may marry whom, *Yevamot* is also the formative tractate for the rabbinic understanding of sexual identity. The tractate discusses the sterile woman (*aylonit*), the eunuch (*saris*, e.g. 8:4), the *androgynos*, and the *tumtum* (8:4–6). And since it is interested in determining when a husband should be deemed dead, in order to permit his wife to remarry, it consists of one of the lengthiest rabbinic discussion of women as witnesses (chapter 15; 16:2; 16:5, 7).

Relationship to Scripture

Broadly speaking, the Mishnah is rooted in the legal discussion of Deuteronomy 25:5–10. However, a variety of issues not addressed in the biblical passage are brought to bear on the question of when the obligation arises and what are the consequences of carrying out levirate marriage or *halitsah*. The Mishnah also imposes its own understanding in significant ways. Unlike the (biblical and Shammaite) understanding of levirate marriage as a fundamental obligation, the Mishnah treats levirate marriage and *halitsah* as alternative options available to the levir. In addition, the "elders of [the levir's] city" who oversee *halitsah* are transformed into a rabbinic "court" (*bet din*); other features of the transaction are formalized as well.

Tractate Yevamot

Chapter One

1:1–2:2 *Co-wives and the Institution of Levirate Marriage*

1 Fifteen women exempt their co-wives and the co-wives of their co-wives forever from *halitsah* and from levirate marriage.
And these are they: (1) his daughter; (2) his daughter's daughter; (3) his son's daughter; (4) his wife's daughter; (5) her son's daughter; (6) her daughter's daughter;[1] (7) his mother-in-law; (8) his mother-in-law's mother; (9) his father-in-law's mother; (10) his sister from his mother;[2] (11) his mother's sister; (12) his wife's sister; (13) the wife of his maternal brother; (14) the wife of his brother who was never alive with him;[3] (15) and his daughter-in-law.
These exempt their co-wives and the co-wives of their co-wives forever from *halitsah* and from levirate marriage;
and all of them, if they died, or refused, or were divorced, or were found to be sterile, their co-wives are permitted.

[1] K, P, and others invert the order of (5) and (6). [2] K, P, and others lack "from his mother."
[3] Lit. "who was not in his world."

1:1–2:2 The tractate begins in 1:1 with a list of close female relatives of a levir. In general, levirate marriage can be fulfilled with any of the deceased brother's wives. Here, the principle is that since the women on the list are themselves prohibited from levirate marriage they "exempt" (more precisely: they prohibit to the levir) any co-wives from levirate marriage as well (see further 1:2). The rules stated in 1:1 are cited and discussed in several of the following traditions. For this phenomenon in *Yevamot* see introduction.

1:1 *co-wives*: Heb. *tsarot*; see 1 Samuel 1:6.

co-wives of co-wives: See below, 1:2.

forever: And any women who might be co-wives to these, and so on successively.

his daughter: See Figure 1A. These women, except for the wife of his brother who was not alive with him (no. 14), are either maternal relations (10, 11, 13), or result from his own marriage. Any of the enumerated women might legally marry the man's brother.

was never alive with him: A brother whose death preceded the levir's own birth. See 2:1.

refused: See 13:1–2. A minor girl whose father had died and who was married off by her mother or brothers may refuse her marriage without divorce when she comes of age.

sterile: Heb. *aylonit* ("deer-like"?). See *Niddah* 5:9.

But you cannot say of his mother-in-law, or his mother-in-law's mother, or his father-in-law's mother, that they were found to be sterile or that they refused.

2 Exempt their co-wives—how?
If his daughter or one of these prohibited relations was married to his brother, and [the brother] had another wife, and he died—
just as his daughter is exempt, so is her co-wife exempt.[4]

[4] One manuscript adds "And how do they exempt their co-wives' co-wives?"

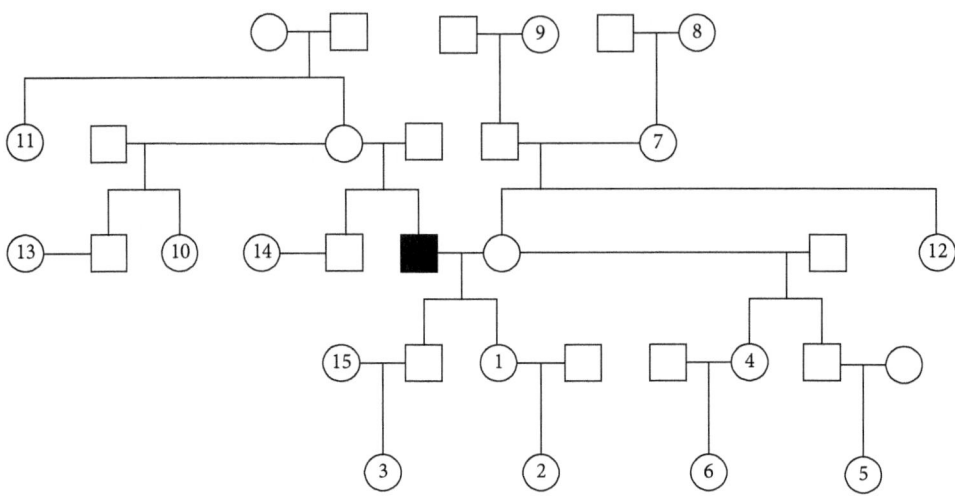

Figure 1A Women in *Yevamot* 1:1

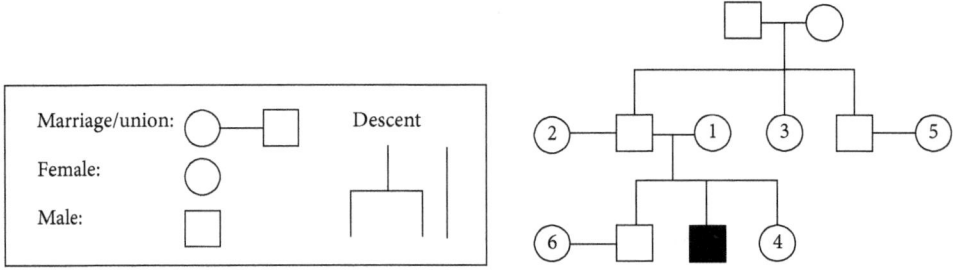

Figure 1B Women in *Yevamot* 1:3

1:2 *Exempt… co-wives—how?* Explicating 1:1.

prohibited relations: Heb. *arayot*, a rabbinic neologism, dependent on Leviticus 18. The reference here is to the fifteen women listed in 1:1.

co-wife of his daughter: Explains how the co-wife of a co-wife may be exempted.

If the co-wife of his daughter went and married his other brother,
and [that brother] had another wife, and he died—
just as his daughter's co-wife is exempt, so is her co-wife's co-wife exempt,
even if there are a hundred.
If they died their co-wives are permitted—how?
If his daughter, or one of these prohibited relations, was married to his brother,
and [the brother] was married to another woman,
and his daughter died, or was divorced,
and then his brother died—
her co-wife is permitted.
And any woman who could have refused but did not refuse—
her co-wife must perform *halitsah* but may not be taken in levirate marriage.

3 Six prohibited relations are more severe than these—
because if they are married to others, their co-wives are permitted:
(1) his mother, and (2) his father's wife, and (3) his father's sister, and (4) his paternal sister, and (5) the wife of his father's brother, and (6) the wife of his paternal brother.

4 The House of Shammai permit co-wives to the brothers;
but the House of Hillel forbid it.
If they were released through *halitsah*—

went and married his other brother: Was divorced from one brother, and married a second.

[that brother] had another wife, now the co-wife of a co-wife. Having once been a co-wife of a prohibited relation, the co-wife of his daughter exempts to the levir any other co-wives in any subsequent marriages to his brothers.

If they died, their co-wives are permitted—how? If the prohibited woman herself predeceased her husband, when that husband dies, her co-wives are "permitted" to undergo levirate marriage (in fact, they are obligated to do so or to perform *halitsah*).

and woman who could have refused: See 1:1. It is not clear whether the Mishnah speaks of a minor who could have refused her husband or a minor who could have refused her levir after her husband died (see 13:1, according to the Hillelite view). The co-wife of a minor who did not "refuse" cannot marry the levir but must be released by him through *halitsah*.

1:3 *Six prohibited relations*: See Figure 1B. These forbidden relations (all prohibited due to a close patrilineal connection) are stricter, because they could not in the first place be married to the man's brother, who stands in the same incestuous relations with them (see Leviticus 18:7–8, 11–12, 14, 16).

because...permitted: The commentaries debate how to construe this sentence. The simplest interpretation is that if the husbands of these six die, a man is then permitted to marry their co-wives. Since they can only marry *others* (i.e. nonbrothers), the prohibition of a brother's wife does not arise, and the levirate obligation in 1:1–2 does not exist.

the wife of his paternal brother: His divorcee or widow left with children, as opposed to the specific case of a widow left childless, who is the subject of *Yevamot*.

1:4 Parallel to *Eduyot* 4:8. The issue between the two Houses is not leniency or stringency but *halitsah* or levirate marriage: the Shammaites uphold levirate marriage, where Hillelites prefer avoiding this kind of marriage by opting to perform *halitsah*. Possibly, the House of Shammai uphold the older practice but, over time, levirate marriage lost its prominent position in favor of *halitsah* as favored by the House of Hillel (see *Bekhorot* 1:7). The avoidance of levirate marriage may be due to increasing preference for monogamous marriages.

permit co-wives to the brothers: The House of Shammai here rule in contradiction to 1:1. The ruling Mishnah is thus according to the House of Hillel.

the House of Shammai deem them unfit for marriage into[5] the priesthood,
but the House of Hillel deem them fit;
if they were taken in levirate marriage—
the House of Shammai deem them fit,
but the House of Hillel deem them unfit.
Even though these forbid and those permit,[6] these deem unfit and these deem fit—
the House of Shammai did not refrain from taking wives from the House of Hillel,
and the House of Hillel did not refrain from taking wives from the House of Shammai.
For all the purities and impurities that these would pronounce pure and these impure—
they did not refrain from making purities together, these relying on those.

Chapter Two

2 The wife of his brother who was never alive with him—how?
Two brothers—
one of them died,
and a brother was born to them,
and afterwards the second took his brother's wife in levirate marriage,
and he died—
the first woman goes out on account of being the wife of his brother who was never alive with him,

---

[5] "Marriage into" added for clarity.   [6] **K** lacks "these...permit."

If they were released through halitsah: Since the surviving brother may marry any of the co-wives of the forbidden relative, if instead he releases them by *halitsah*, the House of Shammai now consider them all divorcees, and as such they may not marry priests (Leviticus 21:7). The House of Hillel, on the other hand, consider these women exempt from the entire levirate procedure, and therefore consider the act of *halitsah* here as of no consequence, and permit these co-wives to marry priests. Conversely, the House of Shammai consider the levirate marriage valid, and *deem* the co-wives *fit* to marry into the priesthood, while the House of Hillel consider it invalid, and *deem* the co-wives *unfit*.

did not refrain from taking wives: An ideological and rhetorical comment on the correct relationship between opponents. Legal divisions should not cause rifts on a personal or societal level, and the Houses of Hillel and Shammai constitute the model. According to the House of Hillel, children born of marriages sanctioned by the House of Shammai would be *mamzerim* (see 4:13), while those born to the co-wives who married into the priesthood after *halitsah* (in this mishnah) would be considered *halalim* (i.e. unfit for the priesthood, see 9:1) by the House of Shammai (see *Qiddushin* 3:12). It is difficult to see how, under such circumstances, members of the two houses could continue to intermarry, yet the mishnah asserts they did.

these relying on those: A continuation of the previous comment on ideal legal cooperation.

2:1 *The wife ....who was never alive with him*—how? See above 1:1.

the second took his brother's wife....and died: We assume that this brother also had an additional wife. Here, the second brother took the widow of the first in levirate marriage after the birth of the third brother (cf. 2:2).

the first woman, i.e. the wife of the first brother, *goes out*, without levirate marriage or *halitsah* with the third brother. "Goes out" is frequently a technical term for exiting a marriage through divorce (e.g. 14:1).

and the second woman on account of being her co-wife.
If [the second brother] verbally betrothed and died—
his wife performs *halitsah* but may not be taken in levirate marriage.

2 Two brothers—
and one of them died,
and the other took his brother's wife in levirate marriage,
and then a brother was born to them,
and [the second brother] died—
the first woman goes forth on account of being the wife of his brother who was never alive with him,
and the second on account of being a co-wife.
If he verbally betrothed her and died—
she undergoes *halitsah* but not levirate marriage.
R. Simeon says:
The levir takes whichever woman that he desires in levirate marriage,
or performs *halitsah* on whichever woman that he wishes.

2:3–4 *Marriage with Forbidden Relations*

3 They stated a general rule regarding a woman awaiting levirate marriage:
If she is a forbidden relation—
she neither performs *halitsah* nor is she taken in levirate marriage;
if her prohibition is a prohibition because of a commandment, or because of holiness—
she must perform *halitsah*, but may not be taken in levirate marriage;

---

his brother who was never alive with him: When the third brother was born, the first brother was no longer in the world, so there is no levirate bond between the first brother's wife (who in the meantime went in levirate marriage to the second) and the third brother. However, the prohibition of taking a brother's wife is still operative.

the second woman: A co-wife to the widow of the first brother, in the marriage with the second.

If....verbally betrothed: Lit. "performed a statement." Levirate marriage is properly contracted only through sexual intercourse; a verbal statement ("You are betrothed to me") creates only a weak legal bond between the levir and the widow, see chapter 5. Therefore, the wife of the second brother both is and is not a full co-wife of the widow of the first brother. As a co-wife, she may not be taken in levirate marriage (because her co-wife is forbidden); as not a full co-wife, she must be released through *halitsah*.

2:2 Unlike the previous mishnah, here, the second brother takes the widow of the first in levirate marriage before the birth of the third brother. According to the anonymous mishnah the legal consequences are the same in both cases.

R. Simeon: When the third brother was born, the widow of the first brother was married to the second brother. According to R. Simeon, for the third brother the status of the widow of the first is just like any other widow of the second brother. He may decide which of the two he will take in levirate marriage or release through *halitsah*, as in the "normal" levirate marriage situation.

2:3 *a general rule*: Cf. Pe'ah 1:4, Ma'aserot 1.1, Tohorot 8.6.

because of a commandment....holiness: These are explicated in 2:4.

her sister, who is also her husband's brother's wife—
may perform *halitsah* or be taken in levirate marriage.
    4 [How:] forbidden because of a commandment?
Relatives once removed, according to the words of the scribes.
Forbidden because of holiness—
a widow to a high priest,
a divorcee and one who has undergone *halitsah* to a regular priest,
a female *mamzer*,
and a female *natin* to an Israelite,
and a daughter of an Israelite to a *natin* or a *mamzer*.

2:5 *Who Is a Brother or a Son for the Purpose of Levirate Marriage?*

    5 Whoever has a brother of any kind, enforces levirate marriage on his brother's wife;
and he is his brother for all purposes,
except one from a female slave or from a gentile woman.
Whoever has a son of any kind—

her sister, who is also her husband's brother's wife: On the result of a special case in which two sisters are married to two brothers, see 3:3; both brothers have died, so both sisters are also sisters-in-law awaiting levirate marriage or *halitsah* from a third brother. If one sister is forbidden to a third brother (as, for example, if he was a priest and she a divorcee), he may undergo *halitsah* with that sister or he may choose to perform levirate marriage or undergo *halitsah* with the other sister who is not prohibited to him.

2:4 *Forbidden . . . . commandment*: Explicating 2:3.

Relatives once removed: Heb. *sheniyot*, "second." The Mishnah here refers to women who are related to the levir, but not mentioned in the list of incest cases found in Leviticus 18. These include, for instance, the man's grandmothers (Tosefta).

Forbidden . . . . holiness: Explicating 2:4.

a widow to a high priest: Leviticus 21:14.

a divorcee . . . . a regular priest: On the divorcee see Leviticus 21:7. The prohibition of a priest to marry a woman who underwent *halitsah* is rabbinic, and derived from a comparison with the divorcee.

a female mamzer: A *mamzer* is the offspring of a forbidden union and prohibited from joining the community of Israel (Deuteronomy 23:3). As a result, neither a *mamzer* nor a *mamzeret* (female *mamzer*, as here) may marry Israelites. See the discussion below, 4:13.

a female natin: *netinah* is the feminine form of *natin*, pl. *netinim*, first mentioned in Ezra as persons who joined the Judaeans when they returned from the Babylonian Exile (e.g. Ezra 2:58, 7:7; Nehemiah 7:72). They are considered a subordinate caste, and may not intermarry with Israelites. More likely, rabbinic legislation about *netinim* reflects a fictitious picture of the Israelite nation.

2:5 *a brother of any kind*: This would seem to refer to brothers sharing a single father whatever the status of the mother. However, the language makes it possible that this includes half-brothers both on the mother's side and on the father's side.

from a female slave or from a gentile woman: Offspring from such sexual unions are not valid kin, see *Qiddushin* 3:12.

a son of any kind: Including a *mamzer* (see below, 4:13).

the son[7] exempts his father's wife from levirate marriage;
and is liable for his beating or his cursing;
and he is his son for all purposes,
except one from a female slave
or from a gentile woman.

2:6–8 Brothers, Sisters, and Levirate Marriage

6 Whoever betrothed one of two sisters,
and does not know which one he betrothed—
gives a writ of divorce to this one and a writ of divorce to that one.
If he died and had one brother—
this one performs *halitsah* for both.
If he had two—
one performs *halitsah* and one takes one in levirate marriage.
If they went ahead and took them in—
one does not take them out of their hands.

7 Two who betrothed two sisters,
this one does not know which he betrothed,
and that one does not know which he betrothed—
this one gives two writs of divorce, and that one gives two writs of divorce.
If they died,
and this one had a brother and that one had a brother—
this one undergoes *halitsah* for both of them,
and that one undergoes *halitsah* for both of them.
This one has one, and that one has two—
the one performs *halitsah* for both;
and the two—

[7] Heb. "he."

---

exempts his father's wife from levirate marriage: The subject of the verb now shifts to the son. The father having produced offspring, even if he dies, his wife need not marry his brother or be released by him.

his beating or his cursing: Exodus 21:15, 17. While the verse mentions father and mother, here, the nouns 'beating' and 'cursing' are in the masculine singular.

2:6–7 Cases where complications arise because siblings have married siblings, as well as because of uncertainties about betrothal. This type of problem is raised again at 3:1–7.

2:6 *Whoever betrothed one of two sisters*: According to Jewish law, betrothal is considered a legally binding relationship that requires divorce to end it (see e.g. *Ketubbot* 2:1; *Gittin* 8:9), even though consummation has not taken place, and is indeed at this point forbidden.

preceded and took them in: Each married one without waiting for the other to undergo *halitsah*. Took in (Hebrew root is *kanas*) is a technical term for a man taking a wife.

one does not take them out of their hands: Despite the formulation of the law which forbids the levirate marriage of both women, the rabbis do not force them to divorce their wives or annul their marriage.

2:7 This passage continues the logical puzzle begun in the preceding: two sisters are each potentially betrothed to two men. In addition, the mishnah adds brothers related to only one of the two deceased husbands.

one performs *halitsah* and one takes one in levirate marriage.
If they preceded and took them in—
one does not take them out of their hands.
This one has two, and that one has two—
the brother of this one performs *halitsah* for one,
and the brother of that one performs *halitsah* for one;
the brother of this one takes in levirate marriage
the one for whom the other had performed *halitsah*,
and that one's brother takes in levirate marriage
the one for whom the other had performed *halitsah*.
If one pair of brothers[8] preceded and performed *halitsah*—
the other pair of brothers[9] should not perform levirate marriage,
but rather, one performs levirate marriage, and one performs *halitsah*.
If they preceded and performed levirate marriage,
one does not take them out of their hands.

   8 The commandment is for the eldest to perform levirate marriage;
yet if the younger preceded him—he has acquired the right.

2:8 cont.   *Sexual Relations with a Slave Woman, a Gentile Woman, or a Married Woman*

One who is accused regarding [sexual intercourse with] a female slave, and then she was released,
or with a gentile woman, and then she converted—
he may not take her in;
and if he took her in, one does not take her out of his hand.
One who is accused regarding a married woman,

---

[8] Heb. "two."   [9] Heb. "two."

2:8–10 This section interrupts two discussions of complex hypothetical cases of a levirate bond involving multiple siblings. After the first tradition in 2:8, which does deal with levirate marriage, the traditions that follow deal neither with levirate marriage nor with *halitsah*, nor are they in any way of a similar literary form as the previous law. They all deal with men and women who are suspected of having engaged in sexual relations out of wedlock, or of taking illegal action in order to make themselves marriageable, and are therefore forbidden to one another.

2:8 *female slave . . . . gentile woman*: See above, 2:5.

released . . . . converted: When a female slave is released from slavery or a gentile is converted, all the laws that apply to Israelite women apply to them.

he may not take her in: For "take in," see above, 2:6. Commentators suggest that the man may not marry a manumitted slave or a converted gentile so as not to substantiate the rumor that he released the maidservant in order to marry her, or so as not to say that the gentile converted for love, which is seen as a false motive for the manumission of a slave or for conversion (Yerushalmi).

accused regarding a married woman: Persons who are suspected of adultery may not marry one another, see *Sotah* 5:1.

and they removed her from under [her husband's] hand,
even if [the accused] has taken her in, he must dismiss her.

2:9–10 *May Witnesses and Judges Marry Women They Released from a Previous Marriage?*

9 One who brings a writ of divorce from abroad, and said:
"In my presence it has been written and in my presence it has been signed"—
he may not marry his wife.
[If he said:]
"He is dead";
"I have killed him";
"We have killed him"—
he may not marry his wife.
R. Judah says:
[If he said]:
"I have killed him"—
his wife may not marry;
"We have killed him"—
his wife may marry.

10 A Sage who forbade a wife to her husband through a vow—
in this case, he may not marry her.

---

dismiss: Heb. *yotsi*, "take out, remove," a technical term for divorce in rabbinic literature, e.g. 4:2, *Ketubbot* 5:5, *Sotah* 6:1.

2:9 *writ of divorce*: Cf. *Gittin* 1:1: one who brings a writ of divorce must be witness to its composition and witnessing. Here it is added that he may not marry the woman to whom he is bringing the writ, for fear that the testimony might have been falsified to gain permissible sexual access to the woman.

He is dead: One who comes from abroad and attests to the death of the husband.

may not marry his wife: Because it may appear as though he killed the man in order to marry the woman.

his wife may not marry, at all. The mishnah could be attempting to prevent self-incrimination. The witness here may be sacrificing himself (for if he killed the husband he deserves to die) to prevent the widow from a lifetime of marital limbo (*aginut* in later sources). Had he known that his words would have no consequences, he would not have incriminated himself. According to Albeck, when the witness calls himself a killer, he disqualifies himself from testifying, according to Exodus 23:1.

2:10 *a vow*: See *Nedarim* introduction. Interpreters assume that in this mishnah the case is of a woman who vowed not to gain any benefit from her husband, which means that they need to be divorced. If her husband did not annul the vow in the proper time, in order to try and release her he must approach a Sage (see, implicitly, *Nedarim* chapter 9) who will look for a loophole in the language of the vow. The case here could also be one of the husband having vowed not to benefit from his wife (see, implicitly, *Nedarim* 2:5). In either case, the Sage has failed to find a loophole and the couple must divorce.

may not marry her: On suspicion that he may have forced their divorce in order to marry the woman.

If she refused him or performed *halitsah* in his presence—
he may marry her,
because he is the court.
And all of these [men] who had wives who then died—
these women are permitted to marry them.
And all of these [women] who were married to other men and were divorced or widowed—
these women are permitted to them.
And all the women are permitted to their sons or their brothers.

Chapter Three

3:1–7 *Brothers, Sisters, and Levirate Marriage*

3 Four brothers, two of them married to two sisters,
and those married to sisters died—
these must perform *halitsah* and may not contract levirate marriage;
and if the brothers preceded and took them in—
they must put them out.

performed halitsah: See below, 12:1.

or performed halitsah in her presence: This may be the link that accounts for the rules of 2:8–10 here in *Yevamot*. Those rulings all dealt with men forbidden to marry certain women because of suspicion of illicit sexual contact, or that the action they took allowed them to marry the woman in question. Here, the woman in question undergoes *halitsah*, which is the subject of our tractate.

because he is the court: Perhaps "For he merely serves as a member of the court."

And all: The rule includes witnesses to the divorce or the husband's death and the judge who, by not releasing a woman from a vow, forced her divorce (2:9). If they were already married, they are not suspected of planning to marry the women for whom they testify or serve as judges. Therefore, when the wife of the witness or the Sage died, they may marry the women they released from marriage through a deed of divorce (2:9) or a vow (2:10). Similarly, if the divorced *women who were married* to some other man after the divorce, once that marriage has ended, the witnesses or Sage is permitted to marry the women in question.

permitted to their sons or brothers: The Mishnah does not suspect that a witness or Sage will falsely force the end of a marriage in order to marry off a relative.

3:1–7 The Mishnah resumes its discussion of complex levirate cases (see above, 2:6–7). Now the Mishnah considers possible cases involving three and four brothers.

3:1 Parallel to *Eduyot* 5:5.

married to two sisters: Leviticus 18:18 forbids a man to marry two sisters. Although this situation does not arise directly here, the two women awaiting the resolution of their levirate widowhood are sisters, and the Mishnah requires that both levirs (also brothers) undergo *halitsah*. However, one might have expected each levir to be permitted to perform levirate marriage. It is not clear why this second option is not allowed, and as we see immediately, the issue is debated between the Houses of Hillel and Shammai.

preceded . . . . they must put them out, in agreement with the House of Hillel (as expressed below). This view invalidates any levirate marriage created in this situation.

R. Eliezer says:
The House of Shammai say:[10]
They may keep their wives,
but the House of Hillel say:
They must put them out.[11]

2 If one of the women was prohibited to one of the levirs:[12]
as a prohibited relation—
he is prohibited with respect to her and permitted with respect to her sister;
and the other is prohibited with respect to both of them;
as a prohibition due to a commandment or a prohibition due to holiness—
she performs *halitsah* and does not undergo levirate marriage.

3 If one of the women was prohibited to one of them as a prohibited relation,
and the other was prohibited to the other as a prohibited relation—
the woman forbidden to this one is permitted to that one,
and the woman who is forbidden to that one is permitted to this one.
It is about this that they said:
Her sister, when she is her husband's brother's wife, either performs *halitsah* or undergoes levirate marriage.

4 Three brothers, two of them married to two sisters,
or to a woman and her daughter,
or to a woman and her daughter's daughter,
or to a woman and her son's daughter—
these women perform *halitsah* but do not undergo levirate marriage;
but R. Simeon exempts.
If one of the women was forbidden to him:
as a prohibited relation—

---

[10] K, P, C: "R. Eliezer said in the name of the House of Shammai."
[11] Lit. "may uphold...must put out."   [12] Heb. "of them."

R. Eliezer reports an earlier dispute between the House of Hillel and the House of Shammai. See n. 10.

They may keep their wives: As in 1:4, the House of Shammai prefer levirate marriage to *halitsah*.

3:2 *as a prohibited relation*: See 2:3.

he is prohibited: Because no levirate bond is created with the widow who is also his own prohibited relation, he is *permitted with respect to her sister*. If the deceased was married to a levir's mother-in-law, for instance, the widow is a prohibited relation of the levir, but her sister is not.

a commandment .... holiness: See above, 2:3, 4. Since a levirate bond is created, but there is also a prohibition, the solution is to end the bond with *halitsah*.

3:3 *forbidden for this one is permitted for that one*: No levirate bond is created between the widow and her prohibited relation, so the other widow is permitted to them (see 3:2).

It is about this: See 2:3.

3:4 *perform halitsah but do not undergo levirate marriage*: The two husbands have died and two sisters are awaiting a levirate marriage. The remaining brother choosing either for levirate marriage also makes the other into a prohibited relation. The rule is therefore to perform *halitsah*, and terminate the levirate bond.

R. Simeon takes the view that no levirate bond is created at all.

he is prohibited with respect to her, and permitted with respect to her sister;
as a prohibition due to commandment or as a prohibition due to holiness—
she performs *halitsah* but does not perform levirate marriage.

5 Three brothers, two of them married to two sisters and one unmarried.
One of the husbands of the sisters died,
and the unmarried brother betrothed the widow verbally,
and then his second brother died—
the House of Shammai say:
His wife remains with him,
but the other woman must go out, since she is the sister of his wife;
but the House of Hillel say:
He must dismiss his wife both by writ of divorce and by *halitsah*,
and his brother's wife by *halitsah*.
It is about this that they said:
Woe to him on account of his wife, and woe to him on account of his brother's wife!

6 Three brothers, two of them married to two sisters,
and one was married to an unrelated woman.[13]
One of the husbands of the sisters died,
and the one married to the unrelated woman took his wife in,
and he died—
the first [widow] goes out as the sister of a wife,
and the second because she is her co-wife.
If [the deceased levir][14] had verbally betrothed her and died—
the unrelated woman performs *halitsah* but does not undergo levirate marriage.

[13] Here and below, lit. "foreign." See annotations.   [14] Here and below, Heb. "he."

---

as a prohibited relation ....commandment ....holiness: As in 3:2. See 2:3, 4;

3:5. Cf. *Eduyot* 4:9.

the House of Shammai ....the House of Hillel: Here, the verbal betrothal has created a defective bond between the first widow and the levir (2:1), so the case falls between one in which a wife's sister becomes a levirate widow and one in which two sisters from two husbands fall to the levir at the same time. Again, the House of Shammai uphold levirate marriage, where the House of Hillel prefer *halitsah* (see above, 1:4 and 3:1). The result in this case is certainly that the House of Shammai offer a more lenient approach.

must go out: See above, 2:1. This is a term often used in the Mishnah for describing the action a woman is forced to take when divorced, see e.g. below 14:1.

dismiss: The same verb, in a different verbal form, as "go out." Here the term refers to the action taken by the husband when divorcing his wife.

It is about this...: Cf. 3:3.

Woe to him on account of his wife. See 13:7 below. The saying follows a popular pattern. Cf. *Kelim* 17:16. Perhaps, however, the reference here is to 14:4.

3:6 *unrelated woman*: Heb. *nokhrit*, often "stranger," "gentile." In 2:5, 8 this word refers to a gentile woman. Yet here, as the text develops, it is clear that the word means a woman who is not related to the other two sisters.

took his wife in: On "taking in" as referring to marriage, see above, 2:6.

Three brothers, two of them married to two sisters and one married to an unrelated woman.
The one married to the unrelated woman died,
and one of the husbands of the sisters took in his wife,
and he died—
the first [widow] goes out as the sister of a wife,
and the second because she is her co-wife.
If the [deceased levir] had verbally betrothed her and died—
the unrelated woman performs *halitsah* but does not undergo levirate marriage.

7 Three brothers, two of them married to two sisters,
and one married to an unrelated woman.
One of the husbands of the sisters died,
and the one married to an unrelated woman took her in,
and the wife of the second died,
and then the one married to an unrelated woman died—
in this case, this woman is forbidden to him forever,
since she had been forbidden to him one hour.
Three brothers, two of them married to two sisters,
and one married to an unrelated woman.
One of the husbands of the sisters divorced his wife,
and the one married to an unrelated woman died,
and the one who had divorced took her in,
and he died—
it is about this that they said:
All those women who died or divorced, their co-wives are permitted.

3:8 Doubtful Betrothal or Divorce

8 And all whose betrothal or divorce was in doubt,
their co-wives perform *halitsah* but do not undergo levirate marriage.
What is doubtful betrothal?

3:7 *and the wife of the second died*: The second brother married to a sister died. When the third brother dies there is no longer a living wife who is a sister of the levir's wife.

since she had been forbidden to him one hour: While married to his brother, as the sister of his wife (Leviticus 18:18).

it is about this that they said: Cf. 3:3.

All those women who…: This probably refers to 1:1. Here, the unrelated woman was never actually the co-wife of the sister.

3:8 *And all whose*: Extends the tradition cited at the end of 3:7. On the legal status of betrothal, see above, 2:6.

perform halitsah but do not undergo levirate marriage: 1:1 above exempted the co-wives of fully married close female relations. In this case there is doubt about whether the marriage was properly formed or ended, so the possible levirate bond is severed by *halitsah*.

What is doubtful betrothal … . Doubtful divorce? For such generalizations, see above, 1:2.

He threw her a writ of betrothal:
if it is doubtful whether it was closer to him or closer to her—
this is doubtful betrothal.
Doubtful divorce?
He wrote a [writ of divorce] in his own handwriting,
but it has no witnesses, [or] it has witnesses but has no date,
[or] it has a date, but only one witness—
this is a doubtful divorce.

3:9–10 *Complex Cases*

9 Three brothers, married to three unrelated women,
and one of them died,
and the second verbally betrothed her,
and he died—
these widows perform *halitsah* but do not undergo levirate marriage,
as it is said: *and one of them dies…her husband's brother shall unite with her*—
with one who has one levirate bond, not one who has two levirate bonds.
R. Simeon says:
He takes whichever he wishes in levirate marriage
and performs *halitsah* with the second.
Two brothers, married to two sisters,
and one of them died,
and then the wife of the second died—
this woman is forbidden to him forever,
since she had been forbidden to him one hour.

threw her a writ of betrothal : Cf. *Gitin* 8:2–3.

[writ of divorce]: See *Gitin* 9:4.

3:9 *and one of them died*: Deuteronomy 25:5.

not one who has two levirate bonds: The verbal betrothal by the second brother did not resolve the status of the widow to whom he made this promise, so the levirate obligation from the first deceased brother still stands. However, the verbal betrothal was sufficiently strong to create a levirate obligation in its own right when the second brother died. Thus one of the widows has two levirate claims on the surviving brother at once.

R. Simeon says: Each of the women is eligible for levirate marriage either as the widow of the first brother (if the verbal betrothal was not effective) or of the second (if it was). He cannot perform levirate marriage with both since the verbal betrothal at least potentially makes one widow the co-wife of the one with whom he performs levirate marriage. But he must perform *halitsah* in case there are actually two levirate claims, one from each deceased brother.

forbidden to him forever: See 3:7.

one hour: When the brother died, the widow was his wife's sister. Even after his wife has died, her sister is prohibited to him.

10 Two who betrothed two women,
and at the time the women entered the marriage chamber, the grooms switched the betrothed[15] of this one with that one, and of that one with this one—
in this case, these are liable because of the prohibition of a married woman;
if they were brothers—
because of the prohibition of a brother's wife;
and if they were sisters—
because of the prohibition of *a woman to her sister*;
and if they were menstruating—
because of the prohibition of a menstruant.
And one segregates them for three months, lest they are pregnant;
and if they were minors who cannot yet[16] give birth, one returns them immediately;
and if they were daughters of priests, they are disqualified from *terumah*.[17]

[15] "Women," "grooms," "betrothed" added for clarity.
[16] Lit. "are not suitable to."   [17] **K** and other manuscripts: "from the priesthood."

3:10 *at the time the women entered*: The situation described may reflect marriages arranged by parents, where the spouses meet on the wedding night, or more broadly the Mishnah's tendency to develop hypothetical cases. Since the betrothal created an inchoate marriage, the exchange of wives has potentially serious consequences (see above, 2:6). The object of these rulings is to bring back order. Each bride will return to the man with which she was betrothed.

a woman to her sister: Leviticus 18:18.

menstruating: Sexual intercourse with a menstruant is always forbidden (see Leviticus 15:24, 18:19). It seems that this prohibition is discussed here, because the prohibition to have sex with a brother's wife, with two sisters, and with a menstruating woman are stated together in Leviticus 18:16, 18, 19, and not because it is relevant to the issue of accidental exchange of wives.

segregates them from their original husbands *for three months*. If betrothed to one man but pregnant by another, the children they will produce will be *mamzerim*, see above, 2:4.

returns them immediately: Since the minors are assumed to be nonreproductive, there is no need to segregate them from their original husbands.

and if they were daughters of priests: A priest's daughter or a priest's wife may eat *terumah*. Here the former is more likely.

terumah: See *Terumot*, introduction. Wives of priests and unmarried, childless daughters of priests were permitted to eat *terumah* as members of a priest's household; Leviticus 22:12–13. Having had sexual relations with a prohibited man, she may not return to her former status in her father's house. Note the reading of the manuscripts (n. 17 and 4:1): the woman would also be ineligible to marry into the priesthood.

Chapter Four

4:1–2 *Valid Levirate Marriage or Halitsah*

4 One who performs *halitsah* for his levirate widow,
and she is found pregnant and gives birth.
As long as the offspring is viable—
he is permitted with respect to her relatives,
and she is permitted with respect to his relatives,
and he has not disqualified her[18] from the priesthood.
If the offspring is not viable—
he is forbidden with respect to her relatives,
and she is forbidden with respect to his relatives,
and he has disqualified her from the priesthood.
  2 One who takes in his levirate widow,
and she is found pregnant and gives birth.
If the offspring is viable—
he must put her out,
and they are liable to bring an offering.
If the offspring is not viable—
he may uphold [the marriage].
If it is doubtful whether it is a nine-month offspring of the first
or whether it is a seven-month offspring of the last[19]—

[18] **K**: "she is not disqualified."   [19] Lit. "…son of nine to the first…son of seven to the last."

4:1–2 deal with boundary cases: valid levirate marriage or *halitsah* may have taken place, and the Mishnah determines the consequences of validity or invalidity. Here and in 4:7–8, the Mishnah treats *halitsah* as analogous in its consequences to divorce.

4:1 *performs halitsah ….and she is found pregnant*: Since his brother now has offspring, valid *halitsah* did not occur.

he is permitted ….she is permitted: There was no valid *halitsah* to cause prohibition regarding close relations of a former spouse (see 4:7).

has not disqualified her from the priesthood. Priests may not marry a divorced woman (Leviticus 27:1). However, in this case the woman is a widow (permitted to priests) since the *halitsah* was invalid.

the offspring is not viable: Consequently, the *halitsah* performed was valid, and as a kind of divorcee the woman cannot marry a priest.

4:2 *liable to bring*: A purgation offering (*hattat*) is brought for unintentionally transgressing a prohibition (Leviticus 24:27–28). The prohibition of a brother's wife is at Leviticus 18:16.

nine-month offspring of the first ….seven-month offspring of the last: The offspring was born seven months after the death of the original husband and could be attributed to either man. (Here and elsewhere, rabbis express the belief that a viable offspring could be born after seven or nine months' gestation, but not after eight).

he must put her out,
and the offspring is fit,
and they are liable to bring an offering for uncertain guilt.

4:3–4 *Property Rights of the Levirate Widow*

3 A woman awaiting her levir to whom property fell—
the House of Shammai and the House of Hillel admit that
she may sell and she may bequeath,
and [the transaction] is valid.
If she died, what does one do with her *ketubbah* payment
and the property that comes and goes with her?
The House of Shammai say:
The husband's heirs divide with the father's heirs.
The House of Hillel say:
The property remains in its presumptive ownership:
ketubbah payment to the husband's heirs,
property that comes and goes with her
belongs to the father's heirs.
  4 If he took her in, she is then like his wife for all purposes,
except that her *ketubbah* payment is against the property of her first husband.

4:5–6 *If Brothers Do Not Wish to Perform Levirate Marriage*

5 It is a commandment for the eldest to perform levirate marriage.
If he did not wish to—

he must put her out: In case the offspring is that of the deceased brother, and *yibbum* is not valid.

the offspring is fit: The child is either the son of the deceased husband, or the child of the levir, whose brother died childless.

offering for uncertain guilt: See Leviticus 5:17–18 and *Keritot* 4:1.

4:3 *to whom property fell*: Inheritance or gift, and not governed by the rules for property brought in at the time of marriage (below).

admit that she may sell .... and it is valid: At *Ketubbot* 8:1 they dispute the general case of such property for married or betrothed women. Here, they agree that a levirate widow may handle her own property.

If she died: A new dispute involving the Hillelites and Shammaites.

ketubbah payment: The money promised in her marriage contract (Heb. *ketubbah*; see *Ketubbot*, introduction).

property that enters and goes out with her: Dowry or trousseau, which her husband manages but returns to her on divorce or on his death.

4:4 *took her in*: Married her; see above, 2:6.

4:5 Surviving brothers might not always view their levirate obligation favorably. The rabbis legislate here for the case where the brothers prefer to forgo the process.

It is a commandment: See 2:8 above.

one approaches all the brothers.
If they did not wish—
one returns to the eldest and says to him:
You are commanded!
Either perform a levirate marriage or perform *halitsah*!

6 If he made his decision dependent on a minor [brother],
[awaiting] when he attains adulthood,
or on an adult, when he returns from abroad,
or on a person who is deaf and mute, or a person who is not legally competent—
one does not listen to him.
Rather, one says to him:
You are commanded!
Either perform a levirate marriage or perform *halitsah*!

4:7–8 *Consequences of Levirate Marriage or Halitsah*

7 One who performs *halitsah* for his levirate widow,
he is thereby like one of the brothers regarding the estate.
If there is a father—
the property belongs to the father.
One who takes in his levirate widow gains possession of the property of his brother.
R. Judah says:
In either case, if there is a father—
the property belongs to the father.
One who performs *halitsah* for his levirate widow—
he is prohibited with respect to her relatives,
and she is prohibited with respect to his relatives.
He is prohibited with respect to her mother, and her mother's mother, and her father's mother, and her daughter, and her daughter's daughter, and her son's daughter, and her sister as long as she is alive;
and his brothers are permitted.
And she is prohibited with respect to his father, and his father's father, and his son, and his son's son, and his brother, and his brother's son.
A person is permitted with respect to the relatives of the co-wife of the woman for whom he performed *halitsah*,
and is prohibited with respect to the co-wife of the relative of the woman for whom he performed *halitsah*.

4:6 *abroad*: See above, 2:9.

deaf and mute .... not legally competent: Elsewhere (Tosefta) we find the view permitting such men to perform *halitsah*; our Mishnah, perhaps, disagrees. No law explicitly refers to them entering a levirate marriage. The elder brother is deferring the decision to a time when the younger brothers become legally competent.

4:7 In view of the reluctance evident in the two previous passages, the rabbis provide a material reward for the brother who enters levirate marriage: the property of the deceased brother.

he is prohibited with respect to her relatives: As with divorce, as a consequence of *halitsah* the levir is not permitted to marry the close relations of the former sister-in-law.

8 One who performs *halitsah* for his levirate widow,
and his brother married her sister, and died—
[the widow] performs *halitsah* but does not undergo levirate marriage.
And so also one who divorces his wife,
and his brother married her sister, and died—
she is thereby exempt from both *halitsah* and levirate marriage.[20]

4:9–11 Additional Rules about Levirate Marriage and Halitsah

9 A woman awaiting levirate marriage,
where [a levir][21] has betrothed her sister.
In the name of R. Judah b. Betera they said:
One says to him: Wait till your elder brother performs the deed.
If his brother performed *halitsah* for her or took her in—
he may take his wife in.
If the levirate widow died—
he may take his wife in.
If the levir died—
he dismisses his wife with a writ of divorce,
and his brother's wife with *halitsah*.

10 The levirate widow does not perform *halitsah* or undergo levirate marriage before three months have passed;[22]
and so too all other women may not become betrothed or marry before three months have passed.
The rule is the same for virgins and nonvirgins,[23] divorcees and widows, married and betrothed.

[20] **K**, **P** lack "from both *halitsah* and levirate marriage."
[21] Lit. "whose brother [i.e. of the deceased]."
[22] Here and below, lit. "until she has three months."
[23] Lit. "having a husband/owner."

4:8 Provides expansion for the final sentence of 4:7.

4:9 For cases of this type, see chapter 2.

wait until your elder brother...: If the elder brother (not betrothed to the widow's sister) performs either levirate marriage or *halitsah*, the betrothed brother is free to marry the sister.

If the levir died: The levir who was not betrothed to the deceased sister. The betrothed brother must divorce the sister (canceling formal betrothal requires divorce) and undergo *halitsah* with her sister (prohibited to him as the sister of his divorced wife). Unlike the last case in 4:8, here levirate obligation to the widow preceded the betrothal of the sister.

4:10 *betrothed*: Here from root *'rs*. Elsewhere (see 2:6), the Mishnah uses verbs on the root *qdsh* ("sanctified"). These terms are used interchangeably in this tractate to denote betrothal. In English, a differentiation in terms is impossible.

three months will determine whether the woman is pregnant. If pregnant, there are no levirate bonds or restrictions on the widow or brothers. The Mishnah rules more generally that all widows must wait three months before marrying again, so that it is known whose child she bears.

virgins .... betrothed: The text presents three pairs, two of opposites, while the third is a complementary pair. *Nonvirgin* (*be'ulot*) literally means "under possession," but can also refer to having been sexually penetrated.

R. Judah says:
The married may be betrothed and the betrothed may marry
except for the betrothed in Judaea,
because he has no shame before her.[24]
R. Yose says:
All women may become betrothed, except the widow,
because of mourning.

11 Four brothers married to four women, and they died.
If the eldest among them wishes to take all of them in levirate marriage—
he is permitted.
Whoever was married to two wives, and died—
intercourse with, or *halitsah* for, one of them exempts her co-wife.
If one of them was fit for marriage and the other unfit:
if he was performing *halitsah*—
he performs *halitsah* with the unfit one;
if he was performing levirate marriage—
he performs levirate marriage with the fit one.

4:12–13 *The Mamzer*

12 One who remarries[25] his divorcee,
or marries the woman for whom he performed *halitsah*,
and one who marries a relative of the woman for whom he performed *halitsah*—
he must put her out, and the offspring is a *mamzer*—
the words of R. Aqiva;
but the Sages say:
The child is not a *mamzer*.
They agree in the case of one who marries the relative of his divorcee,
that the offspring is a *mamzer*.

---

[24] Lit. "his heart is coarse (or 'large') with her."   [25] Lit. "takes back."

R. Judah allows once married women whose status changed to become betrothed (but not yet marry) within three months and he permits the betrothed to marry, within three months, because he does not suspect them of having engaged in illicit sex.

except for the betrothed in Judaea: According to *Ketubbot* 1:5, in Judah betrothed couples used to spend time together before the wedding.

because he has no shame: See n. 24. For the expression, see e.g. *Sotah* 1:6.

R. Yose forbids a widow to become betrothed due to the custom of mourning, rather than the paternity of a child she may be bearing.

4:11 *if the eldest* among the remaining brothers *wished to take all of them, he is permitted*: Unlike the case of the many wives of one deceased brother (3:9).

exempts her co-wife: See 1:1.

unfit: A prohibited incestuous marriage or, for a priest, marriage to a divorcee.

4:12 *mamzer*: The meaning of this term in the Bible (Deuteronomy 23:3; Zachariah 9:6) is derogatory but obscure. See 4:13.

13 Who is a *mamzer*?
Every blood relative who is included in *He may not enter*[26]—
the words of R. Aqiva;
Simeon the Timnite says:
Every [offspring of a union] for which one is liable to *karet*,
and the *halakhah* is according to his words.
R. Joshua says:
Every [offspring of a union] for which one is liable to the death penalty administered by a court.
R. Simeon b. Azzai said:
I found a scroll of genealogies in Jerusalem and it was written therein:
A certain man is a *mamzer* from a married woman,
upholding the words of R. Joshua.
One whose wife died—
he is permitted with respect to her sister;
if he divorced her and she died—
he is permitted with respect to her sister;
if she married another and died—
he is permitted with respect to her sister.
One whose levirate widow died—
he is permitted with respect to her sister;
if he performed *halitsah* for her and she died—
he is permitted with respect to her sister.

[26] K: "The prohibition of entering." See annotations

4:13 *Who is a mamzer?* According to R. Aqiva, a *mamzer* is the offspring of a sexual union between close blood relatives (Heb. *she'er basar*, see Leviticus 18:6, 25:29), who would be included in verses that state explicitly *he may not enter the congregation of the Lord*, see Deuteronomy 23:3-4, 23:3 mentioning *mamzer*. Possibly, R. Aqiva limits *mamzer* status to the offspring of an Israelite and an Ammonite or Moabite, or a castrated man and an Israelite woman specified in these verses (but cf. his view in 4:12). Alternatively: (1) Reading "entering" (as in **K**, see n. 26) and taking it as a euphemism for intercourse (see 6:1), R. Aqiva may refer to sexual unions, and not to scriptural verses at all; or (2) R. Aqiva may include both *every blood relative* and anyone *who is included in He may not enter* (Maimonides).

karet: See *Keritot*, introduction. Leviticus 18:29 specifies *karet* at the end of the list of incestuous and forbidden unions. According to *Simeon the Timnite*, *mamzer* is thus one born of one of those forbidden unions.

the halakhah is according to his words: Such legal determinations are rare in tannaitic literature (only twice more in the Mishnah: *Pe'ah* 3:6, *Shevi'it* 9:5). It is possibly an editorial insertion here, because the passage continues listing other opinions.

death penalty: This view limits the number of *mamzerim*, because there are fewer cases of incest and forbidden intercourse that are punishable by *karet* (see the list in Leviticus 20:10-14) than by death.

R. Simeon b. Azzai: Evidence, such as ancient documents surviving from the Second Temple period (as here), is practically never adduced in tannaitic literature.

One whose wife died: In these cases the Mishnah limits the definition of incest with a wife's sister to the lifetime of the wife.

Chapter Five

5:1–6 *Levirate Marriage, Halitsah, Verbal Betrothal, and Divorce*

5 Rabban Gamaliel says:
There is no writ of divorce [of a levirate widow] after a writ of divorce,
and no verbal betrothal after verbal betrothal,
and no possession after possession,
and no *halitsah* after *halitsah*.
But the Sages say:
There is a writ of divorce after a writ of divorce,
and verbal betrothal after verbal betrothal,
but there is nothing after possession or after *halitsah*.

2 How?
He made a verbal betrothal with his levirate widow and gave her a writ of divorce—
she requires *halitsah* from him.
He made a verbal betrothal and performed *halitsah*—
she requires a writ of divorce from him.
He made a verbal betrothal and took possession of her—
this is according to the commandment.

3 He gave a writ of divorce and made a verbal betrothal—
she requires a writ of divorce and *halitsah*.
He gave a deed of divorce, and took possession of her—

5:1 *There is no writ of divorce...after halitsah*: It is assumed by commentators that the problem discussed is one where the levir performed divorce, verbal betrothal, possession (i.e. act of intercourse, see above, 4:10), or *halitsah* with one levirate widow and followed this with another such act with a co-wife. According to *Rabban Gamaliel*, completing one of these acts with one levirate widow, fully terminates (in the case of divorce or *halitsah*) or fulfills (in the case of verbal betrothal or intercourse) the levirate obligation and further acts with co-wives have no legal effect.

the Sages distinguish between divorce and verbal betrothal on the one hand and possession and *halitsah* on the other. Only in the case of the latter does the first act terminate the levirate obligation.

5:2 *How?* Under what circumstance does a levirate widow require a divorce? In the case of a levir who *made a verbal betrothal and performed halitsah*. Alternatively, and more closely aligned with the commentaries, this passage and those following exemplify the principle of "divorce after divorce," etc. Given the assumption in the commentaries that 5:1 deals with two acts with two women, these examples (involving two acts with the same levirate widow, but see 5:3, end) do not appear to explain 5:1 at all. The commentaries understand this as a freestanding block of material on a related topic—circumstances involving one levir and one levirate widow—rather than an explanation of the preceding.

according to the commandment: An unusual expression, according to which the expected course of action is verbal betrothal of his brother's widow, followed by "taking possession," namely sexual intercourse.

5:3 From here to the end of the chapter, the Mishnah discusses the various possible combinations of the terms mentioned in 5:1. The repeated specification *there is nothing after halitsah* suggests that these passages hold a view closer to that of the Sages in 5:1 than to Rabban Gamaliel's.

she requires a writ of divorce and *halitsah*.
He gave a writ of divorce and performed *halitsah*—
there is nothing after *halitsah*.
He performed *halitsah* and made a verbal betrothal,
or gave a writ of divorce and took possession,
or took possession and made a verbal betrothal,
or gave a writ of divorce and performed *halitsah*—
there is nothing after *halitsah*.
The rule is the same both for one levirate widow and one levir,
and for two levirate widows and one levir.[27]

4 How?
He[28] made a verbal betrothal to this one, and a verbal betrothal to this one—
they require two writs of divorce and *halitsah*.
A verbal betrothal to this one and a writ of divorce to this one—
she requires a writ of divorce and *halitsah*.
A verbal betrothal to this one and took possession of this one—
they require two writs of divorce and *halitsah*.
A verbal betrothal to this one and performed *halitsah* for this one—
the first one requires a writ of divorce.
A writ of divorce to this one and a writ of divorce to this one—
they both require *halitsah* from him.
A writ of divorce to this one and took possession of this one—
she requires a writ of divorce and *halitsah*.
A writ of divorce to this one and a verbal betrothal to this one—
she requires a writ of divorce and *halitsah*.

[27] **K** and other manuscripts: "one levirate widow and for two levirate widows."
[28] The order of the clauses varies in the witnesses.

The rule is the same both for one levirate widow, as in 5:2–3, *and for two levirate widows*, as assumed by the commentaries for 5:1 and exemplified further in 5:4.

5:4 *How?* Exemplifying the closing general rule in 5:3.

verbal betrothal to this one and ....*to this one*: The verbal betrothal to each must be severed by divorce, but only one *halitsah* is required to terminate the levirate obligation.

verbal betrothal .... *writ of divorce*: The woman who was betrothed verbally requires divorce to sever the connection. He must also perform *halitsah* with one of the women.

verbal betrothal .... *took possession*: The logic here is that since when he had intercourse with the second, he had already made a verbal betrothal with the first, the act of intercourse does not successfully create levirate marriage. Again, this requires divorce from each, and one act of *halitsah*.

verbal betrothal .... *halitsah*: Again the *halitsah* has severed the levirate bond, but the first woman must be divorced.

writ of divorce .... *writ of divorce*: The women nevertheless need *halitsah* to sever the levirate bond.

writ of divorce .... *took possession*: The writ of divorce is taken to mean that the levir does not intend to perform levirate marriage. As a result the act of intercourse that follows is not valid for effecting levirate marriage. The levir must divorce her, and perform *halitsah*.

A writ of divorce to this one and performed *halitsah* for this one—
there is nothing after *halitsah*.

5 He performed *halitsah* and performed *halitsah*,
or performed *halitsah* and made a verbal betrothal,
or gave a writ of divorce, or took possession;
or took possession and took possession,
or took possession and made a verbal betrothal,
or gave a deed of divorce and performed *halitsah*—
there is nothing after *halitsah*.
[This is true] both for one levir and for two levirate widows
and for two levirs and one levirate widow.

6 He performed *halitsah* and made a verbal betrothal,
or gave a writ of divorce and took possession,
or took possession and made a verbal betrothal,
or gave a writ of divorce and performed *halitsah*—
there is nothing after *halitsah*,
whether *halitsah* took place[29] in the first place, in the middle, or in the end.
And possession—
when it is in the first place: there is nothing after it;
in the middle or at the end: there is something after it.[30]
R. Nehemiah says:
Both possession and *halitsah*, whether in the first place, in the middle, or at the end:
there is nothing after it.

[29] Added for clarity.   [30] K and others lack this clause.

---

there is nothing after halitsah: The valid *halitsah* terminates the levirate obligation. Unlike some of the preceding cases where both women needed divorce, *halitsah*, or both, here there is no requirement to "fix" the status of the first woman.

5:5 Two women are assumed in each of the cases. Thus *performed halitsah* with one woman *and performed halitsah* with a second woman. In addition, unlike 5:4, there are two sets of cases, one in which *halitsah* was performed with the first woman and another in which intercourse was performed first.

there is nothing after halitsah: Apparently, this should be taken as corresponding to the view of the Sages in 5:1: either *halitsah* or an act of intercourse is final, in that there is no remaining bond between the levir and the other widow.

This is true both for one levir: Cf. 5:3 above.

5:6 *He performed…*: Repeats cases stated in 5:3, although here possibly assuming multiple partners as at the end of 5:5, or a different act with the same woman.

there is nothing after halitsah: If the husband performs *halitsah* with one woman, no further steps are required to either terminate or fulfill the levirate obligation.

And possession: According to this view, intercourse only fulfills the levirate obligation if it is first in the series of possible acts. If it is preceded, for instance, by divorce it cannot fully complete the levirate obligation.

R. Nehemiah, by contrast, views intercourse as effective even if it follows divorce.

Chapter Six

6:1–2   *The Consequences of Intercourse*

6 One who has sexual intercourse with[31] his levirate widow,
whether unintentionally or intentionally,
whether under compulsion or voluntarily,
even if he does it unintentionally, and she intentionally,
he intentionally, and she unintentionally,
he is under compulsion, and she is not under compulsion,
she is under compulsion, and he is not under compulsion,
both he who "pours" and he who "finishes"—
he has acquired.
And there is no differentiation between one intercourse and another.[32]

2   And also one who has sexual intercourse
with any of the prohibited relations in the Torah,
or with those who are unfit—
such as a widow with a high priest,
a divorcee or one who has undergone *halitsah* with a regular priest,
a female *mamzer* or a female *natin* with an Israelite,
a daughter of Israel with a *mamzer* or a *natin*—
he has made her unfit.
And there is no differentiation between intercourses.[33]

---

[31] Lit. "comes to."
[32] Lit. "He did not differentiate between intercourse and intercourse."
[33] Lit. "He did not differentiate between intercourse and intercourse."

6:1 *"pours"*: A euphemism for beginning intercourse, perhaps penetration. *"Finishes"* refers to completing the sex act, so perhaps ejaculation.

acquired: The levir has acquired the levirate widow as a wife. For betrothal as acquisition, compare *Qiddushim* 1:1.

between one intercourse and another: The distinction is either between types of acts, or between intentions (e.g. for the purpose of betrothal or not).

6:2 *unfit*: In this case, a woman who cannot legally enter a marriage with the man in question, as the Mishnah specifies. For the priestly prohibitions, see 2:4.

mamzer: See 4:12.

natin: See 2:4.

made her unfit: Disqualified the women from marrying into the priesthood or, if daughters of priests, from eating *terumah*. Some of these are already invalid (divorcee, *mamzer*, and *natin*) so the mishnah is partly redundant. The mishnah may be using a standard formula that is relevant for the first part, while the last part is simply appended as in other cases.

6:3–5 Marriage to Priests

3 A widow [who had intercourse] with a high priest,
a divorcee and one who has undergone *halitsah* with a regular priest.
If from betrothal—
they may not eat *terumah*;[34]
R. Eliezer[35] and R. Simeon deem them fit.
If they were widowed or divorced:
from marriage—
they are unfit,
from betrothal—
they are fit.

4 A high priest may not marry a widow,
whether a widow from betrothal or a widow from marriage.
And he may not marry a woman who has attained majority;
R. Eliezer[36] and R. Simeon deem her fit
in the case of one who has attained majority.
He may not marry one struck by wood.
If he betrothed a widow, and was appointed high priest—
he may take her in.

[34] **C**: "The words of R. Meir."
[35] So too **C**; **K**, **P**, and others: "Eleazar."
[36] **K**, **P**, and others: "Eleazar."

6:3 For the biblical rules restricting marriage by priests see Leviticus 21:3, 7, 13–14. In addition, Leviticus 22:12–13 prohibits a daughter of a priest who marries outside the priesthood from eating *terumah*, but allows a childless divorcee or widow to eat *terumah* as part of her father's household (see 3:10). This passage deems a daughter of priests who engages in such a marriage as no longer permitted to eat *terumah* either as a wife, or upon dissolution of the marriage as the daughter of a priest.

from betrothal: The anonymous first view of the Mishnah is that this improper betrothal disqualifies the woman from eating *terumah*. R. Eliezar and R. Simeon do not disqualify her. Presumably, both opinions agree that if she was fully married she is disqualified.

were widowed or divorced: The issue is now at what point these women become permanently disqualified from eating *terumah*.

6:4 *A high priest may not marry*: See 2:4. To the biblical rule (Leviticus 21:13) the Mishnah adds the qualification from betrothal or from marriage (see above, 3:10).

a woman who has attained majority: Heb. *bogeret*. The Mishnah is divided about whether majority is attained with the physical changes of puberty or with age (when she becomes twelve years old, *Niddah* 5:6; in later law twelve years and six months). Once an adult and no longer under her father's authority she is disqualified from marrying a high priest, who may only marry a virgin.

struck by wood: A woman who lost her hymen, while still technically a virgin since she had not engaged in sexual intercourse (e.g. *Ketubbot* 1:7).

take her in: Complete the marriage. See above, 2:6.

betrothed a widow: The legal issue is that a rank-and-file priest may marry a widow, but a high priest may not.

And it once happened that Joshua b. Gamla betrothed Martha bat Boethus, and the king appointed him to be high priest, and he took her in.
A levirate widow who fell to a regular priest, and he was nominated high priest, even though he made a verbal betrothal—
in this case he may not take her in.
A high priest, whose brother died,
performs *halitsah* but not levirate marriage.

5 A regular priest may not marry a sterile woman,
unless he has a wife and sons.
R. Judah says:
Even if he has a wife and sons, he may not marry a sterile woman,
because she is the *zonah* spoken of in the Torah.
But the Sages say:
The *zonah* is none other than a female convert, a freed female slave, or she who was sexually possessed in fornication.[37]

6:6 *A Man's Duty to Procreate*

6 A person may not desist from procreation unless he has sons.[38]
The House of Shammai say:
Two males,
but the House of Hillel say:
A male and a female,
as it is written: *male and female he created them.*
If he married a woman and remained with her for ten years,
and she did not give birth—

---

[37] Lit. "who has been possessed in a possession of fornication." [38] Or "children."

---

it once happed to Joshua b. Gamla: Joshua b. Gamla was a high priest toward the end of the Second Temple period. Martha bat Boethus is known only from rabbinic literature.

who fell to a regular priest: For levirate marriage or *halitsah*. In this case the preference is not to perform levirate marriage.

6:5 *sterile woman*: See annotations to 1:1.

zonah: Leviticus 21:7, usually rendered "harlot" or "prostitute" in biblical translations. R. Judah obviously understands the term as applying to a woman who engages in nonreproductive sex.

The zonah is none other than: This view limits the prohibited women to the following categories.

6:6 *A person may not desist*: The Mishnah continues by making it explicit that this law applies only to men.

sons: As the mishnah progresses it becomes clear that according to one opinion, this includes also daughters.

The House of Shammai .... and the House of Hillel: Both houses see the number two as fulfilling the commandment, although they do not agree on the gender of the two. Interestingly, the House of Hillel, who claim that the commandment to procreate also requires daughters, base themselves on a biblical verse (rare in this tractate). Perhaps the House of Shammai deem the requirement to bear sons as self-evident and do not need a verse to support their argument.

male and female: Genesis 5:2.

he is not permitted to desist.
If he divorced her—
she is permitted to marry another;
and the second one is allowed to remain with her ten years.
And if she had a miscarriage she reckons from the time of the miscarriage.
The man is commanded to procreate, but not the woman;
R. Yohanan b. Beroqa says:
Of both of them it says:
God blessed them and God said to them be fertile and increase.

Chapter Seven

7:1–6 *Marriage into the Priesthood and Consumption of Terumah*

7 A widow married to a high priest,
a divorcee or one who underwent *halitsah* married to a regular priest,
if she brought in to him *melog* slaves and Iron Sheep slaves—
her *melog* slaves may not eat *terumah*,
but her Iron Sheep slaves may eat.
And these are *melog* slaves:
if they die, they die for her;
and if they increase in value, they increase in value for her.
Although he is obligated to sustain them,
they may not eat *terumah*.
And these are Iron Sheep slaves:
if they die, they die for him;
and if they increase in value, they increase in value for him.

is not permitted to desist: This law requires a man to make sure he sires children, either by divorcing his sterile wife or by marrying a second wife.

she is permitted to marry another: The woman is allowed to try again with another man.

The man . . . . but not the woman: An explicit statement of what was implicit in the previous clauses.

God blessed them: Genesis 1:28. Again, a dissenting view requires a biblical verse.

7:1 The Mishnah now continues the issues of the priesthood discussed in 6:4–5, and interrupted by 6:6.

melog slaves: The term appears only here in 7:1 and 7:2, and may derive from the Aramaic *melag*, "pluck." Property that the wife owns is not sedentary but plucked, because it goes with her from one man's house (her father's) to another's (her husband's). With *melog* property, any *death* or *increase* is assumed by the wife (*for her*), and they continue to have the status of the wife.

Iron Sheep slaves: See *Bava Metsi'a* 5:6, *Bekhorot* 4:2. The husband is *accountable* for the full value of these slaves, and absorbs any *death* or *increase* they create. As such, they are treated as the husband's for the purposes of *terumah*.

Since he is accountable for them,
they may eat *terumah*.

2 The daughter of an Israelite who was married to a priest,
and brought slaves in to him,
whether *melog* slaves or Iron Sheep slaves—
in this case, they may eat *terumah*.
And the daughter of a priest who was married to an Israelite,
and brought slaves in to him,
whether *melog* slaves or Iron Sheep slaves—
in this case, they may not eat *terumah*.

3 The daughter of an Israelite who was married to a priest,
and he died, and left her pregnant—
her slaves may not eat *terumah*,
because of the portion of the fetus,
because the fetus makes unfit but does not permit eating[39]—
the words of R. Yose.
They said to him:
Since you testified to us about the daughter of Israel to a priest,
the daughter of a priest to a priest, who died, and left her pregnant—
may her slaves not eat *terumah*, because of the portion of the fetus?

4 The fetus, the levir, betrothal, one who is deaf and mute,

---

[39] Lit. "feed."

7:2 The general law on which 7:1 is based.

7:3 *because of the portion of the fetus*: A widowed Israelite mother of a priest may eat *terumah* as the mother of a priest, and a widowed priestly mother of a nonpriest may not. Here, the discussion is about the legal effect of the fetus.

makes unfit: The daughter of a priest who is carrying the unborn child of her late husband, who was not a priest, may not eat *terumah*.

does not permit: Once she has given birth and is the mother of a priest, the widow may eat (7:5), but before the birth, the fetus does permit her to do so. The expression "portion of the fetus" is obscure and it makes the application of the rule to the widow's slaves unclear. One traditional explanation is that only *those that are born into his household* (Leviticus 22:11) are eligible to eat *terumah* and this fetus will not be born into his household. The Tosefta views R. Yose's opinion as unfair.

They said to him: An objection that the rule is not convincing, because it implies that even where the mother was the *daughter of a priest* and the father was *a priest* the slaves cannot eat *because of the portion of the fetus*. In 7:5, though, we learn that a fetus, son of a priest, once born qualifies his mother to eat *terumah*.

7:4 *The fetus, and the levir . . . . and do not permit eating*: This list extends the principle of the previous mishnah.

The fetus: See 7:3.

the levir: A priest's daughter awaiting the decision of the levir may not return to her father's house and partake of *terumah*. Also, a priestly levir of an Israelite woman does not permit her to partake of *terumah*.

betrothal: See above, 2:6. A priest's daughter loses her right to partake of *terumah* when she becomes betrothed to a nonpriest, and an Israelite woman betrothed to a priest, may not yet begin to partake of *terumah*.

one who is deaf and mute: See chapter 14. A speech- and hearing-impaired husband cannot form a fully valid marriage. If he was a nonpriest he disqualifies a priest's daughter from eating *terumah*, and if he was a priest he does not permit his nonpriestly wife to eat *terumah*.

and a male who is nine years and one day old—
these make unfit but do not permit eating.
If it is a matter of doubt whether he is nine years and one day old or not;
a matter of doubt whether he has produced two hairs or not;
if a house fell on him and on his brother's daughter,
and it is unknown which died first—
her co-wife undergoes *halitsah* and not levirate marriage.

5 The rapist, the seducer, and one who is legally incompetent—
neither make unfit nor permit eating.
And if they are not fit to join Israel,
they disqualify.
How?
An Israelite who had intercourse with the daughter of a priest—
she may eat *terumah*;
if she became pregnant—
she may not eat *terumah*.
If the fetus was dismembered in her womb—
she may eat.
A priest who had sexual intercourse with a daughter of Israel—
she may not eat *terumah*;
if she became pregnant—
she may not eat.
If she gave birth—
she may eat.

one who is nine years and one day old: Sexual intercourse from this age on is considered legally meaningful (see 10:6–9). Here, the context is sex with a levirate widow. The woman is unfit to partake of *terumah*, both where she is a priest's daughter and the deceased husband and the levir Israelites, and where she is an Israelite woman and the deceased husband and the levir priests.

If it is a matter of doubt: The cases of doubt either expand on the preceding (their action prohibits a woman from eating *terumah* but does not permit) or introduce a new rule about whether co-wives must undergo *halitsah*.

two hairs: Signs of majority; majority is required whenever proper intention is required.

the house fell: This should be read as if it said. "If the house fell on him and on his brother's daughter to whom he was married," so that the wife is the daughter of a *levir*. Since we are in doubt whether the wife predeceased the husband (and co-wives are subject to levirate marriage or *halitsah*) or the husband predeceased the wife (in which case co-wives are exempt, above 1:1), the co-wife *undergoes halitsah and not levirate marriage*.

7:5 *legally incompetent*: See above, 4:6. Here, he is able to engage in sex but cannot do so with a legally binding intention to marry.

neither make unfit nor permit eating: If one of these had sex with a woman and they were priests they do not make the woman fit to partake of *terumah*. If the woman was the daughter of a priest and they were Israelites, they do not disqualify her from partaking of *terumah*, because their action had no legal force regarding ownership of the woman.

dismembered in her womb: A term for artificial abortion, cf. *Hullin* 4:2.

If she gave birth—she may eat: A pregnant woman does not partake of *terumah* based on the status of the fetus, but once she gives birth, the child determines her status as priestly or not. See above, 7:3.

We find that the power of the son is greater than the power of the father.
The slave disqualifies through sexual intercourse,
but does not disqualify through progeny.
How?
A daughter of Israel to a priest, or a daughter of a priest to an Israelite,
and she had a son from him,
and the son went and became overpowered[40] by a female slave,
and she gave birth to a son from him—
in this case, the offspring[41] is a slave.
If his father's mother was a daughter of Israel to a priest—
she may not eat *terumah*;
a daughter of a priest to an Israelite,
she may eat *terumah*.
A *mamzer* makes unfit and permits eating.
How?
A daughter of an Israelite to a priest,
or a priest's daughter to an Israelite,
and she had a daughter from him,
and the daughter went and was married to a slave, or a gentile,
and had a son from him—
in this case, this is a *mamzer*;
if his mother's mother was a daughter of an Israelite to a priest,
she may eat *terumah*;
a priest's daughter to an Israelite,
she may not eat *terumah*.

[40] Or "conquered."   [41] Heb. "he."

the power of the son: The newborn child of the previous clause.

The slave…: In the examples that follow a daughter of Israel is married to a priest, or a priest's daughter is married to an Israelite. Normally, this would make the former qualified to partake of *terumah* and the latter disqualified. However, if in either case the woman had a son who produced a grandson from a slave woman (who is himself therefore a slave), the grandmother returns to her original status. The priest's daughter is qualified to partake of *terumah* and the Israelite is not. (The examples assume that both the grandfather and the husband have died.)

overpowered: This terminology may suggest that the rabbis see such a relationship as a result of the man not being able to resist the maidservant's allure.

mamzer: See above, 4:13.

makes unfit and permits eating: The *mamzer* is described here as having an opposite effect from the slave on his grandmother. She retains her new status after marriage. The offspring is Israelite, although unmarriageable. Thus a priestly grandmother cannot eat based on her father's status and the nonpriestly grandmother has an offspring from priests.

this is a mamzer: Here the definition is one who is born of an Israelite woman and a slave or a gentile. The union between them is described as marriage and the offspring for these purposes valid (although with legal disqualifications). This definition certainly does not conform to the one suggested and sanctioned in 4.13.

6 A high priest sometimes disqualifies.
How?
A priest's daughter to[42] an Israelite
and had a daughter from him,
and the daughter went and married a priest,
and had a son from him—
in this case, this one is fit to be a high priest standing and serving at the altar,
and feeds his mother,
and disqualifies his mother's mother.
And this one says:
May there not be many like my grandson the high priest[43]
for he disqualifies me from eating *terumah*.

Chapter Eight

8:1–3 *Those Excluded from the Congregation of the Lord*

8 The uncircumcised
and all those who are impure—
may not eat *terumah*;
their wives and slaves—
may eat *terumah*.
One *whose testicles are crushed or whose male member is cut off*—
they and their slaves may eat;
and their wives may not eat.

---

[42] K, P, C explicitly: "who was married to."   [43] Lit. "Not like my son the high priest."

7:6 The outcome described is intentionally counterintuitive. A priest's daughter, married to an Israelite does not partake of *terumah*. Her daughter, an Israelite married to a priest, does partake of *terumah* even after the husband's death, on the strength of her son. That son may become a high priest. However, the grandmother, a former priest's daughter, cannot return to the status she had before she married an Israelite because of this grandson.

8:1 The discussion of eating *terumah* serves as a transition to a digression on those who may "enter the congregation."

The uncircumcised: This rule is not in the Torah, which explicitly prohibits only uncircumcised men from eating the Passover sacrifice (Exodus 12:48), and more generally punishes with *karet* one who forgoes circumcision (Genesis 17:14).

impure: Priests who have contracted impurity, Leviticus 22:4–6.

whose testicles are crushed: Deuteronomy 23:2.

wives may not eat: The wife's right to partake of priestly dues depends on her husband's virility and undeformed purity. If he has become sterile, and has intercourse with his wife, he loses his right to feed her *terumah*. The Mishnah reads Scripture's *may not enter into the congregation of Israel* as prohibiting intercourse with an Israelite woman.

And if he did not have intercourse with her[44] once he became one
whose testicles are crushed or whose male member is cut off—
in this case, these may eat.

2 What is one *whose testicles are crushed*?
Anyone whose testicles have been wounded,
and even just one of them.
And one *whose male member is cut off*?
Anyone whose penis has been severed.
And if just a hair-strand's width[45] of the crown has been preserved—
he is fit.
Those *whose testicles are crushed or whose male member is cut off*
are permitted to a female convert and a freedwoman;
and they are forbidden nothing except being admitted into the congregation,
as it is written: *No one whose testicles are crushed or whose male member is cut off shall be admitted to the congregation of the Lord.*

3 An Ammonite and a Moabite are prohibited,
and their prohibition is forever;
but their females are permitted immediately.
An Egyptian and an Edomite are only prohibited for three generations,
both males and females.
R. Simeon permits the females immediately.[46]
Said R. Simeon:
The matter is a case of lesser and greater:
If in a place where he prohibited the males forever, he permitted the females immediately,
in a place where he prohibited the male only for three generations—
does not logic require that we should permit the females immediately?
They said to him:
If this is *halakhah*, we will accept;

[44] Lit. "did not know her."   [45] **K**: "thread."   [46] Absent in **K**.

And if he did not have intercourse: . This passage introduces a third term, "knowledge," for sexual intercourse after "coming into" (*bi'ah*) and "possessing" (*be'ilah*).

8:2 *whose testicles*: Lit. "eggs." Leviticus 21:20 uses different terminology for one with mutilated testicles, referred to in *Bekhorot* 7:5. The Torah speaks specifically of a mutilated priest whereas *Bekhorot* speaks of a mutilated beast.

penis: Heb. *gid*, generally "sinew, tendon." It is also the term used in Genesis 32:33 and tractate *Zevahim* to refer to the sciatic nerve, whose consumption is prohibited.

crown: A euphemism for the glans which is uncovered by circumcision, see e.g. *Shabbat* 19:6.

fit, as a priest, and to enter the congregation of Israel. On this translation see above, 1:4.

No one...of the Lord: Deuteronomy 23:2.

8:3 *an Ammonite and a Moabite ....An Egyptian and an Edomite*: Deuteronomy 23:4–9.

If this is halakhah, a normative law determined by tradition. See also *Keritot* 3:9. The statement suggests that application of the logical principle is not decisive, and may be challenged. In this case, the discussion does not continue, because R. Simeon claims that this is indeed the law.

but if it is an inference from reason there is a rebuttal.
He said to them:
No, for I state *halakhah*!
The *mamzer* and the *natin* are prohibited and their prohibition is forever;
the rule is one and the same for both males and females.

8:4–6 *Halitsah and a Eunuch, Sterile Woman, Androgynos, and Tumtum*

4 Said R. Joshua:
I heard that the eunuch performs *halitsah*,
and one performs *halitsah* for his wife,
and that the eunuch does not perform *halitsah*,
and one does not perform *halitsah* for his wife;
and I cannot explain.
Said R. Aqiva:
I will explain:
A eunuch due to humans[47] performs *halitsah*,
and one performs *halitsah* for his wife,
because there was a time when he was fit.
A eunuch due to the sun[48] does not perform *halitsah*,
and one does not perform *halitsah* for his wife,
because there was no time when he was fit.
R. Eliezer says:
No, rather: a eunuch due to the sun performs *halitsah*,
and one performs *halitsah* for his wife,
because he is curable.
A eunuch due to humans does not perform *halitsah*,
and one does not perform *halitsah* for his wife,
because he is incurable.
R. Joshua b. Betera testified about Ben Magoset,
who was a eunuch due to humans in Jerusalem,

[47] Lit. "a eunuch of a human."   [48] Lit. "a eunuch of the sun," i.e. since birth.

mamzer (see 4:13) appears in the same biblical context as the prohibition against Ammonites and Moabites (Deuteronomy 23:3). The *natin* (above 2:4) is a rabbinic addition.

8:4 *I heard*: Note the transmission of two seemingly contradictory traditions.

performs halitsah: Here, only the possibility of *halitsah* is discussed. Since the main issue is procreation and a eunuch cannot procreate, levirate marriage is not considered for either the widow of a eunuch or for a eunuch whose brother has died childless.

time when he was fit to be a husband; as opposed to the *eunuch due to the sun*, who was never fit.

curable: Castration performed by humans is irreversible, castration performed by nature is not.

Ben Magoset: For a similar case see 4:13. Note that as opposed to the preceding discussion, which only considered *halitsah*, this story speaks of levirate marriage. This may indicate that it derives from a different legal tradition.

and his wife underwent levirate marriage,
upholding the words of R. Aqiva.

5 The eunuch neither performs *halitsah* nor takes in levirate marriage.
And, so too, the sterile woman neither performs *halitsah* nor is taken in levirate marriage.
The eunuch who performed *halitsah* for his levirate widow,
has not made her unfit;
if he sexually possessed her—
he has made her unfit,
because this is a sexual possession of fornication.
And also the sterile woman for whom the brothers performed *halitsah*—
they have not made her unfit;
if they sexually possessed her—
they have made her unfit,
because the sexual possession of her is one of fornication.[49]

6 A eunuch due to the sun who is a priest who married a daughter of Israel
permits her to eat *terumah*.
R. Yose and R. Simeon say:
An *androgynos* priest who married a daughter of Israel
permits her to eat *terumah*.
R. Judah says:
A *tumtum* who was torn and it was revealed that he is male—
may not perform *halitsah*,
because he is like a eunuch.
An *androgynos* marries, but is not taken in marriage.
R. Eliezer[50] says:
An *androgynos*, one is liable to stoning on his account as with a male.

---

[49] Lit. "the sexual possession of her is the sexual possession of fornication."
[50] K, P, C, and others: "Eleazar."

8:5 *The eunuch*: Compare 8:4.

the sterile woman: See 1:1 and 6:5.

has not made her unfit to marry into the priesthood as a divorcee (*halitsah* being considered equivalent to divorce), Leviticus 21:7 and above, 2:4. Because he is a eunuch, his *halitsah* has no effect on her status, but if he engaged in sex with her, this is *sexual possession of fornication*, making her a *zonah* (see above, 6:5), who is forbidden to a priest.

8:6 *A eunuch . . . . terumah*: See 8:4. Although not capable of reproducing, his marriage is effective and does render the wife eligible to eat terumah.

An androgynos: A Greek term, combining *andro-* (man) and *gyne* (woman). It refers to a person who has the sexual characteristics of both males and females. The rabbis treat the *androgynos* here as male: capable of marrying a woman and, if a priest, making the wife eligible to eat *terumah*.

tumtum: The word is of unknown origin, and refers to someone of indeterminate sex. According to this mishnah, they may have a definite sex (determined by proper genitals), but it is hidden beneath a layer of skin.

An androgynos marries as a male and is *not taken in marriage* as a female.

liable to stoning . . . . as with a male: For R. Eliezer, sex with an *androgynos* is considered a male homosexual act, punishable like other male homosexual acts.

Chapter Nine

9:1–3 *Women Permitted or Prohibited to a Husband or Levir*

9 There are those who are permitted to their husbands and forbidden to their levirs,
permitted to their levirs and forbidden to their husbands,
permitted to both these and these,
forbidden to both these and these.
These are permitted to their husbands and forbidden to their levirs:
a regular priest who married[51] a widow
and has a brother who is a high priest;
a *halal* who married a fit woman
and has a brother who is fit;[52]
an Israelite who married a daughter of Israel[53]
and has a brother who is a *mamzer*;
a *mamzer* who married a female *mamzer*
and has an Israelite[54] brother—
these are permitted to their husbands and forbidden to their levirs.

2 These are permitted to their levirs and forbidden to their husbands:
a high priest who betrothed a widow,
and has a brother who is a regular priest;
a fit priest who married a female *halal*
and has a brother who is a *halal*;
an Israelite who married a female *mamzer*
and has a brother who is a *mamzer*;
a *mamzer* who married a daughter of Israel[55]

---

[51] **K:** "betrothed." [52] **K:** "a fit [priest] who married a fit woman, and has a brother who is a *halal*."
[53] **K:** "an Israelite woman," *yisraelit*.
[54] **K:** "*mamzer*" (probably an error and corrected by a later hand).
[55] **K:** "an Israelite woman," *yisraelit*.

9:1 *permitted to their husbands and forbidden to their levirs*, etc.: At issue in each of the groups in 9:1–2 is levirate marriage: a man, married to a woman who is (or is not) permissible to him, dies without children, and leaves a levir who is (or is not) of similar status with respect to the woman. Thus, *a regular priest* may marry a widow; but *a high priest* may not.

halal: A person born of a priest and a woman forbidden to him, such as a divorcee. A *halal* cannot serve as a priest.

a brother who is fit: This would be a half-brother from the same father. The widow of a *halal* is also prohibited to the priestly brother.

an Israelite brother: Again, a half-brother, who is prohibited from marrying a *mamzer*.

9:2 *betrothed a widow*: In doing so, he has disqualified the widow from marrying a regular priest.

a female halal: The daughter of a priest and a forbidden wife. She is forbidden to her husband the priest, but since the levir is a *halal*, she is permitted to him.

and has an Israelite brother—
these are permitted to their levir and forbidden to their husbands.
Forbidden to both these and these:
a high priest who married a widow and has a brother who is high priest
or a regular priest;
a fit priest who married a female *halal* and has a brother who is fit;
an Israelite who married a *mamzer* and has an Israelite brother;
a *mamzer* who married a daughter of Israel[56] and has a *mamzer* brother—
these are forbidden to both these and these.
All other women are permitted to their husbands and to their levirs.

3 Female relatives once removed according to the words of scribes:
once removed from the husband
but not once removed from the levir—
she is forbidden to the husband and permitted to the levir;
once removed from the levir
but not once removed from the husband—
she is forbidden to the levir but permitted to the husband;
once removed from both this one and this one—
she is forbidden to this one and this one.
She has no *ketubbah* payment,
and no product,[57]
and no maintenance,
and no clothing,[58]
and the offspring is legitimate,
and one forces him to dismiss.
A widow to a high priest,
a divorcee or a woman who underwent *halitsah* to a regular priest,
a female *mamzer* or a female *natin* to an Israelite,
a daughter of Israel to a *natin* or a *mamzer*—
they have a *ketubbah* payment.

[56] K: "an Israelite woman," *yisra'elit*.   [57] Lit. "fruit."   [58] Lit. "that of hers that has worn out."

9:3 *Female relatives....scribes*. See above, 2:4.

She has no ketubbah payment, etc.: Although her husband had written her a marriage contract in which her property rights are listed, and although wives have certain claims of support on their husband, this woman does not.

ketubbah payment: See above, 4:3.

maintenance....clothing: The husband (if he is deceased, the husband's estate) is obligated to provide his wife/widow with food and replace her torn clothing (see e.g. *Ketubbot* 4:4, 5:8–9).

they have a ketubbah payment: In these cases, as opposed to the first set in the mishnah, the prohibition is not kinship related. The traditional explanation for the difference is that the second-degree kin are prohibited "according to the words of the scribes," and need stronger sanction than biblically derived rules.

9:4–6 Israelites, Priests, and Levites

4 A daughter of Israel who is betrothed to a priest,
or pregnant from a priest,
or is the levirate widow of a priest,
and so too the daughter of a priest to an Israelite—
may not eat *terumah*.
A daughter of an Israelite betrothed to a Levite,
pregnant from a Levite,
or is a levirate widow of a Levite,
and so too the daughter of a Levite to an Israelite—
may not eat tithes.
A daughter of a Levite betrothed to a priest,
pregnant from a priest,
a levirate widow of a priest,
and so too the daughter of a priest to a Levite—
may eat neither *terumah* nor tithes.

5 The daughter of an Israelite who is married to a priest may eat *terumah*;
if he died and she had a son from him—
she may eat *terumah*;
if she is married to a Levite—
she may eat tithes;
if he died and she had a son from him—
she may eat tithes;
if she is married to an Israelite—
she may eat neither *terumah* nor tithes;
if he died and she had a son from him—
she may eat neither *terumah* nor tithes.
If her son from the Israelite died—
she may eat tithes;
if her son from the Levite died—
she may eat *terumah*;
if her son from the priest died—
she may eat neither *terumah* nor tithes.

9:4 *may not eat terumah*. See 7:4. If an Israelite woman, her connection to a priest does not qualify her to eat *terumah*, and if the daughter of a priest, she is disqualified by her connection to the nonpriest.

may not eat tithes: Tithes are given to Levites (see Numbers 18:21–26; and *Ma'aserot* introduction). The rules for the wife or mother of a Levite are analogous to those for the wife or mother of a priest (9:5).

9:5 The principle is that as long as the husband lives, she is part of his household and shares whatever status with regard to eating *terumah* or tithes that he has. If she produced a son with this husband, she retains this privilege. If she did not, however, she reverts to her previous status with regard to priestly or levitical gifts.

If her son....died. With no husband, her status with regard to priestly or levitical gifts is determined by her latest living son. If that son died, she reverts to a prior status.

6 A daughter of a priest, who is married to an Israelite, may not eat *terumah*;
if he died, and she had a son from him—
she may not eat *terumah*;
if she is married to a Levite, she may eat tithes;
if he died, and she had a son from him—
she may eat tithes;
if she is married to a priest, she may eat *terumah*;
if he died, and she had a son from him—
she may eat *terumah*.
If her son from the priest died—
she may not eat *terumah*;
if her son from the Levite died—
she may not eat tithes;
if her son from the Israelite died—
she returns to her father's house.
Of this one it is written:
And she returns to her father's house as in her youth; she may eat of her father's food.

Chapter Ten

10:1–3   *A Woman Inadvertently Married to Two Men*

10 A woman whose husband went abroad,[59]
and they came and said to her: "Your husband died,"
and she married,
and afterwards her husband came—
she goes out from this one and that one,
and she requires a divorce from this one and from that one;
and she has no *ketubbah* payment,
and no product,[60]
and no maintenance,
and no clothing,

---

[59] Lit. "to the land of the sea."   [60] Lit. "fruit."

9:6 Analogous to 9:5, but now considering a priest's daughter.

And she returns to her father's house: Leviticus 22:13.

10:1 This group of passages (10:1–3) describes situations in which a woman has married on the assumption that her husband is dead. According to the anonymous view in 10:1, in which the woman remarried on hearsay, the result is that she is penalized in every possible aspect. She is divorced from both men and her children are declared illegitimate, and she is ruined economically.

goes out: For this terminology, see above, 3:5.

terumah: See 9:4.

product .... maintenance .... clothing: See *Ketubbot* 4:4.

neither from this one, nor from that one.
If she took anything from this one or from that one—
she returns it.
And the offspring is a *mamzer* from this one and from that one.
And neither this one nor that one contracts impurity for her.
And neither this one nor that one has the right to what she finds,
or to the labor of her hands,
or to annul her vows.
If she was a daughter of Israel, she becomes disqualified from the priesthood;
and if a daughter of a Levite, from tithes;
and if a daughter of a priest, from *terumah*.
And neither the heirs of this one nor the heirs of that one
inherit her *ketubbah* payment.
And if they died,
this one's brother and that one's brother perform *halitsah* for her
but not levirate marriage.
R. Yose says:
Her *ketubbah* payment is against the property of her first husband.
R. Eleazar says:
The first one owns what she finds and what she earns in the work of her hands,
and is permitted to annul her vows.
R. Simeon says:
Sexual intercourse with her, or *halitsah* by the brother of the first,
exempts her co-wife,
and the offspring from him is not a *mamzer*.
And if she marries without authority she is permitted to return to him.
   2 If she married according to a court—
she goes out and is exempt from a sacrifice.
If she did not marry according to a court—
she goes out and is liable for a sacrifice.
The power of the court is greater:

mamzer from this one and from that one: That is, even should she go back to the first husband, any child from her would be a *mamzer*.

And neither ....contracts impurity: Priests, who are forbidden to become impure, do not participate in funerals except in order to bury their nearest kin (Leviticus 21:1–2). Here, this woman is kin to neither man.

R. Yose ....R. Eleazar ....R. Simeon: Each of these rabbis provides a less severe imposition on the woman on one or several counts, viewing the first marriage as at least in some respects valid.

without authority: This expression is problematic. The implication is that what preceded is "with authority" yet the consequences for the woman are more severe. One might have thought that it meant "by a court," yet 10:2 makes consulting a court advantageous, and rules that in any case she may not return to her first husband. What we certainly see here is that if a woman who thinks, based on witness evidence, that her husband is dead, and marries again without consultation and without external consent, is safer than one who seeks "authority," since without it she may return to her first husband.

10:2 *according to a court*: If the woman married the second man, she must go forth from him, and does not need to bring a purgation offering for having erred, since the error was on the part of the court. On first reading, it appears that all the other consequences of 10:1 are in effect. In 10:2, then, there is at least a modest monetary and ritual advantage in seeking court guidance; however, compare the end of 10:1 and annotations.

it exempts her from a sacrifice.
If the court instructed her to marry,
and she went and acted improperly—
she is liable for a sacrifice,
because they permitted her only to marry.

3 A woman whose husband and son went abroad,
and they came and said to her:
"Your husband died and then your son died,"
and she married,
and afterwards they said to her:
"It was the other way around"—
she goes out,
and the first and last offspring is a *mamzer*.
They said to her:
"Your son died and then your husband died,"
and she underwent levirate marriage,
and afterwards they said to her:
"It was the other way around"—
she goes out,
and the first and last offspring is a *mamzer*.
They said to her:
"Your husband died,"
and she married,
and afterwards they said to her:
"He was alive and then died"—
she goes out,[61]
and the first offspring is a *mamzer* but the last one is not a *mamzer*.
They said to her:
"Your husband died,"
and she became betrothed,
and afterwards her husband came—
she is permitted to return to him.
And even if the latter husband gave her a writ of divorce—
he has not disqualified her from the priesthood.
This is what R. Eleazar b. Matia expounded:

[61] Absent in **K**.

acted improperly: Chose a partner forbidden to her, for instance, a priest if she were a divorcee.

10:3 *she goes out* from her second husband, because her first husband died childless, and she needs levirate marriage or *halitsah*.

first and last offspring is mamzer: If she bore a child when her first husband was still alive, the first child is a *mamzer*. If she bore a later offspring, after he died childless, that child is a *mamzer* because she was a levirate widow and married someone who was forbidden to her as such.

and she became betrothed: Here, the rabbis suggest that the woman's situation is reversible. They even imagine her marrying a priest, because she is not divorced from marriage.

A woman divorced from her husband—
and not from a man who is not her husband.

10:4–5 *A Man Whose Wife Died Abroad*

4 One whose wife went abroad,
and they came and said to him:
"Your wife died,"
and he married her sister, and afterwards his wife came—
she is permitted to return to him.
He is permitted with respect to the relatives of the second,
and the second is permitted with respect to his relatives.
And if the first one died, he is permitted with respect to the second.
They said to him:
"Your wife died,"
and he married her sister,
and afterwards they said to him:
"She was alive, and then died"—
the first offspring is a *mamzer* but the last one is not a *mamzer*.
R. Yose says:
Anyone who disqualifies others disqualifies himself;
and anyone who does not disqualify others does not disqualify himself.

5 They said to him: "Your wife died,"
and he married her sister from the father;

A woman divorced from her husband: Leviticus 21:7. *Eleazar b. Matia* reads the word "husband" as decisive and determines that a divorcee from betrothal had no husband. This supports the preceding anonymous view.

10:4 Mishnah 10:4 and 10:5 continue with cases of a wife who has gone abroad and of a husband who is informed that his wife died. This has completely different consequences, because the husband need not remain monogamous and does not have to undergo levirate marriage if he is childless. Mishnah 10:4 discusses simple situations, but 10:5 goes on to imagine more elaborate (and unlikely) situations.

and he married her sister: This is incest while the wife is alive and thus she was forbidden to him. When the wife returns, the marital relations between the man and the sister are treated as legally ineffective: he can return to his prior status with respect to both his wife and her sister's relations.

the first offspring, conceived when the first wife was still alive so the sister was prohibited, *is a mamzer*. The last was conceived when the man's wife was already dead, so that the sister was permitted to the man and the child is legitimate.

Anyone who disqualifies others: If a person has the capacity to forbid the woman to marry others, he automatically disqualifies her from marrying himself, and vice versa. A case might be where the wife and brother-in-law went abroad and her husband married the wife's sister (who is also the wife of the brother-in-law), because he believed his wife and the husband of her sister dead. When both return, the man has prohibited the sister to her husband (10:1), and being the sister of his living wife, she cannot marry him either.

10:5 In this complicated case, it is assumed that each subsequent marriage is at a further remove from the first wife. The first *sister from her father* does not share parents with the second or the third *sister from her father* (the third or the fifth marriage), and likewise the first *sister from her mother* (the second marriage) does not share any parents with the second *sister from her mother* (the fourth marriage).

they said:[62] "She died,"
and he married her sister from the mother;
they said: "She died,"
and he married her sister from the father;
they said: "She died,"
and he married her sister from the mother,
and they were all found to be alive[63]—
he is permitted with respect to the first, the third, and the fifth,
and they exempt their co-wives;
and he is forbidden with respect to the second and the fourth,
and sexual intercourse with one of them does not exempt their co-wives.
And if he had sexual intercourse with the second after the death of the first—
he is permitted with respect to the second and the fourth,
and they exempt their co-wives;
and he is prohibited with respect to the third and fifth,
and sexual intercourse with one of them does not exempt her co-wife.

10:6–9 *Intercourse with a Brother Nine Years and One Day Old*

6 A [brother] who is nine years and one day old,
makes [levirate widows] unfit for the brothers,
and the brothers make [them] unfit for him;
yet he makes unfit in the first place,
and the brothers make unfit in the first place and at the end.[64]

[62] Here and in what follows, "They said" is added for clarity.
[63] K, P, and others lack this clause.
[64] K: "if the brothers had sexual intercourse with her and betrothed her verbally, gave a writ of divorce, or performed *halitsah*, they have made one another unfit." Our text appears in the margin.

In the first case, the first, third, and fifth are in the position of the wife in 10:4, and are permitted to the man, and the second and fourth, who are sisters to these, are in the position of the sister in 10:4. Similarly, if the husband were to die the regular rules of levirate marriage would apply (and levirate marriage with one of these would exempt her co-wives), but for the second and fourth they do not.

after the death of the first, the second was permitted to him, so the fourth, who is not a sibling to her, is also permitted to him, but not the third or the fifth, who are their siblings. According to the commentaries the case is one where the claim about the first wife's death was in fact true.

10:6 *nine years and one day old*: See above, 7:4. This and the next three mishnayot deal with the consequences of a nine-years-and-one-day-old engaging in sexual intercourse with a levirate bride.

makes unfit for the brothers: Although he cannot marry the levirate widow yet, his act of sexual intercourse disqualifies her as a potential bride for his other brothers.

in the first place and at the end: For this language see 5:6. If one of the other brothers engaged in sex with her after the nine-year-old has done so (*at the end*), she is also disqualified for the nine-year-old (when he attains adulthood).

How?
One who is nine years and one day old
who had sexual intercourse with his levirate widow—
has made [her] unfit for the brothers.
If the brothers had sexual intercourse with her,
or made a verbal betrothal,
or gave her a writ of divorce,
or performed *halitsah*—
they make [her] unfit for him.

7 One who is nine years and one day old
who had sexual intercourse with his levirate widow,
and then his brother who is nine years and one day old
had sexual intercourse with her—
he has made [her] unfit for him.
R. Simeon says:
He has not made [her] unfit.

8 One who is nine years and one day old
who had sexual intercourse with his levirate widow,
and then had sexual intercourse with her co-wife—
has made [her] unfit for himself.
R. Simeon says:
He has not made [her] unfit.
One who is nine years and one day old
who had sexual intercourse with his levirate widow
and died—
she performs *halitsah* but does not perform levirate marriage.
If he married a wife, and then died—
In this case, this one is exempt.

9 One who is nine years and one day old
who had sexual intercourse with his levirate widow,
and when he attained majority married another woman

10:7 Although this passage clearly continues 10:6 it is unclear how the rules in the two texts relate one to the other. The commentaries follow the Babylonian Talmud here which revises 10:6 and introduces categories in 10:7 that are not explicit in the Mishnah. The common thread in all of these is a subsequent sex act by a male who is nine years and one day old. Here, a second act of sexual intercourse by the brother disqualifies the widow from later levirate marriage to the first.

R. Simeon appears in all these cases to question the effectiveness of the sex act of a child.

10:8 In this case by performing sex acts (of incomplete legal effectiveness) with both women he has disqualified the second woman to himself.

If he married a wife, and then died: A child of nine years and one day can perform an effective sex act, but cannot contract a marriage, so there is no levirate obligation after his death.

10:9 *did not have sexual intercourse with the first*: See 8:1. If he did not have sexual relations with the first woman as an adult, her status as a levirate widow is partly in doubt (as in 10:8).

the second was fully his wife, and the regular rules of levirate marriage apply.

and died,[65]
if he did not have sexual intercourse[66] with the first one after becoming an adult—
the first one performs *halitsah* but does not undergo levirate marriage,
and the second one either performs *halitsah* or undergoes levirate marriage.
R. Simeon says:
He takes whichever he wishes in levirate marriage,
and performs *halitsah* for the other.
The rule is one and the same whether he is nine years and one day old
or whether he is twenty years old, who has not yet produced two hairs.

Chapter Eleven

11:1 *Rape and Seduction*

11 One may marry the relatives[67] of a woman who has been raped or seduced.
One who rapes or seduces the relatives[68] of his wife,[69] is liable.
A person may marry a woman raped by his father or seduced by his father;
raped by his son or seduced by his son.
R. Judah forbids a woman raped by his father or seduced by his father.

11:2 *A Woman Who Converts with her Children*

2 The female convert whose sons converted with her—
they neither perform *halitsah*
nor enter a levirate marriage,

---

[65] Absent in **K** and other witnesses. [66] Lit. "know," on which see 8:1.
[67] Lit. "They marry on." [68] Heb. "One who marries on." [69] Lit. "One who is married."

The rule is one...: Male adulthood is judged both by chronological age (nine years and one day) and by anatomical features, in this case the growth of pubic hair. A man needs both, in order to perform legally as an adult (see above, 7:4).

11:1 *One may marry*: See also above 7:5. According to the Torah, the rapist (Deuteronomy 22:28–29) and the seducer (Exodus 22:15–16) are both expected to marry the woman he raped or seduced, unless her father is not interested in the match. In this mishnah, the question is whether such sexual relations prohibit the woman's female relatives to the rapist. The rule is that they do not because the intercourse did not constitute betrothal or marriage.

R. Judah forbids: It seems that incest concerns and reverence for the father, are at issue here.

11:2 *The female convert*: The assumption is that a convert was promiscuous before her conversion and thus there is no knowing whether they really are brothers from the father. Therefore, the levirate obligations are deemed not to apply in their case.

even if the conception of the first is not in holiness, but the birth is in holiness.
and the conception and birth of the second are in holiness.
And so too regarding a freed female slave whose sons were freed with her.

11:3–5   *Mixtures of Offspring of Priests and Other Castes*

3   Five women whose offspring were mixed together,
and the mixed children attained majority, and married women, and died—
four perform *halitsah* on one,
and one takes her in levirate marriage.
He and three perform *halitsah* on another,
and one takes her in levirate marriage.
Thus, each and every wife undergoes four acts of *halitsah*
and enters into one levirate marriage.

4   A woman whose offspring was mixed together with the offspring of her daughter-in-law,
and the mixed children attained majority, and married women, and died—
the sons of the daughter-in-law perform *halitsah* but not levirate marriage,
because it is a case of doubt regarding their brother's wife
and doubt regarding their father's brother's wife;
and the sons of the old woman either perform *halitsah* or perform levirate marriage,
because it is a case of doubt regarding their brother's wife
and doubt regarding their brother's son's wife.
If the fit ones died—

---

not in holiness . . . . in holiness: A pregnant woman, who conceived a child before her conversion but gave birth after conversion. This son is not considered a brother to the second son who was conceived and born within Judaism.

freed female slave: See 6:5.

11:3–5 This section discusses situations where women have children who are raised together, but they do not know which of the children is their son. This hypothetical situation raises several interesting possibilities regarding levirate marriage and regarding marital castes like the priesthood.

11:3 *offspring were mixed together*: Thus, five boys do not know who their mother is, but each of the mothers has another son, who is clearly hers.

four sons whose mothers are certain *perform halitsah on one, and one takes her in levirate marriage*: All of the mixed men are potentially brothers of those whose maternity is certain, thus potentially obligated as levirs. For each of the five whose maternity is not certain, four whose maternity is certain perform *halitsah* on the widow and the fifth may take her as a levirate bride.

11:4 *whose offspring were mixed together with the offspring of her daughter-in-law*: This means that one cannot tell which is the son of the mother-in-law and which her grandson.

sons of the daughter-in-law . . . . doubtfully their brother's wife and the widow is subject to levirate marriage *or doubtfully their father's brother's wife* who is not and who is a prohibited relation.

doubt regarding their brother's son's wife: The old woman is the mother-in-law. In this case, if she is not a levirate widow she is the widow of a nephew, for which no incest prohibition exists, so levirate marriage is permitted.

fit: The sons who are certain.

the sons of the mixtures perform *halitsah* on [the wives of] the old woman's son but do not perform levirate marriage,
because it is a case of doubt regarding his brother's wife
and doubt regarding his father's brother's wife;
and for the sons of the daughter-in-law—
one performs *halitsah* and one performs levirate marriage.

5 The wife of a priest whose offspring was mixed together with the offspring of her maidservant—
in this case, these eat *terumah* and share one portion at the threshing floor
and may not become impure for the dead
and may not marry wives, whether fit or unfit.
If the mixed children attained majority and freed one another—
they marry women suitable for the priesthood,
and they may not contract corpse impurity;
and if they become defiled—
they do not receive forty lashes.
And they may not eat *terumah*;
and if they ate—
they do not pay the principal and fifth.
And they do not share at the threshing floor.

sons of the mixtures, etc.: This situation and what follows mirror the previous case. Again, a critical distinction is that between a father's brother's widow who is always prohibited, and a nephew's widow who is not.

11:5 *The wife of a priest whose offspring was mixed together with the offspring of her maidservant*: A person of the highest caste (the priesthood) is subject to many stringencies, but also enjoys many privileges. The maidservant is of a despised caste that is not or only marginally Jewish. Where their offspring were mixed, *one puts on them the stringencies of the priests and the stringencies of Israelites* (see below). This mishnah details how this is done.

eat terumah: The mixed offspring are either priests or slaves of priests, and permitted to eat *terumah* (3:10).

share one portion at the threshing floor: Numbers 18:27. The Mishnah takes it for granted that tithes and *terumah* are divided among priests and Levites on the threshing floor. The son of the priest and the son of the slave who are mixed receive only one portion because only one of them is a priest.

may not become impure: Since both are doubtful priests (see 10:1).

may not marry wives at all, *whether fit* for marriage (in this case to a priest) *or unfit* to marry an Israelite, as would be the case with another slave.

freed one another: They need to release one another because it is not clear which of them is the priest and master and which of them the slave.

women suitable for the priesthood: They only marry women the priest is permitted to marry and do not allow themselves to *contract corpse impurity* because they are still doubtful priests. However, although willfully contracting impurity is punishable by *lashes* (see Deuteronomy 25:3) for a priest, they are exempt because they are only doubtful priests.

And they may not eat terumah: They are expected to act like nonpriests, but if they act like priests they are not punished like nonpriests. For the penalty of *principal and fifth* for a nonpriest eating *terumah*, see Terumot 6:1. It is derived from the Torah (Leviticus 22:14).

they may sell terumah from their own produce to other priests, since they may not eat it but also cannot be made to give it to another priest.

And they may sell *terumah*, and the proceeds are theirs.
And they do not share the sacred offerings of the Temple,
and one does not give them sacred offerings,
but one does not take theirs out of their hands.
And they are exempt from the shoulder, the two cheeks, and the abomasum.
And their firstborn animal is let out to pasture until it is defiled.
One puts on them the stringencies of the priests and the stringencies of Israelites.

11:6–7 *Doubtful Paternity*

6 A woman who did not wait three months after her husband's death[70]
and married and gave birth,
and it is unknown whether he is a nine-month son of the first, or a seven-month son of the last—
if she had sons from the first and sons from the second:
these perform *halitsah* but do not perform levirate marriage;
and he too performs on them *halitsah* but does not perform levirate marriage.
If he had brothers from the first and brothers from the second who were not from the same mother:
he performs both *halitsah* and levirate marriage;
and they—
one performs *halitsah* and one performs a levirate marriage.[71]

[70] Lit.: "After her husband."   [71] **K**: "and they perform *halitsah* and enter levirate marriage."

sacred offerings of the Temple: Other gifts priests are entitled to such as the hides of the sacrificial animals.

One does not give them sacred offerings, for them to offer sacrifices in the name of the one bringing the sacrifice. For *not take theirs out of their hands*, see 2:6.

shoulder...cheeks....abomasum: In Deuteronomy 18:3 these three parts of a slaughtered animal are set apart for the priests.

And their firstborn animal is let out to pasture till it is defiled: See *Bekhorot* 2:6–8 for this treatment of firstborn animals. If the Temple is standing, the expectation is that the firstborn will be given to a priest immediately to be sacrificed. However, in this case since both may be priests neither is required to do so. Once the animals have been defiled, that is, have sustained an injury and become unfit to be sacrificed, they may be consumed by any Israelite.

11:6 *three months*: See above, 3:10, 4:10.

nine-month son...seven-month son: See above, 4:2.

sons from the first and sons from the second: Sons who are certainly those of the first husband, and sons who are certainly those of the second husband. If the son in the middle, whose paternity is doubtful, marries and then dies childless, the others perform *halitsah* for his widow in case they are the paternal brothers.

brothers...not from the same mother: In this case, the additional brothers are either paternal brothers or not related at all, so there is no bar on levirate marriage.

7 If one was an Israelite and one a priest—
he marries a woman fit for a priest,
and may not contract corpse impurity;
and if he becomes impure, he does not receive forty lashes.
He may not eat *terumah*;
and if he partook—
he does not pay the capital and the added fifth.
And he does not share at the threshing floor,
and sells the *terumah*, and the proceeds are his.
And he does not share the sacred offerings of the Temple,
and one does not give him sacred offerings,
but one does not take his out of his hand.
And he is exempt from the shoulder, the two cheeks, and the abomasum.
And his firstborn animal is let out to pasture until it is defiled.
And one puts on him the stringencies of the priests and the stringencies of Israelites.
If both were priests—
he is bereaved for them, and they are bereaved for him;
he does not become impure for them, and they do not become impure for him;
he does not inherit from them, but they inherit from him.
And he is exempt for his cursing or his beating of this one or that one;
and he is counted[72] in the course of this one and that one,
but does not share.
And if they were both from the same course, he takes one share.

[72] Lit. "ascends."

11:7 *one was an Israelite and one a priest*: The possible fathers in 11:6. The first part of this mishnah extends 11:5 and 11:6. The doubtful paternity corresponds to 11:6, but the special concern of doubtful paternity involving priests corresponds to 11:5. And indeed, the conditions set down are identical to those formulated in 11:5.

If both were priests: Here, the mishnah begins a new situation, where paternity is doubtful but the son is certainly a priest.

bereaved: The status of a mourner before the burial of the deceased.

they are bereaved: for his suspected fathers.

become impure: Priests may only contract corpse impurity in connection with a close family member, see 10:1. Here, the relationship between them is doubtful.

his cursing or his beating of this one or that one: See above, 2:5, and Exodus 21:15, 17 which assigns the death penalty to one who curses or strikes his parent. Here he is not punished because of the two men's doubtful paternity.

course: The priestly courses are the twenty-four families of priests mentioned in 1 Chronicles 24:7–18. The mishnah often imagines the service in the Temple as rotated among them. Since he is not certainly in any one course he does not take a *share* of the sacrificial offerings.

Chapter Twelve

12:1–6 *The Halitsah Ritual*

12 The commandment of *halitsah* is [performed] before three judges, even if all three were laypersons.
If she removed footwear [from her levir's foot],
her *halitsah* is valid;
felt shoes, her *halitsah* is invalid;.
a *sandal* that has a heel, her *halitsah* is valid;
a *sandal* that has no heel, her *halitsah* is invalid.
from the knee down, her *halitsah* is valid;
from the knee up, her *halitsah* is invalid.

2 If she performed *halitsah*
with a *sandal* that is not his,
or with a wooden *sandal*,
or with the left on the right—
her *halitsah* is valid.
If she removed a large one in which he can walk,
or a small one that covers most of his foot—
her *halitsah* is valid.
If she performed *halitsah* at night—
her *halitsah* is valid;
but R. Eliezer deems it invalid.
With the left—
her *halitsah* is invalid;
but R. Eliezer deems it valid.

3 If she removed [the shoe]
and spat

12:1 *three judges, even if all three were laypersons*: The court described here can be an *ad hoc* gathering of persons with no specific training. See *Sanhedrin*, introduction.

removed the shoe: The Torah requires that the woman *remove his shoe from his foot* (Deuteronomy 25:9). In this discussion, the Mishnah is concerned that the footwear comply narrowly with these requirements: that it qualify as a shoe, that it be on his foot, and that the shoe be his.

footwear: Heb. *min'al*, presumably referring to a wrong kind of shoe, or at least a kind of shoe that might be considered wrong. For the Mishnah here the proper shoe for the ritual is a *sandal*.

felt shoes: From the Greek *empilia*, "felt shoes."

12:2 *a sandal that is not his*: See annotation to 12:1.

in which he can walk: Although it is too large, he can still walk in it.

12:3 *removed . . . . spat . . . . did not declare*: All three acts derive from Deuteronomy 25:9.

but did not declare[73]—
her *halitsah* is valid.
If she declared
and spat
but did not remove [the shoe]—
her *halitsah* is invalid.
If she removed [the shoe]
and declared
but did not spit—
R. Eliezer says:
Her *halitsah* is invalid.
R. Aqiva says:
Her *halitsah* is valid.
Said R. Eliezer:
Thus shall be done:
any deed,[74] if omitted, renders invalid.
Said R. Aqiva to him:
Is proof from there?
Thus shall be done to the man—
anything that is done to the man.

4 A deaf-mute man upon whom *halitsah* was performed
and a deaf-mute woman who performed *halitsah*,
and a woman who performed *halitsah* for a minor—
her *halitsah* is invalid.
A minor girl who performed *halitsah* must perform *halitsah* again when she attains majority;
and if she did not perform *halitsah* [again]—
her *halitsah* is invalid.[75]

---

[73] Alt. "read" "recite."   [74] Lit. "thing done."
[75] **K** and other sources read "her *halitsah* is valid."

Said R. Eliezer: Both R. Aqiva and R. Eliezer agree that the decisive action of *halitsah* is the removal of the shoe. They are divided as to what acts left undone invalidate the act. R. Eliezer thinks that the words *thus shall be done* refer to all the actions mentioned in the verse. R. Aqiva, however, thinks that *halitsah* alone, which is *done to the man*, suffices.

Thus shall be done to the man: Deuteronomy 25:9, which continues *who will not build up his brother's house*. This is the declaration referred to above.

12:4 *The man who is deaf and mute*: See above, 4:6.

deaf-mute: The deaf-mute woman is almost exclusively mentioned in *Yevamot*, where she appears thirty times (see also *Gittin* 5:5 and *Eduyot* 7:9, both parallel to 14:2, and *Niddah* 2:1). She is so important in this tractate, especially once *halitsah* rather than levirate marriage is discussed, because this action requires active, verbal participation on the part of the woman, and the rabbis consider the deaf-mute woman unable to do this.

A minor girl: Minors, deaf-mute persons, and the mentally disabled are frequently lumped together in rabbinic literature as lacking legal capacity. Minors are distinct, because they will outgrow their minority. Thus, here the minor and the deaf-mute women are described together, but the minor can repeat her actions, effecting *halitsah*, once she gains majority and they will be considered valid.

5 If she performed *halitsah* before two, or before three,
and one of them was found to be a relative or one who is unfit—
her *halitsah* is invalid.
R. Simeon and R. Yohanan ha-Sandlar deem it valid.
It once happened that [the levir] performed *halitsah* one-on-one[76] in prison,
and the case came[77] before R. Aqiva,
and he deemed it valid.

6 The commandment of *halitsah*:
He and his levirate widow come to a court,
and they give him advice appropriate to him,
as it is written: *The elders of the city shall summon him and talk to him.*
And she says: *My levir refuses to establish a name in Israel for his brother; he will not perform the duty of levir,*
and he says: *I do not want to marry her.*
And they say these in the holy tongue.
His levirate widow shall go up to him in the presence of the elders, pull the sandal off his foot, spit in his face—
spit that is visible to the judges.
And make this declaration: "Thus shall be done to the man who will not build up his brother's house!"
Up to here they read out.
And when R. Hyrcanus read it out under the terebinth in the village Etam[78] and finished the entire section, they decided to read the entire section.
And his name shall be called in Israel "the house of the unshoed one"—

[76] Lit. "between him and her."
[77] **K** and some other witnesses: "and to prison the case came." See annotations.
[78] **K**: "Abus"; **C**: "Akko."

12:5 *unfit*: Someone who cannot serve in a civil court of three; see *Sanhedrin* 3.3–4.

in prison: The *halitsah* itself was performed in prison. The reading of **K** (see n. 77) implies that it is R. Aqiva who was in prison. In either case, the precedent seems to describe an emergency situation. A husband has died; the levir (and perhaps also his levirate bride) perform the *halitsah* ritual without witnesses (and perhaps in prison). R. Aqiva was consulted (in prison according to **K**) and declares the case valid. We are probably speaking here of the situation that ensued in the context of the Bar Kokhba Revolt (132–135 CE), during which R. Aqiva was imprisoned and died.

12:6 *The commandment of halitsah*: What follows is a paraphrase of the biblical chapter on how *halitsah* is performed.

advice: Counsel on whether to perform levirate marriage or *halitsah*.

The elders of the city…: Deuteronomy 25:8.

My levir: Deuteronomy 25:7.

I do not want to marry her: Deuteronomy 25:8.

His levirate widow ….And make this declaration…: Deuteronomy 25:9.

read out: The judges recite the biblical text for the woman to repeat.

section: Deuteronomy 25:5–10.

And his name…: Deuteronomy 25:10.

a commandment for the judges but not a commandment for the disciples.
R. Judah says:
It is a commandment for all who are standing to say: "Unshoed one, unshoed one, unshoed one."

Chapter Thirteen

13:1–6 *Renunciation of marriage by minors*

13 The House of Shammai say:
Renunciation is allowed only for those betrothed;
but the House of Hillel say:
Betrothed and married.
The House of Shammai say:
To a husband but not to a levir;
but the House of Hillel say:
to a husband and to a levir.
The House of Shammai say:
In his presence;
but the House of Hillel say:
in his presence and not in his presence.
The House of Shammai say:
In a court;
but the House of Hillel say:
In a court and not in a court.
Said the House of Hillel to the House of Shammai:
A minor may renounce even four and five times.
Said the House of Shammai to the House of Hillel:
The daughters of Israel are not ownerless.
Rather she renounces,

13:1 *renunciation*: The Mishnah assigns the mother or brothers of a fatherless girl the power to marry her off. However, unlike betrothal or marriage created by a father, contracts arranged by these relatives are subject to renunciation by the girl. See above, 1:1, and the next mishnah.

The daughters of Israel are not ownerless: Perhaps better, "without protection." The term refers to forms of renunciation of ownership and, in association with women, subject to the "taking of liberties."

The *House of Shammai* throughout this mishnah seek to limit the applicability of the girl's renunciation, so as to preserve the patriarchal structure which views a girl with a good name as being one who is protected by a male family member to whom she belongs. The *House of Hillel*, who expand the boundaries of the institution of renunciation, do not do so to empower the minor, but rather in order to limit the authority of a mother and brothers over a girl, relative to a father's patriarchal authority. If a father chose a husband for the minor daughter, she may not renounce him when she attains majority; see also the next mishnah.

and waits[79] till she attains majority,
and renounces,
and marries.

2 Who is a minor who needs to renounce?
One whose mother and brothers married her off with her consent;[80]
if they married her off without her consent, she does not need to renounce.
R. Hanina b. Antigonus says:
Every young girl who cannot safeguard her own betrothal, does not need to renounce.
R. Eliezer says:
The act of a minor does not count as anything,
she is like one seduced:[81]
A daughter of Israel [married] to a priest may not eat *terumah*;
a daughter of a priest to an Israelite may eat *terumah*.

3 R. Eliezer b. Jacob says:
Every postponement that comes from the husband—
it is as if she is his wife;
every postponement that does not come from the husband—
it is as if she is not his wife.

4 One who renounces a husband,
he is permitted with respect to her relatives,
and she is permitted with respect to his relatives,
and he has not disqualified her from the priesthood.

---

[79] Absent in **P**.   [80] Literally: "knowledge."
[81] **K, P, C**: "The act of a minor is only like one being seduced."

13:2 *needs....does not need to renounce*: This mishnah aims at limiting the institution of renunciation from different angles than in 13:1, by limiting the need to take such an action at all. A marriage that the wife "does not need to renounce" had no legal force, and needs no formal act of renunciation.

with her consent: The girl's consent, or perhaps her knowledge, is treated here as a formal requirement. Without this, marriages of minors arranged by their mothers and brothers are invalid to begin with. If she did give her consent, she may renounce, because the rabbis assume that the girl was in no position to know if she consented or not, either because girls who have not come of age are considered mentally immature, or because she was coerced into consenting.

cannot safeguard her own betrothal, does not need to renounce: Mental maturity is required of a minor in order for any sort of pairing to have limited validity. The Sage requires that she be able to preserve her own documents. In other words, a minor girl, according to him, can only be married as a minor if she has the capacity to understand the procedure of betrothal and take it seriously.

The act of a minor....like one seduced: According to R. Eliezer, any marriage to a minor initiated by mother and brothers is of no validity. Thus in the case of a minor, the status consequences for a betrothed or married wife do not take effect. The priest's daughter who is married out maintains her priestly status, the nonpriest who marries a priest does not attain priestly prerogatives.

13:3 *postponement*: In the consummation of the marriage with a minor. The assumption is that if she postpones the consummation, this is like renunciation and the marriage is invalid.

13:4 *One who renounces a man*: Renunciation nullifies the interim marriage of the minor, it does not constitute a divorce. However, if the husband *gave her a writ of divorce* she has the status of a divorcee with all the consequence in terms of incest and priesthood.

If he gave her a writ of divorce,
he is forbidden with respect to her relatives,
and she is forbidden with respect to his relatives,
and he has disqualified her from the priesthood.
If he gave her a writ of divorce and then took her back,
and she renounced him and married another
and she was widowed or divorced—
she is permitted to return to him.
If she renounced him and he took her back,
and gave her a writ of divorce and she married another,
and was widowed or divorced—
she is forbidden to return to him.
This is the rule:
Divorce after renunciation—
she is forbidden to return to him;
renunciation after divorce—
she is permitted to return to him.

5 One who renounces her husband,
was married to another and he divorced her;
to another, and she renounced him;
to another, and he divorced her;
to another, and she renounced him[82]—
any one whom she left through divorce:
she may not return to him;
through renunciation:
she is permitted to return to him.

6 One who divorced a wife, and took her back—
she is permitted to the levir;
but R. Eliezer forbids.
And so too one who divorces an orphan girl, and takes her back—

---

[82] C lacks the second "to another, and he divorced her; to another, and she renounced" and adds, "This is the rule."

---

gave her a writ of divorce .... she is permitted to return to him: A woman who was divorced and remarried may not return to her first husband (Deuteronomy 24:4). Here, the first divorce was undone when the husband allowed the wife to return; she leaves the marriage finally through renunciation, which nullifies the marriage, not through divorce. As a result, when she remarries and that second marriage ends the woman may return to her first husband.

she renounced .... she is forbidden to return to him: The reverse of the preceding. Here, the woman would be returning to a first husband who had divorced her.

This is the rule: This final rule explains the logic according to which the preceding legislation in the mishnah functioned.

13:5 Continues the principles established in 13:4.

13:6 *permitted to the levir*: Normally, the divorcee of a brother who died is forbidden to her levir. As in the preceding discussion, when the husband *took her back*, this removed the status of divorcee. *R. Eliezer* disagrees with this principle.

orphan girl: The minor married off by her mother or brothers (who may renounce, see above, 13:2).

she is permitted to the levir;
but R. Eliezer forbids.
A minor whose father gave her in marriage and was divorced—
she is deemed like an orphan in her father's lifetime;
if he took her back—
all agree[83] that she is forbidden to the levir.

13:7–12   Deaf Women and Minors

7 Two brothers married to two sisters, who are minor orphans,
and the husband of one of them died—
she goes out as the sister of the wife;
and so too, two women who are deaf-mute.
An adult and a minor,
and the minor's husband died—
the minor goes out as the sister of the wife;
if the husband of the adult died—
R. Eliezer says:
They instruct the minor to renounce him.
Rabban Gamaliel says:
If she renounced she renounced;
if not—she waits till she attains majority,
and this one goes out as the sister of the wife.
R. Joshua says:
Woe to him on account of his wife and woe to him on account of his brother's wife—

[83] K, P, C lack "all agree."

---

whose father gave her in marriage: Unlike a brother or mother, a father can create a fully binding marriage for a minor daughter.

an orphan in her father's lifetime: Even though her father lives, because once she is married he has no stake in her (see *Ketubbot* 4:2).

all agree that she is forbidden to the levir: Because she is his brother's divorcee, see previous note.

13:7–12 These mishnayot tackle similarities and differences between deaf-mute people and minor women and between them and adult, hearing women.

13:7 *two minor orphans*: For the law for two sisters see above, 1:2.

goes out: For this terminology for divorce, see above, 3:5. Although the two marriages are not fully valid, they are sufficient to release the widow from a levirate obligation.

two women who are deaf-mute: The Sages treat the deaf-mute as of equal status to minors. See above, 12:4.

minor's husband died: This case is analogous to the ones discussed just above: her marriage has sufficient validity to override the levirate obligation.

Woe to him: This saying already appears above in 3:5. In both cases a man becomes a levir and as a result he loses both his wife and the levirate widow. Here, an adult sister falls as a levirate widow to the husband of her minor sister. *R. Eliezer* thinks that the minor should renounce her husband immediately (according to the House of Hillel see above, 13:1), and thus sanctions the levirate marriage of the adult sister. *Rabban Gamaliel* holds an intermediate position and says that if the minor wife does not renounce one waits for her

he dismisses his wife with a divorce and his brother's wife with *halitsah*.

8   One who was married to two orphan minors, and died—
the sexual intercourse or *halitsah* of either of them
exempts her co-wife;
and so too two women who are deaf-mute.
A minor and a woman who is deaf-mute—
sexual intercourse with either of them does not exempt the other.
One who is legally competent and one who is deaf-mute—
sexual intercourse with the one who is legally competent
exempts the woman who is deaf-mute,
but sexual intercourse with the woman who is deaf-mute
does not exempt the one who is legally competent.
An adult and a minor—
sexual intercourse with the adult exempts the minor,
but sexual intercourse with the minor does not exempt the adult.

9   One who was married to two orphan minors and died:
if the levir had sexual intercourse with the first,
and then had sexual intercourse with the second,
or if his brother had sexual intercourse with the second—
he has not invalidated the first;
and so too two women who are deaf-mute.
A minor and a woman who is deaf-mute:
If the levir had sexual intercourse with the minor,
and then had sexual intercourse with the woman who is deaf-mute,
or his brother had sexual intercourse with the woman who is deaf-mute—
he has not invalidated the minor.
If the levir had sexual intercourse with the deaf-mute woman,
and then had sexual intercourse with the minor,
or his brother had sexual intercourse with the minor—
he has invalidated the deaf-mute woman.

10   One who is legally competent and one who is deaf-mute:
if the levir had sexual intercourse with the one who is legally competent,
and then had sexual intercourse with the deaf-mute woman,

---

to attain majority, and the marriage fully constituted, and then the adult wife would be released as the sister of the wife (see above, 1:1). R. Joshua holds the extreme position (according to the House of Shammai, above 13:1) that a minor does not renounce after marriage. Consequently, he loses both wives: he must divorce the minor wife (only provisionally married) because the levirate widow has a stronger claim, but he must perform *halitsah* with the adult since she is now the sister of his divorcee.

13:8 *A minor and a woman who is deaf-mute*: Although neither is fully legally competent, their statuses are different.

One who is legally competent and one who is deaf-mute . . . . An adult and a minor: In each case, a legal act of the second is compromised in a way that that of the first is not.

13:9, 10, 11 Here the two wives are not sisters. Valid levirate marriage with one prohibits levirate marriage with co-wives, but the sex act of a *minor* or a *woman who is deaf-mute* is not fully valid. The combinations of wives of different statuses are those explored in 13:8.

13:10 *Has (not) invalidated*: By his intercourse with one of the women the levir has (or has not) prohibited the other woman to himself.

or his brother had sexual intercourse with the deaf-mute woman—
he has not invalidated the one who is legally competent.
If the levir had sexual intercourse with the deaf-mute woman,
and then had sexual intercourse with the one who is legally competent,
or his brother had sexual intercourse with the one who is legally competent—
he has invalidated the deaf-mute woman.

11 A minor and an adult:
if the levir had sexual intercourse with the adult,
and then had sexual intercourse with the minor,
or his brother had sexual intercourse with the minor—
he has not disqualified the adult.
If the levir had sexual intercourse with the minor,
and then had sexual intercourse with the adult,
or his brother had sexual intercourse with the adult—
he has not disqualified the minor.
R. Eleazar[84] says:
One instructs the minor to renounce him.

12 A minor levir who had sexual intercourse with a minor levirate widow—
they attain majority one with the other.
If he had intercourse with an adult levirate widow—
she raises him to majority.
A levirate widow who said within thirty days: "I have not been possessed"—
one forces him to perform *halitsah* for her;
after thirty days—
one requests of him to perform *halitsah* for her.
If he admits, even after twelve months—
one forces him to perform *halitsah*.

[84] C: "Eliezer."

13:11 *R. Eleazar*: See n. 84.

One instructs the minor: See above, 13:7.

13:12 *attain majority one with the other*: Before he can enter a legally binding levirate marriage or perform *halitsah*.

raises him to majority: Interpreters suggest this means that she wait till he comes of age. However, the verb here certainly suggests an adult woman raising a child. According to *Niddah* 5:5, a child nine years and one day old who has intercourse with his levirate bride has acquired her but cannot release her (through a writ of divorce) before he comes of age.

I have not been possessed: See above, 4:10 and 5:3. This woman, who was taken in by the levir, had not engaged in sexual intercourse with him and their union has not constituted levirate marriage.

after thirty days: According to the commentaries, after this point her word is no longer fully trustworthy, and the court does not force the husband to perform *halitsah*.

13:13   *Levirate Marriage and Vows*

13 One who vows not to benefit from her levir:
during her husband's lifetime—
one forces him to perform *halitsah* for her;
after her husband's death—
one requests of him to perform *halitsah* for her.
And if she intended this,
even within the lifetime of her husband—
one requests of him to perform *halitsah* for her.

Chapter Fourteen

14:1–4   *Marriage with Deaf People*

14 A man who is deaf-mute who married a woman who is legally competent,
or a man who is legally competent who married a woman who is deaf-mute—
if he wishes, he may dismiss her,[85]
if he wishes, he may keep her.
Just as he brings her in with signs,[86] so too he dismisses her with signs.
One who is legally competent who married one who is legally competent,
and she became deaf-mute—
if he wishes, he may dismiss her,
if he wishes, he may keep her;
If she became legally incompetent—
he may not dismiss her.
If he became deaf-mute or became legally incompetent—
he may not dismiss her ever.

---

[85] Here and throughout chapter 14, "her" is implied and added for clarity.   [86] Or perhaps "gestures."

13:13 This ruling is presented here because of its structural similarity to the end of 13:12.

vows not to benefit from her levir: See *Nedarim* introduction. If a woman vows not to benefit from her husband's brother and this both predated the husband's death and is presumed to have had nothing to do with levirate marriage, the levir can be compelled to free her. If the wife made the vow *after the death of her husband*, so that intention not to undergo levirate can be seen as a major motive for the vow, or if she made this intention explicit, the levir may not be forced to free her through *halitsah*.

14:1–4 This chapter continues to elaborate on marriage with the deaf-mute begun in chapter 13. Deaf-mute persons were thought to have a diminished legal capacity. This creates legal puzzles regarding marriage, divorce, and levirate marriage.

14:1 *dismiss . . . . go out*: For this terminology, see above, 3.5.

signs: The rabbis envision here some sign language employed by the deaf-mute person.

he may not dismiss her ever: See above, 3:7.

Said R. Yohanan b. Nuri:
Why does a woman who became deaf-mute go out
and the man who became deaf-mute may not dismiss?
They said to him:
The man who divorces is not like the woman who is divorced,
since the woman goes out willingly or unwillingly,
and the man does not dismiss unless it is his will.

2 R. Yohanan b. Gudgadah testified:
Concerning a woman who was a deaf-mute
and who was married off by her father—
she may be dismissed by a writ of divorce.
They said to him:
This one is like her.

3 Two deaf-mute brothers married to two deaf-mute sisters,
or to two sisters who are legally competent,
or to two sisters, one who is deaf-mute and one who is legally competent;
or two deaf-mute sisters married to two brothers who are legally competent,
or to two brothers who are deaf-mute,
or to two brothers, one who is deaf-mute and one who is legally competent—
these are exempt from *halitsah* and from levirate marriage.
If they were unrelated women—
they may take them in,
and if they wish to dismiss them—
they may dismiss them.

The man who divorces is not like the woman who is divorced: The explanation given here is the clearest formulation of the gender differences regarding divorce in Jewish law. Men divorce. They decide. Women are divorced. They have no say in the matter. It is strange that this formula is found in this mishnah, which refers specifically to a case where a man may not divorce his wife. This is because when he becomes deaf-mute, he can no longer formulate his will verbally. Here again we see the deaf-mute classified in the same category as the minor and the mentally disabled, who are considered not to be in possession of their full legal faculties and therefore unable to complete a fully valid legal act.

14:2 *R. Yohanan b. Gudgadah testified*, etc.: See *Eduyot* 7:9 (and p. 672 n. 88 for the name of the Sage there). The text in *Eduyot* specifies that the woman was married off by her father. The text is presented here (and also in *Gittin* 5:5) in order to prove the point made in the previous mishnah, that one may divorce a woman who is deaf and mute.

They said to him: Continues the answer presented to Yohanan b. Nuri's question in 14:1. *This one*, the legally competent woman who has become deaf and mute after marriage, *is like* the deaf-mute wife married off by her father.

14:3 A pair of brothers is married to a pair of sisters; either both brothers or both sisters are deaf and mute. In each case, because the marriages and the levirate claims that result from them are weak, but equivalent, the rules are analogous to a case where neither party is impaired: a levirate widow who is the wife's sister is exempt from the laws of levirate marriage.

unrelated women: See above, 3:6. If the two women were not sisters to one another.

take them in: i.e. take in levirate marriage; see 2.6. The widows cannot perform *halitsah* (12:4, above), so the only recourse is to perform levirate marriage. But the marriage may be dissolved subsequently as in 14:1.

4 Two brothers, one deaf-mute and one who is legally competent,
married to two sisters who are legally competent—
if the deaf-mute man, husband to the legally competent woman, died,
what shall the man who is legally competent, husband to the woman who is legally competent, do?
She goes out because of the prohibition of the sister of his wife.
If the man who is legally competent, married to a woman who is legally competent, died,
what shall the deaf-mute man, husband to a woman who is legally competent, do?
He dismisses his wife with a divorce, and his brother's wife is forbidden to him forever.

5[87] Two brothers who are legally competent,
married to two sisters, one deaf-mute and one who is legally competent—
if the one who is legally competent, husband to the deaf-mute woman, died,
what does the one who is legally competent, husband to the woman who is legally competent, do?
She goes out because of the prohibition of the sister of his wife.
If the one who is legally competent, husband to the woman who is legally competent, died, what shall the one who is legally competent, husband to the deaf-mute woman, do?
He dismisses his wife with a writ of divorce and his brother's wife with *halitsah*.

6 Two brothers, one deaf-mute and one who is legally competent,
married to two sisters, one deaf-mute and one who is legally competent—
if the deaf-mute one, husband to the deaf-mute woman, dies, what shall the one who is legally competent, married to the woman who is legally competent, do?
She goes out on account of the sister of his wife.
If the one who is legally competent, married to the woman who is legally competent, died, what shall the deaf-mute one, husband to the deaf-mute woman, do?
He dismisses his wife with a writ of divorce, and his brother's wife is forbidden to him forever.

7 Two brothers, one deaf-mute and one who is legally competent,

[87] Some manuscripts and editions lack the paragraph numeration from here to the end of the chapter.

14:4 This mishnah is a list of all the combinations of deaf and mute and hearing people marrying. It resembles the mishnayot in chapter 3. Unlike the cases of 14:3 these cases juxtapose fully valid marriages (between competent adults) and impaired ones (involving deaf-mute partners). The first group of cases deals with brothers, of whom one is hearing, but where both wives are hearing.

goes out: For this terminology, see above, 3:5. In the first case, since the levirate widow is close kin to the wife of the sole levir and all three parties are legally competent, there is no levirate bond.

dismisses his wife: The deaf-mute man's marriage is only partially valid, so the claim of the levirate widow undermines his own marriage and he must divorce his wife. The deaf-mute man cannot perform *halitsah* (12:4), nor in this case can he perform levirate marriage, so the woman is *forbidden to him forever*.

In the next group of cases there are *two brothers who are legally competent*. Again, the levirate claim created by the marriage of two legally competent people undermines marriage where one partner is deaf-mute; but unlike the preceding case, the competent husband can perform *halitsah* with his levirate bride.

The third group of cases deals with combinations of *two brothers*, only *one* of whom *is deaf-mute*, and *two sisters*, only *one* of whom *is deaf-mute*, assuming that the two competent siblings are married, as are the two deaf-mute siblings.

married to two unrelated women who are legally competent—
if the deaf-mute brother, married to the one who is legally competent, died, what shall the one who is legally competent, married to the one who is legally competent, do?
Either he performs *halitsah* or takes her in levirate marriage.
If the one who is legally competent, married to the woman who is legally competent, dies, what shall the deaf-mute one, married to the one who is legally competent, do?
He takes her in, and does not dismiss her forever.

8 Two brothers who are legally competent,
married to two unrelated women,
one who is legally competent and one who is deaf-mute—
if the one who is legally competent, married to the deaf-mute woman, dies, what shall the one who is legally competent, married to the woman who is legally competent, do?
He takes her in, and if he wishes to dismiss her—he may dismiss her.
If the one who is legally competent, married to the woman who is legally competent, dies, what shall the one who is legally competent, married to the deaf-mute woman, do?
Either he performs *halitsah* or takes her in levirate marriage.

9 Two brothers, one deaf-mute and one who is legally competent,
married to two unrelated women, one deaf-mute and one who is legally competent—
if the deaf-mute married to the deaf-mute woman died, what shall the one who is legally competent, married to the woman who is legally competent, do?
He takes her in, and if he wishes to dismiss her—he may dismiss her.
If the one who is legally competent, married to the woman who is legally competent, died, what shall the deaf-mute, married to the deaf-mute woman, do?
He takes her in and may not dismiss her forever.

unrelated: As in 14:3, at the end of this discussion another factor is added: what happens if the women are not related one to the other? Again, the Mishnah considers situations where both women are competent, where both men are competent, and where one each of the men and women is competent. In these cases the same problem of the competence of deaf-mute people to constitute marriages is at issue, but specific problems posed by sisters do not arise.

may not dismiss her forever, as in 14:1, since the deaf-mute levir cannot sever the marital bond created by levirate marriage.

15:1–16:7 From here to the end of the tractate the Mishnah deals with the issue of ascertaining the death of a husband, in order to allow a wife to remarry. Similar issues had been discussed above, in 10:1–5. A woman may not be married to more than one husband and must therefore be able to prove that she was single, or divorced, or widowed, in order to marry.

Through 16:2 in particular, the discussion revolves around whether the woman is *ne'emenet*, "to be believed" or, better in this context, "trustworthy." This term is used in the Mishnah consistently in order to describe the reliability of a woman's testimony, in most cases concerning her own marital status (aside from this chapter and 16:5 also in *Ketubbot* 1:7–9; 2:5) but not always (see *Bava Qama* 10:2). Compare *Rosh Hashanah* 1:8. Here, the Mishnah treats such testimony as valid in establishing the husband's death for the purposes of remarriage. For other purposes the death is treated as doubtful.

Since polygyny is fully permissible, the parallel question whether a woman is alive or dead does not affect the marriageability of her husband (although it may affect inheritance), because he may marry as many women as he wishes.

Chapter Fifteen

1–3 *A woman testifying to the death of her own husband*

15 A woman who went abroad together with her husband:
if there was peace between him and her and peace in the world,
and she came and said: "My husband died"—
she may marry;
"My husband died"—
she may undergo levirate marriage.
Peace between him and her and war in the world,
a quarrel between him and her and peace in the world,
and she came and said: "My husband died"—
she is not to be believed.
R. Judah says:
She is never to be believed unless she comes weeping with her clothes torn.
They said to him:
Both this one and this one—
may marry.
  2 The House of Hillel say:
The only tradition[88] we have heard
concerns a woman who came from the grain harvest,
and in the same region,
and in accordance with a case that happened.[89]
Said the House of Shammai to them:
A woman who came from the [grain] harvest,
a woman who came from the olive [harvest],
a woman who came from the grape [harvest],
a woman who came from one region to another[90]—

---

[88] The word "tradition" is not in the text but is implied by the verb "heard."
[89] K, P, C lack "and in the same region, and in accordance with a case that happened." Cf. *Eduyot* 1:12.
[90] In place of "grape harvest... to another," K, P, C have only "from abroad." Cf. *Eduyot* 1:12

15:1 *peace*: The assumption here is that at a time of peace, where catastrophes and unexpected tumults are rare, and where the relations between husband and wife are cordial, there is no reason to doubt the woman's testimony.

war in the world: If there is a war, husband and wife may have been separated under strenuous circumstances, and the husband's death is only a likely guess.

quarrel between him and her: The wife may be interested in lying about his death, so as to be released from him, inasmuch as the chances that people will know the truth are very slim.

not to be believed: See annotation to 15:1–16:7.

weeping with her clothes torn: As visible signs of mourning; see *Mo'ed Qatan* 3:7–9.

15:2 Parallel to *Eduyot* 1:12. See also nn. 89, 90.

The only tradition we have heard: The implication is that the rule is based on a received precedent and not on legislation. The House of Hillel here are more restrictive, as *Eduyot* 1:12 maintains: only a woman who returns from the harvest and relates the death of her husband may remarry. This obviously limits women's autonomy and agency.

it is all one and the same.
The Sages spoke of the harvest only because [they spoke] of the usual.
The House of Hillel reversed themselves
and taught according to[91] the House of Shammai.

3 The House of Shammai say:
She may remarry[92] and take her *ketubbah*.
The House of Hillel say:
She may remarry, but she may not take her *ketubbah*.
The House of Shammai said to them:
Since you have permitted
the graver matter of forbidden intercourse,
should you not also permit the lesser matter of property?
Said the House of Hillel to them:
We find that the brothers may not enter into their inheritance on her testimony.
Said the House of Shammai to them:
Should we not deduce [the law] from her *ketubbah* document?
For he writes for her:
"Should you be married to another [after being married to me],
you may take what is prescribed for you."
The House of Hillel reversed themselves
and taught according to the words of the House of Shammai.

[91] P, C, and others: "According to the words of." [92] Here and throughout literally "marry."

Sages .... spoke of the usual: The House of Shammai here demand of the House of Hillel not to be too literal. The *[grain] harvest* is an example not a limiting requirement.

House of Hillel reversed themselves : This is a rhetorical device, used to justify the reason why some rulings in the Mishnah are according to the legal opinion of the House of Shammai. See annotations to *Eduyot* 1:12–14.

15:3 Continues to parallel *Eduyot*.

remarry and take her ketubbah. The rule distinguishes two consequences of the wife's testimony: changing her status to widow and allowing her to collect her marriage settlement, which normally happens after divorce, or after the death of her husband, see *Ketubbot* 1:2–3.

permitted the graver matter of forbidden intercourse: The same term is translated in 1:2 as "forbidden relations."

the brothers: The House of Hillel hold that a woman may remarry on her own testimony of her husband's death, but she is not trusted to declare her husband's death for other purposes. In support of this they point to the shared rule that her testimony cannot dissolve his estate and allow various heirs and creditors, including the woman with her marriage contract, to carve it up. The legal rationale for this (by no means clear) is discussed by the Talmud and commentaries.

"Should you be married .... take what is prescribed for you": Probably a citation from a marriage contract recognized by both the House of Shammai and the House of Hillel, because it persuades the House of Hillel. Surprisingly, the quotation is in Hebrew; cf. *Ketubbot* 4:7–12, in which the document clauses are almost all in Aramaic. This clause is not documented in marriage documents from the second century discovered in the Judaean Desert. Perhaps it is a combination of the two alternative formulations to the clause mentioned in *Ketubbot* 4:12: "You shall dwell in my house and be maintained from my property as long as you are a widow" and "You shall dwell in my house and be maintained from my property till the heirs wish to give you your *ketubbah*."

15:4–5 Testimony Regarding the Death of the Husband

4 All are to be believed to give testimony concerning her
except her mother-in-law,
and the daughter of her mother-in-law,
and her co-wife,
and her husband's brother's wife,
and her husband's daughter.
How does divorce differ from death [of the husband]?
The writ provides proof.
One witness says: "He is dead,"
and she marries,
and another comes and says: "He is not dead"—
this one need not go out.
One witness says: "He is dead,"
and two say: "He is not dead"—
even though she has married—
she must go out.
Two witnesses say: "He is dead,"
and one witness says: "He is not dead"—
even though she has not remarried—
she may remarry.

5 One [co-wife] says: "He is dead,"
and one says: "He is not dead"—
The one who says: "He is dead," may marry and collect her *ketubbah*
and the one who says: "He is not dead," may not marry and may not collect her *ketubbah*.
One says: "He is dead,"
and the other one says: "He was killed"—
R. Meir says:
Since they contradict one another, in this case, these may not remarry.

15:4 *testimony concerning her*: That her husband died and she may remarry.

husband's brother's wife: Cf. 2:3 and 3:3. The idea behind disqualifying all these women as witnesses to the death of a husband is that they may have a grudge against the wife, and maliciously make her commit adultery and produce *mamzerim*.

The writ provides proof: A divorced woman possesses a writ, signed by two witnesses; a widow does not.

go out: For this terminology, see above, 3:5.

15:5 *One [co-wife] says . . . . one says . . .*: Two women, who happen to be co-wives, testify to the death of the same man. In these cases, the evidence is treated separately, and the rabbis do not attempt to get at the truth. They allow the one who maintains he is dead to remarry, collect her marriage contract and its attendant benefits, and take the risk that he is not dead, with all the legal consequences this may have. They "punish" the one who says he is alive, by forbidding her to remarry or benefit from her marriage contract.

Since they contradict one another: Does a woman who says the man has died (presumably of natural causes or accident) sufficiently contradict one who says *he has been killed*? This is the question which the rabbis debate here. R. Judah and R. Simeon think not. R. Meir appears to disagree.

R. Judah and R. Simeon say:
Since both this one and that one admit that he is not living—
they may remarry.
A witness says: "He is dead,"
and a witness says: "He is not dead";
one woman says: "He is dead,"
and another woman says: "He is not dead"—
in this case, she may not marry.

15:6–7   Debates between R. Tarfon and R. Aqiva

6 A woman who went abroad with her husband,
and she came and said: "My husband died"—
she may marry and collect her *ketubbah*,
and her co-wife is prohibited.
If [the co-wife] was a daughter of an Israelite married to a priest—
she may eat *terumah*—
the words of R. Tarfon.
R. Aqiva says:
This is not the way to distance her from transgression;
rather[93] she is forbidden to marry and forbidden to eat *terumah*.

7 If she said: "My husband died, and then my father-in-law died"—
she may remarry and collect her *ketubbah*,
and her mother-in-law is prohibited.
If the mother-in-law[94] were a daughter of Israel married to a priest—
she may eat *terumah*—
the words of R. Tarfon.
R. Aqiva says:
This is not the way to distance her from transgression;
rather[95] she is forbidden to marry and forbidden to eat *terumah*.

[93] Lit. "until."   [94] Heb. "she."   [95] Here and below, "until" as in 15:6.

15:6–7 Four rulings lumped together and formulated similarly, in which R. Aqiva rules harshly, because he considers a harsher ruling as safeguard against sin. The first two continue the discussion of a woman who claims that her husband has died.

15:6 *her co-wife is prohibited . . . . she may eat terumah*: A woman may not testify to the death of her co-wife's husband (see above, 15:4). As a consequence of such testimony, according to R. Tarfon, the co-wife is prohibited from remarrying and does not lose her status as a priest's wife. This is so as not to encourage a wife to maliciously testify to the death of her co-wife's husband.

This is not the way to distance her from transgression: In case the husband really is dead, it would be a terrible thing for her to eat *terumah*.

15:7 *her mother-in-law*: Because a daughter-in-law cannot testify about the death of her mother-in-law's husband, see above, 15:4.

may eat terumah: See previous mishnah.

He betrothed one of five women,
but does not know which one he betrothed,
and each one says: "He betrothed me"—
he gives a writ of divorce to each one,
leaves the *ketubbah* payment between them, and goes away—
the words of R. Tarfon.
R. Aqiva says:
This is not the way to distance him from transgression;
rather he must give a writ of divorce and a *ketubbah* payment to each one.
He robbed one of five persons,
but does not know which one he robbed,
and each one says: "He robbed me"—
he leaves the stolen item between them and goes away—
the words of R. Tarfon.
R. Aqiva says:
This is not the way to distance him from transgression;
rather he must pay [the value of] the stolen item to each one.

15:8–10 *A Wife's Testimony about Herself and Levirate Marriage*

8 A woman who went abroad with her husband
and their son was with them,
and she came and said: "My husband died and then my son died"—
she is to be believed.
"My son died and then my husband died"—
she is not to be believed.
But one is concerned regarding her words,
and she performs *halitsah*
but does not undergo levirate marriage.

writ of divorce to each: He is doubtfully married to each and each requires a writ of divorce (2:6 and *Qiddushin* 3:7, 4:9 and see also *Gittin* 8:9).

leaves the ketubbah payment between them: His one betrothal only obligated him to one settlement. Since each claims it belongs to her, they may share (or fight over) it.

a writ of divorce and a ketubbah payment to each. The man has not fully made right the obligation he created for himself by his statement about betrothal without a full marriage settlement to each woman. The assumption is that a man, who betroths a woman without knowing which, acts rashly and immorally. If he knows that he needs to pay each a marriage contract, he will avoid acting like this.

pay the stolen item to each one: Again, in order to fulfill the obligation he has created through his own statement, the man must provide full compensation for each and every potential victim. Thus, here perhaps, R. Aqiva's suggestion that he pay all those who claim he has robbed them, would have the character of a fine imposed on the thief by society.

15:8 "*My son died and then my husband died*": If her son died first, this would make her a childless widow and thus fit for levirate marriage.

9 A son has been given to me abroad,
and she said: "My son died and then my husband died"—
she is to be believed;
"My husband died and then my son died"—
she is not to be believed.
But one is concerned regarding her words,
and she performs *halitsah* but does not undergo levirate marriage.
10 A levir has been given to me abroad,
and she said: "My husband died and then my levir died,"
or: "My levir and then my husband"—
she is to be believed.
She went abroad with her husband and her levir,
and said: "My husband died,
and then my levir died,"
or "My levir and
then my husband"—
she is not to be believed,
because a woman is not believed to say: "My levir died,"
so that she may marry,
nor: "My sister died,"
so that she may enter the brother-in-law's[96] house.
And a man is not to be believed to say: "My brother has died,"
so that he may take his wife in levirate marriage,
or:" My wife has died," so that he may marry her sister.

[96] Heb. "his."

one is concerned: Adds a qualification to the preceding case: *she performs halitsah but does not undergo levirate marriage*. That is to say, when the Mishnah said *she is not to be believed*, this seems to refer specifically to her status as levirate widow; the fact that she must perform *halitsah* means that we take the testimony about the husband's death as valid. This may reflect the concern that the widow desires her husband's brother, which the rabbis view as a false motive for the levirate marriage (cf. above 2:8).

15:9 *A son has been given to me*: When I was abroad I had a son, but he died. Without this statement about a son we would have assumed that she was a levirate widow. Consequently, *she is to be believed* when her testimony makes her a levirate widow and *not to be believed* when it frees her from that obligation.

one is concerned: See 15:8.

15:10 *A levir has been given to me*: As in 15:9, we only know about the levir from her testimony. *She is to be believed* to be a widow and not to be in need of levirate marriage or *halitsah*.

She went abroad with her husband and her levir: Here, no matter what her testimony, *she is not to be believed* to free herself from the levirate obligation.

Because a woman is not to be believed ….a man is not to be believed, etc.: In all these cases the person is suspected of having a romantic motive for testifying to a death and are therefore forbidden to marry a partner who would have been prohibited without that testimony.

Chapter Sixteen

16:1–2 *Testimony Regarding the Death of a Husband Married to Two Women*

16 A woman whose husband and co-wife went abroad,
and they came and said to her: "Your husband died"—
she may not marry
and may not undergo levirate marriage
until she knows whether her co-wife is pregnant.
If she had a mother-in-law—
she need[97] not be concerned.
If the latter[98] left pregnant[99]—
she must be concerned.
R. Joshua says:
She need not be concerned.

2 Two leviriate widows:
this one says: "My husband is dead,"
and that one says: "My husband is dead"—
this one is prohibited because of the husband of that one,
and that one is prohibited because of the husband of this one.
If this one had witnesses
and that one has no witnesses,
the one who has witnesses is prohibited;
and the one who has no witnesses is permitted.
This one has sons,

[97] Lit. "is…is not."   [98] Heb. "she."   [99] Lit. "full."

16:1 *until she knows whether her co-wife is pregnant*: If her co-wife is pregnant she may not undergo *halitsah* or *levirate marriage* because her husband did not die childless.

need not be concerned: Lest her mother-in-law had given birth to a potential levir.

If the latter left pregnant: Apparently, this refers to the mother-in-law. This means that a potential levir may have been born while the wife was abroad. By contrast, *R. Joshua* does not require the woman to act as if there is a potential levir in this case.

16:2 *Two levirate widows*: Married to two brothers.

prohibited from marrying *because of the husband of that one*: Because the testimony of a wife cannot establish the death of her husband for the purposes of freeing the sister-in-law from the levirate bond.

the one who has witnesses is prohibited: The witnesses make her a widow but, as above, the testimony of the woman alone cannot free her from being a levirate widow.

the one who has no witnesses is permitted: The death of her levir has been attested by witnesses, so she is released from levirate obligations.

This one has sons: The fact that one wife has sons—presumably from the husband—frees herself to remarry; but this fact cannot permit her co-wife because the death of the husband is only established by the co-wife's word.

and this one has no sons,
the one who has a son is permitted,
and the one who has no sons is prohibited.
If they underwent levirate marriage and the levirs died—
they are forbidden to marry.
R. Eliezer says:
Since they were permitted to the levirs, they are permitted to all persons.

16:3–7 Is the Husband Really Dead?

3 One testifies only[100] about the face including the nose,
even if there are distinguishing marks on his body and on his clothing
And one testifies only after[101] his soul departed,
even if they saw him being flayed,
or being crucified,
or that a beast was devouring him.
And one testifies only within three days of death.[102]
R. Judah b. Bava says:
Not all persons, and not all places, and not all times are equal.

4 If he fell into water,
whether those that have limits
or in to those that are limitless—

[100] Lit. "They may not testify except."
[101] Lit. "They may not testify except until."
[102] Lit. "They may not testify except until three days."

underwent levirate marriage: If there were known levirs, the women who attested to the death of their husbands could enter levirate marriage (15:1). If those levirs died, the doubtful deaths of their first husbands (attested only by themselves) make them unable to marry.

R. Eliezer seems to argue for legal consistency: having once been permitted to remarry after the deaths of the first husbands, it makes no sense to limit this only to levirate marriage.

16:3–7 In the remainder of the tractate, the issue is evidence that may establish the death of a husband, hence the permissibility of the wife's remarriage.. We are informed of rough living conditions and of the hazards of declaring one untimely dead.

16:3 The Mishnah sets out three characteristics required to declare a person dead. He was identified by his face including the nose, he was seen dead, and he did not rise within three days.

distinguishing marks: Even if the body had distinctive scars or birthmarks or was found with a certain man's personal belongings, he is not legally identified as the dead man unless the face was visible and recognizable.

flayed .... crucified .... a beast was devouring him: Even if the man was observed in situations which mean certain death, like being crucified, one cannot accept their testimony to his actual death.

R. Judah b. Bava suggests that the above categories are too stringent. If a person was (for example) seen being devoured by a lion (say, in the Roman arena), this would be proof enough that he is dead (Judah b. Bava himself is said to have died at the aftermath of the Bar Kokhba war). Alternatively, following the division of **K** and other early witnesses, this statement introduces the discussion that follows.

16:4 *that have limits*: Like a cistern.

limitless: The sea.

his wife is prohibited.
Said R. Meir:
It once happened that someone fell into a large pit and emerged after three days.
Said R. Yose:
It once happened that a blind man went down to immerse in a cave,
and his escort[103] went down after him,
and they took as long as it takes for their soul to depart,
and they married their wives off.
And again there was the case in Asia of one who was let down into the sea
and all they pulled back was his leg—
the Sages said:
From above the knee—
she may marry;
from below the knee—
she may not marry.

5 Even if he heard from women saying:
"So-and-so died"—
that is enough for him.
R. Judah says:
Even if he heard from little children saying:
"We are going to eulogize and to bury so-and-so."

[103] Lit. "the one who pulls him."

prohibited from marrying because no body was produced and he may yet emerge.

R. Meir: The precedent proves that the *halakhah* legislated above is correct, since once someone did come back after three days.

a large pit: Water that has limits.

R. Yose: The precedent supports the opposite view: although they stayed there only long enough for their souls to depart, certainly shorter than three days, nevertheless they were considered dead and their wives were permitted to remarry.

blind man: Whether the blindness of the subject plays a role in the decision is not spelled out.

to immerse: Ritual immersion. On immersing in *a cave* see e.g. *Shabbat* 22:5; *Nazir* 9:2; *Miqva'ot* 6:1; *Makhshirin* 3:1.

escort: See n. 103. The term is elsewhere used for leading a beast, see e.g. *Bava Qama* 7:6.

Asia. The Roman province or perhaps a local place with that name (e.g. the Biblical site of Etsion Gaver, near present day Aqaba or Eilat).

let down into the sea: Water that is without limit.

all they pulled back was his leg: The rest of him was devoured by fish or other animals.

above the knee . . . . below the knee: If his leg dangling on the rope is from above the knee, one cannot assume that he can swim, and therefore he is dead. If it is only below the knee, he can swim to some shore and emerge alive.

16:5 *Even if he heard*: From this expression onwards, extreme cases of very circumstantial evidence are provided to show to what lengths rabbis were willing to go to release a wife from her absent husband.

to eulogize and to bury so-and-so: The assumption is that children play imitating adults. If adults took part in the burial of a person, came back, and talked about it, children will play such a game.

Whether [the speaker] intended to [testify] or whether he did not intend.
R. Judah b. Bava says:
In the case of an Israelite—
only when he intends;
and in the case of a gentile—
if he intends, his testimony is no testimony.

6 One testifies [to what was seen] in the light of a lamp
and in the light of the moon,
and one marries off based on "a daughter of a voice."
It happened that someone stood on the top of the hill and said:
"So-and-so son of so-and-so from place so-and-so died."
They went and found no one there,
and they married off his wife.
And it happened also in Salmon that someone said:
"I, so-and-so, was bitten by a snake, and now I am dying"—
and they went and did not recognize him,
but they married off his wife.

7 Said R. Aqiva:
When I went down to Nehardea to intercalate the year,
I found Nehemiah, a man of Bet Deli, who said to me:

in the case of a gentile ... his testimony is no testimony: The assumption is that the testimony of a gentile is invalid. This principle is not formulated outright in tannaitic literature but cf. *Makkot* 4:1 mentioning those who are unfit to give evidence.

16:6 *in the light of a lamp and in the light of the moon*: That is, even not in full daylight.

"daughter of a voice": This term is used in many senses in rabbinic literature, from a mere rumor to a heavenly voice, to a personification of God. It is unclear why the feminine "daughter" is used.

They went .... and they married off his wife: Despite the fact that the witness could not be interrogated, his evidence is considered valid.

Salmon: This place is also mentioned in *Kilayim* 4:9. It is identified as Khirbet Salma in Galilee.

"I, so-and-so, was bitten by a snake, and now I am dying": These are the dying words of a person who knows he was bitten by a snake and understands his predicament. Even though he is speaking, and thus not yet dead, his words are taken as evidence for his death.

did not recognize him, but they married his wife off: The assumption here is that a snakebite disfigures a person to the extent that he becomes unrecognizable.

16:7 Parallel to *Eduyot* 8:3, where only the conclusion of this episode is presented.

Nehardea: A large town on the Middle Euphrates and an important center of Jewish presence in Babylonia from an early period.

to intercalate the year: To add a thirteenth month to align the lunar calendar with the solar. See *Rosh Hashanah* introduction.

I heard that in the Land of Israel no one permits the wife to remarry based on the testimony of a single witness, except Judah b. Bava.[104]
And I answered him: So it is.
He said to me: Tell them in my name:
You know that the country is ravaged by soldiers.
I have it on testimony from Rabban Gamaliel the Elder
that one may marry off a woman based on the testimony of a single witness.
And when I came and related these things to Rabban Gamaliel,
he was glad of my words and said:
We have found a companion to R. Judah b. Bava.[105]
From these words Rabban Gamaliel was reminded that men were killed in Tel Arza, and Rabban Gamaliel the Elder permitted their wives to marry based on a single witness, and they accepted that one marries off women based on testimony of a single witness;[106]
and they accepted that one marries off women
based on testimony of a witness from a witness,
based on testimony of a male slave,[107]
based on testimony of a woman,[108]
based on testimony of a female slave.
R. Eliezer and R. Joshua said:
One does not marry off a woman based on the testimony of one witness.
R. Aqiva said:
Not on the testimony of a woman,
and not on the testimony of a male slave,
and not on the testimony of a female slave,[109]
and not on the testimony of relatives.
They said to him:
It happened that the sons of Levi went to Zoar, City of Dates,

[104] **K** (marginal note), **P**, **C**: "Abba."
[105] **P**: "Abba." [106] Lacking in **K**, **P**, **C**, and other witnesses.
[107] **K** and **P** have the male slave before the female slave; **C** lacks the male slave.
[108] **K**, **P**, **C**: "from a woman, from a woman from the words of another woman."
[109] **K**, **P**, **C** do not list the male and female slave here.

no one permits the wife to remarry based on the testimony of a single witness: This tradition contradicts the operative principle in chapters 15 and 16, that allows remarriage on the basis of single witnesses and even of women themselves. The rule that prohibits remarriage on this basis is reversed in this mishnah.

ravaged by soldiers: This is a description of a land at war or under strict military rule, as Palestine was before and after the Bar Kokhba revolt.

Tel Arza is mentioned only here and in parallel traditions. Its location is completely unknown, and the tradition about men killed there is not related elsewhere. We can date the event to before the destruction of the Temple, based on the mention of Rabban Gamaliel the Elder, who appears in the New Testament as Paul's Pharisee teacher (Acts 22:3).

R. Aqiva attempts to assimilate the testimonial basis for permitting a woman to remarry to the laws of testimony present elsewhere in the Mishnah, see *Shevuot* 4:1.

and one of them fell sick on the way,
and they brought him to an inn.
When they came back they said to the [female] innkeeper:
Where is our companion?
She said to them:
He died and I buried him—
and they married off his wife.
They said to him:
And should a daughter of a priest not be equal to an innkeeper?
He said to them:
When the innkeeper is to be believed:
the innkeeper brought out for them his staff[110] and his bag and the Torah scroll he had in his hands.

[110] K, P, C add "and his shoes."

Zoar, City of Dates: Situated southeast of the Dead Sea; see Genesis 19:23. A Jewish community thrived there evidenced by documents from the Judaean Desert from the time of the Bar Kokhba revolt and a large Jewish cemetery from the fourth to the sixth centuries.

They said to R. Aqiva: And should a daughter of a priest not be equal to an innkeeper? May a woman testify alone to the death of a husband (see 15:4), permitting his wife to remarry? This story is of such evidence from (perhaps a gentile) female innkeeper. The rabbis ask of R. Aqiva, how he accepts this evidence while turning down the evidence of trustworthy women, such as a daughter of a priest (*kohen*).

When the innkeeper is to be believed: According to R. Aqiva, the female innkeeper's testimony releasing the woman was not believed as such, but as a result of the man's belongings that she produced (cf. Genesis 38:25). This contradicts 16:3, in which the belongings, without other evidence, are meaningless.

The tractate ends abruptly. The question of a woman's reliability as witness to the death of another woman's husband is not resolved.

Tractate Ketubbot

Robert Brody

Introduction

Overview

Ketubbot ("marriage contracts") is devoted primarily to rules governing the relationship between marriage partners (although it also includes several extensive digressions). These rules are to a considerable extent based on the marriage contract (*ketubbah*, pl. *ketubbot*). In addition to signifying the marriage contract, the word *ketubbah* also has several related meanings, most prominently the basic payment to which the wife is entitled in case the marriage is dissolved by divorce or by the husband's death.

Structure and Organization of the Tractate

The order of discussion of the topics treated in this tractate is roughly chronological, beginning with marriage and its immediate aftermath (chapter 1) and proceeding in chapter 4 to delineate the relative rights of husbands and fathers with respect to women under their authority (4:1–6), followed by a discussion of the normative clauses of the *ketubbah* document (4:7–5:1). Chapters 5 and 6 treat the laws governing relations and monetary arrangements between husbands and wives during the course of their marriage. Grounds for divorce (chapter 7) precede a discussion of rules concerning the wife's property, including property which she inherits before or during the marriage (chapter 8). This is followed by rules governing the collection of monies owed her in the event of her husband's death and of her enjoyment of dower rights if she remains a widow and chooses to remain in her late husband's home (chapters 9–11). Chapter 12 considers the related issue of contractual arrangements to support widows or, especially, daughters. A short appendix (13:10–11) concerns the issue of the married couple's choice of domicile and its implications with regard to marriage and divorce.

There are, in addition, several substantial digressions or appendices: *Ketubbot* 1:6–2:2 and 2:3–10 deal with various issues of trustworthiness that are relevant only in part to this tractate. Chapter 13 contains a long appendix (13:1–9) of disputed rulings from the late Second Temple period, several of which are directly relevant to this tractate.

Chapter 3, dealing with sanctions imposed on a rapist or seducer, is the one exception to the chronological organization. One might perhaps have expected this chapter, which is closely related to biblical texts (see below), to appear at the beginning of the tractate; it is possible that the redactors of the Mishnah chose to begin with more pleasant topics or with topics more directly connected with the central concerns of the tractate.

Main Ideas

Two legal concepts, which rabbis root in Scripture but which are also especially characteristic of rabbinic marriage law, are (1) betrothal (*erusin* or *qiddushin*) as inchoate marriage that can only be severed by divorce and (2) the *ketubbah* payment, a sum promised by the husband and payable in the event of divorce or the husband's death. The default amount in the case of a virgin bride was set at two hundred *zuz* or *dinar*. This could be increased, and according to some opinions could also be decreased, by agreement of the parties. The default amount for a nonvirgin bride was set at half of this sum. In addition, 4:7–5:1 outlines the standard clauses of the *ketubbah* document, stipulating that certain clauses are to be operative ("conditions set by the court") even if they do not appear in the document.

Relationship to Scripture

The lone section of the tractate that is closely related to biblical texts is chapter 3, referring to the sanctions imposed on a rapist or a seducer in Exodus 22:15–16 and Deuteronomy 22:25–29, verses that the rabbis use to derive additional rules. Elsewhere in the tractate, biblical rules stand in the background. Deuteronomy 22:23 treats sexual intercourse with another man after betrothal as adultery punishable by death, providing part of the rationale for treating the arrangement as inchoate marriage. The two-hundred-*zuz ketubbah* was based on exegesis of Exodus 22:15–16 and Deuteronomy 22:28–29, interpreting the fifty *sheqel* mentioned there as corresponding to fifty Roman-era tetradrachms, or two hundred *dinar*. Claims of a bride's nonvirginity (as in chapter 1) refer to the biblical rules about such claims (Deuteronomy 22:13–21).

Special Notes for the Reader

In addition to citing **K** and **P** directly the annotations refer concisely to two main branches of the manuscript tradition of the Mishnah as "Palestinian" and "Babylonian" (although this convention is imprecise). **K** and **P** are, in fact, the earliest complete "Palestinian" manuscripts; "Babylonian" witnesses are those in which the Mishnah is copied along with the Babylonian Talmud. I also refer to the indirect testimony of the Talmudim, especially the Palestinian Talmud, which sometimes cite or presuppose a more original version of the Mishnah even when the two branches of the manuscript tradition are in agreement.

Tractate Ketubbot

Chapter One

1:1–5 *Virginity, Claims of Nonvirginity, and the Ketubbah Payment*

1 A virgin is married on Wednesday and a widow on Thursday.[1]
For the courts sit twice weekly in the towns, on Monday and on Thursday, so that if he had a claim concerning virginity, he would go early to the court.
  2 A virgin's *ketubbah* is two hundred and a widow's one *maneh*.
A virgin who was widowed or divorced or underwent *halitsah* after betrothal—
their *ketubbah* is two hundred and they are subject to a claim of virginity.
A woman who is a convert or was held captive or was a slave,
who was redeemed or converted or manumitted
before the age of three years and a day—
their *ketubbah* is two hundred
and they are subject to a claim of virginity.
  3 An adult male who had intercourse with a female minor,
or a male minor who had intercourse with a female adult,
and a woman who lost her hymen in an accident[2]—
their *ketubbah* is two hundred—
the words of R. Meir;
but the Sages say:

[1] Lit. "fourth day" and "fifth day," counting from Sunday.   [2] Lit. "who was struck by wood."

1:1 *a widow*: Or (presumably) any other bride who is not a virgin.

For the courts: This explanation of the custom of marrying virgins on Wednesdays, although found in all manuscripts of the Mishnah, is an addition to the text (as indicated by the discussion in the Palestinian Talmud).

1:2 *maneh*: One hundred *dinar* or *zuz*, half the amount for a virgin.

subject to a claim of virginity: They are presumed to be virgins at the time of marriage, and therefore their husbands may sue if they claim to have found them nonvirgins. The language is biblical (see Deuteronomy 22:13–21).

A woman, etc.: The underlying presumptions are that non-Jewish women, slaves, and captives are likely to engage in sex (voluntarily or otherwise) outside of marriage, and that sexual activity under the age of three does not cause permanent damage to the hymen.

The *ketubbah* of a woman who lost her hymen in an accident is a *maneh*.

4 A virgin who was widowed or divorced or underwent *halitsah* after marriage—
her *ketubbah* is a *maneh*,
and they are not subject to a claim of virginity.
A woman who is a convert or was held captive or was a slave,
who was redeemed or converted or was manumitted
after the age of three years and a day—
their *ketubbah* is a *maneh*
and they are not subject to a claim of virginity.

5 One who eats at his father-in-law's in Judaea without witnesses
cannot advance a claim of virginity because he is alone with her.
Both widows of Israelites and widows of priests—
their *ketubbah* is a *maneh*;
the court of the priests used to collect four hundred *zuz* for a virgin,
and the Sages did not prevent them.

1:6–2:2 *The Reliability of Claims, Especially in Cases of Personal Status*

6 One who marries a woman and finds she has no hymen:
she says: "I was raped after my betrothal, and your field has been washed away,"
and he says: "No, rather before I married you, and my purchase was made in error"—
Rabban Gamaliel and R. Eliezer say:
She is to be believed.
R. Joshua says:
We do not live from her mouth,
rather, she is presumed to have had intercourse before her betrothal
and to have deceived him,
unless she brings evidence for her assertion.

1:5 *because he is alone with her*: The Mishnah appears to refer to a local custom, one of whose practices left the unmarried couple alone together before marriage. As a consequence, the husband is implicated in any charge of nonvirginity.

zuz: A *dinar*.

did not prevent them: Or perhaps "did not object." The sentence *Both widows...a maneh* was apparently lacking in the version of the Mishnah known to the Palestinian Talmud.

1:6–9 A series of traditions following a parallel pattern. In each case the question under debate is whether a woman's claim about her own sexual activity is to be believed. R. Joshua holds that it is not, and that we presume that her status or that of her offspring is diminished unless she can prove otherwise.

1:6 *your field has been washed away*: Metaphorically: the damage occurred when I was already "your property."

my purchase was made in error: Metaphorically: I contracted marriage on the basis of false information.

We do not live from her mouth: Her word is not to be accepted.

7 If she says: "I lost my hymen in an accident,"
and he says: "No, but rather you have had intercourse with a man"[3]—
Rabban Gamaliel and R. Eliezer say:
She is to be believed;
but R. Joshua says:
We do not live from her mouth,
rather, she is presumed to have had intercourse with a man,
unless she brings evidence for her assertion.

8 If they saw her speaking with someone in the marketplace:[4]
They said to her:[5] "What is the nature of that man?"
"He is so-and-so and a priest"—
Rabban Gamaliel and R. Eliezer say:
She is to be believed;
but R. Joshua says:
We do not live from her mouth,
rather, she is presumed to have had intercourse with a *mamzer* or a *natin*,
unless she brings evidence for her assertion.

9 If she was pregnant and they said to her:
"What is the nature of this fetus?"
"From so-and-so and he is a priest"—
Rabban Gamaliel and R. Eliezer say:
She is to be believed;
but R. Joshua says:
We do not live from her mouth,
rather, she is presumed to be pregnant from a *natin* or a *mamzer*,
unless she brings evidence for her assertion.

10 R. Yose said:
It happened that a young girl went down to draw water from the well and was raped,
and R. Yohanan b. Nuri said:
If most of the residents of the town can give their daughters in marriage to the priesthood,
she may marry into the priesthood.

---

[3] Lit. "You are trodden upon by a man." [4] Absent in most witnesses. [5] Absent in **K, P, C**.

1:8 *mamzer*: The product of an illicit relationship, the exact nature of which is debated (see *Yevamot* 4:13). The *mamzer* has highly restricted marriageability.

natin: A descendant of the Gibeonites (see Joshua 9–10). A priest was prohibited from marrying a woman who had intercourse with a man belonging to one of these categories (see Leviticus 21:7 and *Yevamot* 6:6).

1:10 *she may marry into the priesthood*: The case in question differs from those disputed in the previous passages. The girl presumably could not identify her rapist and so her veracity was not in question. Instead, R. Yohanan b. Nuri relied on the assumption that the rapist belonged to the majority of the local population. Intercourse with a man whose daughter was able to marry into the priesthood would not disqualify the woman from contracting such a marriage.

Chapter Two

2 A woman who was widowed or divorced:
She says: "I was a married as a virgin,"
and he says: "No, but rather I married you as a widow,"
if there are witnesses that she went out with wedding songs[6]
and her head uncovered—
her *ketubbah* is two hundred.
R. Yohanan b. Beroqa said:
The distribution of roasted grains also constitutes proof.

2 And R. Joshua agrees,
that if one says to his fellow:
"This field was your father's and I purchased it from him"—
he is to be believed,
because the mouth which forbade is the mouth which permitted.
But if there are witnesses that it was his father's,
and he says "I purchased it from him"—
he is not to be believed.

2:3–10 *The Reliability of Attestations*

3 Witnesses who say: "This is our handwriting but we were acting under coercion,"
or "We were minors,"
or "We were unfit to testify"—
are to be believed.
If there are witnesses that it is their handwriting,
or if their handwriting goes forth elsewhere—
they are not to be believed.

---

[6] Meaning of Hebrew uncertain.

2:1 *if there are witnesses*: The precise meaning of *wedding songs* (Heb. *hinnuma*) is not clear although it obviously refers to some aspect of her wedding. The translation "wedding songs" (taking it to be a Greek loanword) follows the most common interpretation. A previously married bride would have been expected to cover her hair (see Numbers 5:18 and 7:6 below). In R. Yohanan b. Beroqa's opinion it would suffice to establish certain details of the food served at the wedding, which were customarily offered only at the marriage of virgin brides.

2:2 *R. Joshua agrees* that in this case (in contrast to the cases discussed in 1:6–9) the claimant is to be believed even though he cannot provide evidence to support his claim.

the mouth that forbade is the mouth that permitted: According to this rule, if someone supplies information not known from another source which would tend to his or her disadvantage, but supplements it with additional information which negates the unfavorable implications of the first statement, he or she is to be believed.

2:3 *if their handwriting goes forth elsewhere*: The authenticity of their signatures may be established by comparison with other documents known to be valid.

4 This one says: "This is my handwriting and this is my fellow's handwriting,"
and this one says: "This is my handwriting and this is my fellow's handwriting"—
they are to be believed.
This one says: "This is my handwriting,"
and this one says: "This is my handwriting"—
they must be joined by another—
the words of Rabbi;
but the Sages say:
They need not be joined by another,
rather, a man is believed when he says: "This is my handwriting."

5 A woman who said:
"I was a married woman and am now a divorcee"—
is to be believed,
because the mouth that forbade is the mouth that permitted.
If there are witnesses that she was a married woman,
and she says: "I am now a divorcee"—
she is not to be believed.
A woman who said: "I was taken captive but I am pure"—
is to be believed,
because the mouth that forbade is the mouth that permitted.
If there are witnesses that she was taken captive
and she says, "I am pure," she is not to be believed.
But if the witnesses came after she was married—
the husband is not obligated to divorce her.[7]

6 Two women who were taken captive:
This one says: "I was taken captive, but I am pure,"
and this one says: "I was taken captive, but I am pure"—
are not to be believed.
If each testifies for the other—
they are to be believed.

7 And similarly two men:
This one says: "I am a priest,"
and this one says: "I am a priest"—
they are not to be believed.
If each testifies for the other—
they are to be believed.

8 R. Judah says:
We do not elevate to the priesthood on the basis of a single witness.
R. Eleazar says:
When? Where there are those who contest him.

[7] Lit. "in this case she need not go out."

2:4 *the words of Rabbi*: The text of the Mishnah with which the Palestinian Talmud was familiar does not seem to have included the disagreement between Rabbi (Judah the Patriarch) and the anonymous voice, but that version of the Mishnah cannot be reconstructed with certainty.

2:5 *I am pure*: I did not have sexual relations with my captors.

But where there are none who contest him—
we elevate to the priesthood on the basis of a single witness.
Rabban Simeon b. Gamaliel says in the name of Simeon son of the Prefect:
We elevate to the priesthood on the basis of a single witness.

9 A woman who was imprisoned by gentiles—
on a monetary matter, she is permitted to her husband;
and on a capital matter,[8] she is forbidden to her husband.
A town that was captured by a siege—
all the priestesses found in it are disqualified.
But if they have witnesses—even a male or female slave—they are believed.
A man is not believed with regard to himself.
R. Zechariah son of the butcher said:
By this house! Her hand did not leave my hand
from the time the gentiles entered Jerusalem until they left.
They said to him:
A man is not believed with regard to himself.

10 And these are trusted to testify in their majority
with regard to what they saw as minors:
A man is trusted to say: "This is my father's handwriting,"
and "This is my master's handwriting,"
and "This is my brother's handwriting."
"I remember that so-and-so went out with wedding songs and her head uncovered";
and that "this man used to leave school to immerse himself in order to eat *terumah*";
and that "he used to divide [*terumah*] with us at the threshing floor";
and that "this place is a grave area";
and that "we used to come up to here on the Sabbath."
But a man is not trusted to say:

---

[8] Lit. "on account of lives."

2:8 *Prefect*: Heb. *segan*, a high-ranking priest in the Temple hierarchy. Cf. *Yoma* 4:1, 7:1; *Tamid* 7:3.

2:9 *A woman who was imprisoned*: This section may reflect an ancient rule according to which a married woman who was raped is forbidden to her husband (although other explanations are also possible; for example, that in such circumstances the woman might be suspected of having had sex with her captors voluntarily, perhaps in the hope of securing her release or better treatment).

all the priestesses: Here, the Mishnah reflects the prevailing rule that only a priest's wife is forbidden to her husband in these circumstances, not the wife of a regular Israelite. For "priestess," the wife or daughter of a priest, cf. below 4:8; 7:1-7:2; *Yevamot* 3:10; *Sotah* 3:7.

By this house! An oath formula referring to the Temple, although it had been destroyed by the time this oath was taken.

2:10 *I remember that so-and-so went…*: See 2:1 above.

grave area: an area suspected of being contaminated by corpse impurity. See *Oholot* 17:1-2.

"So-and-so had a right of way[9] in this place";
"So-and-so had a right of standing[10] and eulogizing in this place."

Chapter Three

3:1–3 *Seduction and Rape: Payment of a Fine*

3 These are the young women to whom payment of a fine applies:[11] one who has intercourse with a female *mamzer*, a female *natin*, or a Samaritan[12] woman;
one who has intercourse with a female convert, a woman who was taken captive, or a female slave, who were ransomed, or converted, or manumitted before the age of three years and a day;
one who has intercourse with his sister, or his father's sister, or his mother's sister, or his wife's sister, or his brother's wife, or his father's brother's wife, or a menstruant woman—a fine applies to them.
Even though they are punished by *karet*, they are not put to death by the court.

[9] Hebrew: "had a way" or "had a path."   [10] Hebrew: "had a standing…"
[11] Lit. "who have a fine."   [12] Lit. "Kutite" or "Cuthean."

---

standing and euloguzing: Customs associated with funerals. The witness is not to be believed when he asserts that so-and-so was entitled to make use of a certain location for these customary practices whenever he buried a family member. The underlying rationale of the distinctions made in this mishnah between various subjects of testimony is a matter of dispute; it may be that an adult's memory with regard to childhood experiences is relied upon when these are believed to have been particularly clear and memorable to the child.

3:1–3 These rules concern the fine to be paid by the rapist or seducer of an unmarried virgin according to Exodus 22:15–16 and Deuteronomy 22:28–29.

3:1 *mamzer…natin*: See the annotation to 1:8 above.

Samaritan: The Mishnah uses the (biblical) ethnic name *kuti*, "Kutite" or "Cuthean" (2 Kings 17:24). Various attitudes towards the status of Samaritans may be found in classical rabbinic literature, with later sources generally more negative than earlier ones. This mishnah treats Samaritans as Jews with whom full-fledged Jews should not intermarry.

karet: See *Keritot* introduction.

put to death by the court: The operative principle underlying 3:1–2 is that this fine is to be paid only if the woman may be assumed to have been a virgin prior to the act in question (see the note on 1:2 above) and if the seducer's or rapist's act did not incur the death penalty for (certain categories of) incest. The death penalty supersedes the financial penalty (3:2).

2 And these have no fine:
one who has intercourse with a female convert, or a woman who was a captive or a slave, who were redeemed, or converted, or manumitted after the age of three years and a day.
R. Judah says:
A female captive who is redeemed retains her sanctity even if she is in her majority.
One who has intercourse with his daughter, or his daughter's daughter, or his son's daughter, or his wife's daughter, or her daughter's daughter, or her son's daughter, they have no fine,
because he is liable to the death penalty, for his death is at the hands of the court, and anyone who is liable to the death penalty is not liable to monetary penalty,
as it is said: *And if there is no tragedy, he shall be punished.*

3 A young woman who has been given in betrothal and divorced—
R. Yose the Galilean says:
She has no fine;
R. Aqiva says:
She has a fine, and her fine is hers.

3:4–7 *Seduction and Rape: The Liabilities of Seducers and Rapists*

4 The seducer pays three things and the rapist four:
The seducer pays shame and damage and a fine;
The rapist exceeds him in that he pays suffering.

3:2 The first section of the mishnah concerns cases in which there is no fine because the woman is assumed not to have been a virgin at the time of her rape or seduction. The second section lists cases in which a sexual relationship between the parties is punishable by death (see Leviticus 20) and the monetary punishment is superseded.

R. Judah disagrees with the presumption that a woman in captivity has necessarily engaged in voluntary or coerced intercourse.

anyone who is liable to the death penalty is not liable to monetary penalty: If a single transgression would theoretically be punished both by death and by a monetary penalty, only the death penalty is imposed.

And if there is no tragedy, he shall be punished: Exodus 21:22. The context is one of culpable assault on a pregnant woman: if she dies as a result the man who struck her is put to death and does not pay, but if she does not die he must pay compensation for the loss of the fetus.

3:3 The dispute probably revolves around the interpretation of *who has not been betrothed* in Exodus 22:15 and Deuteronomy 22:28: does this phrase exclude a woman who has been betrothed in the past but is now no longer betrothed?

She has a fine and her fine is hers: Normally (see 4:1 below) the fine is payable to the girl's father, but in this case the father is no longer entitled to the fine; rather, it is paid to her.

3:4–7 The Mishnah distinguishes between seducers and rapists. In the former case, Exodus 22:15–16 assigns compensation to the father in the amount of a brideprice. In the latter, Deuteronomy 22:28–29 requires a fixed fine and permanent marriage. In addition, the Mishnah applies to the rapist or seducer the other penalties for assault in rabbinic law that are relevant in each case (see *Bava Qamma* 8:1).

And what distinguishes the rapist from the seducer?
The rapist pays suffering,
and the seducer does not pay suffering;
the rapist pays immediately,
and the seducer when he divorces;
The rapist "drinks from his planter,"
and the seducer may divorce if he desires to divorce.

5 How does he "drink from his planter"?
Even if she is lame, even if she is blind, even if she is afflicted with boils—
[he must marry her. But]
if a sexual impropriety is found in her or she is unfit to enter Israel—
he is not permitted to keep her,
as it is said: *And she shall be a wife to him*—
a wife who is fit for him.

6 A female orphan who was betrothed and divorced—
R. Eleazar says:
The seducer is not liable but the rapist is liable.

7 What is shame?
It all depends on the one who shames and the one who is shamed.
Damage?
We view her as if she were a slave being sold:
how much was she worth and how much is she worth now?
The fine is the same for all people,
and everything which has a set amount according to the Torah
is the same for all people.

3:8–9 *Seduction and Rape: Additional Rules Involving Fines*

8 Wherever there is sale there is no fine,
and wherever there is a fine there is no sale:

3:5 *drinks from his planter*: An idiom similar in meaning to the English "he has made his bed and now he must lie in it." The rapist may never divorce the woman.

enter Israel: Marry into the Israelite people.

And she shall be a wife for him: Deuteronomy 22:19.

3:6 On the face of it this mishnah deals with the case of a female orphan whose betrothal is arranged by other relatives after her father's death (see 6:6 below) and who was divorced without the marriage being consummated and was later seduced or raped. The basic idea appears to be that the woman's willing participation in the case of seduction causes her to forfeit the right to a fine. Also at issue is presumably the subject of the dispute in 3:3 about whether the rapist or seducer of a formerly betrothed woman, now divorced, is liable. However, it is unclear why here the girl would need to be both an orphan and a divorcee in order to be considered entitled to any fine to be paid. It appears that the Palestinian Talmud was acquainted with a version of the Mishnah which did not include "a female orphan." According to this reading, the simplest explanation would be that R. Eleazar follows the opinion of R. Aqiva in 3:3, ruling that if the girl was raped (but not seduced) the fine would be payable to her and not to her father.

3:8 *sale* refers to the rules of Exodus 21:7–11 dealing with a father's sale of his daughter as a female slave. This mishnah rules that *sale* and *fine* (paid to the father for seduction, above 3:1 and Exodus 22:15–16) apply to a

a female minor may be sold and has no fine,
a young woman has a fine and cannot be sold;
an adult woman—
neither sale nor fine.

9 One who says: "I seduced so-and-so's daughter"—
pays shame and damage on his own account,
and does not pay a fine.
One who says: "I stole and I slaughtered or sold"[13]—
pays the principal on his own account,
and does not pay double payment or four- and fivefold payment.
"My ox killed so-and-so, or so-and-so's ox"—
pays on his own account.
"My ox killed so-and-so's slave"—
does not pay on his own account.
This is the rule:
Whoever pays more than the actual damage does not pay on his own account.

Chapter Four

4:1–2 *The Rights of a Father to His Daughter's Damages and Ketubbah Payment*

4 A young woman who was seduced—
her shame and damage and her fine are her father's,
and her suffering in the case of rape.
If she appeared in court before the father died—

---

[13] "And I slaughtered or sold" is an addition to the text which is lacking in almost all witnesses.

---

minor and a *young woman* respectively. Although *na'arah* in biblical Hebrew does not appear to connote a particular age, in rabbinic Hebrew this status of *young woman* is precisely and narrowly defined, lasting in most cases from age twelve to age twelve-and-a-half. Prior to this period a girl is considered a minor, and after it she is a legally independent adult.

3:9 *on his own account*. On the basis of his own admission, unsupported by witnesses.

slaughtered or sold: This would incur an additional penalty (Exodus 21:37).

killed so-and-so…so-and-so's ox…so-and-so's slave: See Exodus 21:28–36.

Whoever pays more than the actual damage…: A penalty greater than the amount of the damage caused is considered a fine and may be imposed only on the basis of independent testimony.

4:1 *her shame and damage and her fine are her father's*: The fine that the rapist or seducer is obligated to pay by biblical law belongs to the father (Exodus 22:15–16, Deuteronomy 22:28–29).

If she appeared in court: If the trial began with the father alive and the daughter still a minor. As owing to the father, the compensation would be inherited by *the brothers*, his sons (see Numbers 27:8 etc.). However, if she did not come before the court before the death of her father, the compensation payments *are hers*.

they are the father's.
If the father died—
they belong to the brothers;
if she did not have time to appear in court before the father died—
they are hers.
If she appeared in court before attaining her majority—
they are the father's;
if the father dies—
they belong to the brothers.
If she did not have time to appear in court before attaining her majority—
they are hers.
R. Simeon said:
If she did not have time to exact payment before the father died—
they are hers;
but what she produces or finds,
even though she has not had time to exact payment and the father died—
they belong to the brothers.

2 One who gives his daughter in betrothal and he divorced her,
or gave her in betrothal and she was widowed—
her *ketubbah* payment is his.
If he gave her in marriage and he divorced her,
or gave her in marriage and she was widowed—
her *ketubbah* is hers.
R. Judah said:
The first is the father's.
They said to him:
Once he gives her in marriage—
the father has no rights over her.

before attaining her majority: Since a girl's coming of age terminates the father's rights over her, her coming of age during the course of the trial functions analogously to his death. (See annotation to 3:8.) If she appeared in court after attaining majority, the payments are hers; if not they belong to her father or to her brothers.

In *R. Simeon's* opinion this is also true if she comes of age between the end of the trial and the actual payment.

produces or finds: See below 4:4.

4:2 Biblical and rabbinic law distinguish between two stages of marriage, which were normally separated by a considerable interval: betrothal (referred to by forms of the word *aras*, as here, or *qiddesh*) and complete marriage (the root *ns'*), marked by her entry into her husband's home. Betrothal in this scheme was really a kind of inchoate marriage during which the bride was considered to be married (it can only be terminated by divorce or death of the husband) even though she continued to live in her parental home.

The first is the father's: Since the father made the arrangement and provided the dowry.

4:3   A Digression on the Daughter of a Female Convert

3 A female convert whose daughter converted with her and fornicated,
in this case she is [punished] by strangulation;
the door of her father's house and the one hundred *sela* do not apply to her.
If her conception was not in sanctity but her birth was in sanctity,
in this case she[14] is [punished] by stoning;
the door of her father's house and the one hundred *sela* do not apply to her.
If her conception and her birth were in sanctity—
she is like a daughter of Israel in every respect.
If she has a father but no father's door,
if she has a father's door but no father—
she is [punished] by stoning.
The door of her father's house was mentioned only for fulfillment of a commandment.

4:4–6   The Rights and Obligations of Fathers and Husbands

4 The father is entitled with respect to betrothing his daughter,
whether by money, a document, or intercourse,
and is entitled to what she finds, and to the work of her hands, and to annul her vows,
and he accepts her writ of divorce;
but has no usufruct[15] during her lifetime.
If she was married—
the husband exceeds him in that he eats fruits during her lifetime,

---

[14] K adds "like a daughter of Israel."   [15] Lit. "does not eat fruits."

4:3 *A female convert whose daughter converted with her*: The circumstance is a bride whom the husband claims not to have been a virgin at marriage (Deuteronomy 22:13–21). Deuteronomy 22:20–21 provide the punishment of *stoning* if the claim is proven true. According to rabbinic interpretation, those verses refer specifically to an Israelite woman who committed adultery after her betrothal; if she does not meet this condition the penalty is *strangulation*, and the other requirements of these verses are also not carried out. The *daughter who converted* is not fully Israelite so the special rules of this passage do not apply.

her birth was in sanctity: The biblical penalty of *stoning* applies if she was born an Israelite, even if she has no (Israelite) father.

has a father, but no father's door: If the father does not have (or perhaps does not own) a home.

door of her father's house: Deuteronomy 22:21.

for fulfillment of a commandment: If the father's door exists, the authorities are commanded to carry out the execution by this door; but its nonexistence does not exempt the adulterous wife from stoning.

4:4 *The father is entitled*: A woman who has not attained her majority is considered to be under her father's authority (see also 3:8, 4:5). He may give her in marriage regardless of the specific procedure by which the marriage is contracted (*money, document, or intercourse*; *Qiddushin* 1:1). He also holds monetary rights over her but these do not include *usufruct* on property she may own outright (e.g. through inheritance from her mother's family).

the husband exceeds him: In addition to the monetary rights enjoyed by the father, the husband is entitled to the usufruct of his wife's property.

and is responsible for her food, and her redemption from captivity, and for her burial.
R. Judah said:
Even the poorest in Israel may not have less than two flutes and a wailing woman.

5 She is always in the father's authority
until she enters the husband's authority for marriage.[16]
If the father delivered her to the husband's agents—
she is in the husband's possession.
If the father went with the husband's agents,[17]
or if the father's agents went with the husband's agents—
she is in the father's possession.
If the father's agents handed over to the husband's agents—
she is in the husband's possession.

6 The father is not obligated for his daughter's food.
This midrash was expounded by R. Eleazar b. Azariah
before the Sages in the Vineyard at Yavneh:
The sons inherit and the daughters are fed—
just as the sons only inherit after their father's death,
so the daughters are only fed after their father's death.

4:7–5:1 *Clauses of the Ketubbah Document*

7 If he did not write a *ketubbah* for her—
a virgin collects two hundred and a widow a *maneh*,
because it is a stipulation of the court.
If he wrote for her a field worth one hundred in lieu of two hundred *zuz*,
or did not write for her:
"All my property is liable for your *ketubbah*"—
he is liable,
because it is a stipulation of the court.

8 If he did not write for her:
"If you are captured I will redeem you and restore you to be my wife,"

[16] **K, P,** and most witnesses to the Mishnah have instead "until she enters the bridal canopy."
[17] **K, P,** and almost all witnesses lack "If…agents or."

4:5 This mishnah delineates the moment at which control over the young woman passes from the father's to the husband's hands.

4:6 *R. Eleazar b. Azariah's midrash* does not expound a verse from the Torah, but an ancient rule of inheritance law (see 13:3 below and *Bava Batra* 9:1). Alternatively, he interprets the text of the *ketubbah* itself (see the clauses in 4:10 and 4:11). In either event he concludes that a daughter's right to support was to be treated as a form of inheritance and could not be enforced during the father's lifetime.

4:7–12 The Mishnah treats certain clauses in the *ketubbah* document as mandatory, and in effect even if the actual document contradicted (4:7) or omitted (4:8–12) them. Several surviving Jewish marriage documents (but not all) from the early second century CE have clauses like these. The mishnaic clauses are in Aramaic.

4:8 A non-priest is permitted to continue living with his wife if she has been raped, and therefore undertakes to *restore you to be my wife* if she has been captured (see the annotation to 2:9). A priest is forbidden

or for the wife of a priest:
"And return you to your town"—
he is liable,
because it is a stipulation of the court.

9 If she is captured he must redeem her.
If he says: "Here is her writ of divorce and her *ketubbah* payment,
let her redeem herself"—
he is not permitted.
If she falls ill he must cure her.
If he says: "Here is her writ of divorce and her *ketubbah*,
let her cure herself"—
he is permitted.

10 If he did not write for her:
"Male sons that you will have from me shall inherit the money of your *ketubbah*
in addition to their portion with their brothers"—
he is liable,
because it is a stipulation of the court.

11 "Female daughters that you will have from me shall reside in my house
and be fed from my property until they are married to husbands"—
he is liable,
because it is a stipulation of the court.

12 "You shall reside in my house and be fed from my properties
all the days of the extent of your widowhood"—
he is liable,
because it is a stipulation of the court.
The people of Jerusalem wrote thus.
The people of the Galilee wrote like the people of Jerusalem,
But the people of Judaea wrote:
"Until the heirs want to give you your *ketubbah* payment";
therefore, if the heirs want, they give her her *ketubbah* payment and dismiss her.

Chapter Five

5 Even though they said: A virgin collects two hundred and a widow a *maneh*,[18]
if he wants to add even one hundred *maneh*, he may add.

[18] The "Babylonian" witnesses read "A virgin: her *ketubbah* is two hundred…"

to resume married life in these circumstances and therefore undertakes to redeem his wife and *return you to your town*, her place of origin.

5:1 For the distinction between betrothal and marriage see the annotation to 4:2 above.

Even though they said: See n. 18. According to the reading "a virgin collects" this is a reference to 4:7; the reading "a virgin: her *ketubbah* is" refers to 1:2.

If she is widowed or divorced, whether after betrothal or marriage—
she collects everything.
R. Eleazar b. Azariah says:
After marriage she collects everything,
after a betrothal, a virgin collects two hundred and a widow a *maneh*;
for he wrote for her only on condition that he bring her in.
R. Judah says:
If he wants he may write for a virgin a document for two hundred,
and she writes for him: "I have received a *maneh* from you,"
and for a widow [a document for] a *maneh*,
and she writes for him: "I have received fifty *zuz* from you."
R. Meir says:
Whoever gives a virgin less than two hundred and a widow less than a *maneh*—
his intercourse is fornication.

5:2–6:1   *Rights and Responsibilities of Husbands and Wives*

2   One gives a virgin twelve months to prepare herself
from the time her husband has demanded her.[19]
Just as one gives to the woman, one gives to the man to prepare himself.
And thirty days to a widow.
If their time arrives and they have not married,[20]
they eat from his property and eat *terumah*.
R. Tarfon says:
One gives her *terumah* exclusively.
R. Aqiva says:
Half unsanctified produce and half *terumah*.

[19] Or "courted her."   [20] K, P, C add "or if the husbands die."

bring her in: Complete the marriage.

R. *Judah* permits the parties to agree on a smaller amount than the standard *ketubbah* payment, but this cannot be stated explicitly in the marriage document; rather, the bride may write a fictitious receipt for part of the sum promised her.

5:2 *have not married*: The words "or if the husbands die" in **K, P, C** (see n. 20) probably represent an addition to the text.

eat terumah: A woman who is not of a priestly family but marries a priest is entitled to eat *terumah* (*Terumot* introduction; for this rule, see Leviticus 22:10–11). According to this mishnah, betrothed women could eat *terumah* if twelve months have passed since the betrothal without the marriage being consummated. Contrast 5:3.

terumah exclusively... half terumah: According to R. *Tarfon* if the husband is a priest he may supply his wife's food exclusively in the form of *terumah*, which is less expensive than unsanctified produce (because it may be consumed only by priests and their dependents) and which she is prohibited from eating when impure. According to R. *Aqiva* he must provide (at least) half her needs in the form of unsanctified produce.

3 A levir does not give a woman the right to eat[21] *terumah*.
If she passed six months before the husband and six months before the levir,
or even all of them before the husband less one day before the levir,
or all of them before the levir less one day before the husband,[22]
he does not give her the right to eat[23] *terumah*.
This was the first mishnah;
a later court said:
A woman does not eat *terumah* until she enters the marriage canopy.

4 One who consecrates what his wife produces,
she produces and eats.
The remainder—
R. Meir says:
It is sanctified;
and R. Yohanan ha-Sandlar says:
It is unsanctified.

5 These are the labors that a woman performs for her husband:
She grinds and bakes and cooks,
launders and nurses her son[24], makes his bed
and works in wool.
If she brought him one female slave—
she does not grind or bake or launder;
two—she does not cook or nurse her son;
three—she does not make the bed and does not work in wool;[25]
four—she sits on a throne.
R. Eliezer[26] says:

[21] Lit. "A levir does not feed."
[22] K, P, C, and some witnesses to the "Babylonian" tradition lack this line.
[23] Lit. "feed."
[24] Or "child"; so too below.
[25] K, P, C lack "and does not work in wool."
[26] K alone reads "Eleazar."

5:3 *levir*: See *Yevamot* 7:4. The brother of a man who has died without offspring must either marry his widow in levirate marriage (*yibbum*) or release her through *halitsah*. Time spent waiting for a levirate marriage, unlike time spent waiting for complete marriage following betrothal, does not entitle a woman of non-priestly family to eat *terumah*.

or all of them before the levir less one day before the husband: See n. 22. This is probably a later addition.

first mishnah; a later court said…: The rule in 5:2 permitting betrothed women to eat *terumah* was later restricted to married women.

5:4 *produces and eats*: This mishnah assumes a financial arrangement where the wife maintains herself (cf. 5:7, 6:1). She may sell (as unsanctified merchandise) as much of what she produces as necessary in order to provide herself with food.

The remainder: Although the dedication cannot prevent the wife from supporting herself, there remains the question of whether the husband's dedication was effective for what was not used for the woman's maintenance.

5:5 A woman who brings three slaves into her marriage is still obligated to work in wool, while a woman who brings four slaves is excused from all seven of the labors enumerated.

and does not work in wool is probably a mistaken addition (see n. 25).

R. Eliezer requires work even of wealthy women.

Similarly if she brought one hundred female slaves
he may compel her to work in wool,
for idleness leads to lewdness.
Rabban Simeon b. Gamaliel says:
Even one who prohibits his wife from working by means of a vow
must divorce and pay her *ketubbah*,
for idleness is stultifying.

6 One who prohibits his wife from sexual intercourse by a vow—
the House of Shammai say:
Two weeks;
the House of Hillel say:
One week.
Students go out to study Torah without permission—
thirty days,
and laborers—
one week.
The regular time mentioned in the Torah—
men of leisure daily;
laborers twice weekly;
ass drivers once a week;
camel drivers once every thirty days;
and sailors once every six months—
the words of R. Eliezer.[27]

7 One who rebels against her husband—
one reduces her *ketubbah* by seven *dinar* every week.
R. Judah says:
Seven half-*dinar*.
How long does he reduce?
To the amount of her *ketubbah*.
R. Yose says:

[27] **K**, **P**, and a few other manuscripts read "(E)leazar."

prohibits... by means of a vow: For vows, see *Nedarim* introduction; see also 7:1–5.

5:6 According to rabbinic interpretation of Exodus 21:10, a husband is obligated to have sex with his wife with reasonable frequency; our mishnah and some other sources understand this to be the meaning of the word *onah* (usually rendered "duty of marriage" or "marriage rights" in English translations) in that verse. A husband who vows (see 7:1–5) not to have sex with his wife for an extended period is obligated to divorce her and pay her *ketubbah*. The *Houses of Hillel* and *Shammai* disagree as to the maximum period for which such a vow can be made without the husband incurring this obligation.

R. Eliezer specifies the frequency with which a husband is normally expected to have sex with his wife, depending on his occupation.

5:7 *rebels*: Originally a wife's rebellion was probably defined with regard to the labors specified in 5:5, while the husband's "rebellion" concerned the three obligations mentioned in Exodus 21:10 (as understood by the rabbis: food, clothing, and sexual intercourse). Both Talmudim understand the wife's (and presumably also the husband's) rebellion as refusal to engage in sex.

half-dinar: *Tarpe'iqin*, from the Greek name (*tropaikon*) for a Roman coin of the Republican period.

He goes on reducing forever:
perhaps an inheritance will fall to her from elsewhere and he can collect[28] from her.
And similarly, a man who rebels against his wife—
three *dinar* are added to her *ketubbah* weekly.
R. Judah says:
Three half-*dinar*.

8 One who sets his wife up through an intermediary
may not give her less than two *qav* of wheat and four *qav* of barley;
R. Yose said:
Only R. Ishmael allocated barley, because he was near Edom.
He gives her half a *qav* of legumes and half a *log* of oil and a *qav* of dried figs
or a *maneh* of pressed dates.
And if he does not have these he allocates produce for her from elsewhere.
He gives her a bed, a mattress, and a mat.[29]
He gives her a cap for her head and a belt for her hips
and shoes from festival to festival,
and clothes valued at fifty *zuz* annually.
He does not give her new ones in the sunny season
nor worn-out ones in the rainy season;
rather, he gives her clothes valued at fifty *zuz* in the rainy season
and she wears them in worn condition in the sunny season,
and the scraps are hers.

9 He gives her a silver *ma'ah* for her needs,
and she eats with him each Sabbath evening,
and if he does not give her a silver *ma'ah*—what she produces is hers.
And what does she produce[30] for him?
The weight of five *sela* warp thread in Judaea,
which are ten *sela* in the Galilee,
or the weight of ten *sela* weft thread in Judaea,
which are twenty *sela* in the Galilee.
And if she was nursing one reduces what she produces and adds to her food.
In what case is this said?
Regarding the poorest man in Israel,
but as for the dignified man—it is all according to his dignity.

[28] Most witnesses read "he can return and collect from her."
[29] K: "a bed and a mattress; if he has no mattress—a mat."
[30] Lit. "do."

5:8–9 Weekly minimums are given for the wife's provisions in case the husband and wife are living separately and the husband arranges for an intermediary to provide the wife's needs.

5:8 *Only R. Ishmael…near Edom*: In R. Yose's opinion only a Sage who lived near Idumea would have specified a quantity of barley to be given the wife in such circumstances; apparently barley was used primarily as animal feed in other regions.

5:9 The thread used in the weft was twice as heavy as that used in the warp, and the coins used in Judaea were twice as large as those used in the Galilee (cf. *Hullin* 11:2).

Chapter Six

6 What a woman finds and what she produces belong to her husband, and he inherits from her and has usufruct[31] in her lifetime.
Her shame and damage are hers.
R. Judah b. Betera says:
When it is concealed—
she gets two shares and he gets one;
and when it is exposed—
he gets two shares and she gets one.
His is given to him immediately;
hers—
land is to be purchased with it and he has usufruct.

6:2–7 *Monetary Arrangements in Anticipation of Marriage*

2 One who allocates money to his son-in-law and his son-in-law dies—
the Sages said:
He can say:
"I wanted to give to your brother and I do not want to give to you."
3 If she undertook to bring in to him one thousand *dinar*,
he undertakes fifteen *maneh* against them;
and against a valuation—
he undertakes a fifth less.
If the valuation is a *maneh* and it is worth a *maneh*—

---

[31] Here and in the last words of 6:1, lit. "eats produce."

6:1 See above 4:4. According to R. Judah b. Betera, the husband always has a right to part of his wife's damages.

6:2–7 The Mishnah deals with reciprocal monetary arrangements which were customary between the groom's and the bride's sides. Although some details remain obscure, the basic principle is clear: the bride (or her father, at least if she was a minor) normally undertook that she would bring a specified dowry with her when she entered the groom's house, and the groom undertook to add a corresponding (not necessarily identical) sum of money to the basic amount of the *ketubbah* payment (4:7).

6:1 This passage assumes a case of levirate marriage, in a case where the intended groom died after betrothal but before marriage.

6:3–4 Several illustrations of a basic rule that when the woman undertakes to bring money into the marriage the husband is expected to undertake a corresponding obligation of 150% of the amount in addition to the base sum which he is required to undertake in the *ketubbah* (see 1:2). If she undertakes to bring in other property he is only required to undertake an obligation equal to 80% of the assessed value of the property. A *maneh* is worth twenty-five *sela* or one hundred *dinar*.

6:3 *If the valuation is a maneh*: This sentence is quite obscure. The most plausible explanation appears to be that if the woman undertook to bring property assessed at a *maneh and worth a maneh*, the added words *and worth a maneh* imply that the husband is only entitled to property worth a *maneh*.

he has only a *maneh*.
A valuation of a *maneh*—
she gives thirty-one *sela* and a *dinar*;
[of] four hundred—
she[32] gives five hundred.
And when the bridegroom undertakes—
he undertakes a fifth less.

4 If she undertook to bring money in to him,
her *sela* becomes six *dinar*.
The bridegroom undertakes ten *dinar* for[33] a basket for each and every *maneh*.
Rabban Simeon b. Gamaliel says:
All is according to the custom of the land.

5 One who gives his daughter in marriage without specifying
may not give her less than fifty *zuz*.
If he undertook to bring her in naked,
the husband may not say:
"When I bring her in I will clothe her with my clothing,"
rather, he clothes her while she is still in her father's house.
And so, too, one who marries off a female orphan
may not give her less than fifty *zuz*,
and if there is enough in the purse—
they provision her according to her dignity.

6 A female orphan whose mother and brothers gave her in marriage with her consent,[34]
and wrote for her one hundred or fifty[35] *zuz*,

---

[32] K, P: "he."   [33] K, P, and other "Palestinian" witnesses read "and." See the annotation.
[34] K, P, and some other witnesses lack "with her consent."
[35] K, P, C, and some other "Palestinian" witnesses read "one hundred *and* fifty."

---

a valuation…she gives…: The woman's commitment on paper is 80% of what she brings in. A *sela* is four dinar; hence *thirty-one sela and a quarter* are 125 *dinar*.

when the bridegroom: When the bridegroom commits to property he similarly brings in 80% of the official valuation.

6:4 *for a basket*: According to parallel sources a basket of fragrances that the groom commits to providing for each *maneh* the bride brings in. The reading "and a basket" (see n. 33), may also be interpreted as "for a basket."

6:5 A father is expected to provide his daughter with a dowry of at least fifty *zuz* unless he specifies otherwise to the bridegroom.

naked: Without a trousseau or bridal chest of clothing to be used during the marriage.

6:6 *mother and brothers give her in marriage*: Biblical law permits a father to give his (minor) daughter in marriage (Deuteronomy 22: 16); rabbinic law permits her mother and brothers to do so if her father has died while she is still a minor, but in such a case the girl has the option of invalidating the marriage before attaining her majority (see *Yevamot* 13:1–2).

with her consent (see n. 34) is probably a later addition.

one hundred or fifty. The reading "and fifty" (n. 35) may also be understood to mean "or." In any case, the point is that the agreement was for less than *is fitting to be given her*.

when she attains her majority
she can extract from them what is fitting to be given her.
R. Judah says:
If [the father] had given the first daughter in marriage,
the second must be given as much as the first was given.
But the Sages say:
Sometimes a person is poor and becomes wealthy or is wealthy and becomes poor;
rather, we assess the property and give it to her.

7 One who provides money for his daughter through an intermediary,
and she says: "I have confidence in my husband,"
the intermediary must do as he was instructed—
the words of R. Meir;
R. Yose says:
Even if it were a field that she desires to sell,[36]
in such a case, it would be sold as of now!
In what case is this said? Of an adult woman,
but a minor—
the act of a minor is nothing.

Chapter Seven

7:1–5 *Grounds for Divorce: Prohibiting One's Wife by a Vow*

7 One who prohibits his wife by a vow from benefiting from him—
up to a month, he must appoint a provider;
beyond this, he must divorce her and pay the *ketubbah*.
R. Judah says:
For an Israelite—
one month, he maintains;
two months—

---

[36] Lit. "and if this were nothing but a field and…?"

R. Judah and the Sages disagree about how to assess *what is fitting to be given her*.

6:7 If a father seeks to provide for his daughter's future needs but does not fully trust her husband he may deposit funds with a third party who is authorized to disburse them on her behalf. R. Meir and R. Yose disagree as to whether the (adult) daughter may overrule her father's instructions and direct the intermediary to transfer these funds to her husband's safekeeping.

7:1–5 Vows could be used to prevent another person from enjoying any benefit from one's property (see *Nedarim* introduction). The husband's obligation to support his wife could be fulfilled indirectly for a limited time, but if the vow was for a longer period he would be required to divorce her and pay her *ketubbah*.

7:1 R. Judah extends the time granted to a priestly husband because he would be forbidden to remarry his wife if he were to divorce her (see Leviticus 21:7).

he divorces and pays the *ketubbah*;
and for a priestess—
two months, he maintains;
three months—
he divorces and pays the *ketubbah*.

2 One who prohibits his wife by a vow from tasting any one fruit—
he divorces and pays the *ketubbah*.
R. Judah says:
For an Israelite—
one day,[37] he maintains,
two—
he divorces and pays the *ketubbah*;
and for a priestess—
two, he maintains,
three—he divorces and pays the *ketubbah*.

3 One who prohibits his wife by a vow from adorning herself
with any one sort of adornment—
he divorces and pays the *ketubbah*.
R. Yose says:
For poor women—
if he did not set a limit;
and for wealthy women—
thirty days.

4 One who prohibits his wife by a vow from going to her father's house—
when he is with her[38] in the town:
one month—
he must maintain her,
two—
he divorces her and pays the *ketubbah*;
and when he is[39] in another town,
one festival—
he must maintain her,
three[40]—
he divorces her and pays the *ketubbah*.

5 One who prohibits his wife by a vow
from going to a house of mourning or to a house of celebration—
he divorces and pays the *ketubbah*,
because he has locked [the door] before her.

[37] P: "months"; perhaps copied from 7:1.   [38] K: "When they are with her."
[39] K: "they are."   [40] K, P, and others: "two."

priestess: A priest's wife.

7:3 *if he did not set a limit*: A poor woman might not regularly wear adornments; however, a husband could not prevent her from ever adorning herself.

7:4 *in another town...three*: Almost all "Palestinian" versions of the Mishnah have the reading "two," while almost all "Babylonian" versions have the difficult reading "three" (see n. 40).

If he claims: "Because of another matter"—
he is permitted.
If he said to her:
"On condition that you tell so-and-so what you said to me,"
or "what I said to you,"
Or "that she should fill up [a container]
and pour it out on a dungheap,"
he must divorce her and pay the *ketubbah*.

7:6 Grounds for Divorce: Law of Moses and the Jews

6 And these go out without a *ketubbah*:
one who transgresses the law of Moses and the Jews.
What is the law of Moses?
She feeds him that which has not been tithed,
has intercourse with him while a menstruant,
does not separate dough offering,
or vows and does not keep.
And what is the law of the Jews?
She goes out with her head uncovered,
spins in the marketplace, and speaks with every man.
Abba Saul says:
Also one who curses his progenitors[41] in his presence.
R. Tarfon says:
Also one who is loud.
What is "One who is loud"?
Anyone who speaks in her house and her neighbors hear her voice.[42]

---

[41] K (unpointed text): "his children."   [42] See annotations.

7:5 *Because of another matter*: Presumably this refers to improper behavior which he alleges is associated with this venue.

If he said to her: If he makes demands intended to embarrass her.

7:6 *Law of Moses and the Jews*: This formula, which has ancient antecedents, concisely expresses the religious standards that the wife is expected to maintain; it is used in the *ketubbah* document in recording the groom's proposal of marriage.

progenitors: Some manuscripts read "children" (see n. 41), and both Talmudim preserve statements which were apparently intended to reconcile these two traditions.

What is "One who is loud"?...hear her voice: Although found in most witnesses, this discussion is not an integral part of the Mishnah; it was added from the parallel Tosefta.

7:7–8 *Grounds for Divorce: A Wife's Premarital Vows and Blemishes*

7 One who contracts betrothal with a woman
on condition that she has no vows encumbering her
and it is found that there are vows encumbering her—
she is not betrothed.
If he brought her in without specifying
and it was found that there are vows encumbering her—
she goes out without a *ketubbah*.
On condition that she has no blemishes
and she is found to have blemishes,
she is not betrothed.
If he brought her in without specifying
and she was found to have blemishes,
she goes out without a *ketubbah*.
All blemishes that disqualify priests disqualify wives.

8 If she had blemishes when she was still in her father's house—
the father must bring evidence that these blemishes occurred
after she was betrothed,
and his field was swept away.
If she entered the husband's authority—
the husband must bring evidence that these blemishes
occurred before she was betrothed and his purchase was in error—
the words of R. Meir.
But the Sages say:
When does this apply?
In the case of concealed blemishes;
but in the case of exposed blemishes he cannot claim.
If there is a bathhouse in that town
he cannot claim even with respect to concealed blemishes,
because he inspects her by means of his female relatives.

7:7 If the betrothal (or inchoate marriage) is explicitly made conditional on the wife's not having vows or blemishes and it transpires that she does, the marriage would be invalid. Otherwise it would be valid but she would nevertheless be considered so seriously compromised that she would not be entitled to *ketubbah* money. The Mishnah presumes that it is the bride's (or her family's) obligation to inform the groom in advance if she has blemishes or outstanding vows; otherwise he is entitled to assume that she has neither.

blemishes that disqualify priests: See *Bekhorot* 7:1–7.

7:8 *his field was swept away* : See annotations to 1:6 above.

If there is a bathhouse: In this case, the husband would not be entitled to claim that he had discovered his wife's blemishes only after marriage, since he could ask his female relatives to check for concealed blemishes at the communal bathhouse.

7:9–10 Grounds for Divorce: A Husband's Blemishes

9 If a man develops blemishes,
one does not compel him to divorce.
Rabban Simeon b. Gamaliel said:
When does this apply?
With regard to minor blemishes;
but with regard to major ones, one compels him to divorce.

10 These are compelled to divorce:
one who is afflicted with boils,
and one who has polyps,
and the collector,
and the copper smelter,
and the tanner,
whether they had them before they married
or whether they arose[43] after they were married.
And R. Meir said about all of them:
Even though he made a condition with her beforehand
she can say: "I thought I could endure and now I cannot endure";
But the Sages say:
She must accept perforce,
aside from the one afflicted with boils,
because she exacerbates his condition.
It once happened in Sidon that a tanner died
and had a brother who was a tanner,
and the Sages said:
She can say: "I could endure your brother but I cannot endure you."

Chapter Eight

8:1–5 The Wife's Property in the Context of Marriage: Property Inherited by Betrothed or Wife

8 A woman who inherited property before she was betrothed—
the House of Shammai and the House of Hillel agree

---

[43] **K, P, C**, and others: "they learned."

7:10 *collector*: Of feces, used in tanning leather.

I could endure your brother: As above, 6:2, the expression assumes levirate marriage.

8:1 At issue is the question of the circumstances in which a woman may or may not dispose of her property without her husband's consent.

betrothed...married: See annotation to 4:2.

that she sells and gives and it is valid.
If she inherited [property] after she was betrothed—
the House of Shammai say:
She may sell;
but the House of Hillel say:
She may not sell.
These and those agree that if she sold or gave, it is valid.
Said R. Judah:
They said before Rabban Gamaliel:
Since he acquired a wife, has he not acquired the property?
He said to them:
We are ashamed about the new ones and you roll the old ones over us!
If she inherited after she was married:
these and those agree that if she sold or gave—
the husband extracts it from the hands of the buyers.
Before she was married, and then was married:
Rabban Gamaliel says:
If she sold or gave, it is valid.
R. Hananiah b. Aqaviah says:
They said before Rabban Gamaliel:
Since he acquired a wife, has he not acquired the property?
He said to them:
We are ashamed about the new ones and you roll the old ones over us!

2 R. Simeon distinguishes between properties:
Property known to the husband—
she may not sell, and if[44] she sold or gave, it is invalid;
and those not known to the husband—
she may not sell, and if[45] she sold or gave, it is valid.

3 If she inherited money—
let land be bought with it and he eats the produce;
[if it was] produce separated from the ground—
let land be bought with it and he eats the produce;

---

[44] K, P, and others: "that if."   [45] K (before correction), P, and others: "that if."

---

after she was betrothed: the Houses of Hillel and Shammai debate whether she is permitted *ab initio* to dispose of her property although they agree that such a disposition would be legally valid after the fact.

We are ashamed: Rabban Gamaliel expressed discomfort with the existing limitations on a wife's power to dispose of her property and refused to impose any further limitations.

Before she was married, and then was married: If she inherited property before her marriage and sought to dispose of it after her marriage.

8:2 *Property known... not known to the husband*: In R. Simeon's opinion the wife's ability to dispose of property depends on the husband being unaware of her ownership.

8:3 *If she inherited money*: In general, the husband is entitled to the usufruct of his wife's property (see 6:1 above). Here the Mishnah assumes that inheritance in the form of money or wealth as opposed to land will be converted to landed property.

produce attached to the ground—
R. Meir said:
We estimate how much they are worth with produce
and how much they are worth without produce,
and the difference—
let land be bought with it and he eats the produce;
and the Sages say:
Produce attached to the ground is his;
separated from the ground is hers;
let land be bought with it and he eats the produce.

4 R. Simeon says:
Where his power is increased at her entrance,
his power is lessened at her exit;
where his power is lessened at her entrance,
his power is increased at her exit:
Produce attached to the ground—
at her entrance it is his and at her exit, hers;
and detached from the ground—
at her entrance it is hers and at her exit, his.

5 If she inherited elderly male or female slaves—
let them be sold and let land be bought and he eats the produce.
Rabban Simeon b. Gamaliel says:
She may not sell, because they are the praise[46] of her father's house.
If she inherited old olive trees or grapevines—
let them be sold for wood, or let land be bought with them,
and he eats the produce.
R. Judah[47] says:
She may not sell, because they are the praise[48] of her father's house.
One who makes expenditures for his wife's property—
if he expended much and ate little,
expended little and ate much—
whatever he expended he expended, and whatever he ate he ate.
If he expended and did not eat—
he swears how much he expended and takes [that amount].

[46] Alternatively, "profit"; **K, P**: "honor."
[47] **P** and many "Babylonian" witnesses read "R. Simeon b. Gamaliel."
[48] Alt. "profit."

produce attached to the ground: Where she inherits crops already growing on land she inherits, R. Meir and the Sages disagree as to whether the crops are included in the husband's right to usufruct or are to be treated as an additional property which she has inherited and converted into real property.

8:4 *R. Simeon* compares the ways in which attached and unattached produce is treated at the time of marriage (in keeping with the view of the Sages in 8:3) with the way they are treated in the case of divorce, when the wife would reclaim real estate she had brought into the marriage or acquired afterwards.

8:5 *expended and did not eat*: If the husband spent money on his wife's property but did not consume any of its produce.

8:6–8 *The Wife's Property in the Context of Marriage: The Special Case of a Levirate Widow*

6 A woman awaiting her levir who inherited property—
the House of Shammai and the House of Hillel agree
that she sells and gives and it is valid.
If she died, what shall they do with her *ketubbah* payment
and with the property that enters and goes out with her?
The House of Shammai say:
The husband's heirs divide with the father's heirs;
and the House of Hillel say:
The property remains in its presumptive ownership:
the *ketubbah* payment is presumed to belong to the husband's heirs;
property that enters and leaves with her is presumed to belong to the father's heirs.
 7 If the [deceased] brother left money—
Let land be bought with it and he eats the produce.
Produce separated from the land—
let land be bought with it and he eats the produce.
Produce attached to the land—
R. Meir said:
We estimate how much they are worth with produce and how much they are worth without produce,
and the difference—
let land be bought with it and he eats the produce;
But the Sages say:
Produce attached to the ground is his;
separated from the ground, whoever comes first acquires it:
if he came first, he has acquired it;
if she came first, let land be bought with it and he eats the produce.
If he has brought her in, she is like his wife in all respects,
except that her *ketubbah* shall be (incumbent) on the property of her first husband.

8:6–7 See *Yevamot* 4:3–4.

8:6 *woman awaiting her levir*. See *Yevamot* introduction. This is a special case because the bonds between a woman awaiting levirate marriage and her levir are weaker than those between a betrothed couple.

Her *ketubbah payment* probably includes properties which the wife brought into the marriage and were listed in the marriage contract and accepted by the husband at a fixed valuation, while *property that enters and leaves with her* are properties that she brought into the marriage that were not itemized in the marriage contract and continue to be thought of as her property despite the husband's right of usufruct.

8:7 Compare 8:3 above.

separated from the ground: The opinion attribute to the Sages here differs from the analogous passage in 8:3. Here, neither side is granted presumptive ownership of such produce, because the underlying property belonged to the deceased husband.

8 The levir[49] may not say to her:
Your *ketubbah* payment is placed on the table;
rather, all [the brother's] property is liable for her *ketubbah* payment.
And so too, a man may not say to his wife:
Your *ketubbah* payment is placed on the table;
rather, all [the husband's] property is liable for her *ketubbah*.
If [the levir] divorced her, she has only her *ketubbah*.
If he reinstated her, she is like all wives and she has only her *ketubbah*.

Chapter Nine

9:1–3   *Collecting the Ketubbah Payment:*

9 One who writes to his wife:
"I have neither right nor claim with regard to your property"—
he eats produce during her lifetime,
and if she dies he inherits from her.
If so, why did he write to her:
"I have neither right nor claim with regard to your property"?
So that if she sold or gave, it is valid.
If he wrote to her:
"I have neither right nor claim with regard to your property and its produce"—
he does not eat produce in her lifetime,
but if she dies he inherits from her.
R. Judah says:
He always eats the produce of produce unless he writes to her:
"I have neither right nor claim with regard to your property and its produce
and the produce of its produce, forever".
If he wrote to her:
"I have neither right nor claim with regard to your property and its produce

---

[49] Hebrew: "He."

8:8 *The levir... placed on the table*: In a levirate marriage all of the property that the levir has inherited from his brother serves to guarantee the wife's *ketubbah*. The levir may not set aside a particular pot of money or piece of property for this purpose.

so too, a man may not say to his wife: In non-levirate marriage the husband's property is analogously encumbered.

reinstated: If he remarries her, her claim is on his property like that of any other husband: he may alienate property although she has a lien on this property for payment of her *ketubbah*.

9:1 *writes*: Either as part of the marriage document (cf. 4:7–12), or as a separate document renouncing claims to property belonging to the wife (cf. 10:6).

So that if she sold or gave, it is valid. Cf. 8:1–2.

and the produce of its produce, during your life and after your death"—
he does not eat produce during her lifetime and if she dies he does not inherit from her.
Rabban Simeon b. Gamaliel says:
If she dies he inherits from her,
because he has stipulated a condition against what is written in the Torah,
and whoever stipulates a condition against what is written in the Torah,
his condition is invalid.

2 One who died and left a wife and creditors and heirs
and had a deposit or a loan in the hands of others—
R. Tarfon says:
Let them be given to the weakest among them.
R. Aqiva says:
One has no mercy in judgment!
Rather, let them be given to the heirs,
for all of them are required to swear,
but the heirs are not required to swear.

3 If he left produce separated from the ground,
whoever is first acquires it.
If the wife acquires more than the value of her *ketubbah* payment
or the creditor more than his loan—
R. Tarfon says:
Let the excess be given to the weakest among them.
R. Aqiva says:
One has no mercy in judgment!
Rather, let the excess be given to the heirs,
for all of them are required to swear,
but the heirs are not required to swear.

Rabban Simeon b. Gamaliel considers the husband's right to inherit from his wife to be of biblical origin, perhaps on the basis of exegesis of Numbers 27:11. The anonymous first voice disagrees either with this belief or with the principle that any *condition* that contravenes *what is written in the Torah* is *ipso facto* invalid. For this principle see also *Bava Qamma* 7:11 and *Bava Batra* 8:5.

9:2 *a wife and creditors*: Multiple claimants to the estate of the deceased with no clear priority.

a deposit or a loan: Assets belonging to the deceased against which the creditors or the wife had a lien.

R. Tarfon…R. Aqiva: In this mishnah and in 9:3, R. Aqiva holds that the heirs always have precedence over other claimants. Against this R. Tarfon gives priority to the *weakest*, with differing views in the commentaries about what precisely is meant. For oaths in the exaction of payment see *Shevu'ot* introduction.

9:3 *produce separated from the ground*: See above 8:3, 7. Unlike the preceding mishnah, here the property is "up for grabs" and the question of which claimant is to be given preference arises only with regard to any surplus seized by one claimant.

9:4–6   *Laws Connected with Collecting the Ketubbah Payment: Requiring an Oath before Payment*

4   One who sets his wife up as a shopkeeper or appoints her as a guardian
may exact an oath from her any time he wishes.
R. Eliezer says:
Even concerning her spindle or her dough.

5   If he wrote to her:
"I have no right of vow or oath against you,"
he cannot exact an oath from her,
but he can exact an oath from her heirs
or those who come through her.
"I have no right of vow or oath either against you
or against your heirs or those who come through you"—
he cannot exact an oath from her or her heirs
or those who come through her,
but his heirs can exact an oath from her and her heirs
and those who come through her.
"I and my heirs and those who come through me
have no right of vow or oath against you and your heirs
and those who come through you"—
neither he nor his heirs nor those who come through him may exact an oath
from her or her heirs or those who come through her.

6   If she went from her husband's grave to her father's house,
or if she returned to her father-in-law's house and was not made a guardian—
the heirs cannot exact an oath from her.
If she was made a guardian—
the heirs can exact an oath from her with regard to the future,
but they cannot exact an oath from her with regard to the past.

9:4 *exact an oath*: See above, 9:2. According to *R. Eliezer* even a husband who has not set his wife up in a shop may demand that she take an oath that she has not cheated him with regard to the household items entrusted to her.

9:5 As in 9:1, this mishnah contemplates the voluntary renunciation by the husband of some of his or his heirs' rights vis-à-vis his wife, and clarifies the precise implications of various formulas which he may employ for this purpose.

9:6 This mishnah probably represents a continuation of the preceding one, that is to say: the heirs' right to exact an oath of the widow is limited as described in this mishnah because her husband had waived this right on their behalf. Some interpreters, however, understand it to be an independent set of rules which limit the heirs' ability to exact such an oath even if the husband has not waived any of his or his heirs' rights in this regard.

9:7–9 *Collecting the Ketubbah Payment*

7 A woman who detracts from[50] her *ketubbah* may not collect without an oath.
A woman concerning whom one witness testifies that she has been paid
is not permitted to collect without an oath;
from the property of orphans or from encumbered property
or [from the husband] not in his presence—
she may not collect without an oath.

8 A woman who detracts from her *ketubbah*—how?
If her *ketubbah* was one thousand *zuz*
and he said to her:
"You have received your *ketubbah*,"
and she says:
"I have received only a *maneh*"—
she may not collect without an oath.
One witness testifies that she has been paid—how?
If her *ketubbah* was one thousand *zuz*[51]
and he said to her:
"You have received your *ketubbah*,"
and she says:
"I have not received,"
and one witness testifies concerning her that she has been paid—
she may not collect without an oath.
From encumbered property—how?
If he sold his property to others and she is collecting from the purchasers—
she may not collect without an oath.
From the property of orphans—how?
If he died and left his property to orphans and she is collecting from the orphans—
she may not collect without an oath.
And not in his presence—how?
If he went abroad[52] and she is collecting in his absence—
she may not collect without an oath.
R. Simeon says:

[50] Lit. "damages," "causes defects."
[51] "If her *ketubbah* was one thousand *zuz*," lacking in **K** and other witnesses.
[52] Lit. "to the land of the sea."

9:7 *detracts*: See 9:8 for exposition of this and the other issues raised in this mishnah. In the first two cases, the problem is that the effectiveness of the marriage document in establishing a right to collect has been weakened by the woman's admission or the witness's testimony.

from encumbered property, etc.: In these last cases, the right to collect based on the *ketubbah* is pitted against other considerations, namely concern for the rights of third parties or of the absent husband.

9:8 This Mishnah glosses the various possibilities raised in 9:7.

maneh: One hundred *dinar* or *zuz*.

R. Simeon refers back to 9:5–6 and he appears to disagree with the opinion of the anonymous voice presented there with regard to the circumstances in which the husband's heirs may exact an oath from the widow.

Whenever she demands her *ketubbah* payment—
the heirs may exact an oath from her,
and if she does not demand her *ketubbah* payment—
the heirs may not exact an oath from her.

9 If she produced a writ of divorce and it is not accompanied by a *ketubbah*—
she collects her *ketubbah* payment.
A *ketubbah* and it is not accompanied by a writ of divorce—
she says:
"I lost my writ of divorce,"
and he says:
"I lost my receipt";
and similarly a creditor who produces a loan document
that is not accompanied by a *prozbul*—
these are not paid.
Rabban Simeon b. Gamaliel says:
From the danger onward a wife collects her *ketubbah* payment
without a writ of divorce
and a creditor collects without a *prozbul*.
Two writs of divorce and two *ketubbah* documents—
she collects two *ketubbah* payments.
Two *ketubbah* documents and a writ of divorce,
or a *ketubbah* and two writs of divorce,
or a *ketubbah* and a writ of divorce and [the husband's] death—
she collects only one *ketubbah* payment,
for[53] one who divorces a woman and remarries her,
has remarried her on the condition of her first *ketubbah*.
A minor whose father married him off—

[53] K and a few other witnesses lack this word.

9:9 *If she produced a writ of divorce*: A woman who produces a writ of divorce (*get*) is entitled to collect a *ketubbah* payment even if she cannot produce a marriage contract (compare 4:4 above), but a marriage contract without proof of divorce is insufficient. The writ of divorce was normally destroyed upon payment of the *ketubbah*.

and similarly a creditor: The reference is to a creditor who attempts to collect a debt after the seventh (Sabbatical) year. According to biblical law (Deuteronomy 15:1–3) such a debt had lapsed, but a legal innovation attributed to Hillel (*Shevi'it* 10:3) allowed the debt to be collected if the creditor had written a document known as a *prozbul*.

From the danger: From the time of the Hadrianic persecutions, when it could be dangerous to be caught in possession of certain specifically Jewish legal documents.

Two writs of divorce: This section of the mishnah concerns cases in which a couple was divorced and remarried. The default assumption in such cases is that the second marriage is contracted on the basis of the original marriage contract, but if the woman holds two separate marriage contracts and has proof of two marriages having come to an end, she is entitled to collect on both contracts.

A minor… A convert…: Although according to rabbinic law neither a minor nor a non-Jew can contract a legally binding marriage with a Jewish woman, if either marries a Jewish woman and the marriage continues after the husband becomes an adult Jew he is bound by the terms of her *ketubbah* (or, presumably, of a minimal *ketubbah* if he has not written a *ketubbah* for her).

her *ketubbah* is valid,
for he kept her on this condition.
A convert who converted together with his wife—
her *ketubbah* is valid,
for he kept her on this condition.

Chapter Ten

10:1–6 *Multiple Wives, Limited Property*

10 One who was married to two women and died—
the first precedes the second,
and the heirs of the first precede the heirs of the second.
If he married the first and she died, married the second and he died—
the second and her heirs precede the heirs of the first.

2 One who was married to two women and they died and afterward he died,
and the orphans request their mother's *ketubbah* payment,
and there is only enough for two *ketubbah* payments—
they divide equally.
If there is a surplus of a *dinar*—
these take their mother's *ketubbah* and these take their mother's *ketubbah*.
If the orphans said:
"We will add to our father's property an extra *dinar*,"

10:1 *the first precedes the second*: The *ketubbah* establishes a lien against any property belonging to the husband. Here, the earlier lien takes precedence over the later one.

the second and her heirs precede: The second wife is a creditor of the estate since the husband predeceased her, and if she dies before collecting her *ketubbah* payment her heirs inherit her right to it. The heirs of the first wife are not considered creditors: since their mother predeceased their father, she was never entitled to her *ketubbah* payment. Rather, they are considered heirs who seek to inherit from their father.

10:2 *they divide equally*: If the estate is not large enough to allow at least a *dinar* to be divided as inheritance after the two *ketubbah* payments have been made, the heirs divide the estate according to the standard laws of inheritance. (*Equally* does not imply that the firstborn son, if there is one, does not receive a double portion; the intention is to stipulate that the inheritance is divided without regard to the amount of the various *ketubbah* payments.)

surplus of a dinar: As long as there is some surplus after paying out the *ketubbah* payments, the sons of each wife are entitled to collect her *ketubbah* payment (see 4:10 above). Only afterward is the remainder of the estate divided according to the laws of inheritance.

If the orphans said: Presumably one wife's sons stand to gain if the *ketubbah* payments are assigned to each wife's sons, either because their mother's *ketubbah* settlement was larger than the other wife's or because there were fewer sons from this wife, or both. As a result it would be in their interest to artificially increase the value of the estate.

add to our father's estate: Assess the estate at slightly more than its true value and make up the difference, in order to arrive at a situation in which the assessed value of the estate is at least a *dinar* more than the sum of the *ketubbah* payments.

in order to take the *ketubbah* payment owing to their mother—
we do not listen to them;
rather, one assesses the property in court.

3 If there was potential property, it is not like that which is actually held.
R. Simeon says:
Even if there is property that cannot serve as surety—
it counts for nothing,
until there is property that can serve as surety worth a *dinar* more
than the two *ketubbah* payments.

4 One who was married to three women and died:
this one's *ketubbah* payment is a *maneh*,
and this one's two hundred,
and this one's three hundred,
and there is only one hundred there—
they divide equally;
if there were two hundred there—
the one of a *maneh* takes fifty,
and those of two hundred and three hundred each take three gold [*dinar*];
if there were three hundred there,
the one of a *maneh* takes fifty,
and the one of two hundred takes a *maneh*,
and the one of three hundred takes six gold [*dinar*].
Similarly three who put [money] into a purse and gained or lost—
they divide in this way.

one assesses the property in court: Particularly where a small difference in assessment may work to the advantage of one party or another, we require formal assessment by a court.

10:3 *potential property*: Potential property refers to property that the deceased did not actually own at the time of his death, such as property which he stood to inherit.

R. Simeon further restricts the circumstances in which the rule of 4:10 that each wife's sons inherit her *ketubbah* is to be applied.

property that can serve as surety is a common rabbinic expression for real estate, since only real property can be encumbered by a lien.

10:4 *maneh*: One hundred *dinar*. The rule underlying the specific examples considered in the mishnah is as follows: the estate is to be divided equally until the wife with the smallest *ketubbah* has collected half of the sum owed her. At this point the other two divide any remaining property equally until the second has collected half of the amount owed to her. Finally, the wife with the largest *ketubbah* takes the remainder until she too has collected half.

they divide equally: Since there is not sufficient to pay everyone half of the smallest *ketubbah* allotment, they each share the one hundred *dinar* equally.

two hundred: The wife with the smallest *ketubbah* receives half the sum to which she is entitled when 150 *dinar* is divided equally between all three wives. The remaining fifty do not suffice to provide either of the other wives with half the sum owed her, so they are divided equally between the two of them, each receiving three gold [*dinar*] (or seventy-five silver *dinar*).

three hundred: There is enough for each to receive half of their promised allocation. The Mishnah does not consider cases in which the estate is larger than half the total owed to the three wives, but presumably in such a case each would first receive half of the sum owed her, and then the remainder would be divided as described above.

5 One who was married to four women and died—
the first precedes the second,
and the second precedes the third,
and the third precedes the fourth.
The first swears to the second,
and the second swears to the third,
and the third swears to the fourth,
and the fourth is paid without an oath.
Ben Nannas said:
Does she profit because she is last?
She too is paid only with an oath.
If they all were dated[54] on the same day—
whichever precedes its fellow by even an hour takes precedence.
They used to write thus, by hours, in Jerusalem.
If they were dated at the same hour and there was only a *maneh* there—
they divide equally.

6 One who was married to two women and sold his field,
and the first wrote to the purchaser:
"I have neither right nor claim against you"—
the second takes from the purchaser,
and the first from the second,
and the purchaser from the first,
and they go in circles until they compromise between them.
And similarly a creditor,
and similarly a woman who is a creditor.[55]

---

[54] Lit. "went out."
[55] **K**: "a woman and similarly a female creditor"; **P**: "a woman and a female creditor."

10:5 *The first swears to the second*: By collecting the money owing her the first wife leaves less to be divided among the others; she is therefore required to take an oath that this money is in fact due to her and that e.g. her husband did not pay her any of her *ketubbah* money in advance (see above 9:2).

only a maneh ... equally: If all the obligations were contracted simultaneously none takes precedence and all are on an equal footing; if the estate is insufficient to satisfy all these obligations it would presumably be divided according to the procedure described in the previous mishnah.

10:6 The assumption is that there is nothing in the estate from which the wives can collect the monies owed them.

the first wrote to the purchaser: Cf. above 9:1. The first wife has a prior claim (10:1) but has relinquished her right to collect from the buyer. Therefore the second wife may exercise her lien against the buyer. However, the first wife has merely given a personal undertaking to the buyer rather than renouncing any rights to her husband's alienated property. This wife's claim to her husband's property still takes precedence, and she may seize this property from the second wife.

the purchaser from the first: Because she has renounced her right to collect from this property vis-à-vis the buyer.

And similarly a creditor: Presumably the mishnah means to say that this rule is not specific to the case of multiple debts arising from polygamous marriages and would apply equally to debts incurred e.g. by means of loans, where one party has agreed not to exercise a lien against a purchaser.

Chapter Eleven

11:1–6   *The Widow*

11   A widow is maintained from the orphans' property,
and what she produces is theirs,
and they are not responsible for her burial;
her heirs, the heirs to her *ketubbah*, are responsible for her burial.
   2 A widow, whether from betrothal or from marriage, sells without a court.
R. Simeon says:
From marriage, she sells without a court;
from betrothal, she may not sell except in a court,
because she has no entitlement to food,
and anyone who has no entitlement to food may not sell except in a court.
   3 If she sold her *ketubbah* or part of it,
or mortgaged her *ketubbah* or part of it,
or gave her *ketubbah* or part of it to another[56]—
she may not sell the remainder unless in a court.
But the Sages say:
She may sell even four or five times;
and she sells without a court for food,
and she writes:
"I sold these for food."
And a divorcee may not sell except in a court.
   4 A widow whose *ketubbah* payment was two hundred—
if she sold a *maneh* worth for two hundred
or two hundred worth for a *maneh*—

---

[56] K (first hand) lacks: "or gave... to another," probably by homoeoteleuton.

11:1-6 These rules apply to a widow who has not collected her *ketubbah* payment but exercises her dower rights (see 4:12 above).

11:1 *eats... produces... burial*: Compare the rights of a wife, 4:4.

11:2 *sells*: The widow enjoys the unique privilege of being able to sell property belonging to her late husband's estate in order to collect monies to which she is entitled by her marriage contract without having to resort to court proceedings.

R. Simeon limits this right to a fully married woman rather than one who was inchoately married (betrothed).

11:3 *If she sold*: This is the continuation of R. Simeon's opinion.

even four or five times: The widow may sell pieces of property from her late husband's estate on a number of occasions in order to obtain her *ketubbah* payment in installments.

a divorcee is not granted the unique privilege accorded to a widow (11:2).

she has received her *ketubbah* payment.
If her *ketubbah* payment was a *maneh*
and she sold a *maneh* worth and a *dinar* for a *maneh*—
her sale is invalid.
Even if she said:
"I will return the *dinar* to the heirs"—
her sale is invalid.
Rabban Simeon b. Gamaliel says:
Her sale is always valid,
until she leaves the space of nine *qav* in a field
or of half a *qav* in a garden;
and according to R. Aqiva a quarter of a *qav*.
If her *ketubbah* was four hundred and she sold to this one for a *maneh*,
and to this one for a *maneh*,
and to the last one a *maneh*-worth and a *dinar* for a *maneh*—
the sale of the last one is invalid, but those of all the [others] are valid.

5 The assessment of judges that was too low by a sixth or too high by a sixth—
their sale is invalid.
Rabban Simeon b. Gamaliel said:
Their sale is valid.[57]
If so, what is the power of a court worth?
But if they wrote a writ of investigation:
even if they sold a *maneh* worth for two hundred or two hundred worth for a *maneh*—
their sale is valid.

[57] "Their sale is valid" lacking in **K** and other witnesses.

11:4 *she has received her ketubbah payment*: In both of these cases the widow is not entitled to any further payment. In the first case, she has received the full sum of her *ketubbah* payment. In the second, she has sold property belonging to the estate the value of which was equal to her *ketubbah* payment (even though she sold it for less than its true value).

a maneh worth and a dinar... invalid: Because she had no valid claim to property worth more than the sum to which her *ketubbah* entitled her.

always valid, until she leaves the space of nine qav: Rabban Simeon b. Gamaliel disagrees with the preceding anonymous opinion and probably holds that if the widow reimburses the heirs for any excess property she has sold the sale is valid, on condition that the remaining property is large enough to be usable (compare *Bava Batra* 1:6). R. Aqiva disagrees about the minimum size of the field. A *qav* is a measure of volume; what is meant is the sowing area for a *qav* of seed.

If her ketubbah was four hundred: According to the opinion of the Sages in 11:3 the widow may sell parcels of property on several occasions in order to receive her *ketubbah* payments in installments. In the case under consideration each of the earlier sales is valid because the widow exceeded her rights only with the sale of the last parcel.

11:5 *a sixth*: For this proportion as a threshold for over or underassessment compare *Bava Metsi'a* 4:3, *Bava Batra* 7:3.

a writ of investigation: A document issued as part of the process of soliciting bids to purchase a property being sold by the court.

6 One who renounces[58]
or a once-removed relation
or a sterile woman—
has neither *ketubbah* payment,
nor proceeds from usufruct,[59]
nor food, nor worn-out clothes.
If he married her from the beginning
[knowing that she is] a woman incapable of childbearing—
she does have a *ketubbah*.
A widow married[60] to a high priest,
or a divorcee or a woman who has undergone *halitsah* married to a priest,
or a female *mamzer* or *natin* married to an Israelite,
or a *mamzer* or *natin* married to a female Israelite—
they have a *ketubbah*.

Chapter Twelve

12:1–4 *Contractual Obligations to Support Daughters and Widows*

12 One who marries a woman,
and she contracted with him that he would feed her daughter for five years—

[58] K (before correction), P (deleted), C: "female orphan." [59] Lit. "produce."
[60] "Married" here and in the following is supplied for clarity.

11:6 *One who renounces*: A female orphan who had been given in marriage by her mother or brothers, and subsequently renounced the marriage (*Yevamot* 13:1–2). Some Palestinian versions (see n. 58) read "female orphan." If this reading is original and to be interpreted as referring to any orphan married off by her mother or brothers, and not only to one who later renounced her marriage, the author may have believed that this type of marriage, which lacked biblical authority, did not entitle the wife to a *ketubbah*.

once-removed relation: Lit. "second" (*Yevamot* 9:3). A marriage to these rabbinically prohibited relations was denied a *ketubbah* in order to discourage such marriages.

sterile woman: Marriage to a woman incapable of bearing children was considered fundamentally flawed (see 7:7 above; see also *Yevamot* 1:1).

clothes: She is not entitled to recoup after the dissolution of her marriage money she spent on her food or the value of fruits produced by her property which her husband consumed or of property that she brought into the marriage that wore out during that time.

A widow married to a high priest: Although these marriages are biblically prohibited, the marriage contract is considered to be binding, and the women are entitled to the usual property rights.

mamzer…natin. See *Yevamot* 2:4 and annotations there.

12.1 *that he would feed*: Compare the "stipulation of the court" that daughters whose father has died are to be supported from the estate (4:6, 4:11, and 13:3). Here, the mother contracts for support of the daughter from her husband during his lifetime.

he must feed her for five years.
If she was married to another
and contracted with him to feed her daughter for five years—
the first may not say: "When she comes to me[61] I will feed her";
rather, he transports her food to the place where her mother is.
And the two of them may not say: "We will feed her together";
rather, one feeds her, and the other gives her money for food.

2 If she was married—
the husband is liable for her food and they give her money for food.
If they died—
their daughters are fed from unencumbered properties;
but she is fed from encumbered properties,
because she is like a creditor.
The clever ones used to write:
"On condition that I shall feed your daughter for five years, as long as you are with me."

3 A widow who said:
"I do not want to leave my husband's house"—
the heirs cannot say to her:
"Go to your father's house and we will feed you there";
but they feed her in the house of her husband,
and they give her a residence in keeping with her honor.
If she said:
"I do not want to leave my father's house"—
the heirs can say to her:
"If you are with us you are entitled to food
and if you are not with us you are not entitled to food."
If she claims that it is because she is a young woman and they are young men—
they feed her while she is in her father's house.

4 As long as she is in her father's house—
she may collect her *ketubbah* payment forever;

[61] Most "Palestinian" and some "Babylonian" witnesses read "to my house."

If she the mother *was married to another* within the five years of stipulated maintenance, the obligation still holds.

When she comes to me: i.e. as long as the daughter is living with me, but not if she is living with the new husband. Note the assumption that the daughter will live *where her mother is*.

And the two of them may not say: Since each has a contractual obligation to provide the daughter's maintenance, they cannot share the cost, but each must supply it in full, one in kind and one in money.

12.2 *If she* the daughter *was married*: The new husband too is bound to support the wife, so she collects three payments.

because she is like a creditor: As such she collects (if necessary) from property that the deceased husband alienated after contracting this obligation, whereas his heirs are entitled only to collect from property that was his at his death. For *(un)encumbered* property see above 9:7.

12.3 *A widow*: For the contractual obligations to maintain a widow, see 4:12.

and as long as she is in her husband's house—
she may collect her *ketubbah* payment up to twenty-five years,
because twenty-five years is long enough for her to benefit
as much as her *ketubbah* payment—
the words of R. Meir, who said it in the name of
Rabban Simeon b. Gamaliel;
but the Sages say:
As long as she is in her husband's house—
she may collect her *ketubbah* payment forever,
and as long as she is in her father's house—
she may collect her *ketubbah* payment up to twenty-five years.
If she dies, her heirs mention her *ketubbah* payment up to twenty-five years.

Chapter Thirteen

13:1–9 *Admon and Hanan*

13 There were two judges of ordinances[62] in Jerusalem:
Admon and Hanan b. Avishalom.
Hanan said two things and Admon said seven things.
One who went abroad[63] and his wife demands food—
(1) Hanan said:
She swears at the end and does not swear at the beginning.

[62] All "Palestinian" witnesses read "robberies."
[63] Lit. "to the land of the sea."

12:4 *twenty-five years*: It appears that R. Meir and the anonymous Sages offered contrary interpretations of a more ancient ruling, which stated that in one case the widow could collect her *ketubbah* without a time limit while in the other she must claim within twenty-five years. The two views applied the rules to opposite cases. According to R. Meir, a wife who remains in her deceased husband's household eventually receives benefits equivalent to her marriage settlement. According to the Sages, the rationale for the time limit seems to be that a widow who had left her late husband's home for such a long period without claiming her *ketubbah* payment had decided to waive her right to it.

If she dies: The heirs are bound by the same time limit which had applied to the widow, but if they *mention her ketubbah*, i.e. declare their intention to collect, before twenty-five years have elapsed, they are entitled to collect even after this period has passed.

13.1–9 This collection of disputes from the end of the Second Temple period has been inserted here because several of the disputes concern issues relevant to this tractate.

13:1 *judges of ordinances*: This translates the reading of the "Babylonian" witnesses, while the "Palestinian" witnesses have *robberies*. This involves a difference of one letter and is very likely a case of phonetic variation.

She swears that her husband has not left provision for her. According to Hanan she need not take such an oath before the court would supply her with provisions at her husband's expense.

at the end: Most likely, when the husband returns and demands an oath of his wife. An alternative interpretation is, if and when she eventually claims her *ketubbah* payment.

The sons of high priests disputed with him and said:
She swears at the beginning and at the end.
R. Dosa b. Harqinas said according to their words.
Rabban Yohanan b. Zakkai said:
Hanan spoke well: She swears only at the end.

2 One who went abroad[64] and another stood up and supported his wife—
(2) Hanan says:
He has lost his money;
the sons of high priests disputed with him and said:
Let him swear how much he expended and let him take.
R. Dosa b. Harqinas said according to their words.
Rabban Yohanan b. Zakkai said:
Hanan spoke well: He has placed his money on a deer's antler.

3 Admon said seven.
One who died and left sons and daughters,
when the property is great, the sons inherit, and the daughters are fed;
when the property is little, the daughters are fed and the sons must beg at the doors.
(1) Admon said:
Have I lost out because I am a male?
Rabban Gamaliel said:
I approve Admon's words.

4 One who claims jars of oil from his fellow and [the latter] admitted with respect to the jars—
(2) Admon says:
Since he has admitted part[65] of the claim, let him swear;
but the Sages say:
The admission is not of the same type[66] as the claim.
Rabban Gamaliel said:
I approve Admon's words.

---

[64] Lit. "to the land of the sea." [65] C: "of the same *type* as the claim."
[66] K lacks "of the same type"; P and some others: "is not part of."

---

sons of high priests: The members of high priestly families.

13:2 *on a deer's antler*: Idiomatically, he cannot expect ever to see his money again; he has thrown it away.

13:3 *daughters are fed*: Cf. 4:6, 11. According to the first, anonymous opinion, the daughter's entitlement takes precedence over the sons' rights as heirs. Admon presumably considers the sons entitled to be fed along with the daughters until the estate is exhausted.

13:4 *admitted with respect to jars*: Admitted only having received jars but denied having received oil. Anyone who admits part of a monetary claim made against them takes an oath, although someone who denies such a claim entirely is not obligated to take such an oath (see *Shevu'ot* 6:1; the legal principle derives from exegesis of Exodus 22:6–8). Admon and the Sages disagree as to whether a claim to a certain number of jars of oil includes a claim to the jars themselves or whether this is merely a way of describing a certain quantity of oil.

5 One who contracted to give money to his son-in-law and reneged[67]—
she must sit until her head turns white.
(3) Admon says:
She is able to say:
"If I had contracted for myself I would sit until my head turns white;
now that my father has contracted for me, what can I do?
Either marry me or release me!"
Rabban Gamaliel said:
I approve Admon's words.

6 One who disputes the ownership of a field
and he is signed as a witness regarding it—
(4) Admon says:
He is able to say:
"The second is easy for me and the first is more difficult than he."
But the Sages say:
He has lost his right.
If he used it as a marker for another, he has lost his right.

7 One who went abroad[68] and the path to his field was lost—
(5) Admon says:
Let him go by the shortest way;
but the Sages say:
Let him buy a path for one hundred *maneh* or fly in the air.

8 One who produces a loan document against his fellow,
and that one produces [a document] that he has sold him a field—
(6) Admon says:
He is able to say:

[67] Lit. "extended his leg to him."   [68] Lit. "to the land of the sea."

13:5 *she must sit*: The son-in-law now refuses to marry. The woman is now perpetually in a state of inchoate marriage (betrothal). She is neither married nor can she marry anyone else. The groom cannot be forced to either marry or release the woman because his agreement to marry her was made on a condition which has not been fulfilled. By contrast, *Admon* holds that she can demand that the groom resolve her situation.

13:6 *One who disputes the ownership*: Someone has signed as a witness on a deed of sale according to which a second party has purchased a piece of property. The witness later claims to be the true owner of that property.

The second [party, the buyer] is easy for me [to deal with], but the first [party, the seller] is more difficult than he.: According to Admon, the challenger can claim that it was to his advantage to have the property pass to the hands of the buyer before asserting his claim, if, for instance, the seller were a more powerful figure than the purchaser.

the Sages say that by having acted as witness to the sale he has admitted that the seller was the true owner.

used it as a marker for another: It was a standard practice in transactions regarding property to list the adjoining properties and their owners. If the claimant has incidentally confirmed someone else's ownership of the property in question by calling it "so-and-so's field" in describing the boundaries of another property, Admon would agree that he has forfeited any right to assert a claim to the property.

13:7 *path to his field*: A right of way which guaranteed him free passage to his property.

13:8 *produces [a document] that he has sold*: The borrower can show that the creditor subsequently sold him real property.

"If I had owed you, you should have taken what was yours when you sold me the field";
But the Sages say:
This one was clever to have sold him land, because he can distrain it.

9 Two who produced writs of indebtedness against each other—
(7) Admon says:
If I had owed you, how could you have borrowed from me?
But the Sages say:
This one collects his writ of indebtedness,
and this one collects his writ of indebtedness.

13:10–11 Marriage and Residence Choice

10 There are three lands with regard to marriage:
(1) Judaea, (2) Transjordan, and (3) the Galilee.
One does not remove a spouse from a town to a town or from a city to a city.
But within the same land:
one may remove from a town to a town and from a city to a city,
but not from a town to a city or from a city to a town.
One may remove from a bad location to a good location,
but not from a good location to a bad location.
Rabban Simeon b. Gamaliel says:
Not even from a bad location to a good location,
Because the good location is trying.

11 All may bring up to the Land of Israel and none may remove;
all may bring up to Jerusalem and none may remove—
whether men or women.[69]

[69] Almost all "Palestinian" witnesses read: "Whether women or slaves. How so?"

If I had owed you: According to Admon, the prior document in such a case can be argued to have been falsified or already paid. The borrower can claim that if a debt were truly owed it should have been paid when the sale took place.

because he can distrain it: The Sages allow the holder of the loan document to argue that it was in his best interests to make sure that the borrower had collateral to ensure repayment.

13:8 *If I had owed you*: See 13:7. Here, again, according to *Admon*, the later deed can be argued to show that the earlier one is not (or is no longer) valid. By contrast, *the Sages* treat both documents as valid.

13:10 -11 A sort of appendix to the tractate which discusses complications that may arise when there is more than one possible location for a couple's married life.

13:10 *three lands*: Cf. Shevi'it 9:2; Bava Batra 3:2.

Because the good location is trying: Living in a more desirable location may not be a purely positive experience, as it comes with increased expectations.

13:11 *All may bring up*: If the couple is living outside the Land of Israel, either spouse may compel the other to move ("go up") there; but if they are living in the Land of Israel, neither may compel the other to leave.

whether men or women: See n. 69. Both versions are explanatory additions. Furthermore, only the "Palestinian" versions have the words "how so"; this is apparently an addition intended to emphasize the logical connection between the two parts of the mishnah (see below).

If he married a woman in the Land of Israel and divorced her in the Land of Israel—
he gives her the currency of the Land of Israel.
If he married a woman in the Land of Israel and divorced her in Cappadocia—
he gives her the currency of the Land of Israel.
If he married a woman in Cappadocia and divorced her in the Land of Israel—
he gives her the currency of the Land of Israel.
Rabban Simeon b. Gamaliel says:
He gives her the currency of Cappadocia.
If he married a woman in Cappadocia and divorced her in Cappadocia—
he gives her the currency of Cappadocia.

If he married a woman: Normally a debt must be paid in the currency (or according to the value of the currency) of the place in which it was contracted, even if payment takes place elsewhere. *Rabban Simeon b. Gamaliel* believes this rule applies also to the payment of the *ketubbah*. However, the anonymous voice of the Mishnah treats this case as exceptional: because every marriage contracted outside the Land of Israel implicitly includes the desirability or possibility of moving to Israel, if this potential is actualized and the couple is then divorced in Israel, the *ketubbah* is treated as if it had been written there in the first place.

Tractate Nedarim

Robert Goldenberg

Introduction

Overview

In Scripture the primary purpose of a vow (Heb. *neder*, pl. *nedarim*) is to designate an animal as consecrated for sacrifice or to pledge a sacrifice without specifying the animal that will be offered. In rabbinic law this conception was extended: a vow might designate any object or type of objects, or even a person or class of persons, as forbidden to the person making the vow as if these were sacred: in technical language the vow "grasped" an object that was already sanctified and thereby took on its forbidden character. For this reason the basic term for taking a vow upon oneself was *qorban* ("sacrifice"; see Mark 7:11), though in later times the word was often transformed in popular speech to *qonam* and the like.

In practice a vow usually amounted to renouncing all benefit that the indicated object or person might provide, or, by still further extension, all opportunity to provide benefit to a designated person, as if in such a case the target of the vow, rather than the speaker, had uttered it. In contrast to a vow, an oath (*shevu'ah*) obliges the speaker to perform or avoid a specified act. The Mishnah here (2:1–3) sketches some practical differences between the two, but elsewhere (*Sanhedrin* 3:2) it reflects their virtual equivalence in popular speech.

Structure and Organization of the Tractate

The main themes of the present tractate are: distinguishing vow formulations that are binding from those that are not (chapters 1–3), regulating contact between persons when one or both have vowed to provide no benefit to, or derive no benefit from, the other (chapters 4–5), exploring the principle that the language of a vow must be interpreted according to the commonly accepted meaning of the words used (chapters 6–8), setting out procedures for releasing people from vows they regret (chapter 9), and finally defining the power of a father or a husband respectively to nullify the vows of his daughter or wife (chapters 10–11). The Sages' power to *release* people from their vows is designated by various forms of the verb *hittir*, while the power of fathers or husbands to *nullify* the vows of dependent females is designated by forms of the verb *hefer*.

Relationship to Scripture

This power of nullification is the main concern of the Torah's only chapter (Numbers 30) that treats of vows at length, and it explains the location of tractate *Nedarim* in the mishnaic Order of Women (*Nashim*). Other legal passages that deal with vows focus on the requirement of fulfilling them or the obligations that fall on people who fail to fulfill their vows (Leviticus 7:16, 22:21; Numbers 15:3; Deuteronomy 12:17, 23:22). In narrative contexts see Genesis 28:20; Judges 11:30; 1 Samuel 1:11; 2 Samuel 15:8; Jonah 1:16, 2:10. The vows in the latter set were either conditional or expressions of gratitude. Even conditional vows can be understood as expressions of anticipated gratitude, though later commentators occasionally express discomfort at the idea that such vows represent a kind of bargaining with God.

Special Notes for the Reader

As noted, the renunciation of benefit from specified sources is the basic topic of *Nedarim*; this has given rise to a particular textual variation throughout the tractate. The phrase "*Qonam* that I taste figs," for example (see 11:6), amounts to a pledge to abstain from figs. Sometimes the manuscripts provide a positive wording, as given here (this is characteristic of **MB**), but sometimes the wording is negative ("*Qonam* that I not taste figs"); this is more common in **MJ**. The present translation does not indicate all these variations, and translates with or without "not" so as to provide the smoothest and clearest English reading. The meaning is always the same, though commentators have tried to discover a legal difference between the two readings. The difference between the two formulations amounts to a single letter, easily lost or inserted in the process of copying. See especially on 1:4 and 2:2 below.

In addition to the usual abbreviations, for this tractate the following abbreviations also appear in the notes to the translation and in the annotations:

MB The Mishnah text in the Babylonian Talmud (Bavli)
MJ The Mishnah text in the Jerusalem Talmud (Yerushalmi)
TB The Babylonian Talmud (*gemara*)
TJ The Jerusalem Talmud (*gemara*)

Tractate Nedarim

Chapter One

1:1–2 *Circumlocutions and Substitutions*

I All substitutions for vows are as vows,
and for bans are as bans,
and for oaths are as oaths,
and for *nazir* vows are as *nazir* vows.
One who says to his fellow:
"I am forbidden by vow from you,"
"I am separated from you,"
"I am at a distance from you,"
"That I will not eat of yours,"[1]
"That I will not taste of yours"—
he is forbidden.
"I am barred[2] from you":
R. Aqiva[3] was inclined in this case toward stringency.

---

[1] Here and in the next clause, **MB** lacks the negation.   [2] Lit. "excommunicated."
[3] **P**: "Judah," corrected in the margin to "Aqiva."

1:1 *substitutions*: Circumlocutions or euphemisms. The proper formulation of a vow is to forbid oneself from deriving benefit from some object as though it was being dedicated as a sacrifice (*qorban*). A term other than *qorban* but similar to it is called a "substitution" (*kinnui*, or "nickname"), and has the same effect. Examples of such terms appear below, in 1:2.

nazir: Often translated "Nazirite," one who has vowed a term of enhanced religious discipline involving abstention from wine and the grape, avoidance of contact with the dead, and abstention from cutting the hair. See Numbers 6 and *Nazir*.

"I am forbidden... That I will not": Some commentators see these two formulations as constituting a pair, the second ("will not eat") specifying the act that was meant in the first. Others see each of these formulations as a separate possibility. The examples given in this paragraph are circumlocutions that do not include the formal vow. Technically, these are not "substitutions" but "handles" that "grab" at the vow from the outside, as one takes a whole vessel by grasping its handle.

"will not eat": The Babylonian Talmud usually presupposes a reading without the negation; combining this clause with the preceding, the meaning would be "I am forbidden from you... with respect to what I might eat..." Technically such a ban on one's own behavior constitutes an oath and not a vow, but this distinction is often blurred. See further on 2:1 below.

was inclined... toward stringency: Not sure that *I am forbidden from you* constituted a binding vow, but unable to rule more leniently for fear that it did. Alternative translations: "felt pressed," "hesitantly ruled."

"As the vows of the wicked"—
he has vowed with respect to a *nazir* vow, to a sacrifice, or to an oath.
"As the vows of the righteous"—
he has not said anything.
"As their free-will offerings"—
he has vowed with respect to a *nazir* vow or a sacrifice.

2 One who says to his fellow:[4]
Qonam, Qonach, or *Qonas*—
in this case these are substitutions for *Qorban*.
Hereq, Herekh,[5] or *Heref*—
in this case these are substitutions for *Herem*.
Naziq, Naziakh, or *Paziakh*—
in this case these are substitutions for a *nazir*-vow.
Shevutah,[6] *Shequqah;*
or he vowed by *mota*[7]—
in this case these are substitutions for *Shevu'ah*.

[4] **MJ** and **K** lack "to his fellow"; so too many commentaries. The text in **MB** is uncertain.
[5] Certain variants lack this word, but the text provides three examples for the other categories and probably did so here as well.
[6] **K** adds "*Shevuna*" at the beginning of the sequence. [7] Commentaries provide variants for this term.

"the vows of the wicked…of the righteous": Those who lack proper religious scruples are prone to utter impulsive or frivolous vows; therefore one who vows as *the wicked* is deemed to have made a binding vow.

nazir…sacrifice…oath: The Mishnah does not make clear how one of these was created by the statement. The Babylonian Talmud suggests that the context determines which: has a *nazir* walked by, or has someone else just consecrated a sacrifice or spoken an oath? The Palestinian Talmud considers whether a single vow under certain circumstances might entail all three of the indicated obligations. Later commentators show the same diversity of interpretation.

"the vows of the righteous": The truly righteous, however, abstain from making vows altogether; therefore their vows simply do not exist. The righteous do consecrate many voluntary sacrifices; *as their free-will offerings* is therefore a binding formulation.

1:2 *Qonam*, etc.: The Babylonian Talmud identifies these *substitutions* either as foreigners' mispronunciations of Hebrew words that have crept into everyday speech or as nonsense words invented by the rabbis so that people could undertake a vow without actually pronouncing the name of God (see next comment).

Qorban: Lit. "sacrifice." This word is either stated or implied in all vow formulations. In the case of an actual sacrifice, the complete formula of dedication would include the Divine name ("a sacrifice unto God"), and according to the second explanation above the substitutions are designed to avoid this use of the name in nonsacrificial contexts. Widespread use of *qorban* as establishing a vow is suggested by Mark 7:11.

Herem: Lit. "devotion": complete and utter dedication to the deity.

Naziq…nazir vow: See *Nazir* 1:1.

mota: An abbreviated form of *mamota*, Aramaic for "oath." The commentators offer many variants of this word: *momi*, *muma*, etc. The Talmuds presume the form *mohi*, which some explain as a reference to Moses: one who swears "as the oath of Moses" (based on Exodus 2:21) is bound by his oath.

Shevu'ah: "Oath."

1:3–2:1 *Vows of Indirect Reference*

3 One who says:[8]
"Not nonsacral food I shall not eat of yours,"
"Not fit [food I shall not eat of yours],"
"Not clean…,"
"Pure…,"
"Impure…,"
"Left over…,"
"*Piggul*…"—
He is forbidden.
"Like a lamb [is food that I eat of yours]."
"Like the stalls…,"
"Like the wood…,"
"Like the sacrifices…,"
"Like the altar…,"
"Like the Temple…,"
"Like Jerusalem…,"
or if he vowed by any of the altar utensils—
even though he did not mention *Qorban*—
in this case, he vowed by *Qorban*.
R. Judah says:
One[9] who says "Jerusalem" has not said anything.

[8] **K, P** lack "One who says."   [9] **K**: "Even the one who says…"

1:3 *"Not nonsacral food I shall not eat of yours"*: Food that is not "ordinary" (Heb. *hullin*) is sacred. The vow means "I shall treat all your food as sacred and not eat any of it." The second *not* is idiomatic, as often in connection with vows (see annotations to 2:3).

Not fit…: The Mishnah provides variants on the preceding expression.

fit: in other words, normally available for consumption but now forbidden on account of the vow.

clean: Worthy of being offered on the altar, and therefore unavailable to me.

Impure and therefore unavailable for consumption like an impure sacrifice.

Left over: Heb. *notar*. Sacrificial meat left over into the second or third day (this depended on the type of sacrifice) could not be consumed.

Piggul: A sacrifice which the bringer *intended* to eat past the proper time was not merely "left over" but "offensive" and unavailable for consumption at once. See Leviticus 7:18, 19:7, and *Zevahim* introduction.

Like a lamb, etc.: All these items are associated with the sacrificial cult and therefore imply *qorban* even if that word is not actually pronounced. A change in vowels permits reading these phrases as "not a lamb," "not the stalls," etc.; see below 1:4 to "For a sacrifice."

R. Judah: The meaning of the variant in **K** ("Even…") is not clear. Perhaps it should read "Even the one who says: [Like] Jerusalem." In R. Judah's view "Jerusalem" is simply the name of a city, and the presence there of the Temple is not enough to imply the word *qorban* in every mention of the place (see Matthew 23:16). He holds this view even when the comparison "like," which technically enables the vow to "grasp" a sacred object, is included.

4 One who says:
"Sacrifice...,"
"Whole offering...,"
"Grain offering...,"
"Purgation offering...,"
"Thank offering...,"
"Peace offering...,"
"That I will not eat of yours"—
he is forbidden.
R. Judah permits.
"The sacrifice...,"
"Like a sacrifice...,"
"A sacrifice...,"
"Be that I will eat of yours"—
he is forbidden.
"For a sacrifice[10] that I will not eat of yours"—
R. Meir forbids.[11]
One who says to his fellow:
"*Qonam* my mouth from speaking to you,"
"...my hand from working with you,"
"...my foot from walking with you"—
he is forbidden.

[10] **K, P**: "Not a sacrifice..." See annotations. [11] **K** restores "forbids" in the margin.

1:4 *R. Judah permits*: The speaker did not use the preposition "like/as". Without this explicit comparison the vow cannot "grasp" the specified offering, so the intended foods have not received the status of sacred material.

"A sacrifice...that I will eat": In the following (disputed) case *that I will not eat*. The presence or absence of "not" does not matter when the context implies negation. In fact, as in 1:3, textual witnesses often differ over the presence or absence of "not" (see annotation to 2:2).

"for a sacrifice that I will not eat...": In the manuscripts the prefix "for" is replaced by the word "not," which differs by only one letter. This variation too is very common.

R. Meir forbids: By implication the majority opinion holds that "for a sacrifice" is a formula of sanctification, not prohibition: the speaker does not mean to utter a vow of self-deprivation but to dedicate something as a sacrifice. One person cannot sanctify another person's property, however, so R. Meir rejects this interpretation as legally untenable; the words must constitute a vow after all.

"my mouth from speaking": A vow must "grasp" a tangible object and assign it the status of a sacrifice for the one making the vow, but these last vows intend to prohibit intangible actions. Nevertheless, according to this mishnah specifying "mouth" or "hand" or "foot" is deemed sufficient for the vow to "grasp."

Chapter Two

2 And these are permitted:
"Nonsacral food that I will eat of yours is as the flesh of swine,"
"…as idolatry,"
"…as skins with the heart's place cut open,"[12]
"…as carrion,"
"…as animals that died through injury,"
"…as vermin,"
"…as reptiles,"
"…as Aaron's dough portion,"
"…as his *terumah*"—
he is permitted.
One who says to his wife: "You are hereby to me as Mother"—
one opens an opening for him from another place,
in order that he not become frivolous about this.

2:1 cont.–3 *Vows and Oaths*

"*Qonam* that I will not sleep,"[13]
"That I will not speak,"
"That I will not walk";
Or one who says to his wife:
"*Qonam* that I will not have sexual intercourse with you"—
he [falls under the rule] of: *He shall not violate his word.*

---

[12] This item is missing from **K, P**.
[13] Var. "that I will sleep," and so throughout. See annotation on 2:2.

2:1 *"Nonsacral food"*: Nonsacred food (*hullin*) is permitted, so a vow cannot "grasp" it (compare 1:3), and associating it with the items now listed ("flesh of swine…") changes nothing. These items are forbidden by the Torah, not by a vow. For this reason they are not available for a vow to "grasp," and the vow does not become binding.

"skins with the heart's place cut open": If the heart of a living animal has been removed and used in a religious ritual, the skin of that animal is forbidden on account of its association with idolatry (see *Avodah Zarah* 2:3).

opens an opening: Sages should attempt through questioning to find some other reason to release his vow (see chapter 9), but they should not simply tell him the vow was not binding: this might encourage him to utter such vows *frivolously*.

terumah: The word can refer to any offering (see 2:4 below), but it normally denotes the offering given to priests from each year's crop (see *Terumot*).

He shall not violate his word: Numbers 30:3. Strictly speaking these are not binding vows because they have no tangible object to "grasp," but the person who says such a thing should be told to fulfill his expressed intention.

"Oath that I will not sleep,"
"That I will not speak,"
"That I will not walk"—
he is forbidden.

2 "*Qorban* I shall not eat of yours,"
"*Qorban*[14] I shall eat of yours,"
"Not *qorban* I shall not eat of yours"—
[he is] permitted.
"Oath I shall not eat [of] yours,"
"Oath I shall eat [of] yours,"
"Not oath I shall not eat [of] yours"—
he is forbidden;
this is the greater severity of oaths than of vows.
And [there is] a greater severity of vows than of oaths.
How?
If he said:
"*Qonam* a *sukkah*[15] that I will make,"
"A *lulav* that I will take,"
"*Tefillin* that I will put on,"[16]
with vows—
he is forbidden,
with oaths—
he is permitted,
since one may not take an oath to violate commandments.

3 There can be a vow within a vow,[17]
but not an oath within an oath.
How?
If he said:

[14] **K, P** add "and," presumably to be understood as "or." [15] **P** inserts this word between the lines.
[16] **K, P**: "give."   [17] Lit. "there is…"

"Oath that I will…": Heb. *shevu'ah*. Oaths, unlike vows (*nedarim*), do not have to "grasp" a tangible object. The formulation *Oath that* is normally rendered "I swear," but the present awkward translation more sharply displays the contrast between oath and vow, here and in the next two paragraphs as well.

2:2 This paragraph offers a striking demonstration that the presence or absence of a negating particle does not affect the validity or even the meaning of a vow or (below) an oath. Commentators have tried to extract legal consequences from the difference, but the whole point of this text seems to be that in practice there is none.

greater severity of oaths: A vow to abstain from performing a commandment is binding because it can "grasp" the ritual object in question and render it forbidden. Since an oath does not have to "grasp" a tangible object, an oath to abstain from an action is binding.

greater severity of vows: An oath binds the person not the object, and a person cannot sever himself in this way from his Torah-based obligations.

lulav: lit. "palm branch." The term refers here to the bundle of four agricultural products that is used in various rituals during the festival of Sukkot (see *Sukkah* chapters 3–4).

"I shall hereby be a *nazir* if I eat, I shall hereby be a *nazir* if I eat,"[18]
and he ate—
he is liable for each one.
"Oath that I shall not eat, Oath that I shall not eat,"
and he ate—
he is liable for only one.

2:4–5 *Principles of Interpretation*

4 Unspecified vows should be interpreted stringently,
but their specification leniently.
How?
If he said:
"It is hereby to me like salted meat,"
"Like libation wine":
if he vowed that of Heaven[19]—
it is forbidden;
if that of idolatry—
it is permitted;
and if unspecified—
it is forbidden.
"It is hereby to me as if devoted":

---

[18] Both here and in the following clause **P** (as corrected by a second hand) and **K** have a third repetition of the speaker's words. **MJ** has two vows but three oaths.

[19] Var. "of sacrifices of well-being."

2:3 *nazir*: A pledge to become a *nazir* constitutes a vow (see Numbers 6:2).

liable for each one: A vow that is redundant with respect to another vow is nevertheless binding. In the given example he must serve a thirty-day *nazir* term for each broken vow or be *liable to* the penalty for each failure to do so: flogging if the violation was knowing and defiant, a purgation offering if it was not.

liable for only one: If the oath is broken he suffers the prescribed penalty only once.

2:4 *Unspecified vows*: Vows that leave some important detail unclarified must be interpreted according to the most stringent interpretation of the speaker's words; otherwise one cannot be certain that the vow was fulfilled. It does not matter whether the vagueness was intentional or the speaker had simply not realized the words were ambiguous.

specification: On the other hand, if the speaker expressly indicates that his intention was less stringent than might have been the case, that indication is to be accepted.

"salted meat": Sacrificial meat (Leviticus 2:13). There is need to clarify the deity to whom the sacrifice was offered.

if he vowed…: If he clarifies his meaning in one way rather than another, as follows.

Heaven: The Jewish God, worshipped in the Temple. Anything devoted to the Temple is no longer available for human enjoyment and is the model for all vows; its sacrificial status means that a vow can "grasp" it and transfer the prohibition to anything specified. The variant reading "sacrifices of well-being" differs by only one letter and comes to the same thing in practice: a sacrifice of well-being is a particular example of the general idea expressed in the printed version of the text.

idolatry: Anything devoted to idolatry is already forbidden absolutely and cannot be made the subject of a vow.

if as devoted to Heaven—
it is forbidden;
and if as devoted to the priests—
it is permitted;
and if unspecified—
it is forbidden.
"It is hereby to me as tithe":
if he vowed with reference to the cattle tithe—
it is forbidden;
and if with reference to that of the threshing floor[20]—
it is permitted;
and if unspecified,
it is forbidden.
"It is hereby to me as *terumah*":
if he vowed with reference to the *terumah* of the Temple chamber,
it is forbidden,
and if with reference to that of the threshing floor,
it is permitted,
and if unspecified,
it is forbidden—
the words of R. Meir.
R. Judah says:[21]
Unspecified *terumah* in Judaea is forbidden;
in the Galilee it is permitted,
because the men of the Galilee are not familiar with the *terumah* of the Temple chamber.
Unspecified devotions in Judaea are permitted
and in the Galilee are forbidden,
because the men of the Galilee are not familiar with devotions to the priests.

[20] K, P: "tithe of grain." [21] MJ, K, P: "The Sages say."

devoted to the priests: Gifts to the priests are still available for human enjoyment, that is by the recipients, and so the vow has nothing to "grasp."

cattle tithe must be sacrificed; thus a vow can "grasp" it and become binding.

threshing floor: A reference to ordinary tithe, which must be given to the Levites. However, Levites may give or sell tithes to others; no prohibition attaches to them, and therefore a vow in this form has nothing to "grasp." The Mishnah imagines that both tithe and *terumah* (see below) were usually separated at the threshing floor and collected by waiting priests or Levites. See *Ma'aserot* and *Terumot*.

terumah: Since *terumah* (see above 2:1) remains available for human consumption, a vow cannot "grasp" it. However, the term can also refer to the annual gifts of money (see *Sheqalim*) that were collected for the Temple. These funds were no longer available for ordinary use, and a vow made by reference to *the terumah of the Temple chamber* could "grasp" them and become binding.

Unspecified terumah… Unspecified devotions: That is, vows that seek to designate property *terumah* or *devoted*.

familiar: In Judaea, where ordinary people were more likely to do business with the nearby Temple, sacred funds were regularly designated *terumah*. An unspecified vow could therefore "grasp" such funds and become binding. However, in the Galilee, where such funds were not regularly encountered, a vow that sought to "grasp" *terumah* presumably meant the more locally familiar *terumah of the threshing floor* and so could not become binding. The same distinction applies to *devotions*; in Judaea such gifts to the priests were familiar, but in the Galilee people were not likely to have them in mind when pronouncing an ambiguous vow.

5 If he vowed by "devotion" and then said:
"I vowed only by a fisherman's net";
"By sacrifice"[22] and then said:
"I vowed only by tributes to kings";
"I myself am hereby a sacrifice" and then said:
"I vowed only by the bone that I set down for myself that I might vow by it";
"*Qonam* that my wife might have any benefit from me" and then said:
"I vowed only concerning my first wife, whom I divorced"—
one does not [need to] consult about any of these,
though if he did consult,
one should punish him by giving him a stringent ruling—
the words of R. Meir.
But the Sages say:
One opens an opening for him from another place,
and one teaches him that he not treat vows frivolously.

Chapter Three

3:1–3   *Nonbinding vows*

3 The Sages released four vows:
(1) vows of encouragement, and
(2) vows of empty talk, and[23]
(3) vows in error, and
(4) vows unavoidably violated.
Vows of encouragement, how?[24]
If he was selling an object and said:
"*Qonam* that I will reduce for you below a *sela*,"

[22] K, P repeat "If he vowed."
[23] P lacks "and."   [24] K, P lack "how?"

2:5 *"fisherman's net"*: Lit. "the net of the sea." In this and the following cases, a vow that initially appears binding is "specified" (as in 2:4) to mean something nonsacral, often frivolous and trivial. The word *herem*, which normally means "devotion" in the context of vows, can also mean a fisherman's net; see Ezekiel 32:3, Micah 7:2, etc.

"tributes to kings": Lit. "the sacrifices of or for kings."

"I myself": One might vow one's putative value to the Temple. See Leviticus 27:1–8, also *Arakhin*.

"the bone…": The Hebrew word for "myself" literally means "my bone."

one does [not need] to consult…: Such a frivolous vow requires no release by a Sage, but in R. Meir's opinion any request for a release should be treated harshly. The Sages respond as in 2:1 above.

3:1 *released*: In advance; such vows are never binding and do not need release.

four vows: That is, types of vow. Each type is explained as the text goes on.

and the other said:
"*Qonam* that I will add for you above a *sheqel*"—
they both want [to settle] for three *dinar*.
R. Eliezer b. Jacob says:
Even one who places his fellow under a vow
that he should eat with him may say:[25]
"Every vow that I shall speak in the future is void,"
as long as he remembers this at the moment of the vow.

2 Vows of empty talk:
He said:
"*Qonam*[26] if I didn't see along this road as many as those who left Egypt,"
or "...if I didn't see a snake the size of an olive-press beam."
Vows in error:
"If[27] I ate or if I drank,"
and he remembered that he ate or drank;
"That I shall eat or I shall drink,"
and he forgot and ate or drank;
"*Qonam*[28] that my wife will derive any benefit from me,
because she stole my purse,"
or "...struck my son,"
and he became aware that she did not strike him,
or he became aware that she did not steal it.[29]
He saw people eating [his] dates and said:[30]
"They are hereby *qorban* for you,"
and they turned out to be his father and[31] his brothers
and others were with them—
the House of Shammai say:

[25] K: "and said." MJ adds "to him," a clear error.   [26] K, P lack "*Qonam*."   [27] K, P: "He said if…"
[28] K, P: "He said *Qonam*…"   [29] K, P lack "it."   [30] K adds "to them."   [31] K: "or."

---

for three dinar: Both used strong language while negotiating, but neither was really unwilling to accept a compromise; therefore neither has made and broken a binding vow. A *sheqel* is two *dinar*, and a *sela* is four (see glossary): the agreed price splits the difference.

Even one…: A person may explicitly stipulate in advance that a vow not be considered binding. Each Talmud considers an alternative reading without the word "even": in this version R. Eliezer b. Jacob's teaching is unrelated to the foregoing and stands as a separate rule.

3:2 *"Qonam if I didn't see"*: A vow must ."grasp" something tangible, so it must always be understood that the speaker has vowed to forgo the enjoyment of food or other object if what he says is (or is not) true.

"If I ate"… "I shall eat": He said, "may this food be *qonam* to me if I ate such and such";or he said "may this food be *qonam* to me: if I shall eat such and such." The vow can be general or refer to some specific food or drink.

and others: A variant lacks "and." Without that word, the text first provides a straightforward case of a vow made in error and then adds a separate discussion about a complicating circumstance. With "and," the case of the dates is entirely devoted to that more complicated situation.

Shammai… Hillel: The House of Shammai rule that the vow can take effect with respect to the strangers; the owner of the dates may really not wish to share his property with them, but would not prevent his own family from enjoying the fruit. The House of Hillel reject this distinction on the ground that no vow can be partially binding.

They are permitted and those with them are forbidden;
but the House of Hillel say:
Both these and these are permitted.

3 Vows unavoidably violated:
His fellow put him under a vow to eat with him,
and he became ill,
or his son became ill,
or a river delayed him—
these are unavoidably violated vows.

3:4–5   Permitted False Vows

4 One may vow to murderers, and to robbers, and to tax collectors
that it is *terumah*,
even though it is not *terumah*;
that they belong to the royal household,
even though they[32] do not belong to the royal household.[33]
The House of Shammai say:
One may vow about anything, except not by oath;
but the House of Hillel say:
Even by oath.
The House of Shammai say:
He may not begin by vowing for him;
but the House of Hillel say:
He may even begin for him.
The House of Shammai say:
Only by that by which he is forced to vow;
but the House of Hillel say:
Even by that by which he is not forced to vow.
How?

[32] K: "it."   [33] P: "are not theirs."

3:3 *these are unavoidably violated vows*: Only one vow has been mentioned, but see 3:4.

3:4 The vows listed here can be seen as vows conditioned by unavoidable circumstances, and thus a continuation of the category mentioned in 3:3.

robbers: The term used is *haramim*, plural of *herem* (elsewhere in the tractate used for devotion).

terumah: See on 2:1 above. Priestly dues were exempt from tax, so a false affirmation that produce was *terumah* could save it from confiscation. It seems that even criminals and government officials might hesitate to seize priestly food.

royal household: Robbers might not be intimidated by the claim that produce was *terumah*, but they would be less likely to steal royal property.

not by oath: False oaths are condemned in the Decalogue and so carry more severity than vows; even under compulsion one should vow and not swear.

begin: Even a vow should not be offered unless the robbers demand it.

They said to him:
Say "*Qonam* my wife will have no benefit from me,"
And he said "*Qonam* my wife and children will have no benefit from me"—
the House of Shammai say:
His wife is permitted and his children are forbidden;
but the House of Hillel say:
Both are permitted.

5 "These plantings are hereby *qorban* if they are not cut,"
"This cloak is *qorban* if it is not burned"—
they can be redeemed.[34]
"These[35] plantings are hereby *qorban* until they are cut,"
"This cloak is *qorban* until it is burned"—
they cannot be redeemed.[36]

3:6–11 *Clarifying the Language of a Vow*

6 One who vows [to derive no benefit]:
"from those who go down to the sea"
is permitted with respect to those who dwell on the dry land;
"from those who dwell on the dry land"
is forbidden with respect to those who go down to the sea,
since those who go down to the sea are included
among those who dwell on the dry land.[37]

[34] Lit. "they have a redemption."   [35] K restores "these" in the margin.
[36] Lit. "they do not have a redemption."
[37] K corrects "the sea" to "the dry land" in the margin.

His wife is permitted and his children are forbidden: Since the robbers did not insist on including the children, according to the House of Shammai the vow concerning them must be considered voluntary and therefore binding.

3:5 *qorban*: Such objects cannot literally be sacrificed, nor does the speaker pronounce the usual vow formula "to me," which would render the objects forbidden to him alone. Instead, the plantings or the cloak are pledged as a gift to the Temple treasury. The vow is presumably spoken in a situation where the objects are about to be destroyed or stolen, perhaps by government officials as in 3:4; hence the placement of this paragraph immediately after the preceding. Unlike the vows in the previous text, however, this vow is binding and the objects must be redeemed; this is not considered a vow made in error, even if the feared destruction fails to occur.

they can be redeemed: Such objects can be redeemed for 125 percent of their monetary value and then returned to ordinary use; see Leviticus 27:13–15.

they cannot be redeemed: The first part of this mishnah did not specify duration, but here the word "until" implies that the sanctification will remain in effect as long as the objects remain in their present state. The speaker can set aside redemption money over and over again, but each time the object in question returns to its sacred status. The Talmuds consider an alternative explanation: *they cannot be redeemed* after the plantings have been cut or the cloak has been damaged because none is needed. The condition set in the original vow no longer applies, and the consecration is dissolved automatically.

3:6 The rest of the chapter attempts to clarify the usual meaning of common phrases. It is assumed that a vow using any of these phrases should be understood according to their common meaning.

Not like those who travel from Akko to Joppa,
but like one whose way is to sail.

7 One who vows "From those who see the sun"
is forbidden even with respect to the blind,
since he only meant him whom the sun sees.

8 One who vows "From the black-headed"
is forbidden with respect to the bald and those with gray hair,
and is permitted with respect to women and children,
since only men are called black-headed.

9 One who vows:
"From those who have been born"
is permitted with respect to those who may be born;
"From those who may be born"—
is forbidden with respect to those who have been born.[38]
R. Meir permits even those who have been born,
but the Sages say:
He meant only him whose way is to beget.[39]

10 One who vows "From those who rest on the Sabbath"
is forbidden with respect to Israelites and is forbidden with respect to Samaritans;
"From those who eat garlic"—
is forbidden with respect to Israelites and is forbidden[40] with respect to Samaritans;
"From[41] those who go up to Jerusalem"—
is forbidden with respect to Israelites and is permitted with respect to Samaritans.

[38] **MJ, K, P** lack this line. [39] **K, P**: "to be born."
[40] Some witnesses read "permitted." [41] **K, P**: "And from."

Not like those…: Some interpret this last clause with reference to the beginning of the paragraph: *those who dwell on the dry land* includes those who travel short distances by ship but not those who spend most of their time at sea. The more prevalent view is the opposite: even those who spend most of their time on ships are included, since they also maintain homes on land.

3:8 *gray hair*: The vow specified *black-headed* people, but this is presumed to mean any male who might have had black hair at some point.

3:9 The initial opinion distinguishes between *yilodim* ("those who have been born") and *noladim* ("those who are born" and rendered here "who may be born"). In Scripture either word can have both meanings, but the Mishnah tries to assign a different meaning to each: "those who have been born" cannot include those not yet born, but "those who may be born" includes everyone. In the longer **MB** version R. Meir tries to maintain a similar distinction regardless of the word used in the vow (to be sure, this leaves the word "even" unexplained), but the Sages disagree: *noladim* includes any creature that is born or begotten rather than hatched from an egg. In the shorter version found in **MJ** and the manuscripts, "even" means that just as *yilodim* excludes *noladim* so too the opposite is true as well.

whose way is to beget: That is, to produce living young. A variant reads "to be born."

3:10 *Samaritans*: Lit. "Kuthites," see 2 Kings 17:24.

"those who eat garlic": As a Sabbath food (see 8:6). The question is whether Samaritans too cultivate this practice.

"Jerusalem": The Samaritans did not recognize the sanctity of the Jerusalem Temple, and had their own shrine on Mount Gerizim (modern Jabal al-Tur) near Shechem (modern Nablus).

11 "*Qonam,
that I shall derive benefit from the children of Noah*"—
he is permitted with respect to Israelites
and forbidden with respect to the nations of the world.[42]
"*That I shall derive benefit from the seed of Abraham*"—
he is forbidden with respect to Israelites
and permitted with respect to the nations of the world.[43]
"*That I shall derive benefit from Israelites*"—
he buys for more and sells for less.
"*That Israelites shall derive benefit from me*"—
he buys for less and sells for more,
if they listen to him.[44]
"*That I derive benefit from them or they from me*"—
let him derive benefit from gentiles.[45]
"*Qonam that I shall not derive benefit*[46] *from the uncircumcised*"—
he is permitted with respect to the uncircumcised of the Israelites
and forbidden with respect to the circumcised of the nations.
"*Qonam that I shall not derive benefit from the circumcised*":
he is forbidden with respect to the uncircumcised of the Israelites
and permitted with respect to the circumcised of the nations,[47]
because "uncircumcision" is a name only for the gentiles,
as it is said:
*For all the gentiles are uncircumcised
and all the house of Israel are uncircumcised of heart,*
and it says:
This uncircumcised Philistine shall be…,
and it says:
*Lest the daughters of the Philistines be happy,
lest the daughters of the uncircumcised rejoice.*

[42] **K, P** lack "of the world." [43] **K, P** lack "of the world."
[44] **K, P**: "They do not listen to him." [45] **K, P**: "the nations."
[46] **K** restores "benefit" in the margin.
[47] This clause is absent in the body of **K**, but restored in the margin.

3:11 *"children of Noah"*: Strictly speaking Jews too descend from Noah, but in rabbinic legal discourse this is a standard term for gentiles.

"seed of Abraham": According to Genesis, Ishmaelites and Edomites too are the descendants of Abraham, but the vow is interpreted according to common parlance and refers to Jews alone.

"buys for more…": The vow does not preclude doing business with other Jews, but the transaction may not yield a profit.

if they listen: The variant "They do not…" differs in only one to two letters.

For all the gentiles are uncircumcised…: Jeremiah 9:25.

This uncircumcised Philistine: 1 Samuel 17:36, referring to Goliath.

Lest the daughters…: 2 Samuel 1:2.

3:11 cont. *An Excursus on Circumcision*

R. Eleazar b. Azariah said:
The foreskin is repulsive since the wicked are thereby made shameful
as it is said:
For all the gentiles are uncircumcised.[48]
R. Ishmael says:
Great is circumcision, for thirteen covenants were concluded through it.
R. Yose[49] says:
Great is circumcision, for it overrides the severe Sabbath.
R. Joshua b. Qorhah says:
Great is circumcision, for the righteous Moses received no postponement
in its regard for even an hour.
R. Nehemiah says:
Great is circumcision, for it overrides skin afflictions.
Rabbi[50] says:
Great is circumcision,[51]
for despite all the commandments performed by our father Abraham,
he was not called complete until he was circumcised,
as it says:
Go before me and be perfect.
Another matter:
Great is circumcision, since but for it the Holy One who is Blessed
would not have created his world,
as it says:

---

[48] **MJ, K, P** repeat the entire verse.   [49] **MJ, K, P**: "R. Yose the Galilean."
[50] **K**: "R. Meir."   [51] **K** restores this line in the margin.

---

the wicked are thereby made shameful: In standard editions the second half of Jeremiah 9:25, *all the house of Israel are uncircumcised of heart*, is not repeated here even though R. Eleazar b. Azariah's point really derives from that half. (See n. 48.)

thirteen covenants: Genesis 17, which contains the instruction to Abraham that his male descendants be circumcised, contains thirteen occurrences of the word "covenant." See also the comment of Rabbi below.

the severe Sabbath: Violating the law of Sabbath rest generally carries severe penalty (Exodus 31:14; 35:2), but the Torah specifically commands that circumcision take place on the eighth day, even on the Sabbath (see Leviticus 12:3). See also *Shabbat* chapter 19.

Moses received no postponement: The reference is to Exodus 4:25–27, but commentators differ on the precise interpretation: either Moses was punished at once for neglecting his son's circumcision, or he was expected to have carried out the procedure at once but delayed.

skin afflictions: See Leviticus 13. It is forbidden to remove the signs of the disease from one's body, but if such a sign appears on the foreskin it may be removed at the time of circumcision (*Nega'im* 7:4–5).

Go before me…: Genesis 17:1.

Thus says the Lord: If not for my covenant day and night,
I would not have set the laws of heaven and earth.[52]

Chapter Four

4:1–5:6 Vows to Accept No Benefit from Another or to Give No Benefit to Another

4 There is no difference[53] between one from whom his fellow has vowed to accept no benefit
and one from whom he has vowed to accept no food,
except the treading of the foot,
and vessels in which one would not prepare food.[54]
One from whom his fellow has vowed to accept no food[55]—
may not lend him a sifter or a sieve or a millstone or an oven,
but he may lend him a shirt or a ring[56] or a cloak or nose-rings,
and anything in which one would not prepare food.
A place where such are hired out—
he is forbidden.

2 One from whom his fellow has vowed to accept no benefit—

---

[52] MJ, K, and some other medieval witnesses add "Another matter: Great is circumcision, for it is equivalent to all the commandments in the Torah, as it is said, *Behold the blood of the covenant which the Lord has entered with you concerning all these matters*" (Exodus 24:8).

[53] Lit. "There is nothing between…"   [54] P has "life," corrected to "food" between the lines.

[55] MJ: "benefit of food," combining the two terms.   [56] K, P: "rings," placed at the end of the list.

Thus says the Lord…: Jeremiah 33:25. Exodus 24:8, cited in the longer reading (see n. 52) refers to the blood of sacrifices. Here the Mishnah declares the blood of the covenant *par excellence* (blood of circumcision) equal to "all these matters," that is, all the commandments of the Torah.

4:1 *benefit*: In general, the following series of rules understands "benefit" as involving only the direct transfer of value from one person to the other. Financial benefit that is obtained obliquely is generally permitted. Exceptions to this generalization will be noted in their place.

treading of the foot: Access to the other's property. The right to cross another's field constitutes benefit but not nourishment.

nose-rings: Or earrings.

where such are hired out: By sparing his fellow the need to spend money on the hire, he has made it easier for him to obtain food; this violates the vow.

4:2 *contributes his sheqel*: Every male Jew was expected to provide a half-*sheqel* every year to support the Temple in Jerusalem (see *Sheqalim*). If B has vowed to accept no benefit from A, A may nevertheless pay the *sheqel* on behalf of B because no material benefit necessarily comes to B from such an action; even if B completely fails to pay, the Temple will continue to function and B will continue to be included in the public sacrifices.

contributes his *sheqel*, and repays his debt,
and returns his lost property to him.
A place where one takes payment for this—
let the benefit fall to the Sanctuary.

3 And he contributes his *terumah* and tithes with his knowledge,
and offers on his behalf:
the bird sacrifices[57] of *zavim*,
bird sacrifices of *zavot*,
or bird sacrifices of women after childbirth,
or purgation offerings or guilt offerings;
and he teaches him midrash, laws, and legends
but he shall not teach him Scripture.
But he teaches his sons and his daughters[58] Scripture.

[57] Lit. "nests."   [58] K, P lack "his daughters."

repays his debt: No money has passed directly from A to B; the only benefit to B is nonmaterial, in that his creditor will not harass him or threaten to seize his property. If B himself is A's creditor and A repays him, B is merely retrieving his own property.

returns his lost property: The object in question already belongs to B.

takes payment: Returning lost objects is a commandment of the Torah (Deuteronomy 22:3) and one who does so should not expect a reward. Nevertheless, in certain locations those who performed this commandment were customarily paid for their expenses or lost wages.

to the Sanctuary: Despite B's vow A may return B's lost possessions, but if A declines payment for this action B may not keep the money, as that would constitute concrete material benefit which A has conferred on him. Instead, B must deliver the same amount to the Temple treasury.

4:3 *And he contributes*: A continuation of the provisions in 4:2. Agricultural produce in the Land of Israel was subject to various Torah-based taxes; in particular *terumah* (see chapter 2 above, and *Terumot*; a levy of about two percent), ten percent of the remainder to the Levites (this was the so-called "first tithe"; see *Ma'aserot*), and a further ten percent of the reduced remainder given to the poor in some years and kept in other years for consumption in Jerusalem (the "second tithe" and "poor tithe"; see *Ma'aser Sheni*). Despite B's vow, A may meet these obligations on B's behalf. Commentators differ as to whose produce A uses. If he uses B's produce, then B has derived no material benefit from A's action and the vow has not been violated. If A uses his own produce, then the case resembles A's payment of B's debt in the preceding paragraph: B does benefit from A's action, but no material gain passes directly between them. (If A failed to fulfill these obligations on B's behalf, B might simply neglect them.)

with his knowledge: Commentators vary, but the simplest explanations are either that A can use his own produce without B's knowledge but he cannot take B's property, even for a religious purpose, without informing him, or that B knows what A is doing and tacitly consents.

offers on his behalf: A can supply birds which B is obligated to offer as a sacrifice (Leviticus 12:8; 15:14, 29) and any other sacrifices as well; again, no material benefit passes directly from one to the other. The Babylonian Talmud interprets this rule as pertaining to a priest: a priest may offer sacrifices on behalf of one who has vowed to receive no benefit from him. It is true that in some cases he thereby allows the other to consume a portion of the sacrifice, and this is a substantial material benefit, but he is fulfilling his sacred obligation as a priest and not acting on his own initiative.

bird sacrifices: Lit. "nests." See *Qinnim* introduction.

and he teaches him: These were subjects normally taught without a fee.

Scripture: Teachers of Scripture were normally paid. If A teaches B but refuses payment, he has caused material benefit to accrue to B. He may, however, teach B's children; he is only helping B fulfill a commandment (see Deuteronomy 6:7), which is not a material benefit.

And he supports his wife and children,
even though the other is obliged to support them.
But he shall not feed his cattle,
whether pure or impure.
R. Eliezer says:
He feeds the impure,
but he does not feed the pure.
They said to him:
What is the difference[59] between impure and pure?
He said to them:
The pure, its life belongs to Heaven while its body is the owner's;[60]
but the impure, its life and its body belong to Heaven.[61]
They said to him:
Even an impure animal,
its life belongs to Heaven but its body is his,
since if he wishes, he can sell it to gentiles or feed it to the dogs.

4 One from whom his fellow has vowed to accept no benefit,
and[62] he comes in to visit him—
he stands,
but he does not sit.
And he gives him personal healing,[63]

[59] Lit. "What is between…" [60] Lit. "his."
[61] "Soul…Heaven" missing in **K**, and restored in the margin.
[62] Some witnesses lack "and" implying: "he [the other] may enter to visit him."
[63] Lit. "cure of his life."

supports his wife and children: Again, A has saved money for B, but no material benefit has passed directly between them.

feed his cattle: By providing nourishment for B's cattle, A has maintained their value, a future material benefit.

whether pure or impure: It does not matter whether the cattle are of a species permitted to Jews (*pure*) or not (*impure*).

its life belongs to Heaven…: The life of any creature *belongs to Heaven*, but in the case of a permitted species the owner can eat its flesh and so has a material stake in its well-being. He cannot use an impure species in this way, and it seems that R. Eliezer therefore holds that he has no material stake in its nourishment. The anonymous opinion points out an obvious flaw in this reasoning.

4:4 *comes in to visit*: The host is restricted from benefit, and the visitor's activity is limited accordingly. According to the Mishnah, a visit does not confer a material benefit. Some commentators posit that the one receiving the visit is ill, so that the visit fulfills a commandment.

does not sit: As with the return of lost objects in 4:2, the problem is that in certain locations people were paid to spend time with the sick. If the visitor in this case declines such payment, he has rendered a material benefit to the host in violation of the vow. Other commentators simply hold that if the visitor sits down and stays too long the host may receive pleasure, and this would be a forbidden benefit. The term "benefit" would then not refer to anything of substance but simply "pleasure" or "satisfaction." See below for other examples of this usage.

personal healing: The vow may be set aside in view of the commandment to heal one's fellow. This obligation is derived from the commandment (Deuteronomy 22:2) to restore property that is in danger of loss: there is no more valuable "property" than health.

but not financial healing.[64]
And he bathes with him in a large tub,
but not a small one.
And he sleeps with him in a bed.
R. Judah says:
In the sunny season but not in the rainy season,
because he gives him benefit.
And he reclines with him on a bed
and eats with him at a table,
but not from the same plate.
But he eats with him from a plate that goes around.
He does not eat with him from the trough that is before the workers
and[65] he may not work with him in the same furrow[66]—
the words of R. Meir.
But the Sages say:
He does so at a distance from him.

5 One from whom his fellow has vowed to accept no benefit:
before the Seventh Year—
he does not go down into his field,
and he does not eat from the fruit that hangs over;
and during the Seventh Year—
he does not go down into his field,
but he eats from the fruit that hangs over.
If he vowed regarding food:

[64] Lit. "cure of his money." [65] Var. lacks "and." [66] Or "craft."

financial healing: The Talmud suggests this means care of his animals, but the actual language just suggests some kind of financial support. Perhaps the Talmud's proposal was provoked by the odd notion of "curing" material possessions.

but not a small one: A second body in the tub will raise the water level and increase the benefit of the bath.

he gives him benefit: By providing warmth. There is possibly a financial saving involved, but that does not seem to be the concern.

not from the same plate: Lest he intentionally leave the best portions for the other.

a plate that goes around: Lit. "a plate that returns," that is, to the host. If the plate contains so much food that each person will take a portion and food will remain, concern over possible violation of the vow can be set aside.

the trough that is before the workers. Even if many workers share a meal from the same large container, this is not "a pot that goes around" because it will be empty by end of day, and if one takes too little one has left more for another.

he may not work with him: The variant without "and" implies that only this rule belongs to R. Meir; in that case the previous rule about the workers' trough reports an undisputed opinion.

in the same furrow: One person's labor will make the task easier for the other, which is a "benefit."

4:5 This paragraph is based on the distinction in 4:1 and explores the particular circumstances of the Sabbatical year.

fruit that hangs over the boundary of the field, which one can reach without actually entering the field. This fruit remains the property of the owner because it grows from a tree or plant in his field.

before the Seventh Year—
he goes down into his field,
but he does not eat the fruit;
and during the Seventh Year—
he goes down and he eats.

6 One from whom his fellow has vowed to accept no benefit:
he may not lend to him and may not borrow from him,
may not loan to him and may not loan from him,
and may not sell to him and may not buy from him.
If he said to him: "Lend me your cow,"
and he said to him: "It is not available,"
and he said: "*Qonam* if I ever plow my field with it":
if it was his way to plow—
he is forbidden and every [other] person is permitted;
if it was not his way to plow;[67]
he and every [other] person are forbidden.

7 One from whom his fellow has vowed to accept no benefit,
and he has nothing to eat—
he goes to the shopkeeper and says:
"Such-and-such a man is under a vow to accept no benefit from me,
and I don't know what to do."
He gives to him, and he comes and takes from this one.
If his house was to be constructed or his fence to be built or his field to be harvested

[67] "He…plow" absent in **K**, and supplied in the margin.

during the Seventh Year: Reflecting different opinions in the Palestinian Talmud, commentators differ as to whether the oath is uttered during the Seventh (Sabbatical) Year or at any time. During the Seventh Year all produce is legally ownerless and therefore there is no direct benefit that passes from one person to the other. The field itself, however, remains the possession of its owner; in keeping with the general law of private property, the other may not enter it.

vowed regarding food: See 4:1.

4:6 *lend…loan*: The Mishnah distinguishes two kinds of loans: loans of animals or objects for use (*lend*) and loan of money (*loan*).

"Lend me your cow": This begins a new scenario involving two people not yet restricted by a vow.

"Qonam if I ever plow my field with it": Angry at being refused, he vows never to use the cow at all.

if it was his way to plow: If he generally did the plowing himself, the vow ("if *I* ever plow") presumably refers to his own actions only.

if it was not his way: If he generally employed others to plow his field, the vow presumably includes their actions along with his own. The restriction is presumably not universal but limited to the oathtaker's own property and employees.

4:7 *He* the shopkeeper *gives to him* the needy person *and* the shopkeeper *comes and takes from this one*. The other now pays for the food that the needy person has taken. This arrangement was never explicitly established (legally the second is under no obligation to pay), and therefore the vow has not been violated. The same logic applies to the case involving the workers. They provide labor to the one restrained by the vow and the other pays them afterwards, but no such arrangement has ever been openly discussed.

he goes to the workers and says:
"Such-and-such a man is under a vow to accept no benefit from me,
and I don't know what to do."
They work with him, and come and take pay[68] from this one.

8 If they were walking on the way and he had nothing to eat—
he gives to another[69] as a gift,
and that one is permitted with respect to it.[70]
If no one else is with them—
he puts it on a rock or on a fence and says:
"These are hereby now ownerless for anyone who wants them,"
and that one takes and eats.
But R. Yose forbids.

Chapter Five

5 Joint owners who vowed to accept no benefit from one another
are forbidden to enter the courtyard.
R. Eliezer b. Jacob says:
This one enters his own, and that one enters his own.[71]
And[72] both are forbidden to set up a mill or an oven or to raise chickens.
If one of them was forbidden by vow to accept benefit from his fellow
he may not enter the courtyard.
R. Eliezer b. Jacob says:
He may say to him:

[68] K, P: "their pay."   [69] MJ: "to others."   [70] MJ, P: "That one takes and eats and is permitted."
[71] K restores the second half of the sentence above the line.
[72] MJ, K, P lack "and" here and in the last line of the mishnah.

4:8 The opening lines reappear in 5:6.

he had nothing to eat: The one who was forbidden to derive benefit. This further develops the case of 4:7.

he the one from whom the oathtaker may not benefit who has spare food and wants to help *gives to another* someone not bound by the vow, who can give it in turn to the one without anything to eat.

R. Yose forbids: Since no one else is around, the fiction is too transparent.

5:1 *Joint owners*. People who share ownership of a courtyard that is too small simply to be divided.

R. Eliezer b. Jacob holds the opinion that the courtyard can be conceptually divided according to the partners' respective habits of entry and use.

a mill or an oven…: Any partner can refuse to permit such activity in shared property on the ground that it impedes general access. If one partner wishes to do so and the other does not object, he has allowed a benefit to accrue to the first; in the present case this would violate the vow. Uncertainty over the presence of "and" in the text creates uncertainty whether this rule continues R. Eliezer b. Jacob's dissent or represents the common opinion.

"I am entering my own, and I am not entering yours."
And one compels the one who vows to sell his share.

2 If someone from the marketplace was forbidden by vow
to accept benefit from one of them—
he may not enter the courtyard.
R. Eliezer b. Jacob says:
He can say to him:
"I am entering your partner's and I am not entering yours."

3 One forbidden by vow to accept benefit from his fellow
and [the other] owns a bathhouse or olive press rented out in the town:[73]
if he has an interest[74] in them—
[the oath taker] is forbidden;
if he has no interest in them—
he is permitted.
One who says to his fellow:
"*Qonam* that I enter your house or buy your field":
if he died or sold them to another—
he is permitted.
"*Qonam* that I enter this house or buy this field":
if he died or sold them to another—
he is forbidden.

4 "I am hereby banned to you!"—
the one under the oath is forbidden.
"You are hereby banned to me!"—
the one speaking the oath is forbidden.
"I to you and you to me!"—
they both are forbidden.

[73] P lacks "in the town." [74] Lit. "a grip."

And…one compels: Here too uncertainty about "and" creates uncertainty as to whether this continues R. Eliezer b. Jacob's dissent or is a separate, undisputed rule.

5:2 *someone from the marketplace*: Any third party.

one of them: One of the partners.

5:3 *if he has an interest in them*: A percentage of the revenue beyond the fixed rental he receives, or some other right of ownership such as the use of storage space that he has retained. In such a case the facility remains to some degree the property of the owner, and the target of the vow may not use it at all. If the owner has retained no such rights, the facility can be deemed the property of the tenant and the vow no longer applies. This distinction seems to apply whether the target of the vow has paid for the use of the facility or has utilized it at no charge.

if he died…he is permitted: The language of the vow stipulated that the property belong to the object of the vow personally, and ownership has now passed to the buyer or the heirs.

he is forbidden: The language of the vow simply identified the house or the field.

5:4 *banned*: Heb. *herem*. Lit. "dedicated to destruction," thus totally unavailable for ordinary human use.

the one under the oath is forbidden: One person can forbid another to derive any benefit from one's own property.

And they both are permitted with respect to something [established by][75]
those who came up from Babylonia,
and forbidden with respect to something belonging to[76] that same town.

5 And what is something belonging to those who came up from Babylonia?
Such as the Temple Mount, and the Temple Courts,
and the well in the middle of the road.
And what is something belonging to that same town?
Such as the marketplace,
and the bathhouse,
and the synagogue,
and the ark,
and the books,
and one who writes his share over to the *Nasi*.
R. Judah says:
Both one who writes his share over to the *Nasi*
and one who writes his share over to an ordinary person.
What is the difference[77] between one who writes his share over to the *Nasi*
and one who writes his share over to an ordinary person?
One who writes his share over to the *Nasi*,
he need not formally transfer ownership.[78]
But the Sages say:

---

[75] Lit. "belonging to." [76] K: "in that same town." [77] Lit. "What is between…"
[78] K, P add "and one who writes his share over to an ordinary person needs to formally transfer ownership."

---

who came up from Babylonia: The generation that returned from the Babylonian Exile was said to have established public access to certain amenities, and no one can forbid another to use them. These items are identified in the following mishnah.

belonging to that same town: If the town of their common residence has common local amenities, those under this vow may not use them: the one speaking the vow is part owner of these, and they are considered his property for purposes of this vow.

5:5 *the well in the middle of the road*: The returning exiles created wells on public property for the use of pilgrims on the way to Jerusalem.

and one who writes his share over to the Nasi: At first glance this appears to be another item in the list of things belonging to the town, but "one who writes his share over to the *Nasi*" is clearly not such an item. The predominant interpretation, based on the Babylonian Talmud, is that anyone who has by vow forbidden another to enjoy the common town property (see 5:4) can circumvent his vow by transferring his share in that property to the *Nasi*; commentators differ as to whether this is the Patriarch or the president of the local court. The Palestinian Talmud suggests emending the text to "he needs to write his property over…"

ordinary person: In fact he can transfer his ownership to anyone.

formally transfer ownership: Normally ownership in property must be formally transferred (see *Qiddushin* 1:1); the new owner need not be present but can be represented by a third party. R. Judah holds that the *Nasi* by virtue of his office can receive ownership of anything by the present owner's simple declaration, without such formal transfer.

Both this one and this one need to formally transfer ownership;
they spoke of the *Nasi* only in light of the usual practice.[79]
R. Judah says:
The men of the Galilee do not need to write,
for their ancestors have already written for them.

6 One from whom his fellow has vowed to accept no benefit,
and he has nothing to eat—
he gives it to another as a gift,
and that one is permitted with respect to it.
It once happened in Bet Horon that someone's father
was forbidden benefit from him by a vow,
and he was marrying off his son.[80]
He said to his fellow:
The courtyard and the feast are given to you as a gift,
but they are set before you only so that Father will come and eat with us at the feast.
He said to him:
If they are mine, they are hereby consecrated to Heaven.
He said to him:
I did not give you my property in order that you consecrate it to Heaven!
He said to him:
You gave your property to me only in order that you and your father
could eat and drink and become reconciled,
and the sin would hang from his head.
When the matter came before the Sages they said:
Any gift that is not[81] such that if he consecrates it it is not consecrated,[82]
is not a gift.

[79] Lit. "of the present," "of what is." [80] K: "his daughter," corrected in the margin to "his son."
[81] Var. lacks "not." [82] K, P: "it is consecrated."

the usual practice: Even the *Nasi* must formally receive ownership. The rule does not mean to ascribe special legal rights to the *Nasi*, only to indicate that this procedure usually named him when it was carried out.

their ancestors have already written: In the Galilee the local practice always ascribed ownership of common property to the *Nasi*; no special act in any specific case was required.

5:6 *he has nothing to eat*: The rule is quoted from 4:8. Commentators derive two implications from the association of this rule with the incident reported here: the rule also applies in town and not only "on the way," but the gift cannot be transparently false.

his head: A euphemism for "my head."

If he consecrates it it is not consecrated: The present version seems incoherent. According to the variant in the manuscripts, the translation would be: "Any gift which is not [such] that if he consecrates it, it is consecrated is not a gift." The variant that omits the first "not" requires that the second be retained.

Chapter Six

6:1–8:6 *Clarification of Concrete Terms*

6 One who vows [to abstain] from the cooked—
is permitted with respect to the roasted and the potted.[83]
If he said:
"*Qonam* that I taste cooked food"—
he is forbidden with respect to soft food made in a pot
and permitted with respect to thick,
and he is permitted with respect to a soft-cooked egg and a gourd heated in ashes.

2 One who vows from food made in a pot—
is forbidden only from food which is boiled.
If he said:
"*Qonam* that I taste anything lowered into a pot"—
he is forbidden from all foods cooked in a pot.

3 "From the pickled"—
he is forbidden from only pickled vegetables.
"That I taste anything pickled"—
he is forbidden with respect to all pickled foods.
"From the boiled"—
he is forbidden from only boiled meat.[84]

---

[83] Or "boiled."   [84] Var. "vegetables." **MJ**, **P** add "the words of R. Judah."

6:1 The Mishnah returns to the project of clarifying the implications of vows that mention everyday types of food.

potted: Either overcooked or undercooked; commentators differ.

thick: "Cooked food" is food that is soft and eaten with bread, that is, by dipping bread into the dish. Food so thick that it cannot be eaten with a spoon, or would normally not be eaten with bread in this way, is not in this category (Babylonian Talmud).

soft-cooked egg: Or an egg boiled down to so small a size that it can be swallowed whole; these were normally consumed for medicinal purposes, and not eaten with bread as part of a meal. Heb. *teramita* or *tromita*, presumably derived from a Greek term that modern commentators have not successfully identified.

gourd: Or cucumber or pumpkin. These might be softened through burial in hot ash, but this was not considered a form of cooking.

6:2 *food which is boiled*: Foods based on grain that has been softened through thorough boiling (Talmuds); this was apparently the generally accepted meaning of the phrase.

all foods cooked in a pot: And not just the softened grains mentioned in the initial phrase, perhaps other types of food, perhaps foods prepared in a different manner.

6:3 *words of R. Judah*: This phrase normally implies dispute, but the Mishnah reports no other opinion. As noted in n. 84, certain witnesses also contain a reference to R. Judah in the clause about boiled meat.

"That I taste anything boiled"—
he is forbidden with respect to all boiled foods.
"From the roasted"—
he is forbidden from only roasted meat—
the words of R. Judah.
"That I taste anything roasted"—
he is forbidden with respect to all roasted foods.
"From the salted"—
he is forbidden from salted fish.
"That I taste anything salted"—
he is forbidden with respect to all salted foods.

4 "Fish, fishes I shall not taste"—
he is forbidden with respect to them,
both large and small,
both salted and unsalted,
both raw and cooked.
And he is permitted with respect to mashed pickled fish and with respect to brine.
One who vows from chopped mixed fishes—
is forbidden with respect to mashed pickled fish
and permitted with respect to brine and fish sauce.
One who vows from mashed pickled fish—
is forbidden[85] with respect to brine and fish sauce.

5 One who vows from milk—
is permitted with respect to curd.
But R. Yose forbids.
From curd—
is permitted with respect to milk.
Abba Saul says:
One who vows from cheese
is forbidden with respect to it,
both salted and unsalted.

[85] MJ, K, P: "permitted."

6:4 *Fish, fishes*: Commentators differ as to whether the vow must include both the singular and plural forms or merely either of them.

mashed pickled fish: meaning of Heb. *tarit* uncertain. Perhaps herring or sardine, perhaps any species. Since the mash is not recognizable as fish it is excluded from the vow.

brine: Liquid in which fish has been pickled.

chopped mixed fishes: meaning of Heb. *tsahana* uncertain. Others translate "mudfish," a specific species; in that case *tarit* too must be a particular subspecies of *tsahana*.

mashed pickled fish—is forbidden...: Fermented fish and fish mashed or boiled into liquid sauces were widely used as condiments. If the mash is fine enough, it becomes difficult to distinguish from such fluids. But note the variant "permitted," as in the previous sentence.

6:5 *curd*: Or "whey."

6 One who vows from meat
is permitted with respect to the broth and the sediment.
But R. Judah forbids.
Said R. Judah:
It once happened that R. Tarfon forbade me[86] the eggs that had been cooked with[87] it.
They said to him:
And this is so! When?
If he says: "This meat is forbidden to me,"[88]
for[89] one who vows [to abstain] from something
and it becomes mixed with something else,
if there is enough to affect the taste—
it is forbidden.[90]

7 One who vows from wine
is permitted with respect to a cooked dish that has the taste of wine.
If he said:
"*Qonam* that I shall taste this wine"—
and it fell into a cooked dish,
if there is enough to affect the taste,
in such a case it is forbidden.
One who vows from grapes—
is permitted with respect to wine.
From[91] olives—
is permitted with respect to oil.
"*Qonam* I shall not taste these olives or grapes"—
he is forbidden with respect to them and that which emerges from them.

8 One who vows from dates
is permitted with respect to date honey.
From late grapes,
is permitted with respect to late-grape vinegar.
R. Judah b. Betera[92] says:

[86] **MB**: "us."   [87] **MJ, P**: "in."   [88] Lit. "This meat upon me."
[89] **MJ, K, P**: "but." This is almost certainly an error.   [90] **K, P**: "In such a case it is forbidden."
[91] **MJ, K, P** add "and" but **K** crosses it out.   [92] **P** restores "b. Betera" between the lines.

6:6 *broth*: The liquid in which the meat was cooked.

sediment: Or "jelly"; the coagulated material that remains stuck to the pot after it has been emptied.

forbade me: The variant "us" possibly implies that R. Judah himself had not necessarily vowed but R. Tarfon had taught all the disciples this rule.

And this is so! When? R. Judah's interlocutors limit R. Tarfon's ruling to a case where the speaker has vowed to abstain from a particular piece of meat. If that piece then gives its taste to a mixture of foods the whole is forbidden. However, one who simply vows to abstain from "meat" may eat eggs or broth or sediment, because in common speech the term "meat" does not include these.

6:7 *that which emerges from them*: Principally wine and oil, though possibly also any dish prepared with the indicated grapes and olives. In the latter case the rule in 6:6 would apply.

6:8 *late grapes*: Grapes that do not ripen until after the regular season.

Whenever its derivative carries its name and he vows from it,
he is forbidden even with respect to that which emerges from it;
but the Sages permit.

9 One who vows from wine—
is permitted with respect to apple wine;
from[93] oil—
is permitted with respect to sesame oil;
from[94] honey—
is permitted with respect to date honey;
from vinegar—
is permitted with respect to late-grape vinegar;
from leeks—
is permitted with respect to scallions;
from vegetables—
is permitted with respect to wild vegetables,
because this is an attached name.[95]

10 From cabbage[96]—
is forbidden with respect to *ispargos*;
from *ispargos*—
is permitted with respect to cabbage;
from grits—
is forbidden with respect to potted grits,
but R. Yose permits.
From potted grits—
is permitted with respect to grits;
from potted grits—
is forbidden with respect to garlic;
but R. Yose permits.
From garlic—
is permitted[97] with respect to potted grits;
from lentils—

[93] **K, P** have "and from" but **K** crosses out "and."
[94] **MJ, K, P** have "and from" but **K** crosses out "and."   [95] **K** restores "name" in the margin.
[96] **MJ, P**: "One who vows…"   [97] **K**: "forbidden," corrected in the margin to "permitted."

its derivative carries its name: As in the preceding examples, *date* honey or *late-grape* vinegar. A less likely interpretation is the reverse of this: the origin substance is called by the name of its main product, e.g. dates being called "honey." The first part of this paragraph reflects the Sages' permissive opinion.

6:9 *scallions*: Or shallots, or porret; meaning of Hebrew is uncertain.

attached name: The permitted substances all have particular names and are not usually included in the generic category named in the vow. This phrase pertains to the entire paragraph, and not only the distinction between "vegetables" and "wild vegetables."

6:10 The discussion continues the clarifications begun above.

ispargos: Despite the similarity to "asparagus," the Hebrew probably denotes a particular type of cabbage.

potted grits: A mixture of mashed grits (probably beans), onions, and garlic. This explains the rule below that a vow to avoid potted grits entails the avoidance of garlic.

is forbidden with respect to lentil cakes;
but R. Yose permits.
From lentil cakes—
is permitted with respect to lentils.
"Wheat, wheats I shall not taste"—
he is forbidden with respect to them,
both flour and bread.
"Grit, grits I shall not taste"—
he is forbidden with respect to them,
both raw and cooked.
R. Judah says:
"*Qonam* that I taste grits or wheat"—
he is permitted to chew them raw.

Chapter Seven

7 One who vows from vegetables—
is permitted with respect to gourds;
but R. Aqiva forbids.
They said to R. Aqiva:
But is it not like a man who says to his agent:
"Buy me[98] vegetables,"
and he says: "I could find only gourds"?
He said to them:
This is so,
or perhaps he would say: "I could find only beans."
Rather gourds are included in the category "vegetables"

[98] K, P: "us."

---

lentil cakes: Toasted lentils bathed in honey.

"wheats": English has no such word, but the double singular/plural formulation echoes that of "fish, fishes" in 6:4, as does the double formulation "grit, grits," for which again English has no equivalent.

7:1 *"I could find only gourds"*: The agent is either consulting to find out whether gourds will satisfy the request, or reporting why he has bought nothing. In either case the question implies that the language of the vow (*vegetables*) does not normally cover gourds.

"beans": Or "pulses" or "legumes." R. Aqiva counters that the agent might ask a similar question about beans. Perhaps such questions imply that the particular item is included in the general category, but perhaps they imply the opposite. Such hypothetical inquiries do not help in resolving the initial dispute.

gourds are included in the category "vegetables": Having dismissed the usefulness of his interlocutors' hypothetical questions, R. Aqiva simply holds that gourds are indeed vegetables, but the agent has some reason to think they are not the sort of vegetables he was expected to obtain.

and beans are not in the category "vegetables."[99]
And he is forbidden with respect to moist Egyptian beans
and permitted with respect to dry.

2 One who vows from grain—
is forbidden with respect to dry[100] Egyptian beans—
the words of R. Meir;
but the Sages say:
He is forbidden with respect to only the five species.
R. Meir says:
One who vows from produce is forbidden with respect to only the five species,
but one who vows from grain is forbidden with respect to every grain,[101]
but he is permitted with respect to the fruit of trees and vegetables.

3 One who vows from clothing—
is permitted with respect to sackcloth or curtain material or a blanket.
If he said:
"*Qonam* that wool will come upon me"—
he is permitted to cover himself with woolen fleeces.
"That linen will come upon me"—
he is permitted to cover himself with flaxen stalks.
R. Judah says:
It is all according to the one making the vow.
If he was carrying such and sweating and had[102] a bad odor
and he said:
"*Qonam* that wool or linen will come upon me"—
he is permitted to cover himself,
but forbidden to throw them as a bundle over his shoulder.

---

[99] This line is missing from K and P but restored in the margin of K.
[100] MJ and P lack "dry."
[101] Lit. "Everything."
[102] Or "it had…"

---

and beans are not in the category "vegetables": As noted this line is absent from one manuscript and only restored in the margin of another. Retaining the line causes difficulty: whose opinion does it express? The initial dispute has nothing to do with beans, so this final ruling could fit with either opinion expressed there. Omission of the line leaves a clearer text: as noted in the previous paragraph, the assertion about gourds simply reflects R. Aqiva's opinion in his dispute with the others.

Egyptian beans: When still fresh ("moist") these were considered vegetables, but when dry they would be ground into flour and so were considered grain (see 7:2).

7:2 *five species*: Five species embraced by the Torah's rules concerning "grain": wheat, barley, spelt, oats, and rye. The dispute concerns the question whether "grain" or "produce" is the more inclusive term in everyday speech.

every grain: That is, everything that can be prepared as grains are prepared. The particular reference is to dried legumes, which can be ground into flour (as in 7:1 above); according to the variant all legumes are included, presumably because fresh ones can always be dried out. Even R. Meir concedes that other fruits and vegetables are never called "grain."

7:3 *according to the one making the vow*: According to the circumstances when the vow was uttered. The example that follows does not involve wearing.

4 One who vows from a house—
is permitted with respect to the upper floor—
the words of R. Meir;
but the Sages say:
An upper floor is included in "house."
One who vows[103] from the upper floor—
is permitted with respect to the house.

5 One who vows from a bed—
is permitted with respect to a cot—
the words of R. Meir;
but the Sages say:
A cot is included in "bed."
One who vows from a cot—
is permitted with respect to a bed.
One who vows from a town—
is permitted to enter the town Sabbath limit
but forbidden to enter its immediate outskirts;
but one who vows from a house is forbidden beyond the doorframe.

6 "*Qonam* these fruits to me,"[104]
"*Qonam* they are upon my mouth,"[105]
"*Qonam* they[106] are to my mouth"—
he is forbidden[107] with respect to their substitutes or their product.
"...that I eat" or "...that I taste"—
he is permitted with respect to their substitutes or their product,[108]

[103] K restores "one who vows" above the line.
[104] Lit. "on me."
[105] K, P place this example after the next.
[106] K restores "they" between the lines.
[107] K restores "forbidden" in the margin.
[108] K restores this line in the margin.

7:4 *upper floor*: This might have a separate owner and a separate entrance directly from the roof: see *Bava Metsiʿa* 10:1–3.

included in "house": The normal use of the word "house" refers to the entire structure.

7:5 *cot*: A type of stool used to climb onto a bed, or some sort of couch or chaise lounge.

Sabbath limit...immediate outskirts: An imaginary line was drawn around the town slightly more than seventy cubits (ca. thirty-five meters, or 105 feet) beyond its last house; this was called the *immediate outskirts* (*ibbur*) of the town and the vow was considered to cover everything within that line. The Sabbath limit (*tekhum*) was a second such boundary drawn two thousand cubits beyond the first. Those within the town could walk up to this line on the Sabbath and no further, but the territory between the two demarcations was not considered part of the town itself.

beyond the doorframe: The point at which the frame stops the door from swinging. Even though the outer thickness of the walls can be deemed an "extension" of the house, the vow permits access up to the point where the door touches the frame. This is the difference between a vow concerning a town, where the extension is forbidden, and a vow concerning a house; hence the last phrase begins with *but*.

7:6 *substitutes*: Money or other produce for which the forbidden fruits were exchanged.

product: Produce grown from the seeds of the forbidden fruits.

permitted: In the first type of vow, even though he has specified the mouth, it is presumed that he has absolutely renounced all benefit, including commercial benefit, from the fruits in question. The second type is specifically limited to eating or tasting those fruits in particular.

with something the seeds of which perish;
but with something the seeds of which do not perish[109]
even[110] the product of their product is forbidden.

7 One who says to his wife:
"*Qonam* the work of your hands to me,"[111]
"*Qonam* they are upon my mouth,"[112]
"*Qonam* they are to my mouth"—
he is forbidden with respect to their substitutes or their product.
"…that I eat" or "…that I taste"—
he is permitted with respect to their substitutes or their product
with something the seeds of which perish;
but with something the seeds of which do not perish
even[113] the product of their product is forbidden.

8 "That which you make I shall not eat until Passover,"
"That which you make I shall not wear[114] until Passover":
if she made such before Passover—
he is permitted to eat or wear such after Passover.
"That which you make until Passover I shall not eat,"
or "That which you make until Passover I shall not wear":
if she made such before Passover—
he is forbidden to eat or wear such after Passover.

9 "That you derive benefit from me until Passover,
if you go[115] to your father's house until the Festival":
if she went before Passover—
she is forbidden his benefit until Passover;
after Passover—

---

[109] **P** restores "the seeds of which" and "perish" in the margin. [110] **K, P** lack "even."
[111] Lit. "on me."   [112] **K, P** place this example after the next.   [113] **K, P** lack "even."
[114] Lit. "cover myself," and so throughout.   [115] **K** restores "go" in the margin.

---

perish: If the seeds of the forbidden fruit disappear as they sprout, the new plants are considered free of the vow. If the seeds remain, however, they carry the vow with them into all succeeding generations. Commentators differ as to whether this distinction applies to both halves of the paragraph or only the second.

7:7 This paragraph repeats the preceding, now with respect to the product of a wife's labor. The repeated reference to seeds implies that the wife has been engaged in planting or in farm labor of some kind.

7:8 "*I shall not eat until Passover…until Passover I shall not eat*": The distinction between the two parts of the mishnah has to do with whether *until Passover* is taken to refer to the production or the husband's consumption.

7:9 *the Festival*: The autumn Festival of Booths (Sukkot). Both cases presume that the vow is uttered after that festival but before Passover the following spring. The difference between them is that in the first case the time of the condition extends beyond the time of the prohibition while in the second the reverse is true. The first case therefore raises the possibility that she will derive benefit from her husband before the vow is activated but then retroactively activate it later on. In this situation her behavior is no longer subject to regulation, but she has transgressed the law in Numbers 30 and is subject to punishment on that account. Commentators differ as to whether her husband is also guilty for having allowed her to engage in behavior that might later turn out to have been forbidden.

it falls under *he shall not profane his word.*
"That you derive benefit from me until the Festival
if you go to your father's house until Passover":
if she went before Passover—
she is forbidden his benefit until the Festival,
but she is permitted to go after Passover.

Chapter Eight

8 "*Qonam* that I taste wine today"—
he is forbidden only until it grows dark;
"…this week"—
he is forbidden the entire week and the Sabbath [belongs to] the preceding;[116]
"…this month"—
he is forbidden the entire month and the New Moon belongs to the following;
"…this year"—
he is forbidden the entire year,
and the New Year belongs to the future;
"…this Sabbatical cycle"—
he is forbidden the entire Sabbatical cycle,
and the Seventh Year [belongs to] the preceding.[117]
But if he said:
"…one day,"
"…one week, "
"…one month, "
"…one year,"
"[or]…one Sabbatical cycle"—
he is forbidden from day to day.

[116] K, in the margin, corrects to "and the Sabbath belongs to the preceding [week]."
[117] K: "the past Seventh Year," but corrected in margin.

he shall not profane his word: Numbers 30:3.

8:1 *"week"*: Lit. "Sabbath."

the Sabbath [belongs to] the preceding: The language of the standard printed editions and of most witnesses is obscure. The correction in K (see n. 116) conveys the most common interpretation: When one undertakes a vow for *this week*, it refers to a seven-day period ending with Saturday, and the Sabbath day counts as the final day of the preceding week. The same rule applies for the *Sabbatical Year*. On the other hand, *New Moons* and *New Years* are at the beginnings of intervals and are normally associated with the periods that follow them. Commentators vary as to whether these rules apply only to vows spoken at the start of the indicated period or at any later time as well.

from day to day: The formulations *this week*, etc. refer to commonly accepted calendric intervals, but the formulations *one week*, etc. refer to defined numbers of days as measured from the day of the vow to the end of one week, month, and so on.

2 "...until Passover—
he is forbidden until it arrives;
"...until it will be [Passover]"—
he is forbidden until it departs.
"...until before Passover"[118]—
R. Meir says:
He is forbidden until it arrives.
R. Yose says:
He is forbidden until it departs.
   3 "...until the harvest,"
"...until the grape harvest,"
[or] "...until the olive harvest"—
he is forbidden only until it begins.
This is the general rule:
Anything the time of which is fixed
and he said: "...until it will arrive"—
he is forbidden until it arrives.
If he said: "...until it will be"—
he is forbidden until it departs.
And anything the time of which is not fixed,
whether he said "...until it will be," or he said "...until it[119] will arrive"—
he is forbidden only until it arrives.
   4 "...until the summer"
[or] "...until it will be summer"—
until the people start to gather in the baskets;
"...until summer passes"—
until they fold up the knives;[120]

[118] Var. "until the face of Passover."
[119] The words "it...it" were absent in **K** and restored in the margins.   [120] Meaning obscure.

8:2 The Mishnah provides further detailed interpretation of common ways of referring in vows to intervals of time.

"until before Passover": A well-attested variant, different in only one letter, reads "until the face of Passover." This has been variously interpreted to mean the beginning of the holiday, the beginning of its last day, and the end of the last day.

R. Yose: Perhaps he meant until just before the last hour of the holiday. Both the Palestinian Talmud and the Babylonian Talmud find reason to suggest that the attributions to R. Meir and R. Yose should be reversed.

8:3 *"until"*: Under certain conditions this can be taken to mean "up to and including." See the next annotation.

time...is fixed: If the vow specifies an event with predictable onset and predictable duration, the phrase *"until it will be"* can be understood (as above) to include the length of that event. Otherwise the speaker cannot have meant to place himself under a limitation of unknown duration, and the vow is deemed to lapse as soon as the specified event *arrives*.

8:4 The Mishnah proceeds to give examples of intervals "whose time is not fixed."

"fold up the knives": The knives used in cutting figs and preparing them to be pressed into cakes; these knives would be folded up and put away when the summer fig harvest was over. Alternative translations: when the mats for drying the figs have been folded up, or until the figs themselves have been set out in layers.

"…until the harvest"—
until the people start to reap the wheat harvest
but not the barley harvest.
Everything is according to the place of his vow:
if he was in the hill country—
as in the hill country,
and if he was in the valley—
[as] in the valley.
    5 "…until the rains"
[or] "…until the rains will be"—
until the second rains.
R. Simeon b. Gamaliel says:
Until the time of the rains arrives.
"…until the rains stop"—
until Nisan has completely departed,
the words of R. Meir.
R. Judah says:
Until Passover has departed.
"*Qonam* that I taste wine this year"—
if the year is made a leap year,
he is forbidden during the year and its extension.
"…until the beginning of Adar"— [121]
until the beginning of the first Adar.
"…until the end of Adar"—
until the end of the first Adar.[122]

---

[121] This line was missing from **K** and restored in the margin.
    [122] Var. "the second Adar."

---

but not the barley harvest: *Harvest* unclarified means the wheat harvest. Since the barley harvest precedes the wheat harvest, it begins before the condition *until the harvest* has been met.

the place of his vow…the hill country: When he uttered the vow he was in the hill country, where the harvest season begins later; he must honor his vow until that point even if he has moved into the valley.

in the valley: Similarly, if he moves to the hill country he may end his vow when the valley has begun its harvest.

8:5 *the second rains*: The second of three distinct periods of autumn rain in the Land of Israel.

the time of the rains: Even if no rain has in fact come down. The reference is presumably to the aforementioned second rains.

Nisan: The spring month during which Passover falls on the fifteenth day. Cf. *Ta'anit* 1:7.

is made a leap year: At the time of the Mishnah leap years were not set in advance according to a formula. The appropriate authorities would consult during late winter and determine whether an extra month was needed to make sure Passover fell in spring as required by Deuteronomy 16:1 (*Rosh Hashanah* 1:4–2:9). When this was judged necessary, the previous month of Adar was repeated (see below).

its extension: The second Adar.

until the end of the first Adar: Even though a month named Adar must yet run its course, a month with that name has ended. The variant reading (see n. 122) reflects the opposite logic: the time of year called Adar has not yet ended.

R. Judah says:
"*Qonam* that I taste wine until it is Passover"—
he is forbidden only until the night of Passover,[123]
for this one intended only until the hour when it is people's way to drink wine.

    6 If he said:
"*Qonam* that I taste meat until it is the fast,"[124]—
he is forbidden only until the night of the fast,
for this one intended only until the hour when it is people's way to eat meat.
R. Yose his son says:
"*Qonam* that I taste garlic until it is the Sabbath"—
he is forbidden only until the night of the Sabbath,
for this one intended only until the hour when it is people's way to eat garlic.

8:7 Vows Interpreted by Context

    7 One who says to his fellow:
"*Qonam* that I derive any benefit from you unless you come and take for your son[125]
a *kor* of wheat and two barrels of wine"—
in such a case, this one can nullify his vow without the ruling of a Sage,
and say to him:
"You spoke[126] only on account of my honor: this is my honor!"
And so too one who says to his fellow:[127]
"*Qonam* that you derive any benefit from me unless you[128] come and give my son

---

[123] **MB** lacks this line.   [124] **K, P**: "a fast."
[125] **K, P**: "sons."
[126] **MJ, P**: "I spoke to you." **K**: "you spoke to you," but "to you" is marked for deletion.
[127] **K** restores "to his fellow" in the margin.   [128] **P** restores "you" between the lines.

8:6 Continuing the teaching of R. Judah.

"the fast": Perhaps the Day of Atonement, which is often simply called "the fast," perhaps some other scheduled fast day which will come sooner. The variant "a fast" supports this second possibility.

people's way to eat meat: In the large meal preceding the fast.

R. Yose his son: The son of R. Judah.

garlic: See 3:10 above.

8:7 The text moves from interpreting the language of a vow to interpreting the likely intention underlying it.

"kor": Around seven bushels.

nullify: The word normally denotes the right of a father to nullify his daughter's vow or of a husband to nullify his wife's (Numbers 30 and *Nedarim* chapters 10–11), but here the reference is to an encounter between any private individuals. Here, *this one*, the object of the oath, who needed to take a gift of wheat and wine, *can* effect the *nullification of the oath* of the other by his statement.

"this is my honor": The real honor was your eagerness to make such a gift. Alternatively, the greater honor is to refuse gifts that one does not need.

"and give my son": Several modern editions and translations have "son" here. The consonantal text is the same, but **K** and **P** unambiguously have "sons," and there is no reason that this clause should not match the preceding.

a *kor* of wheat and two barrels of wine"—
R. Meir says:
He is forbidden until he gives,
but the Sages say:
Even this one can nullify his vow without the ruling of a Sage,
and say to him: "I am hereby as if I had received."
If they were urging him to marry his sister's daughter
and he said:
"*Qonam* that she derive any benefit from me forever,"
and so too one who was divorcing his wife and said:
"*Qonam* that my wife derive any benefit from me forever,"[129]—
in such a case these are permitted to derive benefit from him,
since this one only meant matters of matrimony.
If he was urging his fellow to eat at his home,
and he said:
"*Qonam* that I enter your house"
[or] "…that I taste a drop of cold water of yours"—
he is permitted to enter his house and drink his cold water,
since this one only meant matters of eating and drinking.

Chapter Nine

9:1–10 *Release from Vows*

9 R. Eliezer says:
One opens for a man with the honor of his father and his mother;
but the Sages forbid.
Said R. Zadok:
Before one opens for him with the honor of his father and his mother

---

[129] K restores this clause in the margin.

"as if I had received" the indicated gift: The one who made the vow can indirectly withdraw the demand which the vow was meant to reinforce.

his sister's daughter: Or anyone else.

matters of matrimony: The vow taker intended to cut off marriage negotiations, not actually to prohibit the woman from benefit.

eating and drinking: A full-scale meal, not a mere sip of water.

9:1 *One opens for a man*: One who has vowed and regrets the vow can approach a Sage or technically even a panel of ordinary people, express his regret at having vowed, and request release from the vow. If such a person requests release without first expressing regret, the Sage or one of the panelists can *open for him* by asking questions designed to elicit an expression of regret. The answer that justifies releasing the speaker of the vow has the form "If I had known…I would not have vowed." See 2:1n.

the honor of his father and his mother: That is: If you had known that your vow would bring dishonor to your parents, would you have desisted? (See 1:1 on *vows of the wicked*.)

one opens for him with the honor of the Omnipresent;
if so there are no vows!
And the Sages agree with R. Eliezer in a matter between him and his father or his mother,
that one opens for him with the honor of his father and his mother.

2 R. Eliezer further said:
One opens with something new,[130]
but the Sages forbid.
How?
If he said:
"*Qonam* that I derive benefit from a certain man,"
and [the other] became a scribe;
or was soon[131] going to marry off his son,
and he said:
"If I had known that he would become a scribe," or
"...that he would soon marry off his son,"
I would not have vowed.
"*Qonam* that I[132] enter this house,"
and it was made a synagogue:
and he said:
"If I had known it would be made a synagogue,
I would not have vowed"—
R. Eliezer permits
but the Sages forbid.

3 R. Meir says:
There are things that are like something new but are not like something new,

---

[130] Lit. "newborn."   [131] **MB** lacks this word, but the meaning seems unaffected.
[132] **K** restores "I" in the margin.

---

the honor of the Omnipresent: Instead of parents, one might mention God: If you had remembered that God takes no pleasure in frivolous vows (Deuteronomy 23:23, Ecclesiastes 5:4), would you still have vowed?

if so there are no vows: Every unnecessary vow brings dishonor to God, and strictly speaking every vow is unnecessary; no vow could withstand this critique. Commentators vary as to whether this comment continues R. Zadok's parenthetical remark, or resumes the Sages' dissent, or represents a separate insertion by the composer of the text.

a matter between him and his father or his mother: His vow will interfere with his obligation to pay them proper respect or make sure they have food and shelter or the like.

9:2 *something new*: The Sage can elicit regret on account of circumstances that did not exist when the vow was made.

"became a scribe," and now the person who vowed needs a scribe's services.

"marry off his son," and now the person who vowed would like to attend the celebration (see 5:6 above).

9:3 *like something new... not like something new*: Commentators differ on the relationship between R. Meir's comment and the preceding dispute between R. Eliezer and the Sages. In one view, R. Meir holds that certain future changes to present circumstances can legitimately allow for releasing the vow because they could well have been anticipated when the vow was spoken and are not altogether *something new*. It is as though the vow was made contingent on the continuation of present circumstances; the speaker intended that the vow lapse if the indicated circumstances ceased to be the case, and it is perhaps not even necessary to obtain

but the Sages do not[133] agree with him.
How?
If he said:
"*Qonam* that I marry a certain woman because her father is bad,"
they said to him: "He has died," or[134] "He has repented";
"*Qonam* that I enter this house, because there is a bad dog inside,"
or "…because there is a snake inside,"
they said to him:
"The dog has died,"
or "The snake has been killed"—
such cases are like something new but they are not like something new,
but the Sages do not[135] agree with him.
  4 R. Meir further said:
One opens for him from what is written in the Torah
and says to him: "If you had known that you were violating
Do not take revenge and
Do not bear a grudge and
Do not hate your brother in your heart and
Love your neighbor as yourself and
That your brother live with you—
lest he grow poor and you be unable to sustain him,"
and he said: "If I had known that this is the case,
I would not have vowed"—
in such a case he is released.

[133] **MJ, K, P** lack "not."   [134] **K** restores "or" in the margin.   [135] **MJ, K, P** lack "not."

the release of a Sage. However, an opposing view understands that R. Meir means that such developments resemble *something new* even though they are not strictly such, and therefore (following the majority opinion in 9:2) the vow cannot be released at all. This ambiguity is compounded by the uncertain text here. If the Sages agree with R. Meir as in **MJ** and the manuscripts, which opinion of R. Meir do they support? If they disagree, as in **MB** and the printed Mishnah, which opinion do they reject, and why? Given the vagueness of R. Meir's statement and the uncertain text of the Sages' response, the matter cannot be resolved. It should be noted that if the Sages do agree with R. Meir the translation should have "and" rather than "but."

9:4 Was the vow motivated by an unworthy sentiment, such as the cited verses aim to suppress? The question "would you have vowed?" is left implied.

Do not take revenge … Do not bear a grudge: Leviticus 19:18.

Do not hate your brother in your heart: Leviticus 19:17.

Love your neighbor as yourself: Leviticus 19:18.

That your brother live with you: Leviticus 25:36.

lest he grow poor: This phrase is not from Scripture, but continues the question one poses to the oath taker: your vow might leave you unable to fulfill these commandments with respect to the person you have excluded from receiving benefit from you. The last-quoted verse appears in the context of the Torah's requirement that Israelites lend without interest to those in need.

5 One opens for a man with his wife's *ketubbah* money.
And it once happened that a man vowed to derive no benefit from his wife,
and her *ketubbah* was four hundred *dinar*;[136]
he[137] came before R. Aqiva,
and he obliged him to give her her *ketubbah*.
He said to him:
Rabbi! Father left eight hundred *dinar*.
My brother took four hundred, and I four hundred;
is it not enough for her that she take two hundred and I two hundred?
R. Aqiva said to him:
Even if you sell the hair on your head,
you must give her her *ketubbah*.
He said to him:
Had I known that this is the case I would not have vowed—
and R. Aqiva released her.[138]

6 One opens with festivals and Sabbaths.
At first they would say:
Those days are permitted and all other days are forbidden,
until R. Aqiva came
and taught that a vow which has been partially released[139] is entirely released.

7 How?
If he said: "*Qonam* that I not derive benefit from all of you":
if one of them was permitted—
they are all permitted.
"...that I not derive benefit from this one and this one,"[140]
if the first one is permitted—
they are all permitted;
if the last one is permitted—

[136] K, P: "four hundred *zuz*," an equivalent amount. [137] MJ, K, P: "she."
[138] MJ, K, P: "him." [139] K, P: "released from its generality." Modern editions vary.
[140] MJ, K, P add an additional "and this one."

9:5 *With his wife's ketubbah*: According to rabbinic law, a marriage must rest on a contract stipulating a payment from a husband to his wife if they divorce or from his estate to his widow if he dies. If a man makes a vow that will entail divorcing his wife (in the present case, that he derive no benefit from her), the Sage can attempt to elicit regret by reminding him of the high cost of discharging this debt.

released her: This reading supports the understanding that it was the wife who brought the case to R. Aqiva, and that he *released her* back to her husband; she had made no vow that had to be released.

9:6 *festivals and Sabbaths*: If a vow imposes fasting or the like, the Sage can attempt to elicit regret over the lost joy of festive times or over the self-imposed sin of fasting on a holy day.

Those days are permitted and all other days are forbidden: Upon eliciting an expression of regret the Sage would release the vow for Sabbaths and other holy days alone.

partially released: The alternative reading "released from its generality" means the same thing: the vow no longer applies as generally as the original language implies.

9:7 *How?* Continues 9:6, illustrating partial release from a vow.

the first one...the last one...the middle one: The vow had identified several individuals in a particular order (compare *Nazir* 4:1, *Shevu'ot* 5:3). "The middle one" is anyone other than the first or the last.

the last one is permitted,
and they all are forbidden;
if the middle one was permitted—
from him downward is permitted,
from him upward is forbidden.[141]
"... that I not derive benefit, *qorban* from this one,[142] and *qorban* from this one"—
one needs an opening for each one.

8 "*Qonam* that I taste wine, because wine is bad for the digestion":
if they said to him:
"But is not old wine good for the digestion?"
he is permitted with respect to old,
and not only old wine is permitted, but all wine.
"*Qonam* that I taste onion, because onion is bad for the heart":
if they said to him:
"Is not wild onion good for the heart?"
he is permitted with respect to wild,
and not only wild onion is permitted, but[143] all onions.
There was a case, and R. Meir permitted him with respect to all onions.

9 One opens for a man with his honor and the honor of his children.
One says to him:
"If you had known that the next day people would say of you,
that is so-and-so's nature: he divorces his wives,"
and they would say of your daughters:
"They are the daughters of divorced women:[144] what caused their mothers to be divorced?"
and he said:
"If I had known this would be case,
I would not have vowed"—
in such a case he is released.

10 "*Qonam* that I not marry so-and-so who is ugly,"
and it turns out[145] she is pretty;
"... dark,"
and it turns out she is fair;

---

[141] "If...forbidden" is missing in **MJ**, **K**, **P** but restored in the margin of **K**.
[142] **K**, **P** add an additional "from this one," but not a third "*qorban*."
[143] **K** restores "but" in the margin.   [144] **K**, **P**: "a divorced woman."
[145] Lit. "behold," and so throughout this paragraph.

---

and they all are forbidden: All except the last, who was permitted.

downward denotes a later point in the sequence, and *upward* an earlier point.

"qorban from this one": By repeating the word *qorban* he has made each refusal of benefit a separate vow, and now each requires its own release procedure.

9:8 *"is not old wine good...?"* Presumably he responded by regretting his vow.

"wild onion": Lit. "village-onion." Alternatively, onion from Cyprus.

9:9 The vow in question entailed divorcing his wife (see on 9:5).

"what caused their mothers...?" Lit. "what did their mothers see" or "how were their mothers worthy" of being divorced?

"…short,"
and it turns out she is tall—
he is permitted with respect to her,
not because she was ugly and became pretty,
dark and became fair
[or] short and became tall,
but because the vow was mistaken.
And[146] there was a case of someone who vowed from benefit from his sister's daughter,
and they brought her into the house of R. Ishmael,
and they made her pretty.
R. Ishmael said to him:
My son, is it about this one that you vowed?
He said to him:
No!
And R. Ishmael released him.
In that same hour R. Ishmael wept and said:
The daughters of Israel are handsome, but poverty makes them ugly.
And when R. Ishmael died the daughters of Israel took up a dirge and said:
Daughters of Israel weep for R. Ishmael.
And so it says of Saul:
Daughters of Israel weep for Saul.

Chapter Ten

10:1–11:12 *Vows of Dependent Females and the Power of Nullification*

10 A betrothed girl:
her father and her husband nullify her vows.

[146] **K, P, MJ** lack "and."

9:10 *his sister's daughter*: He was under pressure to marry a niece whom he found unattractive and therefore made his vow.

and they made her pretty: According to 3:2, a vow based on a mistaken assumption requires no release, but according to the majority opinion in 9:2 a vow cannot be released on the basis of developments subsequent to the time the vow was made. R. Ishmael supports the minority opinion in 9:2 (R. Eliezer) that subsequent developments can be used to release a vow, and turns the present vow into the case of 3:2; it was based on an opinion of the prospective bride that has now become incorrect.

Daughters of Israel weep for Saul: 2 Samuel 1:24.

10:1 *betrothed girl*: A minor girl (Heb. *na'arah*, approaching sexual maturity but not having attained legal majority; see *Niddah* 5:6) still living in her father's house but engaged to marry in a legally binding betrothal (see *Ketubbot* introduction).

nullify her vows: This girl is under double authority in that she has a legal husband but still lives with her father; therefore they must jointly exercise their right to nullify. Neither can do so alone.

If the father nullified and the husband did not nullify,
[or] the husband nullified and the father did not nullify—
it is not nullified.
And there is no need to say, if one of them upheld.

2 If the father died—
authority is not transferred[147] to the husband.
If the husband died—
authority is transferred to the father.
In this way the father's power is stronger than the husband's.
In[148] another matter, the husband's power is stronger than the father's,
in that the husband nullifies during her[149] adulthood,
and the father does not nullify during her adulthood.

3 If she vowed while betrothed:
and was divorced the same day,
and was betrothed the same day,
even to a hundred—
her father and her last husband nullify her vows.
This is the general rule:
Anyone who has not gone out into her own authority for one[150] hour—
her father and her last husband nullify her vows.

4 The way of disciples of the Sages—
before his daughter would leave his premises he would say to her:
"All vows that you uttered in my house, they are hereby nullified."
And so too the husband, before she came into his authority,
would say to her:

---

[147] Lit. "emptied out."   [148] K lacks "in."
[149] "Her" added from context here and in the next clause.   [150] P restores "one" in the margin.

---

upheld: If either man explicitly endorses the vow it can no longer be nullified at all.

10:2 *is not transferred to the husband*: The husband cannot have sole authority over his wife until she has come to live in his house.

adulthood: Heb. *boger*. Once a girl turns twelve and a half years old, she becomes a legal adult (10:5); her father loses several aspects of his parental authority, including the right to nullify her vows.

10:3 *the same day*: The father or the husband can only nullify a vow on the day he hears of it, no later (see 10:8 below).

even to a hundred: During the day when the right to nullify is in force, each successive fiancé receives this right in turn, even though he was not betrothed to the girl at the time she made her vow.

her own authority: By reaching the age of majority while not yet betrothed or married, or by entering at any age into a full marriage and then being widowed or divorced. The inverse "general rule" appears at 11:9 below.

10:4 *All vows that you uttered in my house*: The right to nullify the vow of a daughter or a wife lasts only one day, but that day is measured not from the time of the vow but from the time that the male with authority hears of it. This general act of nullification applies to those vows of which the father had never heard, and allows the daughter to go forth unencumbered.

"All vows that you uttered before you entered my authority, they are hereby nullified."
For[151] once she enters his authority he cannot nullify.

5 An adult woman[152] who waited twelve months or a widow thirty days:
R. Eliezer[153] says:
Since her husband owes her support—
he nullifies.
But the Sages say:
The husband does not nullify until she enters his authority.

6 A woman awaiting her levir:
whether one levir or two levirs—
R. Eliezer[154] says:
He nullifies;
R. Joshua says:
For one but not for two.
R. Aqiva says:

[151] K: "If [he says thus]…"   [152] MJ, K, P: "and one (i.e. a younger girl) who waited…"
[153] Var. "Eleazar."   [154] MJ: "Eleazar" here but "Eliezer" below.

---

once she enters his authority: The husband pronounces a similar blanket nullification during betrothal, because the change in his legal status entails a change in his right to nullify. He acquires a new right as husband, but that right applies only to vows spoken by his wife "in his house" (Numbers 30:11).

he cannot nullify vows made previously.

10:5 *adult woman*: A girl aged twelve and a half years (see above, on 10:2). At that age, the father's right to nullify her vows lapses whether she is betrothed or not. The question here concerns a girl who has been engaged to marry: when does the groom acquire a husband's right to nullify her vows without the father's concurrence?

waited twelve months: Once a couple is betrothed, each of the partners has twelve months to prepare for the marriage celebration and for married life. If the formal marriage is delayed by either party beyond that time, the betrothed woman is nonetheless entitled to support from her husband-to-be (*Ketubbot* 5:2). A widow or divorcee is expected to be ready within thirty days. The reading "and one who" (see n. 152) reflects the view that a female who is betrothed after she enters adulthood is never entitled to more than thirty days' preparation time. The text would then list three categories: such an adult, a widow, or a girl who was betrothed before the age of adulthood but whose marriage has been delayed beyond the normal twelve months.

he nullifies: He has the right to nullify her vows on his sole authority.

enters his authority: Normally by coming to live with him after the marriage is complete. Some commentators hold that it is sufficient that her father or his agent deliver her to agents of her husband-to-be.

10:6 *awaiting her levir*: When a man dies childless his brother must marry the widow through levirate marriage or carry out the ceremony of *halitsah*, "removal of the shoe" (Deuteronomy 25:5–10, and see *Yevamot*). If there are several surviving brothers, any of them may assume this role. A widow in this situation is said to be *awaiting* (lit. "watching") her brother-in-law, to see whether he plans to marry her or release her. The question here is whether a brother-in-law who has not yet taken either action already has the right to nullify her vows.

He nullifies: i.e. he has the power to do so.

For one but not for two: If any brother-in-law acts, the others lose their connection to the widow; meanwhile, therefore, none of them has unambiguous authority over her.

Not for one and not for two.
Said R. Eliezer:
If in the case of a woman whom [a husband] acquired for himself,
he nullifies her vows,
[in the case of] a woman whom they acquired for him in Heaven,[155]
does not logic require that he may nullify her vows?
R. Aqiva said to him:
No. If you have said this about a woman whom he acquired for himself,
over whom others have no authority,
will you say this about a woman who was acquired for him in Heaven,
over whom others have authority?
R. Joshua said to him:
Aqiva! Your words apply to two levirs;
what do you answer about a single levir?
He said to him:
A levirate widow is not so completely tied to the levir[156]
as a betrothed woman is completely tied to her man.

7 One who says to his wife:
"All the vows that you will make from now until I come from such-and-such a place,
they are hereby upheld"—
he has said nothing.
"…they are hereby nullified"—
R. Eliezer says:
It is nullified,
and the Sages say:
It is not nullified.
Said R. Eliezer:
If he nullifies vows that have [already] come under the rule of prohibition,

[155] K, P: "whom Heaven acquired for him." [156] MJ, K, P: "to her man."

Not for one and not for two: R. Aqiva holds that even a single brother-in-law may carry out *halitsah* and lose his potential authority over the widow without ever having possessed it; therefore his right to nullify her vows must be held in abeyance.

acquired for him in Heaven: This woman has become his potential wife without any action on his part at all. She is his predestined wife, so to speak, even more clearly than a woman whom a man has betrothed but not yet married. Should he not be able to nullify her vows as the husband-to-be can do in the more frequent case (as above)?

others have authority: If there is more than one surviving brother, until she has either performed *halitsah* or undergone levirate marriage each of the brothers has some authority over her.

completely tied: A man who has intercourse with the fiancée of another is liable to be put to death on the grounds of adultery (Deuteronomy 22:23–27), but this penalty does not apply in the case of a woman who is "awaiting her levir."

her man: Here the text does not call the fiancé "husband" (*baʾal*) although it did so earlier in the chapter.

10:7 *he has said nothing*: The husband's right to uphold a vow (see 10:1 above) does not extend to vows which have not yet been spoken.

If he nullifies: i.e. if he has the right to nullify.

shall he not nullify vows that have not [yet] come under the rule of prohibition?
They said to him:
Look, it says:[157]
Her husband shall uphold them and her husband shall nullify them—
That which has come under the rule of upholding has comes under the rule of nullifying.
If it has not come under the rule of upholding,
it has not come under the rule of nullifying.

8 Nullification of vows is the whole day.
This has a lenient and a stringent aspect.
How?
If she vowed on Sabbath night—
he nullifies Sabbath night
and on the Sabbath day until dark.[158]
If she vowed as it was growing dark—
he nullifies as long as it is not dark;
for if it grows dark and he has not nullified,[159] he cannot nullify.

Chapter Eleven

11 And these are the vows that he nullifies.
Matters that involve self-affliction:
"If I bathe" or "If I do not bathe,"

[157] K, P lack this introductory phrase.   [158] MJ, P: "After it grows dark," an apparent error.
[159] K, P: "For if he has not nullified and [P: after] it has grown dark."

---

come under the rule Even with vows that have already come into effect and rendered certain objects forbidden to his wife, the husband can nullify the vow and overturn the prohibition; why should he not be able to nullify vows before they come into effect?

Her husband shall uphold them…: Numbers 30:14.

That which comes under the rule of upholding: Both sides agree that the husband cannot uphold vows in anticipation, before they are made. *The Sages* argue from the verse that the same rules that apply to upholding a vow apply to its nullification.

10:8 *the whole day*: A husband or father must nullify a vow the day he hears of it (Numbers 30:6, 9, 13). "The day he hears of it" ends at nightfall, not twenty-four hours later.

lenient…stringent: He can have a relatively long or brief period of opportunity to nullify the vow, depending on when he heard of it.

Sabbath night: The same rule applies to a weeknight as well.

as long as it is not dark: Fully dark.

he cannot nullify any longer.

11:1 *self-affliction*: See Numbers 30:14. Strictly speaking a vow must include a pledge to abstain from something, so *if I bathe* must be understood as shorthand for "*Qonam* that I eat fruit (or use cosmetics, etc.) or if I bathe today…"

"If I put on ornaments" or "If I do not put on ornaments."
Said R. Yose:
These are not matters of self-affliction.

2 And which are vows of self-affliction?
If she said:
"*Qonam* the fruits of the world to me"—
in such a case he can nullify.
"...the fruits of the country to me"—
let him bring her from another country.
"...the fruits from this storekeeper to me"—
he cannot nullify.
And if his supply was only from him,
in such a case he nullifies[160]—
the words of R. Yose.

3 "*Qonam* that I derive benefit from creatures"—
he cannot nullify,
and she can derive benefit from
Gleanings, Forgotten Sheaves, and the Corner of the Field.[161]
"*Qonam* that priests and Levites derive benefit from me"—
they take against his will.
"...these priests and these Levites derive benefit from me"—
let others take.

[160] K adds "returns and" but marks the word for deletion.
[161] K adds "and [other] ownerless property."

"If I bathe": The commentaries differ over whether these examples must be understood as a new question: Does abstention from bathing, etc. for a limited period constitute "self-affliction"?

R. Yose: To abstain from bathing for one day is not self-affliction, so the husband has no right of nullification.

11:2 *And which are...?* This can be read as the continuation of R. Yose's words; the examples in 11:1 do not constitute self-affliction, but *"Qonam the fruits of the world* does. On this reading, the concluding *the words of R. Yose* are hard to understand; the Talmuds understand the repetition to mean that the entire eleventh chapter gives R. Yose's opinions, although alternatively it may mean "R. Yose's words end here."

his supply was only from him: If no other shopkeeper will extend the necessary credit or can provide his household needs.

11:3 *"creatures"*: People.

he cannot nullify: Since the woman can be supported by other means, it is not a vow of "self-denial."

Gleanings, Forgotten Sheaves, and the Corner of the Field: These are gifts to the poor that are mandated by the Torah (Leviticus 19:9, Deuteronomy 24:19). See *Pe'ah*. They are legally ownerless until the poor come to take them, and so do not constitute *benefit from creatures*. Opinions in the Talmud differ as to whether this clause explains why the husband cannot nullify the vow or constitutes a separate consideration.

"priests and Levites": The speaker is a householder, presumably male, who is trying to withhold the gifts from his crops that are due to priests and Levites. This clause has been suggested by the previous reference to agricultural entitlements, but the right of nullification is not relevant to this case.

they take against his will: Again, the Torah has effectively removed his ownership from these items.

4 "*Qonam* that I work for my father,"
or "…your father,"
or "…my brother,"
or "…your brother"—
he cannot nullify.
"…that I work for you"—
he does not need to nullify.
R. Aqiva says:
He may nullify,
lest she earn more than his entitlement.
R. Yohanan b. Nuri says:
He may nullify,
lest he divorce her and she become forbidden to him.[162]

5 If his wife vowed, and[163] he thought it was his daughter;
his daughter vowed, and he thought it was his wife;
she vowed to become a *nazir*, and he thought she had vowed a sacrifice;
she vowed a sacrifice, and he thought she had vowed to become a *nazir*;
she vowed from figs, and he thought she had vowed from grapes;
she vowed from grapes, and he thought she had vowed from figs—
in such a case, he may return and nullify.

6 If she said:
"*Qonam* that I taste these[164] figs or grapes":
if he affirmed concerning the figs—
the entire vow is confirmed;
if he nullified concerning the figs—
it is not nullified unless he also nullifies concerning the grapes.
If she said:

[162] **MJ, K, P**: "…and she become forbidden to return to him."
[163] **K, P** lack all these occurrences of "and," but **K** restores all except the first in the margin or between the lines.
[164] **K** marks "these" for deletion.

11:4 *"work for my father"*: That is, the benefit of the wife's labor must not accrue to the indicated person(s).

he cannot nullify: Based on Numbers 30:17 (*between a man and his wife*), vows that affect relations between husband and wife can be nullified even if they are not vows of self-affliction. But this is not a vow of self-affliction, nor does it directly affect their intimate relation.

he does not need to nullify: A husband has an inalienable right to his wife's labor.

more than his entitlement: A wife is obliged to perform labor worth a set amount of money (see *Ketubbot* 5:9); any excess is her own. She can vow to withhold the benefit of that excess from her husband, so he can nullify the vow.

lest he divorce her: If he divorces her without nullifying the vow, he may never derive any benefit from her again and therefore can never remarry her.

11:5 *return and nullify*: All the cases in this paragraph concern an act of nullification based on an error of fact, leaving the actual vow intact. The husband or father, on learning the true state of affairs, has a second chance to nullify the vow.

11:6 *it is not nullified*: Either the part about grapes or the whole vow; commentators differ.

"*Qonam* that I taste figs and that I taste grapes"[165]—
in this case these are two vows.

7 "I know there are vows, but I did not know there are people who nullify them"—
he may nullify.
"I know there are people who nullify, but I did not know this is a vow"—
R. Meir says:
He may not nullify;
but the Sages say:
He may nullify.

8 One who has vowed that his son-in-law derive no benefit from him,
and he wants to give money to his daughter:
he says to her:
"This money is hereby given to you as a gift,
except that your husband shall have no authority over it;
rather transact with it only for your own enjoyment."[166]

9 *The vow of a widow or divorcee…*[167] *shall stand confirmed over her.*
How?
If she said: "I shall hereby be a *nezirah* starting after thirty days"—
even if she was married within thirty days,
he cannot nullify.
If she vowed while under the husband's authority—
he can nullify.[168]
How?[169]
If she said:
"I shall hereby be a *nezirah* starting after thirty days"[170]—

---

[165] K lacks the words "that I taste grapes" but restores them in the margin.
[166] K: "But [only] for what you put into your mouth."
[167] MJ, P supply the missing words: *all that she has forbidden to herself.*
[168] MJ, K, P: "and he nullified." [169] MJ, K, P lack this question.
[170] K restores "days" in the margin.

---

two vows: And he can nullify either without affecting the other.

11:7 *"I did not know"*: Lit. "I do not know."

"he may nullify": The day he learns of his right to nullify counts as the day he heard of the vow (see 10:8 above).

"this is a vow": The day of the vow had ended before he realized that his wife's or daughter's utterance was such as might be nullified. But the Sages hold as above: the opportunity for nullification begins when he realizes that nullification may be appropriate.

11:8 *One who has vowed*: The text literally means the opposite—one who vowed to derive no benefit from his son-in-law—but the meaning is clear from the sequel. A variant reads "One prevented by vow…from his father-in-law"; another variant corrects to the language reflected in the translation. Property that comes to a married woman is normally at her husband's disposal; this rule provides the background to this discussion (see *Ketubbot* chapter 8).

"your own enjoyment": Lit. "your mouth."

11:9 *The vow of a widow…*: Numbers 30:10.

He cannot nullify: The vow was uttered at a time when no man had the right to nullify it.

even if she was widowed or divorced within thirty days,
in such a case, this is nullified.
If she vowed that day,
and was divorced that day
and he took her back that day—
he cannot nullify.
This is the general rule:
Anyone who has gone out into her own authority for one hour,
he cannot nullify.

10 There are nine girls whose vows must stand:
(1) an adult who is an orphan,
(2) a girl who reached adulthood and is an orphan,
(3) a girl who has not reached adulthood and is an orphan,
(4) an adult whose father died,
(5) a girl who reached adulthood whose father died,
(6) a girl who has not reached adulthood whose father died,
(7) a girl whose father died who reached adulthood after her father died,
(8) an adult whose father is alive,
(9) a girl who reached adulthood whose father is alive.
R. Judah[171] says:
Also one who married off his minor daughter,
and[172] she was widowed or divorced,
and came back to him while she was still a girl.

[171] K: "Meir." [172] Var. lacks "and" and "while": "If she was widowed…she is still a girl."

in such a case, this is nullified: It is presumed that the husband nullified the vow at a time when he had the right to do so. It does not matter that she was no longer attached to him at the time the vow was to take effect.

If she vowed…one hour: Unlike the related passage at 10:3, here the woman was fully married and subsequently divorced, and has *gone out into her own authority*.

he cannot nullify: Vows that preceded his resumption of authority.

11:10 *nine girls*: Normally a "girl" is a female between the ages of twelve and twelve and a half (above, 10:2–5). In the present case, however, commentators differ: some hold that all the listed cases concern girls who were married off before they reached adulthood, while others hold the word here simply means "young woman." In either case the text now lists various categories whose fathers have lost the right to nullify their vows. Despite the apparent complexity of the list, it actually provides parallel sets of categories, reflecting possible changes in a girl's legal status, for three basic types of affected person: girls who have reached full adulthood, girls whose fathers have died, and girls who are "orphans" during their fathers' lives because they have been fully married (that is, not just betrothed) and so have left their fathers' authority. Even if such a girl then ceases to be married through divorce or the death of her husband, she has "gone out into her own authority" (above, 11:9), and there is no male with the power to nullify her vows.

came back to him: Commentators differ as to whether this means returned to her father or remarried her ex-husband.

while she was still a girl: Commentators differ. Some interpret *R. Judah*'s ruling to mean that a minor under the age of twelve who has been married and then unmarried does indeed return to her father's authority; others understand precisely the opposite and apply the general rule of 11:9. The vows of a minor below the age of eleven have no force whatever (*Niddah* 5:6).

11 "*Qonam* that I derive any benefit from my father or[173] your father
if I do anything for you,"
or "…that I derive any benefit from you,
if I[174] do anything for my father or for your father"—
in such a case he can nullify.

12 At first they would say:
Three women go out and collect their *ketubbah*—
one who says:
(1) "I am impure to you," or
(2) "Heaven is between me and you," or
(3) "I am removed from the Jews."
They subsequently said:
Lest a woman set her eyes on another and behave corruptly toward her husband,
rather, she who says:
"I am impure to you"—
must bring proof of her words;
"Heaven is between me and you"—
let them act through pleading.
"I am removed from the Jews"—
let him nullify his portion,
and let her serve him,
and let her be removed from the [other] Jews.

---

[173] Lit. "And."   [174] K restores "I" in the margin.

11:11 Unlike the vows in 11:4 above, these vows directly affect the relation between husband and wife.

11:12 *go out*: The husbands must divorce them. For the expression, see annotations to *Yevamot* 3:5.

collect their ketubbah: Although they have forced an end to the marriage, these women have not forfeited their marriage settlement (compare *Ketubbot* 7:5–6).

"I am impure to you": "I was raped." If the husband is a priest he may no longer live with her.

"Heaven is between me and you": "Only heaven knows that our marriage is unbearable," an implied accusation that the husband is impotent and incapable of fulfilling his marital obligation, while she does not wish to remain childless. Alternatively, the phrase denotes complete mutual estrangement.

"I am removed from the Jews": Sexually.

act through pleading: Commentators differ: perhaps through prayer the husband's virility can be restored, or the couple can be reconciled, or she can be implored to accept the situation, or he can be convinced to quietly give her a divorce.

nullify his portion: The husband has the right to nullify that portion of the vow that affects the marital bond.

let her serve him: Remain sexually available to her husband.

removed from the other Jews: If this marriage ends at some later time, she must indeed abstain from sexual relations with all other Jewish men.

Tractate Nazir

Robert Goldenberg

Introduction

Overview

A *nazir* (often translated "Nazirite"; feminine *nezirah*, plural *nezirim*) is one who has vowed a term of enhanced religious discipline. The Torah devotes a whole chapter (Numbers 6) to this vow and stipulates the types of self-restraint the *nazir* must undertake: all food and drink derived from the grape, as well as all contact with the dead, must be avoided. There is no penalty for drinking wine or eating grapes, other than the general penalties for breaking a vow; on the other hand a *nazir* who contracts corpse impurity, even if accidentally, must offer special sacrifices of purification and begin all over again to fulfill the original vow. Finally, a *nazir* must allow the hair on his head to grow throughout the duration of his vow, and must then shave that hair as part of the completion procedures at the end of his term.

Structure and Organization of the Tractate

Tractate *Nazir* begins by identifying binding vows that vary from the standard "I am hereby a *nazir*": vows that use circumlocutions and vows that refer to known *nezirim* or that mention the rules governing *nezirim* without using the term are also binding. The tractate also offers detailed treatment of the duration of such vows (at least thirty days), of a husband's right to nullify his wife's vows and a father's right to nullify his daughter's, and of complications that may arise in the course of the final ceremonies such as last-minute corpse impurity and unexpected disqualification or loss of the sacrificial animals. Brief treatments of other topics are indicated by the headings in the translation.

It should be noted that the derived term *nezirut* is ambiguous. It can mean "status as a *nazir*" or "duration of a *nazir*'s obligation" or even "vow to become a *nazir*," and has accordingly been translated according to context. Several other terms require explanation as well. As already noted, if a *nazir* contracts corpse impurity he must be purged of the impurity and then start fulfilling his vow from the beginning of its term; the impurity undoes (Heb. *str*) the earlier partial fulfillment, and occurrences of this term in its various forms have been translated with forms of the English word "undo." By contrast, references to a father's or a husband's right to nullify (Heb. *hfr*) his daughter's or his wife's vows (see Numbers 30) have been translated with forms of the word "nullify," and references to the right of Sages to release (Heb. *htyr*) any individual from ill-advised vows are translated with forms of the word "release." (The same word in other contexts has been translated with forms of "permit," its more common meaning.) Finally, references to the *nazir*'s ceremonial haircut on completing his or her term, or on resuming *nazir* status after incurring corpse impurity, are translated as "shave" or "shaving" (Heb. *glh*). In accordance with Hebrew grammar the word *nazir* itself has been taken to designate a male *nazir*, unless the context implies otherwise.

In the traditional sequence of mishnaic tractates, *Nazir* follows immediately after *Nedarim*, where the subject is vows and their fulfillment. The connection is obvious: a *nazir* is one who has taken a very particular vow, and thus represents a specific case of the general topic there treated.

Special Notes for the Reader

The following sigla are used throughout the annotations and the footnotes, in addition to the sigla that are set out in the introduction to the translation:

MB The Mishnah text in the Babylonian Talmud (Bavli)
MJ The Mishnah text in the Jerusalem Talmud (Yerushalmi)
TB The Babylonian Talmud (*gemara*)
TJ The Jerusalem Talmud (*gemara*)

Tractate Nazir

Chapter One

1:1–2 *The Language of a Nazir Vow*

I All substitutions for the *nazir* vow are equivalent to the *nazir* vow[1] itself.
One who says: "I shall be"[2]—
he is thereby a *nazir*.
Or "I shall be handsome"—
a *nazir*.
Naziq or *Naziach* or *Paziach*—
he is thereby a *nazir*.
"I am hereby as this one,"
or "I hereby shall braid,"[3]
or "I hereby shall arrange," or "I must hereby grow wild hair"—
he is thereby a *nazir*.
"I am hereby obliged to offer birds"[4]—
R. Meir says:
A *nazir*;
but the Sages say:
He is not a *nazir*.

[1] K: "*nazir* vows."   [2] See annotations for an alternative reading.   [3] Or "curl."
[4] Or "[grow] nails."

1:1 *All substitutions*: Or circumlocutions, euphemisms, etc. This reflects the general rule at *Nedarim* 1:1.

One who says "I shall be"…a nazir: Both Talmudim explain that something in the situation clarifies the remark, e.g. that a *nazir* has just walked past. Certain witnesses lack "he is thereby a *nazir*"; this would explain the following "or."

Or "I shall be handsome": Again, according to the Talmudim, the situation clarifies: he was curling his hair through his fingers or the like.

Naziq…Naziach…Paziach: The Talmudim identify these either as foreigners' mispronunciations of the word *nazir* that have crept into everyday Hebrew speech or as nonsense words invented by the rabbis as acceptable circumlocutions.

"offer birds": Note the variant "grow nails." In Hebrew "birds" (*tsiporim*) and "nails" (*tsipornayyim*) differ by a single letter, and the text lacks the distinguishing verbs supplied in the translation. The reference to nails arises from Daniel 4:30.

2 "I am hereby a *nazir*[5] from grapeseeds," or
"…from grapeskins,"
or "…from shaving,"
or "…from impurity"—
he is thereby a *nazir*,
and all the details of the *nazir* vow are upon him.
"I am hereby as Samson,"
"…as the son of Manoah,"
"…as the husband of Delilah,"
"…as the one who uprooted the doors of Gaza,"
"…as the one whose eyes the Philistines blinded"—
he is a Samson *nazir*.
What is the difference between a perpetual *nazir* and a Samson *nazir*?
A perpetual *nazir*:
his hair grew heavy—
he lightens it with a razor,
and brings three animals [as sacrifice];
and if he becomes impure he brings the impurity offering.
A Samson *nazir*:
his hair grew heavy—
he does not lighten it,
and if he becomes impure he does not bring the impurity offering.

[5] **MJ, K, P** lack "a *nazir*."

1:2 *"grapeseeds"… "grapeskins"*: The meaning of these two terms (see Numbers 6:4) is obscure; the translation follows R. Yose in 6:2 below.

"impurity": Through contact with the dead.

all the details: It would appear that he has taken on a very limited abstention, but he has made himself a *nazir* in the full sense. (The conjunction here translated "or" can also mean "and.")

"as Samson"… "as the son of Manoah," etc.: References to the biblical judge Samson, his family, or incidents in his life (Judges 13–16). The Talmudim ask whether the speaker must say all these things, in order to avoid the possibility that some other Samson is meant, or any of them. Certain variants lack the recurrences of "as," which supports the first interpretation ("as Samson the son of Manoah, the husband of Delilah, who uprooted…"); others repeatedly add "or," which supports the second.

A perpetual nazir and a Samson nazir: These are special types of *nazir*, as distinct from the common *nazir* treated in 1:1 and the beginning of 1:2. Some of the "details of the *nazir* vow" do not apply to these special categories.

lightens it with a razor: Based on the story of Absalom in 2 Samuel 14:26, this could be done once a year.

three animals: He acts as though his vow has been fulfilled (see Numbers 6:14), but it actually resumes at once.

becomes impure: Contracted corpse impurity.

impurity offering: Numbers 6:9–12.

he does not bring the impurity offering: The Talmudim differ as to whether a Samson *nazir* should avoid the dead but is exempt from the sacrifice for accidental impurity (**TJ**); perhaps a Samson *nazir* need not avoid the dead at all, as Samson himself did not (**TB**).

1:3–7 The Duration of a Nazir's Obligation

3 An unspecified *nazir* vow is thirty days.
If he said: "I am hereby a *nazir* one large,"
"I am hereby a *nazir* one small,"
even "…from now till the end of the world"—
he is a *nazir* for thirty days.
"I am hereby a *nazir* and[6] one day,"
"I am hereby a *nazir* and one hour,"
"I am hereby a *nazir* and a half"—
he is thereby a *nazir* twice.
"I am hereby a *nazir*[7] for thirty days and one hour"—
[he is] a *nazir* for thirty-one days,
because one may not make *nazir* vows by the hour.
  4 "I am hereby a *nazir* as the hairs of my head,"
or "…as the dust of the earth,"
or "…as the sand of the sea—
he is thereby a perpetual *nazir*,
and he shaves [his head] every thirty days.
Rabbi says:
This one does not shave every thirty days.
And who is it who shaves every thirty days?
One who says: "A *nazir* vow[8] is hereby upon me as the hairs of my head,"
or "…as the dust of the earth,"
or "…as the sands of the sea."

[6] K lacks "a *nazir* and." MJ, P lack "and" here and in the next two instances; see annotations.
[7] K lacks "a *nazir* for."   [8] MJ, P: "*nazir* vows" (plural).

1:3 *for thirty days*: None of the foregoing expressions actually indicates a specific duration.

twice: For two consecutive thirty-day periods. In all these cases, he is assumed to have undertaken a standard *nazir* vow for thirty days and then an additional vow as well; that second vow specifies a rather brief period of time, but no *nazir* vow can be for less than thirty days. MJ lacks the "and" in these three clauses, but the meaning appears to be same.

"and one hour": The difference between this vow and the preceding is that the first vow seems to take on a standard thirty-day obligation and then (once that period has elapsed) an additional obligation: this also must last the minimum thirty days. The second vow more clearly intends a single period of time, but "one may not make *nazir* vows by the hour," a rule based on Numbers 6:8 ("the *days* that he is a *nazir*").

1:4 *shaves…every thirty days*: He has accepted as many thirty-day *nazir* vows as the hairs of his head, and so forth.

does not shave every thirty days: But only once every twelve months, like other lifetime *nezirim*.

who is it…? In Rabbi's view the difference between this vow and the foregoing is that the previous vow established a single *nazir* vow to last thirty days for each hair on his head, which means for his whole life. Rabbi's formulation establishes a separate thirty-day *nazir* status for each hair; each vow duly terminates after thirty days but is immediately succeeded by the next.

5 "I[9] am hereby a *nazir* a houseful,"
or "…a basketful"—
one interrogates him:
If he said: "I vowed one great vow"—
he is a *nazir* for thirty days;
and if he said: "I vowed without specifying"—
they consider the basket as if it is full of mustardseeds,
and he is a *nazir* all his days.

6 "I am hereby a *nazir* from here till a certain place"—
they measure how many days it would take to travel from here[10] to that place:
if fewer than thirty days—
he is a *nazir* for thirty days;
and if not—
he is a *nazir* according to the number of days.

7 "I am hereby a *nazir* according to the number of the sun's days"[11]—
he counts a *nazir* vow according to the number of the sun's days.
Said R. Judah:
This once happened; when he finished, he died.

Chapter Two

2:1–4 *Ambiguous or Partial Vows*

2 "I am hereby a *nazir* from dried dates and[12] from pressed figs":
the House of Shammai say:
He is a *nazir*;
but the House of Hillel say:

[9] P has introductory "One who says…"   [10] Lit. "How many days from here to that place."
[11] K, P: "According to the days of the year." See annotations.   [12] Or "or."

1:5 *a houseful*: Alternatively "a barrelful." Here, readings differ by single letter.

If he said: If he clarified his original meaning in this way.

mustardseeds: **TJ** suggests he should get a chance to specify that he meant larger items such as cucumbers. **TB** rejects this option on technical grounds: since we cannot be sure, we must prevent him from bringing the required sacrifices before the proper time, before they could properly be introduced into the Temple.

1:7 *he counts…the sun's days*: A thirty-day *nazir* term for each day of the year for each of the 365 days of the solar year. The reading of **K** and **P** may imply the 354 days of the lunar year.

2:1 *dates…figs*: The specified kinds of fruit are normally permitted to a *nazir*, but here the speaker has taken a vow using the word *nazir*. At first it appears the Houses differ over whether a person making such a vow is in fact a *nazir*: the vow contains the effective word (so the House of Shammai), but it seems to deal with foodstuffs irrelevant to a *nazir*'s vow (so the House of Hillel). R. Judah's comment rejects this interpretation: even the House of Shammai mean only to say that the indicated foods are indeed forbidden as if by

He is not a *nazir*.
Said R. Judah:
Even when the House of Shammai said this,
They only said so about[13] one who says: "They are[14] hereby a sacrifice for me."

2 If he said:
"This cow has said: I am hereby a *nazir* if I stand up,"
"This door has said: I am hereby a *nazir* if I am opened"—
the House of Shammai say:
He is a *nazir*;
but the House of Hillel say:
He is not a *nazir*.
Said R. Judah:
Even when the House of Shammai said this,
they only said so about[15] one who says:
"This cow is hereby a sacrifice to me[16] if it stands up."

3 If they poured him a cup,
and he said: "I am hereby a *nazir* from it"—
he is thereby a *nazir*.
It once happened that a woman was drunk,[17]
and they poured her a cup, and she said:
"I am hereby a *nazir* from it":
the Sages said:
She only meant to say
It is hereby a sacrifice for me.

[13] **K**: "They only said 'this is like one who says…'"
[14] **K, P**: "It is."
[15] **K**: "They only said 'this is like one who says…'"
[16] **MJ, K** lack "to me."
[17] **MJ, K,P** have an alternative spelling that might mean "a drunkard."

a vow (see below), but he is not a *nazir*. This is the simplest reading, but some commentators hold that such a vow does indeed render one a *nazir*. Still other commentators hold the opposite: the vow is ineffective even for dried dates or pressed figs.

a sacrifice: Heb. qorban. The word was routinely used to pronounce a vow; when someone declared that a certain type of food or other substance, or even a certain person, was *qorban*, the effect was to renounce any possibility of enjoying that food or deriving any benefit from the indicated person. See *Nedarim* introduction.

2:2 *"This cow has said"… "This door has said"*: The commentators suggest a situation where a cow refuses to stand up, or a door sticks and cannot be opened, as though they had undertaken *nazir*-like vows to avoid such compliance. The owner therefore says "I too swear *nazir*-like avoidance of them unless they obey me at once." If the owner succeeds, all is well; if others succeed in his place, or if the cow and door simply remain as they were or "comply" without human agency, the question arises, as in 2:1, whether the owner must become a *nazir*. It is taken for granted that the speaker has *not* vowed to offer the cow as an actual sacrifice in the Temple.

a sacrifice: See annotation to 2:1.

2:3 *a cup*: Of wine.

4 "I am hereby a *nazir* on condition that I may drink wine
and[18] become impure through contact with the dead"—
he is thereby a *nazir*,
and he is forbidden with respect to all of these.
"I knew about being a *nazir*,[19]
but I did not know that a *nazir* may not drink wine"—
he is thereby forbidden;[20]
but R. Simeon permits.
"I knew a *nazir* is forbidden with respect to wine,
but I thought the Sages would release me because I cannot[21] live without wine";
or "…because I bury the dead"—
he is thereby permitted,
but R. Simeon forbids.

2:5–6   *Vows on behalf of Others*

5 "I am hereby a *nazir* and obliged to shave a *nazir*,"
and his companion heard and said: "And I, and [I am] obliged to shave a *nazir*":
if they were clever—
they shave one another,
and if not—
they shave[22] other *nezirim*.

[18] Or "or."   [19] **MJ, K, P**: "I know that *nezirim* exist."   [20] **P** adds "[to drink] wine."
[21] **P** restores "cannot" in the margin.   [22] **P** adds "for."

2:4 *"on condition that…contact with the dead"*: A *nazir* must abstain from these activities.

"I knew…I did not know…": The text has present-tense verbs, but in English past-tense language is much more natural. The anonymous view is that he must observe even those aspects of the *nazir* vow that were unknown to him at the time of his undertaking. R. Simeon dissents, either because a vow undertaken in error is never valid (**TJ**) or because a *nazir* vow in particular must be unrestricted to take effect (**TB**), and he had excluded abstention from wine in the intent behind his vow.

"because I bury": Refers to the condition permitting corpse impurity. The implication here is that this is the oath taker's livelihood.

but R. Simeon forbids: This case differs from the preceding in that the vow was undertaken in complete knowledge of the law. The Sages nevertheless accept that this was a vow undertaken in error, while R. Simeon holds that the error was not intrinsic to the vow: the would-be *nazir* expected a certain action by the authorities which did not materialize, but meanwhile his vow has taken effect. One can always petition for release from a vow, but R. Simeon holds that the vow is binding unless and until such a petition is granted.

2:5 *"shave a nazir"*: That is, provide the sacrifices (Numbers 6:13–15) that a *nazir* must bring when his vows are completed.

if they were clever: If each absorbs the other's cost, each must bear the expense of only one set of sacrifices. Otherwise each must pay for his own sacrifices and a second set as well.

6 "I am hereby obliged to shave half a *nazir*,"
and his companion heard and said:
"And I, I am hereby obliged to shave half a *nazir*"—
this one shaves a whole *nazir* and this one shaves a whole *nazir*—
the words of R. Meir;
but the Sages say:
This one shaves half a *nazir* and this one shaves half a *nazir*.[23]

2:7–10   Vows Conditioned on Future Events

7 "I am hereby a *nazir* when a son is born to me,"
and a son is born to him—
he is thereby a *nazir*;
a daughter, a *tumtum*, or an *androgynos* was born to him[24]—
he is not a *nazir*.
If he said: "When I see that a child is born to me"[25]—
even if a daughter, a *tumtum*, or an *androgynos* is born to him,
he is thereby a *nazir*.

8 If his wife miscarried—
he is not a *nazir*.
R. Simeon says:
Let him say: "If it was viable—
I am an obligatory *nazir*;
and if not—
I am a voluntary *nazir*."

[23] **K** twice lacks the second phrase ("and this one...a whole/half a *nazir*").
[24] **K** restores "a daughter" in the margin. **K, P** lack "was born to him."
[25] **MJ, K, P**, and others have only "When I see a child." Still others have only "when a child is born to me."

2:6 *"shave half a nazir"*: Absorb half the cost of a *nazir*'s sacrifices.

the words of R. Meir: Just as one cannot be half a *nazir*, so one cannot subsidize half a *nazir*. The one who utters such a vow must bear the entire cost of the sacrifices; otherwise the vow would remain unfulfilled. The Sages accept the vow as spoken.

2:7 *tumtum*: A person with no visible sex organ. See *Yevamot* 8:6.

androgynos: A person with both male and female sexual characteristics. See *Yevamot* 8:6 and the last chapter of *Bikkurim*.

2:8 *If his wife miscarried*: The Mishnah continues its analysis of the vow described in 2:7.

R. Simeon believes the oath taker should become a *nazir* one way or the other. The actual status of the fetus may be hard to determine, and he must avoid leaving the vow unfulfilled if his condition was in fact satisfied. *If* the fetus *was viable*, R. Simeon holds the condition of the vow to have been fulfilled, and the father is now a *nazir* to fulfill that vow. If not, the anonymous opinion holds that the condition of the vow has not been fulfilled, but R. Simeon would have him become a *voluntary nazir*

If she later gave birth—
he is thereby a *nazir*.
R. Simeon says:
He should say: "If the first was viable—
the first [term as a *nazir*] was obligatory and this one is voluntary,
and if not—
the first was voluntary and this one is obligatory."

9 "I am hereby a *nazir*, and a *nazir* when I shall have a son"—
if he began counting his own [days as a *nazir*] and afterward a son was born to him—
he completes his own [term as a *nazir*]
and afterward counts his son's.
"I am hereby a *nazir* when I shall have a son, and a *nazir*"—
if he began counting his own and afterward a son was born to him,
he sets his own aside
and counts those of his son,
and afterward he completes his own.

10 "I am hereby a *nazir* when I shall have a son,
and a *nazir* for one hundred days"—
if a son was born to him within seventy he has lost nothing.[26]
After seventy, it undoes seventy,
since there is no shaving for fewer than thirty days.

[26] MJ, P: "he will lose nothing."

If she later gave birth: The anonymous opinion sees the live birth as fulfilling the condition of the original vow. R. Simeon requires a second term as a *nazir* but also supplies a clarifying declaration regarding the first. If the first term was in proper fulfillment of the vow this is now a voluntary *nazir* term (there was no further obligation); if not, the vow can now be properly fulfilled.

2:9 *counts his son's*: He begins a new *nazir* term on account of the birth of his son. In the first case he had mentioned his own unconditional vow first; therefore he completes that vow before beginning the second *nazir* period. In the second case the order of the vows was reversed; if a son is born, he must fulfill the conditional vow before anything else. In the first case he shaves and offers the necessary sacrifices before beginning the second term. In the second case one vow remains suspended, its fulfillment begun but not completed; he therefore delays shaving until both vows have been fulfilled, and then he shaves and offers a double set of sacrifices. Some commentators hold that the days of the unfinished term are lost; he may shave after the birth-related term has been completed, but then a new thirty-day period must begin since "there is no shaving for less than thirty days" (see 2:10).

2:10 *within seventy*, so that there are at least thirty days remaining after fulfilling the vow conditional on his son's birth, *he has lost nothing*. Since his conditional vow preceded the unconditional, he must suspend his own *nazir* term and fulfill the term resulting from the birth of his son (see 2:9). He then shaves, offers the necessary sacrifices, and completes his own hundred-day term, picking up where he had left off.

it undoes seventy: He follows the same procedure, except that the second portion of the hundred-day vow must last at least thirty days because *there is no shaving for less than thirty days*. (One needs a full growth of hair in order to "shave.") The days past seventy that he had already fulfilled are lost. This translation follows the most widely accepted reading; a variant supplies the word "undoes up to seventy," which comes to the same thing. Another interpretation, however, holds that the interruption actually undoes the first seventy days, since fewer than the required thirty remain, and the *nazir* must fulfill the entire hundred-day vow after the new term is completed.

Chapter Three

3:1–2 *The End of a Nazir's Term*

3 One who said: "I am hereby a *nazir*"—
he shaves on the thirty-first day,
and if he shaved on the thirtieth day he has fulfilled his obligation.
"I am hereby a *nazir* thirty days"—
if he shaved on the thirtieth day he has not fulfilled his obligation.
  2 One who vowed two *nazir* terms—
he shaves for the first on the thirty-first day,
and for the second on the sixty-first day.
And[27] if he shaved for the first on the thirtieth day,
he shaves for the second on the sixtieth day.
And if he shaved on the fifty-ninth day,[28] he has fulfilled his obligation.
And this is the testimony that R. Papias gave about one who vowed two *nazir* terms:
that if he shaved for the first on the thirtieth day,
he shaves for the second on the sixtieth day;
and if he shaved on the fifty-ninth day,[29] he has fulfilled his obligation,
because the thirtieth day is included in the count.

3:3–6 *Nezirim and Corpse Impurity*

  3 One who said: "I am hereby a *nazir*":
if he became impure on the thirtieth day—
it undoes everything;

---

[27] **MJ,P:** "For if…"   [28] Lit. "on the sixtieth day less one."
[29] Lit. "on the sixtieth day less one."

3:1 *he has not fulfilled his obligation*: The normal rule is that part of the final day counts as the whole. In the second case, the *nazir* has explicitly pledged a thirty-day term and must complete the thirtieth day.

3:2 *included in the count* of the second thirty-day term. Since part of the day counts as the whole, the beginning of the thirtieth day completes the first term and the rest of the thirtieth day can be counted toward the second.

testimony: See the parallel at *Eduyot* 7:5.

3:3 The rule for a *nazir* who incurs corpse impurity normally takes for granted that the impurity took hold some time during the term of the vow. If the *nazir* becomes impure, he must go through the purification ceremony, and then start his *nazir* term over. This paragraph deals with a special case: if the impurity was incurred on the last day of the vow, since the *nazir* can fulfill his sacrificial obligation on that day (3:1).

it undoes everything: The *nazir* must start his *nazir* term over.

R.[30] Eliezer says:
It undoes only seven[31] days.
"I am hereby a *nazir* thirty days":
if he became impure on the thirtieth day—
it undoes everything.

4 "I am hereby a *nazir* one hundred days":
if he became impure on the hundredth day—
it undoes everything;
R. Eliezer says:
It undoes only thirty days.
If he became impure on the 101st day—
it undoes thirty days;
R. Eliezer says:
It undoes only seven.

5 One who vowed to become a *nazir* while in a cemetery:[32]
even if he was there[33] thirty days—
they are not included in the count,

[30] K adds "But…"   [31] P interpolates an extra "thirty."
[32] K, P: "and he is [standing] among graves."   [33] K: "he is there."

R. Eliezer holds that since the *nazir* could have offered the regular sacrifices on the morning of the thirtieth day (see 3:1) he need not start over. Instead he must observe the usual seven-day period of corpse impurity (Numbers 19:11–12), offer the impurity sacrifices on the eighth day, and then just make up the seven days of his impurity. Some commentators interpret differently: in fact he loses no time at all, and his *nazir* vow has been fulfilled, though he must wait until the seven-day purification is over before he can drink wine or come in voluntary contact with the dead.

"I am hereby a nazir thirty days": If the vow had explicitly mentioned thirty (complete) days, however, the *nazir* must indeed start again from the beginning as in 3:1 above.

3:4 This mishnah extends the discussion of the preceding to a longer-term *nazir* vow, adding another special case, namely impurity incurred on the day after the termination of the vow, when a *nazir* would normally offer his sacrifices and undergo shaving.

it undoes everything: The anonymous opinion makes no distinction between the last day of the vow and all the others: a *nazir* who becomes impure in the course of his term loses all the preceding days, undergoes purification, and starts again. The "day of shaving," however, is different: the vow has been fulfilled though its ceremonial closure has not taken place. The *nazir* must indeed start a new term, but under the circumstances a standard thirty-day term will do.

R. Eliezer still maintains the more lenient opinion seen in 3:3 above. In the first case the *nazir* has no choice but to serve out a new term, but the standard thirty days will suffice. In the second case the vow of one hundred days was completed, so the case is no different from that in 3:3 and R. Eliezer's ruling is the same as given there.

3:5 *while in a cemetery*: The vow cannot begin to take effect until he has left the cemetery, so the days *are not included in the count*. For the same reason he is not obliged to offer the purification sacrifices: he is not an impure *nazir* because he was not yet a *nazir* at all.

they, the days prior to his reentering the cemetery, *are included in the count*: One would suppose that the count in any case is interrupted and lost, but mere presence in a cemetery is not included in the list of impurities provided in 7:2–3 below; some commentators therefore hold that once the *nazir* has been purified of cemetery impurity the count can resume from the point when it was interrupted.

and he does not bring an impurity sacrifice.
If he left and reentered—
they are included in the count
and he does bring an impurity sacrifice.
R. Eliezer says:
Not that same day,
as it is said: *The first days shall fall away*—
Until[34] he has *first days*.

6 One who vowed much *nazir* status and completed his term,
and afterward came to the Land—
the House of Shammai say:
He is a *nazir* for thirty days;
but the House of Hillel say:
He is a *nazir* as at the beginning.
It once happened with Queen Helene that her son went to war,
and she said:
"If my son returns from the war in peace I shall be a *nezirah* seven years."
Her son came from the war and she was a *nezirah* seven years,
and at the end of seven years she came up to the Land.
The House of Hillel instructed her that she be a *nezirah* yet another seven years.
At the end of seven years[35] she became impure,

[34] K: "he should have 'first days,'" without "until."
[35] P restores "years" between the lines. K repeats the words "another at the end of seven years."

Not that same day, the day his vow initially took effect. If a *nazir* has not yet completed at least one full day of his term there is nothing to be lost if he becomes impure; hence the Torah's provisions for an impure *nazir* cannot apply to such a person and he need not offer the prescribed sacrifices. Commentators differ as to whether R. Eliezer's rule is limited to the case where the original vow was spoken under conditions of impurity.

The first days shall fall away: Numbers 6:12.

Until he has...: The rule only applies after *days*, in the plural, have transpired.

3:6 This mishnah and the following, with the exception of the Helene material, also appear at *Eduyot* 4:11.

much nazir status: An awkward phrase: commentators understand either a single extended vow or many separate vows. Subtle differences among variant readings support one interpretation or the other.

House of Shammai.... House of Hillel: The entire world outside the Land of Israel ("the land of the nations") was deemed impure. Contact with even a packet of soil from outside the Land of Israel obliged one to go through the ritual of purification that follows corpse impurity, though this impurity did not undo the partial fulfillment of a *nazir*'s vow and make him start over (see below, 7:2–3). Nevertheless, the House of Shammai require an additional thirty-day period of *nazir* status as a penalty for having served out the larger vow(s) on impure territory. The House of Hillel take a stricter view: contact with foreign land would not undo days already counted, but the count cannot begin at all on impure soil. Such a *nazir* is still "at the beginning," and must fulfill the entire vow (or set of vows) all over again.

Queen Helene: Of Adiabene (first century CE, today northern Iraq). Josephus reports that Helene and her son both converted to Judaism.

"in peace": Uninjured.

she became impure: Through corpse impurity.

so she turned out to be a *nezirah* twenty-one years.
Said R. Judah:
She was a *nezirah* for only fourteen years.[36]

3:7 Conflicting Testimony as to a Person's Vow

7 One about whom two sets of witnesses gave testimony—
these testify that he made two *nazir* vows,
and these testify that he made five *nazir* vows:
the House of Shammai say:
The testimony is divided, and there is no *nazir* status here;
but the House of Hillel say:
Two is included in five, so let him be a *nazir* twice.

Chapter Four

4:1 Vows Attached to Other Vows

4 One who said: "I am hereby a *nazir*"—
and his companion heard and said: "And I,"[37] and another said "And I":[38]
they all are *nezirim*.
If the first was released:
they all are released.
If the last was released:
the last is released and they all are bound.
If he said: "I am hereby a *nazir*"—

[36] K lacks "years."   [37] K lacks "and."   [38] Heb. "And I, and I." MJ and P add a third "and I."

---

for only fourteen years: **TB** concludes that R. Judah denies Helene was impure; if she had been, even the House of Shammai would have required an extra thirty days. **TJ** considers this argument and rejects it: the Mishnah simply ignored the one month in the context of so many years. The reason for R. Judah's dissent thus remains unclear. Medieval commentators raise another possibility: she became impure on the last day of her term and added only thirty days in accordance with 3:4 above.

3:7 *The testimony is divided*: Each set of witnesses is contradicted by the other with regard to the crucial fact. Since neither claim is beyond challenge, neither can be accepted.

4:1 *the first was released*: From his vow by a qualified Sage (*Nedarim* 8:7–9:9).

they all are bound: In the first case, all the other vows were dependent on the first ("And I") and could not remain binding if the first was not. In the second case the chain remains sound until the last. The same logic would govern a case where one of the middle links was broken: all vows up to that point remain in force, and all later vows are released. The terms for "released" and "bound" are the usual terms for "permitted" and "forbidden"; see Matthew 18:18.

and his companion heard and said:
"My mouth is as his mouth", or "My hair is as his hair":
he is thereby a *nazir*.

4:1 cont.–5 The Husband's Right to Nullify his Wife's Vow

"I am hereby a *nazir*"—
and his wife heard and said: "And I":
he nullifies hers but his stands.
"I am hereby a *nezirah*"—
and her husband heard and said: "And I":
he cannot nullify.

2 "I am hereby a *nazir*, and you?"
and she said: "Amen":
he nullifies hers but his stands.[39]
"I am hereby a *nezirah*, and you?"
And he said: "Amen":[40]
he cannot nullify.

3 The woman who vowed to be a *nazir*,
and she would drink wine,
or would become impure [through contact] with the dead—
in such a case this person takes forty stripes.[41]

[39] **MJ, K, P**: "and his is void." See annotations.
[40] **MJ, P**: "her husband heard and said 'And I,'" which repeats the final clause of 4:1 but comes to the same thing.
[41] Lit. "absorbs forty."

"My mouth is as his mouth": Anything that he cannot put into his mouth (wine, grapes, etc.) is also forbidden to me.

his wife heard...he nullifies hers: Under certain circumstances a man may nullify the vows of his wife or minor daughter (Numbers 30:4–13; *Nedarim* chapters 10–11). The vows of a man (see Numbers 30:3) offer no such escape.

heard...he cannot nullify: By adding his own vow to his wife's he has ratified hers, and so can no longer nullify it.

4:2 *"and you?"*: In both cases the original speaker addresses his or her spouse. The logic matches that of 4:1 above.

but his stands: Other witnesses read "but his is void" (see n. 39). **TJ** understands the husband's words as a double vow: "I am hereby a *nazir* and so are you." Since no one can be compelled to vow, his wife must now consent; if she demurs, the vow cannot be fulfilled and so is void. **TB** does not share this understanding; the husband has made a vow and invited his wife to join him, but even if she declines his own vow must stand. Neither the oral text nor early written texts provided punctuation, so uncertainty as to whether the husband's words were meant as a question (the only difference is in tone of voice) could easily arise.

4:3 *she would drink wine*: The woman here has willfully violated her vow and thus violated Numbers 30:3 (*he shall not break his word*); therefore she must suffer the penalty.

takes forty stripes: See *Makkot* 3:10.

If her husband nullified her vow,
and she did not know her husband had nullified it,
and she would drink wine or would become impure [through contact] with the dead:
she does not take forty stripes.[42]
R. Judah says:
If she does not take forty stripes,
let her take stripes of rebellion.

4 The woman who uttered a *nazir* vow—
and[43] set aside her animal,
and her husband thereafter nullified her [vow]:
if her animal was his—
it can go out and graze in the flock;
but if her animal was her own—
the purgation offering must die,
and the whole burnt offering should be offered as a whole burnt offering,
and the offering of well-being should be offered as an offering of well-being.
They are to be eaten over one day and do not require bread.
If she[44] had money that was not designated:
it falls into the voluntary offering fund.
Money that was designated:

[42] As above: "absorbs forty." [43] MJ, K, P lack "and." [44] K: "he."

stripes of rebellion: One who intended to violate biblical law but was not technically liable for the penalty of flogging might nevertheless be subject to "stripes of rebellion," corporal punishment inflicted by the authority of the rabbinic court. The woman in question was not strictly guilty of breaking her vow since the vow had in fact been nullified, but she meant to break it and in R. Judah's opinion should be punished for that guilty intent.

4:4 *set aside her animal*: Any of the three animals that would be sacrificed (Numbers 6:14) when her *nazir* term was completed. The reading without "and" tacitly adds "if she" or words to that effect.

go out and graze in the flock: No sanctity attaches to it. The beast belongs to the husband; by nullifying the *nazir* vow he also implicitly denies her right to consecrate the animal.

the purgation offering must die…do not require bread: Although the vow has been cancelled, the various sacrifices are carried out as planned before the vow was canceled, except for certain adjustments. The animal designated as a purgation offering must be allowed to die a natural death, which can be hastened by withholding nourishment until it dies of hunger. The designated offering of well-being need not be accompanied by the baked offerings specified in Numbers 6:15–17, but unlike ordinary offerings of well-being it must be consumed by midnight of the day it is offered.

money that was not designated: She had set aside the funds to buy the necessary sacrifices, but had not divided the money into separate amounts for the three different offerings.

voluntary offering fund: Consecrated money that could not be used for its original purpose was placed in a special account from which animals for whole burnt offering were purchased and sacrificed when occasion allowed. According to *Sheqalim* 6:5–6 there were boxes in the Temple where people might deposit such funds.

money for the purgation offering goes to the Dead Sea;
one may not benefit from it,
though one does not commit sacrilege through their use.[45]
Money for the whole burnt offering:
one brings a whole burnt offering,
and one commits sacrilege through their use.
Money for the offering of well-being:
one brings well-being offerings.
They are to be eaten over one day
and do not require bread.

5 If one of the types of blood was sprinkled on her behalf—
he cannot nullify.
R. Aqiva says:
Even if anyone of all the animals was slaughtered on her behalf—
he cannot nullify.
When does this apply?
With the shaving of purity.
But with the shaving of impurity
he may nullify,
since he can say: "I do not want a degraded wife."
Rabbi[46] says:
Even with the shaving of purity he may nullify,
since he can say: "I do not want a shaven wife."

[45] Lit. "with them."   [46] Variant: "R. Meir," so too in **MB**.

go to the Dead Sea: Money set aside to purchase a purgation offering has the same status as an animal designated for that category. Since the animal must die, the money must "go to the Dead Sea" or be destroyed in some other unproductive fashion.

sacrilege: Leviticus 5:14–16 defines the penalty for unauthorized use of consecrated property.

4:5 *he cannot nullify* her vow: Once the *nazir*'s sacrificial process has begun, the vow is officially terminated and the husband's power to nullify it has lapsed. The anonymous opinion identifies the moment of termination as the first delivery of sacrificial blood to the altar; R. Aqiva moves it earlier, to the slaughter of the first sacrificial beast.

shaving of purity…impurity: A *nazir* must "shave" either when his vow has been successfully fulfilled (*shaving of purity*) or when it was cut short by corpse impurity (*shaving of impurity*).

with the shaving of impurity he may nullify: Even though the sacrifices have been offered the wife's vow remains in effect; in fact she must begin to count her term from the beginning. Therefore the husband's right to nullify the vow has not yet lapsed.

a degraded wife: She is "degraded" by having to avoid activities (drinking wine, styling her hair) that would make her more attractive to her husband.

a shaven wife: Rabbi thinks the husband can cancel the vow even at the last minute, even after the sacrifices have been offered, if he wants to prevent his wife from shaving her head. This discussion presumes that the husband only learns of his wife's vow after it has run its course—at least thirty days—but that is not unimaginable.

4:6 *An Imposed Vow*

6 A man may impose a *nazir* vow on his son,
but a woman may not impose a *nazir* vow on her son.
How?[47]
If he shaved, or his relatives shaved him,
if he objected, or his relatives objected:
if he had designated an animal—
the purgation offering must die,
and the whole burnt offering is to be offered as a whole burnt offering,
and the offering of well-being is to be offered as an offering of wellbeing.
They are to be eaten over one day and do not require bread.
If he had money that was not designated,
it falls into the voluntary offering fund.
Money that was designated:
money for the purgation offering goes to the Dead Sea;
one may not benefit from it, though one does not commit sacrilege through its use.[48]
Money for the whole burnt offering:
one brings a whole burnt offering,
and one commits sacrilege [by using it].
Money for the offering of well-being:
one brings offerings of well-being;
They are to be eaten over one day and do not require bread.

4:7 *Using the Sacrifices of One's Nazir Father*

7 A man may shave on the basis of his father's being a *nazir*,
but a woman may not shave on the basis of her father's being a *nazir*.

---

[47] Numerous medieval authorities delete this word; see annotations.   [48] Lit. "with them."

4:6 *A man...on her son*. Parallel at *Sotah* 3:8.

impose: According to tradition a father, but not a mother, has the authority to declare that his son must become a *nazir*. However, the authority is not absolute; it will soon emerge that the son, or even the son's other relatives, can reject the imposed vow. Commentators vary as to whether the father's right lapses when the son reaches majority.

How? It seems the question means "If the son or the relatives object, what shall the father do with animals or moneys already set aside for the son's sacrifices?" This is awkward, since the possibility of such objection has not yet been raised; many medieval authorities accordingly delete the one-word question.

If he shaved: Unlike the usage elsewhere in the tractate, here the word *shaved* means that the son shaved (or cut his hair in some fashion) in violation of the imposed vow, thereby showing that he rejected it. The same would be the case if his relatives arranged for him to cut his hair, or even if he or they verbally expressed such rejection.

designated an animal: In advance, for the final sacrifices.

4:7 *may shave on the basis*: If the father was a *nazir* who had set aside animals or funds for his sacrifices but died before he could offer them, the son may use those animals or those funds to pay for his own sacrifices if he was a *nazir* as well; by tradition a woman may not do this. Both the text and the particulars of the case are unclear; see further below.

How?
One whose father was a *nazir*,
who had set apart undifferentiated money for his *nazir* obligation and died,
and he said: "I am hereby a *nazir* on condition that I shave with Father's money"—
Said R. Yose:
In such a case this falls to the voluntary offering fund;
this one cannot shave on the basis of his father's being a *nazir*.
Who is it that shaves on the basis of his father's being a *nazir*?
One who was a *nazir* as well as his father,
and his father had set apart undifferentiated money for his *nazir* obligation and died;
that is the one who shaves on the basis of his father's being a *nazir*.

Chapter Five

5:1–2   *Erroneous Consecration*

5 The House of Shammai say:
Erroneous consecration is consecration;
but the House of Hillel say:
It is not consecration.
How?
If he said: "The black ox that comes first out of my house is hereby consecrated,"
and a white one came out—
the House of Shammai say:
It is consecrated;
but the House of Hillel say:
It is not consecrated.
  2 "The gold *dinar* that comes up first into my hand is hereby consecrated,"
and a silver [*dinar*] came up first—
the House of Shammai say:
It is consecrated;

---

undifferentiated money: As above (4:4, 6), the money had not been divided into three parts, each dedicated for a particular sacrifice.

Said R. Yose: Commentators differ as to whether the preceding sentence comes from an unnamed authority (identified in **TJ** as R. Judah) or also comes from R. Yose and indicates the opinion he rejects.

that is the one: Texts vary as to R. Yose's opinion. The translation follows the most widely accepted version, but others reverse his teaching: the one who was already a *nazir* cannot use his father's funds, only one who became a *nazir* after his father had died.

5:1–2 Generally speaking a vow must explicitly state the speaker's intention, but sometimes the intention can be inferred (or presumed) from the language of the vow. In the first case the Houses differ as to the speaker's intention. The House of Shammai hold that the speaker intended to consecrate the first ox that came out of his house. He erroneously predicted that the ox would be black, but that does not matter: the mistake does not undo the basic act of consecration. The House of Hillel take the words more literally: if a black ox came out

but the House of Hillel say:
It is not consecrated.
"The container of wine that comes up first into my hand is hereby consecrated,"
and one of oil came up first—
the House of Shammai say:
It is consecrated;
but the House of Hillel say:
It is not consecrated.

5:3–7   *Erroneous Nazir Vows*

3 One who vowed to become a *nazir*
and then consulted a Sage,[49]
and he bound him—
he counts from the hour that he vowed.
If he consulted a Sage and he released him—
if he had an animal set aside,
it may go and graze in the flock.
The House of Hillel said to the House of Shammai:
Do you not agree in this case that the sanctification was erroneous,
so that it may go and graze in the flock?
The House of Shammai said to them:
Do you not agree in the case of one who erred and declared the ninth to be the tenth

---

[49] **MJ, K**: "the Sages," here and immediately below. **P** is ambiguous.

---

first, it would be consecrated. Since the first ox to appear was white, the vow was based on an error (see *Nedarim* 3:1–2, 9:10) and is void. The House of Shammai were probably guided by the law of cattle tithe in Leviticus 27:32–33 (see below): any attempt to transfer consecration from one animal to another consecrates them both. Here too the attempt to transfer consecration from the putative black ox to the real white one leaves them both consecrated, though only the white ox exists in fact. The logic in the later sets of cases is the same.

5:3 *consulted a Sage*: In the hope of being released from his vow.

bound: The Sage upheld the vow. On "bound" and on "released" in the following clause see above, on 4:1.

he counts: The person in question had already been drinking wine (or perhaps even incurring corpse impurity!) in the expectation that his vow would be released: he is not penalized for having done so, though he must still complete his term. Other views hold that he must now begin the count from the time of the Sage's ruling (**TB**). Still others presume he has not violated the vow (or has done so only inadvertently) but now wishes in any case to be released; in that case he can surely include the days already past in his ongoing count.

Do you not agree…: Continues the preceding discussion. The released *nazir* had consecrated his animals in error, thinking he would have to sacrifice them at the end of his term, but now they are freed of any sanctity. Does this not contradict the position of the House of Shammai?

declared the ninth to be tenth: Ignoring the challenge, the Shammaites respond by referring to Leviticus: each year the crop of newborn animals must be lined up and counted and each tenth animal marked off as part of the tithe, but a miscount that results in declaring the ninth or the eleventh animal to be the tenth is nonetheless effective (Leviticus 27:32–33; *Bekhorot* 9:7–8). The House of Hillel tacitly concede this point but then cite the same Scripture in their turn: the Torah instructs that the ninth or the eleventh animal in line must be added to the tithe, but by implication this rule is not extended to any others. This very specific decree of Scripture can therefore not be used for deriving more general rules about mistaken consecration.

or the tenth to be the ninth or the eleventh to be the tenth,
that it is consecrated?
The House of Hillel said to them:
The staff did not consecrate it.
And what if he erred and placed the staff on the eighth or the twelfth,
would he have been effective?[50]
Rather, it is Scripture, which consecrated the tenth,
that consecrated the ninth and the eleventh.

4 One who vowed to become a *nazir*
and went to fetch his animal
and discovered it had been stolen:
if he vowed before his[51] animal was stolen—
he is thereby a *nazir*;
and if he vowed after his animal had been stolen—
he is not a *nazir*.
And Nahum the Mede[52] made this error
when *nezirim* came up from the exile and found the Temple was destroyed.
Nahum the Mede said to them:
If you had known the Temple was destroyed[53]
would you have become *nezirim*?
They said to him: No!
And Nahum the Mede released them [from their vows].
When the matter came before the Sages,
they said to him:
Anyone who vowed to be a *nazir*:
before the Temple was destroyed—
is a *nazir*,
but [anyone who vowed] after the Temple was destroyed—
is not a *nazir*.

[50] Lit. "had he done anything?" [51] MJ, K, P lack "his," here and immediately below.
[52] MJ, K, P: "Nahum, the man of Media." So throughout, except that P lacks "of Media" in this first occurrence.
[53] K: "was going to be destroyed."

The staff did not consecrate it…Rather, it is Scripture: Merely declaring an animal to be part of the tithe does nothing unless the declaration is made within the framework laid down in Scripture, and Scripture deals only with mistaken identification of numbers nine, ten, and eleven in the counting. The released *nazir*'s mistaken designation of animals for sacrifice falls outside this framework, and the general Hillelite rule (5:1 above) that *erroneous consecration is not consecration* can apply.

5:4 *stolen*: The vow had been offered in the expectation that the animal in question would be part of the post-term sacrifices. If the animal was still available at the time the vow was made, the vow must hold: one who sincerely regrets the consequences of a vow can apply to a Sage for release, but such regret must not be grounded in developments that took place after the vow was made (*Nedarim* 9:2). On the other hand if the animal had already been stolen but the theft was not yet known, the vow is a "mistaken vow" and does not take hold at all (*Nedarim* 3:1–2, 9:10).

came up from the exile: Sometimes "the exile" specifically designates Babylonia, but here it can simply mean that they had come from far away and had not yet heard the Temple was destroyed.

5 If they[54] were walking along the road,
and one came toward them.
One of [the group] said:
"I am hereby a *nazir* if that is so-and-so,"
and another said:
"I am hereby a *nazir* if that is not so-and-so,"[55]
"I am hereby a *nazir* if one of you is a *nazir*,"
"…if one of you is not a *nazir*,"
"…if you are both *nezirim*,"
"…if you are all *nezirim*"—
the House of Shammai say:
They are all *nezirim*;
but the House of Hillel say:
No one is a *nazir* except the one whose words were not fulfilled.
And R. Tarfon says:
Not one of them is a *nazir*.

6 If he suddenly turned away,
he is not a *nazir*.
R. Simeon says:
Let him say: "If it was as I spoke—
I am hereby a *nazir* by obligation,
and if not—
I am hereby a voluntary *nazir*."

[54] Var.: "If six…"   [55] K, P: "if that is not he."

5:5 *"I am hereby a nazir if that is so-and-so"*: Following disagreements in the Talmudim, commentators understand this and the following vows in two opposite ways. According to one opinion, the conditional vow is fulfilled if the approaching person is indeed "so-and-so," and therefore the speaker must become a *nazir*. Alternatively, *I am hereby a nazir* simply expresses the speaker's conviction that the approaching person is "so-and-so": he must now become a *nazir* only if that conviction turns out to have been mistaken. The same pair of interpretations can be applied to the second vow, which is based on the speaker's opinion that the approaching person is *not* "so-and-so," and to all the others as well.

the House of Shammai: This opinion conforms to the previous ruling of the House of Shammai that even a mistaken *nazir* vow is binding (above, 5:1). Once a person says *I am hereby a* nazir, it makes no difference whether his further stipulation is fulfilled or not.

the House of Hillel: In keeping with the first interpretation described above, **TB** offers a proposal to delete the word "not."

R. Tarfon: None of the speakers really intended to become a *nazir*. The vows were meant only to emphasize the strength of their convictions.

5:6 *suddenly turned away*: The individual on whom all the vows in 5:5 depended could not be identified at all.

he is not a nazir: None of the six can know whether his vow was fulfilled or not, so all six vows lose their force.

Let him say: That is, each should say. The anomalous singular language reflects the influence of 2:8 above, where R. Simeon offers the same solution to a similar problem.

7 If he saw a *koy* and said:
"I am hereby a *nazir* if this is a wild animal,"
"I am hereby a *nazir* if this is a not a wild animal,"
"I am hereby a *nazir* if this is a domesticated animal,"
"I am hereby a *nazir* if this is not a domesticated animal,"
"I am hereby a *nazir* if this is a wild animal and a domesticated animal,"
"I am hereby a *nazir* if this is neither a wild animal nor a domesticated animal,"
"I am hereby a *nazir* if one of you is a *nazir*,"
"I am hereby a *nazir*[56] if one of you is not a *nazir*,"
"I am hereby a *nazir* if all of you[57] are *nezirim*"—
they are thereby all *nezirim*.

Chapter Six

6:1–5 *Prohibitions Incumbent on a Nazir*

6 Three categories are forbidden to a *nazir*:
(1) impurity, (2) shaving, and (3) that which comes from the vine.
All that comes from the vine[58] combine,
and he is not liable until he has eaten an olive's bulk of grapes.
(Earlier teaching: Until he has drunk a quarter-*log* of wine.)
R. Aqiva says:
Even if he dipped his bread into wine,

[56] **MJ, K, P** lack this and the next occurrence of "I am hereby a *nazir*."
[57] **MJ, K, P**: "if two of you," "if all of you."
[58] **K** lacks the second "which comes from the vine."

5:7 *saw a koy*: Rabbinic authorities never decided whether the species called *koy*, apparently a kind of deer or goat, was domesticated or wild. See *Bikkurim* 2:8, 11.

they are thereby all nezirim: Each of the first six vows is at least partially true and therefore none of the six conditions is entirely unfulfilled. The ruling that all nine speakers are *nezirim* seems to lead to contradiction: if that is the case, then the statement *I am hereby a* nazir *if one of you is not a* nazir is false and the eighth speaker should not be a *nazir* at all! Commentators resolve this problem by positing that all nine speakers must fulfill their vows out of the uncertainty of their situations, but none of them is a *nazir* outright, beyond all doubt. The eighth speaker must then be understood to have said "I am hereby a *nazir* if one of you is not a *nazir* beyond doubt": none of the other eight is a *nazir* beyond doubt, so even the eighth speaker's condition has been fulfilled.

6:1 *impurity*: From a corpse.

shaving: Includes all cutting of the hair.

liable: To the prescribed penalty for violating his vow.

Earlier teaching: The grapes had to be sufficient to produce a quarter-*log* (about three fluid ounces) of wine; this is several times more than an olive's bulk of grapes. The phrase "earlier teaching" (lit. "first Mishnah") probably refers to an earlier rule, but it may indicate an earlier version of the present text.

and it combines to the bulk of an olive
he is liable.

2 And he is liable for wine by itself,
and for grapes by themselves,
and for grapeseeds by themselves,
and for grapeskins by themselves.[59]
R. Eleazar b. Azariah says:
He is not liable unless he eats two grapeseeds and their skin.
Which are *hartsanim* and which are *zagim*?
Hartsanim are the outer
and *zagim* are the inner—
the words of R. Judah.
R. Yose says:
In order that you not err,
it is like a cattle bell.
The outside is the hood,[60]
and the inside is the clapper.

3 An unspecified *nazir* vow is thirty days:
if he shaved,
or bandits shaved him—
this undoes thirty days.

[59] Grapeseeds: *hartsanim*; grapeskins, *zagin* or occasionally in **K** and **P** *zo/ugin*.   [60] Heb. *zug*.

and it combines: The bread and wine combine to the indicated bulk, even though the bread by itself was not forbidden. R. Aqiva's opinion differs from the earlier, anonymous ruling that the forbidden substances themselves must be of this volume.

6:2 *wine by itself...grapes by themselves*, etc.: A *nazir* who consumes wine and also grapes etc. is flogged for each material separately.

two grapeseeds and their skin: The requirement of two seeds reflects the wording of Numbers 6:4, where the word *hartsanim* appears in the plural as here, while the word *zag* does not.

hartsanim...zagim: The Torah (Numbers 6:4) uses these obscure words, rendered in translation above as "grapeseeds" and "skin," to indicate parts of the grape that are forbidden to a *nazir* beyond the obvious prohibition of the grape flesh or the wine that can be made from it. Here, where the Mishnah asks what the words refer to, the translation supplies the Hebrew terms.

hood: That is the exterior of the bell with its characteristic shape.

6:3 *An unspecified...thirty days*: The introductory clause, quoted from 1:3 above, is repeated here to explain the present rule.

bandits shaved him: against his will.

undoes thirty days: A *nazir* must live according to his vow for at least thirty days (see 2:10 above). If a *nazir* cuts or shaves his hair during this period, he must observe thirty days all over again from that point. If his vow was only for thirty days he starts again. If he vowed for forty days and shaved after twenty, he must serve thirty more, for a total of fifty. If he shaved before ten days had elapsed, however, at least thirty additional days remain; he must therefore only complete the forty days of his original vow. Other interpretations are that he loses the days that have already passed and must start again to complete his original term, or that he must lose thirty days in every case. Similar ambiguity around the phrase "this undoes" can be found above, 3:3–4.

A *nazir* who shaved,
whether with a pair of scissors or a razor,
or who singed[61] his hair
in any amount at all—
is liable.
A *nazir* may rub his hair or untangle it
but he may not comb it.
R. Ishmael says:
He may not rub it with dirt,
because it[62] makes the hair fall out.

4 A *nazir* who drank wine the whole day—
is liable only once.[63]
If they said to him: "Do not drink!" "Do not drink!"
and he drank—
he is liable for each.
If he shaved the whole day—
he is liable once.
If they said to him: "Do not shave!" "Do not shave!"
and he shaved—
he is liable for each.[64]
If he took on corpse impurity the whole day—
he is liable only once.[65]
If they said to him: "Do not become impure!" "Do not become impure!"
and he became impure—
he is liable for each.

5 Three categories are forbidden to a *nazir*:
(1) impurity, (2) shaving, and (3) that which comes from the vine.

[61] The terms in this paragraph are obscure; see annotations. [62] Var. "that makes…"
[63] Here and below, lit. "For one [penalty]." [64] K places this rule after the next.
[65] K adds "etc." as though the text has been abbreviated, but nothing seems missing.

singed…rub…untangle…comb: The precise meaning of these terms is uncertain. The underlying rule is that a *nazir* should not cause any reduction in the hair on his head, and the question here is whether any of the indicated activities would likely cause the loss of hair and should therefore be forbidden. "Untangle" has also been translated "scratch." "Singe" has also been translated "pull out" or "trim." Commentators vary as to whether "rubbing" the hair involves chemicals or other natural materials, or only the *nazir*'s fingers.

6:4 *If he took on corpse impurity the whole day*: That is, he repeatedly exposed himself to corpse impurity but without receiving repeated warnings.

liable for each: Defiance of each warning constitutes a new transgression. The rules in this Mishnah also appear in *Makkot* 3:7–8, in the order found in **K**.

6:5 *Three categories are forbidden*: Quoted from the beginning of the chapter.

Impurity and shaving carry more severity than that which comes from the vine,
in that impurity and shaving undo [the previous days],
and that which comes from the vine does not undo.
That which comes from the vine carries more severity than impurity and shaving,
in that that which comes from the vine provides no exception from its general rule,[66]
and impurity and shaving provide exceptions from their general rule[67]
in the case of a commanded shaving or an abandoned corpse.
And impurity carries more severity than shaving,
in that impurity undoes the whole term[68] and one owes a sacrifice on its account,
and shaving undoes only[69] thirty days and one does not owe a sacrifice on its account.

6:6–11 *Termination Procedures*

6 The shaving for impurity, how?
He would sprinkle on the third and seventh days,
and shave on the seventh,
and bring his sacrifices on the eighth.
And if he shaved on the eighth,
he brings his sacrifices that same day—
the words of R. Aqiva.
R. Tarfon said to him:

---

[66] K adds: "of that which comes from the vine."
[67] K lacks "from their general rule." P repeats the words "that which comes from the wine is permitted"; this insertion produces incoherence.
[68] Lit. "all," "everything."   [69] K adds "up to."

---

impurity and shaving undo [the previous days]: The rule for impurity is explicit in Scripture (Numbers 6:12). The rule for shaving (above, 6:3) is derived from the requirement (Numbers 6:5) that a *nazir* let his hair grow long; by rabbinic determination this required at least thirty days' growth (see 2:10 above). A *nazir* was forbidden to drink wine, but by doing so did not forfeit the completed part of his term.

exception from its general rule: A *nazir* was never permitted to drink wine, even if he had taken a separate oath to do so. The other prohibitions might be set aside under particular circumstances, as explained below.

commanded shaving: A cured person with *tsara'at* had to shave as part of his readmission into the community (Leviticus 14:9). If the one with *tsara'at* was also a *nazir* this requirement was not set aside, even though it meant that some or all of the *nazir* term had to be repeated. Under such circumstances the *nazir* was permitted, in fact required, to shave his head and take the consequences. But see 8:2 below.

abandoned corpse: Lit. *met mitzvah*, "a corpse of religious obligation." If a corpse was found unattended, those who discovered it had to stop whatever they were doing and see to its burial: this requirement took precedence over all other obligations. See further 7:1.

owe a sacrifice: For corpse impurity.

6:6 *how?* What is the procedure when a *nazir* incurs corpse impurity and must be purified and restart his term?

He would sprinkle: In order to remove corpse impurity he would be sprinkled with water containing the ashes of a red heifer (see Numbers 19 and *Parah*).

How is this different from one with *tsara'at*?[70]
He said to him:
This one, his purity depends on his days,
and the purity of one with *tsara'at*[71] depends on his shaving,
and[72] he does not bring a sacrifice unless the sun has set on him.

7 The shaving for purity, how?
He would bring three animals:
a purgation offering, a whole burnt offering, and an offering of well-being,
and[73] he would slaughter the offering of well-being and shave over it—
the words of R. Judah.
R. Eleazar[74] says:
He would shave over the purgation offering only,

[70] Lit. "what is between this and a one with *tsara'at*?"
[71] **MJ** and **P** simply repeat "and this one," but **P** adds "a one with *tsara'at*" between the lines.
[72] **MJ** and **P** lack "and"; see annotations.   [73] **MJ** lacks "and"; see annotations.
[74] Var. "Eliezer."

How is this different from one with tsara'at (Leviticus 14)? Commentators have understood the question in two different ways: (a) Granted that this rule also applies to a person with *tsara'at* who has healed; is there any difference at all between the rules that govern the two cases? If that is the question, R. Aqiva's answer points to a conceptual difference between the two cases, but one without procedural implications. (b) Why can a *nazir* bring his sacrifices the same day he shaves while one with *tsara'at* cannot? On this interpretation, R. Aqiva answers that an impure *nazir* is cleansed of his impurity through the sprinkling on the third and seventh days; he must also shave his head, but he is already purified and therefore can proceed to the sacrifices at once. On the other hand, one with *tsara'at* is cleansed of his impurity precisely by shaving all his hair (Leviticus 14:9), and Scripture clearly indicates the sacrifices must follow the next day (14:10). A parallel rabbinic text appears to suggest that R. Aqiva actually holds that one with *tsara'at* who has healed whose shaving was delayed can also offer his sacrifices without delay, but a variant reading there adds a crucial "not" to the operative phrase.

and he does not bring a sacrifice: **MB** here reads with "and"; in that case the rule can apply to either the one with *tsara'at* who has healed or the impure *nazir*. **MJ** and one manuscript lack the "and," so the reference is presumably to the main subject of the paragraph, the *nazir* who has been impure and then purified. If the rule applies to a *nazir*, the sun must set between the sprinkling and the sacrifices, but not necessarily before the shaving.

6:7 *shaving for purity*: What is the procedure when a *nazir* has successfully completed his term and must now emerge from his *nazir* status?

and he would slaughter: *And* implies continuity; he would bring the three animals to the Temple, begin his offering with the offering of well-being, *and* immediately shave his head. The version in **MJ** allows for the possibility that he would get to the offering of well-being at the end of the process and shave only then. In that case a better translation would be "[when he] slaughtered the offering of well-being [he would] shave over it."

shave over it: Shave the long-grown hair off his head at this point in the procedure, and so too below in the dissenting opinion of R. Eleazar. Commentators differ as to R. Judah's point. The text in Numbers 6:16–17 implies the sequence of sacrifices as given here, and it is possible that R. Judah accepts this sequence but holds that the shaving should be delayed until all three offerings have been completed. Other commentators understand that R. Judah actually requires a different order, with the offering of well-being coming first.

because the purgation offering takes precedence in every situation.
And if he shaved over any one of the three—
he has satisfied his obligation.

8 R. Simeon b. Gamaliel says:
If he brought three animals but did not specify—
the one suitable for a purgation offering should be offered as a purgation offering;
for a whole burnt offering should be offered as a whole burnt offering;
for an offering of well-being should be offered as an offering of well-being.
He would take the hair of his *nazir* head and throw it under the pot,
and if he shaved outside the Temple
he would throw it under the pot.[75]
When does this apply?
For the shaving of purity.
But for the shaving of impurity
he would not throw it under the pot.
R. Meir says:
All throw it under the pot,
Except only for the impure [*nazir* who shaved] outside the Temple.

9 As he was cooking or seething the offering of well-being,
the priest would take *the cooked foreleg from the ram and one unleavened loaf*

---

[75] Var. (so **MB**), "he would not throw it…" This reading seems preferable, for otherwise there is no difference between the Temple and elsewhere.

---

the purgation offering takes precedence in every situation: This is based on Leviticus 5:8, although the context there has nothing to do with a *nazir*.

And if he shaved over any of the three: A separate, uncontested teaching, not part of the conflict between R. Judah and R. Eleazar.

6:8 *R. Simeon b. Gamaliel*: A continuation of the topic in 6:7. Normally when one dedicates an animal as a sacrifice one specifies the type of sacrifice (whole burnt offering, purgation offering, etc.) for which it is intended. In this case, however, even if the animals were consecrated without such specification there is no question as to how each should be handled; the Torah specifies a particular species and a particular sex for each of the *nazir*'s offerings (Numbers 6:14), so each is suitable for only one category of the three.

He would take: This begins a new topic, the proper treatment of the *nazir*'s newly cut hair. There is no reason to ascribe this part of the paragraph to R. Simeon b. Gamaliel.

under the pot: The cauldron in which his offering of well-being was being cooked (see Numbers 6:18).

outside the Temple: Lit. "in the province," or "capital city." The term is ambiguous: it may designate the city of Jerusalem, as opposed to the Temple proper, or it may designate the area outside the city. In the latter case, all of Jerusalem would be included in the sacred precinct.

outside the Temple…under the pot: He would bring the shaved hair with him. With respect to burning the hair under the sacrificial cauldron, the commonly accepted text of the Mishnah does not distinguish among possible locations for shaving, but the **MB** version with "not" limits the described action to those cases where the *nazir* shaves his head at the place where the cauldron is located. This seems to reflect a very old dispute among tannaitic authorities.

6:9 *cooking or seething*: The two words denote different degrees of thorough cooking in a pot, but the precise meaning of each in this context is unclear.

the cooked foreleg…nazir's palms: Numbers 6:19, with various small changes in the word *place* found in variant readings.

*from the basket and one unleavened thin cake,
and place them*[76] *on the nazir's palms*
and wave them,
and after that the *nazir* was permitted to drink wine
and become impure through corpse impurity.
R. Simeon says:
Once the blood of [any] one of the sacrifices[77] had been thrown,
the *nazir* was permitted to drink wine and become impure through corpse impurity.
   10 If he shaved over the offering and it was found to be invalid—
his shaving is invalid,
and his sacrifices are not counted to his credit.
If he shaved over the purgation offering which had not been properly designated,
and thereafter brought his remaining sacrifices[78] properly designated—
his shaving[79] is invalid,
and his sacrifices are not counted to his credit.
If he shaved over the whole burnt offering or the offering of well-being
that had not been properly designated
and thereafter brought his remaining sacrifices properly designated,
his shaving is invalid,
and his sacrifices are not counted to his credit.
R. Simeon says:
That particular offering is not counted to his credit,
but the other offerings are counted to his credit.
And if he shaved over all three and one of them was found to be valid,
his shaving is valid,
but he must bring the remaining sacrifices again.

[76] The witnesses vary in the alteration of "and place them" to fit the context of the Mishnah.
[77] Lit. "One of the bloods."   [78] Here and below, lit. "his sacrifices."
[79] **P**: "his properly designated shaving," presumably a mistaken repetition of the word.

wave them: Leviticus 6:20. A formal act of sacrifice involved "waving" some or all of the sacrificial substance: after placing it in the open hands of the one bringing the offering, the priest would "wave" them in the four directions and also up and down.

blood…had been thrown: In R. Simeon's view, once the blood of any of the three sacrifices had been dashed on the walls of the altar the *nazir's* vow was completed. The restrictions he had undertaken were released at this point.

6:10 *his shaving is invalid*: And he must remain a *nazir* for thirty more days (see on 2:10 above).

properly designated: Lit. "in its name." The validity of a purgation offering depended on its having been designated such before it was slaughtered.

his sacrifices are not counted to his credit: The purgation offering is altogether invalid; the other offerings are valid sacrifices, but they do not fulfill his formal obligation.

R. Simeon holds that the *particular offering* that lacked proper designation when it was slaughtered does not count, but the other sacrifices do fulfill his obligation. Thus he only needs to make up one sacrifice.

11 A person for whom the blood from one of the animals[80] was thrown who then became impure—
R. Eliezer says:
This undoes everything.
But the Sages say:
He must bring the rest of his sacrifices
and become pure.
They said to him:
It once happened with Miriam the Tadmorite[81]
that [after] the blood of one of the animals was thrown for her,
they came and informed her that her daughter was in danger;
she went and found that she had died.
The Sages said:
She must bring the rest of her sacrifices
and become pure.

Chapter Seven

7:1–8:2 *Rules Concerning Corpse Impurity*

7 A high priest and a *nazir* may not become impure for their relatives, but they do become impure for an abandoned corpse.[82]
If they were walking down the road and they found an abandoned corpse—
R. Eliezer says:
Let the high priest become impure, and the *nazir* does not become impure.

[80] Lit. "One of the bloods," as in 6:8.
[81] Var. "Tarmodite" (or "Tarmadite").
[82] This line is missing from **MJ**, **K**, **P**.

6:11 *the blood from one of the animals was thrown* onto the altar as part of the offering. As in 6:8, the Mishnah literally reads "one of the bloods."

This undoes everything: Even the sacrifice that was offered before the *nazir* became impure must be brought again. The phrase does not mean (as it often means in other contexts) that the whole period of *nazir* status is undone and the vow must be fulfilled all over again; it refers only to the sacrificial offerings.

bring the rest ... and become pure: That is, when he becomes pure. The removal of corpse impurity must precede the three sacrifices; otherwise the ex-*nazir* would be barred from entering the Temple.

found that she had died: And contracted corpse-impurity on her account.

Tadmorite: From Palmyra in modern-day Syria. The variant is well attested but only contains a mistaken reversal of two orthographically similar letters.

7:1 *high priest*: See Leviticus 21:11.

abandoned corpse: See on 6:5 above.

But the Sages say:
Let the *nazir* become impure, and the high priest[83] does not become impure.
R. Eliezer said to them:
Let the priest become impure,
because he need not bring a sacrifice on account of his impurity,
but let the *nazir* not become impure,
because he must bring a sacrifice on account of his impurity.
They said to him:
Let the *nazir* become impure,
because his holiness is not permanent,[84]
but let the priest not become impure,
because his holiness is permanent.[85]

2 For which impurities must a *nazir* shave?
For a corpse,
and for an olive's bulk from a corpse,[86]
and for an olive's bulk of liquefied corpse material,
and for a ladleful of decayed flesh;
for the backbone,
and for the skull,
and for a limb from a corpse,
and for a limb from a living body
which has upon it an appropriate amount of flesh,
and for half a *qav* of bones,
and for half a *log* of blood—

[83] P: "ordinary priest." K: "high" is written over erased "ordinary." See annotations.
[84] MJ, K, P: "is temporary" (lit. "for an hour"). [85] Lit. "eternal." [86] K lacks this item.

the Sages say...the high priest should not: The variant reading "ordinary priest" extends the logic of each opinion. Just as R. Eliezer holds that even a high priest should let himself become impure before the *nazir*, so too the Sages hold that a *nazir* should become impure before even an ordinary priest, let alone the high priest.

7:2 A similar list of sources of corpse impurity, without particular reference to *nezirim*, appears at *Oholot* 2:1–2.

must a nazir shave: Numbers 6:9 requires that a *nazir* who contracts corpse impurity must undergo purification as prescribed in Numbers 19, shave the hair already grown, and begin the fulfillment of his vow all over again. The Mishnah now asks: which sources of impurity give rise to this situation?

For a corpse: That is, contact with a corpse, and so throughout. At the end of the list various sorts of contact, not all of them direct physical contact, are identified.

liquefied corpse material: Or coagulated fluid that has seeped from a corpse.

decayed flesh: Moldy dirt into which flesh has decayed.

appropriate amount of flesh: Flesh less than an olive's bulk but sufficient that the limb could heal, were it not severed from the body. A variant reading found in TJ and elsewhere applies this provision to a limb from a corpse as well as a limb from a living body; as though to strengthen this double application, a less common variant reverses the sequence of the two clauses.

Half a qav...half a log: As a dry measure a *qav* measures about two and a half pints. One *log* is a quarter of a liquid *qav*, or about eleven fluid ounces.

for touching or carrying them or sharing a Tent with them,
and for a barley-sized piece of bone,
for touching it or carrying it.[87]
For these a *nazir* shaves,
and sprinkles on the third and seventh days,
and it undoes the previous days;
and he does not begin to count anew until he is purified and brings his sacrifices.[88]

3   But overhanging branches,
and protrusions,
and a plowed-up field,
and the land of the nations,
and a gravestone and its support stone,
and a quarter-*log* of blood,
and a Tent,
and a quarter-*qav* of bones,
and vessels touching a corpse,

[87] MJ, K, P mistakenly repeat "or sharing a Tent with it." In P the word is marked for deletion.
[88] K: "his sacrifice."

carrying them: Even if they are wrapped and not actually touched.

sharing a Tent: According to Numbers 19:14, anyone in the same demarcated space ("tent") with a corpse contracts impurity, even without touching the body or having any effect on it at all. Such a Tent can be an actual room, but it can also be a space such as would be defined by the overhanging branches of a tree.

a barley-sized piece of bone: The size of a single barleycorn (and again in 7:3 immediately below).

and sprinkles: The water of the red heifer, according to Numbers 19:12, 19.

purified: Received the sprinkled water and undergone ritual immersion.

sacrifices: As prescribed in Numbers 6:10.

7:3 The types of impurity listed here entail suspension of the *nazir*'s vow but do not undo earlier partial fulfillment of the vow. The vow can be resumed when the impurity has been properly removed.

overhanging branches: The case here involves uncertainty whether the *nazir* has walked under the particular branches that also overhang a source of impurity (as listed in 7:2).

protrusions: A similar question pertains to stones that protrude from a fence or wall.

a plowed-up field: The field contains a grave that was plowed up, and no one knows whether or where fragments of bone remain.

the land of the nations: See above, 3:6.

gravestone...support stone: A gravestone (lit. "roller") seals the opening to a tomb; a support stone holds the gravestone in place.

and a Tent and a quarter-qav: Commentators differ. Some read these words as identifying two sources of impurity: a *nazir* has touched the outside of a tent containing a corpse but has not entered or has come in contact with a quarter-*qav* of bones. Others read the terms together: a *nazir* has been under a "tent" together with a quarter-*qav* of bones.

vessels touching a corpse: Commentators differ as to whether such vessels convey impurity even after the corpse has been removed or only while the corpse remains.

and the days of his counting,
and the days of his confirmation—
for these a *nazir* need not shave.
He undergoes sprinkling on the third and seventh days,
but it does not undo the previous days.
He begins[89] to count anew at once,
and he has no sacrifice.
Nevertheless they said:[90]
The days of a *zav* or a *zavah*,
and the days on which one with *tsaraʾat* is shut in:
these count for him.

4 Said R. Eleazar[91] in the name of R. Joshua:
Any corpse impurity for which a *nazir* must shave—
one is liable for entering the Temple,
and any corpse impurity for which a *nazir* need not shave—
one is not liable for entering the Temple.
Said R. Meir:
Let this not be lighter than a creeping thing!
Said R. Aqiva:

[89] **MJ** and **P**: "began" (an apparent error).   [90] **K, P** lack "they said."   [91] Var. "Eliezer."

the days of his counting: A person with *tsaraʾat* who has been declared healed must count seven further days and then complete the process of purification (Leviticus 14:8). The case here concerns one who formerly had *tsaraʾat* who is also a *nazir* and is counting these days.

the days of his confirmation: The days while a *nazir* is confirmed with *tsaraʾat* and has not yet been declared healed.

has no sacrifice: Is not obliged to offer an impurity sacrifice before resuming his vow.

Nevertheless they said: This phrase normally introduces an established law that could not have been deduced from other rules. The Talmudim differ as to the presumed origin (Mosaic, rabbinic, etc.) of such a rule. See also *Kilayim* 2:2; *Terumot* 2:1; *Shabbat* 1:3, 10:4.

zav: An individual who suffers from an abnormal flow of sexual fluids (see Leviticus 15) is thereby rendered impure (see tractate *Zavim*), but this particular impurity does not interrupt the fulfillment of a *nazir*'s vow.

shut in: Under certain circumstances, one with a skin condition that may be *tsaraʾat* must be quarantined for seven days and then reexamined (Leviticus 13). If the final judgment is that the condition is not *tsaraʾat*, the person in question can return to normal life and the seven-day period does not interrupt the fulfillment of a *nazir*'s vow; the *nazir* never was formally declared to be with *tsaraʾat* at all.

7:4 *entering the Temple*: It is forbidden for a person with corpse impurity to enter the Temple (Numbers 19:13, 20). Those who do so are liable to the penalty of "cutting off" (*karet*) in some cases but not in others, the distinction corresponding to that in 7:2–3 above.

lighter than a creeping thing: One who enters the Temple having become impure through contact with a "creeping thing" (Leviticus 11:29ff.) is also liable to "cutting off": why should a *nazir* with corpse impurity, even of the lighter varieties listed in 7:3, suffer a lesser penalty than this?

Said R. Aqiva: This begins a separate exchange.

I reasoned before R. Eliezer:
If a barley-sized piece of bone does not render impure a person in a Tent,
but a *nazir* must shave for touching or carrying it,
in the case of a quarter-*log* of blood which renders impure a person in a Tent:
does logic not require that a *nazir* should shave for touching or carrying it?
He said to me:
What is this, Aqiva?
This is not a case where one reasons using lesser and greater.
And when I came and presented the matter before R. Joshua he said to me:
You spoke well, but this is how they have said the *halakhah*.[92]

Chapter Eight

8 Two *nezirim* to whom someone said:
"I saw that one of you became impure, but I do not know which of you"—
they [both] shave,[93]
and they [jointly] bring a sacrifice for impurity and a sacrifice for purity,
and [each of them] says:
"If I am the impure one,
the sacrifice for impurity is mine, and the sacrifice for purity is yours,
and if I am the pure one,
the sacrifice for purity is mine, and the sacrifice for impurity is yours."
They count thirty days,
and they bring a sacrifice for purity,[94] and each says:
"If I am the impure one,

[92] **P**: "this is what the *halakhah* has said."
[93] **MJ**, **P**, and **K** lack "shave."   [94] **K** and **P** end 8:1 here.

---

does logic not require: If a quarter-*log* of blood conveys impurity in more cases than a barley-sized bone, why does it not impose on the *nazir* the need to shave and restart the fulfillment of his vow?

lesser and greater: Heb. *qal va-homer*, inference from a weak case to a strong case, of the sort that R. Aqiva has just proposed.

this is how they have said the halakhah: R. Aqiva's logic cannot be refuted, but the laws pertaining to an impure *nazir* have the authority of tradition (*halakhah*), and are not subject to logical critique.

8:1 *one of you became impure*: Through contact with a corpse.

a sacrifice for impurity and a sacrifice for purity: The two *nezirim* between them bring both the sacrifices due from an impure *nazir* who is ready to start fulfilling his vow anew (Numbers 6:10) and those due from a *nazir* who has successfully completed his vow (Numbers 6:14–15). The text does not say so, but they must wait until the term of their vows has elapsed. Otherwise the one who is not impure is forbidden to cut his hair and the "sacrifice for purity" would be premature.

They count thirty days: This is the minimum term of a *nazir* vow. At this point, the one who was pure has also fulfilled his obligation.

the sacrifice for impurity is mine, and the sacrifice for purity is yours,
and this is my sacrifice for purity;
and if I am the pure one,
the sacrifice for purity is mine, and the sacrifice for impurity is yours,
and this is your sacrifice for purity."
If one of them died:
Said R. Joshua:
Let him request from someone[95] in the marketplace to take a *nazir* vow alongside him,
and he says:
"If I am impure
you[96] are a *nazir* at once,
and if I am pure
you will become a *nazir* in thirty days."
They count thirty days,
and they [jointly] bring a sacrifice for impurity and a sacrifice for purity,[97]
and he says:
"If I am the impure one
the sacrifice for impurity is mine, and the sacrifice for purity is yours,
and if I am the pure one
the sacrifice for purity is mine, and the sacrifice for impurity is of doubtful status."
They count thirty days [again]
and they bring a sacrifice for purity
and he says:
"If I am the impure one
the sacrifice for impurity was mine, and the [earlier] sacrifice for purity was yours
and this is my sacrifice for purity,
and if I am the pure one
the sacrifice for purity was mine, and the sacrifice for impurity was of doubtful status,
and this is your sacrifice for purity."
Ben Zoma said to him:
And who will listen to him to become a *nazir* alongside him?
Rather he brings a bird purgation offering and a cattle whole burnt offering
and says—
"If I was impure:

---

[95] Var. "Let him seek out someone...who will take..." The verb is the same, but the absence of a one-letter preposition changes the nuance.

[96] K has "I," corrected in the margin to "you."   [97] K and P end 8:2 here.

---

alongside him: The word may mean "alongside" the surviving *nazir*, or "coordinated" with his indeterminate needs, or "corresponding to" the deceased *nazir*.

"doubtful status": If the surviving *nazir* was pure the whole time, there was no need for an impurity sacrifice; the birds should be offered but not eaten.

Ben Zoma said to him: To R. Joshua.

a bird purgation offering and a cattle whole burnt offering: These are part of the "sacrifice for impurity" and the "sacrifice for purity" respectively. In either case, the *nazir* shaves at this point: if he was impure he must start again, and if not he has now fulfilled his vow.

the purgation offering is my obligation,
and the whole burnt offering is a free-will sacrifice,
and if I was pure:
the whole burnt offering is my obligation,
and the purgation offering was of doubtful status."
And he counts thirty days
and he brings a sacrifice for purity[98]
and says—
"If I was impure:
the first whole burnt offering was a free-will sacrifice,
and this is out of obligation,
and if I was pure:
the first whole burnt offering was an obligation,
and this is a free-will sacrifice,
and this is the rest of my sacrifice."
Said R. Joshua:
It turns out that he has brought his sacrifices by halves!
But the Sages agreed with[99] Ben Zoma.
2 A *nazir* with doubtful corpse impurity
and with doubtfully confirmed *tsara'at*—
may eat sacred foods after sixty days,

[98] P adds "a sacrifice for impurity." [99] P adds "the words of."

and this is the rest of my sacrifice: In addition to the whole burnt offering brought thirty days previously.

by halves: The three parts of the "sacrifice for purity" should be offered together, and he has separated them by thirty days.

8:2 *doubtful*: A case of doubtful corpse impurity is presented above in 8:1. But the status of one with *tsara'at* is "confirmed" by a priest's formal declaration (Leviticus 13:9-17). How can such a matter be "doubtful"? A simple answer would be that the suspicious lesion disappeared before a priest could inspect it: if it was indeed *tsara'at* the individual in question must undergo the full purification process even though his status as one with *tsara'at* was never confirmed. TJ suggests a case where two persons presented themselves for priestly inspection and one was "confirmed" as someone with *tsara'at*, but then the two individuals' identities were somehow mixed up before the second could be inspected. Thus a person with confirmed *tsara'at* is unquestionably present, but there is no telling who it is. The disease is in any case healed, for otherwise the disqualification would go on indefinitely. The question now concerns the process by which this possible *nazir* with possible *tsara'at* can return to normal activities.

eat sacred foods: Neither one with *tsara'at* nor one with corpse impurity can have any contact at all with the sacred.

sixty days: In order to resume contact with the sacred, a healed person with *tsara'at* must follow the procedures laid down in Leviticus 14. These procedures include two full-body shaves, including of the head, seven days apart. After thirty days, the normal duration of a *nazir* vow, the person with doubtful *tsara'at* may shave once, but because he is a *nazir* must then wait another thirty days to shave the second time: hence, sixty days must pass before his status is resolved. At that point resolution of the *nazir*'s possible impurity can begin, but that process will require two additional periods of thirty days, the first because he may have been impure and must now undergo purification as laid down in Numbers 6:9-11, and the second to complete the vow in purity. (The thirty-day delay after the second offering is needed to allow the *nazir*'s hair to grow back; if the *nazir* was not impure the fourth waiting period was actually unnecessary, but that could not be determined.) The premise is that the original *nazir* vow was for the minimum thirty days, or was unspecified; if the vow explicitly specified a longer period, then four intervals of that greater length must be measured instead.

and drink wine or [voluntarily] acquire corpse impurity after 120 days,
because shaving the affliction overrides a *nazir*'s ban on[100] shaving if it is certain,
but when it is doubtful,
it does not override.

Chapter Nine

9:1 The Power of Nullification

9 *Nezirut* does not apply to gentiles;
nezirut does apply to women and slaves.
The case of women is more severe than that of slaves,
in that one compels his slave
but cannot compel his wife.[101]
The case of slaves is more severe than that of women,
in that one nullifies his wife's vows
but cannot nullify his slave's vows.
If he nullified that of his wife,
he nullified it permanently.
If he nullified that of his slave,
if he went free he must[102] complete his *nazir* term.

[100] Lit. "a *nazir*'s shaving."
[101] K mistakenly shortens to "he compels his wife" but then adds "his slave but does not compel" in the margin.
[102] Var. "He goes free and must complete…" **MJ** and **P** have "he completed"; see annotations.

shaving the affliction overrides … if it is certain: Where there is no doubt about *tsara'at*, the *nazir* may follow these steps immediately upon being declared healed, even if such a leper is also a *nazir*; the fulfillment of the *nazir* vow is suspended or "postponed," the shaving of the head may proceed, and the *nazir*'s status can be resumed or restarted (see 7:3) when the purification after *tsara'at* is complete. However, the 60- and 120-day periods outlined above are necessitated by the fact that *tsara'at* was doubtful. The *nazir* may not have been the one with *tsara'at* and may not need to shave, and therefore the *nazir* ban on shaving the head remains in effect.

9:1 *slaves*: Gentiles enslaved to Israelites were in a quasi-Israelite status that resembled that of women. Here, unlike gentiles to whom the category of *nazir* does not apply at all, slaves, like women, can take on a *nazir* vow. The differences, which the Mishnah now spells out, have to do with the fact that Numbers 30:7–14 gives the husband the right to annul her vow.

one compels his slave: To violate the vow. The vow remains in effect (see below), but the owner may order the slave not to comply. A husband who declines to nullify his wife's vow must allow her to fulfill it.

If he nullified that of his slave: If he compelled the slave to transgress his vow. The language is inexact; strictly speaking the owner has no right to nullify a slave's vow.

if he went free: A variant reading (see n. 102) changes only the vowels in the verb "go free," switching the tense from past to future, and adds "and" before the next phrase. The owner has no right to nullify a slave's vow, and by attempting to do so forfeits his ownership: the ex-slave goes free and may (or, must) now fulfill the vow. The reading "he completed" is an apparent error, though the commentaries and editions do not say so.

If the slave[103] went out of his sight:
R. Meir says:
He may not drink,
but R. Yose says:
He may drink.

9:2–4 *Rules Concerning Presumptive Impurity*

2 A *nazir* who shaved
and then became aware he was impure:
if the impurity was known—
it undoes;
and if it was an impurity from the abyss—
it does not undo.
If he became aware he was impure before[104] he shaved,
in either case it undoes.
How?
If he went down to immerse himself in a cave,
and a corpse was discovered floating at the mouth of the cave—
he is impure.
If it was discovered sunken into the floor of the cave:
if he went down to cool off—
he is pure,
to become purified from corpse impurity—
he is impure.

[103] Lit. "if he went." [104] Lit. "if before."

went out of his sight: Commentators vary: either the slave is simply out of his master's sight and can therefore honor his vow, or he has run away.

9:2 *the impurity was known*: The source of the impurity was known to the public.

it undoes: The completed *nazir* term.

impurity from the abyss: A previously unknown grave or hidden corpse, as though the impurity had suddenly arisen undetected from the deep.

How does the law of *impurity from the abyss* work?

a corpse was discovered floating…impure: A floating corpse is visible to anyone in a position to see it; it therefore constitutes a known impurity even if the *nazir* himself failed to notice it. Being an enclosed space, a cave constitutes a "Tent"; while immersing, the *nazir* shared this "Tent" with the now-discovered corpse (see *Oholot* introduction). It is presumed that the *nazir* was already impure when he entered the cave, but to a degree less severe than corpse impurity and wanted to remove the impurity through this immersion. This presumption will be dropped as the paragraph goes on.

sunken into the floor: The sunken corpse, however, was hidden in the ground beneath the immersion pool, and no one knew it was there until it subsequently emerged *from the abyss*.

For the presumption is that an impure person remains impure,
and the presumption is that a pure person remains pure,
since there are grounds for this.[105]

3 [106] One who initially finds a corpse laid out[107] in its fashion—
he may take it and the affected soil;
if he found two:
he may take them and the affected soil;
if he found three:
if there are between this one and that from four to eight cubits,[108]
in such a case this is a graveyard.[109]
He inspects twenty cubits further from it.
If he found one at the end of twenty cubits
he inspects twenty cubits further from it,
since there are grounds for this:[110]

---

[105] Lit. "the matter has legs."
[106] In **K** and **P** 9:3 and the beginning of 9:4 preceded 9:2; the scribe in **K** has noted the reversal at the end of 9:2.
[107] **K**: "and [it is] laid out…"
[108] **MJ**, **K**, and **P** add "the size of a bier and those who bury it"; commentators vary as to whether the phrase really belongs here. See also *Bava Batra* 6:8.
[109] Lit. "a neighborhood of graves." [110] Lit. "the matter has legs."

---

presumption: Impurity from the abyss does not change the person's current purity status. If a person in a state of purity entered the cave for reasons of personal comfort, the later discovery of the hidden corpse does not render him impure. However, if someone entered the cave while impure, intending to remove the impurity through immersion, the "impurity from the abyss" nullifies the immersion and leaves him as he was when he entered.

9:3 This paragraph is repeated at *Oholot* 16:3.

initially: No other corpse had been found in the vicinity: this is the first. This paragraph applies to anyone, not only to a *nazir*.

in its fashion: In the posture typical of Jewish burials.

he may take it: For reburial elsewhere, so that the place may be used for other purposes.

the affected soil: Soil which the corpse has displaced or which has absorbed blood or other bodily substances from the decaying body. In order to make the location usable for other purposes this too must be removed.

this one and that: Commentators differ as to whether this means from each to the next or from the first to the third.

four: That is, if the discovered graves are between four and eight cubits apart.

a graveyard: The additional corpses may no longer be disturbed since the area cannot successfully be rid of impurity.

twenty cubits further from it: Twenty cubits from the outermost corpse.

at the end of: Within twenty cubits. One must now inspect *twenty cubits further* from the newly discovered corpse.

there are grounds for this: Once a third corpse has been discovered there are grounds for suspecting that even more can be found; therefore the search must continue until twenty cubits of clear ground in every direction have been confirmed.

for if he had found this one first,
he would take it and the affected soil.

4 [111] Any newly arisen doubt concerning skin afflictions
is pure until it is confirmed as impure;
once it is confirmed as impure
its [further] doubt is impure.
One examines a *zav* in seven ways before it is confirmed as *zav* flow:[112]
(1) food, and (2) drink, (3) bearing a load, and (4) jumping,
and (5) illness, and (6) sight, and (7) lustful thought.
Once it is confirmed as *zav* flow
one does not examine him;
his accidental flow, his doubtful flow, and his seminal emission are impure,
since there are grounds for this.[113]
One who strikes his fellow and they judged him [likely] to die,

[111] See textual note to 9:2 (n. 104) for the order in **K** and **P**.
[112] Standard printed editions repeat "abnormal sexual discharge." **K** (as a correction) and **P**: "confirmed as impure," here and immediately below.
[113] Lit. "the matter has legs," here and below.

if he had found: The newly discovered corpse now necessitates a fresh start for the search procedure, just as would have been the case if it had been the first one to be discovered.

9:4 This paragraph contains three separate rules applying the principle that new situations must be evaluated in the light of previously established facts.

skin afflictions: Leviticus 13.

[further] doubt: Newly arisen doubt does not change the existing presumption. A lesion of uncertain status (perhaps it is growing and impure, perhaps it is shrinking and pure), leaves the carrier's personal status unchanged. If not yet confirmed as a person with *tsara'at* he remains free of impurity; if already confirmed he is not rescued by the new possibility that the lesion is shrinking.

One examines: Appears also at *Zavim* 2:2.

before it is confirmed: Any of the seven listed factors might have caused accidental, nonpathological discharge. Since the sufferer has not yet been confirmed as impure, there is motive to write off further incidents as the result of such causes.

food and drink: In excess.

bearing a load: That was too heavy.

illness: Other than of the genitals.

sight: Witnessing others engaged in a sexual act.

there are grounds for this: If the previous examination left no doubt that the genital flow is pathological and impure, there is no point in further examination. Any third occurrence, even one that might previously have been excluded, now entails the additional sacrifice.

One who strikes…grounds for this: Some commentators refer the final clause to the initial ruling (*he is liable*): despite the temporary recovery, there are grounds to suppose the victim died as a result of the blow.

but he recovered from his condition
and afterward grew worse and died—
he is liable.
R. Nehemiah says:
He is exempt,
since there are grounds for this.

9:5 An Aggadic Conclusion

5 Samuel was a *nazir*,
according to the words of R. Nehorai,
as it is said:
And a mora shall not go up on his head.
It is said of Samson:
And a mora,
and it is said of Samuel:
And a mora;
just as the *mora* mentioned in [the story of] Samson means a razor,
so the *mora* mentioned in [the story of] Samuel means a razor.
Said R. Yose:
But does not *mora* refer only to flesh and blood?
R. Nehorai said to him:
But is it not already written:
And Samuel said, "How can I go? Saul will hear and kill me"—
[This shows] that indeed the fear of another man was upon him.

Others refer to R. Nehemiah's dissent: the temporary recovery provides grounds to suppose that the victim's demise was unrelated to the previous blow.

9:5 *Samuel*: When the childless Hannah learned that she was pregnant, she dedicated her unborn child to God and pledged *and a mora shall not go up on his head* (1 Samuel 1:11). *Mora* can mean "razor," and R. Nehorai understands Hannah's words as a pledge that the child would grow up a *nazir*.

of Samson... a mora:: Judges 13:8.

of Samuel... a mora: 1 Samuel 1:11.

flesh and blood: Another meaning of *mora* is "fear." R. Yose interprets Hannah's prayer to mean that no other human being should ever arouse fear in her unborn child.

Saul will hear and kill me: 1 Samuel 16:2. Thus the grown Samuel did indeed fear another man. It cannot be that Hannah's prayer went unanswered, so *mora* must indeed mean "razor" as R. Nehorai understands.

Tractate Sotah

Ishay Rosen-Zvi and Orr Scharf

Introduction

Overview

Tractate *Sotah* broaches two topics, and accordingly, it is divided into two discrete units. Its first six chapters discuss the ritual of the suspected adulteress (*sotah*), beginning with a ritual narrative (up to 3:4), and followed by a series of legal addenda. This unit is followed by its counterpart, chapters 6–9, which discuss a series of rituals that are to be performed in Hebrew only ("the Holy Tongue"), as opposed to rituals that can be recited in any language. The first item on the list of rituals that may be recited in any language (listed but not discussed), is the *sotah* ritual (7:1). It is not exceptional to find in the Mishnah entire units that include a single item that is relevant to the tractate in which they appear. The tractate ends with a reflection on the degenerate reality of recent generations. The formal connection with our tractate again derives from a reference to the annulment of the *sotah* ritual in one of the first items of the narration.

Relationship to Scripture

The *sotah* ritual itself is based on chapter 5 of the book of Numbers, which describes a divine ordeal that jealous husbands may initiate if they suspect that their wives are being unfaithful. The suspected wife is taken to the priest at the Tabernacle, where she is forced to drink "the water of bitterness that brings the curse" (Numbers 5:18), concocted of dirt taken from the Tabernacle floor, and an oath written on a scroll that is then wiped into the water. The reaction of the woman's body to this concoction determines her status: if guilty, the Torah asserts that "her body shall swell, and her thigh shall fall away" (5:27); whereas if innocent, "then she shall be free and shall conceive children" (5:28).

In the tractate's first three chapters, the Mishnah renarrates the biblical ritual. The mishnaic description, however, differs from its biblical source in many ways: the husband's unfounded suspicions in the Bible are transformed by the Mishnah into a complex system of rules of evidence; the closed priestly ritual becomes a public event; and acts of defacement are added to the procedures to be performed before an audience at the Temple gate. Some of these differences derive from the rabbinic midrashic interpretation of the biblical text; some possibly from the actual ritual as performed in the late Second Temple period, and some (probably the majority) from an ideological construct that emerged in the rabbinic post-destruction study house, when the ritual was discussed strictly as a matter of theory.

Main Ideas

Below are some of the main terms and concepts appearing in the tractate:

Warning (qinnui), seclusion (setirah), and *defilement (tume'ah)*: three formal stages that the rabbis add (based on their standard rules of evidence) before deciding whether the wife should undergo the ritual. The husband must prove that his wife was secluded with another man after he warned her specifically not to do so (1:1–2). Only then can he bring her to the priest at the Temple and force her to drink the "water of bitterness." However, if there is even the slightest testimony indicating that the wife actually committed adultery, she cannot undergo the ritual (which is designed only for doubtful cases). Instead, she is divorced and suffers financial sanctions (see below). The tractate discusses this latter case in chapter 6.

Ketubbah: a marriage contract in which the husband undertakes an obligation to pay a sum of money in the case of divorce or death (see *Ketubbot*). Any wife suspected of adultery who cannot or would not undergo the Temple ritual is sanctioned by divorce without receiving her *ketubbah* money. The tractate discusses this in chapter 4.

The Gate of Nicanor: a central gate at the Temple separating the Court of Women (accessible to both men and women; *Middot* 2:5) from the "Israelite" Court (*Kelim* 1:8). The fact that the *sotah* ritual is situated in the Temple's most central location (1:5) attests to the public, spectacular character that the ritual assumes in the Mishnah.

Measure for Measure: a basic principle in the rabbinic concept of divine justice. Only in our case the principle is applied to an actual manmade ritual, as discussed in 1:7–9 (and in much greater detail in Tosefta, *Sotah* chapters 3–4).

Tractate Sotah

Chapter One

1:1–4 *The Evidence Leading to the Sotah Ritual*

1 One who warns[1] his wife—
R. Eliezer says:
He warns her before two and makes her drink based on the testimony of one witness or based on his own testimony,
R. Joshua says:
He warns her before two witnesses and makes her drink based on two witnesses.

2 How does he warn her?
If he said to her before two men,
"Do not speak with so-and-so,"
and she spoke with him, she is still permitted to her husband
and is permitted to eat *terumah*.
If she entered a place of seclusion with him
and remained there long enough to become defiled,
she is forbidden to her husband[2] and forbidden from eating *terumah*.
And if he dies she must perform *halitsah* and may not contract levirate marriage.

[1] Lit. "Is jealous of." See Numbers 5:14.   [2] Lit. "to her house."

1:1 *One who warns*: Lit. "is jealous of," Numbers 5:14. Not to seclude herself with another man (see 1:2).

before two: Lit. "on the basis (or testimony) of." However, there is no testimony before the warning takes place (cf. 6:3; Tosefta 1:2). The Mishnah seeks to preserve the linguistic symmetry with its consequent, "…and makes her drink based on…"

makes her drink: *The water of bitterness that causes the curse*, Numbers 5:18.

one witness: Either the witness or the husband himself saw that she had hid with another.

1:2 *terumah*: Unlike the previous *halakhah* "forbidden unto her husband," which refers to all couples, here the Mishnah refers only to an originally nonpriestly wife married to a priest who is permitted to eat *terumah* by virtue of her marriage. In priestly households, *terumah* constituted a significant portion of the food supply; cf. Leviticus 22:11.

If she entered a place of seclusion, the wife's status as a legitimate wife is in question.

if he dies: Childless. See Deuteronomy 25:5–10.

halitsah…levirate marriage. See *Yevamot* introduction. As above, since her status as legitimate wife is in question, she may only perform *halitsah*, which severs her tie with her husband's kin, and not *levirate marriage*, which continues it.

3 The following are forbidden from eating *terumah*:
She who says:
"I am defiled unto you";
and of whom witnesses have testified that she is defiled;
and she who says:
"I will not drink,"
and she whose husband does not want to make her drink;
and she whose husband has intercourse with her while on the way.
How does he proceed with her?
He takes her to the local court, and they assign to him two disciples of the Sages
lest he have intercourse with her while on the way.
R. Judah says:
Her husband is trustworthy concerning her.

4 They would bring her up to the Great Court in Jerusalem and admonish her
as they admonish witnesses in capital cases,
and say to her,
"My daughter, much sin is wrought by wine, much by frivolity, much by childishness,
and much by evil neighbors;
act for the sake of His great name, written in holiness,
that it be not blotted out by the water."[3]
And they tell her things that she does not deserve to hear;
she and her entire father's house.

1:5–6 *The Opening of the Ritual at the Temple: Humiliation*

5 If she said: "I am defiled"—
she writes a receipt for her *ketubbah* and is divorced.

---

[3] **K, P**: "Do not cause His great name to be blotted out by the water [of bitterness]."

1:3 *"defiled unto you"*: Forbidden to engage in sexual intercourse; cf. Numbers 5:13.

that she is defiled: That she had sexual intercourse with another.

while on the way: To the Temple.

1:4 *Great Court in Jerusalem*: Cf. *Sanhedrin* 11:2.

admonish witnesses in capital cases: See *Sanhedrin* 4:5.

great name: See Numbers 5:23. God's name, the tetragrammaton, was written together with the curse on the scroll whose writing was to be blotted out by the water of bitterness.

things that she does not deserve to hear: Sifre Numbers 12 and the Palestinian Talmud, ad loc. mention in this context stories such as Judah and Tamar (Genesis 38). According to this reading, she is explicitly compared to the nation's forefathers, and the Mishnah thus clarifies that this act is merely a manipulation, devised to make her confess.

1:5 *ketubbah*: Payment from a husband's estate to his wife upon their divorce or his death. Cf. *Ketubbot*.

But if she said: "I am pure"—
They take her up to the Eastern Gate,[4] which is across from the Gate of Nicanor,
where they make suspected adulteresses[5] drink, and purify women after childbirth,
and purify the lepers.
And a priest takes hold of her garments—
if they were torn then they were torn, if they were ripped at the seam then ripped at the seam—
until he uncovers her bosom and loosens her hair.
R. Judah says:
If her bosom was attractive he would not uncover it;
if her hair was attractive he would not loosen it.
6 If she was dressed in white, he would dress her in black.
If she was wearing jewels of gold and chains and noserings and finger rings,
they would be taken from her to deface her.
And then he brings a rope of wicker and ties it above her breasts.
And whoever wishes to watch comes and watches, except her slaves and female slaves,
since with them she feels no shame.
And all women[6] may watch her, for it is written:
That all women may take warning and not commit lewdness as you have done.

1:7–9 *Interlude: The Ritual's Underlying Principle: Measure for Measure*

7 With the measure that one metes out so it is meted out to him:
she adorned herself for transgression—the Omnipresent defaced her;
she uncovered herself for transgression[7]—the Omnipresent uncovered her;

---

[4] **K, P**: "To the Eastern Gates, to the Gates of Nicanor."   [5] Heb. *sotot*.
[6] **K, P**: "all other women."   [7] "For transgression" does not appear in **K, P**.

Eastern Gate...Gate of Nicanor: See n. 4. Both denote the same gate at the Temple separating the women's court and the Israelite court. For the Temple layout see *Middot* and introduction.

purify...after childbirth: See Leviticus 12:1.

purify the lepers: See Leviticus 14:11.

loosens her hair: Numbers 5:18. The rabbis use *satar* instead of the biblical *para*, because in rabbinic Hebrew the latter denotes uncovering rather than loosening.

1:6 *feels no shame*: The same phrase as in *Gittin* 7:4, 8:9; *Yevamot* 4:10; *Ketubbot* 1:4. Rashi, however, interprets it differently, "She is too proud ever to make confession of her guilt before them."

That all women may take warning: Ezekiel 23:48.

1:7 *With the measure*: Unlike the biblical passage, the Mishnah emphasizes the woman's assumed adultery, and interprets the various stages in her treatment as corresponding, "measure for measure" with her alleged transgressions.

the Omnipresent: Hebrew *ha-maqom*, lit. "the place." The expression may also indicate: "the One who dwells in the Temple."

uncovered herself for transgression: See n. 7. The absence of "for transgression" in **K** and **P** may be due to the fact that in rabbinic Hebrew "uncovering" is inherently transgressive.

she began transgression with the thigh first[8] and then with the belly—
therefore the thigh shall suffer first and then the belly;
the rest of her body does not escape unharmed.

8 Samson followed his eyes—
therefore the Philistines gouged out his eyes,
as it is said: *And the Philistines laid hold on him and gouged out his eyes*;
Absalom flaunted[9] his hair—
therefore he was hanged by his hair;
And since he had intercourse with the ten concubines of his father,
therefore they stabbed him with ten spears,
as it is said: *And ten young men, Joab's armor-bearers surrounded him.*
And since he stole away three hearts,[10]
the heart of his father, the heart of the court, and the heart of Israel—
as it is said: *So Absalom stole the hearts of the men of Israel*[11]—
therefore three darts were thrust into him,
as it is said: *And he took three darts in his hand and thrust them through the heart of Absalom.*

9 And so too in favorable matters:
Miriam awaited Moses for a short time,
as it is said: *And his sister stood at a distance*,
therefore Israel stalled for her seven days in the desert,
as it is said: *And the people did not set out on the march till Miriam was brought in again.*
Joseph merited burying his father, and none of his brothers was greater than he,
as it is said: *So Joseph went up to bury his father...and there went up with him both chariots and horsemen.*
Whom have we greater than Joseph, for none other than Moses occupied himself with him.
Moses merited exhuming the bones[12] of Joseph, and none in Israel is greater than he,
as it is written: *And Moses took the bones of Joseph with him.*

---

[8] **K, P**: "Thigh was first to transgress and then the belly."
[9] **K, P**: "prided in the beauty of."
[10] In **K, P**: "committed three thefts."
[11] Absent in **K, P**.
[12] Lit. "gained the bones."

1:8 The principle of "measure for measure" extended to biblical sinners.

Samson followed his eyes: Judges 14:3.

And the Philistines laid hold: Judges 16:21.

And ten young men: 2 Samuel 18:15.

So Absalom stole: 2 Samuel 15:6.

And he took three darts: 2 Samuel 18:14.

1:9 "Measure for measure" applies also to rewards.

And his sister: Exodus 2:4.

And the people: Numbers 12:15.

So Joseph went up: Genesis 50:7, 9.

And Moses took the bones: Exodus 13:19.

Who is greater than Moses! For none other than the Omnipresent[13] occupied himself with him, as it is written: *And he buried him in the valley.*
And not of Moses alone it is spoken thus, but of all the righteous,
for it is written: *Your righteousness shall go before you the glory of the Lord shall be your rear guard.*

Chapter Two

2:1–3:2 *The Ritual Narrative Resumes: Preparations for Forced Drinking*

2 The husband would bring her grain offering in a basket of wicker,
and the priest[14] put it in her hands to tire her.
All other grain offerings are in vessels of ministry from beginning to end,
but this one begins in a wicker basket and ends in vessels of ministry;
all other grain offerings require oil and frankincense,
but this one requires neither oil nor frankincense;
all other grain offerings come from wheat,
but this one comes from barley.
The grain offering of the *omer*, though it comes from barley, comes as sifted flour,
but this one comes as meal.
Rabban Gamaliel says:
Since her deed was the deed of cattle, her offering is the food of cattle.

---

[13] K: "the blessed Omnipresent."   [14] For "husband" and "priest" Hebrew has only "he."

And he buried him: Deuteronomy 34:6.

Your righteousness shall go before you: Isaiah 58:8.

2:1 *grain offering*: Numbers 5:15.

put it in her hands: Scripture narrates the priest's placement of the meal offering in the wife's hands before the oath (Numbers 5:18), while the waving of the offering takes place only after the oath (Numbers 5:25; Sotah 3:1). The Mishnah interprets this long interval as designated to tire her.

from beginning to end: From the time they are first brought by their owner until they are consumed.

ends in the vessels of ministry: Cf. Sotah 3:1.

oil and frankincense: Leviticus 2:1.

wheat: Cf. Exodus 29:2.

sifted flour: Leviticus 2:14; Menahot 10:4.

meal: i.e. unsifted meal, Numbers 5:15.

2 He would bring a new cup of clay and pour into it a half-*log* of water from the laver.
R. Judah says:
A quarter.
As R. Judah[15] lessens the writing so he lessens the water.
He entered the Sanctuary and turned to his right;
and there in a space one cubit by one cubit, was a marble flagstone
on which a ring was fixed.
And when he raises it he takes dust from underneath it
and pours into the cup[16] enough to be visible on the water,
as it is said, *And of the dust that is on the floor of the tabernacle the priest shall take and put it into the water.*

3 He comes to write the scroll.
From which point does he write?
From *If no man has lain with you etc. If you have gone astray, though you are under your husband's authority*,
and he does not write *Let the priest make the woman take the oath.*
And he writes *May the Lord make you an execration and an oath… may this water that brings the curse pass into your bowels and make your body swell and your thigh fall away.*
And he does not write, *And the woman shall say, Amen, Amen!*
R. Yose says:
He would not omit.
R. Judah says:
He writes only *May the Lord make you an execration and an oath etc. May this water that brings the curse pass into your bowels etc.*;
and he does not write, *And the woman shall say, Amen, Amen!*

---

[15] Heb. "he." [16] "Into the cup" added for clarity.

2:2 *pour… water from the laver*: The priest begins preparing the potion (*the water of bitterness that brings the curse*, Numbers 5:18) for the wife to drink. The potion consists of water from the laver, mixed with dust taken from the Temple's floor and ink from the blotted scroll. Cf. Exodus 30:18; *Middot* 3:6.

R. Judah lessens the writing: This is an editorial interpolation, based on a comparison between R. Judah's statements in 2:2 where he requires less water than the anonymous view, and 2:3, where according to R. Judah the priest should write on the scroll a shorter text than what the other Sages rule.

the Sanctuary: *Middot* 4:1.

one cubit by one cubit: Cf. *Middot* 1:9.

And of the dust: Numbers 5:17.

2:3 *If no man has lain*: Numbers 5:19–20.

Let the priest make: Numbers 5:21.

May the Lord make you: Numbers 5:22.

would not omit (lit. "separate") the latter verse, but rather write it in its entirety.

4 He does not write on a tablet nor on papyrus nor on unprepared skin, but only on a scroll,
as it is said: *In a book.*
And he may not write with gum or copperas or anything that leaves a lasting trace, but only with ink,
For it is said: *And he shall blot them out*—script that can be blotted out.

5 What does she say, *Amen, Amen* for?[17]
Amen for the curse, and *Amen* for the oath;
Amen, with respect to this man,
Amen, with respect to another man;
Amen, that I have not gone astray while betrothed, married, awaiting levirate marriage, or after consummation of the levirate marriage;[18]
Amen, that I have not been defiled; and if I have been defiled
may all these curses[19] enter into me![20]
R. Meir says:
Amen, that I have not been defiled; *Amen*, that I will not be defiled.

6 All agree that the condition does not apply to her before becoming betrothed and after becoming divorced.
If she was secluded with another man and became defiled, and later he took her back, the condition does not apply.
The rule is as follows:
In any case in which she has intercourse that does not render her forbidden to him, the condition does not apply.

---

[17] **K, P**: "And why."   [18] Lit. "brought in," i.e. to the levir's house.
[19] Hebrew has only "may they enter me."   [20] **K, P** put this before "*Amen*...levirate marriage."

2:4 *scroll*: Hebrew *megillah*, made from parchment.

In a book: Numbers 5:23. Hebrew *sefer*. In rabbinic usage "book" denotes a scroll rather than a bound codex.

copperas: Iron sulfate, used in the production of ink. Cf. *Megillah* 2:2; *Shabbat* 13:4.

And he shall blot them out: Numbers 5:23.

2:5 *Amen, Amen*: Numbers 5:22. The homilies that follow interpret the wife's double exclamation.

with respect to this man: The man with whom her husband warned not to hide. See 1:2 above.

levirate marriage: Lit. "awaiting her husband's brother [to take her]." Levirate marriage is the duty imposed on a man to marry his brother's childless widow; see. Deuteronomy 25:5–10.

2:6 *All agree*: Even R. Meir who says in the preceding mishnah "*Amen*, that I have not been defiled; *Amen*, that I will not be defiled."

the condition does not apply: Lit. "he does not impose the condition upon her," referring to the oath, Numbers 5:19–22. The priest adjuring her is perceived as the husband's proxy.

was secluded with another man: The same man her husband had warned her from seeing, see 1:2. This clause refers to a case in which the husband divorced the woman, and later remarried her. If in the interim she was secluded with the other man, the oath does not apply.

and became defiled: Had intercourse.

he took her back: Her former husband remarried her.

Chapter Three

3 He would take her grain offering out of a wicker basket and put it in a vessel of ministry and would put it in her hand.[21]
And a priest sets his hand beneath hers and waves the offering.[22]

2 He waved, brought, scooped out, and burnt it, and the rest is consumed by the priests.
He would make her drink and then bring her grain offering.
R. Simeon says:
He brings her grain offering, and then he would make her drink, for it is said:
And afterward he shall make the woman drink the water.
But if he made her drink and then brought her grain offering, it is valid.

3:3–5 *Forced Drinking*

3 As long as the scroll was not blotted out,
if she said: "I will not drink":
her scroll is set aside and her grain offering is scattered on the ash heap.
And her scroll is not valid for use with any other *sotah*.
If the scroll has been blotted out,
and then she said, "I am defiled,"
the water is poured out and her grain offering is scattered on the ash heap.
If the scroll has been blotted out,
and she said, "I will not drink,"
they pour it into her and make her drink against her will.

[21] K, P: "in her hands."   [22] Heb. "it."

3:1 *a priest*: Probably refers to the same priest conducting the entire ritual.

and waves the offering: Elevating the offering as a gesture of dedication to God. According to Numbers 5:25, the priest takes the grain offering from her hands and waves it, whereas here, the *priest sets his hand beneath hers and waves*.

3:2 *brought*: To the altar.

scooped out: Took a handful from the meal offering using his three middle fingers; see *Menahot* introduction.

drink and then bring her grain offering...brings her grain offering and then...drink: The debate arises due to the fact that the instruction to make the woman drink appears both before and after the waving of the offering (Numbers 5:24 and 26–27).

And afterward: Numbers 5:26.

3:3 *set aside*: Lit. "put in *genizah*." The practice of *genizah* is applied to sacred objects put out of use or forbidden for use. See *Shabbat* 16:1.

"I will not drink": The blotting out of the scroll renders the ritual irreversible, whereupon the woman can stop the course of the ritual only by confessing her sin.

4 She hardly finishes drinking until her face turns yellow and her eyes bulge
and her veins swell, and they say,
"Take her away! Take her away!"
so that she not defile the Court.
But if she had any merit it would suspend her punishment.
Some merits suspend punishment for one year,
some merits for two years,
and some merits for three years;
hence Ben Azzai says:
A man must teach his daughter Torah so that if she drinks
she may know that the merit suspends her punishment.
R. Eliezer says:
One who teaches his daughter Torah it is as though[23] he teaches her frivolity.
R. Joshua says:
A woman prefers one *qav* with frivolity over nine *qav* with modesty.[24]
He used to say:
A righteous fool and a cunning knave
and an abstinent woman and tortured abstinent men—
these destroy the world.

5 R. Simeon says:
Merit does not suspend the punishment of the water of bitterness;[25]
for if you say, Merit suspends the punishment of the water of the curse,
you lessen the effect of the water for all the women who drink it;
and you make all undefiled women who have drunk it of ill repute,
for it will be said, They are in truth defiled but merit has suspended their punishment.
Rabbi says:
Merit does suspend the punishment of the water of the curse;
and yet she will not bear children or thrive,
but she will gradually deteriorate and end up dying the selfsame death.

[23] K, P lack: "it is as though."
[24] K, P: "A woman prefers one *qav* of frivolity over nine *qav* of modesty."
[25] K: "the water of the curse."

3:4 This unit details the lethal consequences of the forced drinking.

and they say: The audience, see 1:6.

Court: The inner Court of the Priests. (See *Middot* introduction.) The *sotah* went in to wave the offering, see 3:1 above.

tortured: Lit. "the blows." The idiom is vague and can mean either blows "inflicted by" or "sustained by" the *abstinent*. Vocalized differently: "from the sect of the Pharisees."

abstinent men: Lit. "of the *Perushim*."

3:5 *the selfsame death*: Eventually, the woman whose death is suspended will die the death of the *sotah* narrated above, 3:4.

3:6–8 Ritual Narrative Addenda

6 If her grain offering is defiled before it was sanctified in the vessel—
then it is to be redeemed, like all other grain offerings;
but if after it was sanctified in the vessel—
then it is to be burnt, like all other grain offerings.
The grain offerings of the following are to be burnt:
she who says: "I am defiled unto you,"
and she of whom witnesses have testified that she is defiled,
and she who says: "I will not drink";
and she whose husband does not want to make her drink;
and she whose husband had intercourse with her while on the way;
and all those married to priests—
their grain offerings are to be burnt.

7 A daughter of an Israelite married to a priest,
her grain offering is to be burnt;
a daughter of a priest married to an Israelite,
her grain offering is to be consumed.
How does a priest differ from a daughter of a priest?
The grain offering of the daughter of a priest may be consumed, but a priest's may not be consumed.
The daughter of a priest may become deconsecrated, but a priest may not become deconsecrated.
The daughter of a priest may contract corpse impurity, but a priest may not contract corpse impurity;
a priest may eat of the offerings of the greatest sanctity,
but the daughter of a priest may not eat of the offerings of the greatest sanctity.

3:6 *vessel*: i.e. "of ministry," 3:1.

redeemed: By paying the Temple the value of the offering, the defiled offering is deconsecrated.

It is to be burnt like all other grain offerings that have become impure. See *Menahot* 12:1.

The grain offerings of the following are to be burnt: If one of the following incidents occurs after the offerings are consecrated in the vessels, the grain offering cannot fulfill its purpose and is therefore *burnt* rather than eaten.

all those married to priests: The offering of a priest (or in this case of a woman from a priestly household) is burnt rather than consumed by priests. See Leviticus 6:16.

3:7 *is to be consumed*: i.e. by the priests (3:6).

The daughter of a priest: Lit. priestess. In ancient Judaism, as opposed to Greek and Roman religions, women did not serve as priestesses at the Temple.

deconsecrated: A priestess who had intercourse with a man prohibited to her loses her priestly status and is forbidden from marrying a priest and from eating *terumah* (see Leviticus 21:7). By contrast, a priest who has intercourse with a woman forbidden to him deconsecrates his offspring but not himself (see *Qiddushin* 3:12).

contracts corpse impurity: Leviticus 21:1.

offerings of the greatest sanctity: Purgation offerings, guilt offerings, and the offerings of well-being for the congregation. See *Zevahim* 5:1–5.

may: The mishnaic usage of participles serves three different functions within this passage: (1) normative prescription (*may be consumed*; *may eat of the offerings of greatest sanctity*); (2) permission (*may contract corpse impurity*); (3) potential (*may become deconsecrated*). Similar variations appear in the following mishnah.

8 What are the differences between man and woman?
A man may unbind his hair and rip,
but a woman may not unbind her hair and rip;
a man may impose the *nazir* vow on his son,
but a woman may not impose the *nazir* vow on her son;
a man may shave using *nazir*-offering monies dedicated by his father,
but a woman may not shave using the *nazir*-offering monies dedicated by her father;
a man may sell his daughter, but a woman may not sell her daughter;
a man may give his daughter in betrothal, but a woman may not give her daughter in betrothal;
a man is stoned naked, but a woman is not stoned naked;
a man is hanged, but a woman is not hanged;
a man is sold for committing theft, but a woman is not sold for committing theft.

Chapter Four

4:1–5 Women Who Cannot Drink the Water of Bitterness

4 A woman who is betrothed or awaiting levirate marriage
may not drink and may not take her *ketubbah*;
for it is said: *When a wife under her husband's authority goes astray*,
excluding a woman who is betrothed or awaiting levirate marriage.
A widow married to a high priest,
a divorcee or one who had performed *halitsah* married to a common priest,

---

3:8 *unbind his hair and rip* his clothes, in the case of *tsara'at*. See Leviticus 13:45.

A man may shave: Parallel in *Nazir* 4:6.

shave: The bringing of the *nazir* offering is referred to as *shaving*, since the offerings are brought on the occasion of the completion of the *nazir*'s vow at which time they shave their hair. See *Nazir* 6:7. The Mishnah refers here to a case in which a father allocates money for the offerings at the completion of the vow, but dies before completing his vow. His son, but not his daughter, may use this money to pay for his own nazirite vow. See *Nazir* 3:7.

hanged: After being executed by one of four methods of court executions. See *Sanhedrin* 6:4.

sold for committing theft: To the person whose property he stole if he is unable to pay restitution; see Exodus 22:2.

4:1 *When a wife*: Numbers 5:29.

A widow...or natin: This list specifies cases in which the marriage is forbidden; see *Yevamot* 2:4. Since these women are not considered legal wives they cannot drink the water of bitterness.

a woman *mamzer* or *natin* married to an Israelite,
or the daughter of an Israelite married to a *mamzer* or a *natin*—
may not drink and may not take her *ketubbah*.

2 These also may not drink and may not take their *ketubbah*:
She who says: "I am defiled unto you";
and she about whom witnesses have testified that she is defiled;
and she who says, "I will not drink."
If her husband says: "I will not make her drink";
or she whose husband has intercourse with her while on the way—
she takes her *ketubbah* and may not drink.
If their husbands died before their wives drank,
the House of Shammai say:
They take their *ketubbah* and may not drink;
but the House of Hillel say:
They may not drink and they may not take their *ketubbah*.

3 A woman pregnant with another man's child,
or a woman nursing another man's child,
may not drink and may not take her *ketubbah*—
the words of R. Meir;
but the Sages say:
He may set her apart and take her back after a time.
A sterile woman, an aged woman, and a woman without reproductive organs[26]
may not drink and may not take their *ketubbah*.

[26] Lit. "Ill-equipped to give birth."

---

mamzer: The offspring of prohibited sexual unions, who may not marry Israelites. See *Yevamot* 4:13.

natin: A reference to the biblical Gibeonites, who served the Israelites. See Joshua 9:27; *Qiddushin* 4:1.

may not take her ketubbah: The mishnah refers to women who received warning and were caught secluding themselves with the men whom their husbands warned them about, and are thus forbidden to their husbands (see 1:2 above). The only way for them to become permitted to their husbands is by drinking the water of bitterness. Since all these women may not drink (as Scripture refers only to "a [lawful] wife," Numbers 5:29), they must be divorced, and they also lose their *ketubbah* monies as a sanction.

4:2 *If her husband says*: Since in this case her husband is the party refusing to make her drink, the sanction of losing her *ketubbah* does not apply.

takes her ketubbah and may not drink: See 1:3 and 3:6.

4:3 *pregnant with...nursing another man's child*: The "other man" is the former or deceased husband of a woman who remarried while still pregnant with or nursing her former husband's child, in breach of marriage laws.

He may set her apart: Avoid sexual contact with her. The same root as for "abstinent" above, 3:4–5.

after a time: After the infant is weaned. Therefore, according to the Sages, the husband is not under obligation to divorce her.

sterile woman...without reproductive organs: According to the Sages, these women are forbidden to their husbands because they cannot fulfill the commandment to be fruitful and multiply (Genesis 1:28); see *Yevamot* 6:6. Therefore, they may not be forced to drink, but must be divorced without being able to claim their *ketubbah*.

R. Eliezer says:
He may marry another and be fruitful and multiply by her.
All other women either drink or do not take their *ketubbah*.

4 A priest's wife may drink and be permitted to her husband.
The wife of a eunuch may drink.
One may warn regarding anyone prohibited with respect to sexual unions,
save minors or one who is not a man.

5 The following are warned by a court:
she whose husband has become a deaf-mute or legally incompetent
or has been incarcerated in prison.
They did not say this to make her drink, but only to disqualify her from taking her *ketubbah*.
R. Yose says:
To make her drink as well,
so that when her husband is released from prison he may make her drink.

Chapter Five

5:1–5 *A Series of Homilies Mainly from R. Aqiva*

5 As the water acts upon her so does the water act upon him,[27]
for it is said: *And it shall come*, and again: *And it shall come*.
As she is forbidden to her husband so she is forbidden to her bedmate,

[27] K, P: "so it acts upon him."

R. Eliezer holds that a husband can continue to be married to such a wife, so that in the case of "jealousy" the husband must either have her drink or divorce with her *ketubbah* payment.

4:4 *permitted*: If found innocent. Priestesses who engaged in any sexual activity, even if involuntarily, outside their marriage were forbidden unto their husbands. See *Ketubbot* 2:9; 4:8.

prohibited with respect to sexual unions: Hebrew, *arayot*. The *sotah* rite can be imposed even if the suspected sexual union is prohibited due to kinship. The Mishnah refers to the list of relatives based on Leviticus 18. See *Yevamot* 1:1–3.

one who is not a man: The Talmudim cite three possible explanations to this unique term: animal, gentile, or impotent. In the current context, the third option is the most plausible.

4:5 *They did not say*: The third person plural is used to designate a later mishnah interpreting an older tradition.

5:1 *act upon him*: Her bedmate. Since the man referred to here is already considered her bedmate, the verb translated here as "act" refers not to testing but rather to punishing.

bedmate: Or paramour, Hebrew *boèl*, "one who takes mastery of/has intercourse with." The word is consonant with the word for husband, *baàl*.

for it is said: *And she became defiled...And she became defiled*[28]—
the words of R. Aqiva.
R. Joshua said:
So Zechariah b. ha-Qatsav used to expound.
Rabbi says:
Twice in the section it is said: *If she became defiled...became defiled*:
once for the husband and once for the bedmate.

2 That same day R. Aqiva expounded:
And if any of them falls into any earthen vessel, all that is in it shall become impure;
it does not say *is impure* but *shall become impure*, so that it impurifies another thing. This teaches that a loaf, having contracted second-degree impurity, further impurifies [a loaf] in the third degree.
R. Joshua said:
Who will take away the dust from your eyes, O Rabban Yohanan b. Zakkai!—
for you have said:
A future generation would declare the third-degree loaf insusceptible to impurity, for there is no verse[29] in the Torah designating it impure;
and has not your disciple Aqiva brought a verse from the Torah designating it impure? For it is said: *all that is in it shall become impure*.

3 That same day R. Aqiva expounded:
And you shall measure, outside the city, for the east side two thousand cubits..., while another verse says, *From the wall of the city outward one thousand cubits all around*. It is not possible to say one thousand cubits, since it is also written *two thousand cubits*; and it is not possible to say two thousand cubits, since it is also written *one thousand cubits*.[30]

---

[28] **K, P**: "*If she became defiled.*" Thus it refers to verses 27, 29 as Rabbi's homily below.
[29] **K, P**: this word is missing.
[30] **K, P** add "so why does it say a thousand cubits and why does it say two thousand cubits? Rather..."

And it shall come: Numbers 5:24, 27; the homily is based on the repetition in the biblical wording. Each occurrence is interpreted as referring to a different culprit. (*And it shall come* in verse 22 is probably not counted because it narrates the warning, rather than the act itself.)

And she became defiled: Numbers 5:13 and 14. These words reappear in verse 27 and 29 and Rabbi's second homily may refer to these latter occurrences.

5:2 *And if any of them falls*: Leviticus 11:33. The unusual form of the verb to designate impurity in this verse is read as implying an additional degree of impurity.

second-degree...third-degree loaf: Persons, vessels, or foods that touch one of the sources of impurity (creeping thing, carcass, a person suffering from flux, *tsara'at*, or menstruation, or a person made impure by a corpse), become impure in the first degree and impart second-degree impurity to food through contact. R. Aqiva provides a prooftext to support an old tradition (see *Eduyot* 2:1) whereby food made impure in the second degree can also impart third-degree impurity to other foods through contact. For the degrees of impurity, see *Tohorot* 2:3–5.

5:3 *And you shall measure*: Numbers 35:5. This and the next verse deal with cities and surrounding land set aside for Levites.

From the wall of the city: Numbers 35:4.

How so?

The one thousand cubits are the pastureland, while the two thousand cubits are the Sabbath limit.

R. Eliezer b. R. Yose the Galilean says:

The one thousand cubits are the pastureland and the two thousand cubits are the fields and vineyards.

4 That same day R. Aqiva expounded:

Then sang Moses and the people of Israel this song to the Lord, saying.

The word *saying* does not contain any additional teaching;

what then does Scripture teach by saying *saying*?[31]

It teaches us[32] that Israel responded to each and every utterance of Moses,

as though they were reciting the *Hallel*;[33]

therefore it says *saying*.

R. Nehemiah says:

As though they were reciting the *Shema* and not as though they were reciting the *Hallel*.

5 That same day R. Joshua b. Hyrcanus expounded:

Job served the blessed Holy One out of love alone,

as it is written: *Though he slay me yet will I wait for him.*

Thus far the matter is undecided whether it means

"I will wait for him" or "I will not wait";

but Scripture says: *Till I die I will not put away my integrity from me*,

teaching that he acted out of love.

R. Joshua said:

Who will take away the dust from your eyes, O Rabban Yohanan b. Zakkai!—

for all your life you expounded that Job served the blessed Holy One only out of fear,

---

[31] **K, P**: "and why was it said *saying*."   [32] **K, P**: "It teaches us rather."
[33] **K** adds here "I will sing unto the Lord for he hath triumphed gloriously."

---

pastureland: Of the city.

Sabbath limit: R. Aqiva derives from here the permitted distance for travel outside one's town on the Sabbath. This law predates the Sages, see for example, the Damascus Document (MS A 10.21) and Acts 1:12. The Damascus Document also addresses this contradiction in Numbers 5:4–5 and solves it by assuming two types of Sabbath limit.

R. Eliezer b. R. Yose the Galilean reads the verse as pertaining solely to Levitical cities.

5:4 *Then sang Moses*: Exodus 15:1.

Hallel: Selected chapters from Psalms (113–118) recited on holidays.

as though they were reciting the Hallel: That is, antiphonally. There were two optional reading procedures: if an adult read the *Hallel* the congregation always repeated the first verse of the reading; if a minor read the *Hallel*, the congregation repeated each and every verse (see *Sukkah* 3:10). According to **K** our mishnah is clearly referring to the former option.

Shema: Probably refers to a communal recitation of Deuteronomy 6:4–9.

5:5 *Though he slay me*: Job 13:15.

undecided: The Hebrew homophone *lo* means both "for him" or "not," and both could be spelled identically.

Till I die: Job 27:5.

for it is said: *that was blameless and upright,*
one who feared God, and turned away from evil;
and has not Joshua, your disciple's disciple, now taught that he acted out of love?

Chapter Six

6:1–4 *Testimonies Regarding the Suspected Wife's Defilement*

6 One who has warned his wife and she secluded herself,³⁴
even if he heard it from a flying bird, he must divorce her and pay her *ketubbah*—
the words of R. Eliezer.
R. Joshua says:
Not until the women who spin yarn by the moonlight gossip about her.
  2 If one witness said, I saw her becoming defiled—
she did not drink;
moreover, even a male slave or female slave—
these are trustworthy even to disqualify her from receiving her *ketubbah*.
Her mother-in-law, her mother-in-law's daughter, her co-wife,

---

³⁴ "and she secluded herself": Lacking in **K**.

---

that was blameless and upright: Job 1:1.

6:1 Thus far the tractate discussed two testimony types: regarding warning (*qinnui*); and regarding seclusion (*setirah*). Combined, the two testimonies render her forbidden to her husband until she undergoes the ritual. The current chapter adds a third type of testimony: regarding the "defiling" act itself (*tum'ah*). This testimony, in any shape or form, undermines the doubt, and therefore renders the ritual impracticable, forcing the husband to divorce his wife, sometimes with and sometimes without her *ketubbah* payment, depending on the reliability of the testimony.

warned his wife: Not to be in an intimate situation with a certain person, 1:2 above.

she secluded herself: 1:2 above:

a flying bird: Any source whatsoever (paraphrasing Ecclesiastes 10:20), informing the husband that his wife had sexual intercourse with so-and-so.

he must divorce her and pay her ketubbah: Rather than subject his wife to the ritual. The rumour constitutes sufficient cause to divorce but not to deprive the wife of her *ketubbah*, see above, 1:4; 4:2.

women who spin yarn: The traditional interpretation (first offered by the Yerushalmi ad loc.) of the obscure word *mozrot* or its variant *mutsarot*.

6:2 *she may not drink*: But can be divorced, receiving her *ketubbah*.

disqualify her from receiving her ketubbah: In contrast with the listing of relatives immediately following.

Her mother-in-law, etc.: For this list see *Yevamot* 15:4; *Gittin* 2:7. These are female relations of the husband who are assumed to be antagonistic to the wife, and therefore their testimony is sufficient to prevent the ritual from taking place, but not to trigger financial sanctions.

her husband's brother's wife, and her husband's daughter—
these are trustworthy, not to disqualify her from receiving her *ketubbah*,
but rather to prevent her from drinking.

3 For logic might imply:
if the first testimony, which does not render her forbidden permanently,
is not sustained by fewer than two witnesses,
then the last testimony, which renders her forbidden permanently—
should not logic require that it will not be sustained by fewer than two witnesses?
But Scripture says:
And there is no witness against her—
any testimony[35] against her.
From here there is an argument of lesser and greater to the first testimony:
if the last testimony, which renders her forbidden permanently, is sustained by one witness,
then the first testimony, which does not render her forbidden permanently—
should not logic require that it will be sustained by one witness?
But Scripture says:
Because he has found any matter of indecency in her,
and elsewhere it says, *based on two witnesses*[36] ... *shall any matter be sustained*—
just as the matter spoken of there, must be based on two witnesses,
so, here, it must be based on two witnesses.

4 One witness says, "She was defiled," and another witness says, "She was not defiled";
one woman says, "She was defiled", and another woman says "She was not defiled"—
she would drink.
One says, "She was defiled," and two say, "She was not defiled"—
she would[37] drink.
But if two say, "She was defiled," and one says, "She was not defiled"—
she would not drink.

---

[35] "Testimony" lacking in **K**, **P**. [36] **K**, **P** add "*or based on three witnesses.*"
[37] **K**: "would not."

6:3 *first testimony*: Regarding her entry into a hiding place, see above 1:2.

does not render her forbidden permanently: But only until she drinks the water of bitterness.

last testimony: Regarding her actual sexual intercourse, see above 6:1.

And there is no witness: Numbers 5:13.

any testimony against her is sufficient to prevent her from drinking.

Because he has found: Deuteronomy 24:1.

based on two witnesses: Deuteronomy 19:15.

just as the matter ... based on two witnesses: The midrashic inference here is based on the appearance of the word matter (Hebrew, *davar*) in both verses.

6:4 The mishnah is based on a simple calculation: the testimony of a single witness that the woman was defiled prevents the ritual from taking place, unless it is contradicted by a testimony commensurate with it or of greater magnitude, in which case the ritual goes on.

Chapter Seven

7:1–2 Rituals Performed in Any Language or Only in the Holy Tongue

7 These may be said in any language:[38]
the *sotah* passage,
the declaration over tithes,
the recitation of the *Shema*,
the *tefillah*,
the blessing after meals,
the oath of testimony,
and the oath of deposit.

2 These must be said in the holy tongue:
the recitation for firstfruits,
and *halitsah*,
the blessings and curses,
the priestly blessing,[39]
and the blessing of the high priest,
the passage on the king,

---

[38] **K, P:** *bi-leshonam*—"in their tongue/language," meaning in the vernacular.
[39] In **K** (before emendation): "priestly blessings." See 7:6 below.

7:1 *language*: Lit. "tongue."

sotah passage: Numbers 5:19–22.

the declaration over tithes: Deuteronomy 26:13–15; cf. *Ma'aser Sheni* 5:10–13.

shema … tefillah … blessing after meals: Each of the three liturgical institutions are discussed in this order in *Berakhot*. *Tefillah* refers to the eighteen benedictions (*Amidah* or *Shemoneh Esreh* in contemporary usage) said three times daily; see *Berakhot* 4:1–3.

oath of testimony: Cf. *Shevu'ot* 4:1.

oath of deposit: Cf. *Shevu'ot* 5:1 and following.

7:2 *holy tongue*: Hebrew.

blessings and curses: Deuteronomy 27:15–26 (cf. Deuteronomy 28:2–68, Joshua 8:34). See below 7:5.

priestly blessing: Numbers 6:24–6. See below, 7:6.

blessing of the high priest: A nonbiblical blessing recited, according to the Mishnah, by the high priest on the Day of Atonement. See below, 7:7.

the passage on the king: Deuteronomy 17:14–20. Below, at 7:8, the Mishnah explains that this passage is read as part of the seventh-year rite of gathering (known as *Haqhel*).

the passage on the heifer whose neck is broken,
and the priest anointed for battle when he speaks to the people.

7:3–4   *Exposition of the Preceding Rituals: Firstfruits and Halitsah*

3 The recitation for firstfruits, how?
And you shall answer and say before the Lord your God,[40]
and below it says:
And the Levites shall answer and say;
just as the answer further below is in the holy tongue, so here in the holy tongue.

4 *Halitsah*, how?
And she shall answer and say,[41]
and below it says:
And the Levites shall answer and say;[42]

---

[40] K continues the prooftext: *A wandering Aramaean was my father.*
[41] K, P continue the prooftext: *So shall it be done to the man who does not build up his brother's house.*
[42] K, P continue the prooftext: *to all the men of Israel with a loud voice.*

---

heifer whose neck is broken: Deuteronomy 21:1–9. See below, 9:1–8.

priest anointed for battle: Deuteronomy 20:2–7. The Mishnah understands there to be a special high priest designated ("anointed") for military purposes. See below, 8:1–7.

7:3–9:8 The following passages discuss each of the rituals mentioned in 7:2. In each case, the exposition by the Mishnah is introduced "...how?" The Mishnah then narrates each ritual, excluding the first two items in the list—firstfruits and *halitsah*, which are discussed in their respective tractates (*Bikkurim* and *Yevamot*)—and hence the Mishnah here only cites the prooftext attesting to the necessity of their recitation in the holy tongue.

7:3 *recitation for firstfruits*: Deuteronomy 26:3, 5–10; a passage recited every year by the farmer bringing the firstfruits to the Temple. This biblical passage narrating the people's sacred history from Jacob to the Israelites' entry into the Promised Land is also at the heart of the Passover Haggadah (*Pesahim* 10:4). See *Bikkurim* 3:6.

And you shall answer and say: Deuteronomy 26:5. The Mishnah presents the prooftext as based on a syllogism from the biblical passage on blessings and curses (see note below). The homily may have been based originally on the repetition of two declamatory verbs—*answer* and *say*—implying that the manner of declamation is important as well, not only its content.

And the Levites: Deuteronomy 27:14. The citation is also taken from the biblical passage on blessings and curses discussed below (7:5). The homily does not explain how we know that blessings and curses themselves are restricted to the holy tongue. The Bavli (*Sotah* 33a) offers a complementary prooftext.

7:4 *Halitsah*: Deuteronomy 25:7, 9; *Yevamot* 12:6: the formula recited by the widow whose brother-in-law refuses to enter into levirate marriage with her. See 1:2 above.

And the Levites: Deuteronomy 27:14.

just as the answer further below is in the holy tongue, so here in the holy tongue.
R. Judah says:
And she shall answer and say thus—
she must recite in that same language.

7:5 *Exposition of the Preceding Rituals: Blessings and Curses*

5 The blessings and the curses, how?
When Israel crossed the Jordan and came to Mount Gerizim and to Mount Ebal in Samaria, nearby Shechem, beside the terebinth of Moreh,
as it is said: *Are they not beyond Jordan…*
And below it says:
And Abram passed through the land unto the place of Shechem unto the terebinth of Moreh;
Just as the terebinth of Moreh that is spoken of is at Shechem, so here the terebinth of Moreh that is spoken of is at Shechem.
Six tribes went up to the top of Mount Gerizim and six tribes went up to the top of Mount Ebal.
And the priests and the Levites and the Ark stand below between them;
and the priests surround the Ark and the Levites surround the priests,
and all Israel are on this side and on that,
as it is said: *And all Israel with their elders and officers and their judges, stood on opposite sides of the ark.*
They turned their faces towards Mount Gerizim and began with the blessing:
Blessed be the man that makes not a graven or molten image,[43]
and both answer,[44] Amen!
They turned their faces towards Mount Ebal and began with the curse,
Cursed be the man that makes a graven or molten image,[45]

---

[43] **K, P** adds: "an abomination unto the Lord, the work of a craftsman, and did not place it in hiding."
[44] **K, P**: "answer and say Amen."   [45] **K, P** continues the prooftext: *an abomination unto the Lord.*

And she shall answer and say thus: Deuteronomy 25:9; the homily separates the word "thus" from the clause that follows.

she should recite the biblical passage.

7:5 *Are they not beyond Jordan*: Deuteronomy 11:30.

And Abram passed: Genesis 12:6.

And all Israel: Joshua 8:33.

Blessed be the man: Not a scriptural citation. The rabbis interpret the blessings and curses mentioned in Deuteronomy 27:12–13 as referring to the curses that immediately follow, and therefore added to each biblical curse its respective blessing. Note, however, that the following chapter, Deuteronomy 28, narrates both blessings and curses explicitly.

both: Cf. Deuteronomy 27:15.

and both answer,[46] Amen!—
until they finish the blessings and curses.
And afterward they brought the stones and built the altar and plastered it with plaster.
And they wrote thereon all the words of the Torah in seventy languages,
as it is written: *Very plainly*.
And they took the stones and came and spent the night in their assigned place.

7:6 *Exposition of the Preceding Rituals: Priestly Blessing*

6 The priestly blessing, how?
In the provinces it is said[47] as three blessings, and at the Temple as a single blessing;
at the Temple they say the Name as written, but in the provinces using its epithet;
in the provinces the priests raise their hands shoulder high,
but at the Temple above their heads, excepting the high priest who does not raise his hands above the frontlet.
R. Judah says:
The high priest also raises his hands above the frontlet,
as it is written: *Then Aaron lifted up his hands toward the people and blessed them*.

7:7 *Exposition of the Preceding Rituals: The Blessing of the High Priest on the Day of Atonement*

7 The blessing of the high priest, how?
The minister of the assembly takes a Torah scroll and gives it to the head of the assembly,
and the head of the assembly gives it to the deputy,
and the deputy gives it to the high priest,

---

[46] See note 44 above.   [47] K: "they are said." See 7:1.

Very plainly: Deuteronomy 27:8. The biblical expression is read here as meaning: "fully interpreted."

their assigned place: Joshua 4:3; Joshua 4:20 clarifies that this refers to Gilgal.

7:6 *In the provinces*: As opposed to the city of Jerusalem.

as three blessings: The people respond "Amen" to each of the three verses separately.

say the Name as written: They utter the tetragrammaton as written; *Yoma* 6:2.

epithet: The word *Adonai* (lit. "my Lord[s]") in place of the tetragrammaton.

above the frontlet: Exodus 28:36.

Then Aaron lifted: Leviticus 9:22.

7:7 *blessing of the high priest*: See *Yoma* 7:1, which is probably the source of our mishnah.

minister of the assembly: *Knesset* does not refer here to synagogue (always appearing in the Mishnah as *beit ha-knesset*). See *Makkot* 3:12, where *hazan ha-knesset* (minister of the assembly) performs the flogging, an act executed in any local court (see *Sanhedrin* 1:2).

and the high priest stands and receives it and reads it standing.
And he reads *After the death* and *On the tenth day.*
Then he rolls up the Torah and puts it in his bosom and says:
"More is written here[48] than I have read out before you."
And on the tenth that is in the Book of Numbers he recites by heart,
and he blesses over it eight blessings:
(1) for the Torah, (2) for the temple service, (3) for thanksgiving, (4) for the forgiveness of sin, and (5) for the Temple, and (6) for Israel, and (7) for the priests, and (8) for the remainder of the prayer.

7:8 Exposition of the Preceding Rituals: The Passage on the King at The Ritual of Gathering

8 The passage on the king, how?
After the close of the first Festival day of the Feast, in the eighth year, after the close of the Seventh,
they prepare for him a wooden platform in the Temple Court on which he sits,
as it is said: *At the end of every seven years, at the appointed time.*
The minister of the assembly takes a Torah scroll and gives it to the head of the assembly,
and the head of the assembly gives it to the deputy and the deputy gives it to the high priest,
and the high priest gives it to the king,
and the king stands and receives it and reads it seated.
King Agrippa stood and received it and read it standing, and the Sages praised him.
And when he reached *You may not put a foreigner over you,*[49] his eyes flowed with tears;[50] they said to him:
Fear not, Agrippa! You are our brother! You are our brother! You are our brother![51]

[48] **K, P** lack "here." [49] **K, P** continue the citation: *which is not your brother.*
[50] **K**: "his tears flowed." [51] **K, P** lack the third repetition.

reads it standing: As opposed to the king who would read it seated, see 7:8.

After the death: Leviticus 16:1–34.

On the tenth day: Leviticus 23:26–32.

And on the tenth: Numbers 29:7–11.

for the remainder of the prayer: Asking for the prayer to be accepted. This refers to the benediction "Hear our Prayer" (*Shome'a Tefillah*), the last of the middle unit of the *Tefillah* (on which see the annotation to 7:1).

7:8 *Seventh*: The Sabbatical year; see *Shevi'it*. The ritual reading by the king is based on the Mishnah's understanding of Deuteronomy 31:12, which does not explicitly mention the king. That passage requires the public reading of "this Torah," which according to the Mishnah refers to a series of passages.

At the end of every seven years: Deuteronomy 31:10.

You may not put: Deuteronomy 17:15.

You are our brother: Agrippa the First was the grandson of King Herod, and therefore of Edomite descent. This mishnah may reflect a debate on the status of converts.

He reads from the beginning of Deuteronomy through *Shema*;
And *Shema*,
And it shall come to pass if you shall listen,
You shall surely tithe,
When you complete the tithing,
and the passage on the king,[52]
and the blessings and curses, until he finishes the entire passage.[53]
The blessings that the high priest blesses, the king blesses,
except that he inserts that of the festivals instead of the forgiveness of sin.

Chapter Eight

8:1–7   *Exposition of the Preceding Rituals: Anointed Priest's Speech before a War*

8 When the priest anointed for battle speaks to the people he would speak in the holy tongue,
as it is said: *And when you draw near to the battle, the priest shall come forward*—
this is the priest anointed for battle;
and speak to the people—
in the holy tongue;
and shall say to them, Hear, O Israel, you draw near this day to battle against your enemies—

[52] K, P lack "passage on the king."   [53] K, P: "until he finishes all of them."

Shema: Deuteronomy 6:4.

And it shall come to pass: Deuteronomy 11:13ff.

You shall surely tithe: Deuteronomy 14:22ff.

When you complete the tithing: Deuteronomy 26:12ff.

passage on the king: Deuteronomy 17:14–20.

blessings and curses: Deuteronomy 27:15–26. Cf. Deuteronomy 28:2–68.

until he finishes the entire passage: The king reads a series of passages which together comprise a synopsis of the entire Book of Deuteronomy.

8:1 Deuteronomy 20 gives instructions for the preparations for war, including the speech that "the priest" makes before the assembled soldiers. According to the Mishnah, this is an anointed priest especially for the war. The chapter is a *midrash* on Deuteronomy 20, sometimes in the form of lemma and homily and sometimes by interweaving the verse with the tannaitic narration.

in the holy tongue: Based on the redundancy of *speak* and *saying*. Compare 7:–4 above ("answer and say").

And when you draw near: Deuteronomy 20:2.

against your enemies: The words are seemingly redundant. The homily reads them as a reference to gentiles, as opposed to intra-Jewish feuds.

and not against your brethren—not Judah against Simeon, and not Simeon against Benjamin—

for if you fall into their hands they will have mercy upon you,

as it is said:[54] *And the men who have been mentioned by name rose and took the captives,*[55] *and with the spoil they clothed all that were naked among them; they clothed them, gave them sandals, provided them with food and drink, and anointed them; and carrying all the feeble among them on asses, they brought them to their kinsfolk at Jericho, the city of palm trees. Then they returned to Samaria.*

Against your enemies do you go, for if you fall into their hands they will not have mercy upon you:

Let not your heart faint; do not fear, or tremble, or be in dread of them.

Let not your heart faint at the neighing of horses and the brandishing of swords;

do not fear at the clashing of shields and the multitude of soldiers;[56]

or tremble at the sound of trumpets,[57]

or be in dread at the sound of shouting;[58]

for the Lord your God is he that goes with you—

they come trusting flesh and blood, but you come trusting the Omnipresent.

The Philistines came trusting Goliath. What was his end? In the end he fell by the sword and they fell with him.

The Ammonites came trusting Shobach. What was his end? In the end he fell by the sword and they fell with him.

But it is not so for you, *for the Lord your God is he that goes with you to fight for you*[59]—this is the camp of the ark.

2 *And the officers shall speak to the people, saying, What man is there that has built a new house and has not dedicated it, let him go and return to his house—*

it is all one whether he builds a house for straw, a house for cattle, a house for wood, or a house for stores;

it is all one whether he builds or buys or inherits or whether it is given to him as a gift.

And what man is there that has planted a vineyard and has not enjoyed its fruits[60]—

[54] K, P: "as it is said below." [55] K lacks the remainder of the citation.
[56] K before emendation and others: "tramping." Accordingly *kalgas* should be read as military footwear in accordance with its Latin etymology.
[57] K: "the sound of the trumpets." [58] K: "the sound of the shout."
[59] K, P complete the verse: *to fight for you against your enemies, to save you.*
[60] K, P complete the citation: *let him return to his home.*

And the men who have been mentioned: 2 Chronicles 28:15.

The Philistines came trusting Goliath: 1 Samuel 17:4.

The Ammonites came trusting Shobach: 2 Samuel 10:16.

8:2 *And the officers shall speak*: Deuteronomy 20:5. The instructions in this and the following verses allow certain members of the assembled troops to return home.

to his house: The verse refers to a residential house, and the homily extends its application to nonresidential house types. All three homilies in this mishnah consider the biblical idioms in the verse as casuistic laws that should be extended to additional cases.

And what man is there that has planted a vineyard: Deuteronomy 20:6. The mishnah applies the biblical verse to other forms of produce, and forms of cultivation other than planting.

it is all one whether he plants a vineyard or plants five fruit trees, even if they are of the five kinds;

it is all one whether he plants or sinks them into the ground or grafts them;

it is all one whether he buys or inherits it or whether it is given him as a gift.

And what man is there that has betrothed a wife[61]—

it is all one whether he betroths a virgin or a widow, or even one that awaits levirate marriage;

even if he hears that his brother has died in battle—let him return home.

All of these hearken to the words of the priest from among the ranks of battle;

and they return home and provide water and food and repair the roads.

3 And the following may not return:

one who builds a gate or an exedra or a gallery,

or one who plants only four fruit trees or five fruitless trees;

or one who takes back his divorced wife;

or a widow being married to[62] a high priest,

or a divorcee or a woman who had performed *halitsah* to a common priest,

or a female *mamzer* or *natin* to an Israelite,

or the daughter of an Israelite to either a *mamzer* or a *natin*—

these may not return.

R. Judah says

Also one who rebuilds his house as it was before may not return.

R. Eliezer says:

Also one who builds a house of bricks in the Sharon may not return.

4 And these remain in their places:

one who built a house and dedicated it,

one who planted a vineyard and enjoyed its fruits,

---

[61] K completes the citation: *Let him return to his home.*   [62] Hebrew has only "to."

---

of the five kinds: Of cereals. See *Hallah* 1:1.

And what man is there that has betrothed a wife: Deuteronomy 20:7.

even if he hears: Consequently, his sister-in-law is a levirate widow awaiting his *yibbum*.

and provide water and food and repair the roads: For the military.

8:3 *a widow being married to a high priest…the daughter of an Israelite to either a mamzer or a natin*: All of these are forbidden marriages (cf. *Yevamot* 2:4; and above 4:1).

natin: Refers to the Gibeonites. See Joshua 9:27; *Qiddushin* 4:1.

in the Sharon: The coastal plateau (stretching between Hadera to Herzliyah in contemporary Israel). In the times of the Mishnah, the Sharon was notorious for the poor quality of its building materials, which was the frequent cause of house collapses. Since this is not a viable house it is not included in the exemption of *a man that has built a new house*.

8:4 *remain in their places*: Unlike the previously listed persons who must go to the battlefield and then return (or do not return, depending on their specific status, as detailed above). The mishnah applies the rule of Deuteronomy 24:5, which gives an exemption of one year to the newly married, also to the categories of Deuteronomy 20.

one who married his betrothed,
or one who took in his levirate widow,
as it says: *He shall be exempt one year for the sake of his house:*
For the sake of his house—this is his house;
He shall be—this is his vineyard;
And shall cheer his wife—this is his wife;
Whom he has taken—this is to include also his levirate widow.
These do not provide water and food and do not repair the roads.

5 *And the officers shall speak further to the people and they shall say, What man is there who is fearful and fainthearted?*
R. Aqiva says:
Fearful and fainthearted is meant literally—
one who cannot endure the armies joined in battle or bear to see a drawn sword.
R. Yose the Galilean says:
The *fearful and fainthearted* is one who is afraid for the transgressions that he has committed;
hence the Torah has joined them together with these others, so that he could return because of them.
R. Yose says:
A widow married to a high priest,
or a divorcee or a woman that had performed *halitsah* married to a common priest,
or a female *mamzer* or *natin* married to an Israelite,
or the daughter of an Israelite married to a *mamzer* or *natin*—
this is the *fearful and fainthearted.*

6 *And it shall be when the officers have made an end of speaking unto the people that they shall appoint captains of hosts at the head of the people,*
and at the rearward of the people;
they station guards in front of them and others behind them with axes of iron in their hands, and if any seeks to turn back he may break his legs,
for the beginning of flight is a fall,
as it is said: *Israel has fled before the Philistines, and there has also been a great slaughter among the people.*

He shall be exempt one year: Deuteronomy 24:5.

8:5 *literally*: Lit. "as it is heard."

because of them: According to R. Yose the Galilean, the Torah joins the *fearful and fainthearted* together with the objective reasons for leaving the battlefield detailed above, in order to enable transgressors to save face and provide an alternative explanation for their return home.

A widow married to a high priest: The same list as in 8:3 above. Here the men in these prohibited marriages are the sinful people to whom *fearful and fainthearted* applies.

8:6 *And it shall be*: Deuteronomy 20:9.

at the rearward of the people: The rabbis read *at the head of the people*, as referring to either end of the camp.

as it is said: The mishnah supplements the laws of war from Deuteronomy with the narratives of war from 1 Samuel.

Israel has fled before the Philistines: 1 Samuel 4:17.

and further it says: *the men of Israel fled before the Philistines, and fell slain.*[63]

7 To what do these words refer?
To war of choice;
but in a war that is commanded all go forth,
even *a bridegroom from his room and a bride from her chamber.*
R. Judah said:
What has been said applies to a war that is commanded;
but in an obligatory war all go forth,
even *a bridegroom from his room and a bride from her chamber.*

Chapter Nine

9:1–8 *Exposition of the Preceding Rituals: The Heifer Whose Neck is Broken*

9 The heifer whose neck is broken—in the holy tongue,
as it is said: *If one be found slain on the ground…then your elders and your judges shall come out.*
Three of the Great Court in Jerusalem would come out.
R. Judah says:
Five,
as it is said: *Your elders*, two; and *your judges*, two; and the court must not be even, so they add to them yet one more.

[63] **K, P** complete the citation: *on Mount Gilboa.*

---

the men of Israel fled: 1 Samuel 31:1.

8:7 *war of choice…war that is commanded…obligatory war*: According to the Tosefta the Mishnah is not referring here to a tripartite division, but rather R. Judah is using a different terminology, according to which *mitzvah* is an act of religious piety rather than an obligation.

a bridegroom from his room: Joel 2:16.

9:1 *heifer whose neck is broken*: Deuteronomy 21:1–9 outlines a procedure for resolving the guilt that accrues when a corpse of a murder victim is found between towns and it is not known who is responsible. The ritual involves in part the killing of a heifer by breaking its neck (21:4) and the elders' washing their hands and declaring their innocence (21:7–8).

in the holy tongue: Refers to the text recited by the elders, see Deuteronomy 21:7–8. The homily establishing the requirement of recitation in the holy tongue is not cited here, but is probably based on the duplication of "answer and say"; cf. the homilies above, 7:3–4. *As it is said* refers to the procedure that follows.

If one be found slain: Deuteronomy 21:1.

Three of the Great Court: Cf. *Sanhedrin* 11:2. The involvement of the Great Court is a non-Biblical addition.

2 If it is found hidden in a heap or hung on a tree or floating on the water,
they would not break the neck,
as it is said *in the land*—and not hidden in a heap;
and *lying*—and not hung on a tree;
in the field—and not floating on the water.
If it is found near a frontier, or a town where gentiles[64] were in the majority,
or near a town without a court, they would not break the neck.[65]
They measure only from[66] a town with a court.
If it is found at a like distance from two cities, both bring, two heifers in all.
The words of R. Eliezer.[67]
And Jerusalem does not bring a heifer whose neck is broken.

3 If its head is found in one place and its body in another,
they take the head to the body—
the words of R. Eliezer.
R. Aqiva says:
[They take] the body to the head.

4 Whence did they measure?[68]
R. Eliezer says:
From his navel.
R. Aqiva says:
From his nose.
R. Eliezer b. Jacob says:
From the place where he was slain—from his neck.

5 The elders of Jerusalem departed and went away;
the elders of that city bring *a heifer which has never been worked*
and which has not pulled a yoke,
and[69] a blemish does not disqualify it.

---

[64] **K, P**: "a city wherein gentiles [*goyim*] live."   [65] **K, P** lack "they…neck."
[66] **K**: "to."
[67] **P** adds "and the Sages say: one city brings one broken-neck heifer, but two cities do not bring two heifers."
[68] In **K, P** this mishnah precedes 8:3.   [69] **K**: "and that."

9:2 *frontier…without a court*: All three cases are considered as a legal "no man's land," in which murder is not an anomaly, cf. 9:9 below. According to the reading in **K** and **P** (see n. 65), in these three cases they do not abstain from performing the ritual altogether, but rather measure the distance to the nearest legally functional city.

gentiles: See n. 64. The difference between "where gentiles were the majority" and "where gentiles live" is significant, since mixed cities in Roman Palestine often had a Jewish majority.

Jerusalem does not bring a heifer whose neck is broken: Babylonian Talmud *Sotah* 45b: The Talmud explains that the ritual applies only to land divided among the tribes, thereby excluding Jerusalem.

9:3-4 These two Mishnah units discuss the precise point in the victim's corpse from which the court would measure the distances. Some manuscripts reverse the order of the two units.

9:5 *a heifer which has never been worked*: Deuteronomy 21:3.

And they bring it down *to a mighty stream*,[70]
mighty is to be understood literally; but even if it is not mighty it is valid.
And they break its neck with a cleaver from behind.
And that place is forbidden for sowing and cultivation,
but it is permitted there to comb out flax and to chisel out[71] stones.

6 The elders of that city wash their hands in water at the place where the heifer's neck was broken, saying:
Our hands have not shed this blood, nor have our eyes seen it.
Could it have entered our mind[72] that the elders of the court[73] were shedders of blood?—
Rather, [what the elders mean is] that he did not come into our hands and we sent him away without food,
nor did we see him and leave him without escort.[74]
And the priests say:
Forgive, O Lord, your people Israel, whom you have redeemed and do not set the guilt of innocent blood in the midst of your people Israel, but let the guilt of blood be forgiven them.
They had no need to say:
And the blood shall be forgiven them;
rather, it is the Holy Spirit proclaiming to them:
whenever you do thus *the blood is forgiven them*.

7 If the slayer was found before the heifer's neck was broken, it may go forth and pasture among the flock;
but if the heifer's neck was broken, it must be buried in that place;
for from its beginning it was brought because of doubt,

[70] Or "wadi."   [71] **K, P**: "to clean stones."   [72] **K, P**: "our hearts."
[73] **P**: "that the court."   [74] **K, P** lack "without food" and "without escort."

---

stream: Cf. Deuteronomy 21:4.

mighty: The word could also mean "hard-flowing."

with a cleaver from behind: Imitating the act of murder.

forbidden for sowing and cultivation: See Deuteronomy 21:4.

comb out flax…chisel out stones: Works that do not involve cultivation of the soil, and are therefore permitted.

9:6 The mishnah divided the verses from Deuteronomy 21:7–8 into three parts: the first is recited by the elders, the second by the priests, the third is the answer ascribed to the Holy Spirit; cf. Tosefta *Sotah* 9:2.

Our hands have not shed this blood: Deuteronomy 21:7.

mind: See n. 72. According to the rabbinic worldview thoughts are located in the heart.

without food…without escort: According to the shorter reading in **K** and **P**, the mishnah refers to the murderer (we did not have him in our custody and release him). The longer reading in later editions refers to the victim (announcing that he was not abandoned without offering him assistance).

Forgive, O Lord: Deuteronomy 21:5.

9:7 *doubt*: As detailed in the following mishnah; compare *Sotah* 6:4. Both rituals address cases involving doubt, and therefore are not performed if a legitimate testimony is available. *Sotah* 9:9 discusses the annulment of both rituals together, and the Tosefta ascribes the annulment to the prevalence of transgressions, and hence the termination of doubt.

it atoned for that doubt and fulfilled its purpose.⁷⁵
If the heifer's neck was broken and the slayer was found thereafter, then he shall be slain.

8 If one witness says:
"I saw the slayer,"
and another witness says:
"You⁷⁶ did not see";
If a woman says,
"I saw,"
And another woman says,
"You⁷⁷ did not see,"
they would break the neck.
If one witness says,
"I saw,"
and two say,
"You⁷⁸ did not see,"
they would break the neck.
But if two say,
"We saw,"
and one says to them,
"You⁷⁹ did not see,"
they would not break the neck.

9:9–12 *Termination of the Nation's Legal and Religious Institutions*

9 When the murderers abounded the ritual of breaking the heifer's neck ceased. When Eleazar b. Dinai came and Tehinah b. Parishah was his name⁸⁰ they changed his name to Son of the Murderer.⁸¹

---

75 Literally, "and went on its way." 76 P: "I." See also the next notes.
77 K (before emendation), P: "I." 78 K (before emendation), P: "we." 79 P: "I."
80 K, P: "and Tehinah b. Parishah, and b. Parishah was his name."
81 P before emendation: "House of the Murderer."

---

and the slayer was found thereafter: The duplication in our mishnah is explained by the fact that its first half is taken from *Keritot* 6:2, which discusses the issue of sacrifices for doubted and definite sins.

he shall be slain: By the court. See *Sanhedrin* 9:1.

9:8 *one witness says*: Since the heifer is brought in a case of doubt, the mishnah limits the performance of the ritual to cases in which the testimony regarding the murder does not dispel the doubt.

You did not see: See n. 79. According to the readings with "I," the doubt does not come from a refutation of a testimony but from conflicting testimonies.

9:9–12 The Mishnah presents a series of practices and institutions that ceased as a result of moral decline.

9:9 *Eleazar b. Dinai*: See Josephus, *Antiquities* 20.160–162; cf. *Kelim* 5:10.

When the adulterers abounded the water of bitterness[82] ceased;
and R. Yohanan b. Zakkai caused it to cease,
as it is said: *I will not punish your daughters when they commit whoredom nor your daughters-in-law when they commit adultery, for they themselves* etc.
When Yose b. Yoezer of Tseredah and Yose b. Yohanan of Jerusalem died, the wise men ceased,
as it is written: *There is no cluster to eat,*[83] *my soul desires the first-ripe fig.*

10 Yohanan the high priest abolished the declaration of tithe;
he also abolished the Awakeners and the Stunners;
until his days the hammer used to smite in Jerusalem;
and in his days none needed to inquire concerning *demai*.

11 When the Sanhedrin ceased, singing was abolished at wedding feasts,
as it is said: *They shall not drink wine with a song…*

[82] K, P: "the accursed water."   [83] K: citation ends here.

Tehinah b. Parishah: According to the reading of **K** and **P**, the mishnah is probably speaking about two different persons, Eleazar and Tehinah b. Parishah. The version of the print edition is similar to *Sifre to Deuteronomy*.

I will not punish your daughters: Hosea 4:14. The verse continues *for they themselves go apart with whores*. Cf. the Bavli "If you yourselves are above reproach the water will put your wives to the test; otherwise it will not put them to the test."

Yose b. Yoezer of Tseredah and Yose b. Yohanan: Cf. *Avot* 1:4; *Hagigah* 2:2.

the wise men: Lit. "clusters," *ashkolot*, which is also the meaning of the word in the prooftext from Micah. However, the mishnah appears to make a pun on the Greek *schole*, with the initial vowel functioning as a common pronunciation aid.

There is no cluster: Micah 7:1.

9:10 Parallel in *Ma'aser Sheni* 10:15.

abolished the declaration of tithe: According a tradition in the Tosefta, John Hyrcanus introduced a major reform in the system of tithes, whereby an exemption was granted from bringing nonsacred tithes. This made it impossible to make the declaration of tithe, which asserts that *all* tithes have been set apart.

tithe: The "second" tithe brought to Jerusalem, *Ma'aser Sheni* 5:10–15, based on Deuteronomy 26:13.

Awakeners…Stunners: According to the Tosefta, the *Awakeners* are Levites who recited the verse *Rouse yourself! Why do you sleep, O Lord* (Psalms 44:23), whereas the *Stunners* are priests who beat sacrificial animals before slaughtering them.

the hammer used to smite: Work performed on *hol hamo'ed* (the intermediate days between the first and last holy days of the Sukkot and Passover) according to the Tosefta. See *Mo'ed Qatan*.

demai: Produce regarding which there is doubt whether tithes were allocated (see *Demai*). The annulment of the need to inquire about *demai* is probably due to the reform in the system of tithes narrated above.

9:11 *wedding feasts*: Lit. "house of feasts," a location where wedding feasts are held. Cf. *Eruvin* 8:1; *Ketubbot* 7:5.

They shall not drink: Isaiah 24:9.

12 When the first prophets died, Urim and Thummim ceased.
When the Temple was destroyed the *shamir* and the honeycomb ceased;
and faithful men came to an end, as it is said: *Help, Lord, for the godly man ceaseth.*[84]

9:12 cont.–14   *Lamentation for Destructions*

Rabban Simeon b. Gamaliel says in the name of R. Joshua:
Since the day that the Temple was destroyed there has not been a day without a curse;
and dewfall is without blessing and the fruits have lost their savor.
R. Yose says:
The fruits have also lost their fatness.

13 R. Simeon b. Eleazar says[85]
The [loss of] purity took away the flavour and the fragrance;
the [loss of] tithes took away the fatness of the grain; [86]
and the Sages say,[87]
Fornication and sorceries consumed it all.

14 During the war of Vespasian they decreed against bridegroom wreaths and the *errus*. During the war of Titus[88] they decreed against bridal wreaths and that a person should not teach his son Greek.

---

[84] **K** completes the citation: *for the faithful have vanished from among the sons of men.*
[85] The mishnah is missing from **K** and was added in the margin.
[86] Literally: "Purity took away…tithes took away…"
[87] "And the Sages say" is missing from **K, P**.   [88] **K** reads "Qitos."

9:12 *first prophets*: Cf. *Yoma* 5:2; *Ta'anit* 4:2; *Yadayim* 4:3. According to a tradition in the Babylonian Talmud, this refers to all the Prophets except for Haggai, Zechariah, and Malachi, who were active in the Persian period, at the beginning of the Second Temple period.

Urim and Thummim: Psalms 12:1.

When the Temple was destroyed: Like all other references in the Mishnah to "when the Temple was destroyed," this refers to the Second Temple (destroyed in 70 CE) (see e.g. *Ma'aser Sheni* 5:2; *Rosh Hashanah* 4:3–4.).

the shamir: Name of a hard stone. The Tosefta and the Talmudim interpret it as the worm that cuts through the stone. According to biblical law, the stone blocks from which the Temple's altar is built may not be hewn with iron tools (Exodus 20:21; Deuteronomy 27:6).

honeycomb: Lit. "the sweetness of flower nectar." In mishnaic times honey was produced from fruits (like dates) and honeycomb was considered rare and exotic.

Help, Lord: Psalms 12:1.

9:13 *and the Sages say*. See n. 87. Without this attribution to the Sages, the expression *it all* serves to conclude R. Simon b. Eleazar's statement. According to the printed editions, the Sages offer an alternative explanation for the loss of abundance.

9:14 *war of Vespasian*: 66–70 CE, the great revolt in which Jerusalem and the Temple were destroyed.

decreed against: The rabbinic prohibitions were devised to minimize celebratory expressions within the community. On the theological dimension of these prohibitions see Tosefta.

errus: A musical instrument used in weddings feasts, cf. Yerushalmi and Bavli ad loc.; *Kelim* 15:6.

war of Titus: Reading *qitos* as in **K**, a reference to Lucius Quietus, a military officer who quelled an uprising of Jews in Mesopotamia against the invading Romans (115–117 CE), and was subsequently governor of Palestine.

In the last war they prohibited the bride from going forth in a palanquin inside the town;
but our rabbis permitted the bride to go forth in a palanquin inside the town.

9:15 *Lamentation for the Death of the Sages*

15 When R. Meir died,[89] makers of proverbs ceased.[90]
When Ben Azzai died, diligent students ceased.
When Ben Zoma died, preachers ceased.[91]
When R. Joshua died, the prosperity[92] of the world ceased.
When Rabban Simeon b. Gamaliel died, the locust came and troubles grew many.[93]
When R. Eleazar b. Azariah died, the wealth of the Sages ceased.
When R. Aqiva died, the glory of the Torah ceased.[94]
When R. Hanina b. Dosa died, men of good deeds ceased.
When R. Yose Qatnuta[95] died, the pious ceased.
And why was he called Qatnuta? Because he was of the small remnants of the pious.
When Rabban Yohanan b. Zakkai died, the luster of wisdom ceased.
When Rabban Gamaliel the Elder died, the glory of the Torah ceased and purity and abstinence died.
When R. Ishmael b. Phiabi died, the luster of the priesthood ceased.
When Rabbi died, humility and the fear of sin ceased.[96]

[89] The text beginning with "When R. Meir died" ending with "remnants of the pious" is an insertion from the Tosefta. In **K** it appears after "When R. Meir died," and in **P** it is added at the bottom of the page (clear indications of a later insertion).
[90] **K, P** add "When R. Aqiva died the preachers ceased." See also the notes below.
[91] In **K** (before emendation) and **P** "the students ceased."   [92] Lit. "goodness."
[93] **K** reads only "locust and troubles came."
[94] Missing in **K** (added in a scribal insertion); **P**: "the preachers ceased."
[95] **K**: "Qatontan"; **P**: "Yose ben Qitunta," Qitunta is thus the name of his father or place.
[96] This is where the tractate originally ended (with the death of Rabbi). The remaining units were not originally part of the Mishnah (appearing in **K** but not **P**).

the last war: Bar Kokhba's revolt against Hadrian, 132–135 CE.

9:15 *Ben Azzai…Ben Zoma*: Neither Ben Azzai nor Ben Zoma were appointed as rabbis.

men of good deeds: Cf. *Sukkah* 5:4. May also mean "workers of miracles." Cf. *Berakhot* 5:5.

R. Yose Qatnuta: The Tosefta here reads "of Qetonith," a place name. See also n. 95.

why was he called Qatnuta? A pun: the root *qaton* means "small."

small remnants: The expression denotes the gradual deterioration of the generation.

R. Ishmael b. Phiabi: Variant "Fabi." He was made high priest in 59 CE.

Rabbi: R. Judah the Patriarch, the redactor of the Mishnah. Several mishnah units were introduced by his disciples, as is obviously the case here.

9:15 cont. *Supplements to Tractate Sotah*

R. Phineas b. Jair says:
When the Temple was destroyed, the fellows and the free men were shamed and covered their head and the men of good deeds became feeble;
and the heavy-handed and the loud-mouthed[97] prevailed,
and there is none that searches and none that seeks, and none that inquires.[98]
On whom can we rely? On our Father in heaven.[99]
R. Eliezer the Great says:
Since the day that the Temple was destroyed,
the Sages[100] began to be like the teachers,
and the teachers like the assistants,
and the assistants like the people of the land;
and the people of the land waxed feeble, and there was none that seeks.
On whom can we rely? On our Father in heaven.[101]

9:15 cont. *Eschatological Appendixes*

With the footsteps of the Messiah insolence shall increase and costs shall soar;[102]
The vine shall yield its fruit but the wine shall be costly;
and the empire shall fall into[103] heresy and no reproof.

[97] Literally "men of tongue," probably an abbreviation of the meaning appearing in **K**: "libelers" or "slanderers."
[98] The last phrase is missing from **K**.   [99] **K** reads: "On what can we rely? On our Father in heaven."
[100] The rest of the sentence is given in Aramaic (which is another indication of its late dating).
[101] **K** reads "On what can we rely? On our Father in heaven."
[102] This sentence is in Aramaic. See above. "Messiah" appears in **K** in Hebrew.
[103] **K**: "shall be heresy."

The tractate originally ended with the death of Rabbi. The remaining units are a collection of teachings (appearing also in **K**, but not in **P**) that are not originally part of the Mishnah.

shamed and covered their head: A sign of mourning. See Jeremiah 14:4.

none that searches and none that seeks: Ezekiel 34:6; *searches*, Heb. *doresh*, may also mean "interpreter or preacher" in rabbinic Hebrew.

R. Eliezer the Great: b. Hyrcanus, usually referred to simply as R. Eliezer.

assistants: Or "beadles." The same word is translated "minister" in 7:7, 8.

With the footsteps of the Messiah: The signs which herald the coming of the Messiah at the eschaton.

the empire: Probably a reference to the Christianization of the empire at the beginning of the fourth century, attesting to the late dating of this unit.

The house of assembly shall be given to fornication.
The Galilee shall be laid waste and Golan shall be made desolate;
And the people of the Galilee[104] shall go about from city to city and not be shown compassion.
The wisdom of the Scribes shall rot and the sin-fearing shall be loathed.
And the truth shall be absent.
Youths shall shame the elders,[105] and the elders shall rise up before children,
for the son treats the father with contempt, the daughter rises up against her mother, the daughter-in-law against her mother-in-law; a man's enemies are the men of his own house.
The face of this generation is like the face of a dog.[106]
The son will not be put to shame by his father[107]
and on whom can we rely? On our Father in heaven.
R. Phineas b. Jair says:
Eagerness leads to cleanliness,
and cleanliness leads to purity,
and purity leads to abstinence,
and abstinence leads to holiness,
and holiness leads to humility,
and humility leads to the fear of sin,
and the fear of sin leads to piety,
and piety leads to the Holy Spirit,
and the Holy Spirit leads to the resurrection of the dead,
and the resurrection of the dead comes through[108] Elijah of blessed memory. Amen.

[104] Others, "frontiers."   [105] K: "The youths shall shame."
[106] K: "A generation whose face resembles a dog."   [107] K lacks this sentence.
[108] K: "brings to." Therefore, Elijah's coming is the last stage.

house of assembly: Lit. "a place of gathering." The reference is not necessarily to the central court (see *Rosh Hashanah* 4:4), for any gathering of the Sages may be called *beit va'ad*; see *Avot* 1:4.

And the truth shall be absent: Cf. Isaiah 59:15 with slight grammatical changes.

for the son treats the father with contempt: Micah 7:6.

Tractate Gittin

David Brodsky

Introduction

Overview

Gittin is the plural form of the word *get* which literally means a "legal document," especially a writ of manumission, and, in its generic form, came to refer particularly to the divorce document, given by the husband to his wife. Thus, tractate *Gittin* focuses primarily on divorce between husband and wife.

Relationship to Scripture

Although the Hebrew Bible clearly permits divorce, Deuteronomy 24:1–4 is the only passage in the Torah that describes the process. It is, therefore, the biblical passage that underlies tractate *Gittin*. Those verses do not prescribe divorce, but assume the practice and discuss the case of remarriage after divorce: a husband may not remarry his ex-wife if she married and divorced another man in the interim.

The rabbis of the mishnaic period read these verses prescriptively rather than merely descriptively. In particular, Deuteronomy 24:1 was now understood to provide the reason, conditions, and structure of divorce: a husband whose wife no longer found favor in his eyes over some matter of unseemliness gives her a writ of divorce. Thus, while the Jews of Elephantine in the fifth century BCE permitted men or women to initiate divorce, the Mishnah required that the *man* must give the divorce to his wife. Much of tractate *Gittin* is an exploration of the implications of reading Deuteronomy 24:1 as requiring that the husband must write his wife the bill of divorce and give it in her hand.

Main Ideas

The Mishnah considers a person's agent to have the same status as the person for most purposes, including the writing and giving of the bill of divorce. Much of the tractate deals with the limits and boundaries of such agency. What if the agent is coming from overseas? How can we be sure that the husband actually authorized the bill of divorce if he is not around to verify it? What if he changes his mind after giving the document to his agent but before the agent has delivered the document to his wife? What if the husband builds a condition into the divorce document or the delivery of the document? What if that condition has the divorce begin retroactively at one point in time upon fulfillment of the condition at some later point in time? What if she marries another man in between those two moments? A second important area of focus is the actual writing and witnessing of the document.

The tractate has an extended excursus in the middle of the tractate regarding laws that were changed for the sake of the public welfare and for the sake of peace, many of them having little if anything to do with divorce.

Structure and Organization of the Tractate

Chapter 1 opens with the requirement that someone bringing a writ of divorce from abroad must be able to attest to the writing and signing of the document, together with a discussion of the borders of the Land of Israel and a comparison of deeds of manumission and divorce documents. The bringing of documents from abroad continues into chapter 2 (2:1–2). That chapter then turns to the physical writing of the document extending to the next chapter (chapter 3). A tradition about whether one can assume that the husband was still alive when the document was delivered leads to two digressions about whether things can legally be presumed to be in existence (3:4, 3:7–8). Most of chapter 4 and chapter 5 are not devoted to divorce at all but to innovations or practices that are done "for the public welfare" (4:2–5:7) or "for the sake of peace" (5:8–9). The ability of husbands and wives to appoint agents to deliver or receive the divorce documents is taken up in chapter 6 and the beginning of chapter 7 (through 7:2). The bulk of chapter 7 is devoted to divorce made conditionally. Chapter 8 begins with a divorce (or other) document that is delivered by throwing or under false pretexts (8:1–3) then turns to the physical or formulary matters (8:4–5, 10). The chapter also includes multiple examples in which a woman finds herself improperly divorced and remarried, with dire consequences (8:5–9). The last chapter returns to the formulary and physical characteristics (including multiple divorces written on a single sheet) (9:1–8). The final passage of the tractate (9:10) turns to Deuteronomy 24:1 and presents an apparently early dispute over the grounds for divorce.

Tractate Gittin

Chapter One

1:1–3 *A Divorce Document That Arrives from Outside the Land of Israel*

1 One who brings a divorce document from overseas must say: "It was written in front of me and signed in front of me."
Rabban Gamaliel says:
Even one who brings it from Reqem or from Heger.
R. Eliezer says:
Even from Kefar Ludim to Lod.

1:1 *One who brings*: A messenger.

divorce document: Heb. *get* can refer generically to a deed or a writ but most commonly, as here, used specifically of the deeds of divorce. Rabbis derived the requirement for such a document from Deuteronomy 24:1.

overseas: Lit. "province of the sea." The Bavli questions whether Babylonia would be included as "overseas" or as part of the Land of Israel for these purposes.

must say…in front of me: The divorce document must have the signature of two witnesses testifying to the authenticity of the document, i.e. that the husband either wrote or commissioned the document to be written and sent to his wife. Since this document is being brought from abroad, the signatures alone cannot confirm its authenticity. Therefore, the messenger must also confirm that he was present for the actual transaction. Alternatively, the issue could be that the majority of Jews outside the Land of Israel do not follow rabbinic rules and therefore cannot be trusted to have done it correctly, without the messenger affirming that fact.

Reqem: Josephus identifies this with Petra. Both the targumic literature and the Peshitta translate the biblical Qadesh as Reqem (e.g. Genesis 20:1).

Heger: Also associated with Petra/Reqem/Qadesh, and found as the targumic translation for Shur in Genesis 20:1.

from Kefar Ludim to Lod: These towns were likely quite near one another. It is possible that Lod/Lydda was considered to be on or near the border, though it is north of the southern border town of Ashkelon (see 1:2 below), west of the eastern border town of Reqem, and south of the northern border town of Akko. This statement might be establishing the boundaries of Judaea as opposed to the boundaries of the Land of Israel as a whole which was the subject of the previous part of this mishnah. Cf. *Ma'aser Sheni* 5:2 which places Lod at the boundary of what is considered a day's journey from Jerusalem.

And the Sages say:
Only one who brings it from overseas or takes it out must say:
"It was written in front of me and signed in front of me."
And one who brings it from region to region abroad must say:
"It was written in front of me and signed in front of me."
Rabban Simeon b. Gamaliel says:
Even from province to province.

2 R. Judah says:
From Reqem to the east, and Reqem is like the east.
From Ashkelon to the south, and Ashkelon is like the south.
From Akko to the north, and Akko is like the north.
R. Meir says:
Akko is like the Land of Israel with respect to divorce documents.

3 One who brings a divorce document within the Land of Israel does not need to say:
"It was written in front of me and signed in front of me."
If there are those who contest it—
let it be upheld on the basis of its signatures.
One who brings a divorce document from overseas, and cannot say:
"It was written in front of me and signed in front of me"—
if it has witnesses on it—
let it be upheld on the basis of its signatures.

or takes it out: Out of the Land of Israel. Alternatively, this can be read as part of the next sentence. On that reading, at issue for the Sages is documents brought from abroad and not merely distance or crossing administrative boundaries.

province to province: Between provinces or subregions within a territory.

1:2 *R. Judah* considers Reqem (1:1) to be the eastern boundary of the Land of Israel. Therefore, one who brings a divorce document from there into the Land of Israel must testify that the document was written and signed in front of him.

Reqem is like the east: Reqem, which is on the border, sits outside the border of the Land of Israel and is itself considered beyond the border.

R. Meir disagrees with R. Judah and regards Akko as lying within the Land of Israel for the purpose of divorce documents. Therefore, a messenger coming from Akko would not have to affirm that the divorce document had been written and signed in front of him.

1:3 *within the Land of Israel...upheld on the basis of its signatures*: If the document is contested, the signatures can be verified, rendering the messenger's oral formula unnecessary.

signatures: Lit. "seals"; alternatively, "signatories."

overseas...upheld on the basis of its signatures: If for some reason the messenger is unable to state that it was written and signed in front of him, yet the signatures can be verified, then the signatures really are enough to establish the legitimacy of the document.

1:4–6 *Comparing Divorce Documents with Writs of Manumission*

4 Divorce documents and writs of manumission are one regarding taking them out [from the Land of Israel] and bringing them in.
And this is one of the ways that divorce documents are equivalent to writs of manumission.

5 Any document that has a Samaritan witness is invalid,
except for divorce documents and writs of manumission.
It once happened that they brought a divorce document
before Rabban Gamaliel in Kefar Othnay,
and its witnesses were Samaritan,
and he deemed it valid.
All documents deriving from gentile offices are valid,
even though their signatures are gentile,
except for divorce documents and writs of manumission.
R. Simeon says:
These too are valid;
they only mentioned this regarding when they were issued by laymen.[1]

6 One who says:
"Give this divorce document to my wife,"
or "This writ of manumission to my slave":
if he wanted to retract either—
he may retract—
the words of R. Meir.
But the Sages say:
Regarding divorce documents,
but not regarding writs of manumission,
because one may benefit a person while not in his presence,
but one may only obligate a person while in his presence.
For, if he wishes not to provide food for his slave, he is permitted to do so,

[1] K, P: "for a layman."

1:4 *writs of manumission*: Lit. "manumissions of slaves."

1:5 *Samaritan*: Heb. *Kuti*. In this period, rabbis assigned Samaritans a status between that of a Jew and a gentile.

issued by laymen: Heb. *hedyot*; see n. 1. According to R. Simeon, the anonymous statement above only excluded divorce documents and writs of manumission that were not issued by governmental offices. Those issued from government offices would be valid.

1:6 *if he wanted to retract*: R. Meir holds that so long as it has not yet reached his wife/slave, he may invalidate it.

benefit: The assumption is that a slave gains through manumission, so manumission is valid *not in his presence*, even before it is delivered. By contrast, a divorcee loses the financial benefits of a wife. For the principle see also *Eruvin* 7:11.

but he is not permitted not to provide food for his wife.
He said to them:
But he disqualifies his slave from *terumah* just as he disqualifies his wife!
They said to him:
Because he is his acquisition.
One who says:
"Give this divorce document to my wife,"
or "This writ of manumission to my slave,"
and he dies—
let them not give it after his death.
"Give a *maneh* to so-and-so,"
and he dies—
let them give it after his death.

Chapter Two

2:1–2 *What Witnesses from Abroad Must Witness and Declare*

2 One who brings a divorce document from overseas and said:
"It was written in front of me, but it was not signed in front of me";
"It was signed in front of me, but it was not written in front of me";
"It was written in its entirety in front of me, and half of it was signed in front of me";
"Half of it was written in front of me, and it was signed in its entirety in front of me"—

---

provide food for his wife: See *Ketubbot* 4:4.

terumah: Slaves owned by priests are considered members of their household and are therefore permitted to eat *terumah* (Leviticus 22:11).

Because he is his acquisition: The slave eats *terumah* merely because he is part of the property of the owner. Were the master to sell his slave to a nonpriest, the slave would lose the right to eat *terumah* even without gaining his freedom. Therefore, the slave is different from the wife who eats *terumah* because of her status as a wife.

"Give this divorce document": The wife does not take possession of the divorce document until she has received it (as above).

"This writ of manumission": In apparent contrast to the statement above that a writ of manumission becomes effective when handed to the agent. Possibly, here the owner prescribed that it should be given to the slave. Alternatively, the author of this rule holds that slaves are not manumitted until after they receive the writ of manumission in their hand.

maneh: One hundred *dinar*. Unlike the divorce document and the writ of manumission, when it comes to money or movable property, the utterance of the dead man is followed.

2:1 *One who brings*: Any of these four cases is *invalid*. According to this opinion, the divorce document is only valid if the messenger says that it was written and signed in its entirety before him.

half of it was signed in front of me: One of the two witnesses signed it in front of me.

it is invalid.
If one says: "It was written in front of me,"
and one says: "It was signed in front of me"—
it is invalid.
If two say: "It was written in front of us,"
and one says: "It was signed in front of me"—
it is invalid.
But R. Judah deems it valid.
If one says: "It was written in front of me,"
and two say: "It was signed in front of us"—
it is valid.

2 If it was written and signed during the day;
at night and signed at night;
at night and signed on [the following] day—
it is valid.
During the day and signed at night—
it is invalid.
R. Simeon deems it valid;
for R. Simeon used to say:
All documents that were written during the day and signed at night are invalid except for divorce documents.

2:3–4 *Writing the Divorce Document*

3 One may write with any material:
with ink, arsenic, red chalk, resin, or copper sulfate,
or with anything that is permanent.[2]

[2] **K**, **P**: "with anything that makes a mark."

If one says…it is invalid: Unless the same agent can attest to the validity of the whole process, the deed is invalid.

If two say…and one says…it is invalid: Again a single agent cannot attest to the writing and delivery. By contrast, R. Judah deems it valid, perhaps treating the two who saw it written as legal witnesses.

If one says…and two say…it is valid: As with R. Judah, above, the rationale is perhaps that the pair who attest to the signing can be treated as witnesses, in this case to the signing of the document. The ruling in this case may be related to the principle of validating the document by its signature or signatories (1:3 and elsewhere).

2:2 The day begins at nightfall and continues until the following sunset. If writing and signing took place on the same legal day, the document is valid. If it was written *during the day and signed at night*, it was not written and signed on the same day and is invalid.

2:3 *copper sulfate*: Used in ink and shoemaker's blacking.

anything that is permanent: **K** and **P** read "with anything that makes a mark," which matches the parallel in *Shabbat* 12:4. The variant potentially affects how long-lasting the writing needs to be. For this context (as opposed to that of *Shabbat*), it would seem that the document must be written in permanent ink so that it cannot be forged or altered later. See also *Megillah* 2:2.

One may not write with liquids, or fruit juice,
or with anything that is impermanent.
One may write on anything:
on the leaf of an olive tree;
on a cow's horn, but he must give her the cow;
on a slave's hand, but he must give her the slave.
R. Yose the Galilean says:
One may not write on anything that is alive or on food.

4 One may not write on anything that is attached to the ground.
If he wrote on that which is attached to the ground, detached it, signed it,
and gave it to her—
it is valid.
R. Judah deems it invalid,
until it is written and signed on detached material.
R. Judah b. Betera says:
One may not write on erased papyrus or on unprepared skin,
because it may be forged;
but the Sages deem them valid.

2:5–7 *Who May Write and Deliver the Divorce Document*

5 All are fit to write the divorce document,
even one who is deaf and mute, one who is legally incompetent, and a minor.
A woman may write her divorce document,
and a man may write his receipt—

One may write on anything: Deuteronomy 24:1 states that the man gives his wife a scroll (*sefer*) of divorce. The question addresses how inclusive or limiting the word "scroll" is.

that is alive: Lit. "that has the breath of life": humans or animals. R. Yose not only disagrees with the anonymous author of our mishnah, but he seems to disagree with 2:4 below, which excludes anything that is still attached to the ground.

2:4 *anything that is attached to the ground*: Live plants still rooted in the ground (cf. 2:3 above).

unprepared skin: According to the Bavli, a hide that has been prepared with salt and flour, but not with gallnut.

because it may be forged: In both cases, the surface of the document was such that it would be possible to erase and rewrite sections of the document without anyone being any the wiser.

the Sages were of the opinion that the witnesses to the giving of the document are the ones that make the divorce document valid (Bavli). Moreover, since divorce documents are fairly standardized, the witnesses would remember the details specific to this divorce well enough that they could testify in the event that the document was changed fraudulently after it was given.

2:5 *All are fit to write*: Presumably, anyone could write the document, since what makes it valid are the witnesses' signatures.

A woman may write…a man may write: The woman to whom the document is to be given may write it; similarly the divorcing husband may write the *receipt* expected from the wife to prevent her claiming her settlement a second time. This is because it is the witnesses' signatures that ensure the validity of the documents.

for the document is only upheld by its signatures.
All are fit to bring the divorce document,
except one who is deaf and mute, one who is legally incompetent, a minor,
a blind person, and a gentile.

6 If a minor received it and became an adult [before delivering it],
a deaf-mute person, and he became legally competent,
a blind person, and he became sighted,
a legally incompetent person, and he became competent,
a gentile, and he became a proselyte—
it is invalid.
But if he was sound, and he became deaf and mute, and then he became sound again,
was sighted, became blind, and was sighted again,
was mentally competent, became legally incompetent, and then competent again—
it is valid.
This is the general rule:
Anyone whose beginning and end was capable of intention[3] is valid.

7 Even those women who are not trusted to say that her husband died,
are trusted to bring her divorce document:
her mother-in-law, her mother-in-law's daughter, her co-wife,
her husband's brother's wife, and her husband's daughter.
What is the difference between a divorce document and death?
That the writing acts as proof.
A woman may bring her own divorce document,
provided that she says: "It was written in front of me and signed in front of me."

[3] Lit. "with/in knowledge."

deaf...gentile: The Mishnah regularly considers such people as having diminished legal status because of their lack of legally binding will (see 2:6, end).

2:6 The end of this mishnah articulates the principle that if the person was legally considered capable of will or intention (*da'at*, lit. "knowledge") at the beginning and end of the act, the document is valid. The first examples address cases where someone of diminished legal capacity receives the commission but completes it with full capacity.

gentile is the only case that ostensibly does not seem to fit the general principle that the issue is one of *intention* (i.e. mental competence). Perhaps, the issue is of knowledge of Jewish law, or of trustworthiness to adhere to the rules of Jewish law. Alternatively, the Mishnah denies any legal personhood to gentiles, so their intention has no legal force.

2:7 *Even those women...her husband's daughter*: Cf. Yevamot 15:4, Sotah 6:2. The testimony of the women listed below was suspect if they reported to a wife that *her husband died*. However, these same women would be trusted to bring the divorce document for the wife.

co-wife, in a case of polygyny; *husband's brother's wife*, potentially a future co-wife through levirate marriage (*yibbum*) to the woman being divorced; *husband's daughter*, from another wife.

writing acts as proof: In the case of a distant death, the witnesses are the only proof the court has to go on. In the case of a divorce, while the document has witnesses, the document itself does still act as evidence for its own existence.

A woman may bring her own divorce document: To/from abroad.

Chapter Three

3:1–2 *Divorce Documents Must Be Written Explicitly for the People Getting Divorced*

3 Any divorce document that was not written for a [specific] woman is invalid. How?
If one was passing through the public square, and he heard the voice of the scribes reading out:
"So-and-so is divorcing so-and-so from such-and-such a place,"
and he says:
"That is my name, and that is my wife's name"—
it is invalid to divorce with it.
Furthermore, if he wrote it to divorce his wife, and he changed his mind,
and someone from his town found him and said to him:
"My name is the same as yours,
and my wife's name is the same as your wife's name"—
it is invalid to divorce with it.
Furthermore, if he had two wives by the same name,
and he wrote it to divorce the elder—
he may not divorce the younger with it.
Furthermore, if he said to the scribe:
"Write it for whichever one I will want to divorce"—
it is invalid to divorce with it.

2 One who writes standardized parts of divorce documents—
must leave space for the man and space for the woman and space for the date;
loan documents—must leave space for the lender, space for the borrower,
space for the money, and space for the date;
sale documents—must leave space for the purchaser, space for the seller,
space for the money, space for the field, and space for the date,
because of the enactment.
R. Judah deems them all invalid.

3:1 *"Write it for whichever"*: The document must be written with the woman for whom the document will be used in mind.

3:2 *standardized parts of divorce documents*: The stock formulae of the divorce document did not need to be written with the specific individuals in mind. Scribes, therefore, would write the standardized parts ahead of time and leave space for the names and dates, much like boiler-plate documents today.

because of the enactment: Heb. *taqanah*: The rulings that allow blank forms that can be personalized are all a rabbinic decree that is for the common good. The Yerushalmi explains that the permission to do so is for the sake of the scribes, so that their lives will not be hijacked by work every time someone needs a document. In light of the motif "for the sake of the public welfare" that dominates *Gittin* 4:2–5:7, one might also translate "for the sake of [the public] welfare."

R. Judah requires the entire document to be written for the individual.

R. Eleazar deems them all valid,
except for divorce documents,
as it is said: *and he shall write for her*—
expressly for her.

3:3–4 *Presumption of Continued Existence*

3 One who was bringing a divorce document and he lost it:
if he found it immediately—
it is valid;
but, if not—
it is invalid.
If he found it in a pouch or in a chest:
if he recognizes it—
it is valid.
One who was bringing a divorce document,
and he left [the husband] when he was old or sick—
he gives it to her under the presumption that he is still alive.
The daughter of an Israelite married to a priest whose husband went overseas
may eat *terumah* under the presumption that he is still alive.
One who sends his purgation offering from overseas—
one may offer it under the presumption that he is still alive.

4 R. Eleazar b. Parta said three things before the Sages
and they upheld his opinion.
(1) Regarding a town that was under siege,
(2) a ship that was floundering at sea,
(3) and [a defendant] on his way to be judged,
they are presumed to be alive.

R. Eleazar permits loans and bills of sale to be written in boilerplate language, but he does not permit this for divorce documents.

and he shall write for her: Deuteronomy 24:1. R. Eleazar takes this to mean that the divorce document be written in its entirety with her in mind.

3:3 *bringing*: From abroad.

immediately: If the agent did not find it right away, we cannot be sure that he did not come across another document written for another couple with the same names.

if he recognizes it: The document; alternatively, this could refer to the pouch or chest.

under the presumption that he is still alive: We presume that the husband is still alive until we have definite evidence to the contrary. The divorce document is still given (making her a divorcee rather than a widow).

terumah: See glossary and above 1:6. Since we assume that the husband is still alive, the wife may still eat *terumah* while he is abroad.

purgation offering: If the person has died, the offering may no longer be given (*Temurah* 4:1).

3:4 *Regarding…presumed to be alive*: In each of these cases, even though there is reason to believe that the people involved may be dead, we still presume them to be alive for all legal purposes.

But, regarding a town that was conquered by siege,
a ship that was lost at sea,
and [a convict] going out to be killed,
they have the stringencies of being alive and dead:
if the daughter of an Israelite was married to a [missing] priest
or the daughter of a priest was married to a [missing] Israelite—
she may not eat *terumah*.

3:5–6   *Transmission and Delivery: Documents from within the Land of Israel and Those from Without*

5 One who was bringing a divorce document within the Land of Israel:
and fell ill—
he may send it by means of another;
but if [the husband] said to him: "Take such-and-such object from her for me"—
in such a case, he does not send it by means of another,
since it is not his wish that his property[4] be in the hands of another.

6 One who was bringing a divorce document from overseas:
and fell ill—
he appoints a court to send it,
and he says before them:
"It was written in front of me and signed in front of me."
The final messenger does not need to say:

[4] Lit. "deposit" or "pledge."

But… terumah: In this second set, however, we can no longer presume that they are still alive. Therefore, for legal purposes, we consider them as both alive or dead, depending on which is legally stricter. Thus, *the daughter of an Israelite* whose priest husband falls into one of these cases may no longer eat *terumah* (since we can no longer be certain that he is alive and that she is part of a priestly household). Generally, *the daughter of a priest married to an Israelite* who was widowed may resume eating *terumah* in her father's household. In this case, however, she may not since her Israelite husband may still be alive, making her part of a non-priestly household for the time being.

3:5 *within the Land of Israel*: This is key to the Mishnah's ruling here (cf. 3:6 and above 1:1). So long as the document comes from within the Land of Israel, the messenger's role is not as crucial, since the court can always go back to the original signatories to the document.

does not send it by means of another: If the messenger was tasked with picking something up from the wife when he gave her the divorce document, then he is no longer free to transfer his responsibility to another, since the husband may not trust the other person to handle the object.

3:6 Cf. 3:5. When the document comes from abroad, the agent plays the crucial role of affirming the validity of the document. Therefore, a court is required to allow a new agent to carry the document the rest of the way. This new messenger is now a messenger of the court that has validated the legitimacy of the document rather than a witness to the writing and signing of the document itself.

appoints a court: This seems to imply that he need not go to an official court. If need be, he can establish a "court" from three people and have the "court" appoint someone else to take the divorce document the rest of the way. For this term, see also 4:2 below.

"It was written in front of me and signed in front of me";
rather, he says: "I am a messenger of the court."

3:7–8   Again: Presumption of Continued Existence

7 One who lends money to a priest, a Levite, or a poor person
in order to separate [the gifts] against it from their share—
he separates for them under the presumption that they are still alive,
and he need not worry that the priest or the Levite has died
or that the poor person became wealthy.
But if they died—
he needs to get permission from the heirs.
If he lent the money through the court—
he does not need to get permission from the heirs.

8 One who sets aside produce in order to separate *terumah* and tithe against it,
or money in order to separate second tithe against it—
he separates it under the presumption that they still exist.
If they became lost—
he must be concerned about the prior twenty-four-hour period—
the words of R. Eleazar b. Shamua;
R. Judah says:
At three periods one should check the wine:
during an east wind following the end of Sukkot,
when the grapevines blossom,
and when the liquid begins to enter the unripe grapes.

3:7 *One who lends…from their share*: The creditor lent money under the agreement that instead of the borrower paying the money back, the lender would treat the *terumah* or tithe that he would otherwise have given the borrower as repayment. In the case of *terumah*, the lender sells it to a different priest (since *terumah* may only be consumed by a priest or a member of a priest's household) and the funds received are taken as repayment. For tithe and poor tithe, to a Levite or poor person respectively (see *Ma'aserot* and *Ma'aser Sheni*, introductions), the lender designates the tithe and then may consume it (since the tithes do not have the same restrictions as *terumah*). The Levite or poor person has effectively used the tithe itself as repayment.

[the gifts]: The *terumah* or the Levitical tithe or the poor tithe.

died…became wealthy: The lender need not worry that the borrower has died in the meantime or, in the poor person's case, that he is no longer poor and therefore no longer qualifies for the tithe.

3:8 *under the presumption that they still exist*: We assume that the money and fruit still exist (and presumably the fruit is not spoiled) unless we have evidence to the contrary.

If they became lost: Once we have evidence of nonexistence, however, we presume that the money or fruit may have been lost or spoiled at any time in the *preceding twenty-four-hour period*. The dedication is invalid if it was made during that period, although we need not extend that concern beyond that period.

At three periods one should check the wine: And only at these three periods. At other periods, one may assume that the wine has not gone bad and that one may set aside *terumah* and tithe for it.

Chapter Four

4:1 *More on the Laws of Agency: Until When May the Husband Nullify the Document?*

4 One who sends a divorce document to his wife,
and he reached the messenger, or he sent a messenger after him,
saying to him: "The divorce document that I gave you is null and void"—
in this case, it is null and void.
If [the husband] reached his wife first, or if he sent a messenger,
saying to her: "The divorce document that I sent you is null and void"—
in this case, it is null and void;
if after the divorce document has reached her hand—
he can no longer nullify it.

4:2–5:7 *Measures Instituted for the Public Welfare*

2 Originally, he could appoint a court in another place and nullify it.
Rabban Gamaliel the Elder instituted that one may not do this,
because of the public welfare.
Originally, he might change his name and her name, the name of his city,
or the name of her city.
Rabban Gamaliel the Elder instituted that one write:
so-and-so and every name that he has, so-and-so and every name that she has,
because of the public welfare.

4:1 So long as the husband or his second messenger reach his first messenger or his wife before she receives the divorce document, they may nullify it. Once she has received the document, he may no longer nullify.

4:2–5:7 A series of traditions organized around the idea that they were instituted for the public welfare. The first two (4:2) deal with deeds of divorce.

4:2 *Originally, he could appoint* lit. "make" *a court*: That is, contrary to 4:1, the old law was that the husband did not have to get word to his wife before she received the document that he was nullifying it. Then, in the late Second Temple period, Rabban Gamaliel the Elder changed the law for the public good, presumably because women were assuming they were divorced when they were not, which could result in unintentional adultery. Cf. chapter 8 below.

he might change…Rabban Gamaliel the Elder instituted: The Talmudim and commentaries understand that people might be known by different designations, and that *change* here means to use different names in different documents. According to the decree, the document should state in writing that it was including *every name* that each party had ever been called. (A formula to this effect was conventional in contemporaneous Greek documents.)

3 A widow may not collect payment from the orphans' inheritance except by swearing an oath.
They refrained from making her swear an oath.
Rabban Gamaliel the Elder[5] instituted that she vow to the orphans
whatever they want and collect her *ketubbah* payment.
The witnesses sign the divorce document,
because of the public welfare.
Hillel instituted the *prozbul*,
because of the public welfare.

4 A slave who was kidnapped and they ransomed him:
if he was ransomed to be a slave—
let him be enslaved,
but if to be a freeman—
then let him not be enslaved.
Rabban Simeon b. Gamaliel says:

[5] K, P: "Rabban Simeon ben Gamaliel."

4:3 *A widow*: A widow who continued to live as part of her husband's household would be maintained from his property. If she wished, she could collect her *ketubbah* payment at any time, though to do so she was to swear an oath that she had not previously collected it (cf. *Ketubbot* 9:8).

They refrained: Courts or heirs were reluctant to make her swear for reasons of piety (to avoid the problem of false oaths).

Gamaliel the Elder: See n. 5. Gamaliel the Elder flourished in the early first century (presumably identical with the Gamaliel referred to in Acts of the Apostles). "Simeon b. Gamaliel," the reading of most manuscripts, refers either to his son or to his great-grandson.

vow: In contrast to an oath (here, to certify that she had not received her *ketubbah* already), a vow (*neder*) is a form of binding self-denial (see *Nedarim* introduction). Here, the widow may prohibit herself from benefiting from some good that the heirs chose, with the vow taking effect if she was lying. With that as surety, she could collect her *ketubbah* payment.

The witnesses: Although it is the act of witnessing the document that makes it valid, nevertheless, the witnesses were required to sign the document for the public good as a permanent record verifying the validity of the document. Another explanation is that really, only the witnesses to the *giving* of the document to the wife are needed, and that the witnesses to the writing of the document and its approval by the husband are only an additional stringency, so that the husband cannot claim later that it was done without his approval.

prozbul: A legal procedure whereby lenders may collect their loans even after the Seventh (Sabbatical) Year had arrived, by assigning the loan to the court (the expression is probably the Greek for "before (or to) the council") before the Seventh Year; see *Shevi'it* 10:1–9. Hillel's institution promotes *the public welfare* since the poor found creditors reluctant to lend given that their loans would be cancelled by the Seventh Year (cf. Deuteronomy 15:9).

4:4 *A slave who was kidnapped*: The anonymous author believes that if he was ransomed to be a free person, then he is free, and his debt to his former master has been broken.

Rabban Simeon b. Gamaliel holds that the kidnapping and subsequent ransoming do not affect the slave's relationship to his master. The kidnapping was a violation of the law, and the subsequent ransom only restored the original order.

Either way he is enslaved.
A slave whose master made him security in a loan to others and then freed him—
strictly by law, the slave does not owe anything,
but because of the public welfare, one forces his master to free him,
and he writes a deed [of indebtedness] for his worth.
Rabban Simeon b. Gamaliel says:
He does not write it; rather, he frees him.

5 One who is half-slave and half-free—
he serves his master one day and himself one day—
the words of the House of Hillel.
The House of Shammai said to them:
You have set matters right for his master,
but you have not set matters right for him.
For him to marry a slave woman is impossible;
because he is already half-free,[6]
[to marry] a free woman is [also] impossible,
because he is already half-slave.[7]
Shall he remain childless?[8]
But was not the world created only for fruition and increase

---

[6] K, P, and others lack this clause. [7] K, P, and others lack this clause.
[8] Heb. "refrain."

A slave whose master made him security and who then *freed* the slave before paying back the loan. On one hand, the slave was already mortgaged as collateral to the lender. On the other hand, he has been freed. In the Bavli, it is the lender who has freed the slave.

does not owe anything: Legally, the slave is free, and does not take on any additional obligation (as in what follows).

one forces his master to free him: The lender must free the slave.

and he writes a deed [of indebtedness] for his worth: The slave must compensate the lender for the loss of his property by taking on an obligation to the lender in the amount of his market value in exchange for that freedom. This serves *the public welfare*, either by discouraging people like his former master from playing such tricks, or, for the sake of the former slave, by keeping the lender from claiming the freed slave as his property.

Rabban Simeon b. Gamaliel disagrees with the previous position. As translated here (following the printed editions and in **K** and **P**), the former slave does not hold any responsibility for the collateral that was lost when he ceased being a slave. However, most commentators, following the Bavli, understand the sentence to read *[The slave] does not write it, rather the one who freed him does*. The original master who freed the slave now is (further) indebted to the lender.

4:5 *half-slave and half-free*: Parallel to *Eduyot* 1:13. If he was co-owned by two masters and one of them set him free.

You have set matters right for his master: His half-slave works for him the amount he is owed.

For him to marry ... is impossible: A slave may not marry a free person.

Shall he remain childless? That is, the issue is beyond just his "right" to marry, but his biblical obligation to marry and reproduce.

as it is said: *He did not create it a waste, but formed it to be inhabited*?
Rather, because of the public welfare,
one compels his master to free him,
and he writes a deed [of indebtedness] for half his worth.
And the House of Hillel reversed themselves,
and taught[9] according to the opinion of the House of Shammai.

6 One who sells his slave to a gentile
or [to someone] outside of the Land of Israel—
he goes free.
One does not ransom captives for more than their value,
because of the public welfare.
One does not help the captives escape,
because of the public welfare.
Rabban Simeon b. Gamaliel says:
Because of the welfare of the captives.
And one does not purchase [Torah] scrolls, phylacteries, or *mezuzot* from gentiles
for more than their worth,
because of the public welfare.

7 One who divorces his wife:
on account of rumored adultery[10]—

[9] **K**: "agreed to."   [10] Lit. "for a bad name."

He did not create: Isaiah 45:18.

one compels his master to free him: A slave who has been freed by one co-owner must be freed by the second. The second owner may be compensated for his loss: the slave writes a note for half of his value, a debt he must pay off to the second owner.

4:6 *One who sells*: It is forbidden to sell one's slave to a gentile or to someone who lives outside of the Land of Israel. If someone violated the law and did so anyway, the slave goes free. The reason may be concern over the treatment of the slave or the slaves' quasi-Jewish status, since they would no longer be able to practice Judaism.

help the captives escape: This might have a deleterious effect on future captives. The kidnappers might be harsher in the future. For example, they might take to chaining their future captives to keep them from escaping.

Rabban Simeon b. Gamaliel appears to be concerned about the other captives who are left behind. The kidnappers could be harsher on those left behind.

scrolls, phylacteries, or mezuzot: On one hand, one should make an effort to purchase them back. On the other hand, there is a concern that the gentiles might come to see this as a lucrative prospect and might become encouraged to hold out for ever-increasing sums of money.

4:7 *rumored adultery*: See n. 10; for the expression "bad name" see Deuteronomy 22:14, where it refers to a husband's claim that the wife was not a virgin.

on account of a vow: The anecdote of R. Yose b. Judah below suggests that it is the husband's vow. However, traditionally, it has been understood as the wife's. The vow prohibited the vow-taker from any benefit from the spouse (*Nedarim* introduction).

may not take her back;
on account of a vow—
he may not take her back.
R. Judah says:
Any vow that was known publicly—
he may not take her back,
but that was not known publicly—
he may take her back.
R. Meir says:
Any vow that requires examination by a sage—
he may not take her back,
but that does not require examination by a sage—
he may take her back.
R. Eleazar says:
They only forbade the one on account of the other.
R. Yose b. Judah said:
It once happened in Sidon that a man said to his wife:
Qonam if I do not divorce you,
and he divorced her,
and the Sages permitted him to take her back,
because of the public welfare.

may not take her back: Divorced couples may remarry so long as the wife has not married another man in the interim (Deuteronomy 24:1–4). Here, if the divorce was on account of a rumor of infidelity or the result of a vow, they may not remarry. According to the view that it is due to the wife's vow, if at some point the husband were to realize that he could have annulled her vow, it would throw the validity of the divorce into question, thus disqualifying her future marriage and offspring. Prohibiting the husband ever remarrying the wife means that he cannot disqualify the divorce.

R. Judah is concerned with how public the situation is. According to the Bavli, R. Judah states that he saw the stringency as a way of discouraging the making of vows.

R. Meir: Not all vows require examination by a sage to nullify them (see e.g. *Nedarim* 8:7). For R. Meir, if the vow was one of these lesser vows, then he may remarry her. For vows that a husband can annul, see *Nedarim* chapter 11.

R. Eleazar prohibits remarriage for both types of vows, and considers that divorce due to a vow that does not need examination cannot be reversed *on account of the other* type of vow. According to the Tosefta, R. Eleazar's ruling is for the public welfare.

R. Yose b. Judah brings a story that contradicts the anonymous first position above. Here, it is the husband, not the wife, who makes the vow, suggesting that the entire preceding discussion be read as regarding his vow rather than hers. The Bavli addresses the apparent contradiction.

Qonam: The beginning of a vow formula. The vow makes the wife off limits to himself if he does not divorce her (see *Nedarim* chapters 1–2).

because of the public welfare: The Tosefta and Talmud understand this to refer to all (or at least a number) of the above rulings.

8 One who divorces his wife because she is sterile—
R. Judah says:
He may not take her back.
But the Sages say:
He may take her back.
If she was married to another and had children by him,
and she demanded her *ketubbah* payment,
R. Judah says:
One says to her:
Your silence was better for you than your speech!

9 One who sells himself and his children to a gentile—
one does not ransom him,
but one does redeem the children after their father has died.
One who sells his field to a gentile,
and an Israelite went and purchased it back from him—
the purchaser brings the firstfruits,
because of the public welfare.

4:8 *sterile woman*: Generally taken to be an adult woman who never presented the secondary female sex characteristics. Since a man is obligated to procreate, he may divorce his wife on the grounds that she is sterile, and he does not have to pay her the *ketubbah* payment (*Ketubbot* 11:6).

R. Judah presumably believes that it is best that the husband remain unmarried to her, since he cannot fulfill his obligation to reproduce with her.

But the Sages: According to the Sages, the wife's status as sterile does not prevent her from remarriage to her ex-husband.

demanded her ketubbah payment, from her first husband on the grounds that she was not infertile (*Ketubbot* 11:6).

Your silence was better for you than your speech: Now that the divorcee is requesting her *ketubbah* payment from the first husband, he can argue that he gave her the divorce under false pretenses, thereby negating the divorce and rendering her current marriage adulterous and her children *mamzerim*.

4:9 *One who sells himself*: The obligation to recover Jewish people sold into slavery to gentiles (cf. 4:6 above) does not extend to a person who sold himself.

after their father has died: Presumably, it is the father's responsibility to free his children from the slavery into which he sold them, but, once he has died, that responsibility passes to the community at large.

the purchaser brings the firstfruits: For firstfruits of produce see Deuteronomy 26:1–11 and *Bikkurim* introduction. Produce grown in the Land of Israel is still subject to firstfruits, even if grown by a gentile. Although the Jewish buyer did not plant the produce, he is required to bring the firstfruits. The *public welfare* or rather "repair of the world," here is a stringency: although one might claim an exemption, it is in fact obligatory. Rashi had a shorter, alternative reading: "One who sells his field to a gentile, purchases and brings the firstfruits."

Chapter Five

5 One makes assessments for damages against the highest grade [of land],
creditors against middle grade,
and a woman's *ketubbah* against the lowest grade.
R. Meir says:
Also, the woman's *ketubbah* is against middle-grade land.

2 One does not collect payment from mortgaged[11] property
when nonmortgaged[12] property is available,
even if it is of the lowest quality.
One collects payment from property belonging to orphans
only from the lowest quality.

3 One does not collect payment from mortgaged property
for the consumption[13] of produce,
or for the improvement of property,
or for the maintenance of a widow or orphaned girls,[14]
because of the public welfare.
And one who finds an object does not take an oath,
because of the public welfare.

4 Orphans who were supported by a householder,
or whose father appointed a guardian for them—

---

[11] Lit. "enslaved."   [12] Lit. "free."   [13] K (see also P): "[the wife who] consumes."
[14] Lit. "of a wife and daughters."

5:1 Different types of claims against real property differ over the grade of land the claimant can claim.

damages…highest grade: See Exodus 22:4; *Bava Qamma* 1:1–2.

5:2 *mortgaged property*: If A owes B, B does not collect from A's property that has been used as collateral for a transaction with C, since that is in effect taking from C, rather than A. Rather, B should collect from A's non-mortgaged property even when it is of inferior quality.

5:3 *consumption of produce*: According to the traditional interpretation, this rule deals with theft and resale of a field before harvest. Produce that the purchaser collected after the sale can be recovered from the thief. However, real property that has been mortgaged may not be forced out of the hands of current owners to compensate an owner for fruit of the field that was consumed.

improvement of property: A buyer of sold stolen property who makes improvements to it can be compensated from the thief's property for the loss of the investment, but only from property that is not mortgaged to another party.

maintenance of a widow and orphaned girls: Widows and their unmarried daughters are to be fed and maintained from the estate of the deceased (*Ketubbot* 4:11–12). If need be, property is to be sold to pay for their maintenance, but if this property has already been sold off, it cannot be seized and sold for their maintenance.

one who finds an object: If a person finds an object and returns it, and the owner claims that not all of it was returned, the finder cannot be compelled to take an oath.

5:4 *supported by a householder*: The expression is rare in rabbinic literature. The meaning, therefore, is not entirely clear, but likely implies that the orphans had attached themselves to a home and to the head of that household for advice and perhaps support.

he is obligated to tithe their produce.
A guardian whom their father appointed takes an oath;
if the court appointed him—
he does not take an oath.
Abba Saul says:
The rule is the opposite.
One who makes impure,
who adulterates *terumah*,
or who offers a libation:
if unintentionally—
he is exempt,
if intentionally—
he is liable.
The priests who intentionally caused a sacrifice in the Temple to become *piggul* are liable.

5 R. Yohanan b. Gudgeda testified:
Regarding one who is deaf and mute whose father married her off:
that she goes out through a divorce document;
and regarding an Israelite girl who is a minor who was married to a priest:

to tithe their produce: Even though it is not his produce, the obligation is still his.

A guardian…takes an oath: When the orphans come of age, the guardian swears in court that he has returned all of their property to them.

the opposite: The court-appointed guardian has to take the oath, not the guardian appointed by their father. Presumably, the anonymous author of the first opinion trusts the court to have appointed an honest person and is more skeptical of the trustworthiness of a friend of the family appointed by the father. Abba Shaul is of the opposite opinion: that the father is more likely to have been invested enough in his children's welfare to appoint someone with their best interests at heart than is the court. Alternatively, they may be concerned that the oath could deter one or the other appointee from accepting the position.

makes food belonging to another *impure*, and thereby causes loss to the owner.

adulterates terumah by mixing it with non-sacral food, causing it all to have the status of *terumah* (*Terumot* 4:7–5:9), leading to loss for the owner. (The Mishnah generally assumes that the market value for *terumah* is less than for non-sacral produce since it is restricted in use and has fewer purchasers.)

offers a libation, making the wine unfit for Jews to consume (*Avodah Zarah* 4:8–5:11). In all of these cases, the person who caused financial loss is liable only when it was done intentionally.

piggul: The term is biblical (Leviticus 7:18). However, according to the Mishnah, *piggul* is caused by incorrect intentions about eating the sacrifice at the moment of offering (*Zevahim* introduction). Priests who held the incorrect intention knowingly are likewise liable for the cost of the sacrifice.

5:5 Parallel to *Eduyot* 7:9. The printed editions in *Eduyot* have "Nekhunya b. Gudgeda."

deaf and mute…divorce document: In general, the marriage of a minor daughter married off by her father can only be severed by divorce. The Mishnah assumes that a deaf woman cannot gain full status as a consenting woman; thus she cannot accept a writ of divorce. R. Yohanan b. Gudgeda reported that she may receive her own divorce document since her informed consent is not technically necessary for divorce (*Yevamot* 14:1–2).

an Israelite girl…eats terumah: Although married as a minor, she is considered fully married and eligible to eat *terumah* if her husband is a priest. Some understand the mishnah as referring to a fatherless girl married off by her brother and her mother, who may refuse the marriage when she turns twelve without need for divorce (*Yevamot* 13:1–7). R. Yohanan b. Gudgeda would then report that even in that case she is still married enough to make her eligible to eat *terumah*.

that she eats *terumah*,
and if she died—
her husband inherits from her;
and regarding a stolen beam that was used for a large building:
that [the owner] receive its value,
because of the enactment of the repenters;[15]
and regarding a stolen purgation offering that was not made known to the public,
that it atones,
because of the benefit of the altar.

6 *Siqariqon* was not applied in Judaea [during the time of] those killed in the war. From the time of those killed in the war onward—
siqariqon is applied.
How?
If he purchased [property]:
from the *siqariqon* and then went and purchased it from the owner—
the transaction is invalid;
from the owner and then went and purchased it from the *siqariqon*—
the transaction is valid.
If he purchased:
from the husband and then went and purchased it from the wife—
the transaction is invalid;

[15] **K, P** lack "because of the ... repenters."

if she died: Similarly, the husband inherits in marriage of a minor girl (as above, a fatherless girl married off by her mother or brothers), on R. Yohanan b. Gudgedah's testimony.

stolen beam: Normally, the law would mandate that the beam itself be returned, but since it has been built into the building, the ruling allows a repentant thief to return the monetary value of the beam instead. This enactment is an attempt not to make *repenting* too onerous.

stolen purgation offering: Normally, such offerings would not atone. In this case, since there was no public knowledge that it was stolen, it does atone. This rule seems to be designed to protect the priests from the sin of eating a stolen sacrifice (since the purgation offering is eaten by the priests). Cf. *Eduyot* 7:9. Protecting the priests from this sin is here considered to be a benefit of the altar which warranted changing the law.

5:6 *Siqariqon*: A reference to property that has been confiscated by the Roman authorities. Cf. *Bikkurim* 1:2 and 2:3.

[during the time of] those killed in the war: Likely referring to the Great Revolt against Rome from 66 to 73 CE. *Siqariqon* may then refer to *sicarii* ("dagger bearers") among the rebel groups attested in the writings of Josephus. In the wake of the war, *siqariqon* was applied, that is, Jews were allowed to purchase confiscated land. The ruling may also be responding to the desire to have land ownership in the Land of Israel return to Jewish hands.

from the siqariqon: If the property is purchased first from the confiscator, who has physical possession of the land, *the transaction is invalid*, perhaps because the original owner may feel that he has no choice but to consent to the sale. If, however, the property was bought *from the* original *owner* first, showing his consent, then the sale is *valid*.

from the husband...from the wife: This same general principle applies to the purchasing of property owned by a wife but held in trust by the husband. If the husband is approached for the sale of the wife's property first, the wife might feel pressured into the sale, thus invalidating it.

from the wife and then went and purchased it from the husband—
the transaction is valid.
This is the original teaching.
The later court ruled:
One who purchases property from the *siqariqon* gives a quarter to the owners.
When?
When they do not have the means to purchase it,
but if they do have the means to purchase it, they come first before anyone else.
Rabbi appointed a court, and they voted
that if it had remained with the *siqariqon* for twelve months,
whoever purchases it first acquires it, but he must give the owners one quarter.

7 One who is deaf and mute signals and is signaled to—
and Ben Betera says:
He jumps and is jumped to—
in the case of movable goods:
Young children:
their purchases are purchases and their sales are sales—
in the case of movable goods.

5:8–9   *Rulings Made for the sake of Peace*

8 And these are the things that they said for the sake of peace:[16]
A priest reads first, and after him a Levite, and after him an Israelite,
for the sake of peace.
One makes the *eruv* in an old home,

[16] Lit. "because of the ways of peace," here and throughout 5:8–9.

---

a quarter: Of the purchase price.

When they do not have the means: If the original owners do not have the financial means to purchase back their confiscated land, others may purchase the land from those who confiscated it and give the original owners a quarter of the price. If the original owners do have the means, then they are given priority over all others, and only if they choose not to repurchase their confiscated land may others purchase it.

Rabbi Judah the Patriarch's court added yet another modification of the rule, which sets a time limit of *twelve months* for the original owner's priority.

5:7   *deaf and mute*: See above, 2:5.

signals and is signaled to: To communicate the sale.

Ben Betera seems to want something more than generic signaling with the hands, though it is not entirely clear how exactly he envisions this *jumping*. Some explain this as indicating with his lips, others as literally jumping.

in the case of movable goods only; real-estate transactions would not be valid.

Young children: Minors who are at least old enough to speak and have some understanding of transactions.

5:8   *reads first* from the Torah in the synagogue.

eruv: A symbolic merging of a shared courtyard into a common property enacted through the deposit of food in one of the houses. See *Eruvin* introduction.

for the sake of peace.
The cistern that is nearest the water channel is filled first,
for the sake of peace.
Traps for deer, fowl, and fish have aspects of robbery about them,
for the sake of peace.
R. Yose says:
It is entirely robbery.
That which a deaf-mute, a legally incompetent person, or a minor find
have aspects of robbery about them,
for the sake of peace.
R. Yose says:
It is entirely robbery.
A poor person who shakes[17] at the top of the olive tree,
that which is below it is stealing,
for the sake of peace.
R. Yose says:
It is entirely robbery.
One does not prevent[18] poor gentiles from collecting the Gleanings, Forgotten Things, and Edge of the Field,
for the sake of peace.

9 A woman may lend her fellow,
who is suspected of transgressing the Seventh Year,
a sifter,
a sieve,

---

[17] Or "knocks." [18] Lit. "strike the hands of."

---

in an old home: In the home in which the people have been living the longest. Alternatively, in the home in which they have already been doing it.

Traps…have aspects of robbery: By rabbinic rules of possession, a trap cannot acquire the trapped animal for the trapper, so if another takes the trapped animal, this is not technically stealing, though it is considered akin to stealing *for the sake of peace*.

R. Yose considers taking from a trap to be outright stealing. Presumably, he considers the trap to have acquired the animal for the trapper.

That which a deaf-mute…robbery: People of diminished legal capacity cannot acquire (or dispose of) an object (cf. above 2:5). It is therefore not theft to take those objects that they found from them. Nevertheless, it is like robbery *for the sake of peace*.

R. Yose considers it to be outright robbery.

shakes at the top of the olive tree: By analogy with the preceding, the poor person is trying to gather what had been left in the field for the poor. While shaking the tree does not acquire the olives for the poor person, for another to take them before he descends the tree would be considered akin to stealing *for the sake of peace*. *R. Yose*, however, considers it outright stealing.

One does not prevent: See Leviticus 19:9 and 23:22, and *Peah* introduction. Permission to collect Gleanings is understood to apply only to Israelites. *For the sake of peace*, however, poor gentiles are also permitted to collect this produce.

5:9 Parallel to *Shevi'it* 5:9.

a hand mill
and an oven,
but she may not check [grain] nor grind with her.
The wife of a Fellow may lend the wife of an *am ha'arets*
a sifter
and a sieve,
and she may check, grind, and sift with her.
However, once she adds water,
she may not touch anything with her,
for one may not aid[19] transgressors.
All these laws were said only for the sake of peace.
One may aid gentiles during the Seventh Year,
but not Israelites.
And one may greet them for the sake of peace.

Chapter Six

6:1–7:2   *Agency and Delivery of Divorce Documents*

6 One who says:
"Receive this divorce document for my wife";

[19] Lit. "strengthen the hands of."

Fellow: Heb. *haver*. A member of the rabbinic group, or a pietist subgroup among rabbis. The reference in the second part of this mishnah to the "wife of a Fellow" clearly refers to a member of this group. This reference to "her fellow" may refer to a member of the pietist group or simply to a fellow woman.

Seventh Year: See introduction to *Shevi'it*. The woman may lend the utensils, but she may not check grain or grind with her suspect fellow sectarian so as not to encourage her sinful behavior (as below). Note: a woman may still lend her suspect fellow sectarian these utensils, even though some of her friend's improperly collected Sabbatical produce will inevitably stick to the utensil and thereby get into the woman's food when the utensil is returned.

am ha'arets: Someone who is not a member of the rabbinic group and who does not follow rabbinic practice, especially agricultural laws like tithes and, as here, certain issues regarding purity. Members of the rabbinic fellowship ought not share certain utensils with them.

once she adds water: This makes the produce susceptible to impurity. The wife of a Fellow may no longer work together with the other woman at this point.

aid: Or "encourage." The preceding prohibition about touching suggests that joint work is intended.

aid gentiles during the Seventh Year: Gentiles are not prohibited from working the Land during the Seventh (Sabbatical) Year. Aiding them is not suborning transgression.

greet them: The Bavli understands this as applying even on their holiday, even though that could be seen as abetting idolatry.

6:1 *One who says: "Receive...he may retract"*: The husband makes this third party his own agent. Until the document reaches his wife, it is still in the domain of the husband who may still nullify it.

or "Take this divorce document to my wife"—
if he wished to retract, he may retract.
A woman who said:
"Receive my divorce document for me"—
if he wished to retract, he may not retract.
Therefore, if the husband said to him:
"I don't want you to receive it for her, rather take it to her and give it to her"—
if he wished to retract, he may retract.
Rabban Simeon b. Gamaliel says:
Even the woman who says:
"Take for me my divorce document"—
if he wished to retract, he may not retract.

2 The woman who said:
"Receive my divorce document for me,"
needs two groups of witnesses:
two who say: "She said it before us";
and two who say: "He received it and tore it before us,"[20]
even if the first and the last group are the same,
or one from the first group and one from the last group and another one joins them.
A betrothed young woman[21]—
she and her father receive her divorce document.
R. Judah said:
Two hands do not take possession as one.
Rather, her father alone receives the divorce document.
And any female who cannot preserve her divorce document cannot get divorced.

[20] K (after correction), P: "*She* received it and tore it before us." [21] Heb. *na'arah*.

he may not retract: Where the agent was contracted by the wife, once the document reaches her agent's hand, it is as if it has reached her, and the husband can no longer nullify it.

"I don't want you to receive it…rather take it": If the husband turns her agent into his own, he may nullify the document up until the point it reaches her hand.

Rabban Simeon b. Gamaliel includes this other formula as a valid way for a woman to make this third party her agent.

6:2 *two groups of witnesses*: One group that testifies that she made the third party her agent, and the other that testifies that he received the divorce document.

and tore it: It is not clear why the agent would tear it up. For the Bavli, this passage derives from a time of persecution when there was a need to hide such practices from the authorities. Alternatively, erroneously or by analogy with other documents, the document was torn as a form of cancellation, showing that the document was delivered. Some commentaries explain the mishnah as talking about a case in which it happened to be torn up.

even if…joins them: As long as each group has two members, it does not matter if there is overlap between the groups.

3 A female minor who said:
"Receive my divorce document for me"—
it is not a divorce document until it reaches her hand.
Therefore, if the husband wished to retract,
he may retract,
because a minor cannot appoint an agent.
But, if her father said to him:
"Go and receive my daughter's divorce document for her"—
if he wanted to retract, he may not retract.
One who says:
"Give this divorce document to my wife in such-and-such place,"
and he gave it to her in another place—
it is invalid.
She is in such-and-such place,
and he gave it to her in another place—
it is valid.
The woman who said:
"Receive my divorce document for me in such-and-such place,"
and he received it in another place—
it is invalid.
R. Eliezer[22] deems it valid.
"Bring me my divorce document from such-and-such place,"
and he brought it from another place—
it is valid.

4 [A woman who says:] "Bring me my divorce document"—
eats *terumah* until the document reaches her hand.

[22] K, P: "[E]leazar."

6:3 *A female minor*: A girl under twelve (see *Niddah* 5:6).

it is not a divorce document: Because *a minor cannot appoint an agent*, the divorce becomes effective only when it comes into her possession.

if her father said: The father is able to create agency, so the document has been received once it enters the messenger's hand. Therefore *he*, i.e. the husband, *may not retract*.

"to my wife in such-and-such place": The directive was to give it in that place. It is therefore seen as a condition placed on the document that must be met.

She is in such-and-such place: This is understood as merely descriptive and not interpreted as a requirement for the giving of the document.

The woman who said: "Receive...": A woman's directive to her agent that he *receive* it in a certain place is prescriptive, while the statement to *bring* it from a certain place is not seen as creating a mandate to receive it for her (see 6:4).

6:4 *"Bring me... eats terumah"*: The passage assumes that the woman is a priest's wife and may eat *terumah* as long as she is married. The instruction *bring me* does not make the messenger her agent to receive the document. Consequently, she remains married, and may *eat terumah until the document* is delivered to her.

"Receive my divorce document for me"—
is forbidden to eat *terumah* immediately.
"Receive my divorce document for me in such-and-such place"—
eats *terumah* until the document reaches that place;
R. Eliezer[23] forbids it immediately.

5 One who says:
"Write a divorce document and give it to my wife";
"Divorce her";
"Write a letter and give it to her"—
in such a case, these should write it and give it.
"Dismiss her";
"Support her";
"Do to her as is lawful";[24]
"Do to her as is fitting"—
he has not said anything.
Originally, they used to say:
One who goes out in [a prisoner's] collar and says:
"Write a divorce document[25] for my wife"—
in this case, they write it and give it.
They subsequently said:
Even one who sets sail or sets out in a caravan.
R. Simeon Shezuri says:
Even one who is deathly ill.

[23] **K**, **P**: "[E]leazar."   [24] Or "as is the customary practice."
[25] **K**, possibly **P** before correction, add "and give it."

"Receive": This instruction does commission the agent to receive the document for her. She is potentially not part of the priest's household from the moment the agent is commissioned.

"Receive…in such-and-such place": See 6:3. Since there is a geographical condition on the receipt of the document, she is still considered part of her husband's household *until the document reaches that place*.

R. Eliezer (or Eleazar) treats her as not part of her husband's household for purposes of eating *terumah* from the moment the agent leaves, since we cannot know precisely when the document has arrived and been received.

6:5 *One who says…give it*: In all three cases, his statement is considered a legal declaration of his intent to divorce his wife and creates agency to write and deliver the document.

"Dismiss her…not said anything": Though these statements could imply his intent to divorce his wife, they are not clear enough to create the agency thereby.

Originally: Parallel to *Tevul Yom* 4:5. According to the printed editions, the statement lacks the critical declaration, "and give" (see n. 25); accordingly, the statement would normally not create valid authorization to deliver the divorce document (see 6:5). The Mishnah is lenient in such cases and rules that the divorce should be granted. Originally this ruling was made only for one *going out in [a prisoner's] collar*, i.e. being taken to prison; it was later altered to include other cases with high likelihood of unconfirmed death. The supposition in all of these is that rather than have her being unable to remarry because his death cannot be verified, the husband wishes her to be divorced at this point. Note, however, the inclusion of "and give" in **K** and **P** (before correction) and see *Tevul Yom* 4:5, where **P** again has "and give it."

6 One who was cast into a pit and said:
"Anyone who hears my[26] voice should write a divorce document for my wife"—
in this case, they should write it and give it.
A healthy person who said:
"Write a divorce document[27] for my wife"—
he wanted to toy with her.[28]
It once happened that a healthy person said:
"Write a divorce document[29] for my wife,"
and he went up to the top of the roof, fell, and died.
Rabban Simeon b. Gamaliel said:
The Sages said:
If he fell of his own accord—
in this case this is a divorce document;
if the wind knocked him down—
it is not a divorce document.

7 One who said to two:
"Give a divorce document to my wife";
or to three:
"Write a divorce document and give it to my wife"—
in this case, they write it and give it.
If he said to three:
"Give a divorce document to my wife"—
in this case, they instruct others and [the latter] write it,
because he made them a court—
the words of R. Meir.
And this is the *halakhah* that Hananiah of Ono brought up[30] out of prison:

[26] Printed edition: "his"; **K, P**: "my." [27] **K** adds "and give it." [28] Lit. "play with her."
[29] **K** adds "and give it." [30] **K, P**, and others: "sent."

6:6 *toy*: Since the husband was threatening divorce to toy with his wife but not actually intending to divorce her, the document is not a valid divorce document. As in 6:5, at issue may be that the husband did not say "and give."

of his own accord: If he jumped, then we conclude he indeed did intend to divorce his wife. Since he knew he was going to die, we presume that his intention was not to toy with her, pretending to grant her divorce while leaving her still bound to him. Rather, we presume that his intent was to leave her a divorcee rather than a widow (perhaps to free her from falling to levirate marriage) and that leaving off the proper end of the formula ("and give it") was unintentional. If he fell by accident, however, then he was like one who was healthy when he made that declaration, and we assume he was likely toying with her.

6:7 *to two: Give*. Even though he only told the two to give the document, and he cannot have intended them to constitute a court (which requires three), R. Meir assumes that he intended the two of them both to *write it and give it*.

"Give a divorce document": But did not say to write it.

to three: "Give": Since three people can constitute a court for matters of divorce, R. Meir assumes that he is designating the three as a court but not asking the three to do the writing themselves.

halakhah: Usually translated "law," but here, as frequently, "tradition."

I have received [the tradition] regarding a person who says to three:
"Give a divorce document to my wife"—
that they may instruct others and [the latter] write it,
because he made them a court.
R. Yose said:
We said to the messenger:
We too have received [a tradition] that even if he said to the high court in Jerusalem:
"Give a divorce document to my wife,"
that they should train, write it, and give it.
If he said to ten:
"Write a divorce document[31] for my wife"—
one writes it and two sign it;
"All of you write it"—
one writes it and all of them sign it;
therefore, if one of them died, then the divorce document is invalid.

Chapter Seven

7 One who was seized with delirium
and said: "Write a divorce document for my wife"—
he has not said anything.
If he said: "Write a divorce document for my wife,"
and he was seized with delirium,
and then he rescinded, saying:

---

[31] K, P: "give a divorce document."

---

brought up out of prison: It is not clear what this refers to. Some traditions have it that this was from R. Aqiva when he was incarcerated. Note, however, the reading "sent" (n. 30).

to the messenger: Hananiah of Ono according to the print edition, or his agent according to that of **K**, **P**, and others.

high court in Jerusalem: On the various courts in Jerusalem, see *Sanhedrin* 11:2.

they should train: Telling them to give it is tantamount to telling them to write it, even if they have to learn how to do so.

If he said to ten: "Write a divorce document": This seems to contradict the previous mishnah (6:6) which had made clear that telling people merely to "write" the document was not enough to warrant giving it. **K** and **P** read "give a divorce document…" in this sentence but then "write a divorce document…" in the following sentence, which would fit better with 6:6. Following the printed edition, the Mishnah may simply be stating that they should write and sign the document, not that it should be given yet.

7:1 *delirium*: Interpreted by Maimonides as a kind of mental distress, and by others, following the Talmud, as caused by demonic possession. Some Greek and Latin medical writers refer to mental distress accompanying illness of the heart or stomach, although the term may refer to physical symptoms as well.

he has not said anything…latter words are not anything: What was said while delirious has no legal import.

"Do not write it"—
his latter words are not anything.
If he became mute,
and they said to him:
"Shall we write a divorce document for your wife?"
and he nodded with his head,
they check three times;
if he indicated no for no and yes for yes—
in this case, they should write it and give it.

2 If they said to him:
"Shall we write a divorce document for your wife?"
And he said to them:
"Write it,"
and they told the scribe and he wrote it
and [told] the witnesses and they signed:
even though they wrote it, signed it, and gave it to him and he went back and gave it to her—
in such a case, the divorce document is invalid until he says to the scribe, "Write it";
and to the witnesses: "Sign it."

7:3–9 *Divorce Documents Given to the Wife Conditionally*

3 "This is your divorce document if I die,"
"This is your divorce document if I die[32] from this illness,"
"This is your divorce document after death"—
he has not said anything.
"From today if I die,"
"From now if I die"—
in these cases, this is a divorce document.
"From today and after death"—

[32] K, P lack "if I die."

---

they check three times: To make sure he is understanding and responding accordingly.

7:2 For the divorce document to be valid, the husband must tell the scribes to write and must also tell the witnesses to sign it.

7:3 *he has not said anything*: In each of these cases, the divorce is invalid since his death would already have broken the marital bond and he did not use language with retroactive effect.

"From today if I die": Such a stipulation does not invalidate it. However, the divorce retroactively takes hold after he dies. Unlike the previous case, this is a way for him to make her a divorcee rather than a widow upon his death (if, for example, she wishes not to fall under the category of levirate marriage).

"From today and after death": This leaves ambiguous when the divorce takes hold, whether from now (in which case it would be valid) or only after death (in which case it would be invalid, since death would break the bond of matrimony first). Therefore, should he die without children, she may not enter into levirate marriage with his brother as would normally be required (lest the divorce was valid), but neither is she free to marry another without first breaking her bond to her brother-in-law through *halitsah* (lest the divorce was invalid). For levirate widowhood see Deuteronomy 25:5–9 and *Yevamot* introduction.

this both is and is not a divorce document:[33]
if he dies, she performs *halitsah* rather than entering into levirate marriage.
"This is your divorce document from today if I die from this illness,"
and he arose, went out into the public square, fell ill, and died—
they assess him:
if he died on account of the first illness, it is a divorce document;
but if not, then it is not a divorce document.

4 She may not be alone with him except in front of witnesses—
even a male slave, even a female slave—
except for her own female slave,
because with her own female slave she feels no shame.
What is her status[34] during these days?
R. Judah says:
Like a married woman for all purposes.
R. Yose says:
Divorced and not divorced.

5 "This is your divorce document on the condition that you give me two hundred *dinar*":
in this case, she is divorced and she must give it.
"On the condition that you give it to me from now until thirty days":
if she gave it to him within the thirty days—
she is divorced,
and if not—
she is not divorced.
Rabban Simeon b. Gamaliel said:
It once happened in Sidon regarding a man who said to his wife,

[33] K, P, and others: "this is not a divorce document."   [34] Lit. "what is she."

7:4 *She may not be alone with him*: Apparently, this refers back to the case of divorce "from today if I die" in 7:3. Having already been divorced conditionally, she may not be alone with him in a room behind closed doors, since a divorcee may not be alone with her ex-husband.

witnesses: That is, two people who could verify that they did not have sex.

even a male slave, even a female slave: Although ineligible as witnesses in court, the presence of slaves was a sufficient deterrent against illicit sex.

feels no shame: Lit. "her heart is crude" when it comes to *her own female slave*. Consequently, her slave cannot serve as witness.

during these days: After the statement that she is divorced "from today/now if I die" until he dies.

7:5 *On the condition that*: Conditions may be placed on divorces just as they can on other documents and transactions. If they are met, then the document is valid.

"two hundred dinar": That is the amount of the standard *ketubbah* payment. The Mishnah is allowing the husband to avoid his financial obligation in this way.

"from now until thirty days". A thirty-day time limit for the wife to meet the condition.

It once happened…give him its value: Even though the condition could not be met, the Sages allowed her to pay the value of the cloak.

"This is your divorce document on the condition that you give me my cloak,"
and his cloak was lost,
and the Sages said:
Let her give him its value.

6 "This is your divorce document on the condition that you take care of Father";
"On the condition that you nurse my son"—
How long should she nurse him?
Two years.
R. Judah says:
Eighteen months.
If the son died, or if the father died—
it is a divorce document.
"This is your divorce document on the condition that you take care of Father for two years";
"On the condition that you nurse my son for two years"—
if the son died, or if the father died,[35]
or if the father said: "I do not want you to take care of me,"
even not out of annoyance—
it is not a divorce document.
Rabban Simeon b. Gamaliel says:
In such circumstances it is[36] a divorce document.
Rabban Simeon b. Gamaliel said a general rule:
Any hindrance that does not derive from her,
in such a case, it is a divorce document.

[35] K, P lack "or if the father died." [36] Lit. "such as this is."

7:6 *"take care of"*: Lit. "serve," "attend to." In context of the condition to nurse his child, this likely refers to her taking care of his elderly father, though this need not be the case.

How long should she nurse him? The condition must be met. Now the question is: what is the standard period of nursing a child that would fulfill the condition, assuming the child is alive throughout the period?

If the son or the father died—it is a divorce document: She fulfilled the condition of nursing his child or taking care of his father while he was alive, which is the intent of the condition. Unlike the immediate sequel, here the condition did not specify a particular period of service.

"for two years"… "it is not a divorce document": Since the condition stipulated two years, if the son or father died, or even if the father dismissed her, before the two years were completed, the document would not be valid. K and P lack the words "or if the father died," although from context it would seem that they cannot be differing on the ruling. The clause may have dropped out through repetition.

even not out of annoyance: Since the condition was not met, even through no fault of her own, the document would not be valid.

Rabban Simeon b. Gamaliel considers the divorce document to be valid in all of these cases so long as the woman was not the one hindering fulfillment of the condition.

7 "This is your divorce document if I do not come between now and thirty days,"
and he was going from Judaea to the Galilee, reached Antipatris and returned—
his condition is nullified.
"This is your divorce document if I do not come between now and thirty days,"
and he was going from the Galilee to Judaea, reached Kefar Othnai and returned—
his condition is nullified.
"This is your divorce document if I do not come between now and thirty days,"
and he was going overseas, reached Akko and returned—
his condition is nullified.
"This is your divorce document so long as I am away from your presence[37] thirty days,"
and he went and came, went and came,
so long as he was not alone with her, it is a divorce document.

8 "This is your divorce document if I do not come between now and twelve months,"
and he died within the twelve months—
it is not a divorce document.
"This is your divorce document from now if I do not come between now and twelve months,"
and he died within the twelve months—
it is a divorce document.

9 "If I do not come between now and twelve months,
write and give a divorce document to my wife":
if they wrote the divorce document within twelve months
and gave it after[38] twelve months—

[37] Lit. "pass from opposite your face."   [38] K, P: "within."

7:7 The point of all of these cases is that once the husband puts a condition on the divorce, it is valid only if the condition is met.

Judaea to the Galilee: The condition appears to require both that the husband return within thirty days and also to get to his intended destination. Since he only reached *Antipatris*, he never arrived in the Galilee and failed to fulfill the second part of the condition. The anonymous author would seem to be using this mishnah in part to delineate the borders of Judaea and the Galilee.

Kefar Othnai: Similarly, if he was traveling from the Galilee to Judaea, he would not be deemed to have entered Judaea and would not have fulfilled the condition.

Akko: Cf. above, 1:1.

"so long as I am away from your presence": i.e. I am out of your sight.

he went and came...not alone with her: The Mishnah appears to be narrowing the definition of *your presence* by limiting it to intimate and potentially sexual contact. As in the previous cases, the Mishnah is trying to find the minimum requirement to be considered to have fulfilled his obligation. As long as that is met, the document is valid.

7:8 *"from now"*: This is the only difference between the two statements. In the former case, the divorce would take effect after the twelve months, but he had already died by then, preempting the divorce (see 7:3). In the second case, the divorce takes effect *from now*, so is not preempted by his death.

7:9 *"If I do not come...write and give"*: The stipulation was that nothing should be done until after twelve months, but the agents wrote (**K** and **P**: "and gave") the document within that time.

it is not a divorce document.
"Write and give a divorce document to my wife
if I do not come between now and twelve months":
if they wrote it within twelve months and gave it after twelve months—
it is not a divorce document.
R. Yose says:
Such as this is a divorce document.
If they wrote it after twelve months and gave it after twelve months
and he died—
if the divorce document preceded his death,
then it is a divorce document;
but if his death preceded the divorce document,
it is not a divorce document.
And if it is not known,
this is the case about which[39] they said: she is divorced and not divorced.

Chapter Eight

8:1–3 *The Giving of the Divorce Document*

8 One who throws a divorce document at his wife,
and she is within her house or within her courtyard—
she is divorced.
If he threw it at her within his house or within his courtyard,
even if it[40] is with her in bed—
she is not divorced.
Into her bosom or into her basket—
she is divorced.

[39] Lit. "this is what."   [40] Or "he."

"Write and give"… "if I do not come": The instructions preceded the condition. According to the Bavli, it is this ordering that distinguishes it from the preceding. Alternatively (and noting the reading of the manuscripts in the preceding) in this case, the important distinction is that delivery took place after twelve months although they wrote it earlier. From the end of the mishnah it appears that the anonymous position again holds nothing should be done until after twelve months. *R. Yose* deems the divorce valid at least in this second case.

wrote it after…gave it after: In this scenario, the agents complied with the condition, and the validity of the divorce now depends on whether the divorce or death preceded. If it is uncertain which took place first, then she is *divorced and not divorced*; cf. 7:4.

8:1 *within her house*: Although the document does not reach her person, her property acquires it for her.

within his house: Since the house, courtyard, and bed are his property, she fails to take possession of the document until it reaches her person.

Into her bosom: If it reached her person or her property, then she does acquire the document, even if she is within his property.

2 If he said to her: "Take in this loan document,"
or if she found it behind him, read it, and, behold, it is her divorce document—
it is not a divorce document until he says to her: "This is your divorce document."
If he put it in her hand while she was sleeping; she awoke, read it,
and, behold, it is her divorce document—
it is not a divorce document until he says to her: "This is your divorce document."
If she was standing in the public domain and he threw it at her:
if it is nearer to her—
she is divorced;
if it is nearer to him—
she is not divorced.
if it is halfway—
she is divorced and not divorced.
3 And so regarding the matter of betrothals,
and so regarding the matter of debt:
The creditor[41] said to him: "Throw me my debt,"
and he threw it to him,
if it is nearer to the lender—
the borrower is no longer liable;
if it is nearer to the borrower—
the borrower is liable;
if it is halfway—
they both split it.
She was standing on the top of the roof,
and he threw it to her:
once it reached the airspace of the roof—
she is divorced.
If he was above and she below,

[41] K, P: "He."

8:2 *"loan document"*: The husband must call it a divorce document and say that it is hers.

If he put it in her hand: It is not sufficient that it reached her hand (in this case, while she was unconscious and he had yet to declare it to be her divorce document).

public domain: Unlike the private domain, which acquires on behalf of its owner, the public domain has no owner and therefore does not acquire for anyone except the person who is near the tossed object.

8:3 *betrothals…debt*: The above rule about throwing applies also to these two cases.

"my debt": The money owed.

nearer: Should something happen to the money subsequently, proximity to the parties determines whether the debt has been paid. If *halfway* between them, they share the loss.

on top of the roof: Apparently, it is her roof, which can acquire for her.

he was above: The roof is his and the courtyard hers. Once the document enters her domain she has acquired it. Even if the document becomes irreparably damaged, the divorce has taken place.

and he threw it,
once it left the domain of the roof,
if it became erased or burned—
she is divorced.

8:4–5 *How the Document Must be Written*

4 The House of Shammai say:
A man releases his wife through an old divorce document;
but the House of Hillel prohibit.
And what is an old divorce document?
Any [divorce document] after the writing of which he was alone with her.
5 If he dated[42] it according to an improper kingdom,
according to the kingdom of Media,
according to the kingdom of Greece,
to the building of the Temple,
to the destruction of the Temple;
if he was in the East and he wrote: "In the West";
if he was in the West and he wrote: "In the East"—
she must go out from this one and that one,
and she requires a divorce from this one and from that one;
and she has no *ketubbah* payment,
and no product,[43]
and no maintenance,
and no clothing,
neither from this one, nor from that one.

[42] Lit. "wrote."   [43] Lit. "fruit."

8:4 *after he wrote it for her*, but before giving it to her. The House of Hillel seem to be concerned that the husband may have had intercourse with the wife in the interim.

8:5 *according to an improper kingdom*: That is, the incorrect regime. The date on the divorce document was crucial for establishing when the divorce took place (and, thereby, the legitimacy of subsequent marriages). The date must to according to the official and locally regnant regime.

kingdom of Greece: Presumably the Seleucid Empire, which was conquered by the Romans in 64 BCE. Dating by the Seleucid era (from 312 BCE) remained widespread in the Near East long after.

she must go out: She must get divorced. The Mishnah assumes that she remarried on the basis of one of the improperly executed divorce documents. See *Yevamot* 10:1. She married her second husband while she was still married to her first. She can be married to neither; must receive a divorce from each; has none of the financial rights of a wife such as the *product* of her property held in trust by the husband or *maintenance* to which wives are entitled.

mamzer: The unmarriageable offspring of a severely prohibited union (as here; the mother bore offspring from husband number two while still married to husband number one).

neither this one nor that one: Likewise, the men have none of the rights or ritual or financial responsibilities of husbands.

If she took anything from this one and from that one—
she must return it.
And the offspring is a *mamzer* both from this one and from that one.
And neither this one nor that one may contract impurity for her;
and neither this one nor that one has the right to what she finds,
or to the labor of her hands,
or to annul her vows.
If she was a daughter of Israel, she becomes disqualified from the priesthood;
and if a daughter of a Levite, from tithes;
and if a daughter of a priest, from *terumah*.
And neither the heirs of this one nor the heirs of that one inherit her *ketubbah* payment.
And if they died,
this one's brother and that one's brother perform *halitsah* for her but not levirate marriage.
If his name or her name changed, the name of his city or the name of her city, she separates from each of them, and all of the above policies apply.

8:6–9 *Digression: Second Marriages Undone by Incompletely Severed First Marriages*

6 All of the forbidden sexual relations about which they said that their co-wives are permitted,
if those co-wives went and married,
and were found to be sterile—

contracts impurity: If he is a priest, he may not become impure to bury and mourn for her, as he would were she still his wife (see Leviticus 21:1–4).

what she finds... labor of her hands... to annul her vows: As he would were they married. *Ketubbot* 4:4.

annul her vows: As a husband would; see *Nedarim* chapter 10.

disqualified: As a divorcee she cannot marry a priest. See Leviticus 21:7 and *Yevamot* 2:4 and 6:2. But since she is married, she is not treated as the *daughter of a Levite* or the *daughter of a priest*.

heirs: Under the terms of the marriage contract, the wife's sons inherit her *ketubbah*, but not in this case.

halitsah: Since she is questionably married and questionably divorced, levirate marriage is not performed, but rather the *halitsah* ritual.

8:6 *forbidden sexual relations*: See *Yevamot* 1:1. Envisioned here is a case where a man has married a relation prohibited to his brother, like the mother-in-law of that brother, and died childless. Since the levirate widow is prohibited to the brother she along with all of her co-wives would be exempt from levirate marriage or *halitsah*. See *Yevamot* 1:1.

married other men after their husband died without levirate marriage or *halitsah* being performed on the grounds that it was not needed.

sterile: See above, 4:8. Here, the prohibited relation who exempted the others was found to be sterile, and her marriage to the deceased brother is now invalidated, so she no longer exempts the co-wives. The co-wives are now in the same situation as the cases described in 8:5.

she herself must separate from this one and this one,
and all of these practices[44] apply to her.

7 One who takes in his levirate widow,
and her co-wife went and married another,
and then the former[45] turned out to be sterile,
she must separate from this one and this one,
and all of these practices apply to her.

8 If a scribe wrote a divorce document for a man and a receipt for the woman,[46]
and he erred and gave the divorce document to the woman and the receipt to the man,
and they then gave them to one another,
and after a time, the divorce document was found to be in the possession of the man
and the receipt in the possession of the woman—
she must separate from both of them,
and all of these practices apply to her.
R. Eliezer[47] says:
If immediately—it is not a divorce document;
if after a time—it is a divorce document:
it is not within the first one's power to destroy the right of the second.
If he wrote to divorce his wife and then changed his mind—
the House of Shammai say:
It has disqualified her from the priesthood.
But the House of Hillel say:
Even if he gave it to her conditionally and the condition was not fulfilled—
it has not disqualified her from the priesthood.

[44] Here and below, lit. "ways." [45] Heb. "that one." [46] K, P lack "a divorce...woman."
[47] K, P: "Eleazar."

8:7 *One who takes in his levirate widow*, exempting her co-wives from levirate marriage, and permitting them thereby to remarry as they choose (see *Yevamot* 4:11).

sterile: The levirate widow was found to be sterile. The levirate marriage is annulled. The former co-wife is now obligated either to marry a levir or to or perform *halitsah*.

she must separate from this one and this one: The former co-wife entered a new marriage before her prior marriage was properly terminated, *and all of* the above *practices apply to her* (see 8:5).

8:8 The opening situation is one where it turns out after the fact that a woman was never properly divorced because the scribe gave the parties the wrong documents to give to one another.

all of these practices apply: The strictures of 8:5 above.

it is not within the first one's power: The first husband does not have carte blanche power to trample on the rights of his ex-wife and her new husband. The divorce document was already given and no one came forward with any irregularity; we do not upset the second marriage on this basis. In fact, we may suspect that the first husband is attempting to undo or invalidate what was already done.

disqualified her from the priesthood: For the House of Shammai, the act of writing the divorce document is enough to give her the status of divorcee, at least for purposes of marrying into the priesthood. For the House of Hillel, even an otherwise valid divorce document, if it was given on a condition that was not fulfilled, she is not disqualified.

9 One who divorces his wife
and she spends the night with him at an inn—
the House of Shammai say:
She does not need a second divorce document from him.
But the House of Hillel say:
She does need a second divorce document from him.
When?
When she was divorced from marriage.
But they acknowledge that when she was divorced from betrothal—
she does not need a second divorce document from him,
since in connection with her he does feel shame.
If he took her in on the basis of a bald divorce document,
she must separate from this one and this one—
and all of these practices apply to her.

10 Anyone can complete a bald document.
The words of Ben Nanas.
R. Aqiva says:
Only relatives who are fit to testify elsewhere can complete it.
And what is a bald document? Any document that has more knots than witnesses.

Chapter Nine

9:1–3 *The Essence of the Divorce Document*

9 One who divorces his wife and says to her:
"You are permitted to everyone except for so-and-so"—

8:9 *from marriage*: The fully consummated marriage; distinguished from *betrothal*, an inchoate marriage that requires divorce to sever it.

he does feel shame: The inverse of the expression in 7:4. The House of Hillel do not trust that a fully married couple won't fall back into their prior sexual ways with one another if left to sleep together in the same room.

a bald divorce document: A bound divorce document that lacks enough signatures on the outside attesting to its contents. See 8:10 below; *Bava Batra* 10:1–2.

these practices: Those of 8:5 above. She is questionably married to both her first and second husbands.

8:10 *Anyone can complete a bald document*: Anyone was permitted to add to the signatures on the outer folds to complete the document, even if they would normally be disqualified by virtue of their relationship to the parties involved.

relatives who are fit: Only people who are otherwise qualified to testify, but are disqualified to testify in this case because of their relationship.

more knots than witnesses: According to the traditional interpretation, the document was folded and sewn, folded and sewn, as many times as desired. At least one witness had to sign on the outside of each fold.

R. Eliezer permits,
but the Sages forbid it.
What shall he do?
Let him take it from her and give it back to her and say to her:
"You are permitted to everyone."
But if he wrote it within it—
even though he went back and erased it,
it is invalid.

2 "You are permitted to everyone except to my father,"
or "To your father";
"To my brother";
or "To your brother";
"To a slave";
or "To a gentile";
or to anyone with whom betrothal is impossible[48]—
it is valid.
You are permitted to everyone except a widow to a high priest;
A divorcee or a woman who had performed *halitsah* to a regular priest;
A female *mamzer* or *natin* to an Israelite;
The daughter of an Israelite to a *mamzer* or a *natin*;
or to anyone with whom betrothal is possible,
although through transgression—
it is invalid.

3 The essence of the divorce document is:
You are hereby permitted to everyone.
R. Judah says:

---

[48] Lit. "anyone upon whom she does not have valid betrothal."

9:1 *the Sages forbid*, since the husband has not completely relinquished his exclusive rights to his wife's sexuality.

What shall he do? The husband has made this disqualifying statement orally. Repeating the act of giving without the invalidating statement corrects for the previous mistake.

But if he wrote it: If he wrote the above in the document, a new document needs to be written and given.

9:2 *anyone with whom betrothal is impossible*: In all of the above cases, not only did the rabbis forbid such marriages, but they held that if these people performed inchoate marriage (*qiddushin*, "betrothal"), it would not take hold. See *Qiddushin* 3:12.

a widow to a high priest…: See *Yevamot* 2:4; 6:2. These are all cases of prohibited marriages for which a *betrothal is possible*: if performed, the inchoate marriage is binding. For *halitsah*, *mamzer*, and *natin*, see glossary.

9:3 *The essence*: Lit. "body"; perhaps "the operative clause." The essential part of the divorce document is the statement in which the husband completely frees his wife to remarry whomever she wishes.

R. Judah quotes the operative wording of the divorce document in Aramaic.

And this shall be to you from me a scroll of divorce
and a letter of separation
and a document of dismissal
to go and to be married to any man you wish.[49]
The essence of a writ of manumission is:
You are hereby free. You are hereby your own.[50]

9:4–8 Additional Formal Characteristics of the Divorce Document

4 Three divorce documents are invalid, but if she remarries the offspring is legitimate:
(1) he wrote it in his own hand, but there are no witnesses on it;
(2) it has witnesses on it, but it does not have a date;
(3) it has a date on it, but it only has one witness—
These three divorce documents are invalid, but if she remarries the offspring is legitimate.
R. Eleazar[51] says:
Even though it has no witnesses on it, but he gave it to her before witnesses—
it is valid,
and she may collect from mortgaged property,
because the witnesses only sign the divorce document because of the public welfare.

5 Two men sent two identical divorce documents and they became mixed together—
he gives both to this one and both to the other one.
Therefore, if one of them was lost, the second one is invalid.
Five men wrote jointly in the divorce document:
so-and-so is divorcing so-and-so, and so-and-so [is divorcing] so-and-so,

---

[49] This clause is in Aramaic.   [50] The "you" is feminine.
[51] K: "Eliezer," P: "Eleazar." Modern print editions differ as well.

---

manumission: Note the close connection between divorce and manumission in rabbinic law.

9:4 *legitimate*: Eligible to marry other Jews, as opposed to a *mamzer*. The documents in question are defective in some way, but do not disqualify the offspring of subsequent sexual unions.

R. Eleazar considers a divorce document without witnesses valid if performed before witnesses.

mortgaged property: Above, 5:2 and *Ketubbot* 9:8; 12:2. The divorce is fully valid.

public welfare: Above in 4:2–5:7.

9:5 *identical*: The names of both husbands and wives are the same.

mixed together: And the messenger no longer remembered which one was which.

he gives both: As long as both documents are given to both women, each will assuredly have received her own document.

if one of them was lost: We would be unable to know which woman was intended in the remaining document, so neither can be used.

Five men wrote jointly: The five sets of names may be integrated into one divorce document with the witnesses below testifying to all five divorces. For the divorce to take effect, it must be given to each.

and the witnesses are at the bottom—
they are all valid,
and let it be given to each woman.
If they had written the standard form for each of them,
and the witnesses are at the bottom—
the one with which the witnesses are read is valid.

6 Two divorce documents that were written side by side,
and two Hebrew witnesses run from under this one to under the other one,
and two Greek witnesses run from under this one to under the other one—
the one with which the first witnesses are read is valid.
If one witness is Hebrew and one witness is Greek,
one witness is Hebrew and one witness is Greek,
running from under this one to under the other one—
they are both invalid.

7 If he left over a small part of the divorce document and wrote it on a second sheet,
and the witnesses are at the bottom—
it is valid.
If the witnesses signed at the top of the sheet,
on the side,
or on the back in the case of a simple document—
it is invalid.
If he brought the start of this one next to the start of that one,
and the witnesses were in the middle—
they are both invalid.
The end of this one next to the end of that one,

the standard form for each: If the body (*tofes*, from Greek *typos*) of the document was repeated five times there are technically five documents with only one set of signatures. Consequently, *the witnesses* who *signed at the bottom* would attest only to the last, and only that one is *valid*.

9:6 *Hebrew…Greek witnesses*: Their signatures are in Hebrew, running from right to left, or Greek, running from left to right.

with which the first witnesses are read: If the first witnesses signed in Hebrew, the document on the right would be valid since this is the document read *with the first witnesses*; and the reverse for the Greek signatures and the document on the left.

they are both invalid: The witnesses are staggered with the witness to the other document interpolated in between, so neither document has two witnesses together.

9:7 *If he left over*: Even though the document did not all fit onto a single sheet of parchment, it is valid so long as the witnesses' signatures come at the end.

at the bottom: The witnesses need to sign at the end of the document. This requirement guarantees that nothing was added to the document after the witnesses signed. For *simple document*, see *Bava Batra* 10:1.

the start…next to the start: Two documents were started at the middle of the page with each of the texts extending toward the opposite margins. Having the witnesses sign in the middle would not result in a valid document since they would not appear at the end of either.

The end…next to the end: (Lacking in **K** and **P**; see n. 52.) The ends of the documents meet in the middle, with the witnesses at the end of both. Only the document with signatures facing the same direction as the writing would be valid while the other one would not.

and the witnesses were in the middle—
the one with which the witnesses are read is valid.⁵²
The start of this one next to the end of that one,
and the witnesses were in the middle⁵³—
the one with which the witnesses are read at the end of it is valid.

8 If a divorce document was written
in Hebrew and its witnesses in Greek;
in Greek and its witnesses in Hebrew;
one witness is Hebrew and one is Greek;
he wrote: "Scribe and witness"—
it is valid.
"So-and-so, witness"—
it is valid;
"Son of so-and-so, witness"—
it is valid;
"So-and-so the son of so-and-so," but did not write: "Witness"—
it is valid.
And thus the pure⁵⁴ of mind who were in Jerusalem used to do.
He wrote [only] his byname and her byname—
it is valid.⁵⁵
A coerced divorce document ordered by Israelites⁵⁶—
is valid,
and by gentiles—
is invalid.
And if by gentiles:⁵⁷ they press him and say to him:
Do that which the Israelites say to you—
and it is valid.

⁵² K, P lack "The end...valid." ⁵³ K, P: "below them." ⁵⁴ K, P: "expert" (*beqi'e*).
⁵⁵ In K and P this case precedes "and thus...to do." ⁵⁶ Lit: "in/with/by Israel."
⁵⁷ K (as corrected), P: "And [if] the gentiles..."

The start...next to the end: They were written facing the same direction, one following the other. The witnesses are written *between* the two texts, so the first one is *the one with which the witnesses are read*. The reading of K and P is that the witnesses are below both documents, so the second document is the valid one.

9:8 *written in Hebrew...witnesses in Greek*: Unlike 9:6, there is only one document on the page and no way to confuse to which document the witnesses belong.

"Scribe and witness": At the end of the document, the scribe wrote that he was both the scribe and one of the witnesses. Alternatively: "the scribe wrote [i.e. signed] and a witness [also signed]."

pure of mind: See n. 54. The graphic difference is very slight; in context the reading of K and P seems preferable. Note also that in K and P this comment follows the statement about bynames.

byname: If they used common or nicknames only, the document is still valid.

coerced: While the divorce document must be issued by the husband of his own free will, an Israelite court is authorized to pressure him to give it.

if by gentiles: See n. 57. If a non-Jewish court told the husband to do as the Jewish court had ruled, it would be valid.

9:9 *A Rumored Betrothal and a Rumored Divorce*

9 If her name went out in the town as betrothed—
she is betrothed;
as divorced—she is divorced;
provided that there is no cause for doubt.
What is a cause for doubt?
If so-and-so divorced his wife conditionally,
or if he threw her betrothal at her,
and it was unclear if it was closer to her or to him,
this would be a cause for doubt.

9:10 *Grounds for Divorce*

10 The House of Shammai say:
A man may not divorce his wife unless he finds a matter of unseemliness[58] in her,
as it says: *Because he found in her an unseemly matter.*
But the House of Hillel say:
Even if she ruined his dinner,
as it says: *Because he found in her an unseemly matter.*
R. Aqiva says:
Even if he found another more beautiful than she,
as it says: *And it shall be if she shall not find favor in his eyes.*

[58] Heb. *devar ervah*; **K** (margin): *ervat davar* (the scriptural expression); **P**: *ervah* (without *davar*).

9:9 The Mishnah allows general knowledge about someone's marital status to count as true unless there is reasonable evidence to assume that it is a false rumor.

9:10 *matter of unseemliness*: Echoing the biblical verse that follows (see n. 58).

Because he found in her: Deuteronomy 24:1, the biblical verse that serves as the source of the rules for divorce. The Shammaites read the verse as requiring sexual transgression as a precondition for divorce. Cf. Jesus in Matthew 5:31–32 and Luke 16:18.

House of Hillel take Deuteronomy 24:1 to refer to any "unseemly matter," even ruining his dinner.

R. Aqiva derives from the first part of the verse that all that is necessary for there to be grounds for divorce is for her to fall out of favor with him.

And it shall be: Deuteronomy 24:1.

Tractate Qiddushin

Gail Labovitz

Introduction

Overview

Qiddushin, seemingly from *qaddesh*, "sanctify," is a rabbinic neologism for a binding legal tie between the partners, a state of inchoate marriage during which all laws of adultery are in force, and a formal divorce is needed for the bond to be severed. While this legal institution also exists in biblical law, there it is referred to by the term *aras*. Moreover, though biblical law notes the existence of such a category and mentions some of its legal ramifications (see e.g. Exodus 32:15, Deuteronomy 20:7 and 22:23–28), it does not discuss how betrothal is formed. The initiation of marriage in biblical law is also referred to by the term *laqah*, to take (as in Deuteronomy 24:1, "When a man takes a wife and possesses her…"), but again no actual procedure or ceremony is described, unless perhaps sexual consummation ("possesses her") is understood as the determinative moment.

How early rabbis or their predecessors came to the terms *qaddesh* and *qiddushin* is not known. Only a single rabbinic text, and a late one at that, takes up the question: The Babylonian Talmud compares the act of betrothing (*qiddushin*) to consecrating an item to the Divine (*heqdesh*), "He forbids her to all like that which is sanctified to the Divine." Michael Satlow has suggested that the term might derive from the Greek *ekdosis*, a legal institution very much like rabbinic betrothal.

Structure and Organization of the Tractate

The first chapter can be broken into two parts: (1) a discussion of the acquisition of various living and inanimate forms of property (a woman/wife being the first item, and hence the link to the rest of the tractate) (1:1–6), and (2) various ways of categorizing commandments by factors such as the location in which they apply or the gender of the person obligated to them (1:7–10). The two sections are linked by the use of the formulaic use of "anything/all/anyone" in 1:6 to discuss property transferred by trade, and then in 1:7, 9, and 10 for types of religious obligations and those who do or do not fulfill them. In fact, some scholars have deemed the first part of the chapter to be a very early text that was incorporated whole into the Mishnah by its later editor(s).

Betrothal is the primary topic of chapters 2 and 3, which address betrothals enacted through agents or with various conditions attached (2:1–5; 3:2–6), what items may be used as a means of betrothal (2:6–10), and betrothals in which doubts arise regarding the identities of parties involved (3:7–11). The end of chapter 3 and much of chapter 4

(3:8–4:8) addresses caste status in Israelite society and its implications for who may marry whom, and the status of children born of permitted and forbidden relationships. Chapter 4 also addresses social relations between the genders, expressed largely through the question of what numbers and combinations of men and women may be in a secluded space together (4:12–14). This last concern leads finally into a closing discussion of trades, the worth of labor, and the value of Torah study 4:14). The final sections of 4:14 appear to be additions to the original tractate.

Main Ideas

The primary concept of the tractate is, as already noted, that of *qiddushin*, a binding betrothal/inchoate form of marriage, and more particularly the procedures through which *qiddushin* is enacted, especially the giving of an item of value and a statement of intent. Several other important concepts feature in various sections of the tractate. Chapter 1 addresses the acquisition of property, which encompasses both the various types of property, animate (slaves, animals) and inanimate (land/buildings and movables), and the means by which ownership of each may be legally transferred from the previous owner to the next. Depending on the item, these include transferring the purchase price, transmitting a document that attests to the sale, delivery, lifting the item or drawing the item toward oneself, or acting upon the purchase in a way that indicates ownership over it ("taking possession," sometimes referred to as "usucaption").

Chapters 2 and 3 invoke the ability of a person to perform/participate in certain legal and ritual acts through an appointed agent (*shaliah*); both also take up the means by which legal acts may be undertaken conditionally, how conditions must be worded and how they are or are not fulfilled, and the effects of unfulfilled conditions. The caste statuses of Israelite society figure prominently at the end of chapter 3 and the beginning of chapter 4; especially in need of definition here is the *mamzer* (defined as the offspring of a relationship in which there can be no binding marriage, namely adulterous and incestuous relationships).

Tractate Qiddushin

Chapter One

1:1–6 *Means of Acquisition*

I A woman is acquired in three ways, and acquires herself in two ways.
She is acquired (1) by money, (2) by document, or (3) by sexual intercourse.
By money—
the House of Shammai say:
By a *dinar*, or by the equivalent of a *dinar*;
but the House of Hillel say:
By a *perutah*, or by the equivalent of a *perutah*.
And how much is a *perutah*?
One eighth of an Italian *issar*.
And she acquires herself (1) by a divorce document or (2) by death of the husband.
The levirate widow is acquired by sexual intercourse.
And she acquires herself by *halitsah*, or by death of the levir.

1:1–6 A set of traditions dealing with the acquisition of the rights of ownership.

1:1 *acquired…acquires herself*: Is married, is released from marriage. Cf. *Eduyot* 4:7; note the language of "acquisition" here for wives, as well as for human (slaves) and nonhuman property.

by money…intercourse: By any one of these three.

money: Giving to the woman or her father (if she is a minor) a set amount of money with the express intent of betrothal.

document: Delivery of a document that states his intent to betroth.

dinar…perutah…issar: The relative values of coins is a bit problematic. The *perutah* is the smallest unit of currency recognized in the Mishnah; by a calculation provided in the Tosefta, $1/192$ of a *dinar*. If *Italian issar* means the Roman *as*, valued at $1/16$ of a *denarius*, the *perutah* would here be $1/128$ of a *denarius*. In any case, the Shammaites set the minimum value for betrothal as a coin of some value (perhaps the equivalent of a day laborer's wage) and the Hillelites, the smallest possible coin. In 2:1 below, the Mishnah assumes that the view of the Hillelites is followed.

divorce document: Given to her by her husband or his agent. See *Gittin* introduction.

levirate widow: See Deuteronomy 25:5–10 and *Yevamot* introduction.

is acquired: Becomes the wife of her brother-in-law.

halitsah: See Deuteronomy 25:9–10 and *Yevamot* chapter 12.

2 An Israelite slave is acquired by money or by document.
And he acquires himself by years, or by the Jubilee year, or by reduction of money.
The Israelite female slave exceeds him in that she acquires herself by puberty.[1]
The one with a bored ear is acquired by boring the ear.
And he acquires himself by the Jubilee year, or by death of the master.

3 A Canaanite slave is acquired by money, or by document, or by taking possession.
And he acquires himself by money by the hand of others
or by a document by his own hand—
the words of R. Meir;
but the Sages say:
By money by his own hand,
or by a document by the hand of others;
but only provided the money shall belong to others.

4 Large cattle is acquired by delivery,
and small cattle animal by lifting—
the words of R. Meir and R. Eleazar;
but the Sages say:
Small cattle is acquired by drawing.

[1] Lit. "by signs."

1:2 *Israelite*: A Jewish slave, who sold himself out of poverty, or who was sold by the court to repay a theft. Exodus 21:2 and Deuteronomy 15:12. This sale terminates after seven years, hence *he acquires himself by years*.

by the Jubilee year: See Leviticus 25, particularly verse 40.

by reduction of money: If the slave wishes to gain freedom before the end of the prescribed term, the amount of time the slave has already served is deducted proportionally from his purchase price and he may pay off the remainder.

Israelite female slave: Sold by her father; see Exodus 21:7–11.

exceeds him: Has an additional means of attaining freedom above and beyond those already listed for the male slave.

by puberty: For the "signs" of puberty (see n. 1), see *Niddah* 5:8. According to rabbinic law, a female Israelite may become a slave only while still a minor.

The one with a bored ear: See Exodus 21:5–6 and Deuteronomy 15:16–17.

1:3 *Canaanite slave*: A slave of non-Israelite origins is a chattel slave.

taking possession: Heb. *hazaqah*. By the performance of some act that indicates the purchaser's ownership of the thing or person purchased; compare "intercourse" in the case of marriage.

acquires himself: At issue is the ability of a slave to own property that could be used to free him or to take possession of a deed.

by the hand of others: Someone other than the slave must give the owner money to free the slave.

by his own hand: Given directly to the slave by the owner.

belong to others: While the slave may be the bearer of the money to the master, it cannot belong to the slave.

1:4 *delivery*: From seller to purchaser; again, an act that constitutes taking possession.

drawing: The purchaser draws the animal towards himself.

5 Properties that can serve as surety are acquired
by money, or by a document, or by taking possession;
and those that cannot serve as surety are acquired only by drawing.
Properties that cannot serve as surety are acquired together with properties that can serve as surety, by money, or by a document, or by taking possession.
And properties that cannot serve as surety bind properties that can serve as surety so as to take an oath regarding them.[2]

6 Anything that is used as payment for another thing—
when this one takes possession,
the other becomes obligated with respect to that with which it was exchanged.
How?
One who exchanges an ox for a cow, or a donkey for an ox—
when this one takes possession,
the other becomes obligated with respect to that with which it was exchanged.[3]
Ownership by the Most High is by money,
and ownership by the commoner is by taking possession.
One's statement to the Most High is like one's delivery to the commoner.[4]

1:7–9 *Classifications of Commandments*

7 All commandments regarding the son incumbent on the father[5]—
men are obligated[6] and women are exempt;
and all commandments regarding the father incumbent on the son[7]—

[2] **K** ends instead "and one swears regarding them." **P**: "One binds properties to which a lien applies with properties to which a lien does not apply, in order to swear an oath regarding them."
[3] From "when" through the end of the phrase is missing from **P**.
[4] **K, P**: "my statement ... my delivery."
[5] **K, P**: "commandments of [i.e. incumbent on] the father [regarding] the son."
[6] "Men are obligated" missing from **P**.
[7] **K, P**: "commandments of [i.e. incumbent on] the son [regarding] the father".

1:5 *that can serve as surety*: Land or built property.

together with: If purchased all in the same transaction—for example, in the purchase of a furnished house.

so as to take an oath: Although a court generally may not impose an oath in a case involving the ownership of properties that are subject to surety (e.g. land), an oath may be applied when the properties are joined with movable goods.

1:6 *payment for another*: Used in barter for another item.

Ownership: "Mastery"; "dominion."

Most High: God, in the context meaning a dedication of an item or property to the Temple.

One's statement: One's verbal commitment to dedicate or donate something.

1:7–9 A delineation of to whom (or upon what) various commandments apply.

1:7 *regarding the son incumbent upon on the father*: Of a father toward his child (or more particularly towards his son).

regarding the father incumbent on the son: Of a child toward parents.

men and women are equally obligated.
And all positive commandments that are time-bound—
men are obligated and women are exempt.
And all positive commandments that are not time-bound—
men and women are equally obligated.
And all negative commandments, whether time-bound or non-time-bound—
men and women are equally obligated,
except for the prohibition to *destroy [the side growth of your beard]*,
and the prohibition to *round [off the side growth on your head]*,
and the prohibition to become impure for the dead.

8 Leanings, wavings, bringing near, taking the handful, burnings, pinching the neck, and sprinklings and receivings[8]—
apply to men and not to women,
except for the grain offering of the suspected adulteress and the female *nazir*,
in which the women wave.

9 Any commandment that is dependent on the Land does not apply outside of the Land.
Any that is not dependent on the Land applies whether in the Land or outside of the Land,[9]
except for *orlah* and Mixed Species.
R. Eliezer says:
Even except for new produce.

10 Anyone who does a single commandment—
good is done for him and his days are extended for him and he inherits the Land.

[8] K, P reverse the order of the last two items.   [9] The opening two clauses/cases are reversed in K, P.

positive commandments: Lit. "Commandments of 'You shall do…'"

time-bound: They must be performed on a specific day and/or at a specific time.

negative commandments: Lit. "Commandments of 'You shall not do…'"

destroy…round off: Leviticus 19:27.

become impure: A prohibition for priests. Leviticus 21:2.

1:8 *Leanings, wavings*, etc.: Acts performed in the course of offering an animal or grain sacrifice. See *Zevahim*; *Menahot*. *Leaning* upon the animal to be sacrificed; *waving* of sacrificial portions; *bringing near* and *taking the handful* of grain of the grain offering; *burnings* of the portions offered on the altar; *pinching*, the mode of killing for bird offerings; *sprinklings*, *receivings* of blood.

apply to: May be performed by.

grain offering of the suspected adulteress: Sotah 2:1, 3:1.

and the female nazir: Numbers 6:2 equates men and women.

1:9 *orlah*: Produce from new trees. See Leviticus 19:23; *Orlah* introduction.

Mixed Species planted in the same field. See Leviticus 19:19, *Kilayim* introduction.

new produce: Grain that grows before the offering of the *omer*. See Leviticus 23:14.

1:10 *Mishnah*: Oral Torah, rather than the Mishnah as a work.

And anyone who does not do a single commandment—
good is not done for him and his days are not extended for him and he does not inherit the Land.
Anyone who has Scripture, Mishnah, and Good Conduct[10]—
he will not quickly sin,
as it is said: *A three-fold cord will not quickly be broken.*[11]
And anyone who does not have Scripture, or Mishnah, or Good Conduct—
he is not of the civilized world.[12]

Chapter Two

2:1   *Various Betrothal Rules*

2 The man betroths by himself
and through his agent.
The woman is betrothed by herself
and through her agent.
The man betroths his daughter when she is a girl by himself,
and through his agent.
One who says to a woman:
"Be betrothed to me with this date";
"Be betrothed to me by means of this":[13]
if one of them has the value of a *perutah*—

[10] Or "a trade."   [11] Missing here in **K**, **P**. See next note.
[12] **K**, **P** add "One who does grasp all three of them [**P**: will not quickly sin;] of him the scripture says; *A three-fold cord will not quickly be broken.*
[13] **K**, **P** add "be betrothed to me by means of this."

Good Conduct: Alterntatively, "a trade."

three-fold cord: Ecclesiates 4:12.

civilized world: Lit. "the settlement."

2:1 *through his agent...her agent*: An agent is permitted to act on behalf of the one who designated him.

when she is a girl: Heb. *naʾarah*, generally understood in rabbinic texts to designate a girl during the transitional period of puberty—commonly understood to be between the ages of twelve and twelve and a half—who is no longer considered a minor, but is not a yet a full legal adult. At this age the father still has the legal right to accept a betrothal for the daughter.

One who says to a woman: In each of these cases a man has to give a woman something whose value comes to a *perutah*, as according to the Hillelites in 1:1.

with this date: The difference between this case and the next is whether each date is accompanied by its own betrothal offer or whether a single offer of betrothal accompanies several.

by means of this: See n. 13. According to the reading in **K** and **P** the betrother may be giving a third item, making the phrase parallel with the next case.

she is betrothed;
and if not—
she is not betrothed.
"With this, and with this, and with this":
if all of them together have the value of a *perutah*:
she is betrothed,
and if not,
she is not betrothed.
If she was eating [the dates] one after the other—
she is not betrothed,
until a single of them has the value of a *perutah*.

2:2–5 *Conditional Betrothals*

2 "Be betrothed to me with this cup of wine,"
and it was found to be of honey;
"…of honey,"
and it was found to be of wine;
"With this silver *dinar*,"
and it was found to be of gold;
"…of gold,"
and it was found to be of silver;
"On the condition that I am wealthy,"
and he was found to be poor;
"…poor,"
and he was found to be wealthy—
she is not betrothed.
R. Simeon says:
If he deceived her to her benefit—
she is betrothed.
3 "On the condition that I am a priest,"
and he was found to be a Levite;
"…a Levite,"
and he was found to be a priest;
"…a *natin*,"
and he was found to be a *mamzer*;
"…a *mamzer*,"

---

eating the dates: They do not combine to make up a *perutah* since each one is gone before she takes up the next.

2:2 This Mishnah discusses betrothal made conditionally. According to the initial view, any condition that is not fulfilled invalidates the betrothal. *R. Simeon* deems the betrothal valid if the nonfulfillment is *to her benefit*, if, for instance, the item given to her is more valuable than he claimed.

2:3 Continues 2:2.

natin…mamzer: See 4:1.

and he was found to be a *natin*;
"...a town resident,"
and he was found to be a city resident;
"...a city resident,"
and he was found to be a town resident;
"On the condition that my house is close to the bathhouse,"
and it was found to be far;
"...far,"
and it was found to be near;
"On the condition that I have a daughter or a female servant who is a hairdresser,"
and he does not have;
"On the condition that I do not have..."
and he does have;
"On the condition that I do not have children,"
and he does have;
"On the condition that I do have,"
and he does not have[14]—
in all of these cases,
even though she said: It was in my heart to be betrothed to him despite this[15]—
she is not betrothed.
And similarly when she deceived him.

4 One who said to his agent:
"Go and betroth to me such-and-such woman in such-and-such place,"
and he went and betrothed her in another place—
she is not betrothed.
"Indeed, she is in such-and-such place,"
and he[16] betrothed her in another place—
in this case, she is betrothed.

5 One who betroths a woman on the condition that there are no vows upon her,
and vows were found upon her—
she is not betrothed.
If he brought her in without specifying,

[14] K, P reverse "I have" and "I do not have children."
[15] P lacks "despite this." [16] K, P add "and he went."

when she deceived him: He betrothed her on the condition that she meet one of these (types of) conditions, and she did not.

2:4 Compare *Gittin* 6:3.

Go and betroth...place: The instruction is understood to require that the betrothal take place in the designated location.

Indeed, she is in...place: The instruction is not a requirement but a description.

2:5 *vows*: In the Mishnah, such vows are taken to restrict oneself from something; that thing becomes to the one taking the vow as if it were a sacred item, dedicated to the Temple/Divine and hence forbidden to use or gain benefit from. According to Numbers 30, fathers and husbands have the right to annul vows made by their daughters and wives. See *Nedarim* introduction.

brought her in: Married her.

and vows were found upon her—
she goes out without the *ketubbah* money.
On the condition that there are no blemishes upon her,
and blemishes were found upon her—
she is not betrothed.
If he brought her in without specifying
and blemishes were found upon her,
she goes out without the *ketubbah* money.
All blemishes that disqualify priests disqualify women.

2:6–7   *Goods Given in Betrothal*

6 One who betrothed two women with something of the value of a *perutah*,
or one woman with less than the value of a *perutah*,
even though he sent betrothal presents after that—
she is not betrothed,
because he sent them on account of the original betrothal.
And similarly a minor boy who betrothed.
7 One who betroths a woman and her daughter,
or a woman and her sister,
as one—
they are not betrothed.
It once happened regarding five women,
and among them were two sisters,
that someone collected a basket of figs—
and it belonged to them,
but it was of the Seventh Year—
and said: Behold, you are all betrothed to me with this basket,
and one of them accepted on behalf of all of them—

goes out: Is divorced. Because the betrothal and marriage were not valid, she does not collect her *ketubbah*, the promised marriage settlement.

blemishes that disqualify for priests, and thereby prevent them from serving at the altar, *Bekhorot* 7:1–6.

2:6 *he sent them…original betrothal*: The first gifts did not amount to a *perutah* for each woman. The subsequent gifts were sent assuming the prior ones made a valid betrothal, but in fact, no betrothal had taken place.

a minor boy who betrothed does not create a valid betrothal. If upon reaching majority he were to send gifts to the woman, this would not change her status, because the gifts presume a prior valid betrothal.

2:7 *woman and her daughter…woman and her sister*: Since both cannot be betrothed to the man, and the transaction was *as one*, neither is betrothed.

it belonged to them: The trees from which the figs were taken belonged to one or more of the women. In a normal year this would make them theirs.

of the Seventh Year: Produce of the Seventh (Sabbatical) Year legally belonged to whoever gathered it. The man had sufficient possession of the figs to be able betroth with them.

and the Sages said:
The sisters are not betrothed.

2:8–10 Betrothal with Sanctified and Sacrificial Items

8 One who betroths with his portion,
whether in offerings of the highest sanctity or in offerings of lesser sanctity—
she is not betrothed;
with second tithe,
whether unintentionally or intentionally—
he has not betrothed—
the words of R. Meir.
R. Judah says:
Unintentionally—
he has not betrothed,
intentionally—
he has betrothed.[17]
And with consecrated goods,
intentionally—
he has betrothed,
and unintentionally—
he has not betrothed—
the words of R. Meir.
R. Judah says:
Unintentionally—
he has betrothed,

[17] K, P reverse the order of "unintentionally" and "intentionally."

The sisters are not betrothed, as above. However, this does not invalidate the act of betrothal with respect to the other women.

2:8 *his portion*: The priest's portion of the meat of a sacrifice. These are not for lay consumption and hence a priest cannot use it to effect betrothal. Similarly, *second tithe* does not truly belong to the giver. For R. Meir, the giver does not have the power to use these goods as his own to create a binding betrothal.

intentionally: In knowing and willful violation of the law.

R. Judah: In this first case, the groom has knowingly used restricted goods as his own, and the betrothal is valid; while if he had done so unintentionally the transaction is on some level mistaken. (The commentaries limit R. Judah's statement to second tithe.)

consecrated goods…R. Meir: When done intentionally, the giver desacralizes the sacred goods. He may owe a debt to the Temple, but the betrothal is valid.

R. Judah: According to the commentaries, only where one made use of sacred goods unintentionally can one make restitution consequently. So, only in such a case does R. Judah deem a betrothal made with the goods to be valid. Where it was done intentionally, the sacred goods are never actually his.

intentionally—
he has not betrothed.

9 One who betroths with *orlah*,
with Mixed Species of the vineyard,
with the ox that has been stoned,
and with the heifer whose neck has been broken,
with the bird offerings of one with *tsara'at*,
and with the hair of a *nazir*,
and with the firstborn of a donkey,
and with meat mixed with dairy,
and with nonsacral meat that was slaughtered in the Temple Court—
she is not betrothed.
If he sold them and betrothed with their money—
she is betrothed.

10 One who betroths with *terumah*,
or with tithes,
or with priestly gifts,
or with water of purgation,
or with ashes of a purgation offering—
in such a case, this one is betrothed,
and even if by an Israelite.[18]

[18] K, P: "even though [he is] an Israelite."

2:9 One is prohibited from benefiting from the items listed, so any betrothal using them is invalid.

orlah: Leviticus 19:23 and *Orlah* introduction.

Mixed Species: Leviticus 19:19 and *Kilayim* introduction.

ox: Exodus 21:28, and *Sanhedrin* 1:4. For this and the following see also *Temurah* 7:4.

heifer: Deuteronomy 21:1–9, and *Sotah* 9:1–2.

bird offerings: Leviticus 14:4 and *Nega'im* 14:1–2.

hair: Numbers 6:18 as elaborated by *Nazir* 6:6–11.

firstborn of a donkey: Exodus 34:20 and *Bekhorot* 1:1–7.

meat mixed with dairy: Exodus 23:19; 34:26; Deuteronomy 14:21.

If he sold any of the items listed in the first clause, *their money*, what was received in the sale, does create a valid betrothal.

2:10 Unlike the items in 2:9, these—although restricted in use—have monetary value, and can create a valid betrothal, *even if* done *by an Israelite*.

Chapter Three

3:1 *A Second Betrothal Before the First Is Completed*

3 One who says to his fellow: "Go and betroth to me such-and-such woman,"
and he went and betrothed her to himself—
she is betrothed.[19]
And similarly, one who says to a woman:
"You are betrothed to me after thirty days,"
and another came and betrothed her within thirty—
she is betrothed to the second man.
A daughter of an Israelite to a priest[20]—
she may eat *terumah*.
"From now and after thirty days,"
and another came and betrothed her within thirty days—
she is betrothed and not betrothed.
A daughter of an Israelite to a priest[21] or a daughter of a priest to an Israelite—
she may not eat *terumah*.

---

[19] **K, P** add "to the second [man]."
[20] **P**: "daughter of a priest to an Israelite."
[21] Lacking in **K**.

3:1 As noted in 2:1, an agent can perform a betrothal for the groom. Here the Mishnah deems valid a betrothal of an agent who instead *betrothed her to himself*. Since the betrothal to the sender has not taken place, *she is betrothed* to the agent (see n. 19). Cf. 4:9.

betrothed to me after thirty days: Although an offer of betrothal has been given and received, it has not yet taken effect. A betrothal that takes place in the interim is effective.

A daughter of an Israelite to a priest: If the woman in this case were an Israelite and the second man a priest, the betrothal is entirely binding and she may now eat priests' due as any legitimate wife of a priest may. The reading of **P** here (n. 20) is either an error or, alternatively, could refer to her status during the thirty days, before the betrothal of the first man takes effect, were there to be no intervening betrothal of a second man.

From now and after thirty days: The problem is either that the betrothal is retroactive or, more likely, that it sets two criteria for when the betrothal becomes effective, one before the second betrothal and the other after.

she is betrothed and not betrothed: She is betrothed to one of the two men, but there is doubt as to which.

A daughter of an Israelite to a priest: If either of the two men were a priest, the woman does not eat *terumah* as the wife of a priest.

or a daughter of a priest to an Israelite: If either of the two men were an Israelite, the daughter of a priest also loses the right to eat *terumah* that she had by birth.

3:2–6 *Conditional Betrothals*

2 One who says to a woman:
"Behold, you are betrothed to me, on the condition that I will give you two hundred *zuz*"—
in this case, she is betrothed, provided that he gives it.
"On the condition that I will give it to you within thirty days from now":
if he gave it to her within thirty—
she is betrothed,
and if not—
she is not betrothed.
"On the condition that I have two hundred *zuz*"—
in this case, she is betrothed, provided that he has it.
"On the condition that I show you two hundred *zuz*"—
in this case, she is betrothed, provided that he shows it to her;
but if he showed it to her on the table—
she is not betrothed.
3 "On the condition that I have a *kor*-sized plot of land"[22]—
in this case, she is betrothed, provided that he has it.
"On the condition that I have it in such-and-such place":
if he has it in that place—
she is betrothed,
and if not—
she is not betrothed.
"On the condition that I show you a *kor*-sized plot of land"—
in this case she is betrothed, provided that he shows it to her;
but if he shows it to her in the valley—
she is not betrothed.

[22] Lit. "dust."

3:2 *I will give you*: In the first case there is no time limit set on fulfillment (and no alternative for nonfulfillment; cf. 3:4). The betrothal is effective immediately. In the second, he set a time limit, and if the condition is fulfilled the betrothal then becomes effective.

provided that he has it: Or "as long as he has it." The Mishnah does not specify what happens if the groom does not own the money.

on the table: Presumably the table of a money changer. The money may not be his.

3:3 Continues 3:2.

a kor-sized plot: The sowing area of a *kor* of seed.

provided that he has it: Above, 3:2.

in the valley: Possibly, in a wide open area. As with the money on the table in 3:2, the plot of land may not be his.

4 R. Meir says:
Any condition that is not like the condition of the children of Gad
and the children of Reuben is no condition;
as it was said: *And Moses said to them: If the children of Gad
and the children of Reuben cross over,*
and it is written: *And if they do not cross over armed…*
R. Hananiah[23] b. Gamaliel says:
It was necessary that the matter be stated,
for if it were not so,
the meaning could have been that even in the land of Canaan they would not inherit.

5 One who betroths a woman and said:
"I thought she was the daughter of a priest, and behold she is a Levite";
"A Levite, and behold she is the daughter of a priest";
"Poor, and behold she is rich";
"Rich, and behold she is poor"—
in this case, she is betrothed,
because she did not deceive him.
One who said to a woman:
"Behold, you are betrothed to me after I convert,"
or "After you convert";
"After I am freed,"
or "After you are freed";
"After your husband dies,"
or "After your sister dies";[24]
"After your levir releases you"—
she is not betrothed.
And similarly, one who says to his fellow:
"If your wife gives birth to a female, in this case she is betrothed to me"—

[23] P: "Hanina."   [24] K lacks "After your sister dies."

3:4 *like the condition of the children of Gad*: The two and one half tribes that requested settlement in Transjordan (Numbers 32). The verses set a fulfillable condition as well as what will happen if the condition is not filled.

is no condition: Has no effect as a conditional limitation on the transaction taking place.

And Moses said…And if they do not cross: Numbers 32:29–30.

It was necessary that the matter be stated: That is, without the stipulation of Scripture we might have thought that the children of Gad would not inherit at all; the stipulation makes it clear that if they do not serve as the vanguard they will nevertheless inherit in the Land itself.

3:5 *she did not deceive him*: Rather, the mistake was due to his own misperception.

after I convert…she is not betrothed: One of the parties is not legally capable of betrothal at this point (the as yet unconverted non-Jew, an enslaved person, a woman who is already betrothed or married to another man; see 3:12 below) and/or the condition is not something either party can fulfill of their own volition (the freeing of the slave, the divorce of the wife or her release from the levirate obligation, the death of the sister).

your sister: To whom the betrother is currently married.

she is not betrothed.²⁵
If the wife of his fellow was pregnant and her pregnancy was evident—
his words are binding,
and if she gives birth to a female—
she is betrothed.

6 One who says to a woman:
"Behold, you are betrothed to me
on the condition that I will speak to the governor on your behalf,"
or "I will work with²⁶ you as a laborer":
if he spoke on her behalf to the governor or worked with her as a laborer—
she is betrothed;
and if not—
she is not betrothed.
"On the condition that Father will consent":
if the father consents—
she is betrothed,
and if not—
she is not betrothed.
If the father died—
in this case, she is betrothed;
if the son died—
one instructs the father to say that he does not consent.²⁷

3:7–11   *Confused Betrothals*

7 I betrothed my daughter, but I do not know to whom I betrothed her,
and someone came and said:
"I betrothed her"—
he is believed.
This one said: "I betrothed her,"

---

²⁵ **K, P** read "he has said nothing [of legal substance]"; the rest of the mishnah is absent.
²⁶ Or "for you."   ²⁷ **K, P**: "to say 'I do not want [it].'"

If the wife of his fellow was pregnant: Presumably, then, in the previous case she must not have been (evidently) pregnant. In this case, it is at least likely that the woman will give birth to a viable baby, who may be female.

3:6 *Father*: From the final clause, the father is that of the betrother.

the father died: Before being able to give or refuse consent. This leaves the condition unfulfillable and therefore nonbinding, and *she is betrothed*.

the son died: Before the father gave or withheld consent. The father's assent would make the young woman betrothed and a widow out of uncertainty; his non-consent leaves her status unchanged.

3:7-11 The Mishnah addresses circumstances in which one is uncertain whether or whom one has betrothed. This is kind of discussion is a common one in the Mishnah. See e.g. *Nazir* 8:1; *Bava Metsi'a* 3:3; *Menahot* 13.

and this one said: "I betrothed her"—
both of them give a divorce document.
And if they wanted—
one gives her a divorce document and one marries.

8 "I betrothed my daughter";[28]
or: "I betrothed her and I divorced her while she was a minor,"
and she is a minor—
he is believed.
"I betrothed her and I divorced her while she was a minor,"
and she is of age[29]—
he is not believed.
"She was taken captive and I redeemed her,"
whether she is a minor or she is of age—
he is not believed.
One who said at the time of his death:[30]
"I have children"—
he is believed;
"I have brothers"—
he is not believed.
One who betroths his daughter without specification—
those who have reached majority are not included.

9 One who has two groups of daughters from two wives,
and he said:
"I betrothed my eldest daughter,
but I do not know if it was the eldest of the older ones,
or the eldest of the younger ones,
or the youngest of the older ones who is older than the eldest of the younger ones"—
they are all forbidden,

[28] K, P: "minor daughter". [29] Lit. "big." [30] K: "One who is dying and says".

3:8 In each of the cases regarding a father's claims about his daughter, at issue is the daughter's marriageability to a priest if the father's claim is accepted. Priests are forbidden to marry previously divorced women or those who have had sexual contact, even by rape, with a non-Jew.

and I divorced her: Accepted a bill of divorce for her.

is…is not believed: The issue is her status as a divorcee. Once the daughter is of age, we do not accept the father's statement about her status without proof, although we do when she is a minor.

captive: The assumption is that a female in captivity has been raped by her non-Jewish captors. The father has special rights to attest to her marital status but not to her status as captive.

I have children…brothers: The concern in both cases is levirate marriage. Any children he has will exempt his current wife/wives from the obligation, while the existence of (paternal) brothers will create a levirate obligation.

without specification: Since the father has no power to create a betrothal for an adult daughter, they are certainly not married. The Mishnah is not explicit about the status of the younger daughters. According to R. Meir in 3:9, such daughters would be considered betrothed due to doubt.

3:9 *they are all forbidden*: To be married to someone else absent a divorce document.

except for the youngest of the younger ones—
the words of R. Meir.
R. Yose says:
They are all permitted, except for the eldest of the older ones.
"I betrothed my youngest daughter,
but I do not know if it was the youngest of the younger ones,
or the youngest of the older ones,
or the eldest of the younger ones who is younger than the youngest of the older ones"—
they are all forbidden,
except for the eldest of the older ones—
the words of R. Meir.
R. Yose says:
They are all permitted, except for the youngest of the younger ones.

10 One who says to a woman: "I betrothed you,"
and she says: "You did not betroth me"—
he is forbidden to her relatives,
but she is permitted to his relatives.
She says: "You betrothed me,"
and he says: "I did not betroth you"—
he is permitted to her relatives,
and she is prohibited to his relatives.
"I betrothed you,"
and she says: "You betrothed none other than my daughter"—
he is forbidden to relatives of the older woman,
and the older woman is permitted to his relatives;
he is permitted to relatives of the younger woman,
and the younger woman is permitted to his relatives.

11 "I betrothed your daughter,"
and she says: "You betrothed none other than me"—
he is forbidden to relatives of the younger woman,
and the younger woman is permitted to his relatives;

R. Meir in both cases forbids all but the one daughter who is certainly excluded from the father's utterance.

R. Yose in turn prohibits only the one daughter who must certainly be included in the father's utterance.

3:10 In each of the cases here, a person is held responsible for the consequences of his or her own claim to have betrothed or to have been betrothed—such that one is prohibited from a relationship with relatives of the claimed partner to the betrothal—but is not automatically bound by another's claim.

I betrothed you: His statement is effective enough to make him kin by marriage to her relatives. Her denial is sufficient that she is not kin by marriage to his relations. The Mishnah does not state whether she herself requires a divorce out of uncertainty, but since she is permitted to his relations, we may presume not.

You betrothed... my daughter: By the same logic, the man prohibits himself to the mother's relations, but not those of the daughter. However, neither the daughter nor the woman is restricted. Moreover, according to the commentaries this also has to do with the limited effect of a mother's utterance about her daughter's status, as a woman does not have rights over her daughter's betrothal as does a father.

3:11 Continues 3:10. In this case, the woman's utterance is sufficiently effective to prohibit herself to the man's relations (but see n. 31). Likewise he prohibits himself to the daughter's relations.

he is permitted to relatives of the older woman,
and the older woman is forbidden[31] to his relatives.

3:12–4:8   Caste Status and Marriage

12 Any case where there is betrothal and no transgression—
the offspring follows of the male.
And which is this?
This is a priestly woman, Levite woman, or Israelite woman who was married to a priest, a Levite man, or an Israelite man.
And any case where there is betrothal but there is transgression—
the offspring follows the inferior.[32]
And which is this?
This is a widow to the high priest, a divorcee, or released levirate widow to an ordinary priest,
a female *mamzer* or *natin* to an Israelite man,
the daughter of an Israelite to a *mamzer* or *natin*.
And anyone who cannot have betrothal with him,
but she can have betrothal with others—
the offspring is a *mamzer*.
And which is this?
This is one who has intercourse with any of the forbidden relations that are[33] in the Torah.
And anyone who cannot have betrothal, not with him and not with others—
the offspring is like her.
And which is this?
This is the offspring of a slave woman or a non-Jewish woman.

13 R. Tarfon says:
It is possible for a *mamzer* to be purified.
How?

[31] P: "permitted" (probably a mistake).
[32] Or "blemished." K, P add "among the two of them."
[33] K, P: "that are mentioned in the Torah."

3:12 *betrothal and no transgression*: If the man betroths the woman, the betrothal will take effect and be binding. The marriage is also fully permissible.

betrothal but there is transgression: The marriage is forbidden, but the betrothal is nonetheless legally binding.

the inferior of the two parental statuses. In the case of forbidden priestly marriages, the child does not take the superior status of the father, but is rather a *halal*, a priest of impaired status; see also 4:1 and 6. For the *mamzer* and *natin*, see 4:1.

forbidden relations: See *Yevamot* 1:1.

the offspring is a mamzer: See also *Yevamot* 4:13.

not with him and not with others: One part of the "matrilineal descent" principle: the offspring is a slave or a gentile because the mother is. This passage does not consider the offspring of a Jewish woman and a gentile or a slave; but see *Yevamot* 7:5.

A *mamzer* who married a slave woman,
the offspring is a slave.
If he frees him—
the son is found to be a freedman.
R. Eliezer says:
Behold, this is a slave *mamzer*.

Chapter Four

4 Ten lineages came up from Babylonia: (1) priests, (2) Levites, (3) Israelites, (4) *halalei*, (5) proselytes, and (6) freed persons, (7) the *mamzer*, and (8) the *natin*, (9) *shetuqei*, and (10) foundlings.[34]
Priests, Levites, and Israelites—
they are permitted to marry[35] one another.
Levites, Israelites, *halalei*,[36] converts, and freed persons—
they are permitted to marry one another.[37]
Proselytes,[38] freed persons, the *mamzer*, the *natin*, *shetuqei*, and foundlings[39]—
they are permitted to marry one another.
  2 Who are *shetuqei*?
Anyone who knows his mother and does not know his father.
And foundlings?

[34] P: "and Kuthaeans" (i.e. Samaritans). [35] Lit. "to come among."
[36] The word "*halalei*" is missing from P. [37] This line absent in K.
[38] Absent in K.   [39] P adds here "and Samaritans."

3:13 *the offspring is a slave*: Following the status of the mother, as in 3:12, but treating the *mamzer* father as an Israelite for these purposes.

he frees him: The father frees the slave child, now making him Jewish.

a slave mamzer: Such that he remains a *mamzer* even after being manumitted.

4:1 *lineages*: Alternatively, genealogical groupings, castes.

came up: To the Land of Israel from the Babylonian exile, at the time of Ezra and Nehemiah. The plural forms are Aramaic rather than Hebrew.

priests of impaired status: The offspring of priestly fathers by women whom priests are forbidden to marry (converts, divorcees, freedwomen), who are thereby disqualified from serving as priests (if male) or marrying into priestly families. See the continuation of this mishnah as well as 3:12 above and 4:6 below.

the mamzer: The offspring of an adulterous or incestuous union.

the natin: Rabbinic term for a descendant of the Gibeonites; see Joshua, chapter 9.

shetuqei: Defined in 4:2 as persons of unknown paternity. Lit. "quiet, silent"—this person (or ancestor of this person) is "silent" about his or her unknown paternal lineage.

foundlings: Heb. *asufei*, "gathered in." See 4:2. After *foundlings* P adds "and Samaritans" (see 4:3). Note that this would make eleven categories not ten.

Anyone who was gathered in from the marketplace and does not know either his father or his mother.

Abba Saul used to call the *shetuqei beduqei*.

3 All who are forbidden to marry into the congregation are permitted to one another.

R. Judah prohibits.

R. Eliezer[40] says:

Those who are certain to those who are certain—

it is permitted;

those who are certain to those who are doubtful,

and those who are doubtful to those who are certain,[41]

and those who are doubtful to those who are doubtful—

it is forbidden.

And who are those who are doubtful?

The *shetuqei*, the foundling, and the Samaritan.

4 A man who marries a priestly woman must investigate back from her four foremothers, who are actually eight:[42]

(1) Her mother, and (2) her mother's mother, and (3) her mother's father's mother and (4) her mother, and her (5) father's mother and (6) her mother, and her (7) father's father's mother, and (8) her mother.

A Levite woman or an Israelite woman—

one adds one more to them.

5 One does not investigate from the Altar and beyond,

and not from the Platform and beyond,

---

[40] K, P: "(E)leazar." [41] Absent in some printed editions. [42] K adds "and these are they."

4:2 *beduqei*: Lit. "those examined, investigated." The origins of such people stand in need of being investigated.

4:3 *forbidden to marry into the congregation*: Notably the *mamzer* and *natin*. The language borrows from Scripture; see Deuteronomy 23:3. As in 4:1 they may marry within and between groups.

R. Judah prohibits: In context, he appears to deem these groups unmarriageable, or at a most allows marriages only between members of the same grouping but not between groups.

R. Eliezer: The reading Eleazar, as in **K** and **P**, names a contemporary of R. Judah. With the explication below, he adds a caste (Samaritans) to those of 4:1.

Those who are certain: Those whose prohibition is certain or doubtful. R. Eliezer permits those of known parentage and (therefore) known inferior lineage (*the certain*), i.e. the *mamzer* or *natin*, to marry each other within and across the two groups. He limits the prohibition to the *doubtful* castes—those whose parentage is not known in full or in part, who are therefore unmarriageable. Similarly regarding Samaritans, likely the issue is that they are doubtfully but not certainly of *mamzer* status because the Samaritan community did not practice rabbinic laws of (marriage and) divorce and hence might allow (re)marriages rabbinic law considered adulterous. In practice, the Mishnah elsewhere is concerned primarily with the *mamzer*, and to a much lesser degree the foundling (*Makhshirin* 2:7).

4:4 *four foremothers, who are actually eight*: Four generations of female ancestors on each of the maternal and paternal sides, such that eight actual foremothers are considered.

4:5 *from the Altar and beyond*: If a male ancestor is found to have served as a priest in the Temple, his female ancestors do not need to be further investigated, but are rather presumed to have been fit.

from the Platform: Heb. *dukhan*, whence the Levites sang (*Arakhin* 2:6). Analogously with priests, it is sufficient to point to a male ancestor who was a Levite who served in the Temple.

and not from the Sanhedrin and beyond.
And anyone whose ancestors were known to be among the public officials or alms collectors—
they may marry into the priesthood,
and one does not need to investigate back from them.
R. Yose says:
Even one who had signed as a witness in the old archives of Sepphoris.[43]
R. Hanina[44] b. Antigonus says:
Even one who was recorded in the king's army.

6 The daughter of a male *halal* is disqualified with respect to the priesthood forever.
An Israelite who married a female *halal*—
his daughter is fit with respect to the priesthood.
A *halal* who married the daughter of an Israelite—
his daughter is disqualified with respect to the priesthood.
R. Judah says:
The daughter of a male proselyte is like the daughter of a male *halal*.

7 R. Eliezer b. Jacob says:
An Israelite who married a female proselyte—
his daughter is fit with respect to the priesthood;
and a male proselyte who married the daughter of an Israelite—
his daughter is fit with respect to the priesthood.
But a male proselyte who married a female proselyte—
his daughter is disqualified with respect to the priesthood.
The law is one and the same regarding the proselyte and freed slaves,
even up to ten generations,
until his mother is from Israel.
R. Yose says:
Even a male proselyte who married a female proselyte—
his daughter is fit with respect to the priesthood.

---

[43] P (in error) repeats this statement, attributing the second to Hanina b. Antigonus.
[44] K (P the second time this line appears): "Hananiah."

---

from the Sanhedrin: One has a male ancestor who served as a member of the Sanhedrin.

they may marry into the priesthood: Since the language throughout this sentence is in the masculine, the likely meaning is that men of such lineage may marry their daughters to priestly men.

old archives: Alternatively, "in the archives of Yeshanah of Sepphoris."

4:6 *A halal who…his daughter is disqualified.* This is also the case of the first statement of the Mishnah.

R. Judah adds that the same applies to the daughter of a proselyte.

4:7 *R. Eliezer b. Jacob*: In partial contradiction to R. Judah in 4:6: only the offspring of two proselytes cannot marry into the priesthood.

It is the same…until his mother is from Israel: This statement apparently represents yet another view: as long as the mother is an Israelite, the child can marry into the priesthood.

R. Yose allows the offspring of two proselytes to marry into the priesthood.

8 One who says:
"This son of mine is a *mamzer*"—
he is not believed.
And even if the two of them say[45] of the fetus in her innards: "It is a *mamzer*"—
they are not believed.
R. Judah says:
They are believed.

4:9 Betrothal by Agent

9 One who gave his agent authorization to betroth his daughter,
and [the father] went and betrothed her himself:
if his preceded—
his betrothal is a betrothal,
and if that of his agent preceded—
[the agent's] betrothal is a betrothal.
And if it is not known—
both of them give a divorce document.
And if they wanted—
one gives her a divorce document and one marries her.
And similarly a woman who gave her agent authorization to betroth her,
and she herself went and betrothed herself:
if hers preceded,
her betrothal is a betrothal,
and if that of her agent preceded,
his betrothal is[46] a betrothal.
And if it is not known—
both of them give a divorce document.
And if they wanted—
One gives her a divorce document and one marries her.

[45] P reads "concede" (or "agree").
[46] P: "is not."

4:8 For this kind of discussion, see 3:7.

One who says: A man who says of his child.

the two of them: The pregnant woman and her husband.

4:9 See above, 3:1.

betrothed her himself. The father himself betrothed her to someone other than the man to whom the agent had been instructed to betroth her.

if it is not known: She is potentially betrothed to both and needs a divorce from both, or one needs to cede to the other. See above 3:7.

4:10–11 *Lineage and Families Returning From Abroad*

10 One who went overseas, he and his wife,
and he returned, he and his wife and his children,
and he said: "The wife[47] who went abroad with me,[48] behold this is she, and these are her children"—
he does not need to bring proof regarding either the woman or the children.
"She died, and these are her children"—
he brings proof regarding the children,
but he does not [need to] bring proof regarding the woman.

11 "I married a woman overseas; behold this is she, and these are her children"—
he brings proof regarding the woman,
but does not need to bring proof regarding the children.
"She died, and these are her children"—
he needs to bring proof regarding the woman and regarding the children.

4:12–14 *Gender and Seclusion*

12 A man[49] may not be alone with two women,
but one woman may be alone with two men.
R. Simeon says:
Even one man may be alone with two women[50]
at a time when his wife is with him.
And[51] he may sleep together with them in an inn,
because his wife will guard him.
A person may be alone with his mother and with his daughter,
and he may sleep with them with flesh touching.
And if they had become grown, she sleeps in her[52] clothing and he sleeps in his clothing.

---

[47] **P**: "my wife." [48] **K, P**: "with me."
[49] **K, P**: "one man." [50] **K** begins a new *halakhah* after "women."
[51] **K, P** lack "and." [52] **K, P**: "he…in his."

4:10–11 Whether people returning from abroad need to establish the lineage of family members.

4:10 *The wife who went abroad with him*: He is returning with the same woman, whose lineage was already established prior to going abroad.

She died: Since he is not returning with his wife he must establish that these are her offspring, but her lineage remains in a presumption of fitness as before she went abroad.

4:11 *behold this is she*: The children are presumed hers, but her own lineage is in question.

She died: He must establish both her fitness and that the children are her offspring.

4:12 *at a time*: See nn. 50 and 51. With the reading of the print editions, this gives the justification to R. Simeon's position. Following the division in **K**, an alternative translation links *when his wife is with him* to what follows: "At a time when his wife is with him, he may sleep together with…"

13 An unmarried man may not teach young children,
and a woman may not teach young children.
R. Eliezer says:
Even one who does not have a wife[53] may not teach young children.
  14 R. Judah says:
An unmarried man may not herd animals,
and two unmarried men may not sleep in one cloak.
But the Sages permit.
Anyone whose occupation is with women may not be alone with the women.
And a person should not teach his son a trade among women.

4:14 cont. *God, Trade, and Sustenance*

R. Meir says:
Let a person teach his son a clean and easy trade,
and pray to the One to Whom riches and possessions belong;
for there is no trade that does not have within it both poverty and wealth,
for poverty does not come from the trade, and wealth does not come from the trade,
but all is according to his merit.
R. Simeon b. Eleazar says:
Have you seen in your days a wild animal or bird that has a trade?
Yet they are sustained without trouble.
And were they not created only to serve me,
and I was [not] created to serve my Master?
Does not logic demand that I should be sustained without trouble?
Rather, I have made my deeds evil and ruined my sustenance.
Abba Gurion of Sidon says in the name of Abba Guria:
Let a person not train his son as a donkey driver, a camel driver, a barber, a sailor, a shepherd, or a shopkeeper,
for their trades are the trade of bandits.
R. Judah says in his name:
Donkey drivers, most of them are wicked;
but camel drivers, most of them are fit.
Sailors, most of them are pious.

[53] **K**: "whose wife is not with him."

4:13 *An unmarried man*: In light of R. Eliezer's statement that follows, some interpret this as a man who has never been married.

young children: Lit. "scribes" or "writing."

does not have a wife: Is not presently married. Alternatively (as in **K**), one whose wife is not with him, i.e. is not currently living in the same location.

4:14 *whose occupation is with women*: A trade that is also practiced by and/or involves regular contact with women. This sentence or something like it is the conclusion of the tractate. What follows are supplementary passages. The witnesses differ over exactly what appears. The version of the standard printed editions is given here, with **K** (with **P**) following as an alternative text.

R. Judah says in his name: In the name of Abba Guria.

The best of doctors is for *Gehinom*,
and the most fit of butchers is a partner of Amalek.
R. Nehorai says:
I would put aside all the crafts in the world, and I would not teach my son anything but Torah,
for a person eats from its rewards in this world,
and the capital remains for him for the world-to-come.
And all other crafts are not like this,
for when a person comes to illness, or old age, or sufferings,
and is not able to occupy himself with his work,
he dies of hunger.
But Torah is not like this,
but rather it protects him from all evil in his youth,
and gives him a future and hope for his old age.
Regarding his youth, what does it say?
But they who trust in the Lord shall renew their strength.
Regarding his old age, what does it say?
In old age they still produce fruit.
And so it says regarding our ancestor Abraham, peace be upon him:
And Abraham was old… and the Lord had blessed Abraham in all things.
We have found that our ancestor Abraham performed all of Torah even before it was given,
as it is said:
Inasmuch as Abraham has obeyed my voice and kept My charge, My commandments, My laws, and My teachings.[54]

An Alternative Ending according to Manuscripts K and P

17   R. Meir said:[55]
Let a person not train his son [as] a donkey driver, a camel driver, a barber, a sailor, a shopkeeper, or a shepherd,[56] for their trades are the trade of bandits.

18   R. Meir says:
Let a person teach his son only something[57] from which a person can be sustained. Happy is he who learned a small trade to be sustained by it,

[54] Or "My Torah."   [55] **P**: no attribution.   [56] **P**: order differs.
[57] Lit. "place." So **K. P**: "a small trade."

But they who trust in the Lord: Isaiah 40:31.

In old age they still produce fruit: Psalms 92:15.

And Abraham was old: Genesis 24:1.

Inasmuch as Abraham: Genesis 26:5.

and people's spirits take pleasure in it.

19 R. Judah says:
A person should never teach his son anything but a clean and easy trade,
for there is no trade that does not have within it [both] poverty and wealth,
rather all is according to a person's merit.

20 He used to say:
Have you ever seen a lion that is a load carrier,
a deer that is a fruit picker,
a fox that is a shopkeeper,
a wolf harvesting dates?
And it is a matter of logical inference:
if these, which were created not in order to serve their Master,
are sustained without trouble,
I who was created to serve my Master:
is it not logical that my sustenance should be without trouble?
And who caused me to be sustained with trouble?
It must be said: my sins, because I have made my deeds evil and ruined my sustenance.
R. Nehorai said to them:
I would put aside all the crafts in the world,
and I would not teach my sons anything but Torah,
in order that they eat from its rewards in this world,
and the capital remains for them for the world-to-come.
For there is no trade that you have that lasts for a person,
except in his youth only;
if he falls into illness,
or to a measure of suffering,
or enters into old age and he is not able to stand at his labor,
it is found that he dies of[58] hunger.
But Torah is not like this,
but rather it protects a person from all evil in his youth,
and gives him a future and hope for his old age.
Regarding his youth, what does it say?
But they who trust in the Lord shall renew their strength, they shall rise up with wings like eagles, they shall run and not grow weary, they shall walk and not grow faint (Isaiah 40:31).
Regarding his old age, what does it say?
In old age they still produce fruit, they shall be full of sap and freshness (Psalms 92:15).
And you find regarding our ancestor Abraham,
that he observed the Torah even before it came into the world,
as it was said, *inasmuch as Abraham has obeyed My voice and kept My charge, My commandments, My laws, and My teachings* (Genesis 26:5).
And so you find that the Omnipresent One, blessed be He, blessed him in both his youth and his old age.
Regarding his youth,[59] what does it say?
And Abraham was old...and the Lord had blessed Abraham in all things (Genesis 24:1).

---

[58] P: "is thrown into."   [59] A scribal error? See **P** 4:23.

23 (**P**) And you find regarding our ancestor Abraham,
that the Omnipresent One, blessed be He, blessed him in both his youth and his old age.
Regarding his youth, what does it say?
And I will make of you a great nation and I will bless you and make your name great and you will be a blessing (Genesis 12:2).
Regarding his old age, what does it say?
And Abraham was old… and the Lord had blessed Abraham in all things (Genesis 24:1).

24 (**P**) And you find regarding our ancestor Abraham,
that he observed the Torah (even) before it came into the world,
as it was said, *inasmuch as Abraham has obeyed My voice and kept My charge, My commandments, My laws, and My teachings* (Genesis 26:5).

ORDER OF NEZIQIN

Tractate Bava Qamma 335
Hayim Lapin

Tractate Bava Metsi'a 382
Hayim Lapin

Tractate Bava Batra 439
Hayim Lapin

Tractate Sanhedrin 490
Beth Berkowitz

Tractate Makkot 557
David C. Flatto

Tractate Shevu'ot 584
Elizabeth Shanks Alexander

Tractate Eduyot 628
Shaye J. D. Cohen

Tractate Avodah Zarah 678
Christine Hayes

Tractate Avot 710
Martin S. Jaffee

Tractate Horayot 759
Alyssa Gray

Tractate Bava Qamma

Hayim Lapin

Introduction

Overview

Originally, *Bava Qamma* ("first gate" in Aramaic) was the first of three sections of a single large tractate called *Neziqin*, or "damages." *Bava Qamma* was followed by *Bava Metsi'a* ("middle gate") and *Bava Batra* ("last gate"). Some manuscripts still treat the three tractates as a single unit, and number the chapters of the three tractates sequentially. The division of the single tripartite tractate into three separate tractates or "gates" was known already to the Babylonian Talmud.

Structure and Organization of the Tractate

Bava Qamma deals with injury, damage, and restitution; *Bava Metsi'a* with lost and found property, money, and contracts; and *Bava Batra* with real estate, inheritance, and written deeds. *Bava Qamma* itself may be divided into two large sections: first, 1:1–6:6, damage or injury, generally not caused by humans directly (but see 2:6–3:3), and second, 7:1–10:10, injury and damage by humans directly. The first section makes use of two overarching rubrics: the five "attested sources of damage" (1:1), around which 1:1–3:3 are organized; and the "four primary classes of damages" (1:1), which provide the structure for 3:3–6:6.

Main Ideas

Bava Qamma begins with general concepts (1:1–4), then proceeds to discuss various forms of damage by animals (2:2–5) and humans (2:6–3:7), the goring ox (3:8–5:4), the pit (5:5–7), the animal eating produce (6:1–3), and the fire (6:4–6). The second part of the tractate covers theft of animals (7:1–6), personal injury (8:1–7), robbery (9:1–12), and an assortment of laws on the general topic of theft and restitution (10:1–10).

A number of terms and concepts derive ultimately from the Torah (see below). The owner of a *mu'ad* ox, an ox that is an "attested" source of damage and is presumed to be harmful, pays full compensation and is subject to different rules than the owner of a *tam*, an "innocent" ox, an ox that is presumed harmless, whose owner pays half. A thief pays a two-fold payment and a four- or five-fold payment for having sold or slaughtered a stolen animal. One who injures pays the value of the damage itself as well as several other forms of compensation. A robber (in the Mishnah the term implies violent appropriation) does not pay the extra payments, but in compliance with biblical laws of restitution does pay an added fifth. Concepts that do not derive directly from the Torah include "despair" by the owner of recovering the lost or stolen property, so that the property in effect is no longer owned by the owner; a thief or robber may in some measure come into formal possession of the object and assume liability for it through the performance of certain possessory acts.

In classifying damages as "Pit" or "Horn" or "Foot" or "Tooth" the Mishnah demonstrates a certain amount of theorizing and systematization, so that the terms come to represent types of damage rather than a specific action or body part. Similarly, the notion that certain ritualized acts can establish rights of possession also reflects some measure of conceptualization. However, the Mishnah stands at the inception of such conceptualization, which is much more developed in the Babylonian Talmud and in later rabbinic legislation.

Relationship to Scripture

Of the three sections of the original tractate *Neziqin*, *Bava Qamma* is by far the most dependent upon the Torah. Much of *Bava Qamma*'s legal terminology and many of its concepts are formed in close connection with biblical law. The most significant passage is Exodus 21:18–22:2, which provides specific rules for different types of damage and for compensation after theft, as well as providing the cases that become the "primary classes" themselves of *Bava Qamma* 1:1. Exodus 21:18–19 serves as a source for the rules governing injury and compensation of injury. Leviticus 5:1–26 and Numbers 5:5–10 provide the language and rules for the restitution of a robbed object that a robber wishes to return.

Some mishnaic passages read the biblical verses closely (e.g. 4:4; 5:5–7) even though not framed as commentary, while others have biblical terminology and rules only in the background. The use of Exodus 21:18–22:2 for broad classification is indicative of the way the tractate utilizes the Torah as both a source of authoritative data and as a springboard for the development of its own laws and ideas.

Special Notes for the Reader

In addition to the Kaufmann and Parma manuscripts, the textual notes occasionally cite the Cambridge manuscript of the Mishnah (**C**), and readings from Cairo Genizah fragments (**G**).

Tractate Bava Qamma

Chapter One

1:1–3 *The Four Primary Classes of Damage*

1 There are four primary classes of damage:
(1) the Ox, (2) the Pit, (3) the Crop-Eating Animal, and (4) the Fire.
The Ox is not like the Crop-Eating Animal;
the Crop-Eating Animal is not like the Ox;
and neither this one nor that one, which are alive,
is like the Fire, which is not alive;
and neither this one nor that one, which typically cause damage by moving along,
is like the Pit, which does not typically cause damage by moving along.
The common feature to all of them:
they typically cause damage, and watching over them is upon you,
and when they cause damage,
the one who caused the damage is obligated to make payments for the damage
from the best land.
   2 Everything that I am obligated to guard,
I have made possible the damage that it does.

1:1 *primary classes*: Lit. "fathers." The classification into four categories appears to be based on Exodus 21:28–36; 22:4–5. The classification provides an organizing rubric for the first large section of this tractate (see 3:8, 5:4, 6:1, 6:4).

Crop-Eating Animal: The Hebrew term is obscure. In Exodus, 22:4–5 both seemingly deal with a fire that causes damage. The Mishnah reflects an interpretative tradition that understands 22:4 as dealing with consumption by animals, and 22:5 as discussing *fire*.

is upon you: The second-person formulation is unusual, and one of a number of unusual formulations in 1:1–3.

the one who caused damage: Earlier in the sentence, the focus was on the form the damage takes; here, the focus shifts to the human responsible.

from the best land: The injured party is compensated from real property and has a claim on best-quality land. For the idiom, compare Exodus 22:4: *the best of his field and the best of his vineyard*, and Genesis 47:11. See 1:2.

1:2 *Everything that I am obligated*: A legal aphorism phrased in the first person (another rare formulation).

I have made...possible: Lit. "I have prepared its damage," that is, if it is my responsibility to guard it, whether it is mine or not, it is my actions that are deemed to have caused the damage.

If I have made possible part of the damage that it does,
I am obligated to pay damages as if I had made possible all the damage that it does.
Property not susceptible to sacrilege,
property belonging to members of the covenant,
property that has exclusive ownership,
and in any place except
a domain where the one who caused the damage has exclusive ownership,
or a domain jointly owned by the one who caused the damage
and the one who was damaged.
When[1] he has caused damage,
the one who caused the damage is obligated to make
payments for the damage from the best land.

   3 Assessment in money and monetary equivalent,
before a court,
on the word of witnesses
who are free members of the covenant.
And women are included in the laws of damages.
And the one who was damaged and the one who caused the damage
[share] in payments.

[1] K, P, C: "And when."

If I made part … possible: The classical example is one who partially digs a pit that is completed by someone else.

Property, etc.: Here begins a list of circumstances in which the usual laws of liability for damages apply.

not susceptible to sacrilege: The damaged property does not belong to the Temple, but rather to a lay Israelite.

members of the covenant: See also 1:3. "Israelite" is the more usual term for a Jewish person.

property that has exclusive ownership: Not, for instance, ownerless property.

domain jointly owned: The Babylonian Talmud presents a dispute about whether this clause extends the preceding (damages apply, *except* when in the domain of the one who caused damage *or in the domain* of both jointly) or whether it is one more circumstance when damages apply (*and also in the domain* of both jointly). The problem is both a textual one (whether the next sentence has a conjunction) and a legal one that appears elsewhere: to what extent does liability for damages apply when both parties have a legal right to act there?

When he has caused: Above 1:1. Without the conjunction (see n. 1), this sentence and the preceding can be read as one. This reading fits the second interpretation of the preceding clause. With the conjunction, the statement stands by itself.

1:3 A number of additional qualifications of the application of the laws of damages.

Assessment in money: The assessment of the value of the damages.

and monetary equivalent: According to one early interpretation, this refers to valuation of the liable party's obligation in real property; the commentaries, following the Babylonian Talmud, limit this interpretation to a case where the liable party consisted of orphans whose property is to be protected. This is not the obvious meaning of the Mishnah's wording, and other early traditions (including 1:4, end) assume other forms of payment.

women: Women have full liability for damages they commit, and, if they independently own property that has been damaged, are entitled to full compensation. Cf. 8:4.

[share] in payments: The language is slightly obscure but seems to mean that in the case of half damages (see 1:4) both parties take a loss, following Exodus 21:35; see below 3:9.

1:4–3:7 Sources of Damage: Presumed Harmless or Harmful

4 Five are presumed harmless and five are presumed harmful.
A domestic animal is not presumed to harm by:
(1) goring, (2) butting, (3) biting, (4) squatting, or (5) kicking.
(1) The Tooth is presumed to harm by eating what is appropriate to it.
(2) The Foot is presumed to harm by smashing as it walks.
(3) The Ox that is presumed harmful.
(4) The Ox that causes damage in the domain of the one damaged.
(5) And the Human.
The wolf, and the lion, and the bear, and the leopard, and the panther, and the serpent—these are presumed to harm.
R. Eliezer[2] says:
When they are trained they are not presumed to harm.
But the serpent is always presumed to be harmful.
What is the difference between the presumed harmless and the presumed harmful?
Only that the presumed harmless pays half damages from its own body,
but the presumed harmful pays full damages from the upper story.

[2] K, P: "Eleazar"; C: "[E]liezer."

1:4 *presumed harmless…presumed harmful*: Heb. *tam, muʿad*. The latter term adapts the language of Exodus 21:29, dealing with a goring ox. Biblical law specifies separate penalties in cases involving an ox with a repeated history of violence for both homicide and damage of other animals. The Mishnah extends these rules and considers whether some animals are presumed to be violent or to perform other types of damage even without a prior history of activity. If so, the owner is expected to exercise greater vigilance, and has a higher liability.

A domestic animal is not presumed to harm begins the list of five *presumed harmless* causes of damage.

The Tooth begins the list of presumed harmful sources of damage, ending with *the Human*. In this second list, the Mishnah introduces a typology of damage by animals distinguishing "Tooth," "Foot," and as in 2:5, "Horn." The typology plays an important role in subsequent talmudic discussion.

Tooth…eating: See 2:2.

The Foot: See 2:1.

The Ox: See 2:4. This is the biblical case more narrowly construed.

The Ox that causes…: See 2:5, where the discussion treats this category (and the list of animals presumed harmless in 1:4) as examples of "Horn."

the Human: See 2:6.

The wolf, etc.: See *Bava Metsiʿa* 7:9; *Sanhedrin* 1:4.

Eliezer (or Eleazar; see n. 2); compare the stringent stance of R. Eliezer at *Sanhedrin* 1:4.

but the serpent is always presumed to be harmful: It is not clear whether this is the continuation of R. Eliezer's statement or a new one.

Only that: Heb. "but not." The Mishnah states that there are only two significant differences between animals *presumed to harm* and those *presumed harmless*: that the owner of an animal *presumed harmless* is liable for *half damages* and that payment is *from its own body*. Related traditions include other differences.

from its own body…from the upper story: The body of the damaging animal is to be the source of the payment for animals that are *presumed harmless* (Exodus 21:35), and its value sets the ceiling for liability (3:9). For damage by animals that are *presumed to harm*, there is no such ceiling, and other goods, such as produce stored in *the upper story*, can be used for payment.

Chapter Two

2 How is the Foot "presumed to harm by smashing as it walks"?
The domestic animal is presumed to harm by walking in its typical manner and smashing.
If it was kicking, or if pebbles were sprayed from under its feet, and it smashed vessels—
he pays half damages.
If it stepped on a vessel and broke it, and it fell on another vessel and broke it,
on the first he pays full damages, and on the latter he pays half damages.
Chickens are presumed to harm by walking in their typical manner and smashing.
If a tangle[3] was tied to its feet, or if it was scratching and smashing vessels, he pays half damages.

   2 How is the Tooth "presumed to harm by eating what is appropriate to it"?
The domestic animal is presumed to harm by eating fruit and vegetables.
If it ate garments or vessels he pays half damages.
When does this apply?
In the domain of the one damaged;
but in the public domain, he is exempt.
If it benefited, he pays what it has benefited.
How does he pay what it has benefited?
If it ate from the open square—
he pays what it has benefited;

[3] **K, P, C**: "bucket."

2:1 *How is the Foot*: Chapter 2 expands on each of the presumed harmful causes of damage in 1:4.

Foot: An animal is presumed to cause damage through ordinary walking, but not to *kick* (which would be akin to Horn) or kick up *pebbles*. Given the unspecified location, the rule ought in principle to apply in the public domain, but elsewhere, especially 2:5, the Mishnah assumes that the Foot is not liable in the public domain.

and it fell on: The first vessel, or a fragment of it, broke the second. This is analogous to pebbles.

Chickens: The principle of liability for Foot is applied to other animals.

tangle: Something attached to the bird's leg that causes damage; an example of nonordinary damage.

2:2 *Tooth*: See 1:4, and comment to 2:1. Damage by Tooth refers to the normal eating by an animal, but not the eating of nonfoods.

When does this apply? Owners are not held liable for the damage their animals do by normal eating *in the public domain*, although they are required to repay what they *benefited*, that is, the material benefit owners receive by having their animals fed. If an animal ate valuable produce, what it *benefited* may be considerably less than the *damage*. See 6:2.

How does he pay what it has benefited? Specification of how the payment is determined (cf. 6:2) was expected here. A further qualification that limits the preceding: *the sides of the open square*, where people deposit their goods, or *inside the shop* (a private domain, although open to the public) are places where the exemption of the public domain does not apply.

from the sides of the open square—
he pays what it damaged;
from the doorway to the shop—
he pays what it has benefited;
from inside the shop—
he pays what it has damaged.

3 The dog and the goat that jumped[4] off the roof and smashed vessels—
he pays the full damage because they are presumed to harm.
The dog that took a coal-baked cake, went to the grain stack and ate the cake, and lit the grain stack—
for the cake he pays full damages,
but for the grain stack he pays half damages.

4 Which is presumed harmless, and which is presumed to harm?
Presumed to harm:
any [ox] against whom they testified for three days;
and presumed harmless:
if it refrains for three days—
the words of R. Judah.
R. Meir says:
Presumed to harm:
any ox against whom they have testified three times;
and presumed harmless:
any ox that the children can rub, and it does not gore.[5]

[4] Talmudim discuss the variant "that fell."   [5] K, P, C lack "and it does not gore."

2:3 Two further examples of damages by animals, included as a kind of appendix to the cases discussed so far.

The dog and the goat that jumped: Some animals are expected to climb and jump; damage caused thereby is a species of damage by Foot, for which those animals are *presumed to harm*.

coal-baked-cake: A loaf or cake baked directly on the coals, which may adhere to the loaf. The dog is presumed to harm by eating food it can access (damage by Tooth), so its owner pays full damages for the loaf; but it is not expected to start fires (6:4–6). The Babylonian Talmud and commentaries consider fire damage specific to humans, and the fire damage committed by the animal here to be indirect damage akin to pebbles cast by walking feet (2:1).

2:4 This passage addresses the Ox that is presumed to harm in the list of 1:4. Unlike the other sections of chapter 2, it does not begin with a citation of one of the clauses of 1:4.

three days: Apparently interpreting the characterization of an *ox that has been a goring ox from yesterday or the day before, and attested before its owners* (Exodus 21:29). It is the word "attested" (*mu'ad*) that the Mishnah uses for the "presumed to harm." For *R. Judah*, the three-day period implied by the verse is determinative, so that three incidents over a three-day period make the animal *presumed to harm*, and it reverts to the status of *presumed harmless* after a similar period without incident. According to R. Meir, behavior is determinative: three attestations—over any period—qualify the animal as *presumed to harm*, and its manifest gentleness qualifies it as *presumed harmless*. See 4:2.

5 "The Ox that causes damage in the domain of the one damaged"—how?
If it gored, butted, bit, squatted, or kicked in the public domain,
he pays half damages.
In the domain of the one who was damaged—
R. Tarfon says:
Full damages;
but the Sages say:
Half damages.
R. Tarfon said to them:
If, while the law was lenient in the case of Tooth and Foot in the public domain,
where he is exempt,
it was strict with them in the domain of the one who was damaged,
so that he pays full damages,
where it was strict in the case of the Horn in the public domain,
so that he pays half damages,
does not logic require that we are strict in that case
in the domain of the one who was damaged?
They said to him:
It is enough that what is learned from logical comparison
correspond to what it is compared to.
Just as the liability in the public domain is half damages,
so too in the domain of the one who was damaged the liability is half damages.
He said to them:
Let me not derive Horn from Horn;

2:5 *"The Ox that causes"*: The fourth item on the list of things presumed to harm, see 1:4; *"in the domain of the one damaged,"* where the ox entered private property and caused damage there.

If it gored, butted, etc.: The list of actions is the same as in 1:4. There the animal was said to be "not presumed to harm," that is, not automatically causing liability for full damages. The Mishnah will presently categorize these acts as a variety of damage by Horn. As already in connection with Tooth (2:2), the Mishnah assumes that different rules may apply in the public domain than in the domain of the injured party.

From the fact that *R. Tarfon* assigns *full damages in the domain of the one damaged*, it would appear that the editors, who cite the dispute to illustrate a circumstance of damage caused by something presumed to harm, concur with his view in this dispute.

R. Tarfon said to them: The discussion has R. Tarfon apply a legal analogy (a complex variant of argument of "lesser and greater"). In this first pass, R. Tarfon argues by analogy to the cases of *Tooth and Foot* that we are more lenient in *public domain* than in the *domain of the one who was damaged* (see 2:2), so the same should be the case for *Horn*: if the owner of an animal pays half damages when it gores in the public domain, it should pay full damages in the domain of the one damaged.

It is enough: An aphorism about the application of legal analogies. Where we compare two cases (Horn in the public domain to Horn in the private domain) we should apply the rule in the one case to that of the other. We expect *Horn* damage *in the domain of the one who was damaged* to cause liability for *half damages*; but according to R. Tarfon liability for Horn in the private domain exceeds that of liability in the public domain.

He said to them: In this second pass, R. Tarfon's reasoning is reconfigured to argue: in *the public domain, Horn* is treated more severely than *Tooth and Foot*; so too in *the domain of the one who was damaged, Horn* should be treated more severely.

let me derive Horn from Foot:
if while the law was lenient in the case of Tooth and Foot in the public domain
it was strict in the case of Horn,
where it was strict in the case of Tooth and Foot
in the domain of the one who was damaged,
does not logic require that we are strict in the case of Horn?
They said to him:
It is enough that what is learned from logical comparison
correspond to what it is compared to:
just as the liability in the public domain is half damages,
so too in the domain of the one who was damaged the liability is half damages.
   6 The Human is always presumed to harm:
whether unintentional or intentional, whether awake or asleep.
If he blinded the eye of his fellow or broke his vessels—
he pays full damages.

Chapter Three

3 One who places a jar in the public domain,
and another came and stumbled on it and broke it—
he is exempt.
And if he was damaged by it—
the owner of the jug is liable for his damages.
If his jar broke in the public domain,
and someone slipped on the water
or was injured by its shards—
he is liable.
R. Judah says:
If he acted intentionally, he is liable;
if unintentionally, he is exempt

2:6 *The Human*: The fifth cause of damage that is *presumed to harm* in 1:4. The distinction between half and whole damages never applies to damage that humans do, even if committed *unintentionally* or while *asleep*.

If he blinded... broke his vessels: The Mishnah explicitly includes both damage to other humans and to property.

3:1 The cases beginning in this section deal with at least two kinds of damage: damage done by obstacles placed in a public domain (3:1–5; these are akin to damage by a Pit in 1:1); and damage done by a human more or less directly (3:6–7). They appear here in illustration of damages done by a human (2:6).

One who places... exempt: Placing an obstacle in the public domain was negligent; if a passerby broke it, that person is not liable. Moreover, the owner is *liable for damages* caused by the obstacle.

If his jar broke: This case differs from the preceding in that the creation of the obstacle may be unintentional. R. Judah specifies that owner is only liable *if he acted intentionally*. At issue is the principle that a human is liable even when the damage was inadvertent (2:6).

2 One who pours water in the public domain
and another is damaged by it—
he is liable for the damage he caused.
One who hides thorns or glass,
or makes a fence out of thorns,
or a fence that fell into the public domain,
and others were damaged by them—
he is liable for the damage they caused.

3 One who takes out his straw and his stubble[6] to the public domain
to the dungheaps
and another was damaged by them—
he is liable for the damage he caused.
And anyone who first claims them acquires them.
Rabban Simeon b. Gamaliel says:
All who cause ruin in the public domain and do damage
are liable to pay,
and anyone who first claims them acquires them.[7]
One who turns manure over into the public domain,
and another is injured by it—
he is liable for the damage he caused.

4 Two potters who were walking one after the other,
and the first stumbled and fell, and the second stumbled on the first,
the first is liable for the damage caused to the second.

[6] K (originally): *saqo*, "his sack"; an error for *qasho*, "his stubble"? P, K (marginal reading): "his olive refuse."

[7] Lacking in K, P, C, G. The first printed edition and others place this statement after "one who turns."

3:2 *One who pours*: These variations on the problem of damage do not discuss the possibility of damage to the damager's property.

One who hides, i.e. places and covers them, perhaps by burying, creating a hazard.

or makes a fence: The commentaries, following especially the Babylonian Talmud, understand the thorns to be protruding from the wall into the public domain. While not clearly intended in the Mishnah, this interpretation fits with the broader theme of damage caused in the public domain. However, the interpretation may also reflect ancient disputes about liability in such cases.

3:3 *to the public domain to the dungheaps*: Agricultural refuse was a regular part of the normal cycle of managing waste and fertilization. (For the specific items, note the textual variation in this passage.) The Mishnah here assumes that manuring is done collectively, and that dungheaps are in the public domain, not outside the town or village (see *Bava Metsi'a* 10:7; *Eruvin* 10:7). The specification of waste removal is significant because the activity is both permitted and necessary.

All who cause ruin...: Probably a late addition to the Mishnah (see n. 7) stating a general principle. It is not clear that one either depositing agricultural refuse or turning over manure is "ruining."

turns manure over: Seemingly, a very similar case to the preceding. The commentaries adopt the view from the Talmudim that this statement refers to one seeking to acquire the manure for his or her own use.

3:4 *Two potters...the first is liable*: The human is liable in almost every circumstance (2:6). By falling, the first creates an obstacle, and is liable. The continuation in 3:5 will qualify this principle.

5 One comes with his jar and another comes with his beam,
and the jar of the one is broken by the beam of the other—
he is exempt,
since the one has permission to walk and the other has permission to walk.
If the owner of the beam was first and the owner of the jug was second:
if the jug was broken by the beam—
the owner of the beam is exempt.
If the owner of the beam stood still—
he is liable.
If he said to the owner of the jug: "Stand still"—
he is exempt.
If the owner of the jug was first and the owner of the beam was second,
if the jug was broken by the beam—
he is liable.
If the owner of the jug stood still—
he is exempt.
If [the owner of the jug] said to the owner of the beam: "Stand still"—
he is liable.
And so too if this one comes with his lamp and this one comes with his flax.
 6 Two who were walking in the public domain,
one running and the other walking,
or both running,
and they injured one another—
both are exempt.
 7 One who splits wood in a private domain
and caused damage in the public domain,
or in the public domain
and caused damage in a private domain,
or in a private domain
and caused damage in another private domain—
he is liable.

3:5 *One comes with his jar and another comes with his beam*: A characteristic passage in which the Mishnah explores an issue by altering or reversing the circumstances of the hypothetical case. Here, there are three principles: (1) in simple collisions in the public domain, one is exempt from damage since both parties have *permission to walk* there. (2) When walking in file, the person following carries an additional burden: a potter who failed to keep distance from the carrier of the beam is not eligible for compensation. (3) If the one in front stops, he incurs liability for the collision.

3:6 *one running… or both running*: An expansion of the first principle: running and walking are both permitted, so neither is liable. Both Talmudim record an alternative view that the runner would be liable.

3:7 *One who splits wood*: Analogous to the case of "pebbles" in 2:1, although now caused by a human.

in a private domain: i.e. his own property, and chips flew out into the *public domain*; or was splitting wood *in the public domain*; or was splitting wood *in* his own *private domain* and chips flew into another *private domain*. In all of these cases the person is liable. The issue may be formal (damage that crosses domains; or that occurs in the public domain; or in the domain of the one damaged, 1:2) or substantive (stipulating a level of care and liability, even when the act done is permissible in itself). Where both the work and the damage occur in the public domain, the one committing the damage is presumably liable (3:1–3; 10:5).

3:8–5:4 *The First Primary Form of Damage: The Ox*

8 Two presumed harmless oxen who injured one another—
they pay the half damages from the balance.[8]
If both were presumed to harm—
they pay full damages from the balance.
One was presumed harmless and one presumed to harm:
if the one presumed to harm [caused greater damage] to the one presumed harmless—
he pays full damages from the balance;
if the one presumed harmless [caused greater damage] to the one presumed to harm—
he pays the half damages from the balance.
And so too two humans who injured one another—
they pay full damages from the balance.
A human and an ox presumed to harm or an ox presumed to harm and a human—
he pays full damages from the balance.
A human and a presumed harmless ox or a presumed harmless ox and a human:
if the human [caused greater damage] to the presumed harmless ox—
he pays full damages from the balance;
if the presumed harmless ox [caused greater damage to] the human—
he pays half damages from the balance.
R. Aqiva says:
Even a presumed harmless ox who injured a human
pays the full damages from the balance.

[8] Lit. "with the what is left over."

3:8 The Mishnah begins a discussion of the damaging ox that extends until 5:4.

Two presumed harmless oxen: Both are liable, and the owners of each pay *half damages*. Where the amount owed to each other is not the same, the party with the greater liability pays half the *difference* (lit. "what is left over") between the two amounts.

If both were presumed to harm, and liable to pay *full damages*, the party with the greater liability pays the full *difference* between the two amounts, by the same principle. Note again the practice of modifying features of a hypothetical case to explicate its legal implications.

One was presumed harmless and one presumed to harm: In this variation the two parties have different levels of liability. On the simplest reading, we again subtract the two damage amounts, and when the damage by the ox that is presumed harmless is greater its owner pays half the difference; when damage by the one presumed to harm is greater, that owner pays the full difference. The traditional interpretations are more complicated.

And so too two humans. "A human is always presumed to harm" (2:6), so this is analogous to two presumed harmful oxen above.

A human and an ox presumed to harm: Again, analogous to two presumed harmful oxen.

A human and a presumed harmless ox: Analogous to a harmless ox and an ox presumed to harm.

R. Aqiva holds that injury to a human is always compensated with *full damages*. Other sources connect this view with a specific interpretation of Exodus 21:31.

9 An ox worth one hundred[9] that gored an ox worth two hundred,
and the carcass is not worth anything—
he takes the ox.
An ox worth two hundred that gored an ox worth one hundred,
and the carcass is not worth anything—
said R. Meir:
About this it was said:
And they shall sell the living ox and halve its value in silver,
and they shall also halve the dead [ox].
Said to him R. Judah:
This is indeed the law.
You have upheld *And they shall sell the living ox and halve its value in silver,*
but you have not upheld, *and they shall also halve the dead [ox].*
And which is this?
An ox worth two hundred that gored an ox worth two hundred,
and the carcass is worth fifty *zuz*—
this one takes half of the living ox and half of the dead ox,
and this one takes half of the living ox and half of the dead ox.

10 There is one who is liable for the act of his ox
and exempt from his own act;
exempt from the act of his ox and liable for his own act.
If his ox caused shame—
he is exempt;
but if he caused shame—
he is liable.
If his ox blinded the eye of his slave or knocked out his tooth—
he is exempt;

[9] Heb. *maneh*: see glossary.

3:9 *An ox worth one hundred*: Unlike the preceding, this passage builds on a situation explicitly addressed in Exodus 21:35. The biblical case assumes an animal not known to be a habitual gorer (i.e. presumed harmless, in the language of the Mishnah) that butts another, killing it: *they shall sell the living ox and halve its value in silver, and they shall also halve the dead [ox].*

that gored an ox worth two hundred, and the carcass, the dead animal of the biblical verse, *is not worth anything.* The owner of the goring animal thus owes half the full value of the dead ox, and the injured party *takes the ox* that remains, worth one hundred, as compensation.

An ox worth two hundred: Here, the injured party is owed half of two hundred, and the surviving animal is worth two hundred. According to *R. Meir*, this is what is implied in *And they shall halve...* (Exodus 21:35): the liable party pays half the value of the dead animal (one hundred).

R. Judah responds that the law is indeed as R. Meir stated, but since the carcass of the injured animal was worthless, the preceding case did not correspond to the biblical stipulation that the parties *shall also halve the dead ox* (Exodus 21:35). Such a case would involve animals both *worth two hundred*, while *the carcass is worth fifty*: the injured party receives one hundred from the sale of the living animal, but gives up twenty-five from the value of the carcass, receiving seventy-five in total.

3:10 The owner of an *ox* is exempt from liability when the ox *caused shame* (cf. 8:2) someone, or *blinded the eye of his slave*, while humans who do so are liable. Conversely, oxen make their owners liable when they *injured* their owners' *father or mother* or *lit a grain stack on the Sabbath*, but owners who do so are not liable.

but if he blinded his slave's eye or knocked out his tooth—
he is liable.
If his ox injured his father or mother—
he is liable;
but if he injured his father or mother—
he is exempt.
If his ox lit a grain stack on the Sabbath—
he is liable;
but if he lit a grain stack on the Sabbath—
he is exempt, because he is liable to pay with his life.

11 An ox that was running after another ox and was damaged—
this one says: "Your ox caused damage";
and this one says: "No, it was injured on the rock":
the one who claims property from his fellow,
the burden of proof is upon him.
Two were running after one:
This one says: "Your ox caused damage";
and this one says: "Your ox caused damage"—
they are both exempt.
And if both oxen belonged to one man—
they are both liable.
If one was big and one was small:
the one damaged says: "The big one caused damage,"
and the one causing damage says: "No, the small one caused damage";
if one was presumed harmless and one presumed to harm:
the one damaged says: "The one presumed to harm caused damage,"
and the one causing damage says: "No, the one presumed harmless caused damage":
the one who claims property from his fellow,
the burden of proof is upon him.

because he is liable to pay with his life: The principle is that when an act carries a capital penalty (parents: Exodus 21:15; Sabbath: 31:14), that penalty exempts the transgressor from any monetary penalty that derives from the act.

3:11 *the one who claims…the burden of proof is upon him*: A legal aphorism. Here, the two parties have mutually contradictory claims, so the plaintiff cannot collect damages without proof.

This one says: "Your ox"… and this one says: "Your ox…": Neither animal can be shown to have been responsible so both parties are exempt. But *if both oxen belonged to one man*, the owner of the two animals clearly has liability.

they are both liable seems to mean that, in keeping with Exodus 21:35, if both animals were presumed harmless both may be sold to recover the damages.

If one was big… if one was presumed harmless, and both animals are owned by the same owner. The cases are parallel: possible compensation from a more valuable harmless animal is higher; an animal presumed to harm pays full compensation. The commentaries understand *the one who claims…the burden of proof is upon him* in this case to mean, as above, that no damages are collected at all. A parallel text rules that in such cases the owner of the damaging animals pays the minimal compensation.

If the damaged oxen were two, one big and one small,
and the oxen causing damage were two, one big and one small:
the one damaged says: "The large one damaged the large one,"
and the small one the small one;
and the one causing damage says: "Not so,
the small one damaged the large one, and the large one the small one";
[or] if one was presumed harmless and one presumed harmful:
the one damaged says: "The harmful one damaged the large one,
and the harmless one the small one";
and the one causing damage says: "No, the harmless one damaged the large one,
and the harmful one the small one"—
the one who claims property from his fellow,
the burden of proof is upon him.

Chapter Four

4 An ox that has gored four or five oxen one after another—
he pays to the last of them.
And if there remains a balance to its value,[10]
he goes back to the one before it.
And if there remains a balance to its value,
he returns to the one before that.[11]
And whoever is last benefits—
the words of R. Meir.

[10] Lit. "If there is left over in it."
[11] **P, C** lack this sentence. **K** differs slightly from the printed edition.

If the damaged oxen were two...and the oxen causing damage were two: A modification of the preceding, again with parallel cases presented, but with the added complication that two injured animals of different values also belong to one owner. Each side is assumed to maximize its claim (e.g. claiming that *larger*, harmless animal must pay for the *larger* injured one sets a higher ceiling—half the value of the larger damaging animal—where the damage is greater) or minimize its obligation (e.g. claiming that the *small* harmless animal must pay for damage to the *larger*, setting a lower ceiling where damage is greater). Here, too, the Mishnah rules that *the one who claims...the burden of proof is upon him*.

4:1 *four or five oxen one after another*: The designation "harmful" is here thought to be the result of a formal determination (*muʾad*, "presumed harmful," can literally mean "attested"). As a result, if the animal gored *four or five*, i.e. several, animals in quick succession with no such designation it remains "harmless," and payment is capped at half its value (1:4). This mishnah explores how payment is to be allocated. Both views below share the rule that payment begins with the *last of* the injured parties. The Talmudim address why it is the last party who has the strongest claim. One possibility is that each earlier injured party has assumed some liability for or ownership of the damaging animal.

R. Meir rules that half the value of the damaging animal is a cap on the total damages. *If there remains a balance to* half *its value* (cf. 3:8), payment can be made for damage the preceding animal, *and whoever is last benefits*.

R. Simeon says:
An ox worth two hundred that gored an ox worth two hundred,
and the carcass is not worth anything—
this one takes one hundred, and this one takes one hundred.
If it subsequently gored another ox worth two hundred—
the last one takes one hundred,
and the one before him:
this one takes fifty *zuz* and this one takes fifty *zuz*.
If it subsequently gored another ox worth two hundred—
the last one takes one hundred,
and the one before him takes fifty *zuz*,
and the two first ones take a golden *dinar* each.

2 An ox that is presumed to harm its own kind,
but[12] not presumed to harm those not of its own kind;
presumed to harm humans but not presumed to harm animals;
presumed to harm children, but not presumed to harm adults—
for the one that it is presumed to harm—
he pays full damages;
for the one that it is not presumed to harm—
he pays half damages.
They said before R. Judah:[13]
Then what if it was presumed to harm on Sabbaths,
but not presumed to harm on weekdays?
He said to them:
For the Sabbaths he pays full damages;
for the weekdays he pays half damages.
When is it presumed harmless?
If it refrains for three Sabbaths.

3 An ox belonging to an Israelite that gored an ox

[12] Absent in the first printed edition of the Mishnah; this variant discussed in the Babylonian Talmud.
[13] C: "Aqiva."

According to *R. Simeon*, each time the animal gores, half its remaining value is assigned as damages: the owner of the *last* animal receives *one hundred dinar*, the *one before him* receives *fifty*, and the *two first*, apparently the owner of the first injured animal and the owner, each receive *a golden dinar*, or twenty-five *dinar*.

4:2 *presumed to harm its own kind*: This mishnah examines the possibility that an ox might habitually attack other oxen, or *humans* or *children* only, so that it is possible to be designated "presumed to harm" only that one kind of victim.

They said before R. Judah: This returns us to R. Judah's view in 2:4, that oxen are presumed to harm after goring on three successive days, and are designated harmless after refraining for three successive days. R. Judah is said to respond that refraining for *three* successive *Sabbaths* renders the animal presumed harmless again. This cross-referencing to a dispute elsewhere is rare in the Mishnah.

4:3 The examples discussed in this mishnah and the next include the Temple, a gentile, or an Israelite of diminished capacity (cf. 4:7).

Israelite: The general term for a Jewish person (cf. 1:2). Here it has the additional sense of a lay nonpriest and non-Levite (*Qiddushin* 4:1).

belonging to the consecrated offerings,
or one belonging to the consecrated offerings that gored an ox
belonging to an Israelite—
he is exempt,
as it is said: *The ox of his fellow*—
and not an ox belonging to consecrated offerings.
An ox belonging to an Israelite that gored an ox belonging to a gentile—
he is exempt;
and one belonging to a gentile that gored the ox of an Israelite—
whether presumed harmless or presumed to harm, he pays full damages.

4 An ox belonging to one who is legally competent that gored an ox
belonging to one who is deaf and mute,
or one who is not legally competent,
or a minor—
he is liable.
An ox belonging to one who is deaf and mute,
one legally incompetent,
or a minor
that gored an ox belonging to one who is legally competent—
he is exempt.
An ox belonging to one who is deaf and mute,
one legally incompetent,
or a minor—
the court appoints for them a guardian,
and they testify about them before the guardian.
If the one who was deaf and mute gained full capacities,[14]

[14] Lit. "was opened."

---

consecrated offerings. Literally "that which is sanctified," a term for property dedicated to the Temple.

The ox of his fellow: Exodus 21:35. The full clause is *if the ox of a man should butt the ox of his fellow*. The interpretation here reads *man* and *fellow* as specific, to exclude others: the Temple and, in what follows immediately, non-Jews. Women are not included in this discussion (see 1:3).

one belonging to a gentile: An Israelite is exempt from damages to a gentile although gentiles are liable for damages by their animals. Formally, the gentile is a *man* and so liable for damages, but is not the *fellow* of an Israelite, and so not due compensation for damage suffered. Both Talmudim are aware of the inconsistency and inequity of this legal position. Contrast 4:5.

4:4 *deaf and mute . . . not legally competent . . . minor*: A common triad representing individuals of diminished capacity and legal personhood. This first passage is parallel to that of the Israelite and Temple in 4:3. When the ox of someone of diminished capacity injures that of one of full capacity, or the reverse, the owner of the damaging ox is *exempt*.

the court appoints for them a guardian: In this second passage, the Mishnah appears to contradict itself. Both Talmudim propose that in this passage the ox has an established history of goring; the following passage of our Mishnah does deal with an animal presumed to harm. Alternatively, the Mishnah is drawing on contradictory sources, or shows the traces of editorial revision. According to certain parallel sources, liability of people of diminished capacity for damage done by their oxen was a matter of dispute among rabbis.

If the one who was deaf and mute gained full capacities: The owner has now become fully competent as a legal person. What happens to the status of the animal if it was determined to be harmful? According to *R. Meir*,

the one legally incompetent gained sanity,[15]
or the minor attained majority—
the animal returns to its state of being presumed harmless—
the words of R. Meir.
R. Yose says:
It remains in its prior status.
A stadium ox is not liable to death,
as it is said: *If it should gore*—
and not if they should make it gore.

5 An ox that gored a human and he died:
if it is presumed to harm—
he pays the ransom;
but if it was presumed harmless—
he is exempt from the ransom.
And the one and the other are liable to death.
And so too with a son or a daughter.
If it gored a male slave or female slave—
he pays thirty *sela*,
whether the slave is worth one hundred[16]
or whether he is worth no more than one *dinar*.[17]

6 An ox that was rubbing against a wall and it fell on a person,
[or] it intended to kill an animal and it killed a person;
a gentile, and it killed an Israelite;
a nonviable infant, and it killed a viable person—
it is exempt.

[15] Lit. "became smooth."   [16] K, P: "one hundred *maneh*" = ten thousand *zuz*.
[17] K, P, C: "one golden *dinar*" = twenty-five *zuz*.

---

the animal reverts *to its innocence*. Apparently, because the owner has had a change of status so has the animal. According to *R. Yose* it retains *its prior status*.

A stadium ox: Bulls and other animals were used in Roman public spectacles; here the assumption is that the animal is pitted against a human.

If it should gore: Exodus 21:28. On the basis of this verse the Mishnah concludes that animals forced to gore are exempt from execution.

4:5 *An ox that gored a human*: The Mishnah closely follows Exodus 21:28–32.

if it is presumed to harm: Exodus 21:29–30, although taking it for granted that the owner pays a *ransom* and is exempt from execution. Exodus 21:28, which does not require a ransom, deals, in the Mishnah's terminology, with an ox that is *presumed harmless*.

And so too with a son or a daughter: Compare Exodus 21:31; the text refers to minors.

male slave or female slave: Compare Exodus 21:32. For the Bible's thirty *sheqel*, the Mishnah substitutes thirty *sela*; a *sela* is four *dinar*, or two *sheqel* in the Mishnah's usual monetary system. For the Mishnah, biblical obligations in silver are based on the Tyrian standard; see *Bekhorot* 8:7.

4:6 *rubbing*, so there was no intention of injuring a human; [*or*] *it intended* a nonhuman or a human without full personhood but *killed* a full Israelite instead.

exempt: The Mishnah does not specify whether both execution and ransom (4:5) are included.

7 An ox belonging to a woman,
an ox belonging to orphans,
an ox under the care of a guardian,
a wild ox,
an ox belonging to the consecrated offerings,
or an ox belonging to a proselyte who died and has no heirs—
these are all liable to death.
R. Judah says:
The wild ox,
the ox belonging to the consecrated offerings,
and the ox belonging to the proselyte who died
are exempt from death, since they have no owners.

8 An ox going out to be stoned, and its owner consecrated it—
the consecration is not valid;
if he slaughtered it,
its meat is prohibited.
But if before its trial was finished, he consecrated it—
the consecration is valid;
and if he slaughtered it
its meat is permissible.

9 If he handed it over
to an unpaid guardian or to a borrower,
or to a paid guardian or a renter—
they have entered in the place of the owners:
if the ox was presumed to harm,[18] he pays whole damages;
if presumed harmless, he pays half damages.
If its owner tied it with a halter, or locked [the gate] before it appropriately,
and it went out and did damage—
whether presumed harmless or presumed to harm,
he is liable—
the words of R. Meir.

[18] K, P, C add before this "(And) if it went out and did damage."

4:7 The anonymous portion of the Mishnah views all the listed animals, which have other than free, adult, male Israelite owners (cf. 4:3–4), as *liable to death*. *Belonging to orphans*, in light of 4:4, without a (special?) guardian having been appointed. *Under the care of a guardian*, lit. "of (belonging to) a guardian," but the translation conveys the likely meaning.

R. Judah rules that *wild...consecrated offerings...proselyte who died* without Jewish heirs are all examples of formally ownerless animals. These are excluded by the repetition of "owners" in Exodus 21:28–9.

4:8 *An ox going out to be stoned*: According Exodus 21:28, the meat of the stoned animal cannot be eaten. The Mishnah's view extends this further, treating the consigned animal as ownerless, or perhaps no longer in the world, so that if *its owner consecrated* or *slaughtered* it, the act has no effect. If the owner did these *before its trial was finished*, the act has an effect, and the animal is dedicated or its meat can be eaten.

4:9 *unpaid guardian or a borrower, or to a paid guardian or a renter*, the standard list of bailees (or depositaries) in the Mishnah, connected, ultimately, to Exodus 22:6–14. Here, despite the differences in the guardians' liability for damage to the animal (compare *Bava Metsi'a* chapter 3 and 7:8), the contract of deposit assigns liability for the damage the animal does to the guardian.

R. Meir holds the guardians liable even if they *tied...or locked [the gate] before it appropriately*, R. Judah rules that no more than appropriate care is required.

R. Judah says:
For an ox that is presumed harmless, he is liable,
but for an ox that is presumed harmful, he is not liable,
as it is said: *And its owners have not guarded it*,
and this one was watched!
R. Eliezer says:
There is no guarding it except with a knife.

Chapter Five

5 An ox that gored a cow and its fetus is found at its side,
but it is unknown whether it gave birth before the ox gored it
or whether it gave birth after the ox gored it—
he pays half damages for the cow,
and a quarter damages for the offspring.
And so, too, a cow that gored an ox and its fetus is found at its side,
but it is unknown whether it gave birth before it gored
or whether it gave birth after it gored—
he pays half damages from the cow and a quarter damage from the offspring.

2 A potter who brought his pots to the courtyard of a householder
without permission,
and an animal of the householder smashed them—
he is exempt.
And if it was damaged by them—
the owner of the pots is liable.
But if he introduced them with permission—

And its owners have not guarded it: Exodus 21:36.

R. Eliezer, who states that no standard of care is high enough, would presumably hold that any animal that has gored more than once is liable to stoning. This is an alternative formulation of the definition of an ox that is presumed to harm (cf. 2:4). Parallel texts have a different version of this passage.

5:1 *An ox*: It is clear that the ox is liable for the damage of the *cow*, for which the owner of the ox *pays half damages*. Whether the ox was responsible for the abortion of the *fetus* is in doubt, so the parties split that obligation, and the damager pays *a quarter damages for the offspring*. The discussion is connected to the requirement in Exodus 21:35 to sell the living ox and halve its value in silver. The rule that monetary claims that are in doubt are split is often applied in the Mishnah.

And so, too, in the reverse case: *a pregnant cow that gored an ox*. Here the doubt is whether the offspring is deemed as having been part of the damaging animal at the time of damage, or to have been already separated.

5:2 This mishnah and the next form a unit with three parallel situations, possibly available to the editors as a preexisting unit. The connection to the immediate context is 5:3, dealing with damage done to or by an ox.

A potter: Case 1. *Bava Metsiʿa* 1:2 exempts one from damage if it occurred in one's own domain. Here, if the potter entered *without permission*, the property owner *is exempt* for damage caused by his animal, and in fact *the owner of the pots is liable* for damage to the animal. However, *if he introduced them with permission*, the property owner does assume liability.

the owner of the courtyard is liable.
If he introduced his produce into the courtyard of the householder without permission,
and the animal of the householder ate them—
he is exempt.
And if it was damaged by them—
the owner of the produce is liable.
But if he introduced them with permission—
the owner of the courtyard is liable.

3 If he introduced his ox into the courtyard of the householder
without permission,
and the ox of the householder gored it,
or the dog of the householder bit it—
he is exempt.
If his ox gored the ox of the householder—
he is liable.
If it fell into his cistern and fouled its water—
he is liable.
If his father or his son were in it—
he pays the ransom.
But if he introduced them with permission—
the owner of the courtyard is liable.
Rabbi says:
In all these cases, he is not liable unless he takes it upon himself to guard.

4 An ox that intended to damage his fellow [ox],
and struck a woman and she miscarried[19]—
he is exempt from paying the value of the offspring.
But a human who intended to strike his fellow
and struck a woman and she miscarried—
he pays the value of the offspring.
How does he pay the value of the offspring?
They assess how much the woman is worth before she has given birth,

---

[19] Lit. "and her offspring came out."

If he introduced his produce: Case 2.

5:3 *If he introduced his ox...he is liable*: Case 3. Up to this point case 3 follows 1 and 2. *If it fell* introduces additional complexity. By falling into a *cistern* the ox may *foul its waters* or kill *his father or his son* who were in it.

ransom: Exodus 21:29–30, and above 4:5.

But if he introduced them: The parallel with cases 1 and 2 resumes.

Rabbi rules that in all of the above cases liability arises only when the owner of the property explicitly *takes it upon himself to guard.*

5:4 An ox is treated as having intentionality (in the Talmud, this is the definition of damage by "Horn," 2:5). Its owner is exempt from paying for unintentional damage. A human, however, is always liable (cf. 2:6)

value of the offspring: The damage in question is the precipitation of a miscarriage (see Exodus 21:22–23), invoking a typical mishnaic question of valuation (e.g. 2:2, 6:2, 8:1).

They assess, presumably on the slave market (8:1). This view assumes that a pregnant woman is valued more highly for the potential slave she carries.

and how much she is worth after she has given birth.
Said Rabban Simeon b. Gamaliel:
If so, a woman, once she has given birth, has appreciated in value!
Rather, they assess how much the offspring are worth,
and he gives this to the husband;
and if there is no husband—
he gives it to his heirs.
If she had been a slave and was freed, or a proselyte—
he is exempt.

5:5–7   *The Second Primary Class of Damages: The Pit*

5 One who digs a pit in the private domain and opened it to the public domain;
or in the public domain and opened it to the private domain;
in the private domain and opened it to another private domain—
he is liable.[20]
One who digs a pit in the public domain, and an ox or an ass fell into it—
he is liable.
The rule is the same for[21] one who digs a pit, trench, or cavern, or ditches or channels.
If so, why is it said: *A pit*?
Just as a pit that is capable of causing death is ten handbreadths,
so too any [excavation] capable of causing death is ten handbreadths.
If they were less than ten handbreadths and an ox or an ass fell into it and died—
he is exempt.
But if it was injured by it—
he is liable.

[20] K, P, C: "One who digs … liable" is missing here, and a different version of this rule appears between the end of 5:5 and 5:6.
[21] Lit. "[They are] one."

Rabban Simeon b. Gamaliel objects that the value of a pregnant slave actually increases once she survives delivery due to risks associated with pregnancy and childbirth.

he gives this to the husband: The husband is the owner of the woman's offspring, as in Exodus 21:22.

if there is no husband: If he died; the *heirs* of the husband inherit the damages (*Bava Batra* chapter 8).

a slave and was freed, or a proselyte, so that there is no Jewish husband or husband's heir to receive payment, and the damager is exempt. The Babylonian Talmud's discussion (and hence the commentaries) assume that the woman had had a freed or proselyte husband who has died.

5:5 *One who digs*: Manuscript traditions differ over where this unit appears (see n. 20). Neither Talmud comments on the passage directly, and it was possibly not originally part of the Mishnah. The commentaries are bothered by liability for a pit *opened…to the private domain*, and generally suppose that digger has subsequently renounced ownership of the property (Babylonian Talmud), or that the opening to the pit is adjacent to the public domain.

One who digs…and an ox or an ass fell: The discussion follows Exodus 21:33–34.

The rule is the same…ten handbreadths: Extends the literal rule of the Torah to include any kind of excavation, and derives from the use of *pit* (Exodus 21:33) that liability for death of an animal arises when the excavation is *ten handbreadths* deep.

If it was less than ten, the excavator is liable for injury to the animal.

6 A pit belonging to two partners.
The first one passed it and did not cover it;
the second one, and did not cover it—
the second is liable.
If the first one covered it, and the second came and saw it uncovered
but did not cover it—
the second is liable.
He covered it appropriately, and an ox or an ass fell into it and died—
he is exempt.
He did not cover it appropriately, and an ox or an ass fell into it and died—
he is liable.
It fell forward due to the sound of the digging—
he is liable;
backward due to the sound of the digging—
he is exempt.
If an ox fell into it with its equipment and they were broken;
an ass and its equipment and they were torn—
he is liable for the animal but exempt for the equipment.
If the ox of a deaf-mute person,[22] a legally incompetent person, or a minor
fell into it—
he is liable;
a son or daughter, male or female slave—
he is exempt.

[22] Or "that is deaf-and-mute..."

5:6 *A pit belonging to two partners*: The Mishnah works through liability when one of two owners may be responsible, ruling that the last owner to fail to cover the pit has liability.

and did not cover it: In keeping with Exodus 21:33, where failure to cover determines liability.

He covered: Returns to the general case, referring to the first clause in Exodus 21:33. The owner is liable due to failure to cover the pit, but not if *he covered it appropriately*, even if an animal nevertheless *fell into it and died*.

it fell forward: The Mishnah imagines the animal falling into a pit during excavation (second clause of Exodus 21:33: *or if he should dig a pit*), startled by the sound of the digging. Presumably, the digger is expected to exercise care while an animal is approaching; the digger is liable only when the animal falls *forward*.

If it fell *backward*, while walking away, the digger is not liable.

If an ox...an ass and its equipment: Exodus 21:34 specified that the owner is liable for the animal. The Mishnah concludes that liability does not extend to the yoke or saddle or other equipment.

If the ox of a deaf-mute person: The simplest reading is that the rule distinguishes between damage to an animal belonging to someone lacking legal competence, in which case the owner of the pit is liable, and injury to a son or daughter, male or female slave. The latter, although they do not have full legal personhood, are excluded on the basis of the specification *ox or ass* in Exodus 21:33. Alternatively, as they are not intellectually impaired, they could have been expected to avoid the pit. Note, however, that both Talmudim (and therefore the commentaries) understand the opening phrase to mean "An ox that is deaf, intellectually impaired, or young"; for this possibility cf. *Bekhorot* 7:6. It is also possible to read "ox [or] a deaf person [or]..."

son or daughter, male or female slave appear in Exodus 21:32, immediately preceding the case of pit.

7 The rule is one and the same for an ox as for any animal regarding:
falling into a pit,
separation at Mount Sinai,
double payment,
return of a lost object,
unburdening,
muzzling,
Mixed Species,
and Sabbath.
And so too a wild animal or a bird are like them.
If so, why was it said: *An ox or an ass*?
Only because Scripture spoke of what is usual.²³

Chapter Six

6:1–3 *The Third Primary Class of Damages: The Crop-Eating Animal*

6 One who brings sheep into the sheepfold
and locked it up appropriately, and it got out and did damage—
he is exempt.
If he did not lock it up appropriately, and it got out and did damage—
he is liable.
If it broke out at night,
or if brigands broke it out—
he is exempt.
If the brigands took it out—
the brigands are liable.

---

²³ Lit. "of the present, of that which is." Instead of "Scripture," **P** (corrected by a later hand) has "The Sages."

5:7 *The rule is one and the same*: A final passage addressing the use of *An ox or an ass* in Exodus 21:33. In the cases of *falling into a pit*, *separation* from the mountain at *Sinai* (Exodus 19:13), *double payment* for theft (22:3, 8), a *lost* animal (Exodus 23:4, Deuteronomy 22:1–3), *unburdening* (Exodus 23:5, cf. Deuteronomy 22:4), *muzzling* (Deuteronomy 25:4), *Mixed* forbidden *Species* (Deuteronomy 22:12, see Leviticus 19:19), and *Sabbath* (Exodus 23:12), *Scripture* in specifying an ox or an ass *spoke of what is usual*, that is, about typical animals. The specification does not exclude other animals from these rules.

6:1 The Mishnah now takes up the third primary class of damages: the Crop-Eating Animal.

locked it up appropriately: Compare 4:9.

If it broke out at night: The implication is that the owner could not know or reasonably intervene.

broke it out, made it possible for it to escape, as distinct from *took it out*, where the *brigands are liable* for damage it does.

2 If he left it in the sun or handed it over to a deaf-mute person,
a legally incompetent person, or a minor,
and it went out and did damage—
he is liable;
if he handed it over to a shepherd—
the shepherd assumes liability in his place.[24]
If it fell into the garden and it benefited—
he pays what it has benefited;
if it went down after its typical fashion, and did damage—
he pays what it has damaged.
How does he pay what it has damaged?
They assess the value of a *se'ah*-sized plot of this field before the damage
and after the damage.[25]
R. Simeon says:
If it ate ripe produce, it pays ripe produce;
if a *se'ah*, a *se'ah*; if two *se'ah*, two *se'ah*.

3 One who was making a grain stack in his fellow's field without permission,
and the field owner's animal ate it—
he is exempt;
if it was damaged by them—
the owner of the grain stack is liable.
But if he made a grain stack with permission—
the owner of the field is liable.

6:4–6 *The Fourth Primary Class of Damages: The Fire*

4 One who causes a fire[26] by the hand of a deaf-mute person,
a legally incompetent person, or a minor—

---

[24] Lit. "goes in beneath (i.e. instead) of him."
[25] Lit. "how much it was worth and how much it is worth."
[26] Lit. "sends a fire," or "releases a fire." See Exodus 22:4.

6:2 *left it in the sun... deaf-mute person*: Examples of inappropriate care.

shepherd: A paid guardian (cf. 4:9).

If it fell into the garden: The Mishnah apparently envisions the sheep grazing on a hillside and falling into a terraced plot; *it benefited*: it ate of the produce but otherwise did not cause any damage.

How does he pay what it has damaged? Cf. 2:2. According to this view, one values the damage to the field by estimating the damage to a *se'ah-sized plot*. A *se'ah* is a measure of volume; *a se'ah-sized plot* is the area that can be seeded with a *se'ah* of grain.

R. Simeon estimates damage based on the loss of produce at its present value and the actual amount eaten.

6:3 *One who was making a grain stack*: Parallel with 5:2.

he, the field owner, *is exempt* when his own animal caused damage, since the damage took place where the field owner had exclusive ownership (1:2).

if it was damaged, the grain owner *is liable* for damage done on the field owner's property (cf. 2:5).

6:4 *a deaf-mute person*, etc.: A person of diminished capacity is generally exempt from damages (8:4) and not fully capable of becoming an agent for another.

he is exempt under human law but liable under heavenly law;
if he caused it at the hand of a legally competent person—
the one who is legally competent is liable.
One brought the flame and then another brought the wood—
the one who brings the wood is liable;
one brought the wood and then another brought the flame—
the one who brings the flame is liable.
Another came and fanned it—
the one who fanned it is liable.
If the wind fanned it—
they are all exempt.
One who causes a fire,
and it consumed trees, stones, or soil—
he is liable,
as it is said: *If a flame breaks out and finds thorns,*
and the grain stack or the standing grain or the field is consumed,
the one who sets the fire shall surely pay.
If it spread across a fence that is four cubits high, or a public road, or a river—
he is exempt.
One who lights a fire on his own property, how far may the fire spread?
R. Eleazar b. Azariah says:
They imagine it as if it is in the middle of a *kor*-sized plot.
R. Eliezer says:
Sixteen cubits, as with a public road.[27]
R. Aqiva says:
Fifty cubits.

[27] Or "in the typical manner of the public domain." **K, G** (see also **C**): "as with a public road" as earlier in this mishnah.

liable under heavenly law: And subject to divine punishment.

a legally competent person takes on liability (cf. 4:9). The commentaries view the damage as purposeful and apply the Babylonian Talmud's principle that "there is no agent for commission of a transgression."

brought the flame...the wood...fanned it: The last person to intervene is liable (see 5:9).

wind: According to the discussion of the Yerushalmi, an exceptional wind.

If a flame: Exodus 22:5. The Mishnah reasons, perhaps from the specification "field," that liability for fire applies to a field and its appurtenances: *trees, stones, or soil*. A fire is not expected to cross *a fence...a public road, or a river*, and the one who lit it is *exempt*.

One who lights: Note the shift in language.

how far may the fire spread? At issue is either standards of care or a formal question of how far a fire may be expected to spread.

kor-sized plot: The commentaries estimate the size as 75,000 square cubits, or a square with sides of 274 cubits.

R. Eliezer and *R. Aqiva* give considerably smaller areas.

public road: See *Bava Batra* 6:7.

R. Simeon says:
The one who sets the fire shall surely pay—
it all depends upon the fire.

5 One who lights a grain stack, and there were utensils in it and they caught fire—
R. Judah says:
He pays for what is in it,
but the Sages say:
He pays only for the stack of wheat or of barley.
If a kid was tied to it and a slave nearby, and was burnt with it—
he is liable;
a slave tied to it and a kid nearby, and was burnt with it—
he is exempt.
And the Sages concede to R. Judah in the case of one who lights a large building,
that he pays for all that is in it,
for it is the typical manner of people to leave things in houses.

6 A spark that went out from beneath the hammer, and did damage—
he is liable.
A camel that was laden with flax and passed through the public domain,
its flax went into a shop and was lit by the lamp of the shopkeeper,
and lit the large building—
the owner of the camel is liable.
If the shopkeeper left his lamp outside—
the shopkeeper is liable.
R. Judah says:
In the case of a Hanukkah lamp, he is exempt.

R. Simeon rules that there is no fixed distance (cf. *Bava Batra* 2:2).

The one who set: Exodus 22:5. The midrash is perhaps based on the "superfluous" *the fire*.

6:5 *One who lights*: The language continues the last portion of 6:4.

pays for what is in it: One is liable for items not expected to be hidden in the *grain stack* specified in Exodus 22:5.

If a kid was tied: This may continue the view of R. Judah. The one who set the fire *is liable* because this is a normal agricultural occurrence; but where the *slave* was *tied…and a kid nearby*, he is exempt because this was not to be expected (Maimonides). Rashi explains that he is exempt because one is not liable for monetary payment if the act he committed carries capital liability.

And the Sages concede: Commenting on the debate of R. Judah above: buildings are places where one can expect goods to be stored.

6:6 *A spark that went out…liable*: From context, the damage is in the public domain.

A camel that has transferred a flame, committing damage in the public domain.

its flax went into a shop, so that the lamp was appropriately placed, and the flax extended into the shop, *the owner of the camel is liable*. But if the *lamp* was *left…outside*, the lamp was a public hazard.

Hanukkah: The practice was to light lamps outside so that the placement of the lamp was appropriate, and the shop owner is exempt.

Chapter Seven

7:1–7 *Loss Caused by Humans*

7 The principle[28] of double payment is greater than
the principle of four- or five-fold payment,
for the principle of double payment applies to something that is alive
as well as something that is not alive;
but the principle of four- and five-fold payment applies only to an ox or a sheep,
as it is said: *If a man should steal an ox or a sheep and slaughter it or sell it*, etc.
One who steals stolen property[29] does not pay the double payment;
and one who slaughters or sells stolen property
does not pay the four- or five-fold payment.

2 If one stole on the testimony of two,
and slaughtered or sold on their testimony,
or on the testimony of two others—
he pays the four- or five-fold payment.
If he stole it and sold it on the Sabbath;
stole it and sold it for idolatry;
stole it and slaughtered it on the Day of Atonement;
stole it from his father's property and slaughtered or sold it, and then his father died;
stole it and slaughtered it and then dedicated it to the Temple—
he pays the four- or five-fold payment.
If he stole and slaughtered for medicinal purposes or for dogs;

---

[28] Lit. "measure."
[29] Lit. "One who steals after a thief"; so too in the continuation, "slaughters or sells after a thief."

7:1 *double payment*: Exodus 21:37–22:3; 22:6, 8 mandate double payment by a thief, but a *four- or five-fold payment* in kind for the theft of an ox or a sheep respectively if the thief has slaughtered or sold it.

is greater than: i.e. applies to more cases.

alive: Cf. 1:1 n.

If a man: Exodus 21:37.

One who steals: The rules of multiple payment apply only to the thief who steals from the owner.

7:2 *testimony of two*: A minimum of two witnesses is typically required for effective testimony (Deuteronomy 17:6; *Makkot* 1:7–9) and testimony is required to establish liability. If different witnesses attest to the theft and the slaughter or sale, the thief is still liable.

on the Sabbath...idolatry: Rabbis considered sale on the Sabbath a rabbinic extension of the Sabbath prohibition, and therefore not requiring the death penalty. Similarly, in the other cases there is no death penalty, and the monetary obligation therefore still stands. For the principle at work here, see 3:10 above.

from his father's property...dedicated it to the Temple: In both cases, the obligation to pay arose before a change in status that would have exempted him.

he pays the four- or five-fold payment: As opposed to the cases in 7:4.

for medicinal purposes or for dogs: The slaughter did not render the meat fit to eat (cf. *Hullin* 5:3).

[or] one who slaughtered, and it was found to be *terefah*;
[or] one who slaughtered a nonsacral animal in the Temple Court—
he pays the four- or five-fold payment.
R. Simeon exempts in these two cases.

3 If he stole on the testimony of two,
and slaughtered or sold on their testimony,
and they were found to be plotting witnesses—
they pay the whole.
If he stole on the testimony of two,
and slaughtered or sold on the testimony of others,
and both groups of witnesses[30] were found to be plotting—
the former pay the double payment,
and the latter pay the three-fold payment.
If the latter were found to be plotting—
he pays the double payment,
and they pay the three-fold payment.
If one of the latter is plotting—
the testimony of the latter is nullified;
if one of the former is plotting—
the entire testimony is nullified,
for if there is no theft, there is neither slaughter nor sale.

[30] Lit. "these and these."

terefah: Lit. "a torn animal": a slaughtered animal that was discovered to have been suffering from a fatal disease and therefore not edible (see *Hullin*).

a nonsacral animal in the Temple Court: In this case, the carcass is entirely prohibited. Nonetheless, the thief has carried out "slaughter" and *pays the four- or five-fold payment*.

R. Simeon does not consider *these two cases*, terefah and the animal slaughtered in the Temple Court, to be true slaughter, so the thief *is exempt* from the four- or five-fold payment for slaughter. Cf. *Hullin* 5:3; *Temurah* 7:4.

7:3 *plotting witnesses*, whose testimony is falsified by others who testify that the former were not present to witness the act they claim to have seen (*Makkot* 1:4); they are punished with the same judgment *that he plotted to do to his brother* (Deuteronomy 19:19; see further *Makkot* chapter 1). The Mishnah picks up the topic from 7:2 and continues to 7:4 (beginning) with a number of hypothetical cases involving falsified witnesses. First, both the theft and the slaughter or sale were attested by the same plotting witnesses, so *they pay the whole* when falsified.

stole…on the testimony of others, and both…were found to be plotting: There were two distinct sets of falsified testimony. *The former pay the double payment* for theft alone, *and the latter pay the three-fold payment* over and above the double payment for slaughtering or selling. (Note that in 7:4, the expression "four- and five-fold payment" is retained for this.) When *the latter* alone were falsified, *they pay the three-fold payment*, but the defendant is still liable for the theft itself.

one of the latter is plotting: The defendant pays the double payment as before, because the testimony has been *nullified*, but the plotting witness is exempt unless both witnesses are falsified (Talmudim). If *one of the former* is falsified, the *entire testimony is nullified*, and neither defendant nor witness pays.

4 If he stole on the testimony of two,
and slaughtered or sold on the testimony of one,
or on his own testimony—
he pays the double payment,
but he does not pay the four- or five-fold payment.
If he stole and slaughtered on the Sabbath;
stole and slaughtered for idolatry;
stole from his father and his father died, and afterwards slaughtered or sold;
stole and dedicated to the Temple, and afterwards slaughtered or sold—
he pays the double payment,
but does not pay the four- or five-fold payment.
R. Simeon says:
Sacred offerings for which one is accountable—
he pays the four- and five-fold payment;
and those for which one is not accountable—
he is exempt.

5 If he sold it except for a one-hundredth share in it,
or he had a partnership share in it;
[or] one who slaughters and it became carcass in his hand;
[or] one who stabs or one who tears out—
he pays the double payment but does not pay the four- or five-fold payment.
If he stole it in the domain of the owners, and slaughtered or sold outside their domain;
or if he stole it outside their domain, and slaughtered or sold in their domain;
or if he stole and slaughtered or sold outside their domain—
he pays the four- and five-fold payment.
But if he stole and slaughtered or sold in their domain—
he is exempt.

7:4 *on the testimony of one*, so that there is no effective testimony to the slaughter or sale, *or on his own testimony*, in which case one does not pay a penalty payment (*Ketubbot* 3:9; *Shevuot* 5:4).

stole and slaughtered on the Sabbath…for idolatry: Returns to the first topic of 7:2. Here, the act of slaughter is deemed to carry a death penalty, so the thief does not pay the additional payment for slaughter (3:10).

from his father…and dedicated: Now, the change in status occurred after the liability for *double payment* was incurred, but before the *four- and five-fold payment*, from which the thief is exempt.

R. Simeon qualifies the case of dedication as a sacrifice. The thief is *exempt* only when *one is not accountable* to make restitution by offering a new sacrifice should the one given be disqualified, that is, only if he dedicated the particular animal he stole. In the other case, the thief does not fully relinquish possession of the animal to the Temple. (See *Megillah* 1:6.)

7:5 *except for a one-hundredth share in it*: so that the thief had not fully alienated it.

partnership: According to the commentaries, the thief owned a share in the stolen animal, so that the animal was not entirely stolen when sold; in light of a parallel text it is possible that what is at issue is that a single legal person did not sell the animal.

became carcass: An animal that is slaughtered incorrectly is deemed "carcass" and is prohibited to be eaten; so too if the thief *stabs* or *tears*, which are not acts of correct slaughter.

stole it in the domain of the owners: What constitutes an act of theft is not specified here and difficult to envision (see 7:6), but full liability requires removing the animal from its owner's domain.

6 If he was pulling it and going out, but it died in the domain of the owners—
he is exempt;
if he lifted it up, or removed it from the domain of the owners, and it died—
he is liable.
If he gave it in redemption of his firstborn son or to his creditor,
to an unpaid guardian or a borrower,
or to a paid guardian or a renter,
who was pulling it, but it died in the domain of the owner—
he is exempt.
If the latter lifted it, or removed it from the domain of the owners, and it died—
he is liable.

7 One may not raise small cattle in the Land of Israel,
but one may raise them in Syria and the wilderness areas in the Land of Israel.
One may not raise fowl in Jerusalem, because of the sacrifices;
nor may priests in the Land of Israel, because of purities.
One may not raise pigs in any place.
A person may not raise a dog unless it is tied with a chain.
One may not set snares for pigeons unless it was thirty *ris* from a settlement.

7:6 The first part of this mishnah treats liability for theft as requiring an act of acquisition by the thief.

pulling the animal (cf. *Qiddushin* 1:4, small cattle) does not constitute a possessory act in the domain of the owners; and since the animal *died in the owner's domain*, the thief is exempt (according to many commentators, exempt from the double payment alone).

redemption of his firstborn son: Lit. "his son's birthright," redeeming the firstborn child by paying five biblical *sheqel* to the priest (Numbers 3:40–49).

to his creditor... or a renter, and the animal died while being pulled. In all these cases the latter, lit. "he," that is, the priest, creditor, etc. is exempt, because there was no possessory act. But if he lifted it or removed it, there is a possessory act and the priest, creditor, or guardian is liable.

7:7 A self-contained unit; the connection is to the sheep or goats implied in 7:6.

small cattle: Sheep or goats.

Land of Israel: Territories deemed subject to biblical agricultural laws; *Syria*, nearby territories outside the land (see e.g. *Shevi'it* 6:1). Presumably, because they can damage produce, small cattle are to be raised outside these territories or *in the wilderness areas in the land of Israel*: Geography is not a concern in discussions of animal raising elsewhere (e.g. 6:1; 10:9); one wonders how widely practiced the prohibition was.

fowl may bring dead vermin into contact with holy things in *Jerusalem* or in the homes of *priests* elsewhere.

a dog is a source of danger (*Bava Metsi'a* 7:8).

snares that are too close to a settlement may capture birds belonging to others.

ris: A unit of length; see *Yoma* 6:4.

Chapter Eight

8:1–7 *Personal Injury*

8 One who injures his fellow is liable on its account for five things:
(1) for damage;
(2) for pain;
(3) for healing;
(4) for loss of employment;[31]
(5) and for shame.
For damage, how?
If he blinded his eye, cut off his hand, broke his leg—
they view him as if he were a slave sold in the marketplace,
and they assess his value before the damage and after the damage.[32]
Pain:
if he burnt his fellow with a spit or with a nail,
even on his fingernail where it leaves no bruise,
they estimate how much a person such as this would be willing to receive
in exchange for suffering such pain.
Healing:
if he struck him,
he is liable to provide healing for him.
If growths developed on him—
if due to the blow, he is liable;
if not due to the blow, he is not liable.
If it repeatedly healed and opened,[33] he is liable to provide healing for him;
if it healed fully, he is not liable to provide healing for him.
Loss of employment:
they view him as if he were a guardian of cucumbers,
for the value of his hand or the value of his foot has already been given him.
Shame:
it all depends upon the one shaming and the one shamed.

---

[31] Lit. "sitting," or "abstention from work."
[32] Lit. "how much he was worth, and how much he is worth."
[33] Lit. "It healed and opened, healed and opened."

8:1 *five things*: Exodus 21:19 specifies only "sitting" (perhaps, recuperation; but *loss of employment* according to the Mishnah) and *healing*. A parallel text derives *damage* and *pain* from Exodus 21:24–25, *an eye for an eye…a burn for a burn*. The Mishnah below provides a derivation for *shame*.

The Mishnah outlines the methods to quantify these payments: *damage*, the monetary loss due to injury, as valued on the slave market (cf. 5:4, 6:2). *Pain*, what one would require to willingly endure the pain. *Healing*, the medical care that can be ascribed directly to the injury.

growths are perhaps ulcers or other sores that arise on the body; *healed fully*, even if the wound returns.

Loss of employment, valued as very inexpensive, unskilled, seasonal labor.

Shame: No method is given (cf. 8:6).

One who shames a naked person,
one who shames a blind person,
and one who shames a sleeping person—
he is liable;
but a sleeping person who shames is exempt.
If he fell from the roof and caused damage and shamed—
he is liable for the damage and exempt from the shame.
as it says:
And she stretched out her hand and grasped his shameful parts—
he is not liable for shame unless he has intention.

   2 In this respect, a human is more stringent than an ox:[34]
for a person pays damage, pain, healing, loss of employment, and shame,
and pays the value of offspring;
but the ox pays only damages
and is exempt from the value of offspring.

   3 One who strikes his father or mother and did not cause a bruise on them;
and one who injures his fellow on the Day of Atonement—
he is liable for all of them.
One who injures a Hebrew slave—
he is liable for all of them,
except lost employment, as long as the slave belongs to him.[35]
One who injures a Canaanite slave belonging to others—
is liable for all of them.
R. Judah says:
Slaves have no shame.

---

[34] K, P, C have something to the effect of "and that which is more stringent for a human than an animal is."
[35] Lit. "As long as he is his."

One who shames: Perhaps originally an independent tradition, but here illustrating the absence of a single method for shame.

and grasped his shameful parts. Deuteronomy 25:11, perhaps drawing a connection between the euphemism for testicles and shame.

8:2 Liability of a *human* and an *ox* compared (cf. 1:4, the "sources of damage presumed to be harmful").

offspring: See 5:4.

8:3 *strikes his mother or father*: Exodus 21:15. The Mishnah limits the death penalty to cases involving visible injury, therefore here monetary liability for injury applies.

Day of Atonement: See above 7:2. Since there is no death penalty, there is monetary liability for injury.

slave: Exodus 21:20.

Hebrew slave: That is the indentured servant of Exodus 21:1–5, treated by the Mishnah as a fully free Israelite, and entitled to full compensation *except* for *lost employment*, which is lost to the master who injured him.

Canaanite slave: A chattel slave, legally unfree and the property of the owner; the injurer is liable to the owner. According to *R. Judah*, payment for, and possibly the moral category of, *shame* does not apply to a slave.

4 A deaf-mute,
a legally incompetent person,
a minor—
hostile contact with them is bad.[36]
One who injures them is liable;
and they, if they injure others, are exempt.
A slave,
a woman[37]—
hostile contact with them is bad.
One who injures them is liable;
and they, if they injure others, are exempt.
But they pay after a time:
If the woman is divorced, if the slave is freed—
they are liable to pay.

5 One who strikes his father or mother and causes a bruise on them,
and one who injures his fellow on the Sabbath—
he is exempt from all of them,
because he is judged for capital punishment.
And one who injures his own Canaanite slave
is exempt from all of them.

6 One who strikes his fellow—
he gives him a *sela*.
R. Judah says in the name of R. Yose the Galilean:
One hundred.
If he slapped him—
he gives him two hundred *zuz*.
With the back of the hand—
he gives him four hundred *zuz*.
If he tore his ear,
plucked his hair,
spat and the spittle reached him,

---

[36] Lit. "a blow of theirs is evil." And so also in the next line.   [37] Or "a wife."

8:4 *deaf-mute…legally incompetent…minor*: See 4:4. These individuals cannot assume responsibility for the injuries that they commit, but one is liable for injury to them.

a woman is assumed to be married and without property that she can dispose of autonomously (cf. *Ketubbot* chapter 8).

after a time implies that the *divorced* woman and the *freed* slave are retroactively liable to pay for damage committed while in an impaired legal state. (The status of women is formulated differently in 1:3.)

8:5 The alternative cases to 8:3: injuries where there the injurer is *judged for capital punishment*; injuring one's own *Canaanite slave* (see Exodus 21:20).

8:6 Unlike 8:1, there are conflicting views at work in this mishnah about quantifying penalties for shame.

R. Judah…R. Yose the Galilean: One hundred: Twenty-five times a *sela*. Since the following rules all involve multiples of one hundred *zuz*, these should perhaps be thought of as continuing the tradition of R. Judah.

removed his cloak from him,
uncovered[38] the head of a woman in the marketplace—
he gives four hundred *zuz*.
This is the rule:[39]
It all follows his honor.
Said R. Aqiva:
Even the poorest of Israel—
one views them
as if they are free people who have lost their property,
for they are the children of Abraham, Isaac, and Jacob.
It happened that a man uncovered a woman's head in the marketplace.
She came before R. Aqiva, and he found him liable to give her four hundred *zuz*.
He said to him: Rabbi, give me time
And he gave him time.
He noticed her standing at the entryway to her courtyard,
and he broke a jar before her containing about an *issar*'s worth of oil.
She bared her head,
and was patting [the spill] and putting the oil on her head.
He set up witnesses against her and came before R. Aqiva.
He said to him:
Rabbi, am I to give this one four hundred *zuz*?
He said to him: You have not said anything:
One who injures himself—
even though he is not permitted, he is exempt;
others who injured him—
are liable.
And one who cuts down his own plantings—
even though he is not permitted, he is exempt;
others who cut down his plantings—
are liable.

7 Even though he gives him [payment], he is not forgiven until he asks [the other] for it,
as it is said: *And now, return the man's wife,*

---

[38] Or "loosened." [39] Lacking in **K, P, C**.

It all follows his honor: While not specifying whose honor serves as the criterion (cf. 8:1), this statement reiterates that payment for shame is on a sliding scale.

R. Aqiva, by contrast, holds that all Israelites are of high status, even if poor. The story that follows has R. Aqiva assign four hundred *zuz* as penalty to *a man* who *uncovered a woman's head*, even though she herself was induced to uncover her own head in public.

give me time, to raise the funds; *issar's worth*, a small amount.

One who injures himself: R. Aqiva's response continues in the form of a standard mishnaic passage.

8:7 *He is not forgiven*, and still subject to divine punishment.

And now, return the man's wife: Genesis 20:7. How the verse serves as a prooftext is not self-evident, but Abraham will pray for Abimelech's life and prevent punishment.

And whence do we know that the one forgiving should not be cruel?
As it is said: *And Abraham prayed to God, and God healed Abimelech.*
One who says:
"Blind my eye; cut off my hand; break my foot"—
he is liable;
"[Do so] on condition that you will be exempt"—
he is liable.
"Tear my garment; break my jar"—
he is liable;
"On condition that you will be exempt"—
he is exempt.
"Do so to such and such a person,
on condition that you will be exempt"—
he is liable,
whether [for injury] to his body or to his property.

Chapter Nine

9:1–10:10 *Robbery*

9 One who robs pieces of wood and made them into utensils,
wool and made it into clothing—
he pays according to the time of the robbery.
If he robbed a pregnant cow and it gave birth,
a ewe ready to be sheared[40] and he sheared it—

[40] Lit. "laden."

And Abraham prayed: Genesis 20:17.

One who says…: Two issues intersect: a distinction between injury to body and to property (see the conclusion), and the ability of the injured party to indemnify the injurer at the outset.

"Blind my eye… break my foot": Bodily damage. The injurer is liable even if the one injured said *on condition that you will be exempt*.

"Tear my garment…": Damage to property. In this case the injured party can indemnify the injurer in advance.

"to such and such a person": In the case of a third party, the injurer is liable in all cases.

9:1 *robs*: "Robbery" (*gezelah*) usually implies force, as opposed to "theft" (*genevah*). This mishnah apparently deals with net increases in value, the one following with net decrease.

wood…wool: The raw material has been transformed from its original state.

he pays the value of a cow about to give birth,[41]
a ewe about to be sheared.
If he robbed a cow and it became pregnant in his possession and gave birth;
a ewe and it became ready to be sheared—
he pays according to the time of the robbery.
This is the rule:
All robbers pay according to the time of the robbery.

2 If he robbed an animal and it grew old;
slaves and they grew old—
he pays according to the time of the robbery.
R. Meir says:
In the case of slaves he says to him:
Here, your property is before you.
If he robbed a coin and it split;
produce and it rotted,
wine and it soured—
he pays according to the time of the robbery.
A coin and it was invalidated;
terumah that became impure;
leaven after Passover;
an animal that was used in the commission of a transgression
or that was invalidated from the altar;

---

[41] K, P, G: "pregnant [and ready] to give birth." C has a variant of the printed versions.

---

cow...ewe: The animals still exist, but have produced new products. Even when the entire pregnancy or growth of wool has taken place in *his*, i.e. the robber's, *possession*, the robber pays only the initial value. The Mishnah appears to rule that appreciation or new products become the possession of the robber (although commentaries differ on this point). The Babylonian Talmud (so too the commentaries) understands the robber to formally come into possession of the stolen property.

9:2 *grew old*: Natural and expected depreciation. Here, too, the robber pays *according to the time of the robbery*.

your property is before you is a standard expression for returning the object itself in its present state rather than its value at some other time (cf. 10:5).

R. Meir permits the robber to return the slave, who although depreciated is still in existence. Most commentaries, following the Babylonian Talmud, view this as peculiar to slaves, as a species of real property that does not transfer formally to the possession of the robber. The Palestinian Talmud refers to traditions that would apply such a ruling to animals as well.

coin and it split: Damage to the object itself.

and it was invalidated: A change in status that more or less erases its value.

leaven after Passover may not be used for any purpose (*Pesahim* 2:2).

animal...transgression: Perhaps in the same status as leaven. Cf. commentaries: no longer valid for sacrifice, which requires some distinction between this case and the following.

invalidated: See *Temurah* 6:5. Here, and perhaps in the preceding, the Mishnah entertains a situation in which an animal's appropriateness for the altar may be relevant to its value to the owner.

or that was being taken out to be stoned—
he says to him:
"Here, your property is before you."

3 If he gave something to artisans to repair and they ruined it—
they are liable to pay.
If he gave a box, chest, or cupboard to a carpenter to repair,
and he ruined it—
he is liable to pay.
The builder who undertook to take down a wall
and smashed the stones or caused damage—
he is liable to pay.
If he was taking it down from one side, and it fell on the other—
he is exempt;
but if it was due to the striking—
he is liable.

4 He gave wool to the dyer, and the cauldron burnt it—
he gives him the value of his wool;
if he dyed it badly:
if the appreciation was greater than the outlay—
he gives him the outlay;
if the outlay was greater than the appreciation—
he gives him the appreciation.

taken out to be stoned: See also 4:8.

In all these cases the robber is entitled to say "*Here, your property is before you,*" i.e. to return the property itself.

9:3 The connection between the next two mishnahs and the preceding is damage or change of state to goods in another's possession. Unlike 9:1–2, the Mishnah does not explicitly consider the price at the time of the goods were entrusted to artisans. Most commentaries, following the Babylonian Talmud, again consider whether there has been some binding transfer of possession that affects the standing of the artisan.

artisans…and they ruined goods that needed repair, they *are liable to pay*.

carpenter: An illustrative case; *box, chest, or cupboard*, a common triad of storage objects.

undertook: Perhaps a technical term for a contract in which the owner supplies raw material (cf. *Bava Metsiʿa* 5:4, 6; chapter 9). The artisan is liable for damage he caused, extending to the breaking of building stones.

it fell on the other: Presumably, the wall was being removed because it was a falling hazard. But if it fell *due to the striking*, i.e. as a direct result of the builder's activities, the builder *is liable*.

9:4 *dyer, and the cauldron burnt it*: Singed it or otherwise made it unusable; the dyer repays *value of his wool*. If it was *dyed badly*, the Mishnah considers both *appreciation* in the value of the wool and artisan's *outlay*. The owner is guaranteed the original value along with any increase, less the dyer's expenses. When *appreciation was greater than outlay*, the owner receives the dyed wool, and fully compensates the dyer's expenses. When *outlay was greater*, the owner repays only the increase in value of the wool, and the artisan takes a loss.

[If he gave the wool] to have it dyed red and he dyed it black,
black and he died it red—
R. Meir says:
He gives him the value of his wool;
R. Judah says:
If the appreciation was greater than the outlay—
he gives him the outlay;
if the outlay was greater than the appreciation—
he gives him the appreciation.

5 One who robs his fellow the value of a *perutah* and swore to him—
he must take it to him even to Media.
He may not give it either to his son or to his agent;
but he may give it to the agent of the court.
And if he died, he must give it to his heirs.

6 If he gave him the principal but did not give him the added fifth;
If he forgave him the principal but did not forgive him the added fifth;
If he forgave him this and this
except for less than a *perutah*'s worth of the principal—
he need not follow after him.
If he gave him the added fifth but did not give him the principal;
If he forgave him the added fifth but did not forgive him the principal;
If he forgave him this and this except for a *perutah*'s worth of the principal—
he must follow after him.

7 If he gave him the principal, and he swore to him about the added fifth—
in this case he pays a fifth on the added fifth, until the principal is less than a *perutah*.

---

red and he dyed it black: Here, there was no damage as such, but failure to comply with the contract. According to *R. Meir*, the dyer compensates the owner for *the value of his wool* alone, and any loss or gain accrues to the dyer (cf. the case of the robber in 9:1–2); according to *R. Judah*, gains accrue to the owner, and losses to the dyer.

9:5 See Leviticus 5:21–26, also Numbers 5:5–10. The biblical passages require that a robbery (or other misappropriation) denied by an oath be returned, supplemented by a charge of an additional fifth, and that the robber bring a guilt offering (*Zevahim*, introduction).

perutah: A small coin. Often a minimum standard for a value to have legal significance (cf. *Bava Metsi'a* 4:1).

and swore to him, denying that he owed the owner anything.

even to Media: A region of western Iran; here the expression means roughly "to the ends of the earth."

not…to his, i.e. the owner's *son or his agent*, but to the owner himself or herself (see Leviticus 5:24; compare *Bava Metsi'a* 8:3, where no robbery or oath is involved). However, a *court* may designate an agent to receive the property on behalf of the owner and deliver it. *If he died*, cf. Numbers 5:8.

9:6 *he gave him the principal*: Two series of hypothetical cases to illustrate the law in 9:5. First, the Mishnah does not obligate the robber to follow *after him* "to Media" when the principal is paid, or is *less than a perutah's worth*.

he gave him the added fifth: In this second series, the principal has not been paid, or *a perutah's worth* remains unpaid.

9:7 *he gave him the principal*: A third illustrative situation: the robber under oath denied owing the added fifth, generating a new obligation of a fifth of the fifth. This situation can repeat itself until *the principal is less than a perutah*.

And so with a deposit,
as it is said: *In the case of a deposit,*[42] *or misappropriation*[43] *or robbery or oppressing one's fellow, or if he found a lost object and denied it and swore falsely—*
in this case, this one pays the principal, the added fifth, and a guilt offering.
[If the owner demanded:] "Where is my deposit?"
And he said: "It was lost,
I adjure you,"
and he said: "So be it,"
and the witnesses testify that he consumed it—
he pays the principal.
If he admitted on his own—
he pays the principal, and the added fifth, and the guilt offering.

8 "Where is my deposit?"
And he said: "It was stolen,
I adjure you,"
and he said: "So be it,"
and the witnesses testify that he stole it—
he pays the double payment.
If he admitted on his own—
he pays the principal, and the added fifth, and the guilt offering.

9 One who robs his father and swears to him, and he died—
in this case, he pays the principal and added fifth to his sons or his brothers.
And if he does not wish to or he does not have it—
he may borrow and the creditors come and exact payment.

[42] "As ... deposit" lacking in **K, P, C, G**, and others.   [43] Lit. "reaching out the hand."

In the second half of 9:7 discussion turns to the case of deposit, also dealt with in Leviticus 5:21–26. A *deposit* is an object given to a guardian for safekeeping. The formulation is distinct from 9:5–7, in that it is concerned with obligation for *principal ... added fifth ... and guilt offering.*

a deposit: Leviticus 5:21. For the rules of deposit see *Bava Metsi'a* chapter 3 and 7:8.

"Where is my deposit?" A slightly different version of this passage and 9:8 appears in *Shevu'ot* 8:3. Mini-dialogues involving adjuration are also at *Shevu'ot* 3:11; 5:2, 4–5; 8:2, 5–6.

It was lost: An unpaid guardian is exempt in a case of "loss" (e.g. where an animal wandered off although the guardian took precautions, *Bava Metsi'a* 7:8; *Shevu'ot* 8:1); in this case, the guardian appropriated the deposit, and affirmed that under oath. The Mishnah takes the Bible's rule of added fifth and sacrifice to apply only when *he admitted on his own* (see Numbers 5:7). If *witnesses testify* proving the guardian's guilt, the guardian pays only the principal.

9:8 *It was stolen*: Again, the guardian would be exempt in this case. When *witnesses testify* to the guardian's guilt, the guardian owes *the double payment*. But if *he admitted on his own*, the guardian pays *the added fifth, and the guilt offering.*

9:9 *robs his father and swears to him*: cf. 9:5; *and he died*, and the son wishes to make restitution.

his sons or his brothers: Some commentaries take this to this to mean the father's sons or (in the absence of sons) brothers who would inherit from him; others the robber's sons or brothers. According to either view, the robber must cede the property that he took from his father to an eventual heir of the father in his own absence.

does not wish to give it to his (or his father's) sons or brothers, *or does not have*, i.e. sons or brothers; others, sufficient funds. The robber *may borrow*, and allow the *creditors* to *exact payment* from the father's property

10 One who says to his son: "*Qonam* lest you benefit from me"[44]—
if he died, he may inherit from him.
[If the vow explicitly stated] in his life and in his death[45]—
if he died, he may not inherit from him,
and he must return [his inheritance][46] to his sons or his brothers.
And if he does not have—
he may borrow and the creditors come and exact payment.

11 One who robs a proselyte and swore to him, and then died—
in this case he pays the principal and the added fifth to the priests
and the guilt offering to the altar,
as it is said: *If the man has no redeemer to whom to return the restitution,*
the restitution that is returned belongs to the Lord, to the priest,
in addition to the ram of atonement through which atonement is made for him.
If he was bringing the money and guilt offering up [to the Temple] and he died—
the money is to be returned to his sons,
and the ram of the guilt offering is to graze until it is defiled,
and then it is to be sold and its proceeds are to become[47]
a donation to the Temple.

[44] **K, P, G**: "*Qonam* is that which you benefit from me."
[45] In **K, P**, and others: "in my life and in my death" (continuing the father's oath formula).
[46] For "return" **K, P, C, G** have "give."   [47] Lit. "fall."

---

that the robber possesses. (So Maimonides. Others have the robber use borrowed funds to pay the sons or brothers, with the creditors collecting all or part of the debt from the robbed-and-returned property.)

9:10 "*Qonam*": A circumlocution for *qorban*, "sacrifice," marking the undertaking of a vow, that restricts benefit (*Nedarim* 1:2 and introduction). According to the reading in the manuscripts (see n. 45), the father dedicates as sacrifice, and thus prohibits, any benefit that the son might receive from him. The vow lapses at death, and the son *may inherit*.

and in his death, explicitly extending the vow beyond the father's death, so *he may not inherit*.

return: This implies that *his sons or his brothers* refers to the father's relations (see 9:9). However, the manuscript reading "give" (see n. 46) does not have that implication, and may even suggest the opposite.

If he does not have: See 9:9. Analogously, rather than give away the inheritance, the son may borrow, and the creditor may exact payment from the actual inheritance that the son must not possess. Note that this mishnah lacks "does not wish to."

9:11 A proselyte is assumed to die without heirs; cf. 4:7; 5:4.

robs… and swore: Cf. 9:5. Numbers 5:8, quoted, is the justification for the Mishnah's rules.

priests: And it becomes their lay property.

to the altar: For sacrifice, as distinct from the property of the Temple.

has no redeemer: Close agnate kinsman to stand in for him or his property (cf. Leviticus 25:25–26; Numbers 35; Deuteronomy 19:6, 12; Ruth 3:12; 4:1–12). While the Mishnah lacks the kin structure assumed by the biblical passages, it takes a proselyte to be such a person (but cf. Leviticus 25:47–49).

restitution: i.e. including the added fifth.

he, the robber, *died* before making restitution.

returned to the robber's *sons*, as his heirs (cf. 10:1). The animal was designated as a sacrifice for a designated person and purpose but cannot be offered for that purpose. It is *allowed to graze until it is defiled*, and then sold.

12 If he gave the money to members of the priestly course, and then died—
the heirs may not remove it from their hands,
as it is said: *Whatever the man gives to the priest, it will be his.*
If he gave the money to Jehoiarib and the guilt offering to Jedaiah—
he has fulfilled his obligation;
the guilt offering to Jehoiarib and the money to Jedaiah—
if the guilt offering has not been offered,[48]
the members of Jedaiah offer it;
but if not, he must return it,[49] and bring another guilt offering.
for one who brings his restitution[50] before he brought his guilt offering
has fulfilled his obligation;
if he brought his guilt offering before he brought his restitution,
he has not fulfilled his obligation.
If he gave the principal but did not give the added fifth—
the added fifth does not hinder.

Chapter Ten

10 One who robs and feeds it to his sons[51]
or left[52] it to them—
they are exempt from paying;

---

[48] Lit. "is still in existence." [49] K, P, C, G: "he goes back." [50] Lit. "his robbery."
[51] Or "children." [52] Or "bequeathed."

9:12 *priestly course*: Heb. *mishmar*, that is, the subdivision of priests then in service. Priests were divided into twenty-four hereditary "courses" (literally, "watches," 1 Chronicles 24; *Ta'anit* 4:2), which each served for one week.

died, not having offered the sacrifice. Since the restitution was delivered to the priests, *the heirs* may not reclaim it as in 9:11.

Whatever the man gives: Numbers 5:10.

Jehoiarib…Jedaiah: The first and second "courses" respectively (1 Chronicles 24:7), so that the restitution of the money preceded the sacrifice. If he gave the *guilt offering to Jehoiarib*, i.e. preceding delivery of the property, but it *has not been offered*, it can be offered since the property has been given, that is by *Jedaiah*. If the sacrificial animal has been offered, another animal should be offered.

return: The reading of the manuscripts, "goes back," is preferable. According to the reading *return*, the priests return the property, and the robber brings them back together with a new sacrifice.

one who brings: Perhaps a legal aphorism.

fifth does not hinder: While return of the robbery must precede the sacrifice, the added fifth need not.

10:1 *feeds it to his sons*, so that it is the children who consumed it, *or left it* as inheritance, so that the sons now own it.

exempt, because the robbery was not committed by them.

but if it was something for which he is accountable—
they are required to pay.
One may not change currency either from the chest of the excise collectors
or from the pouch of the tax collectors,
and one may not receive charity from them;
but he may receive from him from his house or the marketplace.

2 If excise collectors seized his ass
and gave him another ass,
if brigands robbed his clothing
and gave him other clothing—
these are his,
because the owners have despaired of them.
One who salvages from a river, or from troops,[53] or from brigands—
if the owners have despaired, then they are his.
And so too a swarm of bees—
if the owners have despaired, then they are his.
Said R. Yohanan b. Beroqa:
A woman or minor is believed to say:
"This swarm came from here."
And he may walk in his fellow's field to save his swarm,

[53] Troops absent in **K**, **P**, **G**; present in **C** in a different order.

---

for which he is accountable: Lit. "that have security"; for another use of the term see 7:4. In connection to contracts, the phrase typically refers to land used to secure a loan, from which creditors may exact payment even if the property has been alienated.

required: Because the owner's claim on the land continues to apply.

One may not change currency: The topic now abruptly shifts to tax collection as state robbery, and the concept of despair. Taxation and seizure of property (see 10:5 below) are among the very few circumstances in which the Mishnah acknowledges the Roman administrative regime.

change currency: Since money was metal, and notions like letters of credit or checks were limited in application, people needed moneychangers or other specialists either to provide small coin or to bulk small amounts into larger coins for longer travel or larger purchases (e.g. *Bava Metsi'a* 4:6, *Ma'aser Sheni* 4:2).

excise collectors…tax collectors: Two distinct kinds of tax collectors. The assumption is that money in the hands of tax collectors in their official capacity is by definition stolen.

his house or the marketplace: That is from the collector as an individual, even though taxation is his source of income.

10:2 *seized his ass*: What is imagined is that the state requisitioned an *ass* for labor or some other purpose but returned an animal that presumably belonged to another; similarly, a case involving *brigands*. The ass or the clothing are presumed stolen, but he may possess them (*they are his*), *because the owners have despaired* of ever receiving them back and have relinquished ownership.

salvages property; *swarm of bees* that create a hive on one's property. In both cases, the property belonged to another. One may possess the property *if the owners have despaired*, but no criterion is given for determining this. According to R. Yohanan b. Beroqa, *a woman or minor is believed*, that is, we relax the rules of evidence in determining the source of the bees.

he, the owner of the hive, *may walk*, i.e. follow the swarm through another's *field*, and is exempt from liability for incidental damage caused. The owner may not *cut off his* fellow's *tree limb* on which the swarm

and if he damages, he pays what he damages,
but he may not cut off his tree limb on condition of giving him the value.
R. Ishmael the son of R. Yohanan b. Beroqa says:
He may even[54] cut and give the value.

3 One who recognizes his utensils or his books in the hands of another,
and he is already known to have suffered a theft[55]—
the buyer swears to him how much he gave,
and he takes it.
But if not—
it is not in his power to do so,
for I say: He sold them to another, and this one bought them from him.

4 One comes with a jug of wine and the other comes with a jar of honey.
If the jar of honey cracked,
and this one poured out his wine and salvaged the honey in [the wine jar]—
he has a claim only to compensation for his labor;[56]
but if he said:
"I will salvage yours and you give me the value of mine"—
he must give it to him.
If a river swept away his ass and his fellow's ass;
his is worth one hundred and his fellow's is worth two hundred:
if this one abandoned his own and salvaged his fellow's—
he has only a claim to compensation for his labor;
but if he said: "I will salvage yours and you give me the value of mine"—
he must give it to him.

---

[54] Lacking in **K, P, C, G**.
[55] Lit. "And the name [i.e. reputation] of theft has gone out about him in the village."
[56] Lit. "he has a claim only to his wage."

---

settled, even stipulating that he will repay the owner of the tree. This is presumably more serious than the damage envisioned in the preceding sentence.

R. Ishmael, the son of R. Yohanan b. Beroqa rules that this, too, is permitted.

10:3 *in the hands of another*, who claims to have bought them, and the victim is *already* publicly *known to have suffered a theft*. Although the *buyer* can be forced to give up the property, absent proof of the purchase the buyer may *swear* to the amount of the purchase *and take* that amount in compensation from the owner (cf. *Shevu'ot* 7:4).

But if not: If the alleged theft was not public knowledge, the victim cannot demand the goods back, even with compensation.

for I say: Marks a reasonable presumption, in this case that the owner was not the victim of a robbery at all.

10:4 Receiving compensation, when one sacrificed one's own property to help another.

One comes: Cf. 3:4–5.

honey…wine: The assumption is that honey is more expensive than wine; cf. the following example.

compensation for his labor: The owner of the wine can claim only a modest amount for the time invested (cf., e.g., 8:1; *Bava Metsi'a* 2:9).

but if he said: "I will salvage," i.e. stipulated at the outset, the owner of the honey *must give* him the value of the wine.

river swept away his ass: An analogous case. River-induced damage appears occasionally (10:2, and below; *Bava Metsi'a* 8:5). In this case the difference between the two parties' property is made explicit. Again, the party that voluntarily gave up property to help the other is entitled only to *labor*, modest compensation for time and effort, unless the alternative arrangement was made explicitly in advance.

5 One who robs a field from his fellow, and oppressors seized it,
if the blow was to the whole region—
he says to him: "Here your property is before you";
but if it was due to the robber—
he must provide him with another field.
If a river swept it away—
he says to him: "Here your property is before you."

6 One who robs his fellow,
or who borrowed from him,
or who had on deposit:[57]
in a settlement—
he may not return it to him in the wilderness;
on condition that he take it to the wilderness—
he may return it to him in the wilderness.

7 One who says to his fellow:
"I robbed you,"
"you lent to me,"
"you deposited with me,"
and "I do not know if I returned it to you or if I did not return it to you"—
he is liable to pay;
but if he said to him:
"I do not know if I robbed you,"
"if you lent to me,"
"if you deposited with me"[58]—
he is exempt from paying.

---

[57] Lit. "[the owner] deposited with him."
[58] K, P, C, G lack "if he said to him"; and add at the end "or if you did not deposit with me."

10:5 *and oppressors seized* the field from the robber. Presumably, these are agents of the government. There may be a general confiscation of property (a *blow...to the whole region*, see too *Bava Metsia* 9:6), or penalizing the robber in particular (*due to the robber*). In the former case the robber may direct the owner to recover the field (*your property is before you*, see 9:5; the expression may reflect sarcasm here). In the latter case, the robber *must provide him with another field*.

a river: A natural occurrence corresponding to a general confiscation. Again, *your property is before you* may carry some sarcasm with it.

10:6 The owner of the property can generally set some conditions on where another repays the property.

robs...borrowed...had on deposit: The three are equivalent in that they involve restitution to the owner (cf. *Bava Metsia* 3:3–4).

in a settlement: If the initial obligation was created in a settled area, the owner cannot be forced to receive payment *in the wilderness*.

on condition that he take it to the wilderness: The initial transaction involved the borrower or guardian taking the property out to the wilderness (e.g. to graze), in which case the owner may be constrained. Alternatively, the owner stipulated payment in the wilderness. (The Babylonian Talmud and most commentaries reject the latter interpretation as obvious.)

10:7 *he is liable to pay*, since the robber admits to the obligation. Both Talmudim cite an amoraic tradition that treats this liability as a "heavenly" one, but not an obligation under the law.

I do not know if I robbed: The speaker is in doubt about whether there is an obligation at all; in this case, *he is exempt*. For the consequences of self-attestation and doubt cf. *Bava Metsia* 3:3; *Yevamot* 15:6.

8 One who stole a lamb from the flock and returned it,
and it died or was stolen—
he is accountable for it.
If the owners did not know either of its theft or its return,
and they counted the flock and it was complete—
he is exempt.

9 One does not buy wool or milk or kids from shepherds,
nor wood or produce from the guardians of produce;
but one may buy from women woolen garments in Judah,[59]
flax garments in the Galilee,
and calves in Sharon.
And all of them, if they said to hide them—
it is prohibited.
And one may buy eggs and fowl in any place.

10 Tufts that the launderer removes—
in this case, these belong to him;
but that the comber removes—
in this case, these belong to the householder.

[59] K, P, and C lack "woolen . . . Judah."

10:8 *stole*; theft is characterized by stealth rather than violence, as in the case of robbery. *Returned it*, from the continuation, presumably without the owner's knowledge, although the owner does know about the theft. The thief is *accountable for it* if something should happen to it. When the owner was not aware of either *its theft or its return*, the thief is exempt from subsequent damage.

they counted: There was an opportunity for the owner to verify that the flock was whole.

10:9 *shepherds* are assumed to be agents, not owners, as are *guardians of produce*; the presumption is that anything they sell is stolen from their employers. By contrast, goods bought *from women, flax garments in the Galilee* (and, according to some readings, *woolen garments in Judah*), and *calves in Sharon*, the coastal plain and foothills south of Haifa, are not under such a presumption. Note the assumption of economic regionalism in this text. The Mishnah's rule may assume that women sell these goods as part of the economic activity managed by a husband (in *Ketubbot* 9:3, "a husband sets up his wife as shopkeeper"), or of her own autonomous economic activity as a divorced or widowed, or even married women (e.g. *Ketubbot* 5:9, when a husband does not provide spending money).

to hide them: To not reveal the source of the goods; the woman is then presumed to be appropriating her husband's property.

10:10 The connection of this passage to 10:9 is not clear. It may have to do with raw material (in this case in the hands of the artisan), or with the textile work mentioned in both passages. That the owner might dismiss small leftover or waste material is also related to "despair," a form of presumed renunciation.

launderer: The passage seems to progress from raw wool, to woven wool, to sewing. Here, *launderer* appears to be the washer of raw wool. Small amounts that are left behind may be taken up by the washer. A *carder* uses combs to pull the fibers into alignment so that they can be spun. In this case tufts of loose wool go to the *householder*, perhaps because they can be aggregated with other wool and recombed or because there is a lot of such "waste."

launderer: Perhaps of newly woven fabric.

The launderer may remove three threads and they belong to him;
more than this—
in that case they belong to the householder.
If there was black thread [woven] over the white,[60]
he takes them all and they are his.
The tailor who left sufficient thread to be able to sew with it,
or[61] a piece of fabric that is three by three—
in this case these are the householder's.[62]
That which the carpenter removes with a plane—
in this case these belong to him;
but with a hatchet—
these belong to the householder.
And if he was working at the premises of the householder—
even the sawdust belongs to the householder.

[60] Lit. "If the black (**K, P, C** lack "the") was over the white (**K, P, C** lack "the")."
[61] **K, P, C, G** lack "or" so that "piece of fabric" is the object of "sew."
[62] **K, P, C, G**: "He must return it to the owners" for: "in this case these are the householder's."

three threads... more than this: More than a negligible number of loose threads must be returned to the *householder*.

black... over the white: An obvious flaw in the weave?

The tailor: For this clause, see n. 61; according to the reading of the manuscripts there is only one case: enough thread to sew a small piece of fabric.

plane... hatchet: The former makes fine, negligible wood waste, which the carpenter can keep; the latter large chips, which belong to the *householder*. If the work took place *on the premises of the householder*, the householder even has a claim to the sawdust.

Tractate Bava Metsi'a

Hayim Lapin

Introduction

Overview

Bava Metsi'a ("middle gate" in Aramaic); some manuscripts designate this tractate *Bava Tinyana* ("the second gate"). The tractate was originally the second part of a larger tractate *Neziqin* ("damages") on civil law (see *Bava Qamma*, introduction).

Structure and Organization of the Tractate

Bava Metsi'a is generally structured in blocks of traditions by subject matter, for example hiring contracts (6:1–9:10). However, there is no clear organizing principle for the order of the blocks of material, or for where individual traditions appear. For instance, deposits are dealt with in chapter 3, but important traditions also appear in 6:6–8, and 7:8–10. At least one cluster of passages appears to be a miscellany (10:4–6). Traditions about some contracts share a common formula, "one who..." (e.g. 3:1–12; 5:1–2; 6:1–5, 7:1–2, 7; 8:1–9:10). In Hebrew, the parallels are built around participial phrases. In two cases, otherwise unrelated topics that appear together in the Torah appear together here (2:9–11; 9:11–13, see below).

Main Ideas

Acquisition of, or care for, lost objects is treated first (1:1–2:11), and the discussion incorporates a passage about caring for a struggling animal. Deposits make up chapter 3. Chapter 4 deals with sale, including wrongful overcharge or underpayment (4:3–9), as well as wrongful speech (4:10) and other rules related to fair practices (4:11). Chapter 5 treats prohibited interest (5:1–3), which extends to types of contracts and practices that result in prohibited gain (5:4–11). The large group of traditions concerning "hire" discusses artisans (6:1–2); animals (6:3–5); day laborers, with specific emphasis on their right to eat in the fields while working (7:1–7); loans for use (8:1–3); lease of houses (8:6-9); and tenant farming (9:1–10). The final sections are about a worker's wage (9:11–12) and pledges (9:13), and disputes over property (10:1–4). This last section marks the transition to real property, dealt with in *Bava Batra*.

Money and markets underlie a number of significant issues in this tractate. Goods are expected to have a market price at any given time, so that one can rescind a sale on the claim of overcharge or underpayment. The definition of sale requires exchange of coin for goods, and the Mishnah attempts to fit barter into this pattern (4:1–2). Similarly, the idea of goods fluctuating in price against coin means that even simple neighborly transactions can potentially be usurious (5:9). Concern with market price further underlies what 5:1 apparently prohibits as "increase" (*tarbit*), an array of investments of capital or prepayment for delayed delivery that might result in unlawful increase for the lender (5:4–10). *Neshekh*, by contrast, refers to the direct charging of interest (5:1).

Perhaps the most interesting set of issues arises around guardians. As noted, the Mishnah reframes the rules of Exodus 22:6–14 around payment. It also adds the category of renter, not explicitly addressed in that passage (7:8). The liability of unpaid or paid guardians is used in turn as a measure of liability in other types of cases (e.g. 6:6–7; see also 2:7).

Relationship to Scripture

Bava Metsi'a demonstrates the complicated relationship between early rabbinic and Torah law. In some cases topics that appear together in the Torah appear together in the tractate. Scripture is the source for key terminology, such as *ona'ah* (literally, "oppression") for wrongful overcharge (e.g. Leviticus 25:17), *neshekh* and *tarbit* for forms of interest on loans (e.g. Leviticus 25:35), or classification of types of damage to property while in the care of another (Exodus 22:6–14). In all of these cases, the Mishnah extends the laws far beyond the biblical verses themselves, treating, for instance, possible permitted and prohibited investments and agricultural contracts (5:4–10). In the Torah, neither the prohibition of overcharge nor the permission for a worker eating in the fields, which the Mishnah attributes to the Torah (7:2; see Deuteronomy 23:25–26; 25:4), appears explicitly. The discussion of deposits in Exodus 22:6–12 makes a primary distinction between deposits of money and animals, but the Mishnah, while clearly utilizing biblical terminology, assumes a distinction between paid and unpaid guardians (7:8).

Special Notes for the Reader

See introduction to *Bava Qamma*. With respect to **C**, see the General Introduction.

Tractate Bava Metsi'a

Chapter One

1:1–2 *Lost Objects: Competing Claims to Found Objects*

1 Two people are holding a cloak:
this one says: "I found it,"
and this one says: "I found it";
[or] this one says: "It is all mine,"
and this one says: "It is all mine"—
this one swears that no less than half of it belongs to him,
and this one swears that no less than half of it belongs to him,
and they split it.
This one says: "It is all mine,"
and this one says: "Half of it is mine"—
the one who says: "It is all mine,"
swears that no less than three parts of it belong to him,
and the one who says: "Half of it is mine,"
swears that no less than one quarter of it belongs to him,
this one takes three parts, and this one takes one quarter.
  2 If two were riding on an animal,
or one was riding and one was leading:
this one says: "It is all mine,"

1:1 *Two people are holding a cloak*: Each claims to have found the object and to own it, but neither has full possession.

"It is all mine": Following the Bavli, most commentaries view this statement as introducing a different dispute (e.g. each claims to have acquired the object by purchase).

swears: In the absence of evidence, the parties must swear to their claim to *no less than half*, and the parties *split* the object (see e.g. *Bava Qamma* 5:1, below 8:4–5; for the oath, *Shevu'ot* 6:1).

"It is all mine"…"Half of it is mine": The one who claims only half is considered to concede the claim of the other party to the other half. Consequently, both the oaths and the assignment of the property divide into *three parts* and *one quarter*.

1:2 *two were riding…one was leading*: Their actions demonstrate ownership of the animal. The Bavli and commentaries understand *riding* and *leading* to be acts that convey ownership (see *Qiddushin* chapter 1 and below 1:3–4).

and this one says: "It is all mine"—
this one swears that no less than half of it belongs to him,
and this one swears that no less than half of it belongs to him,
and they split it.
If they concede or if they have witnesses, they split without an oath.

1:3–5   Lost Objects: Acquiring Ownership of a Lost Object

3 If one was riding on an animal and saw a found object,
and said to his fellow: "Give it to me"—
if he took it and said: "I have gained ownership of it,"
he has gained ownership of it;
if after he gave it to him he said: "I gained ownership of it first"—
his claim is not valid.[1]

4 If he saw the found object and fell upon it and another came and grasped it—
the one who grasped it has gained ownership of it.
He saw them running after the found object,
after an injured gazelle, after unfledged young birds,
and he said: "My field has gained ownership of it for me"—
it has gained ownership for him.
If it was a gazelle running in its typical manner,
or if they were young birds that were fledged,
and he said: "My field has gained ownership of it for me"—
his claim is not valid.[2]

[1] Lit. "He has not said anything."   [2] Lit. "He has not said anything."

If they concede: Presumably this qualifies both 1:1 and 1:2. Concession (e.g. "We found it at the same time") or the presence of witnesses means that *they split without an oath.*

1:3–4 Ownership generally cannot be gained simply by a statement reflecting intention to acquire, but may require an act of taking possession.

1:4 *one was riding...and said to his fellow*: The Mishnah assigns ownership to the rider, who now holds the lost object. The one who picked it up cannot now claim *"I gained ownership of it first."* Implicitly, had the latter held on to it, his claim to ownership would have been supported.

1:4 *fell...grasped*: The claim of the one who grasped the object is stronger.

He saw them running: The owner of a field states his intention to preempt other potential claimants and to acquire the property through its presence in the field.

an injured gazelle...unfledged young birds will stop for a time in the field, which *has gained ownership for him*. A healthy gazelle or *young birds that were fledged* pass through or over the field, so the field owner's *claim is not valid.*

5 That which his minor son or daughter finds,
that which his Canaanite male slave or female slave finds,
that which his wife finds—
in this case these are his.
That which his adult son or daughter finds,
that which his Hebrew male slave or female slave finds,
that which his divorced wife finds, even if he has not given her *ketubbah*—
in this case these are theirs.

1:6–8 Lost Objects: Found Documents

6 If he found loan documents:
if they include a statement of security[3]—
he may not return them,
for the court exacts payment on their basis;[4]
if they do not include a statement of security,
he must return them,
for the court does not exact payment on their basis—
the words of R. Meir.
But the Sages say:
In either case, he may not return them,
for the court exacts payment on their basis.

---

[3] Lit. "If they include security of property."   [4] Absent in **K, P, C**.

1:5 *minor son...these are his*: The individuals in the first group lack full legal personhood and the capacity to acquire the found property in their own right. What they find belongs to the householder. By contrast, the members of the second group do have such rights: what they find belongs to themselves. (According to a tradition in the Bavli, followed by the commentaries, adult children who are dependent on their fathers are "minors" in this respect; cf. 7:6.)

Canaanite slave is chattel, the property of the owner; a *Hebrew slave* is a free but indentured Israelite (*Bava Qamma* 8:3).

1:6 The Mishnah prohibits finders from returning private deeds to their apparent owners (1:6–7), because this might give the holders rights they have not acquired (if the deed was not actually delivered) or no longer have (if they record an obligation subsequently paid). However, documents recording an act of a court are returned (1:8).

loan documents...if they include a statement of security: A clause that guaranteed the lender payment "from what I possess and what I might acquire" (see *Bava Qamma* 7:4). According to R. Meir, *he should not return* these, since a *court* might *exact payment on the basis* of the document. According to the *Sages*, security does not need to be specified in the deed for a *court* to *exact payment*, so the document should not be returned in any case. The concern is that the debt may have already been paid, or perhaps never completed (1:7). The Bavli and commentaries raise the additional concern that the lender and borrower might collude to seize property formerly belonging to the borrower, but now sold to a new owner.

7 If he found divorce documents,[5] emancipations of slaves,
a testament, a gift, or receipts—
in this case, he may not return them,
for I say:
They were written,
and he changed his mind so as not to give them.
8 If he found letters of assessment, letters guaranteeing maintenance,
documents of *halitsah* or of refusal,
documents of selection, or any act of a court—
in this case, he must return them.
If he found a bundle of documents
or a tied bunch of documents in a bag or a chest—
in this case, he must return them.
And how many is a "bundle of documents"?
Three tied to one another.
Rabban Simeon b. Gamaliel says:
One borrowing from three—
he must return it to the borrower;
three borrowing from one—

[5] Lit. "deeds of women."

1:7 *divorce documents* and *emancipations* document change of status from bound to unbound. The word translated "document," *get*, is most commonly used in connection with divorce documents, but can refer to documents more generically (*Bava Batra* 10:1–2).

testament: *Bava Batra* 8:6.

receipts: *Bava Batra* 10:6; in context, perhaps specifically a divorce settlement, cf. *Ketubbot* 9:9; *Gittin* 2:5, 8:8; *Bava Batra* 10:3.

for I say: This formula introduces a presumption.

they were written, and he changed his mind, and the transaction represented by the deed was never put into effect.

1:8 *If he found… or any act of a court*: The documents are all the result of court actions (cf. *Mo'ed Qatan* 3:3). *Letters of assessment*, assessing the property entailed to a creditor (Maimonides, Rashi) or inherited by a minor (Yerushalmi); *maintenance*, support of a widow within her husband's household; *halitsah*, the ritual that severs the ties between a childless widow and her husband's brother (see *Yevamot* 12:1, 6); *refusal*, a minor orphan daughter's refusal of marriage contracted by her brother or mother (see *Yevamot* chapter 13); *selection*, of judges in a civil case (*Sanhedrin* 3:1).

he must return them: It is presumed that these were written and executed, and are either in force or serve as documentary evidence.

a bundle… in a bag or a chest: The commentaries see two separate cases here: (1) documents in a bag or container; and (2) bound documents. They give the rationale (raised in the Bavli) that the bundles or bags have distinguishing marks that allow the owner to identify the documents (see 2:5, 7). Neither is clear in the Mishnah itself, and the following discussion suggests that what is at issue is the identity of the presumptive owner.

Three tied…: This sentence comments on and defines the preceding. *Rabban Simeon b. Gamaliel* further specifies that the identity of the presumptive owner may differ depending on what the documents say.

he must return it to the lender.
If he found a document among his documents,
and he does not know what its nature is—
let it be left until Elijah comes.
If there are among them agreements,
he does what is in the agreements.

Chapter Two

2:1–6 Lost Objects: Obligations of the Finder: Proclaiming the Lost Object

2 These found objects belong to him, and these he is obligated to proclaim.
These found objects are his:
if he found scattered produce, scattered money, loaves in the public domain,
rounds of figs, bakers' loaves, strings of fish, cuts of meat,
shearings of wool as they come from the countryside,[6]
stalks of flax, or tongues of purple—
in this case these are his—
the words of R. Meir.[7]

---

[6] Lit. "that come from their territory." One **G** fragment has "that come from anywhere," replaced with our text in the margins.
[7] Absent in **K, P, C, G**

---

he found...does not know: Although the verb "found" is the same, the discussion is about a *document among* one's own *documents*.

its nature: e.g. whether a lender or borrower deposited it with him (Rashi).

left, i.e. set aside, *until Elijah comes* in the messianic age to resolve uncertainties. Cf. 2:8; 3:4, 5, and see *Eduyot* 8:7.

agreements: Documents specifying what is to be done with the deeds in question (Maimonides); in that case the householder does *what is in the agreements*.

2:1–6 The Mishnah requires finders to proclaim a found object so that its owner may recover it. This section outlines the limits of this responsibility: some objects must be proclaimed; others can be appropriated as ownerless; and still others must be left in place for the loser to recover.

2:1 *these...and these.* Alternatively, these are interrogatives: "Which...belong to him? And which is he obligated to proclaim?"

scattered...these are his. The items listed are not distinctive (see 2:5), or, if distinctive are not unique to a particular owner, so that the owner cannot identify the object.

from the countryside: The expression is difficult to translate (cf. 2:2); translation follows Rashi.

Some witnesses omit *the words of R. Meir* (see n. 7). The preceding does not clearly disagree with the following statement of R. Judah.

R. Judah says:
Anything that has been altered he must proclaim.
How?
If he found a round of figs with a shard in it, a loaf with coins in it.
R. Simeon b. Eleazar says:
Anything that is conventionally traded[8] he is not obligated to proclaim.
  2 And these he is obligated to proclaim:
if he found produce in a utensil or a utensil by itself,
money in a pouch or a pouch by itself,
clusters of produce, clusters of money, three coins on top of one another,
loaves in the private domain, homemade loaves,[9]
shearings of wool as they are bought from the artisan's house,
jars of wine, or jars of oil—
in this case, he is obligated to proclaim them.
  3 If he found tied birds behind the partition or behind the fence,
or on the paths that are in the fields—
in this case, he may not touch them.
If he found a utensil in the dungheap:
if it is covered—
he may not touch it;
if it is uncovered—
he takes it and proclaims.
If he found something in a rubble heap or in an old wall,
in this case, these are his.
If he found it in a new wall—
from its midpoint outward, it is his;
from its midpoint inward, it belongs to the householder.
If he would lease it out to others,
even if it was found inside the house—
in this case, they are his.

[8] Lit. "utensils (or vessels, garments) of trade."   [9] Lit. "loaves of the householder."

altered, so that it is distinctive and can be identified by the owner as in the illustration that follows.

R. Simeon b. Eleazar comments that *conventionally traded* goods (see n. 8) are not distinctive. It is not clear from the Mishnah itself whether *he is not obligated to proclaim* is identical to "these are his," or whether this constitutes an additional category of action.

2:2 *And these he is obligated to proclaim*: The items listed all have something distinctive about them that enables the owner to securely identify them.

2:3 This mishnah introduces a third category of action by the finder: leaving the object in place.

tied birds behind the partition, and covered utensils in dungheaps, were presumably deposited by the owner; moving them is detrimental to the owner's interests.

rubble heap...old wall: The property is assumed to be abandoned and ownerless and the find to belong to the finder.

new wall: The finder stands outside the property reaching into the wall. In the outer part of the wall, *it is his*, i.e. the finder's; in the interior portion, *the householder* is the presumed owner of the found object.

would lease it out: The owner of the property is then not the presumed owner, and the finder may acquire it.

4 If he found it in the shop—
in this case they are his;
between the chest and the shopkeeper—
in this case, they belong to the shopkeeper.
Before the moneychanger—
in this case, they are his.
Between the chair and the moneychanger—
in this case, they belong to the moneychanger.
One[10] who buys produce from his fellow,
or his fellow sent him produce,
and he found money in them—
in this case, they are his.
If they were bound—
he takes them and proclaims.

5 The garment too was included in the general rule of all of these,
so why was it specified?[11]
So that analogy might be made with it,
to tell you:
Just as the garment is distinctive in that it has identifying marks and claimants,
so too everything that has identifying marks and claimants,
he is obligated to proclaim.

6 Until when is he required to proclaim?
Long enough for his neighbors to have heard about it—
the words of R. Meir.
R. Judah says:
Three pilgrimage festivals, and after the last pilgrimage festival, seven days,

[10] Some witnesses read here "R. Judah says: Even one who…"   [11] Lit. "Why did it go out?"

2:4 *shopkeeper*: If found where customers typically go, the object belongs to the finder (the owner is presumed to have despaired of recovering the property, rendering it ownerless; Rashi); if where the proprietor alone goes, it belongs to the proprietor (see Tosefta). Alternatively, here and in the case of a new wall in 2:3, at issue is the ability of the proprietor to automatically acquire possession of found objects (see also 4:1).

chest: Shopkeeper's cash box. The banker's *chair* (or, perhaps, "money pouch," reading Aramaic *kisa*) presumably serves an analogous function.

One who buys… takes them and proclaims: The Mishnah does not assume that the owner is the seller of the produce.

2:5 *garment*: Deuteronomy 22:3 (alternatively, Exodus 22:8). This passage is a rare example of legal midrash in the Mishnah. Deuteronomy 22:1 and 3, which discuss lost property, specify animals, but verse 3 adds also *his garment*. On the basis of this specification, the midrash adds to or extends the general rule: there is an obligation to care for a lost object when it has both *identifying marks* and *claimants*, i.e. that the owners are presumed to still want to recover the property.

2:6 *Until when?* The views in this passage limit the time that the finder is required to proclaim the find. Afterwards, the finder may still be required to care for the object (2:8).

R. Meir gives an apparently short period based on local communication. *R. Judah* requires more than a year, modeled on pilgrimage to the Jerusalem Temple.

seven days: The scenario imagines that the object was lost in Jerusalem, and the owner needs time to learn of the loss and return. Here it is the owner, not the finder, who must *proclaim* the loss (cf. 2:1–4).

so that he may go to his house for up to three days,
and return for up to three days and proclaim for one day.

2:7 Lost Objects: The Owner Must Provide Distinguishing Marks

7 If he identified[12] the lost thing,
but did not identify its distinguishing marks—
he may not give it to him;
and the deceiver, even though he said its distinguishing marks—
he may not give it to him,
as it is said: *Until your brother seeks it*:
until you investigate your brother, whether he is a deceiver or not.

2:7 cont.–11 Lost Objects: Caring for the Lost Object

Anything that produces and eats—
let it produce and eat;
and anything that does not produce and eat—
let it be sold,
as it is said: *And you shall indeed return it to him*.
See, how shall you return it to him?
And what shall happen to the proceeds?[13]
R. Tarfon says:
He may use them;
therefore, if they were lost he is obligated to guarantee their restitution;
R. Aqiva says:
He may not use them;
therefore, if they were lost he is not obligated to guarantee their restitution.

[12] Lit. "said." [13] Lit. "value" or "money."

2:7 *lost thing*: Deuteronomy 22:3. The claimant must prove ownership by saying *its distinguishing marks* (2:5), as well as stating what the object is.

deceiver: i.e. someone already known to be dishonest.

Until your brother seeks it: Deuteronomy 22:2. The midrash plays on two meanings of the verb *darash*, "seek" and "investigate," and creatively treats the subject ("your brother") as the object. Like 2:5 and 2:9–10, this passage is closely tied to exegesis of the Torah. In contrast 2:8 is formulated independently of Scripture.

produces and eats: Such as an animal, which produces milk or wool. The finder may make use of the property to defray the costs of what it *eats*. From the analogous use of this expression in 5:5 and *Ketubbot* 5:4, the animal may be used for labor as well. If it does *not produce and eat* it should be sold.

And you shall indeed return it to him: Exodus 22:2. The doubling of a verb in the verse is taken to limit the obligation of the finder; he can take into account the financial impact of caring for the found property. Cf. 2:9, 10.

R. Tarfon: The proceeds from the sale are treated as a loan: the finder is liable if the money is accidentally lost. According to *R. Aqiva* the funds are a deposit, and the finder is not liable. For liability of borrowers and "guardians" see 7:8 below and *Bava Qamma* 7:4.

8 If he found scrolls,—
he reads from them once in thirty days;
and if does not know how to read—
he rolls them;
but he may not learn for the first time from them,
nor may another read with him.
If he found a cloth[14]—
he shakes it out once in thirty days,
and spreads it out as the object requires,
but not to his own honor.
Silver utensils and copper utensils—
he uses them as they require,
but not so as to wear them down.
Gold utensils and glass utensils—
he may not touch them until Elijah comes.
If he found a sack or a basket
or anything that is not his usual practice to take up[15]—
he may[16] not take it up.

9 What is a lost thing?
If he found a donkey or a cow grazing on the road—
this is not a lost thing;
a donkey with its load overturned,[17]
or a cow running between the vineyards—
in this case, this is a lost thing.
If he returned it and it escaped, he returned it and it escaped,

[14] Or "garment."
[15] **K, P:** "if it is not his usual practice to take [such things] up." **C:** "which it is not…"
[16] Or "need."   [17] Lit. "its vessels/utensils/clothes reversed."

2:8 *scrolls* were objects of considerable value.

rolls: Rolling prevents the leather or parchment from becoming brittle.

for the first time: A text not previously studied. This, or having *another read with him*, may put too much stress on the scroll. This is analogous to using the object *as it requires, but not so as to wear them down*, below. As in 2:7, the finder is not prohibited from gaining benefit through appropriate care of the object.

but not to his own honor: Perhaps, displaying the textile or using it as a furniture covering, to prevent damage to the cloth. Following the Bavli, some commentaries hold that the finder cannot handle the fabric in a way that benefits the finder at all, so as to prevent damage.

Silver…copper: Appropriate use keeps tarnish from building up; but overuse is damaging.

Gold…glass are deemed too fragile for any use.

until Elijah comes: See 1:8.

usual practice: The concern is for the honor of the finder, who is not required to demean himself.

2:9 *What is a lost thing?* Glossing Deuteronomy 22:1–3 (see above 2:7), asking when the Torah rules apply. This passage deals exclusively with animals.

a cow grazing may have been left there by the owner intentionally; one *running between the vineyards* is to be treated as lost property.

even four or five times—
he is obligated to return it,
as it is said: *You shall indeed return them.*
If he lost a *sela*'s income,[18]
he may not say to him: "Give me a *sela*,"
but he gives him his wage as an idle laborer.[19]
If there is a court there, he stipulates[20] before the court;
but if there is no court there, before whom can he stipulate?
His own takes precedence.

10 If he found it in a cattle shed—
he is not obligated to deal with it;
if he found it in the public domain—
he is obligated to deal with it;
and if it was[21] a cemetery—
he does not become impure for it.
If his father said to him: "Become impure,"
or he said to him: "Do not return it"—
he does not listen to him.
If he loosened and loaded, loosened and loaded, even four or five times—
he is obligated,
as it is said: *You shall indeed help.*

[18] Lit. "he was idle with respect to a *sela*." [19] P, and a corrector of K, lack "idle."
[20] K, P, C add "with him." [21] K, P, C: "If it [the animal] was among the tombs."

even four or five times: i.e. repeatedly.

You shall indeed return them: Deuteronomy 22:1. Here and in 2:10 a double form of a verb form is used to extend the application of the biblical rule; cf. 2:7.

lost a sela's income: As opposed to direct expense, as in 2:7. However, this mishnah is in some tension with 2:7, which allows the finder to sell the found property.

idle laborer: The finder is compensated at the rate that out-of-work laborers might take. If we omit "idle" (see n. 19), the compensation is at the going rate. In either case, the finder may not be compensated in full (cf. the wage implied by 7:5).

stipulates before the court: The finder may make caring for the object conditional upon receiving full compensation for outlay. According to the reading *with him* (see n. 20), the condition is made with the owner at the time of return.

if there is no court there, the finder may put his own interests first.

2:10 *cattle shed*, where the animal is under care; *public domain*, where it is presumed lost.

cemetery: Presumably, the finder is a priest, who is supposed to maintain his purity (see Leviticus 21:1).

his father: The obligation to obey one's father does not take precedence over the requirement of purity or over the finder's obligation to return a lost animal.

In the Mishnah, as in Exodus 23:5 and Deuteronomy 22:4, the case of a struggling animal follows immediately after that of a lost one.

even four or five: See 2:9.

You shall indeed help: Exodus 23:5. Again, a duplicated verbal form is taken to extend the application of the rule (2:7, 2:9).

If he went and sat himself down and said:
"Since you have a commandment, if you want to, go ahead and loosen it"—
he is exempt, as it is said: *With him*;
if he was old, or sick—
he is obligated.
It is a commandment from the Torah to loosen, but not to load.
R. Simeon says:
Even to load.
R. Yose the Galilean says:
If it had on it more than its proper load,
he is not duty-bound to deal with it,
as it is said: *Under its load*, a load that it can bear.

11 His lost thing and his father's lost thing—
his lost thing takes precedence;
his lost thing and his master's lost thing—
his own takes precedence.
His father's lost thing and his master's lost thing—
his master's takes precedence,[22]
for his father brought him into this world,
but his master who taught him wisdom
brings him into the life of the world to come.
And if his father is a sage,[23] his father's takes precedence.
If[24] his father and his master were carrying a load—
he sets down his master's load and then he sets down his father's load.
If his father and his master were in captivity—

---

[22] K, P, C add "over his father's."
[23] K, P, C, and other early witnesses: "If his father was equal to his master." Compare the language at the end of this mishnah.
[24] Some medieval witnesses lack all or part of the rest of the mishnah.

With him: Exodus 23:5, taking this expression as requiring the owner's participation in helping the animal. If the owner was *old, or sick*, the passerby is obligated without the help of the owner.

not to load, since the Torah does not specify this. *R. Simeon* requires loading the animal, perhaps based on *You shall indeed raise*, Deuteronomy 22:4. *R. Yose the Galilean* apparently rules that the obligation does not arise at all if the owner overburdened the animal. However, by placing this view here, the Mishnah may treat R. Yose (a generation earlier than R. Simeon) as referring only to reloading the animal.

2:11 The Mishnah now returns to and concludes the discussion of lost objects.

His lost thing… his father's… his master's: One's own property takes precedence over another's (see 2:9), even someone one is obligated to honor. *His master*, his teacher; the same term is used for a slave owner.

his master's takes precedence: A strong statement of the primacy of the master–disciple relationship.

if his father is a sage: See n. 23; according to the reading in the manuscripts, the father must be as learned as the teacher.

If his father and his master were carrying: Similar considerations apply to assisting with a *load*, and with redemption from *captivity*. It is possible that this last discussion was a later addition to the Mishnah (see n. 24).

he redeems his master and then redeems his father;
but if his father is a sage[25]—
he redeems his father and then redeems his master.

Chapter Three

3:1 Deposits: Theft or Loss under the Unpaid Guardian's Care

3 One who deposits with his fellow an animal or utensils,
and they were stolen or lost:
if he paid, and did not want to swear
(for they said: An unpaid guardian swears and is exempt):[26]
if the thief is found—
he pays the two-fold payment;
if he slaughtered it or sold it—
he pays the four-fold or five-fold payment.
To whom does he pay? To the one who has the deposit.[27]
If he swore and did not want to pay:
if the thief is found—
he pays the two-fold payment;
if he slaughtered it or sold it—
he pays the four-fold or five-fold payment.
To whom does he pay? To the owner of the deposit.

[25] **K, P**: "a disciple of sages"; **C**: "the disciple of a sage."   [26] Lit. "and goes out."
[27] **C** provides an expanded and idiosyncratic text at this point.

3:1–12 Deposits are discussed in the Torah especially at Exodus 22:6–14; see also Leviticus 5:23. The Mishnah differs in important respects from the Torah, most notably in treating Exodus 22:6–7 (dealing with inanimate objects) as referring to unpaid guardians, and 9–11 (dealing with animals) as referring to paid guardians. The most concise treatment of "guardians," who for the Mishnah include borrowers and renters, is at 7:8 (parallel at *Shevu'ot* 8:1). Note the repetition of "One who deposits" at the beginning of units in 3:1, 6–11.

3:1 *animal or utensils*: The Mishnah appears to purposely combine cases that are distinct in the Torah.

stolen (Exodus 22:6, 10) *or lost* (analogous to theft, but see also Exodus 22:8): In such a case, the *unpaid guardian* is entitled to *swear* and be *exempt* from paying.

for they said…: A received tradition; its roots are in biblical interpretation (Exodus 22:6, 10).

if he paid… if the thief is found: In the first case, the guardian has paid voluntarily. The Mishnah rules that not only the principal, but also the *two-fold* or *four- or five-fold payments* mandated for the thief (see *Bava Qamma* 7:1) go *to the one who had the deposit*, i.e. the guardian.

he swore and did not want to pay: This is a "normal" case of theft and restitution, and the payment goes *to the owner of the deposit*.

3:2–5 *Deposits: Other Cases of Restitution*

2 One who leases a cow from his fellow, and he lent it to another,
and it died in the typical manner—
the lessee swears that it died in the typical manner,
and the borrower pays the lessee.
Said R. Yose:
How can that one make a profit[28] with the cow of his fellow?
Rather, let the cow go back to the owners.

3 If he said to two:
"I stole one hundred *zuz* from one of you,
but I do not know which of you";
or: "The father of one of you deposited one hundred with me,
but I do not know which he is"—
he gives to this one one hundred and to this one one hundred,
because he has admitted it from his own mouth.[29]

4 If two deposited with one person,
this one one hundred, and this one two hundred.
This one says: "My deposit is two hundred,"[30]
and this one says: "My deposit is two hundred"—
he gives to this one one hundred, and to this one one hundred,
and the rest shall be set aside until Elijah comes.
Said R. Yose:
If so, what has the cheater lost?
Rather, let all of it be set aside until Elijah comes.

---

[28] Lit. "business." Or "How can this be? He is making a profit…!"   [29] Or "voluntarily."
[30] Or, with **K**, **P**, **C**: "The two hundred are mine."

3:2 The cluster of passages in 3:2–5 make up a unit internally linked by objections attributed to R. Yose in 3:2, 4, and 5. Like 3:1, 3:2 deals with a case in which a borrower (a kind of guardian in the Mishnah, see 7:8) receives compensation for loss to the owner. The remaining passages deal with cases where the amount to be repaid is not certain.

One who leases: A lessee is exempt from payment when the animal simply died; but a borrower is not (see 7:8, 10). Here, the lessee who lent the animal out is treated as its owner relative to the borrower and is compensated for the animal. *R. Yose* objects that this is unjust, and rules that *the cow*, i.e. compensation for its value, should *go back to the owners*.

3:3 *"I stole one hundred"*: The same rule will apply to restoring a deposit. The robber, or the son of the guardian, provides the full amount to both parties, since this is the only way to fully compensate the party that is owed the one hundred *zuz* (see also *Ketubbot* 15:6). In contrast to 3:4–5, this mishnah applies only when the robber or son has come forward voluntarily.

3:4 *two deposited with one person*: The parties each claim that the greater amount is owed to them. *he gives to this one…and to this one* the common amount owed to both; compare the division used in 1:1.

Elijah: See 1:8.

According to *R. Yose* it is better that no one receive compensation so that the claimant who cheated not benefit.

5 And so too two utensils,
one worth one hundred and one worth one thousand *zuz*:
this one says: "The valuable one is mine,"
and this one says: "The valuable one is mine"—
he gives the less expensive[31] one to one of them,
and from the proceeds of the sale of the more expensive one,[32]
he gives the value of the less expensive one to the second,
and the rest shall be set aside until Elijah comes.
Said R. Yose:
If so, what has the cheater lost?
Rather, let all of it be set aside until Elijah comes.

3:6–11 Deposits: Depositing Produce, a Utensil, or Money

6 One who deposits produce with his fellow—
even if they are perishing, he may not touch them.
Rabban Simeon b. Gamaliel says:
He sells them before a court,
because he is like one[33] returning a lost thing to its owners.

7 One who deposits produce with his fellow—
in this case he may deduct losses from him:
for wheat and rice, nine half-*qav* to the *kor*;
for barley and millet, nine *qav* to the *kor*;
for spelt and flax seed, three *se'ah* to the *kor*.
It all follows the measure and all follows the time.

---

[31] Lit. "smaller."
[32] Lit. "and from the bigger one"; translation assumes that the guardian sells the deposit to raise the funds to compensate the second owner.
[33] K, P, C: "because of the principle of returning…"

3:5 *And so too two utensils*: The case is almost identical to the preceding, with the exception that there is an item, rather than money, to be divided.

3:6 Produce is subject to spoilage or loss over time. The debate is over whether to intervene at all. 3:6 is in tension with the discussion of acceptable losses in 3:7–8.

even if they are perishing: e.g. souring wine. The view that a guardian should not intervene to prevent spoilage may derive from a literal reading of Exodus 22:7, 10.

Rabban Simeon b. Gamaliel requires the guardian to sell the property to preserve its value, compare 2:7.

returning a lost thing: Perhaps to be taken in a strict sense: applying laws of care for a lost object to a deposit.

3:7 *deduct losses*: Normal loss during long-term storage as opposed to spoilage. The guardian may return less than was actually deposited.

nine half-qav to the kor: One fortieth; *nine qav to the kor*, one twentieth; *three se'ah to the kor*, one tenth.

all follows the measure: Deductions are proportional to the amount.

Said R. Yohanan b. Nuri:
But what does it matter to the mice?
Do they not eat whether there is much or little?
Rather, he deducts losses for a single[34] *kor* alone.
R. Judah says:
If it was a large measure, he does not deduct losses from him,
because they overestimate.[35]

8 He may deduct from him a sixth for wine.
R. Judah says:
A fifth.
He may deduct from him three *log* of oil per one hundred,
a *log* and one half for sediments, and a *log* and one half for absorption.
If the oil was clarified, he does not withhold from him for sediments;
if the jugs were old, he does withhold from him for absorption.
R. Judah says:
Even one selling clarified oil to his fellow any day of the year—
in this case, he accepts upon himself a *log* and one half of sediment per one hundred.

9 One who deposits a jar with his fellow,
and the owners did not designate a place for it, and he carried it and it broke:
if it broke while it was still in his hands,
if it was to serve his own requirements—
he is liable;
if as the jar required it[36]—
he is exempt.
If it broke after he set it down,
whether it was to serve his own requirements or as the jar required it—
he is exempt.

---

[34] K, P, C lack "single." [35] Lit. "exceed."
[36] Here and throughout 3:9: "to serve his own requirements," lit. "if it was for his needs"; "as the jar requires it," lit. "if it was for its needs."

R. Yohanan b. Nuri objects that loss due to *mice* is not proportional.

deducts losses for a single kor: The deductions are proportional for the first *kor*, and then remain fixed.

because they overestimate: According to R. Judah, if the produce was measured for deposit using large measures, we assume that the initial measurement *overestimated* the amount, so no deduction takes place now. Alternatively, with the translation "expand," *expansion* of the grain over time is assumed to balance any loss due to vermin (commentaries, following Bavli).

3:8 *a sixth for wine*: A much higher rate than for oil, below (allowing for evaporation?). This mishnah seems to imply that the wine is in the guardian's vessels and is poured over on delivery.

Even one selling: When purchasing one hundred *log* of clarified wine, the purchaser receives only 98½ *log*. According to *R. Judah* this applies also to clarified wine on deposit.

3:9 *jar*: Cf. 3:12. Since the parties *did not designate a* specific *place*, the guardian's liability is limited to when he handled the jar *to serve his own requirements*, and it broke *while it was still in his hands*. By *his own requirements*, the Mishnah may mean handling without use, for instance, to gain access to something else.

If the owners did designate a place for it, and he carried it and it broke,
whether while still in his hands or after he set it down:
if he moved it to serve his own requirements—
he is liable;
if as the jar required it—
he is exempt.

10 One who deposits money with his fellow:
if he bound them, and cast them behind him,
or[37] if he handed them over to his minor sons or daughters
or[38] did not lock the door before them appropriately—
he is liable,
for he did not guard in the usual manner of guardians.
But if he guarded in the usual manner of guardians—
he is exempt.

11 One who deposits money with a moneychanger:
if they are bound—
he may not make use of them,
therefore, if they were lost, he is not liable to make restitution of them;
if they are loose—
he may make use of them,
therefore, if they were lost, he is liable to make restitution of them.[39]
[One who deposits money] with a householder:
whether bound or loose—
he may not make use of them,
therefore if they were lost, he is not liable to make restitution of them.

---

[37] Conjunction absent in **K**, **P**, **C**.
[38] Heb. *ve-*, can mean "and" or "or."
[39] The versions of this clause, in positive and negative formulation, are absent here and below in **K** and **P**, but present in **C**.

Possibly, if they *did designate a place*, any moving for the guardian's *own requirements* is a breach of the agreement and the guardian is now liable going forward. For *as* [the deposit] *requires it* cf. 2:8.

3:10 Coins are both physical objects requiring care and more or less interchangeable markers of value. Standards of care for money are discussed in 3:10 (cf. 3:6–8). Mishnah 3:11 discusses the use of coinage on deposit.

bound them, and cast them: Carried the pouch about loosely.

or did not lock, so that they were subject to theft. If the guardian's actions led to the damage, but those actions fit *the usual manner of guardians*, i.e. within the understood standard of care, the guardian *is exempt*. Implicit, but not fully developed in the Mishnah, is the category of culpable negligence.

3:11 *moneychanger*: See 2:4.

bound: The moneychanger is responsible for the deposited coins themselves. The distinction between bound and unbound is analogous to the designation of place in 3:10.

lost due to accident; not a failed transaction.

not liable to make restitution: See n. 39, 2:7, and *Bava Qamma* 7:4. Like unpaid guardians who do not pay for loss (3:1, 7:8). With *loose* coins the moneychanger may use the coins professionally, and *is liable to make*

The shopkeeper is like the householder—
the words of R. Meir.
R. Judah says:
The shopkeeper is like the moneychanger.

3:12 Deposits: Misappropriation of the Deposit

12 One who *extends his hand* to the deposit—
the House of Shammai say:
He is to be penalized for appreciation and depreciation.
But the House of Hillel say:
He is to pay according to the time of removal.
R. Aqiva says:
According to the time that repayment is claimed.
One who thinks to *extend his hand* to the deposit—
the House of Shammai say:
He is liable;
but the House of Hillel say:
He is not liable until he *extends his hand* to it,
as it is said: *That he did not extend his hand to the property of his fellow.*[40]
How?
He tipped the jar and took a quarter-*log* from it, and it broke—
he pays only a quarter-*log*;
he lifted the jar and took a quarter-*log* from it, and it broke—
he pays the value of the whole.

[40] Prooftext absent in **K**, **P**, **G**.

restitution of their value, like a paid guardian. With a *householder*, there is never the expectation of use (this would be a kind of loan or hire), so the guardian is not liable for loss.

A *shopkeeper* also serves credit and exchange functions (e.g. 5:4, 9:12, *Shevu'ot* 7:5). The debate is whether the shopkeeper is entitled to use loose coins on deposit.

3:12 *extends his hand*: Exodus 22:7, 13. Uses or appropriates the deposited goods. According to the *House of Shammai*, if there were fluctuations in price, the guardian repays the owner at the most disadvantageous price; according to the *House of Hillel*, the restitution price is set at the moment of use. R. Aqiva sets the restitution price at the moment that the owner claims it.

One who thinks: At issue is the guardian's liability for any future damage or loss that might occur (cf. 3:9). According to the *House of Shammai* intention is sufficient to make the guardian liable; the *House of Hillel* require actual mishandling.

That he did not extend: Exodus 22:7.

How? Exemplifies and expands the Hillelite view by adding that by lifting the jar the guardian has "extended his hand" to the entire jar, and is liable for any subsequent damage or loss to it. This expansion may apply the principle of possessory acts (see *Qiddushin* chapter 1), so that by lifting it the guardian acquires the jar and is now liable for its entirety.

Chapter Four

4:1–2 *Sale and Oppressive Overcharge: Completing the Transaction of Sale*

4 Gold acquires silver; silver does not acquire gold;[41] copper acquires silver; silver does not acquire copper;
bad money acquires good money; good money does not acquire bad money;
the unstamped blank acquires the coin; the coin does not acquire the unstamped blank;
movable goods acquire the coin; the coin does not acquire movable goods.
This is the rule:[42]
All movable goods acquire one another.

2 How?
If he pulled the produce from him, but did not give him money—
he may not withdraw from the sale;[43]
if he gave him money, but did not pull the produce from him,
he may withdraw from the sale.
However, they said:
The One who exacted payment from the men of the generation of the flood

---

[41] **K, P, C, G**: "Silver acquires gold; gold does not acquire silver."
[42] Present in **K, P, C, G**, but absent in some medieval witnesses.
[43] Lit. "he may not go back on it."

4:1–2 These passages address the transaction of sale, which is considered complete when the purchaser takes possession of the merchandise, even if money has not changed hands. The seller has then legally "acquired" the money offered as payment, and the purchaser is bound to pay. Mishnah 4:1 considers how this applies to the exchange of coins. According to 4:2, the significant legal implication is the ability to withdraw from the transaction.

4:1 *Gold acquires silver*: See n. 41. This reading (that of the Bavli), anomalously treats silver as "currency" and gold as "merchandise." According to the reading in the Yerushalmi, less precious metal coins are always "merchandise" with respect to more precious metal coins. The different readings were known in antiquity and both are attributed in the Talmudim to R. Judah the Patriarch.

bad money: Coins that are no longer in circulation (Maimonides, Rashi).

unstamped: Either unstamped molded blanks or bullion.

movable goods...coin: The general case of sale, exchanging goods for money.

movable goods acquire one another: The case of barter. Cf. *Qiddushin* 1:6.

4:2 *How?* Illustrates the general case of sale: *produce* "acquiring" *money*.

pulled the produce: The Mishnah introduces formal taking possession of the merchandise, cf. *Qiddushin* 1:5, *Bava Batra* 5:7. The purchaser *may not withdraw*, and is committed to pay. In the reverse case, the purchaser *did not pull* the merchandise, and *may withdraw* even though *he gave him money*.

The One who exacted payment: Withdrawing is permitted but not proper; the Mishnah warns of divine punishment.

flood: Genesis 6–9; *Tower of Babel*: Genesis 11:1–9.

and of the generation of the Tower of Babel[44]
will in the future exact payment from one who does not stand by his word.
R. Simeon says:
Whoever has the money in his hand, that one has the advantage.[45]

4:3–4 *Sale and Oppressive Overcharge: Overcharge and Reversal of Sale*

3 Wrongful overcharge[46] is four silver *ma'ot*,
out of twenty-four silver *ma'ot* to the *sela*,
one-sixth of the sale price.
Until when is he permitted to return [the purchased item]?
As long as necessary to show it to a merchant or to his relative.
R. Tarfon ruled in Lydda:
Overcharge is eight silver coins to the *sela*,
a third of the sale price.
And the merchants of Lod rejoiced.
He said to them:
It is permissible to return it all day.
They said to him:
Let R. Tarfon leave us as we were before,[47]
and they returned to the words of the Sages.
4 Overcharge applies to both buyer and seller.[48]
Just as wrongful overcharge applies to a private person,

---

[44] Heb. "generation of the dispersion." **K, P, C, G** only refer to the generation of the flood.
[45] Lit. "His hand is higher."   [46] Lit. "oppression."
[47] Lit. "in our place." **K, P, C, G**: "Let him leave us our place," perhaps meaning "would that R. Tarfon would leave us our livelihood."
[48] Lit. they "have overcharge" in all four occurrences in this mishnah.

---

has the advantage: According to *R. Simeon, whoever has the money* can choose to reverse the sale or negotiate new terms (see 4:4). On this view, it is transfer of the money that formalizes the sale.

4:3–4 "Oppression" refers to overcharging or underpaying in the case of sale. (See 4:10 for verbal oppression.) The term derives from Leviticus 25:14, 17, where the context is sale of real property within a jubilee cycle. See 4:9, 10.

4:3 *overcharge* is defined as charging more than *one-sixth* above the appropriate *price*. The purchaser is given sufficient time (from the sequel, less than a day) to consult with others about the price, and to reverse the sale if overcharged. Cf. 4:5.

R. Tarfon allowed higher overcharge before the sale was reversible, but the buyer has *all day* to reverse the sale. The *merchants of Lod* applauded the one but rejected the other.

merchant: The Hebrew *tagar* usually implies a large-scale buyer or seller rather than a peddler or a shopkeeper (see 4:11, 12). *Ruled*, may imply adjudication of a case or some other form of instruction. The responses of the *merchants* may suggest the latter.

4:4 *both buyer and seller*: A seller who finds that the price was too far below the going rate can also reverse the sale.

so wrongful overcharge applies to a merchant.
R. Judah says:
Wrongful overcharge does not apply to a merchant.
Whoever has been overcharged, that one has the advantage:[49]
If he wishes, he may say:
"Give me my money,"
or "Give me the amount by which you have overcharged me."

4:5–6 Sale and Oppressive Overcharge: Reversal of Transactions Involving Bad Coin

5 How much may a *sela* be lacking
and still not have the rule of wrongful overcharge apply to it?
R. Meir says:
Four *issar*, an *issar* to the *dinar*.
R. Judah says:
Four *pondion*, a *pondion* to the *dinar*.
R. Simeon says:
Eight *pondion*, two *pondion* to the *dinar*.
6 Until when is he able to return a coin?
In the cities: as long as necessary to show it to a moneychanger;
and in the villages: until the Sabbath eve.
And if he recognized it—
he accepts it from him even after twelve months,
but the other has grounds only for complaint against him.

[49] Lit. "Whomever it has been laid upon, his hand is higher." **K, C, G**: "Once it has been laid upon him," i.e. "from the time he has been overcharged."

merchant: Even a market professional can claim wrongful overcharge and reverse the sale. *R. Judah* disagrees, presumably because a merchant is expected to know the going price.

Whoever…has the advantage: See n. 49 and 3:2. Advantage (lit. "his hand is higher") here means that the injured party can entirely reverse the sale, or demand compensation for the amount of the over- (or under-) charge.

4:5 If coins were passed as full value and turn out to be under value, similar rules of *ona'ah* apply. The structure of this section partially parallels 4:3.

Four *dinar* made up a *sela*; the other coins mentioned are smaller denominations.

R. Meir…Four issar: one twenty-fourth; *R. Judah…Four pondion*: one twelfth; *R. Simeon…Eight pondion*: one sixth (as in 4:3).

4:6 *In the cities*, where we expect there to be moneychangers, the time is not specified but is presumably short. *Villages* do not have moneychangers, and villagers need until the next Friday in order to go to a local market town that might meet on Fridays (Tosefta) or perhaps Mondays and Thursdays (see *Megillah* 1:1–3; *Ta'anit* 2:9; *Ketubbot* 1:1).

if he recognized it, these time limits do not apply.

only for complaint: The requirement to accept the coins back is not legally enforceable.

And one may give it as second tithe and not be concerned,
for it is only miserliness.[50]

4:7–8 *Sale and Oppressive Overcharge: At Least One Perutah*

7 Wrongful overcharge is at least four silver coins,
a monetary claim is at least two silver coins,
and confession [of monetary obligation] is at least one *perutah*.
There are five cases that require at least one *perutah*:[51]
(1) confession [of monetary obligation] is at least one *perutah*;
(2) and a woman is betrothed with at least one *perutah*;
(3) and one who benefits by at least one *perutah*-worth from Temple property
has committed Temple theft;
(4) and one who finds at least a *perutah*-worth is obligated to proclaim it;
(5) and one who robs his fellow of a *perutah*-worth and swears to him
must take it to him even to Media.

8 There are five cases that require an added fifth:[52]
(1) one who eats *terumah*, or *terumah* from the tithe,

---

[50] Or "for he is only a bad soul." [51] Lit. "There are five *perutot*."
[52] Lit. "There are five fifths."

---

second tithe: See *Ma'aser Sheni*. The produce set aside as second tithe could be exchanged for money, which could in turn be set aside to be used for appropriate food in Jerusalem. The owner of an underweight coin could use it in place of second tithe, since it is valid currency, and refusal to accept the coin is a form of miserliness.

4:7 The Mishnah here includes three sets of rules organized as lists.

Wrongful overcharge: See 4:3; here, the rule is taken to set a minimum, rather than as an example.

monetary claim…confession [of monetary obligation]: These two cases of minimum thresholds are in fact one: when a person claims that another owes money, and the latter confesses to a lesser amount, the judge imposes an oath on the debtor. See *Shevu'ot* 6:1.

five cases: A second list of rules, beginning with the last item of the preceding.

betrothed: Betrothal, or inchoate marriage, is structured as an acquisition, and the groom must transfer a minimum amount. *Qiddushin* 1:1, *Eduyot* 4:7.

benefits: *Me'ilah* 5:1.

Temple theft: Leviticus 5:15–16.

finds: Cf. 2:1.

Media: Cf. *Bava Qamma* 9:5.

4:8 *five cases*: A third list of rules, this one involving payment of the added fifth.

one who eats: These are all mandated gifts for the priests or Levites; a nonpriest or non-Levite who ate them must repay what was eaten and an additional fifth.

terumah: Numbers 18:11–12. See *Terumot* 6:1.

terumah from the tithe: The Mishnah's term for the Levite's obligation to tithe for the priests the tithes he himself receives, Numbers 18:26.

or *terumah* from the tithe of *demai*,
or the dough offering, or firstfruits
adds a fifth;
(2) one who redeems his fourth-year produce or his second tithe
adds a fifth;
(3) one who redeems his Temple property
adds a fifth;
(4) and one who benefits by at least one *perutah*-worth from Temple property
adds a fifth;
(5) and one who robs his fellow of a *perutah*-worth and swears to him
adds a fifth.

4:9 *Sale and Oppressive Overcharge: Special Rules for Slaves, Documents, Land, and Temple Property*

9 These are the things to which wrongful overcharge does not apply:
slaves, documents, land, and Temple property.
Neither double nor four- or five-fold payment applies to them.[53]
An unpaid guardian does not swear on their account,
and a paid guardian does not pay.
R. Simeon says:
Sacrifices for which he has an obligation of restitution—

[53] Lit. "They have neither…"

---

demai: Produce about which it is not certain whether tithes have been removed. The owner must set aside the *terumah from the tithe* in order to make the produce permissible to be eaten; see *Demai*.

dough offering: Hallah 1:9. A portion of the dough set aside for priests.

firstfruits: Bikkurim 2:1.

fourth-year produce: The produce of a tree in the fourth year after planting is brought to Jerusalem for consumption, Leviticus 19:23–24; *Ma'aser Sheni* 5:5.

second tithe: Deuteronomy 14:22–27. See 4:6 and *Ma'aser Sheni* 4:3.

redeems… Temple property one has previously dedicated, Leviticus 27:19. See *Arakhin* 8:2.

benefits… from Temple property: Leviticus 5:16.

robs… and swears, that is falsely. Leviticus 5:24. See *Bava Qamma* 9:6.

4:9 A close parallel to the first part of this mishnah appears at *Shevu'ot* 6:4. Sales involving *slaves, documents*, and *land* differ from transactions involving most movable goods, and either party may have reasons to accept a price well above or below the "normal" price; redemption of *Temple property* is not "sale." The Sifra derives all of these exclusions from Leviticus 25:14.

double… four- or five-fold: See *Bava Qamma* 7:1.

unpaid… paid guardian: See 3:7, 7:8.

R. Simeon applies the rules of overcharge to some cases of sacrifice. Where the dedicator must *make good the provision* if the animal dedicated becomes disqualified (see *Bava Qamma* 7:4), that animal has continued to belong to the dedicator. If it is sold off, the rules of overcharge apply.

overcharge applies to them;
those for which he has no obligation of restitution—
overcharge does not apply to them.
R. Judah says:
Even one who sells a Torah scroll, or an animal, or a pearl—
wrongful overcharge does not apply to them.
They said to him: They said only these.

4:10 *Sale and Oppressive Overcharge: Wrongful Speech*

10 Just as there is wrongful overcharge in purchase and sale,
so there is oppression in speech.[54]
He may not say to him: "How much is this item?" when he does not wish to purchase.
If he was a penitent,
one may not say to him: "Remember your earlier deeds!"
If he was the son of proselytes,
one may not say to him: "Remember the deeds of your forefathers!"
as it is said: *And an alien shall you not wrong, nor shall you oppress him.*

4:11–12 *Sale and Oppressive Overcharge: Rules for the Handling of Merchandise*

11 One does not mix produce with produce, even new with new,
and there is no need to say new with old.
Nevertheless[55], in the case of wine they permitted to mix strong with mild,[56]
because it improves it.

[54] Heb. "Just as there is *ona'ah*...so there is *ona'ah*..."
[55] Lit. "In truth."
[56] Heb. "hard" and "soft."

Even...a Torah scroll, or an animal, or a pearl: In addition to the types of property listed at the beginning of the mishnah, R. Judah adds property of high value for which one might be willing to pay a premium. As a consequence, the purchaser cannot claim overcharge.

They said: The anonymous response is that the list at the beginning of the mishnah is exclusive.

4:10 *Just as*: The formulation suggests that wrongful speech and wrongful overcharge are analogous, or that the rules for speech are an extension from overcharge. The first example given, asking *How much is this? when he does wish to purchase*, fits this formulation. The following two examples are parallel cases of verbal injury: reminding a *penitent* or a *proselyte* of their origins.

And an alien shall you not wrong: Exodus 22:20, reading biblical *ger* as proselyte.

4:11 *One does not mix...even new with new*: A seller agreeing to sell produce from one field should not mix it with produce from another, even if both are from the current crop (Rashi). Alternatively, the Mishnah provides general rules for how produce is marketed.

Nevertheless introduces a qualification in the case of wine. Since the blending of *strong with mild* improves the quality of the milder wine, this is not a deceitful practice and there is no reduction in quality involved.

One does not mix wine sediment with wine,
but he does give him his sediments.
One whose wine became mixed with water—
he may not sell it in a shop,
unless he informs the buyer,
but not to a merchant,
even though he informs him,
for it is only to cheat with it.
In a place where it was customary put water into wine,[57] they may put it in.

12 The merchant may take from five granaries and put them into one bin,
from five winepresses and put them into a single storage jar,
as long as he does not intend to cheat through mixing.[58]
R. Judah says:
A shopkeeper may not distribute parched grain and nuts to children,
because he makes them accustomed to come to him;
but the Sages permit.
And he may not undercut the market price;
but the Sages say:
He is remembered for good.
He may not pick over the pounded beans—
the words[59] of Abba Saul;

[57] K, P, C, G lack "into wine." P, L have *may yam*, "seawater" for *mayim*, "water."
[58] Lit. "does not intend to mix."
[59] K, P, C, G: "in keeping with the words."

sediment: See 3:8. The Mishnah is perhaps considering a seller mixing wine with sediments from another jar. However, the seller can sell wine with its own sediments.

wine...mixed with water diminishes the value of the wine.

unless he informs him: i.e. the buyer. Alternatively, the seller cannot use a shopkeeper as agent without informing the shopkeeper that the wine is mixed. By contrast, a *merchant* (see 4:3) is expected to act dishonestly.

where it was customary to put water: Wine was commonly drunk diluted. The Mishnah is apparently considering places where the wine is sold ready to drink. An alternative reading is "seawater" (see n. 57). Several well-known varieties of wine in the Roman world, e.g. Coan wine, were made with the addition of seawater.

4:12 *merchant*: Again, merchants are suspected of cheating.

as long...mixing: See n. 58. What is prohibited seems to be passing off the mixture as coming from a single, valuable source.

R. Judah: This introduces a freestanding dispute on a new topic. According to R. Judah, distributing *parched grain* constitutes dishonest practice, since it creates incentives beyond proper merchandise offered at a fair price. Any injury would be caused to other sellers rather than the buyers.

may not undercut the market price: Again setting strict limits on incentives for customers, and possibly the continuation of R. Judah above. In this case, *the Sages* commend the practice.

may not pick over the pounded beans: According to the commentaries, the problem is selling the cleaned beans at a significant markup. If we omit *the words of Abba Saul* (see n. 59), this, too, may be a continuation of R. Judah. *The Sages...concede* that picking over only the top layer of beans but leaving the skins with the beans in the rest of the bin is prohibited.

but the Sages permit;
but they concede that he may not pick over at the opening of the bin alone, because that is only deceit.⁶⁰
One may not prettify a person or an animal or utensils.

Chapter Five

5:1 Usury and Increase

5 Which is *usury* and which is *increase*?
Which is *usury*?
One who lends a *sela* for five *dinar*, two *se'ah* of wheat for three,
because he bites.
And which is *increase*?
One who increases through produce.
How?
If he bought wheat from him at a golden *dinar* to the *kor*, and such is the market price:
if wheat then stood at thirty *dinar*,
and he said to him: "Give me my wheat, for I want to sell them and buy⁶¹ wine with them,"

---

⁶⁰ "Alone" is added for clarity. "Deceit": Heb. "stealing the eye."
⁶¹ K, P, C, G: "for I am selling them and buying."

One may not prettify: Translation uncertain. The problem is one of misrepresentation of the quality of the merchandise, as in the Sages' concession.

5:1–11 The Mishnah distinguishes between loans of money or its equivalent and loans of property for use. Chapter 8 deals with the latter. Here, the Mishnah extends the biblical prohibition of lending at interest to instances of sale, where changing market prices or delay in payment might cause a creditor to receive an increase, and to indirect benefits given to a creditor.

5:1 *Which is usury and which is increase?* The Bible uses two terms for interest, *neshekh*, the additional payment a borrower pays as well as repaying the principal, here rendered *usury* (Exodus 22:24; Leviticus 18:17, 25:36, 37; Deuteronomy 23:20; Proverbs 28:8), and *tarbit* (Leviticus 25:36; Ezekiel 18:17; Proverbs 28:8) or *marbit* (Leviticus 25:37), here rendered *increase*. This mishnah, possibly commenting directly on Leviticus 25:36, distinguishes between them.

usury is the explicit charging of interest: *sela* (= four *dinar*) *for five dinar*, a loan of money (the rate is twenty-five percent); *two se'ah…for three*, a loan of produce (the rate is fifty percent).

increase: Based on the illustration that follows, transactions involving changing market values of produce.

How? Illustrates increase.

he bought wheat…you have a claim against me for them in wine: The initial transaction was one for delayed delivery. The purchaser, now a creditor, demands delivery in order to sell at a new, higher price and buy wine. The seller, now a borrower, offers to revalue the obligation at the higher price and to repay in wine. This is prohibited because *he does not have wine*. If the seller had had wine and could have fulfilled the obligation immediately, the contract would have been another sale for delayed delivery (see 5:7, 9).

and he said to him: "Your wheat is hereby valued[62] at thirty *dinar* against me,
and you have a claim against me for them in wine,"
but he does not have wine.

5:2–7 *Transactions That May Result in Prohibited Interest*

2 One who lends to his fellow—
he may not live in his courtyard free of charge,
and may not lease from him at a discount,
because it is interest.
They may increase the hire, but they may not increase the sale price.
How?
If he rented him his courtyard, and said to him:
"If you pay me now, then it is yours for ten *sela* for the year,
but if month to month, for a *sela* a month"—
it is permitted.
If he sold him his field, and said to him:
"If you pay me now, then it belongs to you for one thousand *zuz*,
but if on the threshing floor, for 1,200"—
it is prohibited.
  3 If he sold him a field, and gave him a portion of the price,
and said to him:
"Whenever you want, bring the money and take what is yours"—
it is prohibited.
If he lent to him against his field,
and said to him:
"If you do not pay in full[63] between now and three years from now, then it is mine"—
in this case it is his;
and thus did Boethos b. Zonin do in accordance with the Sages.

[62] Lit. "made."   [63] Lit. "If you do not give me."

5:2 *may not live … may not lease*: Gaining benefit from the borrower in ways that are not directly tied to the value of the loan.

How? If he rented: A series of illustrative cases. The first two correspond to the two parts of the preceding rule. The owner *may* allow the renter to pay *ten sela* up front, but twelve if extended through the year. However, *if he sold* a field, the seller may not allow the buyer the option of paying one thousand *zuz* at the outset, but 1,200 *zuz* if paid after the harvest. As understood by the Bavli and commentaries, this is because rent was due at the end of a contract, so early payment is a discount, but sale price is due from the completion of sale, so delayed payment constitutes interest.

5:3 *If he sold him*: This appears to continue the list of cases introduced in 5:2. The buyer gives a down payment, while the seller retains possession of the field and any income from it until the balance is paid. The benefit to the seller is considered prohibited interest.

lent to him against his field: The borrower has used a field as collateral and stipulated that the lender may seize the field if the loan is unpaid after a three-year term. Since the field and any income remain in the possession of the borrower there is no prohibited material benefit to the lender.

4 One may not set up[64] a shopkeeper at half profit,
and he may not give money by which to buy produce [for resale] at half profit,
unless he gives him his wage as a worker.[65]
One may not set up chickens at half shares,[66]
and he may not assess calves and foals at half shares,
unless he gives him his wage for his labor and his food;
but one does receive calves and foals to raise them until they are tripled in size,
and an ass, until it is ready to bear a burden.

5 One may assess a cow and an ass, and everything that produces and eats, at half shares.
In a place where it was customary to divide the offspring immediately—
they divide it;
in a place where it was customary to raise the animals—
they raise them.
Rabban Simeon b. Gamaliel says:
One may assess a calf with its mother and a foal with its mother.
And one may offer a higher rent[67] for his field,
and he does not worry about interest.

[64] Lit. "seat." [65] K, P, C: "an idle laborer"; cf. 2:9.
[66] Here and in the following cases, lit. "for half."
[67] Hebr. *mafriz*, meaning uncertain. K, P, C: *mafrin*: "they may improve" his field.

5:4 As with sale, profits from investment of funds, raw material, or animals to raise could be considered interest. The Mishnah allows many such transactions, with the constraint that the agent not appear to provide labor in exchange for the use of capital.

One may not set up a shopkeeper: Contracting with someone to sell one's produce. *Half profit* from the sales as the sole compensation. The employer *gives him his wage as a worker* (cf. 2:9 and see n. 65), so that the labor the agent provides is not interest in return for the use of the produce.

One may not set up chickens: Either a contract to raise chickens or eggs or (commentaries, see also Tosefta) providing eggs to the owner of hens in order to hatch them.

assess: A technical designation of a contract (see 5:5), in which the parties assess the current value of the young animals and in which half the difference between the sale price and the original assessment goes to the agent. Again, the one providing the capital must pay the agent *his wage for his labor and his food* (commentaries: the feed for the animals). The precise obligation is slightly different from the preceding case, perhaps because the work is part-time, while the shopkeeper's is full-time.

receive: Another technical term for a contract (5:6, see also 9:1–10) in which the agent assumes less risk than in the preceding, or even no risk (Rashi), although the precise arrangement is not spelled out. It may involve a combination of a fixed per-head payment and a proportion of the appreciation of the animal (Tosefta). A contract of "receipt" is permitted according to the Mishnah.

tripled in size: A very difficult phrase; all intepretations are guesswork. Among the classical commentaries one finds *three years* (Maimonides); *one third its size* (Rashi).

5:5 *One may assess*: This mishnah continues 5:4. An adult ass or cow *produces and eats*, so that the agent receives some compensation for labor (see also 2:7).

where it was customary to divide...to raise: The animals are being maintained for their offspring.

Rabban Simeon allows a contract in which one rolls the assessment of *a calf* in *with* that of *its mother and a foal with its mother*, without separately factoring the labor and feed for the offspring.

may offer a higher rent: See n. 67. The lessee may pay a higher rent in exchange for funds from the lessor to improve the field. Cf. 5:8.

6 One may not receive "iron sheep" from an Israelite,
because it is interest;
but one may receive "iron sheep" from gentiles,
and one may borrow from them and lend to them at interest.
And so too in the case of a resident alien.
An Israelite may lend the money of a gentile,
with the knowledge of the gentile, but not with the knowledge of the Israelite.

7 One may not make a contract of provision for produce
until the market price has been announced.[68]
If the market price has been announced,
one may make a contract for provision,
and even though this one does not have produce, this one does.[69]
If he was the first of the reapers—
he may make a contract of provision with him on the grain stack,
or on the basket of grapes, or on the vat of olives,
or on the lumps of potter's clay,[70]
or on lime, from the time that he has sunk it in the kiln.
And he may make a contract of provision with him for manure all through the year.
R. Yose says:
One may not make a contract of provision for manure,

---

[68] Lit. "goes out."
[69] "If…does" is absent in **K, P, C**, and appears to be an explanatory note from elsewhere.
[70] Lit. "eggs (**K**, or: 'clays,' **P, C, G**) of the potter."

5:6 *"iron sheep"*: A technical expression with roots in ancient Near Eastern law (*Yevamot* 7:1–2; *Bekhorot* 2:4). The value of the animal is held to be immutable (like iron); the agent pays the owner per head and assumes all liability as well as a proportion of any revenue (Tosefta, Yerushalmi). The Mishnah considers the agent to be borrowing the animal and compensating the owner for the loan. For *receive* as a technical term, see 5:4.

but one may receive: One may make contracts with gentiles that carry forms of interest (see Deuteronomy 23:21). The specific permission to *borrow from* gentiles may reflect a prohibition against Israelites borrowing at interest (see 5:11). *Resident alien* is an intermediate biblical category of a non-Israelite who lives among the people and participates in Israelite cult, and is often the subject of protective legislation in the Torah.

knowledge of the gentile, so that the Israelite is acting for the gentile, *but not with the knowledge of the Israelite* alone. Following the Bavli, the commentaries read *but not with the knowledge of the Israelite* as referring to the inverse case in which an Israelite borrowed an Israelite's money from a gentile.

5:7–9 address the problem that all transactions involving produce are potentially interest-bearing, since the value of the produce may fluctuate over time. Similarly, in 5:10 exchange of labor is understood as a loan of a good whose value fluctuates.

5:7 *contract for provision*: Presumably, a contract of advance payment for delayed delivery, or the bulk sale of a crop before it is harvested or processed.

until the market price: Once there is a market price, the transaction is a sale at a discount. As the continuation explains (see n. 68), *even though* the *seller does not have produce* to deliver, the fact of an established market price means that the seller could procure the produce.

If he was the first of the reapers: If the harvest was only beginning, and there was as yet no market price, the seller can make a *contract for provision* for produce once it has been harvested, even if not fully processed. The additional rules about *clay* and *lime* production suggest that these may have been seasonal as well.

until he has manure in the dungheaps;
but the Sages permit.
And he makes a contract of provision with him
according to the cheaper market price.[71]
R. Judah says:
Even though he did not make a contract of provision with him
according to the cheaper market price,
he can say to him: "Give me at this price[72] or give me my money."

5:8–10 *Repayment in Kind or Service*

8 A person may lend his tenant farmers wheat for wheat for seed,
but not for eating.
For Rabban Gamaliel used to lend his tenant farmers wheat for wheat for seed.
Whether it was expensive and became cheaper,
or cheap and became more expensive—
he would take from them at the cheaper market price.
Not because the law is such, but because he wanted to be stringent with himself.

9 A person may not say to his fellow:
"Lend me a *kor* of wheat, and I will give you at the harvest."[73]
But he may say to him:
"Lend me until my son comes,"
or "Until I find the key,"
but Hillel prohibits.

[71] Lit. "high gate," i.e. more merchandise per price
[72] Lit. "like this."
[73] Lit. "at the threshing floor."

he may make a contract…for manure: According to this view, there is a steady supply of manure throughout the year, and no need to have amassed a stock of manure before contracting. *R. Yose* requires the seller to have manure to sell before he can make a contract for provision. *The Sages* appear to hold an identical view to the anonymous one preceding R. Yose.

according to the cheaper market price: The parties can agree that the delivery will be at the lowest price available. According to *R. Judah*, even without such a contract the buyer is in a position to say *Give me at this price or give me my money* (see 4:4), since it is pulling the produce that completes the sale (Rashi; see 4:2).

5:8 *wheat for wheat for seed but not for eating*: A loan of grain to be repaid by an equal measure of grain. This is prohibited, since price fluctuations may result in the lender receiving back a higher value than was given. *For seed* this is permitted. (At harvest time, produce is expected to be at its lowest price.) According to Rashi, this arrangement is effectively a rental with a stipulated higher return for the owner (5:2).

Rabban Gamaliel would avoid this problem by adjusting for price changes and receiving the value of the grain lent, *at the cheaper market price*.

wanted to be stringent: The Mishnah views Rabban Gamaliel's practice as voluntary piety.

5:9 *"Lend me a kor of wheat"*: A short-term loan of produce where the borrower actually has the produce but cannot access it (see 5:1). *Hillel prohibits* such short-term loans, and even prohibits neighborly loans of bread by *a woman…to her fellow* without converting the loan into a monetary one.

And thus would Hillel say:
A woman may not lend a loaf to her fellow until she gives it a monetary value,
lest wheat become more expensive, and they commit prohibited interest.[74]

10 A person may say to his fellow:
"Weed with me and I will weed with you";
"Hoe with me and I will hoe with you."
But he may not say to him:
"Weed with me and I will hoe with you";
"Hoe with me and I will weed with you."
All the days of the dry season are one, and all the days of the rainy season are one.
He may not say to him:
"Plow with me in the dry season and I will plow with you in the rainy season."

5:10 cont.–11 *Additional Rules and Definitions*

10 Rabban Gamaliel says:
There is interest paid in advance, and there is interest paid at the end.
How?
He desired[75] to borrow from him,
and he would send a gift to him and say:
"So that you will lend to me"—
this is interest paid in advance.
If he borrowed from him, and returned his money to him,
and he would send him a gift and say:
"For your money, which was idle with me"—
this is interest paid at the end.
R. Simeon says:
There is verbal interest:
he may not say to him:
"Know that a certain person is coming from a certain place."
11 And these transgress a negative commandment:
the lender, and the borrower, and the guarantor, and the witnesses;

---

[74] Lit. "they will be found to have come into increase."   [75] Lit. "gave his eyes."

5:10 *"Weed with me"*: Exchanges of labor involve the same considerations as loans of produce repaid in kind. Parties can aid each other in the same type of labor in the same season, but not different labors or in different seasons, since the difficulty of the work or the monetary value may differ.

The statement of *Rabban Gamaliel* itself is quite general, and ought to refer to any contract construable as a loan. The illustration addresses, and possibly expands the prohibition to, a non-contractual *gift*, seemingly at the initiative of the borrower.

R. Simeon expands the definition of prohibited interest to *verbal interest*, when the information is of benefit to the lender.

5:11 *these transgress*: The Mishnah interprets the Torah's repetition of the prohibition as addressing each of the parties to the transaction. *You shall not give*: Leviticus 25:37; *You may not take*: Leviticus 25:36; *You shall not be as a creditor*: Exodus 22:24; *You shall not lay interest*: Exodus 22:24, continuing the preceding quotation. The final verse, *And you shall not put a stumbling block before the blind*, Leviticus 19:14, is not specific to loans.

and the Sages say:
Even the scribe.
They transgress due to: *You shall not give [your silver at interest]*;
and due to: *You may not take from him [interest or increase]*;
and due to: *You shall not be as a creditor to him*;
and due to: *You shall not lay interest upon him*.
and due to: *And you shall not put a stumbling block before the blind.*
And you shall fear your God, I am the Lord.

Chapter Six

6:1–2 *Hire of Artisans, Animals, and Laborers: Artisans*

6 One who hires artisans,
and they deceived one another—
they have grounds only for complaint against one another.
If he hired an ass driver or a potter[76] to bring[77] litter bearers or flutes
for the bride or for the dead,
or workers to raise his flax from the steeping vat,
or anything that is subject to loss,
and they withdrew—
in a place where there is no one else,
he hires others at their expense or deceives them.
    2 One who hires artisans,
and they withdrew—
they are at a disadvantage;[78]
and if the householder withdrew—

[76] C: "wagon driver."   [77] "To bring" absent in K, P, C.   [78] Lit. "their hand is lower."

6:1–2 The Mishnah distinguishes the hiring of artisans from the hiring of laborers (see chapter 7). The former may be skilled laborers, or they may be hired on a contract to perform a task.

6:1 *they deceived*: The employer or the workers deceived the other party about terms, and now demand new terms. Following the Bavli, the commentaries also read this as a case when the deceit is between workers, as when a foreman misrepresents the contract.

complaint: See 4:6. Neither party has a legal claim.

subject to loss: Time-sensitive.

withdrew: See 6:2.

or deceives them, falsely promising the workers increased payment.

6:2 *artisans … withdrew*, refusing to work. *If the householder withdrew*, unilaterally cancelling the job. This mishnah may assume that the workers have already begun working, unlike the first case of 6:1.

are … is at a disadvantage: See 4:2, 4.

he is at a disadvantage.
Anyone who alters, that one is at a disadvantage;
anyone who withdraws, that one is at a disadvantage.

6:3–5   Hire of Artisans, Animals, and Laborers: Hire of Animals

3   One who hires an ass
to walk it on the mountain, and he walked it in the valley;
in the valley, and he walked it on the mountain,
even if this one is ten miles and this one is ten miles,
and it died—
he is liable.
One who hires an ass,
and it became blind or was requisitioned for labor[79]—
the owner[80] says to him: "Here, yours is before you";
if it died or broke, [the owner] is obligated to provide him with an ass.
One who hires an ass,
to walk it on the mountain, and he walked it in the valley:
if it slipped—
he is exempt,
if it became overheated—
he is liable;
to walk it in the valley, and he walked it on the mountain:
if it slipped—
he is liable,
if it became overheated,

[79] Lit. "or was made (**K**, **P**, was carried off for) *angareia*,"
[80] Here and in the following clause, where the translation has "the owner" Hebrew has only "he."

Anyone who alters…anyone who withdraws: These are general rules related to the preceding, but not necessarily limited to employment contracts.

6:3–5 The recurring topic in these passages is the renter whose use of the animal differs from that specified in the contract. In general, the renter of an animal is exempt from liability in the case of accidental death, see 7:8. However, divergence from the agreement makes the renter liable.

6:3 *blind*: Alternatively, "became ill" (Maimonides); the term is obscure.

labor: Heb. *angaria*, from Greek *angareia*, a technical term for labor or service requisitioned by the state.

"yours is before you": For the expression, see *Bava Qamma* 9:2. As in *Bava Qamma* 9:5, the animal exists, and the owner is not required to replace it.

died or broke: The language derives from Exodus 22:6–14, on deposits. Not only is the lessee not liable (see 7:8), the owner must provide an animal for the lessee to complete the contract.

mountain…valley…if it slipped: This unit of the Mishnah differs from the first, by qualifying whether the death of the animal was attributable to the change by the renter, and is possibly a revision or an alternative formulation of the previous tradition.

he is exempt;
if on account of the elevation—
he is liable.

4 One who hires a cow,
to plow on the mountain, and he plowed in the valley:
if the plow was broken—
he is exempt;
in the valley, and he plowed on the mountain:
if the plow was broken—
he is liable.
To thresh legumes, and he threshed grain—
he is exempt;
to thresh grain, and he threshed legumes—
he is liable,
for legumes are slippery.

5 One who hires an ass,
to bring wheat with it, and he brought barley with it—
he is liable;[81]
grain, and he brought straw with it—
he is liable;
for volume is difficult to carry;[82]
to bring a *letekh* of wheat, and he brought a *letekh* of barley—
he is exempt;
but if he added to its load, he is liable.
And how much must he add to its load and be liable?
Symmachus says in the name in the name of R. Meir:
A *se'ah* for a camel; three *qav* for an ass

[81] K, P, C lack "he is liable." [82] K, P, C have "is as difficult as weight."

6:4 This mishnah is patterned along the lines of the final portion of 6:3. Interestingly, the Mishnah deals with a *cow* as draft animal rather than an ox.

plowed in the valley, with softer, deeper soil.

if the plow was broken it is not assumed to be due to the renter's alteration. Conversely, if the lessee *plowed on the mountain*, the damage to the plow is ascribed to the change.

thresh legumes…grain: A similar rule applies here, although here the Mishnah explicitly states the reasoning.

6:5 An *ass* is used for transportation rather than traction. *Wheat* is heavier by volume than *barley*, and *grain* is heavier than *straw*. Bringing the same weight—but greater volume—of the lighter product makes the renter liable for damage that occurs, *for volume is difficult to carry* (see n. 82).

to bring a letekh of wheat: Here, the renter has stipulated a specific volume of wheat and is therefore *exempt* from any ensuing damage, because the volume of the barley is the same and the weight less.

added to its load. This is treated in what follows as meaning: if he contracted to bring a volume of wheat and increased the amount of wheat. *Symmachus…in the name of R. Meir* then quantifies permitted amounts. If the volume is assumed to be a *letekh*, the renter is liable if one increases the load by $1/15$ for a camel, or $1/30$ for an ass.

6:6–8   Hire of Artisans, Animals, and Laborers: Rules on Deposits and Guardians

6   All artisans are paid guardians.
And all who have said: "Take what is yours and bring the money,"[83] are unpaid guardians.
"Watch for me and I will watch for you"—
each is a paid guardian;
"Watch for me," and he said: "Leave it before me"[84]—
he is an unpaid guardian.

7   If he lent him against a pledge—
he is a paid guardian.
R. Judah says:
If he lent him money—
he is an unpaid guardian;
if he lent him produce—
he is a paid guardian.
Abba Saul says:
A person is permitted to rent out the pledge of a poor man,
so as to continually credit it to his loan,[85]
because he is like one returning a lost object.

---

[83] K, P, C: "Bring the money and take what is yours."   [84] P, C: "before yourself."
[85] Lit.: "so as to apportion it upon him" (?); The verb is the same as in the contracts of provision in 5:7.

6:6–7 The liabilities of paid and unpaid guardians are used as standards for assessing the liability of people holding others' property as a result of other contracts. The principle appears to be that if both parties receive benefit, the person holding the property is a "paid" guardian; if only the owner receives benefit, the person holding the property is "unpaid." The connection to the present context seems to be the case of artisans (as in 6:1) that begins 6:6.

6:6 *artisans are paid guardians*: Like paid guardians, artisans are liable for theft and loss, although exempt in the case of unavoidable accident (7:8). The artisan receives the benefit of holding the work as collateral against payment (cf. 6:7), and therefore takes on a higher liability.

"Take…and bring the money": The commentaries, following this reading of the Mishnah (see n. 83), explain that the artisan is signaling the owner that he has no intention of holding the object as collateral. For the expression cf. 5:3.

"Watch for me": The mutual benefits make each one a paid guardian.

"Leave it before me": This is taken to be consent, and to make the speaker liable at the level of an unpaid guardian.

6:7 *lent him against a pledge*: The lender is responsible for the object given as pledge as a *paid guardian*. The logic appears to be the same as for artisans. For pledges see further 9:13.

R. Judah: The reasoning for the distinction is not clear. According to the commentaries, for R. Judah the holder of a pledge is not a "paid" guardian in general, but here the lender of produce receives the benefit of disposing of produce that is subject to spoilage.

Abba Saul allows the creditor to actually make business use of the pledge (making the creditor a kind of "renter"), if the financial income goes to reduce the amount owed by the debtor.

credit it to his loan: Precise translation is difficult; the verb is the same as in the contracts of provision in 5:7.

returning a lost object: For the expression see 3:6 and *Shevu'ot* 6:1.

8 One who moves a jar from place to place and broke it,
whether an unpaid guardian or a paid guardian—
he may swear.
R. Eliezer says:
This one and this one may swear,
but[86] I question if this one and this one are able to swear.

Chapter Seven

7:1–8 *Hire of Artisans, Animals, and Laborers: Food for Laborers*

7 One who hires workers,
and told them to come early or stay late:
in a place where it was customary not to come early or not to stay late—
he is not permitted to force them;
in a place where it was customary to feed—
he must feed;
to provide sweets—
he must provide;
all follows the custom of the place.
It happened that R. Yohanan b. Matia said to his son:
Go out and hire workers for us.
He went and agreed to provide food.
And when he came to his father, he said to him:
My son, even if you make a feast for them like that of Solomon in his time,
you have not fulfilled your obligation with respect to them,
for they are the sons of Abraham, Isaac, and Jacob.

[86] K, P, C lack "This one…but."

6:8 *One who moves*: Another passage on moving a jar and the liability of the guardian (3:9, 12).

he may swear and be exempt from payment. Here, the Bavli and the commentaries understand the underlying concern to be negligence in handling the object. Both types of guardian are permitted to swear that they were not negligent.

R. Eliezer concurs that this is the received rule (see n. 86), but questions why either type of guardian might be entitled to an oath denying negligence.

7:1 The discussion now turns to laborers. Unlike artisans (see 6:1–2n.), these are unskilled day laborers. In this mishnah, and those that follow, the worker is generally assumed to be an agricultural worker.

come early or stay late: The employer is expected to follow the custom of the place in both the requirements demanded of the workers and the provision of meals.

R. Yohanan b. Matia said to his son: In light of the comment by Rabban Simeon b. Gamaliel that follows, the story of R. Yohanan b. Matia does not assume that one relies on local custom, as in the preceding tradition.

Rather, before they begin the work go out and say to them:
On condition that you have a claim against me only for bread and legumes alone.
Rabban Simeon b. Gamaliel says:
He did not have to say this; all follows the custom of the land.

2 And these eat according to the Torah:
one who works:
on that which is connected to the ground,
at the time of the completion of the labor;
or on that which is separated from the earth,
before its labor is completed,
on something that[87] grows from the earth.
And these do not eat:
one who works on that which is connected to the ground,
not at the time of the completion of the labor,
and on that which is separated from the earth,
after its labor is completed,
and on something that does not grow from the earth.

3 If he was working with his feet, but not with his hands,
with his hands, but not with his feet,

[87] K: "as long as it."

before they begin: The contract does not formally begin until the labor starts. The stress on the equality of all Israelites as the *sons of Abraham, Isaac, and Jacob* (see Bava Qamma 8:4) coupled with instruction on how to limit workers' entitlements to those of mere laborers, entitled to a meal of *bread and legumes*, points to competing social and economic values within early rabbinic circles.

Rabban Simeon b. Gamaliel's comment coincides with that of the first part of the mishnah: no special stipulations are necessary. Having stipulated to provide meals, the workers' entitlement is still constrained by local custom.

7:2 The Mishnah assumes that workers are entitled to eat produce while working, and considers the right to be granted by the Torah. It is notable that agriculturally focused ritual laws and these laws map onto one another.

eat according to the Torah: In fact, the Torah makes no such explicit permission. Reference may be to Deuteronomy 23:25–26, although these verses do not specify workers, or Deuteronomy 25:4, *Do not muzzle an ox while it threshes*. Permission *according to the Torah* is juxtaposed with benefits governed by "custom" in 7:1, as well as the broadened permission in 7:4. See also 7:8.

connected to the ground... completion of the labor, while picking produce that is not further processed before being used; *separated... before its labor is completed*, while completing further processing, such as threshing of grain.

connected... not at the time of completion, such as weeding; *separated... after its labor is completed*, such as separating dates that have been pressed; *does not grow from the earth*, such as milking cattle. These types of labor do not qualify the worker to eat.

after its labor is completed: Completion of labor is also a significant criterion in other, ritual categories, including when produce becomes liable to gifts for priests and Levites (e.g. *Ma'aserot* 2:4), and *Ma'serot* 2:7 links the legal areas further by exempting from tithes anything a worker is permitted to eat. See further 7:4.

7:3 *working with his feet... carrying on his shoulder*: The first view in the mishnah is that labor that qualifies the worker to eat is relatively loosely defined. According to *R. Yose b. Judah*, the work must involve *hands* and *feet*. This view may stem from midrashic analogy with the "ox" in Deuteronomy 25:6.

even if he was merely carrying on his shoulder[88]—
in this case, this one eats.
R. Yose b. Judah says:
He must[89] work with his hands and his feet.

4 If he was working with figs, he may not eat from the grapes;
with grapes, he may not eat from the figs,
but he may hold himself back
until he gets to the place of the nicer produce and eat.
And in all of these cases they permitted eating only during the time[90] of labor.
But because of the principle of returning a lost object to its owners, they said:
Workers may eat while walking from row to row,
and while they are returning from the winepress,
and in regard to an ass, when it is being unburdened.

5 A worker eats cucumber, even as much as a *dinar*'s worth,
and dates, even as much as a *dinar*'s worth.
R. Eleazar Hisma says:
A worker may not eat more than his wage;
but the Sages permit.
But they teach a person not to be a glutton and close the door before him.

6 A person may stipulate terms for himself,
or his adult son or daughter,
or his adult male slave or female slave,
or his wife,

---

[88] Lit. "even on his shoulder." [89] Lit. "until."
[90] K, P, C: "the time of the completion of the labor," cf. 7:2. "They permitted eating" added for clarity.

7:4 *working with figs*: The worker may eat more from *nicer*, i.e. better quality, produce as long as he is working with that produce. *Ma'aserot* 2:8 contains a near parallel to this rule, where the implicit context is workers' ability to eat without liability to tithes.

only during the time of labor, as opposed to *walking* or *returning* alone. According to the reading *during the time of the completion of the labor* (see n. 90) workers were permitted to eat at the completion of the task or workday rather than during their working activities (Maimonides, *Code*). Alternatively, this reading refers to the specific tasks that complete the labor, as in 7:2, as opposed to ancillary activities. *They said* refers to a prior rule. If the reading including *completion* is correct, this passage may cite 7:2, or both may develop an earlier rule.

principle of returning: Cf. 3:6 and 6:9.

an ass: The application to animals has not been mentioned before, but is specified by Deuteronomy 25:4. Arguably, this passage originated as an exposition of "threshing" in that verse.

7:5 *even as much as a dinar's worth*: a considerable amount of fruit (see *Ma'aserot* 2:6 for comparison; but cf. *Bava Batra* 9:5). This may mean "even an excessive amount," or set a fixed ceiling. R. Eleazar Hisma explicitly sets a ceiling pegged to the wage. The two views may be linked if a *dinar* was the conventional wage to illustrate agricultural day labor (Matthew 20:2).

7:6 *may stipulate terms*: May agree to forgo the right to eat in exchange for higher wages.

adult son, etc.: Adults, regardless of their gender or status, are expected to be able to comply with the stipulation; minors are not. Here, even adult children are imagined as participating in a household governed by a householder; cf. 1:5.

for they have understanding;
but he may not stipulate terms for his minor son and daughter,
nor for his minor male and female slaves,
nor for his animal,
for they have no understanding.

7 One who hires workers to work on his fourth-year produce—
in this case, they may not eat.
If he did not inform them, he redeems it and feeds them.
If his fig rounds broke up or his jars opened—
in this case, they may not eat.
If he did not inform them, he tithes and feeds them.

8 Guardians of produce eat according to the laws of the place,
but not according to the laws of the Torah.

7:8 cont.–10 *Guardians of Property*

There are four guardians:
(1) the unpaid guardian, and
(2) the borrower,
(3) the wage bearer, and
(4) the renter.
The unpaid guardian swears for everything;
the borrower pays for everything;

7:7 *fourth-year produce*: See 4:8 and *Orlah*, introduction; Leviticus 19:23–24. Since the produce must be transported to Jerusalem or redeemed for coin before it can be eaten, the employees *may not eat* while working.

did not inform: Without being informed, the workers have no way of knowing that the produce is prohibited and cannot be said to have agreed to these terms. The owner *redeems* the produce and allows the workers to eat.

fig rounds broke...jars opened: Figs pressed into rounds and jars of wine constitute produce whose work has been completed (cf. 7:2, 4), and are liable to tithes. As in the preceding case, there is no way for the worker to know this.

7:8 *according to the laws of the place*: See 7:1. The rule contrasts with that of 7:2, which addresses the right to eat *according to the Torah*. Guards do not work directly with produce, so are not covered by the rules in the preceding section. This passage serves as the transition to the following section in which the Mishnah returns to guardians.

four guardians: i.e. types of guardians. This concise summary also appears in *Shevu'ot* 8:1. *Wage bearer* is equivalent to "paid guardian" (4:9, 6:6–8).

everything refers to the circumstances specified at the end of the mishnah: *broken...animal* and *loss and theft*. The terminology for these possibilities derives directly from Exodus 22:6–14. However, the Mishnah treats the cases of Exodus 22:6–7 and 7–13 as referring to paid and unpaid guardians. The underlying principle is that liability is tied to benefit to the guardian and owner. An *unpaid guardian* (above, 3:1), gains no benefit but the owner benefits. Consequently liability for the guardian is low. In the case of a *borrower*, the reverse is true and liability is high.

and the wage bearer and the renter swear on the broken, captured, or dead animal,
and pay for loss and theft.

9 A single wolf is not an unavoidable accident;
two wolves are an unavoidable accident.
R. Judah says:
At a time of an infestation of wolves,
even a single wolf is an unavoidable accident.
Two dogs are not an unavoidable accident.
Yadu'a the Babylonian says in the name of R. Meir:
From one direction it is not an unavoidable accident;
from two directions it is an unavoidable accident.
A brigand is an unavoidable accident.
The lion,[91] the bear, the leopard, the panther, and the serpent—
all these are an unavoidable accident.
When?
When they came by themselves.
But if he walked the flocks to a place of bands of wild animals or brigands—
these are not an unavoidable accident.

10 If it died in the typical manner, then it is an unavoidable accident;
if he afflicted it and it died, then it is not an unavoidable accident.
If it went up to the tops of the peaks, and it fell,
then it is an unavoidable accident;
if he brought it up to the tops of the peaks and it fell,
then it is not an unavoidable accident.
An unpaid guardian may stipulate the condition that he be exempt from an oath,
and a borrower that he be exempt from paying;
and a wage bearer and renter that they be exempt from an oath and from paying.

[91] C (and P, as corrected by a second hand) add at the beginning of the list: "The wolf."

In the other two contracts, both parties receive benefit. The *renter* may be derived from the Exodus 22:14b or on analogy with *wage bearer*.

7:9 *unavoidable accident* is a category of damage that has not been explicitly introduced up to this point. The cases imagined correspond to "broken or captured" animal of 7:8 (and Exodus 22:9–14).

R. Judah exempts in the case of an *infestation* (lit. "delegation"), because the animals may be more aggressive (commentaries).

lion…serpent: The list corresponds to the list in *Bava Qamma* 1:4.

if he walked the flocks…these are not an unavoidable accident: Here and in the following passage, the Mishnah adumbrates but does not fully develop the legal category of culpable negligence (see 3:9, 6:8).

7:10 *died in the usual manner*: See 3:2. The case corresponds to "died" in 7:8 and Exodus 22:9–14. Here, and in the case of the animal that *went up* or was *brought up* to a high place from which it fell, the liability depends upon whether the guardian took actions that caused the death or injury.

may stipulate: May undertake a contract on condition that the standard rules do not apply (cf. e.g. 7:6). The cases correspond directly to 7:8. *Exempt from an oath*, but nonetheless remain exempt from paying.

7:11 *Legal Aphorisms regarding Stipulated Conditions*

11 Anyone who stipulates a condition
contradicting[92] what is written in the Torah,[93]
his condition is invalid.
And any stipulated condition that has[94] the dependent act preceding it,
his condition is invalid;
and any stipulated condition that it is possible to fulfill at its end,
and he stipulated the condition from the beginning,
his condition is valid.

Chapter Eight

8:1–3 *Loans for Use*

8 One who borrows a cow,
and borrowed its owner with it,
or[95] hired its owners with it;
or if he borrowed the owners or hired them,
and afterwards borrowed the cow,
and it died—
he is exempt,
as it is written: *If its owners are with him*[96] *he shall not pay.*

---

[92] Lit. "on."
[93] K, P "on (= contradicting) a writing that is in the Torah."
[94] K, P, C: "is."
[95] K, P, instead: "borrowed (C, 'hired') the cow and."
[96] Or "it." So too immediately below.

7:11 *contradicting what is written in the Torah*: The rule appears elsewhere in the Mishnah in conditions related to inheritance: *Ketubbot* 9:1; *Bava Batra* 8:3. There, a father or wife cannot employ a stipulation to prevent a legal heir from inheriting since such a *condition is invalid*.

And any stipulated condition: The translation is a paraphrase. At issue is a transaction in which the outcome is dependent upon a completion of a conditional act (e.g. "If X happens, then Y is yours"). According to Rashi and others, the Mishnah is concerned with the form of the stipulation: for the *stipulated condition* to be valid, it must not precede the *dependent act*. According to Maimonides, the concern is with the performance of the act: One cannot perform a transaction first ("Y is hereby yours") and then stipulate that its validity is contingent upon a condition ("on condition that X happens"). *His condition is invalid*: The act itself is valid, because the limiting condition is not.

To be valid, the *condition* must be *possible to fulfill at its end* and *stipulated…from the beginning*. When the condition is valid, the effectiveness of the act ("Y is yours") depends on the fulfillment of the condition ("If X happens").

8:1 *borrowed…or hired its owners with it*: Exodus 22:13–14a deems a borrower exempt *if its owner was with him/it*. The Mishnah envisions the owner's presence as free ("borrowed") or hired labor. If the owner's engagement was simultaneous with, or preceded, borrowing the animal, the borrower is *exempt* from liability in the case of death.

If its owners are with him, or it: Exodus 22:14.

But if he borrowed the cow, and afterwards borrowed the owners,
or hired them,
and it died—
he is liable,
as it is written: *If its owners are not with him he shall indeed pay.*

2 One who borrows the cow,
if he borrowed it for half a day and rented it for half a day;
borrowed it one day and rented it the next;
rented one and borrowed one,
and it died:
if the lender says:
"The borrowed one died";
"It died on the day it was borrowed";
"It died at the time that it was borrowed,"
and the other says:
"I do not know"—
he is liable;
If the renter says:
"The rented one died";
"It died on the day that it was rented";
"It died at the time that it was rented,"[97]
and the other says:
"I do not know"—
he is exempt.
This one says the borrowed one and this one says the rented one—
the renter may swear that the rented animal died.
This one says: "I do not know"; and this one says: "I do not know"—
let them split it.

3 One who borrows[98] a cow,
and the lender sent it to him by the hand of his son,

---

[97] Lacking in **K**. [98] **K**: "sends."

If the owner was engaged after borrowing, the borrower is *liable*.

If its owners are not with him, or it: Exodus 22:13.

8:2 *borrowed it…rented it*: A borrower is liable for the death of an animal, a renter exempt (7:8).

the lender says: The borrower/renter and the owner dispute whether the animal was borrowed or rented when it died.

the renter says: The reverse of the preceding: the renter makes a positive claim, and the owner does not. The animal is considered rented, and the borrower-and-renter is exempt.

the borrowed one…the rented one: Both parties make positive claims. In this case, the borrower/renter may *swear that the rented animal died* (see 8:1) and be exempt.

"I do not know": Neither party makes a positive claim.

split: Presumably the borrower-and-renter must pay for half.

8:3 Liability as a borrower begins at the moment the borrower takes possession. The Mishnah examines who has possession while the animal is being transferred.

by the hand of his slave,
by the hand of his agent;
or by the hand of the son,
by the hand of the slave,
by the hand of the agent of the borrower,
and it died—
[the borrower] is exempt.
If the borrower said to him:
"Send it to me by the hand of my son,"
"by the hand of my slave,"
"by the hand of my agent";
"by the hand of your son,"
"by the hand of your slave,"
"by the hand of your agent";
or if the lender said to him:
"I am hereby sending it to you by the hand of my son,"
"by the hand of my slave,"
"by the hand of my agent";
or "by the hand of your son,"
"by the hand of your slave,"
"by the hand of your agent,"
and the borrower said: "Send it,"
and he sent it and it died—
he is liable.
And so too at the time when he returns it.

8:4–5 *Exchange or Sale of Animals, Slaves, or Trees*

4 One who exchanges a cow with an ass,
and it gave birth,
and so too one who sells his female slave, and she gave birth,
this one says: "The birth took place[99] before I sold it,"
and this one says: "After I bought it"—
they split it.

[99] Absent in current editions; **P, C**: "It/she gave birth."

And so too: When returning the animal, the borrower remains liable until the moment it enters the owner's possession.

8:4 *exchanges*: By barter. When the new owner takes possession of the ass, the cow automatically transfers to its new owner (*Qiddushin* 1:6). If it were sold, ownership would only transfer when the purchaser takes possession (*Qiddushin* 1:4).

sells his female slave: Unlike movable goods, slaves may transfer to the purchaser at the delivery of the payment (*Qiddushin* 1:3). The parties dispute whether the birth preceded or followed the transfer.

split it: See 1:1.

If he had two slaves, one large and one small,
and so too two fields, one large and one small,
if the buyer says:
"I bought the large one,"
and the latter says:
"I do not know"—
the buyer has gained ownership of the large one.
If the seller says:
"I sold the small one,"
and the latter says:
"I do not know"—
the buyer has only the small one.
This one says: "The big one,"
and this one says: "The small one"—
let the seller swear that he sold the small one.
This one says: "I do not know," and this one says: "I do not know"—
let them split it.
5 One who sells his olive trees for wood,
and they produced less than a quarter-*log* of oil to the *se'ah*—
in this case they belong to the owner of the olive trees.
If they produced a quarter-*log* to the *se'ah*,
this one says: "My olive trees have grown it";
and this one says: "My ground has grown it"—
let them split it.
If a river swept away his olive trees, and put them in the field of his fellow,
this one says: "My olive trees have grown it";
and this one says: "My land has grown it"—
let them split it.

two slaves…and so too two fields: Here the uncertainty is whether the larger or smaller slave or field was sold.

the latter says, I do not know: The party making a positive claim is favored.

let the seller swear: The oath indemnifies the seller against delivering the more valuable property; the buyer gets only the less valuable. Cf. *Shevu'ot* 6:5 where one does not take oaths over slaves and land.

let them split it: They split the difference between the two properties. See 1:1.

8:5 All the examples involve uncertainty about whether the trees or the soil, which belong to different owners, are responsible for the growth of the olives.

sells…for wood, but they still stand on the seller's property.

less than a quarter-log of oil to the se'ah of olives. This expression characterizes the quality of the olives produced (Rashi) rather than the total amount of oil. Below this threshold the olives are negligible and belong to the owner of the trees; above it, and both make positive claims (cf. 8:2, 4), they *split* the oil.

a river swept away: Again, the olive production alone is subject to dispute.

8:6–9 *Lease of Houses*

6 One who leases a house to his fellow during the rainy season—
he cannot expel him from Sukkot[100] until Passover;
during the summer,[101]
thirty days.
And in the cities,
the law is one and the same during the summer or during the rainy season—
twelve months.
And in shops,
the law is one and the same in towns or in cities[102]—
twelve months.
Rabban Simeon b. Gamaliel says:
A shop of bakers or dyers, three years.[103]

7 One who leases a house to his fellow,
the lessor is obligated to provide the door, the bolt, the lock,
and anything that is the work of an artisan.
But anything that is not the work of an artisan,
the renter makes it.
The manure belongs to the householder;
and the renter has only what comes forth from the oven or the stove.

8 One who leases a house to his fellow for a year:
if the year was intercalated, the intercalated month is to the renter's advantage;
if he rented it to him by the month,
if the year was intercalated, the intercalated month is to the lessor's advantage.

---

[100] Lit. "the festival."   [101] Lit. "during the days of the sun."
[102] C: "villages", presumably in error.   [103] P: "twelve months," subsequently corrected.

8:6 *during the rainy season*: The language is a bit awkward, but implies that there is no expulsion at all during the rainy season. The reason may be the difficulty of relocating or the relative paucity of housing. The Mishnah may be setting the minimum or default extent of a lease, or (with commentaries and Bavli) require thirty days' notice at a time before the rainy season begins.

during the summer, thirty days: The standard minimum lease in summer is for one month; the owner may give as little as thirty days' advance notice (Tosefta, Talmud, and commentaries).

cities: The Mishnah's imagined world centers on "towns" (below); cities require special mention. The time limit in cities is longer, perhaps reflecting less availability of housing.

shops have a standard minimum term, or minimum periods of advance notice, of *twelve months*. According to *Rabban Simeon b. Gamaliel*, the term is three years for *bakers or dyers*, because they have considerable outstanding credit that they need to collect (Tosefta).

towns: Settlements with institutions such as shops or synagogues.

8:7 Compare what is conveyed in the sale of a house, *Bava Batra* 4:3.

manure from animals that are kept in the common courtyard.

what comes forth from the oven: Ash and refuse used for fertilizer and other purposes. Cooking too, took place in the courtyard.

8:8 *if the year was intercalated*: i.e. if an extra month was added, see *Rosh Hashanah*.

It happened in Sepphoris, that someone rented a bath from his fellow
for twelve golden *dinar* for a year, a golden *dinar* a month.[104]
The matter came before Rabban Simeon b. Gamaliel and R. Yose;
they said:
Let them split the intercalated month.

9 One who leases a house to his fellow,
and it fell:
He must provide the renter with a house.
If it was small, let him not make it large,
large, let him not make it small;
one, let him not make it two;
two, let him not make it one.
He may neither reduce the number of windows nor increase them,
except with the knowledge of both.

Chapter Nine

9:1–10   *Contracts of Tenant Farming*

9 One who receives a field from his fellow—
in a place where it was customary to harvest by cutting, let him cut;
to uproot, let him uproot;
to plow afterwards, let him plow;

---

[104] C adds "and the year turned out to be intercalated."

It happened in Sepphoris: The contract specified both the yearly and the monthly rent, so the above rule could not be applied.

split intercalated month: See 1:1.

8:9 *must provide*: Compare 6:3, in regard to rental of animals.

small, let him not make it large: The owner must provide as close to an identical dwelling as possible. The following clause, about windows, suggests that both parties may have an interest in retaining the prior conditions.

except with the knowledge of both: For the expression, see 5:6.

9:1–10 The Mishnah knows different kinds of tenant-farming arrangements. In this section, the Mishnah refers generically to these arrangements as "receiving," but they include sharecropping (payment in kind of a proportion of the produce), tenancy for fixed payment in kind, or fixed payment in coin. Above, in connection with raising animals (5:4–6), the verb "receive" is used for a proportionate arrangement, and elsewhere it is used for farming leases as well (*Pe'ah* 5:5).

9:1 *One who receives*: As with the hiring of workers (7:1), the discussion opens with the force of customary practice. See also 4:11, 5:5. Surviving written contracts, especially from Egypt, show that the practices considered here might be specified by the parties (and see *Bava Batra* 10:4; and below 9:3).

all follows the custom of the place.
Just as they split the grain, so they split the fodder and straw.
Just as they split the wine, so do they split the pruned branches and the reeds;
and both of them provide the reeds.

2 One who receives a field from his fellow,
and it is a field dependent on irrigation
or a tree plantation:
if the spring went dry or the tree was cut down—
he does not deduct from his rent due.
If he said: "Lease me[105] this field-dependent-on-irrigation,"
or "this tree plantation":
if the spring went dry or the tree was cut down—
he does deduct from his rent due.

3 One who receives a field from his fellow,
and[106] lets it fallow—
they assess how much the field is likely to have yielded,[107]
and he gives[108] it to him,
for thus does he write[109] to him:
"If I let it fallow and do not work it, I shall pay at the highest rate."

4 One who receives a field from his fellow,
and did not want to weed,

---

[105] Heb. *hakor* (usually, a lease for fixed payment in kind) so too **C**; In contrast **K, P, G** have *haskir*. See annotations.
[106] **K, P, C, G**: "Once he gained possession of it, he let it fallow." **K** lacks "One who receives…fallow."
[107] Or "is capable of yielding."   [108] **K, P, G**: "they give."
[109] **P, C, K** (after correction): "for he says to him"; **G, K** (originally?): "for he writes to him."

Just as they split the grain: The implied lease is a sharecropping one.

both of them provide: They are both responsible for the materials to support the vines at the outset of the labor.

9:2 *spring went dry…tree was cut down*: In the general case, the owner is not responsible for changes to circumstances.

his rent due: Presumably a fixed amount, rather than a percentage.

this field: The tenant stipulated a particular field or tree, and the rent was set based on their condition at that time. Here, the owner *does deduct from his rent due*. Cf. 9:6.

"Lease me": See n. 105. *Hakor* implies payment in kind; *haskir* in money.

9:3 The contract is a sharecropping arrangement. Letting the field *fallow* was part of a known strategy in the Roman Empire for maintaining the quality of the soil (see also 9:8–9). In a one-year lease, however, it would result in no yield from which to pay the owner.

they assess: Typically, this plural form is impersonal. Here it may refer to a court that makes an assessment. Similarly, the alternative reading for *he gives*, "they give" (see n. 108), would imply that the court exacts payment from the tenant.

for thus does he write: See n. 109. A reference to a standard lease formula.

at the highest rate: The payment assumes that the field would have produced high-quality produce.

9:4 Here, the contract is for fixed rent (*hakor*). The owner can require the tenant to *weed* during the tenancy, since failure to do so creates additional labor after its completion.

and said to him:
"What does it matter to you, in as much as I am giving you your rent?"
They do not listen to him,
because the owner can say to him:
"Tomorrow you will leave it, and it will be full of grasses."[110]

5 One who receives a field from his fellow,
and it did not produce:
if there was enough in it to raise a heap—
he is required to care for it.
Said R. Judah:
What fixed amount is a "heap"?
Rather: If there is enough in it for seed.[111]

6 One who receives a field from his fellow,
and it was eaten by locusts or was blighted:
if the blow was to the whole region—
he deducts from his rent;
if the blow was not to the whole region—
he does not deduct from his rent.
R. Judah says:
If he received it from him for money, in neither case does he deduct from his rent.

7 One who receives a field from his fellow,
for ten *kor* of wheat for a year:
if the field was blighted—
he pays him from the produce of the field itself.[112]
If its wheat was good—

---

[110] Lit. "and it produces grasses before me."
[111] Lit. "enough in it for falling"; as vocalized in the manuscripts, perhaps "for casting."
[112] Lit. "he gives him from within it," here and below.

9:5 *did not produce*: The commentaries view the contract as a sharecropping one; if rented for a fixed amount, the owner would in any case receive his rent (but see 9:6). It is possible, though, that the Mishnah is concerned with the tenant following through on the obligation to work the field, as in 9:4.

to raise a heap: Apparently based on a reading of a documentary formula (Tosefta, Bavli).

What fixed amount is a heap? The criterion is too unspecific. *R. Judah* makes the criterion whether the tenant can recover enough to seed the field again (see n. 111).

9:6 Especially given the comment of R. Judah below, the contract here would appear to be for a fixed amount.

blow...to the whole region: A general infestation or blight requires landowners to revise their expectations, but a single field can be attributed to the tenant's own ill fortune (see *Bava Qamma* 10:5).

According to *R. Judah*, if the contract is to pay coin, rather than produce that should derive from the field itself (9:7), even a general infestation or blight does not alter the obligations of the tenant.

9:7 *for ten kor of wheat for a year*: The contract is explicitly one of fixed payment although the principle should apply to sharecropping as well.

blighted, so that the produce was of poor quality. *Good*: Particularly good quality. In both cases, the tenant pays with *produce of the field itself*.

he may not say:
"I am hereby buying from the market,"
but he pays him from the produce of the field itself.

8 One who receives a field from his fellow,
to seed it with barley, he may not seed it with wheat;
with wheat, he may seed it with barley.
Rabban Simeon b. Gamaliel prohibits.
With grain, he may not seed it with legumes;
with legumes, he may seed it with grain.[113]
Rabban Simeon b. Gamaliel prohibits.

9 One who receives a field from his fellow,
for few years—
he may not seed it with flax,
and he has no share in the sycamore beams.
If he received it from him for seven years—
the first year, he may seed it with flax,
and he has a share in the sycamore beams.

10 One who receives a field from his fellow,
for a Sabbatical cycle[114] for seven hundred *zuz*—

---

[113] K, P, G (see also C): "With legumes, he may not seed it with grain; with grain, he may seed it with legumes."

[114] Lit. "a week," i.e. of years. K, P, C reverse the order of the two cases of this mishnah.

"from the market": The tenant may not purchase average-quality wheat to use for payment, and keep all of the good-quality wheat for his own use.

9:8 *wheat...barley*: In this mishnah and 9:9, the underlying agricultural issue is the effect of crops on soil and crop-rotation practices. The tenant may not unilaterally plant *wheat* in place of *barley* but may plant *barley* in place of *wheat*, either because wheat is considered more damaging to the soil than barley (commentaries) or because the greater yield due from barley might sufficiently compensate for any damage (Yerushalmi).

grain...legumes: The reading in the manuscripts (see n. 113) is consistent with awareness of the positive effects of leguminous plants on soil (nitrogen fixing). The Bavli knew both readings and attributed the reading in our printed editions to the ecological conditions of Mesopotamia.

Rabban Simeon b. Gamaliel rules in both cases that the tenant cannot plant a different crop than that stipulated in the contract.

9:9 When the lease was *for a few years*—by implication, fewer than seven—the tenant *may not seed it with flax*, because of the depletion of the soil.

no share in the sycamore beams, presumably because they need a minimum of seven years to reach optimal length. This rule would imply a sharecropping tenancy. A term of *seven years* is long enough for the tenant to plant flax in *the first year*, and similarly to have a *share in the sycamore beams* on vacating the lease.

9:10 *for a Sabbatical cycle*: Lit. "a week" of years, a seven-year period that necessarily includes a Sabbatical year. See *Shevi'it*, introduction.

is included in that number: The tenant is obligated to pay rent during the year when there is no income from the field, and agricultural work is prohibited. Cf. 8:8 for an analogous issue.

the Seventh Year is included in that number;
if he received them from him for seven years for seven hundred *zuz*—
the Seventh Year is not included in that number.

9:11–12 *Paying the Day Laborer His Wage*

11 One hired by day collects his wage during the whole night;[115]
one hired by night collects his wage during the whole day;
one hired by the hour collects the whole night and[116] the whole day.
One hired for the week,
one hired for the month,
one hired for the year,
one hired for the Sabbatical cycle:
if he left by day—
he collects his wage during the whole day;
if he left by night—
he collects his wage during the whole night and the whole day.
12 The law is one and the same for the hire of a person,
the hire of an animal,
and the hire of utensils:
On his day you shall give him his hire, applies to each;
and

---

[115] C: "day" here; and "night" in the following clause.   [116] Alt. "or."

---

for seven years is presumed to mean seven agricultural years, not including the sabbatical Seventh Year.

9:11 Leviticus 19:13 and Deuteronomy 24:14–15 require an employer to pay the worker promptly. Mishnah 9:11 presupposes rules expressed more fully in 9:12.

collects…during the whole night: In part, this mishnah is aligning special rules with the duplication of the law in the Torah (Sifra, and see 9:12). The employee must demand payment over the course of the night, and the employer is compliant with the law as long as payment takes place before morning (Leviticus 19:13).

collects…during the whole day: The corresponding Torah rule is Deuteronomy 24:15.

one hired by the hour, and not for a full day's or night's work.

collects the whole night and the whole day, depending on when the work finished (commentaries). This explanation is somewhat difficult in that the identical expression is used differently in the latter part of this mishnah and one suggestion in the Bavli is that the two parts derive from different sources. Perhaps in both cases, where neither day work nor night work is specified the term is thought to end at the end of a day.

One hired for the week [lit. "Sabbath"]…*for the Sabbatical cycle* [lit. "week"]: The Mishnah extends the biblical rule from day laborers to other contract employees, specifically ones working more than one day or part of a day. The period during which payment is supposed to take place ends with the end of daytime. When the worker *left* the job *by day*, the employer has the remainder of that *whole day* to comply; when the worker *left by night*, the employer has until the end of the following day.

9:12 *one and the same*: The Mishnah applies the Torah's laws to any case involving *hire*. This perhaps reflects a measure of systematization of contract law.

On his day: Deuteronomy 24:15.

You shall not let the wage of the laborer rest with you overnight until the morning applies to each.
When?
When he claimed his hire from him;
but if he did not claim from him,
the employer[117] does not transgress.
If he arranged for credit for him at a shopkeeper or a moneychanger,
he does not transgress.
The hired laborer, at his appropriate time, swears[118] and takes;
if his time has passed, he does not swear and take.
If there are witnesses that he claimed [his hire] from him,
in this case he swears and takes.
A resident alien:
On that day you shall give him his hire, applies to him.
but *You shall not let the wage of the laborer rest with you overnight until the morning* does not apply to him.

9:13 *Rules about Pledges*

13 One who lends to his fellow
may not exact a pledge from him except in court,

[117] Lit. "he." [118] K, P, C: "swears at his appropriate time [lit. at his time] and collects."

You shall not let: Leviticus 19:13. See 9:11.

When he claimed: The employer's transgression of the biblical laws is not automatic, but contingent upon the employee actually claiming payment.

shopkeeper…moneychanger: As in 3:11, both may be engaged in small-scale credit transactions. See also *Shevu'ot* 7:5. The employer *does not transgress*, even if the shopkeeper or moneychanger fails to pay, because he has provided a mechanism for payment.

at his appropriate time: Presumably, the times specified in 9:11 when the employee "collects." Compare *On his day*, Deuteronomy 24:15.

swears and takes: Generally, an oath exempts a claimant from payment in the absence of proof from the testimony of witnesses (e.g. 3:1 above). In a number of cases, including unpaid workers, the Mishnah permits a claimant to *take*, i.e. exact payment, on the basis of an oath. See *Shevu'ot* 7:1.

if his time has passed: If the employee's charge that the employer has not paid is made after the appropriate time, the employee is not given the benefit of the doubt and is not allowed to swear.

If there are witnesses that the employee claimed payment at "his time," the employee is given the benefit of the doubt and may exact payment with an oath.

resident alien: See above, 5:5. Deuteronomy 24:14 explicitly includes *the alien who is in your land in your gates*. By the time of the Mishnah the legal category of resident alien had become largely theoretical.

9:13 The discussion of timely payment of the worker in Deuteronomy 24:14–15 is preceded (24:6, 10–13) and followed (24:17) by rules about pledges. The juxtaposition in the Torah presumably accounts for the placement of these matters together in the Mishnah as well.

in court: The Mishnah requires a court to mediate seizing a pledge. This requirement is not mentioned in the Torah, unlike the rule that he *may not enter his house*.

and may not enter his house to take his pledge,
as it is said: *You shall stand outside.*
If he had two utensils—
he takes one and leaves[119] one.
And[120] he returns the pillow by night and the plow by day.
And if the debtor died, the creditor does not return it to the creditor's heirs.[121]
Rabban Simeon b. Gamaliel says:
Even to the debtor himself[122] he only returns it up to thirty days;
and from thirty days onward he sells it in court.
A widow, whether she is poor or whether she is wealthy—
one does not exact a pledge from her,
as it is said: *And you shall not take a widow's garment in pledge.*
One who seizes a millstone in pledge,
transgresses a negative commandment,
and is liable on account of two utensils,
as it is said: *You shall not take an upper millstone and lower millstone in pledge.*
Not only have they prohibited[123] upper and lower millstones,
but also anything that one uses to sustain life,
as it is written, *for he takes a life as a pledge.*

---

[119] K, P, C: "returns." [120] K, P, C lack "and."
[121] "Debtor…creditor…creditor's": lit. "he," "his." [122] Lit. "himself." [123] Lit. "said."

---

two utensils: This rule should be read as continued in what follows: *he returns the pillow by night* (see textual note to "and," n. 120). The rule regarding the daytime tool is not explicitly in Scripture. Deuteronomy 24:6, prohibiting taking of millstones, does implicitly discuss taking of items used in daily work.

if the debtor died: The special obligations regarding the pledge only apply to the initial borrower; when the borrower dies, the lender may recover payment from the pledge itself.

Rabban Simeon b. Gamaliel rules that the requirement to repeatedly return a pledge is always temporary. Cf. 3:6 for a similar rule attributed to Rabban Simeon b. Gamaliel. The commentaries take thirty days to be a default court-determined time limit.

A widow: The subject of a special verse: *And you shall not take*, Deuteronomy 24:17. The Mishnah reads this as an absolute prohibition regardless of her poverty.

millstone: Also the subject of a special verse: *You shall not take*, Deuteronomy 24:6.

transgresses a negative commandment: The significance is the transgressor's guilt before the deity. The verse specifies both *upper millstone and lower millstone*, and the Mishnah takes this specification to make the lender liable separately for either part of the mill. If he takes both parts of a mill in pledge, he is liable on account of two utensils.

for he takes a life as a pledge: The conclusion of Deuteronomy 24:6. The Mishnah takes these words to extend the rule to any tool for producing the staples of life.

Chapter Ten

10:1–4 *Disputes between Owners of Upper and Lower Storys*

10 If a house and an upper story, belonging to two different people, fell—
the two of them split the wood, and the stones, and the earth;
and they evaluate which stones are likely to have broken.
If one of them recognized some of the stones as his,
he takes them, and they are removed from the reckoning.

2 A house and an upper story, belonging to two different people—
if the upper story became worn down,
and the owner of the house does not want to fix it—
then the owner of the upper story descends and dwells below,
until he repairs the upper story for him.
R. Yose says:
The lower provides the beams, and the upper provides the plaster.

3 If a house and an upper story, belonging to two different people, fell—
if the owner of the upper story told the owner of the house to build,
but he does not want to build,
then the owner of the upper story builds the house
and dwells in it until he gives him his outlay.
R. Judah says:
Even so, he is dwelling in his fellow's property; he would have to pay him rent.

10:1–4 The Mishnah addresses situations in which owners of a lower or upper *story* may have claims upon another. The subject matter is thematically related to the beginning of *Bava Batra*, with which *Bava Metsi'a* was originally continuous.

10:1 *split the wood, and the stones, and the earth*, seemingly on an equal basis. What follows makes the rule slightly more complex.

evaluate which stones: From the damage itself it may be possible to tell whether the stones of the upper or lower story suffered more damage.

recognized…removed from the reckoning: The parties may claim building material that is distinctive, but in that case they take a smaller share in the remaining material.

10:2 *if the upper story became worn down*: From the statement of R. Yose below, it is the floor of the upper story that has worn down. The first, anonymous, view in the Mishnah is that it is the *owner of the house*, i.e. the lower story, who is obligated to make repairs, or allow the *owner of the upper story* to *descend and dwell below*.

R. *Yose* divides the responsibility between the parties, but it is not clear whether he disagrees over the matter of dwelling in the lower story.

10:3 *owner of the upper story builds…and dwells in it*: The logic is approximately that of the first view in the preceding passage: the owner of the upper story is dependent upon the owner of the house to repair his portion. If he does not, the *owner of the upper story* may *build the house and dwell in it*, until reimbursed by the owner of the house.

R. *Judah* objects that the owner of the upper story is benefiting from the property of the other. The commentaries offer two explanations for R. Judah's alternative rule. (1) Since the upper story is ready, the owner

Rather, the owner of the upper story builds the house and the upper story,
and roofs the upper story,
and dwells in the house until he gives him his outlay.

4 And so too the olive press that is built into the rock,
and a[124] garden is built above it,
and it was worn away—
in this case, the owner of the garden goes down and sows below,
until he makes a vault for his oil press.

10:4 cont.–5   *Miscellaneous Rules*

The wall or the tree that fell into the public domain and did damage—
he is exempt from paying.
If they gave him time to cut down the tree or take down the wall,
and it fell within the time—
he is exempt
after the time—
he is liable.

5 One whose wall was near his fellow's garden,
and it fell,
and the garden owner[125] said to him: "Clear your stones";
and the wall owner said to him: "They are yours"—
one does not listen to him.
Once the garden owner accepted upon himself,
and the wall owner said to him:
"Here is your outlay, and I will take what is mine"—
one does not listen to him.
One who hires a worker to work for him in straw and stubble,

---

[124] K, P, C: "belonging to another.".   [125] "Garden owner" and "wall owner" added for clarity.

---

of the lower story does not receive appreciable benefit (Rashi). (2) The owner of the upper story lives in the upper story, but prevents the other from access to the house, so that he is not living in his house at all (Tosafot).

10:4 *And so too*, referring back to 10:2.

a vault: To support the garden atop it; cf. 10:6.

Beginning with the second half of this passage and continuing through 10:5, the Mishnah presents a series of miscellaneous rules. It is difficult to account for the selection of topics and their placement here.

The wall or the tree: This topic would have fit well in *Bava Qamma* 3:2 or 9:4. Here, what the Mishnah adds is the consideration that "they" (a court or village authorities) gave the person time to remove the potential hazard.

10:5 *One whose wall… they do not listen to* the owner of the wall. The owner of the wall has a responsibility to collect the stones, and cannot renounce ownership of or responsibility for them.

Once he accepted upon himself…they do not listen: Once the owner of the garden has agreed to collect the stones and take ownership of them, the other cannot reimburse him and demand the stones.

One who hires a worker: An analogous discussion, this time in connection with hired laborers (cf. 7:1, 9:11–12).

and the worker[126] said to him: "Give me my hire,"
and he said to him: "Take what you have done as your hire"—
one does not listen to him.
Once the worker accepted upon himself,
and the employer[127] said to him:
"Here is your wage, and I will take what is mine"—
one does not listen to him.
One who takes manure out to the public domain—
the one who takes out may take out, and the one who manures may manure.
One may not steep clay in the public domain, nor form bricks;
but one may knead clay in the public domain, but not bricks.[128]
One who builds in the public domain,
the one who brings stones may bring, and the one who builds may build.
And if he does damage, he pays what he damaged.
Rabban Simeon b. Gamaliel says:
He may even prepare his work thirty days before.

10:6 *Conflicts between Owners of Adjacent Gardens*

6 Two gardens, one above the other, and there are vegetables in between:
R. Meir says:
They belong to the upper.

[126] Lit. "he."   [127] Lit. "he."   [128] **K, P, C**: "not for bricks."

---

work...in stubble and straw: The employer cannot require the worker to take the harvested materials as pay in lieu of coin.

accepted upon himself: Agreed to those terms at the outset. The employer cannot now insist on paying in coin and receiving the work product. The principle implicit here is that the parties to a contract cannot unilaterally alter its terms (see 6:2).

One who takes manure: The topic now returns to hazards in the public domain (as in 10:4; see *Bava Qamma* 3:3). Here, the concern is with short-term deposits of materials for immediate use by the receiver.

One may not steep clay...form bricks: Both are part of the processing of building materials. They are prohibited because they would occupy part of the public domain for extended periods.

One may knead clay, for immediate use. *But not bricks*: According to the reading of the manuscripts, "not for bricks," one may not knead clay in order to form bricks.

One who builds: As in the case of manure, one person may bring the stones and another may make use of them.

And if he does damage: See *Bava Qamma* 3:3. The actions are permitted (townspeople cannot prevent the builder), but he remains liable for damage. The rule presumably applies to all of the preceding cases.

may...prepare his work: Rabban Simeon b. Gamaliel allows the builder to gather building materials in advance of construction and be exempt from payment (Rashi). Or, in another interpretation, the builder is permitted to repair the work for thirty days after construction (Maimonides).

10:6 *gardens, one above the other*: The gardens are terraced, and *vegetables* are growing in the terrace wall in between.

R. Meir...R. Judah: In the first statement of their views, the rabbis base their views on steps that the garden owners could have taken that would have prevented growth; by not taking those steps, each can claim to be responsible for the vegetables between terraces.

R. Judah says:
They belong to the lower.
Said R. Meir:
If the upper wants to take away his earth,
there are no vegetables here.
Said R. Judah:
If the lower wants to fill in his garden,
there are no vegetables here.
Said R. Meir:
Inasmuch as each can prevent the other,
they look to see from whose property this vegetable is growing.
R. Simeon said:
Anything that the upper can reach with his hand and take,
it is his,
and the remainder is the lower's.

each can prevent the other: Each can prevent the produce from growing to the other's benefit, or alternatively, can prevent the excavating or filling in of the respective plots.

R. Simeon provides a compromise position in which both have claim to some of the produce, the upper to what he can reach.

Tractate Bava Batra

Hayim Lapin

Introduction

Overview

Bava Batra ("last gate" in Aramaic) is the third of three tractates that originally made up a single tractate on civil law (see *Bava Qamma*, introduction).

Structure and Organization of the Tractate

Broadly, the tractate is organized in four topical sections. The kinds of claims that owners of adjoining or jointly owned properties may make on one another (chapters 1–3) are subjects that pick up where *Bava Metsi'a* left off. The second section deals with sale, especially of real property, and extends from chapter 4 through chapter 7. Chapters 8 and 9 deal with inheritance and other strategies for dividing property in expectation of death. Finally, chapter 10 deals with written documents.

Main Ideas

Most of the tractate deals in one way or another with landed property, both residential and agricultural. The discussion of joint or adjoining properties addresses partitioning them or surrounding them with walls (1:1–6); separating new plants or installations from existing structures, such as trees from cisterns (2:1–12); the legal consequences of extended use or possession, for transfer of ownership (3:1–4) as well as for the permanence of installations in shared space (3:5–8). The first block of materials in the section on sale deals with which appurtenances or attachments are conveyed with the sale (4:1–5:5), followed by traditions dealing with sale of produce (5:6–6:3); minimum sizes in sales and contracts (6:4, 7–8); rights of access (6:5–7a); and the consequences of formulae in the contract of sale for the outcomes of the sale (7:1–4). The section on inheritance opens with the Mishnah's understanding of biblical rules (8:1–4). Methods for the householder to control the division of property after his death (8:5–7; 9:6–7) bracket a discussion of the uses of the estate for surviving sons or daughters (8:7–9:5). The section on deeds considers formal features and scribal practices (10:1–4), as well as other laws that involve written documents (10:5–8).

Not surprisingly, *Bava Batra* deals extensively with questions of possession and acquisition. As elsewhere, we learn that ownership should be mediated by appropriate possessory acts (5:6–6:3; 9:7). In addition, the Mishnah develops the principle of *hazaqah*, literally "holding." Possession for an extended period establishes ownership of property (3:5–6; compare usucaption in Roman law) and bestows sufficient permanence on an installation so that others cannot insist that the owner remove it (3:7–8; compare praedial servitudes in Roman law). In its laws of sale, the tractate analyzes the components of real property (e.g. fields, houses, cisterns, courtyards); some of these components can be assumed to be included in a sale, others not (4:1–5:5). This kind of analysis is applied even to such practices as butchering (5:5). The strategies for dividing property according to the will of the donor rather than fixed rules of inheritance shows how the Mishnah is not always beholden to biblical paradigms. The category of "gifts of one deathly ill" (Hebrew/Aramaic, *matnot shekhiv mera*, 9:6–7) is particularly important as a contribution to later rabbinic legal thinking. Finally, the discussion of legal documents is of both legal and historical significance (10:1–4).

Relationship to Scripture

The rules of inheritance (8:1–2, 5) are closely tied to the rules of the Torah (Numbers 27:8–11; 36; Deuteronomy 21:15–17). The Mishnah takes these for granted, while regulating the strategies that property owners use to evade the structures of these rules. In addition, there are references to the laws of false witnesses (3:4; Deuteronomy 19:5–21). However, much of the material of *Bava Batra* is not directly based on the Torah or more broadly on the Bible. In fact, in the case of the buying and selling of real estate the Mishnah differs significantly from the Torah. Where Leviticus 25:5–16 called for a system of tribal allotments, which for the most part could only be sold temporarily and which returned to their ancestral holdings in the Jubilee, the Mishnah assumes that real property, whether in settlements or used for agricultural work, is bought and sold permanently.

Special Notes for the Reader

See introduction to *Bava Qamma*.

Tractate Bava Batra

Chapter One

1:1–3 *Adjoining Properties: Building a Wall to Divide Adjoining Property*

1 Partners who wished to make a partition in a courtyard—
they build the wall in the middle.
In a place where it was customary to build with unfinished stones, finished stones, half-length bricks, bricks—
they build.
All follows the custom of the region.
With unfinished stones: this one gives three handbreadths
and this one gives three handbreadths;
with finished stones: this one gives two handbreadths and a half,
and this one gives two handbreadths and a half;
with half-length bricks: this one gives two handbreadths
and this one gives two handbreadths;
with bricks: this one gives one handbreadth and a half
and this one gives one handbreadth and a half.
Therefore, if the wall fell, the place and the stones belong to them both.

1:1–6 The discussion in part develops topics introduced in chapter 10 of *Bava Metsi'a*. The participation of adjoining owners in the building of partition walls is discussed in 1:1–4; 1:5–6 may be read as appendices to that discussion: 1:5 on mutual obligations of householders in a courtyard or a town; and 1:6 on minimal sizes for division of property.

1:1 *middle*: Each party cedes some property on either side of the dividing line, as specified below (commentaries).

half-length bricks: Translation uncertain but follows usage in Habakkuk 2:11.

bricks: Dried mud brick. See *Bava Metsi'a* 10:5.

with unfinished stones: Walls made with *unfinished stones* (or perhaps rubble) are widest, and each party must give up *three handbreadths*, to allow a wall of six handbreadths wide. Walls made of the other building materials are progressively narrower. In the sequel, it is assumed that each also provided the raw materials for one side.

if the wall fell: For the dividing of stones, see *Bava Metsi'a* 10:1.

2 And so too in the case of a garden.
In a place where it was customary to build a wall, one requires him.[1]
But in the valley, in a place where it was customary not to build a wall,
one does not require him,
but rather, if he wishes he withdraws into his own and builds,
and he builds a facade on the outside.
Therefore, if it the wall fell, the place and the stones are his.
If they built with the willing participation[2] of both, they build the wall in the middle,
and they make a facade from this side and from this side.
Therefore if the wall fell, the place and the stones belong to them both.

3 One who surrounds his fellow on three sides,
and he built a fence on the first, second, and third—
one does not require the other.
R. Yose says:
If he got up and built a fence on the fourth, they impose[3] upon him the whole.

1:4–5 *Adjoining Properties: Mutual Responsibilities of Joint Owners of a Courtyard*

4 The wall of a courtyard that fell—
one requires him to build it up to four cubits.
He is presumed to have contributed, until the other[4] brings proof that he has not.

---

[1] "One requires him," absent in **K, P**.   [2] Heb. "knowledge."   [3] Lit. "roll."
[4] Heb. "he."

1:2 *And so too in the case of a garden*: The parties provide space from their respective holdings, because it is *a place where it was customary to build*. Others read *required* to mean that the parties can be compelled to build a wall. (See n. 1.) Holdings in a *valley*, by contrast, are not conventionally walled. The party that wants a partition *withdraws... and builds* entirely on his own land.

facade: The precise meaning is unclear; the facade on the exterior of the wall, facing into the neighbor's property, marks ownership; in the event of a collapse *the place and stones* are presumed to be *his*.

willing participation: "Knowledge," "will"; cf. *Bava Metsi'a* 5:6; 8:8. A *facade*, is made on both sides, indicating joint participation in building, and the building materials presumed to be jointly owned.

1:3 *surrounds*: One person owns fields that abut another's on three sides and built a wall around those three sides. *One does not require* the owner of the surrounded field to cede land as in 1:1, or, perhaps, contribute to the construction, see 1:1.

got up and built. According to R. Yose, if the owner of the second field completed the wall, he gets benefit from its presence and is retroactively obligated for cost (in outlay or land owed).

1:4 *wall of a courtyard*: The discussion seems to be in regard to a partition wall in a joint courtyard (1:1), rather than the exterior wall (cf. 1:5).

up to four cubits: To a standard height, but no higher, as specified below.

He is presumed to have contributed: Commentaries: If another owner claims that one owner did not contribute, *he*, the defendant, is presumed to have contributed unless *he*, the one claiming payment, can bring proof to the contrary. Alternatively: *He*, the joint owner, is assumed to have been party to the original construction and liable to pay, unless *he* himself can bring proof that he did not.

From four cubits and up, one does not require him.
If he abutted[5] to it another wall, even if he did not put the roofing on it—
one imposes[6] the whole upon him.
He is presumed not to have contributed, until the other[7] brings proof that he has.

    5 One forces the joint owner of a courtyard[8]
to contribute to[9] a gate house and door for the courtyard.
Rabban Simeon b. Gamaliel says:
Not all courtyards require a gate house.
One forces the town resident[10]
to contribute to[11] a wall and double doors and a bolt for a town.
Rabban Simeon b. Gamaliel says:
Not all towns require a wall.
How long must he be in a town so that he becomes like the people of the town?
Twelve months.
If he purchased in it a house to live in—
in that case he immediately becomes like the people of the town.

1:6 *Adjoining Properties: Dividing a Courtyard or Other Installation*

    6 They do not divide the courtyard unless there are four cubits for this one and four for this one;
nor the field unless it has in it nine *qav* for this one and nine *qav* for this one.
R. Judah says:
Until it has in it nine half-*qav* for this one and nine half-*qav* for this one.
Nor the garden unless it has in it half a *qav* for this one and half a *qav* for this one.

---

[5] Heb. "leaned."   [6] Lit. "roll."   [7] Heb. "he."   [8] Heb. "him."   [9] Heb. "build."
[10] Heb. "him."   [11] Heb. "build."

---

abutted...another wall: Here, one party refused to extend the wall above four cubits but the others extended it (commentaries). *Abutted* connotes a new wall alongside or adjoining the existing one; according to the commentaries, the new wall is parallel to it but at a distance.

roofing: The existing wall and the new wall make an enclosure, even if no roofing was put on.

impose: As in 1:3, by making use of the partition wall at the new height, the owner of the enclosure becomes retroactively liable for its construction.

presumed not to have contributed: As in the second interpretation above, *he*, the builder of the new wall, is presumed not to have been party to the original wall unless *he* can bring proof that he was.

1:5 The terminology in this mishnah differs from the preceding.

1:6 Following on the discussion of dividing properties, the Mishnah presents a series of rules involving the minimal threshold for divisions.

do not divide: The owners cannot force each other to partition the property.

four cubits: A space with a depth of four cubits.

nine qav: The sowing area for nine *qav* of grain, generally calculated as 3,750 square cubits. *R. Judah* allows smaller remaining fields.

R. Aqiva says:
A quarter-*qav*-sized plot.
Neither the hall, nor the watchtower, nor the dovecote, nor the cloak, nor the bath, nor the oil press,
unless it has in it sufficient for this one and sufficient for this one.
This is the general rule:
Anything that is to be split and it retains its name, they may split;
if not, they may not split.[12]
When?
When both are not willing;
but if both are willing, they may split with even less than this.
And holy writings, even if they both are willing, they may not split.

Chapter Two

2:1–4 *Keeping New Installations at Appropriate Distances from Existing Structures: Settlements and Domestic Settings*

2 A person may not dig a cistern adjacent to the cistern of his fellow, nor a trench, nor a cave, nor a water channel, nor a launderer's basin,
unless he removed it three handbreadths from his fellow's wall and plastered it with lime.
They remove olive refuse, manure, salt, lime, and rocks

---

[12] K, P, C lack "This ... may not split."

---

quarter-qav sized plot: There is a slight shift in terminology in the tradition of R. Aqiva.

Neither the hall ... oil press: Most of the items on the list might appear on an enclosed farmstead; the garment is incongruous here.

hall: A formal dining room, although the term may be used more loosely here.

Watchtower: Alternatively, "grand hall" (Maimonides, Rashi).

sufficient for this one: Apparently, with the parts of the property retaining the original function. For minimal sizes, see also 6:4.

retains its name: The name is thought to embody the functional and legal status of the property.

holy writings: Scriptural texts, in the form of scrolls.

2:1 *may not dig ... lime*: The concern is especially with moisture undermining the wall.

trench, cave, water channel: A trio of terms that are treated together several times in the Mishnah and Tosefta.

olive refuse ... lime: Again, the concern is with damaging the soil. In this case, the owner of the hazardous materials applies lime to the wall of the neighbor's wall. Particularly according to the reading "or" (see n. 13), plastering or maintaining proper distance are alternatives.

rocks may compress and weaken the soil (Yerushalmi) or trap moisture.

They remove: This expression repeatedly introduces rules in 2:5–11. The remaining cases require only maintaining distance from the wall, not plastering. The Mishnah adds concerns about roots (seeds), vibrations (mills for grain) or fire (ovens).

three handbreadths from his fellow's wall, and[13] plaster with lime.
They remove seeds, or a plow, or urine three handbreadths from the wall,
and they remove a mill [from the wall so that the wall is]
three handbreadths from the lower millstone,
which is four from the upper millstone,
and an oven [so that the wall is] three from the base, which is four from the lip.

2 A person may not erect an oven in a house unless there is above it a height of four cubits.
If he was erecting it in an upper story, there must be below it plaster of three handbreadths,
and for a stove, one handbreath,
and if he caused damage, he pays what he has damaged.
R. Simeon says:
They only said all these amounts so that if he caused damage he is exempt from paying.

3 A person may not open a bakers' or dyers' shop beneath the storehouse of his fellow,
nor a stall for cattle.
Nevertheless, in the case of wine they permitted, but not a stall for cattle.
A shop in the courtyard—
he can prevent him and say to him:
"I cannot sleep from the sound of those coming and the sound of those going."
He makes utensils and goes out and sells them in the marketplace.
But he cannot prevent him and say to him:
"I cannot sleep from the sound of the hammer, or the sound of the mill,
or the sound of the children."

[13] K, P, C, G: "or."

---

seeds, or a plow: Sowing and plowing are prohibited within three handbreadths.

Urine was used as a cleaning agent.

2:2 *oven*: A large installation made of clay or stone. Food was placed inside the cavity of the oven from above. *Stove*: Typically, smaller, and built to heat a cooking pot.

caused damage: Abiding by these safety procedures does not exempt the owner from liability for damage. See *Bava Metsi'a* 10:5, and for the expression, *Bava Qamma* 3:3, 6:2. It is not clear whether this statement and R. Simeon's that follows comment only on ovens and stoves or include the hazards in 2:1 as well.

R. Simeon holds that complying with the requirements does make one exempt.

all these amounts: The required distances or the thickness of the plaster.

2:3 *storehouse* for grain or produce. The fumes or heat from the installations damage the produce.

wine... but not a stall for cattle: A storage house for wine, but not a cattle stall, can be above these installations because the heat or smoke was deemed beneficial. Alternatively, a wine cellar or shop, but not a cattle stall, could be below a storehouse.

he can prevent: Residents sharing the same courtyard can object to customers coming in at all hours.

But he cannot prevent: The other residents cannot object to the existence of a workshop, if the sale is taking place elsewhere.

children: Commentaries: students reciting lessons, but perhaps also apprentices (Yerushalmi).

4 One whose wall abutted[14] his neighbor's wall,
he may not abut another wall against it, unless he removed it four cubits.
And windows,
whether above them, below them, or opposite them—
four cubits.

2:5–12 *Keeping New Installations at Appropriate Distances from Existing Structures: Agricultural Settings*

5 They remove a ladder four cubits from the dovecote so that a marten not jump;
and the wall four cubits from the drainage gutter so that he be able to erect the ladder.
They remove a dovecote from the town fifty cubits,
and a person may not make a dovecote on his own property
unless he has fifty cubits in every direction.
R. Judah says:
A four-*kor*-sized area, the full length of a dove's flight.
And if he bought it, even if there was only a quarter-*qav*-sized area,
in this case it stands in his possession.

6 A fledgling found within fifty cubits—
in this case it belongs to the owner of the dovecote;
outside of fifty cubits,

---

[14] Here and in the next clause, Heb. "leaned."

2:4 *whose wall abutted*: Compare 1:4. A has a wall joining B's at a right angle. B now wants to abut a new wall to A's running parallel to B's own earlier wall. There must be a space of at least four cubits between B's two walls.

windows: Two different principles are at work here (Tosefta). (1) Walls should be *four cubits* higher or lower than any windows on the facing wall to prevent peering, and (2) windows should open on a space at least *four cubits* wide so that the window receives sufficient light.

he removed it: As with domestic installations, agricultural installations and plants need to be kept at sufficient distance that they do not cause damage. The repeated references to removal involve mentions of wild animals (2:5), chaff (2:8), odors (2:9) and other sorts of taints (2:10), and tree roots (2:6, 11–12).

2:5 *marten*: Precise identification unknown.

from the drainage gutter: A new wall must allow four cubits from the gutter on an older wall opposite it, so that the owner of the gutter has space to erect a ladder. This appears to qualify earlier rules that mandated a space of four cubits between walls.

dovecote: The required distance *from the town* prevents the birds from eating seeds belonging to others (commentaries). Elsewhere, dovecotes appear as installations that are conveyed with the sale of a "town" (see 4:7).

four-kor-sized area: The sowing area for four *kor* of grain, a much larger distance. By the conventional calculation, 75,000 square cubits, yielding a square of slightly fewer than 274 cubits on a side.

the full length: The expected roaming area of the doves.

if he bought an existing dovecote, it retains its status and may be maintained by the purchaser even if it was only separated by a small distance. (There are one hundred eighty *qav* to the *kor*; see also 1:6.)

2:6 *fledgling*: The bird is no longer in the nest but cannot fly long distances or at all. Cf. *Bava Qamma* 1:4.

in this case it belongs to the one who found it.
If it was found between two dovecotes,
if it was closer to the one, it is his;
if it was closer to the other,[15] it is his;
halfway between, the two split it.

7 They remove a tree twenty-five cubits from the town;
and in the case of[16] the carob or sycamore tree—fifty cubits.
Abba Saul says:
Every non-fruit-bearing tree—fifty cubits.
If the town preceded—
he cuts it down, and he does not pay the monetary value;
if the tree preceded—
he cuts it down, and he gives its monetary value.
If it is doubtful which preceded[17]—
he cuts it down, and he does not pay the monetary value.

8 They remove the fixed threshing floor fifty cubits from the town.
A person may not make a fixed threshing floor in his own property
unless he has fifty cubits in every direction.
And he removes it from his fellow's plantings and his plowed land,
so that he not do damage.

9 They remove animal carcasses and graves and tanneries fifty cubits from the town.
They make tanneries only to the east of the town.
R. Aqiva says:
He may make it in any direction except to the west,
and he removes it fifty cubits.

---

[15] Heb. "this one … this one." The second "if it was closer" lacking in **K, P, C**.
[16] Absent in **K, P**.
[17] Heb. "It is doubtful if this one preceded and it is doubtful if this one preceded." **K, P** (**C** is corrupt) construct the sentence differently.

2:7 *remove a tree…from the town*: See 2:11, where the concern appears to be damage by roots. Cf. Bavli (the practice of keeping a treeless area around the town) and Palestinian Talmud (the canopy of the tree is somehow damaging; the Mishnah's rule preserves light).

carob or sycamore: Because of extensive roots (2:11) or canopy (2:13).

If the town preceded: The tree was planted too close to an existing town.

he cuts…does not pay: The active verbs are the singular. Does "he" who cuts down the tree own the "town" (see 4:7)?

If it is doubtful: Unlike other doubtful cases where the Mishnah enjoins splitting the costs in question (e.g. Bava Metsi'a 8:2, 4–5, and above 2:6), here, the owner of the tree is at a disadvantage.

2:8 *threshing floor*: The concern is with chaff and dust from the threshing process.

And he removes: The damage is not only to settled areas and installations, but to agricultural areas.

2:9 *carcasses…graves…tanneries*: The concern is with odor.

only to the east…except to the west: The debate is about prevailing winds carrying odors. According to R. Aqiva, westerly winds are most common (Tosefta). By this reasoning, the first view is that winds are particularly rare from the east, so only that direction should be utilized.

10 They remove soaking vats from vegetables,
and[18] vetches from onions,
and mustard from bees.
R. Yose permits in the case of mustard.
11 They remove the tree twenty-five cubits from the cistern,
and in the case[19] of the carob and the sycamore tree—fifty cubits,
whether from above or from the side.
If the cistern preceded—
he cuts it down and gives the monetary value;
but if the tree preceded—
he may not cut it down.
If it is doubtful which preceded[20]—
he may not cut it down.
R. Yose says:
Even though the cistern preceded the tree, he may not cut it down,
since this one digs in his own property, and this one plants in his own property.
12 A person may not plant a tree adjacent to the field of his fellow,
unless he removed it four cubits;
it is one and the same for vines and for any tree.
If there was a fence between them—
the one may plant up to the fence from one side,
and the other may plant up to the field from the other.[21]
If his roots were going out into his fellow's property—
he removes them to a depth of [22] three handbreadths,

[18] K: "and from vetches (second hand: and)."   [19] Absent in K, P.
[20] Heb. "It is doubtful if this one preceded and it is doubtful if this one preceded," cf. n. 17. K, P, C construct the sentence differently.
[21] Heb. "This one adjoins/leans from here (lacking in K, P, C), this one adjoins/leans from here (lacking in P, C; K corrupt)."
[22] Lit. "he deepens."

2:10 *They remove*: The distance is not specified.

soaking vats: For extracting fibers from the stems of the flax plant. It is not clear why *R. Yose* singles out *mustard* affecting bees. The reasoning may be that each party legitimately acts in their domain (see 2:11). Cf. commentaries, based on the Bavli, it is the responsibility of the injured party (the beekeeper) to remove himself from potential injury.

2:11 *remove the tree…from the cistern*: Compare 2:7. Here, the commentaries assume that the concern is damage from tree roots.

carob…sycamore: Because their roots are more extensive.

If the cistern preceded, etc.: In each case, the owner of the pit has less latitude to cut down the tree than the owner of a "town" (2:7).

this one digs…and this one plants: For R. Yose, each is legitimately acting in his own domain. The Tosefta provides an alternative reason: "the land is given for planting." This might apply to 2:10 as well.

2:12 *unless he removed it*: The owner of the tree must allow sufficient space to tend to the tree without encroaching on the neighboring field.

fence: A dividing wall allows the owners on either side to plant up to the wall.

If his roots…three handbreadths: Presumably this is not limited to the case of plants separated by a wall.

so that it not hinder the plow.
If he was digging a cistern, a trench, or a cave—
he cuts them as he goes down,
and the wood belongs to him.

2:13–14 Assuring Clearance in Cases of Overhanging Trees

13 A tree that is leaning into the field of his fellow—
he cuts down to allow an ox-goad over the plow;
and in the case of a carob and sycamore—
in line with the plumb line.
A field dependent on irrigation—
the whole tree[23] in line with the plumb line.
Abba Saul says:
Any non-fruit-bearing tree—
the whole tree in line with the plumb line.

14 A tree that is leaning into the public domain—
he cuts down so that a camel may pass with its rider.
R. Judah says:
A camel[24] laden with flax or bunches of prunings.
R. Simeon says:
The whole tree in line with the plumb line,
because of impurity.

[23] K, C: "tree plantation" (cf. *Bava Metsi'a* 9:2); P: "and [in the case of] any tree."
[24] K, P, C lack "a camel."

digging a cistern: No distance is specified (see commentaries, and cf. 2:11).

cistern…trench…cave: See 2:1.

he cuts: The one digging may cut through roots, and may keep the *wood*.

2:13–14 Stylistically, these two paragraphs form a pair. They supply additional rules about trees proximate to other property.

2:13 *cuts down to allow*: Cuts back the overhanging branches so that the farmer walking behind the oxen can swing an *ox-goad over the plow*.

carob and sycamore have a dense canopy.

in line with the plumb line: Any branches that extend into the field, up to the top of the tree, are cut off at the boundary line.

the whole tree: See n. 23. According to the reading "tree plantation," the Mishnah distinguishes between a tree overhanging a crop field, and a tree over a field planted with trees.

Any non-fruit-bearing tree: See 2:7. Abba Saul permits more extensive cutting back of non-fruit-bearing trees.

2:14 *camel…with its rider*: As in 2:13, the criterion is clearance beneath the branches.

camel laden: The principle is the same although the specification is different. According to the Talmud, a laden camel is higher than a camel and its rider.

R. Simeon…because of impurity: The concern is that overhanging trees might form a "tent" over a human corpse and transmit impurity to those under the tree. See *Oholot*, introduction.

Chapter Three

3:1–4 *The Legal Consequences of Extended or Continued Use: Ownership through Extended Possession*

3 Possession of houses, cisterns, trenches, vaults, dovecotes, baths, oil presses, fields dependent upon irrigation, slaves, and anything that produces fruit continuously—
possession of them [creates ownership after] three years from the date of inception.[25]
A field dependent upon rainfall—
possession of it [creates ownership after] three years,
but this need not be from the date of inception.
R. Ishmael says:
Three months in the first year, three months in the last year,
and twelve months in the middle, so eighteen months.
R. Aqiva says:
One month in the first year, one month in the last year,
and twelve months in the middle, so fourteen months.
R. Ishmael said:
When does this apply?
In the case of a field that is sown with seed;[26]

---

[25] Lit. " from day to day."   [26] Lit. "a white field."

3:1–6 Extended holding or use of a property or good can establish a right of ownership of the property for the occupant or user (3:14; cf. usucaption in Roman law). It can also confer a kind of permanence on an installation or its use, so that others cannot demand that its owner or user change the use or remove the installation (3:5–6; see also above 2:5, 3:8). The Mishnah also uses the word *hazaqah* to denote a possessory act (not a period of extended use) that conveys ownership of real property (3:3, end).

3:1 *Possession…date of inception*: See n. 25. The items listed are conventional and appear on lists earlier in the tractate.

cisterns…: See 2:1.

dovecotes…oil presses: See 1:6.

fields dependent upon irrigation: See 2:13.

continuously: And not seasonally dormant.

need not be: The description is ambiguous, and appears to be quantified in the views attributed to R. Ishmael and R. Aqiva that follow.

R. Ishmael and *R. Aqiva* agree that the possessor must gain three crops in three calendar years but differ over the minimum length of time this requires. There are fast-growing crops that the possessor could plant at the end of the first possessing year and the beginning of the third possessing year, thus shortening the time.

When does this apply? R. Ishmael is addressing the general principle, not disputing R. Aqiva.

field that is sown with seed: See n. 26. This is in contradistinction to a *tree plantation*. The field is planted with multiple kinds, and three separate harvests constitute *three years*, even if they took place within a single year.

but in the case of a tree plantation,
if he brought in its crop, gathered its olives, and brought in its figs—
in this case these count as three years.[27]

2 There are three lands for possession: (1) Judah, (2) Transjordan, and (3) the Galilee.
If [the owner] was in Judah and [the other] took possession in the Galilee,
in the Galilee and he took possession in Judah—
it is not [effective] possession,
until he is with him in that region.
R. Judah said:
They only said "three years" so that [the owner] might be in Spain,
and [the other] take possession for one year, and they go and inform him over one year,
and he return in the next year.

3 Any possession that does not include a claim is not possession.
How?
If he said to him: "What are you doing on my property?"
and he said to him: "No one has ever said anything to me"—
it is not possession.
"You sold it to me," "You gave it to me as a gift,"
"Your father sold it to me," "Your father gave it to me as a gift"[28]—
in this case, it is effective possession.
And one who inherits[29] does not need a counter claim.
Artisans,[30] partners, tenant farmers, or guardians—
in their case, the rule of possession does not apply.[31]

[27] Lit. "lo, these are three years." [28] K, P, C lack the claims beginning "Your father."
[29] Lit. "comes in through inheritance." [30] Absent in K, P.
[31] Lit. "have no possession," here and in the other cases where this expression appears.

crop: Generally, the term refers to grain, which would imply that the field is intercultivated with grain. However, the commentaries understand the term to refer to the grapes (see Deuteronomy 22:9).

3:2 *three lands*: Heb. *aratsot*, sing. *erets*. A potential challenger needs to have been able to challenge the claim (see 3:3), and therefore needs to be in the same region.

region: Heb. *medinah*. Note the change in terminology. Possibly, we should read this as requiring that owner and possessor be in the same place for the duration of the period.

R. Judah explains the reason behind the three-year rule (3:1) as allowing a challenger to be at a distance of a year's travel and return. If the preceding meant that the challenger must be local, it is implied that R. Judah rejects this limitation.

3:3 *does not include a claim*: For the possessor to claim land through *possession* also requires a positive claim of ownership, as the Mishnah explains.

is not possession: As in 3:2, ownership is not established through extended possession.

inherits: The heir who has been in possession for the requisite time is not required to establish the deceased's right to the property (Rashbam). Alternatively, this applies also if the deceased had claimed ownership through *possession* (see Maimonides). Or perhaps more simply: an heir has presumptive ownership and the requirement that the possessor make a positive claim is not necessary.

Artisans...guardians: People who might regularly be in possession without ownership. Many witnesses omit "artisans": this makes sense, since they are not necessarily in possession of real property.

does not apply: These possessors do not have the ability to claim ownership through possession.

The rule of possession does not apply to a man
with respect to his wife's property;
and the rule of possession does not apply to a woman
with respect to her husband's property;
nor to a father with respect to a son's property;
nor a son with respect to a father's property.
When does this apply?
When one takes possession.
But one who gives a gift,[32]
or brothers who divided [their inheritance],
or one who takes possession of the property of a proselyte,
if he built a door, or fenced, or broke down a fence at all—
in such cases, it is possession.

4 If two testified about someone that he ate the produce for three years
and they were found to be plotting witnesses—
they pay [the owner] the whole.
Two testify as to the first year, and two as to the second, and two as to the third—
they divide it three ways between them.
Three brothers and one other joins them—
in this case these are three testimonies,
but they form one testimony if they are found to be plotting witnesses.[33]

[32] C adds "he gives the whole."   [33] "If... witnesses," absent in **K, P, C**.

---

a man... a father's property: Again, these might regularly be in possession without ownership. The Mishnah clusters members of the household separately from outsiders.

When, going back to 3:1, do the rules of acquisition by possession over an extended period *apply*?

When one takes possession, establishing ownership through extended possession.

one who gives a gift: In this and the following cases ownership takes place immediately.

property of a proselyte after his death. Proselytes without Israelite children have no heirs, and their land is thus ownerless.

built a door... at all: These all demonstrate possession, and serve as possessory acts, and in the case of real property convey acquisition.

it is possession: As noted at annotation to 3.1–6, the term *hazaqah* has a related but different meaning here. See below, 9:7; and *Qiddushin* 1:5.

3:4 *two testified... plotting witnesses*: A series of legal puzzles about assigning liability. In nearly all circumstances, valid testimony must be based on two or more concurring witnesses (Deuteronomy 19:15). A witness whose testimony was falsified is penalized *according to what he plotted to do to his brother* (Deuteronomy 19:15–21, and see *Makkot*, introduction).

the whole: The witnesses sought to alienate the property and are liable for its full value.

three ways: The pairs of witnesses collectively are liable to pay the owner the value of the field.

Three brothers cannot testify together.

three testimonies: The nonbrother together with each of the brothers constitutes a valid pair. The commentaries understand that each brother testified about a different year, so there are three distinct testimonies validating the acquisition.

but they form one testimony: See n. 33. They must all be disqualified to be liable to pay the owner. Or: for payment purposes there is still a single liability and not three separate liabilities.

3:5–6 *The Legal Consequences of Extended or Continued Use: Permanence through Extended Use*

5 To what things does possession apply
and to what things does possession not apply?[34]
If he was setting up an animal in a courtyard,
or an oven, a stove, or a mill;
or raising fowl, or putting his manure in the courtyard—
it is not possession.
But if he built a partition for his animal ten handbreadths high,
or similarly for an oven, or similarly for a stove, or similarly for a mill;
or if he brought fowl into the house,
and made a place for his manure three[35] handbreadths deep or three handbreadths high—
in this case, it is possession.

6 Possession does not apply to a gutter spout,[36]
but it does apply to its place;
possession applies to a gutter.
Possession does not apply to an Egyptian ladder,
but possession applies to a Tyrian ladder.
Possession does not apply to an Egyptian window,
but possession applies to a Tyrian window.
And which is an Egyptian window?
Any into which the head of a person cannot enter.
R. Judah says:

---

[34] Lit. "... have possession ... do not have possession?" [35] C: "ten."
[36] Lit. "does not have possession," here and throughout this passage.

3:5 *to what things does possession not apply*: Does not confer permanence, and the owner of the courtyard can demand that the owner of the installation remove it. The commentaries, following the Bavli, imagine a shared courtyard where the joint owners do not typically prevent each other from engaging in these activities (but see 3:3).

By contrast, building partitions for installations or altering the ground plan of the courtyard are permanent changes. Since the courtyard owner would typically object to these changes, their failure to object is a sign of consent.

brought fowl into the house: Extended use would designate the structure a chicken coop. This entry is slightly anomalous in this list. Possibly, it provides the setting for the two references to manure.

3:6 *gutter spout…gutter*: A building that has had a gutter and gutter spout for an extended period can continue to maintain the gutter. The right to place a spout is also permanent (its *place*), but not its shape or the direction that it pours (commentaries; see 2:5).

Egyptian ladder: Unfixed and smaller. *Tyrian ladder*: Larger and fixed. The extended placement of a fixed ladder with no objection by others is a sign of their consent. Others cannot remove it or build in its space (see 2:5).

Egyptian…Tyrian window: The question is whether another can obscure the window with new construction (2:4). The "Tyrian" type has permanence and others cannot block it.

And which? According to this view, size is the defining characteristic of the *Egyptian window*. According to R. Judah, *a frame* designates the window as having permanent status.

If it has a frame, even though a person's head cannot enter into it—
in this case, it is possession.
Possession applies to a projection from the wall of one handbreadth or more,
and the other can object;
less than this, possession does not apply,
and the other cannot object.

3:7–8 *The Legal Consequences of Extended or Continued Use: Encroaching on a Courtyard or on the Public Domain*

7 A person may not make an opening for[37] his windows
into a courtyard of which he is part-owner.[38]
If he bought a house in another courtyard, he may not make an opening for it
into a courtyard of which he is part-owner.
If he built an upper story above his house, he may not make an opening for it
into a courtyard of which he is part-owner,
but if he wishes, he may build a room within his own house
or build an upper story above his,
and make an opening for it into his house.
A person may not make an opening for a door opposite a door
in a courtyard of which he is part-owner,
or a window opposite a window.

[37] Here and below, lit. "open." [38] Here and below, lit. "the courtyard owned by partners."

projection: A larger overhang from a wall has a formal legal significance; one smaller than a handbreadth lacks it.

the other can (cannot) object. When the owner of the wall builds the projection, the owner of the property into which it projects can object and prevent the building of the projection if it is a handbreadth or more; but not if it is smaller.

3:7–8 The ability of the owners to make new installations that impinge on common spaces. The restrictions on a house owner are greater in a shared courtyard than in a public thoroughfare.

3:7 *windows*: The owners of a shared courtyard (and, all the more so, any other courtyard) are protected from increased visibility (commentaries and see 2:4).

house in another courtyard: The Mishnah envisions two adjoining complexes built around courtyards. The exterior wall of the house in one courtyard complex also serves as a border wall of the other. In this case and in that of an *upper story* the house owner is prevented from changing the activity and patterns of use in the courtyard.

but if he wishes: The owners of the courtyard cannot prevent the house owner from increasing the number of occupants or the intensity of activity within the house, as long as this does not create new access into the courtyard.

may build a room: He may repartition the existing space in the house or expand into open space outside the shared courtyard.

make an opening…into his house, so that the new room or story has access to the courtyard through the existing opening.

door opposite a door…window opposite a window: Again the issue appears to be the ability to peer through existing windows and doors.

If the door or window[39] was small, he may not make it big;
one, he may not make it two.
But he may open a door opposite a door into the public domain,
or a window opposite a window.
If it was small, he may make it big;
one, he may make it two.

8 One may not make a hollow space under the public domain,
such as cisterns, channels, or vaults;
but R. Eliezer permits,
as long as it is strong enough to support a passing wagon laden with stones.
One does not extend projections or balconies into the public domain;
but if he wishes he may withdraw into his own property and extend them.
If he bought a courtyard and it has projections or balconies—
in this case, it remains in its prior status.[40]

Chapter Four

4:1–3 *Appurtenances Included or Not Included with Sale: A House*

4 One who sells a house,
has not sold the side chamber, even though it opens into it,

[39] Heb. "it."   [40] Heb. "it is in its *hazaqah*."

---

may not make it big…may not make it two: Although the householder has the right to maintain openings that are established (3:5–6), he cannot alter existing ones. However, in *the public domain*, these restrictions do not apply.

3:8 *cisterns, channels, or vaults*. For this list see 2:1.

projections: See 3:6.

may withdraw…and extend them: The prohibition is not on such projections, but on their extension into the public domain. The owner may rebuild the front of the property as long as projections remain within the prior building line.

If he bought…it retains its prior status: The purchaser may retain them although they violate the requirements. See 3:5–6 and the headnote to chapter 3.

4:1–7 The section specifies which parts of an installation or item normally are conveyed with the item itself, and which are not. Characteristically the Mishnah attempts to separate properties, objects, or animals into distinct portions that stand alone in some fashion. If 4:7 refers to a "town" (see below), the section first progresses upward from house to courtyard to village, before turning to agricultural and other installations.

4:1 *house*: A self-contained unit.

has not sold: The other units, although attached and although perhaps accessible only through the main house (see 4:2), are deemed distinct from the house itself.

nor the room behind it,
nor the roof, when it has a parapet ten handbreadths high.
R. Judah says:
If it has the form of a doorway, even though it is not ten handbreadths high, it is not sold.

2 Nor the cistern,
nor the walled cellar,
even though he wrote to him "depth and height"
And he must buy a path for himself—
the words of R. Aqiva.
But the Sages say:
He does not need to buy a path for himself.
And R. Aqiva concedes that when he said to him: "Except for these,"
he does not need to buy a path for himself.
If he sold them to another—
R. Aqiva says:
He does not need to buy a path for himself;
but the Sages say:
He must buy a path for himself.

3 One who sells a house,
has sold the door, but not the key;
has sold the fixed mortar, but not the one that is movable;
has sold the *itstrobal* but not the *qelet*;

---

form of a doorway: This is sufficient to formally qualify the roof as a distinct unit, even though the parapet is not ten handbreadths high.

4:2 Continues 4:1 directly.

wrote… "depth and height": A reference to a conventional, but optional, phrase in the sale contract. A sale applies to the "depth and height" of the sold house itself, it does not apply to structures deemed technically separate. The commentaries differ over whether this statement applies to the "roof" (4:1) as well.

R. Aqiva rules that the seller retains ownership of the attached structures but does not have a right of way through the sold property.

For *the Sages*, retention of ownership comes with access.

"Except for these": When the contract stipulates structures that were not sold with the house, R. Aqiva concedes to the Sages that the seller retains a right of way.

sold them to another: If the original owner sold the roof or attached structures but retained the house. According to R. Aqiva, the sale of these implies access for the purchaser; according to the Sages, the purchaser must also acquire access rights. According to the commentaries, here and above, R. Aqiva considers the implicit terms of the sale to be expansive (above, the seller has not retained access rights and must acquire them; here the seller transferred them with the sale), while the Sages consider sale implicitly to be more restricted in scope.

4:3 *One who sells a house*: Parts of the house (a door) and immovable goods convey with the sale; but movables (a key) do not.

itstrobal: Lit. "pine cone." The lower, fixed part of a mill, perhaps with a cone-shaped projection as in one common type of mill.

qelet: Lit. "basket." The rotating, hollow upper stone through which grain was poured.

and not the oven, and not the stove.[41]
When he said to him: "It and all that is in it"—
then they are all sold.

4:4–6 Appurtenances Included or Not Included with Sale: A Courtyard and other Installations

4 One who sells a courtyard,
has sold the houses, cisterns, trenches, and vaults, but not the movable goods.
When he said to him: "It and all that is in it"—
in this case they are all sold.
In either case, he has not sold the bath or the oil press that is in it.
R. Eliezer[42] says:
One who sells the courtyard has sold only the airspace of the courtyard.

5 One who sells an oil press,
has sold the vat, the grindstone, and the posts;
but has not sold the pressing boards,[43] the wheel, or the beam.
And when he said to him: "It and all that is in it"—
in this case, they are all sold.
R. Eliezer[44] says:
One who sells the oil press has sold the beam.

---

[41] K, P, C: "He has sold the oven, he has sold the stove." [42] K, P, and C: "Leazar."
[43] K (after correction): *kidon*; P: *kirim* (possibly underlying K). [44] K, P, and C: "Leazar."

---

oven…stove: See the n. 41. The alternative reading treats both of these as fixed.

"It and all that is in it": A contractual stipulation at the time of sale.

4:4 *houses*, etc.: These items are the fixed structures or installations that are typical in a courtyard and are conveyed with its sale. As with a house, *movable goods* are not conveyed.

"It and all that is in it." See 4:3.

"In either case," whether or not the stipulation was made, the sale does not include a *bath* or an *oil press*. These are considered distinct installations (and in practice might be rarer in courtyards than cisterns or houses); see 4:5, 6.

R. Eliezer: Or Eleazar, two generations later; see n. 42. The dispute is definitional: does selling a "courtyard" mean the open space, or the complex of buildings and installations that it contains?

4:5 *oil press*: The Mishnah apparently envisions a two-stage process of oil production: crushing the olives and pressing them. The *wheel* may refer to a windlass that applies pressure to the *beam*. Since the Mishnah assumes knowledge of the technical terms, their specific meanings are hard to determine. The parts of the press that are deemed embedded in the ground or built into it are sold with it. Those that are removable are not.

"It and all that is in it". See 4:3.

R. Eliezer (see 4:4 and n. 44.) includes the *beam* as an essential part of the *press*.

6 One who sells a bath,
has not sold the boards, or the benches or the hangings.[45]
When he said to him: "It and all that is in it"—
in this case they are all sold.
In either case, he has not sold the reservoirs of water or the stores of wood.

4:7 Appurtenances Included or Not Included with Sale: A Town

7 One who sells a town,[46]
has sold the houses, cisterns, trenches, vaults, baths, dovecotes, oil presses,
and fields dependent upon irrigation,
but not the movable goods.
And when he said to him: "It and all that is in it,"
even if there were in it an animal and slaves—
in this case, they are all sold.
Rabban Gamaliel says:
One who sells the city has sold the caretaker.

4:8–9 Appurtenances Included or Not Included with Sale: A Field

8 One who sells a field
has sold the stones that are necessary for it,[47]

---

[45] K (and P, C?): "bathing clothes" or "towels."   [46] Or "estate."
[47] Here and in the next clause, lit. "that are for its need."

4:6 *boards*, etc.: Again, these are not fixed and not essential.

"It and all that is in it". See 4:3.

reservoirs for replacing or replenishing the water; *stores of wood*, fuel for heating.

4:7 *town*: The Mishnah imagines the possibility that villages might be privately owned. Alternatively, the Hebrew term refers to a farmstead or estate (see 2:5; 2:7).

movable: See 4:3.

"It and all that is in it": See 4:3.

animal and slaves: These are generally classed with immovable rather than movable property. Here, even these are conveyed with the sale of the town.

caretaker: In this case, the caretaker is assumed to be enslaved. According to Rabban Gamaliel, unlike other slaves, the caretaker is always conveyed with the sale of a "town."

4:8–9 Items that are conveyed with the field (4:8) are part of the operation of the field (e.g. stones), or installations that for technical reasons do not have the status of a separate or permanent installation (e.g. the watcher's hut made without clay).

4:8 *stones that are necessary* for fence building and other purposes. For the expression compare *Bava Metsi'a* 3:9.

and the reeds in the vineyard that are necessary for it,
and the grain that is connected to the ground,
and the thicket of reeds that is smaller than a quarter-*qav*-sized plot,
and the watcher's hut that is not[48] made with clay,
and the carob that has never been grafted onto,
and the sycamore that has never been pruned.[49]

9 But he has not sold the stones that are not necessary for it,
nor the reeds in the field that are not necessary for it,
nor the grain that is separated from the ground.
When he said: "It and all that is in it"—
in this case, they are all sold.
In either case, he has not sold the thicket of reeds
that is the size of a quarter-*qav*-sized field;
nor the watcher's hut that is[50] made with clay,
nor the grafted carob,
nor the cropped sycamore,
nor the cistern,
nor the winepress,
nor the dovecote,
whether destroyed or inhabited.[51]
And he must buy a path for himself—
the words of R. Aqiva.
But the Sages say:

[48] Some medieval authorities lack "not" here and include it in 4:9. [49] Heb. "virgin."
[50] See n. 48.   [51] K, P, C: "whole."

---

reeds, planted on the property for use in supporting vines, or perhaps already cut and set aside.

connected to the ground, and therefore part of the field.

thicket: Alternatively, "partition"; see *Kilayim* 4:4.

quarter-qav-sized plot: See 1:7.

not made with clay, or fixed in place. This would give it the status of a distinct installation that is not conveyed with the field. The alternative reading (see n. 48) would take the use of clay to make the field hut a part of the field.

carob...sycamore: When these have not yet been put to use as "installations" of their own, they are part of the field.

4:9 *has not sold*: Although in the field, they are not sold with it, and the seller may remove them.

"It and all that is in it": See 4:3.

thicket...sycamore: See 4:8. These are always considered separate from the field itself.

quarter-qav, or more.

cistern...winepress...dovecote: Fixed installations that are not subsumed into the field. Because the fruit is more fragile, winepresses are out by the fields; olive presses are associated with village or farmstead, 1:6; 3:1, 6; 4:7.

must buy a path: The seller, who retains ownership of installations in the field, must pay for access. For this dispute, see 4:2.

He does not need to buy a path for himself.
And R. Aqiva concedes that when he said to him: "Except for these,"
that he does not need to buy a path for himself.
If he sold them to another,
R. Aqiva says:
He does not need to buy a path for himself;
but the Sages say:
He does need to buy a path for himself.
When does this apply?
In the case of a seller.
But one who gives as a gift, gives all of them.
The brothers who divided,
if they have gained ownership of the field, they have gained ownership of all of them;
one who takes possession of the property of the proselyte,
if he has taken possession of the field, he has taken possession of all of them.
One who dedicates a field has dedicated all of them.
R. Simeon says:
One who dedicates a field has dedicated only the grafted carob
and the cropped sycamore.

Chapter Five

5:1 Appurtenances Included or Not Included with Sale: A Boat

5 One who sells a boat,
has sold the mast, the sail, the anchor, and all the means for steering it;
but he has not sold the slaves, the packing bags, or cargo.
When he said: "It and all that is in it"—
in this case, they are all sold.

When does this apply?: See 3:3. A *seller* does not sell adjunct installations, but one *who gives a gift* does.

brothers...property of the proselyte: See 3:3. In these cases, perhaps, there is no "seller" to retain ownership of installations.

One who dedicates: On analogy with a gift.

the grafted carob and the cropped sycamore: Living plants that draw on the field for sustenance. Consequently, according to R. Simeon, these are dedicated as well.

5:1 *boat*: Various parts are conveyed with sale of a boat but not the workers (*slaves*) or the *cargo*.

"It and all that is in it": See 4:3.

5:1 cont.–3 Appurtenances Included or Not Included with Sale: Work Animals and their Equipment

If he sold a wagon, he has not sold the mules;
if he sold the mules, he has not sold the wagon.
If he sold the yoke, he has not sold the oxen;⁵²
if he sold the oxen, he has not sold the yoke.
R. Judah says:
The price indicates.
How?
If he said to him, "Sell me your yoke for two hundred *zuz*,"
it is known⁵³ that a yoke is not sold for two hundred *zuz*.
But the Sages say:
Price is not proof.
  2 One who sells an ass,
has not sold its equipment.
Nahum the Mede says:
He has sold its equipment.
R. Judah says:
It is sometimes sold [with the ass] and sometimes not sold.
How?
If the ass was in front of him, and its equipment was on it,
and he said to him: "Sell me this ass of yours"—
then the equipment is sold with the ass;
That is your ass⁵⁴—
the equipment is not sold with the ass.
  3 One who sells an ass
has sold the ass foal⁵⁵ [with it];
if he sold a cow, he has not sold its offspring.

⁵² Heb. "bovine cattle."   ⁵³ C in error, or as a rhetorical question: "is it not known?"
⁵⁴ With **K, P, C**, *hahu*: "That ass of yours."   ⁵⁵ **K, P, C**: "has not sold."

---

wagon… yoke: The instrument and the animals with which they are used are distinct from one another.

price indicates the intention to sell the instrument with or without the animals.

"Sell me": R. Judah's opinion is illustrated from the point of view of the purchaser, not the seller. If the purchaser offered an exorbitant for the *yoke*, the implication is that the transaction was for the yoke and its oxen.

price is not proof: The commentaries distinguish this statement from the rules of *overcharge* in *Bava Metsi'a* chapter 4.

5:2 *Nahum the Mede*: A rarely cited sage associated with the pre-70 CE period. For *R. Judah*, as in 5:1, the purchaser's request determines what is sold.

That is your ass: See n. 54. The purchaser specified the ass itself.

5:3 *has sold the ass foal*: The lactating donkey is primarily useful for feeding its own young, so the young donkey is implied; whereas the milk of a lactating *cow* is useful for its milk more generally, so *he has not sold its offspring* (commentaries.) The alternative reading, "has not sold" in the case of the ass foal (see n. 55), makes a donkey equivalent to a cow; in both cases, the adult and the offspring are different entities with respect to sale.

5:3 (cont)–5 *Appurtenances Included or Not Included with Sale: Additional Rules about What Is Conveyed with Sale*

If he sold a dungheap, he has sold the manure in it;
if he sold a cistern, he has sold its water;
if he sold a hive, he has sold the bees;
if he sold a dovecote, he has sold the doves.[56]
One who buys the fruit of a dovecote from his fellow—
he sends out the first pair;
the fruit of a hive—
he takes three swarms and castrates;
honeycombs—
he leaves two combs;
olive trees to be cut—
he leaves two branches per tree.

4 One who acquires two trees in the field[57] of his fellow,
in this case he has not acquired the land.
R. Meir says:
He has acquired the land.
If they grew large, he need not trim them;
and that which grows from the trunk belongs to him;
from the roots belongs to the landowner.

[56] K, P, C put "dovecote" before "hive." [57] K, P, C lack "field."

5:3–5 The beginning of each of the passages below is connected to the problem of what is conveyed with the sale. However, in 5:3–4, the passages go on to discuss other matters, while 5:5 deals with the sale of parts of a single animal. This section may serve as a kind of appendix to the larger section.

dungheap...dovecote: In these cases, the installation is inseparable from the contents.

fruit of a dovecote, etc.: The concern in this passage is to allow the seller to raise new product after the sale. The details presuppose knowledge of practices that are not entirely clear.

sends out the first pair: The purchaser allows it to return to the seller.

the fruit of a hive: Bees; honey is discussed below.

swarms: A population of bees including a queen that propagates a new hive. The purchaser may capture three swarms.

castrates: The Bavli and commentaries suggest two interpretations of the term. (1) The seller inhibits reproduction, so that the original hive produces more honey. (2) Reading the word as "alternates," after three swarms, the purchaser may capture only every other swarm during the term that he is entitled to the fruits of the hive.

branches: The basis for new growth.

5:4 *trees*, and their produce in perpetuity.

has not acquired the land underneath them. See *Bikkurim* 1:6, 11 and *Shevi'it* 1:2. The purchaser *need not trim*, although the increased shade inhibits the growth of crops on the landowner's land. Alternatively (commentaries), the landowner *must not trim*.

roots: The Mishnah associates the roots (that are underground, commentaries) with the land and its owner.

And if they died, he has no land.
If he bought three,
he has acquired land.
If they grew large, he must trim them;
And that which grows from the trunk or from the roots belongs to him.
And if they died, he has the land.

5 One who sells the head of[58] a large animal,
he has not sold the feet;
if he sold the feet, he has not sold the head.
If he sold the windpipe, he has not sold the liver;
if he sold the liver, he has not sold the windpipe.
But in the case of a small animal,
if he sold the head, he has sold the feet;
if he sold the feet, he has not sold the head;
if he sold the windpipe, he has sold the liver;
if he sold the liver, he has not sold the windpipe.

5:6–11   *Sales Practices*

6 There are four rules for sellers:
(1) If he sold him good wheat, and it was found to be bad—
the buyer is able to withdraw;
(2) Bad, and it was found to be good—
the seller is able to withdraw;
(3) Bad and it was found to be bad, good and it was found to be good—

---

[58] **K, P, C, G**: "in the case of."

---

three, he has acquired land: Three trees constitute a minimal field, *Shevi'it* 1:2. Following the Bavli, the commentaries specify the limits on this rule.

must trim: The purchaser must follow the rules of a tree overhanging another's property (cf. 2:13); the commentaries see this as a reference to the seller who *may trim*.

5:5 *sells the head of a large animal*: Cattle. Again, the Mishnah is concerned to delineate what parts of an animal are distinct for purposes of sale. Evidently, the Mishnah refers to standard practices when dividing an animal.

windpipe, perhaps together with the lungs (commentaries); see *Tamid* 4:3, where windpipe, heart, and lungs appear as a unit.

small animal: Sheep or goats. Here, perhaps because the animal is smaller, the *feet* are subordinated to the *head*, and the *liver* to the *windpipe*.

5:6–11 An appendix to the discussion of sale focusing primarily on produce. Note the issue of possessory acts (pulling) in 5:7–8.

5:6 *four rules*: Lit. "measures." The concern here is with the ability of the parties to reverse a transaction of sale. For a related discussion, see *Bava Metsi'a* chapter 4, esp. 4:2, 4.

good…bad…: In the first two cases, the product turned out to be of a different quality than specified. The disadvantaged party can rescind the sale.

neither one is able to withdraw;
(4) Dark and it was found to be white, white and it was found to be dark;
olive wood, and it was found to be sycamore, sycamore and it was found to be olive;
wine and it was found to be vinegar; vinegar and it was found to be wine—
both are able to withdraw.

5:7–8 Determining the Moment of Sale

7 One who sells produce to his fellow,
if he pulled it but did not measure it, he has acquired it;
measured it but did not pull it, he has not acquired it.
If [the buyer] was clever, he may rent its place.
One who buys flax from his fellow—
in this case, he has not acquired it until he has moved it from one place to another;
but if it was still connected to the ground, and he has plucked any amount—
he has acquired it.

8 One who sells wine or oil to his fellow,
and they went up in price or went down in price:
if [the change in price occurred] before the measure was filled—
[the change in price is] the seller's;
if after the measure was filled—
[the change in price is] the buyer's.
If there was a middleman between them, and the jar broke—
it broke with respect to the middleman.

Dark…olive…wine…: Where the agreement was actually for a different product, both the seller and the purchaser can rescind.

5:7 *pulled…but did not measure*: Here, pulling constitutes a possessory act for produce (*Qiddushin* 1:5), while measuring does not.

may rent its place: By temporarily acquiring the place where the produce is located, the purchaser can take possession of the produce immediately, without a formal possessory act.

moved it from one place to another: Executed an act of possession; see *Bava Metsi'a* 6:8. (Commentaries, following the Bavli: technically, "lifting" the object; see *Qiddushin* 1:3; *Bava Metsi'a* 3:12.)

connected…plucked: Formally or symbolically harvested the smallest amount of the crop purchased. (Cf. Commentaries.)

5:8 *before…after the measure was filled*: The Mishnah fixes the moment at which sale is complete, and the parties cannot renegotiate on the basis of price changes. This passage stands in some tension with the requirement of an act of "pulling" (5:7), and already the Tosefta refines this rule in keeping with other principles.

middleman: The measuring is being done by a broker. Until the actual transfer is made (e.g. through the purchaser pulling the produce), the sale has not been completed. Consequently, if *the jar broke*, the middleman, and not one of the principals, bears the cost.

5:8 cont.–11 *Rules Involving Marketers*

And [the seller] must allow three drops to drip for [the purchaser];
if he tipped it and drained it—
then it belongs to the seller.[59]
And the shopkeeper is not[60] liable to allow three drops to drip.
R. Judah says:
He is exempt on the eve of the Sabbath near dark.

9 One who sends his son to a shopkeeper with a *pondion* in his hand,[61]
and [the shopkeeper] measured out an *issar*'s worth of oil for him, and gave him an *issar*,
if the child broke the dish or lost the *issar*—
the shopkeeper is liable.
R. Judah exempts,
because [the father] sent him on this condition.
And the Sages concede to R. Judah that when the dish is in the hand of the child,
and the shopkeeper measured into it,
the shopkeeper is exempt.

10 The grain dealer wipes his measures once in thirty days,
and the householder once in twelve months.
Rabban Simeon b. Gamaliel says:
The matters are reversed.
The shopkeeper wipes his measures twice a week,
and cleans his weights once a week,
and wipes his scales after each and every weighing.

[59] **K, P, G:** "buyer."   [60] **K, P, G:** "is liable."   [61] **K, P, C,** and others lack "With . . . hand."

---

must allow three drops: The seller or broker must allow the measure to drain a reasonable amount. The rule seems to presuppose viscous liquids like oil rather than wine.

tipped it and drained it: If one extracted the very last liquid from the measure, that liquid belongs to the seller.

A *shopkeeper* is too busy to be required to allow the measure to drain.

the eve of the Sabbath, near dark: R. Judah relaxes the rule for shopkeepers only at this time, when time is short. At other times, the shopkeeper must allow the measure to drain.

5:9 *pondion*: See n. 61; according to the reading without this clause, the son may have been sent just to inform the shopkeeper. A *pondion* equals two *issar*.

The *shopkeeper* should have known not to send back the child with the oil or the change, and thus *is liable*. According to *R. Judah*, the shopkeeper is following the father's expectation. *And the Sages concede*: The child has brought a dish from home. In such a case, the shopkeeper is exempt. (Cf. Tosefta, commentaries: the Sages limit the exemption to the dish alone.)

5:10 *grain dealer wipes his measures*: The concern is for accumulation at the bottom of the measure, effectively shrinking its volume.

The matters are reversed: The householder wipes more frequently than the grain dealer.

Elsewhere, the *shopkeeper* occupies a middle ground between a large-scale professional and a householder. See e.g. *Bava Metsi'a* 3:11. The rules for a shopkeeper are here more detailed than for either householder or wholesale marketer.

11 Said Rabban Simeon b. Gamaliel:
When does this apply?
With moist goods.
But with dry goods he need not do so.
And⁶² he must let the scale incline in [the buyer's] favor by a handbreadth.
If he was measuring for him precisely,⁶³
he must give him the customary addition:
one in ten for moist,
and one in twenty for dry.
In a place where it was customary to measure with small measures,
he may not measure with large;
with large, he may not measure with small;
to level the measure, he may not heap up;
to heap up, he may not level.

Chapter Six

6:1–3 *Complications Arising in the Sale of Produce*

6 One who sells produce to his fellow and they did not sprout—
even flaxseed—
he is not liable to make restitution.
Rabban Simeon b. Gamaliel says:
Garden seeds that are not eaten—

---

⁶² K, G (before correction) lack "and."   ⁶³ Lit. "eye to eye."

5:11 A direct continuation of 5:10. *When* do the rules about shopkeepers *apply? Moist…dry goods*: We expect greater buildup with moist goods.

let the scale incline…a handbreadth: Since we do not know what type of scale is assumed, it is difficult to know exactly how much this represents. The clauses that follow *customary addition* suggest that the amount was small, but not negligible. The rule reflects a convention that is not spelled out. The clause that follows give a sense of scale.

must give: Even though the parties stipulated a strict measurement.

one in ten for moist…one in twenty for dry: The commentaries, following the Bavli, understand the implication as *one in one hundred for moist, one in four hundred for dry*.

where it was customary: The Mishnah frequently addresses common practice in this way. See e.g. 1:1, 2.

with small measures…with large: Either one may cause a seller to over- or underestimate the amount of merchandise. See *Bava Metsiʿa* 3:7.

6:1 *even flaxseed*: Singled out because the seeds are edible although generally used for planting, and perhaps, in addition, because the crop was highly valuable and the seeds correspondingly expensive.

not liable to make restitution, assuming he acted in good faith (see 6:3). The agreement did not specify seed for sowing, and the seeds still have a marketable purpose since they are edible. According to *Rabban Simeon b. Gamaliel*, where the *seeds…are not eaten*, and therefore were sold only for planting, the seller *is liable*.

he is[64] liable to make restitution.

2 One who sells produce to his fellow,
in this case [the buyer] accepts upon himself a quarter-*qav* of waste material to the *se'ah*;
figs—
he accepts upon himself ten worm-infested ones to the hundred;
a cellar of wine—
he accepts upon himself ten sour casks to the hundred;
jars in Sharon—
he accepts upon himself one brittle jar to the hundred.

3 One who sells wine to his fellow,
and it went sour—
he is not liable to make restitution.
But if it was known[65] that his wine was going sour—
then it is a purchase made in error.
And if he said to him: "I am selling you spiced wine"—
he must provide wine that will remain good until the Festival of Weeks.
Old wine—
from the year before;
Aged wine—
from three years before.

6:4 Minimum Building Sizes in Sales and Contracts

4 One who sells a space to his fellow,
to build himself a house,

[64] K, C: "they are."   [65] P: "he knows."

6:2 *accepts*: The buyer cannot object to the sale if the amount of waste material or the degree of spoilage falls within an acceptable range. See 7:2 and *Bava Metsi'a* 3:8.

quarter-qav…to the se'ah: A ratio of one in twenty-four.

One who sells…figs…a cellar of wine…jars: Here, the concern is with spoiled produce. The ratio is one tenth.

in Sharon: The region inland of the coastal plain, south of the Carmel. The region may have been associated with the production of storage jars of this type.

6:3 *wine…not liable to make restitution*: Cf. 6:1. The seller did indeed sell wine, so that the sale is valid.

it was known, to the seller at the time of sale. See n. 65.

purchase made in error: Under these circumstances, the purchaser would not have agreed to the contract, and the sale is rescindable.

And if he said: In these following cases, the seller specifies the kind of wine, and takes on certain obligations.

Old…Aged: i.e. if the seller said, "I am selling old wine"… "I am selling aged wine"

Festival of Weeks: Atseret, also called *Shavu'ot*.

6:4 Compare 1:6.

house: Minimally, a single-roomed unit.

and so too one who receives a contract from his fellow,
to build a marital house[66] for his son or a widow's house for his daughter—
he builds four cubits by six—
the words of R. Aqiva.
R. Ishmael says:
This is a cowshed.
One who wishes to build a cowshed,
builds four cubits by six;
a small house,
six by eight;
a large house,
eight by eight;
a dining room,
ten by ten.
Its height is approximately half its length and half its width.
A proof for the matter: the Temple.[67]
Rabban Simeon b. Gamaliel says:
All is[68] according to the construction of the Temple.

6:5–7 *Rights of Access through Agricultural Land*

5 One who has a cistern within his fellow's house,
he goes in at the time when people typically go in,
and goes out at the time when people typically go out,

[66] K, P duplicate "house," with the resulting reading "to build a house—a marital house for his son…"
[67] P adds "and its walls." For this sentence, K has "A proof for the matter: Rabban Simeon b. Gamaliel says: According to the construction of the Temple"; C: "For there is a basis for the matter: Rabban Simeon b. Gamaliel says: According to the construction of the Temple."
[68] P lacks "all is." K, C lack the entire sentence here; see the preceding note.

receives a contract: Bava Metsiʿa 9:1.

marital… widow's house: Perhaps an addition to an existing house.

four cubits by six, approximately two by three meters.

cowshed: It does not meet the minimal requirements of a house.

One who wishes to build: The specifications are in line with the view of R. Ishmael above.

dining room: Heb. *teraqlin*; perhaps merely "hall" (see also 1:6). According to the architectural writer Vitruvius, the length of a *triclinium* should be twice the width. As here, the height was half the sum of the length and width.

the Temple: Heb. *hekhal*. In Solomon's Temple, the *hekhal* (the chamber before the Holy of Holies) was forty cubits by twenty cubits, and thirty cubits in height (see 1 Kings 6:2, 17), matching the Vitruvian proportions. However, the *devir* (the Holy of Holies) was 20 × 20 × 20 (1 Kings 6:20).

All is… Temple: One view in the Talmud reads this as a rhetorical objection: can every construction be based on the Temple?

6:5–7 Compare 4:1–2, dealing with houses and courtyards.

and he does not bring his animal in and give it to drink from his cistern,
but he fills and gives it to drink outside.
This one makes a lock, and this one makes a lock.

6 One who has a garden within his fellow's garden,
he goes in at the time when people typically go in,
and goes out at the time when people typically go out,
and he may not bring merchants into it,
and he may not go from within it into another field.
And [the owner of] the outer [garden] sows the path.
If they gave him a path from the side with the knowledge of both parties,
he goes in at any time he wants,
and goes out at any time he wants,
and brings merchants into it,
but he may not go from within it to another field,
and neither this one nor this one is permitted to sow it.

7 One through whose field a public road passed,
if he seized it and gave to [the public] from the side—
what he gave is given,
and what he took did not enter his ownership.[69]

6:7 cont.–8 *Minimum Sizes Continued: Roads and Burial Caves*

A private road is four cubits;
a public road is sixteen cubits;
the king's road has no measure.

[69] Lit. "and his did not reach him."

6:5 *cistern within…house*: The owner of the house cannot prevent access to the cistern, but the owner of the cistern is restricted in what activities are possible.

lock: The owner of the house prevents access to the cistern; the owner of the cistern, access to the water without approval.

6:6 *garden within…garden*: The first part of the mishnah closely matches 6:5.

sows the path: This is in juxtaposition to what follows. Here, the owner of the outer field owns the land taken up by the path and may sow it, even if the other must walk on the sown plants.

knowledge of both parties: Or "consent." Cf. *Bava Metsiʿa* 5:6. If the parties agree to a path along the side of the outer field, the owner of the inner garden has no restrictions on access, and the owner of the outer garden is restricted from sowing.

6:7 *public road*: An inchoate theory of public property. The owner of a field cannot unilaterally encroach on the public land.

what he gave is given: Either as a legal disincentive to encroachment or because designation as public is effective (Talmud).

private…public…king's road: Compare the Roman classification of *via privata*, *publica*, and *consularis* or *praetoria* (if ordered by a magistrate).

king's road: See *Sanhedrin* 2:4.

A road to the grave has no measure.
A funeral halting place—
the judges of Sepphoris have said:
a four-*qav*-sized area.

8 One who sells a place to his fellow
to make himself a tomb,
and so too one who receives a contract from his fellow
to make him a tomb—
he makes the interior of the cave four cubits by six,
and opens into it eight niches:
three to this side, three to this side, and two opposite them.
And the niches are four cubits in length,
and their height seven [handbreadths] and their width six [handbreadths].
R. Simeon says:
He makes the interior of the cave six cubits by six cubits,
and opens into it thirteen niches:
four to this side, and four to this side, and three opposite them,
and one to the right of the opening and one to the left.
And he makes a courtyard in front of the cave, six by six,
corresponding to the space occupied by the bier and its buriers,
and he opens to it two caves, one to this side and one to this side.
R. Simeon says:
Four, for each of its four sides.
Rabban Simeon b. Gamaliel says:
It all follows the rock.

funeral halting place: A place where the funeral procession pauses. Alternatively, a gathering place for liturgical practices. See *Ketubbot* 2:10, or in another context *Taʿanit* 4:2–3.

judges of Sepphoris: Otherwise unknown.

four-qav-sized area: The area required to sow four *qav*.

6:8 *tomb*: The Mishnah imagines rock-cut tombs with niches (loculi) around a central chamber. The niches were for secondary burial of the bones, either directly in the niches or in special boxes (ossuaries). The bones of the deceased were collected after the soft tissue had decomposed. See *Moʿed Qatan* 1:5–6.

four cubits by six: The anonymous view of the Mishnah and R. Simeon attempts to define the minimum size and standard layout of tombs.

opposite them: On the back wall, facing the entry. The phrasing is slightly awkward.

four cubits: This would be long enough to hold an entire adult human. *R. Simeon* envisions a larger cave.

to the right…left: Seemingly at the entry to the cave, but conventionally understood to refer to the back corners.

courtyard: The burial caves are to be arranged in complexes with a central courtyard. *R. Simeon* again imagines a more elaborate complex.

It all follows the rock: According to Rabban Simeon b. Gamaliel, one cannot dictate the size and shape of burial caves. Cf. the final statement in 4:4, also Rabban Simeon b. Gamaliel.

Chapter Seven

7:1–4 *Sale of a Field: Consequences of Formulae of Sale*

7 One who says to his fellow:
"I am selling you a *kor*-sized plot of soil":
if there were depressions ten handbreadths deep, or rocks ten handbreadths high—
they are not measured with it;
less than this—
they are measured with it.
And if he said to him:
"Approximately[70] a *kor*-sized plot of soil":
even if there were clefts in it deeper than ten handbreadths,
or rocks higher than ten handbreadths—
in this case, they are measured with it.

2 "I am selling you a *kor*-sized plot of soil, measured by rope":[71]
if he underdelivered by any amount—
the buyer may deduct [from the sale price];
if he overdelivered by any amount,
he must return it.
If he said:
"Whether it is lacking or exceeding"—
even if he underdelivered by a quarter-*qav* to the *se'ah*,
or overdelivered by a quarter-*qav* to the *se'ah*—
it has entered [the buyer's ownership];
more than this—

---

[70] K: "within."   [71] G: "with a measure and a rope"; see n. 72.

7:1–4 The Mishnah is concerned with what the "default" sale includes, and what implications specific stipulations might have. Cf. chapter 4. Although the Mishnah frames the transactions as oral, in practice, one expects that the sales would have been transacted with written deeds.

7:1 *"kor-sized"*: Large enough to sow a *kor* of seed.

ten handbreadths: Depressions or outcroppings of this depth or height are treated as self-contained units. The seller specified a precise area "of soil" so these are not subsumed within the *kor*-sized plot. Cf. *Arakhin* 7:1.

less than this, depressions and outcroppings are subsumed within the larger plot.

"Approximately": The lack of precision means that nonsoil is subsumed within the larger plot.

7:2 *measured by rope*: The contract specified precise measurement for a price. The seller who *underdelivered* must accept a lower price; one who *overdelivered* receives some land back.

"Whether it is lacking or exceeding": An alternative clause that stipulated that a precise measure was not required.

quarter-qav to the se'ah: One twenty-fourth. See 6:2. If overage or deficit is less that this amount, the sale is valid. *More than this* requires the additional steps of compensating the parties.

let him make an account.
And what does he return to him?
Money;
but if he wishes, he may return land to him.
And why did they say: "He returns money to him"?
To improve the position of the seller,
so that if he reserved a nine-*qav*-sized plot in the case of a field,
or a half-*qav*-sized plot in the case of a garden—
and according to the view of R. Aqiva, a quarter-*qav*-sized field—
he returns land to him.
And he does not return the quarter-*qav* alone, but the entire overdelivery

3 I am selling to you measured by rope,[72] whether it is lacking or exceeding—
"whether it is lacking or exceeding" has nullified "measured by a rope";
Whether it is lacking or exceeding, measured by a rope—
"measured by a rope" has nullified "whether it is lacking or exceeding"—
the words of[73] Ben Nanas.
With its distinguishing marks and its neighbors:
less than[74] one sixth—
it has entered [the buyer's ownership];
as much as a sixth, he must deduct.

4 One who says to his fellow: "I am selling you half a field"—
they make an assessment between them, and he takes half his field.
"I am selling you the half to the south"—
they make an assessment between them, and he takes the half to the south.

---

[72] G, K (corrected by a second hand), "with a measure and a rope" throughout; see n. 71.
[73] K, P, C, G, "in accord with the words of."   [74] K, P, C, G: "if he underdelivered by."

---

what does the purchaser *return to* the seller?... *if he wishes*: Apparently (see below): if the seller wishes, the purchaser returns land. *Why...? To improve the position of the seller*: If the overage is too small to make up a viable field the seller can demand money in return. If sufficiently large, the seller can require land. The continuation outlines the latter case.

nine-qav-sized plot...: See 1:6. These qualify as viable fields or gardens that can be worked or sold.

does not return the quarter-qav alone: If the overage was greater than one twenty-fourth (a quarter-*qav* to the *se'ah*), the purchaser returns all of the overage, and not only the amount above one twenty-fourth (commentaries, following the Bavli).

7:3 *measured...whether it is lacking...*: The seller used two contradictory stipulations in the agreement. The Mishnah rules that the second stipulation *has nullified* the first and is determinative.

marks...neighbors: Deeds typically specified the boundaries using landmarks or the current owners of the surrounding fields. Here, the seller did this and said "a *kor*-sized field," but the field as marked is less than this. *Less than*: See n. 74. If the difference was smaller than *one sixth*, no additional steps need be taken. *As much as*: One sixth or more. *Deduct*: The seller must refund some of the price.

7:4 *half a field*: Without further marking out the division.

make an assessment: Commentaries, following the Bavli: assess which half is more valuable, and assign the buyer the lesser half.

to the south: Here, there is minimal specification, and the buyer acquires the half of the field that is *to the south*.

And he takes upon himself the space for a fence, and a ditch, and a small ditch.⁷⁵
And how much is a ditch?
Six handbreadths.
And a small ditch?
Three.

Chapter Eight

8:1–4 *Application of Biblical Rules of Inheritance*

8 There are those who receive inheritance and transmit inheritance;
and there are those who receive inheritance but do not transmit inheritance;
transmit inheritance but do not receive inheritance;
neither receive inheritance nor transmit inheritance.
The following receive inheritance and transmit inheritance:
a father vis-à-vis his sons;
sons vis-à-vis their father;
brothers of the same father [vis-à-vis each other]—
these receive inheritance and transmit inheritance.
A man from his mother;
a man from his wife;
and the sons of sisters—
these receive inheritance but do not transmit inheritance.
A woman to her sons;
and a woman to her husband;
and a mother's brothers—
these transmit inheritance but do not receive inheritance.

---

⁷⁵ Lit. "son of a ditch." For "son" (*ben*), **C**, **P** have *beyn* ("between"?) in this occurrence, and **K**, **P**, **C**, **G** in the following.

And the purchaser *takes upon himself*: The space for the new boundaries comes out of the purchaser's half. Some commentaries understand: the seller takes upon himself.

ditch…small ditch: Dug within the fenced area to inhibit rodents (commentaries).

Six handbreadths: In width.

8:1–4 The biblical rules of inheritance pass property through fathers and give priority to sons. In the absence of sons, the daughters inherit. In the absence of any children, property passes to the brothers of the father, and failing that, to the nearest agnatic (patrilineal) kin (Numbers 27:8–11; see also Numbers 36). Where there are sons, the firstborn receives a double allotment (Deuteronomy 21:15–17). The delineation of kin bears comparison to *Yevamot* 1.

8:1 *There are those who receive…and transmit*: This classificatory framework is characteristic of the Mishnah.

A *father* inherits from his sons where they have no children, and his property passes to his *sons*. *Brothers* inherit where none has sons, and the father is deceased.

The cases of *receive…but do not transmit* and *transmit…but do not receive* are correlatives of one another. Marriage or birth makes the mother or wife a possible source of inheritance for the son or husband, but the

And maternal brothers—
these neither receive inheritance nor transmit inheritance.

2 The order of inheritances is thus:
Should a man die and have no son, then you shall transfer his inheritance to his daughter:
The son precedes the daughter,
and all the lineal descendants of the son precede the daughter.
The daughter precedes the brothers,
the lineal descendants of the daughter precede the brothers.
The brothers precede the father's brothers,
the lineal descendants of the son precede the father's brothers.
This is the rule:
Anyone who precedes in inheritance, his lineal descendants precede [as well],
and a father precedes any of his lineal descendants.

3 The daughters of Zelophehad took three shares in the inheritance:
(1) their father's inheritance, who was among those who left Egypt;
(2) and his share among his brothers in the property of Hepher;
(3) and since he was a firstborn, he takes two shares.

4 The law is one and the same for the son and the daughter in inheritance,
except that the son takes a double portion from the property of the father,
but he does not take a double portion from the property of the mother;
and daughters are maintained from the father's property;
but they are not maintained from the mother's property.

women are not in line for inheritance from these men. One's nephews from *sisters* sharing a common father inherit, in the absence of brothers as the patrilineal descendants of the uncle. However, their patrilineal kin receive any inheritance these men leave behind.

maternal brothers with no common father are not patrilineal kin.

8:2 *Should a man die*: Numbers 27:8. The context is the petition of the daughters of Zelophehad to inherit their father's portion in the Land of Israel. Note the formulation as an exposition of a verse from the Torah. A *son* and his *lineal descendants* take precedence, followed by a *daughter* and any of her *lineal descendants*, and then by the father's patrilineal kin. *A father precedes* any of his surviving sons in inheriting from a son with no sons of his own (commentaries).

8:3 *daughters of Zelophehad*: See 8:2.

their father's inheritance…his share…Hepher: The Mishnah assumes that the Land of Israel was divided among those men who left Egypt. Consequently, both father and grandfather, who were alive during the time of the Exodus, received a portion.

8:4 *The law is one and the same*: Already the Talmud noted that this formulation was difficult, given the rule in 8:3. The sense seems to be: "Sons, and when there are no sons, daughters, inherit following the same rules, with the following exceptions" (cf. commentaries).

double share: Deuteronomy 21:17.

daughters are maintained after the father's death. See 9:1 and *Ketubbot* 7:6, 13:3.

8:5–7 *Assignment of Property in Contemplation of Death*

5 One who says:
"So-and-so is my firstborn son, [but nonetheless] may not take a double portion";
or "So-and-so is my son, [but nonetheless] may not inherit with his brothers"—
his statement is not valid,[76]
for he has stipulated in contradiction to[77] what is written in the Torah.[78]
One who distributes his property to his sons according to his own determination,[79]
if he increased for one, or decreased for one, or made the firstborn equal to them—
his words are valid.
But if he said: "As inheritance,"
his statement is not valid.
If he wrote: "As a gift, whether at the beginning, or at the middle, or at the end"—
his words are valid.
If one says: "So-and-so shall inherit from me," where there is a daughter;
or "My daughter shall inherit from me," where there is a son—
his statement is not valid,
for he has stipulated in contradiction to[80] what is written in the Torah.[81]
R. Yohanan b. Beroqa says:
If he said this about one who is eligible to inherit—
his words are valid;
but if about one who is not eligible to inherit—
his words are not valid.

[76] Here and below in this mishnah, lit. "he has not said anything." [77] Lit. "on."
[78] K, C: "on (= contradicting) a writing that is in the Torah."
[79] Heb. "according to his mouth"; alternative translation: "orally." [80] Lit. "on."
[81] K, C: "on (= contradicting) a writing that is in the Torah."

8:5–7 The Mishnah only allows "inheritance" according to the rules of the Torah (8:1–4, headnote). Still, the Mishnah enables householders to dispose of their property in contemplation of death. Here, the key issue is that the disposition must be a "gift" and not an "inheritance." Compare 9:6–7.

8:5 *"So-and-so"*: Heb. *peloni* (cf. Ruth 4:1), used by the Mishnah as a generic name.

firstborn…double portion. Deuteronomy 21:17.

stipulated…the Torah: Ketubbot 9:1; Bava Metsi'a 7:11. In both clauses, the father's statement ran counter to the explicit laws of inheritance and has no effect.

One who distributes: See 9:5–6.

according to his own determination: Alternatively (and more literally): "orally." Although the distribution goes against biblical inheritance rules, it is *valid* as long as it is not formally called *inheritance*.

If he wrote: Here, writing is explicit.

gift: By making the allocation explicitly a gift somewhere in the document, even if the document also describes it as inheritance (Tosefta), the distribution is *valid*.

"So-and-so shall inherit"… or "My daughter shall inherit": In both cases there is a legally mandated heir, so the statement is invalid, as in the first example in this passage.

eligible…not eligible to inherit: R. Yohanan b. Beroqah rules that if the person is capable of being a legitimate heir, the testator may make such changes; but if the person is not capable (e.g. a daughter, when there are sons), the testator not may not.

One who, in writing, cedes his property to others, and left his sons [with nothing]—
what he has done is done,
but the spirit of the Sages[82] is uneasy with him.
Rabban Simeon b. Gamaliel says:
If his sons did not behave[83] properly,
he is remembered for good.

6 One who says: "This is my son"—he is believed;
"This is my brother"—he is not believed,
and he shares his portion with him.[84]
If he died, the property returns to its place;
if property fell to him from another place,
his brothers may inherit along with him.
One who died, and a testament was found tied on his thigh—
in this case, this is nothing.
If he granted acquisition to another by means of the document,[85]
whether among the heirs or whether not among the heirs—
his words are valid.

[82] K (subsequently corrected), C: "wisdom."   [83] C: "toward him."
[84] Lit. "he takes (K, P may/must take) with him from his share."   [85] Heb. "it."

One who, in writing, cedes: Lit. "writes his property," presumably as a "gift," as above. The father can thus effectively prevent legitimate heirs from inheriting.

spirit of the Sages: For the expression see *Shevi'it* 7:9.

If ... remembered for good: According to Rabban Simeon b. Gamaliel, disinheriting unsuitable heirs is in fact meritorious.

8:6 *One who says*: See *Qiddushin* 4:8, where the implication is whether a woman would require levirate marriage or *halitsah* (*Yevamot*, introduction).

shares his portion with him: The brother who affirms the existence of an additional brother takes a share as if the doubtful brother inherits (e.g. one third, if there are two brothers), and cedes the remainder of his share (one half) to the doubtful brother (commentaries).

If he died: i.e. the doubtful brother died without children, so that inheritance next passes to the brothers (8:1). His inheritance *returns* to the brother who gave a share.

property ... from another place: Property not inherited from his putative father.

his brothers may inherit along with him: The brothers who denied the legitimacy of the doubtful brother may nonetheless take a share in his property. (The deceased considered the others brothers, so they may share. Commentaries.)

testament: See *Bava Metsi'a* 2:7.

found tied on his thigh, so there is no doubt of its authenticity (commentaries).

If he granted ... document: If the testament also included a gift of property to someone, *whether among the heirs* or not, that was not a testamentary gift (Albeck; see 5:5), it is *valid*. Alternatively: If the document had been passed to another to complete the transaction (commentaries).

7 One who, in writing, cedes his property to his sons[86] must write,
"From today and after death"—
the words of R. Judah.
R. Yose says:
He does not need to.
One who in writing cedes his properties to his son after his death—
the father cannot sell them because they are written to the son,
and the son cannot sell them because they are in the possession of the father.
If the father sold them, they are sold until his death;
if the son sold, the buyer has no share in them until the father dies.
The father plucks [the property] and feeds whomever he wants;
and whatever he leaves plucked belongs to the heirs.

8:7 cont.–9:2 *Maintenance of Sons and Daughters after Death*

If one left adult and minor sons,
the adults are not provisioned at the expense of the minors,
and the minors are not maintained[87] at the expense of the adults;
but rather they split equally.
If the adults were married, the minors may be married.

[86] C: "son."   [87] Lit. "fed."

8:7 *One who, in writing, cedes*: See 5:5. The goal is to have the property enter the possession of the sons after his death.

"From today": The father must specify that the transfer of ownership is effective immediately, although he will retain use of the property (below).

does not need to: According to R. Yose, the fact that it is a deed of gift (even if it makes specifications for after death) means that the gift occurs as of the execution of the document (see commentaries).

the father cannot sell…the son cannot sell: The father's property is in limbo: assigned to the son but held by the father. Neither has full control over its disposition.

If the father sold…if the son sold: The father can only make a temporary sale; the son, a sale that will be completed after the death of the father. This statement is possibly a gloss on the preceding.

plucks…and feeds: The father has the product of the property and can dispose of it.

belongs to the heirs: What has been plucked is not governed by the deed of gift, which assigned property to one son, but is inherited according to the rules of inheritance.

adult and minor sons, with no daughters. The question is what additional claims the brothers may have on the property.

provisioned: With clothing (commentaries; implicit in the Bavli).

maintained: Lit. "fed." Neither group of sons gets a stipend out of the common fund before the division of the property, or a promise of ongoing support.

adults were married: Received a dowry or marriage gift in the lifetime of the father. (A gloss in the Bavli understands this clause, but not the one following, to refer to a case in which the sons were married after the death of the father, but before the division of the property.) In this case, the *minors* have a claim to be *married* as well.

And if the minors say: "Now, we are to be married in the manner that you were married"—
one does not listen to them,
but rather what their father has given to them he has given.

8 If he left adult and minor daughters,
the adults are not provisioned at the expense of[88] the minors,
and the minors are not maintained[89] at the expense of the adults;
but rather, they divide equally.
If the adults married, the minors may marry.
And if the minors say: "Now, we are to be married in the manner that you were married"—
ones does not listen to them.
In this respect the rule is stricter for daughters than for sons,
that daughters are maintained at the expense of[90] sons,
but are not maintained at the expense of daughters.

Chapter Nine

9 One who dies and left sons and daughters,
when there is much property,
the sons inherit, and the daughters are maintained;
if[91] there is little property,
the daughters are maintained, and the sons may beg in the doorways.
Admon said:
Because I am male, I have lost?
Said Rabban Gamaliel:[92]

---

[88] Lit. "on."   [89] Lit. "fed."   [90] Lit. "on."   [91] K: "when."
[92] G, apparently: "Rabban Gamaliel says."

"in the manner that you were married": The minors are entitled to a "standard" dowry or settlement, and may not exhaust the estate.

8:8 *adult and minor daughters*, and no sons. The rules are parallel to those for sons (see 8:4).

the rule is stricter: There is a restriction when daughters alone inherit that does not exist when there are sons (who inherit) as well as daughters (who do not). Minor *daughters are maintained* by the sons who inherit (see 9:1), but not by adult *daughters* when there are no sons.

9:1 *sons inherit*: As above.

daughters are maintained: Lit. "fed." Daughters who were unmarried at the time of their father's death were entitled to maintenance until they married. For this as a stipulation in the betrothal document, see *Ketubbot* 4:11.

little property: The daughters are given precedence, and *the sons may beg*. Alternatively, "may borrow."

Admon: Remembered as a judge from Second Temple period Jerusalem. See *Ketubbot* chapter 13. Admon and *Rabban Simeon b. Gamaliel* reject the precedence of the daughter, but the Mishnah does not state how they would rule instead.

I agree with the words of Admon.
  2 If he left sons, and daughters, and a *tumtum*,
when there is much property, the males push him among the females;
if[93] there is little property, the females push him among the males.
One who says: "If my wife gives birth[94] to a male, he may take one hundred,"
if she gave birth to a male, he may take one hundred.
"To a female, two hundred,"
if she gave birth to a female, she may take two hundred;
"If to a male, one hundred; if to a female, two hundred,"
if she gave birth to a male and a female—
the male takes one hundred, and the female two hundred;
if she gave birth to a *tumtum*[95]—
he does not take.
If he said: "Whatever my wife gives birth to shall take,"
then this one takes;
and if there is no other heir but him, he inherits all.

9:3–4 *Improvements to and Deductions from Property after Death*

  3 If he left adult and minor sons—
if the adults improved the property,
they have improved for the common holding;[96]
if they[97] said:
"See what our father has left us, we will labor and consume the profits,"

[93] **K**: "when." [94] **K, P, C, G**: "has given birth."
[95] **P** adds *androgynos*, one with sex characteristics of males and females; the word is marked for deletion.
[96] Here and in the sequel, lit. "for the middle." [97] **G** and others: "the adults."

9:2 *tumtum*: Lacking the sex characteristics of both males and females.

push him among the females: The *tumtum* is eligible for maintenance, but not inheritance. *Push him among the males*: Ineligible for maintenance, and with nothing to inherit.

One who says: A digression based on *tumtum*. The commentaries are divided over whether the situation envisioned is any conditional gift of this sort, or specifically one in contemplation of death.

"If my wife…one hundred"…"To a female, two hundred": In the preceding cases, the *tumtum* was not at issue. Here, since the father specified both male and female, the Mishnah considers—and rejects—the claim of the child of indeterminate sex. Where the father said *Whatever my wife gives birth to*, and did not specify sex, the *tumtum* receives the gift.

no other heir: If the *tumtum* is sole heir as well. Offspring take precedence as potential heirs, see 8:2.

9:3 *left adult and minor sons*: Note the assumption here that the estate is as yet undivided when the improvements are made. Cf. 8:8.

if they said…"we will labor and consume": For the expression see *Bava Metsi'a* 2:7. The adults may stipulate that they will gain the benefits of their improvements. The expression suggests that they receive their payment in the form of cash or goods, but the rule could give them a larger share when the inheritance is divided.

they have improved for themselves.⁹⁸
And similarly a wife who improved the property,
she has improved for the common holding;
If she said:
"See what my husband has left me, I will labor and consume the profits,"
she has improved for herself.

    4 Brothers who were partners of whom one fell into imperial service⁹⁹—
his liability is from the common holding;¹⁰⁰
if he became ill, and received medical treatment, the medical treatment is from his own.

9:4 cont.–5   *Rules Involving Marriage Gifts*

The brothers some of whom made groomsmen's gifts during the life of the father—
if the groomsmen's gifts were returned, they have returned to the common holding,¹⁰¹
for groomsmen's gifts are claimed in court.¹⁰²
But one who sends to his fellow jars of wine or jars of oil,
they are not collected in court,
because they are the granting of favors.¹⁰³

    5 One who sends betrothal gifts to the house of his father-in-law,
if he sent there gifts worth ten thousand *dinar*,

⁹⁸ G (in error): "for the middle."   ⁹⁹ Lit. "artisanship."
¹⁰⁰ Lit. "he has fallen to the common holding."
¹⁰¹ For "if . . . holding," C, G have only "the *shushbinut* has returned to the middle."
¹⁰² P lacks "in court."   ¹⁰³ Or "acts of kindness, charity."

---

wife: Or "woman." A widow has a claim on her husband's property for the amount of her marriage settlement. Until the payment is made, she remains a part of the common household. See *Ketubbot* 4:12, 11, 20.

9:4 *Brothers who were partners*: Sharing their inheritance undivided.

imperial service: Lit. "artisanship." The translation assumes that this is a liability, rather than providing a windfall (cf. Tosefta). The brother was chosen at random, or because of the property he shares with his brother, and is not personally responsible.

ill…from his own: The commentaries are bothered by this rule and specify that it applies when the brother actively brought illness upon himself.

groomsmen's gifts: Heb. *shushbinut*. The Mishnah appears to assume a formal gift exchange, so that one who receives such a gift has an obligation to repay it at a later time. Gifts made *during the life of the father* are assumed to have been made out of the father's property. Consequently, they return *to the common holding*. *Claimed in court*: They are like any other outstanding debt owed to the father's estate (commentaries).

sends…jars of wine or…oil: As wedding gifts, but not as formal *shushbinut*.

9:5 *betrothal gifts*: Heb. *sivlonot*. For betrothal (*qiddushin*) see *Qiddushin*, introduction. Unlike the discussion of groomsmen's gifts above, here the issue is whether the groom can recover the gift if the wedding falls through.

gifts worth ten thousand dinar: Lit. "one hundred *maneh*." In what follows the gifts are for use rather than cash.

and ate even a *dinar*'s worth of a betrothal meal—
they may not be claimed;
if he did not eat a betrothal meal—
then they may be claimed.
If he sent many gifts, that might return[104] with her to her husband's house—
then they may be claimed;
few gifts, that[105] she might use in her father's house—
they may not be claimed.

9:6–7 Deathbed Donations

6 One who was deathly ill who gifted all[106] of his property to others in writing
and left over for himself even the slightest bit of land—
his gift is valid;
if he did not leave over even the slightest bit of land—
his gift is not valid.
If he did not write in it "deathly ill":
he says that he was[107] deathly ill, and they say that he was healthy—
he must bring proof that he was deathly ill—
the words of R. Meir.
But the Sages say:
The one who claims property from his fellow has the burden of proof.

---

[104] K, P, G, C: "in order that they might come."   [105] K, P, G, C: "in order that."
[106] K, P, G, C lack "all."   [107] K, P, G, C: "I was."

---

betrothal meal: Lit. "groom's meal." The exchange of gift and food may mark the good faith actions of both parties, or the benefit of the meal may serve to transfer ownership of the gift. (Rashbam: Due to his pleasure at the meal, the groom cedes the gift.) If the groom ate a modest amount, the gifts *may not be claimed*.

gifts, that might return: Contributed to the trousseau, intending that they will enter the marital household.

that she might use in her father's house: Like the wine and oil in 9:4, these are outright gifts, and *may not be claimed* if the marriage fails.

9:6–7 The Mishnah considers the case of gifts by "one who was deathly ill," literally "lying ill." The giver must retain a minimal amount of property, and the gift is effective even should the donor recover. The assumption is that since the donor takes minimal care for the event of recovery, such a gift can be treated as valid. The precise difference between this form of gift and those discussed in 8:5–7 is not made explicit. Presumably, a gift that does not retain property for the donor would have to conform to the rules of 8:5–7 in order to be valid.

9:6 *One who was deathly ill*: See also *Pe'ah* 3:7.

valid … not valid: Presumably, if valid, he permanently transfers ownership of the property distributed, and if invalid, he does not convey ownership at all.

did not write in it "deathly ill": The donor has recovered and wants to retrieve his property. According to R. Meir, the donor claims that he was deathly ill and the document flawed, and the gifts therefore invalid; the recipients that the donor was healthy and the gifts were valid, along the lines of 8:5–7. Assuming that the property would not be distributed during the donor's lifetime, *the Sages* place the onus of proof on the recipients.

one who claims: See *Bava Qamma* 3:11.

7 One who distributes his property according to his own determination,
R. Eliezer says:
Whether he is healthy or in danger of dying—
property to which security applies is acquired by money, deed, or possession;
and that to which security does not apply is acquired only by pulling.
They said to him:
It once happened that the mother of the sons of an itinerant merchant[108] was ill,
and she said: "Give my cloak to my daughter,"
and it cost 1,200,
and she died,
and they upheld her words.
He said to them:
The mother will bury the sons of the itinerant merchant.[109]
And the Sages[110] say:
On the Sabbath, his words are valid, because he is not able to write;
but not on a weekday.
R. Joshua says:
They said it with reference to the Sabbath,
and by argument of lesser and greater with reference to a weekday.
Similarly: one can make acquisition on behalf of a minor,
but not on behalf of an adult.[111]

---

[108] Or, as a proper noun, "the sons of Rokhel."
[109] Or "The sons of Rokhel/the merchant—let their mother bury them!"
[110] The Mishnah in the Babylonian Talmud: "R. Eliezer."
[111] Some medieval witnesses add "The words of R. Eliezer."

9:7 *distributes ... according to his own determination*: Cf. 8:5.

property to which security applies ... does not apply: See *Qiddushin* 1:5. Whether the seller's creditors may claim the sold property in repayment of the seller's debt. The former category consists primarily of land.

is acquired: At issue is the requirement that transfers of ownership take place through formal possessory acts. See also *Bava Metsiʿa* 4:1–2.

R. Eliezer requires a formal act of transfer for any gift in contemplation of death to be valid.

mother of the sons of an itinerant merchant: Alternatively, "of Rokhel."

cloak: Others "girdle" or "veil."

1,200: Lit. "twelve *maneh*."

they upheld: The story shows that an oral gift was treated as valid.

He, R. Eliezer, *said to them: The mother will bury*: Alternatively: "The mother, may she bury," a curse. R. Eliezer's response does not invalidate the gift itself. (Commentaries: The sons were wicked, and the Sages penalized them in this case.)

the Sages allow an oral gift without possessory act *on the Sabbath*. This responds to the statement of R. Eliezer, before the anecdote. According to *R. Joshua* (see n. 110) the view of the Sages is not an exception for the Sabbath: if they allowed the gift on the Sabbath, surely they allowed it on weekdays.

one can make acquisition: A third party can acquire something on behalf of a minor, who cannot do so for him or herself, but not for an adult, who can. In parallel to the preceding, *R. Joshua* maintains that third parties can acquire on behalf of adults as well.

R. Joshua says:
They said it on behalf of a minor, and by argument of lesser and greater also for an adult.

9:8–10 *A Collapsed House and Indeterminate Precedence in Inheritance*

8 If a house fell upon him and his father,
or upon him and one from whom he inherits,[112]
and he had the obligation of a marriage settlement for a wife or a creditor:
the heirs of the father say: "The son died first and afterwards the father died";
the creditors say: "The father died first and afterwards the son died"—
the House of Shammai say:
Let them split it;
but the House of Hillel say:
The property remains in its prior state of possession.[113]

9 If a house fell upon him and upon his wife:
the heirs of the husband say: "The wife died first and afterwards the husband died";
the heirs of the wife say: "The husband died first and afterwards the wife died"—
the House of Shammai say:
Let them split it;
But the House of Hillel say:
The property remains in its prior possession:
the marriage settlement remains in the possession of the heirs of the husband;
property that comes in and goes out with her remains in the possession
of the heirs of the [wife's] father.[114]

---

[112] P adds "upon him and his heir."   [113] C instead: "The property belongs to his wife."
[114] Heb. "of the father." P: "of the wife (marked for deletion) the father." Some witnesses read "of the wife."

9.8–10 A collapsed house creates uncertainty about the direction of inheritance. For the dispute between the Houses of Shammai and Hillel, see also *Yevamot* 4:3; *Ketubbot* 8:6.

9:8 *"The son died first,"* so that his father inherits from him (see 8:1–4), and this passes to *the heirs of the father*.

"The father died first," so that the son inherits, and the *creditors* can claim from a larger estate.

let them split the inheritance of the son. For the principle, see *Bava Metsi'a* 1:1.

prior state of possession: Effectively, father and son do not inherit from one another.

9:9 *"The wife died first,"* so that the husband inherits from her, and this passes to *the heirs of the husband*.

"The husband died first," so that the marriage settlement passes to the wife, and her heirs inherit any property she owned.

marriage settlement: Heb. *ketubbah*, the promised settlement held in trust by the husband for the wife in the case of divorce or the husband's death (*Ketubbot* 1:2).

goes in and out with her: That is, her dowry.

heirs of the…father: See n. 114. The patrilineal heirs of the woman (who does not have sons in this scenario; see 9:10).

10 If a house fell upon him and upon his mother—
these and these concede that they split it.
Said R. Aqiva:
I concede in this case that the property remains in its prior possession.
Said Ben Azzai to him:
We grieve over the cases that are subject to dispute;
but you come to make disputed cases where they hold the same opinion.

Chapter Ten

10:1–4 *Deeds and Documentary and Scribal Practices*

10 A simple deed—
its witnesses are within it;
a bound deed—
its witnesses are on its reverse.
A simple deed whose witnesses wrote on its reverse,
or a bound deed whose witnesses wrote within it—
they are both invalid.
R. Hananiah b. Gamaliel says:
A bound deed whose witnesses wrote within it is valid,
because he can make it a simple deed.
Rabban Simeon b. Gamaliel says:
All follows the custom of the land.

9:10 *Himself and his mother*: At issue is the property of the mother: either the son inherits it, and it passes to his heirs, or it stays in the mother's possession and it passes to her patrilineal heirs.

these and these concede: The Houses of Shammai and Hillel agree that the parties split the wife's property. R. Aqiva holds that in this case the wife's property should remain *in its prior possession* and pass to her heirs.

Ben Azzai: The objection is not on legal grounds but opposes the unsettling of seemingly settled issues.

10:1 *simple* or "flat" *deed*: For "deed" the Mishnah here uses *get*, in its general sense. Cf. 10:3. The body of a "flat" deed is written once, at the top of a sheet, and the witnesses sign below the text. When rolled and sealed, its signatures are *within*.

bound deed: The text is written first at the top of the sheet, and then a second time below; the signatures are on the *reverse*. When the document is rolled, the signatures are on the outside. The inner version, originally the authoritative one, was bound off for security; the outer was accessible for reference.

they are both invalid: The document must conform to a standard form.

can make it a simple deed: It is possible to salvage a formally defective *bound* deed, by treating it as a *simple* one.

custom of the land: Documents must conform to local standards, not absolute ones. See also *Bava Metsi'a* 7:1, *Ketubbot* 6:4.

2 A simple deed, its [attestation] is with two witnesses;
and a bound deed with three.
A simple deed in which one witness is written,
and a bound deed in which two are written—
both are invalid.
If he wrote: "One hundred *zuz*, which are twenty *sela*"—
[the creditor can collect] only twenty;
"One hundred *zuz*, which are thirty *sela*"—
the creditor can collect only one hundred,
"Silver *zuz*, which are," and the rest is erased—
it is no fewer than two.
"Silver *sela*, which are," and the rest is erased—
it is no fewer than two.
"Darics, which are," and the rest is erased—
it is no fewer than two.[115]
If a *maneh* is written above and two hundred is written below,
[or] two hundred above, and a *maneh* below—
it all follows the lower.
If so, why do they write the upper?
So that if one letter should be erased from the lower he may learn it from the upper.

3 One may write a divorce document for a man even though his wife is not with him;
and a receipt for the wife even though her husband is not with her,
as long as the scribe[116] recognizes them,[117]

---

[115] C lacks the clause about darics. [116] Heb. "he." [117] K, P, C, G: "her" (the wife).

10:2 *If he wrote*: See n. 115. Situations in which the scribe made an error or the text became damaged. The creditor receives the minimum claimable amount. *One hundred zuz* or a *maneh* equals twenty-five *sela*. *Silver zuz…sela…Darics*: The denominations are in the plural, so the creditor can collect *no fewer*, but also no more, *than* two.

Darics: Seemingly a reference to a Persian-period gold coin (cf. Ezra 8:27; see also *Sheqalim* 2:1, 4). It was not current at the time the Mishnah was edited.

If a maneh was written…all follows the lower: For the Mishnah, the lower text is determinative (cf. 10:1 n.). In extant examples from the Judaean Desert the upper copy is less carefully written than the lower. *He may learn from the upper*: It can still serve as a point of reference.

10:3 For 10:3–4 compare *Bava Metsi'a* 1:6–8. This mishnah deals with deeds that unilaterally document a status, obligation, or benefit.

for a man to deliver to his wife to effect a divorce.

his wife is not with him: Divorce is effected only upon delivery and does not require the wife's consent.

receipt: Better: "quittance," a statement by the wife that she has received her divorce settlement.

as long as the scribe recognizes them: The concern seems to be misidentification of the recipient. This may imply that the scribe, and not the principal, delivers it. (See nn. 115 and 116; perhaps addressing specifically the case of the wife being divorced.)

and the husband pays the fee.
One may write a deed for the borrower even though the lender is not with him;
but one does not write for the lender unless the borrower is with him,
and the borrower pays the fee.
One may write a deed for the seller even though the buyer is not with him;
but one does not write for the buyer unless the seller is with him,
and the buyer pays the fee.

4 One does not write deeds of betrothal or marriage
except with the knowledge of both,
and the groom pays the fee.
One does not write[118] deeds of sharecropping or agricultural lease,
except with the knowledge of both,
and the tenant[119] pays the fee.
One does not write deeds[120] of selection or any act of a court,
except with the knowledge of both,
and they both pay the fee.
Rabban Simeon b. Gamaliel says:
Both write two documents,[121] this one for himself and this one for himself.

10:5–8 *Laws Involving Deeds*

5 One who has paid part of his debt, and entrusted his deed to a third party, and said: "If I have not paid you from now until such and such a date,

---

[118] "They do not write" lacking in **K, G**.   [119] Lit. "recipient."
[120] "They do not write" lacking in **K, G, C**.
[121] **K, P, C, G**: "They write two for the two of them" (i.e. one each).

---

pays the fee: The commentaries, following the Bavli, seek the reason for one party's responsibility to pay for the deed in some benefit that that party receives from the transactions. The Mishnah may view the bill of divorce as a responsibility of the husband based on the Torah (Deuteronomy 24:1, 3).

for the borrower: A deed of indebtedness to deliver to the lender. Effectively, the borrower may obligate himself.

for the lender, obligating the borrower. This requires that *the borrower* be *with him*.

for the seller: Proof for the purchaser that the sale was made. Such a deed cannot be written without the participation of the *seller*.

10:4 Unlike 10:3, this passage deals with transactions that require mutual consent.

betrothal or marriage: Two distinct, but legally binding transactions.

sharecropping: For the terminology see *Bava Metsi'a* 9:1–10 and 7:5–6.

selection of judges in monetary cases, *Sanhedrin* 3:1.

10.5–8 This section clearly continues the discussion of deeds introduced in 10:1. However, it contains extraneous material as well, especially in 10:7. It possibly originated as an appendix to earlier material.

10:5 *entrusted his deed*: The parties agreed to entrust the loan document to a third party. If the deed is given to the creditor it would allow him to collect the full amount.

give the creditor[122] his deed,"
if the time arrived and he has not paid—
R. Yose says:
He must give it;
R. Judah says:
He must not give it.

6 One whose loan document was erased—
witnesses testify about it, and he comes before a court,
and they issue him a validation [as follows]:
So-and-so the son of so-and-so, his deed was erased on such and such a date,
and so-and-so and so-and-so are his witnesses.
Someone who has paid part of his debt:
R. Judah says:
Let him replace [the deed];
R. Yose says:
Let him write a receipt.
Said R. Judah:
It turns out that this one must guard his receipt from mice.
Said R. Yose:
This is appropriate for the borrower,[123]
so that the power of the creditor[124] is not weakened.

7 Two brothers, one poor and one wealthy,
and their father left them a bath or an olive press—
if he made them for income, the income goes to the common holding;[125]
if he made them for themselves,[126]
then the wealthy brother may say to the poor brother:
"Buy slaves, and they may bathe in the bathhouse," or

[122] Heb. "him." [123] Lit. "him." [124] Lit. "this one." [125] Lit. "to the middle."
[126] K, P, C, G: "for himself."

---

must... must not give: The unspecified concern may be whether a promise of security of this sort is ever valid (commentaries, Bavli).

10:6 *validation*: The claim against the borrower's property from the initial date is affirmed in a new document.

paid part of his debt: This passage returns to the topic of 10:5, with the same disputants.

replace [the deed]: The debtor writes a new deed of indebtedness.

receipt issued by the creditor to the borrower. See 10:3.

R. Judah objects that it is now the debtor's responsibility to protect his property from seizure by preserving his receipts.

so that the power of the creditor is not weakened: By issuing a new document, the creditor's right to seize property alienated by the creditor (10:8), begins only as of the new date.

10:7 *Two brothers*: This unit would fit better with 9:3–4.

for themselves: For the use of himself and those of his household (see n. 126). Since the installations were built for use, the *poor brother* cannot complain that he makes less use of them than a *wealthy brother*.

"Buy olives and prepare them in the olive press."
Two men who were in one town,
the name of one was Joseph the son of Simeon
and the name of the other was Joseph the son of Simeon:
they may not bring a loan document against each other,
and another may not bring a loan document against either of them.
If someone found among his documents "The deed of Joseph the son of Simeon is paid"—
the deeds of both of them are paid.
What do they do?
They add a third generation.[127]
If they had a third generation in common, they write a distinguishing mark.
If they had distinguishing marks in common, they write "priest."
One who says to his son: "A deed among my deeds is paid, and I do not know which"—
all the deeds are paid.
If there were two deeds relating to one person among them—
the larger of the deeds is deemed to be paid, the smaller is not.
One who lends his fellow with a guarantor—
he may not exact payment from the guarantor;
but if he said: "On condition that I can exact payment from whomever I want"—
he may exact payment from the guarantor.
Rabban Simeon b. Gamaliel said:
If the borrower has property, in neither case should he exact payment from the guarantor.
And thus would Rabban Simeon b. Gamaliel say:
One who serves as guarantor for a wife for her marriage settlement,
and her husband was divorcing her:
let him prevent her[128] by a vow from gaining benefit from him,

---

[127] Lit. "triple." [128] K, P, C lack "her."

Two men: The Mishnah considers the problems posed by men of the same name in a single town. Each can claim that the other is the true borrower in any loan document, and so deflect the creditor.

If someone...both of them are paid: Similarly, any notice in the documents that one of them has paid his debts can be argued by each to apply to him.

What do they do? The Mishnah proposes a practical solution: adding additional generations, distinguishing marks, or hereditary classifications.

"A deed...is paid": See also *Bava Metsiʿa* 1:8. Because the creditor has no way of determining which borrower has paid, all the loan documents must be treated as paid.

two deeds: One of the deeds relating to this borrower is deemed to have been paid, but the creditor is allowed to collect on the other.

the larger...is paid: This avoids having the creditor collect more than is his due.

a guarantor puts up his own property as security for the collection of the loan.

may not exact from the guarantor, without first attempting to collect from the borrower. However, the creditor may stipulate that he *may exact payment from the guarantor*, from either party.

Rabban Simeon b. Gamaliel disagrees in any case in which the *borrower has property*. "And thus" in the following sentence may suggest that here, too, the concern is with defrauding the guarantor.

prevent her by a vow from gaining benefit: The commentaries specify: Before collecting from the guarantor, the husband should prevent his wife by means of a vow from gaining benefit from himself. See *Nedarim*, introduction.

lest they conspire against the property of the guarantor,
and he take back his wife.

8 One who lends to his fellow with a deed
may collect from encumbered property;
if by means of witnesses,
he may collect [only] from unencumbered[129] property.
If [the creditor] took out against [the debtor] his own writing that he owed him money—
he may collect [only] from unencumbered property.
A guarantor designated[130] after the witnesses—
May collect [only] from unencumbered property.
A case once came before R. Ishmael and he said:
He may collect [only] from unencumbered property.
Said to him Ben Nanas:
He does not collect from either encumbered or unencumbered property.
He said to him:
Why?
He said to him:
One who is choking someone in the marketplace,
and his fellow found him and said to him: "Leave him alone"—
the guarantor is exempt,
because the lender did not lend to him on the assurance[131] of [the guarantor].
Rather, who is a guarantor who is liable?
"Lend to him, and I will pay you"—
he is liable,
for indeed the creditor lent to him on the assurance[132] of the guarantor.
Said R. Ishmael:
One who wishes to become wise should engage in monetary laws,
for there is no corner of Torah greater than they, for they are a like a spring that flows forth;
and one who wishes to engage in monetary laws should serve Simeon b. Nanas.

[129] Lit. "free."   [130] Lit. "who goes out." Alternative translation: "added to the document."
[131] C (K before correction?): "for his sake."   [132] K, P, C: "for his sake."

against the property of the guarantor: i.e. the wife collects the divorce settlement from the guarantor, and then returns to her former husband.

10:8 *with a deed*: The Mishnah allows the lender the ability to exercise a lien on property only with a properly executed written deed.

encumbered: Lit. "enslaved": subject to collection by the lender even if alienated by the borrower.

witnesses: Duly witnessed, but not recorded in a deed.

his own writing: A promissory note without witnesses.

designated after the witnesses: Appearing below the signatures of the witnesses, thus not technically a witness. The guarantor therefore cannot recover his money from encumbered property alienated by the borrower. According to *Ben Nanas* such a guarantor is not liable to collection by the creditor at all, because, as in the analogy that follows, when the guarantor appears after the witnesses, *the lender did not lend to him on the assurance of [the guarantor]*.

Said R. Ishmael: The statement provides a concluding passage for the entire tractate.

Tractate Sanhedrin

Beth Berkowitz

Introduction

Overview

The Greek word *synedrion* means "council"; in the Gospels and Josephus the word refers to a judicial and deliberative body presided over by the high priest. In this tractate the word, Hebraized as *Sanhedrin*, refers to various judicial bodies consisting of Sages and presided over by Sages.

Structure and Organization of the Tractate

Tractate *Sanhedrin* describes the courts, cases, procedures, and punishments that comprise the rabbinic justice system. It follows the three *Bavot* (*Bava Qamma*, *Bava Metsi'a*, and *Bava Batra*), which deal with the substance of civil law, and is succeeded by *Makkot*, which originally formed one tractate with *Sanhedrin* and which deals further with procedural and penal law. The tractate begins in chapter 1 with an overview of the judiciary and its three types of courts; chapter 2 digresses to laws relating to the high priest and king; and chapter 3 outlines civil procedure. Chapter 4 contrasts civil procedure with criminal procedure and acts as a fulcrum for the tractate, since from that point onward the subject turns from civil law to criminal. Chapters 4 through 7 map a narrative of criminal execution, and chapters 7 through 11 list capital crimes and define the scope of liability for each one.

Narrative is a key element of the tractate, which takes its audience from the first moment in a trial to the last. The matching narratives for civil and criminal cases only underscore the striking differences between them, especially regarding the relative difficulty of producing a criminal conviction and the dramatic nature of execution.

Main Ideas

Tractate *Sanhedrin* offers a virtual primer in rabbinic legal topics, cataloguing a wide variety of cases that could come up in a rabbinic court. Legal areas covered by chapter 1 include monetary disputes and larceny, personal injury, sexual violation and defamation, the fixing of the calendar, public sacrificial offering, dissolution of marriage, redemption of tithes and of consecrated items, oaths and vows, crimes committed by animals, declaration of war, expansion of the boundaries of Jerusalem and the Temple, the establishment of courts, and trials involving the high priest, an entire Israelite tribe, and an idolatrous town. Legal areas covered by chapters 7 through 11 include incest and other forbidden sexual relations, blasphemy, idolatrous worship and inducement of others to it, desecration of the Sabbath, cursing and striking one's parents, sorcery, homicide, Temple violations, kidnapping, rebellion against one's parents, and rebellion against the high court. Courts are categorized according to the number of judges—three, twenty-three, or seventy-one.

The high priest and the king emerge as major figures of public authority alongside the judges who are this tractate's central concern. The most sustained legal discussion in the tractate, however, is its procedural and penal law. The tractate elaborates four execution methods—stoning, burning, decapitation, and strangulation—and, while it lists almost thirty capital crimes, it gives greatest attention to blasphemy, incitement to idolatry, homicide, the rebellious son, the subverted town, and the rebellious elder. The tractate also prescribes procedures and penalties for cases that fall outside the formal four-execution-method framework; these have served as a significant resource in later Jewish law for extralegal or so-called emergency judicial action.

Perhaps surprising for a tractate whose project is the architecture of law, it features some of the most famous *aggadah* in the entire rabbinic corpus: a meditation on the extraordinary value of a single human life (4:5) and a theologically rich treatise on the fate of human beings after death (chapter 10).

The binary terms that structure the tractate are *dine mamonot* and *dine nefashot*, often translated as civil and criminal law. The terms describe not the character of the case itself, however, but the consequence or punishment that follows from it—for *dine mamonot* (literally "cases of money [or property]"), exaction of the defendant's money, for *dine nefashot* (literally "cases of lives"), exaction of the defendant's life. The tractate uses two terms interchangeably for courts, one native Hebrew—*bet din*—and one transliterated from the Greek word for assembly or council—*Sanhedrin*, which the tractate subdivides into the "Small Sanhedrin," the twenty-three-judge court, and the "Great Sanhedrin," the seventy-one-judge court (alternatively called the "Great Bet Din"). The tractate's language of crime and criminality (the Mishnah possesses no precise equivalents to those English words) is normally the generic liable/exempt or guilty/innocent used in conjunction with specific capital crimes, but at times the tractate takes on a more morally charged tone, describing the listed capital crimes as sins and those who commit them as wicked.

Relationship to Scripture

The tractate is heavily imbued with biblical law on the one hand and highly innovative with respect to it on the other. There are few explicit biblical sources for the basic structure of the judiciary, major elements of trial and execution procedure, judicial trials for animals, extralegal measures, the rabbinic prison (*kippah*), and two of the four execution methods (decapitation and strangulation). The tractate radically recasts the other two execution methods, stoning and burning: instead of a collective throwing of stones, the Mishnah requires the witness to push the convicted criminal from a height and, instead of burning at the stake, the Mishnah requires a lit wick to be thrown into the convicted criminal's bowels. The tractate's treatment of the subverted town and rebellious son also relies on creative exegesis: it reads the relevant passages in Deuteronomy (13:13–19; 21:18–21) so as to drastically restrict the scope of liability. The tractate's exegesis of Deuteronomy's laws of the king is likewise innovative, breaching Deuteronomy's limits and thereby expanding the king's prerogatives. That being said, the tractate's list of capital crimes closely follows Torah law and, when the tractate creates new capital crimes (e.g. stealing the libation cup in 9:6), it marks them out clearly as innovations. The frequency of explicit verse citation varies, from no citations in chapter 5 to over twenty in chapter 10, with the average chapter featuring four to six citations.

Historicity of the Sanhedrin

The historicity of the judicial system described in tractate *Sanhedrin* has been much debated. This very tractate presents certain procedures in the past tense. That criminal courts would have belonged to the Mishnah's past and not to its present accords with the broader historical portrait of Roman Palaestina. Early rabbinic traditions do describe a central rabbinic court in the post-destruction period in the town of Yavneh, but the identification of that court with the high court described in this tractate is a later, postmishnaic effort to emphasize the continuity of rabbinic institutions with those of the Second Temple.

An outstanding question regards the historicity of the tractate's three-judge civil courts, which the tractate does not generally formulate as a past-tense phenomenon. Early rabbinic literature almost always features litigants approaching a single rabbinic judge, not a three-judge tribunal. Legal documents discovered in the Judaean desert suggest multiple languages and legal traditions coexisting, all under the aegis of Roman authority; so if the three-judge tribunals described by the tractate did exist, they would have constituted one among a variety of available legal options.

Special Notes for the Reader

The paragraph division and enumeration in manuscripts **K** and **P** frequently vary from that of the standard printed edition. To avoid confusion we have retained the standard numeration without comment.

Tractate Sanhedrin

Chapter One

1:1–3 *Cases That Require Three Judges*

1 Cases of monetary compensation are with three [judges].
Thefts and injuries are with three.
Damage and half-damage, double payments and four-fold and five-fold payments, are with three.
One who rapes, one who seduces, and one who defames are with three—
the words of R. Meir.
And the Sages say:
One who defames—
with twenty-three, since it has in it death-penalty cases.

1:1 *Cases of monetary compensation*: This and its partner term, "cases of the death penalty," introduced in 1:4 below, are often translated as "civil law" and "criminal law," but those categories come from later Roman law. The Mishnah's categories are based instead on the type of penalty that arises from the case.

are with three: "Judges" is implied. Other rabbinic texts call for five, two, or sometimes just one judge to decide monetary cases.

Damage: This refers to cases where the compensation sought corresponds exactly to the reduction in value caused by the damage. "Damage" likely refers to objects, while the previous term "injuries" likely refers to people.

half-damage, double payments and four-fold and five-fold payments: Half-damage: Exodus 21:35. Double payment: Exodus 22:3. Four- and five-fold payments: Exodus 21:37. The laws governing these payments are detailed in *Bava Qamma*, chapters 1–7.

One who rapes, one who seduces, and one who defames: In all these cases a man is required to pay a penalty to the father of a woman whom he has sexually wronged. Rape: Deuteronomy 22:28–29. Seduction: Exodus 22:16–17. Defamation: Deuteronomy 22:13–19. The relevant rabbinic laws are laid out in *Ketubbot* chapters 3–4.

since it has in it death-penalty cases: Depending on whether the husband's accusation that his wife was not a virgin when they wed proves true or false. If it proves false, he pays a monetary penalty, but if it proves true, the woman is stoned to death (see Deuteronomy 22:20–21). Mishnah 1:4 below requires that death-penalty cases—this case could possibly result in a death penalty—be judged by twenty-three judges. The Mishnah has now begun to introduce cases that do not necessarily entail any monetary compensation and for which there is some dispute regarding whether three judges are sufficient.

2 Lashes are with three.
In the name of R. Ishmael they said:
With twenty-three.[1]
Intercalation of the month is with three.
Intercalation of the year is with three—
the words of R. Meir.
Rabban Simeon b. Gamaliel says:
With three they begin, and with five they deliberate, and they close[2] with seven.
But if they closed with three, it is intercalated.

3 Laying hands by the elders and breaking the neck of the heifer are with three—
the words of R. Simeon.
And R. Judah says:
With five.
Halitsah and refusal are with three.

[1] K, P lack "In the name of…twenty-three."   [2] Lit. "finish, conclude."

1:2 *Lashes*: See Deuteronomy 25:1–3 and *Makkot* chapter 3.

In the name of R. Ishmael they said: With twenty-three: Cases with a penalty of lashes do not fall clearly into the category of monetary compensation, which would require three judges, or into the category of the death penalty, which would require twenty-three judges. The Bavli explains that in R. Ishmael's view lashes are a substitute for the death penalty; according to the Yerushalmi's explanation of R. Ishmael, the person flogged may die from his punishment, which would turn it retroactively into a death-penalty case.

Intercalation of the month: Since a lunar cycle lasts approximately twenty-nine and a half days, some months of the rabbinic calendar are twenty-nine days long and some thirty. The Mishnah refers here to a procedure required at the end of every month, based on testimony regarding the new moon, to decide whether the thirtieth day should be added. See *Rosh Hashanah* chapters 1–3.

Intercalation of the year: An extra month is in some years added to the rabbinic calendar in order to coordinate the lunar cycles with the solar year, which is approximately eleven days longer than twelve lunar months. The Mishnah refers here to the annual convening of a court to determine whether the extra month should be added.

With three they begin… and they close with seven: According to a parallel text (which attributes Rabban Simeon b. Gamaliel's position to "the Sages"), the two judges are added in each phase of the procedure when a majority wishes to add the extra month.

But if they closed with three, it is intercalated: The intercalation is post-facto valid.

1:3 *Laying hands by the elders*: Leviticus 4:15 requires elders to lay their hands upon the head of a bull before it is offered by the community in atonement for a mistaken violation of God's commandments. The related rabbinic laws can be found in *Horayot* chapter 1 The Mishnah identifies the elders with its three-judge tribunal.

breaking the neck of the heifer: Deuteronomy 21:1–9. The related rabbinic laws can be found in *Sotah* chapter 9.

And R. Judah says: With five: According to parallel texts, R. Judah's five-judge requirement applies to both laying of hands by the elders and breaking the neck of the heifer.

Halitsah: Deuteronomy 25:5–6 requires that when a man dies childless his brother should marry the deceased's wife. Deuteronomy 25:7–10 provides a procedure, known as *halitsah*, to release the brother if he does not wish to marry her. The rabbinic laws of *halitsah* are found in *Yevamot* chapter 12.

refusal: This refers to a fatherless female minor whose mother or brother has married her to a man to whom she does not wish to stay married. According to *Yevamot* 13:1, she may declare her opposition before the court and be released from the marriage without a formal divorce.

Fourth-year fruit and second tithe whose worth is not known are with three.
Consecrated items are with three.
Evaluations of movable property[3] are with three.
R. Judah says:
One of them [must be] a priest.
And immovable property is with nine and a priest.
And a person is similar to them.

[3] K: "evaluations and movable property."

Fourth-year fruit: The Rabbis interpret Leviticus 19:23–24 to mean that all fourth-year tree fruit must be taken to Jerusalem and eaten there. *Ma'aser Sheni* 5:4 allows the tree's owner to appear before a tribunal of three to assess the worth of the fruit so that he may take money in place of the fruit and then buy provisions once he arrives in Jerusalem. The Mishnah borrows this substitution procedure from the procedure for tithes in Deuteronomy 14:22–26, the next item in this list. The Mishnah has now turned to cases of monetary assessments related to Temple offerings.

second tithe whose worth is not known: The "second tithe," set aside after the *terumah* offering for the priest and the first tithe for the Levites, is brought to Jerusalem and eaten by its owners in the first, second, fourth, and fifth years of the cycle. If the owner wishes to redeem his produce and take money instead, as Deuteronomy 14:22–26 permits, this mishnah and also *Ma'aser Sheni* 4:2 require a three-person tribunal to assess the worth of the produce or the worth of the coins if either is unclear. It is ambiguous here whether the distinction regarding clear and unclear value applies also to the fourth-year fruits mentioned immediately before.

Consecrated items: Leviticus 27 describes the procedures by which individual Israelites may consecrate money, animals, houses, or fields as gifts to the sanctuary. Redemption of certain consecrated items is permitted on the condition that the owner adds one-fifth of the value of the item. The related rabbinic laws are in tractate *Arakhin*.

Evaluations: Leviticus 27:1–8 provides a scale of monetary values for human beings according to their age and gender. A person may vow to make a donation to the sanctuary in the amount of the value of a person based on that scale. Because Leviticus gives monetary amounts only for human beings, the expression in the Mishnah "evaluations of movable property...and of immovable property" is curious and evoked a number of interpretations in the Talmudim. The Mishnah seems to assume a situation in which the patron (who may be a man, woman, or child) gives either movable or immovable property equivalent to the monetary value of the person whose worth they have decided to donate. The anonymous position and R. Judah disagree regarding the composition of the three-person court required to assess the value of the movable property. The version in **K** either is mistaken or suggests a different reading according to which "consecrations" may function as a heading for evaluations, movable property, and immovable property, each of which represent types of donation to the sanctuary.

with nine and a priest: The extent to which the Mishnah marginalizes the priest in these cases is striking, given that he is the exclusive arbiter in Leviticus 27.

And a person is similar: According to *Arakhin* 5:2, a person might vow to donate the value of a person according to the standardized values provided in Leviticus 27 or according to the market value of the person, which is determined by that person's hypothetical price in the slave market (see *Bava Qamma* 8:1). According to the Talmud, the cryptic final line of this mishnah extends the requirement of ten judges, one of whom must be a priest, to the determination of a person's market value when that value is being donated to the sanctuary. The last two lines here are repeated verbatim in *Megillah* 4:3, where the subject is liturgical acts that require a quorum of ten.

1:4 Cases That Require Twenty-Three Judges

4 Death-penalty cases[4] are with twenty-three.
The animal who has active sexual intercourse [with a human being]
and the animal who has passive sexual intercourse
are with twenty-three,
as it is said: *And you shall kill the woman and the animal,*
and it says: *And you shall kill the animal.*
The ox who is stoned is with twenty-three,
as it is said: *The ox shall be stoned and its owner, too, shall be executed*—
as is the execution of the owners,
so too is the execution of the ox.
The wolf,[5] the lion, the bear, the leopard, the panther, and the snake—
their execution is with twenty-three.
R. Eliezer says:
Anyone who proceeds to kill them has done well.

[4] Lit. "cases of lives."   [5] K, P lack "The wolf."

1:4 *Death-penalty cases*: Chapters 7–11 below list capital crimes and methods of execution.

The animal who has active sexual intercourse…and the animal who has passive sexual intercourse: This mishnah requires a capital trial for the animal that plays either an active or a passive role in sexual intercourse with a human being. The Mishnah does not specify that the active animal is necessarily male or that the passive animal is necessarily female; both participles are grammatically masculine.

And you shall kill the woman and the animal…And you shall kill the animal: Leviticus 20:16, 15. Leviticus 20:16 calls for capital punishment for both the animal and the woman who have sexual relations with each other, and Leviticus 20:15 does so for an animal and a man. The Mishnah does not explain exactly how these verses operate as prooftexts for judicial trials for animals.

The ox who is stoned: According to Exodus 21:28–32, an ox who has gored a human being to death should be stoned.

The ox shall be stoned and its owner, too, shall be executed: Exodus 21:29. This verse refers to a case when an ox with a history of goring—generating an obligation for the owner to guard the ox—gores a person to death. In such a case, the owner's negligence makes him liable for the death penalty. The subsequent verse permits the owner to ransom his life with money. According to early rabbinic law, the owner is not executed and should instead pay the ransom money.

as is the execution of the owners, so too is the execution of the ox: The Mishnah reads the verse against its grain, as both Talmudim seem to recognize. Rather than requiring the execution of the ox's owner, the verse according to the Mishnah's reading requires that the ox be executed using the judicial procedures that are typically used for "owners," meaning human beings.

The wolf, the lion, the bear, the leopard, the panther, and the snake: Bava Qamma 1:4 features the same list of animals, where they are characterized as predictably aggressive towards human beings (see also *Bava Metsi'a* 7:9). The translation "panther" is not certain.

Anyone who proceeds to kill them has done well: This praise is for a person who does not wait for a judicial trial but goes ahead and kills one of these "dangerous" animals who presumably has killed a human being. R. Eliezer could possibly refer to killing a "dangerous" animal who has not harmed anyone but is thought to pose a public risk, but then the contrasting position requiring a trial would have to refer to a different case where the animal has already killed.

R. Aqiva says:
Their execution is with twenty-three.

1:5 Cases That Require Seventy-One Judges

5 One does not judge either the tribe or the false prophet or the high priest except according to a court[6] of seventy-one.
One does not lead forth in an optional war except according to a court of seventy-one.
One does not add to the city or to the Temple precincts except according to a court of seventy-one.
One does not make Sanhedrins for the tribes except according to a court of seventy-one.
One does not make a subverted town except according to a court of seventy-one.
And one does not make a subverted town in a border district or three,[7]
but one does make one or two.

[6] K, P: "in a court."
[7] K, P: "There is no subverted town in a border district and there are not three subverted towns, but one does…"

R. Aqiva says: Their execution is with twenty-three: R. Aqiva repeats the anonymous mishnah's original position, but now it seems to function as a retort to R. Eliezer's claim that it is meritorious to skip a capital trial for a homicidal animal.

1:5 *the tribe*: Both Talmudim offer a number of interpretations of the type of legal case the Mishnah has in mind here, but the Mishnah probably means any legal case in which the tribe happens to be the subject. This case and the ones that follow all seem to have a national or collective dimension that lies behind their special status requiring a court of seventy-one.

the high priest: The Mishnah seems to refer to any legal case in which the high priest is the subject, though the Talmud reads the Mishnah to be excluding monetary cases, for which the high priest should be judged by a court of three like anyone else. The next chapter will explain which standard legal procedures apply to the high priest and which do not.

One does not lead forth: The implied object is the nation's soldiers.

an optional war: Sotah 8:7 speaks of three kinds of war: "a war of obligation (or necessity)," "a war of commandment," and "a war of permission" or optional war. According to one opinion in the Yerushalmi, a war of permission is when "we attack them" and a war of obligation is when "they attack us." This line is repeated below (2:4) in the context of rules related to the king, implying that the king initiates an optional war but must have it approved by the seventy-one-judge court in something resembling a separation of powers.

One does not add to the city or to the Temple precincts: See *Shevu'ot* 2:2, which describes an elaborate procedure for adding to "the city" (presumably Jerusalem) or to the Temple precincts. This procedure involves not only the court of seventy-one but also the king, the prophet, and the sacred stones in the high priest's breastplate.

One does not make Sanhedrins for the tribes: Deuteronomy 16:18 calls for the appointment of magistrates for the tribes. This is the first time that the tractate uses the word *Sanhedrin*. The newly introduced language and the new negative formulations ("One does not judge…except according to…") heighten the sense of importance as the Mishnah moves from three-judge to twenty-three-judge to seventy-one-judge tribunals.

a subverted town: A town whose occupants are persuaded to worship other gods; see Deuteronomy 13:13–19, and see below, 10:4–6, for the procedures.

in a border district or three, but one does make one or two: The syntax here is awkward, but the Mishnah appears to be restricting both the location and the number of towns that the court can declare subverted.

1:6 Scriptural Sources for Twenty-Three-Judge and Seventy-One-Judge Courts

6 The Great Sanhedrin consisted of seventy-one,
and the small one of twenty-three.
And from where [in Scripture do we learn] that the great one consists of seventy-one?
As it is said: *Gather for me seventy of Israel's elders*,
and Moses is over them—
Thus there are seventy-one.
R. Judah says:
Seventy.
And from where [in Scripture do we learn] that the small one consists of twenty-three?
As it is said: *The assembly shall judge ... the assembly shall protect*,
an assembly that judges and an assembly that protects—
thus here[8] are twenty.
And from where [in Scripture do we learn] that an assembly consists of ten?
As it is said: *How much longer shall that wicked assembly*—
Joshua and Caleb were left out of the count.
And from where [in Scripture do we learn] to add three more?
By implication,
as it is said: *Do not side with the many to do wrong*,

[8] K, P lack "here."

According to a parallel text, the underlying concern is the stability of Jewish settlement in the Land of Israel. If strategically or demographically significant towns are destroyed (which is the punishment leveled upon the subverted town), "the nations may break through and destroy the land of Israel."

1:6 *The Great Sanhedrin consisted of seventy-one*: The term *Sanhedrin* is applied only to the twenty-three-judge and seventy-one-judge tribunals and not to the smaller ones laid out earlier in the tractate. Here and elsewhere in the tractate the Mishnah uses the past tense for the judicial procedures it describes.

Gather for me seventy of Israel's elders: Numbers 11:16.

R. Judah says: Seventy: R. Judah claims that Moses was counted as one among, not in addition to, the seventy elders, thus leaving the high court's count at seventy.

The assembly shall judge ... the assembly shall protect: Numbers 35:24–25.

an assembly that judges and an assembly that protects—thus here are twenty: The Mishnah here presumes, against the grain of the verses, that there are two assemblies, not one. According to a parallel, the "assembly that judges" argues for conviction, while the "assembly that protects" argues for acquittal. The court must therefore consist of at least ten judges who could argue for conviction and at least ten other judges who could argue for acquittal.

How much longer shall that wicked assembly: Numbers 14:27, using the same word found in Numbers 35:24, 25.

Joshua and Caleb were left out of the count: Moses sent twelve scouts into the land, and all except Joshua and Caleb spread discouraging reports on their return (see 10:3 below). Reading Numbers 14:27 as a reference to the ten wicked scouts, the Mishnah infers that when Numbers 35:24, 25 uses the same term to describe judicial procedure, it must also be referring to a body of ten men.

Do not side with the many to do wrong: Exodus 23:2. This part of the verse is taken to mean that a bare majority is enough for acquittal but not for conviction.

I infer that I should be[9] with them for good.
If so, why is it said, *Side with the many*?
Your siding for good should not be like your siding for evil:
your siding for good is according to one;[10]
your siding for evil is according to two;
and the court[11] is not balanced,
they add to them one more,
Thus here[12] are twenty-three.
And how many should be in a town so that it may be fit for a Sanhedrin?
One hundred and twenty.
R. Nehemiah says:
Two hundred and thirty, corresponding to *chiefs of tens*.

Chapter Two

2:1 Laws Relating to the High Priest

2 A high priest judges and one judges him.
He testifies and one testifies regarding him.

[9] K, P: "I infer that he said that one should be…"
[10] K, P: "according to one witness," which seems to be an error; two witnesses are normally required and the subject of this mishnah is the number of judges. The scribe appears to have had in mind the language of Deuteronomy 17:6.
[11] K: "and if the court is not balanced."   [12] K, P lack "here."

If so, why is it said, Side with the many: Rabbinic exegesis generally attributes to the Bible a principle of conservation of language. Since, according to this mishnah, *do not side with the many to do wrong* teaches that a court should follow a bare majority only for an acquittal, the final phrase of the verse, "side with the many to do good," which might appear to be teaching precisely that rule, must teach something else.

Thus here are twenty-three: The route by which the Mishnah reaches twenty-three is circuitous. Exodus 23:2 is understood to teach that an acquittal can be reached by a majority of one or more judges, while a conviction must be reached only by a majority of two or more (see also 4:1 below). Since the Mishnah earlier claims that a court must include a group of ten judges who argue for acquittal and a group of ten judges who argue for conviction, in order for such a court to issue a conviction, it would require two more judges to take the side of conviction. That brings the count to twenty-two. In its final step, the Mishnah claims that a court cannot have an even number of judges lest it split down the middle (see also *Sotah* 9:1), so one more judge is added to bring the count to twenty-three.

One hundred and twenty: According to the Talmud's explanation, the number 120 covers a host of communal functions that a particular town must supply before the town can be considered eligible for a Sanhedrin.

chiefs of tens: See Exodus 18:21. R. Nehemiah's 230 inhabitants is the twenty-three person court times ten—one judge for ten inhabitants.

2:1 *A high priest*: This chapter's starting point is the interface of nonjudicial figures of authority—the high priest and the king—with the judicial system, but the chapter goes on to give a broad discussion of the parameters of authority of these other figures.

He performs *halitsah* and one performs *halitsah* for his wife.
And one contracts levirate marriage for his wife,
but he does not contract levirate marriage,
because he is forbidden regarding a widow.
If he has a death [in his family],
he does not follow the bier.
But rather they are concealed, and he is exposed;
They are exposed and he is concealed;[13]
and he follows them until the threshold[14] of the town—
the words of R. Meir.
R. Judah says:
He does not leave the sanctuary,
as it is said: *He shall not go outside the sanctuary.*
And when he comforts others,
it is the custom for the entire people to pass by one after the other,
and the appointed one places him between himself and the people.
And when he is comforted by others,
the entire people say to him,
"We are your atonement."
And he says to them,
"You shall be blessed[15] from the heavens."
And when they offer refreshment to him,
the entire people recline on the ground while he reclines on a bench.

[13] K repeats "they are concealed and he is exposed; they are concealed and he is exposed."
[14] Lit. "opening, doorway."   [15] Or "may you be blessed."

He performs halitsah: See note on 1:3 above.

And one contracts levirate marriage: See note on 1:3 above.

he is forbidden regarding a widow: See Leviticus 21:14.

he does not follow the bier: See Leviticus 21:11, and contrast Leviticus 21:1–4 with respect to rank-and-file priests.

they are concealed and he is exposed: This cat-and-mouse game between the high priest and the funerary procession is a strategy for permitting the high priest some limited participation in the funerary rituals.

He shall not go outside the sanctuary: Leviticus 21:12. R. Judah counters that the high priest is not permitted even limited participation in funerary rites. It is unclear whether the verse prohibits the high priest from leaving the sanctuary at all times or only for the purpose of participating in a funeral.

And when he comforts others: This mishnah proceeds chronologically through the phases of a funeral: procession of the coffin, followed by the comforting of mourners, followed by the feeding of mourners (see *Mo'ed Qatan* 3:5–9).

the appointed one: Also called the deputy high priest.

"We are your atonement": Commentators explain that the people comfort the high priest by telling him that they are prepared to accept in his stead the suffering due to him.

refreshment: The special meal of consolation offered to new mourners on their return from the burial.

2:2–5   Laws Relating to the King

2 The king does not judge nor does one judge him.
He does not testify nor does one testify regarding him.
He does not perform *halitsah* nor does one perform *halitsah* for his wife.
He does not contract levirate marriage nor does one contract levirate marriage for his wife.
R. Judah says:
If he wished to perform *halitsah* or to contract levirate marriage,
he is remembered for good.
They said to him:
One does not listen to him.[16]
And one does not marry his widow.
R. Judah says:
The king may marry the king's widow,
for thus do we find with David,
who married the widow of Saul,
as it is said: *I gave you your master's house and possession of your master's wives.*

3 If he has a death [in his family], he does not leave the threshold of his palace.
R. Judah says:
If he wants to follow the bier he may follow,
for thus do we find with David,
who followed the bier of Abner,
as it is said: *And King David walked behind the bier.*
They said to him:
The matter was only to appease the people.[17]

---

[16] K, P: "If he wished to, one does not listen to him."   [17] K, P: "The matter was only to appease."

2:2 *The king does not judge*: The parallels between this mishnah and the previous one serve to contrast the high priest, who participates normally in court procedures, with the king, who does not, thereby shielding king from court as well as court from king.

he is remembered for good: R. Judah considers it praiseworthy for the king to observe the laws of *halitsah* and levirate marriage even though he is not obliged to, while the Sages do not permit the king to observe these laws even if he wishes to. In a parallel text the Sages explain that the honor of the king would be diminished were he to observe these laws.

And one does not marry his widow: The Torah dictates that the high priest cannot marry a widow; this mishnah flips the law for the king, dictating that no one else can marry his widow. According to a parallel text, 2 Samuel 20:3 is the biblical basis for this prohibition.

I gave you your master's house and possession of your master's wives: In 2 Samuel 12:8, God describes giving the wives of King Saul to his successor King David.

2:3 *he does not leave the threshold of his palace*: Notice the parallel between the high priest, who according to one opinion in the previous mishnah may not leave the sanctuary, and the king, who may not leave his palace.

And King David walked behind the bier: 2 Samuel 3:31.

The matter was only to appease the people: David's public expression of grief for Abner, whom Joab and Abishai had treacherously killed, seems designed to dispel any suspicion that David had ordered Abner's death. The Sages challenge R. Judah's claim that the case of David can be generalized to other kings.

And when they offer refreshment to him,
the entire people recline on the ground while he reclines on a couch.

4 And he leads forth in an optional war according to a court of seventy-one.
And he tears down in order to make for himself a road,
and one may not interfere.
The road of the king has no limit.
And when the entire people takes spoils,
they put it before him and he takes the first portion.
And he shall not have many wives, but only eighteen.
R. Judah says:
He may have many so long as they do not turn away his heart.
R. Simeon says:
Even if there is one and she turns away his heart,
in this case he should not marry her.
If so, why is it said: *And he shall not have many wives*?
Even like Abigail.
He shall not keep many horses, but only sufficient for his chariots.[18]
Nor shall he amass silver and gold to excess, but only sufficient to give wages to an army.
And he writes for himself a book of the Torah for his own sake.
When he goes to war, he takes it with him.[19]
When he comes back, he takes it back with him.

[18] P repeats "He shall not keep many wives" by mistake but adds "horses" afterwards.
[19] K, P also have "and it is with him" in the two preceding sentences.

a couch: An obscure term, the subject of talmudic debate.

2:4 *And he leads forth in an optional war*: See note on 1:5 above.

And he tears down in order to make for himself a road: The king exercises eminent domain.

The road of the king has no limit: Bava Batra 6:7, whose subject is public pathways that run through private property, repeats this line.

And he shall not have many wives: Deuteronomy 17:17.

but only eighteen: The Talmudim base the number eighteen on exegesis of the David narrative in 2 Samuel.

so long as they do not turn away his heart: Deuteronomy 17:17 reads: *And he shall not have many wives lest he turn his heart away*. The Sages are debating to what extent and in what way Deuteronomy's rationale (preventing the king's distraction) limits the rule. In R. Judah's opinion, the king need not limit the number of his wives if there is no risk that they will distract him.

If so, why is it said, And he shall not have many wives? This is a challenge to R. Simeon: if the Torah potentially prohibits even a single wife, why does it speak of "many wives"?

Even like Abigail: King David married Abigail after her evil husband Nabal behaved belligerently towards David and later died (1 Samuel 25). She is described as "intelligent and beautiful" (1 Samuel 25:3). R. Simeon applies the limitation even to worthy mates like Abigail.

He shall not keep many horses: Deuteronomy 17:16. It is ambiguous in Deuteronomy whether the restriction on horses applies to the king's personal use or military use or both. The Mishnah seems to apply the restriction to excessive personal use and to permit the king to build a supply of horses for military use.

Nor shall he amass silver and gold: Deuteronomy 17:17.

When he sits in judgment, it is with him.
When he reclines it is next to him,
as it is said: *Let it remain with him and let him read in it all his life.*

5 One does not ride his horse.
And one does not sit on his throne.
And one does not use his scepter.
And one does not see him when his hair is being cut,
nor when he is naked,[20] nor when he is in the bathhouse,
as it is said: *You shall be free to set a king over yourself—*
that the awe of him should be upon you.

Chapter Three

3:1–5 *Procedures for Monetary Cases: Constitution of the Court*

3 Cases of monetary compensation are with three [judges].
One man[21] chooses one [judge] for himself and the other one chooses one for himself,
and the two of them choose for themselves one more—
the words of R. Meir.
And the Sages say:

[20] **K**: "One does not see him naked except when his hair is being cut, and not in the bathhouse." **K**'s scribe appears to have mistakenly written the Hebrew word for "except" rather than "nor" (the two differ by only a single letter), but **K** likely intended the same prohibitions as are found in the printed edition. **P** has the same order as **K** but with the correct Hebrew word "nor." **P** has its own mistake, however, omitting the necessary conjunction "and," which is inserted in a superscript.

[21] Lit. "this one…and this one…," here and throughout this mishnah.

When he sits in judgment: Since 2:2 explicitly prohibits the king from judging, this may refer to a judicial realm unique to the king. It may, on the other hand, represent a contradictory tradition that permits the king to act as a judge within the rabbinic judiciary.

Let it remain with him: Deuteronomy 17:19. According to the Talmud the king makes the Torah into an amulet and affixes it to his arm so that he can carry it around with him always.

2:5 *You shall be free to set a king over yourself*: Deuteronomy 17:15.

that the awe of him should be upon you: On the assumption that every word in the Bible carries distinctive instruction, the Mishnah may be basing its exegesis of Deuteronomy 17:15 on a presumed redundancy in the prepositional phrase "over yourself" or in the doubled verb *som tasim* ("you shall be free to set").

3:1 *Cases of monetary compensation are with three*: This repeats the first line of the tractate, which lists cases that require three-judge courts. Here begins a chronological narrative of civil procedure.

One man chooses one [judge] for himself: Each litigant chooses a judge, and then the two litigants together choose a third judge. This procedure describes rabbinic civil courts as ad hoc rather than as standing institutions.

The two judges choose for them[22] one more.
One man may disqualify the judge of the other one,
and the other one may disqualify the judge of the first—
the words of R. Meir.
And the Sages say:
When?
At the time that he brings against them evidence that they are related or disqualified,
but if they were qualified or expert,[23] he may not disqualify them.
One man may disqualify the witnesses of the other one,
and the other one may disqualify the witnesses of the first—
the words of R. Meir.
And the Sages say:
When?
At the time that he brings against them evidence that they are related or disqualified,
but if they were qualified, he may not disqualify them.

2 If he said to him: "I accept [my] father as reliable,"[24] "I accept your father as reliable," "I accept three cattle-herders as reliable":
R. Meir says:
He may retract it.
And the Sages say:
He may not retract it.
If he owed his fellow an oath,
and he says to him: "Make a vow to me by the life of your head":
R. Meir says:
He may retract it.
And the Sages say:
He may not retract it.

[22] Or "for themselves."   [23] **K, P**: "expert authorized by the court."
[24] Lit. "father is reliable for me," and so throughout.

that they are related or disqualified: The chapter later lists people who are disqualified from serving as judges or witnesses because they are either of unreliable character (3:3) or related by blood or close social relationship to the litigants (3:4–5).

expert: A parallel uses the expression "expert for the many," that is, a recognized expert. On the expert judge, see also *Bekhorot* 4:4–5.

One man may disqualify the witnesses of the other one: Both Talmudim express surprise over the high degree of autonomy that this rule gives to each litigant regarding the choice of judges and witnesses.

3:2 *he said to him: "I accept [my] father as reliable"*: The list of disqualified relatives in 3:4 begins with the father. This mishnah presents a case where one litigant decides to waive the usual disqualifications for judges and witnesses.

He may retract it: The Talmud debates whether this holds true even after the court has delivered a verdict.

If he owed his fellow an oath, and he says to him, "Make a vow to me by the life of your head": Oaths are used often by the Mishnah to determine the outcome of civil cases (see *Shevu'ot* chapters 5–8). A parallel suggests that the basis for retraction here is that the litigant offered his own oath rather than reciting the one prescribed by the judge.

3 And these are the ones who are disqualified:
one who plays with dice, one who loans on interest, those who [bet on] flying pigeons,[25] and dealers of Seventh-Year produce.[26]
R. Simeon said:
At first they would call them gatherers of Seventh-Year produce, but when violent people multiplied, they changed to calling them dealers of Seventh-Year produce.
R. Judah said:[27]
When?
At the time that they have no other trade besides it,
but when they have a trade that is not this they are qualified.

4 And these are the relatives:
His father,[28] his brother, the brother of his father, the brother of his mother, the husband of his sister, the husband of the sister of his father, the husband of the sister of his mother, the husband of his mother, his father-in-law, and his brother-in-law—
they, their sons, and their sons-in-law, and his stepson alone.
R. Yose said:
This is the mishnah of R. Aqiva.
But the first mishnah [was]:
His uncle, the son of his uncle, and anyone who is fit to inherit from him.

[25] Lit. "one who causes pigeons to fly." [26] P adds "and slaves."
[27] "R. Judah said" is added in the margin in P, but the body of the text lacks it.
[28] K, P lack "His father."

3:3 *And these are the ones who are disqualified*: The activities that disqualify a person are all shady business dealings.

one who loans on interest: Exodus 22:24, Leviticus 25:35–37, and Deuteronomy 23:20–21 prohibit lending money on interest. *Bava Mets'ia* chapter 5 elaborates on this prohibition.

those who [bet on] flying pigeons: A parallel defines this as incitement of pigeons against each other for the purpose of betting on them and expands the disqualification to gambling that involves other animal species.

dealers of Seventh-Year produce: Selling Seventh-Year produce is prohibited. See Leviticus 25:4–7 and *Shevi'it* chapters 7–8.

At first they would call them gatherers: According to the Talmud's explanation of R. Simeon, in an earlier period not only dealers but even mere gatherers of Seventh-Year produce were disqualified from judging and testifying. The *violent people* referred to here are tax collectors, and the Sages began to permit the gathering of Seventh-Year produce in order to pay taxes. Selling Seventh-Year produce, on the other hand, was still prohibited.

At the time that they have no other trade: This would seem to refer to all of the activities listed above.

but when they have a trade that is not this: Even if a person engages in these shady businesses, if he also has a legitimate profession his character is considered reliable.

3:4 *And these are the relatives*: Rabbinic exegesis bases the disqualification of litigants' relatives on Deuteronomy 24:16.

they, their sons, and their sons-in-law, and his stepson alone: The disqualification extends also to the sons and sons-in-law of the listed relatives, except for the stepson, whose sons and sons-in-law would be qualified to testify or to judge.

His uncle, the son of his uncle: The "first Mishnah" echoes the language of Leviticus 25:49, which specifies the uncle and uncle's son as first in the chain after brothers responsible for redeeming an Israelite from slavery. The Leviticus passage links kinship with the paternal side only, and this mishnah appears to be following suit.

anyone who is fit to inherit from him: *Bava Batra* 8:1 lists relatives who inherit. Basing disqualification on inheritance law eliminates many of the maternal relatives found on the list, since inheritance goes through

And anyone who is a relative of his at that time.
If he was a relative but then ceased to be, then he is qualified.
R. Judah says:
Even if his daughter dies,
so long as he has sons from her,
then he is a relative.

5 The one who loves and the one who hates:[29]
the one who loves: this is his groomsman.
The one who hates: anyone who has not spoken with him for three days out of enmity.
They said to him:
Israel are not suspected regarding that.

3:6–8 *Procedures for Monetary Cases*

6 How does one examine the witnesses?
They would bring them in and intimidate them.
And they would send every person[30] outside
and leave the greater of them
and say to him:
"Say: How do you know that this one owes that one?"
If he said: "He said to me that I[31] owe him," "Person so-and-so said to me that he owes him,"
he has said nothing,
unless he says:
"Before us he confessed to him that he owes him two hundred *zuz*."

---

[29] K, P: "The one who loves and the one who hates: who is he?"
[30] K: "them."   [31] P (apparently mistakenly): "the second."

---

the male line. Some commentators see this clause as no longer part of the "first Mishnah" but rather as a resumption of the teaching of R. Aqiva.

And anyone who is a relative of his at that time: Presumably at the time that the relative witnessed the statement or came to testify to it.

If he was a relative but then ceased to be: Lit. "became distant" (the Hebrew word for relative means "near to"). When a spouse dies, the in-law relationship is considered to be dissolved for the purposes of testifying or judging.

so long as he has sons from her, then he is a relative: The widowed son-in-law remains disqualified.

3:5 *Israel are not suspected regarding that*: Jews are not suspected of testifying or judging falsely out of friendship or enmity.

3:6 *They would bring them in*: Presumably this means that the judges bring the witnesses into the court.

and intimidate them: According to the Talmud, the intimidation consists of the judges quoting a biblical verse that would serve to discourage the witnesses from false testimony.

And they would send every person outside: Some versions of the Mishnah have "they would send *them* outside," presumably referring to the witnesses. Based on this version, commentators propose that the litigants remain in court and that the witnesses are brought in separately in order to ensure that they do not coordinate their testimony.

"Person so-and-so said to me that he owes him": This is considered hearsay and is inadmissible.

"Before us he confessed to him that he owes him two hundred zuz": Rabbis in the Talmud explain that the borrower must have made clear that he knew that the two bystanders were serving as witnesses and that his admission of debt would have legal weight.

And after that[32] they bring in the second and examine him.
If their words are found consistent, they discuss the matter.
If two say he is innocent, and one says he is guilty, he is innocent.
If two say he is guilty, and one says he is innocent, he is guilty.
If one says innocent, and one says guilty,
and even if two hold innocent or two hold guilty, and one says: "I do not know,"
they should add judges.[33]

7 When they decided the matter, they would bring them in.
The greatest of the judges says, "Person So-and-so, you are innocent"; "Person So-and-so, you are guilty."
And from where [in Scripture do we learn] that when one of the judges[34] leaves,
he should not say,
"I acquit and my colleagues convict, but what could I do, since my colleagues outnumbered me?"
On this it is said:
Do not go about as a talebearer among your countrymen,[35]
and it says: *A talebearer gives away secrets.*

8 Any time that he brings evidence,
he[36] may appeal[37] the case.
If they said to him,

[32] K, P lack "After that."
[33] K: "Two [judges] say innocent, and one says guilty, he is innocent. Two say guilty, and one says innocent, even if two acquit or convict, and one says I don't know…" P: "Two [judges] say innocent, and one says guilty, he is innocent. Two say guilty, and one says innocent, he is guilty. One says innocent, and one says guilty, and one says I don't know—they should add judges. And even if two acquit or two convict, and one says I don't know—they should add judges."
[34] K, P: "when he leaves."   [35] K, P cite only the second verse.
[36] Or "it," that is, the court.   [37] Lit. "undo."

two say he is innocent, and one says he is guilty: As in English, the Mishnah frequently uses different language for outcomes in civil and criminal cases. In *Sanhedrin*, however, the language stays constant, likely in order to sharpen the many parallels between civil and criminal procedure that structure the tractate. In order to preserve the tractate's linguistic consistency, this translation uses "innocent" and "guilty" even in the context of civil procedure where English would normally use "exempt" and "liable."

and even if two hold innocent or two hold guilty: Technically two judges have a majority and could determine the outcome, but the third judge's indecision invalidates the other two judges' majority agreement.

they should add judges: See 5:5 below for the addition of judges two by two in a capital case when there is an undecided judge.

3:7 *they would bring them in*: This would appear to refer to bringing the litigants back into the court, but the Talmud proposes that this line refers to the witnesses and that the litigants would have already been present.

but what could I do, since my colleagues outnumbered me: The judge is trying to curry favor with the liable party by dissociating himself from the verdict.

Do not go about as a talebearer among your countrymen: Leviticus 19:16. The Hebrew is ambiguous and therefore ripe for exegesis. Manuscripts of the Mishnah omit this verse and feature only the one from Proverbs.

A talebearer gives away secrets: Proverbs 11:13. Both this verse and the one from Leviticus use the same ambiguous noun, which is understood here to refer to a judge who exposes the vote of the court.

3:8 *Any time that he brings evidence*: The liable party may appeal the case if he finds new evidence after the verdict has been delivered.

"Any evidence that you have,
bring from now until thirty days":
If he found [it]³⁸ within thirty days,
he may appeal;
After thirty days,
he may not appeal.
Rabban Simeon b. Gamaliel said:
What should this one do that he did not find [it] within thirty,
and he found it after thirty!
If they said to him, "Bring witnesses,"
and he said, "I have no witnesses";
if they said, "Bring evidence,"
and he said, "I have no evidence,"
and after time he brought evidence,
or he found witnesses,
in such a case this is nothing.³⁹
Rabban Simeon b. Gamaliel said:
What should this one do
that he did not know that he had witnesses,
and he found witnesses!
He did not know that he had evidence,
and he found evidence!
If they said to him, "Bring witnesses,"
and he said, "I have no witnesses";
if they said, "Bring evidence,"
and he said, "I have no evidence";
if he saw that he was going to be found guilty in the case,⁴⁰
and he said, "Draw near so-and-so and so-and-so and testify on my behalf,"
or he brought out evidence from within his bag,
in such a case this is nothing.

³⁸ K, P: "he brought."
³⁹ K mistakenly omits the section enclosed in brackets: "If they said to him, 'Bring witnesses' [and he said, 'I have no witnesses,' if they said, 'Bring evidence'] and he said, 'I have no evidence…'" The scribe fills in the missing text in the margins. Both K and P reverse the nouns in the final step: "and after time he found witnesses, or he found evidence."
⁴⁰ K, P lack "in the case."

and he found it after thirty! In Rabban Simeon b. Gamaliel's opinion, the evidence should be admitted even if the liable party has exceeded the court's time limit. Bad luck should not deprive the litigant of a fair decision.

they said to him: During the trial.

and after time he brought evidence: If after the verdict is announced the liable party brings new evidence, after claiming during the trial that he had none, that evidence is treated with suspicion and not considered a legitimate basis for an appeal.

He did not know that he had evidence, and he found evidence! As before, Rabban Simeon b. Gamaliel's opinion is that the evidence should be admitted and the verdict appealed.

or he brought out evidence from within his belt: Apparently Rabban Simeon b. Gamaliel would agree that in this case the last-minute evidence is suspicious and therefore inadmissible.

Chapter Four

4:1–2 *Monetary Cases Compared to Death-Penalty Cases*

4 The law is one and the same in cases of monetary compensation and death-penalty cases,
in that both are conducted with inquiry and investigation,
as it is said: *You shall have one standard.*
What [differences are there] between cases of monetary compensation and death-penalty cases?
Cases of monetary compensation are with three [judges],
but death-penalty cases are with twenty-three.
Cases of monetary compensation:
one opens either for innocence or for guilt,
but death-penalty cases:
one opens for innocence,
but one does not open for guilt.
Cases of monetary compensation:
one inclines according to one [vote] either for innocence or for guilt,
but death-penalty cases:
one inclines according to one for innocence,
but according to two for guilt.
Cases of monetary compensation:
one reverses either for innocence or for guilt.

4:1 *inquiry and investigation*: See next chapter.

You shall have one standard: Leviticus 24:22. In the context in Leviticus, this verse requires that laws be the same for the foreigner and the native. According to the Mishnah's exegesis, the verse requires that monetary cases and death-penalty cases use the same procedures of witness examination.

What [differences are there] between cases of monetary compensation and death-penalty cases? After establishing one similarity between monetary and death-penalty cases, the chapter goes on to list their many differences. The Mishnah does not explicitly articulate the principle underlying the differences, but it is not hard to infer: monetary cases are evenly weighted towards liability and exemption, while death-penalty cases are weighted towards acquittal.

Cases of monetary compensation are with three: Repeated from 1:1 and 3:1. Most of the enumerated features are, like this one, presented elsewhere in the tractate.

one opens either for innocence or for guilt: *Open* refers to the opening words of the judges' deliberations among themselves; the Talmud alternatively proposes that it refers to the judges' first words to the witnesses or to the judges' first words to the accused.

one inclines according to one [vote] either for innocence or for guilt: Voting procedure in civil cases is outlined in 3:6 above: two out of the three judges must agree on the verdict (unless the third judge declares himself undecided, in which case more judges are required). The case is thus decided by a majority of one.

but according to two for guilt: A guilty verdict in a death-penalty case must have at least two more judges voting for it than judges voting for acquittal. See 1:6 above.

one reverses either for innocence or for guilt: They overturn a verdict discovered to be mistaken.

Death-penalty cases:
one reverses for innocence,
but one does not reverse for guilt.
Cases of monetary compensation:
anyone argues innocence or guilt.
Death-penalty cases:
anyone argues innocence,
but not everyone argues guilt.
Cases of monetary compensation:
one who argues guilt argues innocence,
and one who argues innocence argues guilt.
Death-penalty cases:
one who argues guilt argues innocence,
but one who argues innocence cannot reverse to argue guilt.
Cases of monetary compensation:
one judges during the day and one concludes at night.
Death-penalty cases:
one judges during the day and one concludes during the day.
Cases of monetary compensation:
one concludes on the same day,
either for innocence or for guilt.
Death-penalty cases:
one concludes on the same day for innocence,
but on the next day for guilt.
In accordance with that,
one judges neither on the eve of the Sabbath
nor on the eve of a festival.
  2 Cases of impurities and purities:[41]
one begins from the greatest [judge].
Death-penalty cases:

[41] K, P: "Cases of monetary compensation, purities, and impurities."

anyone argues innocence or guilt: This refers to the judges' deliberations, during which each judge argues his opinion. According to the Talmud, the Mishnah is not allowing literally anyone to argue in court but intends to permit the witnesses or judges-in-training to participate in the deliberations (their participation is addressed in 5:4 below).

one who argues guilt argues innocence, and one who argues innocence argues guilt: The judges can change their mind in either direction during their deliberations in a monetary case.

one who argues guilt argues innocence, but one who argues innocence cannot reverse to argue guilt: According to an opinion in the Talmud, this restriction in a capital case applies only to the period of deliberations but not to the period of the vote.

one judges neither on the eve of the Sabbath nor on the eve of a festival: Implied here is that the criminal court does not sit on Sabbaths and festivals (see *Betsah* 5:2). If the judges were to deliberate on Friday and agree on a criminal conviction, they would need to wait until Sunday to issue the verdict.

4:2 *Cases of impurities and purities*: It is unclear why the focus shifts from cases of monetary compensation to cases determining purity status, which are now juxtaposed with death-penalty cases. Some versions of the Mishnah have both: "Cases of monetary compensation and purities and impurities…"

one begins from the greatest [judge]: The most prestigious judge begins the deliberations.

one begins from the side.
Anyone is qualified to judge cases of monetary compensation,
while not everyone is qualified to judge death-penalty cases—
only priests, Levites, and Israelites who may marry their daughters into the priesthood.

4:3–4 *Constitution of the Criminal Court*

3 The Sanhedrin was like half of a round threshing floor,
so that they would be able to see each other.
And two scribes for the judges stand before them:
one from the right and one from the left.
And they write the words of those for acquittal
and the words of those for conviction.
R. Judah says:
There were three: one writes the words of those for acquittal,
one writes the words of those for conviction,
and the third writes the words of those for acquittal and the words of those for conviction.
  4 And three rows of disciples sit before them.
Each one knows his place.
When they would need to ordain, one ordained from the first [row].

one begins from the side: The least prestigious judge would apparently have sat on the side of the court chamber. A parallel explains that the least prestigious judge opens the arguments "so that his heart will not rely on the words of his master."

Anyone is qualified to judge cases of monetary compensation: An opinion in the Talmud understands this specifically to include the *mamzer* (see *Yevamot* 5:12), and commentators add that this intends to include the proselyte. This teaching is repeated in *Niddah* 6:4.

Israelites who may marry their daughters into the priesthood: See *Qiddushin* 4:4–5. A parallel disqualifies also the eunuch and the childless man—and in an additional opinion, the particularly cruel person or the particularly merciful one—from judging death-penalty cases.

4:3 *The Sanhedrin was like half of a round threshing floor*: The Sanhedrin referred to here is clearly the twenty-three judge court for capital cases, and the purpose of the threshing floor analogy is to help visualize the semicircular configuration in which the judges sit. The Mishnah now begins a narrative of procedure for a capital case. The ad hoc selection of judges in a civil case, described in 3:1, contrasts strikingly with the sitting Sanhedrin described here, where the only selection that transpires is of a single disciple selected for promotion to the rows of judges, perhaps in the event of a judge's death.

And two scribes for the judges: According to 5:5 below, the task of the scribe is to correct the judges if they make a mistake.

And they write the words of those for acquittal and the words of those for conviction: According to this position (in contrast to the subsequent position attributed to R. Judah), each scribe transcribes all the arguments he hears, both for acquittal and for conviction.

4:4 *Each one knows his place*: The hierarchy of the judges and disciples is reflected in the seating arrangement. A parallel adds an extra outer row where the police, the accused, and the witnesses stand.

When they would need to ordain: This refers to ordaining a new judge, perhaps because one of the presiding judges dies. The phrase "laying hands by the elders" (1:3 above) uses the same root.

one ordained from the first [row]: The judges are selected from the disciples who sit before them and have been preparing for promotion.

One from the second comes to the first,
and one from the third comes to the second,
and they choose one more from the assembly
and seat him in the third.
And he would not sit in the place of the first,
but he sits in the place that is appropriate for him.

4:5 *Procedures for Death-Penalty Cases: Intimidation of the Witnesses*

5 How does one intimidate the witnesses in capital cases?[42]
They would bring them in and intimidate them:
"Perhaps you will speak from conjecture, or from rumor, or a witness from another witness, or we heard from a trustworthy person."
Or "Perhaps you do not know that our plan is to examine you with inquiry and investigation.
You should know that death-penalty cases are not like cases of monetary compensation:[43]
cases of monetary compensation: a person gives money and atones for himself.
Death-penalty cases: his blood and the blood of his offspring hang over him until the end of the world.[44]
For thus we find with Cain who killed his brother,[45]
as it is said: *Your brother's bloods cry out to me.*
It does not say 'your brother's blood' but 'your brother's bloods'—
his blood and the blood of his offspring.

[42] Some versions have the redundant "How do they intimidate the witnesses for the witnesses of death-penalty [cases]?"
[43] The scribe of **K** writes the word "cases of," crosses it out, and then formulates a shorter version than the standard one that reads less well: "that cases of monetary compensation are not like death-penalty cases: A person gives money…"
[44] **K**: "until the end of the whole world." **P**: "until the end of all the generations."
[45] **K** lacks "who killed his brother." **P**: "who killed Abel."

One from the second comes to the first: The hierarchy of judges and disciples is carefully preserved when a promotion takes place, with each person advancing in the rows by only one seat.

4:5 *How does one intimidate the witnesses*: This is the first step in a criminal trial. The narrative follows the same steps as for civil trial procedure, but gives each step more sustained attention.

"a person gives money and atones for himself": The person who gives money referred to here is the witness who testifies falsely in a monetary case and must later, if found out, rectify the consequences of his testimony by compensating the wronged party.

"his blood and the blood of his offspring": A false witness in a capital case is eternally responsible for the wrongful death of the convicted victim of his perjury and for the offspring he might have produced if he had lived.

Your brother's bloods cry out to me: Genesis 4:10.

"his blood and the blood of his offspring": Genesis 4:10. According to the Mishnah's reading, the plural form suggests that a person who kills another is considered responsible for taking not only that person's life but also the lives of his potential offspring.

Another interpretation:
Your brother's bloods: that his blood was cast over the trees and over the stones.
In accordance with that,
the human being was created singly to teach you[46]
that if anyone destroys one soul from Israel,[47]
Scripture[48] accounts it to him as if he destroyed a full world.
And if anyone preserves one soul from Israel,[49]
Scripture[50] accounts it to him as if he preserved a full world.
And for the sake of peace among people,
so that a person will not say to another,
'My father is greater than your father.'
And so that the heretics[51] will not say,
'There are multiple powers in the heavens.'
And in order to tell of the greatness of the Holy One Blessed Be He:[52]
For a person mints several[53] coins with one mold,
and they all resemble each other,
while the King of Kings of Kings, the Holy One Blessed Be He,
mints each person in the mold of the first person,
yet there is not one who resembles another.
In accordance with that,
each and every person is obligated to say,
'For me was the world created.'
And perhaps you will say, 'What is this distress to us?'

[46] **K, P**: "In accordance with that, the human being was created singly in the world, to teach that…"
[47] **K, P** lack "from Israel."   [48] **K, P**: "They account it to him as if…"
[49] **K, P** lack "from Israel."   [50] **K, P**: "They account it to him as if…"
[51] "Heretics" is erased in **K** but can still be made out.
[52] **K**: "The King of Kings of Kings, the Holy One Blessed Be He"; **P**: "The King of Kings of Kings, Blessed Be He."
[53] **K, P**: "one hundred coins."

"Another interpretation": It is unclear which parts of this material belong in the script that the judges recite to intimidate the witnesses. Most commentators understand this line to be not part of the script.

"that his blood was cast over the trees and over the stones": According to this reading, the plural "bloods" in Genesis 4:10 reflects the splattering of Abel's blood.

"to teach you that anyone who destroys one soul from Israel": The absence of "from Israel" in the manuscripts produces a more universal statement regarding the value of every human life.

"Scripture accounts it to him": "Scripture" presumably refers to the story of human creation in Genesis 1 and 2.

"as if he destroyed a full world": Since according to the biblical account a "full world" descended from a single man, every man is considered to have the potential to produce a full world.

'There are multiple powers in the heavens': If there had been numerous first human beings, heretics would have been able to argue that numerous gods created them.

'For me was the world created': Commentators say that reflection on this principle would discourage a person from sin, in this case the sin of false testimony.

'What is this distress to us?' In impressing upon the witnesses the gravity of taking a life, the judges may discourage them from testifying at all, even if their testimony is valid.

But is it not already said,
Although able to testify as one who has either seen or learned of the matter, he does not give information, etc.
But perhaps you will say,
'What is it to us to become liable[54] for the blood of this person?'
But is it not already said,
And in the destruction of the wicked, there is joy."

Chapter Five

5:1–6:6 *Procedures for Death-Penalty Cases*

5 They would examine them with seven investigations:
(1) In which seven-year cycle?
(2) In which year?
(3) In which month?
(4) On which date of the month?[55]
(5) On which day [of the week]?
(6) At what hour?
(7) In what place?
R. Yose says:[56]

---

[54] K: "to convict."   [55] Lit. "How much in the month?"
[56] In **K**, R. Yose's opinion begins with "even." In **P**, R. Yose does not appear, and the scribe adds R. Yose's material to the previous opinion: "…On which date of the month? On which day? At what hour? In what place? Do you recognize him? Did you warn him? The idolater: What did you worship and with what did you worship?"

Although able to testify: Leviticus 5:1. The Mishnah's citation is as if to say: the Torah obligates a person to give testimony whether he wishes to or not, and it is as much a sin not to give true testimony as it is to give false testimony.

'What is it to us to become liable for the blood of this person?' A witness may be aware of the Torah's obligation to give testimony yet may still feel reluctant to come forward.

And in the destruction of the wicked, there is joy: Proverbs 11:10.

5:1 *They would examine them*: The Mishnah resumes its narrative of criminal procedure, with the examination of the witnesses following their intimidation.

In which seven-year cycle? The rabbinic calendar, following biblical law (see Leviticus 25:8), measures the calendar in seven seven-year cycles, each of which culminates in a Sabbatical year and all of which culminate in a Jubilee year.

In which year? In which year of the seven-year cycle?

R. Yose says: On which day? According to the Talmud R. Yose's abbreviated set of questions refers to when the witnesses declare "He killed him yesterday," since in that case it would be unnecessary to ask about the year and month.

On which day? At what hour? In what place? Do you recognize him? Did you warn him? The idolater:[57] Whom[58] did he worship and with what did he worship?

2 Anyone who increases examinations is praiseworthy.
[There was] an incident when Ben Zakkai examined the stems of figs.
And what [differences are there] between investigations and examinations?
Investigations: if one says, "I do not know,"[59] their testimony is nullified.
Examinations: if one says, "I do not know," and even[60] two say, "We do not know," their testimony stands.
Both investigations and examinations: when they contradict each other, their testimony is nullified.

3 If one says, "On the second of the month,"
and one says, "On the third of the month,"
their testimony stands,
since this one knows about the intercalation of the month
and the other does not know about the intercalation of the month.

[57] Lit. "the one who worships foreign worship," and so throughout the tractate.
[58] K, P: "What…"
[59] K: "One says, 'I do not know,' or two say they do not know—their testimony is nullified."
[60] K lacks "even."

Do you recognize him? This question would seem to be asking whether the witnesses recognize the defendant, but many commentators, following both Talmudim, take it to be asking whether the witnesses recognize the victim of a homicide.

Did you warn him? Makkot 1:9 requires that the witnesses to a capital offense warn the offender before he commits it; otherwise the offender cannot be executed for that offense.

The idolater: That is, in the trial of an accused idolater. The parameters within which a person is punishable for idolatry are defined at 7:6 below.

5:2 *Anyone who increases examinations is praiseworthy*: As Maimonides explains and as the story about Ben Zakkai implies, "examinations" are questions posed by the judge that do not relate directly to the crime but serve only to establish the consistency of the witnesses' accounts, unlike "investigations," which relate directly to the crime.

[There was] an incident when Ben Zakkai examined the stems of figs: The "stems of figs" represent a detail only loosely related to the incident itself. Ben Zakkai is better known as R. Yohanan b. Zakkai. As many scholars have observed this line seems to refer to a version of the story of Susanna in the Apocrypha.

Investigations: if one says, "I do not know," their testimony is nullified: Since "investigations" address basic information about the incident, both witnesses must be able to provide an answer.

Examinations: if one says, "I do not know," and even two say, "We do not know," their testimony stands: Since "examinations" address ancillary information, it is not essential that one or both witnesses be able to provide an answer.

when they contradict each other, their testimony is nullified: The witnesses' inability to answer an examination question does not disqualify the testimony, but contradictory answers do. Both failure to answer and contradictory answers to "investigations" disqualify the testimony.

5:3 *since this one knows about the intercalation of the month and the other does not know about the intercalation of the month*: When the court intercalates the month, it counts the thirtieth day as part of the month that is ending; otherwise, the thirtieth day becomes the first day of the next month (see note on 1:2 above). A person who did not know of the intercalation would be off by one day. Thus two witnesses could legitimately attribute the same incident to two different days.

If one says, "On the third,"
and one says, "On the fifth,"
their testimony is nullified.
If one says, "At two hours,"
and one says, "At three hours,"
their testimony stands.
If one says, "At three,"
and one says, "At five,"
their testimony is nullified.
R. Judah says:
It stands.
If one says, "At five,"
and one says, "At seven,"[61]
their testimony is nullified,
since at five the sun is in the east
and at seven the sun is in the west.

4 And after that they bring in the second,
and they examine him.
If their words are found consistent,
they open with innocence.
If one of the witnesses said:
"I have [evidence] to argue innocence[62] for him,"
or one of the disciples:
"I have [evidence] to argue conviction for him,"
they silence him.

[61] K: "week [or seven-year cycle],") a mistake.
[62] K: "If one of the witnesses said, 'I have [evidence] to argue guilt for him,' they silence him. If one of the disciples said, 'I have [evidence] to argue innocence for him,' they elevate him…"

If one says, "On the third," and one says, "On the fifth," their testimony is nullified: Ignorance regarding the intercalation cannot account for a discrepancy of two days between the witnesses' testimonies.

If one says, "At two hours," and one says, "At three hours," their testimony stands: "Two hours" and "three hours" refer to two and three hours after daylight breaks. The witnesses may have estimated differently regarding which hour of the day it was when the incident occurred.

If one says, "At three," and one says, "At five," their testimony is null and void: A discrepancy of two hours between the testimonies is considered too great to reflect simply a different estimation of the hour.

R. Judah says: It stands: Even a discrepancy of two hours might reflect simply a different estimation of the hour rather than a substantive contradiction between testimonies.

since at five the sun is in the east and at seven the sun is in the west: A person can easily distinguish between five hours and seven hours by the position of the sun.

5:4 *If their words are found consistent*: If the testimonies are found to be inconsistent, the case is discarded. Identical language is used in 3:6 above at the same juncture in civil procedure, sharpening the parallels—and highlighting the contrasts—between civil procedure and criminal procedure.

they open with innocence: According to 3:6 above, judges in a monetary case who reach this juncture proceed to "discuss the matter," while here in a capital case the judges proceed to "open with innocence." This contrast between civil and criminal procedure was articulated in 4:1 above.

If one of the witnesses said, "I have [evidence] to argue innocence for him,"… they silence him: The witnesses cannot participate at all in the arguments. **K** implies that the witness may argue if he argues for innocence.

If one of the disciples said:
"I have [evidence] to argue innocence for him,"
they elevate him and they seat him among them,
and he does not descend from there the entire day.
If there is substance in his words,
they hear him.
And even if he says:
"I have [evidence] to argue innocence for myself,"[63]
they hear him,
so long as there is substance in his words.

5 If they found innocence for him,
they exonerated him.
But if not,
they extend the case to the next day.
They would break up into partners,
and limit food,
and they would not drink wine all day.
And they deliberate[64] the entire night.
And the next day they wake up early and they come to the court.
The one who acquits says,
"I acquit, and I acquit in my place."
And the one who convicts says,
"I convict, and I convict in my place."
One who argues guilt [may] argue innocence,
but one who argues innocence cannot reverse to argue guilt.
If they made a mistake in the matter,
two scribes of the judges remind them.

[63] K: "...for himself."   [64] K: "they deliberate over the matter the entire night."

they elevate him and they seat him among them, and he does not descend from there the entire day: The language of ascent and descent suggests that the court occupies an elevated place, either physically or metaphorically or both. According to a parallel, the disciple who makes an argument for innocence descends at the end of the day only if his arguments prove not to have substance, but otherwise he is granted permanent membership on the court.

"I have [evidence] to argue innocence for myself," they hear him, so long as there is substance in his words: A parallel adds that if the defendant wishes to argue for his own conviction, he is vigorously silenced.

5:5 *But if not, they extend the case to the next day*: See 4:1 above, which also describes the delaying of a guilty verdict until the day after the initial vote.

And they deliberate the entire night: In a parallel, the judges should spend the night discussing the relevant biblical passage—if the offense is homicide, they should discuss the biblical passage dealing with homicide, etc.

"I acquit, and I acquit in my place": The judge declares that he has not changed his mind from the day before.

One who argues guilt [may] argue innocence, but one who argues innocence cannot reverse to argue guilt: This rule repeats from 4:1 above.

If they made a mistake in the matter, two scribes of the judges remind them: The scribes are first mentioned in the geography of the court as described in 4:3 above. Their role here is to remind the judges of the positions they took the previous day.

If they found innocence for him,
they exonerated him.
But if not, they stand for the count.
If twelve acquit and eleven convict,
he is innocent.
If twelve convict and eleven acquit,
and even if eleven acquit and eleven convict
and one says, "I do not know,"
and even if twenty-two acquit or convict and one says, "I do not know,"
they should add judges.[65]
Until how many do they add?
Two by two, until seventy-one.
If thirty-six acquit and thirty-five convict,
he is innocent.
If thirty-six convict and thirty-five acquit,
they judge these against those
until one of those for conviction approves[66] the words of those for acquittal.

Chapter Six

6 Once the verdict has been determined,[67]
they take him out to stone him.

[65] K, P more briefly: "If twelve convict and eleven acquit, and even if twenty-two acquit or convict and one says, 'I do not know,' they should add judges."
[66] Lit. "sees." [67] Lit. "once the trial has been completed."

If they found innocence for him, they exonerated him: The repetition of this line both at the beginning of this mishnah and here in the middle seems to emphasize the repeated opportunities for acquittal.

If twelve acquit and eleven convict, he is innocent: An acquittal requires a majority of only one. The principle of determining the verdict according to the votes is set forth above in 1:6 and 4:1. Here the most ambiguous voting patterns are addressed.

If twelve convict and eleven acquit: A conviction requires a majority of two, but here the conviction has a majority of only one.

and even if twenty-two acquit or convict and one says, "I do not know": As in the account of civil procedure at 3:6 above, if one of the judges is undecided a verdict cannot be issued.

Two by two, until seventy-one: If the next two judges are divided in their opinion, they add another two judges and so on until they can reach the necessary majority. The cap of seventy-one is so that the "Small Sanhedrin" (as a criminal court is called in 1:6 above) does not surpass the "Great Sanhedrin" of seventy-one judges.

until one of those for conviction approves the words of those for acquittal: One of those who initially voted for conviction must ultimately reverse his opinion so that the court has the majority of one needed for acquittal.

6:1 *Once the verdict has been determined, they take him out to stone him*: This chapter gives the narrative of execution that is set into motion when a guilty verdict is delivered. Stoning is used as the paradigm, and the next chapter will go on to describe, in less detail, the three other methods of execution.

The stoning house was outside the court house,
as it is said: *Take out the blasphemer.*[68]
One [person] stands at the entrance to the court house and a handkerchief is in his hand,
and one person rides[69] a horse at a distance from him,
such that he can see him.
If someone says, "I have [evidence] to argue innocence for him,"
that one waves the handkerchief,
and the horse runs and stops him.
And even if he says, "I have [evidence] to argue innocence for myself,"
they bring him back,
even four or five times,
so long as there is substance in his words.
If they found innocence for him,
they exonerated him.
But if not, he goes out to be stoned.
And the herald goes out before him:
"Person so-and-so son of so-and-so goes out to be stoned
because he transgressed transgression such-and-such,

[68] K, more fully: "Take the blasphemer outside the camp."   [69] K, P lack "one person rides."

The stoning house was outside the court house: According to 6:4 below the "stoning house" was the height of two men; there is no further information about its appearance. The phrase echoes the "burning house" that appears numerous times in the Mishnah; this was the place where disqualified sacrifices were burnt since they could not be offered on the altar. "House" is used flexibly in rabbinic literature to describe various kinds of spaces. The Talmud gives two explanations for the distance between the stoning house and the court house: "so that the court should not appear to be murderers" and "so that he should have [a possibility of] rescue."

Take out the blasphemer: Leviticus 24:14. The verse directs the blasphemer to be taken outside the *camp*, not the court as the Mishnah would have it.

One [person] stands at the entrance to the court house: Now begins a dramatic rescue effort akin to modern last-minute stays of execution. The court solicits exonerating evidence, while a horseman waits at a distance ready to race to the execution to halt it if such evidence should be found.

If someone says, "I have [evidence] to argue innocence for him": The hypothetical argument for exoneration (it is not clear who makes it) repeats language from the prior deliberation phase (5:4). Whereas the parallel appeal phase in civil procedure is indefinite (3:8: "any time that he brings evidence, he may appeal the case"), the appeal phase in capital procedure is necessarily cut short by the convicted criminal's execution.

that one waves the handkerchief, and the horse runs and stops him: The horseman is close enough to the court to see the handkerchief and close enough to the execution site to halt the execution.

And even if he says: The possibility of the convicted man's arguing for his own exoneration is repeated from the previous chapter's deliberation phase (5:4).

even four or five times: Not literally; this is a common idiom in the Mishnah equivalent to "many times." Here it seems to highlight the convicted man's capacity to halt his own execution, albeit on the condition that his arguments have "substance."

If they found innocence for him, they exonerated him: This line is repeated verbatim from the previous chapter (5:5) and emphasizes the continuing opportunities for exoneration.

And the herald goes out before him: The herald both publicizes the execution and solicits last-minute exonerating evidence.

and so-and-so and so-and-so are his witnesses.
Anyone who knows [evidence] of innocence for him,
let him come and argue for him!"

2 When he was[70] ten cubits away from the stoning house, they say to him:
Confess, for thus it is the way of those who are executed to confess,
for all who confess possess a portion in the world to come.
For thus do we find with Achan,
to whom Joshua said: *"My son, pay honor to the Lord, the God of Israel, and make confession to him,"* etc.
And Achan answered Joshua, *"It is true, I have sinned against the Lord, the God of Israel. And this is,"* etc.
And from where [in Scripture do we learn] that his confession atoned for him?
As it is said: *And Joshua said, "What destruction you have brought upon us! The Lord will bring destruction upon you this day"*—
on this day you are destroyed,
but you are not destroyed for the world to come.[71]
And if he does not know to confess,
one says to him, "Say 'May my execution be atonement for all my sins.'"
R. Judah says:
If he knew that he was conspired against,
he says, "May my execution be atonement for all my sins except for this sin."
They said to him:
If so, every person will say this in order to clear themselves.

[70] K, P lack "when he was."   [71] K, P: "the future to come."

6:2 *When he was ten cubits away*: The Mishnah now narrates a gradual approach to the execution site.

Confess: The Mishnah does not here dictate the substance of a confession (as it will do for the person who "does not know to confess"), but the Mishnah's use of the biblical Achan as a model, who admits the details of the transgressions for which he will be executed, suggests that this is what is intended.

for thus it is the way: The Mishnah does not make clear where the quotation ends, or in other words how much of this material is meant to be recited to the convicted person.

My son, pay honor to the Lord: Joshua 7:19. The Mishnah continues to quote this chapter until verse 25.

on this day you are destroyed, but you are not destroyed for the world to come: This interpretive strategy—the biblical text is read to signal a character's fate in the world to come—appears with frequency in chapter 10 below. The irony here is that the biblical text is explicit that Achan will be forever remembered for his sin (Joshua 7:26).

And if he does not know to confess: Either that the convicted person does not see the good in confessing his crime, or is too unnerved to be able to, or does not know the standard format.

May my execution be atonement for all my sins: The Mishnah is ambiguous regarding whether the confession effects atonement ("And from where [in Scripture do we learn] that his *confession* atoned for him?") or the execution itself does so ("May my *execution* be atonement…").

If he knew that he was conspired against: Deuteronomy 19:16–21 describes a malicious witness who has fabricated testimony in order to produce a false conviction (and see *Makkot* chapter 1). Here the case concerns a person who knows he has been wrongly condemned to death on the basis of maliciously fabricated testimony.

If so, every person will say this in order to clear themselves: The Talmud explains that the Sages prohibit such a confession "so as not to cast aspersions on courts and on the witnesses."

3 When he was[72] four cubits away from the stoning house,
they remove his clothing from him.
The man: they cover him in front.
And the woman: in front and in back,
The words of R. Judah.
And the Sages say:
The man is stoned naked,
but the woman is not stoned naked.

4 The stoning house was the height of two men.
One of the witnesses pushes him on his hips.
If he flips over onto his chest, he flips him back over onto his hips.
If he thereby dies, he has fulfilled [his obligation].
But if not, the second takes the stone and puts it on his chest.[73]
If he thereby dies, he has fulfilled [his obligation].
But if not, his stoning is with all of Israel,
as it is said: *Let the hand of the witnesses be the first against him to put him to death, and the hand of the people thereafter.*
All who are stoned are hanged—

[72] **K, P** lack "when he was."
[73] **P**: "the first witness pushes, etc., the first witness then takes the stone, etc., the second witness then takes the stone, etc, and then stoning is with all of Israel." This is either an accidental scribal repetition or a different version of the procedure with an additional step in which the taking of the stone is done first by the first witness and then again, if the convicted man survives, by the second witness.

6:3 *And the woman: in front and in back*: A parallel text explains "because the woman is all *ervah* (indecency or impropriety)."

The man is stoned naked, but the woman is not stoned naked: The Sages' rejoinder to R. Judah is ambiguous as to whether their use of the word "naked" includes the genital coverings that R. Judah prescribes. The simplest way to read the dispute is that both sides agree that a man is stoned largely naked, though with his genitals covered, while they disagree regarding a woman. R. Judah argues that a woman is stoned largely naked, though with minor coverings, while the Sages argue that a woman should be fully clothed.

6:4 *One of the witnesses pushes him on his hips*: The Bible's stoning procedure—each person hurls a stone and the combined force of the group's stones causes death—contrasts strikingly with the Mishnah's interpretation of it, according to which the witness pushes the condemned man from a high platform and kills him by force of the fall.

If he flips over onto his chest, he flips him back over onto his hips: Explanations offered for the flip to face-up are to check whether he is dead, to drop the stone on his chest, or to preserve his dignity.

he has fulfilled [his obligation]: The next chapter of the Mishnah will refer to a "commandment of those who are stoned," making sense of the language of fulfillment here.

the second takes the stone and puts it on his chest: The Mishnah describes a tag-team procedure: the first witness pushes the condemned man from a height; if the fall does not kill him, the second witness drops a stone on top of the fallen man in order to crush him; if that does not succeed, all of Israel stones him in the conventional sense. A parallel has only the second step and implies that the two witnesses together drop a heavy stone.

Let the hand of the witnesses: Deuteronomy 17:7. The passage instructs Israel to stone to death a person who is determined upon legal investigation to have worshipped other gods.

All who are stoned are hanged: Deuteronomy 21:22–23 describes the practice of hanging (or impaling) executed criminals.

the words of R. Eliezer.
And the Sages say:
Only the blasphemer and the idolater are hanged.
A man: they hang him facing the people.
And a woman: facing the tree—
the words of R. Eliezer.
And the Sages say:
A man is hanged, but a woman is not hanged.
R. Eliezer said to them:
Did not[74] Simeon b. Shetah hang women in Ashqelon?
They said to him:
He hanged eighty women,
but one does not judge two on the same day.
How do they hang him?
They sink the beam into the ground,
and the wood extends from it,
and he encircles one hand on top of the other,
and he hangs him.
R. Yose says:
The beam is inclined against the wall,
and he hangs him the way that butchers do.[75]
And one loosens him immediately.[76]
And if he remains overnight one transgresses a negative commandment with respect to him, as it is said: *You must not let his corpse remain on the stake but must bury him the same day. For an impaled body is an affront to God*, etc.
As if to say, why is he hanged?
Because he "blessed"[77] the Name,
and the name of Heaven was found profaned.

[74] **K, P**: "There was an incident..." rather than "did not?"
[75] **K**: "The way that the butchers hang."   [76] **P**: "One hangs and loosens him immediately."
[77] Instead of the euphemistic "he blessed," **K, P** have "he cursed."

Only the blasphemer and the idolater are hanged: According to the Talmudim, the blasphemer and the idolater are singled out because each has "stretched his hand out against" (Yerushalmi) or "denied the essence" (Bavli).

A man is hanged, but a woman is not hanged: See 6:3 for an analogous debate between the Sages and R. Judah.

He hanged eighty women, but one does not judge two on the same day: In other words, Simeon b. Shetah's actions were irregular and cannot be used to establish legal precedent.

They sink the beam into the ground: Noting the resemblance between the Mishnah's hanging and Roman crucifixion, some have suggested that the Mishnah's post-mortem hanging represents a rejection of crucifixion as a means of execution.

You must not let his corpse remain: Deuteronomy 21:23.

Because he "blessed" the Name, and the name of Heaven is found profaned: "Bless" is a euphemism for "curse." The Mishnah may understand the noun "curse" (or "affront") in Deuteronomy 21:23 to refer both to the initial sin of the executed person—cursing God, or blasphemy—as well as to the effect that the hanging of the corpse has upon God. A parallel text builds on the biblical idea that man is created in the image of God to imagine a king with an identical twin who, when hanged for his crimes, gives the public the impression that the king himself has been hanged. This would explain how God could be cursed by the hanging corpse.

5 R. Meir said:
At the time a person suffers,
the divine presence,[78] what does the tongue say?
As it were,[79] I am lighter than my head, I am lighter than my arm.
If thus does the Place[80] sorrow over the blood of the wicked that is spilled,[81]
how much the more so over the blood of the righteous.
And not only this,
but anyone who causes his dead to remain overnight transgresses a negative commandment.
If he caused him to remain overnight for his honor,
to bring him a coffin and shrouds,
he does not transgress with respect to him.
And they did not bury him in the burial site of his fathers,
but rather two cemeteries were instituted for the court house,
one for those who were decapitated and for those who were strangled,
and one for those who were stoned and for those who were burned.[82]

6 Once the flesh is decomposed,
one collects the bones and buries them in their place.

[78] K, P lack "the divine presence."   [79] K, P lack "As it were."
[80] K, P: "if thus Scripture said, I sorrow over…"
[81] K, P lack "that is spilled" with respect to the blood of the wicked and place it at the end referring to the blood of the righteous.
[82] In K, P the order of the couplets is reversed.

6:5 *the divine presence, what does the tongue say?* The syntax of this sentence, which provides another midrash on Deuteronomy 21:23, is similarly awkward in the Hebrew.

As it were: This expression is used to mute the anthropomorphism of this midrash.

I am lighter than my head, I am lighter than my arm: "I am lighter" is an enigmatic wordplay on Deuteronomy 21:23 whose meaning was debated in the Talmud. One possibility offered is that God is complaining that his head and arm feel heavy when a person is hanged.

the Place: A standard rabbinic term for God.

And they did not bury him in the burial site of his fathers: "One does not bury a wicked person next to a righteous person" (Talmud).

decapitated…strangled…stoned…burned: The four execution methods are set out at the beginning of the next chapter. The Mishnah features a two-way dispute there between R. Simeon and an anonymous consensus about the relative severity of the methods, but the sides agree that stoning and burning are for more severe crimes than are decapitation and strangulation. With that in mind, the Talmud explains the Mishnah's burial groupings here by saying that one does not bury the severely wicked (stoned and burned criminals) next to the moderately wicked (those decapitated or strangled).

6:6 *Once the flesh is decomposed, one collects the bones*: Secondary burial of bones in an ossuary was a common Jewish practice in Roman Palaestina. According to a parallel text representatives of the court are directed to collect the bones.

and buries them in their place: The Talmud interprets "in their place" to refer to a final burial in the ancestral tomb and infers that the executed criminal is considered to have gained atonement for his sins once his flesh has decomposed. But a parallel text is explicit that the executed criminal is permanently buried in the separate graveyard set aside by the court, and the Mishnah likely also has the separate graveyard in mind when it speaks of "their place."

And the relatives come and greet the judges and the witnesses,[83]
as if to say, that we have in our hearts nothing against you,
that you judged a verdict of truth.
And they did not mourn with full rites but with initial rites,
since initial rites are private.

Chapter Seven

7:1–3 *The Four Methods of Execution*

7 Four execution methods were transmitted[84] to the court:
Stoning, burning, decapitation,[85] and strangulation.
R. Simeon says:
Burning, stoning, strangulation, and decapitation.
This is the commandment of those who are stoned.

---

[83] K, P: "the witnesses and the judges."
[84] Lit. "transmitted, delivered."   [85] Lit. "killing."

And the relatives come and greet the judges and the witnesses: The relatives of the executed man must show support for the court's decision to execute. The chronology seems to backtrack to the day of the execution, since the mourning rites described here are those that apply in the period between death and burial.

And they did not mourn with full rites but with initial rites, since initial rites are private: The "initial rites" entail exemption from positive commandments and abstention from certain physical pleasures. The Mishnah's motivating concern for prohibiting the relatives from the full rites of mourning may be that those rites would appear to dignify the criminal and potentially to challenge the court's actions. According to an explanation in the Talmud, the Mishnah prohibits full mourning because it is predicated on the dead person's atonement; since atonement is granted to the executed criminal only after the conventional period of mourning has already passed, the mourning is permanently canceled rather than delayed.

7:1 *Four execution methods were transmitted*: According to the Talmud these four methods are an oral tradition.

Stoning, burning, decapitation, and strangulation: The Yerushalmi provides a biblical prooftext for the first three execution methods: stoning—*and you shall stone them to death* (Deuteronomy 17:5); burning—*both he and they shall be put to the fire* (Leviticus 20:14); decapitation—*I will bring a sword against you to wreak vengeance for the covenant* (Leviticus 26:25). The Yerushalmi further says that strangulation has no explicit source in the Torah and should be applied in cases when the Torah does not specify an execution method.

R. Simeon says: Burning, stoning, strangulation, and decapitation: R. Simeon disagrees on the order of severity of the four methods. The logic of R. Simeon and of the anonymous position is expanded upon in 9:3 below.

This is the commandment of those who are stoned: This sentence looks backward to the previous chapter's description of stoning. The Mishnah will go on to describe the other three methods (in the order that they are presented by the anonymous Sages). The mention of all four penalties at this point causes an awkward interruption of the description of each penalty's procedure.

2 The commandment of those who are burned:
they would sink him into manure up to his knees,
And they put a rough handkerchief within a soft one,
and he surrounds his neck.
This one pulls in his direction, and that one pulls in his direction, until he opens his mouth,
and he lights the wick and throws it into his mouth,
and it descends into his belly and burns his bowels.
R. Judah says:
Even he, if he died by their hand,
they would not have upheld the commandment of burning with respect to him.
Rather, they should open his mouth with a pair of tongs against his will,[86]
and he lights the wick and throws it into his mouth,
and it descends into his belly and burns his bowels.[87]
R. Eleazar b. Zadok said:
There was an incident with one daughter of a priest who prostituted herself,
and they surrounded her with bundles of vines and burned her.
They said to him:
Because the court of that time was not expert.

[86] Lit. "not for his good."
[87] In **P**, R. Judah's entire opinion is absent in the main text and written instead into the margins.

7:2 *they would sink him into manure up to his knees*: The purpose of the manure may be both to hold the convicted man in place and to degrade him.

they put a rough handkerchief within a soft one: It seems odd that the Mishnah would be concerned with protecting the skin of a man about to be executed. This along with other features of Mishnaic execution has led some to speculate that the procedures are designed to preserve the human form, which, it is proposed, was taken by the Rabbis to be created literally in the image of God.

and he surrounds his neck: The verbs shift from plural to singular, but it is not clear who is meant to perform any of these actions.

This one pulls in his direction, and that one pulls in his direction: Based on the stoning procedure elaborated in the previous chapter, one would assume that the two people pulling on the handkerchief are the witnesses.

he lights the wick and throws it into his mouth, And it descends into his belly and burns his bowels: Unlike burning at the stake, the Mishnah's burning is inside the body. According to both Talmudim, the wick is made of lead or tin, and the burning is caused by hot metal.

Even he, if he died by their hand, they would not have upheld the commandment of burning: Strangulation and burning as the Mishnah lays them out are almost identical procedures. R. Judah's concern is that the man will die from strangulation before he dies from burning, his proper penalty. The "even he" that begins the sentence is syntactically awkward.

Rather, they should open his mouth with a pair of tongs against his will: The tongs prevent strangulation.

daughter of a priest: See 9:1 below and Leviticus 21:9.

And they surrounded her with bundles of vines and burned her: R. Eleazar b. Zadok challenges the Mishnah's method of internal burning with an incident in which the more familiar method of burning at the stake was employed.

Because the court of that time was not expert: The Talmud specifies that the court was Saducean. In a parallel, R. Eleazar b. Zadok claims to have witnessed the execution himself when he was a child, and his testimony is dismissed on the grounds that children's testimony is invalid.

3 The commandment of those who are decapitated:[88]
they would chop off his head with the sword,
the way that the kingdom does.
R. Judah says:
This is a disgrace.[89]
Rather they lay his head on the chopping block,
and he cuts it off with an axe.
They said to him:
There is no death more disgraceful than that.
The commandment of those who are strangled:
they would sink him into manure up to his knees,
and put a rough handkerchief within the soft one,
and he surrounds his neck.
This one pulls in his direction,
and that one pulls in his direction,
until his life departs.

7:4–11 *Violations with a Penalty of Stoning*

4 These are the ones who are stoned:
one who has sexual intercourse with his mother;[90]
one who has sexual intercourse with the wife of his father;
with his daughter-in-law;
with another male;
with an animal;

---

[88] Lit. "killed."   [89] A variant adds "to him."
[90] Lit. "the one who comes upon the mother," and so on for similar violations.

7:3 *the way that the kingdom does*: "Kingdom" in tannaitic texts frequently refers to Roman imperial authority.

This is a disgrace: To the body of the executed man. According to other sources R. Judah objects to the Sages' sword method because it is borrowed from Roman authorities.

7:4 *These are the ones who are stoned*: The capital violations that follow all appear in biblical verses, but the penalty of stoning is explicit for only a few. The talmudic commentary fills in the exegetical holes, frequently interpreting the biblical phrase *his/their bloodguilt is upon him/them* to indicate stoning. The Mishnah will proceed to give lists of violations also for the penalties of burning (9:1), decapitation (9:1), and strangulation (11:1). In each case, after the list is initially presented, the Mishnah goes on to provide details about the items on the list. Tractate *Makkot* will continue with lists for those who are exiled (2:1) and those who are flogged (3:1). These lists contain a great deal of overlap with the violations punished with *karet* listed in *Keritot* 1:1.

one who has sexual intercourse with his mother: Based on Leviticus 18:7. The first violations on the list deal with sexual intercourse and follow the order of prohibitions found in Leviticus 18.

one who has sexual intercourse with the wife of his father: His stepmother, based on Leviticus 18:8 and 20:11.

with his daughter-in-law: Based on Leviticus 18:15 and 20:12.

with another male: Based on Leviticus 18:22 and 20:13.

with an animal: Based on Leviticus 18:23 and 20:15.

the woman who causes an animal to have sexual intercourse with her;
the blasphemer;
the idolater;[91]
one who gives of his seed to Molekh;
one who possesses *ov* and *yid'oni*;
one who profanes the Sabbath;
one who curses his father or his mother;
one who has sexual intercourse with a betrothed girl;
the enticer;
the subverter;
the sorcerer;
and the stubborn and rebellious son.
One who has sexual intercourse with his mother:

[91] Lit. "the one who worships foreign worship," here and below.

the woman who causes an animal to have sexual intercourse with her: The Mishnah uses the causative verb because it presumes that a woman does not play the active role in sexual intercourse. The Bible likewise specifies both men and women when it prohibits sexual intercourse with an animal; see Leviticus 18:23 and 20:16.

the blasphemer: The list of violations now turns towards crimes against God. Leviticus 24:10–16 prescribes stoning as the punishment for blasphemy though the particular language used for the offense here derives from Numbers 15:30.

the idolater: Based on Deuteronomy 17:2–5, which prescribes stoning for an Israelite who worships other gods.

one who gives of his seed to Molekh: Based on Leviticus 18:21, Leviticus 20:2–5, and Deuteronomy 18:10.

one who possesses ov and yid'oni: Based on Leviticus 19:31; 20:6, 27; and Deuteronomy 18:10–11. These are forms of necromancy; see 7:7 below.

one who profanes the Sabbath: Based on the narrative of the woodgatherer on the Sabbath in Numbers 15:32–36.

one who curses his father or his mother: Based on Exodus 21:17 and Leviticus 20:9.

one who has sexual intercourse with a betrothed girl: Based on Deuteronomy 22:23–24, which holds betrothal to be equivalent to matrimony for the purposes of defining prohibited sexual status. The man and the betrothed girl are considered to have committed adultery.

the enticer: Based on Deuteronomy 13:7–12, which describes an Israelite secretly inducing his intimate family or friends into idolatry.

the subverter: Based on Deuteronomy 13:13–19, which describes an Israelite who turns an entire town towards idolatry. The penalty for the townspeople is discussed below, 10:4–6. The difference between this violation and the previous one (the "enticer") is debated in both Talmudim.

the sorcerer: Exodus 22:17 declares that a sorceress—the feminine noun is used—should not be "let live." Deuteronomy 18:10 lists the sorcerer—the male noun is used—among other practitioners of divination and magic who should not be "found among you."

the stubborn and rebellious son: Based on Deuteronomy 21:18–21. The stubborn and rebellious son will be discussed in the next chapter.

One who has sexual intercourse with his mother: The Mishnah now backtracks and gives details regarding the listed violations.

he is liable for her under the category of "his mother"[92] and under the category of "the wife of his father."
R. Judah says:
He is liable only under the category of "his mother."
One who has sexual intercourse with the wife of his father:
he is liable for her under the category of "the wife of his father" and the category of "another man's wife,"
whether it is during the life of his father or after the death of his father,
whether it is from [the time of] the betrothal or from the nuptials.
One who has sexual intercourse with his daughter-in-law:
he is liable for her under the category of "his daughter-in-law" and the category of "another man's wife,"
whether it is during the life of his son or after the death of his son,
whether it is from [the time of] the betrothal or from the nuptials.
One who has sexual intercourse with another male or with an animal,
and the woman who causes an animal to have sexual intercourse with her:
if a human sinned, did the animal sin?
Rather, since temptation came to the person by means of her,
therefore Scripture said she should be stoned.
Another interpretation: so that the animal should not pass in the market, and they will say, "This is the one on account of which so-and-so was stoned."
   5 The blasphemer:
he is not liable unless he explicitly says the Name.

[92] K: "the father," an apparent mistake.

He is liable for her: The Yerushalmi asks about the peculiar double indemnity here ("Can you say...that he is stoned and then stoned again?") and explains it in terms of the warning required by the witnesses. If the witnesses give the potential capital criminal the requisite warning using either of these categories, that man will be capitally liable for the act of intercourse. The word here translated as "he is liable" is the same word translated elsewhere as "he is guilty." The change reflects the change in context—while the earlier chapters use the term to describe the judges' final determination in a particular case, here and henceforth it is used to describe the potential scope of liability for each criminal violation.

and the category of "another man's wife": i.e. adultery. Adultery appears in 11:1 below as one of the violations penalized with strangulation.

whether it is during the life of his father or after the death of his father: Even if the father has died and the father's wife might no longer technically be considered the man's stepmother, or even if the father has only betrothed but not wed the woman who will become the man's stepmother, that man is nevertheless considered to have violated this prohibition if he were to have sexual intercourse with her. The same stringencies repeat for the prohibition against a man's sexual intercourse with his daughter-in-law.

If a human sinned, did the animal sin? The Mishnah's question relates to the death penalty for the animal. See 1:4 above, which discusses the judicial trial of the animal.

Rather, since temptation came to the person by means of her: The animal is executed not because the animal herself sinned, claims the Mishnah, but because she was the means of sin for a human being.

So that the animal should not pass in the market: The Talmud calls this "degradation" for the person who has been executed.

7:5 *he is not liable until he explicitly says the Name*: On the names of God for which one is liable, see *Shevu'ot* 4:13.

R. Joshua b. Qorhah said:
Throughout the day they judge the witnesses with a substitute word:
Yose should strike Yose.
Once the verdict is delivered, one does not kill with a substitute word,
but rather one takes every person outside
and asks[93] the greatest among them,
saying to him, "Say explicitly what you heard."
And he says.
And the judges stand on their feet and tear [their clothing] and do not mend.
And the second says, "I too am like him."
And the third says, "I too am like him."

6 The idolater:
the law is one and the same whether one worships,
one sacrifices,
one burns incense,
one pours a libation,
one bows down,
one accepts upon himself its divinity,
or one who says to it, "You are my god."
But one who embraces,
kisses,
makes an offering to it,[94]

[93] K, P: "they leave remaining."
[94] Alternatively, "honors the idol" or "sweeps the space" surrounding it.

throughout the day they judge the witnesses with a substitute word: Trying a person for blasphemy poses the problem of not repeating the crime in the course of testifying to it.

Yose should strike Yose: This is the expression that should substitute for the blasphemy during the course of the trial. The Yerushalmi explains that the letters in *Yose* have the same total numerical value as those in *Elohim*, one of God's names. On the form "Yose should strike Yose," the Bavli explains that blasphemy must involve cursing the divine name using the divine name.

Once the verdict is delivered, one does not kill with a substitute word: A person should not be executed based on testimony that is not entirely precise.

but rather one takes every person outside and asks the greatest among them: The blasphemy should be heard by as few people as possible. This line repeats the initial procedures of witness examination described in 3:6 above.

And the judges stand on their feet and tear: Numbers 14:6, 2 Kings 18:37 and 19:1 describe characters who tear their clothing upon hearing a challenge to God's authority, as do Mark 14:63, Matthew 26:65, and Acts 14:14.

I too am like him: The second witness should not repeat the blasphemy but should corroborate it.

And the third says: Only two witnesses are required, but this line suggests that more may testify.

7:6 *worships…sacrifices*, etc.: These worship practices are considered conventional and therefore fall under the category of idolatry.

But one who embraces, kisses, etc.: These acts of honor or affection towards an idol have a lesser status than worship and do not incur the death penalty but are nevertheless prohibited. According to R. Judah in another source, kissing an idol incurs "execution at the hands of Heaven."

sprinkles,⁹⁵
cleanses,
anoints,
dresses, or
puts shoes on—
he transgresses a negative commandment.
One who makes a vow in its name
and one who makes an oath⁹⁶ in its name—
he transgresses a negative commandment.
One who opens wide to Ba'al Pe'or—that is its worship.
One who throws a stone at Merqolis—that is its worship.

7 One who gives of his seed to Molekh—
he is not liable unless he delivers to Molekh,
and he passes [him] through the fire.
If he delivered to Molekh but did not pass through the fire,⁹⁷
or if he passed through the fire but did not deliver him to Molekh—
he is not liable unless he delivers to Molekh and he passes through the fire.
One who possesses *ov*—
this is the necromancer who speaks from his armpit.⁹⁸
And a *yid'oni*—

⁹⁵ P inserts "hugs" between "makes an offering to" and "sprinkles."
⁹⁶ Lit. "upholds" or "testifies."
⁹⁷ K lacks "If he delivered to Molekh but did not pass him through the fire, or."
⁹⁸ K, P: "This is the necromancer and one who speaks from his armpit."

One who makes a vow in its name and one who makes an oath in its name: Like the acts mentioned above, making a vow or an oath in an idol's name is not considered worship and does not incur the death penalty, but it is still prohibited.

One who opens wide to Ba'al Pe'or—that is its worship: Pe'or or Ba'al Pe'or is a Moabite god that the Israelites are described as being seduced into worshipping (Numbers 25 and other passages). The Mishnah probably understands the name to refer to exposing oneself, though the Talmud seems to understand the Mishnah to be referring to defecation. The Mishnah's claim here is that bodily exposure (or defecation), even if it is conventionally considered an act of degradation, in this context constitutes idolatrous worship and, as such, is penalized with stoning.

One who throws a stone at Merqolis: See *Avodah Zarah* 4:1–2 for further discussion. Merqolis worship entails placing ("throwing") stones next to an image of the god Merqolis, a Hebraization of the Latin *Mercurius* (Mercury), the Roman god of travel and commerce. The Mishnah here combines discussion of ancient biblical gods (Pe'or) with contemporaneous Roman ones (Mercury) and in both cases declares acts conventionally considered insults to paradoxically constitute worship.

7:7 One who gives of his seed to Molekh: The Mishnah combines Leviticus 18:21 and 20:2–5, which describe giving and passing one's seed to *Molekh*, with Deuteronomy 18:10, which describes passing one's son or daughter through the fire.

he passes [him] through the fire: Since this is not spelled out by the Mishnah, the Talmud imagines different ways in which passing one's child over the fire would have transpired: in one, a pile of bricks is set up with fires lit on both sides of it and, in another, a ring is suspended from a frame over a bonfire. Modern scholars are no more sure than the Talmud is on the subject.

This is the necromancer who speaks from his armpit: The Mishnah blends the biblical version of divination with a contemporaneous Roman pagan version.

this is one who speaks from his mouth.
They are by stoning,
and one who inquires of them is by biblical admonition.

8 One who profanes the Sabbath [is liable]—
if by an act for which one is liable to *karet* for intentional action
and liable for a purgation offering for accidental action.
One who curses his father and his mother—
he is not liable unless he curses them with the Name.
If he cursed them with a substitute word:[99]
R. Meir deems him liable, but the Sages deem him exempt.

9 One who has sexual intercourse with a betrothed girl—
he is not liable unless the girl is a betrothed virgin and she is in her father's house.
If two have had sexual intercourse with her,
the first is with stoning and the second with strangulation.

10 The enticer—
this is the common person who entices the common person;
he said to him, "There is awe in Place Such-and-such; thus does it eat, thus does it drink, thus does it cause good, thus does it cause evil."
Of all those liable for execution in the Torah

[99] K here has an extra clause, "if he cursed them with the Name," which appears to be a scribal error.

this is one who speaks from his mouth: According to parallels, the practitioner places a bone in his mouth. This and the previous technique are methods of asking the dead to speak and to predict the future.

one who inquires of them is by biblical admonition: "Biblical admonition" refers to practices that the Torah instructs Israel not to do but for which in this case there is no capital punishment.

7:8 *if by an act…karet…purgation*: This principle is laid out in *Keritot* 1:2 and the liable categories of labor on the Sabbath are laid out in *Shabbat* 7:2. A violator of the Sabbath is punished by stoning if he was forewarned; if not forewarned, by *karet*.

If he cursed them: Cf. *Shevu'ot* 4:13.

7:9 *he is not liable unless the girl is a betrothed virgin and she is in her father's house*: Deuteronomy 22:23 describes a "virgin who is betrothed to a man." The Mishnah seems to be excluding cases involving a female who is either too old or too young, a girl who has had sexual intercourse already, and a girl who has already departed from her father's domain.

the first is with stoning and the second with strangulation: In such a case, the first man who has sexual intercourse with the betrothed virgin is given Deuteronomy 22:23–24's punishment of stoning. Because at that point the woman is no longer a virgin, the second man who has sexual intercourse with her is punished with the normal penalty for adultery, strangulation (see 11:1 below), even though she still has not consummated the marriage with the man betrothed to her.

7:10 *this is the common person who entices the common person*: The connotations of "common person" here are ambiguous. The Talmud proposes that the Mishnah's use of the same word regarding both the subject and the object of the enticement is intended to differentiate that violation from the false prophet and the subverter; in the former case the subject is not a common person, and in the latter the object is an entire town. The enticer is characterized as particularly pernicious in the procedure that follows in that he operates in secret, making it difficult to come up with the requisite two witnesses.

"There is awe in Place Such-and-such": "Awe" refers here to a deity.

one entraps only this [case].
If he spoke to two,
and they are his witnesses,
they bring him to the court house and they stone him.
If he spoke to one,[100] he says:
"I have friends wanting this."
If he was tricky and[101] he [says that he] cannot speak in front of them,[102]
one entraps him with witnesses[103] behind the fence,
and he says to him: "Say what you said to me in private."
And the other one says [the enticement] to him, and he says to him:[104]
"How can we leave our God who is in the heavens and go and worship trees and stones?"
If he retracts,
indeed that is best.
But if he said: "Thus is our obligation, and thus it is good for us,"
those standing behind the fence bring him to the court and stone him.
One who says: "I will worship"; "I will go and I will worship"; "Let us go and let us worship"; "I will sacrifice"; "I will go and I will sacrifice"; "Let us go and let us sacrifice"; "I will burn incense"; "I will go and I will burn incense"; "Let us go and let us burn incense"; "I will pour a libation"; "I will go and I will pour a libation"; "Let us go and let us pour a libation"; "I will bow down"; "I will go and I will bow down"; "Let us go and let us bow down."
The subverter—
this is one who says, "Let us go and let us worship foreign worship."

11 The sorcerer—
one who performs an action is liable[105] but not one who tricks the eyes.

[100] K, P: "If he spoke to one, and he says…"
[101] "And" absent in K and added in a superscript in P.   [102] K, P add "Rather."
[103] "With witnesses" absent in K, P, both of which have instead "they entrap them."
[104] K: "and he" is crossed out; "the other one says to him" appears next; "and he says to him" after that is absent. P: "And he says to him, and the other one says to him." The repetition and vagueness of the referents no doubt caused the variations here.
[105] K, P lack "is liable."

one entraps only this [case]: Entrapment procedures are required to produce a conviction for this devious crime. A parallel text lists a variety of other procedural exceptions for the enticer.

"I have friends wanting this": The object of the enticement should try to engineer another witness by pretending to have friends who might also be interested in idolatry.

If he was tricky and he [says that he] cannot speak in front of them: The enticer is particularly devious and manages to evade the entrapment plot.

If he retracts, indeed that is best: The Mishnah makes clear that its entrapment procedure, while designed to produce a conviction, is not motivated by the hope that it will.

One who says, "I will worship…": One is liable as an enticer for any of the formulations that follow. These formulations repeat and expand upon the catalog of worship practices in 7:6 above, but here the person is liable not for engaging in the worship itself but for speaking about it and encouraging others to engage in it.

This is one who says, "Let us go and let us worship foreign worship": The subverter overlaps with the enticer, since the formulation "Let us go…" is associated with both.

7:11 *one who performs an action is liable, but not one who tricks the eyes*: The Mishnah distinguishes between sleight of hand and a substantive act of sorcery (clearly presuming that sorcery can be efficacious).

R. Aqiva says in the name of R. Joshua:
Two gather cucumbers:
one gatherer is exempt and one gatherer is liable:
the one who performs an action is liable;
the one who tricks the eyes is exempt.

Chapter Eight

8:1–5 *The Stubborn and Rebellious Son*

8 The stubborn and rebellious son:
at what point does he become a stubborn and rebellious son?
From the time that he grows two hairs
until the time when he grows a "beard" all round.
The lower [beard] and not the upper one,
but the Sages spoke in clean language.
As it is said: *If a man has a stubborn and rebellious son—*
A son and not a daughter.
A son and not a man.
A minor is exempt since he has not come within the scope of the commandments.

Two gather cucumbers: One gatherer is exempt and one gatherer is liable: The one who makes it appear as though he has gathered cucumbers is exempt, but the one who uses sorcery actually to gather cucumbers is liable for execution.

8:1 *The stubborn and rebellious son*: The last item on the list of violations punished with stoning (see 7:4).

From the time that he grows two hairs: This refers to pubic hair and, according to other passages in the Mishnah, is a sign in both girls and boys that puberty has begun. *Niddah* 6:11 says that a boy who has grown two hairs is responsible for all the commandments in the Torah and repeats the age range given here for the rebellious son.

The lower [beard] and not the upper one: The Mishnah clarifies that the beard of which it speaks refers not to facial hair (the "upper beard") but to pubic hair (the "lower beard"). The two hairs mark the onset of puberty, while a full "beard" marks the end stage. According to an opinion in the Bavli, the window of liability for a rebellious son is only three months long; according to an opinion in the Yerushalmi, the time span is six months.

A son and not a daughter: A parallel text calls this restriction a "decree of the king" or, in other words, a law justified by authority rather than by logic. The Yerushalmi declares that many aspects of these laws run counter to logic.

A son and not a man: "Son" is being read restrictively to exclude people of the wrong gender (women) and of the wrong age (children or full adults).

A minor is exempt since he has not come within the scope of the commandments: The boy cannot be considered to be violating commandments if he is not yet liable for them.

2 At what point does he become liable?
From the time that he eats a *tartemar* of meat and drinks a half-*log* of wine of the Italian [measure].¹⁰⁶
R. Yose says:
A *maneh* of meat and a *log* of wine.
If he ate in the course of a gathering for a commandment;¹⁰⁷
if he ate in the course of [a gathering] for the intercalation of the month;
if he ate the second tithe in Jerusalem;
if he ate animals discovered to be forbidden after proper slaughtering or not slaughtered properly;
vermin and reptiles;
(if he ate untithed produce or first tithe from which *terumah* had not been taken, or second tithe or sanctified produce that had not been redeemed);¹⁰⁸
if he ate a thing that is a commandment or a thing that is a violation;

¹⁰⁶ The printed editions suggest that the wine is Italian, while the manuscripts suggest that the half-*log* goes according to Italian measure, which seems to be correct.
¹⁰⁷ K lacks this example.   ¹⁰⁸ K, P lack the material in parentheses.

8:2 *From the time that he eats a tartemar of meat and drinks a half-log of wine*: The word *tartemar* appears nowhere else in the Mishnah, and the Talmudim are not sure what it means. *Log*, on the other hand, is a common mishnaic measure of volume approximately equal to a third of a liter.

of the Italian [measure]: Numerous other mishnayot speak of Italian measures, suggesting that "Italian" refers here not to the type of wine, as most commentators understand it based on the printed edition, but to the type of measurement; this accords with the manuscript text and with broader usage in the Mishnah.

A maneh of meat and a log of wine: R. Yose's standard of consumption (a full *log* of wine versus the anonymous position's half-*log*) makes it more difficult for a boy to become liable as a rebellious son.

If he ate in the course of a gathering for a commandment: This and the next two scenarios involve eating in the course of celebrating the fulfillment of a commandment. In all the following cases the boy's gluttony would not make him liable, according to the Talmud, because action in such circumstances was deemed unlikely to become habit.

if he ate in the course of [a gathering] for the intercalation of the month: According to the Talmud, such a feast involves at least ten men setting out bread and beans. On intercalation of the month, see note on 1:2 above.

if he ate the second tithe in Jerusalem: See note on 1:3 above.

if he ate animals discovered to be forbidden after proper slaughtering or not slaughtered properly: This and the next scenario involve foods that are forbidden because particular circumstances invalidate them. This list of forbidden foods, including the part omitted from the manuscripts, is found in *Makkot* 3:2 in a list of acts of eating for which a person is flogged.

vermin and reptiles: The language is a standard rabbinic hendiadys for animals forbidden for consumption.

if he ate untithed produce ... had not been redeemed: This grouping occurs verbatim in *Berakhot* 7:1 for meals over which one does not say the full grace because these foods are forbidden (see the annotations there). The grouping is omitted by the manuscripts here, probably because the consumption of these foods does not in fact confer the status of rebellious son.

if he ate a thing that is a commandment or a thing that is a violation: While the Bavli understands this line to be adding scenarios, it more likely furnishes a general principle meant to encompass the previously listed scenarios as well as other potential ones: liability for the rebellious son is restricted to food and drink that are legally neutral. The Yerushalmi's articulation of the principle links it to Scripture: *He does not listen to our voice* (Deuteronomy 21:20)—that is, not even to the voice of his Father who is in the heavens.

if he ate any food but did not eat meat;
if he drank any drink but did not drink wine:
he does not become a stubborn and rebellious son unless he eats meat and drinks wine,
as it is said: *He is a glutton and a drunkard.*
And even though there is no proof for the matter, there is a hint of the matter,
as it is said: *Do not be of those who guzzle wine, or glut themselves on meat.*

3 If he stole that which belongs to his father and ate in the domain of his father,
that which belongs to others and ate in the domain of others,
that which belongs to others and ate in the domain of his father:
he does not become a stubborn and rebellious son
unless he steals that which belongs to his father
and eats in the domain of others.
R. Yose b. Judah says:
Unless he steals that which belongs to his father
and that which belongs to his mother.

4 If his father wished but his mother did not wish,
if his father did not wish but his mother did wish:[109]
he does not become a stubborn and rebellious son unless both of them wish it.
R. Judah says:
If his mother was not fit for his father,
he does not become a stubborn and rebellious son.
If one of them had a stumped arm,
was lame of foot, mute, blind, or deaf,
he does not become a stubborn and rebellious son,
as it is said: *His father and his mother shall take hold of him*—and not those who have a stumped arm.
And they bring him out—and not those who are lame of foot.
And they shall say—and not those who are mute.

[109] K, P reverse the order in the second line.

And even though there is no proof for the matter, there is a hint of the matter: This is standard rabbinic phraseology (e.g. *Shabbat* 8:7) to indicate evidence from a nonlegal, non-Pentateuchal scriptural source.

Do not be of those who guzzle wine, or glut themselves on meat: Proverbs 23:20, which uses the same verbs as Deuteronomy 21:20 but specifies wine and meat.

8:3 *unless he steals that which belongs to his father and eats in the domain of others*: The Talmud explains that this is the only case where he has resources readily available to him (his father's) yet does not fear discovery of his gluttony (because he eats outside his home).

8:4 *If his mother was not fit for his father*: The Talmud rejects the possibility that this refers to legal fitness and proposes instead that it refers to likeness between the parents in their voice, appearance, and height.

His father and his mother shall take hold of him: Deuteronomy 21:19. The subsequent citations follow the order of the Deuteronomy passage. The principle behind the Mishnah's interpretations is that if the ritual cannot be carried out in precisely the way that Deuteronomy prescribes then it should not be carried out at all. The Talmud calls this principle "we require the verse to be as it is written."

And they bring him out: Deuteronomy 21:19. The Mishnah presumes that a parent who has a limp would not be able to "bring him out."

And they shall say: Deuteronomy 21:20. The Mishnah presumes that a parent who is mute would not be able to speak these words.

This son of ours—and not those who are blind.
He does not listen to our voice—and not those who are deaf.
They warn him before three and they flog him.
If he returned to his corruption,
he is judged with twenty-three.
But he is not stoned unless the first three are there,
as it is said: *This son of ours*—this one who was flogged before you.
If he fled before his verdict was delivered,
and after that his lower beard grew all round,
he is exempt.
If he fled after his verdict was delivered,
and after that his lower beard grew all round,
he is liable.

5 The stubborn and rebellious son is judged according to his end:
he should die innocent
and he should not die guilty.
For the death of the wicked is a benefit to them
and a benefit to the world.
But for the righteous,
it is evil for them
and evil for the world.

This son of ours: Deuteronomy 21:20. The Mishnah presumes that a parent who is blind would not be able to identify the boy as "this son of ours."

He does not listen to our voice: Deuteronomy 21:20. The Mishnah presumes that a deaf parent could not claim to hear the son's disobedient remarks.

They warn him before three: The nature and agent of this warning is debated by commentators, since warning typically requires two witnesses, yet this Mishnah associates warning with three.

they flog him: The flogging of the boy is not explicit in Deuteronomy but is based by the Talmud on the phrase, *even after they discipline him* (Deuteronomy 21:18). On a court of three for flogging, see 1:2 above.

If he fled before his verdict was delivered, and after that his lower beard grew all round, he is exempt: Because he is no longer suitable to be a rebellious son.

If he fled after his verdict was delivered, and after that his lower beard grew all round, he is liable: Once the verdict is delivered, it no longer matters if his status changes. According to the Talmud, "Once his verdict is delivered, he is a dead (lit. "killed") man."

8:5 *The stubborn and rebellious son is judged according to his end*: He is judged according to the violations he will commit rather than those he already has. Gluttony and drunkenness are not in themselves capital crimes but presumably will lead to them.

he should die innocent and he should not die guilty: Therein lies the principle underlying the rebellious son as the Mishnah construes it: the boy is executed despite the fact that he is innocent of any capital crimes, precisely in order to keep him that way. The Talmud imagines that the son is destined to use up all his parents' resources and then to harass people and eventually to commit murder.

For the death of the wicked is a benefit to them and a benefit to the world: In the Mishnah's thinking, the rebellious son's death is a boon to him, saving him from the sins he would have someday committed. The Mishnah goes from there into a digression on differences between the righteous and the wicked that present a paradox: experiences generally considered negative—like death and dispersal—are in fact a benefit for the wicked.

Wine and sleep for the wicked is a benefit to them
and a benefit to the world.
But for the righteous,
it is evil for them
and evil for the world.
Dispersal for the wicked is a benefit to them
and a benefit to the world.
But for the righteous,
it is evil for them
and evil for the world.
Assembly for the wicked is evil for them
and evil for the world.
But for the righteous,
it is a benefit for them
and a benefit for the world.
Rest for the wicked is evil for them
and evil for the world.
But for the righteous,
it is a benefit for them
and a benefit for the world.

8:6–7 *Those Killed for Crimes Not Yet Committed*

6 One who breaks in is judged according to his end.
If he broke in and broke a jug:
if there is blood guilt in his case, he is liable.
If there is no blood guilt in his case, he is exempt.

Assembly for the wicked is evil for them and evil for the world: The pattern reverses at the end, with the Mishnah listing things that are evil for the wicked and a benefit for the righteous.

8:6 *One who breaks in is judged according to his end*: According to Exodus 22:1–2, a householder can kill a nighttime burglar with impunity if he catches him red-handed. If it happens in the daytime, however, the situation is thought to present no imminent danger to the householder's life, the principle of self-defense becomes insufficient, and the householder incurs blood guilt if he kills the burglar. The burglar is discussed in connection with the rebellious son since both are killed (the rebellious son by formal execution, the burglar by the householder in self-defense) on the basis of crimes they presumably will commit.

If he broke in and broke a jug: if there is blood guilt in his case, he is liable: Because the daytime (or otherwise not life-threatening) burglar is not, in effect, capitally liable, he becomes civilly liable for any damage he might cause.

If there is no blood guilt in his case, he is exempt: If the householder has no blood guilt for killing the burglar, it means that the burglar is, in effect, capitally liable, and thus he becomes exempt from any civil liabilities he may incur. See the theory spelled out in *Ketubbot* 3:2 and *Bava Qamma* 3:10 and 8:5 that one cannot simultaneously incur criminal and civil liabilities.

7 And these are the ones whom one saves [by taking] their lives:
one who pursues another man to kill him,
another male,
or a betrothed girl.
But one who pursues an animal,
or who profanes the Sabbath,
or who worships foreign worship—
one does not save them with their lives.

Chapter Nine

9:1–2 *Violations with Penalties of Burning and Decapitation*

9 And these are the ones who are burned:
one who has sexual intercourse with a woman and her daughter,
and the daughter of a priest who prostituted herself.[110]
In the category of "a woman and her daughter" are:

[110] K, P lack "Who prostituted herself."

8:7 *And these are the ones whom one saves [by taking] their lives*: This line could be read as referring either to "saving" the pursuer from future sins by taking his life, or to saving the life of the victim by taking the life of the pursuer. Since the Mishnah goes on to mention some cases when no other human life is at stake, the former reading seems more likely.

one who pursues another man to kill him, another male to have sexual intercourse with him, *or a betrothed girl*: A parallel text expands this law to one who pursues a woman for any forbidden sexual relationship.

But one who pursues an animal to have sexual intercourse with her, *or who profanes the Sabbath, or who worships foreign worship—one does not save them with their lives*:

Maimonides explains that observing the Sabbath and shunning idolatry are singled out because they are foundations for the entire Torah. The Mishnah's point is that these sins, grave as they are, have the same status as any other when confronting a person about to commit them. That person may be executed only *after* he has been convicted by the court for committing the sin, not to *prevent* him from doing so. R. Eleazar son of R. Zadok in a parallel text dissents and offers the opinion that one should "save," i.e. preemptively kill, a man poised to commit idolatry.

9:1 *And these are the ones who are burned*: The Mishnah has completed its discussion of violations punished with stoning and moves on to violations punished with burning (see annotation on 7:4 above).

one who has sexual intercourse with a woman and her daughter: Based on Leviticus 18:17 and 20:14. While Leviticus 18:7 formulates the prohibition in terms of "a woman and her daughter," Leviticus 20:14 formulates it in terms of "a woman and her mother."

and the daughter of a priest who prostituted herself: Based on Leviticus 21:9 (see also 7:2 above). A parallel text specifies that the priest's daughter in question must be married and features a dispute regarding the penalty for the priest's daughter who is betrothed.

In the category of "a woman and her daughter": Sexual intercourse with any of the listed female relatives falls under the rubric of this violation.

his daughter; the daughter of his daughter; the daughter of his son; the daughter of his wife; the daughter of her daughter; the daughter of her son; his mother-in-law; the mother of his mother-in-law; and the mother of his father-in-law.[111]

And these are the ones who are decapitated:

the murderer and the people of the subverted town.

A murderer who struck his neighbor with a stone or with an iron implement,

or held him down under water,

or in a flame,

such that he was not able to emerge from there,

and he died,

is liable.

[111] P lacks the last three relatives.

his daughter; the daughter of his daughter: The daughter is famously absent from the incest taboos of Leviticus, but the Mishnah subsumes it under this prohibition.

the daughter of his son: Prohibited explicitly by Leviticus 18:10, which the Mishnah here assimilates with Leviticus 18:17.

the daughter of his wife; the daughter of her daughter; the daughter of her son: These three relations are explicitly prohibited by Leviticus 18:17.

his mother-in-law: Sexual intercourse between a man and his mother-in-law is explicitly prohibited by Leviticus 20:14 and cursed by Deuteronomy 27:23. It is also implied by the prohibition of "a woman and her daughter" (Leviticus 18:17), if one works backward instead of forward through the generations.

the mother of his mother-in-law; and the mother of his father-in-law: These are the backward-looking equivalents of "daughter of her daughter" and "daughter of her son" of Leviticus 18:17. In the case of sexual intercourse with the mother of his mother-in-law, he would be having sexual intercourse with "a woman and the daughter of her daughter," and in the case of the mother of his father-in-law, he is having sexual intercourse with "a woman and the daughter of her son."

And these are the ones who are decapitated: The Mishnah has now covered violations penalized with stoning and burning and moves on to the execution method of decapitation, the next lower degree of severity.

the murderer: Laws of homicide are given in Exodus 21:12–14, Numbers 35, and Deuteronomy 19. Decapitation is not the explicit penalty for homicide in any of these sources. Indeed, decapitation is not represented in the Bible as a formal judicial penalty, though midrashic commentary does find textual roots for it there.

and the people of the subverted town: Deuteronomy 13:13–19 describes an entire town being incited to idolatry. The instruction in Deuteronomy 13:16 to "put the inhabitants of that town to the sword" is taken by the early Rabbis to be a reference to the penalty of decapitation, though Deuteronomy is describing not judicial execution but something more like a holy war.

A murderer who struck his neighbor with a stone or with an iron implement: In mentioning these implements, the Mishnah follows the lead of Numbers 35:16–17, which presents these as typical deadly weapons.

or held him down under water or in a flame: The Mishnah now imagines deadly scenarios that are alternatives to the biblical ones. The verb used here, "held down," is meant to contrast with the verb in the subsequent and parallel scenario, "pushed," where a fatal outcome is not necessarily intended.

such that he was not able to emerge from there: The liability pattern in the cases that follow is that both intent to kill as well as direct causation must be present. Liability may be established, even if the homicide entails some degree of error or ambiguity, so long as those two ingredients are both present. The cases in 9:1 seem concerned more with causation, while the cases in 9:2 seem concerned more with intention. In fact, in the case of drowning or burning to death where a person is not able to escape, intent to kill and direct causation would both seem relatively easy to establish.

If he pushed him into the water or into flame,
such that he was able to emerge from there and he died,
he is exempt.
If he set a dog on him or set a snake on him,
he is exempt.
If he caused the snake to bite him:
R. Judah deems him liable,
but the Sages deem him exempt.
One who strikes another,
whether with a stone or with a fist,
and they conjectured that he will die,
but he improved from his former condition,
but after that he got worse and died,
is liable.
R. Nehemiah says:
He is exempt,
since there is a basis for the matter.[112]

2 If he intended to kill an animal and he killed a human being,
a gentile and he killed an Israelite,
nonviable babies and he killed a viable baby,
he is exempt.

[112] Lit. "the thing has legs."

If he pushed him…such that he was able to emerge from there: Intent to kill and direct causation would both be difficult to establish if the victim could have escaped. According to midrash, the cases in these instances and the ones that follow are "handed over to Heaven."

If he set a dog on him or set a snake on him, he is exempt: The animal and not the person who incited him might be seen as the direct cause of death.

If he caused the snake to bite him: R. Judah deems him liable, but the Sages deem him exempt: According to commentaries, this scenario differs from the previous one in that the person goes so far as to place the snake's teeth on the body of the victim. Presumably the difference of opinion between R. Judah and the Sages regards whether the animal and not the person might still be seen as the direct cause of death.

whether with a stone or with the fist: The Mishnah mimics the language of Exodus 21:18 regarding compensation for injury.

and they conjecture that he will die…he is liable: This is a boundary case, since causation is complicated by the temporary recovery of the victim. The key to the homicide's ultimate liability is that the victim's injuries were initially assessed to be fatal.

He is exempt, since there is a basis for the matter: R. Nehemiah argues that direct causation is not sufficiently clear in such a case, since one could argue that the patient's poor health, and not the initial blow from which the victim temporarily recovered, caused his death. In an alternative tradition in the Yerushalmi, "there is a basis for the matter" is attached to the consensus opinion and not to R. Nehemiah's. This rule also appears in *Nazir* 9:3.

9:2 *If he intended to kill an animal…he is exempt*: The Mishnah moves on to cases in which intent to kill, rather than causation, is ambiguous. In these cases, the agent intended to kill a being for whom there is criminal liability (human being, Israelite, viable baby) but instead killed a being for whom there is no criminal liability (animal, gentile, nonviable baby). The Mishnah presumes that liability for homicide is based on a generalized intent to kill and that the victim need not be the intended individual so long as the victim belongs to a liable category. This presumption will be contested later by R. Simeon. The same set of misdirected homicides is attributed to an ox in *Bava Qamma* 4:6.

If he intended to strike him on his hips,
and there was not sufficient force in [the blow] to kill on his hips,
and it landed on his chest and there was in it sufficient force to kill on his chest,
and he died,
he is exempt.
If he intended to strike him on his chest,
and there was in it sufficient force to kill on his chest,
and it landed on his hips and there was not in it sufficient force to kill on his hips,
and he died,
he is exempt.
If he intended to strike an adult,
and there was not in it sufficient force to kill the adult,
and it landed on a child and there was in it sufficient force to kill the child,
and he died,[113]
he is exempt.
If he intended to strike a child,
and there was in it sufficient force to kill the child,
and it landed on an adult and there was not in it sufficient force to kill the adult,
and he died,
he is exempt.
But if he intended to strike him on his hips,
and there was in it sufficient force to kill on his hips,
and it landed on his chest,
and he died,
he is liable.

[113] K, P have the ruling "he is exempt" only here. K also has an extra line that appears to be mistaken (see italics): "If he intended to strike an adult and there was not in it sufficient force to kill an adult, *and it landed on a child and there was in it sufficient force to kill an adult*, and it landed on the child and there was in it sufficient force to kill a child, and he died."

If he intended to strike him on his hips: This case problematizes intention, while the subsequent case returns to causation. This agent of homicide presumably did not have intent to kill—though he did have intent to injure—since the blow he aimed at the hips did not have fatal force. The blow accidentally landed on a more vulnerable part of the body, i.e. the chest, where it had an unintended fatal impact.

If he intended to strike him on his chest: This aggressor did have clear intent to kill, but he cannot be considered the direct cause of the homicide since the blow he landed on the less vulnerable part of his victim's body, i.e. the hips, should not have had a fatal impact. The implication is that poor health or bad luck contributed significantly enough to the fatality to release the aggressor from criminal liability.

If he intended to strike an adult: The adult/child binary plays a role parallel to that of hips/chest in the previous case, since in both cases the first entity is less vulnerable than the second. The mistake in this case involves striking the wrong person rather than the wrong body part. Like the first hips/chest case above, this agent of homicide presumably did not have intent to kill.

If he intended to strike a child: Like the second hips/chest case above, this aggressor had clear intent to kill but cannot be considered the direct cause of the homicide since the blow that landed on the less vulnerable person should not have had a fatal impact.

But if he intended to strike him on his hips…he is liable: The Mishnah arrives finally at cases that combine intent to kill with direct causation to produce criminal liability, yet even these cases contain some degree of error. The agent is liable for homicide in this case because he had intent to kill and put sufficient power into the strike to make it incontrovertibly the direct cause of death, even though the strike did land on a body part for which it was not intended.

If he intended to strike an adult,
and there was in it sufficient force to kill the adult,
and it landed on a child,
and he died,
he is liable.
R. Simeon says:
Even if he intended to kill this one and he killed that one,
he is exempt.

9:3–4 *Mixed Death Penalties*

3 A murderer who was mingled with others:
All of them are exempt.
R. Judah says:
They gather them into prison.
Criminals convicted of all the death penalties who were mingled with each other are judged with the lightest.
Those who are stoned with those who are burned:
R. Simeon says:
They are judged with stoning,
since burning is more severe.
And the Sages say:
They are judged with burning,
since stoning is more severe.
R. Simeon said to them:

If he intended to strike an adult…he is liable: Because the agent had intent to kill and was the direct cause of death, he is liable even though the strike landed on a person for whom it was not intended.

R. Simeon says: Even if he intended to kill this one and he killed that one, he is exempt: R. Simeon argues that intent to kill cannot be generalized even when the intended victim and the actual victim both belong to categories of people for whom there is criminal liability. R. Simeon's statement is best read as an objection to the first statement in this Mishnah dealing with categories of people for whom there is no criminal liability (animal, gentile, nonviable baby), since the word "even" in his statement suggests that he is treating a more extreme case, whereas the immediately preceding case conforms precisely to his description (the victims are of comparable liability). In another version of R. Simeon's statement in the Talmud, the murderer must announce "My intention is for so-and-so" in order for him to become liable.

9:3 *A murderer who was mingled with others*: Commentaries discuss whether this murderer is suspected for murder or has already been convicted.

They gather them into prison: Presumably until it can be sorted out which man is the murderer. The word for prison, *kippah*, from a Hebrew root that means bend, bow, or force, may refer either to the domed ceiling of the cell or to the coercive character of the incarceration. According to the Talmud, the cell's height was limited to that of an average person and would have been an uncomfortable space in which to be confined.

Criminals convicted of all the death penalties who were mingled with each other are judged with the lightest: The situation is that convicted criminals are mixed together and it is not known who was sentenced with which death penalty. The Mishnah requires that the lightest penalty be applied to all.

Those who are stoned with those who are burned: The Mishnah now gives examples illustrating the principle it has just set forth.

If burning were not more severe,
it would not have been given to the priest's daughter who prostituted herself.
They said to him:
If stoning were not more severe,
it would not have been given to the blasphemer and to the idolater.[114]
Those who are decapitated with those who are strangled:
R. Simeon says:
With the sword.
And the Sages say:
With strangulation.

4 Someone who is liable for two execution methods of the court is judged with the more severe.
If he committed a violation that has associated with it two execution methods,
he is judged with the more severe.
R. Yose says:
He is judged according to the first legal restriction that fell upon him.

[114] Literally, "the one who worships foreign worship."

If burning were not more severe, it would not have been given to the priest's daughter who prostituted herself: In order to determine the degrees of severity of the execution methods, the Rabbis work backward from the violation to which the Torah applies them. Since R. Simeon considers the case of the priest's daughter to be the gravest capital violation, he infers that burning, which the Torah applies to that violation, must be the gravest execution method. The Mishnah here fills in some of the reasoning behind the positions of R. Simeon and the Sages set forth in 7:1 above. The Mishnah does not here address the logic underlying R. Simeon's and the Sages' positions on the relative severity of decapitation and strangulation as it does for stoning and burning, probably because the biblical sources for decapitation and strangulation are less clear.

If stoning were not more severe, it would not have been given to the blasphemer and to the idolater: In the Sages' view, blasphemy and idolatry are the gravest violations and therefore stoning, which the Torah applies to them, must be the gravest execution method.

With the sword: In other words, decapitation. Here R. Simeon and the Sages rehearse their positions about the relative severity of strangulation and decapitation. Since R. Simeon considers decapitation less severe, he applies it in the case of mixed penalties, following the principle articulated above that the lighter penalty is applied to all.

9:4 *Someone who is liable for two execution methods of the court is judged with the more severe*: A person who committed two capital crimes that incur two different types of execution. People with different penalties who have been mixed together are judged with the less severe, but a single person to whom two penalties apply is judged with the more severe.

If he committed a violation that has associated with it two execution methods, he is judged with the more severe: In the previous case a single person has committed two capital violations, while in this case a single person has committed a single violation associated with two execution penalties. The example given in a parallel text is a man who has sexual intercourse with his married mother-in-law: he violates the prohibition on adultery, whose penalty is strangulation, as well as the prohibition on sexual intercourse with one's mother-in-law, whose penalty is burning.

He is judged according to the first legal restriction that fell upon him: R. Yose dissents, advocating not the more severe penalty but the first penalty that applies to the act. The parallel just cited spells out the implications in the sample case of intercourse with one's married mother-in-law. If a man's mother-in-law was widowed or divorced at the time that he married her daughter, and then later the mother-in-law was

9:5–6 *Irregular Penalties*

5 Someone who was flogged and repeated:
the court[115] puts him in prison and feeds him barley until his stomach bursts.
One who kills a person[116] without witnesses:
they put him into prison and feed him *meager bread and scant water*.
  6 One who steals a libation vessel,
one who curses [God] by the name of another god,
and one who sexually possesses an Aramaean woman:
zealots may attack him.
A priest who served while impure:

---

[115] K, P have the preposition "in" before the word "court," suggesting the following translation: "Someone who was flogged repeatedly in the court, they gather him…" This version makes the line more tightly parallel with what follows.

[116] K, P: "One who kills people…"

---

married and the son-in-law subsequently had sexual intercourse with her, the first legal restriction that applied to the man would have been that regarding the mother-in-law. If she was married at the time that he married her daughter, however, then the first legal restriction that would have applied to the man was adultery.

9:5 *Someone who was flogged and repeated*: The Mishnah turns from mixed and multiple penalties to irregular penalties for cases where either the penalty is considered insufficient or there is no formal penalty. In the case of a repeat offender for a violation penalized with flogging, the Mishnah considers the formal penalty to be insufficient and devises a more severe one. The subject of "repeated" is ambiguous and could refer either to the offender's repetition of his offense or to the court's repetition of its flogging; in the manuscript version the subject is clearly the court.

the court puts him in prison and feeds him barley until his stomach bursts: Commentators discuss the meaning, both practical and symbolic, of the force-feeding of barley and if it constitutes a form of execution.

One who kills a person without witnesses: The Talmudim address the obvious question of how it is known that the man killed a person if there are no witnesses. It would seem that the evidence is sufficient to convince people of the crime but not to produce a formal conviction.

They put him in to prison and feed him meager bread and scant water: The phrase "meager bread and scant water" is taken from Isaiah 30:20. Commentators discuss whether the meager feeding described here, which contrasts with the overfeeding described in the previous case, is intended to starve the homicide to death or only to inflict deprivation. Another possibility is that it is meant to require the prison to provide him with adequate nourishment. A parallel text applies this penalty to the case where a capital criminal is warned before he commits the crime but does not respond clearly to the warning, thereby precluding a conviction.

9:6 *One who steals a libation vessel*: The Talmud searches for a biblical verse to explain why the Mishnah would call for such a severe penalty for this theft.

one who curses [God] by the name of another god: This translation follows the talmudic interpretation, but the meaning is unclear.

one who sexually possesses an Aramaean woman: "Aramaean woman" probably acts as a catch-all term for non-Israelite women. Commentators restrict the zealots' attack only to the time of sexual intercourse and only when it is performed in public.

zealots may attack him: Uncomfortable with the vigilante justice condoned by the Mishnah, the Bavli qualifies it: if the zealot seeks counsel before he launches his attack, he should be discouraged. The Yerushalmi, along similar lines, comments that such zealotry is "not according to the will of the Sages."

A priest who served while impure: The Talmud bases the penalty on Leviticus 22:2.

his priestly brothers do not bring him to the court,
but rather the young priests take him outside the Temple precinct,
and they split[117] his skull with clubs.
A nonpriest who served in the sanctuary:
R. Aqiva says:
With strangulation.
And the Sages say:
By the hands of heaven.

Chapter Ten

10:1–3 *Who Has a Portion in the World to Come?*

10 All of Israel possesses a portion in the world to come,
as it is said: *And your people, all of them righteous, shall possess the land for all time; they are the shoot that I planted, my handiwork in which I glory.*[118]

---

[117] **K, P** repeat "take out" instead of "split," but **P** corrects it in the margins.
[118] **K** lacks these lines. That absence may be due to a page break. In **P** the opening line is present but not the biblical prooftext.

---

his priestly brothers do not bring him to the court: The Mishnah explicitly directs this procedure to be conducted extra- or nonjudicially.

but rather the young priests: The young priests (literally "the blossoms of the priesthood") are mentioned a number of times in rabbinic literature.

take him outside the Temple precinct: Presumably to avoid it being contaminated by a corpse.

A nonpriest who serves in the sanctuary: The instruction that *any outsider who encroaches shall be put to death* is repeated in Numbers 1:51, 3:10, 3:38, and 18:7.

R. Aqiva says: With strangulation: The underlying question is how to interpret the verb *shall be put to death* in the biblical instruction. According to R. Aqiva, this term calls for judicial execution (and, since the method is unspecified, strangulation is applied). According to the Sages, however, the word signals divine, not human, punishment. The precise meaning of the rabbinic expression "death by the hands of heaven" is difficult to pin down, as is its relationship to the punishment known as *karet*. A parallel text adds other Temple- and purity-related transgressions to those punished with death by the hands of heaven.

Manuscripts of the Mishnah contain as chapter 10 a chapter traditionally called *Pereq Heleq*—the "Portion Chapter"—because of its discussion of who possesses a portion in the world to come (10:1–4). In the standard printed edition of the Babylonian Talmud, however, it is the eleventh and last chapter. The inclusiveness towards all Jews expressed in this mishnah's initial statement is belied by the subsequent teachings that deny a portion in the world to come to various Jewish heretics and biblical figures. This chapter has therefore been read, on the one hand, as a grand statement of Jewish inclusiveness and, on the other, as a blueprint for rabbinic orthodoxy. Commentators have inferred from the denial in 10:2 of a portion in the world to come to Balaam, the gentile prophet, that the Mishnah presumes that other gentiles can possess a portion in the world to come. The Mishnah does not explain exactly what is meant by "a portion in the world to come," a phrase that occurs also in *Avot* 3:11.

10:1 *And your people, all of them righteous*: Isaiah 60:21. The emphasis is on the verse's description of the entire people of Israel as righteous. Possession of the land seems to be understood as a reference to possession of a portion in the world to come.

And these are the ones who do not possess a portion in the world to come:
one who says that [the doctrine of] the resurrection of the dead is not from the Torah,[119]
[one who says that] there is no Torah from the heavens,
and [the] Epicurean.
R. Aqiva says:
Even one who reads the noncanonical books,[120]
and one who whispers over a wound and says: *All the diseases that I brought upon the Egyptians I will not bring upon you, for I the Lord am your healer.*
Abba Saul says:
Even one who pronounces the Name by its letters.

2 Three kings and four commoners do not possess a portion in the world to come.
Three kings: Jeroboam, Ahab, and Manasseh.
R. Judah says:
Manasseh does possess a portion in the world to come,
as it is said: *He prayed to him, and he granted his prayer, heard his plea, and returned him to Jerusalem to his kingdom.*
They said to him:
He returned him to his kingdom,

---

[119] K, P lack "from the Torah." [120] Lit. "outside books."

---

resurrection of the dead: The Talmud comments that the punishment here is measure for measure: one who denies resurrection of the dead is himself denied a share in the resurrection of the dead, which is understood to be equivalent to a portion in the world to come. The variant in the manuscripts—that is, the absence of "from the Torah"—changes the stakes in the discussion: now the question is not one of scriptural exegesis but the more fundamental question whether the resurrection of the dead is to be affirmed at all.

there is no Torah from the heavens: If this refers to the oral Torah, then it would rehearse one of the major points of difference, besides resurrection, that Josephus ascribes to the Sadducees and Pharisees.

Epicurean: Heb. *Apiqoros*: A follower of the school of the Greek philosopher Epicurus, which the early Rabbis associate with a rejection of divine providence. *Avot* 2:24 instructs: "Know what to answer an Epicurean." The term Epicurean in rabbinic literature came to refer to any Jewish heretic or dissenter, and Rabbis in both Talmudim offer a variety of interpretations of the term that emphasize insufficient respect for rabbinic authority and/or the Torah.

the noncanonical books: The Yerushalmi understands this to refer to the books of Ben Sira and the otherwise unknown La'ana. The Bavli understands this to refer to the "books of the heretics."

one who whispers over a wound: According to the Talmudim's explanation for this severe punishment, this healer also spits on the wound, and "one should not mention the name of Heaven while spitting."

All the diseases that I brought upon the Egyptians: Exodus 15:26.

Even one who pronounces the Name by its letters: The Yerushalmi says that this refers to the manner in which the Samaritans swear.

10:2 *Three kings and four commoners do not possess a portion in the world to come*: The Mishnah now turns to biblical figures, first individuals and then collectives, each set according to the order of the biblical narrative. The Talmudim ask why various other biblical figures who exhibited evil behavior did not land on this list.

Jeroboam, Ahab, and Manasseh: All three are vilified in the biblical narrative. Jeroboam—1 Kings 11:26–14:20. Ahab—1 Kings 16:28–22:40. Manasseh—2 Kings 20:21–21:18. A parallel text mentions four kings instead of three and adds to the list Ahaz, father of Hezekiah (2 Kings 15:38–16:20).

He prayed to him: 2 Chronicles 33:13. A parallel text cites 2 Chronicles 33:19. The portrait of Manasseh in 2 Chronicles is more sympathetic than that in 2 Kings.

but he did not return him to life in the world to come.
Four commoners: Balaam, Doeg, Ahitophel, and Gehazi.

3 The generation of the flood does not possess a portion in the world to come,
and they do not stand in judgment,
as it is said: *My breath shall not abide in man forever—*
neither judgment nor breath.[121]
The generation of the dispersal does not possess a portion in the world to come,
as it is said: *Thus the Lord scattered them from there over the face of the whole earth.*
Thus the Lord scattered them—in this world.
And from there the Lord scattered them—in the world to come.[122]
The people of Sodom do not possess a portion in the world to come,
as it is said: *Now the inhabitants of Sodom were very wicked sinners against the Lord.*
Wicked—in this world.
Sinners—in the world to come.[123]
But they stand in judgment.
R. Nehemiah says:
Neither these nor those stand in judgment,
as it is said: *Therefore the wicked will not survive in judgment, nor will sinners in the assembly of the righteous.*
Therefore the wicked will not survive in judgment—this is the generation of the flood.
Nor will sinners in the assembly of the righteous—these are the people of Sodom.
They said to him:
They do not stand in the assembly of the righteous,
but they stand in the assembly of the wicked.
The spies do not possess a portion in the world to come,

[121] K, P lack "neither judgment nor breath."
[122] K, P lack reference to the generation of the dispersal.
[123] K, P lack the verse and its midrash.

Balaam: Numbers 22:2–24:25. *Doeg*: 1 Samuel 21:8–22:23. *Ahitophel*: 2 Samuel 15:12–17:23. *Gehazi*: 2 Kings 4:12–5:27; 8:1–6.

10:3 *The generation of the flood*: The Mishnah turns to the primeval history of Genesis.

My breath shall not abide in man forever: Genesis 6:3.

neither judgment nor breath: According to the exegesis, the people in the biblical narrative obtain neither future judgment nor future life. The interpretation rests on a series of Hebrew puns.

The generation of the dispersal: This is a common rabbinic trope referring to the people who build the Tower of Babel, as described in Genesis 11.

Thus the Lord scattered them: Genesis 11:8.

And from there the Lord scattered them: Genesis 11:9. The Mishnah reads the repetition in Genesis 11:8–9 as a reference to the characters' fates in both this world and the next. The cases that follow conform to a similar pattern in which biblical verses teach about the ultimate fate of the characters.

Now the inhabitants of Sodom: Genesis 13:13.

Therefore the wicked will not survive in judgment: Psalm 1:5.

Nor will sinners in the assembly of the righteous: The word "sinners" in Psalm 1:5 is used also in Genesis 13:13 regarding Sodom, facilitating the link between the two.

The spies do not possess a portion in the world to come: Numbers 13–14.

as it is said: *Those who spread such calumnies about the land died of plague, by the will of the Lord.*
Died—in this world.
Of plague—in the world to come.[124]
The generation of the wilderness does not possess a portion in the world to come, and they do not stand in judgment,
as it is said: *In this very wilderness they shall meet their end, and here they shall die*—the words of R. Aqiva.
R. Eliezer says:
About them it says: *Bring in my devotees, who made a covenant with me over sacrifice.*
Korah's assembly will not rise up in the future,
as it is said: *The earth closed over them*—in this world.
And they vanished from the midst of the congregation—in the world to come—[125]
the words of R. Aqiva.
R. Eliezer says:
About them it says, *The Lord deals death and gives life, casts down in Sheol and raises up.*
The ten tribes will not return in the future,
as it is said: *And He cast them into another land, as it is to this day.*
Just as this day goes and does not return,
so too they go and do not return—
the words of R. Aqiva.
R. Eliezer says:
Just as the day darkens and brightens,
so too the ten tribes,

[124] K, P lack the section on the spies. [125] K, P quote the verse without midrashic interruption.

Those who spread such calumnies: Numbers 14:37. A parallel cites Numbers 14:23 instead.

The generation of the wilderness: Numbers 14:11–38.

In this very wilderness: Numbers 14:35. In a parallel: *In this very wilderness they shall meet their end*—in this world; *and here they shall die*—in the world to come.

the words of R. Aqiva: This is the first of three disputes between R. Aqiva and R. Eliezer in which R. Aqiva takes the more punitive position regarding the biblical characters in question.

Bring in my devotees: Psalm 50:5. R. Eliezer links Psalm 50:5 with the generation of the wilderness on the basis of Exodus 24:5–8, which describes the Israelites in the wilderness offering sacrifices to ratify their covenant with God.

Korah's assembly: Numbers 16.

The earth closed over them: Numbers 16:33.

The Lord deals death and gives life: 1 Samuel 2:6.

The ten tribes will not return in the future: 2 Kings 17:1–23 describes the exiling of the northern tribes by the Assyrian king. R. Aqiva here declares that this fate is final.

And He cast them into another land: Deuteronomy 29:27.

so too they go and do not return: R. Aqiva and R. Eliezer differ on the implications of "this day." For R. Aqiva, the key feature of a day is evanescence, which in turn characterizes the fate of the tribes to live in eternal exile. For R. Eliezer, the key feature of a day is the turn from darkness to light; that turn points to the future return of the tribes from exile.

who have become dark,
in the future will be brightened.

10:4–6 *Continuation: Violations with a Penalty of Decapitation*

4 The people of the subverted town do not possess a portion in the world to come,[126] as it is said: *Some scoundrels from among you have gone out and subverted the inhabitants of their town.*
And they are not decapitated unless its subverters are from that town and from that tribe,
and unless the majority of it is subverted,
and unless men subvert them.
If women or children subverted it,
or if a minority of it was subverted,
or if its subverters are outside it,
in such cases these are like individuals
and they require two witnesses and a warning for each one.
This is more severe regarding individuals than regarding groups:
since the individuals are with stoning,
their property is spared.
But groups are with decapitation,
so their property is destroyed.
   5 *Strike*, etc.:
the caravan of donkey drivers and the caravan of camel drivers who travel from place to place:

---

[126] K, P lack "do not possess a portion in the world to come."

10:4 *The people of the subverted town*: The Mishnah now returns to the list of violations penalized with decapitation (see 9:1 above) and proceeds to give details for the next item on the list, the people of the subverted town (discussed briefly also in 1:5 above).

Some scoundrels from among you: Deuteronomy 13:14. The treatment of the subverted town in chapter 10 features a great deal of midrash, echoing the treatment of the rebellious son in chapter 8. Both chapters read the relevant biblical passages as highly specific legal models. A parallel text says about both the rebellious son and the subverted town that they never have been or will be.

from that tribe: Commentators say this restriction is based on *from among you* (Deuteronomy 13:14).

unless men subvert them: This restriction arises from the word *men* in Deuteronomy 13:14.

these are like individuals: All the normal legal procedures of warning and testimony, which are apparently suspended for each individual in a subverted town, are applied to every "subverted" individual if the requirements for a subverted town are not met.

This is more severe regarding individuals than regarding groups: Deuteronomy 13:16 instructs that the property of the subverted town be destroyed. This mishnah creates a kind of balance sheet between the individual idolater, who is punished with stoning (7:6), and the people of the subverted town, who are punished with the sword: the individual idolaters who receive the more severe execution method are permitted to pass on their property, while the collective idolaters who receive the less severe execution method are not.

10:5 *Strike, etc.*: Deuteronomy 13:16.

these save it.
Doom it and all that is in it to destruction, etc.—from here they said:
The property of righteous people that is inside it is destroyed;
that which is outside it is spared.
The property of wicked people,
whether it is inside it or outside it,
is destroyed.

6 As it is said:[127] *Gather all its spoil inside the open square,* etc.—
if it does not have an open square, one makes for it an open square.
If its open square was outside it, one brings it inside.[128]
And burn the town and all its spoil as an entire burnt offering to the Lord your God: [129]
its spoil—and not the spoil of heaven.
From here they said:
The consecrated items that are in it should be redeemed and the tithes should be let spoil;

---

[127] K, P lack "As it is said."   [128] K, P add "as it is said: *inside the open square*."
[129] K, P introduce the verse citation with "as it is said," and P's citation starts with "inside the open square."

---

these save it: This law can be read as either counting or not counting vagrants as part of the resident population for the purposes of declaring a subverted town. Both readings rely on the previous mishnah's requirement that the majority of the inhabitants of the town be implicated. In the reading where vagrants count, the Mishnah would be describing a situation where vagrants who are longtime residents (thirty days or more, according to other texts) join with a significant portion of the nonsubverted population; in this case, they "save" the town from being declared subverted by helping to form a nonsubverted majority. In the reading where vagrants do not count, the Mishnah would be describing a situation where short-term vagrants make up a significant portion of the subverted population; in this case, they "save" the town from being declared subverted because without them only a minority of the population can be considered subverted.

Doom it and all that is in it: Deuteronomy 13:17.

The property of righteous people that is inside it is destroyed: A parallel text elaborates that the property of the righteous is destroyed because it caused them to live among the wicked. This law is derived from the phrase *and all that is in it* (Deuteronomy 13:17).

The property of wicked people, whether it is inside it or outside it, is destroyed: This law is derived from *all its spoil* (Deuteronomy 13:17)—"all" teaches that the property of the wicked even outside the town is destroyed. The Mishnah thereby shifts the emphasis from punishment of the town to punishment of the wicked.

10:6 *Gather all its spoil*: Deuteronomy 13:17.

if it does not have an open square, one makes for it an open square: The law must be executed exactly according to the details of Scripture. According to an alternative opinion in the Talmud, if the town has no square, then it may not become a subverted town.

If its open square was outside it, one brings it inside: Perhaps by rebuilding the walls of the town to include the square.

its spoil—and not the spoil of heaven: Based on the word *its spoil*, the Mishnah excludes consecrated items and tithes, i.e. "the spoil of heaven," from the destruction.

The consecrated items that are in it should be redeemed and the tithes should be let spoil: As the property of a condemned town, the consecrated items can no longer be used for the Temple and must be redeemed instead. On the redemption of consecrated items, see notes on 1:3 above. The tithes should not be eaten by the priests, but as sacred food the tithes should not be burned along with the other property. Thus they are left to rot.

the second tithe and holy writings should be hidden.
As an entire burnt offering to the Lord your God—
R. Simeon said:
The Holy One Blessed Be He said:[130] "If you do justice to the subverted town, I will credit you as though you had offered[131] an entire burnt offering before me."
And it shall remain an everlasting ruin, never to be rebuilt—
it should not be made even into gardens and orchards—
the words of R. Yose the Galilean.
R. Aqiva says:
Never to be rebuilt—it should not be rebuilt as it had been,
but it may be made into gardens and orchards.
Let nothing that has been doomed stick to your hand—
for any time that wicked people are in the world,
God's wrath is in the world;
When wicked people are destroyed from the world,
God's wrath ceases from the world.

Chapter Eleven

11:1–6 *Violations with a Penalty of Strangulation*

11 1 These are the ones who are strangled:
one who strikes his father or his mother;
one who kidnaps[132] a person from Israel;

---

[130] K, P lack "The Holy One Blessed Be He said."
[131] K: "offered upon it…"
[132] Lit. "steals," here and below.

---

the second tithe and holy writings should be hidden: On the second tithe, see note on 1:3 above. According to commentators, the second tithe is hidden rather than left to spoil like the other tithes because the second tithe is normally eaten by the owners themselves rather than by the priests, and therefore by force of habit they might be tempted to dig into the stock.

I will credit you as though you had offered an entire burnt offering before me: This statement creates a wordplay with a root that is used for offering a sacrifice, for crediting, and for the burnt offering. Here R. Simeon imagines God encouraging the court to punish the subverted town.

And it shall remain an everlasting ruin: Deuteronomy 13:17.

Let nothing that has been doomed stick to your hand: Deuteronomy 13:18. The Mishnah means to invoke the continuation of the verse: *in order that the Lord may turn from His blazing anger and show you compassion*.

11:1 *These are the ones who are strangled*: The Mishnah presents the fourth and final list of capital crimes, those punished with strangulation. According to the Mishnah, strangulation is the mode of execution when the Torah does not specify otherwise.

One who strikes his father or his mother: Based on Exodus 21:15.

one who kidnaps a person from Israel: Based on Exodus 21:16 and Deuteronomy 24:7. The purpose of kidnapping is assumed by the Bible and by the Mishnah to be human trafficking. Deuteronomy restricts liability to the capture and sale of fellow Israelites, and the Mishnah follows suit.

an elder who rebels against the court;
a false prophet;
one who prophesies in the name of[133] idolatry;
one who has sexual intercourse with another man's wife;
witnesses who conspire against a priest's daughter;
and the man who sexually possesses her.
One who strikes his father or his mother
is not liable unless he makes a wound in them.
This is more stringent for the one who curses than for the one who strikes,
for the one who curses after death is liable,
but the one who strikes after death is exempt.
One who kidnaps a person from Israel
is not liable unless he brings him into his domain.
R. Judah says:
Unless he brings him into his domain and uses him,
as it is said: *And he enslaved him or sold him.*
One who kidnaps his own son:

[133] Instead of "in the name of," **K, P** have "for the sake of," which differs by only one letter.

an elder who rebels against the court: Based on Deuteronomy 17:8–13, which instructs that a case too difficult for local courts be brought to a high court of referral, whose decision is final. According to Deuteronomy 17:12, anyone who disobeys the high court's decision is put to death. The Mishnah understands this verse to refer not to the litigants but to a judge who decides a case in opposition to the ruling of the high court.

a false prophet; one who prophesies in the name of idolatry: Based on Deuteronomy 18:20–22. According to 1:5 above, the false prophet is judged by a court of seventy-one.

one who has sexual intercourse with another man's wife: i.e. adultery, based on Leviticus 20:10.

witnesses who conspire against a priest's daughter: Deuteronomy 19:19 dictates that a malicious false witness be given the same punishment that he sought to inflict. This mishnah makes an exception for the case of the priest's daughter who commits harlotry (see 9:1 above) who, if found guilty, is punished by burning. Even though technically the false witness in such a case should be burned, this mishnah says that the false witness (as well as the sexual partner involved in a case where she is in fact guilty) should be punished by strangulation (and see 11:6 below). Since the first chapter of tractate *Makkot* deals at length with the laws of conspiring witnesses, this last item in tractate *Sanhedrin* serves as a transition from this tractate to the next; in fact the two were originally one tractate.

is not liable until he makes a wound in them: The Mishnah here restricts the scope of this severe biblical legislation.

the one who curses after death is liable, but the one who strikes after death is exempt: In the Mishnah's view, the parents cannot be physically wounded after they die, and therefore the son or daughter who strikes a dead parent is not liable for execution. Since the parents can still be cursed even after they have died, the son or daughter who curses a dead parent is liable for execution.

is not liable until he brings him into his domain: Midrash bases this restriction on *he is found in his hand* (Exodus 21:16).

unless he brings him into his domain and uses him: It is ambiguous in Exodus but clear in Deuteronomy that enslavement or sale has already taken place. R. Judah's position emphasizes Deuteronomy's formulation. See Deuteronomy 24:7.

One who kidnaps his own son: The Talmudim offer an exegetical basis for the two positions. According to the Yerushalmi, R. Yohanan b. Beroqa reads *from the children of Israel* (Deuteronomy 24:7) to include one's own son within the scope of liability, while the Sages read *his fellow* (Deuteronomy 24:7) to exclude him.

R. Ishmael the son of R. Yohanan b. Beroqa[134] deems him liable,
but the Sages deem him exempt.
If he kidnapped someone who is half-slave and half-free,
R. Judah[135] deems him liable,
but the Sages deem him exempt.

2 An elder who rebels against the court,
as it is said: *If a case is too baffling for you to decide*, etc.
There were three courts:
one sitting at the entrance to the Temple Mount,
and one sitting at the entrance to the Temple precinct,
and one sitting in the Chamber of Hewn Stone.
They come to the one that is at the entrance to the Temple Mount
and he says: "Thus did I interpret and thus interpreted my colleagues; thus did I teach and thus taught my colleagues."
If they had a tradition, they say it to them.
But if not, they come to those at the entrance to the Temple precinct,
and he says: "Thus did I interpret and thus interpreted my colleagues; thus did I teach and thus taught my colleagues."
If they had a tradition, they say it to them.

---

[134] **K, P** lack "R. Ishmael son of."
[135] **P**: "R. Yohanan b. Beroqa." **P** places the section on the half-free/half-slave victim in the margins rather than in the body of the text.

According to the Bavli, the Sages read *if a man is found to have kidnapped* (Deuteronomy 24:7) to exclude a person who is commonly found [in the proximity of the kidnapper], such as one's own son.

If he kidnapped someone who is half-slave and half-free: R. Judah deems him liable, but the Sages deem him exempt: According to the Yerushalmi, R. Judah reads "his fellow" (Deuteronomy 24:7) to include within the scope of liability even a "part-fellow," that is to say, even a partially free man, while the Sages read "his fellow" to include only a "full-fellow," that is to say, only a fully free man. It is reasonable to infer, as the Bavli does, that according to all opinions a "full" slave is not within the scope of liability for kidnapping.

11:2 *If a case is too baffling*: Deuteronomy 17:8.

There were three courts: This Mishnah shifts to the past tense to describe the Temple judiciary, thus returning full circle to the theme of chapter 1, the structure of the judiciary. Like the rabbinic judiciary described in chapter 1, the Temple judiciary consisted of three courts of ascending gravitas, though that gravitas was linked not to the number of judges, as it for the rabbinic courts, but to their location within the Temple. A parallel describes a court at the *Hel* (see *Middot* 1:5). The parallel also describes the promotion of judges from the local courts to the court at the *Hel* up to the "Supreme Court" in the Chamber of Hewn Stone, which reportedly sat from morning until afternoon and on Sabbaths and festivals. According to a parallel tradition in the Talmud, the court in the Chamber of Hewn Stone had seventy-one judges, while the courts at the Temple Mount and Temple precinct each had twenty-three, matched by twenty-three-judge courts in every town in Israel. According to this reconstruction (imbued with a strong nostalgia for a past it characterizes as one of unity and clear lines of authority), a difficult case would first go to the local court, then to the court in the neighboring town, and then to the three highest Temple Courts. The historicity of these courts, like the history of the Sanhedrin itself, is highly debatable.

the entrance to the Temple Mount: See *Middot* 2:1–4.

the entrance to the Temple precinct: See *Middot* 2:5–6.

But if not, these and those come to the high court in the Chamber of Hewn Stone
from which Torah goes out to all of Israel,
as it is said: *From that place that the Lord will choose.*
If he returned to his town, and he again taught in the way that he had taught, he is exempt.
But if he instructed action he is liable,
as it is said: *Should a man act presumptuously*—
He is not liable unless he instructs action.
A disciple who instructed action
is exempt;
his stringency proves to be his leniency.

3 There is greater stringency regarding the words of the scribes
than regarding the words of the Torah.
One who says there is no *tefillin*, in order to transgress the words of the Torah,
is exempt.

---

the Chamber of Hewn Stone: See *Middot* 5:3–4, which describes a court in the Chamber of Hewn Stone, though that court's role is represented as being the examination of priests for disqualifications from service. *Pe'ah* 2:6 and *Eduyot* 7:4 describe questions being brought to a court in the Chamber of Hewn Stone.

they come: In a parallel version, "he and the instructing judge among them" come to the court at the Temple Mount.

If they had a tradition, they say it to them: According to a position in the Talmud, a judge is liable as a rebellious elder only when he represents his decision as a matter of his own opinion and the high court represents their opinion as received tradition. Another position expands the liability, however, to include even the reverse, where the high court's position is based on opinion, while the dissenting judge's position is based on tradition.

From that place that the Lord will choose: Deuteronomy 17:10. The Mishnah identifies the unnamed site in Deuteronomy with the Second Temple.

But if he instructed action he is liable: Instructing action is contrasted with merely teaching; the judge is liable as a rebellious elder only for the former.

Should a man act presumptuously: Deuteronomy 17:12. The emphasis is on the word "act." While the verse's concern is the litigant's action, the Mishnah's reading applies the verse to the local judge's instruction of action.

his stringency proves to be his leniency: Since a disciple is not yet authorized to instruct, his instruction cannot make him liable for this violation. Thus "his stringency," his lack of authorization to instruct, becomes "his leniency," his exemption for the death penalty.

11:3 *regarding the words of the scribes than regarding the words of the Torah*: "Words of the scribes" refers to pre- and protorabbinic rulings and appears a number of times in Mishnah and Tosefta partnered with "words of the Torah." The words of the scribes carry a greater stringency probably because they are considered more vulnerable to dispute or neglect and their observance hinges on respect for rabbinic authority.

One who says there is no tefillin: Tefillin is an ironic example of "words of the Torah" since the biblical verses in question (Exodus 13:9, 16; Deuteronomy 6:8, 11:18) must be creatively interpreted in order to arrive at the practice of donning *tefillin*. Similar examples of efforts to uproot the Torah's law are given in *Horayot* 1:3.

in order to transgress the words of the Torah, is exempt: An instruction that baldly negates a commandment considered explicit in the Torah does not constitute a rebellion against the high court's authority.

[One who says there are] five *tefillin* sections, in order to add to the words of the scribes, is liable.

4 One executes him neither in the court in his town nor in the court in Yavneh;
rather, one takes him up to the high court in Jerusalem,
and keeps guard over him until the festival,
and executes him on the festival,
as it is said: *All the people will hear and be afraid and will not act presumptuously again*—
the words of R. Aqiva.
R. Judah says:
One does not delay the case of this person;
rather, one executes him immediately,
and writes and sends out messengers to[136] all the places:
"Person so-and-so son of Person so-and-so was sentenced to execution by the court."

5 The false prophet:
one[137] who prophesies about what he has not heard or what was not said to him:
His death is by the hands of man.[138]

[136] Lit. "in."   [137] K, P: "The false prophet *and* the one who prophesies..."
[138] K, P lack "His death is by the hands of man."

[One who says there are] five tefillin sections in order to add to the words of the scribes, is liable: This refers to the text compartments of the *tefillin* case for the head. Tradition established that there should be four such compartments, one for each of the verses where *tefillin* are said to be commanded. A judge who instructs people to make five compartments would be liable for the death penalty as a rebellious elder. The Talmudim discuss whether liability lies specifically in adding to the words of the scribes or simply in any amendment. One position in the Talmud understands *tefillin* to be the only case to which the law of the rebellious elder pertains.

11:4 *nor in the court in Yavneh*: The mention of the court in Yavneh confuses the chronological setting, which so far has been in the Second Temple past, since Yavneh represents the location of the rabbinic movement after the Second Temple was destroyed. Commentators struggled to understand this reference, which seems to involve the retrojection of a Yavneh court into the Second Temple period.

But one takes him up to the high court in Jerusalem: The execution procedure mimics the judicial procedure, both of which culminate in the high court in Jerusalem. As in the previous mishnah and the first chapter of the tractate, the courts are presented as a set of three with ascending gravitas (the local court; the Yavneh court; the high court in Jerusalem).

keeps guard over him until the festival…executes him on the festival: The execution is delayed until the festival and performed in Jerusalem so that the maximum number of people will witness it.

All the people will hear and be afraid: Deuteronomy 17:13. The execution functions as a public deterrent.

writes and sends out messengers in all the places: According to midrash, the crux of the debate is how to read *all the people will hear and be afraid* in Deuteronomy 17:13. The root of "be afraid" is similar to the root of "see," and R. Judah's argument is that R. Aqiva has confused the two—it is not seeing the execution but hearing about it that Deuteronomy directs. R. Judah therefore proposes that messengers deliver news of the execution, and he prohibits any delay in the execution.

11:5 *one who prophesies about what he has not heard or what was not said to him*: The Mishnah's description of the false prophet is based on Deuteronomy 18:20. According to commentators on the Mishnah, "what he has not heard" refers to a completely fabricated prophecy, while "what was not said to him" refers to a prophecy that was given to someone else but which the false prophet claims to be his own. Other sources link the descriptions to specific biblical exemplars: *One who prophesies about what he has not heard* is exemplified by Zedekiah son of Kenaanah (1 Kings 22), and *one who prophesies about what was not said to him* is exemplified by Hananiah son of Azzur, Jeremiah's opponent (Jeremiah 28).

His death is by the hands of man: i.e. judicial execution.

But one who suppresses his prophecy,
one who ignores the words of the prophet,
and a prophet who transgresses his own words:
His death is by the hands of heaven,
as it is said: *I myself will call him to account.*

6 One who prophesies in the name of idolatry and says, "Thus said idolatry":
Even if he conformed with the law so as to declare impure the impure or to declare pure the pure.
One who has sexual intercourse with another man's wife:
once she entered the domain of the husband in marriage,
even if she was not sexually possessed,
one who has sexual intercourse with her:
in such cases [he dies] by strangulation.
And the witnesses who conspire against a priest's daughter
and the man who sexually possesses her:
For all conspiring witnesses may anticipate the same execution method [they sought to inflict]
except for witnesses who conspire against a priest's daughter and the man who sexually possesses her.

But the one who suppresses his prophecy: This category and the next two (another source adds a fourth, "one who changes his prophecy") are based on the first half of Deuteronomy 18:19, *And if anybody fails to heed the words he speaks in My name*. The biblical exemplar provided by other sources for "one who suppresses his prophecy" is Jonah.

one who ignores the words of the prophet: According to the Talmud, a biblical example of a person ignoring the words of a prophet can be found in 1 Kings 20:35–36.

a prophet who transgresses his own words: The biblical exemplar is the prophet described in 1 Kings 13, who was identified by later tradition as Ido.

His death is by the hands of heaven: See note on "death by the hands of heaven" in 9:6 above.

I myself will call him to account: Deuteronomy 18:19. The Mishnah takes this to mean that the human court should not act because God Himself will "execute" the offender.

11:6 *One who prophesies in the name of idolatry*: Based on Deuteronomy 18:20.

"Thus said idolatry": Whereas 7:6 above deals with a person who worships other gods, and 7:10 deals with a person who entices people to worship other gods, this mishnah deals with someone who prophesies in the name of other gods.

so as to declare impure the impure or to declare pure the pure: A person is liable for prophesying in the name of idolatry even if the substance of the prophecy is in accordance with God's law.

in such cases [he dies] by strangulation: Sexual intercourse with another man's wife is considered adultery even if the marriage in question has not yet been consummated.

for all conspiring witnesses may anticipate the same execution method: Based on Deuteronomy 19:19.

except for witnesses who conspire against a priest's daughter and the man who sexually possesses her: Midrash bases these exceptions—that the sexual partner and the conspiring witnesses are not burned as the priest's daughter is—on the word "she" in *it is her father whom she defiles; she shall be put to the fire* (Leviticus 21:9). "She," and not her sexual partner, "she," and not her conspiring witnesses, is to be burned.

Tractate Makkot

David C. Flatto

Introduction

Overview

Tractate *Makkot* (lit. "floggings") is named after a specific form of punishment—the corporal punishment of lashes (also referred to as *malkot*)—which is administered to violators of numerous Torah prohibitions. This punishment is referred to in 1:1–3, and elaborated upon in detail in the third chapter. More generally, the subject of punishments spans the latter half of the previous tractate, *Sanhedrin* (chapters 6–11), and continues throughout this tractate, with successive sections delineating the regulations pertaining to each form of punishment. The same literary formula ("These are the ones [that are punished with punishment X]...") is used to mark the opening of each section (see *Sanhedrin* 7:4, 9:1, 11:1 and *Makkot* 2:1 and 3:1). There are additional continuities between these two tractates: *Sanhedrin* 11:6 (the last mishnah in the tractate) discusses perjured witnesses who cannot be punished in a talionic manner (measure for measure), which directly segues into the subject matter of *Makkot* 1:1; *Sanhedrin* 4–5 records rules of testimony that are also analyzed in *Makkot* 1; and *Makkot* 1:10 delineates the jurisdiction of the Sanhedrin. In fact, in the Kaufman, Parma, and Cambridge Mishnah manuscripts these constitute a single tractate (i.e. the three chapters of *Makkot* comprise the final chapters of tractate *Sanhedrin*, which consists in total of fourteen chapters devoted to courts, witnesses, and punishments).

Structure, Organization, and Main Ideas of the Tractate

Tractate *Makkot* is composed of three chapters, each largely devoted to a discrete topic.

Chapter 1: In biblical and rabbinic jurisprudence, oral testimony constitutes the leading form of evidence, and is ordinarily afforded absolute credibility when admitted by the court (a confession, by contrast, is explicitly disqualified according to later rabbinic sources). Certain regulations are specified in this chapter regarding the impact and responsibility of each of the witnesses within a set; the requirement that the witnesses warn the perpetrator in advance of a transgression; and (arguable) differences between witnesses in monetary and capital cases.

The centrality of oral testimony in rabbinic jurisprudence helps explain the heightened focus in rabbinic literature on the topic of *hazamah*, perjury. Conferring absolute credibility on the oral testimony of witnesses poses a substantial risk of perjury. Accordingly, the Mishnah codifies the biblical rule that perjured testimony is not just invalidated, but punished harshly with a talionic form of punishment; if this is impossible, then , lashes.

According to tractate *Makkot*, a charge of perjury can only be made by a second set of respondent witnesses who present a specific kind of testimony against the first set of witnesses (see 1:4). Limiting the rule of perjury in this manner may be due to a concern that the first set of witnesses be punished only if they are lying, rather than if they are mistaken. In any event, why the second set of respondent witnesses should be believed rather than the first set of witnesses, is not obvious. The Talmud remarks that the rule of perjury is a novelty.

At the conclusion of the first chapter (1:10) the Mishnah describes the leniency of rabbinic courts in enforcing capital punishment (in contrast with the stringency of biblical law). This striking passage calls into question whether rabbinic penology can function effectively on a practical level (or whether it was ever intended to function in such a manner).

Chapter 2: Only an accidental killer must go into exile to a refuge city as a penalty, as opposed to an intentional murderer who is subject to capital punishment (2:6). Rabbinic jurisprudence also evidently operates with a third, subordinate, category of an unaware or involuntary killer who is not even required to go into exile to a refuge city. The specific rulings recorded throughout the chapter, which distinguish cases where exile is required from those where it is not, however, do not overtly depend on whether a killing is accidental or not. Instead, the Mishnah lists various exemptions from exile that are based on scriptural hermeneutics, without disclosing a reason for each exemption (see annotation on 2:1).

Chapter 3: Although Scripture does not specify when penal lashes are to be administered, according to rabbinic interpretation they constitute the default punishment for the violation of most prohibitions recorded in the Torah, including many prohibitions with an unspecified punishment. In all, Maimonides enumerates 207 prohibitions that are punishable by lashes. According to this calculation, the list of around fifty prohibitions recorded in this mishnaic chapter is not exhaustive, notwithstanding the sweeping formulation of 3:1 ("And these are the ones who are lashed…"). Indeed, classic commentators understand the Mishnah's list to be not exhaustive, but selective, focused upon a subset of novel cases.

Relationship to Scripture

Chapter 1: The prohibition of perjury is enumerated in the Decalogue. See Exodus 20:16 and Deuteronomy 5:17. The punishment for perjury is recorded in Deuteronomy 19:16–21. The plain sense of the verses arguably refers to a single perjuring witness, who is challenged by the person whom he is trying to frame. The judges examine the witness to ascertain whether he is honest or a perjurer. When an inconsistency is found in his testimony, he is declared to be a perjurer. According to our Mishnah, however, a charge of perjury requires a second set of witnesses who provide ad hominem testimony against the first set.

Chapter 2: Although several biblical passages form the basis of the Mishnah's treatment of the laws of an accidental killer (Exodus 21:12–14, Numbers 35:9–34, Deuteronomy 4:41–43 and 19:1–13, and Joshua 20:1–9), the Mishnah conceptualizes these laws in a novel manner. Whereas in the Bible the cities of refuge offer a safe haven to the accidental killer where he or she can escape the vengeance of the avenger of blood (and perhaps gain atonement), in the Mishnah their role is to serve as a remote destination where the killer is banished as a punishment. Understood in this way, the laws of exile fit alongside the other punishments delineated in the latter half of *Sanhedrin* and *Makkot*.

Chapter 3: The administration of lashes is recorded in a single passage in the Torah, Deuteronomy 25:2–3, where the underlying offense is unspecified. Rabbinic tradition, however, interprets this as the standard punishment for most Torah prohibitions, as described above.

Special Notes for the Reader

In writing the annotation, I have consulted the classical sources and the medieval commentators, as well as Hanoch Albeck's Mishnah commentary. I have profited from the scholarship of Aharon Shemesh, Shlomo Naeh, Shamma Friedman, David Henshke, and Devora Steinmetz.

Tractate Makkot

Chapter One

1:1–3 *The Punishment of Witnesses Found to Be Perjurers*

I How do witnesses become [liable as] perjurers?
[If the witnesses falsely declare:]
"We testify that so-and-so is the son of a divorcee"
or "The son of a released woman"—
We do not state that he shall instead be treated like a son of a divorcee
or a son of a released woman,
but rather he is to receive forty lashes.
[If the witnesses falsely declare:]
"We testify that so-and-so is obligated to go into exile"—
we do not state that he shall instead go into exile,
but rather he is to receive forty lashes.
[If the witnesses falsely declare:]
"We testify that so-and-so divorced his wife but has not paid her *ketubbah*"—

1:1 *perjurers*: The basis of this law is Deuteronomy 19:19, which delineates a talionic form of punishment: the perjurers are punished measure for measure. The Rabbis construe the verse as referring to perjury that was exposed by a second set of witnesses. See 1:4. The Mishnah addresses the kind of punishment perjurers receive in cases where a talionic form of punishment is impossible or inapplicable. This Mishnah continues the topic of *Sanhedrin* 11:6.

so-and-so: Who is a priest.

"*the son of a divorcee*": A priest may not marry a divorcee. See Leviticus 21:7. The progeny of such a union does not have the sacred status of a priest.

"*a released woman*": Heb. *halutsah*; a childless woman whose husband has died retains a levirate tie to her husband's brother. The latter may sever this tie through a *halitsah* ceremony. See Deuteronomy 25:5–10. Under rabbinic law, she has the same legal status as a divorcee.

forty lashes: The standard penalty for violating a Torah prohibition, in this case, perjury. See 1:3 and 3:10; Deuteronomy 25:2–3.

"*exile*": The penalty for an accidental homicide (chapter 2).

ketubbah: the financial obligation imposed by a *ketubbah*, a marriage contract. The contract obligates the husband or husband's estate to pay a base amount of two hundred *zuz* to his wife when he divorces or predeceases her. If the wife predeceases her husband, there is no financial obligation (the husband inherits the *ketubbah*). See *Ketubbot*.

even though today or tomorrow he will ultimately pay her *ketubbah*—
[nevertheless]
we estimate how much a person is willing to pay for her *ketubbah*,
[knowing that he will receive payment only] in case she becomes widowed or divorced,
but if she dies, her husband will inherit it.
[If the witnesses falsely declare:]
"We testify that so-and-so owes his fellow one thousand *zuz*,
on condition that he will repay him within thirty days,"
but he says [the condition is that he will repay him] within ten years—
we estimate how much a person is willing to pay[1]
in order that he will have in hand one thousand *zuz*,
[the difference] between repaying within thirty days and repaying within ten years.

2 [If the witnesses falsely declare:]
"We testify that so-and-so owes his fellow two hundred *zuz*,"
and they are found to be perjurers—
they are flogged and must pay
since the category[2] for which he incurs a flogging
is not the same as the one for which he incurs a payment—
the words of R. Meir.
But the Sages say:
All those who pay are not flogged.

3 [If the witnesses falsely declare:]
"We testify that so-and-so is liable [to be flogged] with forty lashes,"
and they are found to be perjurers—
they are flogged with eighty [lashes],
on account of[3] *You shall not bear false witness against your neighbor*,
and on account of[4] *You shall do to him as he schemed to do to his fellow*—
the words of R. Meir.
But the Sages say:
They are only flogged with forty [lashes].

---

[1] K lacks "to pay."   [2] Lit. "the name."
[3] K, P: "due to the category of."   [4] K, P: "due to the category of."

---

even though today or tomorrow he the husband *will ultimately pay her ketubbah*: This statement is inaccurate since if she dies first the husband does not pay her *ketubbah*.

we estimate how much a person is willing to pay for her ketubbah: The talionic form of punishment requires the perjurers to pay the amount of which they tried to deprive the husband by their false testimony. That amount is not the face amount of the *ketubbah* (since the husband may need to eventually make such a payment anyway), but instead is calculated based on the present value of the *ketubbah*. Commentators debate whether the perjurers must pay the present value, or the difference between two hundred *zuz* and the present value.

1:2 *the category*: the underlying verse in Scripture.

1:3 *You shall not bear false witness*: Exodus 20:13.

You shall do to him as he schemed to do to his fellow: Deuteronomy 19:19.

One may divide a payment, but not a punishment of flogging.
How so?
If they testified that one owes his fellow two hundred *zuz*,
and[5] they were found to be perjurers—
they divide the payment among themselves,
But if[6] they testified that one is liable to be flogged with forty lashes,
and they were found to be perjurers—
each and every one [of the perjurers] is flogged with forty [lashes].

1:4–6 *The Procedure for Determining Perjury*

4 Witnesses become perjurers only when they themselves are [directly] perjured.[7]
How so?
If the witnesses [falsely] declare:
"We testify that so-and-so murdered a man,"
[and] they respond to them:
"How do you testify [in this manner],
since the victim or the murderer was with us on that day in such-and-such a place?"—
these are not deemed perjurers.
But if they respond to them:
"How do you testify [in this manner],
since you were with us on that day in such and such a place?"—
These are deemed perjurers, and are executed based on their words.[8]

5 If others came and perjured them,
and [still] others came and perjured them,
even a hundred [sets of witnesses]—

---

[5] K lacks "and."   [6] K, P lack "But if."
[7] Alt. "Witnesses only become perjurers when they perjure themselves."   [8] Lit. "their mouths."

One may divide a payment penalty, *but not a punishment of flogging*: Each set of witnesses is comprised of two or more witnesses. See 1:7.

1:4 *Witnesses become perjurers only when they themselves are [directly] perjured*: A foundational principle in the rabbinic rule of perjury: a second set of respondent witnesses must present ad hominem testimony (as specified in the Mishnah's continuation) in order to charge the first set of witnesses with perjury.

"How do you testify [in this manner], since the victim or murderer was with us"…these are not deemed perjurers: Since the testimony of the second set of respondent witnesses is not ad hominem, the rule of perjury will not apply, and the first set of witnesses will not be punished (even though the contradictory testimony of the second set of respondent witnesses negates the testimony of the first set of witnesses).

1:5 The details of the case envisioned by the Mishnah are obscure. Some commentators explain as follows. The first set of witnesses testify that person X is guilty of murder, but a second set perjures that first set (by declaring "you were with us," see 1:4); a third set testifies that person X is guilty of murder, but the second set perjures that set too; a fourth set testifies that person X is guilty of murder, but the second set perjures that set too; and so on—all the sets of witnesses that testify against person X are perjured by the second set. The Mishnah rules that all of these sets of witnesses, who are perjured by the second set, are to be executed

they are all executed.
R. Judah says:
This is a collusion[9] of conspiring factions,
and only the first set of witnesses is executed.

6 Perjured witnesses are executed only [if they are perjured]
after conclusion of the trial [in which they testified].
For the Sadducees say [that perjurers are executed]
only after the [falsely accused] person has been executed,
as it is said: *a life for a life*.
The Sages responded to them:
But it already states, *You shall do to him as he schemed to do to his fellow*,
thus implying that his fellow is [still] alive.
And if so, why does it state, *a life for life*?
Could it be that they are executed the moment
after their [false] testimony has been admitted?
[No.]
Scripture teaches *a life for a life*—
Thus, they are executed only after conclusion of the trial.

---

[9] Text and meaning uncertain.

---

for their false testimony against person X (and person X is not executed). R. Judah demurs, arguing that the second set can be believed to perjure the first set, but not any additional set. Other commentaries offer other explanations.

collusion: The word is *istasis*, here translated "collusion"; it is spelled variously in the printed editions and manuscripts and is of uncertain meaning. The collusion is presumably between the second set of respondent witnesses and the suspect (who is shielded from incriminating testimony by the response of the second set of witnesses against all the subsequent sets of witnesses).

1:6 *after conclusion of the trial [in which they testified]*: According to the Pharisees, the perjurers can only be considered to have schemed against their fellow if their perjured testimony led to a verdict against him. Once a punishment has been meted out, however, the Pharisees maintain (according to the Talmud) that the perjurers can no longer be punished.

conclusion of the trial: The Talmud debates whether the conclusion of the trial refers to the announcement of the verdict or the subsequent instruction to implement the verdict. According to both opinions it precedes the actual implementation. See *Sanhedrin* 6:1.

Sadducees: Second Temple sectarian opponents of the Pharisees, who argued on various legal matters with the Pharisees. See *Yadayim* 4:6–8.

a life for a life: Exodus 21:23, cf. Deuteronomy 19:21.

You shall do to him as he schemed to do to his fellow: Deuteronomy 19:19.

the moment after their [false] testimony has been admitted: Which precedes the conclusion of the trial.

Thus, they are executed only after conclusion of the trial: Evidently, once the trial has been concluded with a verdict against the suspect that they framed, it is as if the suspect's life has been forfeited.

1:7–9　*Multiple Witnesses in a Set*

7 *A person shall be put to death on the testimony of two witnesses or three witnesses*—
if the testimony is valid with two [witnesses], why does Scripture specify three [witnesses]?
In order to link three [witnesses] to two [witnesses]:
just as three [witnesses] can incriminate two [witnesses] as perjurers,
so too two [witnesses] can incriminate three [witnesses] as perjurers.
And how do we know that [this is so] even [with] a hundred [witnesses]?
Scripture teaches *witnesses*.
R. Simeon says:
Just as two [witnesses] are executed only if both [witnesses] are perjurers,
so too three [witnesses] are executed only if all three [witnesses] are perjurers.
And how do we know that [this is so] even [with] a hundred [witnesses]?
Scripture teaches *witnesses*.
R. Aqiva says:
The third [witness] comes [in the biblical verse only to teach
that he is] to be treated stringently,
and to make his legal punishment the same as the others.[10]
And if Scripture thus punishes as a transgressor
one who attaches himself to those who are transgressors,
all the more so[11] will it reward as meritorious
one who attaches himself to those who are meritorious.[12]

8 Just as [in the case of] two [witnesses],
if one of them is found to be a relative or disqualified—
their testimony is nullified,

---

[10] Or "and to equate how he is regulated to the way others are treated."　　[11] **K, P**: "all the more."
[12] Lit. "…as performers of commandments…those who perform commandments"; **K** and **P** change to singular.

1:7 *A person shall be put to death*: Deuteronomy 17:6, cf. 19:15.

And how do we know…: How do we know that two witnesses can incriminate even a hundred witnesses as perjurers?

witnesses: Deuteronomy 17:6.

only if both [witnesses] are perjurers: As defined in 1:4.

And how do we know that [this is so] even [with] a hundred [witnesses]? How do we know that even a hundred witnesses are not executed until all hundred are found to be perjurers?

R. Aqiva says: Most commentators assume that R. Aqiva agrees with R. Simeon; a minority position contends that they are in dispute.

The third [witness] comes: The third witness will also be punished as a perjurer.

1:8 *a relative*: See *Sanhedrin* 3:4.

disqualified: See *Sanhedrin* 3:3.

nullified: The joint testimony of this set of witnesses is impeached if one witness within the set is found to be a relative or disqualified.

So too [in the case of] three [witnesses],
if one of them is found to be a relative or disqualified—
their testimony is nullified.[13] How do we know that [this is so] even [with] a hundred [witnesses]?
Scripture teaches *witnesses*.
R. Yose says:
When are the [above] teachings applicable?
In capital trials,
but in monetary trials,
the testimony is valid on the basis of the remainder [of eligible witnesses].
Rabbi says:
The law is one and the same whether in monetary trials or capital trials—
when [the witnesses] warned [the perpetrators].
However, when they did not warn them,
what should two brothers do who saw one[14] who murdered a person?

9 If two [witnesses] saw [the perpetrator] from this window,
and another two [witnesses] saw him from that window,
and one warned him from the middle—
if some among them can see one another,
they are considered a single testimony.
Otherwise,
they are considered two testimonies.
Therefore, if one [set] of them is found to be perjurers—

---

[13] This line ("So…nullified") is missing from **K**. [14] **K**: "at once."

---

witnesses: Deuteronomy 17:6.

When are the [above] teachings applicable? In capital trials: Rashi explains this as a special leniency that is invoked to protect defendants in capital trials.

whether in monetary trials or capital trials: In both, the joint testimony is nullified if one witness within the set is found to be a relative or disqualified.

when [the witnesses] warned [the perpetrators]: This line seems to qualify the rule in the first part of this mishnah, only the witnesses who warn a perpetrator constitute members of a single set, such that their joint testimony is nullified if one witness within the set is found to be a relative or disqualified.

warned them: Rabbinic law requires witnesses to issue an advance warning to a perpetrator about to commit a prohibited act. See 3:7 and *Sanhedrin* 5:1. Otherwise, the perpetrator cannot be punished in court (in cases of capital or corporal punishment).

what should two brothers do who saw one who murdered a person? Without the qualification(s) cited above for identifying the witnesses who constitute members of a single set, any time a pair of family members witnesses a crime all eyewitness testimony would automatically be impeached (since two witnesses to the crime are relatives to one another).

1:9 *they are considered a single testimony*: The witnesses in both windows constitute members of a single set that offers a single testimony.

they are considered two testimonies: The witnesses in each window constitute members of discrete sets. The two sets offer discrete testimonies. The ramification of this bifurcation is explained in the continuation of the mishnah.

[the perpetrator] and [the perjurers] are executed,
but the second [set] is exempt.
R. Yose[15] says:
[The perpetrator] is never executed,
unless he is orally[16] warned by his two witnesses,
as it is said: *on the testimony of two witnesses*
Another interpretation:
on the testimony of two witnesses—
[this teaches] that a Sanhedrin may not hear [testimony] through[17] a translator.

1:10 *The Finality of a Court Verdict; the Jurisdiction and Practice of a Sanhedrin*

10 One whose trial has concluded [with an adverse judgment],
and who has then escaped, and now appears before the same court—
they may not repeal his judgment.[18]
Any[19] place where two [witnesses] stand and proclaim:
"We testify concerning so-and-so,[20] that his trial has concluded [with an adverse judgment]
in the court of so-and-so, and so-and-so were his [opposing] witnesses"—
he is to be executed.
A Sanhedrin has jurisdiction in the Land [of Israel] and outside the Land [of Israel].
A Sanhedrin that executes [a perpetrator] once every seven years is called destructive.
R. Elazazar b. Azariah says:
Once in seventy years.

---

[15] K, P: "R. Yose b. Judah."   [16] P lacks "orally."
[17] Lit. "from the mouth of a translator"; K: "as if from the mouth of a translator."
[18] Alt. "trial."   [19] K: "In any place."   [20] K lacks "so-and-so."

[the perpetrator] and [the perjurers] are executed: The perpetrator is executed as a murderer (based on the valid testimony of the second set of witnesses); the perjurers, who schemed to frame a suspect with a murder charge (notwithstanding the fact that he incidentally was a murderer), are executed.

but the second [set] is exempt: their testimony that the perpetrator committed murder is valid.

orally warned by his two witnesses: R. Yose disputes the above position that validates the warning from an individual standing in the middle.

on the testimony of two witnesses: Deuteronomy 17:6.

a Sanhedrin: The term can refer to the high court, or an intermediate capital court. See *Sanhedrin* 1:6.

1:10 *One whose trial has concluded*: See 1:6.

and who has then escaped: In order to avert the implementation of the adverse judgment.

they may not repeal his judgment: This is a kind of *res judicata* rule. Contrast this with the conditions for repealing judgment specified in *Sanhedrin* 3:8.

place: Court.

R. Tarfon and R. Aqiva say:
If we had been members of a Sanhedrin, nobody would have ever been executed.[21]
Rabban Simeon b. Gamaliel says:
They would have also multiplied the number of murderers in Israel.

Chapter Two

2:1–3 Who Is Obligated to Go into Exile

2 These[22] are the ones who go into exile:
one who kills someone by accident.
If one was rolling [the roof] with a roller,
and it fell upon another and killed him;
[or] if one was lowering a barrel,
and it fell upon another and killed him;
[or] if one was descending a ladder,
and fell upon another and killed him—
in these cases, he goes into exile.
However, if one was pulling up a roller,
and it fell upon another and killed him;
[or] if one was drawing up a barrel, and the rope snapped,
and it fell upon another and killed him;
[or] if one was ascending a ladder,
and fell upon another and killed him—
in these cases, he does not go into exile.
This is the general rule:
Whenever [a person causes a death] in his downward motion,[23]
he goes into exile,
And when it is not in his downward motion,
he does not go into exile.
If the iron blade slips from the handle,[24] and kills [another]—

[21] **K, P** add "within it" (i.e. within its proceedings). [22] **K** adds "And."
[23] According to the punctuation of **K, P**: "whenever [an object causes a death] while being lowered."
[24] **K**: "from its barrel," **P**: "from its mount."

2:1 *exile*: To the cities of refuge described in 2:4.

lowering: By a rope.

if one was descending a ladder, and fell upon another: Here the person, rather than an object, falls directly on the victim and kills him.

This is the general rule: Throughout 2:1–3, the Mishnah lists various exemptions from exile that are rooted in scriptural hermeneutics. Here the Mishnah articulates a broader principle, which seems to be animated by a legal rationale.

If the iron blade slips from the handle: The debate between Rabbi and the Sages, in this case and the next, revolves around their different interpretations of the verse: *the ax flies off the wood* (Deuteronomy 19:5).

Rabbi says:
He does not go into exile.
But the Sages say:
He goes into exile.
From the tree that is being chopped—
Rabbi says:
He goes into exile.
But the Sages say:
He does not go into exile.

2 One who throws a stone into a public domain and kills [another]—
in this case, he goes into exile.
R. Eliezer b. Jacob says:
If after the stone was released from his hand,
the other stuck out his head and was struck,
in this case, he is exempt.
One who threw a stone into his own courtyard and killed [another]—
if the victim has permission to enter there,
he goes into exile.
But if not, he does not go into exile.
As it is said: *when a man goes with his neighbor into a forest*—
just as in the forest both the victim and the assailant have permission to enter there—
this excludes the courtyard of a householder,
where the victim and the assailant[25] do not [equally] have permission to enter there.
Abba Saul says:
Just as chopping wood is a voluntary act—
this excludes a father who strikes his son,
and a master who beats his pupil,
and an agent of the court.

3 A father goes into exile because of[26] his son,
and a son goes into exile[27] because of his father.

[25] K, P lack "and the assailant."   [26] Alt. "on account of."   [27] P lacks "goes into exile."

From the tree that is being chopped: The iron blade was loosened upon impact with the tree that was being chopped, and the blade flew off and killed somebody. Alternatively, a wood splinter flew off from the tree that was being chopped and killed somebody.

2:2 *when a man goes with his neighbor into a forest*: Deuteronomy 19:5.

the victim and the assailant: Lit. "the injured and the injurer." The formulation may be borrowed from the tort context.

the victim and the assailant do not [equally] have permission: where the victim does not have permission to enter. The alternative reading of K and P is preferable.

this excludes a father...and a master: Since their actions are obligatory.

an agent of the court: Who delivers lashes. See 3:12. The Tosefta distinguishes between an agent who lashes with permission of the court (who goes into exile) and one who lashes without permission (who does not).

2:3 *because of*: Due to the accidental killing of.

A father goes into exile because of his son: If this teaching is consistent with Abba Saul's teaching in 2:2, we must assume that this mishnah refers to a father who accidentally kills his son, while not in the course of disciplining him.

All go into exile because of an Israelite,
and an Israelite goes into exile because of them,
except because of a resident alien.
And a resident alien does not go into exile,
except because of a resident alien.
A blind person does not go into exile—
the words of R. Judah.
R. Meir says:
He does go into exile.
An enemy does not go into exile.
R. Yose b. R. Judah says:
An enemy is executed, because he is like an habitual danger.
R. Simeon says:
There is an enemy who goes into exile,
and there is an enemy who does not go into exile.
This is the general rule:[28]
When it can be said that he killed knowingly,[29]
he does not go into exile,
but when he killed unknowingly,
in these cases, he goes into exile.

2:4–8 *Cities of Refuge*

4 To where does one go into exile?
To cities[30] of refuge.
To the three that are beyond the Jordan, and to the three that are in the land of Canaan,
as it is said: *Three cities you shall designate beyond the Jordan,*
and three cities you shall designate in the land of Canaan, etc.
Before the three in the Land of Israel were chosen,
the three beyond the Jordan did not provide refuge,

[28] **K, P** lack "This is the general rule."   [29] Alt. "intentionally and unintentionally."
[30] **K**: "city."

a resident alien: According to one opinion in the Talmud, this is a gentile who resides in the Land of Israel and accepts upon himself or herself the seven Noachide laws.

except because of a resident alien: An alternative recension reads, "except a resident alien," in which case this line refers to a resident alien who kills by accident, rather than one who is a victim of an accidental killing.

A blind person: See *Megillah* 4:6.

An enemy: Defined as one who does not speak to another person out of hatred for three (consecutive) days. See *Sanhedrin* 3:5.

An enemy does not go into exile: The Tosefta adds that an enemy is also not punished as an intentional murderer either—unless there are witnesses and he or she was duly warned.

R. Yose b. R. Judah…danger: He is treated like an intentional murderer that is subject to capital punishment.

2:4 *beyond the Jordan*: The Transjordan, a region east of the Jordan river settled by two and a half of the twelve tribes of Israel. See Numbers 32.

Three cities you shall designate beyond the Jordan: Numbers 35:14.

as it is said: *There shall be six cities of refuge*,
on condition³¹ that all six provide refuge at once.

5 And pathways were directed to them, from one to the other,
as it is said: *You shall prepare the pathway, and divide into three parts*, etc.
And they provide them³² two disciples of the Sages,
lest he kill him on the way,
and they will speak to him.
R. Meir says:
He too³³ may speak for himself,
As it is said: *And this is the matter of the manslayer.*³⁴

6 R. Yose b. Judah says:
Initially, both an accidental and an intentional [killer]
would go immediately to the cities of refuge,³⁵
and the court would [then] send and summon him³⁶ from there.
One who is condemned to capital punishment by the court³⁷—
they execute him;
but one who is not condemned to capital punishment—
they release him.
one who is condemned to exile—
they return him to his place,
As it is said: *And the assembly shall restore him to his city of refuge*, etc.
The [high priest] anointed with the oil of anointment,
and the one with many garments,

---

[31] K lacks "on condition." [32] K, P: "provide him." [33] K lacks "too."
[34] Alt. "murderer." [35] K: "city." [36] K, P: "them." [37] K, P lack "by the court."

There shall be six cities of refuge: Numbers 35:13.

2:5 *You shall prepare the pathway*: Deuteronomy 19:3.

And they: Judges of the court.

provide them: To the accidental killers.

lest he kill him on the way: Lest the avenger of blood kill the accidental killer.

they will speak to him: Two disciples of the Sages accompany the accidental killer on his journey to the city of refuge in order to dissuade the avenger of blood from killing the accidental killer.

He too may speak for himself: **K** (and other sources) omit the word 'too,' suggesting that the accidental killer does not need the accompaniment of two scholars.

And this is the matter (Heb. *davar*, which can mean "matter" or "word") *of the manslayer*: Deuteronomy 19:4.

2:6 *Initially, both an accidental and an intentional [killer]...*: See Numbers 35:11–12, 15–34.

One who is condemned to capital punishment by the court—they execute him: See *Sanhedrin* 9:1.

to his place: The refuge city that he immediately went to after the accidental killing.

And the assembly shall restore him to his city of refuge: Numbers 35:25.

The [high priest]: These all have the status of a high priest; see *Horayot* 3:4.

the one with many garments: See *Yoma* 7:5.

and the one who passed from his anointment—
the law is one and the same:
[by their death] they return the murderer [to his home].[38]
R. Judah says:
Even the [high priest] anointed for battle returns the murderer [to his home].
Therefore, the mothers of the [high] priests would supply them with sustenance[39] and clothing,
in order that they should not pray that their sons should die.
If the high priest dies after his trial has concluded,
in that case he does not go into exile.
[But] if the high priest dies before his trial has concluded,
and they appoint another [high priest] in his stead,
and afterwards his trial concludes—
he returns [to his home] upon the death of the second [high priest].

7 If his trial concludes when there is no high priest,
[or] if one kills a high priest,
or if a high priest killed—
he may never leave from [the refuge city].
Nor may he leave
for compulsory[40] testimony;
nor for testimony concerning monetary matters;
nor for testimony concerning capital matters.
And even if the Israelites need him,
and even if he is a military commander of Israel such as Joab b. Zeruiah—
he may never leave from there.
As it is said, *there, to which he fled*—
there shall be his dwelling,
there shall be his death,
there shall be his burial.
Just as the city grants refuge,
So too its boundary grants refuge.

[38] **K, P** lack this line.   [39] Alt. "a livelihood."   [40] Alt. "religious."

the one who passed from his anointment: The priest who temporarily replaced the high priest when he became impure. See *Yoma* 1:1.

the [priest] anointed for battle: Deuteronomy 20:1–9 and *Sotah* 8:1.

trial has concluded: See 1:6.

2:7 *compulsory testimony*: See Leviticus 5:1. Alternatively, this refers to religious testimony, such as testimony relating to the lunar calendar. See *Rosh Hashanah* 1:9.

And even if the Israelites need him: Similar formulation in *Yoma* 7:5.

Joab b. Zeruiah: The military commander under King David. See 2 Samuel 8:16.

there, to which he fled: Numbers 35:25.

there: In the Tosefta R. Eliezer b. Jacob derives this ruling from the three-fold repetition of the word *there* in Numbers 35:25 and Deuteronomy 19:3–4..

boundary: 2,000 cubits. See Numbers 35:5 and *Sotah* 5:3.

A murderer that exited beyond the boundary,
and the avenger of blood found him—
R. Yose the Galilean says:
It is the duty of the avenger of blood [to kill him],
and the right of any person.
R. Aqiva says:
It is the right of the avenger of blood,
and any person is not culpable for [killing] him.
A tree that is standing within the boundary
and its foliage extends beyond the boundary,
or [a tree that is] standing outside the boundary
and its foliage extends to within the boundary—
everything follows the foliage.
If one killed [accidentally] within that [refuge] city—
he goes into exile from [one] neighborhood to [another] neighborhood,
but a Levite [who killed accidentally within a refuge city] goes into exile
from [one refuge] city to [another refuge] city.

8 Similarly, a murderer who went into exile to his[41] refuge city,
and the men of the city wished to honor him—
he should say to them: "I am a murderer."
If they say to him: "Nevertheless…,"
he may accept [honor] from them.
As it is said: *And this is the matter of the manslayer.*
They would pay rent to the Levites—
the words of R. Judah.
R. Meir says:
They would not pay rent to them.
And he returns to his previous post

[41] P lacks "his."

A murderer that exited beyond the boundary: See Numbers 35:26–27.

and any person is not culpable for [killing] him: Not to be punished in court, but such action is nevertheless prohibited.

everything follows the foliage: If the branches extend outside the boundary, then even the trunk within does not provide refuge; and if the branches extend inside the boundary, then even the trunk outside does provide refuge.

If one killed [accidentally] within that [refuge] city: An accidental killer, who is already in exile in a refuge city, killed somebody else within the refuge city by accident. The midrash derives this ruling from Numbers 35:28.

but a Levite [who killed accidentally within a refuge city]…: The six refuge cities are Levite cities. In addition, there are another forty-two Levite cities. See Numbers 35:6–7.

2:8 *Similarly, a murderer…of the manslayer*: Parallel text in *Shevi'it* 10:8. The opening word ("Similarly"), and perhaps the entire clause, is transferred from *Shevi'it* to here.

And this is the matter of the manslayer: Deuteronomy 19:4; on Heb. *davar* see 2:5n.

rent: For dwelling in the refuge city.

[after being released upon the death of the high priest]—
the words of R. Meir.
R. Judah says:
He would not return to his previous post.

Chapter Three

3:1–6 *Transgressors Punishable by Lashes*

3 And[42] these are the ones who are lashed:
one who has intercourse with his sister,
or his father's sister,
or his mother's sister,
or his wife's sister,
or his brother's wife,
or his father's brother's wife,
or a menstruant;
a widow to a high priest,
a divorcee or released woman to a common priest;

[42] K, P lack "And."

3:1 *And these are the ones who are lashed*: these are the transgressors who are liable to be punished with lashes. Penal lashes can only be administered if a transgressor has been warned. See 3.7.

one who has intercourse with his sister…: Most of the prohibitions enumerated here are subject to the heavenly punishment of *karet* (the exceptions will be specified below). See 3.15. See also *Keritot* 1:1 and *Ketubbot* 3:1 for similar lists of such prohibitions.

intercourse with his sister: Leviticus 18:9 and Leviticus 20:17.

or his father's sister: Leviticus 18:12 and Leviticus 20:19.

or his mother's sister: Leviticus 18:13 and Leviticus 20:19.

or his wife's sister: Leviticus 18:18.

or his brother's wife: Leviticus 18:16 and Leviticus 20:21.

a menstruant: Leviticus 18:19 and Leviticus 20:18.

a widow to a high priest: A high priest is prohibited from marrying a widow. See Leviticus 21:14. The Talmud records a dispute about whether this prohibition is violated upon marriage, or only if the marriage is subsequently consummated.

a divorcee…to a common priest: A common priest is prohibited from marrying a divorcee. See Leviticus 21:7. The prohibition is also reiterated for a high priest. See Leviticus 21:14. According to most commentators, the same talmudic debate referred to in the previous paragraph applies to this prohibition as well.

released woman: Under rabbinic law, she has the marital status of a divorcee. See 1:1.

or released woman to a common priest: The Mishnah records this prohibition alongside the other biblical prohibitions that are punishable with lashes. But the last line of this Mishnah implies that it is an inferior

a female *mamzer* or female *natin* to an Israelite,
or the daughter of an Israelite[43] to a *natin* or *mamzer*.[44]
A widow who is [also] a divorcee—
[a high priest] is liable for her on two counts.
A divorcee who is [also] a released woman—
[a priest] is liable on only one count alone.

2 One who while impure ate sacred [food],
or one who comes to the Temple while impure,
or one who eats [prohibited animal] fat, or blood,
or leftover [sacrificial meat], or that which is disqualified,
or that which is impure;[45]
one who slaughters or offers [a sacrifice] outside [of the Temple];
or one who eats leavened bread on Passover,
or one who eats or does work on the Day of Atonement;
or one who prepares the oil [of anointment],

---

[43] Alt. "an Israelite woman." [44] K, P lack these clauses (beginning with "a female *mamzer*").
[45] K lacks "or that which is impure."

---

prohibition, and the Talmud plainly understands this to be only a rabbinic prohibition. The inaccurate listing of this prohibition here is only due to its common association with the previously listed item.

mamzer: The offspring of an illicit sexual relationship. See *Qiddushin* 3:12 and *Yevamot* 4:13.

natin: A caste category usually associated with a *mamzer*. See *Qiddushin* 4:1. In Ezra 2:43–54 and Nehemiah 10:29 *netinim* are listed as members of the Jerusalem community in good standing, but by rabbinic times *netinim* had become a group with an impaired status. Note that the entire line, which does not appear in the Mishnah manuscripts, is likely interpolated from *Qiddushin* 3:12 or *Yevamot* 2:4.

[a priest] is liable on only one count alone: A *halutsah* is prohibited to a common priest like a divorcee.

3:2 *One who while impure ate sacred [food]*: Leviticus 7:20.

or one who comes to the Temple while impure: Leviticus 12:4, Numbers 5:3 and 19:13.

or one who eats [prohibited animal] fat: Leviticus 3:17 and 7:23–25.

or blood: Leviticus 3:17, 7:26–27.

or leftover [sacrificial meat]: Each sacrifice has a set timeframe within which it must be eaten, ranging up to two days. See Exodus 29:34 and Leviticus 19:6–8.

or that which is disqualified: Leviticus 7:18 and 19:6–8. A sacrifice becomes disqualified if any part of the ritual is conducted with intention to eat or offer the sacrifice outside its proper timeframe. See *Zevahim* 2:3.

or that which is impure: Leviticus 7:19. This line is missing in K and in the parallel list in *Keritot* 1:1.

one who slaughters...outside [of the Temple]: Leviticus 17:3–7, Deuteronomy 12:13.

or one who eats leavened bread on Passover: Exodus 12:15, 19 and 13:3.

or one who eats...on the Day of Atonement: Leviticus 23:27 and 29.

or one who...does work on the Day of Atonement: Leviticus 23:28 and 30–31.

or one who prepares the oil [of anointment]: It is a prohibition to replicate the oil of anointment that was used in the Tabernacle/Temple. See Exodus 30:32–33.

or one who prepares the incense,
or one who lathers [himself] with the oil of anointment;
or one who eats carcasses or *treifot*,
vermin or crawling creatures;
one who ate untithed produce,
or first tithe whose *terumah* was not removed,
or second tithe or consecrated [food] that were not redeemed.
How much must one eat from untithed produce so as to be liable?
R. Simeon says:
The slightest amount.
But the Sages say:
An olive's bulk.
R. Simeon responded:
Do you not concede to me that one who eats an ant,
however small, is liable?
They responded to him:
This is because it is in the form in which it was created.

or one who prepares the incense: It is a prohibition to replicate the incense that was used in the Tabernacle/Temple. See Exodus 30:37–38.

incense: Special incense that is prepared in the Temple and offered twice daily by the priest on the Golden Altar, and offered in the inner chamber of the Temple by the high priest on the Day of Atonement. See Exodus 30:1–8 and Leviticus 16:12–13.

or one who lathers [himself] with the oil of anointment: Exodus 30:32–33. The Tosefta states that this prohibition refers to one who lathers with the original oil of anointment that Moses prepared in the desert.

or one who eats carcasses or treifot, vermin or crawling creatures: Traditional commentators interpret these four terms as specific references to discrete prohibitions, as delineated in the next notes. Aharon Shemesh, however, argues that this phrase serves as a shorthand for all forbidden foods. See *Sanhedrin* 8:2 and *Shevu'ot* 3:4.

carcasses: The meat of animals that are not ritually slaughtered. See Deuteronomy 14:21.

treifot: Plural of *terefah*: the meat of animals afflicted by certain fatal ailments. See Exodus 22:30 and *Hullin* 3:1.

vermin or crawling creatures: Leviticus 11:11–13 and 41–44. The prohibition on eating carcasses, *treifot*, vermin and crawling creatures, and all the other prohibitions listed below, are not punishable by *karet*.

one who ate untithed produce: The Talmud derives this prohibition from Leviticus 22:15 or Deuteronomy 12:17.

or first tithe whose terumah was not removed: A Levite who receives a first tithe is obligated to separate *terumah*, which is to be given to a priest; see Numbers 18:26–28.

terumah: Numbers 18:11–12.

or second tithe...that were not redeemed: Deuteronomy 12:17. Commentaries debate why second tithe is listed again in 3:3. Some have suggested that the duplication is the result of second tithe's common association with the next listed item. See e.g. *Berakhot* 7:1.

or consecrated [food] that were not redeemed: This constitutes a form of misappropriation of Temple property.

consecrated [food]: For example, an animal that is consecrated as a sacrifice that becomes blemished and therefore unsuitable to be offered, must be redeemed before it is consumed. The source of the prohibition is unclear.

one who eats an ant...is liable: Leviticus 11:42.

He responded to them:
So too a single grain of wheat is in the form in which it was created.

3 One who eats:
firstfruits before [the owner] had recited [the liturgical recitation] over them,
[or] offerings of the highest sanctity outside of the [Tabernacle] curtains,
[or] offerings of lesser sanctity or second tithe outside the wall [of Jerusalem];
one who breaks the bone of a Passover [sacrifice] that is pure—
in these cases, he is lashed forty.
But one who leaves over from a pure[46] [sacrifice]
or breaks [a bone] of an impure [Passover sacrifice]—
he is not lashed forty.

4 One who removes [from a nest] a mother [bird] together with[47] the fledglings—
R. Judah says:
He is lashed, but need not release [her].

[46] K, P lack "from a pure." [47] Lit. "on top of."

3:3 *One a priest who eats first fruits*: See *Bikkurim* 2:1.

before [the owner] had recited: Deuteronomy 26:5–10 and *Bikkurim* 3:6.

offerings of the highest sanctity: Certain sacrifices, including purgation and guilt offerings, have a relatively high degree of sanctity. They must be eaten within the Temple. See *Zevahim* 5:1–5. The Talmud derives this prohibition from Exodus 22:30.

the [Tabernacle] curtains: The Tabernacle in the wilderness was surrounded by curtains. See Exodus 27:9. In the Mishnah "curtains" designates the outer boundaries of the Temple.

offerings of lesser sanctity: Can be eaten anywhere within Jerusalem. See *Zevahim* 5:6–8.

second tithe outside the wall [of Jerusalem]: Deuteronomy 12:17. According to the Talmud the second tithe in question has already been brought to Jerusalem, and then is subsequently eaten outside of its walls.

one who breaks the bone of a Passover [sacrifice]: Exodus 12:46. Paralleled by *Pesahim* 7:11.

or breaks [a bone] of an impure [Passover sacrifice]: The Talmud derives this from the wording of Exodus 12:46.

he is not lashed forty: Why is one who leaves over from a pure sacrifice not lashed? Commentators have proposed various explanations, the most likely of which is as follows. Exodus 12:10 states that leftover sacrificial meat must be burnt. Thus, even if one violates the prohibition not to leave over sacrificial meat beyond the set timeframe, there is an affirmative duty that can be fulfilled, thus removing the penalty. See the principle in the next mishnah (3.4).

3:4 *One who removes [from a nest] a mother [bird] together with the fledglings*: Scripture prohibits somebody from acting in this manner, and instead instructs the person with an affirmative duty—to release the mother bird and then take the young fledglings. See Deuteronomy 22:6–7. See the parallel passage in *Hullin* 12:4.

a mother [bird] together with the fledglings: The formulation in certain parallel versions of this passage is "a mother [bird] from on top of the young." The commentaries, likewise, debate whether the prohibition refers to the removal of the mother bird along with the young fledglings (similar to another prohibition recorded in Leviticus 22:28), or her removal from on top of them.

R. Judah says: He is lashed, but need not release [her]: R. Judah interprets the affirmative duty in the latter Deuteronomy verse as an instruction as to what should be done a priori. In the Mishnah's case, he has already violated the prohibition, and there is no legal efficacy in now releasing the mother bird.

But the Sages say:
He must release [her], but is not lashed.
This is the general rule:
Any negative commandment that has an affirmative duty[48]—
one is not liable for [violating] it.

5 One who shaves smooth a part of his head,[49]
or one who rounds off the sidegrowth of his head,
or one who destroys the sidegrowth of his beard,
or one who makes one gash [in mourning] over a deceased [person]—
he is liable.
If he made one gash [in mourning] over five deceased [people],
or five gashes over one deceased [person]—
he is liable for each and every one.
For[50] the head—
twice: one from here, and one from there.
And[51] for the beard—
two from here, and two from there,[52] and one from below.
R. Eliezer says:
If he removed it all at once, he is liable only once.
And he is liable only if he removed it with a razor.
R. Eliezer says:
He is liable even if he gathered it with tweezers or with a plucker.[53]

[48] Lit. "arise, do"; **K**, **P**: "arise and do."
[49] Alt. "One who makes a baldness on his head."
[50] **K** adds "He is liable" before "For the head."
[51] **K** lacks "And."
[52] **K** lacks "and two from there."
[53] Alt. "planes" or "pincers."

But the Sages say: He must release [her], but is not lashed: The Sages interpret the latter verse as an affirmative duty that serves as a corrective to the prohibition. Thus, even releasing the mother bird post facto can correct the prohibited act, as explained in the following principle.

3:5 *One who shaves smooth a part of his head*: Leviticus 21:5 and Deuteronomy 14:1. This act is an ancient mourning practice.

the sidegrowth of his head . . . beard: Leviticus 19:27.

or one who makes one gash [in mourning] over a deceased [person]: Leviticus 19:28.

he is liable for each and every one: five times, corresponding to each deceased person he is mourning, or to the multiple number of gashes he makes in mourning over one deceased person.

For the head…: Different sections of the head may not be rounded off.

And for the beard…: Different sections of the beard may not be destroyed.

two from here…: One on the upper cheekbone, and one on the lower cheekbone.

one from below: On the chin.

And he is liable only if he removed it with a razor: The Talmud derives the source of this opinion by linking the word "cut" in Leviticus 21:5 to the word "destroy" in Leviticus 19:27, to conclude that the prohibition forbids a "cut that destroys," i.e. with a razor.

6 One who writes with incisions[54] [on his skin]—
if he writes but does not incise,
or incises but does not write,
he is not liable, unless he writes and incises
with ink, or blue dye, or any substance that makes a mark.
R. Simeon b. Judah, in the name of R. Simeon, says:
He is not liable unless he writes the name of God,
as it is said: *You shall not incise any marks on yourselves: I am the Lord.*[55]

3:7–9 Multiple Sets of Lashes

7 If a *nazir* was drinking wine throughout the day—
he is liable only once.
If they told him, "Do not drink! Do not drink!" but [nevertheless] he drinks—
he is liable for each and every one.
8 If he was impurifying himself
by [contact with] corpses throughout the day—
he is liable only once.
If they told him, "Do not impurify yourself! Do not impurify yourself!"
but [nevertheless] was impurifying himself—
he is liable for each and every one.
If he he was shaving throughout the day—
he is liable only once.
If they told him, "Do not shave! Do not shave!"
but [nevertheless] he shaves—
he is liable for each and every one.
If one was wearing [a garment made of] a prohibited mixture throughout the day—
he is only liable once.
If they told him, "Do not wear [it]! Do not wear [it]!"

---

[54] Lit. "writes a writing of incision."
[55] P adds "in your land" in the citation of the verse, which seems to be an error.

3:6 *One who writes with incisions [on his skin]*: A tattoo, Leviticus 19:28. The Mishnah interprets the verse to refer to two actions: writing and incising.

3:7–8 Paralleled by *Nazir* 6:4.

3:7 A *nazir* is prohibited from drinking wine; see Numbers 6:3–4.

If they told him, "Do not drink! Do not drink!" but [nevertheless] he drinks: Unlike the first scenario where he was warned only once, here he is repeatedly warned, but continues to drink following each and every warning.

he is liable for each and every one: he is liable once for each warning that he violates.

3:8 A *nazir* is prohibited from contracting corpse impurity; see Numbers 6:6.

A *nazir* is also prohibited from shaving his head; see Numbers 6:5.

a prohibited mixture: All Israelites are prohibited from wearing a mixture of wool and linen; see Leviticus 19:19 and Deuteronomy 22:11. For all forms of prohibited mixtures, see *Kilayim*.

but [nevertheless] he strips and [then] wears [it again]—
he is liable for each and every one.

9 It is possible that one person can plow a single furrow
and be liable on its account for [the violation of] eight prohibitions—
one who plows:
(1) with an ox and a donkey [together];
(2–3)[56] that are consecrated;
(4) a prohibited [seed] mixture in a vineyard;
(5) and during[57] the Seventh Year;
(6) and during a festival;
(7) and he is a priest;
and (8) a *nazir* plowing in an impure field.
Hananiah b. Hakinai says:
Also (9) if he is wearing [a garment made of] a prohibited mixture [while plowing].
They said to him:
This is not within the same category.
He said to them:
The *nazir* too is not within the same category.

[56] There are different ways of counting the eight prohibitions. See the annotations.
[57] **K**, **P** lack "during."

3:9 *an ox and a donkey*: Another type of prohibited mixture, see Deuteronomy 22:10.

that are consecrated: Plowing with a consecrated ox that is designated to be offered as a sacrifice violates a biblical prohibition. See Deuteronomy 15:19. According to some commentators, the Mishnah specifically refers to a firstborn ox that has innate sanctity (which is the literal subject of this biblical verse). Commentators debate whether there is also a second prohibition that is violated here. Some suggest that the Mishnah refers to a firstborn donkey that has quasi-sanctity (Exodus 13:13); or a consecrated sheep (imprecisely called here a donkey). According to others, the Mishnah refers to a donkey that belongs to the Temple, so plowing with it is a violation of the biblical prohibition of misappropriating Temple property. See Deuteronomy 12:17. A demurring opinion counts only one prohibition, and instead enumerates a second prohibition related to plowing a vineyard, as described in the next note.

a prohibited [seed] mixture in a vineyard: Sowing a vineyard with other seed (for example, wheat and barley) is another prohibited mixture. See Deuteronomy 22:9. The Talmud states that the act of plowing covers the vine and seed with dirt, which is the legal equivalent of sowing. According to some commentators (the demurring opinion referred to in the previous note), there is an additional prohibition that is violated here by plowing with mixed seed. See Leviticus 19:19.

during the Seventh Year: Leviticus 25:4.

during a festival: See Leviticus 23:7. The Mishnah refers to a holiday, rather than the Sabbath, because plowing on the latter would be punishable by capital punishment (or *karet*), not lashes.

he is a priest, and a nazir plowing in an impure field: A priest is prohibited from becoming defiled. See Leviticus 21:1. A *nazir* is also prohibited. See 3.8.

an impure field: A burial site.

Also if he is wearing [a garment made of] a prohibited mixture: See 3.8.

This is not within the same category: The prohibition of wearing a *kilayim* garment is unrelated to the act of plowing.

The nazir: a priest or a *nazir*.

The nazir too is not within the same category: A priest or *nazir* becoming defiled has no intrinsic connection to plowing either.

3:10–14 The Process of Administering Lashes

10 How many [times] do they lash him?
Forty less one.
As it is said, *by[58] count forty*—
a number that is proximate to forty.
R. Judah says:
He is lashed[59] forty [times] in full.
And where is he lashed the additional one?
Between his shoulders.

11 They estimate[60] his capacity to endure [lashes]
only with[61] [a number of] floggings that[62] can be divided by three.[63]
If they estimate that he can endure forty [lashes],
but while he was being lashed they said that he cannot endure forty—
he is exempt [from the remainder].
If they estimate that he can endure eighteen [lashes],
but after he was lashed they said that he can endure forty—
he is exempt.
If he committed a transgression involving [the violation of] two prohibitions:
if they estimate him with a single estimate [for both]—
he is lashed and is then exempt.
But[64] if not—
he is lashed, and then heals, and then is lashed again.

12 How do they lash him?
He binds his two hands on the pillar, here and there,
and the attendant of the assembly grips his clothes—
if they tear, they tear; and if they unravel, they unravel—

---

[58] K lacks "by." [59] K, P lack "He is lashed."
[60] K: "elevate" or "make him stand" or "establish". [61] K lacks "with." [62] K lacks "that."
[63] In K, this line is better translated as "floggings divisible by three." [64] K lacks "But."

3:10 *by count forty*: Deuteronomy 25:2–3, combining the last word from verse 2 with the first word from verse 3.

And where is he lashed the additional one? The initial thirty-nine lashes are administered in accordance with the procedure described in 3.13.

3:11 On dividing the number of lashes by three, see 3.13.

forty [lashes]: i.e. thirty-nine (a number that can be divided by three).

he is exempt: from receiving any more lashes.

If he committed a transgression involving [the violation of] two prohibitions: He deserves to be punished with two sets of lashes, but the total number of lashes he will actually receive depends on how the estimation is done.

if they estimate him with a single estimate [for both]: Combining the prohibitions into a single estimation will lead to a leniency for the transgressor.

3:12 *here and there*: on both sides of the pillar.

until he exposes his chest.⁶⁵
And the stone [platform] is placed behind him.
The attendant of the assembly stands upon it,
And a strap of calf [hide] is in his hand—
it is doubled over, one into two, and two into four,
and two straps are ascending and descending [within] it.
13 Its handle is a handbreadth, and its width is a handbreadth,
and its tip⁶⁶ reaches onto⁶⁷ his core.⁶⁸
And he flogs him⁶⁹ one-third [of the lashes] from his front,
and two-thirds⁷⁰ from his rear.
And he does not flog him either standing, or sitting,
but rather when he is inclined,
as it is said, *And the magistrate shall have him lie down.*
And the one who flogs, flogs with one hand with all his might.
14 And the reciter recites:
If you fail to observe faithfully, etc.
and the Lord will inflict extraordinary plagues upon you and your offspring, etc.,
and he returns to the beginning of the recitation.
(*Therefore observe faithfully the terms of this covenant,* etc.,
and he concludes,
But He, being merciful, forgives iniquity, etc.,
and he returns to the beginning of the recitation.)⁷¹
And⁷² if he dies under his hand—

⁶⁵ Lit. "until he exposes his heart"; **K** lacks this clause.   ⁶⁶ **K, P** lack "its tip."
⁶⁷ **K** lacks "on."   ⁶⁸ Or "belly."   ⁶⁹ **P** lacks "him."   ⁷⁰ Lit. "two portions."
⁷¹ **K, P** lack these parenthetical verses.   ⁷² **K** lacks "And."

---

until he exposes his chest: The same formulation appears in *Sotah* 1.5.

and two straps: two separate straps.

3:13 *and two-thirds from his rear*: Some commentators interpret this to mean one-third on each of his shoulders.

he does not flog him neither standing, or sitting, but rather when he is inclined: The recipient of the lashes (the transgressor) is inclined..

And the magistrate shall have him lie down: Deuteronomy 25:2.

3:14 *And the reciter recites*: While the penal lashes are being administered. According to the Talmud, a third court official counts aloud the number of lashes.

If you fail to observe faithfully, etc. and the Lord will inflict extraordinary plagues (Heb. makkot) upon you and your offspring, etc.: Deuteronomy 28:58–59. The verses refer to the plagues God will inflict on the unfaithful; but when recited as part of the penal procedure they refer to the lashes (or floggings, i.e. *makkot*) being administered by the court against the unfaithful transgressor.

and he returns to the beginning of the recitation: Upon completion of the scriptural recitation the reciter starts over, if the administration of lashes is still ongoing.

Therefore observe faithfully the terms of this covenant, etc.: Deuteronomy 29:8.

But He, being merciful, forgives iniquity, etc.: Psalms 78:38. This is likely a later interpolation.

he is exempt.
If he added one extra[73] [lash of the] strap, and he dies—
in this case,[74] he goes into exile because of him.[75]
If he is soiled either by excrement or by urine—
he is exempt.
R. Judah says:
The man, by excrement; and the woman, by urine.

3:15–16 *Punishments and Rewards*

15 All those liable for *karet* who are lashed—
are exempted from their *karet*,
as it is said: *And your brother be degraded before your eyes*—
once he is lashed he thereby becomes like your brother—
the words of R. Hananiah b. Gamaliel.
R. Hananiah b. Gamaliel said:
If the one who commits one transgression
forfeits his life for it,
how much more so the one who performs one commandment
shall have his life restored to him?
R. Simeon says:
This is derived from its [scriptural] context—

[73] P lacks "extra."   [74] Alt. "in these cases."   [75] Alt. "on his account."

---

he is exempt: From exile. See 2.2.

If he added one extra [lash of the] strap: The Talmud attributes this to a confusion in the counting, but this is not the implication of the parallel Tosefta passage.

in this case he goes into exile because of him: He is punished as an accidental killer.

If he is soiled . . . he is exempt: from further punishment because he has suffered public degradation.

3:15 *exempted from their karet*: Whereas 3.1 states implicitly that those who are liable for *karet* are also liable for lashes, this mishnah significantly adds that one who is punished with lashes is exempt from *karet*.

karet: Lit. "excision." The exact meaning of this biblical term is not clear. In rabbinic literature the term connotes a divinely inflicted punishment for violation of certain particular prohibitions. See *Keritot* 1:1, which enumerates thirty-six such prohibitions.

And your brother be degraded before your eyes: Deuteronomy 25:3.

once he is lashed he thereby becomes like your brother: he is your equal in stature; he is fully reinstated into the community.

R. Hananiah b. Gamaliel said: If the one who commits one transgression . . .: This is a discrete homiletic teaching about *karet* by the same Sage. See 1.7 for a similar teaching.

If the one who commits one transgression forfeits his life for it: if one violates a prohibition whose punishment is *karet*. Alternatively, Aharon Shemesh interprets this line to mean that if one deliberately transgresses any Torah prohibition the punishment is *karet*.

This is derived from its [scriptural] context: Leviticus 18. A verse from within this biblical chapter that delineates numerous prohibitions that are punished with *karet* describes the reward of life granted to those who act in an upright manner.

as it is said: *Such persons shall be cut off*, etc.
and it says: *By the pursuit of which a person shall live*—
thus, anyone who sits [passively] and does not violate a transgression,
is given a reward like one who performs[76] a commandment.
R. Simeon b. Rabbi says:
Behold it says:
But make sure that you do not partake of blood; for the blood is the life, etc.
Now if blood—from which a person's soul is repulsed[77]—
[nevertheless] one who refrains from it receives a reward,
theft and illicit sexual relations—
which a person's soul desires and lusts [after]—
how much more so will one who refrains from them merit [reward]
for himself and his next generation and his subsequent generations,
until the end of all generations.

16 R. Hananiah b. Aqashiah says:
The Holy One[78] Blessed Be He wanted to merit Israel,
therefore He increased for them Torah and commandments,
as it is said: *The Lord desires His [servant's] vindication,
that he may magnify and glorify [His] Torah.*

[76] Or perhaps "as if he had performed."   [77] K, P: "afraid."
[78] K, P use a different euphemism for God, "Hamakom" (lit. "The Place").

Such persons shall be cut off, etc.: Leviticus 18:29.

By the pursuit of which a person shall live: Leviticus 18:5.

R. Simeon b. Rabbi says: A related teaching, which describes the reward that one is granted for refraining from violating prohibitions.

But make sure that you do not partake of blood; for the blood is the life, etc.: Deuteronomy 12:23.

[nevertheless] one who refrains from it receives a reward: See Deuteronomy 12:25.

3:16 *The Holy One Blessed Be He wanted to merit Israel, therefore He increased for them Torah and commandments*: This teaching continues along the lines of the above theme—God, who rewards those who fulfill commandments (and refrain from the violation of prohibitions), increased the number of commandments in order to enlarge the reward that Israel will receive. The Talmud in this context records the famous opinion of R. Simlai that there are 613 commandments. Scholars debate whether R. Hananiah's teaching is a post-Mishnaic addition.

Torah and commandments: A biblical idiom. See Exodus 24:12.

The Lord desires His [servant's] vindication, that he may magnify and glorify [His] Torah: Isaiah 42:21. According to R. Hananiah's teaching, God magnifies the Torah by increasing the number of commandments.

His [servant's] vindication: Israel's vindication. See Isaiah 42:19.

Tractate Shevu'ot

Elizabeth Shanks Alexander

Introduction

Overview

The tractate's name (*Shevu'ot*) means "oaths." Accordingly, the majority of the tractate (chapters 3–8) surveys laws related to the practice of swearing an oath. Chapters 1–2, however, treat a completely different topic: the inadvertent violation of the holy precincts of the Temple or of holy food by impurity, and its ritual rectification. The two topics, which at first appear unrelated to each other, are joined in a single tractate for two reasons, one substantive and one rhetorical. Substantive: the two topics are rooted in the rabbinic interpretation of adjacent verses in Leviticus 5:1–4. Verses 1 and 4 concern oaths, verses 2 and 3 concern impurity. Rhetorical: the Mishnah presents both topics (impurity and oaths) under the rubric of "two kinds that are in fact four" (1:1, 2:1, 3:1).

Structure, Organization, and Main Ideas of the Tractate

Chapter 1 deals with the procedure of ritual atonement for the unknowing violation of holy spaces or holy food through impurity. Chapter 2 describes how one in fact may unwittingly violate holy spaces or holy food. Leviticus 5:2–3 lies in the background of both chapters concerning impurity.

The remaining chapters in the tractate deal with oaths. The unity of most chapters is determined by the biblical source that lies in the background. Most of the chapters are structured around biblical passages that feature the terms "oath" or "swear." Considered as a whole, the tractate provides a comprehensive treatment of its subject matter by collecting in a single place laws derived from various scriptural passages, even if the passages are not cited.

Chapter 3's discussion of rash and vain oaths derives from Leviticus 5:4. Chapter 4 discusses the testimonial oath, which is imposed on potential witnesses to ensure that they do not withhold relevant testimony from the court (derived from Leviticus 5:1). Chapter 5 discusses the oath of deposit, which is imposed on the defendant to confirm that he is not in possession of goods or money that by rights belong to the claimant (derived from Leviticus 5:20–26). Chapter 6 clarifies the conditions under which a court may impose an oath on the defendant. Chapter 7 lists an exceptional set of circumstances in which the court imposes an oath on the claimant so that he can extract payment from the defendant. Chapter 8 discusses the oath that is imposed upon guardians when an owner's property has been lost or damaged while in their care. The purpose of this oath is to exempt the guardian from liability (derived from Exodus 22:6–14).

Relationship to Scripture

Leviticus 5:2–3, which sets the stage for the discussion in chapters 1 and 2, describes a scenario that unfolds in three stages: first, an individual becomes impure; second, he forgets about his impure state; and third, he later recalls it. The Mishnah focuses on the fact that the biblical verse imputes "guilt" to the individual. Whence the guilt? The Mishnah assumes that the individual did something he should not have done while he was in an impure state, namely, he must have entered the holy precincts of the Temple or eaten holy food. The Mishnah, then, assumes an ever so slightly revised sequence of events: first, one has knowledge of one's impurity; second, one forgets about one's impurity *and transgresses inadvertently* (i.e. enters a holy precinct or eats holy food), and third, one recalls the initial impurity, which causes one to "realize his guilt" in transgressing. The mishnaic term "knowledge of impurity" refers to this scenario.

The Mishnah modifies the biblical scenario in yet another way. Biblical language suggests that the transgressor has *no knowledge whatsoever* of his impurity when he violates the sanctity of the holy with his impurity (step two). By contrast, the Mishnah envisions a situation in which the transgressor at step two has knowledge of some, but not all, of the information necessary to prevent his impure body from coming into contact with the holy. Either he recalls that he is impure but forgets he is doing an activity that requires a pure state, or he recalls that the activity he is doing requires a pure state, but he forgets that he is in an impure state. The term "knowledge" in the phrase "knowledge of impurity" refers not to the transgressor's knowledge of his impurity at the beginning of the sequence (step one), but to his *incomplete* knowledge when he transgresses inadvertently (step two).

Tractate Shevu'ot

Chapter One

1:1 "Two Kinds Which Are Four"

I Oaths are of two kinds, which are in fact four.
Knowledge of impurity is of two kinds, which are in fact four.
Transport on the Sabbath[1] is of two kinds, which are in fact four.
Skin afflictions appear[2] in two manners, which are in fact four.

---

[1] Lit. "The goings-out of the Sabbath are two, which are four."
[2] Lit. "Appearances of afflictions are two, which are four."

1:1 This mishnah is a short catalog of legal phenomena that can be conceptualized as two primary types, each of which itself manifests in two additional ways.

Oaths: See below, chapter 3.

two kinds, which are in fact four: 3:1 offers illustrative examples. The Sifra implies that the two primary categories are rash oaths regarding future action (1 and 2), while the two derivative categories are vain oaths regarding the past (3 and 4).

Knowledge of impurity: See below, chapter 2.

two kinds, which are in fact four: See below, 2:1.

Transport on the Sabbath: See *Shabbat* 1:1.

two kinds: Or ways to envision the transport of an object between two individuals, each standing in a different domain: (1) one person performs both of the transactions involved, moving the object from hand to hand (A to B) and domain to domain (A′ to B′), or (2) they "share" the work of transporting, with one moving the object from hand to hand (A to B) and the other moving the object from domain to domain (A′ to B′), each performing one of the transactions needed to move the object from domain to domain and hand to hand.

Skin afflictions: See Leviticus 13:2–8. The Mishnah assumes that discoloration and swelling are the two primary forms of whiteness, and that each one of those primary forms of whiteness has a *sapaḥat*, that is, a secondary appearance. There are therefore only two major kinds of skin abnormalities (discoloration and swelling), but four varieties of whiteness in which those abnormalities can appear. See *Nega'im* 1:1.

1:2–1:4   *Ritual Atonement for Violating Holy Spaces or Holy Food*

2 All situations in which there is awareness[3] initially, awareness at the end,
but lack of awareness in the intervening period—
behold, this one is liable to a sliding-scale offering.[4]
If there is awareness initially, but no awareness at the end—
the goat that is offered inside, together with the Day of Atonement,
temporarily suspends his guilt;
at such point as it becomes known to him,
he brings a sliding-scale offering.

3 If there is no awareness initially, but there is awareness at the end—
the goat that is offered outside, together with the Day of Atonement, atones,
As it says: *In addition to the purgation offering of atonement.*
That for which this one atones, the other also atones:
Just as the inside goat[5] atones only for transgressions of which he is aware,

---

[3] Lit. "knowledge."   [4] Lit. "rising and falling offering."   [5] Lit. "the inner one."

1:2 This mishnah and the next prescribe ritual remediation for an individual who while impure inadvertently enters a holy precinct of the Temple or eats holy food. The transgression can occur with varying degrees of awareness.

awareness initially: At the time that it happened, he was aware that he had become impure.

awareness at the end: He remembered his impurity at some point after he had eaten holy food or entered a holy precinct.

lack of awareness in the intervening period: He was unaware of either his impurity or the fact that he was entering a holy precinct or eating holy food.

sliding-scale offering: Which is determined according to one's financial means. See Leviticus 5:6–12

no awareness at the end: He forgets completely that he is impure, never realizing that he transgressed by eating holy food or entering a holy precinct. Unaware of the transgression, he cannot take steps to atone for it by bringing the proper offering.

becomes known to him: When he remembers that he had been impure and realizes he had inadvertently transgressed.

the goat that is offered inside: Leviticus 16:5 prescribes the sacrifice of a goat on the Day of Atonement whose purpose is to atone for violations of the Holy Sanctuary and holy food by the nation as a whole. This goat is called "the goat that is offered inside" because its blood is sprinkled in the innermost chamber of the Temple, the Holy of Holies (*Yoma* 5:4).

1:3 *no awareness initially… awareness at the end*: He was not aware at the time he became impure and could not have prevented his consumption of holy food or his entrance into a holy precinct. At some point in the future he realizes that he was impure and inadvertently transgressed.

the goat that is offered outside: This goat is offered in the Court of the Priests and its blood is sprinkled on the altar there as part of the additional (*musaf*) offerings on the Day of Atonement. See *Yoma* 7:3.

As it is says: Numbers 29:11.

Just as…so too: The inside goat atones for violations of the Holy Sanctuary and holy food of which the transgressor has limited awareness, being aware at the beginning but not the end. Likewise, the outside goat

so too the outside goat atones only for transgressions of which he is aware.

4 And for those [transgressions] about which there is awareness neither initially nor at the end—
the goats offered on festivals and the goats offered on the New Moon atone—
these are the words of R. Judah.
R. Simeon says:
The goats offered on the festivals atone, but not the goats offered on the New Moon.
For what, then, do the goats offered on the New Moon atone?
For the pure person who ate impure food.
R. Meir says:
All the goats atone equally—
all atone for the impurification of the Temple and its holy things.
R. Simeon used to say:
The goats offered on the New Moon atone for the pure person who ate impure food;
those offered on the festivals atone for transgressions
in which there was awareness neither initially nor at the end;
and that offered on the Day of Atonement atones for transgressions
in which there was no awareness initially, but there was awareness at the end.

1:4 cont.–5 *Are the Goats Interchangeable?*

They said to him:
May one goat be offered in place of the other?

atones for transgressions of the Holy Sanctuary and holy food of which the transgressor has limited awareness, being aware at the end but not the beginning

1:4 *the goats offered on festivals*: The additional (*musaf*) offerings for the three pilgrimage festivals (Passover, Shavu'ot, and Sukkot) include a sin-offering goat to atone for Israel's transgressions. See Numbers 28:22, 30; and 29:16, 19, 22, 25, 28, 31, 34., 38.

the goats offered on the New Moon: The additional (*musaf*) offerings for the New Moon include a sin-offering goat to atone for Israel's transgressions. See Numbers 28:15.

the pure person who ate impure food: Up to this point, the chapter deals with transgressions involving an *impure* person who encounters *holy* items (food or Sanctuary). The mishnah now turns to the related, but inverse case of a *pure* person who eats *impure food*.

the impurification of the Temple and its holy things: This category encompasses all situations described in 1:3–4; the cases of 1:2 end with awareness, and therefore do not require the "catch-all" atonement provided by the additional (*musaf*) goat offerings of the holidays/New Moon.

R. Simeon says... used to say that there is a high level of coordination between goats and transgressions: each goat atones for a different type of transgression.

R. Meir asserts that any of the goats can atone for any of the transgressions listed in 1:3–4.

May one goat be offered in place of the other? A goat that has been designated for an occasion other than the current one. For example, may they offer a goat that had been designated for the Day of Atonement on

He said to them:
They may.
They said to him:
Since [you believe that] the goats do not atone equally,
how can one be offered in place of the other?
He said to them:
They all come to atone for the impurification of the Temple and its holy things.
5 R. Simeon b. Judah says in his name:
The goats offered on the New Moon atone for the pure person who ate impure food.
Those offered on the Festivals atone for even more;
they atone for the pure person who ate impure food,
and for transgressions in which there was awareness neither initially nor at the end.
Those offered on the Day of Atonement atone for even more;
they atone for the pure person who ate impure food,
for transgressions in which there was awareness neither initially nor at the end,
and for transgressions in which there was no awareness initially,
but there was awareness at the end.
They said to him:
May one be offered in place of the other?
He said: Yes.
They said to him:
If so, the goats of the Day of Atonement may well be offered
in place of the goats of the New Moon.
But how can the goats of the New Moon be offered
in place of the goats of the Day of Atonement,
as this grants it an atoning power that it does not properly possess.
He said to them:
They all come to atone for the impurification of the Temple and its holy things.

the occasion of the New Moon, given that each goat atones for a different transgression in the view of R. Simeon?

1:5 *his name*: R. Simeon b. Judah (ca. 170–200 CE) in the name of R. Simeon [bar Yohai] (ca. 135–170 CE).

The goats associated with different holidays have distinct degrees of potency and atone for an increasingly greater number of transgressions.

They said to him: Because R. Simeon b. Judah understands R. Simeon's position differently from the anonymous Sages in 1:4, he also understands the Sages' challenge to R. Simeon differently.

If so: Regarding the goats as interchangeable makes sense when a Day of Atonement goat stands in for a New Moon goat, since the more potent Day of Atonement goat atones for transgressions for which the less potent New Moon goat also atones.

But how can the less potent New Moon goat stand in for a Day of Atonement goat, as the former does not atone for the transgressions covered by the latter?

1:6–7 *Intentional Violation of the Sanctity of the Temple*

6 For one who intentionally impurifies the Temple and its holy things—
the goat offered inside, together with the Day of Atonement, atones.
For all other transgressions in the Torah—
the light and the serious, the intentional and the unintentional,
the known and the unknown, the positive commands and the negative commands,
those punishable by *karet* and those punishable by death by the court—
the scapegoat[6] atones.

7 The law is one and the same for Israelites, priests, and the anointed priest.
What is the difference between Israelites, priests, and the anointed priest?
The bull's blood atones for priestly impurification of the Temple and its holy things.
R. Simeon says:
Just as the blood of the inner goat atones for Israel,
so too the blood of the bull atones for the priests.
Just as the confession over the scapegoat atones for Israel,
so too the confession over the bull atones for the priests.

[6] Lit. "the sent goat."

1:6 *intentionally impurifies*: In contrast to 1:1–5 that treat *unintentional* violations of the Holy sanctuary and holy food.

impurifies the Temple: By entering in a state of ritual impurity.

[Or impurifies] holy things: By consuming holy food in a state of ritual impurity.

the goat offered inside: The goat whose blood is sprinkled in the Holy of Holies (Leviticus 16:5 and *Yoma* 5:4) atones for Israel's intentional transgressions of the Holy Sanctuary. Also offered as an "inside offering" is a bull, which atones for priestly violations of the Holy Sanctuary (Leviticus 16:3, 6 and *Yoma* 4:2–3 and 5:3).

karet: Death at the hands of heaven.

death by a human *court*: According to set legal procedures involving presentation of evidence, testimony by witnesses, and deliberation by judges.

the scapegoat: Leviticus 16:8–10, 21–22 and *Yoma* 6.

1:7 *one and the same for…*: All social classes achieve atonement for the transgressions listed in the previous mishnah (light/serious, positive/negative, etc.) by the scapegoat.

Israelites: The nonpriestly caste.

the anointed priest: The high priest, who is anointed with oil at his installation.

The bull's blood atones for inadvertent transgressions by the priests/high priest. Israelite atonement for comparable transgressions is achieved by the blood of the inner goat.

blood of the inner goat…blood of the bull: Observing that the inner goat atones for the Israelites' transgressions without the aid of a confession, R. Simeon concludes that the blood of the bull atones for priestly transgressions without the aid of a confession as well. R. Simeon avers that the high priests' confession upon slaughtering the bull achieves atonement for something other than violations of the holy Sanctuary and holy food with impurity. In his view, it atones for priestly sins encompassed by the list in 1:6. In other words, priestly atonement for these transgressions is not accomplished by the scapegoat.

confession…confession: Just as the confession on the scapegoat's head atones for Israel's transgressions unrelated to the Holy Sanctuary, the confession on the bull's head atones for the priests' transgressions unrelated to the Holy Sanctuary.

Chapter Two

2:1–4 *Unwitting Impurification of the Temple and Its Holy Things*

2 Knowledge of impurity is of two kinds, which are in fact four:
If one became impure and was aware[7] of it, but then,
(1) forgot the impurity, but recalled the holiness of the food,
or (2) forgot the holiness of the food, but recalled the impurity,
or forgot both this and this,
and he ate holy food without awareness.
If, after eating, he became aware—
behold, such a one is liable to a sliding-scale offering.
If one became impure and was aware of it, but then,
(3) forgot the impurity, but recalled the holiness of the Temple,
or (4) forgot the holiness of the Temple, but recalled the impurity,
or forgot both this and this,
and he entered the Temple without awareness.
If, after exiting, he became aware—
behold, such a one is liable to a sliding-scale offering.

2 The law is one and the same whether one enters the Temple Court or whether one enters an addition to the Temple Court,

---

[7] Lit. "and he knew," and so throughout.

2:1 *Knowledge of impurity*: If an individual becomes impure and forgets either that he is impure or that he is entering a holy precinct/eating holy food, he must bring an offering when he later realizes he transgressed (1:2). The term "knowledge" in the phrase "knowledge of impurity" refers not to the transgressor's initial awareness of his impurity, but to his incomplete understanding of the situation at the time that he transgresses.

and was aware of it: When he becomes impure, he realizes what has happened and recalls the requirement to avoid eating holy food and entering holy precincts in such a state.

forgot both that he is impure and that the food is holy. This scenario does not figure in the count of the four situations in which the transgressor has incomplete "knowledge of impurity."

he became aware: After eating he recalls that which he forgot. He now realizes he inadvertently ate holy food in a state of impurity.

forgot both that he is impure and that he is in a holy space. This scenario does not figure in the count of the four situations in which the transgressor has incomplete "knowledge of impurity."

A *sliding-scale offering* is determined according to one's financial means. A sheep or goat for those with substantial resources, two turtle doves or pigeons for those with moderate resources, and a tenth of an *ephah* of fine flour for those with limited resources. See Leviticus 5:6–12.

If, after exiting, he became aware of his transgression. Scenarios (1) and (2) resolve when the transgressor leaves the sanctuary and recalls what he had earlier forgotten. After a brief digression (2:2), the text addresses the situation in which one becomes impure *while in* the sanctuary (2:3).

2:2 *The law is one and the same*: Entrance to Court additions requires the same level of purity as to the original Court.

given that they make an addition[8] to the city and Temple Courts
only [on the authority of] a king, a prophet, the *urim v'tumim*, and the Sanhedrin of seventy-one,
and [only when accompanied] by two thanksgiving offerings and by song.
The [members of the] court proceed, the two thanksgiving offerings follow behind them,
and all Israel follows behind them.
The inner loaf is eaten and the outer loaf is burned.
Any addition for which each of these things was not done:
one who enters there—he is not liable for it.

3 If one became impure while in the Court,
and then forgot about the impurity but remembered the holiness of the Temple,
Or forgot about the holiness of the Temple, but remembered the impurity,
Or forgot about both this and this—
If he prostrated, or stayed long enough to prostrate, or went out the long way,
he is liable;
[If he went out] the short way,
he is exempt.

[8] Lit. "they do not add."

given the high standards imposed when expanding, additions have the same degree of sanctity as the original.

urim v'tumim: This term refers to the twelve stones on the breastplate of the high priest that were consulted for advice on difficult questions.

two thanksgiving offerings: Leviticus 7:11–15 outlines a ritual procedure for expressing gratitude for God's beneficence. The thanksgiving offering is accompanied by cakes and wafers, both leavened and unleavened. The Mishnah here refers to two leavened loaves that accompanied the thanksgiving animal offering and were part of a procession at the dedication of the expanded city or Court.

The [members of the] court proceed around the perimeter of the addition. The certifying ceremony appears to be modeled after Nehemiah's celebration upon completing the new walls of Jerusalem. See Nehemiah 12:31–43.

two thanksgiving offerings follow behind them: Nehemiah's celebration included two large "thanksgivings" (Nehemiah 12:31) circling the new walls. In Nehemiah, the term references two large "thanksgiving choirs." The Mishnah understands the two large "thanksgivings" to be two large loaves that accompanied the thanksgiving offering.

inner loaf… outer loaf: According to their position in the procession around the perimeter of the addition.

for which each of these things was not done: Since the additional space was not properly authorized, entering it in a state of impurity is not a transgression and carries no penalty.

2:3 *If he prostrated…stayed long enough…went out the long way*: If he did not leave as expeditiously as possible after recalling what he earlier forgot.

went out the long way: One typically exits the Sanctuary by walking counterclockwise three-quarters of the way around the perimeter of the Court. For example, if one enters through an eastern gate, one walks north along the eastern perimeter, turns west and continues along the northern perimeter, turns south and continues along the western perimeter, and finally turns east in order to exit from a southern gate (*Middot* 2:2).

the short way: The most expeditious way to leave the Holy Sanctuary is to walk clockwise one-quarter of the way around the perimeter from where one enters. For example, if one enters through an eastern gate, one should walk south and turn west at the southern perimeter in order to exit from a southern gate (*Middot* 2:2).

This is a positive commandment regarding the Temple,
for which [the members of the high court] are not liable [if they err].

4 And what is a positive commandment regarding the menstruant,
for which [the members of the high court] are liable [if they err]?
If one was having relations with a pure woman, and she said to him, "I have become impure,"
And he withdrew immediately—
he is liable, since exiting is as pleasurable to him as entering.

2:5 Scriptural Sources for "Knowledge of Impurity"

5 R. Eliezer says:
The creeping thing... and the fact escaped him:
one is liable for forgetting the creeping thing,
but one is not liable for forgetting the holiness of the Temple.
R. Aqiva says:
And though he had become impure, the fact escapes him:
one is liable for forgetting impurity [of any sort],
but one is not liable for forgetting the holiness of the Temple.

positive commandment regarding the Temple: The requirement to leave the Temple in the most expeditious manner possible.

for which [the members of the high court] are not liable [if they err]: Typically, a high court that causes the nation to sin by inadvertently misrepresenting the law brings a bull to atone on its own and on the people's behalf. See Leviticus 4:14 and *Horayot* 1:4. In two exceptional cases, including the present one, the Court does not bring a bull of expiation even though it misled the people. See *Horayot* 2:4.

2:4 *positive commandmen... the menstruant... is liable*: If a man's wife tells him during intercourse that she has begun menstruating, he must conclude the act in the most expeditious manner possible, that is, without further enjoyment or stimulation. Proper protocol requires that he let his member go limp before withdrawing. If the Court inadvertently and erroneously instructs him to withdraw from her immediately, they atone with a bull. See *Horayot* 2:4.

I have become impure: I have begun menstruating.

2:5 *R. Eliezer* disagrees with the view assumed throughout chapters 1 and 2, namely that one becomes liable for forgetting *either* one's own state as impure *or* the holiness of the Sanctuary.

the creeping thing... and the fact escaped him: Leviticus 5:2.

one is liable for forgetting the creeping thing... not... the holiness of the Temple: The phrases *creeping thing* and *and the fact escaped him* appear in close proximity to each other in the scriptural verse. In contrast, the verse says nothing about forgetting one's location relative to the Holy Sanctuary.

And though he had become impure, the fact escapes him: Leviticus 5:2.

R. Aqiva: Like R. Eliezer, he imposes liability only for forgetting one's own state of impurity. Whether R. Eliezer and R. Aqiva disagree is not clear. The Bavli suggests two explanations. One is that the two views do not differ; the two Sages learn the same rule from different phrases within the same verse. A second possibility is that the two Sages differ in the level of awareness required in order to be liable. R. Eliezer rules that one must know the source of the impurity. R. Aqiva rules that knowledge of impurity is sufficient; one need not know the source.

R. Ishmael says:
And the fact escapes him … and the fact escapes him:
[the phrase is written] two times,
in order to create obligation when one forgets the impurity
and when one forgets the holiness of the Temple.

Chapter Three

3:1–6   *Oaths about the Future and about the Past*

3   Oaths are of two kinds, which are in fact four:
[If one said:] "I swear[9]
(1) that I will eat," or
(2) "that I will not eat,"
(3) "that I ate," or
(4) "that I did not eat."
[If one said]: "I swear I will not eat,"
and ate any amount whatsoever—
he is liable—
the words of R. Aqiva.
They said to R. Aqiva:
Where else have we found [an instance of] someone eating any amount whatsoever who is liable, such that this one would be liable?
R. Aqiva said to them:
Well then, where else have we found [an instance of] someone [merely] speaking

[9] Lit. "It is an oath that …," and so throughout.

And the fact escapes him … and the fact escapes him: Leviticus 5:2–3.

3:1 *Oaths are of two kinds*: See note on 1:1.

two … which are … four: The two basic categories are positive ("I will") and negative ("I will not") oaths, which become four when they are framed in the future ("I will") and the past ("I did"). See 1:1. The four categories are generated by an interpretation of Leviticus 5:4, *when a person blurts out an oath to bad or good purpose*.

and ate any amount whatsoever: The consumption of food is generally considered legally significant only upon consuming an olive's bulk of food. See, for example, *Hallah* 1:2. According to R. Aqiva, oaths impose a unique type of prohibition, for which one is liable upon eating even less than an olive's worth ("anything whatsoever").

such that this one would be liable: The Sages demand consistency among the laws that prohibit food consumption.

this one: Someone who ate even the smallest amount after taking an oath not to eat.

Well then: R. Aqiva responds by showing that the eating prohibitions imposed by oaths are a class unto themselves.

someone [merely] speaking: A person who swears to eat a given food or to eat on a given day, and then fails to do so is liable for transgressing the rash oath. Though the person never performs a concrete action that

who must bring an offering, such that this one [merely] speaks and must bring an offering?
[If one said:] "I swear that I will not eat,"
and then ate and drank—
he is liable on only one count.
[If one said:] "I swear that I will not eat and that I will not drink,"
and then ate and drank—
he is liable on two counts.

2 [If one said:] "I swear that I will not eat,"
and then ate wheat bread, barley bread, and spelt bread—
he is liable on only one count.
[If one said:] "I swear that I will not eat wheat bread, barley bread, and spelt bread,"
and then ate [them]—
he is liable on each and every count.

3 [If one said:] "I swear that I will not drink,"
and then drank diverse types of drinks—
he is liable on only one count.
[If one said:] "I swear that I will not drink wine, oil, and honey,"
and then drank [them]—
he is liable on each and every count.

4 [If one said:] "I swear I will not eat,"
and then ate edible things that are not suitable for eating,
or drank liquids that are not suitable for drinking—
he is exempt.
[If one said:] "I swear I will not eat,"
and then ate carrion or torn flesh, vermin or creeping things—

renders him liable, he incurs guilt requiring expiation through an offering nonetheless. If one who performs no action whatsoever incurs guilt for violating his oath, then certainly one who eats only a small amount should also incur guilt.

this one: Someone who took an oath to not eat and subsequently ate less than an olive's bulk.

and then ate and drank: i.e. performed two distinct actions that can be construed as eating. The Mishnah assumes that the original oath ("I swear I will not eat") prohibits both eating and drinking.

on only one count: The transgression is evaluated on the basis of the stated intent. Having stated the oath in a general fashion, the oathtaker is not separately liable for diverse types of consumption ("eating and drinking").

3:2 *on only one count*: Since wheat, barley, and spelt (if that indeed is the correct translation) are all varieties of grain (*Hallah* 1:1).

3:4 *edible things that are not suitable for eating*: Like dust, which is unpalatable and has no nutritional value.

or drank: As in 3:1, the Mishnah assumes it is possible to transgress an oath not to eat when one drinks.

liquids that are not suitable for drinking: Like urine from an animal.

he is exempt from any liabilities incurred for transgressing the oath. Ingesting nonedibles and nonpotables does not violate the oath's stated intent.

carrion or torn flesh, vermin or creeping things: These meats are suitable for eating, though prohibited by Jewish law.

he is liable.
R. Simeon exempts.
[If one said:] "May any benefit that my wife have from me be *qonam* if I ate today,"
and he ate carrion or torn flesh, forbidden beasts or creeping things—
his wife is forbidden [to have any benefit from him].

5 The law is one and the same for matters regarding oneself and matters regarding others,
and for matters that are material, and matters that are immaterial.
How so?
If one said: "I swear
that I will give to such and such a person,"
or "that I will not give [to such and such a person],"
or "that I did give [to such and such a person],"
or "that I did not give [to such and such a person]";
"that I will sleep,"
or "that I will not sleep,"
or "that I did sleep,"
or "that I did not sleep";
"that I will throw a pebble into the sea,"
or "that I will not throw [a pebble into the sea],"
or "that I did throw [a pebble into the sea],"
or "that I did not throw [a pebble into the sea]"—
[all of these oaths are binding].
R. Ishmael says:
One is liable only regarding [oaths] that concern the future,

he is liable: Foods prohibited by Jewish law belong to the generic category of edibles since a gentile considers them food; eating them violates the stated intent of the oath.

R. Simeon exempts because he thinks that the oathtaker would not have intended the oath to prohibit forbidden consumables..

qonam: This term is a substitute for the word *qorban*, meaning "offering"; see *Nedarim* 1:2. The classic vow formula likens a specified item to an offering (*qorban*) that has been dedicated to the Temple and is thus unavailable for general use. Rash oaths differ from vows in that rash oaths prohibit an activity ("I swear I will not eat") and vows prohibit an object ("That loaf is like a *qorban* to me").

3:5 *The law is one and the same*: Rash and vain oaths take force in equal measure.

oneself… others: Irrespective of whether the oath concerns oneself or others.

material…immaterial: Irrespective of whether the prescribed action makes a substantive impact on the world.

"I will give to such and such a person": This is an example of an oath that concerns another.

"I will give"… "will not"… "did give"… "did not give:" The rubric of four related oaths (positive and negative, future and past) echoes the rubric presented at the beginning of the chapter (3:1). As there, the Mishnah moves seamlessly between rash and vain oaths, since both derive from the same scriptural source (Leviticus 5:4).

"I will throw a pebble into the sea": This is an example of an oath that has no substantive impact on the world.

as it is written:
To do evil or to do good.
R. Aqiva said to him:
If so, I have only [oaths] that concern doing evil and doing good;
whence can we derive [oaths] that concern things other than doing evil and doing good?
[R. Ishmael] said to him:
From scriptural hints regarding additional meanings.
[R. Aqiva] said to him:
If Scripture hinted regarding this additional meaning,
then it hinted regarding the other additional meaning.

6 One who swore
to violate a commandment, but did not violate it—
he is exempt;
to perform a commandment, but did not perform it—
he is exempt.
[This, in spite of the fact] that logic dictates that one should be liable [in the second instance],
in accordance with the words of R. Judah b. Betera.
R. Judah b. Betera said:
If one is liable for oaths concerning voluntary actions,
these being actions for which one did not take an oath at Mount Sinai,
Doesn't logic dictate that one should be liable for oaths concerning commandments,
these being actions for which one did take an oath at Mount Sinai?
[The Sages] said to him:
No.
Just because you drew a conclusion about oaths that concern voluntary actions,

---

To do evil or to do good: Leviticus 5:4. R. Ishmael disagrees with the presumptive position of this chapter that oaths regarding the past can be derived from this verse.

If so: R. Aqiva demonstrates that a truly literal reading of the verse would limit oathtaking to actions that have a negative and positive impact.

whence: In Scripture.

From scriptural hints regarding additional meanings: R. Ishmael does not reveal what the scriptural hints are.

If Scripture hinted regarding…then it hinted regarding…: If some of Scripture's prescriptions are merely implied, there is no reason to accept R. Ishmael's extension of the verse (to include actions that are neither for evil nor good) while rejecting R. Aqiva's (to include past, as well as future, actions).

3:6 *to violate a commandment*: See 3:8.

is exempt: From the penalties exacted from those who violate a rash oath (for penalties, see 3:7).

to perform a commandment: Whereas in the first case the oath undermines the authority of the commandment, in this case the oath reinforces the authority of the commandment.

logic dictates that one should be liable: For failing to perform an oath to uphold a commandment.

Doesn't logic dictate: R. Judah b. Betera reasons as follows: If an oath about ordinary matters ("voluntary actions") creates obligation where none previously existed, then surely an oath to uphold a commandment can reinforce an obligation that is already in force.

these being actions to which one can just as easily say "no," as "yes,"
does not mean you can draw the same conclusion about oaths that concern commandments,
these being actions to which one cannot just as easily say "no," as "yes,"
Indeed, if one swore to violate [a commandment] and did not violate [it]—he is exempt.

3:7–11   Rash and Vain Oaths

7 [If one said:] "I swear I will not eat this loaf, I swear I will not eat it, I swear I will not eat it,"
and ate it—he is liable on only one count.
This is a rash oath,
for which one is liable to lashes for intentional transgressions, and
a sliding-scale offering for unintentional transgressions.
[For] a vain oath,
one is liable to lashes for intentional transgressions, and
for unintentional transgressions—one is exempt.
   8 What is a vain oath?
If one swore to reverse what is known by all:
[for example,] if one said of a stone column that it is made of gold, or
of a man, that he is a woman, or
of a woman, that she is a man;
[Or] if one swore about something that is impossible:

actions to which one can just as easily say "no," as "yes": The Torah is neutral regarding voluntary actions. It matters not whether one takes on a new obligation (says "yes") or not (says "no").

actions to which one cannot just as easily say "no," as "yes": The Torah is not neutral regarding one's performance of commandments. One is not free to say "no" to a commandment.

is exempt: From liability for the violation of the oath. Though an oath that aims to reinforce an existing commandment does not take effect, the obligation to perform the commandment itself remains.

3:7 *I swear I will not eat it, I swear I will not eat it*: If one made the same oath about the same loaf three times. This mishnah examines issues already explored in 3:1 (multiple counts of liability) and continued in 3:9 (the impact of repeating oaths that affirm or contradict each other).

he is liable on only one count: Commentators offer various reasons for the single count of liability in the face of multiple articulations of the oath. The most straightforward explanation is that from the moment that the first oath is uttered, the second and third oaths are not legitimate oaths because the action to which they refer is already the subject of an oath.

A *rash oath* declares one's intent to perform, or refrain from performing, a particular action. Though one may eventually fulfill the oath, it is considered rash, reflecting both the biblical and rabbinic disapproval of using oaths in this manner. The rabbinic term "rash oath" derives from Leviticus 5:4.

vain oath: See definition and examples in 3:8. Vain oaths are discussed in the same context as rash oaths because both types derive from Leviticus 5:4.

3:8 *If one said to witnesses: Come and testify on my behalf*: A litigant has the legal right to require potential witnesses to appear in court. See 4:3.

[for example, if one said:]
"If I didn't see a camel flying through the air," or
"If I didn't see a snake like the beam of an olive press";
If one said to witnesses: "Come and testify on my behalf,"
[And they said:]
"We swear we will not testify on your behalf";
If one swore to violate[10] a commandment:
[for example, if one said]
"I won't make a *sukkah*," or
"I won't take the *lulav*," or
"I won't put on *tefillin*"—
this is a vain oath,
for which one is liable to lashes for intentional transgressions, and
for unintentional transgressions—one is exempt.

9 [If one said:] "I swear I will eat this loaf, I swear I will not eat it"—
The first is a rash oath, and
the second is a vain oath.
If he ate it, he transgressed the vain oath.
If he did not eat it, he transgressed the rash oath.

[10] Lit. "to cancel" or "to annul."

"*We swear we will not testify on your behalf*": Potential witnesses can refuse to appear in court only if they are ignorant of testimony relevant to the litigant's case. In this scenario they try to avoid appearing in court by fiat—they simply do not wish to testify. Since declining to testify in this manner is a violation of Leviticus 5:1, their oath of refusal has no legal standing.

If one swore to violate a commandment: As noted in 3:6, an oath to violate a commandment has no legal standing as a rash oath. Should one fail to fulfill the oath to violate a commandment, one is not liable for a *rash oath*. The moment one utters an oath to violate a commandment, one is, however, guilty of a *vain oath*.

sukkah: See Leviticus 23:42 and *Sukkah* chapters 1–3.

lulav: Leviticus 23:40.

tefillin: Phylacteries, little boxes containing the biblical passages to "bind [these words] as a sign upon your hand and let them serve as a symbol between your eyes" (Deuteronomy 6:8, 11:18, see also Exodus 13:9, 16).

3:9 "*I swear I will eat…I swear I will not eat it*": The oathtaker makes two rash oaths that directly contradict each other. Fulfilling one oath requires violating the other.

rash oath: Before the second oath is articulated, the first oath is a rash oath like any other. It fortifies one's desire to perform a voluntary action with the force of an oath.

vain oath: The second oath has the exterior form of a rash oath since it expresses the desire to refrain from a particular action. Insofar as it contradicts the terms of the first oath, it is a vain oath (see 3:8). According to the Tosefta, the oathtaker becomes liable for the second oath in its capacity as vain oath as soon as he utters it.

If he ate it: By fulfilling the stipulations of the first oath ("to eat this loaf"), the oathtaker violates the terms of the second oath ("not to eat it").

he transgressed the vain oath: That is, the second oath. Though the second oath ("not to eat it") is a vain oath from the moment it is uttered, it retains its form as a rash oath. When the oathtaker eats the loaf, he incurs additional guilt for violating the terms of his second rash oath ("I swear I will not eat it").

he transgressed the rash oath: That is, the first oath, in its capacity as rash oath. The second oath ("I swear I will not eat it") retains its status as a vain oath, for which he is liable immediately upon uttering it.

10 The [law of the] rash oath is applicable to men and women,
nonrelatives and relatives,
those fit [to testify] and those unfit,
before a court and not before a court,
when one utters the oath of one's own accord.
And one is liable to lashes for intentional transgressions, and
for unintentional transgressions—[one is liable to] a sliding-scale offering.

11 The [law of the] vain oath is applicable to men and women,
nonrelatives and relatives,
those fit [to testify] and those unfit,
before a court and not before a court,
when one utters the oath of one's own accord.
One is liable to lashes for intentional transgressions, and
for unintentional transgressions—one is exempt.
The law is one and the same for the one as for the other—
one who is submitted to an oath by someone else is liable.
How so?
If one said:
"I did not eat today," or
"I did not put *tefillin* on today,"
[And another said:]
"I submit you to an oath,"
And the first one said:
"I accede to the oath."[11]
[If he swore falsely]—he is liable.

Chapter Four

4:1–13 *Testimonial Oaths*

4 The [law of the] testimonial oath is applicable to men, but not to women;
To nonrelatives, but not to relatives;

[11] Lit. "amen," and so throughout.

3:10–11 Women, close relations, and those guilty of shady practices (*Sanhedrin* 3:3–4, *Rosh Hashanah* 1:8) are not allowed to testify in rabbinic courts and their testimonial oaths have no legal standing (4:1). Their rash and vain oaths are valid.

when one utters the oath of one's own accord: One says: "I swear…" on one's own initiative. The other possibility is that an outside party submits one to an oath, as at the end of 3:11.

3:11 *the one…the other*: Rash and vain oaths.

tefillin: See note on 3:8.

4:1 *testimonial oath*: Imposed upon potential witnesses as a means of confirming that they are not withholding evidence relevant to a case (4:3). See Leviticus 5: See note to 3:10–11.1.

To those fit [to testify], but not to those unfit;
and it is applicable only to those capable of giving testimony;
before a court and not before a court,
when one utters the oath of own's accord.
[When submitted to the oath] by someone else,
they are not liable [for swearing falsely]
unless they deny [knowing testimony] in court—
these are the words of R. Meir.
The Sages say:
No matter whether [one utters the oath] of one's own accord
or [was submitted to the oath] by someone else,
they are not liable [for swearing falsely]
unless they deny [knowing testimony] in court.

2 They are liable for [falsifying] the oath intentionally,
and for inadvertently swearing regarding testimony that they intentionally [withheld],
but they are not liable for [testimony] they unintentionally [withheld].
And to what are they liable when [falsifying] intentionally?
A sliding-scale offering.

3 The testimonial oath, how so?
If one said to two men:
"Come and testify on my behalf,"
[And they replied:]
"We swear we know no testimony on your behalf."
Or they said:
"We know no testimony on your behalf,"
and he [the litigant] said,
"I submit you to an oath,"
and they said,
"We accede to the oath."
In this case [if they swore falsely] they are liable.
If one submitted them to an oath five times not before a court,
and then they went to court and admitted [to knowing testimony],
they are exempt.

only to those capable of giving testimony: According to *Sanhedrin* 2:2, a king does not testify.

by someone else: The litigant requiring testimony initiates the process by pronouncing a formula that introduces the oath (see 4:3); the potential witness accepts the terms of the oath by responding "amen."

4:2 *for inadvertently swearing regarding testimony that they intentionally [withheld]*: Though the potential witnesses did not realize that the oath would be binding, they intentionally withheld testimony from the litigant.

A sliding-scale offering: See Leviticus 5:6–12.

4:3 *"I submit you to an oath"*: The oath is initiated "by someone else" (see language in 4:1). Potential witnesses must verbally accept the terms of the oath in order for it to take force.

they are exempt: For having sworn falsely when they were not in the presence of the court. The fact that they admitted to knowing testimony once they arrived at court suggests that they did not take the oaths out of court seriously.

If they denied [knowing testimony]—
they are liable for each and every [false oath outside of court].
If one submitted them to an oath five times before a court,
and they denied [knowing testimony each time],
they are liable on only one count.
R. Simeon said:
What is the reason [for only one count of liability in the last case]?
Since they are not able to retract [after the first false oath] and admit [to knowing testimony].

4 If two [potential witnesses] together denied [knowing testimony],
both are liable.
If they denied one after the other,
the first is liable and the second is exempt.
If one denied and the other admitted [knowing testimony],
the one who denied is liable.
If there were two pairs of witnesses,
and the first pair denied [knowing testimony],
and then later the second pair denied [knowing testimony]—
both pairs are liable,
since the testimony could have been established by either pair.

5 [If a litigant said:] "I submit you to an oath to come and testify on my behalf that I have a deposit, a loan, a stolen item, and a lost item in so-and-so's custody,"
[And they responded:] "We swear we know no testimony on your behalf"—
[if they swore falsely] they are liable on only one count.

If they denied knowing even after they arrived in court. This scenario builds on the previous one and envisions the potential witnesses denying five times out of court before persisting in their denial in court.

they are liable for each and every [false oath outside of court]: The fact that they persisted in their denial once at court suggests that each of the earlier denials was intentional.

What is the reason for only one count of liability when potential witnesses swear falsely at the conclusion of five imprecations in court?

Since they are not able to retract...and admit: Having made the initial oath in court, it takes force immediately. Once the initial oath has been made, subsequent pronouncements have the external form of an oath, but do not qualify as distinct oaths. Repeated testimonial oaths take force only when the oathtaker has had an opportunity to retract each one. In the former case, all five testimonial oaths stand because the oathtaker could have come to court at any point to retract or affirm them. The possibility of retracting each of the five oaths uttered outside of court renders each one distinct and valid once ratified by the final oath in court.

4:4 *the first is liable and the second is exempt*: Once the first witness has denied knowing testimony, the second witness's testimony is useless to the court. If the second witness takes a testimonial oath where no obligation exists, he is exempt even when he falsely denies knowing information relevant to the case.

the one who denied is liable since his actions are directly responsible for impeding the court's assessment of the case.

since the testimony could have been established by either pair: Since testimony by either pair of witnesses can stand in court, each pair is equally liable for obstructing the court's proceedings by falsely denying testimony.

4:5 *they are liable on only one count...they are liable on each and every count*: When the potential witnesses deny knowing testimony relevant to each one of the litigant's claims, each denial is regarded as a separate oath with its own count of liability in the event they swear falsely.

[If they responded:] "We swear we know nothing
regarding a deposit, a loan, a stolen item, or a lost item of yours in so-and-so's custody"—
[if they swore falsely] they are liable on each and every count.
[If a litigant said:] "I submit you to an oath to come and testify on my behalf
that I have a security consisting of wheat, barley, and spelt in so-and-so's custody,"
[And they responded:] "We swear we know no testimony on your behalf"—
[if they swore falsely] they are liable on only one count.
[If they responded:] "We swear we know no testimony on your behalf
regarding your wheat, barley, and spelt in so-and-so's custody"—
[if they swore falsely,] they are liable on each and every count.

6 [If a litigant said:] "I submit you to an oath to come and testify on my behalf
that [any of the following payments] are due to me from the hand of so-and-so:
a damage payment, or a half-damage payment,
or a two-fold payment, or a four- or five-fold payment,
[Or payment due me on account of the fact]
that so-and-so raped my daughter,
or that so-and-so seduced my daughter,
or that my son hit me,
or that my fellow injured me,
or that he set fire to my grain pile on the Day of Atonement,"
[If potential witnesses swear falsely that they know no such testimony]—
they are liable.

4:6 *"damage payment"*: Owed by defendant to the claimant.

"half-damage payment": This refers to cases where compensation corresponds to half the reduction in value caused by the damage. Examples include damage caused by a goring ox with no prior goring history (*Bava Qamma* 1:4), as well as damage caused in an unusual manner (*Bava Qamma* 2:1).

"a two-fold payment" is extracted from the thief who still possesses the object that he stole. In addition to the payment, he is also required to return the original object. See Exodus 22:3 and *Bava Qamma* 7:1.

"a four- or five-fold payment" is extracted from the thief who has sold or slaughtered the stolen animal such that it cannot be returned. See Exodus 21:37 and *Bava Qamma* 7:1.

"so-and-so raped my daughter" and is obligated to make payments to the victim's father; see *Ketubbot* 3:4.

"so-and-so seduced my daughter" and is obligated to make payments to the victim's father; see *Ketubbot* 3:4.

"my son hit me" and is obligated to pay a fine. Though Exodus 21:15 stipulates that hitting one's parents is a capital offense, *Sanhedrin* 11:1 restricts the death penalty to cases where the child's blow is sufficient to inflict a wound. Our mishnah presumes that a wound is not inflicted and a fine, rather than the death penalty, is levied on the child.

"my fellow," that is my social equal, *injured me* and is obligated to make payments; see *Bava Qamma* 8:1.

"set fire to my grain pile on the Day of Atonement" and is obligated to damage payments. One who lights a fire on the Day of Atonement is liable to *karet* (death at the hands of heaven) for performing one of the prohibited labors (see *Shabbat* 7:2). The punishment of *karet*, unlike a death penalty inflicted by a human court, does not cancel payments for damages (*Bava Qamma* 3:10 and 8:5).

they, the potential witnesses, *are liable*: The principle at work here is that witnesses are held accountable for swearing falsely only when their testimony, if given truthfully, would have resulted in monies paid to the claimant.

7 [If a litigant said:] "I submit you to an oath to come and testify on my behalf that I am a priest,
or that I am a Levite,
or that I am not the son of a divorced woman,
or that I am not the son of a woman who performed *halitsah*,
or that so-and-so is a priest,
or that so-and-so is a Levite,
or that he is not the son of a divorced woman,
or that he is not the son of a woman who performed *halitsah*,
or that so-and-so raped his daughter,
or that so-and-so seduced his daughter,
or that my son injured me,
or that my fellow injured me or set fire to my grain pile on the Sabbath,"[12]
[If potential witnesses swear falsely that they know no such testimony]—
they are exempt.

8 [If a litigant said:] "I submit you to an oath to come and testify on my behalf that so-and-so said he would give me two hundred *zuz*,
and then never gave me [the money]";
[If they swear falsely that they know no such testimony]—
in this case they are exempt,
since one is liable only for monetary claims that are like a deposit.

[12] **P, K**: "Or that my fellow's son injured him, or that he set fire to my grain pile on the Sabbath."

4:7 *"That I am a priest…a Levite"*: The litigant in this case wants the witnesses to confirm his entitlement to the rights and privileges of his caste.

"the son of a divorced woman": Leviticus 21:7 prohibits marriage between a priest and a divorcee; their offspring is disqualified from the priesthood and may not receive *terumah* and other priestly gifts.

"the son of a woman who performed halitsah": Deuteronomy 25:9. For the rabbis a woman who has performed *halitsah* has the same legal status as a divorcee.

"that so-and-so raped…seduced his daughter": The Hebrew is ambiguous. Most interpreters assume that the situation implied here involves the rapist/seducer assaulting his own daughter. One who rapes/seduces his own daughter is punished with the death penalty (*Sanhedrin* 9:1) rather than damage payments. Rashi prefers to read that phrase as implying that the rapist/seducer assaults the daughter of a third party, in which case the person imposing the oath acts for someone else's financial benefit. According to 4:12, the testimonial oath must be imposed directly by the claimant.

"that my son injured me": For which the son receives the death penalty, as per Exodus 21:15.

"that my fellow," i.e. one of the same social class, *injured me or set fire to my grain pile on the Sabbath*: Since the fellow receives the death penalty for violating the Sabbath, damage payments are waived.

they are exempt: Even if they swore falsely. The witnesses are not held accountable for swearing falsely when their testimony, if given truthfully, would not have resulted in monies paid to the one imposing the oath.

4:8 *monetary claims that are like a deposit*: Insofar as the disputed sum is legally the property of the claimant but is understood to be temporarily in the possession of the defendant.

4:9 *since the oath preceded the testimony*: At the time of the oath, the witnesses knew no information related to the claimant's case. The testimonial oath can be imposed to solicit only information *already* known by the witnesses.

9 [If a man said to potential witnesses:]
"I submit you to an oath affirming that, when you know testimony on my behalf,
you will come and testify on my behalf"—
in this case they are exempt,
since the oath preceded the testimony.

10 [If a man] stood in the synagogue, and said:
"I submit you to an oath affirming that, if you know testimony on my behalf,
you will come and testify on my behalf"—
in this case they are exempt,
unless he directs his [request] at them [who ostensibly know testimony].

11 [If a man] said to two others:
"So-and-so and so-and-so, I submit you to an oath affirming that,
if you know testimony on my behalf, you will come and testify on my behalf."
[And they responded:] "We swear we know no testimony on your behalf,"
but they did know secondhand testimony on his behalf,
or one of them was a relative or unfit [to give testimony]—
in this case they are exempt.

12 [If the claimant] sent a message through his servant,
or if the defendant said to them:
"I submit you to an oath affirming that, if you know testimony on his behalf,
you will come and testify on his behalf."
[If they swear falsely,] they are exempt,
unless they hear [the oath] from the mouth of the claimant.

13 [If one said:]
"I submit you to an oath," or
"I command you," or
"I obligate you"—

4:10 *"I submit you"*: The oath is addressed indiscriminately to all those present in the synagogue.

they are exempt even though, knowing relevant information, they swore falsely to not knowing.

unless he is directing his [request] at them: In order to take force, the oath needs to be addressed to two specified individuals.

4:11 *secondhand testimony*: Information, though relevant to the case, if learned by hearsay is inadmissible as evidence in court. See *Sanhedrin* 4:5.

a relative of the claimant, and therefore disqualified from testifying on his behalf even if he knows information relevant to the case. See *Sanhedrin* 3:4.

unfit [to give testimony]: *Sanhedrin* 3:3.

4:12 *unless they hear*: Only the claimant has the right to submit potential witnesses to an oath, and he must do so in person.

4:13 *[If one said]*: This mishnah distinguishes between acceptable and unacceptable formulas when imposing a testimonial oath.

"I command you" to take an oath.

"I obligate you" to take an oath.

[if they swear falsely,] they are liable.
[If one says:]
"By heaven and by earth"—
[If they swear falsely]—
they are exempt,
[If one says:]
"By *alef dalet*,"
"By *yod heh*,"
"By *Shaddai*,"
"By the Hosts,"
"By the Gracious and Merciful One,"
"By the One Who Is Long Suffering and of Great Kindness,"
Or by any of the substitutions for God's name—
[If they swear falsely,] they are liable.
[Likewise,] one who curses [God] with any of them is liable—
the words of R. Meir.
But the Sages exempt him.
One who curses his father and mother with any of them is liable—
the words of R. Meir.
But the Sages exempt him.
One who curses himself or his fellow using any of them,
transgresses a negative commandment.
[If one said:]
"May God smite you,"
or "May God smite you thus"—

"By heaven and by earth"... they are exempt: Since the phrase "Heaven and Earth" is not one of God's names.

"By": i.e. in the name of…, I submit you to an oath.

"alef dalet": The first ("a") and fourth ("d") letters of the Hebrew alphabet; an abbreviation for the divine name *Adonai*. The Mishnah uses an abbreviation to avoid writing out God's name.

"yod heh": The tenth ("y") and fifth ("h") letters of the Hebrew alphabet; an abbreviation for the Tetragrammaton ("YHWH").

"Shaddai": often translated as *The Almighty*; another name of God.

"Hosts": The Lord of Hosts; another of God's names.

One who curses... with any of them is liable: One who curses God employing any of these names incurs guilt for blasphemy (Leviticus 24:15-16). See *Sanhedrin* 7:5.

But the Sages exempt him from the death penalty for blasphemy.

One who curses his father and mother... is liable: Exodus 21:17 and Leviticus 20:9 impose the death penalty for children who curse their parents. The rabbis interpret this to mean death by stoning (*Sanhedrin* 7:4).

the words of R. Meir... the Sages exempt: The same dispute is recorded in *Sanhedrin* 7:8. There it is explained that the Sages exempt because these curses do not employ God's name directly.

"May God smite you" if you do not testify on my behalf. Here the Mishnah returns to the subject of testimonial oaths.

"May God smite you thus": Specifying a particular malady. Rashi understands the phrase to refer to a scenario in which one person is reading aloud the biblical passage that enumerates the curses with which

this is the *curse* written in the Torah.
[If one said:]
"May he not smite you,"
"May he bless you,"
"May he bring about good things for you"—
R. Meir declares him liable,
but the Sages exempt him.

Chapter Five

5:1–5 *Oath of Deposit*

5 The [law of the] oath of deposit is applicable to men and women,
nonrelatives and relatives,
those fit [to testify] and those unfit,
before a court and not before a court,
when one utters the oath oneself.
[When the oath is imposed] by someone else,
one is not liable unless one swears falsely in court—
the words of R. Meir.
But the Sages say:
No matter whether [one utters the oath] of one's own accord
or [was submitted to the oath] by someone else,
as long as one swears falsely—
one is liable.

God will smite the people Israel if they do not obey the terms of the covenant (Deuteronomy 28). With this phrase, the claimant threatens the curses that have just been read.

this is the curse written in the Torah: in Leviticus 5:1. R. Meir considers these formulas valid for the purpose of the testimonial oath, even though they do not invoke God's name directly.

"May he not smite you, May he bless you, May he bring about good things for you," if you do provide testimony. These formulas offer divine blessing to potential witnesses who agree to provide testimony. Since they implicitly invoke divine wrath ("May he smite you," "May he curse you," "May he bring about bad things for you") on potential witnesses who decline to testify, R. Meir considers these formulas valid for the purpose of the testimonial oath.

5:1 The *oath of deposit* is imposed when the claimant holds that the defendant owes him money or goods. The disputed sum is regarded as a "deposit" that one claimant has left in the hands of the defendant. The oath is imposed in order to get the defendant to return what rightfully belongs to the claimant. See 5:2 for details, and Leviticus 5:20–26.

women...relatives...and those unfit to testify: See note on 3:10–11 and 4:1.

[When the oath is imposed] by someone else: See 5:2.

And one is liable when the [false] oath is intentional,
and when one swears unintentionally
while [misrepresenting the state of] the deposit intentionally.
but one is not liable when it is unintentional.
And for what is one liable when it is intentional?
A guilt offering worth *silver sheqels*.

2 The oath of deposit, how so?
One says to another: "Give me my deposit which is currently in your possession,"
[and the second replies:] "I swear nothing of yours is in my possession."
Or [the second] says: "Nothing of yours is in my possession,"
[and the first replies:] "I impose an oath upon you,"
And [the second] says: "I accede to the oath"—
this one is liable.
If one imposed an oath upon him five times,
no matter whether he was before a court or not before a court,
if he denied [having the deposit]—
he is liable on each and every count.
R. Simeon said:
What is the reason?
Since he can return and admit [to having the deposit].

3 If five individuals were making a claim against him,
and they said to him: "Give us our deposit that is in your possession,"
[and he replied:] "I swear I have nothing of yours [plural] in my possession"—
he is liable on only one count.
[If he replied:] "I swear have nothing of yours [singular]

---

when the [false] oath is intentional, and when one swears unintentionally while [misrepresenting the state of] the deposit intentionally: The Mishnah assumes the capacity for intention on two levels: (1) as regards the oath, and (2) as regards the facts of the deposit. In the first scenario ("the false oath is intentional"), the oathtaker acts with intention on both levels: he willfully misrepresents the facts while knowingly and willfully employing the oath formula. In the second scenario ("swears unintentionally while intentionally misrepresenting the facts"), the oathtaker acts with intention on the second level only: he willfully misrepresents the facts, but does not understand that he is making an oath. The Mishnah considers him liable in both cases.

not liable when it, the oath, *is not intentional*: The Mishnah assumes that the oathtaker did not willfully misrepresent the facts.

for what is one liable: Leviticus 5:24–25 states that one who swears falsely regarding a "deposit" must repay the monies owed, plus a fifth, in addition to the guilt offering mentioned here.

silver sheqels: A phrase drawn from Leviticus 5:15 where it delineates the currency in which the value of a guilt offering is measured. The Mishnah uses the phrase as shorthand to indicate the minimum value of a guilt offering, understood as the kind of silver *sheqel* used in the Temple rather than the kind of silver *sheqel* in general circulation when the Mishnah was composed. See *Zevahim* 10:5 for additional requirements of the guilt offering.

5:2 *Since he can return and admit [to having the deposit]* at any point between the oaths, each oath is distinct and he is fully liable for it.

5:3 *Only if he states the oath formula at the end*: i.e. after indicating each of the three defendants distinctly, making clear his intention that the oath concerns each one as an individual.

or yours [singular] or yours [singular] in my possession"—
[If he swore falsely] he is liable on each and every count.
R. Eliezer says:
Only if he states the oath formula at the end.
R. Simeon says:
Only if he states the oath formula for each and every one.
[If one says:] "Give me the deposit, the loan, the stolen item, and lost item
that I have in your possession,"
[and the other replies:] "I swear I have nothing of yours in my possession"—
he is liable on only one count.
[But if the other replies:] "I swear I do not have your deposit, loan, stolen item, and lost
item in my possession"—
he is liable on each and every count.
[If one says:] "Give me the wheat [plural], barley [plural], and spelt [plural]
that I have in your possession,"
[and the other replies:] "I swear I have nothing of yours in my possession"—
he is liable on only one count.
[But if the other replies:] "I swear I do not have
your wheat [plural], barley [plural], and spelt [plural] in my possession"—
he is liable on each and every count.
R. Meir says:
Even if he said: wheat [singular], barley [singular], and spelt [singular]—
he is liable on each and every count.

4 [If the claimant says:] "You raped my daughter, or you seduced my daughter,"
and [the defendant] says: "I did not rape [her], or I did not seduce [her],"
[and the claimant says:] "I submit you to an oath,"
and [the defendant] said: "I accede to the oath"—
[if he swore falsely] he is liable.
R. Simeon exempts him, since one does not pay a fixed fine
[when one admits to wrongdoing] of his own accord.

Only if he states the oath formula for each and every defendant, leaving no room for confusion regarding his intention to make three separate oaths.

Even if he said: wheat [singular]...: Using slightly different language to indicate the same referent. In this example, the claimant stipulates that he is owed wheat, barley, and spelt using the plural form, as per conventional rabbinic usage. The defendant denies having the contested property in his possession using the singular form, as per the usage in Exodus 9:31–32.

5:4 "*You raped... or you seduced my daughter*" and therefore you owe me four (for rape) or three (for seduction) payments (Exodus 22:15–16; Deuteronomy 22:28–29). These payments, to which the victim's father is legally entitled, constitute the disputed "deposit." See *Ketubbot* 3:4.

R. Simeon exempts him, since one does not pay a fixed fine... of own's accord: R. Simeon's ruling is based on the principle that if one admits to wrongdoing, one pays only for the damage inflicted; all penalties beyond that are waived (see *Ketubbot* 3:9). In the case of a woman who has been raped or seduced, the fixed fine is waived when the aggressor confesses, as it constitutes payment above and beyond damage inflicted. Basic damage in the case of rape and seduction is assessed as shame, devaluation, and pain (in the case of rape) payments. In R. Simeon's view, the oath of deposit is imposed only when the disputed sum is definite. Since

They [the Sages] said to him:
Even though one does not pay a fixed fine
[when one admits to wrongdoing] of one's own accord,
one pays for shame and devaluation [when one admits to wrongdoing] of own's own accord.

5 [If the claimant says:] "You stole my ox,"
and [the defendant] says: "I did not steal,"
[and the claimant says:] "I submit you to an oath,"
and [defendant] said: "I accede to the oath"—
[if he swore falsely,] he is liable.
[If the defendant replies:] "I stole, but I did not slaughter or sell,"
[and the claimant says:] "I submit you to an oath,"
and [the defendant] said: "I accede to the oath"—
[if he swore falsely,] "he is exempt.

it is unclear in advance whether the defendant will admit to or deny wrongdoing, the disputed sum is unclear and an oath of deposit cannot be imposed. If the oath is nonetheless imposed and the defendant falsely denies the accusation, he is not liable since the oath was inappropriately administered.

Even though ... one pays for shame and devaluation: The assailant pays for shame and devaluation both when he admits wrongdoing and when he initially denies and subsequently is exposed as lying (though in the latter case, he pays a fixed fine in addition to shame and devaluation). The Sages stress that payments will be assessed either way if the violation occurred. Since what is at stake between the claimant and defendant is whether the violation occurred, the Sages assume there is a disputed sum at stake.

5:5 This mishnah alternates between cases in which factual dispute does and does not entail financial dispute. While the oath of deposit is imposed when factual dispute entails financial dispute, it is not imposed when factual dispute does not entail financial dispute.

"*You stole my ox*": The thief is obligated to return the ox, as well as to pay a penalty equivalent to the ox's value (Exodus 22:3). If the defendant admits to having stolen the ox, he is not required to pay the additional penalty, though he remains obligated to return the ox (or pay the owner its value).

he is liable in the event that he swore falsely. The oath is a valid oath because there is a disputed sum irrespective of whether the defendant admits initially to the theft or not. If, under the pressure of an oath, he admits to the theft, the dispute is limited to the value of the ox. If he persists in his denial to the point of swearing that he did not steal the ox, the dispute concerns double the ox's value. In any event, there is a disputed sum. The oath is valid and, if sworn falsely, incurs liability.

[If the defendant replies]: If, instead of denying the entire accusation, the defendant admits part (stealing) and denies part (slaughtering or selling).

"*I stole, but I did not slaughter or sell*": By admitting to stealing the ox, the defendant admits to owing the owner the value of the ox. The dispute is limited to whether the defendant slaughtered and sold the ox.

"*slaughter or sell*": See Exodus 21:37.

he is exempt: Though this case involves a factual dispute between the litigants (was the ox slaughtered /sold?), it does not necessarily involve a financial dispute. If, under pressure of the oath, the defendant admits to having sold and slaughtered the ox, the defendant will not owe the owner anything beyond the value of the ox, which he admitted to owing even before the oath was administered. Since it is impossible to know before the oath is imposed whether the factual dispute will also entail a financial dispute, the oath of deposit may not be imposed. If imposed, it is not valid, and the defendant is not liable though he misrepresented the facts while under oath.

[If the claimant says:] "Your ox killed my ox,
and [the defendant] says: "It did not kill,"
[and the claimant says:] "I submit you to an oath,"
and [the defendant] said: "I accede to the oath"—
[if he swore falsely,] he is liable.
[If the claimant said:] "Your ox killed my slave,"
and [the defendant] says: "It did not kill,"
[and the claimant said:] "I submit you to an oath,"
and [the defendant] said: "I accede to the oath"—
[if he swore falsely,] he is exempt.
[If the claimant says:] "You injured me or inflicted a wound, "
and [the defendant] says: "I did not injure you or inflict a wound,"
[and the claimant says:] "I submit you to an oath,"
and [the defendant] said: "I accede to the oath"—
[if he swore falsely,] he is liable.
If one's slave said to one: "You caused my tooth to fall out or you blinded me,"
and he says: "I did not cause it to fall out," or "I did not blind,"
[and slave as claimant says:] "I submit you to an oath,"
and [master as defendant] said: "I accede to the oath"—
[if he swore falsely,] he is exempt.

"*Your ox killed my ox*": The amount of the damage payment depends on whether the ox was in the habit of goring. The owner of the aggressor ox pays the victim ox's full value for a habitual gorer, and half the ox's value if the ox is a first-time offender (Exodus 21:35–36).

he is liable because the oath was imposed in an appropriate manner. The factual dispute (did the ox kill?) entails a financial dispute irrespective of whether the defendant admits or denies wrongdoing under pressure of the oath. The owner will pay in any event, whether half or full value.

"*Your ox killed my slave*" and therefore you owe me thirty *sheqel* (Exodus 21:32).

he is exempt because the oath was imposed in circumstances that do not necessarily involve a financial dispute. In the event that the defendant admits that his ox killed the slave, the damage payment is waived on account of the fact that it is assessed in a manner that is independent of the value of the damage.

"*You injured me or inflicted a wound*": One who injures his fellow must pay five damage payments: for damage, pain, medical expenses, time out of work, and shame. See *Bava Qamma* 8:1 for the assessment of these payments. The five damage payments are paid irrespective of whether the assailant admits to wrongdoing or not.

he is liable because the factual dispute necessarily entails a financial dispute. The assailant is obligated to pay damage reparations even when the defendant admits to wrongdoing. It is appropriate to impose an oath of deposit in these circumstances, so the defendant who falsely denies wrongdoing under oath is liable for the false oath.

"*You caused my tooth to fall out or you blinded me*": The master who injures his slave must grant the slave his freedom (Exodus 21:26–27).

he is exempt: The reasoning here is difficult to understand. Medieval commentators explain that the slave's freedom is regarded as a fixed fine above and beyond the value of the damage to the eye or tooth, for which the master is not responsible if he volunteers his admission of wrongdoing.

This is the rule:
Anyone who pays when he admits [to wrongdoing] of his own accord is liable.
Anyone who does not pay when he admits [to wrongdoing] of his own accord is exempt.

Chapter Six

6:1–7 *Judges' Oath*

6 The judges' oath:
the claim must be [a minimum of] two silver coins,
and the admission must be [at least] the equivalence of one *perutah*,
and if the admission is not of the same kind as the claim—
he is exempt.
How so?
[If the claimant said:] "You have two silver coins of mine in your possession,"
[and the defendant said:] "I have only one *perutah* of yours in my possession"[13]—
he is exempt.[14]
[But if the claimant said:] "You have two silver coins and one *perutah* of mine in your possession,"
[and the defendant said:] "I have only one *perutah* of yours in my possession"—
he is liable.

[13] K, P: "I have nothing of yours in my possession."
[14] K adds "[If the claimant said:] You have two silver coins and a *perutah* of mine in your possession, [and the defendant said:] I have nothing of yours in my possession—he is exempt."

Anyone who pays … is liable; does not pay … is exempt: One who volunteers a confession of guilt does not pay fixed fines though he remains responsible for the value of the damage (*Ketubbot* 3:9). Since it is always possible that the defendant will admit to wrongdoing of his own accord and the fixed fine will be waived, the scenarios resolved by fixed fines alone do not necessarily entail a financial dispute. One may not impose an oath of deposit concerning such disputes, and if imposed the defendant incurs no liability for misrepresenting the facts under oath.

6:1 *The judges' oath*: Judges in a civil dispute may impose an oath on the defendant in order to determine his liability to the claimant.

the claim must be: The claimant must be suing for money or goods equal in value to two silver coins known as *ma'ah*, which are coins of intermediate value. Thirty-two *perutah* make a *ma'ah*. Six *ma'ah* make a *dinar*.

the admission must be: The defendant must admit in some degree to the debt in order for the judges' oath to be imposed. The judges' oath does not adjudicate cases of outright denial on the defendant's part. Rather, it is used to adjudicate cases where there is a disparity between the claimant's claim and the defendant's admission.

"You have two silver coins" … "I have only one perutah": This scenario meets one of the two stated conditions for imposing the judges' oath. The defendant admits to owing the claimant one *perutah*, but the disparity between claim (two silver coins = sixty-four *perutah*) and admission (one *perutah*) is just shy of two silver coins (sixty-three *perutah*). This scenario makes clear that when the Mishnah speaks of a minimum "claim," it refers to the *disparity* between claim and admission and not the value of the claim per se.

[If the claimant said:] "You have a *maneh* of mine in your possession,"
[and the defendant said:] "I have nothing of yours in my possession"—
he is exempt.
[But if the claimant said:] "You have a *maneh* of mine in your possession,"
[and the defendant said:] "I have only fifty *dinar* of yours in my possession"—
he is liable.
[If the claimant said:] "You have a *maneh* belonging to my father in your possession,"
[and the defendant said:] "I have only fifty *dinar* of his in my possession"—
he is exempt, since he is regarded as one who returns a lost object.

2 [If the claimant said:] "You have a *maneh* of mine in your possession,"
And he said to him in the presence of witnesses:[15] "Yes."
And the next day he said to him: "Give it to me,"
[And if the defendant said:] "I [already] gave it to you"—
he is exempt.
[But if he said:] "I have nothing of yours in my possession"—
he is liable.
[If the claimant said:] "You have a *maneh* of mine in your possession,"
and he said: "Yes."
[And the claimant then said:] "Give it to me only in the presence of witnesses,"

[15] K, P lack "in the presence of witnesses."

---

he is exempt: The judges' oath may not be imposed for a case exhibiting these features. If the oath is nonetheless imposed and the defendant swears falsely, he is not liable for his false oath.

"You have two silver coins and one perutah"… "I have only one perutah"… he is liable: The judges' oath can be imposed because the disparity between claim (sixty-five *perutah*) and admission (one *perutah*) is equal to two silver coins (sixty-four *perutah*).

"You have a maneh"… "I have nothing"… he is exempt: The judges' oath cannot be imposed because the defendant does not admit in some degree to the claim.

"maneh": A very large unit of currency equal to six hundred of the silver coins discussed above (*ma'ah*).

"maneh"… "fifty dinar:" A *maneh* is worth one hundred silver *dinar*. The disparity between claim and admission is fifty silver *dinar*.

"You have a maneh"… "I have only fifty dinar"… he is liable: Even though the claim and the admission are expressed in different units of currency, they are regarded as being alike in kind such that the judges' oath can be imposed.

"You have a maneh belonging to father"… "I have only fifty dinar"… he is exempt: The Talmud assumes this case refers to an instance where the father has died and the son believes, but is not certain beyond a doubt, that the defendant has an outstanding debt to his father. Though the defendant admits to part of the claim, the strength of the son's claim is uncertain and the judges' oath may not be imposed.

since he, the defendant, could have denied the entirety of the debt, he *is regarded as one who returns a lost object* voluntarily rather than as a defendant in a case of competing claims.

6:2 *he said to him in the presence of witnesses: Yes*: The defendant admits to the debt in a legally binding manner (i.e. in front of witnesses).

"I have nothing of yours in my possession"—he is liable: In this scenario the defendant contradicts his statement of the previous day. The fact that he admitted to the debt initially in front of witnesses, however, gives his earlier statement legal standing. The judges' oath can be imposed because the defendant "admitted" to his debt on the previous day.

and the next day he said to him: "Give it to me,"
[and the defendant said:] "I [already] gave it to you"—
he is liable, since he was supposed to give it to him in the presence of witnesses.

3 [If the claimant said]: "You have a *litra* of gold belonging to me in your possession,"
[and the defendant said:] "I have only a *litra* of silver belonging to you in my possession"—
he is exempt.
[But if the claimant said:] "You have a gold *dinar* of mine in your possession,"
[and the defendant said:] "I have only a silver *dinar* of yours in my possession,"
or a *trisit*, or a *pundion*, or a *perutah*—
he is liable, since all types of coin are one and the same.
[If the claimant said:] "You have a *kor* of grain of mine in your possession,"
[and the defendant said:] "I have only a *letekh* of legumes of yours in my possession"—
he is exempt.
[But if the claimant said:] "You have a *kor* of produce of mine in your possession,"
[and the defendant said:] "I have only a *letekh* of legumes of yours in my possession"—
he liable, since legumes are included in the category of produce.
If one claims wheat from him, and the other admits to having barley—
he is exempt.
But Rabban Gamaliel deems him liable.[16]
If one claims jugs of oil from his fellow, and the other admits to having containers:
Admon says:
Since he admitted in part to the same kind as the claim—

[16] K, P add: "as in [the following teaching]."

6:3 "*You have a litra of gold*"... "*I have only a litra of silver*"... *he is exempt*: Though both the claim and admission are stated in terms of a *litra*, they are not alike in kind. The claimant demands a pound of gold and the defendant admits to possessing a pound of silver. The judges' oath cannot be imposed.

litra: A measure of weight, equivalent approximately to one pound or 450 grams.

gold dinar: A coin similar in appearance to the silver *dinar*, but worth twenty-five times as much.

trisit: A coin equal in value to twenty-four *perutah*.

pundion: A Roman coin equal in value to sixteen *perutah*.

perutah: A copper coin, the smallest unit of currency.

kor of grain... letekh of legumes—he is exempt: Both the claim and admission are expressed using comparable units that measure volume (*kor* and *letekh*). Nonetheless, the claim and admission concern different substances (grain as opposed to legumes); the judges' oath cannot be imposed.

kor: A large unit of volume equal to two *letekh*.

grain: Wheat, barley, spelt, etc.

letekh: A unit of volume equal to half a *kor*.

legumes: Peas, beans, lentils, etc.

Rabban Gamaliel deems him liable: On the assumption that wheat and barley are alike in kind; both are grains.

Admon... Rabban Gamaliel: Parallel in *Ketubbot* 13:4.

he swears.
But the Sages say:
The admission is not of the same kind as the claim.
Rabban Gamaliel said,
I see the merit of Admon's words.
If one claims from him utensils and land,
and the other admitted to the utensils but denied having land,
or [admitted] to having land but denied having utensils—
he is exempt.[17]
If he admitted to having a portion of the land—
he is exempt.
[But if he admitted to having] a portion of the utensils—
he is liable, since property that cannot serve as surety
implicates property that can serve as surety for the purposes of an oath.

4 One does not swear in response to the claim of a deaf-mute,
a legally incompetent person, or a minor,
And one does not impose an oath upon a minor,

---

[17] K, P: "If he admitted to having utensils, but denied having land, or if he admitted to having land, but denied having utensils, or if he admitted to a portion of the utensils—he is liable. If he admitted to a portion of the land—he is exempt."

---

admitted to the utensils, but denied having land...he is exempt: Since the defendant admits to having the claimant's utensils in his possession, the dispute is limited to land. The judges' oath may not, however, be imposed when the dispute concerns land (6:5). The version in manuscripts **P** and **K** rules differently in both this case (admits to utensils, but denies land) and the next (admits to land, but denies utensils). They rule that the defendant is liable in both cases, presumably on the logic that land and utensils together constitute a single claim. For them, admitting to either land or utensils meets the threshold of a partial admission.

[admitted] to having land, but denied having utensils—he is exempt: Since the dispute concerning land cannot be adjudicated with a judges' oath, the dispute is limited to utensils. The defendant, however, denies possession of even a portion of the utensils, and fails to meet the criteria for imposing the judges' oath. He does not admit to a portion of the claim.

since property that cannot serve as surety, the utensils, *implicates property that can serve as surety*, the land, *for the purposes of an oath*: This case is an exception to the principle in 6:5 that the judges' oath is not imposed for disputes concerning land. This provision is also stated in *Qiddushin* 1:5. **P** and **K** use this principle to adjudicate the first two cases as well, where they rule that the defendant is liable. Utensils, which are subject to the judges' oath, implicate land, which is not, and therefore admitting either land or utensils constitutes a partial admission.

property that cannot serve as surety: For a debt. This phrase is shorthand for movable property, i.e. the utensils.

property that can serve as surety: For a debt. This phrase is shorthand for immovable property, i.e. the land.

6:4 One, the defendant, *does not swear*, the judges' oath, *in response to the claim of a deaf-mute, a legally incompetent person, or a minor* because these individuals do not have independent legal standing as claimants.

one does not impose the judges' oath *upon a minor* if he is the defendant because, being underage, he is not considered legally competent.

but one does swear [when making a claim] against a minor
or regarding consecrated offerings.
  5 These are the things about which one does not swear:
slaves, documents, land, and consecrated offerings.
They are also not subject to [the penalty of] two-fold payments,
or of four-fold or five-fold payments.
The unpaid guardian does not swear [regarding them].
The wage bearer does not pay [for them].
R. Simeon says:
One swears regarding sacred offerings for which one is accountable.
And one does not swear regarding sacred offerings for which one is not accountable.
  6 R. Meir says:
There are things that are on the land,[18] but are not regarded like land,

[18] K has "like land."

---

but one does swear [when making a claim] against a minor: Under normal circumstances, the judges' oath is imposed on the defendant. When the defendant is a minor who cannot swear, the oath is imposed upon the claimant instead. In order to extract funds from a minor, the claimant must attest to his claim under oath. This provision protects minors from fraudulent claims. See also 7:7.

consecrated offerings have been dedicated to the Temple and are typically no longer available for profane use. When the claimant has a case against someone who dedicated his property to the Temple before repaying the debt, the only available recourse for the claimant is to collect his debt from the consecrated property. Though the judges' oath is usually imposed upon the defendant, in this case the judges' oath is imposed on the claimant. If he swears that he has not otherwise collected his debt, he may collect it from the dedicated property though it must be redeemed so that it is no longer sacred. See also *Arakhin* 6:3

6:5 This mishnah lists items that do not warrant having the judges' oath imposed on the defendant when he admits to a portion of the claim. In *Bava Metsi'a* 4:9 the same items are represented as exceptions to the rules of overcharge.

two-fold payments…four-fold or five-fold payments: See 4:6.

the unpaid guardian takes care of his fellow's property as a favor to the owner and receives no compensation. Should the property be lost or damaged while in his care, he has no liability provided he swears that he did not appropriate the property. See 8:1 (and *Bava Metsi'a* 7:8) based on Exodus 22:6–8.

does not swear [regarding them]: If these items are in the care of an unpaid guardian, he does not swear in order to be released from financial responsibility for them.

The wage bearer takes care of his fellow's property for a fee. Should the property become lost or damaged while in his care, he has limited liability. He must pay to replace the property if it is lost or stolen. See 8:1 (and *Bava Metsi'a* 7:8) based on Exodus 22:9–10.

One swears regarding sacred offerings for which one is accountable: Under certain circumstances an animal must be replaced if, having been set aside for sacrifice, it was lost before having been offered. The judges' oath is imposed when the dispute involves such animals, as they remain within the owner's jurisdiction.

one does not swear regarding sacred offerings for which one is not accountable: In other circumstances an animal need not be replaced if, having been set aside for sacrifice, it was lost before being offered. The judges' oath is not imposed when the dispute involves such animals, as they fall outside the owner's jurisdiction.

6:6 *but are not regarded like land*: That is, one does take an oath to resolve a dispute over such items.

But the Sages do not assent.
How so?
[If the claimant said:] "I delivered ten vines laden [with fruit] to you,"
and the other says: "There were only five,"
R. Meir requires an oath,
but the Sages say:
Anything that is attached to the land—
it is like land.
One swears only about something that can be specified by size, by weight, or by number.
How so?
[If the claimant said:] "I delivered a full house to you,"
or [if he said:] "I delivered a full purse to you,"
and the other says: "I don't know, but whatever you left, you may take"—
he is exempt.
[If the claimant said: "I delivered a full house] up to the molding over the window,"
and the other says: "Up to the window"—
he is liable.

7 When one extends a loan to his fellow that is secured by a pledge,
and he loses the pledge:
If [the lender] said to [the borrower]:
"I lent you a *sela* against it, and [the pledge] was worth a *sheqel*,"
and the other says: "Not so.
Actually you lent me a *sela* against it,
and [the pledge] was worth a *sela*"—
he is exempt.
[If the lender said to the borrower:]
"I lent you a *sela* against it, and [the pledge] was worth a *sheqel*,"
and the other says: "Not so.
Actually you lent me a *sela* against it, and [the pledge] was worth three *dinar*"—
he is liable.
[If the borrower said to the lender:]
"You lent me a *sela* against it, and [the pledge] was worth two *sela*."

full house: Commentaries understand this as a house full of produce.

6:7 *sela*: A coin worth two *sheqel* or four *dinar*.

sheqel: A coin worth two *dinar*, or half a *sela*. According to the lender, the loan (one *sela* = four *dinar*) is worth more than the lost pledge (one *sheqel* = two *dinar*), and the borrower still owes the lender one *sheqel* (= two *dinar*).

and the other says: According to the borrower, the loan (one *sela*) is equal in value to the lost pledge (one *sela*). In his version of events, the borrower owes the lender nothing.

he, the borrower, *is exempt*: from the judges' oath, which is imposed only when the defendant admits to part of the claim (6:1). Here the defendant (borrower) denies the entire claim.

[If the lender said]: The lender claims that the borrower owes him one *sheqel* (= two *dinar*), which is the value of the loan (one *sela* = four *dinar*) minus the value of the lost pledge (one *sheqel* = two *dinar*).

and the other says: The borrower admits to owing the lender one *dinar*, which is the value of the loan (one *sela* = four *dinar*) minus the value of the lost pledge (three *dinar*).

and the other says: "Not so.
Actually I lent you a *sela* against it, and [the pledge] was worth a *sela*"—
he is exempt.
[If the borrower said to the lender:]
"You lent me a *sela* against it, and [the pledge] was worth two *sela*,"
and the other says: "Not so.
Actually I lent you a *sela* against it, and [the pledge] was worth five *dinar*"—
he is liable.
And who swears?
The one in whose custody the deposit resides, lest one swear and the other take the deposit out.

Chapter Seven

7:1–7   *Oaths to Extract Payment*

7 Everyone for whom the Torah prescribes an oath swears in order to refrain from paying.
But the following individuals swear in order to collect [money owed]:
the hired worker,
one who has been robbed,

he, the borrower, is liable: The judge's oath can be imposed in this case because the defendant (borrower) admits to part (one *dinar*) of the claim (two *dinar*). See 6:1.

"You lent me a sela"… "[the pledge] was worth two sela": According to borrower, the lender owes him one *sela* (= four *dinar*), which is the value of the lost pledge (two *sela* = eight *dinar*) minus the value of the loan (one *sela* = four *dinar*).

and the other says: According to the lender, there is no outstanding debt since the value of the lost pledge (one *sela* = four *dinar*) is equal in value to the loan (one *sela* = four *dinar*).

he, the lender, is exempt: The judge's oath is imposed only when the defendant admits to part of the claim (6:1). Here the defendant (the lender) denies the entire claim.

the other says… "[the pledge] was worth five dinar": According to the lender, he owes the borrower one *dinar*, which is the value of the lost pledge (five *dinar*) minus the value of the loan (one *sela* = four *dinar*).

he, the lender, is liable: The judge's oath can be imposed because the defendant (the lender) admits to part (one *dinar*) of the claim (four *dinar*).

The one in whose custody the deposit resides: i.e. the lender.

lest one, the borrower, swear and the other, the lender, take the deposit out: The concern is that the lender can produce the pledge after the borrower swears (falsely) about the value of the pledge. The Mishnah presumes that the lender will not swear to having lost an object that he later intends to introduce as evidence.

7:1 *Everyone for whom the Torah prescribes an oath*: In order to be released from financial liability. Examples include the oath of deposit (5:1–5), the judges' oath (6:1–7) and the guardian's oath (8:1). The defendant swears that he does not owe money, which suffices to exonerate him.

one who has been wounded,
one engaged in a suit against someone whose oath is suspect,
and the shopkeeper with respect to [what is written in] his ledger.
The hired worker, how so?
If one said to [one's employer]:
"Give me my wages, which are in your possession,"
and he says: "I gave them,"
and the other says: "I did not collect them."
He swears and collects [the wages].
R. Judah says,
Only if there is at least a minimal admission.
How so?
If one said to [one's employer]:
"Give me my wages, amounting to fifty *dinar*, which are in your possession,"
and the other says: "You received a gold *dinar*."

2 One who has been robbed, how so?
If they testified that one entered another's house without permission to take a pledge,
and one says: "You took my utensils,"
and other says: "I did not take [them]"—
this one may swear in order to collect [the stolen utensils].
R. Judah says,
Only if there is at least a minimal admission.
How so?
If one said to the other: "You took two utensils,"
And the other says: "I took only one."

3 One who has been wounded, how so?
If they testify regarding him that he entered the presence of the other intact and left wounded,
and one said to the other: "You wounded me,"
and the other says: "I did not wound [you]"—

---

someone whose oath is suspect: As a result of engaging in the shady business practices listed in 7:4.

a minimal admission: The right to swear in order to collect is extended to the hired worker only if the employer admits to having paid a portion of the wages.

gold dinar: Twenty-five silver *dinar* are equal in value to one gold *dinar*. The worker's claim (fifty silver *dinar*) minus what the employer says he already paid (one gold dinar = twenty-five silver *dinar*) is the amount that the employer admits to owing the worker (twenty-five silver *dinar*).

7:2 *If they testified*: There needs to be some external basis for crediting the claim.

a pledge: An object belonging to the defendant that was serving as security for a loan extended to the claimant. The witnesses testify that the defendant was seen entering the claimant's home with empty hands and exiting with something in his hand.

this one, the person whose house was broken into, *may swear in order to collect* restitution for the stolen items.

Only if there is at least a minimal admission by the one who entered without permission.

7:3 *this one*: The wounded person.

this one may swear in order to collect [monies owed].
R. Judah says,
Only if there is a minimal admission.
How so?
If one says to the other: "You inflicted two wounds on me,"
and the other says: "I inflicted only one wound on you."

4 One [engaged in a suit] against someone whose oath is suspect, how so?
The law is one and the same whether for the testimonial oath or the oath of deposit,
and even for a vain oath.
If one of them was one who plays with dice,
one who loans on interest,
one of those who bet on flying pigeons,
or one of those who trade in Seventh-Year produce—
his opponent may swear in order to collect [monies owed].
If both of them were suspect,
the oath returns to its proper place—
the words of R. Yose.
R. Meir says:
Let them split it.

5 The shopkeeper with respect to [what is written in] his ledger, how so?
Not the case where he says to [the customer]:
"It is written in my ledger that you owe me two hundred *zuz*."
Rather, if one said to [the shopkeeper]:
"Give my son[19] two *seah* of grain," or
"Give my worker[20] small coins in exchange for a *sela*,"
and [the shopkeeper] says: "I gave it [already]."
But they say: "We did not collect it [from the shopkeeper]."

[19] K, P: "my sons."   [20] K, P: "my workers."

---

in order to collect the payments due to one who has sustained personal injury at the hand of another. See *Bava Qamma* 8:1.

7:4 *testimonial oath*: See 4:3.

oath of deposit: See 5:2.

If one of them: That is, if the defendant is suspect on account of participating in the following shady business practices. See *Sanhedrin* 3:3 and *Rosh Hashanah* 1:8.

the oath returns to its proper place: The defendant takes the oath, as per the usual convention.

7:5 *Not the case*: The shopkeeper does not have an unconditional right to swear in order to collect monies owed.

zuz: A silver coin, also sometimes called a silver *dinar*.

Seah: A measure of volume.

"Give my worker small coins in exchange for a sela" that I will later give you. Here the householder requests that the shopkeeper extend him a *sela*'s worth of credit, and pay his workers directly so that the householder not violate the requirement to compensate workers in a timely manner. See *Bava Metsi'a* 9:12.

He swears and collects, and they swear and collect.
Ben Nanas said:
How so?
[Requiring both sides to swear] brings these and these to the brink of a vain oath.
Rather, he collects without swearing, and they collect without swearing.

6 If one said to the shopkeeper: "Give me a *dinar*'s worth of produce,"
and [the shopkeeper] gave it to him.
And [the shopkeeper] said to him: "Give me the *dinar*,"
and [the householder] said: "I already gave it to you,
and you put it in the money chest"—
the householder swears.
If [the householder] gave [the shopkeeper] the *dinar* and said to him:
"Give me the produce,"
and [the shopkeeper] said to him: "I already gave it to you,
and you carried it into your house"—
the shopkeeper swears.
R. Judah says,
Whoever is in possession of the produce has the upper hand.
If one said to a moneychanger: "Give me a *dinar*'s worth of small coins,"
and [the moneychanger] gave [the small coins] to him.
And [the moneychanger] said to him: "Give me the *dinar*,"
and [the householder] said to him: "I already gave it to you,
and you put it in the money chest"—
the householder swears.
If [the householder] gave the *dinar* to him, and said to him: "Give me the small coins,"
and [the moneychanger] said to him: "I gave them to you,
and you thrust them into your purse"—

He swears and collects, and they swear and collect: Both the shopkeeper and the son/worker collect their due from the householder.

[Requiring both sides to swear] brings these and these to the brink of a vain oath: Ben Nanas reasons that one of the parties has to be lying since their claims conflict. If both parties are required to swear concerning the truth of their claim, one will inevitably make a vain oath. For the definition of a vain oath, see 3:8. Ben Nanas suggests that the householder rectify the financial shortfalls to both parties without requiring them to confirm their claim under oath.

7:6 *the householder swears* that he paid the money already and is released from having to pay for the produce a second time.

the shopkeeper swears that he delivered the produce and is released from having to make a second delivery of produce.

Whoever is in possession of the produce has the upper hand: In the first scenario, the householder has the upper hand because the produce has already been delivered. In the second scenario, the shopkeeper has the upper hand because he authorizes the delivery of produce. If he claims he already delivered, he will not authorize a second delivery. According to R. Judah, an oath is superfluous for one who already has the upper hand.

the householder swears that he already gave the *dinar* and is released from the obligation to give the moneychanger a second *dinar*.

the moneychanger swears.
R. Judah says:
It is not the practice of a moneylender to give [even] an *issar* until he collects his *dinar*.
7 Just as they said:
A woman who reduces the value of her *ketubbah* [by admitting that part has already been paid]
may not collect without an oath,
and [a woman about whom] one witness testifies that she was paid [her *ketubbah*]
may not collect without an oath,
and [a woman whose *ketubbah* is paid] from encumbered property
or from the property of orphans
may not collect without an oath,
and [a woman whose *ketubbah* is paid] not in the presence of the one [who divorced her]
may not collect without an oath—
so too orphans may not collect without an oath.
[The oath is as follows:]
We swear that father did not command us,
and that father did not tell us,
and that we did not find among father's papers,
that this debt had been paid.
R. Yohanan b. Beroqa says,
Even if the son was born after the father died,
He must swear in order to collect.

the moneychanger swears that he already gave the small coins and is released from the obligation to give the small coins a second time.

It is not the practice of a moneylender to give [even] an issar: This principle suggests that the householder should be believed without an oath when he claims that the moneylender already took his *dinar* and placed it in the money chest.

7:7 *they said*: In *Ketubbot* 9:7–8. A divorcee or widow must swear in order to collect the unpaid portion of her *ketubbah*.

[a woman about whom] one witness testifies: Two witnesses are required to establish that her *ketubbah* was paid out already. One witness suffices only to cast doubt upon her claim that she was not paid, which is confirmed by having her swear that she did not.

encumbered property: Property that her former husband sold to a third party. If the former husband does not have additional property from which to pay the *ketubbah*, the woman is entitled to reclaim the sold property, provided she swear that she has not otherwise collected payment.

property of orphans: When a man dies, leaving all of his property to his sons (his heirs), his widow is entitled to collect her *ketubbah* payment from the orphans' inheritance provided she swears that she has not received it from other sources.

so too orphans do not collect a debt owed to their father, the rights to which they inherit at his death.

Even if the son is born after the father died and could not have been instructed by his father to collect the debt or been told by his father that the debt had been collected.

Rabban Simeon b. Gamaliel said:
If there are witnesses who testify
that the father at the moment of death said that this debt was not paid,
[the orphan] collects without an oath.

8 The following individuals may be submitted to an oath [even] without a [definite] claim:
business partners,
tenant farmers,
a household administrator,
a wife who negotiates within the household,
and the "son of the house."
If one [of these individuals]
said to him [who is concerned that there may have been misappropriation]:
"What is your claim against me?"
[And the other replies:] "I want you to swear to me"—
he is obligated.
If business partners or tenant farmers have already divided their assets—
one may not submit him to an oath.
If an oath was imposed on account of a different claim,
they can roll onto him [an oath] about everything.
But the Seventh Year cancels the oath.

7:8 *without a [definite] claim*: The individuals listed have routine access to property and resources belonging to others. They can be subjected to an oath at any time in order to confirm that they have not misappropriated the property or resources of others.

tenant farmers owe a portion of their yield to their landlord.

a household administrator or manager with access to the household's financial resources.

a wife who negotiates: i.e. manages financial affairs associated with the household.

the "son of the house": One son who serves as executor of his deceased father's estate, settling all debts, collecting all claims, and distributing the assets among the surviving sons.

"I want you to swear" that you did not misappropriate property belonging to me.

he is obligated to swear. The business partner must swear that he split the profits appropriately, the tenant farmer that he did not keep more than his share of the yield, the household administrator and the wife that they did not misappropriate household resources, and the "son of the house" that he did not withhold for himself more inheritance than is his due.

If an oath was imposed on account of a different claim ... everything: If another dispute arose between business partners or between the tenant farmer and landlord, and the new dispute occasions an oath, it may be extended so that it mediates not only the new conflict, but also verifies that the past division of assets was appropriate.

the Seventh Year cancels the oath: Every seven years all debts are canceled and the land is not farmed for a year. The Seventh Year imposes a statute of limitations on financial disputes and the ability to adjudicate them by means of an oath. One cannot impose an oath based on a suspicion that preceded the Seventh Year.

Chapter Eight

8:1–6 *Oaths That Release Guardians from Liability*

8 There are four [types of] guardians:
(1) the unpaid guardian,
(2) the borrower,
(3) the wage bearer, and
(4) the renter.
The unpaid guardian swears for everything,
and the borrower pays for everything.
The wage bearer and the renter swear regarding the broken, the captured, and the dead [animal],
and they pay for loss and theft.

2 If one said to an unpaid guardian: "Where is my ox?"
And [the unpaid guardian] said to [the owner]:
"It died," but actually it was broken, or captured, or stolen, or lost;
"It was broken," but actually it died, or was captured, or stolen, or lost;
"It was captured," but actually it died, or was broken, or stolen, or lost;
"It was stolen," but actually it died, or was broken, or captured, or lost;
"It was lost," but actually it died, or was broken, or captured, or stolen;
[If the owner said to the unpaid guardian:] "I submit you to an oath,"
and [the unpaid guardian] said: I accede to the oath—
he is exempt.

3 [If the owner said to an unpaid guardian:] "Where is my ox?"
And [the unpaid guardian] said to [the owner]:
"I don't know what you are talking about,"

8:1 *There are four [types of] guardians*: These rules are derived from Exodus 22:6–14.

the unpaid guardian watches over someone else's property as a favor (free of charge) and has no liability in the event of loss or damage.

the wage bearer is financially compensated for watching over someone else's property. If the property is lost or damaged while in his care, he is responsible for cases that were easily preventable, but not for cases deemed out of his control.

the renter pays for the privilege to use someone else's property. Like the wage bearer, he is responsible for cases that were easily preventable, but not for cases deemed out of his control.

The unpaid guardian swears for everything: In order to be freed of liability for all the forms of damage listed at the end of the mishnah (loss, theft, death, breakage, capture), the unpaid guardian must swear that he did not have a hand in the loss.

8:2 *"It died," but actually…*: The unpaid guardian misrepresents the circumstances by which the ox was lost.

he is exempt from having to bring a guilt offering (5:1). Though he misrepresents the truth under oath, he has no financial gain thereby.

8:3 *"I don't know what you are talking about"…he is exempt* from having to bring a guilt offering (5:1). Though he misrepresents the truth under oath, he has no financial gain thereby.

but actually it died, or was broken, or captured, or stolen, or lost;
[if the owner said to the unpaid guardian:] "I submit you to an oath,"
and [the unpaid guardian] said: "I accede to the oath"—
he is exempt.
[If the owner said to an unpaid guardian:] "Where is my ox?"
and [the unpaid guardian] said to [the owner]: "It was lost";
[if the owner said to the unpaid guardian:] "I submit you to an oath,"
And [the unpaid guardian] said: "I accede to the oath,"
and then witnesses testify that he ate it—
he pays the value [of the ox].
If he admits of his own accord—
he pays the value [of the ox] and a fifth [of the value of the ox], and [brings] a guilt offering.
[If the owner said to an unpaid guardian:] "Where is my ox?"
and [the unpaid guardian] said to [the owner]: "It was stolen,"
[If the owner said to the unpaid guardian:] "I submit you to an oath,"
and [the unpaid guardian] said: "I accede to the oath,"
and then witnesses testify that he stole it—
he pays two-fold [the value of the ox].
If he admits of his own accord—
he pays the value [of the ox] and a fifth [of the value of the ox], and [brings] a guilt offering.

4 If one said to someone in the marketplace:
"Where is my ox that you stole?"
and he says: "I didn't steal it,"
and witnesses testify that he stole it—
he pays two-fold [the value of the ox].
[If witnesses testify that] he slaughtered or sold it—
he pays the four-fold or five-fold payment.
If he saw witnesses that were approaching slowly, and said:
"I stole it, but I did not slaughter or sell it"—
he pays only the value [of the ox].

witnesses testify…admits of his own accord: In both cases, the unpaid guardian repays the value of the ox that he appropriated. He does not, however, pay the penalty for his false oath (an additional fifth of the ox's value and a guilt offering) unless he admits to having sworn falsely of his own accord. The penalties prescribed in Leviticus 5:21–26 (the value, an added fifth, and a guilt offering) obtain only when the transgressor "admits his guilt." See also *Bava Qamma* 9:7.

witnesses testify that he stole it…two-fold: He is regarded as a thief and pays the penalty assessed upon all thieves (Exodus 22:6). This case and the next appear in slightly modified form in *Bava Qamma* 9:8.

If he admits of his own accord: His penalty is assessed as one who has sworn the oath of deposit falsely (5:1).

8:4 *slaughtered or sold it—he pays four-fold or five-fold payment*: The value of the stolen animal. The Torah prescribes a higher penalty for the theft of an animal that cannot be returned because it was slaughtered or sold by the thief (Exodus 21:37).

"I stole it"…pays only the value [of the ox]: If the thief admits to his crime before the witnesses arrive to testify against him, he returns the stolen item (or pays its value). He is not penalized for his initial mistruth, since it was not made under oath.

5 If one said to a borrower:
"Where is my ox?"
and [the borrower] said to [the owner]:
"It died," but actually it was broken, or captured, or stolen, or lost;
"It was broken," but actually it died, or was captured, or stolen, or lost;
"It was captured," but actually it died, or was broken, or stolen, or lost;
"It was stolen," but actually it died, or was broken, or captured, or lost;
"It was lost," but actually it died, or was broken, or captured, or stolen;
[if the owner said to the borrower:] "I submit you to an oath."
And he [the borrower] said: "I accede to the oath"—
he is exempt.

6 [If the owner said to the borrower:] "Where is my ox?"
and [the borrower] said to [the owner]:
"I don't know what you are talking about,"
but actually it died, or was broken, or captured, or stolen, or lost;
[if the owner said to the borrower:] "I submit you to an oath,"
and [the borrower] said: "I accede to the oath"—
he is liable.
If one said to a wage bearer or a renter: "Where is my ox?"
and [the wage bearer or renter] said to [the owner]:
"It died," but actually it was broken, or captured;
"It was broken," but actually it died, or was captured;
"It was captured," but actually it died, or was broken;
"It was stolen," but actually it was lost;
"It was lost," but actually it was stolen;
[if the owner said to the wage bearer or the renter:] "I submit you to an oath,"
and [the wage bearer or the renter] says: "I accede to the oath"—
he is exempt.
[If the wage-bearer or the renter said]:
"It died," "It was broken," or "It was captured," and actually it was stolen or lost,

8:5 *If one said to a borrower* who is financially responsible for all cases of loss and damage (8:1).

"It died," but actually...: The scenarios listed misrepresent the truth in a manner that does not financially benefit the borrower, since he has to pay in all cases.

he is exempt from having to bring the guilt offering associated with a false oath of deposit (5:1). Though he misrepresented the truth under oath, he experienced no financial gain thereby.

8:6 *"I don't know what you are talking about"...he is liable* for the penalty associated with swearing an oath of deposit falsely (5:1). The borrower stands to gain financially by his misrepresentation of the facts. Had he admitted to the circumstances of loss or damage, he would have been obligated to reimburse the owner.

said to a wage bearer or a renter who are liable for preventable circumstances (loss and theft), but not for circumstances beyond their control (death, breakage, capture).

"It died," but actually it was broken, or captured...: The wage bearer/renter misrepresents the truth in a manner that has no financial repercussions. He need not reimburse in the case of death, breakage, or capture.

[if the owner said to the wage bearer or the renter:] "I submit you to an oath,"
And [the wage bearer or the renter] says: "I accede to the oath"—
he is liable.
[If the wage bearer or the renter said:]
"It was stolen," or "It was lost," and actually it died, was broken, or was captured,
[if the owner said to the wage bearer or the renter:] "I submit you to an oath,"
and [the wage bearer or the renter] said: "I accede to the oath"—
he is exempt.
This is the general rule:
Anyone who replaces an obligation with an obligation,
an exemption with an exemption,
or an exemption with an obligation,
is exempt.
[Anyone who replaces] an obligation with an exemption is liable.
This is the general rule:
Anyone who swears [falsely] in order to lighten his liability is liable.
Anyone who swears [falsely] his liability is exempt.

"It was lost," but actually it was stolen...: The wage bearer/renter misrepresents the truth in a manner that has no financial repercussions. He reimburses the owner in cases of both loss and theft.

he is exempt from the penalties associated with the oath of deposit (5:1), since his misrepresentation does not redound to his financial benefit.

"It died," "It was broken," or "It was captured": The wage bearer/renter claims that the loss occurred in circumstances beyond his control, for which he has no financial responsibility.

and actually it was stolen or lost: These being circumstances that he could have prevented and for which he is financially responsible. The wage bearer/renter's misrepresentation of truth under oath has clear financial benefit: it releases him from a payment that he otherwise owes.

he is liable for having sworn the oath of deposit falsely.

"It was stolen," or "It was lost": The wage bearer/renter claims that the loss occurred in circumstances that he could have prevented, for which he bears financial responsibility.

and actually it died, was broken, or was captured: The true circumstances of loss, which are beyond the guardian's control, do not entail financial responsibility for the wage bearer/renter. His false oath does not benefit him financially.

he is exempt from the penalties associated with his false oath of deposit (5:1).

replaces an obligation with an obligation: The guardian claims that the loss occurred under one set of circumstances, which impose financial liability, but the loss actually occurred under a different set of circumstances, which impose the same level of financial liability.

an exemption: Circumstances that do not require payment from the guardian.

an exemption with an obligation: The guardian claims that the loss occurred in circumstances that require payment ("an obligation") when the actual circumstances would not have required payment ("an exemption").

he is exempt from penalties associated with his false oath of deposit (5:1) since no financial benefit accrues to the guardian when he misrepresents the truth under oath.

[replaces] an obligation with an exemption: The guardian's claim entails no payment ("exemption") while the actual circumstances of loss do entail payment ("obligation").

Tractate Eduyot

Shaye J. D. Cohen

Introduction

Overview

Eduyot is one of two mishnaic tractates not devoted to the exposition of a given legal or ritual topic (the other is *Avot*). *Eduyot*'s content is overwhelmingly legal, but is topically diverse. Its statements are grouped together on the basis of some common denominator which has nothing to do with the subject matter (e.g. the tractate groups together cases in which Shammai disagrees with the House of Shammai, leniencies of the House of Shammai and severities of the House of Hillel, cases in which the House of Hillel retracted its view in favor of the view of the House of Shammai).

Among the criteria which serve to organize the statements within this tractate is the phrase "R. *x* testified" or "R. *x* and R. *y* testified." What exactly "testified" means is not explained (see notes on 1:3 and 5:6), but the prominence of this rubric seems to have given the tractate its name, since the most likely explanation of the word *Eduyot* is "testimonies." (A possible alternative is to repoint the name as *Idiyot* and to parse it as "the best" or "the best ones," an explanation which seems to be confirmed by the Babylonian Talmud which refers to this tractate as *Behirta* or *Behirata*, Aramaic for "the chosen," or "the chosen ones," that is, exemplary statements.)

About two-thirds of the statements in *Eduyot* appear elsewhere in the Mishnah in their appropriate topical context; sometimes these parallels are identical with what is in *Eduyot*, other times the parallels reflect different versions of the same material. Most of the parallels are statements in the orders *Zera'im*, "Seeds" (concerning tithes and other payments to priests, the illicit mixing of grain and grapes, gifts to the poor from the harvest, second tithe, the Seventh Year) and *Tohorot*, "Purities" (concerning the transfer of impurity, Tent impurity, the susceptibility of various objects to impurity, purification pools, the waters of the red heifer). Less frequent are the parallels in the other orders. There are almost no parallels in *Neziqin*. The unparalleled material in *Eduyot*, about one third of the whole, has roughly the same topic profile as the paralleled material: statements that might have belonged to *Zera'im* and *Tohorot* are the most numerous, followed by statements that might have belonged to the other orders. Once again, *Neziqin* is barely represented.

There is no Talmud to *Eduyot*, although various parts of it, both the paralleled and the unparalleled, are cited and discussed in the Talmud. Adding to the anomalousness of the tractate is the fact that many Sages cited here appear nowhere else in rabbinic literature. *Eduyot*, like *Avot*, is located in the order *Neziqin*; why, we do not know.

Structure and Organization of the Tractate

There is no discernible plan or structure in the tractate. Statements are grouped together in clusters, but the clusters are loosely connected with each other, if at all, and do not seem to be arranged in a purposeful manner. Here is an outline of the tractate:

1:1–3 The Sages reject both Shammai and Hillel
1:4–6 Why the Mishnah records views that are rejected
1:7–11 Shammai is more severe than the House of Shammai
1:12–14 The House of Hillel reverse themselves and follow the House of Shammai
2:1–3 Four testimonies of R. Hanina the Prefect of the Priests
2:4–10 Statements of R. Ishmael and R. Aqiva
3:1–6 The leniencies of R. Dosa b. Harqinas are rejected by the Sages
3:7–9 The severities of R. Joshua and R. Zadok are rejected by the Sages
3:9–11 Severities and leniencies of Rabban Gamaliel
3:12 A statement of R. Eleazar b. Azariah
4:1–5:5 Leniencies of the House of Shammai, severities of the House of Hillel
5:6–7 Testimony and dramatic tale of Aqavya b. Mahalalel
6:1–8:5 Testimonies
8:6–7 I heard/received a tradition

Main Ideas

What might be the point of this odd tractate and this odd assortment of material has long intrigued scholars. Some have suggested that *Eduyot* is the earliest tractate of the Mishnah; before the Sages hit upon the idea of arranging material topically, they grouped material by other criteria (e.g. all the statements of R. *x*), and *Eduyot* is the sole survivor (along with other bits and pieces scattered here and there in the Mishnah) of the old way of doing things. This view handily explains why so much of *Eduyot* is repeated elsewhere in the Mishnah: as the topical arrangement took hold, numerous statements were extracted from *Eduyot* and repeated in their proper topical context. Although this explanation makes sense, it is not likely to be correct. In many of the parallels, the version in *Eduyot* appears to be secondary to the one that appears elsewhere; that is, it appears that the editor of *Eduyot* found material elsewhere in the Mishnah and copied it (with modifications).

A more likely explanation is that *Eduyot* (like *Avot*) is one of the latest tractates, in which the Mishnah reflects on itself, in particular on the phenomenon of debate and discord among the Sages (see especially 1:4–6, a passage unique to *Eduyot*). A recurrent theme in *Eduyot* is that Sages should not "stand on their words," that is, they should not oppose the majority when the majority asserts itself (1:4; 5:6–7). Nor should Sages be doctrinaire in their opinions; sometimes the Sages are stringent, sometimes lenient (chapter 3); the House of Gamaliel were strict with themselves but lenient with the rest of Israel (3:10); the House of Shammai usually are more stringent than the House of Hillel, but sometimes they are not (4:1–5:5); the Hillelites reversed themselves on more than one occasion and accepted the view of the Shammaites (1:12–14); rabbinic legal debate is civil and rational (1:12–14; chapter 6). The Mishnah comments disapprovingly that R. Yose b. Yoezer was "Yose the permitter," on account of his consistently lenient views (8:4). According to the final mishnah in the tractate, when the prophet Elijah returns at the end of days he will put an end to social injustice and legal discord (8:7).

This, perhaps, is the purpose of *Eduyot*: to sketch the implicit rules by which rabbinic society manages to cohere in spite of a culture that fosters legal disagreement. (4:8, with its claim that the Houses of Hillel and Shammai did not refrain from dining with each other or marrying each other, in spite of their numerous disagreements in purity law and marriage law, fits this theme too, but our two main manuscripts, **K** and **P**, omit it. Its original home is *Yevamot* 1:4.)

Relationship to Scripture

Since *Eduyot* treats a wide range of legal and ritual subjects, each paragraph has its own relationship with the laws of the Torah. The tractate cites a verse from the Torah only once (2:9), and that in a nonlegal context.

Special Notes for the Reader

I am grateful to my friend Rabbi Leonard Gordon for his criticisms and suggestions.

Tractate Eduyot

Chapter One

1:1–3   *The Sages Reject Both Shammai and Hillel*

1 Shammai says:
All women—
it is enough [that their impurity begins only from] the moment
[that they see menstrual blood and onward].
Hillel[1] says:
[A woman's impurity extends]
from [her previous] self-examination to [her present] self-examination,
even if [the interval is of] many days.
But the Sages say:
[The law] follows the words of neither this one nor that one;
but [a woman is deemed impure either] during the preceding twenty-four hours,
if this is less than [the time] from [her previous] self-examination
to [her present] self-examination,
or from [her previous] self-examination to [her present] self-examination,
if this is less than twenty-four hours.[2]
Any woman who has a regular menstrual cycle—
it is enough [that she is deemed impure only from] the moment
[that she sees menstrual blood and onward].
If she had sexual intercourse and used test rags,
this counts as a self-examination

---

[1] **K**: "House of Hillel."
[2] Lit. "she reduces the [retroactive impurity of] time-to-time by means of examination-to-examination, or she reduces [the retroactive impurity of] examination-to-examination by means of time-to-time."

1:1 Parallel to *Niddah* 1:1.

All women: A woman who does not know exactly when her menstrual flow began has no retroactive impurity, says Shammai; she is deemed impure only from the moment that she became aware of her flow. According to Hillel, however, she is impure retroactively up to the last point when she knew for certain that her flow had not yet started. According to the Sages she is impure retroactively but only up to a maximum of twenty-four hours.

test rags: To check for blood before and after intercourse.

[and[3]] may lessen either the interval of twenty-four hours,
or [the interval] from [the previous] self-examination
to [the present] self-examination.

2 Shammai says:
[Bread dough made from more] than one *qav* [of flour] is liable to *hallah*.
And Hillel says:
[More than] two *qav*.
But the Sages say:
[The law] follows the words of neither this one nor that one;
but [dough must be made from at least] one *qav* and a half [of flour
in order to be] liable to *hallah*.
When the measures increased in size, they said:
Five-quarters of a *qav* are liable.
R. Yose says:
[Exactly] five are exempt, but five and a little bit are liable.

3 Hillel says:
One full *hin* of drawn water renders an immersion pool unfit.
[Hillel used the word *hin*] only[4] because
a person must use the same language as his teacher.
And Shammai says:
Nine *qav*.
But the Sages say:
[The law] follows the words of neither this one nor that one.
But when two weavers came from the Dung Gate in Jerusalem
and testified in the name of Shemaiah and Avtalyon

[3] K has "and."   [4] K, P lack "only."

1:2 *qav*: A measure of volume.

hallah: Dough offering, given to a priest (Numbers 15:20).

five quarters: Hallah 2:6.

1:3 *full hin*: Twelve *log* (a *log* is a measure of volume).

renders an immersion pool unfit: An immersion pool (a *miqvah*) becomes fit to be used for purification once it contains forty *se'ah* = 960 *log* of "flowing" water, that is, water that has never been collected in a container. If while the *miqvah* is being filled, not yet having reached the forty-*se'ah* mark, an amount (debated in this mishnah) of "drawn water" is added, then the entire amount is deemed as if it were drawn water and thus unfit to be made into a proper *miqvah*. (The unfit water may be used for other purposes, of course; it simply cannot be used for a *miqvah*.) See *Miqva'ot*.

[Hillel used the word hin]: A biblical, archaic term.

Nine qav: Thirty-six *log*.

came before the Sages, location unstated, *and testified*: This is the first occurrence in our tractate of the verb "testified," which will recur frequently (2:1, 3; 5:6; 6:1–2; chapters 7–8); the verb conveys more authority than the plain "said," but what it means exactly the Mishnah never explains. "Testimonies" are found in other tractates too (*Eruvin* 3:4, *Sheqalim* 1:4, *Yevamot* 14:2). Here it is striking that the testimony of two anonymous nonelites overturns the teaching of two "fathers of the world" (1:4), one of whom was even careful enough to retain the archaic wording of his teacher.

Shemaiah and Avtalyon: *Avot* 1:10; below 5:6. Shammai and Hillel are reputed to have been their disciples (*Avot* 1:12).

that three *log* of drawn water render an immersion pool unfit—
[the Sages] confirmed their words.

1:4–6   Why the Mishnah Records Views That Are Rejected

4   And why do [the Sages] record the words of Shammai and Hillel for no purpose?[5]
To teach future generations that no one should stand on his words,
for the fathers of the world did not stand on their words.
   5   And why do they [the Sages] record the words of an individual
against[6] that of the majority,
inasmuch as the law always follows the words of the majority?
So that if a court approves the words of the individual,
it may rely upon him.[7]
For a court cannot annul the words of another court
unless it exceeds it both in wisdom and in number;
if it exceeded it in wisdom but not in number,
or in number but not in wisdom,
it cannot annul its words;
unless it exceeds it both in wisdom and in number.
   6   R. Judah said:
If so, why do they [the Sages] record the words of an individual
against that of the majority for no purpose?
So that if one shall say, "I have received such a tradition,"[8]
[another] may reply to him,
"What you heard was in accordance with the words of so-and-so."

   [5] Or " to no avail"; lit. "for annulment." **K, P**: "And why do [the Sages] record the words of Shammai and Hillel? To annul them." The same in 1:8 below.
   [6] Lit. "amidst."
   [7] So **P; K** and the printed edition could also be translated "and if it relies upon him."
   [8] The word "tradition" is not in the text but is implied by the verb "received."

three log: Miqva'ot 2:4 and 3:1.

1:4 *stand on their words*: Insist on the rectitude of their opinions. This mishnah assumes that Shammai and Hillel, having been corrected by the Sages (1:1–3), retracted their own views and accepted the ruling of the Sages. Contrast the behavior of Aqaviah b. Mahalalel (5:6–7).

fathers of the world: Sages of old or founding figures, in this case Shammai and Hillel. Cf. the title of tractate *Avot* (Fathers).

1:5 The commentators debate the syntax and structure of this mishnah, as well as the precise meaning of "wisdom" and "number" (number of judges? age of judges?). As translated here, the Mishnah says that a later court can overturn the decision of an earlier court only if the later court exceeds the earlier in wisdom and number; and/or unless the later court is relying on what had been a minority opinion of the earlier court. Some scholars have argued that the provision *for a court cannot annul the words of another court* etc. is a later addition designed to limit the judicial freedom of the previous sentence.

1:6 R. Judah disagrees with 1:5.

What you heard was in accordance with the words of so-and-so and consequently without authority, since it has already been considered and rejected.

1:7–11 *Shammai Is More Severe Than the House of Shammai*

7 The House of Shammai say:
A quarter-*qav* of bones—
any bones, whether from two [corpses] or from three—
[convey Tent impurity].
But the House of Hillel say:
A quarter-*qav* of bones [convey Tent impurity,
only if the bones are] from a [single] corpse,
[and] from the greater part of the skeleton[9]
or the greater part of the number [of bones].
Shammai says:
Even [a quarter-*qav*] from one bone [conveys Tent impurity].

8 Vetches of *terumah*—
the House of Shammai say:
One must soak and rub them in purity,
but one may feed them [to animals] in impurity.
But the House of Hillel say:
One must soak them in purity,
but one may rub them and feed them [to animals] in impurity.
Shammai says:
They may be eaten [only] dry.
R. Aqiva says:
Whatever is done to them may be done in impurity.

---

[9] Lit. "building," "frame."

1:7 Partial parallel to *Oholot* 2:1. According to Numbers 19 a human corpse in an enclosed space (a "Tent") imparts impurity to persons and objects inside that space, even without direct contact. Corpse impurity so transmitted is known as "Tent impurity." See *Oholot*. The transmission of such impurity did not require an entire corpse; even parts of a corpse would suffice. See 3:1 and chapter 6 below, also *Oholot* 2:1. Here the two Houses and Shammai debate the minimum number/amount of bones required to impart Tent impurity. All agree that the minimum volume is a quarter-*qav* of bones but disagree as to the details. This Mishnah speaks of dry bones with no attached flesh; 6:2 below speaks of bones with flesh attached.

greater part of the skeleton: The greater part of the skeleton in bulk; *greater part of the number [of bones]*: The human body has 248 bones (*Oholot* 1:8); consequently the greater part is 125 (*Oholot* 2:1). See end of chapter 6 below.

1:8 Parallel to *Maaser Sheni* 2:4. Vetches (a class of flowering plants of the legume family) were grown for animal feed; they would be used after being soaked and rubbed (*Shabbat* 20:3). In an emergency they could also be consumed by people, and therefore were regarded as liable to *terumah*, the agricultural offering given to the priest (Numbers 18:11–13). *Terumah* had to be protected from impurity, from the time of its designation until its consumption by the priest. But because vetches were liable to *terumah* only because of legal severity, and because vetch *terumah* would seldom be actually given to a priest, the degree of purity required was the subject of debate.

One must soak and rub them in purity: Because there is still potential they will be used as human food, at these two stages vetch *terumah* should be treated as regular *terumah*. When they are fed to animals the vetches lose their status as human food, and no requirement of purity remains.

One must soak them in purity because the act of soaking renders them susceptible to impurity (see *Makhshirin*). But after they have been soaked, the vetches are no longer treated as regular *terumah* because they are not regular food, say the House of Hillel.

They may be eaten by animals *[only] dry* and thus are not susceptible to impurity.

9 One[10] who changes a *sela*'s worth of second-tithe copper coins [outside of Jerusalem[11]]—
the House of Shammai say:
He may change them for a whole *sela* [of silver].
But the House of Hillel say:
A *sheqel*'s worth of silver and a *sheqel*'s worth in copper coin.
R. Meir says:
One may not exchange [second-tithe] silver
and [second-tithe] produce [together] for [other] silver.
But the Sages permit it.
 10 One who changes a *sela* of second tithe in Jerusalem—
the House of Shammai say:
[He must[12] change] the whole *sela* into copper coin.
But the House of Hillel say:
[He may take] one *sheqel*'s worth of silver
and one *sheqel*'s worth in copper coin.
Those who argue before the Sages say:
Three *dinar*'s worth of silver and one of copper.
R. Aqiva says:
Three *dinar*'s worth of silver
and from the fourth silver, a quarter in copper coin.[13]
R. Tarfon says:

[10] Entire mishnah originally lacking in **P** but supplied in the margin.
[11] **K** adds "in Jerusalem," probably a mistake derived from 1:10.
[12] Alt. "He may."
[13] Translation uncertain.

1:9 Parallel to *Ma'aser Sheni* 2:8. This mishnah is included here only because it parallels the next mishnah, which features a debate between Shammai and the House of Shammai.

second tithe: The Israelite farmer is to bring a tithe of his crops and all his firstborn animals to the central sanctuary (Jerusalem) where he is to consume them. If he wishes, while at home he can convert ("redeem") the produce into money ("silver"), with which he can purchase provisions when he arrives at the central sanctuary. See Deuteronomy 14:22–26.

A *whole sela* is a large silver coin, equivalent to two silver *sheqel* (= four *dinar*), and worth many copper coins. While journeying to Jerusalem a pilgrim would prefer to carry a few large-denomination coins rather than many small-denomination coins. But when he arrives at Jerusalem he will need small-denomination coins for daily use. In this mishnah the Houses are arguing how to balance these two needs.

R. Meir prohibits converting second-tithe silver coin into larger-denomination silver coin, even if one adds value ("produce") to the transaction.

1:10 Parallel to *Ma'aser Sheni* 2:9. See previous mishnah.

One silver *sela* = two silver *sheqel* = four silver *dinar*.

[He must change] *the whole sela into copper coin* to encourage him to spend his money and to minimize moneychanging fees.

Those who argue before the Sages: A unique expression in the Mishnah.

and from the fourth silver, a quarter in copper coin: Translation uncertain; the commentaries debate how to interpret R. Aqiva's ruling. As translated it seems to mean that three and three-quarter *dinar* are to be kept in silver, and that one-quarter *dinar* only is to be exchanged into copper coins.

Four *asper* in silver.
Shammai says:
Let him deposit it in a shop and [gradually] consume its value.

11 A bride's chair whose seat boards[14] were removed—
the House of Shammai declare it [still] susceptible to impurity;
but the House of Hillel declare it not susceptible.
Shammai says:
Even the frame of a chair is susceptible to impurity.
A chair that one affixed to a kneading trough[15]—
the House of Shammai declare it [still] susceptible to impurity,
but the House of Hillel declare it not susceptible.
Shammai says:
Even a chair that was made inside a trough[16] [is susceptible to impurity].

1:12–14 The House of Hillel Reverse Themselves and Follow the House of Shammai

12 [In] these matters the House of Hillel reversed themselves
and taught according to the words of the House of Shammai:
if a woman came from the land beyond the sea and said:
"My husband is dead"—she may [re]marry;
"My husband is dead"—she may[17] contract levirate marriage—
[the words of the House of Shammai].[18]
But the House of Hillel say:
The only tradition[19] we have heard

---

[14] Meaning uncertain. Other possible translations: "cushions," "coverings," "protruding arms."
[15] Or: "a chair to which one affixed a kneading trough." [16] Lit. "even that which was made in it."
[17] Or "must." [18] Lacking in **K** and printed editions; present in **P**.
[19] The word "tradition" is not in the text but is implied by the verb "heard."

Four asper in silver: The meaning of the word *asper* and the meaning of R. Tarfon's ruling are uncertain, debated by the commentators.

1:11 Parallel to *Kelim* 22:4; see also below 2:8.

If parts of a chair are removed, is the remainder still usable as a chair? If yes, it remains a chair and *susceptible to impurity* if sat upon by a *zav* (see *Zavim* 2:4); if not, it is no longer a chair and no longer *susceptible to impurity* if sat upon by a *zav*. "A bride's chair" is mentioned also in *Kelim* 22:7 and 23:4.

Even though it is now affixed to a kneading trough, the *chair* remains a chair, and therefore susceptible to impurity if sat upon by a *zav*. Thus the House of Shammai. According to Shammai, even if the chair never existed independently as a chair but from the beginning of its existence had been attached to a kneading trough, nevertheless, it is to be regarded as a chair and susceptible to impurity if sat upon by a *zav*. But the House of Hillel say that the attachment of a kneading trough removes a chair from the category of "chair."

1:12 Parallel to *Yevamot* 15:1–3.

she may [re]marry: Normally two male witnesses are required to establish a legal fact, but in the case of missing husbands the Sages were lenient. See below 6:1 and 8:5.

levirate marriage: Deuteronomy 25:5–10.

concerns a woman who came from the [grain] harvest
[and said "My husband is dead"].
The House of Shammai said to them:
A woman who came from the [grain] harvest,
a woman who came from the olive [harvest],
a woman who came from the land beyond the sea—
it is all one and the same.
They spoke of the [grain] harvest only because [they spoke] of the usual.
The House of Hillel reversed themselves
and taught according to[20] the House of Shammai.
The House of Shammai say:
She may [re]marry and take her *ketubbah*.
But the House of Hillel say:
She may [re]marry but she may not take her *ketubbah*.
The House of Shammai said to them:
Since you have declared permissible
the graver matter of forbidden intercourse,
should you not also declare permissible the lesser matter of property?
The House of Hillel said to them:
We find that the brothers may not enter into their inheritance on her testimony.
The House of Shammai said to them:
Should we not deduce [the law] from her *ketubbah* document?
For he writes for her [as follows]:
"Should you be married to another [after being married to me],
you may take what is prescribed for you."
The House of Hillel reversed themselves
and taught according to the words of the House of Shammai.

13 One who is half-slave and half-free—
he serves his master one day and himself one day—
the words of the House of Hillel.
The House of Shammai said to them:

[20] K adds "the words of."

ketubbah: Upon the inception of a marriage a husband gives his wife a document, known as a *ketubbah*, in which he obligates himself and/or his estate to make certain payments to the wife and her children if the marriage is terminated through divorce or his death. These payments are often called, as here, the *ketubbah*.

We find: We know the law.

the brothers: The heirs to the missing/dead man. They do not assume title to their father's property on the basis of this woman's testimony.

ketubbah document: For other standard clauses in a *ketubbah*, see *Ketubbot* 4:6–12.

"you may take what is prescribed for you": The wife may take her financial settlement (her *ketubbah*) when she is free to remarry. The *ketubbah* document thus implies a linkage between the right of remarriage and the receipt of the *ketubbah* payment.

1:13 Parallel to *Gittin* 4:5.

half-slave and half-free: For example, a man dies and leaves a slave to his two sons, one of whom frees the slave, while the other one does not. The result is a person who is half-slave and half-free.

You have set matters right for his master,
but you have not set matters right for him.
For him to marry a slavewoman is impossible,
[to marry] a freewoman is [also] impossible.
Shall he remain childless?
But was not the world created only for fruition and increase,
as it is written: *He did not create it a waste, but formed it to be inhabited*?
But to set matters right for the world,
one compels his master to set him free,
and he writes a bond [of indebtedness] for half his value.
The House of Hillel reversed themselves
and taught according to[21] the House of Shammai.

14 An earthenware vessel protects everything [within it from contracting Tent impurity]—
according to the words of the House of Hillel.
But the House of Shammai say:
It protects only foodstuffs and liquids and [other] earthenware vessels.
The House of Hillel said to them:
Why?
The House of Shammai said to them:
Because vis-à-vis an *am haʾarets* it is impure,
and a vessel that is impure cannot interpose
[between the corpse impurity in the Tent and the vessel's contents].
The House of Hillel said to them:
But have you not pronounced pure the foodstuffs and liquids within it?

---

[21] **K** adds "the words of."

---

to marry a slavewoman is impossible because a free Israelite may not marry a slave (*Qiddushin* 4:1); *[to marry] a freewoman is [also] impossible* because a slave may not marry an Israelite.

He did not create it a waste, but formed it to be inhabited: Isaiah 45:18.

he, the former slave, *writes a bond [of indebtedness]* to his former owner.

1:14 Partial parallel to *Kelim* 10:1 and *Oholot* 5:3.

On *Tent impurity* see above 1:7. From Numbers 19:15 the Sages deduced that a sealed earthen vessel protects its contents from Tent impurity. Thus, if a sealed earthenware vessel is in the same enclosure ("Tent") as a corpse, everything in the enclosure is impure via Tent impurity except for the sealed vessel and its contents, which, if pure to begin with, remain in a state of purity.

It protects only foodstuffs and liquids and [other] earthenware vessels but not vessels of wood or metal.

An *am haʾarets* is a farmer who is suspected by the Sages of not following the purity rules governing the production and processing of food, especially agricultural produce. (The *am haʾarets* was also suspected of not separating tithes properly, but that is not our concern here.) Consequently those Sages, known as *haverim*, "Associates," who punctiliously observed the purity rules, would not partake of food prepared by an *am haʾarets*, and would not borrow food-preparation utensils from an *am haʾarets* unless they had first been purified. See *Demai*.

vis-à-vis an am haʾarets it is impure: The *haverim* regarded as impure all foodstuffs and all utensils of the *am haʾarets*.

The House of Hillel and the House of Shammai agree that *a vessel that is impure cannot interpose*, that is, cannot protect its contents from Tent impurity, but disagree (at first) on its application.

The House of Shammai said to them:
When we pronounced pure the foodstuffs and liquids within it,
we pronounced them pure for himself [alone];
but when you pronounced the vessel pure,
you pronounced it pure for yourself as well as for him.
The House of Hillel reversed themselves
and taught according to[22] the House of Shammai.

Chapter Two

2:1–3 Four Testimonies of R. Hanina the Prefect of the Priests

2 R. Hanina,[23] the Prefect of the Priests, testified concerning four things.
(1) Never in all their days did the priests refrain
from burning [sacrificial] meat
that had become impure by a derived source of impurity,
together with [sacrificial] meat
that had become impure by a primary source of impurity,

---

[22] K adds "the words of." [23] K, P: "Hananyah," here and in 2:2 below.

---

we pronounced them pure for himself the *am ha'arets [alone]*: In no case will *haverim* share the foodstuffs, or borrow an earthenware vessel, of an *am ha'arets*, so even if an *am ha'arets* knows the ruling that a sealed earthenware vessel *protects foodstuffs and liquids and [other] earthenware vessels*, no harm will come to a *haver* as a result. A *haver* will not borrow an *am ha'arets*'s earthenware vessel because an earthenware vessel cannot be purified (Leviticus 11:33).

but when you pronounced the vessel pure: When you Hillelites pronounced pure the wood or metal vessel within the sealed earthenware vessel, *you pronounced it pure for yourself*, the purity-observing *haver*, as well *as for him*, the non-purity-observing *am ha'arets*. The *haver* might wish to borrow the *am ha'arets*'s wood or metal vessel, intending to purify it in the normal manner (by immersion). But the *haver* does not realize that this vessel is impure to a much higher degree, since it had been in a sealed earthenware vessel in a Tent with a corpse, and the sealed earthenware vessel provides only the illusion of protection from impurity, since it itself is impure. Consequently the impurity of the wood or metal vessel is corpse impurity (transmitted via the Tent with a corpse), which is far more severe than the statutory impurity of the vessels of an *am ha'arets*. (The removal of corpse impurity requires sprinkling with the waters of purgation on the third and seventh days, as specified in Numbers 19). If the Hillelite ruling is allowed to stand, say the House of Shammai, a *haver* might be misled into borrowing from an *am ha'arets* a metal or wood vessel that he otherwise would never have borrowed.

2:1 Parallel to *Pesahim* 1:6–7.

the priests of the Jerusalem Temple.

derived source of impurity…primary source of impurity: A "primary source of impurity" (lit. "father of impurity") is, for example, a menstruant or a dead creeping thing (*Kelim* 1:1–4). A person or object rendered impure by coming into contact with a primary source of impurity becomes impure to a lesser degree ("first-degree impurity"). Objects and foodstuffs that have the status of "first-degree impurity" can transfer impurity

even though they were adding impurity to its impurity.
R. Aqiva added:
Never in all their days did the priests refrain
from burning oil
that had been rendered unfit by a *tevul yom*,
in a lamp that had become impure by one who had contracted corpse impurity,
even though they were adding impurity to its impurity.

2 (2) R. Hanina, the Prefect of the Priests, said:
Never in my days did I see a hide taken out[24] to the place of burning.
R. Aqiva said:
From his words we learn
that if one flayed a firstborn, and it was found to have been a *terefah*,
the priests may [nonetheless] use its hide.
But the Sages say:
"We have not seen" is no proof;
but, rather, [such a hide] must be taken out[25] to the place of burning.

---

[24] Lit. "go out." Absent in **P** (probably a mistake).   [25] Lit. "must go out."

---

to other objects and foodstuffs (but not persons), which as a result become impure to a second degree and which in turn can create impurity to a third degree. Fourth-degree impurity is the end of the chain. With each further remove from the original source, the impurity becomes weaker and less transferable. Only food that is *terumah* (agricultural offering to the priest, Numbers 18) is susceptible to third-degree impurity, and only sacrificial meat is susceptible to fourth-degree impurity. A *derived source of impurity* (lit. "offspring of impurity") is any level of impurity below primary, that is, all levels of impurity from first degree to fourth.

oil that is *terumah*, designated for a priest (Numbers 18:12).

rendered unfit by being made impure.

a *tevul yom* (lit. "one who immersed that day") is a person who has completed the process of purification but is awaiting nightfall for the purification to be completely effective (Leviticus 22:7, Deuteronomy 23:12). A *tevul yom* is impure vis-à-vis *terumah* and sacrificial meats, but pure vis-à-vis everything else. See *Tevul Yom*.

2:2 Parallel to *Zevahim* 12:4.

the place of burning: The place outside the Temple to which the carcasses of unfit sacrifices were taken and burnt (*Sheqalim* 7:3; *Yoma* 3:2; *Menahot* 2:2). R. Hanina says that hides were never burnt there, because they were always available for use by the priests.

firstborn: The firstborn males of flock and herd were to be brought as sacrifices (Exodus 13:11–13; Deuteronomy 15:19–23).

terefah: A defective animal whose defect could not have been detected before being slaughtered (and, in this case, flayed). If slaughtered for food, the animal may not be eaten; if slaughtered for the altar, the animal may not be sacrificed.

the priests may [nonetheless] use its hide in spite of the fact that it was not sacrificed on the altar. The priests may use the hide of a firstborn animal in any case.

"We have not seen": In other words, an argument from silence.

3 (3) He testified also of a little village beside Jerusalem
in which lived an old man who used to lend money
to all the people of the village and write [the promissory notes] in his own hand,
and others would sign [as witnesses];
and when the matter[26] came before the Sages, they declared it permissible.
[From this] you may naturally learn
that a woman may write her own bill of divorce and a man his own receipt,
because a document['s validity] is established only by its signatories.
(4) [He testified also] that [if][27] a needle is found in [sacrificial] meat,
the knife and the hands are pure but the meat is impure;
but if it is found in the excrement, everything is pure.

2:4–8 *Tripartite Statements*

4 Three things did R. Ishmael say before the Sages in the vineyard at Yavneh.
(1) Concerning a beaten egg placed upon vegetables of *terumah*—
that it is a connective;
but if it is like a cap—that it is not a connective.
(2) Concerning an ear of wheat [left uncut] during the harvest

---

[26] Lit. "incident", "event."
[27] It is not clear whether R. Hanina is reporting an incident that happened (as in 2:1–3) or a freestanding law. The formulation of "the knife and the hands are pure but the meat is impure" suggests the latter, hence I have supplied "[if]."

2:3 *permissible*: If a lender writes out his own promissory note, the note is valid and enforceable provided that it is signed by valid witnesses.

[From this] you may naturally learn: Apparently an anonymous comment of the Mishnah, not a continuation of the testimony of R. Hanina. See *Gittin* 2:5.

receipt: After a man has paid off his wife's *ketubbah* (see 1:12n.), he receives a *receipt* from her.

a document['s validity] is established only by its signatories: Its witnesses, and not by its scribe. Therefore even if a document was written out by a person who stands to gain from that document and thus may be suspected of falsification, if the document bears the signatures of valid witnesses, it is valid.

a needle: The commentators debate whether the needle was known to be impure or not.

the knife and the hands that touched the meat *are pure* because there is doubt whether they touched the needle, and doubtful impurity in a public place is deemed to be pure (*Tohorot* 4:4).

but the meat is impure: because the meat has certainly contacted the needle.

in the excrement: in the animal's intestines.

2:4 (1) parallel to *Tevul Yom* 3:2; (2) parallel to *Pe'ah* 5:2.

vineyard: The name of the rabbinic academy *at Yavneh*: a town west-north-west of Jerusalem, where the Sages are said to have gathered after the destruction of the temple in 70 CE. The Greek name is Yamnia.

terumah: Agricultural offering to the priest, which must be kept in a state of high purity.

connective: So that if a source of light impurity (e.g. a *tevul yom*, 2:1n.) touches the egg, even though the egg itself does not become impure, it conveys impurity to the *terumah* beneath.

cap: When cooked the egg covers the vegetables but is not integrated with them.

and whose top reaches the standing wheat—
if it can be harvested together with the standing wheat,
in this case it belongs to the householder;
otherwise it belongs to the poor.
(3) Concerning a small garden surrounded by trellised vines—
if there is room enough on the one side for a grape gatherer and his basket,
and room enough on the other side for a grape gatherer and his basket,
[the middle of the garden] may be sown [with grain];
otherwise it may not be sown.

5 Three things did they say before R. Ishmael.
In response he stated neither prohibition nor permission,
but R. Joshua b. Matia interpreted them.
(1) One who lances an abscess on the Sabbath—
if in order to make an opening in it, he is culpable;
but if in order to take out pus, he is not culpable.
(2) Concerning one who traps a snake on the Sabbath—
if his purpose is to prevent it from biting him, he is not culpable;
but if to obtain medicine, he is culpable.
(3) Concerning stewpots made of white clay[28]—
that they remain pure if in a Tent with a corpse,

[28] Translation uncertain.

---

whose top reaches the adjacent *standing wheat*: Raising the possibility that the two, the passed-over one and the standing one, could be harvested together, that is, held with one hand and cut together.

otherwise: If the two cannot be held by one hand and cut together, the passed-over ear of wheat *belongs to the poor*: in consonance with Deuteronomy 24:19.

a small garden: The commentators supply additional details on the basis of *Kilayim* 4:1, 6:1, 7:3. The issue here is that grapevines must be kept separate from grain (Deuteronomy 22:9). Cf. 5:2 (3).

2:5 *In response he stated neither prohibition nor permission*: This heading does not quite fit what follows. In none of the three cases in this mishnah is the legal question framed in terms of prohibition or permission; the questions rather are framed in terms of culpable vs. not culpable, or impure vs. pure.

but R. Joshua b. Matia interpreted them: In the three paragraphs that follow, the statement of the case was recited by the Sages before R. Ishmael, and the elaboration of the law was delivered by R. Joshua b. Matia.

if in order to make an opening in it, he is culpable: Why this should be culpable is not clear. A parallel text explains that the opening "is made like the opening that physicians make."

one who traps a snake: Trapping is prohibited on the Sabbath (*Shabbat* 7:2 no. 25).

if his purpose is to prevent it from biting him, he is not culpable: Shabbat 16:7.

if to obtain medicine: Presumably not an immediate need on the Sabbath.

Concerning stewpots made of white clay: The commentators explain that these were pots that were made of hollowed-out balls of clay. After being fired they were split in half, yielding two pots (or a pot and a cover). In this mishnah the pots have not yet been fired and split.

that they remain pure even *if in a Tent with a corpse*: The stewpots are not susceptible to "Tent impurity" (see 1:14n.) because they are sealed.

but that they are impure if carried by a *zav*.
R. Eleazar b. Zadok says:
Even if carried by a *zav* they are pure,[29]
since their manufacture is not complete.

6 Three things did R. Ishmael say but R. Aqiva did not agree with him:
(1) Garlic or (2) unripe grapes or (3) undeveloped ears [of grain]
that one was crushing while it was still day [on the eve of the Sabbath]—
R. Ishmael says:
He may finish them after nightfall.
But R. Aqiva says:
He may not finish them.

7 Three things did they say before R. Aqiva,
two in the name of R. Eliezer
and one in the name of R. Joshua.
Two in the name of R. Eliezer:
(1) A woman may go out [on the Sabbath] wearing a "city of gold"; and
(2) Pigeon flyers are unfit to give testimony.
And one in the name of R. Joshua:
If a weasel with a [dead] creeping thing in its mouth
walked upon loaves of *terumah*,
and there is doubt whether it touched them or did not touch them—
the doubt is pure.

8 Three things did R. Aqiva say;
concerning two of them they agreed with him
and concerning one they did not agree with him.

[29] K lacks everything after "that they remain pure" up to and including "they are pure," an omission caused by homeoteleuton.

but that they are impure if carried by a zav: Because even in their unfired state they are deemed utensils, and thus susceptible to impurity if carried by a *zav* (Leviticus 15:12).

since their manufacture is not complete: Not having been fired, they are not yet deemed utensils, and thus are not susceptible to impurity (*Kelim* 4:4).

2:6 *He may finish them after nightfall*: He may leave the weight in place to finish crushing them on the Sabbath, and he may use the liquid that is extracted. Cf. *Shabbat* 1:9.

He may not finish them: He may not extract the liquid on the Sabbath; if he does, he may not use the liquid on the Sabbath. See *Shabbat* 22:1.

2:7 *"city of gold"*: A tiara shaped like the city of Jerusalem (*Kelim* 11:8); wearing such a tiara on the Sabbath is prohibited according to *Shabbat* 6:1.

pigeon flyers: *Sanhedrin* 3:3. Their malfeasance is either gambling or pigeon stealing.

a weasel: Parallel to *Tohorot* 4:2.

a [dead] creeping thing: One of eight creatures listed in Leviticus 11:29–31.

the doubt is pure: Even though doubtful impurity in a private space is normally deemed impure, nevertheless, the loaves of *terumah* are regarded as pure because the source of impurity (the dead creeping thing) was in motion. Cf. 3:7.

Concerning the sandal of limeworkers—
that it is susceptible to *midras* impurity;
concerning the remains of an oven—
[that it must be] four [handbreadths high
in order to continue to be susceptible to impurity]—
whereas [formerly] they had said three [handbreadths].
[Concerning these two] they agreed with him.
And concerning one they did not agree with him:
concerning a chair two of whose seat boards[30] were removed,
one beside the other—
R. Aqiva declares it [still] susceptible to impurity,
but the Sages declare it not susceptible.

2:9–10   *Two More Statements of R. Aqiva*

9 He used to say:
A father endows his child with beauty, strength, riches, wisdom, and years;
and[31] with the number of the generations before him, which is the end [of days],
for it is said: *Calling the generations from the beginning*;
even though it is said: *And they shall serve them;
and they shall afflict them four hundred years,*
it is also said:[32] *But the fourth generation shall return here again.*

---

[30] Meaning uncertain. Other possible translations: "cushions," "coverings," "protruding arms."
[31] "And" lacking in **P**.   [32] **P**: "as it is said."

2:8 *the sandal of limeworkers*: The sandal that limeworkers wear over their regular shoes to protect their feet from the lime. For purposes of purity law these sandals are to be treated as regular sandals.

midras impurity: If a *zav* (a man or woman with an abnormal sexual discharge; see Leviticus 15:1–15) steps or sits or reclines or leans or rides upon an object upon which people customarily sit or recline or ride, the *zav* transfers his impurity to that object; this type of impurity is called *midras* impurity.

four [handbreadths high]: If a broken oven stands at least four handbreadths high upon the ground, it is still an oven, hence still susceptible to impurity. But if it is not that high, it is no longer an oven and no longer susceptible to impurity. See *Kelim* 5:1.

[formerly]: 7:7, 8.

a chair: See 1:11n.

[still] susceptible to impurity: Because it is still a chair.

2:9 *and with the number of generations before him*: Before the son. The meaning is ambiguous, referring either to generations past or generations future. The reference to *the end [of days]* suggests the latter. The meaning of this paragraph, especially the relationship of the three biblical citations to each other and to the opening sentence, is most obscure.

Calling the generations: Isaiah 41:4.

And they the Israelites *shall serve them* the Egyptians: Genesis 15:13.

But the fourth generation shall return here: i.e. to the land of Canaan: Genesis 15:16.

10 He also used to say:
Five things are of twelve months:
(1) the judgment of the generation of the Flood—twelve months;
(2) the judgment of Job—twelve months;
(3) the judgment of the Egyptians—twelve months;
(4) the judgment of Gog and Magog in the time to come—twelve months;
(5) the judgment of the wicked in Gehenna—twelve months,
for it is written: *It shall be from month to month.*
R. Yohanan b. Nuri says:
[Only as long as] from Passover to the Festival of Weeks,
for it is written: *And from Sabbath to Sabbath.*

Chapter Three

3:1–6 *The Leniencies of R. Dosa b. Harqinas Are Rejected by the Sages*

3 All [parts of a corpse] that impart Tent impurity:
if they were divided in half and brought[33] into a house—
R. Dosa b. Harqinas declares [everything in the house to be] pure,

---

[33] Lit. "and one brought them."

2:10 *Flood—twelve months*: Cf. Genesis 7:11 and 8:14.

Job—twelve months: Cf. Job 7:3.

Gog and Magog: Ezekiel 38–39.

the wicked in Gehenna: The Mishnah understands the last part of Isaiah 66:24 to mean that the worm and the fire of Gehenna will last *from month to month*, that is, when the same month comes round again, a year.

from Passover, which is called a "Sabbath" in Leviticus 23:15 *to the Festival of Weeks*, which is celebrated the day after a Sabbath in Leviticus 23:16, a total of seven weeks.

for it is written in that same verse, Isaiah 66:24.

3:1 Parallel to *Oholot* 3:1.

All [parts of a corpse] that impart Tent impurity: Any part of a human corpse equal to, or larger than, the minimums stated in *Oholot* 2:1 (and above 1:7). This mishnah is speaking of corpse flesh.

Tent impurity: See above 1:7. The Sages understood Numbers 19 to imply that a person or object, not in an enclosed space, could nevertheless contract Tent impurity by overshadowing or "tenting over" a corpse or by having the corpse tent over them. That is, if a person is located directly over a corpse or directly under a corpse, the person contracts corpse impurity even though the person has not touched the corpse.

if they were divided in half: For a piece of corpse flesh to impart Tent impurity, or to confer impurity by touch or by carriage, it must be at a minimum in bulk the size of an olive. Below this minimum it does not impart impurity. The question addressed by this mishnah is whether two halves can be deemed to constitute a minimum whole.

According to *R. Dosa b. Harqinas* an olive's bulk of corpse flesh, if divided in two, does not confer impurity; the two halves do not constitute a whole.

but the Sages declare it impure.
How so?
If one touched or carried two pieces of carrion, each in bulk a half-olive;
or, in the case of a corpse,
if one touched one half-olive's bulk
while tenting over another half-olive's bulk;
or if one touched one half-olive's bulk
while another half-olive's bulk tented over him;
or if one tented over two [pieces, each a] half-olive's bulk;
or if one tented over one half-olive's bulk while another half-olive's bulk tented over him—
[in all these cases] R. Dosa b. Harqinas declares him pure,
but the Sages declare him impure.
But if one touched one half-olive's bulk [of a corpse]
and some other thing tented over both him and another half-olive's bulk;
or if one tented over one half-olive's bulk
and some other thing tented over both him and another half-olive's bulk—
he is pure.
R. Meir said:
In these cases too R. Dosa declares him pure, and the Sages declare him impure.
[Because according to the Sages] all [of these combinations make the person] impure,
except for [a combination of] contact impurity and carriage impurity,
or carriage impurity and Tent impurity.
This is the general rule: If [the sources of impurity are] of one category,
[the person is] impure;
if of two categories, he is pure.

2 Bits of food[34] do not combine—
the words of R. Dosa b. Harqinas.[35]
But the Sages say:
They do combine.

[34] Or "separated food".
[35] P: "the words of R. Meir" (corrected to "Dosa"). Both P and K lack "son of Harqinas."

one touched or carried two pieces of carrion: Leviticus 11:39–40. Carrion does not impart Tent impurity. This case is mentioned here because the same principle is involved.

he is pure: Even according to the Sages.

contact impurity and carriage impurity: If a person touches a half-olive's bulk of corpse flesh in one hand, and carries (without touching) another half-olive's bulk of corpse flesh in the other.

or carriage impurity and Tent impurity: If a person carries (without touching) a half-olive's bulk of corpse flesh while simultaneously tenting over, or being tented over by, another half-olive's bulk of corpse flesh.

This is the general rule: A continuation of the view of R. Meir. The commentators explain that according to the Sages contact impurity and Tent impurity are understood to be one category.

3:2 *Bits of food*: Parallel to *Tohorot* 8:8 (contrast *Me'ilah* 4:5). *One may exchange second tithe*: Parallel to *Ma'aser Sheni* 1:2. *One must immerse one's hands*: Parallel to *Hagigah* 2:5.

Bits of impure *food do not combine* to constitute the minimum amount of impure food required to transmit impurity to other food. That minimum amount is the bulk of an egg (*Tohorot* 1:5).

One may exchange second tithe for unminted metal—[36]
so R. Dosa.
But the Sages say:
One may not exchange[37] it.
One must immerse one's hands before [contact with the ashes of] purgation—
so R. Dosa.
But the Sages say:
If one's hands become impure the whole body is impure.

3 The innards of a melon or the trimmings of a vegetable
that are *terumah*—
R. Dosa permits them to nonpriests,
but the Sages forbid them.
Five shorn ewes—if [the weight of each fleece] is a *maneh, maneh,* and a half,
they are liable to the first shearing—
so R. Dosa.
But the Sages say:
Five ewes—no matter how much [their fleeces may weigh].

4 All mats are susceptible to corpse impurity [but not to *midras* impurity]—
the words of R. Dosa.
But the Sages say:
[Also] to *midras* impurity.

[36] Or perhaps "coin blanks."   [37] **K, P:** "But the Sages forbid it."

---

second tithe: Deuteronomy 14:22–26. This debate turns on the interpretation of *kesef* in Deuteronomy 14:25: does it mean "money" or "silver"? See 1:9 above.

[ashes of] purgation: Water containing the ash of the red heifer, in accordance with Numbers 19. This water had to be prepared and administered in the state of highest purity.

If one's hands become impure the whole body is impure: Consequently, immersion of hands is insufficient. In context this is not a general rejection of the impurity of hands (5:6 below; see *Yadayim*) but an affirmation of the high degree of purity required of those preparing the water of the red heifer.

3:3 *innards…trimmings*: The parts that are usually not eaten.

R. Dosa permits them to be eaten by *nonpriests* because they are not regarded as regular food, hence they never became *terumah*.

Five shorn ewes: Parallel to *Hullin* 11:2.

maneh, maneh and a half: A *maneh* in weight equals one hundred *dinar*. The commentators understand this phrase to mean the weight of 150 *dinar* each.

the first shearing: Deuteronomy 18:4, an offering to the priest.

Both R. Dosa and the Sages agree that a minimum of *five* sheep is required to establish an obligation of "first shearing"; less than five is not a "flock."

3:4 *All mats*: The issue here is whether mats constitute bedding upon which a person might recline or sit. If yes, they are susceptible to *midras* impurity; if not, they are not susceptible.

midras impurity: See 2:8.

No nettings are susceptible to impurity except that which is used for a belt—[38]
so R. Dosa.
But the Sages say:
They are all susceptible to impurity except that used by wool dealers.[39]

5 A sling whose pouch is woven is susceptible to impurity.[40]
But if it is of leather—
R. Dosa b. Harqinas declares it not susceptible to impurity,
but the Sages declare it susceptible.
If the place for the finger is severed, it is not susceptible to impurity;
but if the place for the strap is severed, it is susceptible to impurity.[41]

6 A woman who was taken captive may eat *terumah*—
the words of R. Dosa.
But the Sages say:
There is a captive who may eat and there is a captive who may not eat.
How so?
If a woman said, "I was taken captive, yet I am pure," she may eat,
since the mouth that forbade is the mouth that permitted;[42]

---

[38] Or "girdle." The word is variously transmitted in the manuscripts.
[39] Or "woolworkers."
[40] Lit. "impure."
[41] The scribe of P originally wrote "If the place for the finger is severed, it is susceptible to impurity; but if the place for the strap is severed, it is not susceptible to impurity" and then corrected it.
[42] K, P lack "Since the mouth that forbade is the mouth that permitted."

No nettings: The issue here is whether cloth made of netting constitutes a garment. If yes, it is susceptible to impurity; if not, it is not susceptible.

a belt: A garment.

except that used by wool dealers, which is more like a rope than a garment.

3:5 *A sling* is a length of cord to which a *pouch* (lit. "receptacle") is attached. A missile (typically a stone) is placed in the pouch. One end of the cord is looped around the *finger* of one hand, while the other end of the cord is held by the other hand by means of a tab or a *strap* that is attached to the cord. The pouch is twirled around over the head and the missile is released when the hand lets go of the strap.

A sling whose pouch is made of *woven* material *is susceptible to impurity* because the presence of the pouch makes the sling a vessel for the purposes of purity law. See *Kelim* 15:1.

leather: Separate rules may apply; see *Kelim* 27:1–3.

If the place for the finger is severed, it is not susceptible to impurity because it can no longer function as a sling; *but if the place for the strap is severed, it is susceptible to impurity* because it can still function as a sling.

3:6 The view of the Sages appears in *Ketubbot* 2:5.

A woman of nonpriestly stock married to a priest may eat *terumah* received by her husband (Leviticus 22:11). However, if she has intercourse with a gentile man, even unwillingly, she may no longer remain with her priestly husband (*Ketubbot* 4:8) and consequently may no longer eat his *terumah*. R. Dosa says that an Israelite woman married to a priest may continue to eat *terumah* even if she had been kidnapped by gentiles and redeemed, since we do not know for a certainty that she was violated.

the mouth that forbade is the mouth that permitted: A principle that is elaborated in *Ketubbot* 2:1–5. This woman is the sole source for the information that she had been taken captive by gentiles; she is also the sole source for the information that she had not been violated during her captivity. If we are to believe her first statement, we should also believe her second.

but if there are witnesses to the fact that she was taken captive,
and she says, "I am pure,"
she may not eat.

3:7–9 *The Severities of R. Joshua and R. Zadok Are Rejected by the Sages*

7 Four cases of doubt[ful impurity]—
R. Joshua declares them impure,
but the Sages declare them pure.
How so?
(1) If an impure person is standing and a pure person passes by; or
(2) if a pure person is standing and an impure person passes by; or
(3) if what is impure is in a private domain
and what is pure[43] is in a public domain; or
(4) if what is pure is in a private domain
and what is impure is in the public domain;
and [in all these cases] there is doubt
whether one contacted the other or not,
or whether one tented over the other or not,
or whether one moved the other or not—
R. Joshua declares them impure,
but the Sages declare them pure.

8 Three things R. Zadok declares susceptible to impurity,
but the Sages declare not susceptible:
(1) the nail of a moneychanger,
(2) a grist dealer's chest, and
(3) the nail of a sundial.
R. Zadok declares them susceptible to impurity,
but the Sages declare them not susceptible.

[43] P: "and what is impure and what is pure in the public domain," probably a mistake.

if there are witnesses to the fact of her captivity, she needs witnesses to establish the fact that she was not violated.

3:7 Parallel to *Tohorot* 6:2.

Doubtful impurity in *a public domain* is deemed pure, but doubtful impurity in *a private domain* is deemed impure (2:3n).

tented over: That is, overshadowed. A corpse, or bits of a corpse, imparts impurity to persons or objects that share an enclosure or an overhang with the corpse (see 3:1).

3:8 Parallel to *Kelim* 12:5. What is at issue here and in the following mishnah is whether or not any of the indicated objects is a utensil in and of itself, and consequently susceptible to impurity.

The identification and function of the *nail of a moneychanger* and *a grist dealer's chest* are not clear and are debated by the commentators.

The *nail of a sundial* is the gnomon, the vertical piece that casts the shadow.

3:9–11 *Severities and Leniencies of Rabban Gamaliel*

9 Four things Rabban Gamaliel declares susceptible to impurity,
but the Sages declare not susceptible:
(1) the metal basket cover of householders,
(2) the hanger of a strigil,
(3) the blanks of metal utensils, and
(4) a tray[44] broken in two.
But the Sages agree with Rabban Gamaliel
in the case of a tray that was broken in two pieces,
the one large and the other small—
that the larger is susceptible to impurity
but the smaller is not susceptible to impurity.

10 In three things Rabban Gamaliel is stringent,
following the words of the House of Shammai:
(1) one may not stow [a container of] hot food on a Festival day for the Sabbath;
(2) nor may one right a [fallen] lampstand on a Festival day;
(3) nor may one bake bread in large loaves [on a Festival day],
but only small cakes.[45]
Rabban Gamaliel said:
Never in all their days did the people of my father's household
bake bread in large loaves, but only small cakes.[46]
They said to him:
What proof can be brought from your father's household?[47]
They were accustomed to be stringent with themselves, but lenient to Israel,
so that they might bake bread both as large loaves and as thick cake.

[44] Or "board." Some translate "plate."
[45] Or "twisted loaves…flat cakes."
[46] Or "twisted loaves…flat cakes."
[47] Lit. "What can we do to [or for] your father's household?"

3:9 Parallel to *Kelim* 12:6.

householders: But metal basket covers of physicians are susceptible to impurity even according to the Sages (*Kelim* 12:3).

the hanger of a strigil: the handle of a scraper used in the bath.

the blanks of metal utensils: The blank pieces of metal that are to be shaped into utensils.

3:10 Parallel to *Betsah* 2:6.

on a Festival day that falls on a Friday.

a [fallen] lampstand: The Talmud explains that righting the lampstand is prohibited because it was constructed out of numerous pieces that would need reassembling after falling. (If, in contrast, it were a single piece, then righting it would be permissible.)

large loaves…small cakes: Large loaves (or, in the alternative rendering, twisted loaves) are prohibited to be made on a festival day because making them is a lot of work, and it is certain that there will be leftovers for the morrow.

thick cake: See *Shabbat* 1:10.

11 In contrast[48] in three matters he was lenient:[49]
(1) one may sweep between couches, and
(2) one may put incense [on the fire] on a Festival day, and
(3) one may prepare a "helmeted" kid on Passover night.
But the Sages forbid these things.

3:12 R. Eleazar b. Azariah

12 Three things did R. Eleazar b. Azariah permit and the Sages forbid:
(1) his cow would go out [on the Sabbath] with a strap between its horns, and
(2) one may scrape cattle on a Festival day, and
(3) grind peppers in their mill.
R. Judah says:
One may not scrape cattle on a Festival day since it might cause a wound,
but one may rub them.
But the Sages say:
One may not scrape them and one may not even rub them.

Chapter Four

4:1–12 Leniencies of the House of Shammai, Severities of the House of Hillel

4 The following things are among those in which the House of Shammai are lenient,

[48] Lit. "Moreover" or "Even he."
[49] Lit. "[in] three things he said [a legal opinion] that was lenient."

3:11 Parallel to *Betsah* 2:7.

One may not *sweep between* the dining *couches on a festival day* because the Sages fear fear that in doing so the householder may try to even out holes or pits in the earthen floor.

The Sages forbid *incense on a festival day* because it is not necessary.

a "helmeted" kid: The Paschal lamb (or goat) was roasted on a spit, with the internal organs removed from the carcass and placed over the head so that they would roast at the same speed as the rest of the meat (*Pesahim* 7:1). This gave the lamb (or goat) the appearance of wearing a helmet. Rabban Gamaliel permits preparing a kid in this manner on Passover eve as a memorial to the Paschal sacrifice that had been offered when the Temple stood. The Sages forbid doing so, for it looks as if one is preparing the Paschal sacrifice outside the Temple.

3:12 Parallel to *Betsah* 2:8.

his cow would go out: *Shabbat* 5:4.

scrape...rub: Exactly what actions are meant by these verbs is not certain and is debated by the commentators. Danby translates "curry...comb."

4:1 Parallel to *Betsah* 1:1.

The following things are among those...: This is not a complete list; see 5:1–5 and *Oholot* 11:3–6; *Shabbat* 21:3 (according to the printed editions).

and the House of Hillel are stringent.
If an egg was laid on a Festival day—
the House of Shammai say:
It may be eaten.
But the House of Hillel say:
It may not be eaten.
The House of Shammai say:
An olive's bulk of leaven and a date's bulk of that which is leavened
[violates the prohibition of possessing leaven on Passover].
But the House of Hillel say:
An olive's bulk of either.

2 If an animal was born on a Festival day—
all agree that it is permitted,
and if a chick emerged from an egg [on a Festival day]—
all agree that it is forbidden.[50]
If one slaughtered a wild animal or a bird on a Festival day—
the House of Shammai say:
He may dig with a spade and cover [the blood].
But the House of Hillel say:
He may not slaughter unless he had earth prepared in advance
[to cover the blood].
But they agree that if he slaughtered,
he may dig with a spade and cover [the blood];
[moreover, they agreed] that the ash of a double-stove is prepared in advance.

[50] K, P lack entire sentence.

If an egg was laid on a Festival day: The issue here is whether the newly laid egg is deemed to be "prepared" or not. Only food that was prepared in advance of the holiday may be processed or eaten on the holiday. (If the egg was laid on the Sabbath, all would agree that it is prohibited on the Sabbath.)

Exodus 13:7 prohibits the possession of leaven and that which is leavened (the distinction between the two is not clear) during the seven days of Passover. The Houses debate the minimum amount required to violate the prohibition. A *date's bulk* is larger than an *olive's*.

4:2 *If an animal...all agree that it is forbidden*: An addition to the Mishnah drawn from the Talmud.

If a domesticated *animal*: Cow, sheep, or goat.

permitted: To be slaughtered and eaten.

all agree, even the House of Hillel, *that it is permitted*.

all agree, even the House of Shammai, *that it is forbidden*.

The difference between a chick and a newborn animal is that the former was not ready to be eaten on the day before the festival day, hence was not "prepared," whereas the latter was.

If one slaughtered: Parallel to *Betsah* 1:2.

a wild animal or a bird...cover [the blood]: Leviticus 17:13.

But they agree: The House of Hillel concedes to the House of Shammai.

is deemed to be *prepared in advance*.

3 The House of Shammai say:
Renunciation of ownership [of produce] for the benefit of the poor [alone]
is [a valid] renunciation of ownership.
But the House of Hillel say:
Renunciation of ownership [of produce] is valid
only if ownership is renounced for the benefit of the wealthy as well,
as is the case in the year of release.
If all the sheaves in a field were each one *qav* but one was four *qav*,
and [this is the one] that he forgot—
the House of Shammai say:
It is not Forgotten Sheaf;
but the House of Hillel say:
It is Forgotten Sheaf.
   4 A sheaf that one forgot
near a wall or a stack of grain or the oxen or the tools—
the House of Shammai say:
It is not Forgotten Sheaf.
But the House of Hillel say:
It is Forgotten Sheaf.
   5 [The produce of] a fourth-year vineyard—
the House of Shammai say:

4:3 Parallel to *Pe'ah* 6:1.

Renunciation of ownership: A landowner is obligated by the Torah to leave behind some of his harvest for the poor (Leviticus 19:9–10; 23:22; Deuteronomy 24:19) and to pay tithes to the Levite and *terumah* to the priest. A landowner, willing to support the poor but hoping to avoid the obligation of tithes and *terumah*, renounced his ownership of a certain part of his produce, but did so with the proviso that the ownership be renounced only for the sake of the poor. According to the House of Shammai, the renunciation is valid, and he has thus avoided the obligation of *terumah* and tithes on that part of his produce (hence the House of Shammai are said to be "lenient"). The House of Hillel, however, say, that renunciation of ownership only for the benefit of the poor is not a valid renunciation, hence the produce is still liable to *terumah* and tithes (hence the House of Hillel are said to be stringent).

the year of release: Every seventh year, crops may be harvested by all and not only by the poor (Exodus 23:10–11).

qav: A unit of volume (1:2).

Forgotten Sheaf: Deuteronomy 24:19.

4:4 Parallel to *Pe'ah* 6:2.

not Forgotten Sheaf: By leaving the sheaf next to items of value the landowner has acquired ownership of the sheaf. Even though he subsequently forgot it, the sheaf does not have the status of Forgotten Sheaf (Deuteronomy 24:19); consequently the sheaf belongs to the landowner, not the poor (and from the landowner's perspective the ruling of the House of Shammai is lenient).

4:5 Parallel to *Pe'ah* 7:6 and *Ma'aser Sheni* 5:3. Fruit that matures in the fourth year after a fruit tree has been planted (Leviticus 19:24) is treated like second tithe: the produce is to be brought to Jerusalem and consumed there, or it may be redeemed for money, and the money brought to Jerusalem and spent there (see above 1:9n.). The Houses debate whether two other rules that apply to second tithe also apply to fourth-year produce: *Added Fifth* and *Removal*.

Neither the law of Added Fifth nor the law of Removal applies.
But the House of Hillel say:
The law of Added Fifth and the law of Removal apply.
The House of Shammai say:
The law of Separated Grape and the law of Defective Cluster apply,
and the poor must redeem the grapes for themselves.
But the House of Hillel say:
All of it goes to the winepress.

6 A jar of pickled[51] olives—
the House of Shammai say:
One need not pierce it.
But the House of Hillel say:
One needs to pierce it.
But they agree that if one pierced it and the lees plug it,
it is not susceptible to impurity.
One who anoints oneself with pure oil, then becomes impure,
descends [to the immersion pool] and immerses—
the House of Shammai say:
Even though [the oil] drips [from his body], it[52] is pure.
But House of Hillel say:
[It is pure if there remains on his body just] enough [oil] to anoint a small limb.

[51] Lit. "rolled."   [52] Or "he" and so on for the rest of the mishnah.

Added Fifth: If second-tithe produce is redeemed and converted into money, the landowner must add a fifth to its value (Leviticus 27:31; *Bava Metsi'a* 4:8).

Removal: Leftover second-tithe produce must be removed from the house and destroyed on the day before Passover of the fourth and seventh years of the seven-year Sabbatical cycle (Deuteronomy 26:13; *Ma'aser Sheni* 5:6).

Separated Grape...Defective Cluster: Leviticus 19:10; Deuteronomy 24:21; *Pe'ah* 7:3–4. These belong to the poor; since the produce is of a fourth-year vineyard, the poor are responsible for redeeming the produce and bringing its value to Jerusalem. (From the landowner's perspective the ruling of the House of Shammai is lenient, since the landowner has that much less fourth-year produce to take to Jerusalem.)

All of it goes to the winepress: The landowner owns, and is responsible for, all of it.

4:6 *One* the owner *need not pierce it*: To let out the liquid that exudes from the fruit (what we may call olive juice). Produce is susceptible to impurity only if it was first moistened (Leviticus 11:34, 38) by one of seven liquids (*Makhshirin* 6:4), and only if it was moistened with the owner's knowledge and desire. At issue here is whether the owner of the olives, if he is to keep his olives insusceptible to impurity, needs to give a palpable demonstration that he is indifferent to the olive juice that is rendering his olives moist. According to the *House of Shammai* he does not, perhaps because the House of Shammai do not regard olive juice as one of the select seven liquids (cf. *Makhshirin* 6:5).

The *House of Hillel* demand of the owner a palpable demonstration that he is indifferent to the olive juice; piercing the jar is such a demonstration. The House of Hillel do not demand, however, the drainage of the liquid. If the hole gets stopped up by the lees, the House of Hillel concede to the House of Shammai that the owner may let the olives remain in their juice in the jar, all the while remaining insusceptible to impurity.

House of Shammai say...it is pure: Since the person has become pure, so has the oil.

a small limb: The little finger. More oil than that retains its impurity, since an immersion pool cannot purify liquids other than water.

But if the oil was impure at the outset—
the House of Shammai say:
[It is pure if there remains on his body just] enough [oil] to anoint a small limb.
But the House of Hillel say:
[It is pure if there remains on his body just] enough [oil] to be a moist liquid.
R. Judah says in the name of the House of Hillel:
[The oil is pure if] it is moist and moistens other things.

7 A woman is betrothed by [receipt of] a *dinar* or a *dinar*'s equivalent—
according to the words of the House of Shammai.
But the House of Hillel say:
[She is betrothed] by a *perutah* or a *perutah*'s equivalent.
And how much is a *perutah*?
One eighth of an Italian *issar*.
The House of Shammai say:
A person may divorce his wife with an old bill of divorce.
But the House of Hillel forbid it.
What is an old bill of divorce?
Any case in which he spent time alone with her after he had written it for her.
One who divorces his wife and she then lodges with him in an inn—
the House of Shammai say:
She does not need another bill of divorce from him.
But the House of Hillel say:
She needs another bill of divorce from him.
When does this apply?
Only if she was divorced after cohabitation;
but[53] if she was divorced after betrothal,
she does not need another bill of divorce from him,
since he is not bold with her.[54]

[53] K, P: "but they [the House of Hillel] concede that."
[54] Lit. "since his heart is not (yet) big/proud with her." K lacks "not."

[just] enough [oil] to be a moist liquid: Which is less than the amount needed to anoint a little finger.

it is moist and moistens other things: More than "just enough to be moist" but less than "just enough to anoint a little finger."

4:7 *A woman is betrothed*: Parallel to *Kiddushin* 1:1; *old bill of divorce*: Parallel to *Gittin* 8:4; *one who divorces his wife*: Parallel to *Gittin* 8:9.

dinar...perutah...issar: An *issar* is a twenty-fourth of a *dinar*, a *perutah* is ⅛ of an *issar*, so a *perutah* is a ¹⁄₁₉₂ of a *dinar*. In the three debates in this mishnah, the House of Hillel make it easier to contract a valid marriage, and harder to divorce, than do the House of Shammai; this is a severity because a woman not deemed to be married according to the House of Shammai is deemed to be married according to the House of Hillel and therefore susceptible to a charge of adultery.

When does this apply? Under what conditions do the Hillelites require a second bill of divorce?

since he is not bold with her: That is, we may assume that they did not have sexual relations in the inn.

8 The House of Shammai permit co-wives
to [be married in levirate marriage to any of] the brothers.
But the House of Hillel forbid it.
If[55] they were released through *halitsah*—
the House of Shammai declare them unfit for marriage into the priesthood,
but the House of Hillel declare them fit.
If they were married in levirate marriage—
the House of Shammai declare them fit
[for subsequent marriage into the priesthood],
but the House of Hillel declare them unfit.
Even though these declare unfit and these declare fit,
yet the House of Shammai did not refrain
from taking wives from the House of Hillel,
and the House of Hillel did not refrain
from taking wives from the House of Shammai.
And [in spite of] all the purities and impurities
that these would pronounce pure and these impure—
they did not refrain from making purities together, these with those.

9 If there were three brothers,
two of them married to two sisters, and one unmarried,
and one of the married brothers died,
and the unmarried brother betrothed the widow verbally,

[55] K, P lack the rest of this mishnah here but include it in the parallel in *Yevamot*.

4:8 Parallel to *Yevamot* 1:4. According to Deuteronomy 25:5-10, the law of levirate marriage, a man must marry his deceased brother's widow if the brother died without issue. If the surviving brother refuses to marry the widow, she performs the ritual of *halitsah* ("release") and becomes a *halutsah* ("a released woman"). The Houses debate the following situation: if brother #1 marries two (or more) wives, one of whom is a permissible spouse for him but a prohibited spouse for brother #2 (for example, brother #1 marries the daughter of brother #2), may/must brother #2 take in levirate marriage one of the other wives of deceased brother #1, or does the presence of the prohibited widow render all the widows prohibited? The House of Shammai permit levirate marriage in this instance, thus their position is lenient.

If they were released through halitsah: That is, if one of the widows performed *halitsah*, all the widows have the status of "released women," according to the House of Shammai, and thus are *unfit for marriage into the priesthood* because a "released woman" is of the same legal status as a divorcee. The House of Shammai treat the *halitsah* as legally meaningful, since the surviving brother could have performed levirate marriage instead. The House of Hillel treat the *halitsah* as legally meaningless since in this situation levirate marriage is prohibited; the widows do not have the legal status of "released women."

If they one or more of the widows *were married in levirate marriage*: Upon the death of their levir they may marry a priest, since they have the status of widows and their levirate marriage was legitimate, according to the House of Shammai. According to the House of Hillel, however, these women are *unfit* for subsequent marriage with a priest, because their levirate marriage was illegitimate—the marriage of a man with his brother's wife, outside of levirate marriage, is prohibited (Leviticus 18:16)—and a woman who has had illicit intercourse may not be married to a priest (*Yevamot* 6:5).

4:9 Parallel to *Yevamot* 3:5. Cf. 5:5 below.

two of them married to two sisters: But childless.

betrothed her verbally: Levirate marriage is properly contracted only through sexual intercourse; a verbal statement ("You are betrothed to me") creates a legal bond between the levir and the widow, but a weak one. See *Yevamot* 5.

and then his second brother died—
the House of Shammai say:
His wife may remain with him but the other woman must leave,
since she is the sister of his wife.
But the House of Hillel say:
He must dismiss his wife both by bill of divorce and by *halitsah*,
and his brother's wife by *halitsah*.
This is what [they meant when] they said,
"Woe to him on account of his wife,
and woe to him on account of his brother's wife!"

10   One who prohibits his wife by oath
from having sexual intercourse with him—
the House of Shammai say:
[He may abide by his oath] for two weeks.
But the House of Hillel say:
For one week [only].
A woman who miscarries on the night of the eighty-first day—
the House of Shammai declare her exempt from an offering.
But the House of Hillel declare her liable.
A linen sheet vis-à-vis the obligation of *tsitsit*—
the House of Shammai declare it exempt,
but the House of Hillel declare it liable.
A basket [of fruit] intended for the Sabbath—

the other woman must leave without either *halitsah* or a divorce, *since she is the sister of his wife* and therefore prohibited (Leviticus 18:18). The verbal betrothal was sufficient to contract levirate marriage with the first sister.

He must dismiss his wife…and his brother's wife: Because verbal betrothal was not sufficient to make an unambiguous levirate marriage with the first sister. He is now confronted by two sisters, each of whom prevents him from marrying the other.

they said: R. Joshua in *Yevamot* 13:7.

"Woe to him": Through no fault of his own he is unable to keep his wife or marry her sister. He remains without a wife.

4:10 *One who prohibits his wife*: Parallel to *Ketubbot* 5:6; *A woman who miscarries*: Parallel to *Keritot* 1:6; *A basket [of fruit]*: Parallel to *Ma'aserot* 4:2. (The paragraph about *tsitsit* has no parallel in the Mishnah.)

on the night of the eighty-first day: At the inception of the eighty-first day after the birth of a girl. When night turns to day, the eighty-first day, the mother is obligated to bring a sacrifice (Leviticus 12:5–6) to mark the birth. The question here is whether the miscarriage requires her to bring an additional sacrifice. *Keritot* 1:6 gives a full presentation of the debate between the Houses.

tsitsit: The "fringe" that is to be affixed to the "corners" of a garment according to Numbers 15:38 and Deuteronomy 22:12. The issue here seems to be whether a linen sheet is considered a "garment."

basket [of fruit] intended for the Sabbath: Before the fruit can be eaten on the Sabbath tithes must be separated; this must be done before the Sabbath (*Shabbat* 2:7). The question here is whether the intention to eat of the fruit on the Sabbath mandates that tithing must precede any eating from the basket, no matter when (on the Sabbath or before) or under what circumstances (formal eating or snacking). The House of Shammai permit pre-Sabbath snacking even without tithing. See introduction to *Ma'aserot*.

the House of Shammai declare it exempt [from tithes],
but the House of Hillel declare it liable.

11 One who vowed an extended period of being a *nazir*,
completed it, and afterward came to the Land [of Israel]—
the House of Shammai say:
[He needs to be] a *nazir* for [only] thirty days.
But the House of Hillel say:
He is a *nazir* as at the beginning.
One who is the object of the testimony of two groups of witnesses,
these testifying that he had vowed two [periods of being a *nazir*],
and those testifying that he had vowed five—
the House of Shammai say:
Their testimony is divided, and there is no *nazir* status here.
But the House of Hillel say:
Two are included within five, so let him be a *nazir* for two periods.

12 If a person was located below a crack [in the roof]—
the House of Shammai say:
He does not give passage to the impurity.
But the House of Hillel say:
A person is hollow, and his upper side gives passage to the impurity.

4:11 Parallel to *Nazir* 3:6–7.

nazir: Numbers 6:1–21 and *Nazir*.

extended period of being a nazir: Greater than thirty days or multiple periods of thirty days. A vow to become a *nazir*, if the duration is unspecified, is assumed to have a duration of thirty days.

completed it: He fulfilled his vow in the Diaspora and has now come to the Land of Israel, perhaps to bring the sacrifice required at the end of a *nazir* period (Numbers 6:14–15).

thirty days: A single period of being a *nazir*.

as at the beginning: He must be a *nazir* for multiple periods of thirty days, in accordance with his original vow. The Hillelites believe that one cannot truly be a *nazir* outside the Land of Israel because of impurity concerns.

4:12 Parallel to *Oholot* 11:3. According to Numbers 19 a human corpse in an enclosed space (a "Tent") imparts impurity to persons and objects inside that space, even without direct contact. See 1:7n. Here the Mishnah is speaking of a corpse on one side of a roofed area, and vessels on the other side; the roof, however, has a crack, so that the corpse and the vessels are not in a common enclosed space and the vessels do not contract impurity. If the crack is bridged, however, the impurity will extend from the corpse to the vessels. The crack can be bridged by a person or object either lying atop the crack or lying under the crack, provided in the latter case that the person or object is suspended at least one handbreadth above the floor (and thus is a "Tent" in its own right; see *Oholot* 11:2). Here the Houses debate whether a (living) human body, lying on the floor under the crack, can serve as a conduit for the impurity. The House of Shammai say no, because the body is not suspended one handbreadth above the floor, but the Hillelites say yes, because a human body is treated as hollow, and the part of the body farthest from the floor is as if suspended above the floor.

upper side: Not the part resting on the floor, but the part at least one handbreadth above the floor.

Chapter Five

5:1–5 More Leniencies of the House of Shammai, Severities of the House of Hillel

5 R. Judah says:
[The following] six things are among those in which the House of Shammai are lenient, and the House of Hillel are stringent.
(1) The blood of carcasses—
the House of Shammai declare it pure, but the House of Hillel declare it impure.
(2) An egg from a [bird's] carcass—
if one similar to it can be found for sale in the market, it is permitted; otherwise it is forbidden.
[This is the law] according to the words of the House of Shammai.
But the House of Hillel forbid it.
But they [the House of Shammai] concede that an egg from a bird that is *terefah* is forbidden, since it grew in what is forbidden.
(3) The blood of a gentile woman and (4) "the blood of purification" of a leprous woman—
the House of Shammai declare it pure;
but the House of Hillel say:
It has the same status as her spittle or her urine.

5:1 (3) and (4) parallel to *Niddah* 4:3 (see below 5:4); (5) parallel to *Sheviit* 4:2; (6) partially parallel to *Kelim* 26:4.

The blood of animal *carcasses*: The carcass itself is impure (Leviticus 11:39–40), and the question here is whether the blood is deemed to be part of, or separate from, the carcass. The commentators debate whether the House of Shammai mean that the blood is not impure at all, or only that the blood is not as impure as the carcass. A testimony is provided in 8:1 endorsing the view of the House of Shammai.

An egg from a [bird's] carcass: That is, an egg found in the carcass of a bird that would have been permissible for eating had it been properly slaughtered, *is permitted* to be eaten if eggs in a similar state of development, that is, fully developed, are *for sale in the market*; if they are, then this egg too is deemed to be fully developed. Since it grew inside a bird that could have been fit for eating, it itself may be eaten; since it is fully developed, the death of the mother bird does not affect its status as permissible. If it is not yet fully developed, it is deemed to be part of its mother and therefore forbidden to be eaten, since the mother bird cannot be eaten, not having been slaughtered. If, however, the mother bird is *terefah*, that is, if it was slaughtered properly but was found to be diseased (*Hullin* 2:4, 3:3), then the egg may not be eaten, no matter what its state of development, since it grew inside a mother bird that could not have been eaten. So the House of Shammai.

The menstrual or post-partum *blood of a gentile woman* does not impurify according to the House of Shammai, because gentiles are outside the Torah's purity system. The *"blood of purification"* is post-partum bleeding on days 8–40 after the birth of a boy, or days 15–80 after the birth of a girl (Leviticus 12:4–5). This blood does not impurify. Even though the bodily fluids of one with *tsara'at* normally impurify, the House of Shammai argue that the law of "the blood of purification" applies even to such a woman. The House of Hillel argue that just as the Sages decreed that the spittle and urine of gentiles impurify (when wet, not dry; *Niddah* 7:1), so too did they decree concerning the menstrual or post-partum blood of gentiles. And while the House of Hillel concede that "the blood of purification" of a woman with *tsara'at* does not impurify to the same degree as menstrual blood, it does impurify to the same degree as spittle and urine.

(5) One may eat Seventh-Year produce either with or without permission [of the field's owner]—
according to the words of the House of Shammai.
But the House of Hillel say:
One may eat it only with permission.[56]
(6) A waterskin—
the House of Shammai say:
[It is susceptible to impurity only] if it is knotted [and] remains [knotted].
But the House of Hillel say:
Even though it is not knotted.

2 R. Yose says:
[The following] six things are among those in which
the House of Shammai are lenient, and the House of Hillel are stringent.
(1) Fowl may be served on[57] the table together with cheese
but may not be eaten [with it]—
according to the words of the House of Shammai.
But the House of Hillel say:
It may not be served[58] [with it] and it may not be eaten [with it].
(2) One may separate *terumah* from olives for oil, or from grapes for wine—
according to the words of the House of Shammai.
But the House of Hillel say:
One may not separate *terumah* thus.

[56] K: "One may not eat it either with or without permission." P (and the punctuator of K): "One may not eat it with permission."
[57] Lit. "ascend."   [58] Lit. "ascend."

with or without permission: According to Torah law (Exodus 23:11; see above 4:3n.), Seventh-Year produce is akin to ownerless property and is available freely to all. The Houses debate whether the Sages, in order to ensure that people do not develop the habit of descending on fields belonging to others when it is not the Seventh Year, demanded that Seventh-Year foragers obtain permission from the field owner first. The variant readings suggest that the tradition was not certain how to construe this debate.

waterskin: A bag for water made from an animal skin whose openings are tied up to create a watertight seal.

[only] if it is knotted [and] remains [knotted]: For the House of Shammai a waterskin is deemed to be a utensil and susceptible to impurity only if it has been permanently knotted, allowing it to hold water. According to the House of Hillel it is susceptible to impurity even if not knotted, presumably because it is still able to hold some water.

5:2 (1) parallel to *Hullin* 8:1, (2) parallel to *Terumot* 1:4 (with significant changes), (3) parallel to *Kilayim* 4:5, (4) is parallel to *Hallah* 1:6, (5) parallel to *Miqva'ot* 5:6, (6) parallel to *Pesahim* 8:8.

Fowl may be served on the table together with cheese: The prohibition of mixing meat with dairy was deduced by the Sages from the three-fold repetition of the prohibition of boiling a kid in its mother's milk (Exodus 23:19; Exodus 34:26; Deuteronomy 14:21). Some Sages argued that fowl should not be included in this prohibition since fowl do not have mother's milk (*Hullin* 8:4), but ultimately fowl were included. The House of Shammai state that the separation of fowl from dairy does not need to be as strict as the separation of meat from dairy. The House of Hillel disagree.

olives for oil…grapes for wine: The question here is whether *terumah* can be separated from unprocessed produce (olives, grapes) on behalf of processed produce (oil, wine).

(3) One who sows seed within four cubits of a vineyard—
the House of Shammai say:
He has "sanctified" one row.
But the House of Hillel say:
He has "sanctified" two rows.
(4) Flour paste—
the House of Shammai declare exempt [from dough offering],
but the House of Hillel declare it liable.
(5) One may immerse [impure utensils] in rainwater runoff—
according to the words of the House of Shammai.
But the House of Hillel say:
One may not immerse [utensils] thus.
(6) A convert who converted on Passover eve—
the House of Shammai say:
He may immerse himself and eat his Passover offering in the evening.
But the House of Hillel say:
One who separates from the foreskin is like one who separates from the grave.

3 R. Ishmael[59] says:
[The following] three things are among those in which the House of Shammai are lenient, and the House of Hillel are stringent.
(1) The book of Ecclesiastes does not render the hands impure—
according to the words of the House of Shammai.
But the House of Hillel say:
It renders the hands impure.

[59] K, P: "Simeon."

One who sows grain *seed within four cubits of a vineyard*: Deuteronomy 22:9 prohibits sowing grain in a vineyard; the Sages calculated that there needs to be a separation of at least four cubits. See above 2:4 (3) and *Kilayim*. If grain is planted within four cubits of a vineyard, then one or two rows of vines fronting the grain have been "sanctified" (the language of Deuteronomy 22:9), that is, rendered unfit for use.

Flour paste: Flour cooked in hot water.

[dough offering]: Numbers 15:17–21, tractate *Hallah*.

rainwater runoff: Rainwater running down a slope. The rainwater runoff in its totality amounts to forty *se'ah*, the minimum amount required for an immersion pool (1:3n.). The House of Shammai permit the immersion of utensils in any part of the runoff; the House of Hillel demand that the entire forty *se'ah* collect in one place before any immersion can take place.

A convert or proselyte *who converted* to Judaism *on Passover eve*: on 14 Nisan, the day on which the Paschal lamb is slaughtered. *He may immerse himself* to remove any impurity that may inhere in him and then proceed to join native Jews in consuming the Paschal sacrifice that evening. This immersion is not part of the ritual process of conversion; rather, it is a postconversion rite that allows the convert to participate in the eating of the Paschal sacrifice. The Mishnah does not explain what rituals exactly are meant by the phrase *a convert who converted*; the comment of the House of Hillel shows that circumcision at least is intended.

One, a gentile male, *who separates from the foreskin* through circumcision *is like one who separates from the grave*: Consequently, the immersion required by the House of Shammai would not suffice, say the House of Hillel, to make the convert ready for the Paschal lamb in the evening. The convert needs to wait seven days and be sprinkled with the waters of the red heifer (Numbers 19).

5:3 (3) parallel to *Uqtsin* 3:6.

render the hands impure: Sacred scrolls, when touched, render the hands impure (*Yadayim* 3:5). If a scroll "renders the hands impure," it is sacred (scholars debate whether this sanctity is coterminous with our

(2) Waters of purgation that fulfilled their purpose—
the House of Shammai declare them pure;
but the House of Hillel declare them impure.
(3) Black cumin—
the House of Shammai declare it insusceptible to impurity;
but the House of Hillel declare it susceptible.
And likewise concerning tithes.
    4 R. Eliezer[60] says:
[The following] two things are among those in which
the House of Shammai are lenient, and the House of Hillel are stringent.
(1) The blood of a post-partum woman who has not yet immersed—
the House of Shammai say:
It has the same status as her spittle or her urine.
But the House of Hillel say:
[It conveys impurity] whether wet or dry.
But [the House of Shammai] concede that if a woman gave birth
while in a state of impurity caused by abnormal flow of blood,
[the blood] conveys impurity whether wet or dry.
    5 (2)[61] If there were four brothers,
and two of them married two sisters and then died—
the sisters must perform *halitsah*

    [60] K, P: "Eleazar."   [61] K, P add "and."

category of "canonical"); if it does not render the hands impure it is not sacred. Our mishnah, which has the Houses debate the status of the book of Ecclesiastes, agrees with R. Simeon in *Yadayim* 3:5.

Waters of purgation: The waters of the red heifer (Numbers 19) *that fulfilled their purpose* that were sprinkled on an impure person and that then dripped off onto another person or an object.

the House of Shammai declare them pure: That is, they do not impart impurity. See *Parah* 12:4.

insusceptible to impurity: Because it is not deemed to be food.

And likewise concerning tithes: If black cumin is food, it is susceptible to impurity and liable to tithes; if not, not.

5:4 Parallel to *Niddah* 4:3 (see above 5:1).

post-partum woman: A woman after childbirth. Seven days after giving birth to a son, or fourteen days after giving birth to a daughter, she is to immerse, after which any genital bleeding for the next thirty-three/sixty-six days is deemed to be "blood of purification," which imparts no impurity. See 5:1. At issue here is the status of her post-partum bleeding in days 8–40 or 15–80; since she did not immerse at the close of day 7 (in the case of a boy) or day 14 (in the case of a girl), the Houses agree that her blood does not have the status of the "blood of purification," but debate what degree of impurity it does have.

It has the same status as her spittle or her urine: It renders impure when wet, but not when dry. See *Niddah* 7:1.

whether wet or dry: The blood has the same status as menstrual blood and as the blood of days 1–7 (or, in the case of the birth of a girl, 1–14).

if a woman gave birth while in a state of impurity caused by abnormal persistent noncyclical *flow of blood* (Leviticus 15:25), that is, if the woman was a *zavah* when she gave birth, *[the blood]*, even the blood she has in days 8–40 (or 15–80), which normally would be "the blood of purification," *conveys impurity whether wet or dry*, like menstrual blood.

5:5 Parallel to *Yevamot* 3:1. Cf. 4:9 above.

and may not contract levirate marriage.
And if the brothers went ahead and married them,[62]
they must divorce them.
R. Eliezer[63] says in the name of the House of Shammai:
They may keep their wives.[64]
But the House of Hillel say:
They must divorce them.

5:6–7 *Aqaviah b. Mahalalel*

6 Aqaviah b. Mahalalel testified concerning four things.
They said to him:
Aqaviah, reverse yourself in the four things that you have said,
and we will make you Head of the Court in Israel.
He said to them:
Better that I be called a fool all my days
than that I be made wicked[65] before God even for a moment.
Let them not say of me:
He reversed himself for the sake of office.
He declared impure (1) "sentinel hair" and (2) yellow[66] blood;
But the Sages declare them pure.
(3) Hair that was shed by a blemished firstling and

---

[62] Lit. "gathered them in."   [63] K, P: "Eleazar."   [64] Lit. "they may uphold [their marriages]."
[65] Lit. "and not to be made wicked."   [66] Or "green."

---

halitsah… levirate marriage: See 4:8–9 above. The issue here is the same as in 4:9: the presence of two sisters in the levirate marriage pool prevents the surviving brothers from marrying either of them. In 4:9 there is one surviving brother, here there are two.

went ahead: Ignored the law.

5:6 *Aqaviah b. Mahalalel testified*: This is the only "testimony" that Mishnah *Eduyot* rejects. Cf. 8:5n.

Head of the Court: Lit. "Father of the Court," *Hagigah* 2:2.

"sentinel hair": This is explained in *Nega'im* 5:3 as follows. A discoloration in the skin, within which a hair has turned white, is impure (Leviticus 13:3). If the discoloration abates, leaving behind just the white hair, the hair has become a "sentinel," a watchman posted by the discoloration, as it were. If the discoloration returns, it is the same discoloration as before, says Aqaviah; consequently the person is impure as before. The "sentinel hair" links the two episodes of discoloration into one episode of impurity. The Sages, however, argue that the two episodes are separate, and that the second is not impure because in it the white hair preceded the discoloration, and in such a case the discoloration is not impure. This hair is not a "sentinel."

yellow blood: In *Niddah* 2:6 the Sages and Aqaviah debate whether yellow blood is a kind of menstrual blood and therefore impure (Aqaviah) or not (Sages).

All male *firstlings* of animals that may be eaten belong to the priest; if it is without blemish it is sacrificed by the priest and eaten in a state of holiness; if it is blemished the priest may slaughter it and use it as he wishes. Blemished or no, a firstling must not be sheared or otherwise provide benefit to its original owner or to the priest until it has been slaughtered. This is how the Sages squared Numbers 18:15–18 with Deuteronomy 15:19–23; see *Bekhorot*. Aqaviah and the Sages debate a case in which the animal's owner, presumably a priest, collected and stored the wool that the living animal shed. As long as the animal is alive, its shed wool is as prohibited as its unshed wool. Since the animal is blemished, it is to be slaughtered, after which its meat may be consumed and its hide and wool may be used. Does the slaughter retroactively permit the use of the

that one placed in a wall niche—
he permitted it [for use] after the animal was slaughtered.
But the Sages forbid it.
(4) He said:
One may not give[67] [the water of bitterness] to either a female convert
or a freed slavewoman to drink.
But the Sages say:
One may give her[68] to drink.
They said to him:
It once happened to Kharkemit, a freed slavewoman who was in Jerusalem,
that Shemaiah and Avtalyon gave her to drink.
He replied:
Only in show[69] did they give her to drink.
So they banned him;
and because he died during his banishment, the court stoned his coffin.
R. Judah said:
God forbid that it was Aqaviah who was banned!
The Temple Court would never be shut in front of any person in Israel
so wise and sin-fearing as Aqaviah b. Mahalalel.[70]
But whom did they ban?
Eliezer b. Enoch,[71] because he doubted the purification of hands.
And when [Eliezer b. Enoch] died, the court sent and laid a stone on his coffin;
which teaches that if anyone is banned and dies during his banishment,
his coffin must be stoned.[72]

7 At the moment of Aqaviah's death he said to his son:
My son, reverse yourself in the four things that I said.
He answered:
Why did you not reverse yourself?

---

[67] Or "They do not give."   [68] Or "they give her."
[69] Translation uncertain; the word is variously spelled and variously explained.
[70] Or "For even when the Temple Court was packed with all Israel [no one could be found] like Aqaviah b. Mahalalel in wisdom or fear of sin." This is how traditional commentators understand the text.
[71] K: spelling of patronymic uncertain.   [72] Lit. "they stone his coffin."

---

wool that the animal had shed before it was slaughtered? Aqaviah says yes, the Sages say no. This is R. Judah's version of the debate in *Bekhorot* 3:4.

wall niche: Or anyplace else for safekeeping.

[the water of bitterness]: Numbers 5:24. It is not clear whether Aqaviah and the Sages are debating a law in the abstract (whether the Temple authorities may or may not administer the water of bitterness to a given woman) or are debating the Temple procedure of old (did the priests administer the water of bitterness to a given woman or not?). Similar uncertainty in 6:1.

he doubted the purification of hands: He rejected the rabbinic law that under certain circumstances the hands can become impure independently of the rest of the body. See *Yadayim* 3:2 and 3:2 above. Cf. Gospel of Mark 7:1–12.

5:7 *I…they*: The Sages, my opponents.

He said to him:
I heard my tradition from a majority,
and they heard their tradition from a majority.
I stood by what I heard, and they stood by what they heard.
But you have heard a tradition from the mouth of an individual
and a tradition from the mouth of a majority.
It is better to abandon the words of the individual
and to hold to the words of the majority.
He said to him:
Father, give your colleagues instructions concerning me.
He said to him:
I shall not.
He said to him:
Have you perhaps found in me some cause for complaint?
He said to him:
No. Your deeds will bring you near [to them],
and your deeds will keep you far [from them].

Chapter Six

6:1–2   *More Testimonies*

6 R. Judah b. Bava testified concerning five things:
(1) that one may instruct [married] girls to exercise their "right of refusal";
(2) that one may marry off a woman based on the testimony of a single witness;

I heard my tradition from a majority, and they heard their tradition from a majority: Logically this is impossible, since two opposing positions cannot both represent the majority. Presumably we are meant to understand that each side believed its position to represent the view of the majority.

I stood by what I had heard: Something that the individual sage is not supposed to do (1:4).

give your colleagues instructions concerning me: A recommendation.

6:1 *"right of refusal"*: A father has the right to marry off his minor daughter. If the father dies, a girl can be married off by her mother or brother, except that in that case she has "the right of refusal," which allows her to renounce her marriage at any point prior to achieving maturity (she does not require a divorce; see *Yevamot* 13:1). In some cases of levirate marriage, the Sages felt that a wife who was a minor when married off by her mother or brother and is still a minor should be instructed to exercise her right of refusal so that her husband could marry one of the grown-up women in the levirate marriage pool. See *Yevamot* 13:7, 11.

single witness: Normally two witnesses are required to establish a legal fact, but the Sages wished to expedite a wife's remarriage, so they required the testimony of only a single witness to establish the husband's death. In 8:5 below this testimony is attributed not to Judah b. Bava but to Nehemiah a man of Bet Deli; *Yevamot* 16:7 gives credit to both.

(3) that a cock was stoned in Jerusalem because it killed a human being;[73]
(4) that [only] wine [at least] forty days old
may be[74] poured out as a libation on the altar; and
(5) that the morning *Tamid* sacrifice may be[75] offered [even] at the fourth hour.

2 R. Joshua and R. Nehuniah b. Elinatan,[76] a man of Kefar ha-Bavli,[77]
testified that [a single] limb from a corpse is impure.
Whereas R. Eliezer says:
[When] the Sages said [that a single limb is impure, they meant]
only a limb from a living person.
[The Sages] said to him:
Is it not an inference from the less to the greater?
If a limb separated from a living person, who is pure, is impure,
how much more so should a limb separated from the dead,
which is impure, be impure!
He answered:
They said only a limb from a living person.
Another explanation:
The impurity of the living is more manifold than the impurity of the dead,
since the living conveys impurity by lying down or sitting,
so that whatever is beneath him transmits impurity to persons and garments;

[73] Lit. "soul." [74] Or "was." [75] Or "was." [76] K: "R. Nehemiah b. Elnatan."
[77] "Babylonian Village."

cock was stoned: With reference to stoning an animal that killed a person, Exodus 21:28 speaks only of an ox, but the Sages understood "ox" expansively, to include any animal. Cf. *Bava Qamma* 5:7.

a human being: A baby.

wine not [at least] forty days old is not deemed to be wine.

Tamid sacrifice: The whole burnt sacrifice offered daily, morning and evening (Exodus 29:39; Numbers 28:4).

the fourth hour: Each day of twenty four hours is divided into twelve hours of daylight and twelve hours of darkness. From day to day and season to season hours do not have fixed length. On a perfectly symmetrical day with twelve hours of daylight and twelve of darkness, the fourth hour in the morning would be (in our reckoning) 10 a.m.

6:2 *[a single] limb* no matter how small, even less than an olive's bulk, provided that it is a whole limb and that the flesh is still attached. See 1:7 and 3:1 above; *Oholot* 1:7 and 2:1; *Kelim* 1:5. It is *impure* and conveys impurity, as does a corpse, to persons and objects via contact, carriage, and Tent.

a limb from a living person... is impure: R. Eliezer agrees with R. Joshua and R. Nehuniah on this point; their disagreement concerns solely the impurity of a limb from a corpse.

Another explanation: The editor of the Mishnah, apparently not happy with R. Eliezer's refusal to engage in a debate with R. Joshua and R. Nehuniah, gives R. Eliezer a response (perhaps inspired by 6:3 and parallel to *Zavim* 4:6).

The impurity of the living is more manifold than the impurity of the dead: Therefore it is perfectly logical for R. Eliezer to say that a single limb from a living person is impure but that a single limb from a corpse is not.

The impurity of the living: The *zav*, the man with an abnormal sexual discharge, transmits impurity via sitting or lying down. See Leviticus 15:5–6. If a *zav* sits upon a stack of cushions, his impurity penetrates even to the lowest cushion, so that if someone touches any of them, even the lowest, that person, and the clothing that he is wearing, become impure. See *Zavim* 2:4.

and further, the living conveys *madaf* impurity to whatever is above him
so that it transmits impurity to foodstuffs and liquids;
but a corpse does not convey impurity [in either of these manners].

6:3 The Impurity of Flesh and Bone

3 If an olive's bulk of flesh separates from the limb of a living person—
R. Eliezer declares it impure,
but R. Joshua and R. Nehuniah declare it pure.
If a barleycorn's bulk of bone separates from the limb of a living person—
R. Nehuniah declares it impure,
whereas R. Eliezer and R. Joshua declare it pure.
They said to R. Eliezer:
Why have you seen fit to declare impure
an olive's bulk of flesh separated from the limb of a living person?
He said to them:
We find that a limb from a living person is like a whole corpse.
Just as in the case of a corpse,
if an olive's bulk of flesh separated from it is impure,
so, too, in the case of a limb of a living person,
an olive's bulk of flesh separated from it should be impure.
They said to him:
No!
If you declare impure an olive's bulk of flesh separated from a corpse,
[your position is consistent] when you also declare impure
a barleycorn's bulk of bone separated from it;
but if you declare impure an olive's bulk of flesh
separated from the limb of a living person,
[how is your position consistent] when you declare pure
a barleycorn's bulk of bone separated from it?
They said to R. Nehuniah:
Why have you seen fit to declare impure a barleycorn's bulk of bone
separated from the limb of a living person?
He said to them:
We find that a limb from a living person is like a whole corpse.
Just as in the case of a corpse,

the living conveys madaf impurity to whatever is above him: The etymology and precise meaning of *madaf* are debated; it designates the reception of impurity by overshadowing a *zav*. Whatever objects are directly above a *zav*, no matter how many layers they may be, become impure and transmit impurity to foodstuffs and liquids, but not to people or garments. See *Zavim* 5:2.

a corpse does not convey impurity: If one sits or lies on a cushion that had formerly been occupied by a corpse, no impurity is contracted. Overshadowing a corpse will contract impurity, but not if a Tent intervenes; in that case the impurity is confined to the Tent. In contrast *madaf* impurity of the *zav* bursts upward.

6:3 *a limb from a living person is like a whole corpse*: Oholot 2:1.

you also declare impure a barleycorn's bulk of bone separated from a corpse: Oholot 2:3.

a barleycorn's bulk of bone separated from it is impure,
so, too, in the case of a limb from a living person,
a barleycorn's bulk of bone separated from it should be impure.
They said to him:
No!
If you declare impure a barleycorn's bulk of bone separated from a corpse,
[your position is consistent] when you also declare impure
an olive's bulk of flesh separated from it;
but if you declare impure a barleycorn's bulk of bone
separated from the limb of a living person,
[how is your position consistent] when you declare pure
an olive's bulk of flesh separated from it?
They said to R. Eliezer:
Why have you seen fit to apply your rules inconsistently?
Declare them both impure or declare them both pure!
He said to them:
The impurity of flesh is more manifold than the impurity of bones,
since [the impurity of] flesh applies both to carcasses and creeping things,
which is not so in the case of [the impurity of] bones.
Another explanation
[to show that the impurity of flesh is more manifold than the impurity of bones]:
a limb that has its proper flesh conveys impurity
by contact, by carriage, and by Tent.
If any flesh is lacking it is [still] impure,
but if any bone is lacking, it is pure.
They said to R. Nehuniah:
Why have you seen fit to apply your rules inconsistently?
Declare them both impure or declare them both pure!
He said to them:
The impurity of bones is more manifold than the impurity of flesh,
since flesh separated from a living person is pure,
but a limb separated from it is impure, provided that it is in its natural state.[78]

[78] Lit. "as it was created."

Why have you seen fit to apply your rules inconsistently? In another context (*Sheqalim* 4:7) R. Eliezer is praised for applying his rules consistently.

both: An olive's bulk of flesh separated from the limb of a living person and a barleycorn's bulk of bone separated from the limb of a living person.

carcasses and creeping things: Leviticus 11:35, 39.

a limb that has its proper flesh conveys impurity by contact, by carriage (even without direct contact), *and by Tent*: Oholot 2:1 and see below.

If any flesh is lacking it is [still] impure and conveys impurity by contact and by carriage, but not by Tent (*Oholot* 2:3).

if any bone is lacking, it is pure: See *Oholot* 2:5. The commentators debate whether our mishnah is speaking of a limb from a corpse or a limb from a living person, and whether of an olive's bulk or less than an olive's bulk.

in its natural state: With its flesh, vessels, ligaments, etc.

Another explanation
[to show that the impurity of bones is more manifold than the impurity of flesh]:
an olive's bulk of flesh [from a corpse] conveys impurity
by contact, carriage, and Tent;
and the greater part of the skeleton [of a corpse] conveys impurity
by contact, carriage, and Tent;
but if any of the flesh is lacking, it is pure,
while if any of the greater part of the bones is lacking,
it yet conveys impurity by contact and carriage,
although it is pure in that it does not convey impurity by Tent.
Another explanation
[to show that the impurity of bones is more manifold than the impurity of flesh]:
if the entire flesh of a corpse is less than an olive's bulk—
it is pure;
but if the bones constitute the greater part of the skeleton[79]
or the greater part of the number [of bones],
they are impure, even if they are less than a quarter-*qav*.
They said to R. Joshua:
Why have you seen fit to declare both pure?
He said to them:
No!
If you have said that [flesh and bone are impure when separated from] a corpse,
to which apply "the greater part," "a quarter," or "decomposition,"
shall you say the same thing of [flesh and bone separated from] a living person,
to which "the greater part," "a quarter," or "decomposition," do not apply?

Chapter Seven

7:1–4 *Testimonies of R. Zadok*

7 R. Joshua and R. Zadok testified
concerning the [animal used for the] redemption of the firstborn of an ass—
if it died, the priest has no claim whatever to it.
Whereas R. Eliezer says:

[79] Lit. "building," "frame."

---

greater part of the skeleton...greater part of the number [of bones]...quarter-qav: see 1:7.

or "decomposition": The dust of a decomposing corpse (*Oholot* 2:1–2).

7:1 Parallel to *Bekhorot* 1:6.

the [animal used for the] redemption of the firstborn of an ass: The Torah demands that every firstborn of an ass be "redeemed" by a sheep, which must then be given to a priest for sacrifice; see Exodus 13:13; 34:19–20.

One is still liable for it, like the five *sela* of a [firstborn] son.
But the Sages say:
One is not liable for it, like the redemption of second tithe.

2 R. Zadok testified concerning the brine of impure locusts—that it is pure.
For the First Mishnah [taught in contrast]:
If impure locusts were pickled together with pure locusts—
they do not render their brine unfit.

3 R. Zadok testified concerning [a pool]
in which the flowing water was more plentiful than the dripping water—
that it is fit.
[This] once happened at Birat-ha-Piliyya;
when the case came before the Sages, they declared it fit.

4 R. Zadok testified concerning flowing water—
if one directed it[80] through [a channel made from] foliage[81] of nuts, it is fit.

[80] Lit. "if one caused them to gush." [81] K, P: "leaves."

---

like the five sela of a [firstborn] son: Numbers 18:15–16. If the father designated five *sela* for the redemption of his firstborn son and then lost them, he is obligated to replace them (*Bekhorot* 8:8).

the redemption of second tithe: Deuteronomy 14:22–26. If a landowner redeemed his second tithe and then lost the money of redemption, he is not obligated to replace it.

The testimony of R. Joshua and R. Zadok supports the Sages against R. Eliezer.

7:2 Parallel to *Terumot* 10:9.

brine: The pickling liquid that may contain fluid exuded by the locusts.

impure: Forbidden to be eaten.

pure: Permitted to be eaten. Some varieties of locust may be eaten (8:4 below; Leviticus 11:22).

brine of impure locusts—that it is pure: Because the forbidden locusts have not contributed substantively to the brine.

the First Mishnah: An earlier form of the Mishnah's teaching. Other references to "the First Mishnah" are found in *Ketubbot* 5:3, *Gittin* 5:6, *Nazir* 6:1, *Sanhedrin* 3:4.

the forbidden locusts *do not render the brine* of the permitted locusts *unfit* to be eaten:

The *First Mishnah* taught that the brine of the forbidden locusts may be consumed when produced in a mixture with permitted locusts. R. Zadok is more lenient: the brine of forbidden locusts may be consumed even by itself.

7:3 Parallel to *Miqva'ot* 5:5.

flowing water: A river or stream; these waters purify from impurity even if the amount of water in which the bather has immersed is less than forty *se'ah*.

dripping water: Rainwater; these waters purify from impurity only when amassed in the amount of at least forty *se'ah* (1:3n.).

If a pool of water contains more *flowing water . . . than dripping water*, then the law of flowing water applies, and the pool is fit for purification even if it does not contain forty *se'ah*. This testimony is supported by the report of an actual case.

7:4 *foliage of nuts*: *Parah* 6:4.

it is fit: In spite of being redirected by human artifice, the water retains its "natural" power of purification.

This once happened at Ahaliyya;[82]
when the case came before the Chamber of Hewn Stone, they declared it fit.

7:5–7 Testimonies of R. Joshua and R. Papias

5 R. Joshua and R. Yaqim a man of Haddar testified
concerning a jar containing [the ashes of] purgation—
if one set it on top of a [dead] creeping thing, it is impure.
Whereas R. Eliezer declares it pure.
R. Papias testified concerning a man who vowed two Nazirite vows—
if he shaved off his hair [on the completion of the] first on the thirtieth day,
he may shave off his hair [on the completion of the] second on the sixtieth day;
and if he shaved off his hair on the fifty-ninth day,
he has fulfilled his obligation,
since the thirtieth day counts for him as part of the prescribed number of days.
6 R. Joshua and R. Papias testified
concerning the offspring of [an animal designated] an offering of well-being—
that it must be offered as an offering of well-being.
Whereas R. Eliezer says:
The offspring of [an animal designated] an offering of well-being
may not be offered as an offering of well-being.
But the Sages say:
It is offered.
R. Papias said:
I testify that once we had a heifer that was an offering of well-being;
we ate it at Passover
and ate its offspring as an offering of well-being at the festival.

[82] P: "Uliyyah" (vocalization uncertain).

Chamber of Hewn Stone: The seat of the high court in the Temple (*Sanhedrin* 11:2, *Middot* 5:4).

7:5 First part parallel to *Parah* 10:3, second part parallel to *Nazir* 3:2.

[the ashes of] purgation: Numbers 19; see 3:2 above and 8:1 below. The ashes of the red heifer need to be prepared in the highest state of purity.

[dead] creeping thing: Leviticus 11:29–38.

it is impure: Even though the jar does not transmit impurity to the ash within, nevertheless the ash is impure, because the Torah said to store the ash *in a pure place* (Numbers 19:9).

if he shaved off his hair: This is part of the ritual that marks the completion of a *nazir*'s vow (Numbers 6:18). Since the standard vow of a *nazir* is for a period of thirty days (above 4:11n.), the standard rule is that he may shave on the thirty-first day. The point of R. Papias's testimony is that if he shaves on day 30, the ritual is valid; furthermore, day 30 can count both as the final day of the first vow and the first day of the second, thus allowing him to complete his second vow on the fifty-ninth day.

7:6 Parallel to *Temurah* 3:1.

the festival: Either Sukkot (Booths), six months after Passover, or the Festival of Weeks, seven weeks after Passover.

7 They testified concerning the long-boards[83] of bakers—
that they are susceptible to impurity;
Whereas R. Eliezer declares them insusceptible.
They testified concerning an oven—
if one cut it into rings and put sand between each ring,
that it is [nonetheless] susceptible to impurity.
Whereas R. Eliezer declares it insusceptible.
They testified that the Sages[84] can extend the year any time during Adar;
Whereas they had [formerly] said: Only until Purim.
They testified that the Sages[85] can extend the year conditionally.
It once happened that
Rabban Gamaliel went to receive authority from the governor in Syria,
and his return was delayed; so they extended the year
on condition that Rabban Gamaliel should consent.
When he returned he said "I consent,"
and the result was that the year was extended.[86]

7:8–8:5   More Testimonies

8 Menahem b. Signai[87] testified concerning the rim extension of a cauldron—
if of olive seethers, it is susceptible to impurity,
but if of dyers, it is not susceptible;
whereas they had [formerly] said the contrary.
9 R. Nehuniah[88] b. Gudgada testified:
concerning a woman who was a deaf-mute—

[83] K: "basins" or "troughs."   [84] Lit. "They."   [85] Lit. "they."
[86] K: "He said to them 'I consent—extended.'"   [87] K, P: "Sangai."   [88] K, P: "Yohanan."

7:7 First part parallel to *Kelim* 15:2, middle part parallel to *Kelim* 5:10.

long-boards... insusceptible: Because they are plain pieces of wood and therefore not regarded as utensils for purposes of purity law.

oven: Made of clay. The purpose of this maneuver was apparently to attempt to create an oven impervious to impurity (cf. *Kelim* 5:8). This is the "oven of Akhnai" (*Kelim* 5:10).

extend the year: By adding a leap month, Second Adar.

[formerly]: 2:8.

until Purim: The fourteenth of Adar.

What *authority* Rabban Gamaliel received from the Roman *governor in Syria* is a matter of speculation.

7:8 Parallel to *Kelim* 5:5.

the clay *rim extension of a* metal *cauldron* is supposed to prevent the boiling water from spilling over. The issue here is whether the extension is part of the cauldron, and consequently liable to impurity like the cauldron itself, or not.

[formerly]: 2:8.

7:9 Parallel to *Gittin* 5:5, first clause also parallel to *Yevamot* 14:2, second clause also parallel to *Eduyot* 8:2.

if she was given in marriage by her father,
she may be dismissed by a bill of divorce;
concerning the minor daughter of an Israelite—
if she was married to a priest, she may eat of his *terumah*;
and if she dies, her husband is her heir;
concerning a beam—
if one stole it and built it into a large house, he must give [the owner] its value;
concerning a purgation offering—
if [the animal] was stolen property, and this was not known publicly,
[nevertheless] it effects atonement.
[It does so] for the betterment of the altar.

Chapter Eight

8 R. Joshua b. Betera testified concerning the blood of carcasses—
that it is pure.
R. Simeon b. Betera testified concerning the ashes of purgation—
that if an impure person touches part of it, he renders the whole of it impure.
R. Aqiva added [a testimony]
concerning fine flour, incense, frankincense, and coals—

she was given in marriage by her father: While yet a minor (6:1).

she may be dismissed by a bill of divorce: In spite of the fact that she is incompetent; see *Yevamot* 14:1.

if she was married to a priest: *Terumah* may be consumed only by the priest and his family, not by lay Israelites. If a minor daughter of an Israelite is given by her father to a priest in marriage, there is no question that she would eat her husband's *terumah* and he would inherit her estate. She is his wife. Therefore the commentators explain that the novelty of this mishnah is that a minor is deemed to be fully the priest's wife even if she were given to him in marriage by her mother and/or brothers, her father having died (6:1 above). A father has the right under Torah law to marry off his minor daughter, whereas a mother and brothers have that right only under rabbinic law. Nevertheless, she may eat [at least some of] her husband's *terumah* and her husband inherits her estate. This testimony is attributed to different sages and given a different ending in 8:2 below.

he must give [the owner] its value: But is not obligated to destroy the house in order to return the beam.

purgation offering: Leviticus 4, for inadvertent sin.

for the betterment of the altar: If the sacrifice is retroactively declared null and void, the priests will regret having placed a nonsacrifice on the altar and as a result may hesitate in processing future sacrifices. As long as the priests are working in good faith, not having any reason to suspect that a sacrificial animal is stolen (or otherwise unfit), their work is deemed valid.

8:1 *the blood of animal carcasses*: The carcass itself is impure (Leviticus 11:39–40); the blood is pure because it is regarded as separate from the carcass. The position here endorsed is ascribed in 5:1 to the House of Shammai.

ashes of purgation: Ashes of the red heifer (Numbers 19). See 7:5 above.

fine flour…frankincense: Ingredients in the meal offering (Leviticus 2:1, 6:8).

incense: Exodus 30:34–38.

coals: Leviticus 16:12.

that if a *tevul yom* touches a part of any one of them,
he renders the whole of it unfit.

2 R. Judah b. Bava[89] and R. Judah the Priest testified
concerning the minor daughter of an Israelite—
if she was married to a priest,
she may eat of his *terumah* once she has entered the bridal chamber,
even though she has not yet had intercourse.
R. Yose[90] the Priest and R. Zechariah b. ha-Qatsav[91] testified
concerning a young girl who had been given[92] as a pledge in Ashqelon—
that the members of her family kept her distant from them [upon her return],
although she had witnesses who testified
that she had neither spent time alone[93] [with a man] nor been defiled.
The Sages said to the members of her family:[94]
If you believe [the witnesses] that she was given[95] as a pledge,
you should believe also that she neither spent time alone[96] [with a man]
nor was defiled;
but if you do not believe [the witnesses]
that she neither spent time alone[97] [with a man] nor was defiled,
you should not believe that she was given[98] as a pledge.

3 R. Joshua and R. Judah[99] b. Betera testified
concerning the widow of a "dough" family—

[89] K, P: "Abba." [90] K: "Joseph"; P: "Yosah." [91] Lit. "the butcher." [92] Or "taken."
[93] Lit. "hidden herself." [94] Lit. "them." [95] Or "taken." [96] Lit. "hid herself."
[97] Lit. "hidden herself." [98] Or "taken." [99] K, P: "Joshua."

tevul yom: Lit. "one who immersed that day," is a person undergoing purification who has completed the entire process but is awaiting nightfall for the purification to be completely effective (Leviticus 22:7, Deuteronomy 23:12). A *tevul yom* is deemed impure vis-à-vis *terumah* and sacrificial meats, but pure vis-à-vis everything else. See 2:1n. and *Tevul Yom*. R. Aqiva argues that the same high level of purity required for the ashes of the red heifer should also be required for other temple materials. The *tevul yom* by his touch does not render any of these substances impure but he does render them unfit for use.

8:2 The commentators debate whether the testimony of *R. Judah b. Bava and R. Judah the Priest* is identical with that of R. Nekhuniah b. Gudgada in 7:9. Each has a final clause not in the other.

who had been given to (or taken by) gentiles *as a pledge* against a loan. The girl was not kidnapped or held for ransom; she was given in pledge by her family. What the girl thought of this is not stated.

the members of her family were either priests or pedigreed Israelites acting like priests.

kept her distant: They neither married her themselves nor did they give her away in marriage. A woman who has had sex with a gentile may not be married to a priest (the rabbinic understanding of Leviticus 21:7).

It is not clear where the testimony of *R. Yose the Priest and R. Zechariah b. ha-Qatsav* ends: are they endorsing the view of the family or of the Sages? In the simplest reading, the words of the Sages to the family constitute the testimony of R. Yose and R. Zechariah.

spent time alone lit. "hidden herself" [with a man].

defiled: The language of Numbers 5:13.

8:3 *"dough" family*: A family that, like a dough, is a mixture of various things; in this case the family is rumored to have among its members a man suspected of being a *hallal*, a priest of blemished ancestry (the offspring of a priest and a divorcee, Leviticus 21:7). If a *hallal* marries or has sex with an Israelite woman, even if she is of unblemished ancestry, she becomes unfit for subsequent marriage to a priest.

that she is fit for marriage into the priesthood,
because[100] a "dough" family is fit to declare impure or pure,
to keep at a distance or to bring near.
Rabban Simeon b.[101] Gamaliel said:
We accept your testimony, but what shall we do,
for Rabban Yohanan b. Zakkai decreed not to have courts go into session for cases such as this?
The priests will listen to you to keep at a distance but not to bring near.

4 R. Yose b. Yoezer a man of Tseredah testified concerning the *ayal* locust—
that it is pure;
and concerning the liquid of the [Temple] slaughterhouse—
that it is pure;
and that one who draws near to[102] a corpse becomes impure.
And they called him Yose the Permitter.

5 R. Aqiva testified in the name of Nehemiah a man of Bet Deli
that one may marry off a woman based on the testimony of a single witness.
R. Joshua testified concerning [human] bones
that were once found in the woodshed [of the Temple]

---

[100] K lack "because" (the sentence ends with "priesthood" and a new sentence begins with "A 'dough' family"); P: "and."
[101] K, P lack "Simeon b."   [102] Or "touches."

A *widow of a "dough" family* is a widow whose late husband belonged to such a family. The rumor that this family has a *hallal* among its members may or may not be true, and even if it be true, her late husband may or may not have been that *hallal*. But if her husband was that *hallal*, she, now a widow, is not fit for marriage to a priest.

a "dough" family is fit to declare impure or pure: The exact meaning is not clear. Apparently it means that even "dough" families can be trusted to keep track of the lineages of its members, so that they know who is and who is not a *hallal*, who is and who is not marriageable to a priest, who is and who is not of the highest marital pedigree. The variant readings show that the tradents of this mishnah were not sure how this line connected with what came before it. See 8:7 below.

The priests will listen to you to keep a widow of a "dough" family *at a distance*, that is, to declare her unmarriageable, *but not to bring near*, not to declare her fit for marriage.

8:4 R. Yose's testimony is in Aramaic, which is highly unusual.

the ayal locust...pure: Fit to be eaten; according to Leviticus 11, some locusts may be eaten. See 7:2.

the liquid of the [Temple] slaughterhouse...pure: This means either that it is not susceptible to impurity or that it is not one of the moistening agents that make food capable of receiving impurity (4:6). See *Kelim* 15:6.

one who draws near to or touches *a corpse becomes impure*: This line has long puzzled commentators. Corpse impurity is stated explicitly in the Torah (Numbers 19)—what has R. Yose added? Furthermore, how does R. Yose's affimation of corpse impurity contribute to his reputation as a "permitter"? The commentators explain that by upholding impurity caused by direct contact with a corpse, R. Yose is denying that corpse impurity can be transferred by indirect contact, and therein lies his leniency.

Yose the Permitter: A pejorative appellation.

8:5 *Nehemiah a man of Bet Deli*: See 6:1 above and *Yevamot* 16:7.

woodshed [of the Temple]: *Middot* 2:5.

[that] the Sages said:
One may collect them bone by bone and everything is pure.

8:6–7   *I Heard a Tradition*

6   R. Eliezer said:
I heard a tradition[103] that while they were building[104] the Sanctuary,
they made curtains for the Sanctuary and curtains for the courtyards,
but they built the Sanctuary from outside, and the courtyards from within.
R. Joshua said:
I heard a tradition[105] that one may[106] offer sacrifices
although there is no Temple,
and eat the Holiest of the Holy [Offerings] although there are no curtains,
and the Lesser Holy [Offerings] and the second tithe although there is no wall;

[103] The word "tradition" is not in the text but is implied by the verb "heard."
[104] K: "I heard that they will build the Sanctuary."
[105] The word "tradition" is not in the text but is implied by the verb "heard."
[106] Or "one offers…and eats…"

[that] the Sages said: In the text translated here R. Joshua's testimony is the statement of the Sages. This is difficult (for the closest analogue see 8:2). Some later witnesses to the text supply additional words as follows: "R. Joshua testified concerning [human] bones that were once found in the woodshed [of the Temple]—*that they are impure* [and consequently that the woodshed and all within it, or perhaps the entire Temple Mount, are impure]. But the Sages said: One may collect them bone by bone and everything is pure." This version is also difficult because in no other instance (except in the story of Aqaviah, 5:6) is a testimony rejected by the Sages. In any event the Sages thought that the bones were not evidence of a burial ground inside the Temple.

8:6 *they were building*: The people who returned from Babylonia to Judaea in the Persian period (sixth and fifth centuries BCE in our chronology).

Sanctuary: The inner part of the Temple, comprising the Holy and the Holy of Holies.

curtains: Apparently to prevent outsiders from looking in.

from outside: The curtains were between the workers and the Sanctuary.

from within: The curtains were between the workers and the general public.

although there is no Temple: The Temple was destroyed in 70 CE by the Romans. It is not clear whether R. Joshua is prescribing law or is describing contemporary practice (see alternative translation).

the Holiest of the Holy [Offerings]: Purgation offerings and guilt offerings, sacrifices (*Zevahim* 5:1–5) that are to be eaten by male priests in the Temple.

although there are no curtains: The word for "curtains" is the same as used above in the statement of R. Eliezer, except that here the reference is to the walls of the Temple (word derived from Exodus 27:9).

Lesser Holy [Offerings]: Various sacrifices listed in *Zevahim* 5:6–8.

second tithe: 1:9 above; Deuteronomy 14:22–27.

although there is no wall: Lesser Holy [Offerings] and second tithe are to be consumed within the city of Jerusalem, even if the city no longer has a wall.

since its first sanctification sanctified it
both for its own time and for the time to come.

7 R. Joshua said:
I received a tradition[107] from Rabban Yohanan b. Zakkai,
who heard it from his teacher, and his teacher from his teacher,
as a *halakhah* given to Moses from Sinai,
that Elijah will come not to declare impure or pure,
to keep distant or to bring near,
but to keep distant those that were forcibly brought near,
and to bring near those that were forcibly kept distant.
The family of Bet Tserephah was in the land beyond Jordan,
and Ben Zion forcibly kept it distant;
and yet another [family] was there, and Ben Zion forcibly drew it near.
[Families] such as these will Elijah come to declare impure or pure,
to keep distant or to bring near.
R. Judah says:
To bring near but not to keep distant.
R. Simeon says:
To settle[108] legal disputes.[109]
But the Sages say:
Neither to keep distant nor to bring near,
but to make peace in the world,
as it is said:
Behold I am sending you Elijah the prophet…
and he shall turn the heart of the fathers to the children
and the heart of the children to their fathers.

[107] The word "tradition" is not in the text but is implied by the verb "received."
[108] Lit. "to even out."   [109] Or "social discord."

its first sanctification by Solomon who built the first Temple.

and for the time to come: The city of Jerusalem and the Temple Mount retain their sanctity forever, even after the Temple has been destroyed. The commentators debate whether this is the view of R. Joshua alone or also of R. Eliezer.

8:7 *halakhah*: Usually translated "law" or "normative law," but here there is no legal content to R. Joshua's tradition. Perhaps here the word means "received truth."

halakhah given to Moses from Sinai: Pe'ah 2:6, Yadayim 4:3.

to declare impure and pure, to keep distant and to bring near: In context apparently a reference to marital eligibility; see 8:3. Or perhaps it is a reference to maintaining one's status in the world of the Sages; see 5:6–7.

The identity of *Ben Zion*, and the nature of the events alluded to here, are unknown.

as it is said: Malachi 4:5–6.

Tractate Avodah Zarah

Christine Hayes

Introduction

Overview

The eighth tractate of order *Neziqin* is *Avodah Zarah*, lit. "foreign worship," the rabbinic term used to denote idolatry. The tractate does not contain rules concerning Jews who engage in idolatrous acts or forbidden customs (for which see tractates *Sanhedrin* and *Makkot*); rather, the tractate contains regulations designed to make it possible for Jews to deal with non-Jews in a manner that does not endanger the Jew or lead to a violation of Jewish law and custom.

Traditional commentators observed that *Avodah Zarah* is a combination of two tractates. The first runs from 1:1 to 4:7 and regulates business dealings connected with idolatry, the use of images, objects, and appurtenances associated with idolatry, as well as the food items of non-Jews. This unit concludes—as many tractates do—with an aggadic mishnah (4:7). A second tractate begins at 4:8 and runs through 5:12. This section deals almost entirely with rules regarding libation wine.

Main Ideas

Despite the Bible's complete ban on idolatry in the Land of Israel, the Mishnah lacks any normative command to wage war against idolaters or idolatry in the Land of Israel. The rabbinic approach has been contrasted with that of the Hasmoneans, who did destroy idolatrous temples and images and force non-Jews in the Land of Israel to convert, and with that of separatists who lived in voluntary self-exile until such time as Israel's deity would bring an end to the dominion of the nations. Forced to accept the entanglement of Israelite and pagan society in the Land of Israel, the rabbis adopted a two-fold strategy of passive resistance by (i) distancing themselves from idolatry through various avoidance mechanisms and (ii) creating legal definitions that removed certain objects and actions from the biblical prohibition of idolatry and allowed interaction with non-Jews to occur.

To ensure that Jews avoid idolatry, the rabbis ruled that they may not benefit from it directly (personal consumption or use) or indirectly (through sale or indirect use), or support it by engaging in certain transactions in the days prior to an idolatrous festival that might facilitate idolatrous worship (1:1). They may not sell to a non-Jew specific items commonly known to be used in idolatrous worship (1:5), nor may they confer a benefit on idolatry through construction activities (1:7; 3:6) or patronage at places of business (1:4; 4:3) associated with idols. In many instances, they must take pains to avoid even the appearance of supporting idolatry (1:4; 1:9). Libation wine (which includes even wine merely under the suspicion of having been used for libation) is prohibited to a Jew (2:3; chapters 4 and 5) as are the fragments of images (3:2), any worshipped object (4:4–7), and cultic offerings or appurtenances (2:3–5; 3:5; 3:7). Parallel rulings for Christians appear in Tertullian's *De Idololatria* (ca. 200 CE).

The second strategy employed by the rabbis to enable existence in an environment saturated with idolatry is the legal principle that only that which is *treated* as a deity (worshipped or revered) is defined as an idol. Thus, images need not be avoided if they are merely aesthetic (3:4), are depicted on common household utensils (3:4), or are otherwise treated as profane by non-Jews (3:7; 3:10; 4:4–7).

While most of the prohibitions and regulations contained in tractate *Avodah Zarah* are motivated by the concern to neither benefit from nor contribute to idolatry, some are motivated by a concern for the observance of Jewish dietary laws. Chapter 2 lists foods of a non-Jew that are prohibited because of the possibility of mixture with, absorption of, or defilement by impure or forbidden substances, as well as foods to which no such anxiety attaches. The vessels of non-Jews are forbidden to Jews because they may have absorbed particles of prohibited flesh or liquid (e.g. fat or libation wine) and may exude those particles into the liquid or food placed into the vessel by the Jew (2:3; 5:12).

Finally, some regulations are motivated by a desire to prevent landholding by idolaters in the Land of Israel (1:8) or by a general distrust of non-Jews as dangerous and/or morally licentious. In cases of potential sexual assault, bestiality, and murder, the rabbis prefer to err on the side of suspicion and stringency (see 1:7; 2:1–2). In lower-stakes areas—commercial interactions, ritual purity—the rabbis often prefer to err on the side of trust and leniency.

There is little evidence for the claim by some scholars that rabbinic regulation of interactions with non-Jews was based originally on an ancient conception of non-Jews as *intrinsically* ritually impure and that the alternative rationales articulated in the rabbinic sources as laid out above are later inventions designed to counteract an excessive separatism. A communicable ritual impurity—either intrinsic or because of failure to observe the ritual purity laws of Leviticus 12–15—is not attributed to living non-Jews in biblical sources, as the rabbis explicitly acknowledge (*Nega'im* 3:1, 7:1, 11:1, 12:1, *Niddah* 4:3, 7:3, *Miqva'ot* 8:3–4, *Zavim* 2:1, 2:3). (By contrast, anxiety about consuming non-kosher foods when in the company of non-Jews and a preference for endogamy are verifiably ancient concerns attested in biblical and post-biblical texts.) While a few sources attribute an unusual and statutory ritual impurity to gentiles, ritual impurity occurs mostly in connection with comestibles coming into contact with vessels or winepresses that have previously absorbed impure food stuffs or libation wine.

The goal of the mishnaic sages was not to prohibit all interaction with non-Jews, but to preserve the religious integrity of Jews who must live and work and trade and shop among persons whose ignorance of, or even hostility towards, Jewish law compromised that integrity. Tractate *Avodah Zarah* contains regulations that make it possible for a Jew to deal with non-Jews with the confidence that one is not violating Jewish law. Thus, there is no conflict between the simultaneous existence of a wealth of regulations that govern interaction between Jews and non-Jews and evidence of extensive commercial, business, legal, and even social interactions.

Relationship to Scripture

The main biblical verses that underlie the rabbinic discussion of idolaters, idols, and idolatry are: (1) Exodus 34:12–16, which commands the Israelites to destroy the seven

Canaanite nations and to make no covenant with them lest fraternization and intermarriage lead the Israelites into idolatry; (2) Deuteronomy 7:2–5, which repeats this prohibition and also calls for the utter destruction of and lack of mercy towards the seven nations, as well as the complete obliteration of their cult objects; (3) Deuteronomy 7:25–26, which adds to this a prohibition against coveting and taking the gold and silver on idolatrous images and against bringing such an abomination into one's home; (4) Deuteronomy 12:2–3, which commands the destruction of those places where the seven nations worship their gods, as well as their altars and other cult objects; and (5) Deuteronomy 13:18, which in connection with the annihilation of an idolatrous city, commands that nothing of the forbidden items "cleave to your hand."

Special Notes for the Reader

Mishnah *Avodah Zarah* has been preserved in two versions—a version that served as the basis for the discussions in the schools of the Land of Israel and a version that served as the basis for the discussions in the schools of Babylonia. Some of the important divergences between these two versions are pointed out in the notes and comments. For a full presentation of the evidence see the critical edition of this tractate by David Rosenthal (PhD diss., Hebrew University, 1980).

As is the case throughout this translation, in this tractate too the term *Yisrael* is translated "Israelite," and the terms *goy* and *nokhri*, are translated "gentile." However, in the annotations, as in this introduction, in order to ease comprehension and enhance appreciation for the text's sense of Self and Other, the translator has chosen to use "Jew" and "non-Jew."

Tractate Avodah Zarah

Chapter One

1:1–4 *Business Dealings with Gentiles on Specified Occasions*

1 For three days prior to the festivals of gentiles it is prohibited:
to do business[1] with them,
to lend objects to or borrow objects from them,
to lend money to or borrow money from them,
to repay a debt or to collect a debt from them.
R. Judah says:
One may collect a debt from them because it distresses him.
They said to him:
Even though it distresses him now, he is happy about it later on.
  2 R. Ishmael says:
Three days before them and three days after them, it is prohibited
[to engage in transactions with them].
But the Sages say:
Before their festivals it is prohibited; after their festivals it is permitted.

[1] Lit. "to buy and sell."

1:1 The purpose of this law, like others in the tractate, is to ensure that a Jew does not contribute in any way to idolatrous worship by either enabling a non-Jew's idolatry (supplying necessary materials) or motivating it (providing a reason for the non-Jew to worship an idol). The Talmudim debate which of these considerations (enabling or motivating) is primary in this first mishnah.

festivals: In view of the festivals listed in 1:3, the prohibition is probably intended to apply to the main public festivals of the pagan calendar.

to do business: Some commentators limit the meaning of the phrase here to the sale of, for example, sacrificial animals, items that directly enable idolatrous acts; others apply the phrase to the sale of perishable goods or the purchase of durable goods because both of these transactions inspire gratitude.

They the Sages *said to him*: Impersonal subject, traditionally attributed to "the Sages" generally.

1:2 *Three days before them and three days after them*: The Talmud discusses whether the number three is inclusive or exclusive of the festival.

3 And these are the festivals of gentiles:
the Kalends, the Saturnalia, the Kratesim, the *genesia* of the emperors,
[that is,] the day of birth and the day of death [of the emperor]—
the words of R. Meir.
But the Sages say:
Any death in which there is burning features idolatry,
but one in which there is no burning does not feature idolatry.
The day of shaving his beard and his forelock,
and the day on which he returns from the sea,
and the day on which he is released from prison[2]—
it is not prohibited [to engage in transactions with them]
except in connection to that day and that person.[3]

---

[2] The Babylonian text tradition contains an additional line: "and a gentile who prepares a feast for his son"—this is a later insertion based on a passage in the Talmud.

[3] The Babylonian text tradition adds the word "only" at the end of this line.

1:3 The list of affected events, which reflects the reality of Roman Palaestina and Syria in the first centuries CE, includes public and private events.

the Kalends: The New Year's Day festival celebrated publicly on January 1 and featuring public sacrifice.

the Saturnalia: A celebration stretching from December 17 to December 23.

the Kratesim: More accurately *kratesis*, a holiday decreed by the Roman Senate to commemorate the conquest of Alexandria by Octavian in 30 BCE.

the genesia of the emperors: Probably, the anniversary of the emperor's birth and apotheosis, in which case the next clause ("the day of birth and the day of death") was originally a gloss explaining the foreign term rather than an independent item in the list.

the day of birth and the day of death [of the emperor]: This translation assumes that the phrase glosses the term *genesia*, and that the anniversary of the birth and the death of the emperor only are intended. However, the Talmudim view this phrase as an independent item referring to the anniversary of the birth and the death of any person, not only the emperor. R. Meir includes these celebrations in his list because in his view they are occasions for idolatrous customs and rituals.

The day of shaving: According to most commentators, the list of private festivals and celebrations that do not fall under the full prohibition in 1:1 begins here. Some commentators maintain that "the day of shaving the beard and forelock" still refers to the emperor. However, the limitation of the prohibition "to that person" in the final line of the mishnah implies a private individual and poses a challenge to this reading.

forelock: In rabbinic texts, the term used here denotes a forelock of hair that is considered a foreign fashion associated usually with young boys and generally indicative of idolatry.

The day of shaving his beard and his forelock: The Talmudim and later commentators debate whether "the day of shaving his beard and his forelock" refers to (a) a single ritual in which both beard and forelock are shaved; (b) a single ritual in which the beard is shaved and a forelock is formed; (c) two rituals, one in which the beard is shaved and one in which the forelock is shaved; or (d) two rituals, one in which the beard is shaved and one in which the forelock is formed. Interpretation (c) is to be preferred. There is a classic Greek ritual of cutting the forelock upon attaining puberty/majority and dedicating the hair to a god, and there are a few indications that young Romans dedicated hair to a god, perhaps in fulfillment of a vow. In addition, it was common Roman practice to shave the first beard as a sign of passage into manhood, and public festivals accompanied the first beard shaving of the emperors. Classical sources do not attest to a ritual involving the shaving of both beard and forelock. These appear to be separate rituals.

4 A town in which there is idolatry—
it is permitted [to engage in transactions with them] outside the town;
a town outside of which there is idolatry—
it is permitted [to engage in transactions with them] inside the town.
What about traveling there?
When the road goes to that place only, it is prohibited,
but if it is possible to travel by that road to another place, it is permitted.
A town in which there is idolatry,
and in which there are shops that are decorated and shops that are not decorated—
such a case happened in Bet Shean, and the Sages said:
The decorated [shops] are prohibited and those that are not decorated are permitted.

1:5–9 *Articles That May or May Not Be Sold or Rented to Gentiles*

5 These items are prohibited for sale to gentiles:
fir cones and "pine cones,"[4] frankincense, and a white cock.
R. Judah says:
It is permitted to sell him a white cock among other cocks.
If a cock is [sold] by itself, one should cut off its spur and sell it to him,
because they do not sacrifice defective animals to idolatry.
As for all other objects:
if no specification [that it is for idolatrous use] is made,
it is permitted [to sell to them];
but if specification is made,
it is prohibited [to sell to them].
R. Meir says:
It is also prohibited to sell to gentiles fine dates, or Hazab or Nicolaus dates.

[4] The Palestinian text tradition reads "white" followed by a gloss in Greek: a small pine. The phrase "white figs, [i.e.] small pines" was misconstrued in the Babylonian tradition as two distinct items: "white figs and [their] stems."

1:4 This mishnah moves from the public festivals and individual idolatrous rituals of 1:3 to consider local festivals, particularly those associated with market days in a given town.

1:5 This mishnah distinguishes between items which carry a presumption of idolatrous use (pine cones, white cocks, and frankincense) and which may be sold if there is reason to believe that they will not be so used, and all other items which do not carry a presumption of idolatrous use and which may not be sold if there is reason to believe that they will be so used.

fir cones and "pine cones": The Mishnah prohibits the cones of two types of pine, a white cock, and frankincense. Pine cones were widely used in several cults in Roman-period Asia Minor, as were white cocks (the regular offering of the poor) and frankincense.

R. Judah says: R. Judah makes a concession in cases where it is unlikely or precluded that the cock is being purchased for idolatrous sacrifice.

Nicolaus dates: Probably named for Nicolas of Damascus, the first-century BCE Greek historian and philosopher and friend of Herod the Great; he is recorded in Greek sources as sending fine dates to the emperor Augustus. Already in amoraic times, there was confusion over all three of the terms employed in R. Meir's teaching and each was interpreted as a distinct type of date.

6 Where it is customary to sell small cattle to gentiles, one may sell them.
Where it is customary not to sell small cattle to gentiles, one may not sell them.[5]
And under no circumstance may one sell them large cattle, calves, or foals, whole or maimed.
R. Judah permits a maimed animal and Ben Betera permits a horse.

7 One may not sell them:
bears, lions, or anything that may injure the public.
One may not build with them:
a basilica and gallows, a stadium and a tribunal;
but one may build with them bathhouses.[6]
When one reaches the niche in which the idol is placed
it is prohibited to build [with them].

---

[5] A variant adds "a man should not alter this [i.e. local custom] for fear of creating conflict." This addition appears to be based on *Pesahim* 4:1.

[6] Early printed editions of the Talmud contain the variant "theaters."

1:6 This mishnah is repeated verbatim in *Pesahim* 4:3 as one in a list of examples of divergent customs (though here it is recommended that one follow local custom rather than the more stringent custom; cf. *Pesahim* 4:1). Other rabbinic texts consider two distinct rationales for the prohibitions in this mishnah. Some connect the ban on selling large cattle to the biblical commandment of Sabbath rest even for labor animals. The ban on selling even small cattle in some locales is thus an added stringency to protect against the sale of large working animals. Others connect the ban on selling large cattle to the desire to withhold from non-Jews weapons or anything that might pose a public danger (in line with 1:7).

a maimed animal...a horse: In R. Judah's view, a maimed animal is unlikely to be put to work and in Ben Betera's view, a horse does not perform a kind of labor on the Sabbath that involves liability.

1:7 The historical reality behind the ban on the sale of bears and lions is the use of such animals in theatrical exhibitions and gladiatorial contests. The continuation of the mishnah bans Jews from assisting non-Jews in the construction of the stadia which housed these violent games, where humans were often killed for sport.

anything that may injure the public: In their discussions of the ban on selling large animals, both domestic and wild, other rabbinic texts also prohibit the sale of weapons or weapon accessories to non-Jews. The Mishnah contains no such explicit weapons ban, but may allude to one in this general prohibition of "anything which may injure the public."

a basilica and gallows, a stadium and a tribunal: All four of these places are associated with unjust or violent death, for which reason Jews may not assist in their construction.

basilica: A large, high building used as a market and also as a court of law.

gallows: A small platform used in trial proceedings on which the accused was questioned/tortured or on which the court tribunal sat.

stadium: The site of wild-beast hunts and gladiatorial contests. There were stadia at Tiberias and Caesarea. In the latter, thousands of Jewish captives were slaughtered in contests at the end of the Jewish war.

tribunal: The term refers to a special tribunal or platform on which the magistrate sat and which was erected when there was no regular law court (hence the term "basilica" does not cover this kind of special tribunal).

bathhouses: The Hebrew has two terms, but here again the second term should be understood as a gloss explaining the first term (which is Greek), so that the mishnah permits only one item—bathhouses. Commentators who assume two distinct entities draw a distinction between them by distinguishing between public and private bathhouses. Idols were often found in bathhouses (see 3:4 below).

niche: The term may include a chamber that housed an idol.

8 One may not make ornaments for an idol:
necklaces, or earrings, or finger rings.
R. Eliezer says:
For a fee it is permitted.[7]
One may not sell to them anything attached to the ground,
but after it has been detached [from the ground] one may sell it.
R. Judah says:
One may sell it on the condition that it will be detached.
One may not rent houses to them in the Land of Israel and, needless to say, fields,
and in Syria one may rent houses to them, but not fields,
and outside the Land of Israel one may sell houses to them and rent fields—
the words of R. Meir.
R. Yose says:
In the Land of Israel one may rent houses to them but not fields,
and in Syria one may sell houses to them and rent fields,
and outside the Land of Israel one may sell both.

9 But even in a place where they permitted renting
they did not refer to a place of residence,
because [the gentile] will bring an idol into the house, as it is said:
And you shall not bring an abomination into your house.
Under no circumstance may one rent a bathhouse to him
because it is called by the [Israelite] owner's name.

[7] The entire rule about ornaments is lacking in numerous manuscripts.

1:8 This mishnah prohibits the sale or lease to non-Jews of fields and even houses in the Land of Israel. According to the Talmudim, the ban on selling lands is in fulfillment of Deuteronomy 7:2 *you shall not be gracious to them* (as interpreted by the rabbis: "you shall grant them no encampment") in the Land of Israel.

For a fee it is permitted: R. Eliezer may hold that when a fee is received, the motivation for making the ornaments is purely commercial and not reverential.

attached to the ground: Referring specifically to the Land of Israel. For the rabbis, the divine apportionment of the land to the Jews precludes the possibility of ownership of the land by non-Jews who will not observe the many laws of agriculture, tithing, and Sabbatical and jubilee years associated with the land. Non-Jews may reside in the land as resident aliens.

One may not rent houses…and, needless to say, fields: Throughout this mishnah, the rules regarding fields are a degree more severe than those regarding houses. The reason is that while the sale of both houses and land gives non-Jews a "foothold" in the land, the sale of land also entails the loss of tithes and first-fruit offerings, which the non-Jew will not offer.

in Syria: According to the Talmud, this refers to areas conquered by David not at the behest of God. While possessing some holiness, these lands are not as holy as the Land of Israel.

1:9 *And you shall not bring an abomination into your house*: Deuteronomy 7:26, in reference to an idol or graven image.

because it is called by the [Israelite] owner's name: The concern is that the non-Jewish renter will operate the bath on the Sabbath and, because the bath is known to belong to the Jew, the latter will appear to be violating the Sabbath prohibition against taking money.

Chapter Two

2:1–2 *Prohibitions on account of Danger*

2 One may not place an animal in the inns of gentiles,
because they are suspected of bestiality;
and a woman may not be alone with them,
because they are suspected of sexual immorality;
and a man may not be alone with them,
because they are suspected of bloodshed.
An Israelite woman may not serve as midwife for a gentile woman,
because she gives birth to a child for idolatry,[8]
but a gentile woman may serve as midwife for an Israelite woman.
An Israelite woman may not suckle the child of a gentile woman,
but a gentile woman may suckle the child of an Israelite woman
in the latter's premises.

  2 One may accept from them healing of one's property
but not healing of one's body.

---

[8] This motive clause does not appear in many witnesses. It is likely an insertion from the Talmud.

2:1 As in 1:7 above, some of the rulings in this and the following mishnah are motivated by fear of harm by non-Jews. Jews are warned against situations that provide an easy opportunity for a non-Jew to commit sexually immoral acts with animals or Jewish women or to harm or kill a Jew.

inns: Assumed by rabbinic authors to be places of ill repute.

a man: Hebrew *adam* can refer to humans generally or males specifically. Presumably all Jews should fear violence at the hands of a hostile non-Jew, but women have the additional fear of sexual violation as indicated in the preceding clause.

An Israelite woman may not serve as midwife: The Talmud overrules the Mishnah and rules that Jewish women may serve as midwives for non-Jewish women if the service is performed for a wage. This halakhic change is supported by a widespread aggadic tradition depicting rabbinic uneasiness over inequitable rulings that might offend non-Jews.

but a gentile woman may serve as midwife…may suckle: The Mishnah is here more lenient than parallel tannaitic teachings that prohibit non-Jewish midwives and wetnurses on the suspicion that they will seek to harm the Jewish infant.

in the latter's premises: The Hebrew term refers to domain but in the strong sense of authority, dominion, and control. The idea here is that the non-Jew may suckle the Jewish infant only when she is within the Jewish mother's (physical) domain and, therefore, under her supervision and control. The Talmudim extend this condition to the preceding clause that permits a non-Jewish midwife to assist with a birth.

2:2 The rulings in this mishnah also warn against situations that provide an easy opportunity for a non-Jew to harm or kill a Jew. Seeking physical healing at the hands of a non-Jew and patronizing a non-Jewish barber (who handles sharp implements) are deemed to expose the Jew to an unacceptable level of risk.

one's property: Here the likely meaning is one's living property, i.e. animals and possibly slaves. The Jew may take his animals or slaves to a non-Jew to be healed because he risks injury to his property only, but he may not risk injury to his own life. Cf. *Nedarim* 4:4.

And one may not have one's hair cut by them in any place—
the words of R. Meir.
But the Sages say:
In a public place it is permitted,
but not when they are alone.

2:3–6   Food and Food-Related Items

3 The following items of gentiles are prohibited
and their prohibition extends to all benefit:
the wine or the vinegar of gentiles that was formerly wine;
and Adriatic earthenware;
and skins perforated at the heart—
Rabban Simeon b. Gamaliel says:
It is prohibited only when the perforation is circular,

one may not have one's hair cut: The Yerushalmi exempts the Patriarch and his entourage from the prohibition against having one's hair cut by a non-Jew because these individuals need to adopt the manners and dress appropriate to their official duties in the Greco-Roman world.

In a public place: As in the previous mishnah, the factor of supervision lowers the risk of injury. Thus, against R. Meir's blanket prohibition, the Sages permit a non-Jewish barber in a public setting. The Talmud is more lenient still.

when they are alone: That is, the barber and the client.

2:3 While many of the rulings in chapter 1 prohibited transactions that might provide some benefit *to* idolatry, the rulings in this mishnah and those immediately following are concerned to prevent Jewish benefit *from* idolatry. These rules assume degrees of prohibition of benefit from idolatry. The less severe prohibition bans consumption only (eating and drinking) while a more severe prohibition bans not only consumption but also any mode of profit through sale or use.

their prohibition extends to all benefit: This phrase indicates the most severe degree of prohibition.

the wine or the vinegar: Wine is prohibited lest it had been offered as a libation to a foreign deity, and vinegar that was formerly wine in the possession of a non-Jew is prohibited for the same reason (it may have been offered while yet wine). The legal definition of prohibited libation wine and the rules regarding it are spelled out in greater detail in chapters 4 and 5.

Adriatic earthenware: Unfired jars from the Adriatic coast that were filled with wine that would be absorbed into the clay. The jars were subsequently broken into portable wine-infused shards that could be placed in water, extracting the wine and creating a beverage. According to the Bavli, the name derives from the emperor Hadrian rather than the jars' Adriatic provenance.

skins perforated at the heart: The perforation at the heart appears to indicate that the animal was killed in an idolatrous sacrificial ritual. Based on an elaboration in the Yerushalmi, it has been suggested that the Mishnah refers to the sacrifice of the bull performed as part of the mysteries of Mithras, a cult popular among Roman soldiers, officials, and aristocrats in the first to fourth centuries CE. In depictions of the sacrifice, the bull is stabbed in the torso (the more typical method of ritual slaughter in antiquity is the slitting of the throat).

perforation: According to Rabban Simeon b. Gamaliel the shape of the perforation indicates whether or not the animal was indeed killed in an idolatrous ritual. According to the Yerushalmi, the ritual entailed removal of the heart while the animal was yet alive. The skin would rebound and form a circular hole. Thus an oblong hole indicated that the skin did not originate from an animal sacrificed in this idolatrous ritual. However, these appear to be imaginative elaborations.

But [when it is] oblong,
it is permitted.
Meat that is being brought in to an idol is permitted,
but that which is being brought out is prohibited,
because it is like *sacrifices to the dead*—
the words of R. Aqiva.
It is prohibited to do business with those on the way to "debauchery,"
but with those returning,
it is permitted.

4   Skin bottles and jars of gentiles,
and the wine of an Israelite that has been placed in them,
are prohibited
and their prohibition extends to all benefit.
But the Sages say:
Their prohibition does not extend to all benefit.
The grape pits and grapeskins of gentiles,
are prohibited
and their prohibition extends to all benefit—
the words of R. Meir.
But the Sages say:
They are prohibited if moist but permitted if dry.[9]

[9] Instead of this line **K** and some other manuscripts have "their prohibition does not extend to all benefit."

sacrifices to the dead: Psalms 106:28 refers to the Israelites' offerings to Baal-Peor (Numbers 25:1–2) as *sacrifices to the dead*, reflecting the biblical assessment of idols as "lifeless" or inert. The verse is cited in rabbinic sources as the source for the prohibition of consuming or benefiting from food offered to idols.

"debauchery": Understood by the Talmudim to be an abusive term for an idolatrous market or festival. The prohibition of transactions with those on their way to such a market place may be compared to 1:1 and 1:4 above, and the rationale is the same—the prohibition of enabling or motivating idolatry. This does not apply to those leaving the market.

2:4 This mishnah lists items prohibited because of the presence of substances that may derive from an idolatrous libation or sacrifice: either non-Jewish wine (which is subject to the suspicion that it has been used for libation) or marrow taken from the bones of an animal sacrificed to an idol. The degree of the prohibition is disputed in two of the three cases, with the rabbis adopting the more lenient position against R. Meir.

Skin bottles and jars: Such containers absorb some of the wine they hold. This wine would leech into fluids later placed in the container. Thus, the vessels are prohibited if used by non-Jews because the Jew will consume the libation wine that is exuded into the contents from the vessels' walls.

the wine of an Israelite that has been placed in them: Similarly, if the vessels formerly held libation wine it will leech into the Jew's wine that has been placed in them.

grape pits and grapeskins: This refers to the pits and skins that remain after the treading of the grapes for wine. The basis of the prohibition is unclear. It may be that the prohibition of non-Jewish wine is extended to pits and skins on the model of Numbers 6:3–4, which prohibits a *nazir* from consuming anything from the grapevine, including the pits and skins. However, it is possible that R. Meir considers the pits and skins to be ritually impure.

prohibited if moist but permitted if dry: Following the pattern of the other two cases in this mishnah we might expect the Sages to state that "their prohibition does not extend to all benefit." This is indeed the reading

The *muries* and Bithynian cheese of gentiles
are prohibited
and their prohibition extends to all benefit—
the words of R. Meir.
But the Sages say:
Their prohibition does not extend to all benefit.
　5　R. Judah said:
R. Ishmael inquired of R. Joshua while they were walking on the road.
He said:[10]
Why did they prohibit the cheese of gentiles?
He said to him:
Because they curdle it with the rennet of an animal that has died of natural causes
[and has not been properly slaughtered].
R. Ishmael replied to him:
But isn't the rennet of a whole burnt offering a more stringent case
than the rennet of an animal that has died of natural causes,
and yet they said:
A priest with a strong disposition may suck it out raw,
(but they[11] did not agree to this;

[10] Absent in several witnesses.　　[11] K adds "the Sages."

of K and should perhaps be preferred. The view that these items are prohibited if moist but permitted if dry transfers the prohibition from the realm of idolatry to the realm of ritual impurity since food items are susceptible to impurity only after becoming moist. However, the source of the ritual impurity in this instance is not clear. Alternatively, the line may be inserted on the model of Numbers 6:3–4, which prohibits the *nazir* from consuming grapes whether "moist or dry." If so, the rabbis are objecting to R. Meir's use of the *nazir* wine prohibition as the model for the prohibition of non-Jewish wine, asserting that the prohibition of the latter does not extend to dried grape by-products.

muries and Bithynian cheese: Muries was a fish-based brine used for pickling or as a condiment. *Muries* may be objectionable because of the use of a small amount of wine in its preparation (raising the possibility of consuming libation wine). The text as it stands is understood to refer to Bithynian cheese (named for a region in Asia Minor), which, judging from the next mishnah, may have been curdled with rennet taken from the bones of an animal sacrificed to idolatry. However, the word "Bithynian" is subject to much textual variation and scholars suggest an original form related to the Syriac name for a kind of white cheese; in this case the word may be a gloss on "cheese."

2:5 This mishnah questions the previous mishnah's prohibition of Bithynian cheese for consumption only, rather than all benefit. In answer to an inquiry from R. Ishmael, R. Joshua attributes the prohibition of non-Jewish cheese to the fact that it is curdled with the rennet of an animal that has died naturally rather than being properly slaughtered (see *Hullin* 8:5). R. Ishmael argues that the rennet of such an animal is not in fact prohibited, since the rennet of a whole burnt offering is not prohibited to priests and a whole burnt offering is a more stringent case than this. R. Joshua, persuaded by this argument, offers an alternative explanation: the cheese is curdled with rennet from animals sacrificed to idolatry. This too is challenged. The rennet of an animal sacrificed to idolatry should be prohibited for all benefit yet in the case of non-Jewish cheese, the Sages prohibit consumption only (2:4). Stymied, R. Joshua distracts R. Ishmael to another topic of discussion: how to read an ambiguous suffix ending in Song of Songs 1:2.

but they did not agree to this: The section in parentheses is a later editorial addition that disrupts R. Ishmael's proof. It points out that, contrary to R. Ishmael's assertion, the rabbis hold that the rennet of a whole burnt offering is prohibited; however, *ex post facto* a priest who consumes it is not liable for sacrilege. R. Joshua, however, accepts R. Ishmael's objection as it stands.

rather they said:
No benefit may be derived from it
though the law of sacrilege[12] does not apply)?
[R. Joshua] retracted[13] and said:
Because they curdle it with the rennet of calves [sacrificed to] idolatry.
He replied:
If so, why didn't they prohibit all benefit from it?
[R. Joshua] distracted him with another matter, saying:
Ishmael, my brother,[14] how do you recite this verse
for your[15] *love is better than wine* or
for your[16] *love is better than wine*?
He replied to him:
For your[17] *love is better than wine.*
He [R. Joshua] said to him:
No, it is not so,
because the parallel verse
your ointments[18]
instructs us regarding it.

6 The following items of gentiles are prohibited
but their prohibition does not extend to all benefit:
milk that was milked by a gentile without Israelite supervision,
and their bread and oil
(Rabbi and his court permitted oil),

[12] Or "misappropriation of the sacred." [13] Other witnesses lack this.
[14] Several witnesses lack "my brother." [15] Masc. *dodekha*. [16] Fem. *dodayikh*.
[17] Fem. *dodayikh*. [18] Masc. *shemanekha*.

---

retracted: The Talmudim explain the contradiction between *Hullin* 8:5 and our mishnah by saying that the law was retracted, but the earlier version of the law was not removed from *Hullin* 8:5 because "a mishnah does not move [i.e. is not removed] from its place [even if the ruling is later retracted]."

distracted him: The Talmudim understand R. Joshua's effort to distract R. Ishmael from his line of questioning as indicating not that he could not provide an explanation but that he did not wish to reveal the real reason for the prohibition. Both Talmudim refer to the custom of not revealing the reason for a new ruling for fear that people will find fault with it and come to treat the prohibition lightly.

for your love is better than wine: Song of Songs 1:2. R. Joshua's question concerns the grammatical gender of the possessive suffix "your" in the phrase *your love*: is this line uttered by the female lover in praise of the male lover or by the male lover in praise of the female? Elsewhere this verse is expounded to mean that the words of the Sages are more precious than the words of Torah, which may be R. Joshua's way of saying that the ordinances of the Sages should be esteemed and accepted regardless of the reason.

2:6 The items listed in this mishnah are prohibited to a lesser degree than the items listed in 2:4; they are prohibited for consumption only rather than all benefit.

without Israelite supervision: The concern is that the milk might be mixed with milk from a forbidden animal.

bread and oil: The Talmudim explain that commensality is prohibited lest it lead to intermarriage.

Rabbi and his court permitted oil: This parenthetical phrase is a later addition to the Mishnah and refers to R. Judah II, not R. Judah the editor of the Mishnah. The Talmudim justify the revocation of the prohibition of non-Jewish oil on the grounds that "we make no decree upon the community unless the majority is able

and boiled and pressed preserves into which they customarily put wine or vinegar,
and pounded *terit*,
and fish brine that has no fish (there is no *kilbit* floating in it),[19]
and *hilek* fish,
and drops of asafetida,
and sal conditum.
These are prohibited
but their prohibition does not extend to all benefit.

2:7 Permitted Food Items

7 The following are permitted for eating:
milk that was milked by a gentile under Israelite supervision,
and honey,
and overripe grapes even though they are exuding liquid
since they do not come under the rule of food rendered susceptible to impurity by liquids,
and preserves into which they do not customarily put wine or vinegar,

---

[19] Several witnesses lack the parenthetical phrase.

---

to abide by it." The historical merit of this statement cannot be assessed, but Josephus and a talmudic tradition attest to the zealous observance of the prohibition in an earlier period.

boiled and pressed preserves: Fruits and vegetables preserved by boiling or pressing. Evidently the small quantity of wine or vinegar added to these preserves was not deemed to warrant a ban on all benefit. The Bavli adds a second reason to the prohibition on boiled preserves—the ban on foods cooked by a non-Jew. Thus, pressed preserves lacking wine or vinegar are permitted (see m. 2:7 below) but boiled preserves remain prohibited (hence their omission from 2:7 below).

pounded terit: A species of small fish. When pounded it is impossible to ensure that no prohibited species is present.

fish brine that has no fish: The absence of fish makes it impossible to ensure that no prohibited species of fish was used in making the brine.

there is no kilbit floating in it: The term *kilbit* is traditionally understood to refer to various small fish, some prohibited and some permitted. This clause is an explanatory gloss on the previous clause.

hilek fish: According to commentators, a fish that is easily confused with nonkosher fish. One modern commentator maintains that this word is a gloss on "pounded *terit*" that entered the text at the wrong place.

asafetida: According to commentators, the juice from this plant was extracted by cutting with a knife. If the knife has fat from a forbidden animal on it, the forbidden substance may be absorbed by the bitter juice.

sal conditum: According to the Bavli and commentators, the intestines of nonkosher fish were mixed with this digestive aid.

2:7 While the items listed in 2:4 are subject to a full prohibition (consumption and all benefit) and the items in 2:6 are subject to a prohibition of consumption only, the items in this mishnah are subject to no prohibition.

overripe grapes: Despite the liquid exuding from these grapes they are not considered to be susceptible to defilement by a source of impurity in the non-Jew's domain. Variant readings lead some commentators to interpret this word as "honeycombs."

and *terit* that is not pounded,
and fish brine that has fish in it,
and the leaf of asafetida,
and rolled olive cakes.
R. Yose[20] says:
Those dropping their stones are forbidden.
Locusts that come from a basket are prohibited,
but those from the store are permitted.
The same is true of *terumah*.

Chapter Three

3:1–4 *Prohibited and Permitted Images*

3 All images are prohibited because they are worshiped once a year—the words of R. Meir.
But the Sages say:
Only that which holds in its hand a staff, a bird, or a sphere is prohibited.
R. Simeon b. Gamaliel says:
That which holds anything in its hand.
   2 If one finds fragments of images,
these are permitted.

[20] K: R. Judah.

---

the leaf of asafetida: The leaf was not subject to the concerns mentioned in 2:6 in connection with the juice from the asafetida.

Those dropping their stones are forbidden: Olive cakes moistened to the extent that the stones drop out are likely to have been soaked in wine.

from a basket…from the store: Locusts in the seller's basket were sprinkled with wine as a preservative while those in the store were not.

terumah: Analogously, priests who violate the law and sell *terumah* as if it were not sacred are more likely to violate the law with a small quantity than risk discovery and lose the value of an entire storehouse of produce.

3:1–4 operate under the assumption that not all images are used in worship and therefore not all images are subject to the laws concerning idolatry.

3:1 *prohibited*: From all benefit.

a staff, a bird, or a sphere: The Talmudim understand these items to be symbols of authority and assume that the ruling pertains to royal images that are worshiped. Statues and images depicting figures holding these items are attested from this period.

That which holds anything: According to R. Simeon b. Gamaliel an image holding any object is worshiped and thus prohibited.

3:2 Fragments of images are not used in the cult and therefore are not subject to the laws concerning idolatry. By contrast a complete model of a body part is so used and subject to the biblical ban on idolatry.

If he found the model of a hand or the model of a foot,
these are prohibited
because objects of this type are worshiped.

3 One who finds utensils bearing the figure of the sun, the figure of the moon,
or the figure of a dragon
must throw[21] them into the Dead Sea.
R. Simeon b. Gamaliel says:
Those on utensils of value are prohibited;
those on utensils of no value are permitted.
R. Yose says:
One grinds it up and scatters [the dust] to the wind or casts it into the sea.
They said to him:
Even so, it would become fertilizer, and it is written,
And nothing of the devoted thing shall cleave to your hand.

4 Proqlos the son of Plaslos[22] asked Rabban Gamaliel in Akko
while he was bathing in the Bath of Aphrodite, and said to him:
It is written in your Torah:
And nothing of the devoted thing shall cleave to your hand,
so why do you bathe in the Bath of Aphrodite?
He said to him:
One may not answer in a bath.
And when he went out he said to him:[23]
I did not come into her space, she came into mine;
people don't say:

---

[21] Lit., "bring," "deliver."
[22] Likely a corruption of *philosophos*. The name is transmitted variously in the manuscripts.
[23] K lacks "We do not answer in a bath. And when he went out he said to him."

---

model: This mishnah may refer to figures of body parts given as votive offerings to a healing god, attested for this period.

3:3 This mishnah draws a distinction that will be illustrated in the next between images that are purely ornamental and thus not subject to the biblical ban on benefit, and those that are genuinely cultic.

dragon: A possible reference to the pagan worship of a sea-monster attested in this period. The Talmudim consider the dragon an idolatrous image and mention its appearance on the standards of Trajan's cohort.

fertilizer: The ground-up item may combine with and enrich the soil with the result that a Jew who benefits from vegetation grown in this soil will derive benefit from idolatry.

And nothing of the devoted thing: Deuteronomy 13:18, concerning the idolatrous city that is to be completely destroyed. The term "devoted" in this verse means forbidden for human use and transferred to the sacred realm through total annihilation. This verse is the biblical source for the idea that a Jew may derive absolutely no benefit from an idol but must completely destroy it.

3:4 Proqlos is represented as possessing some knowledge of Jewish law; Rabban Gamaliel gives him a three-part response.

One may not answer in a bath: One does not discuss matters of Torah in the presence of nudity.

her space: The first part of Rabban Gamaliel's answer is that the bath was intended from the outset as a bath and that the statue of Aphrodite was introduced only secondarily. See 3:7 for an elaboration of this idea.

The bath was made as an ornament[24] for Aphrodite,
but rather they say:
Aphrodite was made as an ornament for the bath.
Moreover, if you were given a great deal of money,
you would not go in to your idol naked or after an emission of semen,
nor would you urinate before her!
Yet this [image] stands at the mouth of the sewer
and everyone urinates before her!
It is written only *their gods*—
that which is treated as a god is prohibited,
but that which is not treated as a god is permitted.

3:5 *Mountains and Hills Worshiped by Idolaters*

5 Gentiles who worship mountains and hills:
[the mountains and hills] are permitted,
but what is on them is prohibited, as it is written:
You shall not covet the silver or the gold that is upon them nor take it.
R. Yose the Galilean says:
Their gods on the mountains and not "the mountains [that are] their gods";
Their gods…upon the hills and not "the hills [that are] their gods."
And why is an *asherah* prohibited?[25]

---

[24] Several witnesses lack "as an ornament."   [25] K lacks this line.

---

ornament: The reason for the introduction of the statue is addressed in the second part of Rabban Gamaliel's response: because Aphrodite's statue served a purely decorative and not a cultic function in the bathhouse, the bath retained its original noncultic status.

their gods: Deuteronomy 12:2–3. These verses demand the destruction of their gods.

treated as a god: Rabban Gamaliel's third statement bolsters his claim that the statue's purpose is decorative and not cultic by pointing out that the statue is not *treated* as an idol and only that which is treated as an idol (worshiped or accorded the proper respect) falls under the biblical prohibition of idolatry.

3:5 This mishnah introduces a limitation on the ability of a non-Jew to render objects prohibited to Jews through worship. Specifically, a non-Jew's worship of certain natural formations, such as mountains and hills, does not render them prohibited. Prohibition attaches only to objects located on or under these natural sites.

what is on them: In view of the prooftext that follows, the phrase probably refers to gold and silver items that are worshiped on the mountain; later tradition understands this statement as prohibiting even things attached to mountains and hills.

You shall not covet: Deuteronomy 7:25. The verse orders the destruction of the graven images of gods, and proscribes coveting or taking the gold and silver that covered the image.

Their gods on the mountains: Deuteronomy 12:2. This verse orders the destruction of all places where the nations worship their gods. R. Yose cites this verse as proof that only their gods on the mountains and hills must be destroyed and not the mountains and hills themselves, and according to later tradition, not that which is attached to mountains and hills.

asherah: A living tree worshiped by non-Jews (in contrast, the biblical *asherah* was likely a wooden post symbolic of a tree). By offering this additional prooftext (Deuteronomy 12:2), R. Yose creates a problem. The

Because it has been handled by human hands,
and whatever has been handled by human hands is prohibited.
R. Aqiva said:
I will explain and expound it to you:
Wherever you find a high mountain or a lofty hill or a green tree,
know that there is an idol there.

3:6–7 Houses and Stones

6 If a person's house adjoins idolatry, and the house collapses,
rebuilding it is prohibited.
What should he do?
He must withdraw four cubits[26] into his own domain and rebuild.
If the wall belonged jointly to him and the idol,
it is deemed to belong half to each.
Its stones, wood, and earth defile like a creeping thing, as it is written:
You shall utterly abominate it.
R. Aqiva says:
[They defile] like a menstruant, as it is written:

[26] Several witnesses lack "four cubits."

verse orders the destruction of "their gods" on the mountains and hills and under leafy trees. If it means "their gods" on the mountains and hills and not the mountains and hills themselves, then it must also mean "their gods" under the leafy trees and not the leafy trees themselves. However, the rabbis understand "leafy trees" to refer to an *asherah* and Deuteronomy 12:3 orders the destruction of every *asherah*. Thus, R. Yose's exegesis leads to a contradiction.

handled by human hands: It is not a fully natural object, like a mountain or hill; the latter are insusceptible to becoming prohibited through worship.

know that there is an idol there: R. Aqiva understands Deuteronomy 12:2 as listing the likely location of idols.

3:6 This mishnah prohibits rebuilding the collapsed wall of one's house if in so doing one restores the wall of an idolatrous shrine. By retreating and building the wall within his own domain, the Jew separates his house from idolatry. The second clause of the mishnah introduces a new concern: impurity. Biblically, idols and idolatry are associated with non-communicable moral impurity rather than communicable ritual impurity. The ritual impurity of idols is a postbiblical innovation based on different biblical similes for idols and idolatry (e.g. an idol is likened to a corpse, a menstruant, and other sources of ritual impurity).

adjoins: The house and the idolatrous shrine share a wall.

If the wall belonged jointly: The joint ownership divides the wall down the middle. The materials on the homeowner's side (from the center inward) are permitted for use and benefit, while the materials on the shrine's side (from the center outward) are prohibited for use and benefit.

like a creeping thing: A creeping thing has a low level of impurity and defiles only by actual contact, not by carrying or by overhang.

You shall utterly abominate it: Deuteronomy 7:26. The verse prohibits Jews from bringing a graven image into the home. The image is to be abominated and detested, terms that in the Bible are usually applied to morally reprehensible, rather than ritually impure, actions and objects.

like a menstruant: A menstruant possesses a higher level of impurity and defiles by contact and carrying but not by overhang. The mishnah implies that the analogy extends only to the question of defilement by carrying and does not include the many other characteristic features of menstrual impurity.

You shall cast them away like a rejected thing; you will say to it, "Get out!"
Just as a menstruant defiles by carriage,
so an idol defiles by carriage.

7 There are three kinds of houses:
(1) a house that was built from the outset for idolatry—it is prohibited;
(2) if one plastered it and paneled it for the sake of idolatry, and renovated it—
one removes what was renovated;
(3) if someone brought an idol in [to the house] and took it out again—
it is permitted.
There are three kinds of stones:
(1) a stone that was hewn from the outset as a pedestal [for an idol] is prohibited;
(2) if one plastered it and paneled it for the sake of idolatry, and renovated it,
one removes what was renovated;
(3) if one set up an idol on it and then took it away—it is permitted.

3:7 cont.–10 *Asherah*

There are three kinds of *asherah*:
(1) a tree that was planted from the outset as a pedestal [for an idol] is prohibited;
(2) if one chopped or trimmed it for the sake of idolatry, and it sprouted anew,
one removes what sprouted;
(3) if one set up an idol under it and then annulled it, it is permitted.
Which is an *asherah*?
Any [tree] under which is an idol.
R. Simeon says:
Any [tree] that is worshiped.
It once happened in Sidon,
in connection with a tree that was worshiped,
that they found a heap [of stones] under it.

You shall cast them away: Isaiah 30:22. This verse states that Israel will defile images covered with gold and silver, and then cast them away like a rejected thing. The biblical simile illustrates the repulsive nature of idols. R. Aqiva exploits the allusion to menstruation in the verb "to cast away" (the Hebrew word for menstruant is from the root "to cast out") and establishes an analogy between the idol and the menstruant not merely in terms of the requirement of expulsion, but in terms of ritual impurity.

3:7 The mishnah conveys additional rules regarding benefit from idolatry in three parallel sets of three rulings each. Concerning houses, stones, and *asherah*, three categories are distinguished: permitted, permitted after restoration of an earlier status, and prohibited. The role of intention is significant. The mishnah also includes a dispute over the definition of an *asherah*.

Which is an asherah? This line introduces a dispute that has ritual-purity implications as will become clear in the next mishnah. The first anonymous view identifies an *asherah* as any tree under which an idol is located. If so, the source of the impurity is the idol that conveys impurity by the overhang created by the branches of the tree that houses it. But in R. Simeon's view an *asherah* is any tree that people worship. Thus, the tree itself, as a worshiped object or idol, conveys impurity and, because of its particular shape, probably conveys that impurity by overhang.

It once happened in Sidon: The story supports R. Simeon's view. It was not the tree that was worshiped but an idol under it, and thus the tree was permitted.

R. Simeon said to them:
Check this heap.
And they checked it and they found an image in it.
He said to them:
Since it is the image that they are worshiping,
we will permit the tree for them.

8 One may not sit in an *asherah*'s shade,
but if one sat, one is pure;
and one may not pass under it,
but if one passed, one is impure.
If it encroached on the public way
and one passed under it, one is pure;
and they sow vegetables under it in the rainy season,
but not in the dry season,
but lettuce—not in the dry season and not in the rainy season.
R. Yose says:
Also not vegetables in the rainy season,
because the foliage falls and serves as fertilizer.

9 If one took pieces of wood from an *asherah*,
it is prohibited to benefit from them.
If one heated an oven with them—
if a new oven, it is taken apart,
but if an old oven, it is allowed to cool.

3:8 The prohibition of benefit from an *asherah* includes benefit derived from its shade. Thus, sitting or passing under its shade is prohibited, as is taking advantage of its shade to protect vegetables from the heat of the summer sun and lettuce from damage by winter rains. R. Yose would prohibit even winter vegetables grown in its shade because the falling leaves provide a benefit as fertilizer.

pure: The language of prohibition in the first clause of the first two rulings (one may not sit…one may not pass…) implies that the purpose of the ruling is to prevent benefit from idolatry (consistent with chapter 3 as a whole). However, the language of ritual impurity in the second clause (one is pure…one is impure…) implies that the purpose of the ruling is to prevent ritual defilement (a topic first introduced in 3:6).

impure: Persons who pass under the overhanging branches of an *asherah* are ritually defiled. The precise reason for the *asherah*'s defiling power (see the dispute in the previous mishnah) is not indicated.

encroached on the public way: The fact that ritual impurity is not imposed when it is impossible to avoid passing under the overhanging branches of an *asherah* indicates that the impurity is rabbinically, not biblically, decreed.

lettuce: Lettuce is delicate and in the winter the *asherah* would benefit it by shielding it from the winter rains.

3:9 Benefit from the detached wood of an *asherah* is also prohibited. This mishnah indicates the steps to be taken if the wood of an *asherah* is used to heat an oven for baking bread or deployed as a shuttle for weaving.

if a new oven, it is taken apart: Clay ovens were sealed at the first heating. Because a new clay oven heated for the first time with the wood of an *asherah* would derive a benefit from idolatry, it must be disassembled.

it is allowed to cool: An older oven that is already sealed receives no such benefit from heating with the wood of the *asherah* and does not become prohibited. However, it must be allowed to cool before use so that no bread is baked in the heat produced by the *asherah* wood.

If one baked bread in [the oven],
it is prohibited to benefit from [the bread];
if it was mixed with other [loaves],
it is prohibited to benefit from any of them.
R. Eliezer says:
He should throw[27] any benefit he has derived from them into the Dead Sea.
They said to him:
There is no redemption price in regard to idolatry.
If one took [wood for] a shuttle from [an *asherah*],
it is prohibited to benefit from it.
If he wove a garment with it,
it is prohibited to benefit from the garment;
if it was mixed with other [garments],
and those others with others,
it is prohibited to derive benefit from any of them.
R. Eliezer says:
He should throw any benefit he has derived from it into the Dead Sea.
They said to him:
There is no redemption price in regard to idolatry.

   10 How does one annul an *asherah*?
If he took from it a stick or a twig, even a leaf,
it is annulled.
If he trimmed it—
for the sake of [the tree it remains] prohibited;
not for the sake of the tree, it is permitted.

[27] Lit. "bring," "deliver," here and below.

mixed with other [loaves]: The presence of one prohibited loaf with others prohibits all of them. Because the loaves are discrete items, someone will end up consuming a fully prohibited loaf. Thus, the principle of dilution, which would permit, for example, a liquid in which is mingled a tiny amount of a prohibited liquid, does not apply.

He should throw…into the Dead Sea: R. Eliezer envisages the substitution of a monetary equivalent, which is then destroyed, as a device for rendering the bread (or garment) permitted.

There is no redemption price in regard to idolatry: The Sages object that the legal remedy of redemption money does not apply in the case of idolatry.

If he wove a garment: The same principles apply to a garment woven with a shuttle made from the wood of an *asherah*.

3:10 The Mishnah distinguishes between a kind of pruning and trimming that annuls the sacred status of the *asherah*, rendering it permitted for use and benefit by a Jew, and one that does not. Presumably this mishnah refers to actions undertaken by the worshiper.

annul: Actions that diminish the tree in some way have the effect of annulling its sacred status.

for the sake of [the tree]: If the pruning and trimming are intended to enhance the tree's growth, then it does not serve to annul its sacred (and therefore prohibited) status.

Chapter Four

4:1–2 *Merqolis*

4 R. Ishmael says:
Three stones beside one another—
if beside a *Merqolis*, they are prohibited;
but two stones are permitted.
But the Sages say:
Those which appear to be associated with it are prohibited;
those which do not appear to be associated with it are permitted.
 2 If one found coins, clothing, or utensils on top of [the *Merqolis*],
these are permitted.
Bunches of grapes, garlands of wheat, wine, oil, fine flour,
and anything that is similarly offered on an altar,
are prohibited.

4:3 *Property Owned by an Idol*

 3 A garden or a bathhouse that belongs to an idol:
one may use them if it does not advantage [the idol],
but one may not use them if it advantages [the idol].

4:1 *Merqolis*: Statues of Hermes (Roman Mercury) were erected on the roadside and near boundaries. Travelers would pay homage to Hermes by placing stones near the statues to form cairns. Jews are prohibited from deriving any benefit from these stones because of the idolatrous connection. This mishnah presents two views of the criteria for determining whether stones found near the statue fall under the prohibition or not.

Three … two: R. Ishmael's criterion for determining the status of a given stone is numerical. A minimum of three stones is required to form a pile (or, perhaps, a dolmen consisting of two upright stones with a third stone laid on top). Thus, one or two stones are exempt from the prohibition, because it is unlikely that they have been intentionally placed for an idolatrous purpose.

associated with it: The Sages' criterion for determining the status of a given stone is its connection to the statue regardless of number. Stones that appear to be associated with the statue (referring perhaps to proximity) are likely to have been placed or tossed to form a cairn.

4:2 draws a distinction between the objects found at a Hermes shrine. Those objects intended for use by fellow travelers (coins, clothing, or utensils) are not associated with idolatry and are permitted for use by Jews, while those intended as votive offerings are associated with idolatry and are thus prohibited for use by Jews.

4:3 prohibits the use of a garden or bathhouse that belongs to an idol (presumably the priests or cult of the idol) if such use gives an advantage or benefit of any kind to the idol. The prohibition is removed if the garden or bathhouse is only partly owned by an idol.

advantage: Commentators supply various explanations ranging from monetary payment to an expression of thanks or homage.

If it belonged to the idol and to others jointly,
one may use them whether it is to the idol's advantage or not.

4:4–7 *Annulment of Idols*

4 The idol of a gentile is prohibited immediately;
that of an Israelite is not prohibited until it is worshiped.
A gentile can annul his own idol and his fellow's,[28]
but an Israelite cannot annul the idol of a gentile.
If one annuls an idol, he has [thereby also]
annulled its appurtenances.
If he annulled its appurtenances,
they are permitted,[29]
but [the idol] itself is prohibited.
5 How does one annul it?
If one cut off the tip of its ear,

[28] Var. "A gentile can annul his own idol and an Israelite's." See annotations.
[29] Several witnesses read "annulled."

jointly: In the case of joint ownership, the benefit (whether monetary or not) is regarded as directed to the human co-owner.

4:4–7 are concerned with the annulment of idols. Annulment occurs when a pagan performs some desecrating action on or with the idol (e.g. damaging or defacing it), indicating its profane status in his eyes. Such annulment converts forbidden images and idols into cultically neutral objects that may legitimately be used by Jews for various purposes. These mishnayot address the following questions: Who has the power to annul idols and when (4:4)? What is the extent of the annulment (4:4)? How are idols annulled (4:5)? From what actions can annulment be inferred (4:6)? Why doesn't God annul (i.e. destroy) idols (4:7)?

4:4 *prohibited immediately…prohibited until it is worshiped*: In tannaitic texts, the issue of the annulment of an idol is connected with the time at which an idol's prohibited status is initiated. According to one view an idol made by a Jew is prohibited immediately—even before he worships it. Just as he is powerless to initiate its prohibited status by worshiping it, he is powerless to end its prohibited status by annulling it. By contrast, a non-Jew who makes an idol initiates its prohibited status by worshiping it and is equally empowered to end its prohibited status by annulling it. Whether the non-Jew's power of annulment extends to the idols of others, even Jews, is a matter of controversy. However, our mishnah adopts the position of R. Aqiva according to which the idol of a Jew is prohibited only once it has been worshiped, whereas that of a non-Jew is prohibited immediately. On this view, there is no logical connection between the power to initiate an idol's prohibited status by worship and the power to initiate an idol's permitted status by annulling it. Non-Jews are powerless regarding the onset of prohibited status (their idols are prohibited immediately) and yet they retain the power to annul their idols.

A gentile can annul…an Israelite cannot annul: Manuscript evidence as well as talmudic discussions indicate that R. Judah originally taught that "A gentile can annul his own idol and an Israelite's," then retracted the ruling and taught that "A gentile can annul his own idol and his fellow's (that is, the idol of his fellow gentile)." The latter ruling was preserved in Babylonia and became the basis of the Babylonian Talmud's discussion. The former ruling was later reinstated in Palaestina and became the basis for the discussion in the Palestinian Talmud. Other rabbinic texts indicate that the change is connected to Rabbi's adoption of the minority view that the idol of a Jew is insusceptible to annulment.

4:5 This mishnah considers what acts may be taken as sure signs that an idol has been annulled. Physical mutilation is a sure sign of annulment while acts of contempt or degradation are not. Acts of alienation (sale or pawn) are subject to a dispute.

the tip of its nose,
the tip of its finger,
or defaced it even without reducing it,
one has annulled it.
If one spat before it,
urinated before it,
dragged it,
or threw excrement at it,
it is not annulled.
If one sold it or gave it as a pledge—
Rabbi says it is annulled,
but the Sages say it is not annulled.

6 An idol whose worshipers abandoned it:
in a time of peace is permitted;
in a time of war is prohibited.
The pedestals of kings are permitted
because they set [an idol] on them [only] when kings pass by.

7 They asked the elders in Rome:
If God is displeased by idolatry, why doesn't he destroy[30] it?
They said to them:
If [idolaters] worshiped an object that the world does not need,
he would destroy it;
but look, they worship the sun, the moon, the stars, and the constellations;[31]
shall he destroy his world because of fools?
They said to them:
If so, let him destroy whatever the world doesn't need
and leave that which the world needs!

---

[30] The same verb translated above as "annul."
[31] Certain witnesses lack "constellations"; others add "mountains and hills."

---

it is not annulled: Such acts may be performed in a moment of pique and do not necessarily indicate a genuine or permanent defection from the idol.

sold it or gave it as a pledge: Sale and pawn are considered sure signs of annulment by Rabbi, but not by the Sages. The Talmudim explain that if the idol is sold to another worshiper it might not be annulled first. The identity and intention of the purchaser is thus a relevant consideration.

4:6 This mishnah continues to consider whether certain acts may be taken as sure signs that an idol has been annulled.

abandoned: Voluntary abandonment of an idol indicates that it is no longer revered and may therefore be taken as a sign of annulment. Thus, idols abandoned in a time of war are not permitted, since their abandonment may be due to the exigencies of war rather than an intentional annulment.

pedestals of kings: The Mishnah envisages pedestals upon which an idol was temporarily erected as a king's procession passes by—perhaps to honor the king or to enable the king to bow to the idol, though such activity has only a weak correspondence to known practices in late antiquity.

4:7 This aggadic text addresses the deeper question: why doesn't God simply uproot idols and idolatry from his world? The text takes advantage of a pun—the term for "annul" can also mean "destroy." Thus, the questioners ask why God does not *annul* idols himself, but the Sages who answer mobilize the other meaning of the word and explain why God does not *destroy* objects worshiped by idolaters.

elders in Rome: Perhaps the four who traveled to Rome according to *Eruvin* 4:1.

They said to them:
We would [thereby] only confirm those who worship them, [for they] would say:
Know that [the sun, moon, etc.] are gods, because they were not destroyed.

4:8–5:11 *Libation Wine*

8 One may buy from gentiles a winepress that was trodden,
even though [the gentile] takes [the grapes] in his hand
and puts them on the heap.
And it does not become libation wine
until it flows down into the vat.
If it flows into the vat—
what is in the vat is prohibited
and the rest is permitted.

9 One may tread in a winepress with a gentile,
but one may not gather grapes with him.
An Israelite who works in a state of impurity:
one may not tread or gather grapes with him,
but one may help him convey the jars to and from the winepress.

4:8–5:11 is an extended unit concerning libation wine, i.e. wine that has been poured as a libation or otherwise dedicated to an idol. The Mishnah prohibits all wine of a non-Jew for fear that it may have been used in this way and so involve a Jew in a violation of the prohibition against deriving benefit from idolatry. The rules of prohibited wine distinguish between contact in which no libation is deemed to have occurred, so that the wine is permitted to a Jew, and contact in which libation might have occurred, rendering the wine prohibited. In the Mishnah, libation wine is generally classified as prohibited rather than impure, since deriving benefit from idolatry rather than contracting ritual impurity is the primary legal concern (though impurity language is employed in connection with non-Jewish winepresses in 5:11).

4:8 *a winepress*: A winepress and its contents. The press consisted of two troughs. An upper trough in which the grapes are heaped for treading was connected by a pipe to a lower trough in which the exuded juice collected.

[the gentile] takes … and puts them on the heap: The non-Jew piles the grapes on the heap for pressing but this contact does not create a prohibition, either because the contact is deemed noncultic or because the grapes are not yet susceptible to the status of prohibited wine.

until it flows down: Only the exuded juice is susceptible to becoming forbidden should the non-Jew then touch it and potentially dedicate some drops to an idol.

the rest is permitted: That which is in the upper trough is not susceptible.

4:9 This mishnah considers three cases in which a Jew must beware of providing aid to someone involved in a violation: a non-Jew who is suspected of pouring wine as a libation, a Jew who prepares wine without concern for ritual impurity, and a baker who prepares bread in a state of ritual impurity. In each instance, the Jew may not enable the violation, but once the violation has occurred he is permitted to assist the other in his work.

One may tread … but one may not gather: According to commentators, one cannot assist with gathering since the grapes will be defiled when placed in impure vessels. This mishnah permits a Jew to tread the grapes with a non-Jew because (1) if the concern is impurity then they are already defiled by the impurity of the non-Jew's vessels or (2) if the concern is libation, the juice is not susceptible to the prohibition until it descends into the lower vat. According to the Talmudim, a different version of this mishnah permitted gathering grapes with a non-Jew.

but one may help him convey the jars: Although one may not assist a fellow Jew who defiles his grapes, once the deed is done one may assist him in conveying his wine jars since no further violation is incurred.

A baker who works in a state of impurity:
one may not knead the dough or roll it with him,
but one may help him convey the bread to the shopkeeper.

10 If a gentile is found standing next to a vat of wine:
if he has a lien upon it, it is prohibited.
if he does not have a lien upon it, it is permitted.³²
If he fell into the vat and came up,
or measured it with a rod,
or flicked out a hornet with a rod,
or was tapping the rim of a frothing cask—
all of these cases have occurred,
and the Sages said:
Let the wine be sold.
But R. Simeon permits it.
If he took a jar and threw it into the vat [of wine]—³³
this happened and they declared it fit [even for drinking].

11 One who prepares the wine of a gentile in a state of purity
and leaves it in his premises, in a house open to the public domain—

---

³² K: "if he has a lien upon it, it is permitted"—an evident error.
³³ The Babylonian recension of this mishnah reads "If he took a jar and threw it into the vat [of wine] *in anger.*"

4:10 This mishnah considers cases of a non-Jew's proximity to and contact with wine.

if he has a lien upon it: The non-Jew may consider himself entitled to handle the wine as if it is already his, hence it is prohibited under the suspicion of libation wine.

If he fell: In this case, the non-Jew's contact is unintentional and there is no intention to pour a libation. The Babylonian Talmud understands the mishnah to refer to a case in which the non-Jew drowns and his body is brought out by others (because if he emerged alive he would offer libation in thanks to his idol, rendering the wine prohibited). This is, however, a forced and grammatically untenable reading.

or measured it with a rod: In this case there is intentional but indirect contact and with no intention to offer libation.

or flicked out a hornet with a rod: In this case, there is intentional but indirect contact and even though drops are sprinkled, there is no intention to offer libation.

or was tapping the rim of a frothing cask: In this case, there is intentional but indirect contact to settle the froth, with no intention to offer libation.

Let the wine be sold: In all of these cases, the Sages declare a partial prohibition—the Jew may not drink the wine, but he can benefit indirectly by selling it.

threw it into the vat: Tossing an object into a vat of wine from a distance, even though it creates a sprinkling, does not render the wine prohibited. The words "in anger" in the Babylonian recension of the Mishnah are a late addition.

4:11 The case imagined here is one in which a Jew ensures that the wine of a non-Jew has been prepared in such a way that it is permitted to Jews—it has not been used for libation and no ritual impurity has befallen it. The wine is now left in the non-Jew's house—under what conditions is the wine's permitted status preserved?

in a state of purity: No disqualification—defilement or libation—has befallen it.

house open to the public domain: Where it is exposed to public view and accessible.

if in a city in which are both gentiles and Israelites,
it is permitted;
if in a city which is entirely gentile,
it is prohibited unless he installs a watchman.
The watchman does not need to sit and watch it;
even though he goes in and out, the wine is permitted.
R. Simeon b. Eleazar says:
The domain of gentiles is all one and the same.

12 One who prepares the wine of a gentile in a state of purity
and leaves it in his premises, and the latter writes for him:
"I have received money in payment from you"—
[the wine] is allowed.
But if the Israelite should want to remove it
and [the gentile] does not allow it until he gives him his money—
this happened in Bet Shean and the Sages prohibited it.

Chapter Five

5 If one hires a laborer to assist him in preparing libation wine,
his wages are prohibited;
but if one hired him to assist him with other work,
even if he told him:
"Move for me that jar of libation wine from this place to that place,"
his wage is permitted.
One who hires an ass to carry libation wine,
his hire is prohibited;

in a city in which are both gentiles and Israelites: The wine is permitted in such a city because the possibility of being observed by a Jew deters the non-Jewish owner from tampering with the wine. In a city with no Jews, the wine is permitted only if a watchman is hired as a deterrent against tampering.

even though he goes in and out: The watchman need not be continuously present; the threat of being observed deters the non-Jewish owner from tampering with the wine.

The domain of gentiles is always one and the same: In R. Simeon's view, a watchman is always necessary, without exception.

4:12 *is allowed*: Since the money has been paid, the wine is the property of the Jew and will not be handled by the non-Jew.

and the Sages prohibited it: Since the money has not been paid and the Jew wants to nevertheless remove it, the non-Jew may treat it as a pledge and feel entitled to handle it.

5:1 This mishnah prohibits a Jew from deriving benefit—specifically, earning a wage—from libation wine. However, if a Jew is hired to perform other labor, that is, if his wage is earned for performing another task, then he may agree to an employer's request that, in addition, he move jars of libation wine.

If one hires a laborer: A non-Jewish employer hires a Jewish laborer.

One who hires an ass: The mishnah speaks of a non-Jew who hires an ass from a Jew.

but if he hired it for riding,
even if he rested his flagon on it,
its hire is permitted.

2 If libation wine fell on grapes,
one washes them and they are permitted;
but if they are split open they are prohibited.
If it fell on figs or on dates,
and there is sufficient in them to impart a flavor,
[they are] prohibited.[34]
It once happened to Boethos b. Zonin that he conveyed dried figs on a ship
and a jar of libation wine broke and fell on them,
and he asked the Sages and they permitted them.
This is the general rule:
Anything that derives benefit by means of an imparted flavor is prohibited,
anything that does not derive benefit by means of an imparted flavor is permitted,
for example, vinegar on pounded beans.

3 A gentile who was helping an Israelite convey jars of wine from place to place—
if on the presumption that the wine was watched, it is permitted;
if [the Israelite] told him that he was going away,
[it is forbidden] if there was time for him to bore a hole and stop it up again,

[34] Several witnesses lack this sentence.

for riding: If the animal is hired for the express purpose of riding, the money is permitted because the conveyance of a flask of libation wine is incidental. The hire is prohibited only if the animal was hired for the express purpose of transporting libation wine.

5:2 This mishnah enunciates the principle according to which contact with libation wine renders a food prohibited: if the libation wine improves the flavor it is deemed to have conferred a benefit and the food item is prohibited.

split open: When the grapes are split, the libation wine is absorbed into them and cannot simply be washed off.

they permitted them: The figs are allowed despite the libation wine. The previous line contradicts this ruling, supporting the manuscript evidence that it is a late addition. The Talmudim are forced to distinguish the two cases (for example, in the first case an improving flavor is imparted to the figs, but in the case of Boethos ben Zonin, the flavor of the figs is adversely affected).

derives benefit by means of an imparted flavor: If the libation wine is sufficient to impart a flavor and that flavor is an improvement, then the food is prohibited.

vinegar on pounded beans: The vinegar is derived from libation wine.

5:3–5 This unit discusses the conditions under which a sealed jar of wine comes under the suspicion of having been opened for libation by a non-Jew. The possibility that a Jew will enter and catch the non-Jew in the act of tampering with a Jew's wine is deemed a sufficient deterrent and thus the wine is permitted.

5:3 *presumption*: When a non-Jew and a Jew together process jars of wine, the legal presumption is that the non-Jew will not tamper with the wine because he cannot do so unobserved.

if [the Israelite] told him that he was going away: When a period of absence is specified the non-Jew may feel emboldened to tamper with the wine knowing that he will not be observed, and so the wine is forbidden.

if there was time: The announced absence must be long enough for the non-Jew to bore a hole, pour some wine as a libation, repair the hole with new clay, and let the clay dry.

and for the clay to dry.
Rabban Simeon b. Gamaliel says:
If there was time for him to open it[35] and close it up
and for it to dry.

4 One who leaves his wine on a wagon or a boat—
if he took a shortcut and entered the town and bathed,
[the wine] is permitted.
But if [the Israelite] told him that he was going away,
[it is forbidden] if there was time for him to bore a hole and stop it up again,
and for the clay to dry.
R. Simeon b. Gamaliel says:
If there was time for him to open it and close it up
and for it to dry.
One who leaves a gentile in his shop,
even though he goes in and out,
[the wine] is permitted.
But if [the Israelite] told him that he was going away,
[it is forbidden] if there was time for him to bore a hole and stop it up again,
and for the clay to dry.
R. Simeon b. Gamaliel says:
If there was time for him to open it and close it up,
and for it to dry.

5 If [an Israelite] was dining with [a gentile]
and [the Israelite] placed flagons of wine on the table
and flagons of wine on the side table,
and left and went out—
what is on the table is prohibited,
and what is on the side table is permitted.
If he said to him, "Mix some wine and drink,"
even that which is on the side table is prohibited.
Open jars are prohibited;
sealed jars [are prohibited] if there was time for him to open it and close it up
and for it to dry.

[35] Certain witnesses add "the jar," here and in the next mishnah (twice).

R. Simeon b. Gamaliel says: According to R. Simeon b. Gamaliel, the announced absence must be long enough for the non-Jew to remove the jar's stopper, pour some wine as a libation, replace and reseal the stopper, and let the clay dry.

5:4 This mishnah considers two instances in which a non-Jew is left alone with the wine and without a watchman. Here again, the wine is allowed because of the deterrent effect of the non-Jew's imminent return. But when the period of the non-Jew's absence is announced the same rules apply as in 5:3.

on a wagon or a boat: That is, in the care of a non-Jew on a wagon or boat.

5:5 *side table*: A small, round, three-legged table that held extra dishes and wine.

what is on the table is prohibited: It is presumed that the non-Jewish guest would help himself to the wine on the table and not the side table.

"Mix some wine and drink": The invitation to mix some wine (dilute it with water) may be interpreted as an invitation to take freely from all available wine, hence even that on the side table is prohibited.

6 If a gentile[36] troop entered a city—
if in peacetime, open jars are prohibited
and sealed jars are permitted;
if in wartime, both are permitted
because they are not at leisure to offer libation.

7 Israelite artisans to whom a gentile has sent a jar of libation wine[37]—
they are permitted to say to him, "Give us its value in cash."
Once it has entered their possession, it is prohibited.
One who sells wine to a gentile—
if he fixed a price before measuring it out,
the money is permitted;
if he measured it out before fixing a price,
the money is prohibited.
If he took a funnel and measured out [wine] into the gentile's flask,
and then measured out [wine] into an Israelite's flask—
if some wine [from the first] remained [in the funnel],
[the wine in the Israelite's flask] is prohibited.
One who empties out [wine] from one vessel into another vessel—
what remains in the one from which [he poured] is permitted,
but what remains in the one into which [he poured] is prohibited.

8 Libation wine is prohibited
and renders prohibited in the smallest quantity.
Wine mixed with wine,
water mixed with water,
the smallest quantity [of the prohibited substance renders the whole prohibited].
Wine mixed with water,
and water mixed with wine,
[is prohibited if the prohibited substance is sufficient] to impart a flavor.

[36] Several witnesses lack "gentiles."   [37] A few witnesses add the gloss "as a wage."

5:6 *troop*: The Hebrew word implies that these soldiers intend to loot the population.

5:7 *Once it has entered their possession*: Workers can request from their non-Jewish employer payment in cash rather than libation wine, up until the wine enters their premises and is accepted as payment. Once accepted as payment it cannot be exchanged for money, as this is tantamount to selling libation wine.

if he fixed a price before measuring it out: Fixing the price is tantamount to a sale while measuring the wine into the non-Jew's vessels renders it prohibited. Thus, the price must be fixed before the wine is rendered prohibited (i.e. before measuring it out); if after, then the Jew will be guilty of selling, i.e. deriving benefit from, prohibited wine.

empties out [wine] from one vessel into another vessel: i.e. from a Jew's vessel into a non-Jew's vessel. There is no concern that the formation of a continuous stream "transfers" the prohibition from the wine in the lower, receiving vessel to the wine in the upper, pouring vessel.

5:8 This mishnah, like the next, contains specific illustrations of a general principle and a statement of that principle.

renders prohibited in the smallest quantity: When mixed with other wine, libation wine prohibits by the smallest quantity. The same is true of prohibited water mixed with water.

to impart a flavor: When mixed with water, libation wine prohibits only when in sufficient quantity to impart a flavor. The same is true of prohibited water mixed with wine.

This is the general rule:
A species mixed with the same species,
the smallest quantity [of the prohibited substance renders the whole prohibited];
a species mixed with a different species,
[is prohibited if the prohibited substance is sufficient] to impart a flavor.

9 The following are prohibited and render prohibited in the smallest quantity:
libation wine, and an idol,
skins with an incision at the heart,
the stoned ox, the heifer whose neck is broken,
the sacrificial birds of one with *tsara'at*, the hair of a *nazir*,
the firstborn of an ass, meat boiled in milk,[38]
nonsacred animals slaughtered in the Temple courtyard—
these are prohibited and render prohibited in the smallest quantity.

10 If libation wine fell into a vat,
all of it is prohibited for any benefit.
R. Simeon b. Gamaliel says:
He may sell it all to a gentile
minus the value of the libation wine that is in it.

11 A stone winepress which a gentile has covered in pitch—
[an Israelite] scours it and it is ritually pure.

[38] Two witnesses add "the scapegoat."

5:9 This mishnah has a tripartite structure: a general statement that the items listed in the mishnah are prohibited and render other items prohibited by the smallest quantity; an illustrative list of prohibited items that, when mixed with like items, render them prohibited by the smallest quantity; a recapitulation of the first general statement.

skins with an incision at the heart: See 2:3 above. If mixed with other skins, this skin renders them prohibited in the smallest amount.

the stoned ox: The ox referred to in Exodus 21:28. Meat from such an animal is prohibited and when mixed with other meat renders it prohibited in the smallest amount. The same principle applies to the items below.

the heifer whose neck is broken: The heifer referred to in Deuteronomy 21:4.

the sacrificial birds of one with tsara'at: The birds offered as part of the purification ritual for a person with scale-disease ("leprosy"); see Leviticus 14:4–7.

the hair of a nazir: Offered at the completion of the Nazirite vow; see Numbers 6:18.

the firstborn of an ass: Prohibited until redeemed; see Exodus 13:13, 34:20.

meat boiled in milk: The prohibition derives from a rabbinic reading of Exodus 23:19, 34:26, and Deuteronomy 14:21.

nonsacred animals slaughtered in the Temple courtyard: A prohibition inferred from Deuteronomy 12:20ff., which permits profane slaughter outside the sanctuary.

5:10 The previous mishnah appears to deal with a jar of libation wine that has become unrecognizably mixed among other jars of wine, while this mishnah appears to deal with libation wine that has been poured into a vat of wine.

5:11 Winepresses were lined with pitch, which absorbed some of the wine. A Jew must ensure that the pitch lining of a non-Jew's winepress contains no prohibited wine before using it.

A stone winepress: Because there is no fear of absorption by the stone, it is sufficient to scour the pitch lining to remove the prohibited wine.

A wooden one—
Rabbi says:
He must scour it,
but the Sages say:
He must scrape off the pitch.
A clay one—
even though he scraped off the pitch
it is prohibited.

5:12 Utensils Purchased from a Gentile

12 One who purchases utensils from gentiles—
that which is usually purified by immersion, let him immerse it;
by scalding, let him scald it;
by making it white hot in fire, let him make it white hot in fire.
One makes a spit or a gridiron white hot in fire.
One polishes a knife and it is pure.

A wooden one: Because wood absorbs liquid, the pitch lining of a wooden press was thicker than that of a stone press. Therefore, the rabbis held that the lining must be completely removed.

A clay one: In a clay press the wine is absorbed into the walls of the press itself so that removal of the pitch is insufficient and the winepress is prohibited.

5:12 Utensils purchased from a non-Jew may have absorbed prohibited food items or come into contact with ritual impurities and must therefore be cleansed and purified. The prescribed methods are derived from Numbers 31:22–23, which describes the process for purifying the vessels taken as war booty from the Midianites. The first step is rinsing and scalding or heating in fire (depending on the constitution of the utensil) in order to remove prohibited substances (see Leviticus 6:21 and 11:32 where the same methods remove prohibited substances that cling to Jewish vessels). The second step is sprinkling with the waters of purgation, presumably to remove corpse impurity from the battlefield. In rabbinic times, when waters of purgation were no longer available, this step was replaced by immersion in a *miqveh*.

by immersion: This applies to metal and glass utensils.

by scalding: This applies to metal pots and pans.

by making it white hot: This applies to metal utensils used on the fire.

Tractate Avot

Martin S. Jaffee

Introduction

Overview

Avot literally means "fathers." This title is perhaps intentionally ambiguous. On the one hand, it calls to mind the "Fathers of the World," the Sages whose instruction is epitomized in its traditions (*Eduyot* 1:4). On the other, the term *avot* may allude to this instruction itself, as a body of generative or first principles (*Shabbat* 7:2 is an example of this usage).

In addition to circulating in manuscripts and printed texts of the Mishnah, there is a second, expanded textual tradition of this tractate that circulated in prayer books. This is due to the custom that arose by the early Middle Ages to recite *Avot* on Sabbath afternoons (in some places only in the six weeks between the festivals of Passover and Weeks (Shavu'ot). This liturgical version of the tractate is commonly entitled *Pirqei Avot*, translated as "Chapters of the Fathers" or "Ethics of the Fathers."

Structure and Organization of the Tractate

Chapters 1–4 are concerned with documenting the unfolding of the Torah tradition chronologically through its great historical exemplars, beginning with Moses. The tractate begins (1:1) with its famous assertion that "Moses received Torah from Sinai, and transmitted it to Joshua, and Joshua to the elders, etc." Nearly all of the first two chapters are preoccupied with naming the leaders of each generation of Sages and assigning to each of them three characteristic teachings (1:2–2:16). Chapters 3 and 4, too, are organized roughly chronologically, first presenting the sayings of the teachers who formed the core of Sages associated in rabbinic historiographical tradition with Yavneh, and then the Sages of the following generation.

Chapter 5 departs from this chronological presentation. Its traditions are arranged into groups of teachings organized by descending number, e.g. "by ten utterances was the world created" (5:1), "seven are the traits of a clod" (5:7).

The version of *Avot* that reflects liturgical recitation appends a sixth chapter, called *Pereq Qinyan Torah* (the "Chapter on the Acquisition of Torah"). The chapter is clearly postmishnaic. It is substantially identical to chapter 8 of *Kallah Rabbati* and chapter 17 of the *Seder Eliyahu Zuta*, both post-Talmudic rabbinic works. The teachings of chapter 6 about the life of Torah are entirely congruent with those of the first five chapters of *Avot*. The chapter may have been added so that the tractate would have six chapters, reflecting the practice (see above) of studying one chapter of the tractate on each of the six weeks between Passover and Shavu'ot. For the sake of completeness chapter 6 is included here.

Main Ideas

Avot combines a general concern with ethics, right-mindedness, and right practice that shares much with Hellenistic and Roman moral philosophy, with a sense of sacred history and divine judgment that might have been common to many ancient Jews and Christians, a commitment to observing commandments, and with specifically rabbinic values of piety and above all study and discipleship. The annotations to the translation address the character of the tractate as an anthology of sayings that encourage the pursuit of the rabbinic ideal of Torah study and the embodiment of its values.

For the compilers of *Avot*, "Torah" is more than the Five Books of Moses or even the entire collection of Scripture. It is a body of knowledge that is passed on in a living tradition transmitted by masters to their disciples. In order to acquire knowledge of Torah one must become an apprentice of a Torah Sage, imitate his way of life, and attend to his teachings. While most of the Mishnah explores the halakhic obligations binding upon Jews in general, *Avot* explores the extrahalakhic domain of attitudes, values, inner dispositions, and moods appropriate to a disciple of rabbinic Sages. *Avot* attempts to capture in language what the Sage embodies in his very life.

Relationship to Scripture

Avot quotes widely from the Bible. The quotations of a verse from Proverbs (see 4:19) and Ben Sira (4:4; a book that was not included in the rabbinic canon of Scripture) as the content of a Sage's tradition, are especially curious (see 4:14). Although not a tractate on a topic of law, the laws that are mentioned may be an index of the kind of piety embraced by the editors. These include the festivals (3:11), tithes (1:16; 3:13; 5:8, 9); vows (3:13; 4:18); Seventh Year (5:8, 9), and, surprisingly, sacred offerings (3:11). See also 1:8 (textual notes) and 3:18.

Special Notes for the Reader

The text of chapter 6 (*Qinyan Torah*), which does not appear in the Kaufmann or Parma manuscripts, has been checked against the versions of *Kallah Rabbati*, *Seder Eliyahu Zuta*, and *Avot* as printed in the Vilna edition of the Babylonian Talmud in 1886. The annotations to the text throughout are informed by the late talmudic-period compendium, *Avot of Rabbi Nathan*, other mishnaic and talmudic passages, and, for chapter 6 in particular, on the so-called *gemara* that accompanies *Kallah Rabbati*'s version.

Tractate Avot

Chapter One

1:1–3 *Torah Transmission from Moses Through Antigonus, a Man of Sokho*

I Moses received Torah from Sinai and transmitted it to Joshua.
And Joshua to the elders.
And the elders to the prophets.
And the prophets transmitted it to the members of the Great Assembly
And they taught three things:
(1) Be careful in rendering judgment;
(2) and nurture many disciples;

1:1 The opening passage establishes Moses as the originator of the Torah-study tradition. The principal successors follow in the form of notices that the successors "received" the Torah together with statements given in their names.

Moses received Torah: "Torah," here, is the authoritative instruction by a Master of both the scriptural text and its corresponding oral interpretive tradition. The audience of *Avot* would have understood Torah to include the Written and Oral Torah. This conceptualization of Torah makes its earliest literary appearance in midrashic texts edited by the late third century CE.

Joshua to the elders: An oblique reference to "the elders who extended their days after the death of Joshua" (Joshua 24:31).

elders...to members of the Great Assembly: This list ignores the biblical and postbiblical priesthood as transmitters of the Torah tradition. Individual participants in the Torah lineage may have been priests, such as Simeon the Righteous (1:2) or Yose b. Yoezer (1:4; based on traditions elsewhere), but their priestly status is not mentioned here.

the members of the Great Assembly: Rabbinic historical memory places this group early in the Persian-era postexilic community in the environs of Jerusalem. Compare Nehemiah 10. No ancient writers outside of rabbinic circles mentions a governing council of this name during Persian rule; there may have been a *gerousia* (council of elders) from the era of Ptolemaic and Syrian rule (ca. 220–167 BCE).

three things: The grouping of traditions into sets of three dominates *Avot*'s introductory list of teachings. See *Avot* 5:1–16 for groupings based on the numbers ten, seven, and four.

Be careful in rendering judgment: In the Second Temple period, this judicial role could have been filled by local elders, scribes of the various communities known from the Judaean sectarian landscape, or by official Temple functionaries. By the time of the Mishnah's compilation ca. 220 CE, rabbinic Sages served as judges as well. Cf. 4:7–8.

nurture many disciples: Scribes were cultivated to think of themselves as an elite social class, pursuing a divine calling. One task of the Sage is to direct the disciple in the construction of this new identity.

(3) and create a hedge for the Torah.

2 Simeon the Righteous was among the survivors of the Great Assembly.
He used to teach:
The world exists for the sake of three things—
(1) for the sake of the Torah;
(2) and for the sake of the cult;
(3) and for the sake of reciprocity.

3 Antigonus, a man of Sokho, received from Simeon the Righteous.
He used to teach:
Do not act like servants who attend their Master expecting to receive an allotment.
Rather, act like servants who attend their Master without expecting to receive an allotment.[1]
And may the awe of Heaven subdue you!

[1] **K, P**: "act like servants who attend their Master expecting to receive no allotment."

create a hedge: In the context of *Avot* and the Mishnah as a whole, the metaphor probably refers to a protective barrier of rules and principles that prevent the Torah of Moses from being ignored or violated. Presumably, cultivating this "hedge" would be an essential part of discipleship training. For other implications of "hedge," see 3:13.

1:2 *Simeon the Righteous* is the only high priest to be recalled as a transmitter of rabbinic tradition during the Second Temple period. Talmudic historiography places him in the time of Alexander the Great (336–323 BCE). Nonrabbinic sources refer to a high priest of that name early in the second century BCE.

The world exists: Lit. "stands." Cf. 1:18.

three things: See annotation to 1:1.

the Torah: In its broader sense. See 1:1.

the cult: Lit. "the service." In the Second Temple milieu, this term would imply the sacrificial cult presided over by the Temple priesthood. In the post-Temple era, the meaning of the term extends to the entire life of rabbinic piety, including prayer and Torah study.

reciprocity: Lit. "returning kindness."

1:3 *Antigonus* clarifies the nonpriestly conception of "cultic service" (1:2). What is the proper attitude of the servant whose Master is the Creator of the World? The answer is a simile drawn from the world of indentured servitude, a familiar institution of the Greco-Roman world.

a man of: The term *ish* is probably an honorific, designating a "patron" of the community and not merely a common resident of the town. Most men designated in this way are recalled as predestruction figures who appear only once or twice in mishnaic traditions.

Sokho: See Joshua 15:35.

an allotment: Lit. "a measure (of bread)," as remuneration for a service. The disciple should serve God out of a sense of infinite obligation rather than from a sense of entitlement.

awe of Heaven: Respect for the majesty of God encourages compliance with even the most apparently insignificant commandments. Awe of Heaven is a major virtue cultivated in rabbinic disciple circles (2:2, 3:17, 4:12).

1:4–15 Torah Transmission Through the Pairs

4 Yose b. Yoezer, a man of Tseredah, and Yose b. Yohanan, a man of Jerusalem, received from them.[2]
Yose b. Yoezer says:
Let your home be a gathering place for Sages.
And may you be filthy with the dust of their feet.
And may you thirstily drink in their words.

5 Yose b. Yohanan, a man of Jerusalem, says:
Let your home be open wide for hospitality;
and may the poor be like members of the household;
but do not indulge in idle conversation with a woman.
They said this about a man's own woman[3]—
this applies by inference of lesser and greater the more so to his friend's woman!
For this reason the Sages said:
Whenever a man indulges in idle conversation with the woman[4]
he does harm to himself,
wastes time he could be using to learn Torah,
and, in the end, he will inherit Gehenna.

6 Joshua b. Perahiah and Nittai[5] of Arbel received from them.
Joshua b. Perahiah says:
Appoint for yourself a Master;

---

[2] K, P: "from him." [3] P adds "when she is a menstruant."
[4] K adds "When she is a menstruant." [5] K, P: "Mattai."

1:4–15 In this series, traditions are passed to pairs of Sages. Rabbinic historiography knows this as the period of the "Pairs." A closely related list appears in *Hagigah* 2:2, where one of the pair is said to be *Nasi* (prince, or patriarch; see 2:1, 2) and the other "head of the court."

1:4 *a man of*: See 1:3.

Tseredah: See 1 Kings 11:26.

1:5 *Yose b. Yohanan* picks up the third theme of the teaching of the Great Assembly—reciprocity and generosity.

a woman: Or "a wife."

They said this . . .: An editorial or scribal comment about the danger of intimate socializing with women.

lesser and greater: See 6:3. The addition amplifies the original statement by taking *ha-ishah* there to refer specifically to one's own wife.

idle conversation with the woman: Any woman. The glosses "while she is a menstruant" in the manuscripts (see n. 4) temper the tradition by restricting its application: one need not avoid conversation with *all* women.

Gehenna and its alternative, *Sheol* (see 4:22), designate a kind of postmortem purgatory where departed souls are purified from transgressions committed while embodied.

1:6 *of Arbel*: In contrast to "a man of" (1:3), this expression signals geographical origin. For Arbel see Hosea 10:14, but there were several ancient sites by that name.

Appoint . . . a Master: Lit. "make." A single guide in all his studies. The identical teaching is ascribed to Rabban Gamaliel at 1:16.

acquire for yourself a study partner;
and judge each person more kindly than he deserves.

7 Nittai of Arbel says:
Avoid a bad neighbor;
and do not associate with the wicked;
and do not abandon hope in retributive justice!

8 Judah b. Tabbai and Simeon b. Shatah received from them.
Judah b. Tabbai says:
Do not act like one who advocates.[6]
And when litigants stand before you in a case, assume they are guilty.
But when they are dismissed from court, treat them as innocent,
for they have accepted the judgment upon themselves.

9 Simeon b. Shatah says:
Examine witnesses extensively,
and be careful with your words,
for these might teach them how to lie.

10 Shemaiah and Avtalyon received from them.
Shemaiah says:
Love work,
and hate arrogance,
and do not become a familiar of the civil authority.

11 Avtalyon says:
Sages, choose your words with care!

[6] **P** has *arkhe*, with an aleph.

acquire: Or "create." See 6:10.

a study partner: Hebr. *haver*; here, an intimate codisciple (*Avot of Rabbi Nathan* A).

more kindly than he deserves: Lit. "on the merit side of the scale."

1:7 *bad neighbor...retributive justice*: Second Temple texts such as the Wisdom of Ben Sira offer similar advice.

1:8 Rabbinic tradition associates *Judah b. Tabbai* and especially *Simeon b. Shatah* with the reign of Alexander Jannaeus (103–76 BCE), and his successor, Queen Salome Alexandra (ruled 76–67 BCE). Simeon b. Shatah is traditionally associated with the Pharisees, who, Josephus says, strongly influenced Salome.

one who advocates: When judging, one should avoid prompting witnesses to shade the truth. Alternatively, the expression may mean "a head judge" (taking the reading of **P** to be the Greek word *arkhe*, "head").

1:10 *Shemaiah* and *Avtalyon* may be identical with Pollion the Pharisee and his disciple Samaias who are mentioned by Josephus in connection with events early in the reign of Herod.

Love work: In the context of this passage, physical labor is evidence of humility.

arrogance: Lit. "lordship."

civil authority: Lit. "power." The reference is probably to the Roman government.

1:11 *choose your words with care*: The social context is the circle of disciples (*bet midrash*). This is the first of many teachings in *Avot* that employ the rhetorical features of parable or allegory.

For you might be exiled to a place of evil waters.
And the disciples coming after you might drink and die,
and thus the name of Heaven would be profaned.

12 Hillel and Shammai received from them.
Hillel says:
Be among Aaron's disciples,
loving peace and pursuing peace,
loving humankind and drawing them close to Torah.

13 He used to teach:
Seeking a name, he loses his name.
And whoever does not add detracts.
And whoever does not learn deserves death;[7]
whoever exploits the Crown will come to nothing.

14 He used to teach:
If I'm not mine, who will be mine?

[7] **K** adds "Whoever does not practice [Torah] is worthy of execution."

exiled: Expelled from the circle of discipleship as a consequence of false teachings. Contrast the image of exiling oneself *to* a "place of Torah" (4:14).

to a place of evil waters: The foul waters of corrupted teaching.

disciples…might drink and die: Your own disciples might teach your errors and perpetuate them in their own disciples.

profaned: Lit. "made common," "exhausted of sanctity"; idiomatically "desecrated." Actions arising from false teachings interpreted as Torah would profane God's name.

1:12 *Hillel and Shammai* are presumed to have been active during and shortly after the reign of Herod the Great (37–4 BCE). They are the first figures from *Avot*'s chain of tradition whose legal rulings were formulated for oral transmission elsewhere in the Mishnah. In addition, they are the eponymous founders of "houses" or "schools" whose traditions play a significant role in the Mishnah and elsewhere.

Be among Aaron's disciples: According to a passage in the Tosefta, the foundation of the tradition of Aaron as peacemaker is Malachi 2:6.

loving humankind: Lit. "creatures."

1:13 These and a few other traditions of Hillel are framed in Aramaic instead of the usual Hebrew. Quite possibly these are popular sayings of the folk tradition that came to be ascribed to founding figures in the Pharisaic-rabbinic lineage. This may also explain why many such sayings appear in the mouths of several figures.

Seeking a name, he loses his name: Seeking fame risks losing one's reputation.

whoever does not add detracts: One who is not expanding his knowledge of Torah is perforce losing it.

whoever does not learn deserves death: If one separates from Torah, "the Tree of Life" (Proverbs 3:11), one might as well die.

whoever exploits the Crown of Torah (see 4:5, R. Zadok).

1:14 The editor resumes the practice of arranging teachings in triplets.

If I'm not mine: The aphorism has an echo in the first-century CE Stoic philosopher, Epictetus. The *Avot of Rabbi Nathan* paraphrases the triplet: "If I do not acquire merit in this life, who will acquire it for me? If I do not acquire merit on my own, what is my merit worth? If I do not acquire merit during my life, who will acquire it after my death?"

But when I am mine, what am I?
And if not at this moment, when?

15 Shammai says:
Make your Torah study a discipline.
Say little, but do much.
And greet everyone with a cheerful expression.

1:16–2:7 *Torah Transmission in the Gamalielian Lineage*

16 Rabban Gamaliel says:
Appoint for yourself a Master.
And rise beyond doubt.
And do not tithe by too much guesswork.

17 Simeon, his son, says:
I have grown up among Sages my entire life,
and I have found that nothing benefits a body more than silence;
and deeds are the main thing, not interpretation;
and whoever chatters on invites sin.

18 Rabban Simeon b. Gamaliel says:

1:15 *your Torah study*: Lit. "your Torah."

a discipline: Lit. "fixed."

1:16 A new lineage tradition emanating from the politically influential family of Gamaliel (1:16–2:4) interrupts the list of successors to Moses through Hillel and Shammai (1:1–15; 2:8–16). Members of this family were part of the Jerusalem aristocracy of the late Second Temple period, and the rabbinic Patriarchs traced their lineage from them.

Rabban: This title seems to indicate honor and communal leadership. It is normally restricted to figures in the Gamalielian lineage; Rabban Yohanan b. Zakkai (2:8) is an exception. *Rabban Gamaliel* "the Elder" is the son or grandson of Hillel in later rabbinic historiography; he is also mentioned in the Acts of the Apostles.

Appoint for yourself a Master: See 1:6 (Joshua b. Perahiah).

rise beyond doubt: Apprentice yourself to a Master of rabbinic Torah.

And do not tithe by too much guesswork: According to biblical and rabbinic law agricultural offerings (tithes) must be removed from crops raised by Jews in the Land of Israel (see *Ma'aserot* and *Ma'aser Sheni*). While tithes separated by estimation ("guesswork") are permitted, the practice is here discouraged (see *Terumot* 4:6). Instruction in the proper method of tithing is one of the doubts resolved by acquiring a Master.

1:17 *Simeon, his son*: A principal figure in Pharisaic circles prior to and during the war against Rome (66–73 CE).

nothing benefits a body: Idiomatically "a person."

interpretation: Heb. *midrash*. Compare "say little but do much" (Shammai, 1:15).

chatters on: Lit. "multiplies words." This applies not only to conversations with women (1:5), but presumably in all social settings, including the discipleship circle.

1:18 *Rabban Simeon b. Gamaliel* is probably the grandson of the previous authority of the same name. He is recalled as among those who reconstructed rabbinic learning after the Bar Kokhba rebellion. *Avot* apparently omits Rabban Simeon's father, Rabban Gamaliel II, who succeeded Rabban Yohanan b. Zakkai as the main figure of the Yavnean disciple community at the end of the first century CE.

The world exists[8] for the sake of three things—
(1) for the sake of judgment;
(2) and for the sake of truth;
(3) and for the sake of peace.
As it is said: *Truth, justice, and peace shall establish you in your gates.*[9]

Chapter Two

2 Rabbi says:
Which is the virtuous path a person should choose for himself?
Whichever a person respects and draws respect from others.
And be as diligent about a minor commandment as you are about a major commandment,
for you cannot know the reward of a commandment.
And you should calculate the cost of a commandment against its reward, and the reward of a transgression against its cost.
And if you consider three things, you will not fall into transgression:
Know what is above you—
(1) an eye that sees;
(2) and an ear that hears;
(3) and all your actions are written in a book.

[8] **K, P**: "is sustained."   [9] **K, P** lack the prooftext; added in **K** by a second hand.

The world exists: Compare 1:2. The manuscripts read *qayam*, "is sustained," here (see n. 8). The distinction is between those activities that justify the creation of the world (*omed*) and those forces necessary to sustain the world's operation (*qayam*) once it has been brought into being.

judgment: That is, judicial impartiality.

truth: Fair and honest dealings.

peace: In the heavenly and earthly realms.

Truth, justice, and peace shall establish you: Zechariah 8:16.

establish you: Lit. "shall you establish." The verse is read to mean that these virtues will sustain the community even as the community works to embody them.

2:1 R. Judah the Patriarch was the son of Rabban Simeon b. Gamaliel II (1:18). By tradition the editor of the Mishnah, his impact upon rabbinic tradition is so great that he is simply referred to as *Rabbi*, "my master." The editor of our tractate honors Rabbi with three thematically distinct teachings, mirroring the prestige accorded to Hillel (1:12–14).

Which is the virtuous path: Lit. "straight," but also "upright." Cf. 2:9.

the reward of a commandment: The divine calculation of reward and punishment is beyond human knowledge. The best attitude, then, is to put a full effort into every commandment for which one is obligated.

a book: The book that will be opened in the eschatological future.

2 Rabban Gamaliel, the son of R. Judah the Patriarch, says:
Torah study goes best with a worldly occupation,
for labor in both blots out the thought of wickedness.
And any Torah study unaccompanied by work will eventually be wasted
and arouse wickedness.
And all who toil for the community should toil for the sake of Heaven—
for the merits of their ancestors works in their favor,
and their righteousness stands forever.
And as for you, I ascribe a reward for you as if you had done it all by yourself!
 3 Be cautious of the civil authority,
for they only get close to people for ulterior motives.
They appear friendly when the hour benefits them,
but they do not stand by a person at the hour of his crisis.
 4 He used to teach:
Do His will as if it were your will,
so that He does your will as if it were His will.
Nullify your will before His will,
so that He nullifies the will of others before your will.
Hillel[10] says:
Do not withdraw from the community.
And do not trust yourself until the day you die.
And do not judge your friend until you reach his place.
And do not say a thing that should not be heard[11]—

[10] **K, P**, and others: "R. Hillel."
[11] Prior to emendation **K** reads "a thing that should be heard."

2:2 Rabban Gamaliel (III), *the son of R. Judah the Patriarch*: Apparently, the latest authority to appear in *Avot*'s first five original chapters (but see 2:4). Like his father, and Hillel before him, he is here honored with the distribution of his teaching among three distinct passages (2:2–4).

a worldly occupation: Lit. "way of the world." The term has a wide semantic range in rabbinic literature, including "a trade," "proper etiquette," and "sexual relations." Here, the first meaning seems most appropriate. The ideal Torah scholar is self-sufficient and capable of supporting his studies by his labor. Compare 3:5 (R. Nehuniah b. ha-Qanah). For an example of the second meaning, see 3:17.

Torah . . . unaccompanied by work: See 1.10. Not only is Torah study improved by labor, but Torah study without labor will itself weaken the character.

for the sake of Heaven: Communal leaders should abandon self-interest in service of the interests of the community. For an application of this term to purely interpersonal relations, see 2:12.

And as for you: A congratulatory statement ascribed to God promising communal leaders reward even for work that could not be completed. See also 2:16.

2:3 Continues the charge to those who labor for the community. Compare 1:10 (Shemaiah).

2:4 *Avot* now returns the tradition history back to its crucial Herodian-era hero. This draws in its wake four further teachings (2:5–7) that link Hillel to Rabban Yohanan b. Zakkai (2:8). The alternative reading, "R. Hillel" (see n. 10) would refer to the fourth-century Patriarch, Hillel II. This would make him the latest figure mentioned in chapters 1 through 5 of *Avot*.

do not withdraw from the community: Lit. "do not separate from."

do not say a thing that should not be heard, for in the end it will be heard: Perhaps a counsel against gossip. Some commentaries construe "be heard" as "be understood" and see here the reassurance that the most difficult teachings of Torah will eventually be explicated and grasped.

for in the end it will be heard.
And do not say, "When I have time I will learn"—
for you may not have time.

5 He used to teach:
A coarse person has no fear of sin;
and an ignorant person cannot be pious;
and a shy person cannot learn;
and an impatient person cannot teach;
and not everyone who amasses capital is thoughtful;
and where there are no people, engage yourself in becoming a person.

6 Also, once he saw a certain skull floating in the water.
He said to it:
Because you drowned others, they drowned you,
and in the end those who drowned you will be drowned.

7 He used to teach:
More flesh? More maggots!
More property? More worry![12]
More wives? More bewitching!
More maidservants? More immorality!
More manservants? More theft![13]
More Torah? More life![14]
More study? More wisdom!
More advice? More insight![15]
More charity? More peace!

---

[12] K, P: "More property? More litigation!"   [13] K lists "more wives" after "more manservants."
[14] K lacks "more study," "more advice," and "more charity."   [15] P: "More advice? More courage!"

2:5 Hillel lists five traits of mind that impede the pursuit of five principal virtues. The sixth teaching summarizes the foregoing.

an ignorant person: Heb. *am ha'arets*. Lit. "a peasant" (as in Ezra 9:11, Nehemiah 9:30). In mishnaic idiom it denotes a Jew who fails to observe the laws of tithing properly, cf. 1:16.

cannot be pious: Without rabbinic discipleship training, true piety is impossible.

not everyone who amasses capital is thoughtful: Presumably, a person immersed in trade has neither time nor desire to learn Torah.

and where there are no people: Even if all around you lack virtue, you can embody virtue yourself. *People*: Lit. "men." The passage is possibly to be read as a comment about true masculinity.

2:6 The teaching is in the form of a *chreia*, a Greco-Roman rhetorical device in which a brief narrative sets the context for a trenchant observation. The content here is likely a bit of proverbial folk wisdom to the effect that "what goes around comes around."

Because you drowned others: A vivid illustration of the rabbinic principle of divine justice: "measure for measure" (cf. 4:9, 5:8–9). See comments to 1:13 and 5:22–23.

2:7 Hillel's final teaching in this series consists of two perfectly balanced lists in the pattern "the more X, the more Y." The two lists contrast with one another.

More flesh, etc.: Five principal signs of this-worldly well-being all carry the seeds of death or decay within them.

More Torah…More study, etc.: By contrast, Torah, and the virtues proceeding from its study, all carry with them this-worldly benefits.

He acquired a good name? He acquired it for himself!
He acquired Torah? He acquired for himself the life of the World to Come.

2:8–14 Transmission to Rabban Yohanan b. Zakkai and His Disciples

8 Rabban Yohanan b. Zakkai received from Hillel and from Shammai.
He used to teach:
If you have learned much Torah, do not think too highly of yourself,
for this is why you were created!
Rabban Yohanan b. Zakkai had five disciples.
And they are:
(1)   R. Eliezer b. Hyrcanus;
(2)   R. Joshua b. Hananiah;
(3)   R. Yose the Priest;[16]
(4)   R. Simeon b. Nathaniel;
(5)   and R. Eleazar b. Arakh.
And this is how he would recount their praises:
R. Eliezer b. Hyrcanus: A plastered cistern that does not lose a drop!
R. Joshua b. Hananiah: How fortunate is his mother!
R. Yose the Priest: A model of piety!
R. Simeon b. Nathaniel: He fears sin!
And R. Eleazar b. Arakh: An overflowing fountain!
He used to teach:
If all the Sages of Israel were on one pan of a scale,
and Eliezer b. Hyrcanus were on the other,
he would outweigh them all!

---

[16] **K**: "R. Joseph"; "the Priest" is added by a second hand. Yose is the diminutive form of Joseph.

He acquired: This concluding coda follows the form of the primary list, but abandons the symmetry of elements.

World to Come refers primarily to life after the resurrection and eschatological judgment. See 2:14, 2:16, 3:1, 3:11, 4:16–17. Compare Gehenna at 1:5 and Sheol at 4:22.

2:8 *Rabban Yohanan b. Zakkai received from Hillel and from Shammai*: The formula of transmission that dominates 1:2–14 (*X received from Y*) skips over the Gamalielian lineage (1:15–2:4) and resumes with Rabban Yohanan b. Zakkai. In later rabbinic historiography, he is assigned an essential role in the founding of the academy of Yavneh. Elsewhere, the Mishnah places Rabban Yohanan in the direct lineage of Torah traditions from Sinai, although without mentioning Hillel and Shammai (e.g. *Eduyot* 8:7, *Yadayim* 4:3).

this is why you were created: Torah study brings the disciple to the highest form of human perfection.

five disciples: The description of the Torah lineage transmitted to his primary disciples occupies most of the remainder of our chapter (2:9–14). The number is conventional.

A plastered cistern: R. Eliezer forgot none of the Torah he had learned.

A model of piety: Lit. "pious" (Heb. *hasid*).

An overflowing fountain: The sources of his teaching never run dry.

Abba Saul said in his name:
If all the Sages of Israel were on one pan of a scale,
and R. Eliezer b. Hyrcanus were with them, but R. Eleazar were on the other,
he would outweigh them all!

9 He said to them:
Go out and discover
which is the straight[17] path a person should follow.
R. Eliezer says: A good eye!
R. Joshua says: A good fellow!
R. Yose says: A good neighbor!
R. Simeon says: The sense to see what is coming!
R. Eleazar says: A good mind!
He said to them:
I prefer the words of Eleazar b. Arakh,
for in his words are your words included.
He said to them:
Go out and discover which is the evil path a person should avoid.
R. Eliezer says: An evil eye!
R. Joshua says: An evil fellow!
R. Yose[18] says: An evil neighbor!
R. Simeon says: One who borrows and does not repay!
One who borrows from people is like one who borrows
from the Omnipresent, blessed be He,

[17] K, P: "good."   [18] K: "Joseph."

Abba Saul said in his name: Abba Saul offers a version of Rabban Yohanan's praise that singles out R. Eleazar b. Arakh, rather than R. Eliezer b. Hyrcanus, as the foremost disciple. This may reflect conflict in later generations over the succession to Rabban Yohanan.

2:9 The Master asks a pair of starkly dichotomous questions and the disciples' answers reflect this, balancing a virtuous ("good") trait against its corresponding vice ("evil"). The responses of R. Simeon are an exception.

which is the straight path…evil path: The questions ask about styles of life rather than a personality trait or a specific virtue or vice (as in e.g. 5:10–15).

A good eye…An evil eye: A generous spirit devoid of envy as opposed to a jealous spirit. Here and at 2:11, *an evil eye* is a metaphor for jealousy. Elsewhere, "*the* evil eye" (*ayin hara*) is a kind of curse that has its source in envy of another's good fortune.

A good fellow…An evil fellow: The word *haver* can imply a fellow disciple (1:6). Thus: be a disciple in order to have a good fellow disciple.

The sense to see what is coming: Lit. "who sees what emerges."

A good mind…An evil mind: Lit. "a good/evil heart." The heart is understood here as the seat of intellectual and moral faculties as opposed to the passions.

One who borrows: Psalms 37:21. The scriptural verse is construed to imply that it is God himself who makes good on bad loans. Thus one who fails to repay a debt might as well be stealing from God.

the Omnipresent, blessed be He: This common rabbinic divine epithet literally means "the Place" (cf. 2:13, 3:3, 3:10, 3:14). Its theological usage in Judaism is documented in Greco-Jewish literature in the first century CE.

as it is said:
An evil person borrows but does not repay, but the righteous one is generous in giving.
R. Eleazar says: An evil mind!
He said to them: I prefer the words of Eleazar b. Arakh,
for your words are included in his words.

10 Each taught three things.
R. Eliezer says:
Let your fellow's honor be as precious to you as your own.[19]
And do not be easily angered.
And repent one day before you die.
And warm yourself in the fire of the Sages,
but beware of being burned by their coals!
For they bite like foxes, sting like scorpions, hiss like serpents,
and all their words are like fiery cinders![20]

11 R. Joshua says:
The evil eye,[21] the evil desire, and hatred of people
drive a person from the world.

12 R. Yose[22] says:
Let your fellow's property be as precious to you as your own;
and discipline yourself to study Torah, for it is not your birthright;
and may all your actions be for the sake of Heaven.

---

[19] **K**: "as your own soul." **K**'s glossator adds "as your own" as "another version."
[20] Some commentators delete "but beware…cinders" as an addition. It is present in Version A of *Avot of Rabbi Nathan*, but not Version B.
[21] **K**: "An evil eye."
[22] **K**: "R. Joseph."

An evil person: Psalms 37:21

I prefer: Lit. "I see."

2:10 *Each taught three things*: The traditions extend to 2:14. R. Eliezer is assigned four traditions.

Let your fellow's honor: The identical teaching is ascribed to R. Eleazar b. Shammua at 4:12 where it is the first of three teachings. Cf. 2:12, where "property" replaces "honor."

repent one day before you die: Lit. "return (to the correct path)."

And warm yourself: An unusually sharp observation about the dangers of associating with Sages.

2:11 One tripartite teaching, rather than three distinct teachings. *The evil eye*: Better "an evil eye" as at 2:9 (see n. 21). *The evil desire*: The source of desire. Normally expressed as the urge to trespass limits established by the commandments (*Avot of Rabbi Nathan* A 16; cf. Romans 7:21–25), the evil desire can also be figured as the source of human creativity. See 4:1 and 4:22.

2:12 *Let your fellow's property*: Cf. 2:10.

for it is not your birthright: The disanalogy is to land, which one can inherit without working or living on it. In contrast, Torah can be an inheritance only to one who labors in it.

for the sake of Heaven: Cf. 2:2.

13 R. Simeon says:
Be very careful in reciting the *Shema* and the Prayer;[23]
and when you pray, do not make it a rote practice,
rather, an appeal for graciousness and compassion[24]
from the Omnipresent, blessed be He,
as it is said:
For He is compassionate and gracious, patient and generous, renouncing evil;
and do not consider yourself wicked!

14 R. Eleazar says:
Be diligent to study Torah;[25]
and know how to respond to an *apiqoros*;
and know before whom you labor,
for your employer can be trusted to pay you exactly what your work is worth.[26]

2:15–16 *Teachings of R. Tarfon*

15 R. Tarfon says:
The day is short, the work is heavy, and the workers are lazy—
but the pay is great, and the householder is in a hurry!

16 He used to teach:
It is not up to you to finish the work,

---

[23] K lacks "the Prayer."   [24] K lacks "and compassion."
[25] K, P lack "Torah," merging this clause and the following.
[26] P and K replace this clause with "and who is your employer."

2:13 *the Shema*: The twice-daily liturgical recitation of Deuteronomy 6:4–9, 11:13–17, and Numbers 15:37–41. See *Berakhot* chapters 1–3. For the Prayer (n. 23) see *Berakhot* 4–5.

a rote practice…an appeal for graciousness: Lit. "do not make it fixed; rather make it graciousness…" Cf. *Berakhot* 4:4.

the Omnipresent, blessed be He: See 2:9.

For He is compassionate: Joel 2:13.

do not consider yourself wicked: Excessive self-criticism engenders despair of the power of repentance to repair the divine-human relationship. Compare 4:17.

2:14 *Torah; and know*: See n. 25. The words are required to bring the number of teachings to three.

apiqoros: This is probably an Aramaicized form of the Greek name *Epikouros*, for "disciple of Epicurus." In early rabbinic literature the epithet is usually applied to Jews who publicly defy the authority of the Sages.

for your employer: The phrase upsets the schematic of three teachings and seems to have been added to establish a thematic connection to R. Tarfon's teaching at 2:16. See n. 26.

2:15 *The day is short*: The parable compares Torah study by analogy to physical labor. Compare Hippocrates, *Aphorisms* 1.1, on the difficulty of mastering medical knowledge: "Life is short, the art long, the opportunity fleeting, the experiment treacherous, and the crisis of the disease dangerous."

is in a hurry: The accounting of the reward in the World to Come is imminent.

2:16 *not up to you to finish*: As the wisdom of Torah is infinite, no one can plumb its depths.

but you are not free to give it up.
And if you have learned much Torah, you will get a great reward,
for[27] your employer can be trusted to pay you exactly what your work is worth.
And know this: the reward of the righteous is in the World to Come.[28]

Chapter Three

3:1–2 *Teachers of the Predestruction Generation*

3 Aqaviah b. Mahalalel says:
Contemplate three things and you will not fall into the clutches of transgression:
Know (1) from where you came;
(2) and toward what you are headed;
(3) and before whom you will eventually give an account of yourself.
From where did you come?
A stinking drop!
And toward what are you headed?
To the place of dust, the worm, and the maggot!
And before whom will you eventually give an accounting?
Before the King of Kings of Kings, the Blessed Holy One!
  2 R. Hananiah,[29] the Prefect of the Priests, says:
Pray for the well-being of the Empire,

[27] "You...for" does not appear in **K**.
[28] Statement does not appear in **K**, **P** or *Avot of Rabbi Nathan B*.
[29] So **K, P**; ed. Vilna: "Hanina." The names are easily confused, as in R. Hananiah/Hanina b. Teradion below.

not free to give it up: Nevertheless, it is up to the disciple to make the effort.

your employer: Lit. "the master of your labor," God.

the reward...in the World to Come: See 2:7, and *Pe'ah* 1:1.

3:1–4:5 Compositionally, 3:1–2 opens a lengthy parenthesis, closing at 4:5, in which a collection of "Yavnean" traditions (3:2–4:4), ascribed to the post-70 CE era when traditionally the center of the rabbinic movement was at the coastal town of Yavneh (see *Ketubbot* 4.7; *Eduyot* 2.6), is framed at either end by traditions of predestruction teachers.

3:1 *Aqaviah b. Mahalalel*: See *Eduyot* 5:6–7, including the tradition of his banishment. His teaching about human destiny dovetails with R. Tarfon's emphasis on the promise of the World to Come (2:16).

King of Kings of Kings: The epithet is a polemical allusion to the Roman imperial cult. If the Roman emperor is the "King of Kings" (a title adopted by the king of Persia) then the God of Israel is the "King of Kings of Kings."

3:2 *Prefect of the Priests*: See *Yoma* 7:2, *Tamid* 7:3.

Pray for the well-being of the Empire: See Jeremiah 29:7: "pray for the well-being of the city to which I have exiled you." The current conquering city is Rome.

but for the fear of it,
people would eat each other alive.

3:2 cont.–18: *Yavnean Masters in the Lineage of R. Yohanan b. Zakkai and R. Aqiva*

R. Hananiah b. Teradion says:
Two who are sitting without words of Torah between them—
this is indeed the *seat of the mockers*,
as it is said: *And he did not sit in the seat of the mockers.*
But, two who are sitting and sharing words of Torah—
they encounter the divine Presence between them,
as it is said:
Then those in awe of the Lord spoke with each other,
and the Lord attended and heard,
and the Book of Remembrance was written before him,
for those in Awe of the Lord and those contemplate his name.
From this I learn about only two people.
How do I know that even one who sits and engages in Torah,
the Blessed Holy One grants him a reward?
For it is said:
One who sits alone and meditates in silence, it is placed upon him.[30]
   3 R. Simeon says:
Three who ate at a single table and did not share words of Torah—
it is as if they have eaten sacrifices for the dead,
as it is said: *For all tables are full of vomit and filth, there is no place.*
But if three ate at a single table and shared words of Torah—

---

[30] Lacking in **K**, **P**.

---

people…alive: The phrase uses biblical language and syntax.

3:2-18 Nearly all of the Sages quoted here were disciples of Rabban Yohanan b. Zakkai or of R. Aqiva.

3:2 *seat of the mockers*: Psalms 1:1.

the divine Presence: Heb. *shekhinah*. This epithet for God stresses divine intimacy as opposed to, e.g. the *Omnipresent*, which stresses ontological primacy.

those in awe: Malachi 3.16, is taken to refer to God's Presence ("the Lord attended and heard") among those who meditate and discourse upon Torah ("those in awe…spoke with each other"), namely disciples.

One who sits: Lamentations 3:28. *It is placed upon him*: "It" is implied in the Hebrew and taken in reference to God's granting of a reward to the individual.

3:3 The form and substance of this teaching here are continuous with 3:2 (R. Hananiah b. Teradion).

For all tables: Isaiah 28:8. The Mishnah places the "tables" in a sacrificial context; by implication, the meal shared by disciples is sacrificial as well. *No place*: The tradition mobilizes this scriptural prooftext in service of a pun. The word *maqom* ("place") is identical to the divine epithet, *ha-maqom*, "Omnipresent." Without the presence of God, as invoked in words of Torah, the table is defiled.

it is as if they ate at the table of the Omnipresent, blessed be He,
as it is said: *And he said to me, this is the table that is before the Lord.*

4 R. Hanina b. Hakhinai says:
One who awakens at night,
or one who walks in isolated[31] paths,
or one who turns his thoughts to trivialities—
indeed, he brings disaster upon himself.

5 R. Nehuniah b. ha-Qanah says:
All who accept upon themselves the yoke of Torah study
are released from the yoke of the kingdom and the yoke of a worldly occupation.
But all who unburden themselves of the yoke of Torah study
are burdened with the yoke of the kingdom and the yoke of a worldly occupation.

6 R. Halafta, a man of Kefar Hananiah, says:
If ten sit and engage in Torah study—
the divine Presence will descend upon them,
as it is said: *God is present in the congregation of God.*
How do we know this applies even to five?
As it is said: *He has established his bundle on the earth.*[32]
How do we know this applies even to three?
As it is said: *Among God He shall render judgment.*[33]
How do we know this applies even to two?
As it is said: *Then those in awe of the Lord spoke with each other,*

[31] Lacking in **K, P**. [32] **K, P** have Psalm 82:1. [33] **K, P** have Amos 9:6.

the Omnipresent, blessed be He: See 2:9n.

And he said to me: Ezekiel 41:22.

3:4 *he brings disaster upon himself*: Literally, "he is obliged to forfeit his soul." The references seem to be to forms of ritual practice rejected by rabbis.

3:5 Contrast this tradition with 1:10; 2:2.

yoke of the kingdom: Perhaps, political leadership.

worldly occupation: See 2:2.

3:6 *R. Halafta* is later than most of the Sages included here. In view of the similarity in topic and form to 3:2–4, the tradition may have been included out of mnemonic and thematic considerations.

a man of: See comment on 1:3.

divine Presence: See 3:2.

God (Elohim) *is present*: Psalms 82:1. *Congregation of God*: The exegesis assumes that a "congregation" consists of a minimum of ten, e.g. *Sanhedrin* 1:6.

He has established: Amos 9:6. The prooftext for this and the next clause are reversed in important witnesses (see n. 32). *His bundle*: In the context of the verse, "his vault."

Among God: Psalms 82:1. Here, as elsewhere, the plural *Elohim* is taken as a reference to a court of human scholars, of which the minimum number is three members.

Then those in awe of the Lord spoke with each other: Malachi 3:16. A two-way conversation invoking God's response.

and the Lord attended and heard, etc.
How do we know this applies even to one?
As it is said: *In every place I hear my name mentioned*
I will come to you and bring you blessings.

7 R. Eleazar,[34] a man of Bartota, says:
Give Him what is His, for you and yours are His.
And this is what it says in connection with David:
For everything comes from You, and from Your very hand do we give You offerings.
R. Simeon[35] says:
One who is going along repeating traditions,
and he breaks off his repetition, exclaiming:
"How lovely is this tree! How lovely is this furrow!"—
Scripture regards him[36] as if he brings disaster upon himself.

8 R. Dostai b. R. Yannai in the name of R. Meir says:
Any who forgets a single lesson from his repetition—
Scripture regards him as if he brings disaster upon himself,
as it is said:
Only be careful and preserve your soul, lest you forget these words
that your eyes have seen.
Is it possible that this applies even if his repetition overwhelms him?
The teaching says: *Lest these things pass from your mind all the days of your life.*

---

[34] **K, P** add "b. Judah."   [35] **K, P**: "R. Jacob."
[36] Here and at 3:8, **P** and **K** have "they regard him." The terms are interchangeable.

In every place . . . I will come to you (sing.) *and bring you* (sing.) *blessings*: Exodus 20:21.

3:7 *a man of*: See 1:3.

Give Him what is His, for you and yours are His: Compare Gospel of John 17:9–10.

For everything comes from You: 1 Chronicles 29:14.

Simeon: Alternatively, "Jacob." See n. 35. R. Simeon b. Yohai was traditionally a disciple of R. Aqiva, one generation later than the "Yavnean" period. "Jacob" could be the Yavnean Jacob b. Qorshai (see 4:16) and might be the preferable reading.

repeating traditions: Reciting oral traditions to fix them in memory. See 3:8.

his repetition: Lit. "his mishnah."

Scripture regards him: Avot 3:8 will inform us that the relevant verse is Deuteronomy 4:9.

brings disaster: See 3.4. Interrupting oral recitation in order to appreciate the visible world risks forgetting Torah and, thus, losing its worldly and otherworldly rewards.

3:8 *R. Dostai*. Another late figure included among earlier Sages. This tradition is closely connected to that of R. Simeon at 3:7. The sayings in *Avot* 3:8–10 share a common basic pattern of formulation.

Only be careful: Deuteronomy 4:9.

even if his repetition overwhelms him? This anonymous addendum softens the catastrophic implications imagined by R. Simeon and R. Dostai.

The teaching says: Heb. *Talmud lomar*, lit. "the study text states." A midrashic formula for introducing a prooftext from Scripture.

Lest these things pass: Deuteronomy 4:9.

Thus, disaster will not befall him
unless he intentionally dismisses them from his mind.

9 R. Hanina b. Dosa says:
Any whose fear of sin precedes his wisdom—
his wisdom will endure.
But any whose wisdom precedes his fear of sin—
his wisdom will not endure.
He used to teach:
Any whose deeds exceed his wisdom—
his wisdom will endure.
But any whose wisdom exceeds his deeds—
his wisdom will not endure.

10 He used to teach:
Any in whom the spirit of people takes pleasure—
the spirit of the Omnipresent takes pleasure in him.
But any in whom the spirit of people takes no pleasure—
the spirit of the Omnipresent takes no pleasure in him.[37]
R. Dosa b. Harqinas says:
Morning sleep, noontime wine, childish talk,
and loitering at the gathering houses[38] of the ignorant
drive a person from the world.

11 R. Eleazar of Modi'in says:
One who profanes sacred offerings,
or one who demeans the festivals,
or one who shames[39] his friend in public,
or one who voids the covenant of Father Abraham,

---

[37] Clause missing in **K**, and added in the margin.   [38] **K**, **P**: "gatherings."
[39] Hebrew, *ha-malbin*, "causes pallor"; **K**: *ha-ma'adim*, "causes blushing." Absent in **P**.

3:9 *R. Hanina b. Dosa*: In other traditions, a miracle worker. See *Berakhot* 5:5, *Sotah* 9.15 (a postmishnaic addition). Retention of wisdom is contingent upon either the psychological condition of awe of God or the behavioral condition of performing commandments.

3:10 *Omnipresent*: See 2:9.

Morning sleep: The disciple should greet the dawn with the morning *Shema* and prayer.

noontime wine: Wine disrupts the ability and desire to spend the day in Torah study.

loitering: Lit. "sitting." This sitting contrasts with "sitting" for the study of Torah, 2:7. These "gatherings" (see n. 38; perhaps "synagogues") are, therefore, the mirror opposite of the gatherings of the disciples.

ignorant: Heb. *amme ha'arets*, see 2:4.

from the world: The only world that matters, that of the disciple circle.

3:11 *profanes sacred offerings*: An animal designated by its owner for a sacrifice can no longer be used in any way that benefits the former owner, for example, as a beast of burden.

demeans the festivals: The reference is to the intermediate days of the festivals of Sukkot (Booths) and Pesah (Passover). These are neither entirely profane nor entirely holy days of rest (see *Mo'ed Qatan*, introduction).

voids the covenant: Neglect of, or possibly surgical concealment of, circumcision.

or one who discloses aspects of the Torah against accepted legal tradition[40]—
even if he possesses Torah study and commandments—
he has no share in the World to Come.

12   R. Ishmael says:
Hasten to[41] superiors;
and be fair to[42] subordinates;
and greet everyone with joy.

13   R. Aqiva says:
Laughter and silliness accustom a person to lewdness.
Tradition[43] is a hedge for the Torah;
tithes are a hedge for wealth;[44]
vows are a hedge for self-control;
the hedge for wisdom is silence.

14   He used to teach:
Beloved is Adam, having been created in the image.
And even more beloved is he,
in that it was disclosed to him that he is created in the image,
as it is said: *In the image of God He made the Adam.*[45]
Beloved is Israel, having been called children of the Omnipresent.
And even more beloved are they,

---

[40] K, P lack "against the tradition."   [41] K, P lack "to."   [42] K, P lack "to."
[43] Hebrew: *masoret*. K: "tithes," *ma'aserot*; P: "traditions," *mesorot*.   [44] Absent in K.
[45] Prooftext lacking in K, and added in the margin.

---

discloses: Interprets and teaches the Torah "against the grain" of its traditional rabbinic meanings. See n. 40. Following the manuscripts: "One who acts insolently towards the Torah" (lit. "reveals the face").

no share in the World to Come: See *Sanhedrin* 10:1.

3:12 *Hasten to superiors*: Lit. "Be quick (or light) to the head."

fair to subordinates: Lit. "Be easy to the black-haired" (i.e. the young).

greet everyone with joy: Cf. 1:15 (Shammai); 4:15 (R. Matia b. Heresh).

3:13 *R. Aqiva*: After Rabban Yohanan b. Zakkai, the major figure in "Yavnean" circles.

silliness: Lit. "light-headedness." This is similar to R. Ishmael's expression in 3:12, with a different meaning.

Tradition: The traditional orthography and vocalization of the scriptural text. However, see n. 43. *Hedge* links R. Aqiva to the members of the Great Assembly, 1:1.

tithes: The payment of agricultural offerings ensures the fertility of the fields and herds.

vows: Vows to prohibit oneself from benefiting from even permitted pleasures aid in developing abstinence. But see 4:18.

the hedge for wisdom is silence: See also 1:17.

3:14 Three teachings built upon an identical mnemonic formula.

Adam: The reference is clearly to humanity as a whole. See also *Sanhedrin* 4:5.

In the image: Genesis 9:6.

the Omnipresent: See 2:9.

in that it was disclosed to them that they are called children of the Omnipresent,
as it is said: *You are children of the Lord your God.*
Beloved is Israel, having been given a desirable[46] tool.[47]
And even more beloved are they,
in that it was disclosed to them that they had been given a desirable[48] tool
through which the world was created,
as it is said: *For a good teaching have I given you, My Torah, do not abandon it.*[49]

15 Everything is foreseen, yet choice is still possible;
and for good is the world judged;
and everything depends on the majority of actions.

16 He used to teach:
Everything is given for collateral,
and a snare is spread over all living things.
The shop is open, and the shopkeeper is keeping accounts;
the account book is open, and the hand is writing;
anyone who wants to borrow may borrow,[50]
and the collectors make their rounds each day;
they collect from a person whether he agrees or not,
and they have plenty of proof;[51]
the judgment is a true one,
and everything is prepared for the meal.

17 R. Eleazar b. Azariah says:
Without Torah there is no decency, without decency there is no Torah,

---

[46] K lacks "desirable." [47] K, P add here "through which the world was created."
[48] K lacks "desirable." [49] Prooftext lacking in K, and added in the margin.
[50] K, P lack this clause. [51] K lacks this clause.

You are children: Deuteronomy 14:1.

tool through which the world was created: For Torah as a cosmogonic agent compare Philo of Alexandria and the *logos*/Word in Gospel of John. The theme is further developed in later rabbinic literature.

a good teaching: Proverbs 4:2. The Mishnah reads this as "an acquisition" or "a good."

3:15 *for good is the world judged*: i.e. mercifully.

the majority of actions: Whether good or evil, they are all totaled up and figure in the judgment.

3:16 *Everything is given for collateral*: Everything may be claimed by the creditor, God.

a snare is spread over all living things: All are at risk of unexpected death and punishment.

shopkeeper…account book: God expects eventual payment of the debt. Cf. 2:1. For shopkeeper as creditor see *Bava Metsiʿa* 3:11; *Shevuʿot* 7:5.

the collectors: The troubles of life, or perhaps divine emissaries, exact their punishment.

have plenty of proof: See n. 51. They can document the exaction of the security.

prepared for the meal: A heavenly banquet, after all are judged.

3:17 *R. Eleazar b. Azariah*: Elsewhere connected with R. Aqiva and Rabban Gamaliel II. The tradition provides pairs of mutually dependent principles.

decency: "The way of the world," see 2:2. Here, context demands rendering as "moral decency" rather than as "pursuit of a livelihood" (see below). Torah is a complete pedagogical system that mediates its moral values through behaviors learned via emulation of acknowledged Masters.

Without wisdom there is no awe, without awe there is no wisdom.
Without discernment there is no knowledge, without knowledge there is no discernment.
Without flour there is no Torah, without Torah there is no flour.
He used to teach:
Anyone whose wisdom exceeds his deeds, what is he like?
He is like a tree with many branches and few roots.
And the wind will come to uproot and overturn it,
as it is said:
He shall be like a bush in the desert, not knowing that good is coming;
and it dwells in a scorched wilderness, a parched land, and uninhabited.[52]
But anyone whose deeds exceed his wisdom, what is he like?
He is like a tree with few branches and many roots.
For even if all the winds in the world come upon it, they will not uproot it from its place,
as it is said:
And he shall be like a tree planted near water,
spreading its roots toward the stream,
not knowing that heat is coming; and its leaves will be green,
and in years of drought he will have no worry,
and he will never lack for fruit.[53]

18 R. Eleazer b. Hisma says:
Bird offerings and the onset of menstrual precautions—
these are the essence of the received tradition.[54]
Turning points of the year and geometry—
appetizers for wisdom.

[52] Prooftext lacking in **P**.   [53] Prooftext lacking in **P**.   [54] So ed. Vilna and **K**. **P**: "Torah."

wisdom... awe: Intellectual mastery is the foundation of awe at the complexity of God's world and the wisdom that created it. And without awe there is no desire to amass intellectual mastery.

discernment... knowledge: Analytical skills and discursive knowledge are mutually dependent.

flour... Torah: The body must be sustained, while without merit acquired through Torah study, the disciple's pursuit of a livelihood will suffer. See 2:2, and cf. above in this mishnah.

wisdom exceeds his deeds... deeds exceed his wisdom: Cf. 3:9 (R. Hanina b. Dosa). This tradition adds a colorful metaphor drawn from the arborist's experience.

He shall be like a bush: Jeremiah 17:10.

And he shall be like a tree: Jeremiah 17:8.

3:18 *Bird offerings*: Lit. "nests," the smallest animal offering in the Temple. See *Qinnim*.

the onset of menstrual precautions: See *Niddah*.

the essence of the received tradition: Lit. "the body of the laws." Compare *Hagigah* 1:8. The point is that these are neglected or highly technical subjects.

Turning points of the year: Calculating the equinoxes and solstices on the solar calendar.

geometry: Heb. *gematria*. Alternatively, an early reference to the midrashic method of calculating the numerical equivalents of scriptural terms.

appetizers for wisdom: While topics like geometry and meteorology may be of interest to the disciple, they are not the key topic of study.

Chapter Four

4:1–5 *Later Yavnean Figures*

4 Ben Zoma says:
Who is wise?
One who learns from each person,
as it is said: *From all my teachers have I learned.*
Who is heroic?
One who quells his passion,
as it is said:
Better one who is patient than a hero,
and one who rules his spirit than one who conquers a city.
Who is rich?
One who finds joy in his situation,
as it is said:
When you eat the yield of your hands, you shall rejoice and be happy.
You shall rejoice—in this world;
and be happy—in the world to come.[55]
Who is honorable?
One who honors people,
as it is said:
Those who honor Me I shall honor, but those who spurn Me shall come to ruin.

2 Ben Azzai says:
Run to perform a minor commandment as you would for a major commandment.[56]
And flee from transgression—
for a commandment brings with it another commandment,

---

[55] K lacks the glosses on the biblical verse. [56] K, P lack "as...commandment."

4:1 These later Yavnean figures form a transition generation between that associated with Yavneh and the post-Bar Kokhba period associated in some traditions with the village of Usha.

From all my teachers: Psalms 119:99. Lit. "I have learned more than all my teachers." The saying midrashically inverts the meaning of the verse.

his passion: Heb. *yetser*, "urge, desire" (see 2:11, 4:22). The dictum has echoes in Roman-era moral philosophy.

Better one who is patient: Proverbs 16:32.

When you eat: Psalms 128:2.

people: Lit. "creatures."

Those who honor: 1 Samuel 2:30. God is the speaker. By implication, one must honor the divine image in each human being (see 3:15).

4:2 *as you would for a major commandment*: See 2:1, and n. 56.

a commandment brings...a transgression brings: Habit works both to encourage more good deeds as well as evil deeds.

while a transgression brings with it another transgression,
since the reward of a commandment is another commandment,
and the reward of a transgression is another transgression.

3 He used to teach:
Do not despise any person
or dismiss any object,
for there is no person without his hour
and no object without its place.

4 R. Levitas, a man of Yavneh, says:
Be exceedingly humble of spirit, for the human hope is the worm.
R. Yohanan b. Beroqa says:
Whoever profanes the name of Heaven in secret will be punished in public. The rule is[57] one and the same for unintentional and intentional transgression in regard to profanation of the Name.

5 R. Ishmael his son[58] says:
One who learns in order to teach receives the strength to learn and to teach;
but one who learns in order to do receives the strength to learn and to teach, to observe and to do.
R. Zadok says:
Do not make of them a crown to elevate yourself, nor a spade to dig with.

---

[57] Heb. "It is one...it is one."   [58] K lacks "his son."

since the reward: Virtue, in the form of performing commandments, is its own reward. Cf. 1:3.

4:3 *there is no person...no object*: God creates all creatures and plots out their destinies; there are no "insignificant" creatures.

4:4 *Levitas*: Apparently the only mention of this figure in tannaitic literature.

a man of: See 1:3.

Yavneh: The coastal town at the center of much rabbinic historiographical tradition.

Be exceedingly humble: Nearly a verbatim quotation from Ben Sira 7:17. See 4.19, quoting Proverbs 24:17. For the sentiment, see 3:1.

profanes the name of Heaven: See comment to 1:11 and 3:11.

punished in public: Lest the community doubt that sin is punished and obedience is rewarded.

4:5 *his son*: See n. 58. Without this designation the Sage referred to is perhaps R. Ishmael b. Elisha; see 3:12 and 4:7.

to teach...to do: The distinction broadly corresponds to the Greek categories of theoretical knowledge (*episteme*) and practical skill (*tekhne*).

to learn and to teach: Those who teach "theory" devoid of practical application are enabled to succeed in that task.

to learn and to teach, to observe and to do: In contrast, one who masters "theory" in order to act in accord with the Torah's knowledge, gains the ability to teach as well. Thus the performance of the Torah's commandments is the most exemplary goal of learning. See also 3:9, and the following tradition.

R. Zadok: If the earlier of two Sages by this name is meant, this tradition, supplied with a citation of a teaching of Hillel, closes the parenthesis opened at 3:1.

Do not make of them: The words of Torah. *A crown*: A means of self-aggrandizement. *A spade to dig with*: Idiomatically, to "earn a livelihood with."

And this is what Hillel used to teach:
Whoever exploits the Crown will come to nothing
Learn from this:
Whoever enjoys benefit from words of Torah removes his life from the world.

4:6–22 Traditions of Later Masters

6 R. Yose says:
Whoever honors the Torah is himself honored among people;
but whoever dishonors the Torah is himself dishonored among people.

7 R. Ishmael, his son, says:
One who recuses himself from a case
unburdens himself of hostility, theft, and false oaths.
And one who is arbitrary in instruction is foolish, wicked, and morally coarse.

8 He used to teach:
Do not render judgment in isolation,
for only One renders judgment in isolation;
and do not say "Accept my opinion!"
for they have the presumption of truth—not you!

9 R. Jonathan says:
All who fulfill the Torah in poverty will in the end fulfill it in wealth.
And all who neglect it in wealth will in the end neglect it in poverty.

10 R. Meir says:
Minimize business and busy yourself with Torah.
And be humble of spirit before each person.

And this is what Hillel: An editorial insertion. See 1:13.

enjoys benefit: The benefit envisioned may be material, as in the taking of fees for judging; see *Nedarim* 4:3.

4:6 These traditions are associated with Sages of the mid- to late second century, the "generation of Usha."

is himself: Lit. "his body is."

4:7 *R. Ishmael*: See n. 58. and and annotation on 4:5. The several R. Ishmaels are easily confused with one another.

recuses himself: Lit. "spares himself from judgment." The talmudic tradition reflects ambivalence about Sages serving as judges.

arbitrary in instruction: Lit. "is coarse-minded in instruction."

4:8 *judgment in isolation*: *Sanhedrin* 1 mandates a panel of three judges for most monetary matters.

"Accept my opinion!" Do not try to sway other judges in a panel to your view in an arrogant manner.

they have the presumption of truth: Truth resides with the majority.

4:10 *Minimize business*: In the rabbinic controversy over how to divide the disciples' time between Torah study and worldly matters, R. Meir takes the middle road (cf. 2:2).

humble of spirit. See e.g. 3:1, 4:4, 4:8.

And if you have neglected Torah study, there are[59] many forms of neglect.
And if you have labored in Torah study, He has[60] great reward to give you.

11 R. Eliezer b. Jacob says:
One who performs a single commandment creates for himself a single advocate.
And one who commits a single transgression creates for himself a single prosecutor.
Repentance and good deeds are a shield against retribution.
R. Yohanan ha-Sandlar says:
All gatherings convened for the sake of Heaven will in the end endure.
But those not convened for the sake of Heaven will not in the end endure.

12 R. Eleazar b. Shamua[61] says:
May your disciple's honor be as precious to you as your own,
and the honor of your fellow like the awe of your Master,
and the awe of your Master like the awe of Heaven.

13 R. Judah says:
Be very careful in study, for forgetfulness in study is regarded as intentional.
R. Simeon says:
There are three crowns—
(1) the crown of Torah,
(2) the crown of priesthood,
(3) and the crown of royalty.
But the crown of good repute surpasses them all.

[59] K, P: "I have"; K as vocalized: "he has."
[60] The whole phrase lacking in K (later added) and other witnesses. K (addition), P: "I have"; K (addition as vocalized) "he has."
[61] K lacks the patronym.

many forms of neglect: Perhaps "God will provide you with many occasions to neglect Torah." See n. 59. Another example of "measure for measure" (see 2:6).

4:11 *advocate*: A Greek word meaning "intercessor." Cf. Gospel of John 14:26.

prosecutor: A Greek word meaning "accuser." Each good and bad deed makes an "argument" in the final judgment of the individual.

ha-Sandlar: The name means "the shoemaker."

for the sake of Heaven: Communal leaders must subordinate any personal agendas to divine service (2:2; cf. 5:17). For "gatherings" see 3:10 and n. 38.

4:12 *your disciple's honor*: Cf. 2:10, R. Eliezer b. Hyrcanus.

and the awe of your Master like the awe of Heaven: God is venerated by the reverence offered the Master as an embodiment of God's Torah. See 1:3.

4:13 *study*: Heb. *talmud*. The reference is to the analytical study of oral traditions.

forgetfulness in study: Alternatively "For inadvertent errors in study are deemed intentional."

crown of Torah, earned through labor in Torah study.

of Priesthood, ascribed by birth and family lineage. Priests retained prestige in the postdestruction era.

of Royalty, conferred upon those of Davidic lineage.

of Good Repute: Lit. "of a good name." This fourth crown, accessible to all, *surpasses* the traditional measures of status.

14 R. Nehorai says:
Exile yourself to a place of Torah.
And do not think, "It will follow me!" or that your friends will sustain it for you.
And *do not rely on your own insight*.

15 R. Yannai says:
We cannot comprehend either the peace of mind of the wicked
or the suffering of the righteous.
R. Matia b. Heresh says:
Be the first to offer a greeting to each person.
And be a tail to lions rather than a head to foxes.

16 R. Jacob[62] says:
This World is like a vestibule to the World to Come—
prepare yourself in the vestibule so that you can enter the banquet hall!

17 He used to teach:
One hour of repentance and good deeds in This World
is worth more than the entire life of the World to Come.
But one hour of bliss in the World to Come
is worth more than the entire life of This World.

[62] K reads "Aqiva." The names are orthographically similar.

4:14 *Exile yourself*: One should move to a place where discipleship in Torah is thriving. For the tradition compare 1:11.

It will follow me! Having joined a discipleship community and taken a Master, the disciple must actively engage in the learning community.

friends will sustain it: Learning must be a personal acquisition on the part of the disciple.

do not rely on your own insight: Proverbs 3:5. A biblical quotation is here presented as the teaching of a rabbinic Sage. See 4.19. In context the implication is that Torah requires the society of the Sages, and not individual *insight* alone.

4:15 *cannot comprehend*: Lit. "have not in our hands." There is ultimately no explanation for this classic problem of theodicy (see Ecclesiastes 8:14).

Be the first to offer a greeting: See also 1:15, 3:12.

a tail to lions rather than a head to foxes: The disciple should strive to be a minor figure in a great community of learning rather than a major figure in a mediocre community.

4:16 *World to Come*: See 2:7.

prepare yourself with Torah study and commandments.

banquet hall: From the Greek *triklinion*. For the World to Come as banquet see also 3:16, R. Aqiva.

4:17 *One hour of repentance*: The moment of repentance acquires for the penitent the eternity of the World to Come.

bliss: Lit. "pleasure of spirit."

more than the entire life of This World: The blessedness of life in the World to Come exceeds any transient pleasure in This World.

18 R. Simeon b. Eleazar says:
Do not appease your friend in the hour of his rage;
and do not comfort him in the hour his dead lies before him;
and do not interrogate him in the hour of his vow;
and do not try to see him in the hour of his disgrace.

19 Samuel ha-Qatan says:
When your enemy falls, do not exult,
and in his stumbling let your heart not rejoice,
lest the Lord take notice and find it evil in his sight,
and turns His anger away from him.

20 Elisha b. Avuyah says:
One who learns as a boy, what is this like?
Ink inscribed on new paper.
One who learns as an old man, what is this like?
Ink inscribed on reused paper.
R. Yose b. R. Judah, a man of Kefar Ha-Bavli, says:
One who learns from youngsters, what is this like?
Eating unripe grapes and drinking wine straight from the press.
One who learns from elders, what is this like?
Eating ripe grapes and drinking aged wine.
Rabbi[63] says:

---

[63] **K**: "Rabbi Meir."

4:18 *Do not appease...*: Each statement illustrates the general principle that where human emotion is concerned, timing is everything.

do not interrogate him in the hour of his vow: A vow refers to a formal declaration to forswear any benefit from or to an individual or class of persons or things. The vow can be released by a Sage if, upon interrogation, the vowmaker declares that had he foreseen the implications of the vow, he would not have taken it at all. (See *Nedarim* introduction and chapter 9). Here, the advice is to allow one who vows in anger to calm down, lest he insist he understands and accepts the consequences of the vow, and thus forecloses the possibility of nullification.

do not try to see: A person who suffers public humiliation must be given time to recover self-respect.

4:19 *Samuel ha-Qatan* ("the small"): Recalled as a Yavnean throughout rabbinic tradition. The presence of his teaching in the midst of later Sages is anomalous.

When your enemy: Proverbs 24:17. This is the only instance in *Avot* of a Sage whose entire teaching constitutes a scriptural citation. See also 4:4 (R. Levitas); 4:14 (R. Nehorai).

4:20 *Elisha b. Avuyah*: Elsewhere in rabbinic tradition, he is said to have become a heretic after entering "the Orchard" (or "Paradise," perhaps a reference to esoteric study) with R. Aqiva, Ben Zoma (4:1), and Ben Azzai (4:2).

inscribed on new paper...reused (lit. "erased") *paper*: The Hebrew term does not actually refer to paper, but to another writing medium such as papyrus. Rabbinic oral tradition imagined the process of memorizing as "writing" on the surface of the memory.

a man of: See 1:3.

unripe grapes...wine straight from the press: i.e. insufficiently mature.

Rabbi: R. Judah the Patriarch (see 2:1).

Do not consider the jug, but rather its contents.
There are new jugs filled with aged wine,
and old ones that do not even contain new wine.
   21 R. Eliezer[64] ha-Qappar says:
Envy, appetite, and honor drive a person from the world.
   22 He used to teach:
The born are destined to die,
and the dead are destined to be revived,
and the revived are destined for judgment—
in order to know, to declare, and to confess that:
He is God,
He is the Shaper,
He is the Creator,
He is the Discerner,
He is the Judge,
He is the Witness,
He is the Plaintiff,
and He alone will pass future judgment.
Blessed is He![65]
For before Him there is neither flaw nor forgetting,
neither favoritism nor bribery,
for everything is His.
And know this: Everything is perfectly calculated.
And do not let your desire convince you that Sheol is a refuge.
For without consent were you conceived,
and without consent were you born,
and without consent you live,

[64] K (after correction), P: "Eleazar."   [65] Absent in K.

Do not consider the jug: Cf. the saying of Jesus, Mark 2:18–22, Matthew 9:17, Luke 5:33–39. The age of a student or teacher offers no sure guide. The three traditions in this mishnah form an interesting juxtaposition.

4:21 *Envy, appetite, and honor*: Desires pit one against one's community, and this leads to social isolation.

drive a person from the world: See 2:11.

4:22 *The born...destined for judgment*: Birth, death, resurrection, and judgment are the common lot of humanity.

to know, to declare, and to confess: The Hebrew infinitives are all built on the same root. Seven specific affirmations follow.

He alone will pass future judgment: He alone will preside over the eschatological drama.

Blessed: See n. 65. A new set of attributes follows.

Everything is perfectly calculated: Lit. "according to the accounting." See 3:16.

do not let: An admonition to the disciple.

your desire: Heb. *yetser*. See 2:11, 4:1.

Sheol: In biblical thought, Sheol is a world of shades (see 1 Kings 2:6). In rabbinic usage, it becomes, like Gehenna, the place of punishment after death (see 1:5).

and without consent you die,
and, without consent, you shall eventually account for yourself before the King of Kings of Kings, the Blessed Holy One.

Chapter Five

5:1–6 *Number Lists and Puzzles: The Number Ten*

5 With ten utterances was the world created.
What does this teaching convey?[66]
Could not one utterance have sufficed to create it?
Rather, to impose retribution upon the wicked,
who destroy a world created with ten utterances,
and to give a worthy reward to the righteous,
who sustain a world created with ten utterances.

2 Ten are the generations from Adam till Noah.
This shows His forbearance,
for each generation was insolent before Him,
until He brought the floodwaters upon them!
Ten are the generations from Noah till Abraham.
This shows His forbearance,
for each generation was insolent before Him,

---

[66] K, P: "What is this teaching?"

King of Kings of Kings: See 3:1. This passage ties together many themes of chapters 3 and 4, especially divine majesty, human creatureliness, and the inevitability of death.

5:1 The editorial method of chapter 5 radically departs from that of earlier chapters. There are no named Sages (excluding additions at the end), and consequently, no chronological organization. Instead, numbered lists undergird the chapter's traditions. In several cases, they constitute what might be called "number puzzles." The chapter concludes with teachings in which the words "all" or "every" are basic to the formulation of the tradition (5:16–19).

ten utterances: The traditions trace the covenantal history of Israel from the creation of the world (5:1–5), and concludes with the final acts of creation (5:6). In 5:1–4, the audience is required to supply the references. In Genesis 1, God creates by speech.

What does this teaching convey? See 3:8.

retribution…worthy reward: Destroying the world through neglect of Torah enhances the punishment of the wicked; while sustaining it through Torah study enhances the reward of the righteous.

5:2 *Adam till Noah*: See Genesis 5.

insolent: Lit. "continually angering." The responsibility for the flood rests not only on that generation (cf. Genesis 6:1–8), but also on all preceding generations.

Noah till Abraham: See Genesis 10:1–32; 11:10–30.

until Father Abraham came and received the reward of all of them.

3 Ten are the trials imposed upon Father Abraham, peace be upon him,[67] and he withstood them all.
This teaches how precious to Him was Father Abraham, peace be upon him.[68]

4 Ten are the miracles worked for our ancestors in Egypt,
and ten at the sea.
Ten are the plagues that the Blessed Holy One inflicted on the Egyptians in Egypt,
and ten at the sea.
Ten are the trials our ancestors imposed upon the Omnipresent, blessed be He in the wilderness,
as it is said: *And they tried Me these ten times and did not hear My voice!*.

5 Ten are the miracles worked for our ancestors in the Temple:[69]
(1) no woman ever miscarried from the aroma of the sanctified meat;
(2) and no sanctified meat ever stank;
(3) and no fly ever appeared in the butchering place;
(4) and no seminal emission ever befell the high priest on the Day of Atonement;
(5) and no rain ever drowned the fires of the pyres;
(6) and no wind ever dispersed the pillar of smoke;
(7) and no blemish ever befell the Sheaf, the Two Loaves, or the showbread.[70]

---

[67] K, P lack "Peace...upon him."   [68] K, P lack "Peace...upon him."
[69] K preserves a slightly different order of the same items.
[70] Lit. "Bread of the Holy Presence."

---

reward of all of them: Perhaps, whatever merit might have accrued to any of them.

5:3 *trials*: See 5:4. Each trial tests Abraham's trust in the covenant promises made to him by God, and he prevails. Commentaries differ on the precise enumeration.

5:4 *Ten...in Egypt, and ten at the sea*: There is no specific enumeration in the biblical narrative.

miracles: Lit. "signs." The Hebrew word sounds like the word for "trials" in 5:3.

plagues: Lit. "blows." See Exodus 8–11.

ten at the sea: Again, there is no specific enumeration in the biblical record.

trials...in the wilderness: In contrast to the case of Abraham, here, Israel tests God, cf. 5:3.

And they tried Me: Numbers 14:22.

5:5 *Ten...miracles* witness to divine oversight of the Temple, as a visible symbol of the continuity of the covenant.

no seminal emission, which would have disqualified the high priest from his sacrificial duties. See *Yoma* 1.

Sheaf: The *omer* (barley sheaf) offered on the second day of Passover. See Leviticus 23:11 and *Menahot* 10:1–9.

Two Loaves from the new wheat harvest in late spring are offered on the pilgrimage festival of Shavu'ot (Weeks). See Leviticus 23:17 and *Menahot* 11:1.

the showbread: Twelve unleavened loaves placed in the sanctuary on Sabbath eve and are replaced on the following Sabbath eve, when the bread is divided among the priests. See Leviticus 24:5–9 and *Menahot* 11:1–5.

(8) they stood crowded but prostrated in comfort;
(9) and no snake or scorpion ever caused harm in Jerusalem;
(10) and no one ever said to his friend: "I have no place to sleep in Jerusalem."

6 Ten are the things created on Sabbath eve at twilight.
And here they are:
(1) the mouth of the earth;
(2) and the mouth of the well;
(3) and the mouth of the ass;
(4) and the rainbow;
(5) and the manna;
(6) and the staff;
(7) and the worm;
(8) and the script;
(9) and the text;
(10) and the tablets.
And some add:
Also the demons.
And the grave of Moses.
And the ram of Father Abraham.
And some add:
Also the tongs made with tongs.

stood crowded but prostrated in comfort: Despite the crowding at pilgrimage festivals, all worshipers at the Temple had room for prostration.

no place to sleep: Much like the Temple Court, *Jerusalem* itself expanded to provide pilgrims with lodging.

5:6 A final list of ten. Virtually all the items listed here have a place in the rabbinic understanding of divinely guided covenantal history.

Sabbath eve: The first Sabbath eve at the conclusion of the six days of creation.

at twilight: Literally, "between the suns," a liminal period set aside as the framework for redemptive events contemplated for future embodiment.

mouth of the earth that swallowed Korah and his followers, Numbers 16:32; cf. 5:17. *Mouth of the well*: Miriam's well during the wandering in the wilderness, Numbers 21:16–18. *Mouth of the ass* that spoke to Balaam, Numbers 22:28. *The rainbow* marking God's covenant at the end of the flood, Genesis 9:13. *Manna*: Food provided by God in the wilderness, Exodus 16:15. *The staff* of Moses, Exodus 4:17. *The worm*: Heb. *shamir*. In one talmudic interpretation, a legendary stone-eating worm that was used, in lieu of prohibited iron tools, to build the Temple. *script . . . text . . . tablets*: The letter forms, text, and writing surface for the Ten Commandments. *Text* or stylus.

the demons: Lit. "destroyers."

grave of Moses, unknown to humans, Deuteronomy 34:6.

the ram that replaced Isaac as a sacrificial victim, Genesis 22:13.

tongs: Although obscure as phrased, this may refer to the tradition elsewhere that since tongs require others to make them, the first tongs must have been specially created.

5:7–9   Number Lists and Puzzles: Two Lists of Seven

7 Seven are the traits of a clod and seven of a Sage:
(1) a Sage never speaks in the presence of one greater than him in wisdom;
(2) and he does not interrupt his fellow's discourse;
(3) and he is in no hurry to reply;
(4) he asks relevant questions and replies appropriately;[71]
(5) and he discusses first things first and last things last.
(6) and when he does not know, he says: "I have not heard";
(7) and he concedes to the truth.
And it is just the opposite with a clod.

8 Seven kinds of retribution befall the world on account of seven principal transgressions:
if some offer tithes, but some do not offer tithes,
(1) famine by drought ensues—
some go hungry, but some are sated.
If it was concluded:
not to offer tithes—
(2) famine by civil unrest and drought ensues.
not to remove the dough offering—
(3) famine by wasting away ensues.
(4) Pestilence befalls the world—
on account of death sentences mandated by the Torah that were not remanded to the court, and on account of Seventh-Year produce.
(5) The sword befalls the world—
on account of corruption of justice, and on account of those who rule in regard to the Torah without reference to the tradition.

---

[71] **K**: "He asks appropriately and gives relevant answers."

5:7   *traits*: Lit. "things."

clod: Heb. *golem*, "unformed clay"; referring to common person who has not mastered the Sages' Torah.

appropriately: Lit. "according to tradition". *First things first and last things last*: Arranges thoughts cogently. *Does not know*: Lit. "has not heard." He possesses intellectual humility.

5:8   *retribution…transgressions*: Given the rabbinic understanding of retributive justice (see 2:6), commentators address the puzzle of correlating a specific type of punishment with a specific category of transgression. Thus, *some offer tithes…famine by drought* might mean that uneven performance is matched by uneven famine caused by intermittent, unreliable rains. For tithes see *Ma'aserot* and *Ma'aser Sheni*.

concluded: See e.g. *Sanhedrin* 1:2; 3:7, *Yadayim* 3:5; 4:1, 3. By consensus, people entirely stopped performing these commandments.

dough offering: See Numbers 15:17–21 and *Hallah*. Cf. *Shabbat* 2:6.

wasting away: Some commentators interpret cannibalism; see Leviticus 27:29.

Seventh-Year produce: Agriculture was prohibited in every seventh year, and produce that did grow was not to be appropriated exclusively by the landowner. See *Shevi'it* introduction. Item 7 of this list (5:9) addresses failure to observe the Sabbatical year more generally.

without reference to the tradition: See 5:7. A theological foundation of *Avot* is that the Torah cannot be implemented without the guidance of the tradition stemming from Moses at Sinai.

9 (6) The marauding beast befalls the world—
on account of vain oaths and profanation of the Name.
(7) Exile befalls the world—
on account of idolatrous worship, and on account of illicit sexual acts, and on account of bloodshed, and on account of releasing the land.

5:9 cont.–15 *Number Lists and Puzzles: Lists of Four*

At four junctures pestilence increases:
(1) In the Fourth Year;
(2) and in the Seventh Year;
(3) and at the departure of the Seventh Year;
(4) and at the departure of the Festival each and every year.
In the Fourth Year—
because of the poor tithe of the Third Year.
In the Seventh Year—
because of the poor tithe of the Sixth Year.
And at the departure of the Seventh Year—
because of Seventh-Year produce.
And at the departure of the Festival each and every year—
because of theft of the poor gifts.

10 Four are the types among people:

5:9 Continues the list of seven punishments. The witnesses differ over where to break the mishnah, suggesting uncertainty about the enumeration.

profanation of the Name: See 1:11; 4:4.

Exile…on account of idolatrous worship: See Deuteronomy 29:23–27. *Illicit sexual acts*: Lit. "uncovered nakedness." See Leviticus 18:28. *Bloodshed*: See Numbers 35:33. In other tannaitic and posttannaitic texts, these three form a triad of serious sins. Compare Acts 15:20.

releasing the land during the Seventh Year. Here, the reference is to engaging in prohibited agriculture; cf. 5:8. See Leviticus 26:43.

pestilence increases: Repeated epidemics are responses to the failure to set aside the agricultural gifts for the poor, which are due in various years of the Sabbatical cycle.

Fourth Year…Seventh Year—because of the poor tithe: Deuteronomy 28:38–39, as interpreted by rabbis, required householders to give over their tithes to the poor in the third and sixth years of the Sabbatical cycle. See *Ma'aser Sheni*, introduction. The penalty in the form of pestilence would come in the following year.

because of Seventh-Year produce: Cf. 5:8.

departure of the Festival: Sukkot (Booths). Sukkot coincides with the fall harvest, at the end of which various offerings for the poor, such as gleanings or the corners of the field, are to be left in the fields (Leviticus 19:10). See *Pe'ah*, introduction.

5:10–15 Six lists defining common personality traits and human types, each containing four traits apiece, evenly divided between positive and negative, and each characterized by an appropriate epithet. 5:11–14 are especially close in pattern.

5:10 *types*: Lit. "measures."

(1) one who says: "Mine is mine and yours is yours"—
this type is the mean.
But some say: this is the type of Sodom.
(2) "Mine is yours and yours is mine"—
a simpleton!
(3) "Mine is yours and yours is yours"—
pious!
(4) "Mine is mine and yours is mine"—
wicked!

11 Four are the types among moods:
(1) easy to anger, easy to appease—
his gain is canceled by his loss;
(2) hard to anger, hard to appease—
his loss is canceled by his gain;
(3) hard to anger, easy to appease—
pious!
(4) easy to anger, hard to appease—
wicked!

12 Four are the types among disciples:[72]
(1) quick to grasp, quick to lose—
his gain is canceled by his loss;
(2) slow to grasp, slow to lose—
his loss is canceled by his gain;
(3) quick to grasp, slow to lose—
a Sage!
(4) slow to grasp, quick to lose—
this one received a bad portion.

[72] **K, P**: *lemedim*, "learners."

---

type of Sodom: For the disputing view, this type is tolerant of the poverty of others as long as one can keep one's own possessions. See Ezekiel 16:49.

a simpleton: Heb. *am ha'arets*. Here, the expression does not appear to conform to its usual meaning in the Mishnah (see 2:5). The issue is ignorance of the customary desire of a person to retain control of one's own possessions. Perhaps the literal meaning, "a rustic," is intended here.

pious: Heb. *hasid*. The piety of one who knows that all possessions are given "on pledge" (3:16). Such a person "finds joy in his situation" (4:1) and is truly rich.

5:11 *moods*: Lit. "thoughts," or "minds." We might say "personality types."

his gain is canceled by his loss: The benefit of being easily calmed is canceled by submission to frequent rages. *his loss is canceled by his gain*: The benefit of being difficult to anger more than compensates for the occasional loss of control associated with anger.

5:12 *disciples*: Better, "learners," as in **K**, since at issue is receptiveness to learning rather than depth of knowledge or study skills per se. Cf. 2:8 (Rabban Yohanan b. Zakkai).

quick to grasp: Lit. "quick to hear." Perhaps, "commit to memory." *Quick to lose*: Forgets easily. Whatever is *gained* from rapid comprehension is soon *lost* from a poor memory. *Slow to grasp, slow to lose*: A retentive mind will benefit from the knowledge it is able to absorb over a lifetime.

13 Four are the types among givers of charity:
(1) he wants for himself to give, but others should not give—
he is stingy with others' wealth.
(2) Others should give, but he should not give—
he is stingy with own wealth.
(3) He should give and others should give—
pious!
(4) He should not give and others should not give—
wicked!

14 Four are the types among those who attend the house of study:
(1) he attends, but does not act—
he keeps the reward of attending;
(2) acts, but does not attend—
he keeps the reward of action;
(3) attends and acts—
pious!
(4) does not attend and does not act—
wicked!

15 Four are the types among those who sit before Sages:
the (1) sponge and the (2) funnel; the (3) strainer and the (4) sieve.
The sponge—
which absorbs everything.
The funnel—
what goes in one side, comes out the other.
The strainer—
which lets out the wine and keeps the sediment.
The sieve—
which lets out the flour and keeps the semolina.

5:13 *stingy with others' wealth*: Lit. "his eye is evil concerning theirs." This person wants the prestige of being a great philanthropist, but at the expense of the poor. *Pious*: Piety here lies in the desire to maximize what is available to those in need. *Wicked*: Such "having" while others "have not" is unjust and will lead to social turmoil that strikes at the heart of society. For the idea of retributive justice that underlies these sentiments, see 5:9.

5:14 *attend*: Lit. "go to."

house of study: Probably to be understood as a discipleship group rather than a formal academy.

does not act: The disciple who has yet to act upon his lessons.

keeps the reward of action: Embodying the norms of discipleship, even without knowing their deeper significance, is itself a source of merit.

5:15 *Four are the types among those who sit before Sages*: Torah disciples who do attend the study circle (5:14) are here likened to common household tools for the production of staple foods, the sustaining qualities of which are likened to Torah itself. See 2:8.

5:16–19 *Teachings about "Any"*

16 Any[73] love that depends upon a thing—
when the thing is lost, the love is lost.
But one that doesn't depend upon a thing—
it will never be lost.
What is an example of love that depends upon a thing?
The love of Amnon and Tamar.
And one that doesn't depend upon a thing?
The love of David and Jonathan.

17 Any[74] dispute joined for the sake of Heaven will in the end endure.
But one not joined for the sake of Heaven will not in the end endure.
What is an example of a dispute for the sake of Heaven?
This is the dispute of Hillel and Shammai.
And one not for the sake of Heaven?
The dispute of Korah and his people.

18 Any who bring virtue to the community will not fall into sin.
But any who cause the community to sin will not even have a chance for repentance.
Moses was virtuous and brought virtue to the community.
Thus, the virtue of the community is accredited to him,

---

[73] P reverses the order of 5:16 and 5:17.   [74] See preceding note.

5:16–19 The superscription of each of the next traditions is built on the form "any N that is X... but one that is not X...," in which each clause represents a moral absolute embodied by an historical hero or villain. Chapter 5 probably concluded at one time with a version of 5:19 that opened with the example of the disciples of Balaam and concluded with Abraham and the World to Come. See textual notes to 5:19.

5:16 *love*: Here in the Greco-Roman sense of *agape*. Compare 1 Corinthians 13:4–7.

when the thing is lost, the love is lost: If love is based upon some instrumental purpose, other than the well-being of the beloved, it will evaporate with the loss of the ulterior motive.

Amnon and Tamar: A son of King David who first "loved" then raped and subsequently "hated" his half-sister Tamar (2 Samuel 13:15).

David and Jonathan: The future King David and the son of the current king, Saul (1 Samuel 18:1). Jacob's love for his son, Benjamin, is similarly described (Genesis 44:30). Ideal love is figured as the selfless love of a father for a son or, in the context of *Avot*, the love of a Master for his disciple.

5:17 *Any dispute*: Alternatively, "party" or "group." Cf. 4:11, where "gathering" is used in virtually an identical teaching.

will in the end endure: That is, a dispute grounded in honest search for truth will yield principles that have permanent value within the tradition. *Eduyot* 1:4–5 is an illustration. A strikingly similar sentiment is ascribed to the Pharisee, Gamaliel, at Acts of the Apostles 5:38–39.

Hillel and Shammai: Tannaitic literature is rich in disputes between Hillel and Shammai, and especially the schools founded in their names.

Korah and his people: Numbers 16. See above 5:6.

5:18 *virtue*: Alternatively "merit." Here, equated with obedience to rabbinic teaching.

the virtue of the community is accredited to him: The virtuous leader is credited with the deeds he elicits from others. See also 2:2.

as it is said:
He performed righteous deeds for the Lord, and his statutes remain with Israel.
Jeroboam sinned and caused the community to sin.
Thus, the sin of the community is accredited to him,
as it is said:
And for the sins of Jeroboam that he committed, and which he caused Israel to commit.

19 Any with these three traits are among the disciples of Father Abraham.
But any with three other traits are among the disciples of Balaam the wicked.
(1) A good eye, (2) a humble character, and (3) a low spirit—
among the disciples of Father Abraham.
(1) An evil eye, (2) a haughty character, (3) and a high spirit—
among the disciples of Balaam.
And what distinguishes disciples of Father Abraham from disciples of Balaam the wicked?
Disciples of Father Abraham[75] enjoy This World
and inherit the World to Come,[76]
as it is said:
I will bequeath substance to those who love Me, and their treasuries I will fill.
But disciples of Balaam the wicked inherit Gehenna
and descend into the Pit of Destruction,
as it is said:
And You, O God, will bring them down to the Pit of Destruction—
those men of blood and lies will not live out half their days, but I trust in You.

---

[75] **K, P**, and other important witnesses have "disciples of Balaam" before "disciples of Abraham."
[76] For "enjoy...World to Come" **K** has "will inherit the Garden of Eden."

He performed righteous deeds: Deuteronomy 33:21.

Jeroboam: The founder of the northern Kingdom of Israel who established sacrificial shrines in Dan and Bethel.

And for the sins: 1 Kings 15:30.

5:19 *Balaam*: A prophet who sought to curse Israel (Numbers 22–24).

A good eye: 2:9. *Humble character*: As at 4:4.

An evil eye: 2:9. *Haughty spirit*, the remedy for which is at 4:22.

what distinguishes disciples of Father Abraham: See n. 75. With the reading of the manuscripts this passage might have made a suitable conclusion to the chapter. The material that follows appears to be a later copyist's addition.

enjoy This World and inherit the World to Come: See n. 76. The Garden of Eden as an epithet for "eternity" (as in **K**) is attested elsewhere in the entire Mishnah solely at 5:20 below.

I will bequeath: Proverbs 8:21. *Substance*: Heb. *yesh*, here read midrashically as that which abides forever.

Gehenna: 1:5, 5:20; see also Sheol (4:22).

And You, O God: Psalms 55:24.

5:20–23 *An Exhortation and Addenda*

20 Judah b. Tema says:
Be bold as the leopard, swift as the eagle, fleet as the deer, and ferocious as the lion in doing the will of your Father in Heaven.
He used to teach:
The bold-faced belong to Gehenna, but the shame-faced to the Garden of Eden.
May it be Your will, Lord, our God, that You rebuild Your city speedily in our days, and place our destiny with Your Torah.

21 He[77] used to teach:
aged five, Scripture;
aged ten, Mishnah;
aged thirteen, commandments;
aged fifteen, study;
aged eighteen, the marriage canopy;
aged twenty, pursuing;
aged thirty, strength;
aged forty, insight;
aged fifty, counsel;
aged sixty, an elder;
aged seventy, old age;
aged eighty, heroic age;
aged ninety, stooped over;
aged one hundred, as though dead and gone and no longer in the world!

[77] **K, P** lack all of 5:21.

5:20 With its concluding benediction 5:20 may once have formed the final passage of *Avot*. However, the medieval witnesses typically include some form of 5:20–23.

The bold-faced: The repetition of "bold" may signal that boldness in divine service is a virtue, while a vice in interpersonal relations.

Gehenna…Garden of Eden: See annotations to 5:19.

May it be Your will: A ubiquitous petition formula in rabbinic prayer.

5:21 *Mishnah*: Lit. "recitation"; "oral repetition." The noun probably refers to the type of study rather than to the Mishnah as a completed text.

commandments: Able to understand the commandments well enough to be obliged to fulfill them.

study: Heb. *talmud*. Again, a reference to a textual practice rather than to a completed text by that name.

pursuing: A livelihood. See 2:2; 3:17.

strength…insight…counsel…an elder: The terms signal progressive deepening of wisdom until it reaches its most profound expression at age sixty. *Ziqnah*, translated "an elder" can convey both age ("old age") and acquired status ("elderhood").

heroic age: An allusion to Psalm 90:10.

stooped over: Perhaps, vocalized slightly differently, "to pray," or even "to babble."

22 Ben Bag-Bag says:
Turn it every which way, for everything is in it;[78]
and meditate on it;[79]
and grow old and worn with it;[80]
and never abandon it—for there is no lot better than this.

23 Ben Heh-Heh says:
As the pain, so the gain.

Chapter Six

6:1–11 *On the Acquisition of Torah*

The Sages transmitted in the idiom of the Mishnah.
Blessed is the One Who chose them and their teaching!

6 R. Meir says:
Anyone who engages in Torah study for its own sake acquires many distinctions.
And what is more, the entire world is equivalent to him in value.
He is called: intimate; beloved; lover of the Omnipresent; lover of humankind; rejoicer of the Omnipresent; rejoicer of humankind.

---

[78] **K** (after correction): "for all of it is in you and all of you is within it"; **P**: "for everything is in it and all of you is in it."

[79] *Tekheze*, "gaze"; others *tehege*, "meditate." Phrase is lacking in **P** and (apparently) **K**. **K**, marginal reading, *u-vah teheve*, "and be in it," or perhaps "and expound upon it."

[80] Lacking in **P** and **K**.

5:22 *Turn it…for everything is in it*: Study of the Torah can never exhaust its contents.

meditate on it: Lit. "gaze into it"; see n. 79.

lot: Measure, quality.

5:23 *As the pain, so the gain*: Unlike other endeavors, the rewards of Torah study are always commensurate with whatever effort is invested in it.

Chapter 6 is a later addition to the tractate, as its prologue already acknowledges, and appears to be drawn from posttalmudic rabbinic compilations. See the introduction.

in the idiom "tongue, language" *of the Mishnah* suggests that those who appended it knew that it was not from the Mishnah.

6:1 *Torah study for its own sake*: The reference is to study whose purpose is simply to know God's revelation and to live accordingly.

distinctions: Lit. "things."

the entire world: See also 5:1.

lover of the Omnipresent: See 2:9.

lover of humankind: For the expression see 1:12. To love God is to love the divine image in the human (3:14).

rejoicer: The fruits of one's own beloved status brings joy to both God and humanity.

And it clothes him in humility and awe;
and conditions him to be righteous, and pious, and upright, and faithful;
and distances him from sin;
and brings him near to merit.
And through him one enjoys counsel, and wisdom, insight, and courage,
as it is said: *Mine are counsel and wisdom! I am insight! Courage is mine!*
And it accords him kingship, and authority, and penetrating judgment.
And they disclose to him the mysteries of the Torah.
And he becomes a gushing fountain, and like a river that never ceases to flow.
And he shall be modest, and long-suffering, and forgiving of insult.
And it makes him great, and exalts him beyond all deeds.

2 Said R. Joshua b. Levi:
Each and every day a voice proceeds from Mount Horeb, announcing and declaring:
Woe to humankind for insulting the Torah!
For anyone who fails to engage in Torah study is called contemptible,
as it is said:
Like a golden ring in a pig's snout is a lovely woman with no sense.
And it says:

---

it: The Torah.

righteous: Heb. *tsadiq*, rendered "righteous," has a broad semantic range. Here, it seems to refer to proper behavior in ritual obligations to God.

pious: Heb. *hasid*. The inner quality of devotion to God.

faithful: Heb. *ne'eman*. Trusting in God's conduct of the world.

through him one enjoys counsel: Humanity benefits from the Sage's grasp of the world's ways.

Mine are counsel and wisdom! Proverbs 8:14. The speaker is Wisdom, personified. The verse provides the sequence of forms of wisdom "counsel, wisdom, insight, and courage."

it accords: As above, the Torah.

kingship: See Proverbs 8:15. The master of Torah is worthy of kingship, since *by me* [Wisdom] *do kings rule*.

penetrating judgment: As a Master of Torah, the Sage is renowned as a judge.

mysteries of the Torah: Perhaps a reference to cosmology ("the workings of the heavenly chariot") and cosmogony ("the workings of creation"). See *Hagigah* 2:1.

a gushing fountain...a river: Imbibing the mysteries of the Torah, the Master of Torah is transformed into an inexhaustible source of life-giving teaching. Cf. 1:11, 6:2. See also Ben Sira 24:23–31.

exalts him beyond all deeds: The "deeds" refer to the actions that sustained the world. The Master of Torah sustains the world merely by acting within it (cf. 1:18, 6:2). Alternatively, "beyond all created things."

6:2 *a voice*: Lit. "a derived voice, echo." This is commonly understood as the voice of God suitable to an age in which prophecy is no longer possible.

Mount Horeb: The mountain of revelation according to Deuteronomy 5. (In Exodus 19–20 the name is Mount Sinai, as in *Avot* 1:1.)

Woe to humankind: Lit. "creatures" (1:12).

for insulting the Torah! The insult of neglect.

Like a golden ring: Proverbs 11:22.

And the tablets were the work of God, and the writing was the writing of God, engraved upon the tablets.
Do not pronounce the word as "engraved," but rather "freedom."
For no one is as free as one who engages in study of Torah!
And anyone who engages in study of Torah regularly—
he is indeed exalted,
as it is said:
From Midbar to Mattanah, and from Mattanah to Nahaliel, and from Nahaliel to Bamot.

3 One who learns from his fellow a single chapter, or a single tradition, or a single verse, or a single explanation, even a single letter—
must treat him with honor.
For so do we find of David, King of Israel,
who learned from Ahithophel only two things,
that he called him his master, his teacher, and his companion,
as it is said: *And you, a person of my rank, are my teacher and my companion.*
Now, is this not an inference of lesser and greater?
Just as David, King of Israel,
who learned from Ahithophel only two things,
called him his master, his teacher, and his companion—
one who learns from his partner a single chapter, or a single tradition, or a single verse, or a single explanation, even a single letter—
all the more so must he treat him with honor!
Now "honor" is nothing but Torah,
as it is said: *Sages will inherit honor,*

And the tablets: Exodus 32:16.

Do not pronounce: This common form of rabbinic exegesis plays with the ambiguity of the consonantal text of the Bible. Here, the word for "engraved," *harut*, is revocalized *herut*, "freedom," to make a point about the liberating character of Torah study.

From Midbar: Numbers 21:19. The verse details the migrations of the movable spring of water from which Israel drank during its travels. The midrashist identifies water with Torah, and interprets each of the place names accordingly: "From the gift of Torah to the divine bequest, and from the divine bequest to the heights."

6:3 *One who learns…must treat him with honor*: Torah, even in the most minute amount, is of infinite value. The debt incurred by the student is repaid by the honor and respect accorded to the teacher of Torah.

tradition: Heb. *halakhah*; alternatively, "law."

explanation: Heb. *dibbur*; alternatively, "statement, clause."

David: Biblical King David is a role model of the Torah Sage.

Ahithophel: An advisor to David who betrayed the king to support Absalom's insurrection (2 Samuel 15:10–12; 30–31).

only two things: These are not specified here or in the biblical text.

And you, a person of my rank: Psalms 55:14.

lesser and greater: See also 2:5. A standard from of rabbinic argument. Here, if David accorded to the wise but wicked Ahithophel great honor for teaching him only two traditions, all the more so should lowly disciples bestow honor upon even the most humble teacher.

Sages will inherit: Proverbs 3:35.

and *The perfect will inherit goodness.*
Now "goodness" is nothing but Torah,
as it is said: *For a good teaching have I given you; my Torah, do not abandon it.*
   4 This is the path of Torah:
You will eat your bread with salt, and drink water in measured amounts,
and sleep on the ground and live a life of troubles, and you shall labor in Torah.
And if you do this, *You are fortunate and you will prosper.*
You are fortunate—in This World.
And you will prosper—in the World to Come.
Do not seek greatness for yourself,
and do not covet honor.
More than merely study, do.
And do not hunger after the tables of kings,
for your table is greater than their table,
and your Crown is greater than their crown,
and your employer can be trusted to pay you exactly what your work is worth.

6:5–6   *The Attributes of a Torah Sage*

   5 Torah is greater than the Priesthood and Royalty,
for Royalty is acquired with thirty virtues, and the Priesthood with twenty-four,
but Torah is acquired with forty-eight things:

The perfect: Proverbs 28:10. Lit. "innocent."

For a good teaching: Proverbs 4:2. Cf. 3:14. The exposition of the verses place Torah at the true center of social values.

6:4 A series of independent traditions all of which present discipleship in Torah as a kind of ascetic discipline (cf. 6:5).

This is the path of Torah: This is what the life of Torah study may exact from the disciple.

You are fortunate: Psalms 128:2.

Do not seek greatness: A commonplace theme in *Avot*, e.g. 1:13. Cf. 6:5.

More than merely study, do: Translation is slightly loose. The point is the significance of performing the commandments. See e.g. 3:9.

your Crown is greater than their crown: Cf. 1:13, 4:13.

your employer: 2:16 (R. Tarfon).

6:5 This list of traits and virtues of the Torah master is patched together from smaller units of tradition. This is obvious from the various formulas for presenting the traits. While the items of 6:5 are identical in pattern, those of 6:6 break into smaller formal units.

royalty…priesthood…Torah: See 4:13, the three "Crowns."

thirty…twenty-four: *Kallah Rabbati* provides lists.

virtues: Lit. "ascents, degrees." Perhaps "distinctions."

forty-eight things: In contrast to royalty and the priesthood, the qualities of the Sage are internal states of being, cultivated and inculcated by discipleship training. "Things" or "words" refers to behavioral traits associated with moral self-formation. As formulated the list has forty-nine items.

(1) by study;⁸¹ (2) by paying attention; (3) by preparing the lips; (4) by an insightful mind; (5) by clarity of mind; (6) by shuddering; (7) by awe; (8) by humility; (9) by joy; (10) by serving the Sages;⁸² (11) by examining fellows; (12) by drilling disciples; (13) by sitting; (14) by Scripture; (15) by Mishnah; (16) by limiting sleep; (17) by limiting conversation; (18) by limiting pleasure; (19) by limiting laughter; (20) by limiting worldly pursuits; (21) by patience; (22) by a good disposition; (23) by trust in Sages; (24) by accepting troubles.

6 (25) One who knows his place; (26) and one who finds joy in his situation; (27) and one who makes a hedge for his words; (28) and one who does not think highly of himself; (29) beloved; (30) a lover of the Omnipresent; (31) a lover of humankind; (32) a lover of righteous deeds; (33) a lover of rebuke; (34) a lover of clear moral vision; (35) he distances himself from honor; (36) he does not become arrogant because of his studies; (37) he is not gratified by adjudication; (38) he shares the yoke with his partner; (39) he judges his friend more kindly than he deserves; (40) he restores him to the truth; (41) he restores him to peace; (42) his mind is organized when he studies; (43) he asks and answers; (44) he understands and adds; (45) one who learns in order to teach; (46) and one who teaches in order to do; (47) one who brings wisdom to his master; (48) and one who draws connections among traditions he has heard; (49) and one who cites an opinion in the name of its transmitter.

⁸¹ *Kallah Rabbati*: *yishuv*, "sitting (in study)."
⁸² *Seder Eliyahu Zuta*: "by imitation of the Sages."

study: Heb. *talmud*. *Preparing the lips*: Commentators suggest that this is a reference to memorization of the oral tradition. *Shuddering...joy*: Each of these terms refers to a psychological consequence of Torah study. Each stems from an enhanced capacity of the disciple to intuit the closeness of the divine Presence.

serving the Sages: Joining the disciple circle of a Torah master included not only "classroom hours" but living and traveling with the Sage so as to learn how he embodied the ideals of Torah. *Sitting* in Torah study.

Scripture: Or "reading." *Mishnah*: Repeating and memorizing rabbinic teaching.

limiting sleep...conversation...pleasure...laughter...worldly pursuits: All these reflect the ascetic ethos of certain strands of rabbinic tradition. Cf. 6:4. *Worldly pursuits*: Heb. *derekh erets*. Alternatively, considering the ascetic context, this could be a reference to limiting sexual activity. Cf. 2:2, 3:17.

good disposition: Lit. "a good heart." See annotations to 2:8. *Accepting troubles*: Lit. "discipline" or "suffering." Whatever challenges one faces in life are divinely given opportunities for moral growth (4:22).

6:6 *One who knows his place*: This refers not only to a person in a subordinate social position. Cf. 4:3.

finds joy in his situation: Cf. 4:1. *Makes a hedge*: See 1:1, 3:13. *And one who does not think highly of himself*: See 2:8.

beloved, etc.: This series of six items is simply a more ample version of the series included at 6:1. *Of rebuke*: In the rabbinic sense, this refers to welcoming constructive criticism offered out of concern for one's well-being. *A lover of clear moral vision*: Lit. "uprightness." See 2:1.

distances himself from honor: See 4:21. *Does not become arrogant because of his studies*: Cf. 4:8. *Not gratified by adjudication*: A person engaged in judging should approach the task with trepidation, because the consequences of error are so great. Cf. 1:11, 4:7 *Yoke*: Probably shorthand for "the yoke of the Torah," or "of the kingdom of Heaven." See 3:5; *Berakhot* 2:2. *More kindly than he deserves*: Cf. 1:6. *Restores him to peace*: When friends come into conflict the imperative is to recreate harmony. Alternatively, if students of Torah dispute its meaning it is crucial to restore peace among them. *His mind is organized...adds*: Cf. 5:7. *Learns in order to teach...in order to do*: Cf. 4:5. *Draws connections*: Lit. "directs what he has heard."

Indeed, now you learn: Anyone who cites a statement in the name of the one who said it
brings redemption to the world,
as it is said: *And Esther told the king in the name of Mordecai.*

7 Great is Torah! For it gives life to its devotees in This World and the World to Come,
as it is said: *For they are life to those who find them, healing for his entire body.*
And it says: *It will be a cure for your body, a tonic for your bones.*
And it says: *It is a tree of life to those who seize it, and those who rely upon it are blessed.*
And it says: *They are a graceful wreath upon your head, a necklace about your throat.*
And it says: *She will adorn your head with a graceful wreath, crown you with a glorious diadem.*
And it says: *In her right hand is length of days, in her left, riches and honor.*
And it says: *For they will bestow upon you length of days, years of life and well-being.*

8 R. Simeon b. Menasya[83] says in the name of R. Simeon b. Yohai:
Good looks, and strength, and wealth, and honor, and wisdom, and old age,[84] and gray hair, and offspring—
adorn the righteous and adorn the world,
as it is said: *Gray hair is a crown of glory, it is attained by the way of righteousness.*
And it says: *The crown of the wise is their wealth.*

---

[83] Some witnesses: "R. Simeon b. R. Judah."   [84] Some witnesses lack this item.

cites a statement: This key virtue is important not only for interpreting what the masters say, but also serves mnemonic interests in keeping the various teachings well-preserved.

And Esther told: Esther 2:22. The point seems to be that the redemptive events described in Esther depended upon Esther's fidelity to tradition transmitted by an acknowledged master.

6:7 *its devotees*: Lit. "its doers."

For they are life: Proverbs 4:22. "They," "it," and "she" in this and the following verses are taken to refer to the Torah. The first stich in each verse is taken to refer to This World, the second in the World to Come.

And it says: With this formula, a series of verses is adduced to make a single point. The practice is pursued at other junctures of 6:8–10 as well, constituting a refrain that unifies the sources into a single unit.

It will be a cure: Proverbs 3:8.

It is a tree of life: Proverbs 3:18.

They are a graceful wreath: Proverbs 1:9.

She will adorn your head: Proverbs 4:9.

In her right hand: Proverbs 4:16.

For they will bestow: Proverbs 3:2.

6:8 *Good looks ... adorn the righteous*: These worldly benefits come to the righteous by virtue of their piety, and the impact of the righteous on the world is enabled by these virtues as well.

as it is said: The prooftexts neither address the seven qualities in the listed sequence, nor do they address all the qualities.

Gray hair is a crown of glory: Proverbs 14:24: gray hair.

And it says. See 6:7n.

The crown of the wise: Proverbs 14:24: wealth.

And it says: *The crown of old age is grandchildren, and the glory of children is their parents.*
And it says: *The glory of the young is their strength, and the majesty of the old is gray hair.*
And it says: *Then the moon shall be shamed, and the sun abashed, for the Lord of Hosts will reign on Mount Zion and in Jerusalem, and His Glory will be revealed to His elders.*
R. Simeon b. Menasya says:
These seven qualities, which the Sages ascribed to the righteous, were all embodied in Rabbi and his sons.

9 Said[85] R. Yose b. Qisma:
One time I was walking on the road and a certain person encountered me.
He greeted me, and I returned the greeting.
He said to me:
Rabbi! Where are you from?
I replied: From a great city of Sages and scribes am I!
He said to me: Rabbi! Would you not like to live among us in our place? For I would give you many thousands of golden *dinar*, fine gems, and pearls.
I replied: My son! If you were to give me all the silver, gold, fine gems, and pearls in the world, I would only live in a place of Torah study.
For at the hour of a person's passing, nothing accompanies him—
not silver, not gold, not fine gems, and not pearls—
other than Torah study and good works alone,
as it is said:
When you walk it will lead you, when you lie down it will watch over you, and when you are awake it will be your conversation.
When you walk it will lead you—
in This World.
When you lie down it will watch over you—
in the grave.
When you are awake it will be your conversation—
in the World to Come.
And so is it written in the Psalter, by David, the King of Israel:

[85] Entire passage lacking in *Kallah Rabbati* and *Seder Eliyahu Zuta*.

The crown of old age: Proverbs 17:6.

The glory of the young: Proverbs 20:29.

Then the moon shall be shamed: Isaiah 24:23. Perhaps referring to "adorn the world."

seven qualities: Our version has eight. See n. 84.

were all embodied in Rabbi and his sons: See 2:1.

6:9 The story of R. Yose b. Qisma is a fitting conclusion to a chapter that begins the theme of Torah study for its own sake.

When you walk: Proverbs 6:22. The concluding exegesis artfully applies the verse even after death.

I delight in the Torah of Your mouth more than in thousands of gold and silver.
And it says:
Mine is the silver and mine is the gold, says the Lord of Hosts!

6:10–11 *Testimonies to God as Creator*

10 Five creations did the Blessed Holy One create for Himself in His world:
And here they are:
(1) Torah, one creation.
(2) The heaven and earth, one creation.
(3) Abraham, one creation.
(4) Israel, one creation.
(5) The Holy Temple, one creation.
Torah, one creation.
How do we know?
For it is written: *The Lord created me at the beginning of His course, as the first of his primordial works.*
Heaven and earth, one creation.
How do we know?
As it is said: *Thus said the Lord: the heavens are My throne and the earth is My footstool. What house can you build for Me? And where is My resting place?*
And it says: *How great are Your deeds, O Lord, all of them that you created in wisdom, the entire world is filled with your creations!*
Abraham, one creation.
How do we know?
For it is written: *And He blessed him, saying: Blessed is Abram to the Highest God, Creator of heaven and earth.*
Israel, one creation.
How do we know?
For it is written: *Until Your people passes, O Lord.*
Until this people—your creation—passes.

I delight: Psalms 119:72.

And it says: See 6:7.

Mine is the silver: Haggai 2:8. The citations return attention to the story of R. Yose b. Qisma.

6:10 *Five creations* or "acquisitions" or "possessions."

How do we know? Lit. "from where?" This common term in rabbinic exegesis usually calls for a verse as prooftext.

The Lord created me: Proverbs 8:22.

Thus said the Lord: the heavens are My throne: Isaiah 66:1.

How great are Your deeds: Psalms 104:24.

And He blessed him, saying: Blessed is Abram: Genesis 14:19. Here, Abraham is a special possession of God.

Until Your people passes: Exodus 15:16.

And it says: *As to the holy ones who are in the land, and the mighty, all of My desire lies in them.*
The Holy Temple, one creation.
How do we know?
As it is said: *The Temple of the Lord have Your hands established.*
And it says: *He brought them to His holy realm, the mountain His right hand had acquired.*

11 All that the Blessed Holy One created in His world,
He created only to honor Himself,
as it is said: *Everything that is called in My Name and My Honor, I have created it, I have formed it, and I have made it.*
And it says: *The Lord will reign for all eternity.*
R. Hananiah b. Aqashiah said:
The Holy One, blessed be He, wished to bring virtue to Israel.
Therefore he gave them the Torah and commandments.
As it says:
*The Lord desires, for the sake of his righteous ones,
to make his Torah great and to make it glorious.*[86]

---

[86] Passage lacking in some witnesses.

As to the holy ones: Psalms 16:3. Here, again, the sense of "special possession" is operative.

The Temple of the Lord: Exodus 15:17.

He brought them to His holy realm: Psalms 78:54.

6:11 *created*: Heb. *bara*, as in Genesis 1:1. The word *qanah* having been mined for its midrashic significance at 6:10, other semantically overlapping terms are explored here.

Everything that is called in My Name: Isaiah 43:7.

created: Heb. stem *bara*. *Formed*: Heb. stem *yatzar*. *Made*: Heb. stem *asah*.

And it says: See 6:7.

The Lord will reign: Exodus 15:18.

R. Hananiah b. Aqashiah: See n. 86.

The Lord desires: Isaiah 42:21.

Tractate Horayot

Alyssa Gray

Introduction

Overview

Horayot, more commonly written *hora'ot*, means "legal rulings." Tractate *Horayot* deals with legal rulings—actually, unintentionally erroneous legal rulings—made by the Great Court (the Sanhedrin) or the anointed ("high") priest for themselves and/or for the people Israel, and unintentional violations of law committed by the *Nasi* (whom the rabbis identify as the king of Israel; in the rabbis' own time this was the title of the Patriarch) and by individuals. A key issue in the tractate is clarification of the circumstances in which the Great Court must bring an expiatory sacrifice on its own and the entire people's behalf or when the circumstances of its erroneous ruling are such that only individual expiatory sacrifices are to be brought. The subject matter of *Horayot* makes it a logical part of Order *Neziqin* (like the larger, related tractate *Sanhedrin*), although none of the institutions it discusses still existed during the rabbinic period. Indeed, the Great Court as portrayed in the Mishnah may never have existed at all. The reader should keep an eye on two ideas: (1) the conviction of *Horayot*—based on biblical law—that the leaders of Israel are not a law unto themselves, but can err as to the law and must atone for their errors; and (2) how *Horayot* constructs "Israel." *Horayot* posits an intimate connection among the people, the high priest, the *Nasi*, and the Great Court, and even ponders the relation of part to whole in the Israelite tribal structure in chapter 1.

Structure and Organization of the Tractate

Horayot consists of three chapters. Chapter 1 deals entirely with erroneous rulings of the Great Court, on the basis of which the Court and people unintentionally commit transgressions. The first two paragraphs deal with the individual who acts according to the erroneous ruling, and establish the point that awareness of the Court's error renders any transgressive action taken pursuant to its ruling *intentional* transgression. The third paragraph clarifies the point that only a ruling as to part of an area of law will trigger the Court's obligation to atone for itself and the entire people. A ruling that nullifies an entire area of law—e.g. denying that there is a Sabbath in the Torah—is an outrage against common sense that no one could take seriously, and thus the Court need not bring an atoning sacrifice for the people. This paragraph's implicit theme of identifying situations in which the Court's erroneous ruling will not trigger an obligation of collective atonement continues into the next. This one establishes that the improper composition of a Court or transgressions committed intentionally also nullify the Court's obligation of collective atonement. Chapter 1 closes with a lengthy fifth paragraph in which different opinions are presented about a situation in which most but not all of the people follow the Court's erroneous ruling. This paragraph interestingly also invokes the Israelite tribal structure, implicitly pondering the relation of these smaller "peoples" to the larger people Israel.

Chapter 2 opens with two paragraphs that deal with an unintentionally erroneous ruling by the anointed priest, on the basis of which he unintentionally commits a transgression. The third, fourth, and fifth paragraphs shed additional light on the types of laws for which the Court's ruling will trigger an obligation of collective atonement, and on differences between the culpability and modes of atonement of the Court, anointed priest, *Nasi*, and individual.

Chapter 3 opens with three paragraphs that explore situations in which an individual sins in one status—whether that of private individual, *Nasi*, or anointed priest—and then changes his status. These considerations of status logically lead to definitions of the *Nasi* (the king) in the third paragraph and of the anointed priest (the high priest anointed with oil) in the fourth. The fourth paragraph also ponders other classifications of high priests and the legal distinctions between them: the high priest of many garments, the serving high priest, and the high priest who has passed from active service. The focus in chapter 3 on status and classification is broadened in the fifth paragraph to include consideration of some legal differences between the high priests and ordinary priests. The sixth, seventh, and eighth paragraphs are united by the theme of what (or who) takes precedence over what (or whom), a theme that is logically related to the chapter's overall focus on status and classification. In light of the tractate's interest in the anointed priest and the chapter's intense focus on status and precedence, the end of the eighth paragraph is an unexpected, albeit characteristically rabbinic inversion: a scholarly *mamzer* is declared to rank higher than an ignorant high priest. This is the note on which tractate *Horayot* ends.

Relationship to Scripture

The principal biblical bases of the tractate are Leviticus 4 and Numbers 15:22–31, although there is much other scriptural citation and interpretation throughout. Leviticus 4:2 refers to *a person*, 4:3 to the *anointed priest*, 4:13 to the *entire congregation of Israel*, and 4:22 to the *Nasi*. The rabbis understand the *entire congregation of Israel* to be the Great Court; an unsurprising exegetical move for the rabbis. Numbers 15:22–31 refers neither to the *Nasi* nor the anointed priest and explicitly includes the non-Israelite convert (*ger*) among inadvertent transgressors who require atonement equally with Israel. The gaps in Numbers 15:22–31 may account for the rabbis' sense that Leviticus 4 is the principal scriptural source for *Horayot* and Numbers 15:22–31 secondary to it.

Tractate Horayot

Chapter One

1:1–5 *When a Court Erroneously Permits Transgression*

1 If the court ruled [permitting the community] to transgress one of the commandments stated in the Torah,
and an individual went and acted inadvertently according to their ruling:
whether they acted and he acted with them;
whether they acted and he acted after them;
whether they did not act and he acted—
he is exempt,
because he relied upon the court.
If the court ruled,
and one of them knew they had erred,
or a student worthy of issuing rulings [knew they had erred],

---

1:1 *If the court ruled*: "Court" refers to the Sanhedrin of seventy-one members, located according to rabbinic tradition in the Chamber of Hewn Stone of the Jerusalem Temple. See the end of 1:5, below.

[permitting the community] to transgress one of the commandments stated in the Torah: The Talmud emphasizes that the court is not liable for its erroneous ruling until it explicitly permits the community to perform the transgressive act. The commandment must be one the intentional violation of which is punishable by *karet*, and the unintentional violation of which entails a purgation offering (see 2:3, below). For a definition of "one of the commandments stated in the Torah," see 1:3.

whether they acted and he acted with them: If the members of the court followed their own erroneous ruling and the individual acted along with them.

whether they acted and he acted after them: If the members of the court acted in accordance with their own erroneous ruling and the individual followed suit afterwards.

whether they did not act and he acted: The members of the court did not act on their own erroneous ruling, but the individual did so.

he is exempt, because he relied upon the court: In all three instances, the individual is exempt from the obligation to bring his own expiatory sacrifice. Whether he acted with, after, or without the court, he acted in total reliance upon its ruling. Consequently it is the court that is obligated to bring the expiatory sacrifice.

and one of them knew they had erred: One of the members of the court knew that the court's ruling was erroneous.

or a student worthy of issuing rulings [knew they had erred]: The "student" has the appropriate level of knowledge and skill in the law to issue legal rulings, although he is not (yet) authorized to do so.

and that one went and acted according to their ruling:
whether they acted and he acted with them;
whether they acted and he acted after them;
whether they did not act and he acted—
in such a case this one is culpable,
because he did not rely upon the court.
This is the general rule:
The one who relies upon himself is culpable,
and the one who relies upon the court is exempt.

2 If the court ruled,
recognized they had erred,
and reversed themselves—
whether or not [the members of the court] had brought their atoning sacrifice—
and [someone] went and acted according to their ruling:
R. Simeon exempts,
and R. Eliezer says:
Doubt.
What is the doubt?[1]
If he was sitting in his house,
he is culpable.

---

[1] **P** lacks "doubt."

---

and that one: The member of the court or the student aware of the court's error.

went and acted according to their ruling: The previous statement about the individual reads "went and acted inadvertently according to their ruling." "Inadvertently" is logically missing from this statement about the member of the court and the student. Their awareness of the court's error renders *intentional* their transgressive performance in apparent obedience to the court.

in such a case this one is culpable, because he did not rely upon the court: The member of the court or student aware of the court's error is obligated to bring an individual expiatory sacrifice. His awareness of the court's error shows that he was not "relying" upon the court in transgressing the Torah law.

The one who relies upon himself is culpable: The one who relies on his own view, and not that of the court. The juxtaposition of this clause to the previous one shows that a member of the court or student who is aware of the court's error is considered to be one who relies upon himself and not the court.

1:2 *If the court ruled*: The Sanhedrin ruled to permit the forbidden, and most of the people followed their ruling.

recognized they had erred, and reversed themselves: The court realized its error after issuing the ruling, and went back on it.

and [someone] went and acted according to their ruling: The individual acted on the erroneous ruling after the court recognized its error and reversed itself. He was presumably unaware of the reversal.

R. Simeon exempts, and R. Eliezer says: Doubt: R. Simeon holds that the individual is exempt from bringing his own expiatory sacrifice because he did not know of the court's reversal. He is therefore considered to be one "who relies upon the court." R. Eliezer is in doubt as to whether this individual is one who "relies upon the court" or upon himself. Perhaps the individual should have known of the court's reversal; if he could and should have known, he should not be considered one "who relies upon the court."

If he was sitting in his house, he is culpable: This individual should have known about the court's reversal.

If he had gone to a province of the sea,
he is exempt.[2]
R. Aqiva said:
I acknowledge as to this one [the latter case]
that he is closer to exemption than to culpability.
Ben Azzai said to him:
How is this one different from the one who sits in his house?
It is possible for the one who sits in his house to have heard,
but this one—it was not possible for him to have heard.

3 If the court ruled to uproot the entire body [of a commandment];
if they said:
There is no law of the menstruant in the Torah,
there is no Sabbath in the Torah,
there is no law of idolatry in the Torah,[3]
then these are exempt.
If they ruled to nullify part [of a commandment] and to uphold part,
then these are culpable.
How?
If they said:
There is a law of the menstruant in the Torah,

[2] K, P lack "exempt."   [3] P lacks "in the Torah."

If he had gone to a province of the sea, he is exempt: Had the individual been far away from home at the time of the court's reversal, he is considered to be one who "relies upon the court." He would not necessarily have had access to information about the court's reversal.

R. Aqiva said…that he is closer to exemption than to culpability: The one who travels away from home is closer to exemption than liability because he may not have been able to learn of the court's retraction.

Ben Azzai said to him: How is this one different from the one who sits in his house? Why is the individual who sits in his house culpable (as per R. Eliezer) while the one who travels to a province of the sea exempt?

It is possible for the one who sits in his house to have heard, but this one—it was not possible for him to have heard: Logic (and an alternative version of the mishnah) suggest that this is R. Aqiva's response to Ben Azzai.

1:3 *If the court ruled to uproot the entire body [of a commandment]*: An entire area of the law, as the Mishnah goes on to explain. The court says that there is no law of the menstruant in the Torah, no Sabbath in the Torah, or no law of idolatry in the Torah.

then these are exempt: It being common knowledge that there are menstrual restrictions, prohibited Sabbath labors, and prohibitions connected to idolatry in the Torah, individuals who follow the court's erroneous and complete uprooting of any of these laws cannot be said to "rely upon the court." Consequently the court is exempt from having to bring a bull to atone on behalf of the entire community (Leviticus 4:14). Rather, transgressing individuals will be required to bring individual expiatory sacrifices.

If they ruled to nullify part [of a commandment] and to uphold part, then these are culpable: The Mishnah will shortly clarify what it means for the court to "nullify" and "uphold" part of a commandment. In the event the court does so, and most of the people act on the erroneous ruling, the court is liable to offer a bull on behalf of the entire people.

How? What does it mean for the Court to "nullify" part of a commandment and "uphold" part?

but someone who has intercourse with [a woman]
who watches herself for a day corresponding to a day
is exempt;
there is a Sabbath in the Torah,
but the one who brings out from the private domain to the public domain
is exempt;
there is a law of idolatry in the Torah,
but the one who bows [to an idol] is exempt—
then these are culpable,
as it is said: *a matter escapes notice*;
a matter, and not the entire body [of the commandment].

4 If the court ruled,
and one of them knew they had erred
and said to them:
You are erring,
or had the court's legal expert not been there,
or had one of them been a *mamzer*, a *natin*, or an elderly man who had never had children,[4]
then these are exempt [from offering an expiatory sacrifice on behalf of the entire community].

[4] **K**: "who had not had [children]"; **P** and the printed editions: lit. "who had not seen for himself [children]."

but someone who has intercourse with [a woman] who watches herself for a day corresponding to a day is exempt: A woman is to count at least seven days for her menstruation, and more if she menstruates beyond seven days. These days are followed by an eleven-day period separating one menstruation from the next. If she sees blood during one of these eleven days, she immerses on the morning following the sighting of the blood. If she does not see blood again that day, she is pure in the evening; if she saw blood two days running she must wait two "clean" days before immersing, and so on. Between the time of her immersion and sunset, she is legally considered to be a menstruant, and intercourse with her is forbidden on penalty of *karet*. In this case, the court's erroneous ruling is that one who has intercourse with such a woman is not culpable.

then these are culpable: In cases like these three, the court itself is liable to bring a bull on behalf of the entire people, for fear that most have acted on the court's erroneous ruling.

a matter escapes notice; a matter, and not the entire body [of the commandment]: This is the rabbinic interpretation of Leviticus 4:13.

1:4 *one of them knew they had erred, and said to them: You are erring*: One of the members of the court pointed out the error and yet the court went ahead and ruled, erroneously permitting that which is forbidden.

or had the court's legal expert not been there: The term here rendered as "legal expert" may refer to a figure whose role was to be a legal resource for the court, reciting the legal material on which they would base their decisions. Commentators also hypothesize that this term could refer to the president or vice president of the court.

a convert, a mamzer, a natin, or an elderly man who had never had children: All of these categories of people are ineligible to serve on courts (see *Sanhedrin* 4:2). The *mamzer* is a product of a forbidden sexual relationship. According to rabbinic tradition the *natin* is a descendant of the biblical Gibeonites, whom Joshua had designated to be *hewers of wood and drawers of water* (Joshua 9:27). The elderly man who never had children is not considered worthy to judge because, having never had children, he is seen as apt to be cruel.

then these are exempt [from offering an expiatory sacrifice on behalf of the entire community]: If the court's legal expert was not there, or if the court included one of the categories of persons just listed, the court is exempt from having to bring a bull to atone for the people. The improper composition of the court invalidates its judicial action and the transgressing individuals must bring the expiatory sacrifices appropriate for individuals.

For it is said here, *congregation*
and it is said there, *congregation*.
Just as the *congregation* mentioned there
means that all of them must be worthy to issue rulings,
so the *congregation* mentioned here
means that all of them must be worthy to issue rulings.
If the court ruled in error
and the entire congregation acted inadvertently—
[the members of the court] bring a bull.
[If the court ruled] knowingly,
and [the entire congregation] acted in error—
[the individual members of the congregation] bring a lamb or a goat.
[If the court ruled] in error,
and [the entire congregation] acted knowingly—
then [all of] these are exempt.
   5 If the court ruled
and all or most of the congregation acted according to their ruling:
[the members of the court] bring a bull;
as to idolatry, [the members of the court] bring a bull and a goat—

For it is said here, congregation and it is said there, congregation: The word "congregation" is used in Leviticus 4:13 with respect to the court's erroneous ruling, and the same word is used in Numbers 35:24 with respect to capital punishment. Just as the "congregation" (understood as the court) of Numbers 35:24 cannot impose capital punishment unless all of them are worthy to issue legal rulings, so the "congregation" of Leviticus 4:13 cannot offer the expiatory bull on behalf of the entire people unless all of them are worthy to issue legal rulings.

[the members of the court] bring a bull: If the court inadvertently permitted that which is forbidden, and most of the people relied on their ruling not knowing it was in error, then the court brings a bull on its own and the people's behalf (Leviticus 4:14).

[the individual members of the congregation] bring a lamb or a goat: If the court knowingly permitted that which was forbidden, the consequence of their having acted consciously is that they cannot offer a bull on their own and the people's behalf. Even if most of the community had relied on the ruling, the members of the community are nevertheless considered to be individual transgressors, each person individually liable to bring his own lamb or goat. The sex of the sacrificial animal is specified in the Torah (Leviticus 4:28, 32).

then [all of] these are exempt: If the court inadvertently permitted the forbidden, and most of the community knew the ruling was erroneous and acted on it anyway, then neither the court nor the individual members of the community bring an expiatory offering. The court does not offer a bull on its own and the community's behalf because the community did not rely upon its ruling (since they knew it was erroneous). The individual members of the community do not bring expiatory offerings of goats or lambs because they knew of the court's error and therefore sinned knowingly. Expiatory offerings may not be brought for intentional sins.

1:5 *as to idolatry, [the members of the court] bring a bull and a goat—the words of R. Meir*: R. Meir's view is that in the event the court inadvertently permits the violation of a law pertaining to idolatry—and most of the community relies and acts on the court's ruling—the court must offer a goat as well as a bull on its own and the community's behalf. R. Meir's view is based on a rabbinic interpretation that Numbers 15:24 refers to idolatry. Again, the sex of the animals is specified in the Torah (Leviticus 4:23).

the words of R. Meir.
R. Judah says:
Twelve tribes bring twelve bulls,
and as to idolatry, they bring twelve bulls and twelve goats.[5]
R. Simeon says:
Thirteen bulls,
and as to idolatry, thirteen bulls and thirteen goats:
a bull and a goat for each and every tribe,[6]
and a bull and a goat for the court.
If the court ruled,
and seven tribes—
or most of them—
acted according to their ruling,
[the members of the court] bring a bull;
as to idolatry, they bring a bull and a goat—
the words of R. Meir.
R. Judah says:
Seven tribes that transgressed bring seven bulls,
and the other tribes that did not transgress bring a bull on their behalf,
for even those that did not transgress bring [expiatory sacrifices] on behalf of the transgressors.
R. Simeon says:
Eight bulls,

[5] K, P render R. Judah's view as being that "twelve tribes" bring "twelve goats" only.
[6] K, P: "for each tribe," unlike the printed "each and every tribe." The same difference appears in R. Simeon's words immediately following.

R. Judah says: Twelve tribes bring twelve bulls, and as to idolatry, they bring twelve bulls and twelve goats: R. Judah's view is that *congregation* (Leviticus 4:13) refers to the community and not to the court. Moreover, the tribes of Israel are referred to as *congregation* (e.g. Genesis 48:4; 2 Chronicles 20:5). Thus in the event the court—which is the Sanhedrin—inadvertently permits a violation of law and most of the community acts on that ruling, each individual tribe must bring its own bull, and, in the case of idolatry, its own bull and goat.

R. Simeon says: Thirteen bulls, and as to idolatry, thirteen bulls and thirteen goats: a bull and a goat for each and every tribe, and a bull and a goat for the court: R. Simeon's view is similar to R. Judah's, except that he holds that the court must bring its own bull, or, in the case of idolatry, its own bull and goat.

If the court ruled, and seven tribes—or most of them—acted according to their ruling, [the members of the court] bring a bull; as to idolatry, they bring a bull and a goat—the words of R. Meir: Seven discrete tribes or the majority of the population of seven discrete tribes (or, according to another view, most of the community, even if that is not most of the tribes) followed the court's inadvertent ruling permitting the forbidden. According to R. Meir, the court brings a bull on their behalf, or a bull and a goat in the case of idolatry, because as long as most of the community sinned by following the court's ruling, the court is obligated to bring the atoning sacrifice.

and the other tribes...on behalf of the transgressors: In R. Judah's view, even tribes that did not transgress in reliance on the court's erroneous ruling bring sacrifices on behalf of those that did.

R. Simeon says: Eight bulls, and as to idolatry—eight bulls and eight goats: a bull and a goat for each and every tribe, and a bull and a goat for the court: R. Simeon notes, as he did earlier, that the court must bring its own bull, or, in the case of idolatry, its own bull and goat. He disagrees with R. Judah about the innocent tribes, holding that they do not have to offer sacrifices on behalf of the transgressors.

and as to idolatry,
eight bulls and eight goats:
a bull and a goat for each and every tribe,
and a bull and a goat for the court.
If the court of one of the tribes ruled [erroneously],
and that tribe acted according to their ruling,
that tribe is culpable,
and all the other tribes are exempt—
the words of R. Judah.
And the Sages say:
There is only culpability as to a ruling of the Great Court,
as it is said, *If it is the whole community of Israel that has erred*—
and not the *community* of that tribe.

Chapter Two

2:1–3 *Rulings of the Anointed Priest*

2 If the anointed priest ruled for himself:
[if he ruled] in error
and acted unwittingly [on the ruling],
he brings a bull.
[If he ruled] in error
and acted knowingly,
or [if he ruled] knowingly
and acted unwittingly [on the ruling],

If the court of one of the tribes ruled [erroneously] to permit a partial violation of the Torah.

that tribe is culpable, and all the other tribes are exempt: R. Judah holds that an individual tribe is obligated to offer a bull for relying on the inadvertent ruling of its own court.

And the Sages say: There is only culpability as to a ruling of the great court: The court's offering of a bull to atone for the community's reliance on its erroneous ruling only applies to a ruling of the great court for the entire community, not to the ruling of an individual tribe's court for that tribe. This is derived from Leviticus 4:13: *If it is the whole community of Israel that has erred*—the *whole* community, and not just the community of a particular tribe. The great court represents the entire community of Israel.

2:1 *If the anointed priest*: The priest anointed with oil; the high priest.

[if he ruled] in error and acted unwittingly [on the ruling], he brings a bull: If the erroneous ruling was inadvertent and the anointed priest acted on that ruling unaware of the error, then he offers a bull in expiation as per Leviticus 4:3.

[If he ruled] in error and acted knowingly on the ruling, or [if he ruled] knowingly and acted unwittingly [on the ruling], he is exempt: In neither of these cases does the anointed priest bring a bull in expiation. In the first case he ruled unintentionally but acted intentionally. In the second case he intentionally ruled to permit himself something unlawful, but ultimately committed the transgression inadvertently. When intention is introduced into the mix, an expiatory offering cannot be brought.

he is exempt,
for the anointed priest's ruling for himself
is like the court's ruling for the community.[7]

2 If he ruled and acted by himself,
he achieves atonement by and for himself.
If he ruled and acted with the community,
he achieves atonement for himself with the community.
For the [members of the] court are not culpable
unless they rule to nullify part [of a Torah commandment]
and uphold part [of a commandment],
and likewise the anointed [priest].
Nor [are they culpable for a ruling] concerning idolatry,
unless they rule to nullify part [of a Torah commandment]
and uphold part [of a commandment].

2:3–7 *Parameters of Culpability and Modes of Atonement*

3 [The members of the court] are only culpable for legal error
[together] with unwitting action,
and likewise the anointed [priest].
And as to idolatry they are only culpable[8] for legal error with unwitting action.
The [members of the] court[9] are not culpable
until they rule on a matter
the punishment for intentional violation of which is *karet*,

---

[7] K: "the anointed priest's ruling for himself *is* the court's ruling 'over' the community."
[8] K, P lack the explicit reference to culpability.   [9] K, P lack "the court."

---

for the anointed priest's ruling for himself is like the court's ruling for the community: Just as the court does not offer a bull in expiation unless it issues an inadvertent ruling followed by an inadvertent transgression committed in reliance on the ruling, neither does the anointed priest.

2:2 *If he ruled and acted by himself, he achieves atonement by and for himself*: If the anointed priest ruled inadvertently to permit himself a violation of part of a commandment and transgressed inadvertently pursuant to that ruling, he brings a bull for himself.

If he ruled and acted with the community [the court]*, he achieves atonement for himself with the community*: If the anointed priest ruled inadvertently along with the court and then acted inadvertently with a majority of the community, he does not bring his own bull. He achieves atonement together with the court and community.

Nor [are they culpable for a ruling]: That is, the members of the court or the anointed priest.

2:3 *legal error… unwitting action*: The members of the court and the anointed priest are only liable to bring a bull in the event that an erroneous ruling permitting the forbidden is followed by an inadvertent transgressive action taken pursuant to the ruling.

The [members of the] court are not culpable…Likewise the anointed [priest]: Inadvertence in issuing an erroneous ruling and in acting in accordance with it is necessary but not sufficient to trigger an obligation of collective atonement. The legal matter at issue must be one for which, in general, knowing violation is punishable by *karet* (in the absence of witnesses) and inadvertent violation entails a purgation offering. The

and for the unwitting violation of which is a purgation offering.
Likewise the anointed [priest].
And they are not [culpable] as to [a ruling pertaining to] idolatry,
until they rule[10] on a matter the punishment for the advertent violation of which is *karet*,
and the punishment for the unwitting violation of which is a purgation offering.

4 [The members of the court] are culpable
neither for [an erroneous ruling concerning] a positive [commandment]
nor a negative commandment pertaining to the Temple.
And [individuals] do not bring an offering for uncertain guilt either for [a possible violation of] a positive commandment or a negative commandment pertaining to the Temple.
But [the members of the court] are culpable

[10] K, P lack "they rule."

precise nature of *karet* is uncertain, except that it is not a punishment administered by human beings. *Karet* may mean dying before one's time, dying without children, or some other form of divinely administered punishment.

2:4 *[The members of the court] are culpable...pertaining to the Temple*: "Pertaining to the Temple" means pertaining to the purity or impurity of the Temple and the holy things within it. The court does not bring a bull for an erroneous ruling pertaining to the purity or impurity of the Temple and its holy things. The reason is that an individual's mandatory expiatory offering for inadvertently violating the Temple's purity is not a purgation offering of fixed value (see 2:3, above), but a sacrifice of fluctuating value, calibrated according to the wealth of the penitent (Leviticus 5:6–13). Since the individual's sacrifice in this case is not the typical purgation offering, the court is not required to offer a bull. The following paragraphs provide illustrations of the kinds of commandment intended.

a positive [commandment]: Numbers 5:2 instructs that *anyone with an eruption or a discharge and anyone defiled by a corpse* must be removed from the camp. If such a person finds himself within the Temple, he must exit by the shortest possible route. The court's hypothetical erroneous ruling is that this person is permitted to exit the Temple by a longer route. See *Shevu'ot* 2:3. Should the court issue such an erroneous ruling, it does not bring a bull in atonement.

a negative commandment: An impure person is forbidden to enter the Temple (e.g. Leviticus 12:4). Should the court permit such a person to enter the Temple through an inadvertently erroneous ruling, the court does not bring a bull in atonement.

offering for uncertain guilt: The rabbis interpret Leviticus 5:17–19 as referring to the bringing of a sacrifice by individuals who suspect, but are not certain, that they have sinned. The rabbis call this sacrifice a "hanging" (guilt) offering. The doubt as to the violation of law causes the question of guilt to remain "hanging."

And [individuals] do not bring an offering for uncertain guilt either for [a possible violation of] a positive commandment or a negative commandment pertaining to the Temple: An individual is only obligated to bring such an offering if he suspects that he has violated a law for which, in general, an undoubted and inadvertent violation entails a purgation offering. Since individuals are required to bring an offering of varying value (lit. "offering that ascends and descends")—and not a purgation offering—for inadvertent violations of the Temple's purity, they are not required to bring an offering for uncertain guilt if they suspect they may have committed such a violation.

But [the members of the court] are culpable [for an erroneous ruling] concerning a positive or negative commandment pertaining to the menstruant: The case of the menstruant is likely singled out because it is a case of purity/impurity as to which the court *is* culpable for an inadvertent erroneous ruling. The court is culpable because the law of the menstruant is within the category of laws the knowing violation of which is punishable by *karet* and the inadvertent violation of which entails a purgation offering.

[for an erroneous ruling] concerning a positive or negative commandment pertaining to the menstruant.
And [individuals] do bring an offering for uncertain guilt
for [a possible violation of] a positive or negative commandment pertaining to the menstruant.
What is a positive commandment pertaining to the menstruant?
Separate from the menstruant.
And a negative commandment?
Do not approach a menstruant.

5 [The members of the court] are not culpable[11] for
"hearing the voice,"
or "pronouncement of the lips,"
or for [an erroneous ruling concerning] the impurity of the Temple and its holy things,
nor is the *Nasi*—
the words of R. Yose the Galilean.

[11] P: "are only culpable."

And [individuals] do bring an offering of uncertain guilt for [a possible violation of] a positive or negative commandment pertaining to the menstruant: Individuals are liable to bring such an offering if they suspect they have inadvertently violated a menstrual prohibition. This is so because they are required to bring purgation offerings if they have inadvertently and without a doubt committed such a violation.

Separate from the menstruant: See *Shevu'ot* 2:4. If a man's wife tells him during intercourse that she has become impure [= begun menstruating], he must separate from her. If he separates immediately, he is liable, since this separation is as pleasurable to him as their coming together. If the court inadvertently and erroneously rules that he is permitted to separate from her immediately, then this is an error for which they must atone with a bull.

Do not approach a menstruant: If the court issues an erroneous ruling pertaining to this negative commandment about the menstruant (Leviticus 18:19), they must offer a bull.

2:5 *[The members of the court] are not culpable*: The court is not liable to offer a bull for an inadvertent ruling permitting a violation of the law in the listed situations, even if a majority of the community acts inadvertently in accordance with their ruling. This is because individuals who transgress these listed laws are liable to bring an offering of fluctuating value (see 2:4, above) but not a purgation offering.

"hearing the voice": Leviticus 5:1 requires one who is aware of information to testify to it. The rabbis understand this verse as the basis of the "oath of testimony" (see *Shevu'ot* 4:3). This is an oath whereby persons swear that they do not have information that would be helpful to a party in a judicial proceeding.

"pronouncement of the lips": This is a type of oath whereby a person swears that he will not do something that he then proceeds to do or that he will do something and then fails to fulfill his oath. See Leviticus 5:4, Numbers 30:7-13, *Shevu'ot* 3:7.

or for [an erroneous ruling concerning] the impurity of the Temple and its holy things: See 2:4 above.

nor is the Nasi—the words of R. Yose the Galilean: The title *Nasi* is often applied to the Patriarch of talmudic times, but the rabbis in this tractate understand the biblical *Nasi* to be the king (see 3:3, below). In this tractate, therefore, the title is left untranslated. The Talmud understands the scriptural language *which by the commandment of the Lord his God ought not to be done* (Leviticus 4:22) as referring to "one who has only God above him," namely, the king. Unlike the court, the king can be liable for an inadvertent act in violation of the law even without his having issued a ruling. R. Yose holds that the king never brings an offering of fluctuating value—since he is not someone who can become poor—and thus he brings no sacrifice at all for an inadvertent violation of one of these laws (the violation of which, as noted earlier, is atoned for by offerings of fluctuating value).

R. Aqiva says:
The *Nasi* is culpable as to all of them
except "hearing the voice,"
because the king neither judges nor is judged,
neither testifies nor is the subject of testimony.[12]

6 All the commandments of the Torah
the intentional violation of which entails *karet*
and the unwitting violation of which entails a purgation offering:
an individual brings a [female] lamb or [female] goat;
the *Nasi*, a [male] goat,
and the anointed [priest] and the court bring a bull.
And as to idolatry:
an individual, the *Nasi*, and the anointed [priest] bring a [female] goat,
and the court brings a bull and a [male] goat:
a bull for a burnt offering,
and a [male] goat for a purgation offering.

7 An offering for uncertain guilt:
an individual and the *Nasi* are liable [to bring it],

[12] K lacks the clause about testimony.

R. Aqiva says: The Nasi is culpable as to all of them except "hearing the voice," because the king neither judges nor is judged, neither testifies nor is the subject of testimony: Unlike R. Yose the Galilean, R. Aqiva holds that the king is liable to bring an offering of fluctuating value as to all of the listed laws except for "hearing the voice." The latter is an exception because kings neither judge nor are judged; neither testify, nor are the subject of testimony (see *Sanhedrin* 2:2).

2:6 *karet*: See the annotations to 2:3, above.

an individual brings a [female] lamb or [female] goat: As per Leviticus 4:27–28.

the Nasi, a [male] goat: As per Leviticus 4:22–23.

and the anointed [priest] and the court bring a bull: Unlike the individual and the *Nasi* (king), the anointed priest and the court are liable for an inadvertent, erroneous ruling followed by an inadvertent transgression committed in reliance on the ruling. Thus they bring a bull as per Leviticus 4:3 (the anointed priest) and 4:13–14 (the court).

And as to idolatry: an individual, the Nasi, and the anointed [priest] bring a [female] goat: Numbers 15:27 mandates that the individual who has sinned inadvertently must bring a female goat in expiation. Numbers 15:29 declares that *you shall have one ritual for anyone who acts in error*. The rabbis interpret this to mean that an ordinary individual, the *Nasi*, and the anointed priest offer the same purgation offering—a female goat—for an inadvertent violation of idolatry.

and the court brings a bull and a [male] goat: a bull for a burnt offering, and a [male] goat for a purgation offering: As per Numbers 15:24. See also 1:5, above.

2:7 *offering for uncertain guilt: an individual and the Nasi are liable [to bring it]*: This offering is brought when there is doubt as to whether a transgression has been committed (Leviticus 5:17–19 and 2:4). Moreover, it is brought for doubtful violation of a law for which, in general, a purgation offering is brought for an undoubted inadvertent violation of the law. The view in this mishnah that the *Nasi* brings an offering for uncertain guilt in appropriate circumstances is an anonymous statement of the view attributed earlier (2:5) to R. Aqiva.

and the anointed [priest] and the court are exempt.
An offering for definite guilt:
an individual, the *Nasi*, and the anointed [priest] are liable [to bring it],
and the [members of the] court are exempt.
For "hearing the voice," "the pronouncement of the lips,"
and for [an erroneous ruling concerning] the impurity of the Temple and its holy things:
the [members of the] court are exempt,
and the individual, the *Nasi*, and the anointed [priest] are liable,
except that the high priest is not culpable for [an erroneous ruling concerning] the impurity of the Temple and its holy things—
the words of R. Simeon.[13]
And what do [the *Nasi* and the anointed] bring [in these cases]?
An offering of varying value.
R. Eliezer says:
The *Nasi* brings a [male] goat.

---

[13] **K** lacks "except that" and reads that the "Great Court" is not culpable for an erroneous ruling concerning the impurity of the Temple and its holy things. **K** also lacks the reference to R. Simeon.

---

and the anointed [priest] and the court are exempt: In the case of the anointed priest and the court, the doubt would be as to whether they had in fact erred in their legal ruling.

offering for definite guilt: There are five such offerings, as per *Zevahim* 5:5. One who denies a monetary claim against him and later admits to it must bring the guilt offering of robberies (Leviticus 5:21–26). One who makes improper, profane use of holy objects must bring the guilt offering of misuse of sacred property (Leviticus 5:14–16). One who has intercourse with a female slave betrothed to a Hebrew slave must bring the guilt offering of the designated female slave (Leviticus 19:20–22). One who becomes ritually impure during a period of *nezirut* must bring the guilt offering of the *nazir* (Numbers 6:9–12). Finally, one who has recovered from *tsara'at* and is purified after being declared a *metsora* must bring the guilt-offering of the *metsora* (Leviticus 14:10–12).

an individual, the Nasi, and the anointed [priest] are liable [to bring it]: An ordinary individual, the *Nasi*, and the anointed priest are liable to bring an offering of definite guilt in the five instances set out in *Zevahim* 5:5.

and the [members of the] court are exempt: The court is only liable to bring an offering in a situation in which the intentional violation of a law entails the punishment of *karet*. Since none of the five cases that require an offering of definite guilt entail *karet*, the court does not bring this offering—even if it inadvertently rules to permit a violation in one of these areas.

For "hearing the voice"... the individual, the Nasi, and the anointed [priest] are liable: R. Aqiva holds in 2:5 that the *Nasi* is not liable for "hearing the voice." The view in this mishnah is that he is liable; the same rule applies to him, the ordinary individual, and the anointed priest as per Leviticus 4:27 (*any person*).

except that the high priest is not culpable for [an erroneous ruling concerning] the impurity of the Temple and its holy things—the words of R. Simeon: R. Simeon derives this from Numbers 19:20, which speaks of *anyone*, interpreted to exclude the high priest. See also *Parah* 12:4.

An offering of varying value: As per Leviticus 5:6–13, the individual will bring what he can afford, and the *Nasi* and high priest—being of greater means—will bring a sheep or a goat.

Chapter Three

3:1–3 When the Sinner Changes His Status; Defining the "Nasi"

3 An anointed priest who sinned
and afterwards passed from his anointed status,
and likewise the *Nasi* who sinned
and afterwards passed from his greatness—
the anointed priest brings a bull,
and the *Nasi* brings a [male] goat.

2 An anointed priest who passed from his anointed status
and sinned afterwards,
and likewise the *Nasi* who passed from his greatness
and sinned afterwards—
the anointed priest brings a bull,
and the *Nasi* is like an ordinary person.

3 If they sinned before they were appointed
and were afterwards appointed,
then they are like ordinary persons.
R. Simeon says:
If [the sin] was known to them before they were appointed,
they are culpable;

3:1 *An anointed priest who sinned*: He sinned in permitting himself the violation of a commandment the intentional violation of which is punished with *karet* and the inadvertent violation of which is punished with a purgation offering. He also acted on his ruling.

and afterwards passed from his anointed status: He ceased to be the high priest after issuing and following his ruling, but before bringing the expiatory sacrifice.

the Nasi who sinned and afterwards passed from his greatness: Similarly, the *Nasi* who permitted himself such a violation and who ceased to be the ruler before bringing his expiatory sacrifice.

the anointed priest brings a bull, and the Nasi brings a [male] goat: The anointed priest and the *Nasi* offer the sacrifice appropriate to their positions at the time of the sin: a bull for the anointed priest, and a male goat for the *Nasi*.

3:2 *the anointed priest brings a bull, and the Nasi is like an ordinary person*: If the anointed priest permits himself such a violation *after* he ceases to serve as high priest, he nevertheless offers a bull in expiation since he still retains the sanctity of the high priesthood (see 3:4). In the same situation, the erstwhile *Nasi* expiates his sin like an ordinary person, because the Torah stresses (Leviticus 4:22) *In case it is a chieftain who incurs guilt*—the "chieftain" (*Nasi*) only brings a male goat in expiation if he is still the *Nasi*; if not, he is no different than any person.

3:3 *If they sinned before they were appointed and were afterwards appointed, then they are like ordinary persons*: As 3:1 makes clear, the timing of the sin is what matters. If the men sinned prior to assuming the positions of high priest or *Nasi*, then they atone like any other person.

R. Simeon says: If [the sin] was known to them before they were appointed, they are culpable: R. Simeon holds that not only is the timing of the sin critical, but also the timing of the sinner's awareness of it. The now-anointed high priest and *Nasi* are only liable to atone like ordinary persons if they sinned and became aware of the sin prior to their appointments.

if from when they were appointed,
[they are] exempt.
And who is the *Nasi*?
This is the king,
as it is said: *doing unwittingly any of the things which by the commandment of the Lord his God ought not to be done*—
a *Nasi* over whom there is none but the Lord his God.

3:4–5 Defining the "Anointed Priest"

4 And who is the anointed [priest]?
The one anointed with the oil of anointing,
not the one of many garments.
The only difference between[14] a [high] priest anointed with the oil of anointing and [the high priest] of many garments
is the bull that comes [to atone] for error concerning "all the commandments."
The only difference between the serving [high] priest

[14] Lit. "There is nothing between…" here and below.

---

if from when they were appointed, [they are] exempt: If they sinned as ordinary persons but only became aware of it after their appointment, they are exempt from bringing any atoning sacrifice. They cannot now offer the sacrifices appropriate for ordinary persons, nor can they offer the expiatory sacrifices appropriate to their station—since they were ordinary persons at the time they sinned.

And who is the Nasi? Who is the *Nasi* who is obligated to offer a male goat in expiation (Leviticus 4:22) rather than the ordinary person's offering?

a Nasi over whom there is none but the Lord his God: This is the rabbinic interpretation of Leviticus 4:22. A *Nasi* over whom there is none but God is none other than the king of Israel, as opposed to the head of one of the twelve tribes.

3:4 *And who is the anointed [priest]?* The Mishnah seeks to identify which high priest it is whose atonement is a bull as per Leviticus 4:3.

The one anointed with the oil of anointing, not the one of many garments: According to rabbinic tradition, high priests were not anointed with oil during the Second Temple period (and perhaps even late in the period of the first temple). High priests were distinguished from ordinary priests by wearing eight, rather than four, priestly garments. See *Yoma* 7:5; *Megillah* 1:9.

The only difference between a [high] priest anointed with the oil of anointing and [the high priest] of many garments is the bull: Leviticus 4:3 directs that if the "anointed priest" sins so as to cast guilt upon the people, he atones by offering a bull. In the same situation, the high priest of multiple garments offers the same sacrifice as that offered by an ordinary Israelite. See *Megillah* 1:9.

error concerning "all the commandments": This refers to the inadvertent ruling by the great court permitting a transgression of part of one of all the commandments of the Torah. See above, 1:1–3.

the serving [high] priest: Should the high priest become temporarily unfit for service, another will be appointed. The priest currently serving as high priest is referred to as "the serving [high] priest." See *Megillah* 1:9.

The only difference … is the bull of the Day of Atonement and the tenth of an ephah: On the bull of the Day of Atonement, see Leviticus 16:6. The offering of a tenth of an *ephah* of fine flour is mentioned at Leviticus

and the [high] priest who has passed [out of priestly service]
is the bull of the Day of Atonement and the tenth of an *ephah*.
Both are equal with regard to the sacrificial service of the Day of Atonement,
and [both] are commanded concerning the virgin,
forbidden concerning the widow,
do not incur impurity as to their [deceased] relatives,
neither grow their hair nor tear [their garments],
and cause the return of the murderer.

5 The high priest tears from the bottom
and the ordinary [priest] from above.
The high priest offers sacrifice while an *onen*
and does not eat,
and the ordinary [priest] neither offers sacrifice nor eats.

3:6–8 Rules of Precedence

6 Everything more frequent than something else
takes precedence over the other thing,

6:13–15. It was first offered during the dedication of Aaron and his sons as priests during Israel's wandering in the desert, and was thereafter to be offered by the high priest every day. In the cases of both the bull of the Day of Atonement and the tenth of an *ephah*, these offerings might only be performed by the serving [high] priest. See *Megillah* 1:9.

the [high] priest who has passed [out of priestly service]: This refers to the [high] priest removed from service; either the anointed priest who was (temporarily) removed on account of some ritual unfitness or his replacement who was removed so that the anointed priest could resume his service once his unfitness ceased. See *Megillah* 1:9.

and [both] are commanded concerning the virgin: Both the serving priest and the priest who has passed from the high priestly state are commanded to marry only virgins (Leviticus 21:13).

forbidden concerning the widow: Both are forbidden to marry widows (Leviticus 21:14).

do not incur impurity as to their [deceased] relatives: Neither the serving priest nor the priest who has passed from the high priestly status is permitted to incur impurity for the sake of tending to his deceased close relatives: see Leviticus 21:11.

neither grow their hair nor tear [their garments]: In mourning (Leviticus 21:10).

and cause the return of the murderer: Perpetrators of unintentional homicide who fled to cities of refuge may return to their homes upon the death of either the serving priest or the priest who has passed from high priestly status. See Numbers 35:25; *Makkot* 2:6.

3:5 *The high priest tears from the bottom and the ordinary [priest] from above*: The prohibition in 3:4 of the high priest's tearing his clothes in mourning for a deceased relative is understood here as a prohibition against tearing in the same way that other priests do, not as an absolute prohibition against tearing. Thus like an ordinary Israelite, the ordinary priest tears from the collar, while the high priest tears his clothes from the bottom of his garment.

while an onen: An *onen* is a mourner prior to the burial of the deceased. Despite being in this difficult situation, the high priest offers sacrifice pursuant to Leviticus 21:12: *He shall not go outside the sanctuary . . .*

and does not eat: Of the sacrifice.

3:6 *Everything more frequent*: Any religious act that is practiced more frequently must be performed prior to a religious act that is practiced less frequently. See also *Zevahim* 10:1–2.

and everything of greater sanctity than something else
takes precedence over the other.
If the anointed [priest]'s bull and the congregation's bull are standing [awaiting sacrifice],
the anointed [priest]'s bull precedes the congregation's bull
as to all its [necessary sacrificial] acts.

7 A man precedes a woman[15] as to saving life
and returning a lost object,
and a woman precedes a man as to clothing
and being rescued from captivity.[16]
When both of them are vulnerable to disgrace,
the man takes precedence over the woman.

8 A priest precedes a Levite,
a Levite an Israelite,
an Israelite a *mamzer*,
a *mamzer* a *natin*,
a *natin* a convert,

---

[15] P lacks "a woman."
[16] Lit. "the house of captivity," except that P lacks "captivity."

---

everything of greater sanctity: The Talmud points out that Leviticus 21:8 says of the priests *and you must treat them as holy*. This is understood to mean that the priests—who are of greater sanctity than lay Israelites—are to read first from the Torah during public Torah reading, among other firsts.

the anointed [priest]'s bull precedes the congregation's bull: If the high priest is required to offer a bull to atone for a ruling in which he permitted himself a violation of a commandment and he also acted on his ruling, his offering must take precedence over the great court's offering of a bull to atone for the congregation's obedience to such a ruling. The Talmud explains that the atonement of the high priest—who makes atonement for the people—must take precedence over the atonement of those for whom he does this. Leviticus 16:6 stresses that Aaron, the original high priest, was *to make expiation for himself and for his household*—understood as *first* himself, and *then* his household.

3:7 *A man precedes a woman as to saving life*: If both a man and a woman are in danger of their lives, the man's life is to be saved first.

returning a lost object: Similarly, if both a man and a woman have lost objects, the man's lost object is to be returned first. Cf. Deuteronomy 33:3; *Bava Metsi'a* 2:11.

a woman precedes a man as to clothing: If both a man and woman are in need of clothing, the woman should be clothed first.

and being rescued from captivity: A woman is to be rescued from captivity prior to a man, given the greater likelihood that the woman will be subjected to sexual degradation.

When both of them are vulnerable to disgrace: If both the man and woman are equally likely to be sexually abused in captivity, then the man should be rescued first.

3:8 *A priest precedes a Levite*: This list establishes precedence for the purposes of honor.

an Israelite a mamzer: The Israelite precedes the *mamzer*, who is born of a forbidden sexual relationship and excluded from regular membership in the community: see Deuteronomy 23:3.

a mamzer a natin: The *natin* is understood to be a descendant of the biblical Gibeonites, whom Joshua had designated to be *hewers of wood and drawers of water* (Joshua 9:27).

and a convert a freed slave.
When?
When all of them are [otherwise] equal.
But if the *mamzer* is a scholar and the high priest an ignoramus—
the scholarly *mamzer* takes precedence over the ignorant high priest.

a freed slave: This is the "Canaanite" or gentile slave, not the "Hebrew" slave.

When? When all of them are [otherwise] equal: "Equal" refers to equality in knowledge of Torah.